GLENCOE

Introduction to Business

In partnership with BusinessWeek

TEACHER WRAPAROUND EDITION

FIFTH EDITION

Betty J. Brown
Ball State University

John E. Clow
State University of New York, College at Oneonta
National Council of Economic Education, New York, NY

www.introbus.glencoe.com

Glencoe
McGraw-Hill

New York, New York   Columbus, Ohio   Chicago, Illinois   Peoria, Illinois   Woodland Hills, California

ABOUT THE AUTHORS

Dr. Betty J. Brown is Professor of Business Education and Office Administration at Ball State University, Muncie, Ind. She was formerly Associate Professor of Technological and Adult Education, Business Education, and Office Systems Management, at the University of Tennessee, Knoxville. In addition to teaching at the secondary and postsecondary levels, Dr. Brown has written numerous articles, delivered speeches, and conducted workshops on the teaching of business.

Dr. John E. Clow is the Director of Leatherstocking Center for Economic Education at the State University of New York, College at Oneonta. He also serves as the National Program Consultant of the National Council on Economic Education in New York. Prior to that he was President of Berkeley College of Manhattan. Dr. Clow has taught at both secondary and postsecondary levels and has to his credit numerous speeches and publications in the areas of business and economic education.

Glencoe/McGraw-Hill

A Division of The McGraw-Hill Companies

Printed in the United States of America.

Send all inquiries to:
Glencoe/McGraw-Hill
21600 Oxnard Street, Suite 500
Woodland Hills, CA 91367

X 035743

ISBN 0-07-825868-5

2 3 4 5 6 7 8 9   027   06 05 04 03 02

Contents for Teacher Wraparound Edition

GREAT IDEAS FROM THE CLASSROOM OF...

Chapter 1
Gwen Alsburry
Business Education Teacher
Oakdale High School
Oakdale, La.

Chapter 2
Stephanie Andrejcak
Business Teacher
Burnt Hills-Ballston Lake Central School District
Burnt Hills, N.Y.

Chapter 3
Mary Warnke
Business Education Instructor
Brillion Public School
Brillion, Wis.

Chapter 4
Bill Paden
Teacher and Coach
Cleveland High School
Reseda, Calif.

Chapter 5
Beth Patzke
Business Education Department Chair
Baldwin-Woodville High School
Baldwin, Wis.

Chapter 6
Angel Gonzalez
Teacher
A.B. Miller High School
Fontana, Calif.

Chapter 7
Susan Case
Business Teacher
South Beloit High School
South Beloit, Ill.

Chapter 8
Joe Ree, Ph.D.
Professor, Modern Language and Linguistics
Florida State University
Tallahassee, Fla.

Chapter 9
Michelle Walker, Ph.D.
Assistant Professor, Education
University of North Texas
Denton, Tex.

Chapter 10
Jay S. Brown
Business Education Teacher
Pleasant Valley High School
Brodheadsville, Pa.

Chapter 11
Phillip Schwenk
Teacher
Grover Cleveland High School
Reseda, Calif.

Chapter 12
Vincent Tesi
Business Teacher
Colts Neck High School
Colts Neck, N.J.

Chapter 13
Greg Gregoriou
Business Teacher
Parkside High School
Dundas, Ontario, Canada

Chapter 14
Keith A. Schneider
Business Education Instructor
Cambridge High School
Cambridge, Wis.

Chapter 15
Linda R. Burkett
Business Ed. Teacher
South Vermillion High School
Clinton, Ind.

Chapter 16
Janet Fisher
Business Department Chair
Beavercreek High School
Beavercreek, Ohio

Chapter 17
Edward J. Murphy
Business Education Teacher
John Jay High School
Hopewell Junction, N.Y.

Chapter 18
Miranda Nixon Blocker
Business Educator
Heyward Career and Technology Center
Columbia, S.C.

Chapter 19
Gail Sobel
Business Teacher
DeRuyter High School
DeRuyter, N.Y.

Chapter 20
Jane Keegan
Business Department Chair
Franklin County High School
Brookville, Ind.

Chapter 21
Luis F. Varela
Assistant Principal
Oconee County High School
Watkinsville, Ga.

Chapter 22
Tej Bhatia, Ph.D.
Professor of Linguistics
Syracuse University
Syracuse, N.Y.

Chapter 23
Paul Richmond
Business Department Chair
Thomas Edison High School
Elmira Heights, N.Y.

Chapter 24
Sharon Larson
Business Technology Teacher
Prairie Ridge High School
Crystal Lake, Ill.

Chapter 25
Larry M. Condra
Business Education Teacher
Abilene High School
Abilene, Tex.

Chapter 26
Cheryl A. Moore
Business Education Teacher
Ellison High School
Killeen, Tex.

Chapter 27
Therese Velasquez
Teacher
Patrick Henry High School
San Diego, Calif.

Chapter 28
Gloria Farris
Business Teacher
Seneca High School
Louisville, Ky.

Chapter 29
John Bucci
Teacher
Arvada High School
Arvada, Colo.

Chapter 30
Barry Danziger
Business Teacher
Franklin High School
Somerset, N.J.

Chapter 31
Claudia Harris
Business Teacher
Delta High School
Clarksburg, Calif.

Chapter 32
Jennifer Harrison
Teacher
Cleveland High School
Reseda, Calif.

Chapter 33
Robert D. Madison, Ph
Assistant Principal
Boys & Girls High Sch
Brooklyn, N.Y.

Chapter 34
Mary Valigur
Teacher
Sandia High
Albuquerq

Chapte
John ol
Tea
D
rtune, Ph.D.

ek School
, Colo.

EDUCATIONAL REVIEWERS

Doug Ahlers
Business Teacher
Sutter Union High School
Sutter, Calif.

Gwen Alsburry
Business Education Teacher
Oakdale High School
Oakdale, La.

Stephanie Andrejcak
Business Teacher
Burnt Hills-Ballston Lake Central
School District
Burnt Hills, N.Y.

Jane Babcock
Business Education Teacher
Petoskey High School
Petoskey, Mich.

chael Baker
ness Teacher
rier High School
ka, Ill.

Paul
Busind
Chippcher
Doyles h School
hio

Angela B.
Business Te
Technical C
West County
Park Hills, M ool

Sandy Blackma
Business Teacher
Benton High Sch
Benton, Ill.

Marilyn Blum
Business Department
Santiago High School
Garden Grove, Calif.

Ron Bonhaus
Business Education Teacher
Taylor High School
North Bend, Ohio

Teresa Boulds
Business/Computer
Education Teacher
Eldorado High School
Eldorado, Ill.

Jeremy Brady
Business Teacher
Coleman High School
Coleman, Wis.

Jay Brown
Business Education Teacher
Lincoln Way High School East
Campus
Frankfort, Ill.

Jay S. Brown
Business Education Teacher
Pleasant Valley High School
Brodheadsville, Pa.

Ruby Bullen
Chairperson, Business and
Computer Education
Thornwood High School
South Holland, Ill.

Linda Burkett
Business Ed. Teacher
South Vermillion High School
Clinton, Ind.

Susan Case
Business Teacher
South Beloit High School
South Beloit, Ill.

Becky Ceniceros
Business Teacher
Forsan ISD
orsan, Tex.

Genie Chaney
Business/Computer
Education Teacher
Edmond North High School
Edmond, Okla.

Janene B. Chisek
Business Instructor
Freeland High School
Freeland, Mich.

Todd Christman
Business Teacher
Monroe Central High School
Woodsfield, Ohio

Susan Cleavenger
Business Teacher
Waynesburg Central High School
Waynesburg, Pa.

Sharon Clem
Business, English, and
Speech Teacher
Pleasant Valley School District
Brodheadsville, Pa.

Margaret Colvin
Business Teacher
Southern Regional High School
Manahawkin, N.J.

Larry M. Condra
Business Education Teacher
Abilene High School
Abilene, Tex.

Richard Corbo
Business Teacher, Dean
James Monroe Academy for
Business & Law
Bronx, N.Y.

Rosalynd Cravin
Business Teacher
Northbrook High School
Houston, Tex.

Janice Curtis
Business Teacher
Plymouth High School
Plymouth, Ind.

Nancy Dague
Business Teacher
Chippiwa Hills High School
Remus, Mich.

Barry Danziger
Business Teacher
Franklin High School
Somerset, N.J.

Chandra Darr
Instructional Technology
Specialist (ITS)
East Davidson High School
Thomasville, N.C.

Elizabeth Deaton
Business Teacher
Hamshire-Fannett ISD
Hamshire, Tex.

Jimmie Dedmon
Business Teacher
Walters High School
Walters, Okla.

William Delaney
Business Education Teacher
Penn Cambria
Cresson, Pa.

Cora DeMott
Business Education Teacher
Thomas County Central
High School
Thomasville, Ga.

Donnajean deSilva
Business Teacher
Grandview Heights High School
Columbus, Ohio

Melissa S. Dornbusch
Business Teacher
Milton-Union High School
West Milton, Ohio

JoAnn Dotson
Entrepreneurial Business
Academy Director
Hanford West High School
Hanford, Calif.

Brian Dudley
Business Teacher
Wapahani High School
Selma, Ind.

Michael Duncan
Business Teacher
Castle High School
Newburgh, Ind.

Lonney Evon
Business and Mathematics Teacher
Quincy High School
Quincy, Mich.

Wil Farrell
Business Department Chair
McHenry High School—West
McHenry, Ill.

Gerald Finsen
Business Education Teacher
Rancocas Valley
Regional High School
Mt. Holly, N.J.

Kimberlee S. Fish
Business Teacher
Davison High School
Davison, Mich.

Janet Fisher
Business Department Chair
Beavercreek High School
Beavercreek, Ohio

Joyce Fleming
Accounting Teacher
Alexandria High School
Alexandria, Ala.

Renee Flory
Business Education Teacher
Donegal High School
Mount Joy, Pa.

Jane Foreman
Vocational Work Study Instructor
Porter County Career Center
Valparaiso, Ind.

Holly Gast
Business Teacher
Danbury Local Schools
Marblehead, Ohio

Charlotte Gibson
Business Teacher
Madison Cons. High School
Madison, Ind.

Joyce Hagen
Business Teacher
Newburg High School
Newburg, Mo.

Kim Hancock
Business Educator
Blanchard High School
Blanchard, Okla.

Claudia Harris
Business Teacher
Delta High School
Clarksburg, Calif.

Susan Harshbarger
Business Teacher
Graceville High School
Graceville, Fla.

Madeline Hatcher
Business Education Teacher
Waskom High School
Waskom, Tex.

Lisa Heid
Business Teacher
Noblesville High School
Noblesville, Ind.

Ellen Heim
Business Education
Wheeling High School
Wheeling, Ill.

Evelyn Holderieath
Business Teacher
Northwestern R-I
Mendon, Mo.

Lynda Johnson
Business Teacher
Mooreland
Mooreland, Okla.

Thelma K. Jones
Cooperative Office Education
Coordinator
Capitol High School
Baton Rouge, La.

Jane Keegan
Business Department Chair
Franklin County High School
Brookville, Ind.

Connie Kelley
Business Teacher
Graham High School
Graham, Tex.

Tommy G. Kindig
Business Education Teacher
Big Pasture School
Randlett, Okla.

Jayne Klingel
Business Teacher
River Valley High School
Marion, Ohio

Brenda Knight
Chairperson, Business and
Technology
Cedar Park High School
Cedar Park, Tex.

Brad Knoche
Business Department Chair
South Milwauhu High School
South Milwauhu, Wis.

James Kramer
Business Teacher
Baker Co. Middle School
Marrlenny, Fla.

Wayne L. Kurlander
Business Instructor
Minisink Valley High School
Statehill, N.Y.

Sharon Larson
Business Technology Teacher
Prairie Ridge High School
Crystal Lake, Ill.

Sally Layman
Business Department Chair
John Glenn High School
Norwalk, Calif.

Arlene Lent
Business Teacher
Clyde-Savannah High School
Clyde, N.Y.

Bob Lieber
Business Education Instructor
Westfield
Houston, Tex.

Donna Lyde
Business Education Instructor
Petersburg High School
Petersburg, Tex.

Robert D. Madison, Ph.D.
Assistant Principal
Boys & Girls High School
Brooklyn, N.Y.

Alan Magee
Business Teacher
C-P.P.West High School
Painted Post, N.Y.

Teresa Marcella
Business Department Chair
Bensalem High School
Bensalem, Pa.

Tamera McCarthy
Business Education Instructor
Oconto High School
Oconto, Wis.

Patricia McRobert
Teacher Emeritus
Park Hill High School
Kansas City, Mo.

Joan Miller
Business Teacher
Darlington High School
Darlington, Wis.

James Monroe
Business Education Teacher
Greene Central High School
Snow Hill, N.C.

Cheryl A. Moore
Business Education Teacher
Ellison High School
Killeen, Tex.

Helen Morris
Business Education Teacher
Burl Co. Inst. Tech.
Westhampton, N.J.

William Morrison
Business Teacher
Windber Area
Windber, Pa.

Joyce Muhlenkamp
Business and Computer Science
Teacher
St. Henry High School
St. Henry, Ohio

Edward J. Murphy
Business Education Teacher
John Jay High School
Hopewell Junction, N.Y.

Rachel Nichols
Business/Computer Education
Teacher
Ridgewood Junior High
Arnold, Mo.

Angie Niebrugge
Business Education
Charleston High School
Charleston, Ill.

Susan Nunnally
TCP Dept. Chair,
Business Education Teacher,
Tech Prep Site Team Leader
Forsyth Central High School
Cumming, Ga.

Debby Odom
Business Teacher, Technology
Coordinator
Gruver High School
Gruver, Tex.

Azzie Olds
Business Teacher
North Caddo Magnet High School
Vivian, La.

Beth Patzke
Business Education Department
Chair
Baldwin-Woodville High School
Baldwin, Wis.

Jan Payne
Business Education Department
Head
Beaver Schools
Beaver, Okla.

Elaine Peeters
Business Teacher
North Rose-Wolcott High School
Wolcott, N.Y.

John R. Pehle
Vocation Department Chair
Lincoln-Way High School
East Campus
Frankfort, Ill.

Bobbi Pulver
Business Instructor
Three Lakes High School
Three Lakes, Wis.

Olivia Ramirez
Business/Computer Educator
Tornillo High School
Tornillo, Tex.

Lynn Retz
Business Instructor
Auburndale High School
Auburndale, Wis.

Paul Richmond
Business Department Chair
Thomas Edison High School
Elmia Heights, N.Y.

Marlene Roberts
Business Education
Teacher/School-to-Work
Coordinator
Gr. Johnstown High School
Johnstown, Pa.

Tim Rohlinger
Business Education Teacher
Kewaskum High School
Kewaskum, Wis.

Teri Roscka
Business Teacher
Twin Lakes High School
Monticello, Ind.

Sherry Rouner
Business Education
Mt. Vernon High School
Mt. Vernon, Mo.

Jason Russell
Business and Social Studies Teacher
Springs Valley
Frenchlick, Ind.

William Sanderson
Applied Academics Chairperson
Homewood-Flossmoor High
School
Flossmoor, Ill.

Keith A. Schneider
Business Education Instructor
Cambridge High School
Cambridge, Wis.

Sandra Schroeder
Business Education Teacher
New Lisbon Schools
New Lisbon, Wis.

Bernice Scozzafave
Business Education Teacher
Eastern High School
Lansing, Mich.

Katie B. Shaw Clements
Business Technology Ed.
Department Chair
Havana Northside High School
Havana, Fla.

Mary Shroyer
Business Department Chair
Northridge High School
Middlebury, Ind.

Susan Siler
Business/Computer Teacher
Huntley High School
Huntley, Ill.

Gail Sobel
Business Teacher
DeRuyter High School
DeRuyter, N.Y.

Joan Sountis
Business Education Department
Chairperson
Cliffside Park High
Cliffside Park, N.J.

Kathy Speichinger
Business Teacher
Belle High School
Belle, Mo.

Lois Stadtmiller
Business Department Head
Curwensville High School
Curwensville, Pa.

Diane Stefanisko
Business Teacher
Octorara High School
Atglen, Pa.

Deborah Surnbrock
Department Head, Business
Department
East Central High School
St. Leon, Ind.

Sandra Talley
Business Teacher
Sunny Hill
Fullerton, Calif.

Karen Teach
Business Education Teacher
Clear Springs High School
Clear Springs, Md.

Vince Tesi
Business Teacher
Colts Neck High School
Colts Neck, N.J.

Brandi Thomas
Computer Education Teacher
Soledad High School
Soledad, Calif.

Jim Tiedeman
Business Education Teacher
Benton High School
Benton, Wis.

Scott Truelove
Business Teacher
Hilltop High School
W. Unity, Ohio

Tresa Twenter
Business Teacher
Green Ridge High School
Green Ridge, Mo.

Joe Ward
Business Teacher
Tomlinson High School
Jackson, Mich.

Mary Warnke
Business Education Instructor
Brillion Public School
Brillion, Wis.

Libbey Watkins
Business Teacher
Sibley High School
Sibley, La.

Tracy Weller
Business Education Instructor
Albany R-III High School
Albany, Mo.

Diana White
Business Teacher
Holt County R-2
Mound City, Mo.

Lance White
Business Teacher
Round Lake High School
Round Lake, Ill.

Ruth Ann White
Business Teacher
White's Jr/Sr High School
Wabash, Ind.

Judy Williams
Business Teacher
N.Knox High School
Bicknell, Ind.

Nancy Yankee
Accounting and Business Teacher
Holden High School
Holden, Mo.

Table of Contents

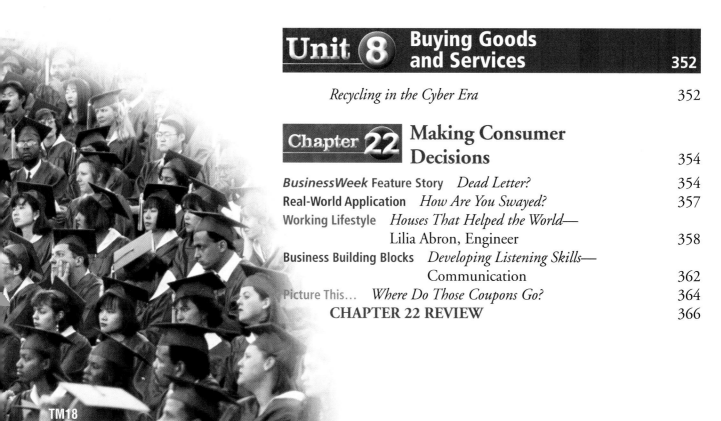

Understanding the Unit

Unit Structure

Introduction to Business is divided into 11 units, each beginning with a unit opener. The unit opener utilizes trivia to engage you in an introductory account of topics to come in the following chapters.

INTRODUCTION
The unit overview offers a real-world squib, with accompanying factoids about concepts covered in the unit. It introduces the concepts that will be explored, acting as a preview for what is to follow.

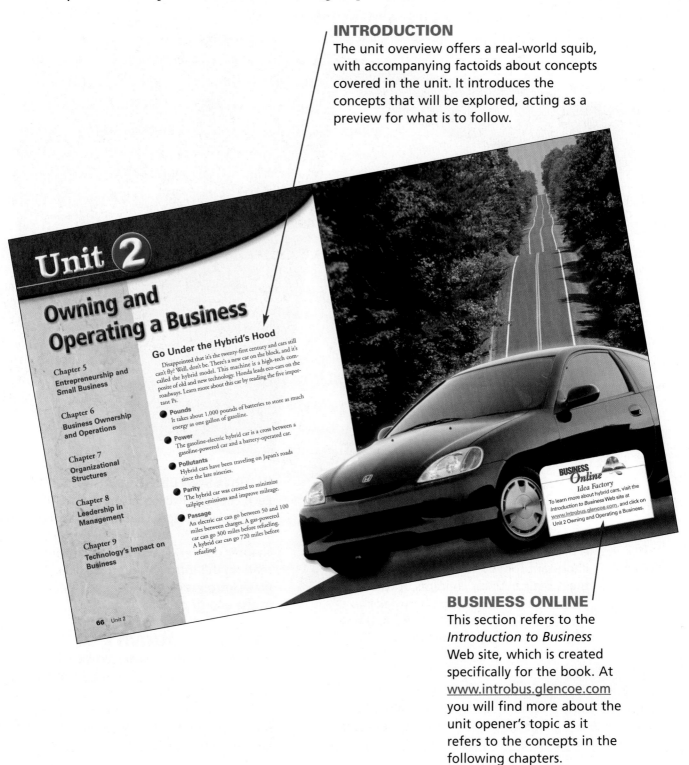

Unit 2

Owning and Operating a Business

Chapter 5
Entrepreneurship and Small Business

Chapter 6
Business Ownership and Operations

Chapter 7
Organizational Structures

Chapter 8
Leadership in Management

Chapter 9
Technology's Impact on Business

Go Under the Hybrid's Hood

Disappointed that it's the twenty-first century and cars still can't fly? Well, don't be. There's a new car on the block, and it's called the hybrid model. This machine is a high-tech composite of old and new technology. Honda leads eco-cars on the roadways. Learn more about this car by reading the five important Ps.

● **Pounds**
It takes about 1,000 pounds of batteries to store as much energy as one gallon of gasoline.

● **Power**
The gasoline-electric hybrid car is a cross between a gasoline-powered car and a battery-operated car.

● **Pollutants**
Hybrid cars have been traveling on Japan's roads since the late nineties.

● **Parity**
The hybrid car was created to minimize tailpipe emissions and improve mileage.

● **Passage**
An electric car can go between 50 and 100 miles between charges. A gas-powered car can go 300 miles before refueling. A hybrid car can go 720 miles before refueling!

BUSINESS Online
Idea Factory
To learn more about hybrid cars, visit the *Introduction to Business* Web site at www.introbus.glencoe.com, and click on Unit 2 Owning and Operating a Business.

66 Unit 2

BUSINESS ONLINE
This section refers to the *Introduction to Business* Web site, which is created specifically for the book. At www.introbus.glencoe.com you will find more about the unit opener's topic as it refers to the concepts in the following chapters.

Understanding the Chapter

Chapter Structure

The chapter opener gives you a brief introduction to the new material that will be covered in the chapter. Each chapter begins with a list of the skills and knowledge you can expect to have mastered once you have completed the chapter. Photographs expand and reinforce the business and economic concepts presented in each chapter.

LEARNING OBJECTIVES
These direct your reading as you progress through the chapter. Use these as a tool for test review.

WHY IT'S IMPORTANT
A brief paragraph explains why it is important for you to learn and understand these basic business concepts. It will help you to make a connection between the specific concepts being discussed and how they fit into the larger picture.

KEY WORDS
This is a list of the key words that are introduced throughout the chapter. Key words are printed in boldface and highlighted the first time that they are introduced and defined within the text.

BUSINESSWEEK FEATURE STORY
Each chapter incorporates a different *BusinessWeek* story that applies to the chapter. The first part of the story is introduced in the chapter opener. The story in its entirety may be read on the *Introduction to Business* Web site at www.introbus.glencoe.com. It reappears again at the end of each chapter.

EXTENSION ACTIVITY
After reading the BusinessWeek Feature Story, you're presented with a real-world situation. You'll be called on to apply common sense and business knowledge. Each activity is different.

Understanding the Features

Introduction to Business Features

Each chapter contains a selection of the features you'll read about on the following pages. Each varies in length and focus. They help you understand the practical and real-world application of the concepts that you master throughout this book. While they vary in content, they all show a realistic and creative approach to business. Each feature ends with a question that asks you to expand on what you learned with critical and creative thinking.

Technology Toolkit

You'll find this in the margin in particular chapters. It informs you about a specific aspect of a technology gadget used in the business world. It expands the scope of technology to illustrate its impact on culture, language, ethnic heritage, political philosophy, social and economic systems, shared history, multinational economic unions, international trade, competition of resources, job specialization, and environmental factors. The Critical Thinking question in each feature asks you to analyze, interpret, and apply a concept in the feature.

Consider This...

You'll find this in the margin in particular chapters. Each highlights real-world companies or situations in the business world. Topics may encompass technology, community development, international business development, business's influence on the environment, contemporary business culture, sociological and environmental influences on business, economic development, and so on. The Analyze question at the end will allow you to tackle a business problem using your own unique critical- and creative-thinking skills.

Business Building Blocks

You'll find this feature in various chapters. This presents important skills that are necessary for success in school and on the job. Each feature focuses on communication, math, or analytical skills. First the topic is introduced and then you

Math

have an activity to practice the skill.

Usually the adjoining box includes tips or a how-to list. Often it is important to read the material in this box before completing the Practice.

Understanding the Features

Working Lifestyle

What are you doing at 10 A.M.?

This career profile appears in different chapters. Each chapter features a different person, one person representing an occupation from 1 of the 16 career clusters outlined by the U.S. Department of Education. The narrative is based upon what each person does on the job at 10 A.M. in the morning.

The "Salary" gives you the average income of an occupation profiled as well as the salary range. "Outlook for This Career" offers a few words about the particular position's future. The final question, "Connecting Careers Activity," focuses on recent developments in business and asks you to speculate how these might affect the career in an ever-changing world.

Health Science

CAREER PATH

You Make the Call

You'll find this in a variety of chapters in this book.

This is a short feature, which poses an ethical quandary. You're asked a few follow-up questions about how to react to the situation. This takes into account many of the concepts you'll learn in the unit and its chapters. Often this is about weighing personal gain versus social responsibility.

Writing for Business

Portfolio Activity

You'll find this in a variety of chapters. This new, interdisciplinary skills feature asks you to plot and write your own original story. Creativity is highly encouraged in research and writing. The first paragraph introduces you to the subject and offers directions. It's important to carefully read this paragraph. Then you'll "Pick a Path."

This is your chance to select which story you want to pursue. Each is a little different, but only choose one. "The Setting" gives you the place of the story; "Rising Action" offers specific events you'll need to take into account; and the two-step process is how to work your way to a climax, or conclusion (which you control).

Lastly, the "Conclusion" will ask you to evaluate your story by completing a specific language arts task in order to give your story structure and shape. This feature integrates and applies reading comprehension, written communication, application of business vocabulary, and the decision-making process.

Understanding the Features

Visual Narratives

REAL-WORLD APPLICATION

In every chapter you'll find a real-world photo essay on a company, a person, or contemporary issue. Each is a four-part photo essay, which falls at the top, right-hand corner of every page between the chapter opener and chapter review. This is a visual way of studying the concepts that are addressed in the chapter.

GLOBAL ECONOMY

This narrative uses a map and squibs to expound on a concept presented in a chapter.

PICTURE THIS...

There are seven of these visual narratives in the book. Each describes a particular technological process. People often take for granted how things work without really breaking down and understanding the construction. This gives you a deeper understanding of the world around you.

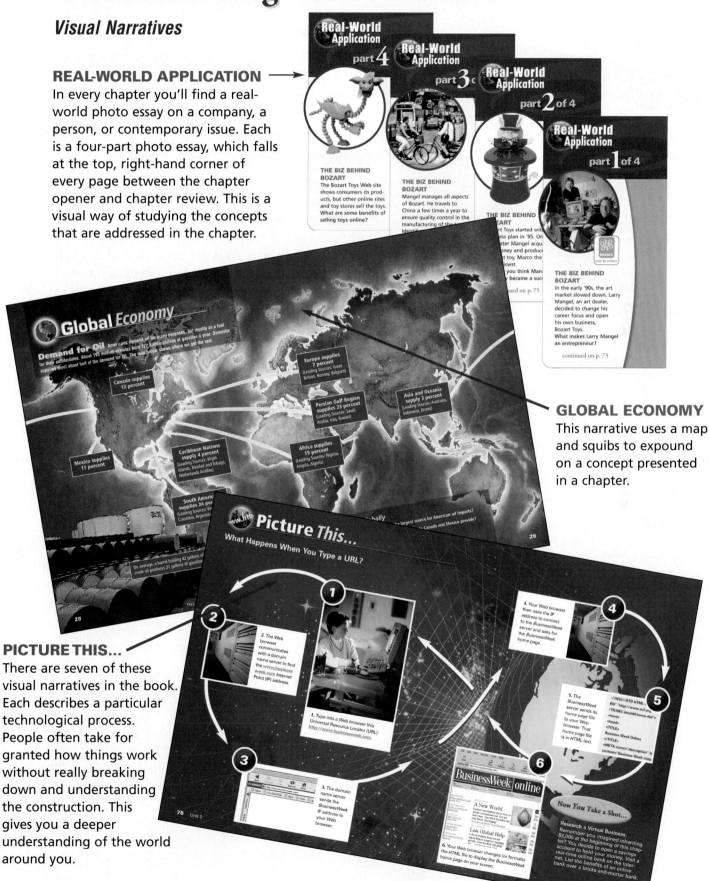

Understanding Assessment

Review Structure

Each major concept in each chapter ends with a section called Fast Review. The section assessment is a brief version of the Chapter Review found at the end of the chapter. This gives you an opportunity to review the major concepts just covered. Activities and questions help you review important business and economic terms and concepts.

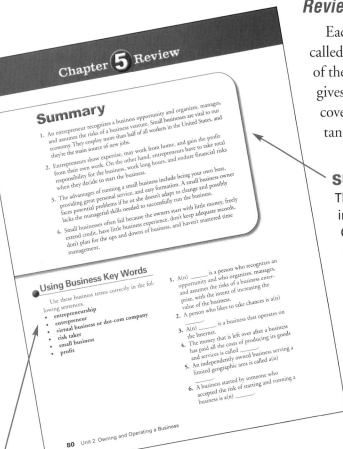

SUMMARY

This reinforces the Learning Objectives that were introduced in the chapter opener. Each Learning Objective is summarized point by point in this small section. You may use this as a study tool to remind yourself of major concepts in the chapter. This is a list of the main ideas of the chapter for quick review and recall.

CRITICAL THINKING

These questions offer you the chance to show your application and more in-depth understanding of the concepts in the chapter. You'll be asked to interpret, analyze, compare, or make judgments based on ideas from the chapter.

USING BUSINESS KEY WORDS

This activity will call on your recollection of the vocabulary words introduced throughout the chapter. You'll be asked to complete the sentences or match the key word to its definition.

REVIEW WHAT YOU LEARNED

This exercise requires recall of information found in the text.

UNDERSTANDING BUSINESS CONCEPTS

This section asks you to apply the concepts and skills learned in the chapter.

VIEWING AND REPRESENTING

This section asks you to use your visual literacy skills to deconstruct an image, which relates to business and economics. The photograph may be metaphorical or straightforward. Use the concepts you have learned in a chapter to complete this activity.

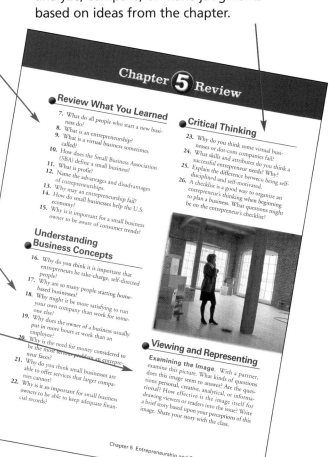

Understanding Assessment

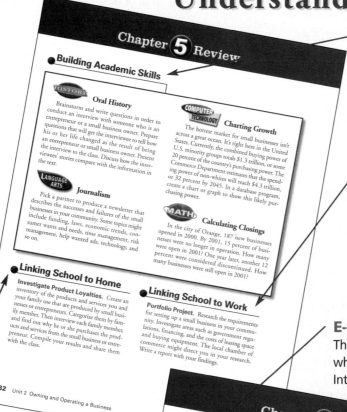

BUILDING ACADEMIC SKILLS
This section is an interdisciplinary approach to business and economics concepts. Language arts, computer technology, math, history, social science, and science are the subjects you might be asked to explore in this section in order to complete an activity.

LINKING SCHOOL TO WORK
These activities ask you to explore your work experiences, or the specific work experiences of community leaders or business owners. You may interview someone who is employed to gain his or her perspective. The principles in this activity relate to the business and economics concepts covered in the chapter.

E-HOMEWORK
This element consists of two activities which are designed to enhance your Internet and technology skills.

BUSINESSWEEK ANALYZING THE FEATURE STORY
The BusinessWeek Feature Story introduced at the beginning of the chapter closes the Chapter Review. This activity asks you read the entire feature article before answering the questions in this section.

LINKING SCHOOL TO HOME
The activity is designed to relate business principles to your home environment. You may be asked to apply practical and analytical skills of business concepts to your home life.

CONNECTING ACADEMICS
This activity places you in a hypothetical situation where you have to make a decision. Math, computer technology, language arts, science, social science, and history are all subjects you might be asked to explore in conjunction with business concepts presented in the chapter.

BUSINESS ONLINE
"The Full Story" heading contains a Web-based version of the *BusinessWeek* Feature Story. Read the entire article at **www.introbus.glencoe.com.**

CREATIVE JOURNAL ACTIVITY
This may be used as a portfolio activity, which offers you the opportunity to demonstrate the skills that you master after you have read the chapter. A portfolio or journal contains pieces of successful projects and samples of your

Understanding Unit Assessment

BusinessWeek Seminar

A four-page *BusinessWeek* Seminar asks you to explore career, small business, technology, or global business in-depth. Each seminar asks you to research a topic by using news magazines, newspapers, and the Internet. It requires research, exploration, interaction, critical thinking, analysis, and assessment.

INVESTIGATE THE IMAGES
These questions will focus on analyzing your observations when looking at photographs on the *BusinessWeek* Seminar opening page. Then you will think critically about the media and how it represents culture and newsworthy trends.

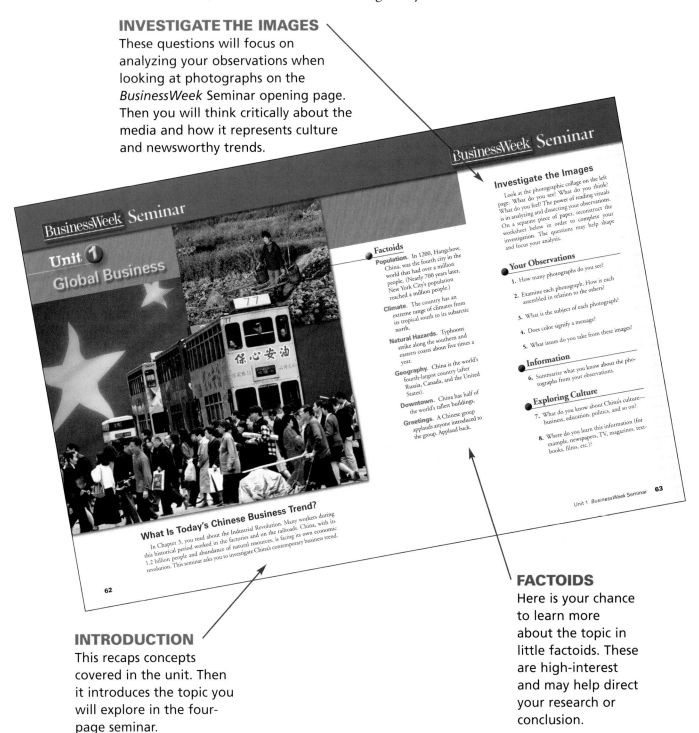

INTRODUCTION
This recaps concepts covered in the unit. Then it introduces the topic you will explore in the four-page seminar.

FACTOIDS
Here is your chance to learn more about the topic in little factoids. These are high-interest and may help direct your research or conclusion.

Understanding Unit Assessment

BusinessWeek Seminar

PREPARATION
This section offers a brief summary of the topic covered in the seminar and actual materials needed for completion. It introduces the concepts that will be explored in-depth, acting as a preview of what is to come.

PROCEDURES
This step-by-step process informs you of how the seminar will be completed in an organized manner.

CHART IT
A brief paragraph explains how to create a graphic organizer about your topic. The illustration is also an example of how your version might look. Often this is an individual and group discussion activity. It requires you to use your conceptual and analytical skills.

ANALYZE AND CONCLUDE
After analyzing, discussing, and studying "Chart It," this section presents you with critical thinking questions. These will ask you to examine all of your research and to give conclusive answers.

BECOMING AN INFORMED CONSUMER
This is the last section of the four-page *BusinessWeek* Seminar. Here is your chance to polish your business knowledge by applying it to your own life. Evaluate the concepts you explored in the unit and the seminar. Make decisions based on ideas from the unit.

BUSINESSWEEK ONLINE
This element consists of further research about the topic you explored in the seminar. The "Further Exploration" heading contains the Web site and specific topic for you to enhance your knowledge and Internet skills.

BusinessWeek Seminar

Taking Aim at Global Business

Preparation

Find out why Chinese workers are migrating from farming villages to industrial cities, and how their moves affect business trends in China.

Objective

In this *BusinessWeek* Seminar, you will:

- **Research** the media to find articles on Chinese workers' migration patterns.
- **Investigate** the topic by using a journalist's arsenal of key questions—who, what, where, when, why, and how.
- **Interview** a classmate who poses as a migrant worker.

Materials Needed
- ✓ Recent copies of *BusinessWeek*, the *Wall Street Journal*, or Internet access
- ✓ Paper
- ✓ Pencil
- ✓ Small tape recorder (if it's available)
- ✓ Poster board
- ✓ Markers

Procedures

1. Choose a research partner.
2. Find and read a recent article written about the migration of Chinese workers. If possible, use the Internet to access the Web site of a business publication. For example, access the *BusinessWeek* Web site at **www.businessweek.com**. Click on the tab labeled "Global Business" or use the internal search engine to locate the topic.

64   Unit

BusinessWeek *BONUS: THE NEW SOFTWARE STARS*

BusinessWeek

Taiwan Banks

India

Daimler's Board

LVMH

100 million rural workers have flooded into China's cities, and millions more may be on the way. Here is the story of one family, the Miss of Hongshuasen

THE GREAT MIGRATION

3. Consider the following issues:
   - Why are people migrating to the cities?
   - What problems do they encounter?
   - Are the benefits worth the risks?
   - How does this affect China's economy?

4. Create a role-play in which one partner plays a newspaper reporter interviewing a migrant worker, and the other plays the worker. In your role-play, you should describe why the worker left his or her village and what his or her feelings are about living and working in a big city. Make sure to discuss living conditions in the village versus living conditions in the city. The role-play should be two to three minutes long. Present it to the class.

BusinessWeek Seminar

Chart It

With your partner make two lists: "Advantages of Migrating to the City" and "Disadvantages of Migrating to the City," and list what you think are the three most important of each. As a class, reproduce the table that is below and create a comprehensive list on the board.

Migrating to the City

Advantages	Disadvantages

Analyze and Conclude

After studying the comprehensive list on the board, answer the questions below:
1. **Making Inference.** What is the most important reason a worker has for migrating to a city in China?
2. **Recognizing Cause and Effect.** What are the dangers of migrating?
3. **Interpreting the Facts.** How will the migration of workers influence the economy of China and, therefore, business in China?

Becoming an Informed Citizen

Congratulations, you finished the seminar. Now it's time to reflect on the decisions you made.

Critical Thinking. Why did you choose to report certain aspects of your research and not other parts of the information? Did an article's images play any part in your decision making? Or did you pick an article based on its title?

Analyzing Your Future. How will China's migration patterns affect you as a citizen of the world?

BUSINESS Online

Further Exploration

To find out more about workers' migration patterns in other countries, visit the Glencoe *Introduction to Business* Web site www.introbus.glencoe.com.

TM31

Why It's Important

Why Study Business?

It's Thursday evening, and you're watching the local news. A reporter talks about the price of consumer goods. A little later she mentions an online company just went bankrupt. The federal government just announced a change in interest rates. What does this mean? What difference does it make? More than ever before, you need to understand the world. What happens in business and government will make a difference in your life. Change comes faster and faster. Companies come and go, and new types of companies appear. Now is an exciting time to study business.

THE DECISION-MAKING PROCESS. At the core of your everyday life is the ability to choose. To make a choice you have to follow a decision-making process. This process may be decided instantly or over the course of time, with strategic planning. The process has these essential steps:

Step 1. Identify the problem.
Step 2. List the alternatives.
Step 3. Determine the pros and cons.
Step 4. Make the best decision.
Step 5. Evaluate your decision.

Whether you're buying a T-shirt to support a charitable cause or making a decision to acquire a multi-billion dollar company, this five-step process is used every day. (Chapter 1 gives an in-depth discussion about each step.)

You hear news about the ups and downs of the economy, the closing of some companies, the formation of others, and the future of industries. All of you are affected by business. All of you are consumers, most of you will have several jobs during your lifetime.

THE VALUE OF KNOWLEDGE. You'll probably have several jobs during your lifetime. The more education you have, the better your income. So you're very smart to choose to study business. This course features careers and business opportunities that are available to you. The business world has all types of jobs, and you'll learn about those jobs and the businesses that furnish employment to the millions of workers in the economy.

What Do the Concepts in Introduction to Business Mean?

1. **Government and Democracy.** Understanding the workings of government helps you become a better citizen.

2. **Economic Factors.** Understanding production, distribution, and consumption helps you see how economic factors influence your daily life.

3. **Global Connections.** Being aware of global interdependence helps you make decisions and deal with the difficult issues you'll encounter.

4. **Science and Technology.** Understanding the roles of science and technology helps you see their impact on the society today and the roles they'll play in the future.

5. **Geography and History.** Geography helps you understand how humans interact with their environment.

6. **Civic Rights and Responsibilities.** Recognizing democratic principles will help you claim and fulfill your own civic duties.

7. **Groups and Institutions.** Identifying how political and social groups and institutions work helps you work with others.

8. **Continuity and Change.** Recognizing historic roots helps you understand why things are the way they are today.

9. **Culture and Traditions.** Being aware of culture differences and diversity issues helps you better understand yourself and others.

10. **Individual Action.** Recognizing the contributions you can make to the world will influence the world.

Unit Planning Guide

The information in the Unit Planning Guide gives you a comprehensive overview of the unit content along with the background information, which will help you provide the best possible learning situation for your class. On the first two pages of each unit planning guide, you can easily identify unit objectives and unit enrichment resources.

You'll also find program resources available to you for each chapter in the unit. Refer to these pages as you plan each lesson in order to make the most of the numerous instructional materials included with *Introduction to Business.*

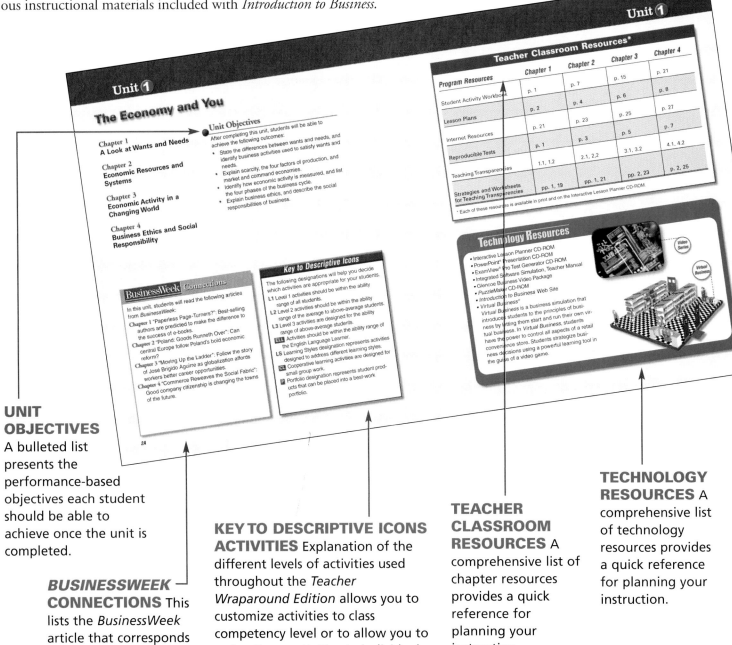

UNIT OBJECTIVES
A bulleted list presents the performance-based objectives each student should be able to achieve once the unit is completed.

BUSINESSWEEK CONNECTIONS This lists the *BusinessWeek* article that corresponds with each chapter. A brief synopsis follows each article title.

KEY TO DESCRIPTIVE ICONS ACTIVITIES Explanation of the different levels of activities used throughout the *Teacher Wraparound Edition* allows you to customize activities to class competency level or to allow you to assign these activities to individual students on the basis of personal ability.

TEACHER CLASSROOM RESOURCES A comprehensive list of chapter resources provides a quick reference for planning your instruction.

TECHNOLOGY RESOURCES A comprehensive list of technology resources provides a quick reference for planning your instruction.

Scope and Sequence

If you're using, or plan to use, the Academic Standards of Learning to guide changes in your business education curriculum, you can be assured that *Introduction to Business* aligns the disciplines. On the second two-page layout of each unit planning guide, you'll find a table presenting correlations between *Introduction to Business* and the Academic Standards of Learning.

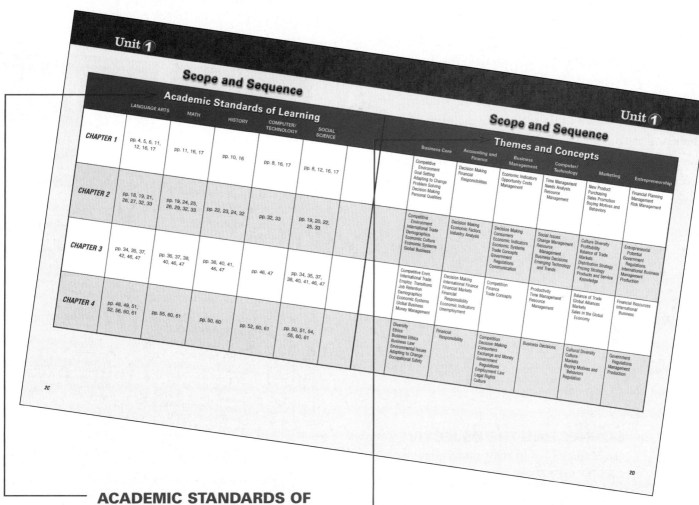

ACADEMIC STANDARDS OF LEARNING In-text content, activities, and assessment related to the disciplines are detailed in each chapter.

THEMES AND CONCEPTS Scope and Sequence aligns *Introduction to Business* with the six major themes and concepts in business. Review the Scope and Sequence at the beginning of the unit in order to review each chapter's inclusion of important business concepts.

Introduction

Today business students bring to the classroom a variety of learning styles and needs. The *Teacher Wraparound Edition* of *Introduction to Business* provides you and your students with a wide range of activities to fit your classroom needs. Designed to assist both new and experienced teachers by providing a wealth of teaching suggestions, resources, and professional notes, the *Teacher Wraparound Edition* has been designed as a convenience for you and to allow you to maximize the program's effectiveness.

The Four-Step Teaching Plan

The structure of the *Teacher Wraparound Edition* places a four-step teaching plan, text answers, critical thinking activities, discussion questions, cooperative learning

Focus

The Focus introduces new material. You first need to gain students' attention and interest. Therefore, the first step in the four-step process is to focus the students' interest through an activity that makes the material relevant to them and encourages them to want to continue to explore the chapter. Complete the Focus activity within the first several minutes of class; it provides a motivational lead-in to the concepts that will be presented later in the section.

INTRODUCING THE CHAPTER
gives you a synopsis of what is to come in the chapter.

CONNECTING THE OBJECTIVES
raises questions in relation to chapter objectives.

BUSINESSWEEK FEATURE STORY
briefly describes the article at the beginning of the chapter, which should be read in its entirety before the end of the chapter. The entire article is available on the *Introduction to Business* Web site or in the *Teacher Resource Binder.*

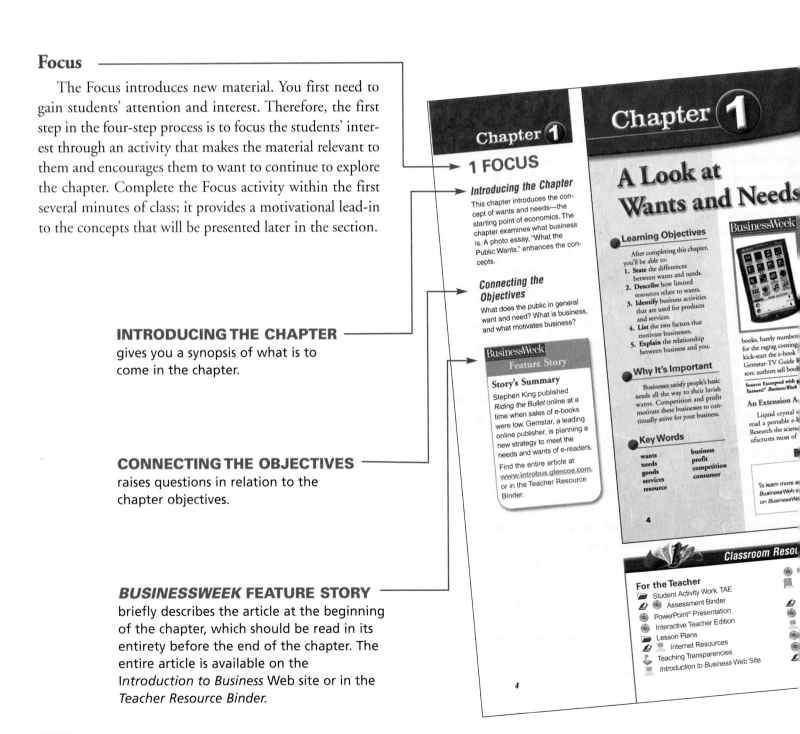

activities, as well as additional teaching notes on the same page as the related student text. Each section of each chapter in the *Teacher Wraparound Edition* is divided into four instructional sections according to a master approach designed to help you develop the chapter concepts and materials in an organized, consistent manner. This widely accepted instructional method develops students' understanding of subject matter while providing a consistent framework that makes it easy for you to teach the material. The four steps in the plan are Focus, Teach, Assess, and Close.

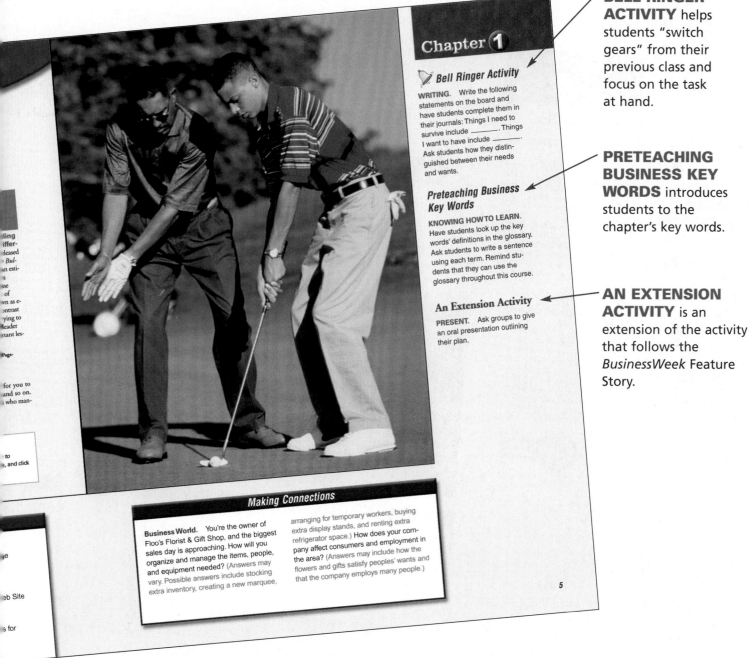

Chapter 1

Bell Ringer Activity

WRITING. Write the following statements on the board and have students complete them in their journals: Things I need to survive include ———. Things I want to have include ———. Ask students how they distinguished between their needs and wants.

Preteaching Business Key Words

KNOWING HOW TO LEARN. Have students look up the key words' definitions in the glossary. Ask students to write a sentence using each term. Remind students that they can use the glossary throughout this course.

An Extension Activity

PRESENT. Ask groups to give an oral presentation outlining their plan.

Making Connections

Business World. You're the owner of Floo's Florist & Gift Shop, and the biggest sales day is approaching. How will you organize and manage the items, people, and equipment needed? (Answers may vary. Possible answers include stocking extra inventory, creating a new marquee, arranging for temporary workers, buying extra display stands, and renting extra refrigerator space.) How does your company affect consumers and employment in the area? (Answers may include how the flowers and gifts satisfy peoples' wants and that the company employs many people.)

5

BELL RINGER ACTIVITY helps students "switch gears" from their previous class and focus on the task at hand.

PRETEACHING BUSINESS KEY WORDS introduces students to the chapter's key words.

AN EXTENSION ACTIVITY is an extension of the activity that follows the *BusinessWeek* Feature Story.

Teach

The Teach section contains the central core of the lesson, encompassing a teaching plan designed to give you maximum flexibility to meet the learning needs of your class. The suggestions offered in this section employ a wide variety of approaches to support your classroom instruction. For example, you'll find discussion starters to get the class involved in cooperative learning activities and critical thinking activities. Appropriate teaching activities at three different levels relate the chapter content to other key subjects such as math, communications, problem solving, decision making, and human relations. In addition, other activities suitable for independent practice are here for you to assign as needed.

BUSINESS CONNECTION applies a real-world example to the concepts introduced in the chapter.

DEVELOP CONCEPTS activity offers students a chance to engage in the concepts.

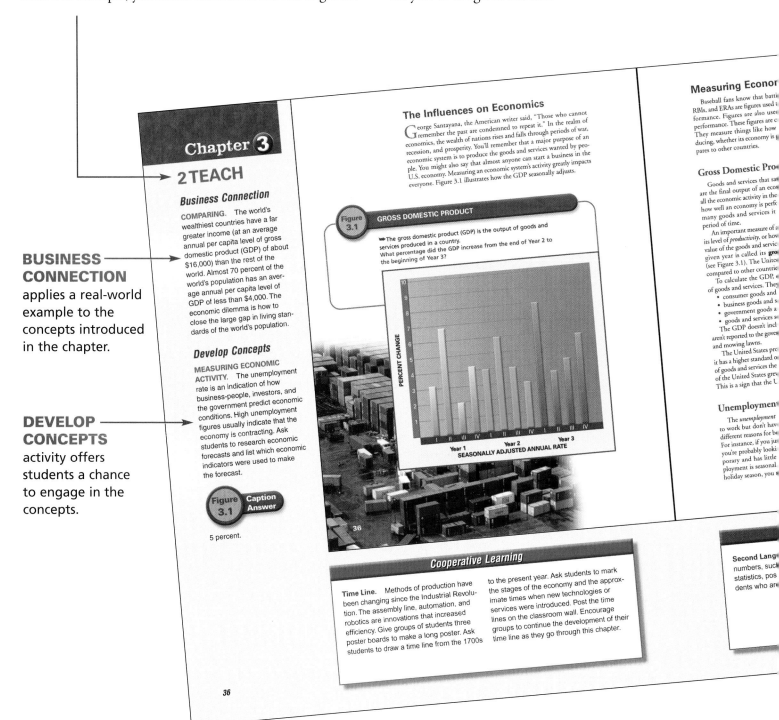

Chapter 3

2 TEACH

Business Connection

COMPARING. The world's wealthiest countries have a far greater income (at an average annual per capita level of gross domestic product (GDP) of about $16,000) than the rest of the world. Almost 70 percent of the world's population has an average annual per capita level of GDP of less than $4,000. The economic dilemma is how to close the large gap in living standards of the world's population.

Develop Concepts

MEASURING ECONOMIC ACTIVITY. The unemployment rate is an indication of how business-people, investors, and the government predict economic conditions. High unemployment figures usually indicate that the economy is contracting. Ask students to research economic forecasts and list which economic indicators were used to make the forecast.

Figure 3.1 Caption Answer

5 percent.

The Influences on Economics

George Santayana, the American writer said, "Those who cannot remember the past are condemned to repeat it." In the realm of economics, the wealth of nations rises and falls through periods of war, recession, and prosperity. You'll remember that a major purpose of an economic system is to produce the goods and services wanted by people. You might also say that almost anyone can start a business in the U.S. economy. Measuring an economic system's activity greatly impacts everyone. Figure 3.1 illustrates how the GDP seasonally adjusts.

Figure 3.1 **GROSS DOMESTIC PRODUCT**

The gross domestic product (GDP) is the output of goods and services produced in a country. What percentage did the GDP increase from the end of Year 2 to the beginning of Year 3?

PERCENT CHANGE

Year 1   Year 2   Year 3
SEASONALLY ADJUSTED ANNUAL RATE

36

Cooperative Learning

Time Line. Methods of production have been changing since the Industrial Revolution. The assembly line, automation, and robotics are innovations that increased efficiency. Give groups of students three poster boards to make a long poster. Ask students to draw a time line from the 1700s to the present year. Ask students to mark the stages of the economy and the approximate times when new technologies or services were introduced. Post the time lines on the classroom wall. Encourage groups to continue the development of their time line as they go through this chapter.

Measuring Econom

Baseball fans know that batti RBIs, and ERAs are figures used t formance. Figures are also use performance. These figures are c They measure things like how ducing, whether its economy is g pares to other countries.

Gross Domestic Pro

Goods and services that sa are the final output of an eco all the economic activity in the how well an economy is perfo many goods and services in period of time.

An important measure of a its level of *productivity*, or how value of the goods and servic given year is called its **gro** (see Figure 3.1). The Unite compared to other countrie

To calculate the GDP, of goods and services. They
- consumer goods and
- business goods and s
- government goods a
- goods and services s

The GDP doesn't incl aren't reported to the gover and mowing lawns.

The United States pro it has a higher standard o of goods and services the of the United States grev This is a sign that the U

Unemploymen

The *unemployment* to work but don't hav different reasons for be For instance, if you ju you're probably looki porary and has little ployment is seasonal holiday season, you

Second Lang numbers, suc statistics, pos dents who ar

TECHNOLOGY RESOURCES directs you to a technology resource applicable to teaching the chapter.

INDEPENDENT PRACTICE includes activities in which students work by themselves to demonstrate and rehearse new knowledge.

THINKING CRITICALLY activities offer students the chance to demonstrate a more in-depth understanding of the chapter's concepts.

DISCUSSION STARTER helps you involve students in chapter material. This promotes learning by encouraging students to use dialogue as a tool to enhance thinking and understanding.

INDIVIDUALIZED PRACTICE includes activities which have graduated levels of difficulty. You may assign one of the three activities depending on students' abilities.

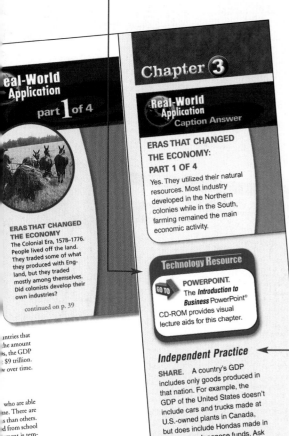

Chapter 3

Real-World Application part 1 of 4

ERAS THAT CHANGED THE ECONOMY
The Colonial Era, 1578–1776. People lived off the land. They traded some of what they produced with England, but they traded mostly among themselves. Did colonists develop their own industries?

continued on p. 39

Real-World Application Caption Answer

ERAS THAT CHANGED THE ECONOMY: PART 1 OF 4
Yes. They utilized their natural resources. Most industry developed in the Northern colonies while in the South, farming remained the main economic activity.

Technology Resource

GO TO POWERPOINT. The *Introduction to Business* PowerPoint® CD-ROM provides visual lecture aids for this chapter.

Independent Practice

SHARE. A country's GDP includes only goods produced in that nation. For example, the GDP of the United States doesn't include cars and trucks made at U.S.-owned plants in Canada, but does include Hondas made in Ohio using Japanese funds. Ask students to share other examples and to write these in their journals. **LS**

Thinking Critically

CONTEMPLATING. You're daydreaming and you start thinking about your career choices. You've heard people talking about automation replacing humans in the workplace. How does this affect the unemployment rate? The GDP?

37

3 Economic Activity in a Changing World **37**

(left partial column)
...ntries that ...he amount ...s, the GDP ...$9 trillion. ...w over time.

...who are able ...ne. There are ...s than others. ...d from school ...yment is tem- ...ype of unem- ...tail during the ...t of the year.

ividual Needs

English speakers tend to say the numbers very quickly and blur the sounds. To help students understand the meaning of the numbers, write them on the board.

Chapter 3

2 TEACH (Cont.)

Develop Concepts

THE BUSINESS CYCLE. Ask students to think about their favorite sports team. Does the team always win? Discuss winning and losing streaks, and compare them to how the economy has its ups and downs. Ask students what phase they think the economy is in now. What economic activity—prosperity, recession, depression, or recovery—they hear discussed in the media? (Answers will vary.)

Discussion Starter

MEANING. Call on students, and ask them what *standard of living* means. Ask them to compare the standard of living in the United States with that of other countries.

Figure 3.2 Caption Answer

Prosperity, recession, depression, and recovery.

40

The Business C

Once you enter the work... over the years. You could m... animation studio, get laid... copy shop. You could go b... and then get a job doing sp... of the changes you go thro...

Economies go through... petition, and changes in... changes seem to form pa... through slumps in the 19... nomic activity were alway... rise and fall of economic... The business cycle has f... and recovery. Figure 3.2.

Figure BUSINESS CYCLE MODEL

Chapter 5

2 TEACH (Cont.)

Discussion Starter

SMALL BUSINESSES. Have students list all the people they know who work for small businesses. Then discuss the types of jobs people hold at small businesses. These people work in what industries?

Individualized Practice

Tell the students that the market for small businesses is getting better.

L1 Divide students into pairs to discuss how the economy affects small business owners.

L2 Have students prepare a graph to show how small business ownership will look over the next 40 years.

L3 Have students research how big companies are teaming up with small companies to better serve the marketplace.

Figure 5.2 Caption Answer

Home furnishing stores, furniture stores, and paint, glass, and wallpaper stores. **CL**

74

Assess

The Assess section provides a variety of evaluation and reteaching activities designed to accommodate a wide range of learning abilities. Reteaching provides a means of presenting the same concept in a different manner, allowing you to help students who might have difficulty understanding the material. Enrichment activities found here will allow you to enhance the learning experience for those who have mastered the section content and are ready for more in-depth, experiential learning. The activities in this category provide you with a method of assessing students' comprehension before continuing with new information. The evaluation found in this section supplies you with a complete testing program that includes reproducible tests.

RETEACHING activities help reinforce section concepts.

ENRICHMENT activities extend students' understanding of the section.

EVALUATION refers you to the Section Assessment.

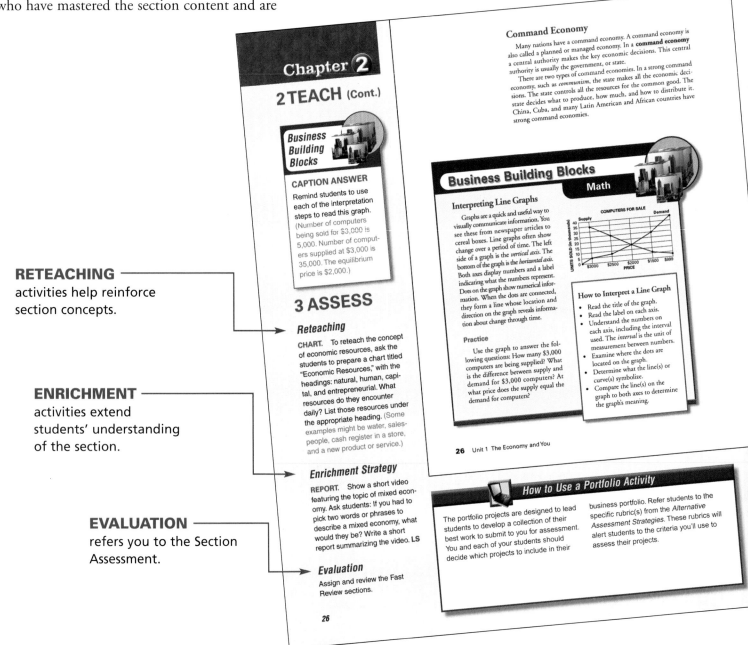

Close

The final step in the teaching plan, Close, allows students to demonstrate to you what they've learned. This is accomplished through a wide variety of activities including vocabulary review, review questions, and answering questions and solving problems about the material in the chapter. Close provides you with an activity to summarize the chapter's contents and to be sure students have retained the key points.

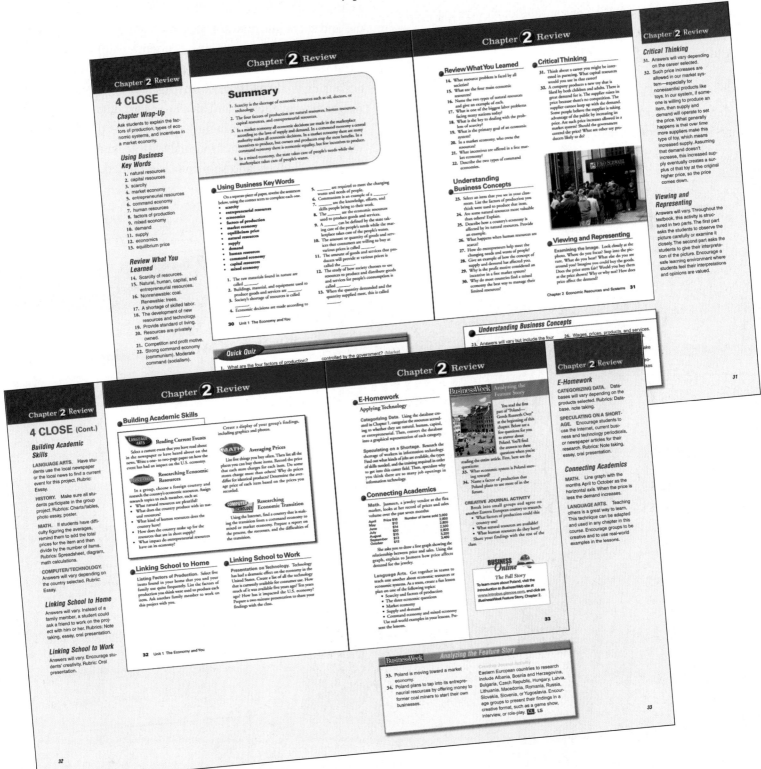

Reinforcement

The *Introduction to Business* program offers a complete selection of teacher support materials. Used in conjunction with the *Teacher Wraparound Edition*, these materials will enable you to tailor this program to meet the specific needs of your classes. The program resources are specifically developed to assist you in meeting your course objectives and maximizing student learning.

STUDENT ACTIVITY WORKBOOK provides students with reinforcement of problems and activities to review the content learned throughout each chapter.

INTEGRATED SOFTWARE SIMULATION, STUDENT EDITION

This simulation offers activities in Microsoft Works 6.0 for Windows, Microsoft Office 2000 for Windows, and AppleWorks 6 for Macintosh. In this real-world simulation, students learn how to use an integrated software program, such as Microsoft Office 2000. Students learn to use and share information between word processor, spreadsheet, and database programs. Students assume the role of a trainee in a media store and perform various job-related activities within the accounting, advertising, human resources, inventory, and sales departments. A series of Quickstart activities is included for each of the three software versions. A teacher manual with teaching tips, evaluation guidelines, and solutions is included.

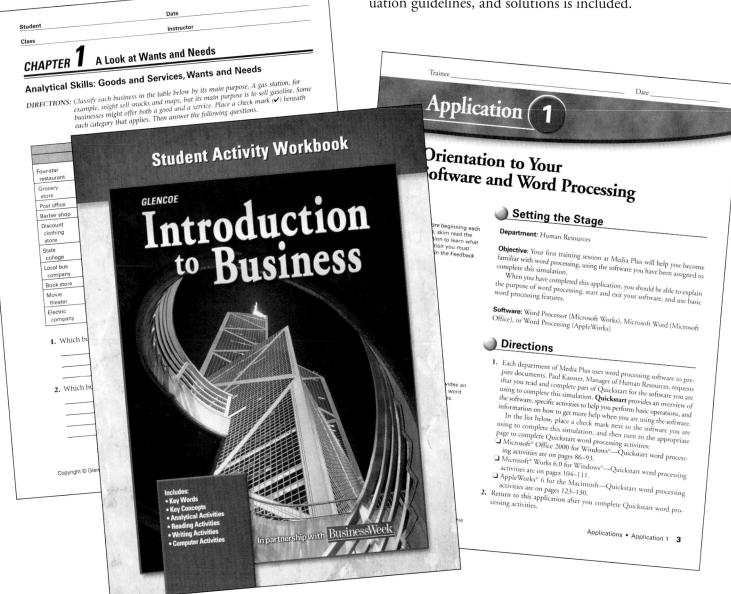

The Teacher Resource Binder

This contains the complete collection of excellent resources and teaching aids to support you:

The **STUDENT ACTIVITY WORKBOOK** with **TEACHER ANNOTATED EDITION** provides key word reviews, fact and idea reviews, computer applications for spreadsheet, database, presentation, and word processing programs.

Student _____ Date _____

Instructor _____

Class _____

CHAPTER 1 A Look at Wants and Needs

Analytical Skills: Goods and Services, Wants and Needs

DIRECTIONS: *Classify each business in the table below by its main purpose. A gas station, for example, might sell snacks and maps, but its main purpose is to sell gasoline. Some businesses might offer both a good and a service. Place a check mark (✔) beneath each category that applies. Then answer the following questions.*

	CATEGORIES					
	Good	Service	Want	Need	Public	Private
						✔
Four-star restaurant	✔	✔		✔		✔
Grocery store	✔		✔		✔	✔
Post office	✔	✔	✔			
Barber shop		✔				✔
Discount clothing store			✔		✔	
State college		✔	✔		✔	
		✔	✔			✔
			✔			✔
		✔	✔			
		✔			✔	✔

...ses fulfill wants that are still important to your daily life?
...ght not be necessary, but is important for communication. A college education
...ty, but is important for a promising future. Taking the bus might not be necessity,
...t transportation is important.

...nesses focus equally on goods and services?
...r offers food (a good) and someone to prepare and serve the food (a service). The
...not only sends mail, but sells mail supplies and stamps. Movie theaters screen
...service), but also sell goods such as popcorn and soda. Most retail stores, such as
...s, clothing stores, and grocery stores, offer some form of customer service.

Introduction to Business Chapter 1 **3**

...lencoe/McGraw-Hill

Teacher Annotated Edition
Student Activity Workbook

GLENCOE

Introduction to Business

Includes:
• Key Words
• Key Concepts
• Analytical Activities
• Reading Activities
• Writing Activities
• Computer Activities

In partnership with BusinessWeek

LESSON PLANS

provides a checklist of components for each chapter and cross-references all of the *Introduction to Business* resource materials. Using Lesson Plans allows you to organize and customize each lesson to your needs, allowing you to focus on the important task of teaching instead of planning.

INTERNET RESOURCES

will help you and your students understand the basics of the Internet and how it can be used as a source of information. Internet Resources includes 35 chapter-related activities that will help your students connect the Internet to their business education.

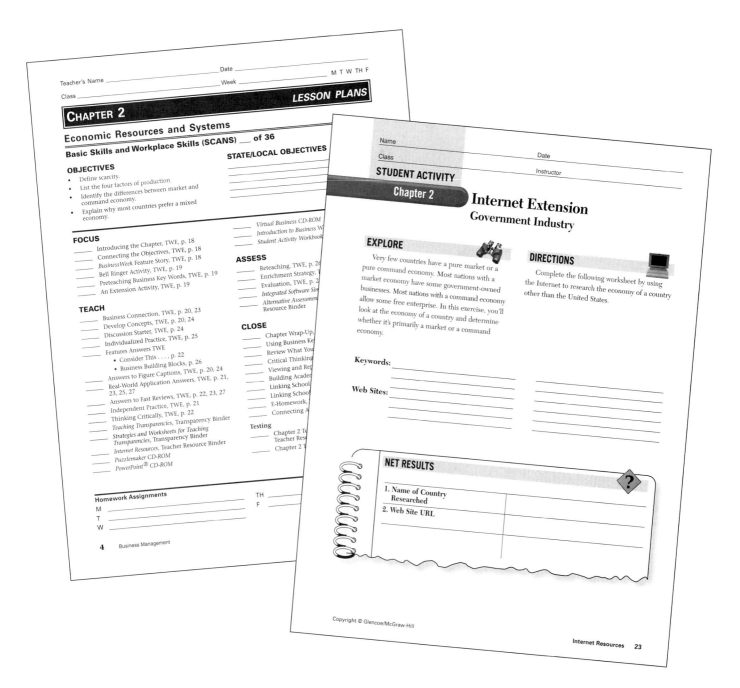

A *BUSINESSWEEK* **FEATURE STORY** found at the beginning of each chapter introduces the concepts as they appear in the real world. Copies of the entire stories are available on the *Introduction to Business* Web site and in the Teacher Resource Binder.

POWERPOINT® CD-ROM

The *Introduction to Business* **PowerPoint Presentations** provides over 1,400 high interest, visually-motivating slides that allow you to introduce each text section visually. Each chapter presentation includes text highlights, charts, graphs, and figures, as well as a graphic organizer that helps students conceptually structure a major business concept.

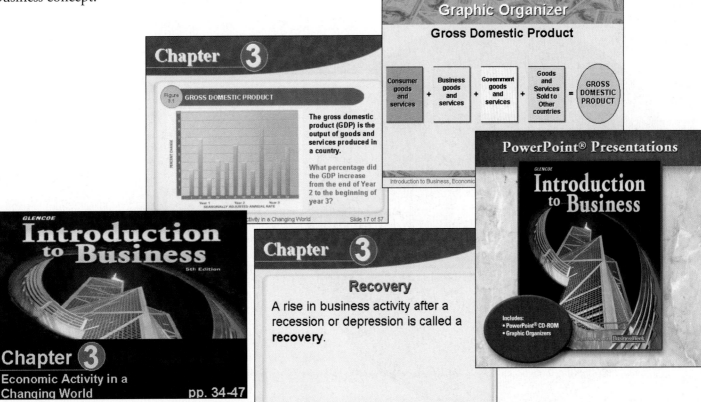

Assessment Binder

REPRODUCIBLE TESTS includes tests you can photocopy and hand out to your students. Find the answer key in the back of the book. Chapter, mid-term, unit, and final exams are included.

The **EXAMVIEW® PRO CD-ROM** is one of the most comprehensive test packages on the market. It provides an accurate and exhaustive source of text items for a wide variety of examination styles. It contains more than 1,500 questions, organized around learning objectives and categorized by chapter and unit.

Name _____ Date _____

CHAPTER *17* TEST

Managing Business Finances

A. TRUE/FALSE: In the left-hand space, write **T** if the statement is true or **F** if the statement is false.

_____ **1.** To run a business successfully, you must be able to put together a financial plan, budget, and keep track of your income and expenses.

_____ **2.** The first step in financial management is purchasing assets like equipment and supplies.

_____ **3.** One of the responsibilities of a financial manager is to find additional sources of funds.

_____ **4.** A cash budget tells you how much money your business will need over the long run.

_____ **5.** Your financial records are confidential so you don't have to show them to banks or investors.

B. MULTIPLE CHOICE: Choose the correct answer and write the letter in the left-hand space.

_____ **1.** Which of the following helps you predict how much money you'll need and how to control your spending?
    a. budget   **c.** owner's equity
    b. cash reserves   **d.** asset

_____ **2.** What is a one-year accounting period called?
    a. balance sheet   **c.** financial forecast
    b. operating costs   **d.** fiscal year

_____ **3.** Cash, equipment, buildings, supplies, inventory, and land are all examples of this.
    a. financial plan   **c.** assets
    b. accounting   **d.** budget

_____ **4.** Which is a report of net income or net loss over an accounting period?
    a. budget   **c.** balance sheet
    b. income statement   **d.** financial forecast

_____ **5.** What is the report of the financial state of your business on a certain date called?
    a. operating budget   **c.** income statement
    b. cash budget   **d.** balance sheet

         Reproducible Tests 33

GLENCOE

Introduction to Business

ExamView® Pro Test Generator

McGraw Hill **Glencoe McGraw-Hill**

Copyright © 2003 by the McGraw-Hill Companies 0-07-825859-6 P/N G7513X.10

Transparency Binder

TEACHING TRANSPARENCIES includes figures, charts, and graphs from *Introduction to Business* in a simple to use format.

Give the **STRATEGIES AND WORKSHEET FOR TEACHING TRANSPARENCIES** to students as you review graphs, charts, and figures from the Student Edition. Each worksheet asks the students to think critically about the visual information.

INTEGRATED SOFTWARE SIMULATION WITH TEACHER MANUAL

The simulation offers activities in Microsoft Works 6.0 for Windows, Microsoft Office 2000 for Windows, and AppleWorks 6 for Macintosh. In this real-world simulation, students learn how to use an integrated software program, such as Microsoft Office 2000. Students learn to use and share information between word processor, spreadsheet, and database programs. Students assume the role of a trainee in a media store and perform various job-related activities within the accounting, advertising, human resources, inventory, and sales departments. A series of Quickstart activities is included for each of the three software versions. A teacher manual with teaching tips, evaluation guidelines, and solutions is included.

Student _____ Class _____ Instructor _____

Date Assigned _____ Date Completed _____

WORKSHEET: Transparency 24-1 Consumers' Choices Require Caution

Directions: *Refer to Transparency 24-1 and answer the questions below.*

1. What are the steps to consider when joining a health club?

2. When is the best time to visit the club you are considering joining?

3. What are some questions to ask when visiting the club?

4. What are some questions to ask when considering its contract?

Copyright © Glencoe/McGraw-Hill

Integrated Software Simulation

GLENCOE

Integrated Software Simulation Teacher Manual

GLENCOE

Introduction to Business

In partnership with **BusinessWeek**

GLENCOE

Introduction to Business

Integrated Software Simulation

Mc Graw Hill **Glencoe McGraw-Hill**

Copyright © 2003 by the McGraw-Hill Companies 0-07-825859-6 P/N G75105.10

GLENCOE BUSINESS VIDEO PACKAGE
includes ten videos on various business topics like global business, forms of ownership, marketing, business etiquette, human resources management, personal finance, and so on. They introduce or reinforce concepts in *Introduction to Business.*

TEACHER MANUAL AND ACTIVITY GUIDE includes
original articles and *BusinessWeek* articles, with accompanying worksheets about the stories. Additionally, specific questions about the videos are also included, which aid students in their understanding.

Student	Class	Instructor
Date Assigned	Date Completed	

BusinessWeek Article Questions

1. According to this article, what is the small business edge? How does it affect marketing strategy?

Student	Class	Instructor
Date Assigned	Date Completed	

VIDEO 4: Marketing: Customer as a Stakeholder (11:11)

BusinessWeek Article: Help for Do-It-Yourself Marketers

point game plan for using materials you already have to find out more about your customers. Look at credit-card information to see where they live. Ask callers where they're from and

and Activity Guide **23**

The **_BUSINESSWEEK_** **BUSINESS POSTER PACKAGE** includes seven posters that are appropriate for business-related concepts. At the beginning of each unit you can put up a new poster and use it as a visual aid for classroom discussions.

The **PUZZLEMAKER CD-ROM** helps students review the key words in the book.

Program Resources

The **INTERACTIVE LESSON PLANNER** is easy-to-use software for course management. It combines electronic lesson plans with the convenience of the complete teacher resources package on the CD-ROM.

Introduction to Business Web site

ONLINE RESOURCES FOR TEACHERS, STUDENTS, AND PARENTS. The *Introduction to Business* Web site provides teachers, students, and parents with a wide range of materials. On the student site, chapter links bring a world of relevant business resources to enrich and extend classroom learning. The student site provides a fun-format concentration game to reinforce key words as well as homework hints, real-world applications, career information, and *BusinessWeek* articles.

The teacher site contains professional development resources, file downloads to *Virtual Business*, high school exit exam preparation materials, and senior project preparation materials, as well as real-world applications and *BusinessWeek* articles.

Glencoe's **TEACHING TODAY WEB** site features daily teaching tips, free downloadable materials, annotated Web resources, educational news, and more! The site contains a wealth of information on topics from high stakes testing to classroom management.

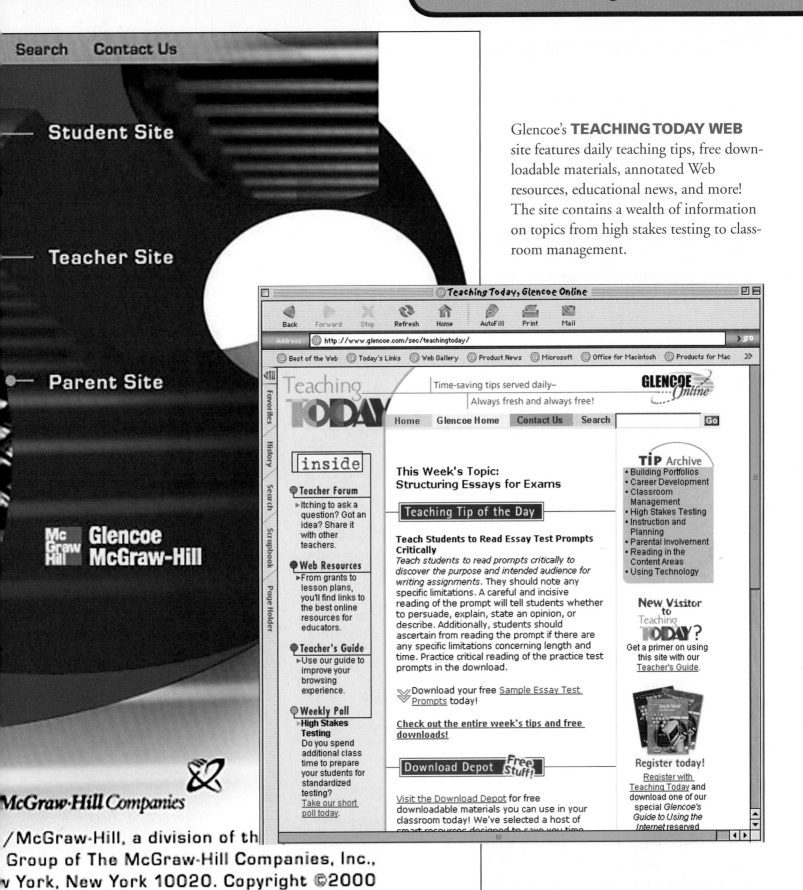

Virtual Business® and *Introduction to Business*

What Is Virtual Business?

Virtual Business is a fully visual marketing and business simulation that introduces students to the principles of marketing by letting them start and run their own businesses. Clearly relevant and truly exciting, *Virtual Business* will attract students to your class. *Virtual Business* is designed to complement, not replace, the current teaching model. *Virtual Business* is designed and developed based on research conducted by Knowledge Matters, Inc. for the U.S. Department of Education.

Unlike previous business simulations, *Virtual Business* is highly visual. Students learn by literally seeing how their decisions affect the business. In *Virtual Business* students have the power to control all aspects of a retail convenience store.

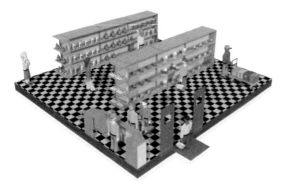

What You Get

The *Virtual Business* classroom package contains everything you need to get your students excited, motivated, and eager to learn about marketing. It also makes prep time a breeze.

The CD-ROM contains the *Virtual Business* software, an interactive tutorial, 21 pre-saved modular activities with lesson plans, and the *Virtual Business* Analyzer companion software for post-activity classroom analysis and discussion. Now you can have your students actually making business decisions including merchandising, pricing, promotion, and market research. It doesn't get any closer to the real thing. Your students can even utilize an exciting set of online tools located at **www.knowledgematters.com.**

Find a simulation solution by using *Virtual Business—Retailing* and/or *Virtual Business—Management*. Each has a slightly different angle on the world of running a business. The following is a list of what each simulation covers.

Virtual Business®—Retailing	Virtual Business®—Management
Introduction to Business	**Introduction to Business**
• Supply and Demand	• Running a Business
• Taking Business	• Starting a Business
• Business Writing	• International Issues
• Management Report	• Warehouse Design
• Business Cycles	• Fleet Management
• Monopoly Pricing	• Purchasing
	• Capital Equipment
Marketing	
• Pricing	**Information Technology**
• Promotion	• E-Commerce
• Merchandising	• Geographic Info Systems
• Staffing	• Telecommuting
• Purchasing	
• Market Research	**International Business**
• Target Marketing	• Country Selection
	• Exchange Rates
Finance	• Tariffs and Protectionism
• Financial Statements	
• Forecasting	**Management**
• Financial Alternatives	• Recruiting and Hiring
• Venture Capital	• Organizing
	• Employee Evaluation
Entrepreneurship	• Wages and Employment
• Start-up Basics	• Training
• The Business Plan	
• The Annual Report	
• Turnaround	
• Uncertainty	

Your students can enter the Future Business Leaders of America (FBLA) Virtual Business Challenge. Teams use *Virtual Business—Management* to compete on this online competitive event. You can find out more about the competitive event at **www.knowledgematters.com**. *Virtual Business—Management* is correlated to *Introduction to Business*. Using this business program helps your students get prepared for the event. You can find the activities and lesson plans created for the FBLA Virtual Business event on the course's Web site at **www.introbus.glencoe.com**.

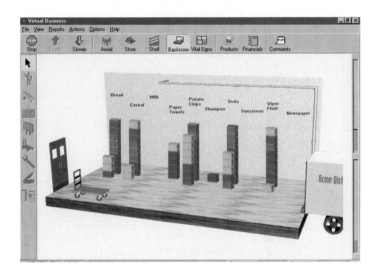

The "Multiplayer" Add-On

Students love competitions. With the multiplayer add-on you can have head-to-head competitions over a network. Students compete in the same virtual economy LIVE against other students in your school via your local area network or against other students anywhere in the world using the Internet.

The Virtual Business CyberConsultant

The *Virtual Business* CyberConsultant is your tireless helper in succeeding with *Virtual Business*. She is, in fact, an expert system packed with artificial (and real) intelligence on how to run a business. She will review eight aspects of your business and give you critical advice to increase market share and profits. As a teaching tool she will individually grade the eight aspects of the business and assign an overall grade. Have students upload their virtual business simulations for review by the CyberConsultant. She even assigns grades!

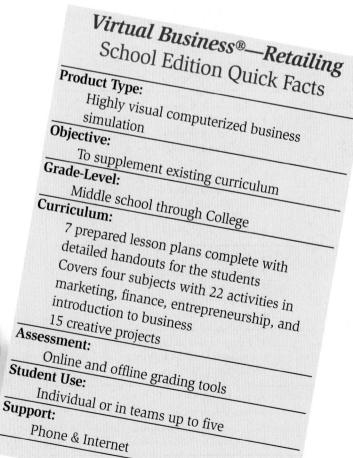

Virtual Business®—Retailing
School Edition Quick Facts

Product Type:
Highly visual computerized business simulation

Objective:
To supplement existing curriculum

Grade-Level:
Middle school through College

Curriculum:
7 prepared lesson plans complete with detailed handouts for the students
Covers four subjects with 22 activities in marketing, finance, entrepreneurship, and introduction to business
15 creative projects

Assessment:
Online and offline grading tools

Student Use:
Individual or in teams up to five

Support:
Phone & Internet

SCANS CORRELATIONS

A variety of student text features and instructional tools located in the *Teacher Wraparound Edition* provide opportunities for your students to improve foundation and workplace skills identified by the U.S. Secretary's Commission on Achieving Necessary Skills. The Commission's fundamental purpose is to encourage a high-performance economy characterized by high-skill, high-wage employment.

Foundation Skills

Basic Skills

Skill	*Introduction to Business Activity*
Reading	▸ Learning Objectives ▸ Why It's Important ▸ Key Words ▸ Business Online ▸ Real-World Application ▸ Technology Toolkit ▸ Writing for Business ▸ Business Building Blocks ▸ Consider This… ▸ Working Lifestyle ▸ You Make the Call ▸ Picture This… ▸ Global Economy ▸ Fast Review ▸ Chapter Review ▸ *BusinessWeek* Seminar
Writing	▸ Writing for Business ▸ Chapter Review 　　Using Business Key Words 　　Viewing and Representing 　　Building Academic Skills 　　Linking School to Home 　　Linking School to Work 　　E-Homework 　　Connecting Academics ▸ *BusinessWeek* Seminar
Math	▸ Chapter Review ▸ Building Academic Skills ▸ E-Homework ▸ Connecting Academics ▸ Appendix: Math Review
Listening	▸ Chapter concepts and procedures 　　lecture and discussion ▸ Teamwork Activities
Speaking	▸ Fast Review ▸ You Make the Call ▸ Teamwork Activities ▸ Critical Thinking Questions

Thinking Skills

Skill	*Introduction to Business Activity*
Creative Thinking	▸ An Extension Activity ▸ Real-World Application ▸ Technology Toolkit ▸ Writing for Business ▸ You Make the Call ▸ Consider This… ▸ Picture This… ▸ Global Economy ▸ Chapter Review 　　Understanding Business Concepts 　　Critical Thinking 　　Building Academic Skills 　　E-Homework 　　Connecting Academics 　　Creative Journal Activity
Decision Making	▸ Writing for Business ▸ You Make the Call ▸ Picture This… ▸ Global Economy ▸ Working Lifestyle ▸ *BusinessWeek* Seminar ▸ Critical Thinking Problems ▸ Chapter Review
Problem Solving	▸ *BusinessWeek* Seminar ▸ Chapter Review ▸ You Make the Call ▸ Consider This…
Seeing Things in the Mind's Eye	▸ You Make the Call ▸ Consider This… ▸ Technology Toolkit ▸ Working Lifestyle ▸ An Extension Activity ▸ Chapter Review
Knowing How to Learn	▸ Fast Review ▸ Learning Objectives ▸ Key Words ▸ Why It's Important ▸ Chapter Review
Reasoning	▸ An Extension Activity ▸ Creative Journal Activity ▸ Writing for Business ▸ Real-World Application ▸ Chapter Review ▸ *BusinessWeek* Seminar

Personal Qualities

Quality	Introduction to Business
Responsibility	▶ Learning Objectives ▶ Fast Review ▶ Chapter Review ▶ Real-World Application
Integrity/Honesty	▶ You Make the Call ▶ An Extension Activity ▶ Creative Journal Activity ▶ Fast Review ▶ Chapter Review

Quality	Introduction to Business
Self-Management	▶ Writing for Business ▶ Fast Review ▶ Chapter Review
Self-Esteem	▶ Writing for Business ▶ You Make the Call ▶ Chapter Review
Sociability	▶ *Business Week* Seminar ▶ Chapter Review ▶ Picture This…

Workplace Competencies

Interpersonal Skills

Participating as Members of a Team	▶ *Business Week* Seminar ▶ Chapter Review
Teaching Others	▶ Picture This… ▶ Global Economy ▶ Real-World Application ▶ Chapter Review ▶ You Make the Call
Serving Clients	▶ Chapter Review ▶ Writing for Business ▶ You Make the Call ▶ *Business Week* Seminar ▶ Picture This…
Exercising Leadership	▶ *Business Week* Seminar ▶ Chapter Review ▶ You Make the Call ▶ Working Lifestyle
Negotiating to Arrive at a Decision	▶ *Business Week* Seminar ▶ You Make the Call
Working With Cultural Diversity	▶ *Business Week* Seminar ▶ Global Economy ▶ Picture This…

Resources

Allocating Time	▶ Writing for Business ▶ Chapter Review ▶ *Business Week* Seminar
Allocating Money	▶ Business Building Blocks ▶ Academic Building Skills
Allocating Material and Facility Resources	▶ *Business Week* Seminar ▶ Picture This… ▶ Global Economy
Allocating Human Resources	▶ Chapter Review ▶ You Make the Call ▶ Writing for Business

Information

Acquiring and Evaluating Information	▶ Fast Review ▶ Chapter Review ▶ *Business Week* Seminar
Organizing and Maintaining Information	▶ Chapter Review ▶ Fast Review
Interpreting and Communicating Information	▶ Fast Review ▶ Technology Toolkit ▶ Consider This… ▶ You Make the Call ▶ Writing for Business ▶ Business Building Blocks
Using Computers to Process Information	▶ Technology Toolkit ▶ Chapter Review ▶ *Business Week* Seminar ▶ Integrated Software Simulation ▶ *Introduction to Business* Web site ▶ *Business Week* Feature Story ▶ *Virtual Business*® ▶ Student Activity Workbook

Systems	
Understanding Systems	▶ Technology Toolkit ▶ Chapter Review ▶ Picture This… ▶ Integrated Software Simulation ▶ Student Activity Workbook
Monitoring and Correcting Performance	▶ Key Words ▶ Learning Objectives ▶ Why It's Important ▶ Fast Review ▶ Chapter Review ▶ Student Activity Workbook
Improving and Designing Systems	▶ Integrated Software Simulation ▶ Technology Toolkit ▶ Picture This

Technology	
Selecting Technology	▶ Integrated Software Simulation
Applying Technology to Task	▶ Integrated Software Simulation ▶ *BusinessWeek* Seminar ▶ Writing for Business ▶ *Virtual Business*® ▶ *Introduction to Business* Web site
Maintaining and Troubleshooting Technology	▶ Integrated Software Simulation ▶ Technology Toolkit ▶ Picture This…

Academic Standards of Learning

Integrating Academics Into Your Business Program

Integrating academics takes principles from other subjects and concretely and metaphorically relates these to business education. This enrichment will engage students who understand and learn best by a variety of examples.

LANGUAGE ARTS Business couldn't happen without interaction. In order to learn the content in this course, students must read the textbook and critically listen. Students should be encouraged to read the textbook with a paper and  notebook in hand. This way they can work through solutions, write questions, or take notes about the concept. Give special emphasis to reading directions and questions. What exactly is being asked? How do you get to the solution? It's difficult to arrive at a correct answer without knowing the question. A major step in finding the answer is to read and understand the question. Stress the importance of reading for understanding throughout the course.

Introduction to Business encourages language growth through reading, responding, writing, and reflecting. In any business environment all of these skills are required.

This textbook provides a framework for each student's growth toward full language maturity. Language arts assignments empower the students to draw on their experiences and business knowledge.

MATH In this course, writing mathematics means solving problems and doing computations. It can also  mean writing brief reports on business topics you assign for research projects. In solving problems and doing computation, legibility and neatness are essential. Mistakes are often the result of the careless placement of letters, numbers, or symbols. It's impossible for students to find the correct solution to a problem if the computation is illegible.

Help students to realize the importance of correct alignment in computations. In addition and subtraction exercises, the correct place-value alignment of digits is essential, both in copying an exercise and in writing the answer. In multiplication, the focus is on correct alignment of the partial products. In division, correct alignment of the first digit in the quotient is important. Also, stress the importance of the alignment of decimals when applicable.

Writing brief research reports give students an opportunity to formulate, organize, internalize, evaluate, and share their work and ideas. Expect to find a wide range of responses from your students in their written reports, and be prepared to take the time that will be necessary for students to improve their writing skills. Reading students' work will provide you with a valuable method for evaluating their progress.

HISTORY/SOCIAL SCIENCE History and social science furnish a wealth of material that can help stu-

dents appreciate the cultural diversity in the United States and in a global marketplace. By reading *Introduction to Business*, students receive a broad view of the people and events that have contributed to the foundation and improvement of business.

Diversity expands culture. As immigration continues to make the United States a society with a wide variety of cultural perspectives, it's increasingly important for students to see people different from themselves as interesting business leaders who have different ideas, customs, and languages, but who also share many of the same values. By studying all aspects of diversity in business, students gain a keen understanding of the roles that all business people have played and continue to play today.

COMPUTER/TECHNOLOGY Economic society changed from an industrial to an information-based soci-

ety. As a result, your students' future business careers will be touched by computer technology. Technology changes the way you work, play, and live. Access to the Internet allows people to do research and exchange ideas with others from all over the world. Telecommuting allows people to work from home. Teaching technology in business helps the global marketplace.

The *Introduction to Business* program helps you integrate technology into your classroom through computer-based activities. Business Online, Technology Toolkit, Building Academic Skills, and E-Homework are sections in the Student Edition where students practice various computer applications. These features and activities ask students to apply their business knowledge using various types of technology. The *Internet Resources* supplement presents an overview of the Internet as well as 35 Internet activities, which are correlated to each chapter in the textbook.

The *Student Activity Workbook* supplement of *Introduction to Business* includes a computer activity for each chapter in the textbook. This supplement and the *Integrated Software Simulation* asks students to use commercial software to complete the computer activities, which include using word processing, database, or spreadsheet applications. In addition, activity questions require students to interpret their calculations or activity results and to extrapolate the information to broader marketing situations.

SCIENCE By today's projections, seven out of ten American jobs will be related to science, mathematics, or electronics. According to the experts, if students haven't grasped the fundamentals, they probably won't

advance in science and may not have a future in a global job market.

In *Introduction to Business*, the link to science may not always be obvious but you might think about their relationship in a larger sense. How do the fundamentals of science relate to business? By using the four themes that unify science—energy, systems and interactions, scale and structure, and stability and change—you can apply these concepts to business education. Here is a synopsis of each scientific theme:

Energy. Physical sciences surround you. Energy sources are crucial in the interactions among science, technology, and society. In business the use of physical energy propels technology, which is revolutionizing the global marketplace.

System and Interactions. A system can be incredibly tiny or complex. By defining the boundaries of a system, you can study the interactions among its parts.

Scale and Structure. Structure emphasizes the relationship among different arrangements. Scale defines the focus of the relationship. As the focus is shifted from a system to its components, the properties of the structure may remain constant. Business constantly challenges opportunities of scale and structure on literal and metaphorical levels.

Stability and Change. A system that is stable is constant. Often stability is the result of a system being in equilibrium. If a system isn't stable, it undergoes change. Changes in an unstable environment may be characterized as trends, cycles, or irregular changes. Business is the daily ebb and flow of commerce, finance, and technology.

SCOPE & SEQUENCE

Academic Standards of Learning

	LANGUAGE ARTS	MATH	HISTORY	COMPUTER/ TECHNOLOGY	SOCIAL SCIENCE	
CHAPTER 1	pp. 4, 5, 6, 11, 12, 16, 17	pp. 11, 16, 17	pp. 10, 16	pp. 8, 16, 17	pp. 8, 12, 16, 17	
CHAPTER 2	pp. 18, 19, 21, 26, 27, 32, 33	pp. 19, 24, 25, 26, 29, 32, 33	pp. 22, 23, 24, 32	pp. 32, 33	pp. 19, 20, 22, 25, 33	
CHAPTER 3	pp. 34, 35, 37, 42, 46, 47	pp. 36, 37, 38, 40, 46, 47	pp. 36, 40, 41, 46, 47	pp. 46, 47	pp. 34, 35, 37, 38, 40, 41, 46, 47	
CHAPTER 4	pp. 48, 49, 51, 52, 56, 60, 61	pp. 55, 60, 61	pp. 50, 60	pp. 52, 60, 61	pp. 50, 51, 54, 55, 60, 61	

Themes and Concepts

Business Core	Accounting and Finance	Business Management	Computer/ Technology	Marketing	Entrepreneurship
Competitive Environment Goal Setting Adapting to Change Problem Solving Decision Making Personal Qualities	Decision Making Financial Responsibilities	Economic Indicators Opportunity Costs Management	Time Management Needs Analysis Resource Management	New Product Purchasing Sales Promotion Buying Motives and Behaviors	Financial Planning Management Risk Management
Competitive Environment International Trade Demographics Economic Culture Economic Systems Global Business	Decision Making Economic Factors Industry Analysis	Decision Making Consumers Economic Indicators Economic Systems Trade Concepts Government Regulations Communication	Social Issues Change Management Resource Management Business Decisions Emerging Technology and Trends	Culture Diversity Profitability Balance of Trade Markets Distribution Strategy Pricing Strategy Products and Service Knowledge	Entrepreneurial Potential Government Regulations International Business Management Production
Competitive Envir. International Trade Employ. Transitions Job Retention Demographics Economic Systems Global Business Money Management	Decision Making International Finance Financial Markets Financial Responsibility Economic Indicators Unemployment	Competition Finance Trade Concepts	Productivity Time Management Resource Management	Balance of Trade Global Alliances Markets Sales in the Global Economy	Financial Resources International Business
Diversity Ethics Business Ethics Business Law Environmental Issues Adapting to Change Occupational Safety	Financial Responsibility	Competition Decision Making Consumers Exchange and Money Government Regulations Employment Law Legal Rights Culture	Business Decisions	Cultural Diversity Culture Markets Buying Motives and Behaviors Regulation	Government Regulations Management Production

Academic Standards of Learning

	LANGUAGE ARTS	MATH	HISTORY	COMPUTER/ TECHNOLOGY	SOCIAL SCIENCE	
CHAPTER 5	pp. 68, 69, 71, 72, 77, 82, 83	pp. 82, 83	pp. 73, 75, 82	pp. 71, 72, 73, 77, 78, 79, 82, 83	pp. 69, 70, 74, 75	
CHAPTER 6	pp. 84, 85, 87, 88, 90, 92, 93, 96, 97	pp. 87, 96, 97	p. 91	pp. 87, 93, 96, 97	pp. 85, 86, 90, 91, 96	
CHAPTER 7	pp. 98, 99, 100, 101, 102, 104, 105, 106, 107, 110	pp. 103, 105, 110, 111	pp. 104, 110	pp. 101, 107, 110, 111	pp. 98, 99, 100, 103, 104, 107	
CHAPTER 8	pp. 112, 113, 114, 115, 116, 117, 118, 119, 120, 121, 122, 123	pp. 122, 123	pp. 116, 119, 122	pp. 115, 118, 120, 121, 122, 123	pp. 112, 113, 114, 115, 116, 177, 118, 119	
CHAPTER 9	pp. 126, 127, 129, 133, 135, 138	pp. 138, 139	pp. 127, 128, 129, 130, 131, 134, 138	pp. 126, 127, 128, 129, 130, 131, 132, 133, 134, 135, 138, 139	pp. 127, 128, 130, 131, 132, 133, 134, 135	

Themes and Concepts

Business Core	Accounting and Finance	Business Management	Computer/ Technology	Marketing	Entrepreneurship
Methods of Communication Ethics Business Ownership Entrepreneurial Concepts Environmental Issues Business Operations	Decision Making Financial Analysis Budgeting	Competitive Environment Decision Making Basic Management Functions Technology	Computer Applications Supervision Time Management Technological Innovations Telecommunications Bussiness Model	E-commerce Market Research Purchasing Electronic Marketing Risk Management Merchandising—Color Theory	Entrepreneurial Potential Management Marketing Analysis Research and Development Technology
Effectiveness Methods of Comm. Business Ownership Competitive Envir. Goal Setting Retention Money Management Adapting to Change	Cash Management Decision Making Financial Responsibility	Competition Consumers Business Organizations Basic Management Functions Research and Development	Business Environment Business Management Supervision Business Models Customer Service Resource Management	Profitability Distribution Strategy Risk Management	Business Image Management Production Research and Development
Business Ownership Entrepreneurial Concepts Goal Setting Business Relationships Conflict Resolution Teamwork Decision Making	Decision Making	Business Organizations Basic Management Functions Research and Development	Project Management Business Environment Business Management Change Management Business Models	Culture Infra Structure	Risk Management Research and Development
Business Ethics Competitive Environment Business Operations Goal Setting Interest Assessment Teamwork Motivation Personal Qualities	Ethics	Competition Decision Making Opportunity Costs Business Organization	Basic Management Functions Time Management Business Decisions	Culture Risk Management	Entrepreneurial Potential Research and Development
Environmental Factors Employment Transitions Interest Assessment Adapting to Change Planning	Decision Making Computer Accounting Systems Budgeting	Competition Opportunity Costs Research and Development	Project Management Business Management Computer Applications Time Management Business Decisions Emerging Technology and Trends Resource Management	E-Commerce Culture	Business Image Entrepreneurial Potential Management Research and Development

Academic Standards of Learning

	LANGUAGE ARTS	MATH	HISTORY	COMPUTER/ TECHNOLOGY	SOCIAL SCIENCE	
CHAPTER 10	pp. 146, 147, 148, 150, 158	pp. 158, 159	pp. 147, 149, 152, 154, 158, 159	pp. 155, 158, 159	pp. 147, 148, 150, 152, 153, 158	
CHAPTER 11	pp. 160, 161, 162, 164, 167, 168, 172, 173	pp. 165, 172, 173	pp. 166, 172, 173	pp. 163, 169, 172, 173	pp. 162, 163, 164, 168, 172	
CHAPTER 12	pp. 174, 175, 177, 178, 181, 188, 189	pp. 176, 178, 180, 181, 188, 189	pp. 174, 179, 185, 188	pp. 177, 183, 188, 189	pp. 176, 177, 188	
CHAPTER 13	pp. 196, 197, 199, 200, 202, 203, 208, 209	pp. 198, 201, 202, 208, 209	p. 208	pp. 197, 199, 200, 204, 205, 208, 209	pp. 197, 198, 202, 208	
CHAPTER 14	pp. 210, 211, 214, 216, 217, 218, 224, 225	pp. 222, 224, 225	pp. 213, 216, 224	pp. 213, 214, 219, 224, 225	pp. 217, 224	

Themes and Concepts

Business Core	Accounting and Finance	Business Management	Computer/ Technology	Marketing	Entrepreneurship
Competitive Environment International Trade Economic Culture Exchange Rates Global Business Adapting to Change Global Communications Planning	Decision Making International Finance Financial Markets Trade Finance	Competition Economic Incentives Exchange and Money Productivity Trade Concepts International Regulations	Business Environment Emerging Technology and Trends	Global Alliances Trade Barriers Distribution Strategy Sales in a Global Economy Regulation	International Business Financial Resources
Business Law Interrelations of Business Operations Adapting to Change	Governing Agencies Financial Responsibility Intellectual Property	Economic Institutions Economic System Ethics Government Regulations Sources of Law Legal Rights	Project Management Security Productivity Supervision Business Decisions	Risk Management Information Technology Industry Ethics Regulation	Government Regulations Management Risk Management
Business Law Business/Finance Relationships Investments	Financial Services Investment Analysis	Economic Institutions and Incentives Government Regulations Source of Law	Safety and Security Technical Resources Business Environment Records Management Monitoring and Investigation	Customer Service Infra Structure Financial Institutions Regulation	Collections Government Regulations Legal Considerations and Control
Competitive Environment Entrepreneurial Concepts Demographics Global Business Teamwork Presentation Communications	Decision Making Economic Factors Budgeting Cost Behavior	Consumers Competition Decision Making Opportunity Costs Policy and Strategy Formulation	Project Management Computer Applications Systems Selection	Customer Service Profitability Culture Marketing Mix Markets Market Analysis Research and Development	Business Image Capital Budgeting Entrepreneurial Concepts Marketing Plan Pricing Strategies Production Promotion
Competitive Environment Interest Assessment Demographics Culture Diversity Adapting to Change Communication	Decision Making Ethics Costing Methods	Competition Consumers Decision Making Technology	Program Design Social Issues Business Decisions Media Types	Cultural Diversity Markets Branding Packaging Positioning Advertising Public Relations/ Publicity Promotion	Business Image Location and Property Analysis Research and Development Technology

Academic Standards of Learning

	LANGUAGE ARTS	MATH	HISTORY	COMPUTER/ TECHNOLOGY	SOCIAL SCIENCE	
CHAPTER 15	pp. 232, 233, 234, 235, 236, 238, 239, 240, 241, 244	pp. 234, 244, 245	p. 244	pp. 235, 241, 244, 245	pp. 233, 234, 237, 238, 239, 245	
CHAPTER 16	pp. 247, 248, 249, 250, 252, 253, 254, 255, 260	pp. 260, 261	pp. 251, 260	pp. 249, 255, 260, 261	pp. 246, 247, 248, 249, 251, 252, 253, 254, 261	
CHAPTER 17	pp. 269, 271, 272, 274, 276, 280	pp. 268, 270, 273, 275, 280, 281	pp. 274, 280	pp. 271, 277, 280, 281	pp. 269, 270, 271, 272, 274, 275, 276, 277, 281	
CHAPTER 18	pp. 283, 285, 286, 287, 289, 296, 297	pp. 284, 296, 297	pp. 282, 288, 292, 296	pp. 282, 283, 284, 285, 286, 287, 288, 290, 291, 292, 296, 297	pp. 282, 284, 285, 286, 287, 288, 290, 291, 292	
CHAPTER 19	pp. 299, 305, 310, 311	pp. 301, 303, 310, 311	p. 299	pp. 298, 299, 300, 301, 302, 303, 304, 305, 306, 307, 310, 311	pp. 300, 301, 302, 304, 305, 307, 310	

Themes and Concepts

Business Core	Accounting and Finance	Business Management	Computer/Technology	Marketing	Entrepreneurship

Career Exploration
Employment
  Transitions
Interest Assessment
Job Acquisition
Job Retention
Adapting to Change
	Technological
	  Applications
	Internal Control
		Decision Making
		Unemployment
		Business
		  Organizations
		Communication
			Business Environment
			Supervision
			Operating Systems
			Human–Computer
			  Interfaces
			Training
				Cultural Diversity
				Logistics
				Technology
					Business Image
					Human Resources
					  Management
					Research and
					  Development

Employee Transitions
Retention
Demographics
Economic Culture
Adapting to Change
Diversity
Teamwork
Work Ethics
Social Issues
	Decision Making
	Ethics
	Economic Factors
	Technology
		Competition
		Ethics
		Human Resource
		  Development and
		  Management
		International
		  Relationships
		Technology
			Business and
			  Technology Ethics
			Business Environment
			Emerging Technology
			  and Trends
				Cultural Diversity
				Customer Relations
				Culture
				Public Relations
					International Business
					Research and
					  Development

Business Law
Interrelationships in
  Business Operations
Financial Statements
Financial Systems
Money Management
	Accounting Principles
	Cash Management
	Financial Analysis
	Payroll
	Financial Responsibility
	Budgeting
	Internal Control
	Revenue and Expense
	  Recognition
		Decision Making
		Opportunity Costs
		Finance
			Records Management
			Systems Analysis
				Profitability
				Industry Ethics
				Policies and
				  Procedures
					Collections
					Contracts
					Inventory Management

Business Ethics
Business Law
Employment
  Transitions
Technological
  Inventions
Telecommunications
	Decision Making
	Technological
	  Applications
		Consumers
		Productivity
			Communications
			Technology
				E-Commerce
				Technology
				Information
				  Technology
				Electronic Marketing
					Management
					Research and
					  Development
					Risk Management

Adapting to Change
Conflict Resolution
Time Management
Applications
Computer Operations
Technology
  Innovations
	Computer Accounting
	  Systems
	Technological
	  Applications
		Opportunity Costs
		Technological
		  Applications
			Ethics
			Information
			  Technology
			Computer
			  Applications
			Computer and
			  Communication
			  Systems
				Security
				Systems Analysis
				  and Design
				Resource Management
					Entrepreneurial
					  Potential
					Legal Considerations
					Management
					Technology

Academic Standards of Learning

	LANGUAGE ARTS	MATH	HISTORY	COMPUTER/ TECHNOLOGY	SOCIAL SCIENCE	
CHAPTER 20	pp. 319, 320, 323, 325, 327, 330, 331	pp. 318, 330, 331	pp. 321, 324, 325	pp. 321, 327, 330, 331	pp. 319, 320, 321, 323, 324, 326, 327, 330	
CHAPTER 21	pp. 333, 334, 336, 338, 339, 345, 346, 347	pp. 337, 346, 347	pp. 343, 346	pp. 335, 341, 342, 346, 347	pp. 333, 334, 335, 336, 338, 339, 341, 342	

	LANGUAGE ARTS	MATH	HISTORY	COMPUTER/ TECHNOLOGY	SOCIAL SCIENCE	
CHAPTER 22	pp. 355, 361, 363, 368	pp. 359, 361, 365, 368, 369	pp. 356, 358, 368	pp. 354, 357, 363, 364, 368, 369	pp. 356, 357, 358, 360, 362, 367	
CHAPTER 23	pp. 371, 375, 377, 382, 383	pp. 378, 382, 383	pp. 371, 374, 377	pp. 370, 371, 373, 379, 382, 383	pp. 370, 371, 372, 373, 375, 376, 378, 379, 382	
CHAPTER 24	pp. 385, 387, 388, 391, 392, 393, 396, 397	pp. 396, 397	pp. 385, 386, 390, 396	pp. 387, 389, 393, 396, 397	pp. 385, 386, 387, 388, 390, 391, 393, 396	

Themes and Concepts

Business Core	Accounting and Finance	Business Management	Computer/ Technology	Marketing	Entrepreneurship
Competitive Envir. Career Exploration Employ. Transitions Goal Setting Job Acquisition Job Retention Teamwork Motivation Personal Qualities	Decision Making Competition	Unemployment Employment Law Contracts Human Resources Development and Management	Program Design and Development Business Management Business Decisions Culture	Motives and Behavior Policies and Procedures	Business Image Entrepreneurial Potential Human Resources Management Technology
Entrepreneurial Concepts Career Exploration Employment Transitions Goal Setting Interest Assessment Job Acquisition Retention	Decision Making Technology	Competition Consumers Decision Making Productivity Unemployment Employment Law Ethics Environmental Factors	Computer and Communication Systems Program Design Social Issues	Cultural Diversity Risk Management	Entrepreneurial Concepts Management

Business Core	Accounting and Finance	Business Management	Computer/ Technology	Marketing	Entrepreneurship
Business Law Competitive Environment Interrelations of Business Operations Economic Culture Demographics Adapting to Change Communications	Decision Making Accounting Principles	Competition Consumers Decision Making Opportunity Costs Productivity Communication	Knowledge Management Business Procedures Social Issues Business Decisions Customer Support	Customer Relations Customer Service E-Commerce Culture Marketing Strategy and Planning Buying Motives and Behaviors Customer Transactions	Business Image Contracts Pricing Strategies Production Promotion
Business Law Business Ethics Competitive Environment Adapting to Change Information Resources	Decision Making Ethics	Competition Consumers Decision Making Change Research Communications	Knowledge Management Change Management Needs Analysis	Customer Relations Customer Service Pricing Strategy Buying Motives and Behaviors	Management Product Pricing Strategies
Business Law Business Ownership Problem Solving Communications Decision Making Governing Agencies	Revenue and Expense Recognition	Competition Consumers Decision Making Government Regulations Legal Rights Sources of Law	Security Technical Resources Business Environment Business Management Safety	Customer Relations Customer Service Regulation Policies and Procedures	Contracts Government Regulations Management Purchasing and Inventory Management

Academic Standards of Learning

	LANGUAGE ARTS	MATH	HISTORY	COMPUTER/ TECHNOLOGY	SOCIAL SCIENCE	
CHAPTER 25	pp. 405, 408, 410, 412, 413, 416	pp. 410, 416, 417	p. 409	pp. 405, 406, 413, 416, 417	pp. 405, 406, 407, 409, 415, 416, 417	
CHAPTER 26	pp. 419, 421, 422, 423, 425, 426, 432	pp. 420, 421, 423, 424, 425, 426, 432, 433	pp. 424, 432	pp. 421, 426, 432	pp. 418, 419, 420, 424, 425, 426, 427, 433	
CHAPTER 27	pp. 435, 436, 437, 438, 439, 440, 441, 442, 443, 446, 447	pp. 446, 447	pp. 436, 438, 441, 446	pp. 435, 437, 439, 443, 446, 447	pp. 436, 437, 438, 440, 441, 443	

Themes and Concepts

Business Core	Accounting and Finance	Business Management	Computer/ Technology	Marketing	Entrepreneurship

Business Ethics
Business Law
Financial Statements
Decision Making
Planning
	Decision Making
	Payroll
	Credit Analysis
	Financial Services
	Risk Analysis
		Consumers
		Decision Making
		Opportunity Costs
		Policy & Strategy
		   Formulation
			Business and
			   Technology Ethics
			Safety and Security
			Risk Analysis
				Risk Management
				New Product/Service
				Purchasing
					Contracts
					Collections

Competitive
   Environment
Financial Statements
Money Management
Adapting to Change
Decision Making
	Financial Systems
	Money Management
	Adapting to Change
	Document
	   Processing
	Information
	   Resources
	Decision Making
		Technological
		   Applications
		Credit Analysis
		Financial Services
		Consumers
		Exchange and Money
		Management
			Security
			Change Management
			Risk Analysis
			Business Decisions
				Purchasing
				Product/Service Mix
				Buying Motives and
				   Behaviors
					Collections
					Contracts
					Research and
					   Development
					Sales

Business Law
Business/Financial
   Relationships
Planning
Personal Qualities
	Ethics
	Financial Analysis
	Governing Agencies
	Credit Analysis
	Revenue and Expense
	   Recognition
		Consumers
		Decision Making
		Contracts
		Government
		   Regulations
		Sources of Law
			Business Environment
			Safety and Security
			Social Issues
			Needs Analysis
				Customer Relations
				Risk Management
				Products and Service
				   Knowledge
				Credit Review
				Financial Institutions
				Regulation
					Contracts
					Collections
					Financial Resources
					Government
					   Regulations
					Human Resources
					   Management

Academic Standards of Learning

	LANGUAGE ARTS	MATH	HISTORY	COMPUTER/ TECHNOLOGY	SOCIAL SCIENCE	
CHAPTER 28	pp. 455, 457, 459, 461, 462, 463, 468, 469	pp. 455, 458, 459, 460, 462, 468	p. 468	pp. 457, 461, 463, 468, 469	pp. 454, 460, 463, 464, 465, 469	
CHAPTER 29	pp. 471, 473, 474, 476, 477, 479, 482, 483	pp. 472, 477, 482, 483	p. 470	pp. 473, 479, 482, 483	pp. 470, 471, 474, 476, 482	
CHAPTER 30	pp. 485, 486, 487, 488, 489, 490, 491, 492, 493, 496, 497	pp. 485, 487, 488, 489, 496, 497	p. 496	pp. 487, 493, 496, 497	pp. 486, 488, 490	
CHAPTER 31	pp. 499, 501, 503, 505, 506, 507, 510, 511	pp. 502, 503, 504, 510, 511	pp. 502, 510	pp. 498, 501, 507, 510, 511	pp. 499, 503, 504, 506, 509	
CHAPTER 32	pp. 513, 514, 515, 516, 519, 520, 521, 524	pp. 513, 516, 518, 524, 525	pp. 513, 520, 524	pp. 515, 521, 524, 525	pp. 513, 514, 516, 518, 519	

Themes and Concepts

Business Core	Accounting and Finance	Business Management	Computer/ Technology	Marketing	Entrepreneurship

Goal Setting
Interest Assessment
Communication
Decision Making
Personal Qualities
Planning
	Cash Management
	Decision Making
	Financial Analysis
	Revenue and Expense
	  Recognition
	Taxation
		Consumers
		Decision Making
		Communication
		Time Management
		Needs Analysis
			Records Management
			Business Decisions
				Profitability
				Risk Management
				Purchasing
				Buys Motives and
				  Behaviors
				Credit Review
					Contracts
					Entrepreneurial
					  Potential
					Financial Resources
					Management

Environmental Issues
Goal Setting
Business/Financial
  Relationship
Financial Statement
Financial System
Money Management
	Cash Management
	Decision Making
	Technological
	  Applications
	Financial Statements
	Budgeting
	Cost Behavior
		Consumers
		Decision Making
			Computer Applications
			Security
			Records Management
			Needs Analysis
				Risk Management
				Security and Loss
				  Prevention
					Financial Planning
					Management

Business Law
Competitive
  Environment
Financial Statements
Money Management
Document Processing
Decision Making
Planning
	Cash Management
	Decision Making
	Industry/Market
	  Analysis
	Risk Analysis
	Budgeting
		Decision Making
		Competition
		Economic Indicators
		Research and
		  Development
		Policy and Strategies
		  Formulation
		Comparative
		  Advantages
			Security
			Time Management
			Risk Analysis
				Market Analysis
				Risk Management
				Products and Service
				  Knowledge
				Financial Institutions
					Collections
					Contracts
					Financial Resources
					Financial Planning
					Government
					  Regulations
					Pricing Strategies
					Management

Business Ethics
Business Law
Business Ownership
Business/Financial
  Relationships
Economic Culture
Economic System
Investments
	Decision Making
	Financial Analysis
	International Finance
	Governing Agencies
	International Finance
	Economic Factors
	Investment Analysis
		Economic Indicators
		Decision Making
		Ethics
		Research and
		  Development
		Comparative
		  Advantage
			Needs Analysis
			Resource
			  Management
			Risk Analysis
				Risk Management
				Branding
				Positioning
				Purchasing
				Product/Service
				  Classification
				Policies and
				  Procedures
					Management
					Property Analysis
					Risk Management

Business Law
Entrepreneurial
  Concepts
Economic Culture
Investment
Money Management
	Cash Management
	Decision Making
	Financial Analysis
		Decision Making
		Contracts
		Finance
			Records Management
			Needs Analysis
			Risk Analysis
				Buying Motives and
				  Behaviors
				Customer
				  Transactions
				Financial Institutions
				Risk Management
				Policies and
				  Procedures
				Regulation
					Contracts
					Entrepreneurial
					  Potential
					Financial Resources
					Financial Planning
					Location and Property
					  Analysis

Academic Standards of Learning

	LANGUAGE ARTS	MATH	HISTORY	COMPUTER/ TECHNOLOGY	SOCIAL SCIENCE	
CHAPTER 33	pp. 533, 534, 535, 536, 537, 538, 539, 540, 541, 546	pp. 533, 538, 546, 547	p. 534	pp. 532, 534, 535, 541, 546, 547	pp. 533, 536, 538, 539, 540, 542, 543, 546, 547	
CHAPTER 34	pp. 549, 550, 551, 552, 553, 555, 560	pp. 549, 552, 560, 561	pp. 554, 560	pp. 551, 557, 560, 561	pp. 549, 550, 553, 554, 557, 561	
CHAPTER 35	pp. 563, 564, 566, 567, 568, 569, 570, 574, 575	pp. 564, 566, 570, 574, 575	p. 564	pp. 565, 571, 574, 575	pp. 563, 568, 569, 574	

Themes and Concepts

Business Core	Accounting and Finance	Business Management	Computer/ Technology	Marketing	Entrepreneurship

Business Law
Occupational Safety
Communication
	Decision Making
	Governing Agencies
	Financial Responsibility
	Risk Analysis
	Technology
	Costing Methods
		Consumers
		Decision Making
		Contracts
		Government
		  Regulations
		Legal Rights
		Sources of Law
			Systems Analysis and
			  Design
			Security
			Social Issues
				Customer Relations
				Risk Management
				Technology
				Salesmanship
				Policies and
				  Procedures
				Regulation
					Contracts
					Collections
					Financial Resources
					Government
					  Regulations
					Location and Property
					  Analysis

Business Law
Occupational Safety
Communication
	Decision Making
	Financial
	  Responsibility
	Risk Analysis
	Technology
		Consumers
		Decision Making
		Contracts
		Legal Rights
		Sources of Law
			Security
			Social Issues
				Risk Management
				Technology
				Salesmanship
				Policies and
				  Procedures
				Regulation
					Contracts
					Collections
					Financial Resources
					Location and Property
					  Analysis

Business Ethics
Business Law
Investment
Money Management
Document Processing
Information
  Resources
Communication
	Decision Making
	Financial
	  Responsibility
	Risk Analysis
	Technology
		Decision Making
		Financial
		  Responsibility
		Risk Analysis
		Technology
			Computer and
			  Communication
			  Systems
			Records Management
			Needs Analysis
			Business Decisions
				Customer Relations
				Risk Management
				Technology
				Policies and
				  Procedures
				Regulation
					Contracts
					Collections
					Financial Resources
					Government
					  Regulations
					Location and Property
					  Analysis

Integrating Cultural Diversity

Your students will be faced with a diverse marketplace in which people of many different cultures are both workers and consumers. Cultural knowledge may be the difference between success and failure in global business. For students to become productive workers and responsible citizens, they must be open to cultural differences.

As students learn about skills needed to be successful in a business career, they should keep in mind the wide diversity of the people they are likely to encounter in every aspect of their working and personal lives. In the classroom and in one-on-one conferences, you can help your students consider the diversity of the U.S. population, not only in terms of ethnicity, but also in terms of customs, attitudes, religious beliefs, language backgrounds, and physical capabilities. High school students need to understand that ability and success aren't related to skin color or gender.

Multicultural Education

Multicultural education incorporates the idea that all students—regardless of their gender and social class, and their ethnic, racial, or cultural characteristics—should have an equal opportunity to learn in school. Learning about other cultures concurrently with their own culture helps children recognize similarities and appreciate differences, without perceiving inferiority or superiority of one or the other. To foster cultural awareness you might:

- Recognize that all students are unique, have special talents, abilities, etc.

- Promote uniqueness and diversity as positive.

- Know, appreciate, and respect cultural backgrounds of your students.

- Use authentic situations to provide cultural learning and understanding.

- Make sure that historical information is accurate and nondiscriminatory.

- Make sure people from all cultures are represented fairly and accurately.

- Make sure there is gender equity.

- Welcome parent and community involvement.

Use current news stories and advertisements to call students' attention to cultural differences that influence business.

Using Cooperative Learning

Studies show that students learn faster and retain more information when they are actively involved in the learning process. Studies also show that in a classroom setting, adolescents often learn more from each other about subject matter than from a traditional teacher-led lecture and discussion. Cooperative learning is one method that gets students actively involved in learning and at the same time allows for peer teaching.

Using Cooperative Learning

Your business course provides many opportunities for students to learn and apply the skills necessary for positive interpersonal relationships. Through the use of cooperative learning, the teacher can offer a structured method of teaching team-building, collaborative social skills, and team decision making while teaching basic concepts—essential skills for the workplace. This learning structure is especially effective for more difficult learning tasks, such as problem solving, critical thinking, and conceptual learning.

The Benefits of Cooperative Learning

- Cooperative learning emphasizes working toward group goals as opposed to the traditional emphasis on individual competition and achievement.

- Students discover that not only must they learn the material themselves, but also they are responsible for helping everyone in the group learn the material.

- Cooperative learning increases academic achievement and develops essential social skills.

- Students discover how to work with people of all types.

- Students learn valuable problem-solving, team-building, and creativity skills that transfer to real-world occupations and work environments.

- People who help each other and work together toward a common goal generally begin to feel more positive about each other and interact constructively when performing collective tasks.

- Students don't feel as isolated, and they gain self-esteem.

- Students have the opportunity to perceive other students as colleagues rather than competitors. As a result, they recognize the value of helping others rather than working competitively.

Cooperative Learning in this Text

In *Introduction to Business*, students and teachers have a variety of materials to assist with cooperative learning activities. Many of the features and chapter assessment activities can be completed in a cooperative learning environment. These activities include the Chapter Review, *BusinessWeek* Seminar, Business Building Blocks, and You Make the Call.

Alternative Assessment Strategies

The teaching and learning process relies upon accurate assessments to gauge students' knowledge of subject matter. The traditional method of assessment measures students' progress by objective written tests. This type of formal assessment is satisfactory for evaluating mastery of content topics. However, these kinds of tests are not enough in today's business curriculum. New business curriculum objectives focus on communication, human relations, problem solving, and critical thinking skills. Written tests alone cannot fully evaluate a student's acquisition and mastery of these skills. Therefore, alternative performance assessment strategies are encouraged.

Performance Assessment

Performance assessment is based on judging the quality of a student's response to a specific task. The student is placed in a real-world, business-related situation that corresponds to classroom learning, and then evaluated on how she or he performs in that situation. The *Introduction to Business* program provides you with many activities, projects, and situations that create opportunities for performance assessment.

At the end of each chapter, in the review, students write or demonstrate responses to real-life situations. Through their responses, students develop skills such as decision making and strategy formulation. Students also have the opportunity to improve their public speaking skills. Building Academic Skills provides cross-curricular links to important lesson objectives.

Formal Assessment

Glencoe also provides a complete package of assessment instruments to measure your students' skills and content knowledge.

The **ASSESSMENT PACKAGE** includes Exam-View®Pro software that allows you to print out multiple versions of chapter mid-term, final, and unit tests. Answers are provided. You can also use the Reproducible Tests to hand out to students.

At the end of each major heading in a chapter, you'll find a Fast Review, which immediately quizzes the students' reading comprehension. **CHAPTER REVIEW** provides students with immediate reinforcement to review key concepts and improve critical thinking skills. In addition, students develop decision-making abilities through case analyses.

The Chapter Review at the end of every chapter can be used to assess your students' mastery of business concepts and chapter objectives.

***BUSINESSWEEK* FEATURE STORY REVIEW** asks real-world questions about the article just read by students. These can be used to evaluate students' understanding of business concepts and procedures.

Assessment Strategies

Teaching the wide range of skills and knowledge required for business management requires different forms of assessment. Individual students respond differently to various types of assessment. The chart on the next page can help you determine which strategies will work best for your students.

STRATEGIES	ADVANTAGES	DISADVANTAGES
• Objective measures • Multiple choice • Matching • Item sets • True/False	• Reliable, easy to validate • Objective, if designed effectively • Low cost, efficient • Automated administration • Lends to equating	• Measures cognitive knowledge effectively • Limited on other measures • Not a good measure of overall performance
• Written measures • Essays • Restricted response • Written simulations • Case analysis • Problem-solving exercises	• Face validity (real life) • In-depth assessment • Measures writing skills and higher level skills • Reasonable developmental costs and time	• Subjective scoring • Time consuming and expensive to score • Limited breadth • Difficult to equate • Moderate reliability
• Oral measures • Oral examinations • Interviews	• Measures communications and interpersonal skills • In-depth assessment with varied stimulus materials • Learner involvement	• Costly and time consuming • Limited reliability • Narrow sampling of content • Scoring difficult, need multiple raters
• Simulated activities • In-basket • Computer simulations	• Moderate reliability • Performance-based measure	• Costly and time consuming • Difficult to score, administer, and develop
• Portfolio and product analysis • Work samples • Projects • Work diaries and logs • Achievement records	• Provides information not normally available • Learner involvement • Face validity (real life) • Easy to collect information	• Costly to administer • Labor and paper intensive • Difficult to validate or equate • Based toward best samples or outstanding qualities
• Performance measures • Demonstrations • Presentations • Performances • Production work • Observation	• Job-related • Relatively easy to administer • In-depth assessment • Face validity	• Rater training required • Hard to equate • Subjective scoring • Time consuming if breadth is needed
• Performance records • References • Performance rating forms • Parental rating	• Efficient • Low cost • Easy to administer	• Low reliability • Subjective • Hard to equate • Rate judgment
• Self-evaluation	• Learner involvement and empowerment • Learner responsibility • Measures dimensions not available otherwise	• May be biased or unrealistic

Developing Critical Thinking Skills

As your students emerge into the world of business, they'll be required to process, analyze, interpret, and communicate financial information. Successful employees possess the ability to make insightful decisions, solve problems creatively, and interact with diverse groups.

Basic Elements of Critical Thinking

Critical thinking is the process of logically deciding on a course of action or a conclusion to a question or scenario. It involves the ability to

- compare and contrast,

- solve problems and make decisions,

- analyze and evaluate,

- synthesize and transfer knowledge,

- conduct metacognitive exercises.

Problem-Solving Strategies

1. Define the problem. Work through the following questions: What is the situation or the context of the problem? Can the problem be separated into various elements? Students should understand that the way a problem is perceived defines the problem. To define the problem clearly, state the problem in one or two sentences.

2. Gather information and facts. Next, it is necessary to make certain that you have all the necessary information about the situation. Ask questions and observe.

3. Go from the general to the specific. Look at the big picture as you gain a general understanding of the context of the problem. Think of a more general situation. Break the problem down into its smaller parts.

4. Develop a plan. Problem-solvers formulate a potential plan of action based on the information gathered. Outline your plan step-by-step. Evaluate how the problem will be affected if your plan is enacted.

5. Make connections. Elements of the problem create a framework of relationships and connections to each other and to outside information. If students can learn to connect what they have learned in other classes or in life experiences to the problem at hand, they will become successful problem-solvers.

6. Be flexible and creative. Problems often have a variety of acceptable outcomes. Students should approach the situation from different viewpoints and directions, exploring options. Speculation, intuition, and estimation are important in this process.

Benefits of Critical Thinking

Critical thinking skills are important to:

- help students investigate their own methods for solving problems and resolving issues creatively,

- lead students to investigations that compare and contrast knowns and unknowns, and

- allow students to make decisions about their own learning and to make them aware of the processes they use.

How to Teach Critical Thinking

Since all learning requires thinking, your students will benefit from exposure to a variety of thinking exercises. Benjamin Bloom's Taxonomy of the Cognitive Domain is widely recognized for its schema of levels of thinking. Each of Bloom's cognitive categories includes a list of thinking skills and indicates the kinds of behavior students are expected to perform at the objectives of goals of specific learning tasks. Here are some examples:

THINKING SKILL	BEHAVIORS REQUIRED
Knowledge	Define, recognize, recall, identify, label, understand, examine, show, collect
Comprehension	translate, interpret, explain, describe, summarize, extrapolate
Application	apply, solve, experiment, show, predict
Analysis	connect, relate, differentiate, classify, arrange, check, group, distinguish, organize, categorize, detect, compare, infer
Synthesis	produce, propose, design, plan, combine, formulate, compose, hypothesize, construct
Evaluation	appraise, judge, criticize, decide

Stress the importance of critical thinking in daily life. Students should learn to focus their efforts on sound decision-making processes, not snap judgments.

Critical Thinking in the Introduction to Business *program*

Both the student text and the *Teacher Wraparound Edition* provide numerous activities and suggestions to help you incorporate and integrate critical thinking skills into your course.

- **UNIT AND CHAPTER INTRODUCTIONS.** Each unit and chapter opens with information on a real-world tidbit and story related to the business topic. After reading these your students will be asked to answer questions about what they have read.

- **TECHNOLOGY TOOLKIT.** This feature offers technology-related topics that are integral to business. Students will respond to a critical thinking question related to the technology topic addressed.

- **CAREERS IN BUSINESS.** Students will gain exposure to all career clusters established by the U.S. Department of Education in Working Lifestyle. Each feature offers an inside look at a person's profession—it focuses on what each person does at ten o'clock in the morning. The Connecting Academic Careers question at the end of each profile helps students extend the career information.

- **AN EXTENSION ACTIVITY.** This builds off of the *BusinessWeek* Feature Story. By recalling and utilizing learned information, students hypothesize about or appraise newly introduced data to formulate conclusions.

- **CRITICAL THINKING PROBLEMS.** This appears in the Chapter Review of each chapter. Students might review business concepts before applying them to the questions. After synthesizing and organizing the information presented, students compare alternatives, present potential solutions, and appraise outcomes.

- Critical thinking skills extend to every sector of our lives. In the feature You Make the Call, students are asked to apply solid decision-making processes to work through ethical situations.

- In the feature called Real-World Application, your students review questions provoked by thought, research, and analysis of the concepts from real-world businesses and their applications.

- **BUSINESS BUILDING BLOCKS.** This teaches students how to analyze and evaluate information presented in business. They practice a variety of critical thinking skills such as problem solving, analyzing, evaluating, decision making, and synthesizing information.

Integrating Ethics

During their business careers, your students will encounter many situations that will require them to make decisions about their own actions. Helping students learn about ethical behavior and considering the effects of a decision before it's made are important topics for your business course.

The goal of introducing ethics into your course is not to teach values, but rather to help students clarify their ethical beliefs and to learn how to evaluate ethical situations in light of their personal beliefs. Students need to learn how to evaluate their actions and to ask themselves questions such as, "Will I think well of myself if I take this action?" "Would I want others to know about my actions?"

The Ethical Decision Model

Your students will learn to analyze ethical situations better if they have a model to use when deliberating the issues and the people affected by a decision. Several decision models exist, but the basic steps for an ethical decision model are as follows:

1. Determine the ethical issue.

2. Identify the actions for handling the situation.

3. Identify the people affected by the situation.

4. Analyze how the situation affects the people involved.

5. Decide which of the actions to take.

Classroom Strategies

Several methods may be used to integrate discussions of ethical issues into your business course. You may use various *Business Week* feature stories found throughout the book, use You Make the Call, use *Business Week* Seminar, or collect articles that portray ethical dilemmas. Have students analyze the situations in class or write short reports of their analyses and conclusions.

BUSINESSWEEK SEMINARS. Using unit ending seminars from the textbook, have the entire class use the ethical decision model to analyze the issues and possible actions to take. Make sure your students feel free to voice their opinions. If a full-class discussion becomes unwieldy, you may want to use small groups in a cooperative learning activity.

COOPERATIVE LEARNING GROUPS. Small groups of students are especially well suited to discussing cases and sharing their ideas about ethical issues. Divide students into groups of four to five. Observe groups to be sure that all students are participating. Allow each group to reach its conclusions, then ask a member of each to share that group's ideas with the class.

ROLE-PLAYS AND DEBATES. Have your students role-play ethical situations, using their own ideas about how to respond to a given situation. Discuss class responses to the role-play, guiding students in using the ethical decision model. Set up debate teams to present different sides of an ethical issue.

You Make the Call

Benefiting Your Employees

The small business you launched last year is doing so well you want to hire an assistant. The law requires you to pay workers compensation insurance. Workers compensation provides some financial assistance to an employee who is injured on the job. You want to offer your new assistant additional benefits, such as health insurance and a retirement plan. Also, you would like to offer childcare assistance, or tuition assistance for job-related training. As a new entrepreneur, however, you don't know if you can afford the expense of additional benefits.

Making an Ethical Decision

1. Are all employees—even those in small businesses—entitled to job benefits?
2. If you were an employee, what kinds of benefits would you want?
3. If you were an employer, what benefits would you want to offer and why? What other job "perks" could you offer your employees that would not directly cost money?

The textbook contains You Make the Call, which asks students to answer the questions in Making an Ethical Decision. You may want to use this feature for class discussions or have your students develop their writing and communication skills by requiring short reports analyzing the ethical aspects of the scenarios.

Meeting Individual Needs and Learning Styles

One of your greatest challenges as a teacher is to provide a positive learning environment for all students in your classroom. Because each student has his or her own unique set of abilities, perceptions, and needs, learning styles and physical abilities of your students may vary widely.

Assisting Students With Individual Needs

In order to help you provide all your students with a positive learning experience, this text provides a variety of activities. This diversity will stimulate student interest, motivate learning, and facilitate understanding. The *Teacher Wraparound Edition* also provides Individualized Practice activities. These activities reinforce chapter learning by allowing students to progress at their own pace.

Teaching Students With Special Needs

Students in your classroom may have orthopedic impairments. They may have hearing or vision impairments, learning disabilities, or behavior disorders—all of which may interfere with their ability to learn. The learning styles of your students may also vary. Some students may be visual learners; others may learn more effectively through hands-on activities. Some students may work well independently, while others need the interaction of others. Students may come from a variety of cultural backgrounds, and some may be second language learners.

Once you determine the special needs of your students, you can identify the areas in the curriculum that may present barriers to them. In order to remove those barriers, you may need to modify your teaching methods.

On the following pages are two charts. The first chart, Meeting Special Needs, describes some of the special needs you may encounter with students in your classroom and identifies sources of information. Also provided are tips for modifying your teaching style to accommodate the special needs of your students.

The second chart, Eight Ways of Learning, will help you identify your students' learning styles. The chart gives a description of each type of learner; describes the likes of each type, what each type is good at, and how each learns best; and names some famous learners. Once you have identified each student's learning style, you can modify your teaching strategies to best suit his or her needs.

Meeting Special Needs

Subject	Description	Sources of Information
Second Language Learners	Certain students often speak English as a second language, or not at all. Customs and behavior of people in the majority culture may be confusing for some of these students. Cultural values may inhibit some of these students from full participation in the classroom.	• *Teaching English as a Second Language* • *Mainstreaming and the Minority Child*
Behavior Disorders	Children with behavior disorders deviate from standards or expectations of behavior and impair the functioning of others and themselves. These children may also be gifted or have learning disabilities.	• *Exceptional Children* • *Journal of Special Education*
Visual Impairments	Children with visual impairments have partial or total loss of sight. Individuals with visual impairments are not significantly different from their sighted peers in ability range or personality. However, blindness may affect cognitive, motor, and social development.	• *Journal of Visual Impairment and Blindness* • *Education of Visually Handicapped* • *American Foundation for the Blind*
Hearing Impairments	Children with hearing impairments have partial or total loss of hearing. Individuals with hearing impairments are not significantly different from their peers in ability range or personality. However, the chronic condition of deafness may affect cognitive, motor, social, and speech development.	• *American Annals of the Deaf* • *Journal of Speech and Hearing Research* • *Sign Language Studies*
Physical Impairments	Children with physical impairments fall into two categories—those with orthopedic impairments (use of one or more limbs severely restricted) and those with other health impairments.	• *The Source Book for the Disabled* • *Teaching Exceptional Children*
Gifted	Although no formal definition exists, these students can be described as having above average ability, task commitment, and creativity. They rank in the top 5 percent of their classes. They usually finish work more quickly than other students and are capable of divergent thinking.	• *Journal for the Education of the Gifted* • *Gifted Child Quarterly* • *Gifted Creative/Talented*
Learning Disabilities	All students with learning disabilities have a problem in one or more areas, such as academic learning, language, perception, social-emotional adjustment, memory, or ability to pay attention.	• *Journal of Learning Disabilities* • *Learning Disability Quarterly*

Tips for Instruction

- Remember that students' ability to speak English does not reflect their academic ability.
- Try to incorporate students' cultural experiences into your instruction. The help of a bilingual aide may be effective.
- Include information about different cultures in your curriculum to help build students' self-image.
- Avoid cultural stereotypes.
- Encourage students to share their cultures in the classroom.

- Work for long-term improvement; do not expect immediate success.
- Talk with students about their strengths and weaknesses, and clearly outline objectives.
- Structure schedules, rules, room arrangement, and safety for a conducive learning environment.
- Model appropriate behavior for students and reinforce proper behavior.

- Modify assignments as needed to help students become independent.
- Teach classmates how to serve as guides for the visually impaired.
- Tape lectures and reading assignments for the visually impaired.
- Encourage students to use their sense of touch; provide tactile models whenever possible.
- Verbally describe people and events as they occur in the classroom for students with visual impairments.

- Limit unnecessary noise in the classroom.
- Provide favorable seating arrangements so students with hearing impairments can see speakers and read their lips (or interpreters can assist); avoid visual distractions.
- Write out all instructions on paper or on the board; overhead projectors enable you to maintain eye contact while writing.
- Avoid standing with your back to the window or light source.

- With the student, determine when you should offer aid.
- Help other students and adults understand students with physical impairments.
- Learn about special devices or procedures and if any special safety precautions are needed.
- Allow students to participate in all activities including field trips, special events, and projects.

- Emphasize concepts, theories, relationships, ideas, and generalizations.
- Let students express themselves in a variety of ways including drawing, creative writing, or acting.
- Make arrangements for students to work on independent projects.
- Make arrangements for students to take selected subjects early.

- Provide assistance and direction; clearly define rules, assignments, and duties.
- Allow for pair interaction during class time; utilize peer helpers.
- Practice skills frequently. Distribute outlines of material presented to class.
- Allow extra time to complete tests and assignments.

Eight Ways of Learning

Type	Description	Likes to...
Verbal/Linguistic Learner	Intelligence is related to words and language, written, and spoken.	read, write, tell stories, play word games, and tell jokes and riddles
Logical/Mathematical Learner	Intelligence deals with inductive and deductive thinking and reasoning, numbers, and abstractions.	perform experiments, solve puzzles, work with numbers, ask questions, and explore patterns and relationships
Visual/Spatial Learner	Intelligence relies on the sense of sight and being able to visualize an object, including the ability to create mental images.	draw, build, design, and create things, daydream, do jigsaw puzzles and mazes, watch videos, look at photos, and draw maps and charts
Naturalistic Learner	Intelligence has to do with observing, understanding, and organizing patterns in the natural environment.	spend time outdoors and work with plants, animals, and other parts of the natural environment; good at identifying plants and animals and at hearing and seeing connections to nature
Musical/Rhythmic Learner	Intelligence is based on recognition of tonal patterns, including various environmental sounds, and on sensitivity to rhythm and beats.	sing and hum, listen to music, play an instrument, move body when music is playing, and make up songs
Bodily/Kinesthetic Learner	Intelligence is related to physical movement and the brain's motor cortex, which controls bodily motion.	learn by hands-on methods, demonstrate skill in crafts, tinker, perform, display physical endurance, and challenge self—physically
Interpersonal Learner	Intelligence operates primarily through person-to-person relationships and communication.	have lots of friends, talk to people, join groups, play cooperative games, solve problems as part of a group, and volunteer help when others need it
Intrapersonal Learner	Intelligence is related to inner states of being, self-reflection, metacognition, and awareness of spiritual realities.	work alone, pursue own interests, daydream, keep a personal diary or journal, and think about starting own business

Is good at...	Learns best by...	Famous Learners
memorizing names, dates, places, and trivia; spelling; using descriptive language; and creating imaginary worlds	saying, hearing, and seeing words	Maya Angelou—poet Abraham Lincoln—U.S. President and statesman Jerry Seinfeld—comedian Mary Hatwood Futrell—international teacher, leader, orator
math, reasoning, logic, problem solving, computing numbers, moving from concrete to abstract, thinking conceptually	categorizing, classifying, and working with abstract patterns and relationships	Stephen Hawking—physicist Albert Einstein—theoretical physicist Marilyn Burns—math educator Alexa Canady—neurosurgeon
understanding the use of space and how to get around in it, thinking in three-dimensional terms, and imagining things in clear visual images	visualizing, dreaming, using the mind's eye, and working with colors and pictures	Pablo Picasso—artist Maria Martinez—Pueblo Indian famous for black pottery Faith Ringgold—painter, quilter, and writer I.M. Pei—architect
measuring, charting, mapping, observing plants and animals, keeping journals, collecting, classifying, participating in outdoor activities	visualizing, hands-on activities, bringing outdoors into the classroom, relating home/classroom to the natural world	George Washington Carver—agricultural chemist Rachel Carson—scientific writer Charles Darwin—evolutionist John James Audubon—conservationist
remembering melodies; keeping time; mimicking beat and rhythm; noticing pitches, rhythms, and background and environmental sounds	rhythm, melody, and music	Henry Mancini—composer Marian Anderson—contralto Midori—violinist Paul McCartney—singer, songwriter, musician
physical activities such as sports, dancing, acting, and crafts	touching, moving, interacting with space, and processing knowledge through bodily sensations	Marcel Marceau—mime Jackie Joyner-Kersey—Olympic gold medalist in track and field Katherine Dunham—modern dancer Dr. Christian Bernard—cardiac surgeon
understanding people and their feelings, leading others, organizing, communicating, manipulating, mediating conflicts	sharing, comparing, relating, cooperating, and interviewing	Jimmy Carter—former U.S. President and statesman Eleanor Roosevelt—former first lady Lee Iococca—president of Chrysler Corporation Mother Teresa—winner of Nobel Peace Prize
understanding self, focusing inward on feelings/dreams, following instincts, pursuing interests, and being original	working alone, doing individualized projects, engaging in self-paced instruction	Marva Collins—educator Mara Montessori—educator and physician Sigmund Freud—psychotherapist Anne Sexton—poet

COURSE PLANNING GUIDE

Block Scheduling

(90-minute periods for nine weeks, meeting alternate days, or meeting every day for 90 minutes a day for nine weeks)

GRADING PERIOD	CHAPTERS	CLASS PERIODS
UNIT 1	**THE ECONOMY AND YOU**	
Chapter 1	A Look at Needs and Wants	2
Chapter 2	Economic Resources and Systems	2
Chapter 3	Economic Activity in a Changing World	2
Chapter 4	Business Ethics and Social Responsibility	2
BusinessWeek Seminar, Global Business, What Is Today's Chinese Business Trend?		2
UNIT 2	**OWNING AND OPERATING A BUSINESS**	
Chapter 5	Entrepreneurship and Small Business	2
Chapter 6	Business Ownership and Operations	2
Chapter 7	Organizational Structures	2
Chapter 8	Leadership in Management	2
Chapter 9	Technology's Impact on Business	2
BusinessWeek Seminar, Small Business, Discovering Small Business		2
UNIT 3	**GROUPS AFFECTING BUSINESS**	
Chapter 10	Business in a Global Economy	2
Chapter 11	The Role of Government in Business	2
Chapter 12	Money and Financial Institutions	2
BusinessWeek Seminar, Careers, Discovering Business Careers		2
UNIT 4	**MARKETING TO THE CONSUMER**	
Chapter 13	Marketing in Today's World	2
Chapter 14	Advertising: The Art of Attracting an Audience	2
BusinessWeek Seminar, Technology, Discovering Technology in Marketing		1
UNIT 5	**THE HUMAN RESOURCES ADVANTAGE**	
Chapter 15	Human Resources Management	2
Chapter 16	Culture and Diversity in Business	2
BusinessWeek Seminar, Careers, Using Resources to Find the Right People		2
UNIT 6	**MANAGING FINANCIAL AND TECHNOLOGICAL RESOURCES**	
Chapter 17	Managing Business Finances	2
Chapter 18	Technology Advancements in the Workplace	2

GRADING PERIOD	CHAPTERS	CLASS PERIODS
Chapter 19	Basics of Computers	2
BusinessWeek Seminar, Technology, Applying Technology to New Business Ideas		2
UNIT 7	**CAREER PLANNING IN A GLOBAL ECONOMY**	
Chapter 20	Developing a Career Plan	2
Chapter 21	Getting a Job	2
BusinessWeek Seminar, Global Business, Career Options in a Global Economy		2
UNIT 8	**BUYING GOODS AND SERVICES**	
Chapter 22	Making Consumer Decisions	2
Chapter 23	Consumer Rights and Responsibilities	2
Chapter 24	Protecting Consumers	2
BusinessWeek Seminar, Global Business, Understanding OPEC		1
UNIT 9	**CREDIT**	
Chapter 25	What Is Credit?	2
Chapter 26	How to Get and Keep Credit	2
Chapter 27	Your Credit and the Law	2
BusinessWeek Seminar, Small Business, Using Credit to Start a Small Business		2
UNIT 10	**MONEY MANAGEMENT**	
Chapter 28	Planning a Budget	2
Chapter 29	Checking Accounts	2
Chapter 30	Savings Accounts	2
Chapter 31	Investing in Stocks	2
Chapter 32	Bonds and Real Estate	2
BusinessWeek Seminar, Technology, Tracking Investments on the Internet		2
UNIT 11	**RISK MANAGEMENT**	
Chapter 33	Vehicle Insurance	2
Chapter 34	Property Insurance	2
Chapter 35	Life and Health Insurance	2
BusinessWeek Seminar, Careers, Investigating Business Schools		2

Six-Week Grading Period

GRADING PERIOD	CHAPTERS	CLASS PERIODS
1	**UNIT 1 THE ECONOMY AND YOU**	
	Chapter 1 A Look at Needs and Wants	4
	Chapter 2 Economic Resources and Systems	4
	Chapter 3 Economic Activity in a Changing World	4
	Chapter 4 Business Ethics and Social Responsibility	4
	BusinessWeek Seminar, Global Business, What Is Today's Chinese Business Trend?	2

GRADING PERIOD	CHAPTERS	CLASS PERIODS
	UNIT 2 OWNING AND OPERATING A BUSINESS	
	Chapter 5 Entrepreneurship and Small Business	4
	Chapter 6 Business Ownership and Operations	4
	Chapter 7 Organizational Structures	4
2	Chapter 8 Leadership in Management	5
	Chapter 9 Technology's Impact on Business	5
	BusinessWeek Seminar, Small Business, Discovering Small Business	4

CONTINUED AT TOP OF THE NEXT PAGE

Six-Week Grading Period (continued)

GRADING PERIOD	CHAPTERS	CLASS PERIODS
	UNIT 3 GROUPS AFFECTING BUSINESS	
	Chapter 10 Business in a Global Economy	4
	Chapter 11 The Role of Government in Business	4
	Chapter 12 Money and Financial Institutions	5
	Business Week Seminar, Careers, Discovering Business Careers	3
3	**UNIT 4 MARKETING TO THE CONSUMER**	
	Chapter 13 Marketing in Today's World	6
	Chapter 14 Advertising: The Art of Attracting an Audience	5
	Business Week Seminar, Technology, Discovering Technology in Marketing	4
	UNIT 5 THE HUMAN RESOURCES ADVANTAGE	
	Chapter 15 Human Resources Management	5
	Chapter 16 Culture and Diversity in Business	6
	Business Week Seminar, Careers, Using Resources to Find the Right People	4
4	**UNIT 6 MANAGING FINANCIAL AND TECHNOLOGICAL RESOURCES**	
	Chapter 17 Managing Business Finances	5
	Chapter 18 Technology Advancements in the Workplace	5
	Chapter 19 Basics of Computers	4
	Business Week Seminar, Technology, Applying Technology to New Business Ideas	3
	UNIT 7 CAREER PLANNING IN A GLOBAL ECONOMY	
	Chapter 20 Developing a Career Plan	5
	Chapter 21 Getting a Job	5

GRADING PERIOD	CHAPTERS	CLASS PERIODS
	Business Week Seminar, Global Business, Career Options in a Global Economy	3
5	**UNIT 8 BUYING GOODS AND SERVICES**	
	Chapter 22 Making Consumer Decisions	4
	Chapter 23 Consumer Rights and Responsibilities	4
	Chapter 24 Protecting Consumers	4
	Business Week Seminar, Global Business, Understanding OPEC	3
	UNIT 9 CREDIT	
	Chapter 25 What Is Credit?	4
	Chapter 26 How to Get and Keep Credit	4
	Chapter 27 Your Credit and the Law	4
	Business Week Seminar, Small Business, Using Credit to Start a Small Business	3
6	**UNIT 10 MONEY MANAGEMENT**	
	Chapter 28 Planning a Budget	3
	Chapter 29 Checking Accounts	3
	Chapter 30 Savings Accounts	3
	Chapter 31 Investing in Stocks	3
	Chapter 32 Bonds and Real Estate	3
	Business Week Seminar, Technology, Tracking Investments on the Internet	3
	UNIT 11 RISK MANAGEMENT	
	Chapter 33 Vehicle Insurance	3
	Chapter 34 Property Insurance	3
	Chapter 35 Life and Health Insurance	3
	Business Week Seminar, Careers, Investigating Business Schools	3

Nine-Week Grading Period

GRADING PERIOD	CHAPTERS	CLASS PERIODS
1	**UNIT 1 THE ECONOMY AND YOU**	
	Chapter 1 A Look at Needs and Wants	4
	Chapter 2 Economic Resources and Systems	5
	Chapter 3 Economic Activity in a Changing World	4
	Chapter 4 Business Ethics and Social Responsibility	4
	Business Week Seminar, Global Business, What Is Today's Chinese Business Trend?	3
	UNIT 2 OWNING AND OPERATING A BUSINESS	
	Chapter 5 Entrepreneurship and Small Business	5
	Chapter 6 Business Ownership and Operations	4
	Chapter 7 Organizational Structures	4
	Chapter 8 Leadership in Management	4
	Chapter 9 Technology's Impact on Business	5
	Business Week Seminar, Small Business, Discovering Small Business	3
2	**UNIT 3 GROUPS AFFECTING BUSINESS**	
	Chapter 10 Business in a Global Economy	5
	Chapter 11 The Role of Government in Business	5

GRADING PERIOD	CHAPTERS	CLASS PERIODS
	Chapter 12 Money and Financial Institutions	5
	Business Week Seminar, Careers, Discovering Business Careers	3
	UNIT 4 MARKETING TO THE CONSUMER	
	Chapter 13 Marketing in Today's World	6
	Chapter 14 Advertising: The Art of Attracting an Audience	5
	Business Week Seminar, Technology, Discovering Technology in Marketing	3
	UNIT 5 THE HUMAN RESOURCES ADVANTAGE	
	Chapter 15 Human Resources Management	5
	Chapter 16 Culture and Diversity in Business	5
	Business Week Seminar, Careers, Using Resources to Find the Right People	3
3	**UNIT 6 MANAGING FINANCIAL AND TECHNOLOGICAL RESOURCES**	
	Chapter 17 Managing Business Finances	4
	Chapter 18 Technology Advancements in the Workplace	4

CONTINUED AT TOP OF THE NEXT PAGE

Teaching Strategies

Nine-Week Grading Period (continued)

GRADING PERIOD	CHAPTERS	CLASS PERIODS
	Chapter 19 Basics of Computers	4
	Business Week Seminar, Technology, Applying Technology to New Business Ideas	3
	UNIT 7 CAREER PLANNING IN A GLOBAL ECONOMY	
	Chapter 20 Developing a Career Plan	5
	Chapter 21 Getting a Job	5
	Business Week Seminar, Global Business, Career Options in a Global Economy	4
	UNIT 8 BUYING GOODS AND SERVICES	
	Chapter 22 Making Consumer Decisions	5
	Chapter 23 Consumer Rights and Responsibilities	4
	Chapter 24 Protecting Consumers	4
	Business Week Seminar, Global Business, Understanding OPEC	3
4	**UNIT 9 CREDIT**	
	Chapter 25 What Is Credit?	4
	Chapter 26 How to Get and Keep Credit	4

GRADING PERIOD	CHAPTERS	CLASS PERIODS
	Chapter 27 Your Credit and the Law	3
	Business Week Seminar, Small Business, Using Credit to Start a Small Business	2
	UNIT 10 MONEY MANAGEMENT	
	Chapter 28 Planning a Budget	4
	Chapter 29 Checking Accounts	4
	Chapter 30 Savings Accounts	3
	Chapter 31 Investing in Stocks	3
	Chapter 32 Bonds and Real Estate	4
	Business Week Seminar, Technology, Tracking Investments on the Internet	2
	UNIT 11 RISK MANAGEMENT	
	Chapter 33 Vehicle Insurance	3
	Chapter 34 Property Insurance	3
	Chapter 35 Life and Health Insurance	3
	Business Week Seminar, Careers, Investigating Business Schools	3

One-Semester Course Emphasizing Personal and Business Finance

UNIT 1 THE ECONOMY AND YOU
Chapter 1 A Look at Needs and Wants
Chapter 2 Economic Resources and Systems
Chapter 3 Economic Activity in a Changing World
Chapter 4 Business Ethics and Social Responsibility
Business Week Seminar, Global Business, What Is Today's Chinese Business Trend?

UNIT 2 OWNING AND OPERATING A BUSINESS
Chapter 5 Entrepreneurship and Small Business
Chapter 6 Business Ownership and Operations
Chapter 7 Organizational Structures
Chapter 8 Leadership in Management
Chapter 9 Technology's Impact on Business
Business Week Seminar, Small Business, Discovering Small Business

UNIT 3 GROUPS AFFECTING BUSINESS
Chapter 10 Business in a Global Economy
Chapter 11 The Role of Government in Business
Chapter 12 Money and Financial Institutions
Business Week Seminar, Careers, Discovering Business Careers

UNIT 6 MANAGING FINANCIAL AND TECHNOLOGICAL RESOURCES
Chapter 17 Managing Business Finances
Chapter 18 Technology Advancements in the Workplace
Chapter 19 Basics of Computers
Business Week Seminar, Technology, Applying Technology to New Business Ideas

UNIT 7 CAREER PLANNING IN A GLOBAL ECONOMY
Chapter 20 Developing a Career Plan

Chapter 21 Getting a Job
Business Week Seminar, Global Business, Career Options in a Global Economy

UNIT 8 BUYING GOODS AND SERVICES
Chapter 22 Making Consumer Decisions
Chapter 23 Consumer Rights and Responsibilities
Chapter 24 Protecting Consumers
Business Week Seminar, Global Business, Understanding OPEC

UNIT 9 CREDIT
Chapter 25 What Is Credit?
Chapter 26 How to Get and Keep Credit
Chapter 27 Your Credit and the Law
Business Week Seminar, Small Business, Using Credit to Start a Small Business

UNIT 10 MONEY MANAGEMENT
Chapter 28 Planning a Budget
Chapter 29 Checking Accounts
Chapter 30 Savings Accounts
Chapter 31 Investing in Stocks
Chapter 32 Bonds and Real Estate
Business Week Seminar, Technology, Tracking Investments on the Internet

UNIT 11 RISK MANAGEMENT
Chapter 33 Vehicle Insurance
Chapter 34 Property Insurance
Chapter 35 Life and Health Insurance
Business Week Seminar, Careers, Investigating Business Schools

One-Semester Course Emphasizing Entrepreneurship

UNIT 1 THE ECONOMY AND YOU
Chapter 1 A Look at Needs and Wants
Chapter 2 Economic Resources and Systems
Chapter 3 Economic Activity in a Changing World
Chapter 4 Business Ethics and Social Responsibility
BusinessWeek Seminar, Global Business, What Is Today's Chinese Business Trend?

UNIT 2 OWNING AND OPERATING A BUSINESS
Chapter 5 Entrepreneurship and Small Business
Chapter 6 Business Ownership and Operations
Chapter 7 Organizational Structures
Chapter 8 Leadership in Management
Chapter 9 Technology's Impact on Business
BusinessWeek Seminar, Small Business, Discovering Small Business

UNIT 3 GROUPS AFFECTING BUSINESS
Chapter 10 Business in a Global Economy
Chapter 11 The Role of Government in Business
Chapter 12 Money and Financial Institutions
BusinessWeek Seminar, Careers, Discovering Business Careers

UNIT 4 MARKETING TO THE CONSUMER
Chapter 13 Marketing in Today's World
Chapter 14 Advertising: The Art of Attracting an Audience
BusinessWeek Seminar, Technology, Discovering Technology in Marketing

UNIT 5 THE HUMAN RESOURCES ADVANTAGE
Chapter 15 Human Resources Management
Chapter 16 Culture and Diversity in Business
BusinessWeek Seminar, Careers, Using Resources to Find the Right People

UNIT 6 MANAGING FINANCIAL AND TECHNOLOGICAL RESOURCES
Chapter 17 Managing Business Finances
Chapter 18 Technology Advancements in the Workplace
Chapter 19 Basics of Computers
BusinessWeek Seminar, Technology, Applying Technology to New Business Ideas

UNIT 9 CREDIT
Chapter 25 What Is Credit?
Chapter 26 How to Get and Keep Credit
Chapter 27 Your Credit and the Law
BusinessWeek Seminar, Small Business, Using Credit to Start a Small Business

UNIT 11 RISK MANAGEMENT
Chapter 33 Vehicle Insurance
Chapter 34 Property Insurance
Chapter 35 Life and Health Insurance
BusinessWeek Seminar, Careers, Investigating Business Schools

One-Semester Course Emphasizing Economics

UNIT 1 THE ECONOMY AND YOU
Chapter 1 A Look at Needs and Wants
Chapter 2 Economic Resources and Systems
Chapter 3 Economic Activity in a Changing World
Chapter 4 Business Ethics and Social Responsibility
BusinessWeek Seminar, Global Business, What Is Today's Chinese Business Trend?

UNIT 2 OWNING AND OPERATING A BUSINESS
Chapter 5 Entrepreneurship and Small Business
Chapter 6 Business Ownership and Operations
Chapter 7 Organizational Structures
Chapter 8 Leadership in Management
Chapter 9 Technology's Impact on Business
BusinessWeek Seminar, Small Business, Discovering Small Business

UNIT 3 GROUPS AFFECTING BUSINESS
Chapter 10 Business in a Global Economy
Chapter 11 The Role of Government in Business
Chapter 12 Money and Financial Institutions
BusinessWeek Seminar, Careers, Discovering Business Careers

UNIT 10 MONEY MANAGEMENT
Chapter 28 Planning a Budget
Chapter 29 Checking Accounts
Chapter 30 Savings Accounts
Chapter 31 Investing in Stocks
Chapter 32 Bonds and Real Estate
BusinessWeek Seminar, Technology, Tracking Investments on the Internet

The Economy and You

● Unit Objectives

After completing this unit, students will be able to achieve the following outcomes:

- State the differences between wants and needs, and identify business activities used to satisfy wants and needs.
- Explain scarcity, the four factors of production, and market and command economies.
- Identify how economic activity is measured, and list the four phases of the business cycle.
- Explain business ethics, and describe the social responsibilities of business.

BusinessWeek Connections

In this unit, students will read the following articles from *BusinessWeek*:

Chapter 1 "Paperless Page-Turners?": Best-selling authors are predicted to make the difference to the success of e-books.

Chapter 2 "Poland: Goods Runneth Over": Can central Europe follow Poland's bold economic reform?

Chapter 3 "Moving Up the Ladder": Follow the story of José Brigido Aguirre as globalization affords workers better career opportunities.

Chapter 4 "Commerce Reweaves the Social Fabric": Good company citizenship is changing the towns of the future.

Key to Descriptive Icons

The following designations will help you decide which activities are appropriate for your students.

L1 Level 1 activities should be within the ability range of all students.

L2 Level 2 activities should be within the ability range of the average to above-average students.

L3 Level 3 activities are designed for the ability range of above-average students.

ELL Activities should be within the ability range of the English Language Learner.

LS Learning Styles designation represents activities designed to address different learning styles.

CL Cooperative learning activities are designed for small group work.

P Portfolio designation represents student products that can be placed into a best-work portfolio.

Teacher Classroom Resources*

Program Resources	Chapter 1	Chapter 2	Chapter 3	Chapter 4
Student Activity Workbook	p. 1	p. 7	p. 15	p. 21
Lesson Plans	p. 2	p. 4	p. 6	p. 8
Internet Resources	p. 21	p. 23	p. 25	p. 27
Reproducible Tests	p. 1	p. 3	p. 5	p. 7
Teaching Transparencies	1.1, 1.2	2.1, 2,2	3.1, 3.2	4.1, 4.2
Strategies and Worksheets for Teaching Transparencies	pp. 1, 19	pp. 1, 21	pp. 2, 23	p. 2, 25

* Each of these resources is available in print and on the Interactive Lesson Planner CD-ROM.

Technology Resources

- Interactive Lesson Planner CD-ROM
- PowerPoint® Presentation CD-ROM
- ExamView® Pro Test Generator CD-ROM
- Integrated Software Simulation, Teacher Manual
- Glencoe Business Video Package
- *PuzzleMaker* CD-ROM
- *Introduction to Business* Web Site
- *Virtual Business*®
  Virtual Business is a business simulation that introduces students to the principles of business by letting them start and run their own virtual business. In *Virtual Business*, students have the power to control all aspects of a retail convenience store. Students strategize business decisions using a powerful learning tool in the guise of a video game.

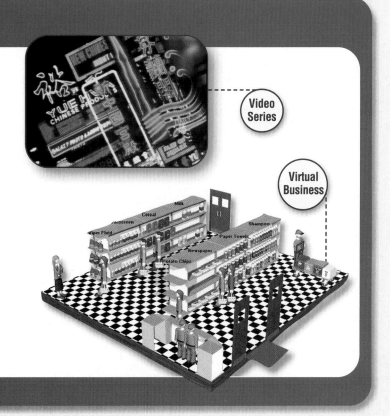

Video Series

Virtual Business

Scope and Sequence

Academic Standards of Learning

	LANGUAGE ARTS	MATH	HISTORY	COMPUTER/ TECHNOLOGY	SOCIAL SCIENCE
CHAPTER 1	pp. 4, 5, 6, 11, 12, 16, 17	pp. 11, 16, 17	pp. 10, 16	pp. 8, 16, 17	pp. 8, 12, 16, 17
CHAPTER 2	pp. 18, 19, 21, 26, 27, 32, 33	pp. 19, 24, 25, 26, 29, 32, 33	pp. 22, 23, 24, 32	pp. 32, 33	pp. 19, 20, 22, 25, 33
CHAPTER 3	pp. 34, 35, 37, 42, 46, 47	pp. 36, 37, 38, 40, 46, 47	pp. 36, 40, 41, 46, 47	pp. 46, 47	pp. 34, 35, 37, 38, 40, 41, 46, 47
CHAPTER 4	pp. 48, 49, 51, 52, 56, 60, 61	pp. 55, 60, 61	pp. 50, 60	pp. 52, 60, 61	pp. 50, 51, 54, 55, 60, 61

Scope and Sequence

Themes and Concepts

Business Core	Accounting and Finance	Business Management	Computer/ Technology	Marketing	Entrepreneurship
Competitive Environment Goal Setting Adapting to Change Problem Solving Decision Making Personal Qualities	Decision Making Financial Responsibilities	Economic Indicators Opportunity Costs Management	Time Management Needs Analysis Resource Management	New Product Purchasing Sales Promotion Buying Motives and Behaviors	Financial Planning Management Risk Management
Competitive Environment International Trade Demographics Economic Culture Economic Systems Global Business	Decision Making Economic Factors Industry Analysis	Decision Making Consumers Economic Indicators Economic Systems Trade Concepts Government Regulations Communication	Social Issues Change Management Resource Management Business Decisions Emerging Technology and Trends	Culture Diversity Profitability Balance of Trade Markets Distribution Strategy Pricing Strategy Products and Service Knowledge	Entrepreneurial Potential Government Regulations International Business Management Production
Competitive Envir. International Trade Employ. Transitions Job Retention Demographics Economic Systems Global Business Money Management	Decision Making International Finance Financial Markets Financial Responsibility Economic Indicators Unemployment	Competition Finance Trade Concepts	Productivity Time Management Resource Management	Balance of Trade Global Alliances Markets Sales in the Global Economy	Financial Resources International Business
Diversity Ethics Business Ethics Business Law Environmental Issues Adapting to Change Occupational Safety	Financial Responsibility	Competition Decision Making Consumers Exchange and Money Government Regulations Employment Law Legal Rights Culture	Business Decisions	Cultural Diversity Culture Markets Buying Motives and Behaviors Regulation	Government Regulations Management Production

Unit Overview

Unit 1 gives information about economic activity that affects everyday life.

CHAPTER 1 explains wants and needs and examines what business is.

CHAPTER 2 introduces scarcity and the four factors of production, and describes economic systems.

CHAPTER 3 describes types of economic measurements and explains the four phases of the business cycle.

CHAPTER 4 focuses on business ethics and describes the social responsibility of business.

Introducing the Unit

Ask students to list things they want and things they need. Ask how businesses provide for these wants and needs. Then have students give examples of companies they feel are good, socially responsible businesses. Explain to students that many of the goods we buy to satisfy our wants and needs come from other countries. Our country also sells many products to other countries.

Technology Resource

INTRODUCTION TO BUSINESS WEB SITE. To find out more about content in Unit 1, visit the Glencoe *Introduction to Business* Web site. **www.introbus.glencoe.com**

The Economy and You

Confectionary Consumption

Valentine's Day. Halloween. You've all seen the bins and bins full of chocolate ready for sale and consumption until your gut aches. The story of chocolate goes back as far as the discovery of America. Columbus came back from America with the main ingredient of chocolate—cocoa beans—and delivered them to the Court of King Ferdinand and Queen Isabella. Around 1765 the first chocolate factory was established in New England and gained much attention and interest from cocoa bean growers, manufacturers, and consumers. Chocolate's a want for some and for others it's their livelihood.

- **Lavish Lands**
  Cocoa beans are only cultivated in land no more than 20 degrees north or south of the equator.

- **The Average Danish**
  Denmark consumes the most sugar per capita in the world.

- **Sweet Sales**
  The chocolate industry sells $13 billion of product per year.

- **The World's Nuts**
  Chocolate manufacturers use 40 percent of the world's almonds and 20 percent of the world's peanuts.

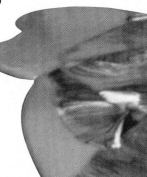

- **Essential Nutrients**
  The U.S. Army food rations include three 4-ounce chocolate bars.

Field Trip Suggestion

Local Business. Take students for a bus tour around the community. Before the trip have students mark the planned route on a local map. On the trip, stop and point out commercial areas, business parks, large businesses, and small businesses. Have students mark their map with symbols, such as letters or numbers, as a key for each stopping point. On the trip ask questions relevant to this unit about wants and needs, economic resources and systems, changing economic activity, and business ethics and social responsibility. This local business tour will give students awareness of the vast business activity in the community. This will form a foundation of knowledge to use throughout this course. **LS, CL**

BUSINESS
Online
Idea Factory
To learn more about the chocolate industry, visit the *Introduction to Business* Web site at **www.introbus.glencoe.com**, and click on Unit 1 The Economy and You.

Unit 1

Bulletin Board

Glencoe Poster Teaching Tip

Before introducing the poster, ask students who have jobs if coworkers ever report unethical behavior. Let students know that in Chapter 4 of this unit they'll be discussing business ethics and social responsibility. Then have the students take the quiz on the poster. Lead a class discussion by asking students: Do you think ethical behavior is important in business? Why or why not? Encourage students to give examples.

⏱ Out of Time?

If time doesn't permit teaching each chapter in this unit, you may use the chapter's "Preteaching Business Key Words" activity and the summary to focus on the business vocabulary and main points.

Portfolio Activity

Interview and Report. Have students choose a local business (possibly one of the businesses they saw on this unit's field trip) and arrange to interview a manager or executive. The interview may be a phone interview. Students should prepare questions to find out what services or goods the company provides, how the current economy and government are helping or hindering the company's success at the present time, and examples of how the company is socially responsible. Students should ask for company brochures. Have students create a report on the interview illustrated with cut outs from the company brochures, or magazines. **P**, **LS**

SCANS Correlation Chart*

Foundation Skills

Basic Skills	Reading	Writing	Math	Listening	Speaking	
Thinking Skills	Creative Thinking	Decision Making	Problem Solving	Seeing Things in the Mind's Eye	Knowing How to Learn	Reasoning
Personal Qualities	Responsibility	Self-Esteem	Sociability	Self-Management	Integrity/ Honesty	

Workplace Competencies

Resources	Allocating Time	Allocating Money	Allocating Material and Facility Resources	Allocating Human Resources		
Information	Acquiring and Evaluating Information	Organizing and Maintaining Information	Interpreting and Communicating Information	Using Computers to Process Information		
Interpersonal Skills	Participating as a Member of a Team	Teaching Others	Serving Clients/ Customers	Exercising Leadership	Negotiating to Arrive at a Decision	Working With Cultural Diversity
Systems	Understanding Systems	Monitoring and Correcting Performance	Improving and Designing Systems			
Technology	Selecting Technology	Applying Technology to Task	Maintaining and Troubleshooting Technology			

*This chart's highlighted blocks indicate the chapter's content coverage in the Student Edition and the Teacher Wraparound Edition.

Resource Manager

Teaching Transparencies

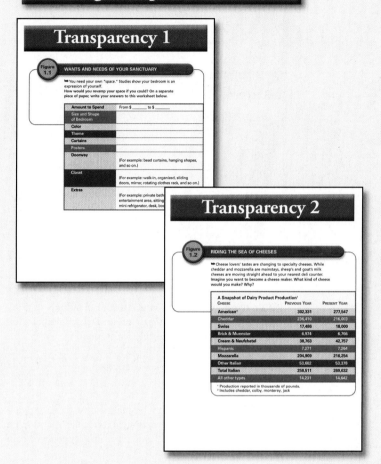

Transparency 1

Figure 1.1 WANTS AND NEEDS OF YOUR SANCTUARY

➡ You need your own "space." Studies show your bedroom is an expression of yourself.
How would you revamp your space if you could? On a separate piece of paper, write your answers to this worksheet below.

Amount to Spend	From $ _____ to $ _____
Size and Shape of Bedroom	
Color	
Theme	
Curtains	
Posters	
Doorway	(For example: bead curtains, hanging shapes, and so on.)
Closet	(For example: walk-in, organized, sliding doors, mirror, rotating clothes rack, and so on.)
Extras	(For example: private bath, entertainment area, sitting mini refrigerator, desk, boo

Transparency 2

Figure 1.2 RIDING THE SEA OF CHEESES

➡ Cheese lovers' tastes are changing to specialty cheeses. While cheddar and mozzarella are mainstays, sheep's and goat's milk cheeses are moving straight ahead to your nearest deli counter. Imagine you want to become a cheese maker. What kind of cheese would you make? Why?

A Snapshot of Dairy Product Production[1]

CHEESE	PREVIOUS YEAR	PRESENT YEAR
American[2]	302,331	277,547
Cheddar	236,410	216,003
Swiss	17,486	18,000
Brick & Muenster	6,974	6,766
Cream & Neufchatel	38,763	42,757
Hispanic	7,271	7,264
Mozzarella	204,909	216,254
Other Italian	53,602	53,378
Total Italian	258,511	269,632
All other types	14,231	14,642

[1] Production reported in thousands of pounds.
[2] Includes cheddar, colby, monterey, jack

Application and Enrichment

- 🖊 Lesson Plans
- 📕 *BusinessWeek* Poster Package
- 🔧 Teaching Transparencies
- 💿 🖊 Integrated Software Simulation
- 📼 🖊 Glencoe Business Video Package

Review and Reinforcement

- 💿 *PuzzleMaker*
- 💻 🖊 Internet Resources
- 🖊 Student Activity Workbook
- 🖊 Strat. and Work. for Teaching Transparencies

Assessment and Evaluation

- 🖊 Reproducible Tests
- 🖊 Alternative Assessment Strategies
- 💿 ExamView® Pro Test Generator

Technology

- 💿 *PuzzleMaker*
- 💿 ExamView® Pro Test Generator
- 📼 Glencoe Business Video Package
- 💿 PowerPoint® Presentation
- 💿 🖊 Integrated Software Simulation
- 💿 Interactive Lesson Planner
- 💿 *Virtual Business*®

KEY	🖊 Printed	💾 Software	📼 Videocassette	📕 Poster
	🔧 Transparency	💿 CD-ROM	💻 Internet	

Visit www.introbus.glencoe.com, the Web site companion to *Introduction to Business.* The student's page includes:

- interactive tutor
- additional *BusinessWeek* articles and activities
- business Web links
- homework hints
- real-world application activities
- additional career path activities

Information on how to prepare your students for the high school exit exam and special projects are also included.

Use the Glencoe Web site for additional resources. All essential content is covered in the Student Edition.

1 FOCUS

Introducing the Chapter

This chapter introduces the concept of wants and needs—the starting point of economics. The chapter examines what business is. A photo essay, "What the Public Wants," enhances the concepts.

Connecting the Objectives

What does the public in general want and need? What is business, and what motivates business?

BusinessWeek
Feature Story

Story's Summary

Stephen King published *Riding the Bullet* online at a time when sales of e-books were low. Gemstar, a leading online publisher, is planning a new strategy to meet the needs and wants of e-readers.

Find the entire article at www.introbus.glencoe.com, or in the Teacher Resource Binder.

Chapter 1

A Look at Wants and Needs

● Learning Objectives

After completing this chapter, you'll be able to:
1. **State** the differences between wants and needs.
2. **Describe** how limited resources relate to wants.
3. **Identify** business activities that are used for products and services.
4. **List** the two factors that motivate businesses.
5. **Explain** the relationship between business and you.

● Why It's Important

Businesses satisfy people's basic needs all the way to their lavish wants. Competition and profit motivate these businesses to continually strive for your business.

● Key Words

wants	business
needs	profit
goods	competition
services	consumer
resource	

4

BusinessWeek Feature Story

Paperless Page-Turners?

Gemstar Hopes Best-Selling Authors Will Make the Difference. When Stephen King released his 66-page novella *Riding The Bullet* exclusively in digital form, an estimated 400,000 computer users downloaded copies. At the same time, though cumulative sales of paperback-sized gizmos, known as e-books, barely numbered in the thousands. It was a sad contrast for the ragtag contingent of companies that have been trying to kick-start the e-book business since 1998. But industry leader Gemstar-TV Guide International Inc. learned an important lesson: authors sell books, whizbang formats don't.

Source: Excerpted with permission from "Will E-Books Be Real Page-Turners?" *BusinessWeek Online*, October 23, 2000.

An Extension Activity

Liquid crystal display (LCD) makes it possible for you to read a portable e-book, a wristwatch, a calculator, and so on. Research the science behind liquid crystal display and who manufactures most of it.

BUSINESS Online
The Full Story

To learn more about e-books, visit the *Introduction to Business* Web site at www.introbus.glencoe.com, and click on *BusinessWeek* Feature Story, Chapter 1.

Classroom Resources

For the Teacher
- 📁 Student Activity Work. TAE
- 📒 💿 Assessment Binder
- 💿 PowerPoint® Presentation
- 💿 Interactive Lesson Planner
- 📁 Lesson Plans
- 📒 💻 Internet Resources
- 🖨 Teaching Transparencies
- 💻 *Introduction to Business* Web Site

- 💿 Integrated Soft. Sim. TM
- 📄 *BusinessWeek* Poster Package

For the Student
- 📒 Student Activity Workbook
- 💿 *Virtual Business®*
- 💻 *Introduction to Business* Web Site
- 💿 Integrated Soft. Sim.
- 💿 *PuzzleMaker*
- 📒 Strategies and Worksheets for Teaching Transparencies

Making Connections

Business World. You're the owner of Floo's Florist & Gift Shop, and the biggest sales day is approaching. How will you organize and manage the items, people, and equipment needed? (Answers may vary. Possible answers include stocking extra inventory, creating a new marquee, arranging for temporary workers, buying extra display stands, and renting extra refrigerator space.) How does your company affect consumers and employment in the area? (Answers may include how the flowers and gifts satisfy peoples' wants and that the company employs many people.)

2 TEACH

Business Connection

Customers want low prices and great service. The marketing strategy of Home Depot consists of offering prices 20 to 30 percent lower than those of its competition. Low prices often go hand in hand, with minimal levels of customer service, but at Home Depot employees are trained in home-repair techniques and are encouraged to educate customers. As an extra service, stores offer free clinics for customers on topics ranging from plumbing to decorative tiling. Home Depot offers the great service that customers want because workers get stock shares in the company, so they have a personal interest in the company. Stores display a variety of products in no-frills, warehouse-style stores.

Develop Concepts

CLASSIFY. Ask students to list the things they need between the time they leave their house in the morning and lunchtime. (Examples: transportation, food, clothing, shelter, etc.)

Figure 1.1 Caption Answer

Answers will vary.

Economics' Starting Points: Wants and Needs

Look at the tag on your shirt or the label on your backpack. You make choices about the clothes you buy and music you download. When you buy snacks from the vending machine, you choose a product based on cost, taste, brand recognition, and supply. Guess what? You've just made business decisions. New products, higher prices, and the supply of products affect your family, friends, and you.

Business in Today's World

Suppose you have $10. You could use it to buy lunch, buy a magazine, or go to a movie. What is the difference between what you want and what you need? How can you satisfy wants and needs with the money you have available? Figure 1.1 asks you to think and write about your wants and needs.

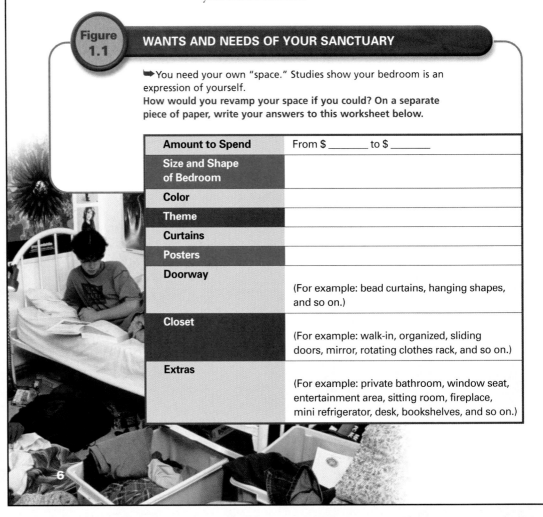

Figure 1.1

WANTS AND NEEDS OF YOUR SANCTUARY

➡ You need your own "space." Studies show your bedroom is an expression of yourself.
How would you revamp your space if you could? On a separate piece of paper, write your answers to this worksheet below.

Amount to Spend	From $ _____ to $ _____
Size and Shape of Bedroom	
Color	
Theme	
Curtains	
Posters	
Doorway	(For example: bead curtains, hanging shapes, and so on.)
Closet	(For example: walk-in, organized, sliding doors, mirror, rotating clothes rack, and so on.)
Extras	(For example: private bathroom, window seat, entertainment area, sitting room, fireplace, mini refrigerator, desk, bookshelves, and so on.)

6

Cooperative Learning

A Better Service or Product. Students often carry everything for the whole day— books, lunch, school supplies, cell phones, handheld organizers, and even jackets and shoes. JanSport developed backpacks with compartments designed to fit new technology products; straps and lanyards carry extras. As a consumer you affect business by buying certain products or services.

Business can also affect you by offering certain products or services. Ask students to work in groups of four to decide on a product or service to make their lives easier and better. Have them draw a poster-size blueprint of the product or a diagram representing the service. Call on each group to share its poster, and explain the product or service. **LS**

An Abundance of Wants

Wants are the things you wish you could have. Each person has wants. You might want a mountain bike, while your best friend may want a road bike. A group of people may also share the same wants. A family may want a new car, a company may want a more advanced computer system, or an athletic club may want to add a swimming pool. Although these wants are shared, they are considered *private wants*.

On the other hand, some wants are widely shared by many people. These wants are no longer considered private but become *public wants*, such as highways, drinking water, and education. For the most part local, state, and federal governments satisfy public wants.

Satisfying Wants and Needs With Goods and Services

Necessary wants are **needs**. Food, shelter, and clothing are basic needs. Whether private or public, necessary or optional, some type of good or service can satisfy most of your wants and needs. **Goods** can be physically weighed or measured. Bicycles and skates are goods, as are groceries and telephones. Goods satisfy your wants and needs for material things that you *can* see or touch.

At some point, your mountain bike may need a tune-up. Although you could try to do this yourself, it's more likely that you will take it to a bike shop for maintenance. If you pay a bike shop to repair your bike, you're buying a service. **Services** are tasks that people or machines perform. Services also satisfy some of your wants for things you *cannot* see or touch. Many services such as cutting hair or teaching guitar lessons are provided for a fee.

Not all business activities satisfy wants. People want things that cannot be valued in terms of money. For example, individuals want love and respect. In a business context wants are *not* about these intangible kinds of desires. Businesses please those wants that can be satisfied by goods and services.

Unlimited Wants, Limited Resources

Most people have unlimited wants for goods and services. In the United States, Canada, England, and Japan, the majority of consumers have satisfied their lower-order needs, so marketers promote goods and services that will appeal to higher-order needs. Take Marie Van de Mark, a young entrepreneur, who started Jam Enterprise. She created a $2 million company from making promotional items from metal. Amazon.com and A/X Armani Exchange like her products. The more money you make, the more goods

Chapter 1 A Look at Needs and Wants **7**

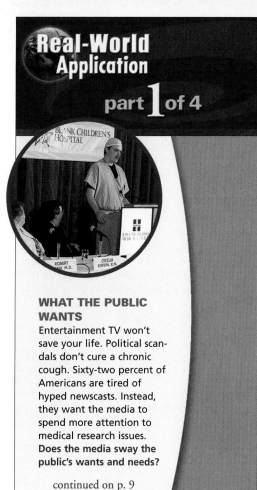

Real-World Application

part 1 of 4

WHAT THE PUBLIC WANTS
Entertainment TV won't save your life. Political scandals don't cure a chronic cough. Sixty-two percent of Americans are tired of hyped newscasts. Instead, they want the media to spend more attention to medical research issues. **Does the media sway the public's wants and needs?**

continued on p. 9

Chapter 1

Real-World Application
Caption Answer

WHAT THE PUBLIC WANTS: PART 1 OF 4

Not necessarily. According to a survey commissioned by Research America, over 50 percent of adults stated that the government doesn't spend enough money on medical research. In fact, the federal government spends less than 1 percent on medical research.

Technology Resource

 POWERPOINT. The *Introduction to Business* PowerPoint® CD-ROM provides visual lecture aids for this chapter.

Independent Practice

LIST. Make a list of classroom resources. (The list might include audiovisual equipment, books, desks, computers, tables, board, and so on.) How does each resource help satisfy your style of learning? (Answers will vary. Styles of learning include visual, auditory, kinesthetic, spatial, interpersonal, and intrapersonal.) **LS**

Meeting Individual Needs

Students With Visual Impairments.
Due to the visual nature of this textbook, you may want to plan for some of the challenges faced by students with visual impairments in your class. In discussing illustrations, photographs, or charts, it may be useful to describe aloud the photograph, giving verbal descriptions of the shapes and sizes in the picture along with clear descriptions of the whole picture.

2 TEACH (Cont.)

Technology
Toolkit

Caption Answer

Answers will vary and might include computers in tennis shoes or sunglasses for transmitting data, music, games, and e-mail. Wearable computers are potentially invaluable in many areas, including medicine, the military, and underwater exploration.

Thinking Critically

DECISION MAKING. You're at a theme park with a friend for the day. You found a special on the ticket—just $35. You both have only $65. You want to buy the ticket and lunch. You also have a choice of snacks, arcade games, pictures, souvenirs, and gifts. How much will you spend, what will you spend it on, and why? (Remind students to use the decision-making process. Answers and situations will vary.)

Technology Toolkit

Listen to Your Ring, Watch Your Watch

Wristwatch cameras have been standard equipment for action heroes. Today, this "smart jewelry" is a reality for anyone. Pervasive computing inserts silicon chips in your jewelry so you can listen to the radio, phone friends, take pictures, download music, or withdraw money from your bank account.

Students in a Florida high school already use the personal computer rings to record their attendance, gain entrance to classrooms, and even pay for cafeteria meals.

Critical Thinking
What other kinds of wearable computers might enhance people's wants and needs?

or services you want. However, few have enough resources to satisfy all of their wants. A **resource** is anything that people can use to make or obtain what they need or want. Examples of resources include fuel, timber, labor, and money. The problem of unlimited wants and limited resources affects individuals, companies, and nations.

Resources limit the number of wants people can satisfy. For example, you may want a new pair of jeans and a new camera, but you may only have enough money to buy one of these things. You may also want to earn a lot of money, but you have only so much time to work between school and family responsibilities. Businesses and government are influenced by the same problem. They lack the resources to do all the things that they want to do. It is important for individuals, businesses, and nations to make the best use of limited resources.

Deciding on Your Resources. Every day you have opportunities to make choices about how you'll act, how you'll treat others, and what you'll do. You should make these important decisions carefully. People make the most of their resources by making the right choices about what to buy. The decision-making process is a step-by-step method to carefully consider alternatives that result in better choices. The decision-making process is a procedure for carefully considering alternatives and their consequences before you make a final decision. The process has these essential steps:

Step 1. Identify the problem. Whether the decision-making problem is one that occurs daily or comes up only a few times in a lifetime, this is the first step. It is often the easiest.

Step 2. List the alternatives. Take time to think through the problem, so you can come up with a good range of alternatives. Try to include all the important ones.

Step 3. Determine the pros and cons. Write down and weigh the advantages and disadvantages of each alternative. Your values and goals now become part of the decision-making process.

Step 4. Make the best decision. Determining the best alterative is the key step in the process. Rank the alternatives according to their pros and cons. After you pick a winner, ask yourself what you'll lose if you give up your second choice. Do you really want to give that alternative?

Step 5. Evaluate your decision. After you've put your decision into effect, ask yourself whether you achieved the results you expected. Would you make the same choice again?

Social Science   Curriculum Connection

Community Wants. What are some wants of the local community that aren't universally agreed upon? For example, some people may think the community needs another elementary school; others may think it isn't necessary. Have students choose a community issue and discuss why community members take different sides on the issue and what resources are involved. How much of the disagreement is about the use of the community's resources?

You may not use all of the steps of the process every time you buy something. For example, when you decide to buy orange juice, you may always buy the same brand. However, many decisions need more careful thought. A bike can be an important purchase because you're likely to keep it for some time. A bike can also cost anywhere from $100 to $2,000. When you consider what type of bike to buy (mountain bike or road bike) and what brand (Gary Fisher or Trek) you'll probably use all five steps of the decision-making process.

 Fast Review

1. Define wants, needs, goods, services, and resources.
2. What is the difference between public wants and private wants?
3. List the steps in a decision-making process.

What Is Business?

Whether you're deciding what movie to see or what bike to buy, your wants and needs are usually satisfied by business. **Business** is any activity that seeks profit by providing goods or services to others. Businesses provide you with necessities such as food, clothing, housing, medical care, and transportation, as well as things that make your life easier and better. Businesses also provide people with the opportunity to become wealthy. For instance, take the late founder of Wal-Mart Stores, Inc., Sam Walton. In 1962 Walton opened the first store in Arkansas. Today, the company sells about $200 billion worth of goods and services. To become a successful company, it had to figure out that its customers wanted low prices and genuine customer service.

What Business Does

You might be surprised about all the things that happen before you see a product in the store. What happens before your favorite soft drink is available to buy? The company conducted taste tests to make sure enough people liked the flavor of the soft drink. Chances are you saw an ad for that soft drink on TV. Someone else made sure that your local grocery store had enough of the soft drink on hand so that it is available when you go to buy it.

Levi Strauss and Jacob Davis successfully responded to people's wants and needs. The two became business partners in 1873 and began selling work pants to miners, surveyors, cowboys, and other hard-working westerners. Early buyers called the denim pants "Levi's" and the name stuck. Today, Levi Strauss & Company dominates the world of manufacturing jeans.

Chapter 1 A Look at Needs and Wants **9**

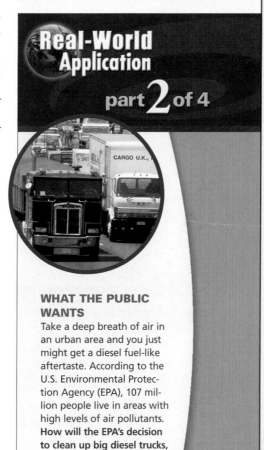

WHAT THE PUBLIC WANTS

Take a deep breath of air in an urban area and you just might get a diesel fuel-like aftertaste. According to the U.S. Environmental Protection Agency (EPA), 107 million people live in areas with high levels of air pollutants. **How will the EPA's decision to clean up big diesel trucks, buses, and diesel fuel influence some businesses?**

continued on p. 11

WHAT THE PUBLIC WANTS: PART 2 OF 4

This decision will protect the public health and would prevent more than 360,000 asthma attacks each year. The EPA is requiring that business use high-tech pollution devices to refine the air from highway diesel fuel. This may increase businesses' costs for cleanup equipment.

Fast Review Answers

1. Wants are things you wish you could have. Needs are things you must have to survive. Goods can be physically weighed or measured. Services are tasks that people or machines perform. People use resources to obtain something.
2. Public wants are widely shared by many people; a small group of people hold private wants.
3. Identify the problem, list the alternatives, determine the pros and cons, make the best decision, and evaluate your decision.

Business Connection

Growers of chili peppers in New Mexico have competition from Mexico farmers. Labor and farming costs are lower in Mexico, and U.S. processors often buy the lower-priced imports. For example, jalapeño growing costs $172 per ton in Delicias, Chihuahua, compared to $340 per ton in Doña Ana County, New Mexico.

Great Ideas From the Classroom of...

Gwen Alsburry
Oakdale High School
Oakdale, La.

Motivation. MOTIVATION = Movement, Oral, Time, Interaction, Visualize, Action, Technique, Involve, Output, Now. Every student is unique. Different strategies can be used to reach individual learning styles. I motivate students by bringing outside sources into the classroom related to the lesson—current news articles, magazines, Internet, and TV news. I encourage students to discuss the issues presented and allow time for them to develop ideas of their own to solve the issues or problems.

2 TEACH (Cont.)

Develop Concepts

RECOGNIZING COMPETITION. Ask students to give specific and general examples of how competition affects businesses. List these examples on the board. Then discuss the effects of competition. *(A specific example could be when there are two gas stations across the street from each other; one gas station might lower its prices to draw customers away from the other station. General examples will include price wars, customer service, and cost cutting.)*

Discussion Starter

DOING BUSINESS. Ask students to think of a local retail store and ask what the store does to make the merchandise available? *(Answers will include stocking inventory, organizing and training sales staff, advertising, maintaining a comfortable environment, and displaying merchandise in an attractive way.)*

Figure 1.2 Caption Answer

Answers will vary according to factors such as taste and trends.

Similar business activities happen for every product or service that is offered. A business must *organize* the people and equipment to provide the product. People within the organization *manage* the company's resources to *produce* the product. The company then *markets* the product or service by deciding where to sell it and how to advertise it. Every business uses some combination of these activities.

Businesses' Motivations

Why would a person or a business supply the goods and services you want? It comes down to turning a profit. **Profit** is the amount of money left over after a business has paid for the cost of producing its goods and services. Without profit, a company cannot survive in a competitive business world where each strives for a chunk of the market's business. Profit is the motivation for taking the risk to start a business. It's the reward for satisfying the needs and wants of consumers. A business is profitable when sales are high, and costs are kept low.

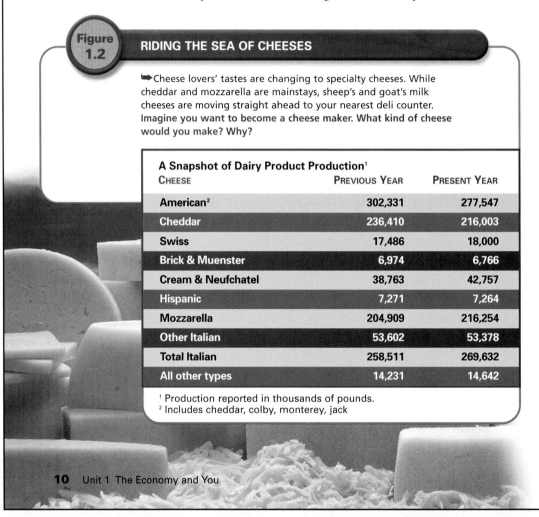

Figure 1.2

RIDING THE SEA OF CHEESES

➡ Cheese lovers' tastes are changing to specialty cheeses. While cheddar and mozzarella are mainstays, sheep's and goat's milk cheeses are moving straight ahead to your nearest deli counter. Imagine you want to become a cheese maker. What kind of cheese would you make? Why?

A Snapshot of Dairy Product Production[1]

CHEESE	PREVIOUS YEAR	PRESENT YEAR
American[2]	302,331	277,547
Cheddar	236,410	216,003
Swiss	17,486	18,000
Brick & Muenster	6,974	6,766
Cream & Neufchatel	38,763	42,757
Hispanic	7,271	7,264
Mozzarella	204,909	216,254
Other Italian	53,602	53,378
Total Italian	258,511	269,632
All other types	14,231	14,642

[1] Production reported in thousands of pounds.
[2] Includes cheddar, colby, monterey, jack

10 Unit 1 The Economy and You

Global Perspective

Needs and Environment. Someone living in a rain forest doesn't have the same needs as someone living in Northern Canada. Discuss how needs vary depending on environment. Have groups of students choose a country or a region of the world and speculate about the climate and economic conditions of that area. Have them develop a list of needs for survival in that climate based on what they have discussed.

When consumers' wants and needs change then businesses are motivated to change along with them. In order to change with consumers' wants and needs the companies thrive on **competition**, or the contest between businesses to win customers. For example, people are very interested in buying cellular telephones. Motorola offers cell phones with access to the Internet, digital operating systems, and an FM stereo. The Finnish pioneer of wireless telecommunications, Nokia, offers you the power to personally design your own cell phone cover in the company's online studio.

When there is more than one kind of cellular phone to choose from, you can buy the cheapest one, the one that is the right size, the right shape, the right color, or has the right high-tech capabilities. Competition is a direct response to consumers' wants and needs. Figure 1.2 asks you to make a business decision based upon the consumer's tastes. Will competition and profit wager into your decision?

Business and You

Businesses make many decisions that impact you. They decide what products and services to produce. However, you also affect business. You decide what kind of products and services you want and where you will buy them. This mutual relationship relies on each partner making a decision.

You as a Consumer. A **consumer** is a person who selects, purchases, uses, or disposes of goods or services. Business is aware of your changing needs and wants. For instance, take electrical engineer Jeff Hawkins who is the original creator and designer of the Palm™Pilot, a handheld computer product. The handheld device has changed the way people communicate and organize their lives. A compact handheld computing device allows you to electronically organize your to-do list, calendar, e-mail, address book, and download software.

Businesses also affect you when they discontinue products. The decision to stop manufacturing products is often because there is a decreasing demand. When a company is slow to respond to customers' complaints and doesn't communicate very well, then customers usually find another company's product to buy. When customers behave this way the company doesn't make much money. Either the company makes some changes to satisfy its customers or the company folds.

You as a Wage Earner. Businesses affect you as a wage earner. In order to make products and provide services, businesses hire people to work. In order to produce a product, the business decides how it will be produced. For example, if Gene's Pizza decides to deliver pizzas to its customers, it needs to hire pizza-delivery drivers.

Chapter 1 A Look at Needs and Wants **11**

Real-World Application

part 3 of 4

WHAT THE PUBLIC WANTS
According to 81 percent of those surveyed by a team of researchers from Washington State University, learning is a lifelong pursuit for a successful career. More adults are enrolling in continuing education courses. **How are colleges and universities changing to meet this demand?**

continued on p. 13

Real-World Application
Caption Answer

WHAT THE PUBLIC WANTS: PART 3 OF 4
They must create more off-campus sites to support adult learners. More institutions are also offering distance learning.

Individualized Practice

MANAGING BUSINESS.
Tell students to imagine they own and manage a large store. They've been invited to the local chamber of commerce to give a talk to new entrepreneurs about what is involved in the day-to-day running of a business.

L1 Divide students into pairs and have each discuss aspects of the day-to-day operations of running a business.

L2 Their audience wants to hear about a priority list of tasks a business owner must do on a day-to-day basis. These will include steps toward short-range and long-range business goals. Have students write the prioritized task list.

L3 Have students write a brief essay about what they do in a typical business day. The day will include activities toward short-range and long-range business goals and plans to beat the competition.

Curriculum Connection

Fund-Raising. Provide students with the following problem: Yeong and Christopher need to raise $100 for their school choir trip. They plan to make and sell chocolate-chip cookies at their school. They spend $22 on ingredients and price the cookies at 75 cents apiece. How many cookies do they need to sell to make a $100 profit? ($122 ÷ 0.75 = 163 cookies [rounded up].)

2 TEACH (Cont.)

Working Lifestyle

Caption Answer

Help people, meaningful work, paid well, on the cutting edge, etc.

✓ **Fast Review Answers**

1. Any activity that seeks profit by providing goods and services to others.
2. Organizing, managing, producing, and marketing.
3. Provides things you need and want. Business provides you with a job.

3 ASSESS

Reteaching

DECISION MAKING. Apply the decision-making model to the following problem: Customers at Yuri's Yogurt Shoppe want soup and sandwiches. A new bistro opened nearby and Yuri is afraid he'll lose business. Expanding the menu means hiring workers and remodeling.

Enrichment Strategy

READ. Read an article from the newspaper's business section. Ask them to specify the company's activities. **LS**

Evaluation

Assign and review the Fast Review sections.

In business today, workers have more input about how business is done. A business you work for may ask you to think of ways to improve the production process. When you're an employee, decision-making skills, quality of work, and input to problems help a business flourish. IDEO is a product-design company responsible for innovating Polaroid's I-Zone instant camera and Crest's stand-up toothpaste tube. The small company attracts passionate people who have fun and work hard as a team to produce its products every day.

 Fast Review

1. Define business.
2. List the business activities that happen behind every product or service.
3. How does business affect you as a consumer and as a wage earner?

Working Lifestyle

What are you doing at 10 A.M.?

Curing Children

"A lot of doctors go into pediatrics because they want to work with kids," says pediatrician Eric Lau. "Then they find you treat the parents as much as the children. When kids are sick, parents are really stressed out!"

Lau always wanted to work with kids, so when he volunteered at a hospital and became interested in medicine as a college student, pediatrics was a perfect fit for him as a career. Since graduating medical school, going through residency, and joining a small practice, he hasn't been disappointed.

Appointments at Lau's office begin at 8:45 in the morning, so by 10:00 he is diagnosing coughs, colds, and ear infections. Lau says, "It's sort of like what I expected, but you never really know what it's like until you're there.

The pace is always changing. You're faced with situations where you're not sure what's going on, but you have to make decisions. You're always thinking."

Lau is always making on-the-spot decisions, but the most rewarding aspect of his job is long-term. He says, "I treat kids, make them better, and, over the course of time, watch them grow."

Salary

The median income of physicians is about $164,000, with a range between $120,000 and $250,000 a year.

Outlook for This Career

This profession is expected to grow faster than average due to a growing population. This drives the overall growth of healthcare services.

Connecting Careers Activity

Education and training to become a doctor takes longer than any other occupation. What are the benefits of choosing a medical career path?

 Health Science

CAREER PATH

12   Unit 1 The Economy and You

How to Use a Portfolio Activity

The portfolio projects are designed to lead students to develop a collection of their best work to submit to you for assessment. You and each of your students should decide which projects to include in their business portfolio. Refer students to the specific rubric(s) from the *Alternative Assessment Strategies*. These rubrics will alert students to the criteria you'll use to assess their projects.

Self-Discovery in Business

Before dinner you start watching the local news. A broadcast journalist talks about the price of consumer goods. A little later, the reporter mentions that a major online company filed for bankruptcy. The federal government announces a change in interest rates. What does this mean to you? What difference does it make? Will it influence your life, your friends, or your family? Do the actions of the government and businesses have any impact on you?

More than ever before, you need to understand the world you live and work in. What happens in business and government will make a difference in your life. Change comes faster and faster. Companies come and go, and new types of companies continually appear.

The Value of Knowledge

What do you need to be a wise consumer, a good employee, or a successful business owner? Everyone is a consumer. Learning how to get the most from your spending now is important, but getting the most from your future income is even more important.

When you become a business owner, manager, or employee, you'll need business knowledge. You'll probably have several jobs during your lifetime. The more education you have, the better your income. Business in today's world has all types of jobs, and you'll learn and understand the role of those jobs, which influence the millions of workers in all economies.

What Do You Like?

You may not know yet whether you would like to work for someone else or whether you would like to have your own business. Explore the world of business. Learn as much now in order to make an informed decision in the future.

If you like to work outside, for example, you could explore businesses in forestry, gardening or landscaping, ranching, or animal care. If you prefer to take risks on new ventures then being an entrepreneur may appeal to you. If you like to create ideas, you might like to be a writer or an actor. If you like to work with numbers and solve problems, you may find yourself drawn to being an accountant, an engineer, or a mathematician. Explore all the business opportunities in order to see what is available to you in order to satisfy your wants and needs.

 Fast Review

1. Why is it important to understand business today?
2. How will knowledge help your career?

Real-World Application
part 4 of 4

WHAT THE PUBLIC WANTS
Diversity is the core of the U.S. public. More minorities are attending college, which feed the workforce. **Why is diversity an important stimulant for the workforce?**

Real-World Application
Caption Answer

WHAT THE PUBLIC WANTS: PART 4 OF 4
Global business increases your chances of working with people from different cultures and races. Positive relationships with your coworkers affect a business's productivity and efficiency.

Technology Resource

 GO TO **VIRTUAL BUSINESS.** Introduce wants and needs using Knowledge Matters' *Virtual Business* interactive simulation. Go to the *Introduction to Business* Web site **www.introbus.glencoe.com** to download the *Virtual Business* Activity. Run the *Virtual Business* tutorial before beginning this activity.

Fast Review Answers ✓

1. What happens in business and government will make a difference in you and your family's lives as consumers and as workers.
2. The more education you have, often the better your income. Knowledge helps you understand the role of jobs in today's economy.

Meeting Individual Needs

Students With Physical Disabilities. Have students with physical disabilities that affect their dexterity prepare assignments electronically, if possible. If computers are available, consider having students prepare lists, graphic organizers, charts, or paragraphs using appropriate software.

4 CLOSE

Chapter Wrap-Up

Ask students to explain the significant factors of wants and needs, the things a business does, and business's motivations.

Using Business Key Words

1. needs
2. business
3. resources
4. competition
5. wants
6. consumer
7. services
8. goods
9. profit

Review What You Learned

10. A family might want a DVD, a business might want new phones, and a photography club might want a digital camera.
11. Local, state, and federal governments.
12. Wants include a new pair of jeans or a computer. Needs are food and shelter.
13. Goods are items like bricks and milk. Services are tasks like giving a haircut or repairing a computer.
14. All wants will never be satisfied.
15. Yes.
16. Results in better choices.
17. A business organizes, manages, markets, and advertises.
18. Businesses offer goods and services based upon what people need and want.
19. You affect productivity and quality of work.

Summary

1. Wants are those things you wish you could have. Needs are things you need for survival, like food, shelter, and clothing. Goods satisfy your wants and needs for material things that you can see or touch, whereas services satisfy some of your wants for things you cannot see or touch.

2. Limited resources affect the number of wants.

3. Business activities include producing and distributing goods and services to consumers. Every business organizes, manages, produces, and markets a product or service.

4. Both profit and competition motivate businesses to meet wants and needs.

5. Business affects consumers by the products or services it decides to offer. You affect business by what products and services you buy. Business also affects you as a wage earner by determining the types of jobs that will be available. You also affect business by how you work.

● Using Business Key Words

In today's business world, people often use the following terms. See if you can match each term to its definition.

- **wants**
- **services**
- **needs**
- **resource**
- **goods**
- **business**
- **competition**
- **consumer**
- **profit**

1. Things we must have to survive.
2. Any activity that seeks profit by providing goods or services to others.
3. Anything that people can use to make or obtain what they want or need.
4. The contest between businesses to win customers.
5. Things we wish we could have.
6. A person who selects, purchases, uses, or disposes of goods or services.
7. Tasks that people or machines perform.
8. Material things that can be weighed or measured.
9. The amount of money left over after a business has paid for the cost of producing its goods and services.

Quick Quiz

1. What is the difference between needs and wants? (Needs are things you must have to survive, like water and shelter. Wants are things you would like to have but don't need to survive.)

2. How do consumers' changing wants affect business? (As consumers develop different wants, new businesses start-up to meet those wants; existing businesses lose business if they don't change.)

3. How do wage earners affect business? (When they work slow or fast and meet or miss deadlines they affect production or output. Productivity and quality help profitability.)

Review What You Learned

10. Explain how a family, a business, or a group could have private wants.
11. Who satisfies most of the public wants shared by many people?
12. Describe the difference between wants and needs. Give two examples of each.
13. Explain the major difference between goods and services. Give two examples of each.
14. Describe the problem of unlimited wants and limited resources.
15. Is time an example of a resource? Explain your answer.
16. Why is the decision-making process important to use when making choices about what to buy?
17. Describe the business activities that happen for every product or service that is offered for sale.
18. How do the decisions that businesses make affect you as a consumer?
19. How do the decisions that you make as a wage earner affect a business?

Understanding Business Concepts

20. Give a personal example of a private want, a public want, and a need.
21. Do you think it's possible to have all your wants satisfied? Explain.
22. Think about a purchasing decision you'll have to make in the next few weeks. Use the five-step process to carefully consider your alternatives.
23. How does business provide people with the opportunity to become wealthy?
24. Describe how business decisions determine the jobs that you and other wage earners have.

Critical Thinking

25. Why do you think Wal-Mart has been so successful?
26. What would you do if a product you like to buy was no longer offered by the business?
27. List three situations in which decision making has greatly influenced your life.
28. How have you improved the production process of something?

Viewing and Representing

Examining the Image. Pair up with a partner and take turns asking each other these questions: What exactly do you see in this photo? What people and objects are pictured? Thinking about wants and needs, what do you think is going on? What would you want if you were in this situation? Would you really need it or them?

Critical Thinking

25. Answers will vary but might include the fact that Wal-Mart understands what people want to buy, prices their products fairly, and opens stores where there is a need.
26. Answers will vary. Students might write letters to the company or look for a different brand to purchase.
27. Answers will vary depending on goals chosen by students.
28. Answers will vary.

Viewing and Representing

Advertising, television, movies, and other visual media have a great impact on students' lives—often without them realizing it. The Viewing and Representing activity increases students' awareness of media's powerful and subtle effects and promotes critical thinking skills. Students' answers will vary.

Chapter 1 A Look at Needs and Wants **15**

● *Understanding Business Concepts*

20. Answers will vary. A private want might be a new motorcycle; a public want might be better roads; and a need might be tonight's dinner.
21. Most students will say no; since their resources (money) are limited, all their wants won't be satisfied.
22. Answers will vary, but make sure students use all five steps.
23. By figuring out what people want to buy, businesses are successful and their owners become wealthy.
24. If a business decision is made to offer different services, people with the necessary skills would need to be trained or hired.

4 CLOSE (Cont.)

Building Academic Skills

LANGUAGE ARTS. Students will find the most information using the Yellow Pages, newspaper advertisements, or local flyers. Rubrics: Oral presentation, note taking.

HISTORY. Students will find information in the library or on the Internet. There have been several books written about Sam Walton and the success of Wal-Mart. Rubric: Two-page paper.

MATH. Budgets will vary. Let students choose the method they use to share their budgets. Possible rubrics: Spreadsheet, diagram.

COMPUTER/TECHNOLOGY. Remind students that there are numerous magazines showcasing emerging technology. The Internet is a good resource as well. Encourage students to use their imagination and creativity. Rubrics: Essay, poster.

Linking School to Home

Answers will vary. Your needs on the island would be for necessities such as food, clothing, and shelter. You would not be able to purchase goods and services from others. You would have to satisfy your wants in other ways.

Linking School to Work

Answers will vary but should include various sources of information and a discussion of the decision-making process. Rubric: Essay.

Building Academic Skills

 Grouping

List five businesses you're familiar with in your community. Identify whether the business provides goods or services? Do any provide both? For example, many hair salons not only provide the service of cutting and styling hair but also sell hair-care products, which are goods. List the kinds of decisions that the business might have made in choosing what to provide for its customers.

 Researching

Research the history of Wal-Mart. Include information about how Sam Walton became one of the richest people in America. Find out how many stores are currently located in the United States and if there are any located outside the United States. Write a two-page paper with your findings.

 Budgeting

Imagine you've been given $100 for next month's expenses. Create a budget showing how you would spend the money. Determine how much of the $100 would be spent on needs and how much would be spent on wants. Compare your budget with another member in your class.

 Predicting

Handheld computer devices, like the Palm™Pilot, are becoming very popular. Research another emerging technological device and predict when you think it will become as popular as handheld computers. Write a 100-word paragraph about the device and include a picture if possible.

Linking School to Home

Compare and Contrast. Suppose you're stranded on a small, uninhabited tropical island. Do you think your wants and needs would be different on the island than at home in your own community? Would satisfying those wants and needs be different on the island? Describe how the resources available on the island would impact your wants and needs.

Linking School to Work

Evaluating Information. Interview the manager or owner of a local small business. Find out about the sources of information he or she uses in making business decisions. Ask how he or she evaluates the information before acting upon it. Does he or she use the decision-making model described in this chapter? Write a 200-word report about the ways that person evaluates information.

E-Homework

Applying Technology

Create a Database. As a class, research all the resources that were used to build and furnish your school. Create a database of the resources used. Save this database to be used in Chapter 2.

Online Research. Using the Internet, research a business that sells a product that you use. Who started the business? When and why was it founded? Find out what resources were used to create the product the business sells. Is the product a want or need for you?

Connecting Academics

Math. At the baseball park you pay a lot if you want to buy food at the concession stand. You could satisfy your need for food and drink by bringing healthy snacks from home that cost less. If you buy a hot dog, peanuts, and soda from the concession stand it could cost you $5. Let's say instead, you bring a homemade ham sandwich, grapes, and a soft drink, and they only cost you $3. What's your percentage savings?

Social Science. When there are limited resources, you need to make decisions. Imagine you're managing the concession stands at the major league baseball park nearest to you. You need to make a profit. Here are possibilities on how to run the concession stands:

- Research concessions at ball parks and then brainstorm about your concessions.
- List the materials, equipment, and labor you'll need. If possible, use a spreadsheet program.
- Write your five steps in the decision-making process.
- What other information, if any, do you need to make an informed decision?

You read the first part of "Paperless Page-Turners?" at the beginning of this chapter. Below are a few questions for you to answer about the article. You'll find the answers to these questions when you're reading the entire article. First, here are the questions:

29. What is Gemstar predicting about the wants of people who buy books?
30. How do the decisions of Gemstar and publishers affect consumers who buy books?

CREATIVE JOURNAL ACTIVITY

Plan your own pizzeria by answering these questions.

Organize: How many people will work in the restaurant? Where will the equipment be located?

Manage: Who will supervise the pizza makers? Who will make sure the pizzas are made with quality ingredients?

Produce: How will the pizzas be made? Who will make the pizzas?

Market: How will you advertise? Will coupons be given away?

BUSINESS Online

The Full Story

To learn more about e-books, visit the *Introduction to Business* Web site at **www.introbus.glencoe.com**, and click on *BusinessWeek* Feature Story, Chapter 1.

E-Homework

CREATE A DATABASE. Help students think about not only the bricks and mortar, but the furnishings as well. Rubrics: Database, note taking.

ONLINE RESEARCH. Students' answers will vary. Rubrics: Note taking, essay, oral presentation.

Connecting Academics

MATH. $5.00 - $3.00 = $2.00. $2.00 ÷ $5.00 = 0.4 or 40%

SOCIAL SCIENCE. Students' choices of concessions will vary. Answers should include all five steps in the decision-making process. To make an informed decision as to whether they can make a profit, students need information about fees ballparks charge vendors.

29. Publishers are predicting that consumers will take to reading books on liquid crystal display screens. Bonus answer: They're also predicting that they'll spend as much as $300 to buy reading devices.

30. Downloadable titles may be offered before the books actually publish.

Creative Journal Activity

Students' pizzeria plans will vary. Students might draw a diagram to show the organization of their planned pizzeria. Students' decisions about management and pizza production will vary and should include supporting reasoning. **CL**, LS

SCANS Correlation Chart*

Foundation Skills

Basic Skills	Reading	Writing	Math	Listening	Speaking
Thinking Skills	Creative Thinking	Decision Making	Problem Solving	Seeing Things in the Mind's Eye	Knowing How to Learn
Personal Qualities	Responsibility	Self-Esteem	Sociability	Self-Management	Integrity/ Honesty

					Reasoning

Workplace Competencies

Resources	Allocating Time	Allocating Money	Allocating Material and Facility Resources	Allocating Human Resources	
Information	Acquiring and Evaluating Information	Organizing and Maintaining Information	Interpreting and Communicating Information	Using Computers to Process Information	
Interpersonal Skills	Participating as a Member of a Team	Teaching Others	Serving Clients/ Customers	Exercising Leadership	Negotiating to Arrive at a Decision / Working With Cultural Diversity
Systems	Understanding Systems	Monitoring and Correcting Performance	Improving and Designing Systems		
Technology	Selecting Technology	Applying Technology to Task	Maintaining and Troubleshooting Technology		

*This chart's highlighted blocks indicate the chapter's content coverage in the Student Edition and the Teacher Wraparound Edition.

Resource Manager

Teaching Transparencies

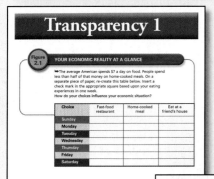

Transparency 1

Figure 2.1

YOUR ECONOMIC REALITY AT A GLANCE

➡ The average American spends $7 a day on food. People spend less than half of that money on home-cooked meals. On a separate piece of paper, re-create this table below. Insert a check mark in the appropriate square based upon your eating experiences in one week. How do your choices influence your economic situation?

Choice	Fast-food restaurant	Home-cooked meal	Eat at a friend's house
Sunday			
Monday			
Tuesday			
Wednesday			
Thursday			
Friday			
Saturday			

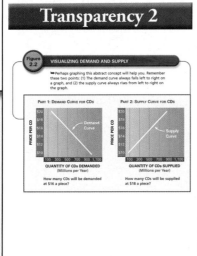

Transparency 2

Figure 2.2

VISUALIZING DEMAND AND SUPPLY

➡ Perhaps graphing this abstract concept will help you. Remember these two points: (1) the demand curve always falls left to right on a graph, and (2) the supply curve always rises from left to right on the graph.

PART 1: DEMAND CURVE FOR CDs

PART 2: SUPPLY CURVE FOR CDs

QUANTITY OF CDs DEMANDED (Millions per Year)

QUANTITY OF CDs SUPPLIED (Millions per Year)

How many CDs will be demanded at $16 a piece?

How many CDs will be supplied at $18 a piece?

Application and Enrichment

- Lesson Plans
- *BusinessWeek* Poster Package
- Teaching Transparencies
- Integrated Software Simulation
- Glencoe Business Video Package

Review and Reinforcement

- *PuzzleMaker*
- Internet Resources
- Student Activity Workbook
- Strat. and Work. for Teaching Transparencies

Assessment and Evaluation

- Reproducible Tests
- Alternative Assessment Strategies
- ExamView® Pro Test Generator

Technology

- *PuzzleMaker*
- ExamView® Pro Test Generator
- Glencoe Business Video Package
- PowerPoint® Presentation
- Integrated Software Simulation
- Interactive Lesson Planner
- *Virtual Business*®

KEY	🖉 Printed	💾 Software	📼 Videocassette	🖼 Poster
	🕹 Transparency	💿 CD-ROM	🖥 Internet	

BUSINESS Online

Visit www.introbus.glencoe.com, the Web site companion to *Introduction to Business.* The student's page includes:

- interactive tutor
- additional *BusinessWeek* articles and activities
- business Web links
- homework hints
- real-world application activities
- additional career path activities

Information on how to prepare your students for the high school exit exam and special projects are also included.

Use the Glencoe Web site for additional resources. All essential content is covered in the Student Edition.

Chapter 2

1 FOCUS

Introducing the Chapter

This chapter introduces scarcity and the four factors of production. It describes economic systems. This chapter is enhanced with a real-world photo essay, "How the Hearth Saved You Money," about the manufacturer of the corn-burning appliance.

Connecting the Objectives

What kinds of problems do all countries face because of scarce economic resources? What do these phrases mean to you: supply and demand, capitalism or market economy, and communism or command economy?

BusinessWeek
Feature Story

Story's Summary

Poland's economic system is in transition. Evidence of the new, successful economy was seen at a fair in Warsaw's Old Town one recent Sunday afternoon. Luxury goods from cosmetics to candies were on sale.

Find the entire article at **www.introbus.glencoe.com**, or in the Teacher Resource Binder.

Economic Resources and Systems

● Learning Objectives

After completing this chapter, you'll be able to:
1. **Define** scarcity.
2. **List** the four factors of production.
3. **Identify** the differences between market and command economies.
4. **Explain** why most countries prefer a mixed economy.

● Why It's Important

Understanding economic resources and systems is essential to lessening economic problems.

● Key Words

scarcity
factors of production
natural resources
human resources
capital resources
entrepreneurial resources
economics
market economy
demand
supply
equilibrium price
command economy
mixed economy

18

BusinessWeek Feature Story

Poland—Goods Runneth Over

Poland Is an Inspiration for the Rest of Europe. For a newcomer, it was quite a scene. Merchants, artisans, and even bankers lined the streets to offer their products at a fair in Warsaw's Old Town on a recent Sunday afternoon. As a band played Louis Armstrong's "Wonderful World" and other tunes, prosperous-looking Poles shopped for private pension funds as well as locally made goods ranging from candies to cosmetics. What a change from a decade ago when voters ended communist rule by supporting Solidarity candidates in Poland's first competitive elections. Within months, communism had collapsed across Eastern Europe.

Source: Excerpted with permission from "Poland: A Beacon for the Rest of Europe," *BusinessWeek Online*, June 21, 1999.

An Extension Activity

Research the brainchild behind the theories of the Communist movement. Then find out which Soviet leader modified it and lead the Revolution of October 1917.

BUSINESS
Online
The Full Story
To learn more about Poland, visit the *Introduction to Business* Web site at **www.introbus.glencoe.com**, and click on *BusinessWeek* Feature Story, Chapter 2.

Classroom Resources

For the Teacher
📁 Student Activity Work. TAE
📝💿 Assessment Binder
💿 PowerPoint® Presentation
💿 Interactive Lesson Planner
📁 Lesson Plans
📝💻 Internet Resources
🔦 Teaching Transparencies
🖥 *Introduction to Business* Web Site

💿 Integrated Soft. Sim. TM
📕 *BusinessWeek* Poster Package
For the Student
📝 Student Activity Workbook
💿 *Virtual Business*®
🖥 *Introduction to Business* Web Site
💿 Integrated Soft. Sim.
💿 *PuzzleMaker*
📝 Strategies and Worksheets for Teaching Transparencies

Bell Ringer Activity

SPEAKING. Scarcity is shortage of resources, which is a basic economic problem for any society. Ask students to talk about their shopping experiences. Did a store ever run out of an item they wanted to buy? Did a store ever discontinue an item they liked? What did they do? Why was the store out of the item?

Preteaching Business Key Words

LISTENING. Read aloud the chapter's key words from the glossary. Ask volunteers to repeat in their own words the definition of each key word. **LS**

An Extension Activity

POSTER. Ask groups to create a poster summarizing their findings. **LS**, **CL**

Making Connections

Economics. Imagine that you have a new teacher who has decided that no matter how clear (or unclear) a report is, how many answers are correct (or incorrect) on a quiz, or how good (or bad) a student project is, the student will receive an average grade. How do you feel? What will you do? Describe how this knowledge will affect the effort you put into a report, quiz, or project.

How well will you retain information? How will this affect your future? Suppose this happened to you in a job? What economic system does this describe? (Answers will include how a lack of advancement and increased wage incentive in a strong command economy might affect job performance, productivity, morale, and quality.)

2 TEACH

Business Connection

CHANGING ECONOMIC SYSTEMS. China's command economy began economic reform in 1979. The government lessened its control of the economy, allowing in some aspects of a market economy and encouraging foreign investment. As a result of this reform, China's economy grew and achieved one of the highest growth rates in the world. Industrial activity (e.g., manufacturing, mining, and construction) contributes the largest percentage of the country's economy. Transportation, commerce, and services together contribute 33 percent of the economy. Agriculture, forestry, and fishing account for 18 percent.

Develop Concepts

FACTORS OF PRODUCTION. Leng tells Andrew she thinks they should set up a smoothie bar at school as a fund-raiser for their track team. What four factors of production are involved? (Answer includes natural resources: fruit, yogurt, orange juice, and ice; human resources: Leng and Andrew; capital resources: table, signs, blender, pitchers, and cups; entrepreneurial resources: Leng's idea for the bar.)

Figure 2.1 Caption Answer

Answers will vary. Your choices are influenced by your situation.
CL

What Is Economics?

You're gearing up for a weekend trip to the boardwalk with your friends. You take out your in-line skates from the back of your closet. Just by looking at the scratches and dust on them you suppose they need a wheel rotation. Unfortunately, you don't have the parts to do it. You also don't know how to switch the wheels yourself, and you don't have enough money to get it done. You have a shortage of resources. Just as individuals have to deal with a shortage of resources, so do societies.

Factors of Production

A society might not have enough oil, doctors, or technology to satisfy the wants and needs of its people. This shortage of resources is called **scarcity**. A basic economic problem for any society is how to manage its resources. Figure 2.1 illustrates how your choices between wants and needs influence your economic situation.

To meet the wants and needs of its people, a society must produce goods and services. The means to produce them are called economic resources, or **factors of production**. Factors of production include things like the wheat that grows in the ground, the tractor that harvests it, and the labor that turns it into flour.

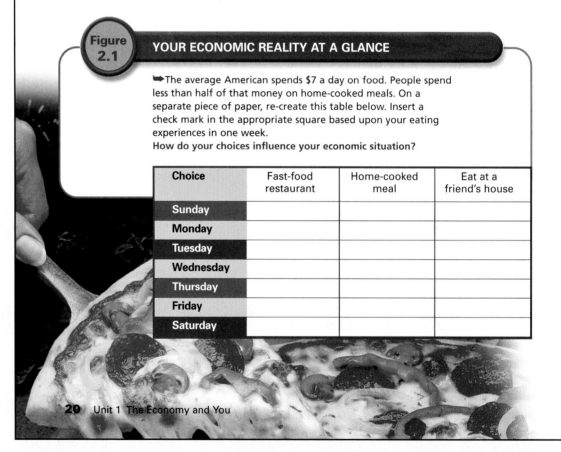

Figure 2.1

YOUR ECONOMIC REALITY AT A GLANCE

➡The average American spends $7 a day on food. People spend less than half of that money on home-cooked meals. On a separate piece of paper, re-create this table below. Insert a check mark in the appropriate square based upon your eating experiences in one week.

How do your choices influence your economic situation?

Choice	Fast-food restaurant	Home-cooked meal	Eat at a friend's house
Sunday			
Monday			
Tuesday			
Wednesday			
Thursday			
Friday			
Saturday			

20 Unit 1 The Economy and You

Cooperative Learning

Motivation in Economic Systems. Ask students to form groups of four. Groups will create a point and counterpoint segment for a television newsmagazine. Have each group discuss the ways in which people are motivated to produce goods and services in each economic system—market, command, and mixed. The segment should give what each team thinks are the good and bad aspects of each system. Suggest that a chart will help them keep track of the points made during the discussion.

Natural Resources

The raw materials found in nature are called **natural resources**. Natural resources become factors of production when used to produce goods. The trees used to make paper and the fish harvested for food are factors of production. Natural resources are often basic elements that can be combined in various ways to create goods. Even synthetic or artificially produced materials are made by combining or changing natural resources. For example, nylon is a synthetic material derived from coal, water, and air.

The economy of many countries is based on its natural resources. For example, the economy of Saudi Arabia depends on its oil production. Many Latin American countries rely on their coffee crops. Other countries, such as Japan, have few natural resources and must get them from somewhere else.

Some resources, like wheat and cattle, are *renewable*. They can be reproduced. Other resources are limited, or *nonrenewable*, like coal, iron, and oil. The amount of natural resources available to a society has a direct effect on its economy.

Human Resources

To produce goods and provide services requires the work of many people. The knowledge, efforts, and skills people bring to their work are called **human resources**, or labor. Teachers, coal miners, bank managers, and farmworkers are all human resources. Whether you're a cashier or a news anchor, you're a human resource. Human resources are needed for everything from drilling oil out of the ground to selling gasoline at a service station.

Labor can be skilled or unskilled, physical or intellectual. One of the biggest problems facing many nations today is not a shortage of labor but a shortage of skilled labor. Many developing nations have plenty of human and natural resources but lack the training or technology to use them. In the United States there is a shortage of nurses, which is problematic since 78 million baby boomers begin turning 65 in a decade. A shrinking hospital staff threatens their future care as well as for all patients.

Capital Resources

Another factor of production is capital resources. Capital resources are not the same as capital, or money. **Capital resources** are the things used to produce goods and services, like buildings, materials, and equipment. They include delivery trucks, supermarkets, cash registers, and medical supplies. A Deere & Company tractor that a farmer uses to

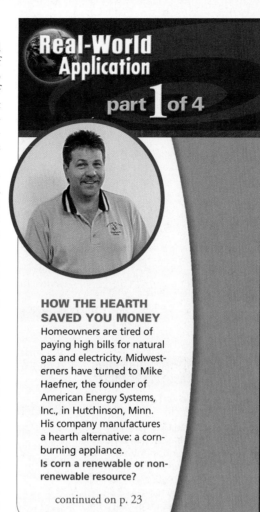

Real-World Application

part 1 of 4

HOW THE HEARTH SAVED YOU MONEY
Homeowners are tired of paying high bills for natural gas and electricity. Midwesterners have turned to Mike Haefner, the founder of American Energy Systems, Inc., in Hutchinson, Minn. His company manufactures a hearth alternative: a corn-burning appliance.
Is corn a renewable or nonrenewable resource?

continued on p. 23

Chapter 2 Economic Resources and Systems **21**

Chapter 2

Real-World Application
Caption Answer

HOW THE HEARTH SAVED YOU MONEY: PART 1 OF 4
Renewable.

Technology Resource

GO TO

POWERPOINT.
The *Introduction to Business* PowerPoint® CD-ROM provides visual lecture aids for this chapter.

Independent Practice

DESIGN. Ask students to design and create posters illustrating several examples of both nonrenewable and renewable resources. Display the posters in the classroom and discuss the problems presented by the limited supplies of some of the resources shown. **LS**

Meeting Individual Needs

Students With Learning Disabilities. Some students with learning disabilities have trouble with sequential tasks involving numbers and in following step-by-step instructions. For example, they may have trouble completing a worksheet or chart. Allow these students extra time to complete the assignment. Assign a peer to help the student complete his or her assignment.

Consider This...

Caption Answer

Answers may vary. The issues surrounding the rights of indigenous cultures and multinationals are vastly complex. Historically around the world there have been two main issues. First, one or two top government officials have made large personal gains. Second, the indigenous people often don't want the companies to leave, but want fair treatment.

Thinking Critically

PROBLEM SOLVING. Your state has had long, hot summers for a few years and now there's a drought in your area. Your local water authority is having trouble maintaining supplies. The news reports that people are to conserve water from 6 A.M. to 8 P.M. tomorrow. What will you do to cope through this water shortage? (Answers will vary and may include buy bottled water, don't use the washing machine and dishwasher, and so on.)

✔ Fast Review Answers

1. The shortage of economic resources such as oil, doctors, and technology.
2. Natural resources, human resources, capital resources, and entrepreneurial resources.
3. Delivery trucks, supermarkets, cash registers, medical supplies, and computers.

Consider This...

Blood Is Thicker Than Oil

Occidental Petroleum Corp. is exploring for oil in Colombia. However, the U'wa people oppose oil exploration on the land they have lived on for thousands of years. For them, oil is the "blood of Mother Earth." The problem is more complex because the Colombian government supports the oil production, which will bring development to the country.

ANALYZE

Who has the right to the land—the U'wa people, the corporation, or the Colombian government?

harvest wheat is a capital resource. The headquarters of IBM is a capital resource. If you're a writer or an accountant, the computer you use is a capital resource.

As the wants and needs of people change, so do the needs for capital resources. In developing nations such as Zimbabwe, there is still a great need for agricultural equipment.

Entrepreneurial Resources

To meet the changing wants and needs of people requires **entrepreneurial resources**. Entrepreneurs recognize the need for new goods and services. They improve on ways to use resources, or create and produce new ones. Henry Ford perfected the factory assembly line method of mass production. Computer industry pioneers William Hewlett and David Packard developed the programmable scientific calculator.

A key to dealing with scarcity is to develop new resources and technologies. For example, researchers at Pioneer Hi-Bred and DuPont are developing and improving insect resistant corn to protect against corn rootworm, which is a costly expense to farmers.

✔ Fast Review

1. What is scarcity?
2. What are the four factors of production?
3. What are some examples of capital resources?

Making Decisions About Production

The problem of scarcity forces societies to answer some basic economic questions. No society has enough productive resources available to produce everything people want. Every society must, therefore, make choices.

Basic Economic Questions

Rules and regulations determine choices. A society makes the choices by answering the following three economic questions: What should be produced? How should it be produced? Who should share in what is produced?

What Should Be Produced? Every country must decide how to use its resources to meet the needs of its people. It has to determine what to produce and how much to produce. The resources used for one purpose can't also be used for something else. For example, a piece of land could be used to grow wheat or corn. It could also be used as the site of a factory, a housing development, or a park. However, the land can only be used for one of these things at a time. Deciding to use it for one purpose means giving up the opportunity to use it for something else.

Science · Curriculum Connection

A Natural Resource. Pair students to research a natural resource. For example: coal, petroleum, natural gas, sulfur, water, or trees. Students could explore renewal practices for renewable resources, conservation efforts made for nonrenewable resources, products made from the resource, environmental problems connected with the resource, and the role of the resource in our economy. Ask pairs to share a report with the class. **CL**, **LS**

How Should It Be Produced? When a society decides what to produce, it must also address other types of questions, such as what methods will be used, how many people will work on the production, and what will be the quality of the items produced? The answers to these questions depend on two factors. One factor depends on how goods are to be produced. Another important factor is the quantity of available resources. In a country where there are workers but very little capital resources, it's probable that little equipment and larger amounts of labor are used in producing goods. The opposite would be true in a country with capital resources but relatively few workers.

Who Should Share in What Is Produced? This question focuses on the concept that people can't get everything that they want because the society doesn't have enough resources. Thus, who gets the limited number of goods that are produced? Although the first two basic economic decisions are important, choosing how goods and services are distributed probably interests people most. In most societies, people can have as many goods and services as they can afford to buy. Thus, the amount of income people receive determines how many goods and services they can have. Then the question arises as to how does the society determine the income earned by each individual in that society?

 Fast Review

1. When a society chooses to use a resource for one purpose and gives up the opportunity to use it for some other purpose, what cost is involved?
2. What happens to production methods when a country discovers new ways to combine economic resources?
3. In most countries, what determines how many goods and services a person can buy?

Types of Economic Systems

Economics studies how society chooses to use resources to produce and distribute goods and services for people's consumption. Businesses may contribute to an economic system by inventing products that use available resources.

To use its limited resources effectively, every nation needs an economic system. An economic system determines how resources will be used. The primary goal of an economic system is to provide people with a minimum standard of living, or quality of life.

To answer the basic economic questions just discussed, two basic and opposing economic systems have been developed. They are commonly referred to as a market economy and a command economy.

HOW THE HEARTH SAVED YOU MONEY
The Countryside Multi-Fuel Corn/Pellet Stove burns corn (and it doesn't smell like popcorn). Burning corn saves the homeowner ten times more money than electricity or heating oil. **Based upon the cost savings, do you think the price of corn is high or low?**

continued on p. 25

HOW THE HEARTH SAVED YOU MONEY: PART 2 OF 4
Low.

Business Connection

Bertil Hult founded E. F. Education—an organization providing language learning, intercultural exchange, and educational travel—in Stockholm in 1965. Socialist Sweden, with its moderate command economy, did not support entrepreneurship and by the 1970s Hult left Sweden and built his business in the United Kingdom, Germany, and the United States. Now, the E. F. Education organization provides employment for over 17,000 people. In Sweden by 1991 the economy was slow and jobs were harder to find. Then in early 1995, Sweden realized entrepreneurs were needed to bring new business and employment. The nation started to develop a mixed economy, liberalizing state-dominated markets such as banking and telecommunications, and the Swedish economy started to grow.

Fast Review Answers

1. Opportunity cost.
2. The equation of capital resources versus human resources changes.
3. The amount of income they receive.

Global Perspective

Survey. Most of the world's economies are converging toward the market economy system. One of the most promising of these seems to be Mexico, whose economy is transforming from a closed economy to an open, market economy. Suggest that students survey recent news periodicals in the library or on the Internet for articles detailing with events in Mexico's economic progress. What change has there been in state-owned enterprises, opportunities for national and foreign investment, regulatory management and accountability, laws governing competition, choices for Mexican consumers, and elimination of red tape? Encourage students to share their findings on a poster exhibit.

2 TEACH (Cont.)

Develop Concepts

SPECIFY. Have students research the economy in Hungary, Mexico, or Peru. Ask them to share specific words used in articles to describe the economy and changes in the economy. Make a list of words and phrases on the board. (Words and phrases may include a standard of living, privatization, revitalization, state companies, socialist, slowed growth, inflation, state spending, private sector, liberalize, rebuild, stimulate growth, create jobs, market economy, and mixed economy.)

Discussion Starter

DIFFERENTIATING. Ask students to describe government. (Government refers to the system of political institutions, laws, and customs that a society uses to determine its code of conduct.) Ask students to describe an economic system. (An economic system describes a way of producing and distributing goods and services.) Ask students to create a mnemonic device to help them remember the difference between a government and an economic system. **LS**

Figure 2.2 Caption Answer

Demand Curve, 500. Supply Curve, 700.

Market Economy

In a **market economy** economic decisions are made in the marketplace according to the laws of supply and demand. Mobil gas stations, Fantastic Sam's hair salons, Federal Express offices, and the New York Stock Exchange are all marketplaces. The marketplace is anywhere money changes hands.

The Market and Prices. Price plays an important role in the market economy. Price is the amount of money given or asked for when goods and services are bought or sold. If producers think the price consumers will pay for a good or service is too low, and the price does not earn them a profit, they will produce little or none of the product. If they think the price is high enough to earn a profit, they will produce the good and service.

Consumers are the ones who determine the demand of an item. **Demand** is the amount or quantity of goods and services that consumers are willing to buy at various prices. Generally, the higher the price, the

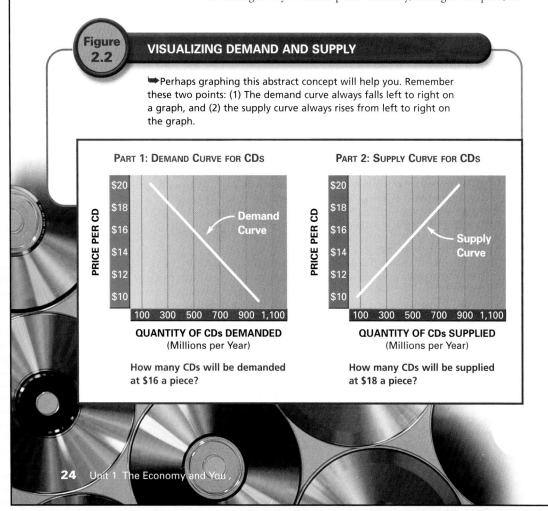

Figure 2.2

VISUALIZING DEMAND AND SUPPLY

➡Perhaps graphing this abstract concept will help you. Remember these two points: (1) The demand curve always falls left to right on a graph, and (2) the supply curve always rises from left to right on the graph.

PART 1: DEMAND CURVE FOR CDs

PRICE PER CD: $20, $18, $16, $14, $12, $10

Demand Curve

QUANTITY OF CDs DEMANDED (Millions per Year): 100 300 500 700 900 1,100

How many CDs will be demanded at $16 a piece?

PART 2: SUPPLY CURVE FOR CDs

PRICE PER CD: $20, $18, $16, $14, $12, $10

Supply Curve

QUANTITY OF CDs SUPPLIED (Millions per Year): 100 300 500 700 900 1,100

How many CDs will be supplied at $18 a piece?

Great Ideas From the Classroom of...

Stephanie Andrejcak
Burnt Hills-Ballston
Lake Central School District
Burnt Hills, N.Y.

Supply and Demand. When I teach supply and demand, I hand out random amounts of play money to the students in class. Then I hold up a lollipop and ask them how much they're willing to "pay" for the lollipop. Naturally, the student with the most money purchases the lollipop. Then I hold up six lollipops and again ask how much they would pay. The price students are willing to pay decreases because there is more of a supply. It's a good way to teach the students the relationship between supply, demand, and price.

fewer consumers will buy an item. The opposite also applies: The lower the price, the more consumers will buy.

Suppose you walk into a store with $15 to buy a CD. The store is having a "two for one" sale on CDs. You decide to buy two CDs for the price of one. Chances are many other customers will do the same thing. This results in more CDs being sold. The sale encourages consumers to buy more.

Producers are influenced to supply goods or services by the prices in the market. **Supply** is the amount of goods and services that producers will provide at various prices. Producers want to receive a price for their goods and services that will cover their costs and provide a profit.

Suppose the price for eggs rises from $2 to $4 a dozen. The price will probably increase because egg-producing businesses will see more profits to be made at $4. At that price, producers are encouraged to produce more eggs.

Demand and supply work together. Figure 2.2 illustrates demand and supply. When the quantity demanded and the quantity supplied meet, this is called the **equilibrium price**. Equilibrium, then, is the price at which the amount supplied and the amount demanded meet.

A market economy is also called *capitalism*, or private enterprise. In a capitalist system, resources are privately owned. You can own your own home, your own land, and your own business. You decide how your business will be run, what to sell, and how much to charge. As a consumer, you decide where to live, where to shop, and what to buy. If you need shampoo, you can buy the name brand for dry, unmanageable hair, or the store brand that's on sale. Government control of the marketplace is minimal. The primary role of government is to support the marketplace by removing obstacles such as trade barriers. The United States and Japan are examples of capitalist countries.

The Market's Motivations. A market economy also offers incentives, such as competition and the profit motive, to produce more. The *profit motive* is simply the desire to make more money. You have an incentive to work harder and longer if you can make more money. Businesses compete for customers by producing better and cheaper products. The constant demand for new goods and services encourages entrepreneurship.

The problem with a market economy is that owners and producers reap the most rewards. Unskilled workers and older adults are often unable to afford basic needs such as health care. In the United States, for example, the average chief executive officer makes almost 500 times as much as the average blue-collar worker. A small number of large companies can join forces to control the supply of products and manipulate prices. The profit motive can become an end in itself rather than a means to improve the product for all.

Chapter 2 Economic Resources and Systems **25**

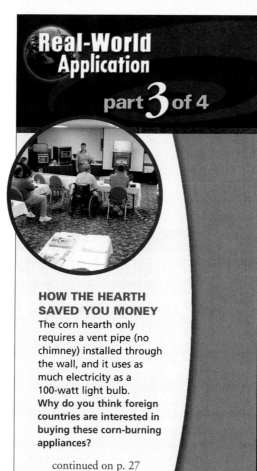

Real-World Application
part 3 of 4

HOW THE HEARTH SAVED YOU MONEY
The corn hearth only requires a vent pipe (no chimney) installed through the wall, and it uses as much electricity as a 100-watt light bulb. **Why do you think foreign countries are interested in buying these corn-burning appliances?**

continued on p. 27

Real-World Application
Caption Answer

HOW THE HEARTH SAVED YOU MONEY: PART 3 OF 4

The answer will vary. It might help countries save money, capitalize on utilizing natural resources, and protect the environment.

Individualized Practice

SUPPLY AND DEMAND. Ask students how many soft drinks they would buy at the following single-can prices: 25¢, 50¢, $1, $1.50, $2.00, $2.50, and $3.00. Make a chart to record the quantities of soft drinks students would purchase at each price. Ask students to create a bar graph using the information in the chart.

L1 Pair students to work together to make the bar graph. Have students share reasons why prices may go up or go down. (Answers will vary but may include changes in supplies of materials or increases in labor costs needed to make the product.)

L2 Ask students to give other examples of price and demand in a brief discussion.

L3 Ask students to write three paragraphs discussing the relationships between price and demand, supply and price, and supply and demand.

Social Science   *Curriculum Connection*

Communication. Group students in pairs to discuss the following: Should our society use scarce resources to produce different versions of one product? (An example is plastic toys for children.) What are the resources used? Would society be better off if fewer versions of some products were made, particularly if they use resources that are difficult or impossible to recycle or renew? Have groups share their conclusions in a brief discussion of the use of scarce resources.

Business Building Blocks

CAPTION ANSWER

Remind students to use each of the interpretation steps to read this graph. (Number of computers being sold for $3,000 is 5,000. Number of computers supplied at $3,000 is 35,000. The equilibrium price is $2,000.)

3 ASSESS

Reteaching

CHART. To reteach the concept of economic resources, ask the students to prepare a chart titled "Economic Resources," with the headings: natural, human, capital, and entrepreneurial. What resources do they encounter daily? List those resources under the appropriate heading. (Some examples might be water, salespeople, cash register in a store, and a new product or service.)

Enrichment Strategy

REPORT. Show a short video featuring the topic of mixed economy. Ask students: If you had to pick two words or phrases to describe a mixed economy, what would they be? Write a short report summarizing the video. **LS**

Evaluation

Assign and review the Fast Review sections.

Command Economy

Many nations have a command economy. A command economy is also called a planned or managed economy. In a **command economy** a central authority makes the key economic decisions. This central authority is usually the government, or state.

There are two types of command economies. In a strong command economy, such as *communism*, the state makes all the economic decisions. The state controls all the resources for the common good. The state decides what to produce, how much, and how to distribute it. China, Cuba, and many Latin American and African countries have strong command economies.

Business Building Blocks

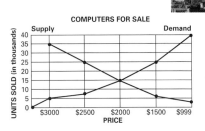

Math

Interpreting Line Graphs

Graphs are a quick and useful way to visually communicate information. You see these from newspaper articles to cereal boxes. Line graphs often show change over a period of time. The left side of a graph is the *vertical axis*. The bottom of the graph is the *horizontal axis*. Both axes display numbers and a label indicating what the numbers represent. Dots on the graph show numerical information. When the dots are connected, they form a line whose location and direction on the graph reveals information about change through time.

COMPUTERS FOR SALE

UNITS SOLD (in thousands) — Supply / Demand
PRICE: $3000, $2500, $2000, $1500, $999

Practice

Use the graph to answer the following questions: How many $3,000 computers are being supplied? What is the difference between supply and demand for $3,000 computers? At what price does the supply equal the demand for computers?

How to Interpret a Line Graph

- Read the title of the graph.
- Read the label on each axis.
- Understand the numbers on each axis, including the interval used. The *interval* is the unit of measurement between numbers.
- Examine where the dots are located on the graph.
- Determine what the line(s) or curve(s) symbolize.
- Compare the line(s) on the graph to both axes to determine the graph's meaning.

How to Use a Portfolio Activity

The portfolio projects are designed to lead students to develop a collection of their best work to submit to you for assessment. You and each of your students should decide which projects to include in their business portfolio. Refer students to the specific rubric(s) from the *Alternative Assessment Strategies*. These rubrics will alert students to the criteria you'll use to assess their projects.

In a moderate command economy, also called *social-ism*, there is some form of private enterprise. The state owns major resources, such as airlines and steel, and makes the key economic decisions. However, individuals may own some businesses. France and Sweden are countries that have moderate command economies.

The primary advantage of a command economy is that it guarantees everyone an equal standard of living. The state provides you with a job, a place to live, and health care. Goods and services are distributed evenly. The state also takes care of things like utilities, transportation, and defense. There is usually less crime and poverty because everyone's needs and wants are equally met.

There are some disadvantages to a command economy. In a strong command economy since the state provides all goods and services there is little choice of what to buy. Goods that aren't considered necessities like fashion clothing and VCRs are often unavailable. Prices are fixed by the state, so there is no incentive to produce a better product. Wages are fixed by the state. If you're a highly skilled worker, like a doctor or a lawyer, you often earn the same wage as an unskilled worker. There is no incentive for entrepreneurship when you can't run your own business.

Mixed Economy

A free market economy and a command economy are great ideas in principle but don't always work in practice. In a market economy, there can be great poverty in the midst of great wealth. In a command economy, everyone is economically equal. In reality, few nations have an economy based totally on one model or the other.

Most nations have a **mixed economy**, a combination of a market and command economy. The state takes care of people's needs while the marketplace takes care of people's wants. In the United States, for example, the government provides things like defense and education. The marketplace provides things like cars, computers, and fast food. There is some government regulation of business.

In every country, one type of economy is dominant. However, most countries find a mixed economy is the best way to manage their limited resources.

 Fast Review _____

1. What is an economic system?
2. What is the difference between a market economy and a command economy?
3. What are the advantages and disadvantages of a command economy and a market economy?

Chapter 2 Economic Resources and Systems **27**

HOW THE HEARTH SAVED YOU MONEY
The average home using a multi-fuel corn stove will burn 150 to 200 bushels of corn a season. Imagine a command economy that only allows 100 bushels of corn per household.
How might this affect the people?

Real-World Application
part **4** of 4

Chapter 2

Real-World Application
Caption Answer

HOW THE HEARTH SAVED YOU MONEY: PART 4 OF 4
Answers will vary. It affects people's standard of living.

Technology Resource

 VIRTUAL BUSINESS. Introduce supply and demand using Knowledge Matters' *Virtual Business*. Go to the *Introduction to Business* Web site **www.introbus.glencoe.com** to download the *Virtual Business* activity. Run the *Virtual Business* tutorial before beginning this activity.

Fast Review Answers ✓

1. Determines how resources will be used.
2. Market economy— economic decisions are made according to supply and demand. Command economy—economic decisions are made by a central authority.
3. Command economy offers few incentives to produce. A market economy offers incentives to produce.

Meeting Individual Needs

Students With Learning Disabilities. For students who find the written text difficult to use, you may wish to make chapter audiotapes so they can listen and read simultaneously. The tapes can be made with the help of other students in the class.

Set a relaxed pace for the reading, and use a clicker to signal when to turn pages. This idea may be extended by students cooperating to produce videotapes of the reading of chapter material.

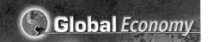

Demand for Oil

1 FOCUS

Tell students that the Middle East contains more than half of the world's known oil reserves. (In contrast, the United States has only 2 percent of the world's supplies.) However, the region accounts for only about one-third of the world's oil production. This is because the Organization of Petroleum Exporting Countries (OPEC)—the oil cartel—exercises considerable control over production in the region.

2 TEACH

Direct students to study the map annotations and to note the sources of the oil consumed in the United States. Then discuss the significance of U.S. dependence on oil from other countries. What events could obstruct the flow of foreign oil to the United States? How would that affect the American economy? (Students may suggest that political unrest, wars, terrorism, and changing trade relations all might interrupt the flow of imported oil. This could disrupt activity in the U. S. economy, because nearly half of the country's oil consumption is met by foreign sources.)

Global *Economy*

Demand for Oil Americans demand oil for many purposes, but mostly as a fuel for their automobiles. About 193 million vehicles burn 122 billion gallons of gasoline a year. Domestic supplies meet about half of the demand for oil. The map below shows where we get the rest.

Canada supplies 13 percent

Mexico supplies 11 percent

Caribbean Nations supply 4 percent (Leading Sources: Virgin Islands, Trinidad and Tobago, Netherlands Antilles)

South America supplies 24 percent (Leading Sources: Venezuela, Colombia, Argentina)

On average, a barrel holding 42 gallons of crude oil produces 21 gallons of gasoline.

28

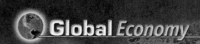

**Europe supplies
7 percent**
(Leading Sources: Great
Britain, Norway, Belgium)

**Persian Gulf Region
supplies 23 percent**
(Leading Sources: Saudi
Arabia, Iraq, Kuwait)

**Asia and Oceania
supply 3 percent**
(Leading Sources: Australia,
Indonesia, Brunei)

**rica supplies
5 percent**
g Sources: Nigeria,
, Algeria)

Thinking Globally

1. Which region of the world is the largest source for American oil imports?

2. What percentage of American oil imports do Canada and Mexico provide?

29

3 ASSESS

Have students answer the Thinking Globally questions.

4 CLOSE

Have students assume that they are experts assigned to study the United States' dependence on foreign oil. Ask them what recommendations they might make to the government to protect the country from oil shortages due to a disruption of the flow of foreign oil.

? Did You Know?

The United States accounts for only about 5 percent of the world's population. However, it consumes close to 25 percent of the world's oil.

 **Thinking Globally**
Caption Answer

1. South America

2. 24 percent

4 CLOSE

Chapter Wrap-Up

Ask students to explain the factors of production, types of economic systems, and incentives in a market economy.

Using Business Key Words

1. natural resources
2. capital resources
3. scarcity
4. market economy
5. entrepreneurial resources
6. command economy
7. human resources
8. factors of production
9. mixed economy
10. demand
11. supply
12. economics
13. equilibrium price

Review What You Learned

14. Scarcity of resources.
15. Natural, human, capital, and entrepreneurial resources.
16. Nonrenewable: coal. Renewable: trees.
17. A shortage of skilled labor.
18. The development of new resources and technology.
19. Provide standard of living.
20. Resources are privately owned.
21. Competition and profit motive.
22. Strong command economy (communism). Moderate command (socialism).

30

Summary

1. Scarcity is the shortage of economic resources such as oil, doctors, or technology.

2. The four factors of production are natural resources, human resources, capital resources, and entrepreneurial resources.

3. In a market economy all economic decisions are made in the marketplace according to the laws of supply and demand. In a command economy a central authority makes all economic decisions. In a market economy there are many incentives to produce, but owners and producers reap the most benefits. In a command economy there is economic equality, but few incentives to produce.

4. In a mixed economy, the state takes care of people's needs while the marketplace takes care of people's wants.

● Using Business Key Words

On a separate piece of paper, rewrite the sentences below, using the correct term to complete each one.

- **scarcity**
- **entrepreneurial resources**
- **economics**
- **factors of production**
- **market economy**
- **equilibrium price**
- **natural resources**
- **supply**
- **demand**
- **human resources**
- **command economy**
- **capital resources**
- **mixed economy**

1. The raw materials found in nature are called _____.
2. Buildings, material, and equipment used to produce goods and services are _____.
3. Society's shortage of resources is called _____.
4. Economic decisions are made according to _____.

5. _____ are required to meet the changing wants and needs of people.
6. Communism is an example of a _____.
7. _____ are the knowledge, efforts, and skills people bring to their work.
8. The _____ are the economic resources used to produce goods and services.
9. A _____ can be defined by the state taking care of the people's needs while the marketplace takes care of the people's wants.
10. The amount or quantity of goods and services that consumers are willing to buy at various prices is called _____.
11. The amount of goods and services that producers will provide at various prices is called the _____.
12. The study of how society chooses to use resources to produce and distribute goods and services for people's consumption is called _____.
13. When the quantity demanded and the quantity supplied meet, this is called _____.

30 Unit 1 The Economy and You

Quick Quiz

1. What are the four factors of production? (Natural, human, capital, and entrepreneurial resources.)
2. How can a change in supply increase a price? A change in demand? (A decrease in supply or an increase in demand will increase a price.)
3. In what economic system are the resources privately owned? Owned and controlled by the government? (Market economy; strong command.)
4. Which economic system is most often associated with communism? Capitalism? Socialism? (Strong command; free market; moderate command.)

Review What You Learned

14. What resource problem is faced by all societies?
15. What are the four main economic resources?
16. Name the two types of natural resources and give an example of each.
17. What is one of the biggest labor problems facing many nations today?
18. What is the key to dealing with the problem of scarcity?
19. What is the primary goal of an economic system?
20. In a market economy, who owns the resources?
21. What incentives are offered in a free market economy?
22. Describe the two types of command economies.

Understanding Business Concepts

23. Select an item that you see in your classroom. List the factors of production you think were used to produce that item.
24. Are some natural resources more valuable than others? Explain.
25. Describe how a country's economy is affected by its natural resources. Provide an example.
26. What happens when human resources are scarce?
27. How do entrepreneurs help meet the changing needs and wants of people?
28. Give an example of how the concept of supply and demand has affected you.
29. Why is the profit motive considered an incentive in a free market system?
30. Why do most countries find a mixed economy the best way to manage their limited resources?

Critical Thinking

31. Think about a career you might be interested in pursuing. What capital resources would you use in that career?
32. A company produces a new toy that is liked by both children and adults. There is great demand for it. The supplier raises its price because there's no competition. The supplier cannot keep up with the demand. Some people believe the supplier is taking advantage of the public by increasing its price. Are such price increases allowed in a market system? Should the government control the price? What are other toy producers likely to do?

Viewing and Representing

Examining the Image. Look closely at the photo. Where do you focus? Step into the picture. What do you hear? What else do you see around you? Imagine you could buy the goods. Does the price seem fair? Would you buy them at the price shown? Why or why not? How does price affect the demand?

Chapter 2 Economic Resources and Systems **31**

Chapter 2 Review

Critical Thinking

31. Answers will vary depending on the career selected.
32. Such price increases are allowed in our market system—especially for nonessential products like toys. In our system, if someone is willing to produce an item, then supply and demand will operate to set the price. What generally happens is that over time more suppliers make this type of toy, which means increased supply. Assuming that demand doesn't increase, this increased supply eventually creates a surplus of that toy at the original higher price, so the price comes down.

Viewing and Representing

Answers will vary. Throughout the textbook, this activity is structured in two parts. The first part asks the students to observe the picture carefully or examine it closely. The second part asks the students to give their interpretation of the picture. Encourage a safe learning environment where students feel their interpretations and opinions are valued.

Understanding Business Concepts

23. Answers will vary but include the four factors of production.
24. Yes.
25. If the natural resources found in a country are very valuable or vital, then the economy of that country flourishes. If there are few natural resources the country relies on other countries.
26. Wages, prices, products, and services.
27. Recognize new goods and services.
28. Answers will vary.
29. The profit motive is the desire to make more money.
30. When the state takes care of the people's needs and the marketplace takes care of the people's wants.

4 CLOSE (Cont.)

Building Academic Skills

LANGUAGE ARTS. Have students use the local newspaper or the local news to find a current event for this project. Rubric: Essay.

HISTORY. Make sure all students participate in the group project. Rubrics: Charts/tables, photo essay, poster.

MATH. If students have difficulty figuring the averages, remind them to add the total prices for the item and then divide by the number of items. Rubrics: Spreadsheet, diagram, math calculations.

COMPUTER/TECHNOLOGY. Answers will vary depending on the country selected. Rubric: Essay.

Linking School to Home

Answers will vary. Instead of a family member, a student could ask a friend to work on the project with him or her. Rubrics: Note taking, essay, oral presentation.

Linking School to Work

Answers will vary. Encourage students' creativity. Rubric: Oral presentation.

Building Academic Skills

 Reading Current Events

Select a current event that you have read about in the newspaper or have heard about on the news. Write a one- to two-page paper on how the event has had an impact on the U.S. economy.

 Researching Economic Resources

In a group, choose a foreign country and research the country's economic resources. Assign research topics to each member, such as:
- What natural resources are plentiful?
- What does the country produce with its natural resources?
- What kind of human resources does the country have?
- How does the country make up for the resources that are in short supply?
- What impact do entrepreneurial resources have on its economy?

Create a display of your group's findings, including graphics and photos.

 Averaging Prices

List five things you buy often. Then list all the places you can buy those items. Record the price that each store charges for each item. Do some stores charge more than others? Why do prices differ for identical products? Determine the average price of each item based on the prices you recorded.

 Researching Economic Transition

Using the Internet, find a country that is making the transition from a command economy to mixed or market economy. Prepare a report on the process, the successes, and the difficulties of the transition.

Linking School to Home

Listing Factors of Production. Select five items found in your home that you and your family use quite frequently. List the factors of production you think were used to produce each item. Ask another family member to work on this project with you.

Linking School to Work

Presentation on Technology. Technology has had a dramatic effect on the economy in the United States. Create a list of all the technology that is currently available for consumer use. How much of it was available five years ago? Ten years ago? How has it impacted the U.S. economy? Prepare a two-minute presentation to share your findings with the class.

E-Homework

Applying Technology

Categorizing Data. Using the database created in Chapter 1, categorize the resources according to whether they are natural, human, capital, or entrepreneurial. Then, convert the database into a graphical representation of each category.

Speculating on a Shortage. Research the shortage of workers in information technology. Find out what kinds of jobs are available, the types of skills needed, and the training required in order to get into this career field. Then, speculate why you think there are so many job openings in information technology.

Connecting Academics

Math. Jasmeen, a jewelry vendor at the flea market, looks at her record of prices and sales volume over the past seven months:

	Price	Number of items sold
April	$10	3,000
May	$12	2,900
June	$14	2,800
July	$20	2,500
August	$15	2,800
September	$13	3,200
October	$12	3,400

She asks you to draw a line graph showing the relationship between price and sales. Using the graph, explain to Jasmeen how price affects demand for the jewelry.

Language Arts. Get together in teams to teach one another about economic resources or economic systems. As a team, create a fun lesson plan on one of the following topics:
- Scarcity and factors of production
- The three economic questions
- Market economy
- Supply and demand
- Command economy and mixed economy

Use real-world examples in your lessons. Present the lessons.

 Analyzing the Feature Story

You read the first part of "Poland—Goods Runneth Over" at the beginning of this chapter. Below are a few questions for you to answer about Poland. You'll find the answers to these questions when you're reading the entire article. First, here are the questions:

33. What economic system is Poland moving toward?

34. Name a factor of production that Poland plans to use more of in the future.

CREATIVE JOURNAL ACTIVITY

Break into small groups and agree on another Eastern European country to research.
- What factors of production could this country use?
- What natural resources are available?
- What human resources do they have?

Share your findings with the rest of the class.

The Full Story

To learn more about Poland, visit the *Introduction to Business* Web site at **www.introbus.glencoe.com**, and click on *BusinessWeek* Feature Story, Chapter 2.

E-Homework

CATEGORIZING DATA. Databases will vary depending on the products selected. Rubrics: Database, note taking.

SPECULATING ON A SHORTAGE. Encourage students to use the Internet, current business and technology periodicals, or newspaper articles for their research. Rubrics: Note taking, essay, oral presentation.

Connecting Academics

MATH. Line graph with the months April to October as the horizontal axis. When the price is less the demand increases.

LANGUAGE ARTS. Teaching others is a great way to learn. This technique can be adapted and used in any chapter in this course. Encourage groups to be creative and to use real-world examples in the lessons.

BusinessWeek Analyzing the Feature Story

33. Poland is moving toward a market economy.

34. Poland plans to tap into its entrepreneurial resources by offering money to former coal miners to start their own businesses.

Creative Journal Activity

Eastern European countries to research include Albania, Bosnia and Herzegovina, Bulgaria, Czech Republic, Hungary, Latvia, Lithuania, Macedonia, Romania, Russia, Slovakia, Slovenia, or Yugoslavia. Encourage groups to present their findings in a creative format, such as a game show, interview, or role-play. **CL**, **LS**

SCANS Correlation Chart*

Foundation Skills

Basic Skills	Reading	Writing	Math	Listening	Speaking	
Thinking Skills	Creative Thinking	Decision Making	Problem Solving	Seeing Things in the Mind's Eye	Knowing How to Learn	Reasoning
Personal Qualities	Responsibility	Self-Esteem	Sociability	Self-Management	Integrity/ Honesty	

Workplace Competencies

Resources	Allocating Time	Allocating Money	Allocating Material and Facility Resources	Allocating Human Resources		
Information	Acquiring and Evaluating Information	Organizing and Maintaining Information	Interpreting and Communicating Information	Using Computers to Process Information		
Interpersonal Skills	Participating as a Member of a Team	Teaching Others	Serving Clients/ Customers	Exercising Leadership	Negotiating to Arrive at a Decision	Working With Cultural Diversity
Systems	Understanding Systems	Monitoring and Correcting Performance	Improving and Designing Systems			
Technology	Selecting Technology	Applying Technology to Task	Maintaining and Troubleshooting Technology			

*This chart's highlighted blocks indicate the chapter's content coverage in the Student Edition and the Teacher Wraparound Edition.

Resource Manager

Teaching Transparencies

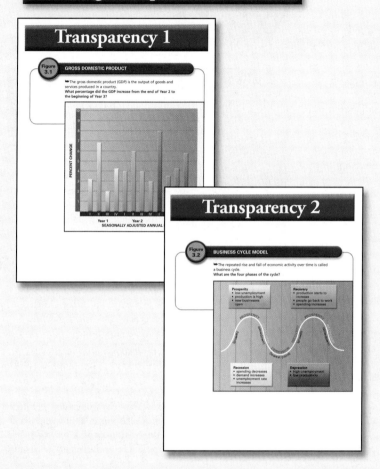

Transparency 1

Figure 3.1 GROSS DOMESTIC PRODUCT

The gross domestic product (GDP) is the output of goods and services produced in a country.
What percentage did the GDP increase from the end of Year 2 to the beginning of Year 3?

PERCENT CHANGE

Year 1   Year 2
SEASONALLY ADJUSTED ANNUAL

Transparency 2

Figure 3.2 BUSINESS CYCLE MODEL

The repeated rise and fall of economic activity over time is called a business cycle.
What are the four phases of the cycle?

Prosperity
• low unemployment
• production is high
• new businesses open

Recovery
• production starts to increase
• people go back to work
• spending increases

Recession
• spending decreases
• demand increases
• unemployment rate increases

Depression
• high unemployment
• low productivity

Application and Enrichment

- Lesson Plans
- *BusinessWeek* Poster Package
- Teaching Transparencies
- Integrated Software Simulation
- Glencoe Business Video Package

Review and Reinforcement

- *PuzzleMaker*
- Internet Resources
- Student Activity Workbook
- Strat. and Work. for Teaching Transparencies

Assessment and Evaluation

- Reproducible Tests
- Alternative Assessment Strategies
- ExamView® Pro Test Generator

Technology

- *PuzzleMaker*
- ExamView® Pro Test Generator
- Glencoe Business Video Package
- PowerPoint® Presentation
- Integrated Software Simulation
- Interactive Lesson Planner
- *Virtual Business*®

KEY	✎ Printed	💾 Software	📼 Videocassette	📕 Poster
	🕹 Transparency	💿 CD-ROM	🖥 Internet	

BUSINESS Online

Visit **www.introbus.glencoe.com**, the Web site companion to *Introduction to Business.* The student's page includes:

- interactive tutor
- additional *BusinessWeek* articles and activities
- business Web links
- homework hints
- real-world application activities
- additional career path activities

Information on how to prepare your students for the high school exit exam and special projects are also included.

Use the Glencoe Web site for additional resources. All essential content is covered in the Student Edition.

1 FOCUS

Introducing the Chapter

This chapter describes types of economic measurements. It introduces the four phases of the business cycle—prosperity, recession, depression, and recovery. A photo essay, "Eras That Changed the Economy," explores the economy from a historical perspective.

Connecting the Objectives

How does a country measure its economy? What terms do you hear when people talk about the rise and fall of the economy?

BusinessWeek

Feature Story

Story's Summary

José Aguirre, a 25-year-old factory technician, brings home less than $135 a week. Home is a small house with seven other family members in Ciudad Juarez, a bustling town on the U.S.–Mexico border. Aguirre is happy that his standard of living has improved since the new economic era has helped careers, benefits, housing, and training. How has this come about? (It has much to do with both the U.S. and Mexican governments.)

Find the entire article at www.introbus.glencoe.com, or in the Teacher Resource Binder.

Economic Activity in a Changing World

Learning Objectives

After completing this chapter, you'll be able to:
1. **Identify** how economic activity is measured.
2. **Explain** how inflation and deflation work.
3. **Discuss** the four phases of the business cycle.

Why It's Important

Economic activity affects everyday life. The history of the economy affects industries and people of today and tomorrow.

Key Words

gross domestic product (GDP)
standard of living
inflation
deflation
budget deficit
national debt
budget surplus
business cycle
prosperity
recession
depression
recovery

BusinessWeek Feature Story

Moving up the Ladder

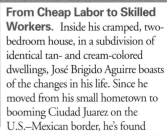

From Cheap Labor to Skilled Workers. Inside his cramped, two-bedroom house, in a subdivision of identical tan- and cream-colored dwellings, José Brigido Aguirre boasts of the changes in his life. Since he moved from his small hometown to booming Ciudad Juarez on the U.S.–Mexican border, he's found employment as a technician in a factory. Thanks to a mortgage he lined up through a program funded by the government and his employers, Delphi Automotive Systems Corp. in Tory, Mich., Aguirre, 25, now supports three generations—eight people in all—under one roof on $135 a week before taxes.

Source: Excerpted with permission from "Moving up the Ladder: From Cheap Labor to Skilled Workers," *BusinessWeek Online*, November 6, 2000.

An Extension Activity

Imagine your friend from Mexico City just landed an internship with Southwest Airlines in Dallas, Texas. Your friend is a little nervous about living in a new country with new etiquette. Research business etiquette tips that he or she might use to fit in.

The Full Story

To learn more about globalization, visit the *Introduction to Business* Web site at www.introbus.glencoe.com, and click on *BusinessWeek* Feature Story, Chapter 3.

Classroom Resources

For the Teacher
📁 Student Activity Work. TAE
📓💿 Assessment Binder
💿 PowerPoint® Presentation
💿 Interactive Lesson Planner
📁 Lesson Plans
📓💻 Internet Resources
🔦 Teaching Transparencies
💻 *Introduction to Business* Web Site

💿 Integrated Soft. Sim. TM
📓 *BusinessWeek* Poster Package
For the Student
📓 Student Activity Workbook
💿 *Virtual Business*®
💻 *Introduction to Business* Web Site
💿 Integrated Soft. Sim.
💿 *PuzzleMaker*
📓 Strategies and Worksheets for Teaching Transparencies

🔔 Bell Ringer Activity

ACQUIRING AND EVALUATING INFORMATION. Make copies of a current magazine or newspaper article about economic conditions and distribute it to students. (See www.businessweek.com) Ask students: How would you describe today's economy? What terms might you use? What factors mentioned in the article indicate the state of the economy? If you needed to find other reliable sources of information on economic conditions, what resources could you use?

Preteaching Business Key Words

TEACHING OTHERS. Pair students. Each pair splits the key word list in half. Instruct students to find the definition of their words in the glossary and then take turns teaching each other. For example, read the definition of the key word, and then ask the other student to write how a journalist might use the key word in a sentence. **LS**

An Extension Activity

ROLE-PLAY. Generally, Americans are conversational and casual. Handshakes are usually used upon first introductions and then rarely used again. Role-play behavior differences you might see depending on the workplace (i.e., a corporate office or a manufacturing plant). **LS**, **CL**

Making Connections

Assembly Line. In groups of five or six, experiment with assembly-line techniques using a simple product and process, such as assembling booklets. (For example, illustrated instruction booklets on how to do research on the Internet.) Select one group as the control group, which doesn't use assembly-line methods. All the other groups should organize its own assembly line. The groups assemble as many booklets as possible in five minutes. At the end of the experiment, compare the efficiency of the methods of all the groups. How did the groups' outcomes compare to the control group? How does efficiency affect production?

2 TEACH

Business Connection

COMPARING. The world's wealthiest countries have a far greater income (at an average annual per capita level of gross domestic product (GDP) of about $16,000) than the rest of the world. Almost 70 percent of the world's population has an average annual per capita level of GDP of less than $4,000. The economic dilemma is how to close the large gap in living standards of the world's population.

Develop Concepts

MEASURING ECONOMIC ACTIVITY. The unemployment rate is an indication of how business-people, investors, and the government predict economic conditions. High unemployment figures usually indicate that the economy is contracting. Ask students to research economic forecasts and list which economic indicators were used to make the forecast.

Figure 3.1 Caption Answer

5 percent.

The Influences on Economics

George Santayana, the American writer said, "Those who cannot remember the past are condemned to repeat it." In the realm of economics, the wealth of nations rises and falls through periods of war, recession, and prosperity. You'll remember that a major purpose of an economic system is to produce the goods and services wanted by people. You might also say that almost anyone can start a business in the U.S. economy. Measuring an economic system's activity greatly impacts everyone. Figure 3.1 illustrates how the GDP seasonally adjusts.

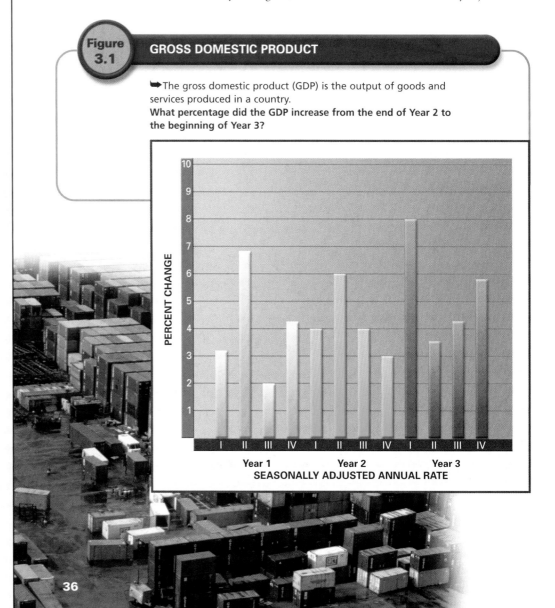

Figure 3.1

GROSS DOMESTIC PRODUCT

➡ The gross domestic product (GDP) is the output of goods and services produced in a country.
What percentage did the GDP increase from the end of Year 2 to the beginning of Year 3?

Chart: PERCENT CHANGE vs. Year 1, Year 2, Year 3 (quarters I, II, III, IV)
SEASONALLY ADJUSTED ANNUAL RATE

Cooperative Learning

Time Line. Methods of production have been changing since the Industrial Revolution. The assembly line, automation, and robotics are innovations that increased efficiency. Give groups of students three poster boards to make a long poster. Ask students to draw a time line from the 1700s to the present year. Ask students to mark the stages of the economy and the approximate times when new technologies or services were introduced. Post the time lines on the classroom wall. Encourage groups to continue the development of their time line as they go through this chapter.

Measuring Economic Activity

Baseball fans know that batting averages, strikeouts, RBIs, and ERAs are figures used to measure a player's performance. Figures are also used to measure economic performance. These figures are called *economic indicators*. They measure things like how much a country is producing, whether its economy is growing, and how it compares to other countries.

Gross Domestic Product (GDP)

Goods and services that satisfy your wants and needs are the final output of an economy. They're the result of all the economic activity in the country. One way of telling how well an economy is performing is to determine how many goods and services it produces during a certain period of time.

An important measure of a country's economic health is its level of *productivity*, or how much it produces. The total value of the goods and services produced in a country in a given year is called its **gross domestic product (GDP)** (see Figure 3.1). The United States has a very high GDP compared to other countries.

To calculate the GDP, economists compute the sum of goods and services. They include four main areas:

- consumer goods and services
- business goods and services
- government goods and services
- goods and services sold to other countries

The GDP doesn't include the goods and services that aren't reported to the government, like daycare, babysitting, and mowing lawns.

The United States produces so much more than other countries that it has a higher standard of living. The **standard of living** is the amount of goods and services the average citizen can buy. In the 1990s, the GDP of the United States grew from about $5.5 trillion to almost $9 trillion. This is a sign that the U.S. economy has continued to grow over time.

Unemployment Rate

The *unemployment rate* measures the number of people who are able to work but don't have a job during a given period of time. There are different reasons for being unemployed, some more serious than others. For instance, if you just quit your job or you just graduated from school you're probably looking for work. This type of unemployment is temporary and has little effect on the economy. Another type of unemployment is seasonal. If you harvest crops or work in retail during the holiday season, you may only work during a certain part of the year.

Real-World Application

part 1 of 4

ERAS THAT CHANGED THE ECONOMY
The Colonial Era, 1578–1776. People lived off the land. They traded some of what they produced with England, but they traded mostly among themselves. **Did colonists develop their own industries?**

continued on p. 39

Meeting Individual Needs

Second Language Learners. Large numbers, such as budget deficit or surplus statistics, pose a special challenge to students who are learning English. Fluent English speakers tend to say the numbers very quickly and blur the sounds. To help students understand the meaning of the numbers, write them on the board.

Real-World Application
Caption Answer

ERAS THAT CHANGED THE ECONOMY: PART 1 OF 4

Yes. They utilized their natural resources. Most industry developed in the Northern colonies while in the South, farming remained the main economic activity.

Technology Resource

GO TO **POWERPOINT.** The ***Introduction to Business*** PowerPoint® CD-ROM provides visual lecture aids for this chapter.

Independent Practice

SHARE. A country's GDP includes only goods produced in that nation. For example, the GDP of the United States doesn't include cars and trucks made at U.S.-owned plants in Canada, but does include Hondas made in Ohio using Japanese funds. Ask students to share other examples and to write these in their journals. **LS**

Thinking Critically

CONTEMPLATING. You're daydreaming and you start thinking about your career choices. You've heard people talking about automation replacing humans in the workplace. How does this affect the unemployment rate? The GDP?

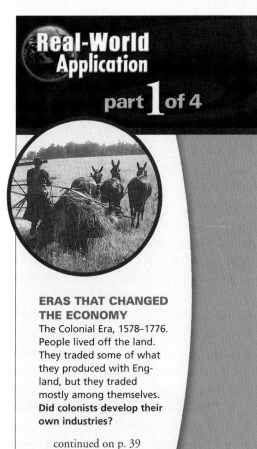

Caption Answer

1. This situation presents two social groups—the population afflicted with the disease and the government of Cuba. Students must recognize that what they consider moral and ethical may shift according to variables such as the severity of a disease and the number of its victims.

2. After they decide whether the vaccine should be sold, students may discuss the relationship between the individual and the other company executives. Do ethics shift depending on the roles you are in? Is it ethical to take a stand that conflicts with your personal moral views?

3. What other avenues might be taken to accomplish the "right" end? Could the company work through American diplomats? The United Nations? Non-governmental or nonprofit organizations?

A more serious type of unemployment is caused by changes in industry. New technology can replace workers or require new skills. Companies merge or restructure and "downsize," laying off thousands of workers. These types of workers can remain unemployed for a long period of time unless they're retrained or a company finds them new jobs. The worst type of unemployment occurs when the entire economy slows down. Millions of people in every industry can lose their jobs because there isn't enough work. This type of unemployment lasts until the economy recovers, which can take years.

Changes in the unemployment rate show whether an economy is picking up or slowing down. For example, in 1999, the unemployment rates in Japan and the United States were almost the same, about 4.4 percent. Between 1990 and 1999, however, the unemployment rate in the United States steadily decreased while in Japan it almost doubled. This shows that the U.S. economy was actually growing while the Japanese economy was declining.

Rate of Inflation

Another important measure of economic strength is the rate of inflation. **Inflation** is a general increase in the cost of goods and services. Inflation can happen when an economy actually becomes too productive. The more people are employed, the more people spend. As the demand for goods goes up, producers raise their prices. To pay the higher

You Make the Call

Dealing With Different Economic Systems

You're the president of a large biotechnology company that produces new vaccines for several tropical diseases. The communist government of Cuba has requested that you sell the vaccine to help stop a serious disease. Only your company has developed the vaccine. Personally, you're opposed to communist societies.

Making an Ethical Decision

1. Should you encourage other company executives to approve sale of the vaccine?
2. Does it matter if the disease is deadly? What if it wasn't fatal but caused blindness and was highly infectious?
3. If the United States doesn't allow its citizens to trade with Cuba, would you still discuss the topic with executives? If the executives want to help, how else could your company get the vaccine to those who need it?

MATH — *Curriculum Connection*

Price Comparison. Group students and assign each an item such as a loaf of bread, a gallon of milk, a dozen eggs, or a pound of sugar. Have them find the current price for the item and then its price 5, 10, and 25 years ago. Have each group graph its findings and make an oral presentation to explain the graph and inflation.

prices, workers demand higher wages. When wages go up, producers raise prices again to pay for the higher wages, and so on. This situation might spiral out of control and lead to *hyperinflation*.

Many other factors can lead to inflation, such as the government printing too much money. When the supply of goods is greater than the demand it can result in deflation. **Deflation** is a general decrease in the cost of goods and services. When an economy produces more goods than people want, it has to lower prices and cut production. As a result, people have less money to buy goods so the demand continues to go down. This is what happened to some of the Asian nations in the 1990s. Manufacturing countries like Japan and Taiwan over-produced goods such as TVs and VCRs, which led to an economic collapse.

The United States tries to maintain a slow but steady rate of economic growth to avoid both inflation and deflation. This is done by controlling productivity and keeping a certain number of people unemployed. That way there is less risk of producers making too many goods or workers demanding higher wages.

National Debt

Countries can run up large debts. The main source of income for a government is taxes. It uses the tax money to pay for social programs like defense, education, and social security. When the government spends more on programs than it collects in taxes, the difference in the amount is called the **budget deficit**. The U.S. government ran up a huge deficit in the 1980s when it cut taxes while increasing spending on programs. To pay for the difference, the government borrows money from the public, banks, and even other countries. The total amount of money a government owes is its **national debt**. If the debt gets too large, a nation can become dependent on other nations or unable to borrow any more money. This is the case in many developing nations.

On the other hand, a situation when a government's revenue exceeds its expenditures during a one year period is a **budget surplus**. The government will probably use a surplus to cut taxes, reduce the national debt, or increase spending for certain programs. For the most part, a surplus is a rarity.

 Fast Review _____

1. What are some reasons for unemployment?
2. What is the difference between inflation and deflation?

Real-World Application
part **2** of 4

ERAS THAT CHANGED THE ECONOMY
The Industrial Revolution, 1861–1914. Society transitioned from an agricultural economy to one relying on complex machinery. Farming still ruled most industry even with the invention of Eli Whitney's cotton gin. How did factories influence the workforce?

continued on p. 41

Real-World Application
Caption Answer

ERAS THAT CHANGED THE ECONOMY: PART 2 OF 4
Rapid industrialization allowed more immigrants to arrive and flock to urban areas. The increase in workers allowed America to produce more than twice as much iron and steel as Germany and England combined.

Fast Review Answers ✓

1. Quitting a job, seasonal unemployment, layoffs within industries, and widespread layoffs due to economic slumps.
2. Inflation is a general increase in the cost of goods and services. Deflation is a general decrease in the cost of goods and services.

Business Connection

FASHION DESIGNERS. A few years ago a recession-leery climate had fashion designers scaling back on trendy lines because buyers had a tight budget. Many of the top-name designers, such as Ralph Lauren, brought out classic lines and colors to satisfy people's need to buy clothes that would stay fashionable for three or four years.

Great Ideas From the Classroom of...

Mary Warnke
Brillion High School
Brillion, Wis.

Run a Resource Center. Students run our Teacher Resource Center. Students copy, transcribe, pre-proof, and offer software services to staff members by creating programs for events. Prior to opening the center, students are taught basic office machines and software. They appoint an office manager of the week who is responsible for helping class members correctly complete assigned tasks in a timely manner. The position requires motivation and integrity.

Develop Concepts

THE BUSINESS CYCLE. Ask students to think about their favorite sports team. Does the team always win? Discuss winning and losing streaks, and compare them to how the economy has its ups and downs. Ask students what phase they think the economy is in now. What economic activity—prosperity, recession, depression, or recovery—do they hear discussed in the media? (Answers will vary.)

Discussion Starter

MEANING. Call on students, and ask them what *standard of living* means. Ask them to compare the standard of living in the United States with that of other countries.

Figure 3.2 Caption Answer

Prosperity, recession, depression, and recovery.

The Business Cycle

Once you enter the workforce, you'll experience many ups and downs over the years. You could make a lot of money drawing cartoons for an animation studio, get laid off, and take a temporary job managing a copy shop. You could go back to school to study computer graphics, and then get a job doing special effects, or start your own business. Some of the changes you go through will be due to changes in the economy.

Economies go through ups and down as a result of wars, foreign competition, and changes in technology. Over long periods of time these changes seem to form patterns. For example, the U.S. economy went through slumps in the 1930s, the 1950s, and the 1970s. Slumps in economic activity were always followed by a new wave of productivity. This rise and fall of economic activity over time is called the **business cycle**. The business cycle has four phases—prosperity, recession, depression, and recovery. Figure 3.2 shows the ebb and flow of the business cycle.

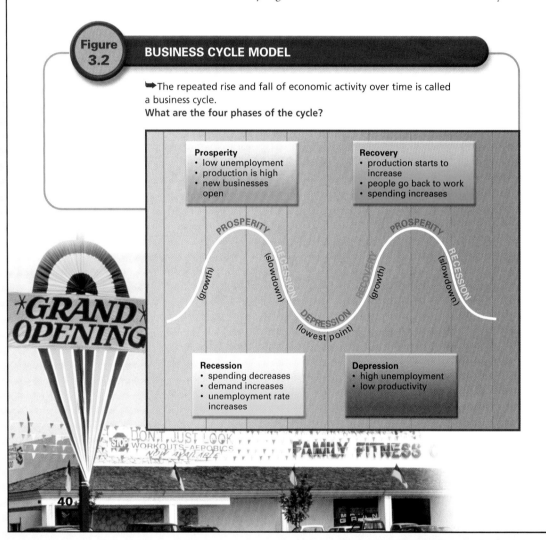

Figure 3.2

BUSINESS CYCLE MODEL

➡ The repeated rise and fall of economic activity over time is called a business cycle.
What are the four phases of the cycle?

Prosperity
- low unemployment
- production is high
- new businesses open

Recovery
- production starts to increase
- people go back to work
- spending increases

PROSPERITY (growth)
RECESSION (slowdown)
PROSPERITY
RECOVERY (growth)
RECESSION (slowdown)
DEPRESSION (lowest point)

Recession
- spending decreases
- demand increases
- unemployment rate increases

Depression
- high unemployment
- low productivity

40

Global Perspective

Economic Fluctuation. Assign groups to find and analyze another country's economic fluctuations over the past ten years. How did the fluctuations affect, if at all, the U.S. economy? Ask each group to explain why some of the economic fluctuations occurred and how the country responded to them.

Every phase indicates changes to an economy, to industries, and to working people. Changes in the economy can affect some industries, such as the manufacturing industry or the health-care industry, as well as working people. A period of expansion or economic growth affecting the auto industry may mean more job opportunities and higher employment in that industry.

The economic ups and downs of one country can affect other countries too. In a global economy, in which several countries are trading goods and services with one another, one country's economy can affect its other trading partners. If the U.S. economy is in a period of economic expansion, the United States may purchase goods and services from other countries—promoting expansion in those countries. In today's global economy, most countries are interdependent (that is, their economies are linked together).

Prosperity

Prosperity is a peak of economic activity. Unemployment is low, production of goods and services is high, and new businesses open. This condition spreads throughout the economy. Wages are usually higher so there is a greater demand for goods to be produced. More people can buy houses, so the building industry is busier. People also want to buy more goods from other countries, so those countries benefit as well.

The 1990s was a record period of prosperity in the United States. Much of it was due to the low rate of inflation and the Internet creating new business opportunities. Prosperity, however, doesn't last. Any number of things can change. Companies produce too much, people stop buying, or inflation starts to rise.

Recession

During a **recession**, economic activity slows down. Spending decreases and so does the demand for products. Businesses produce less so they need fewer workers. The unemployment rate then increases so people have less to spend. There is a general drop in productivity and the GDP declines.

A recession can affect only one industry, related industries, or spread to the entire economy. For example, if there is a recession in the auto-making industry, it leads to a recession in industries that make parts for cars, like steel and rubber. When this happens, it's called the *ripple effect*. In the 1970s an oil shortage in the United States caused gas prices to increase. Gas is used for every kind of economic activity, from driving

Real-World Application
part 3 of 4

ERAS THAT CHANGED THE ECONOMY
The Era of Mass Production, 1914–1995. World War I (WWI) was the first mechanized war. It created a demand for massive resources. By the end of WWI, Henry Ford had perfected the assembly line. **How did the assembly line change American society?**

continued on p. 43

Real-World Application
Caption Answer

ERAS THAT CHANGED THE ECONOMY: PART 3 OF 4
Production increased and industry growth soared.

Individualized Practice

RECESSION. Ask students to review a *BusinessWeek* article and then complete one of the options below. The topic should be about the economy

L1 Have pairs of students discuss what measures businesses can take to protect themselves in times of recession in the business cycle.

L2 Ask pairs of students to role-play the question-and-answer session in their own words.

L3 Group students to make a chart summarizing the author's comments on business and the economy. Ask groups to present the charts to the class.

Chapter 3 Economic Activity in a Changing World **41**

HISTORY — Curriculum Connection

Ice Cream Production. Ask students to investigate the history of Dreyer's ice cream company and to write an essay detailing changes in ice cream production, marketing, and the company itself under each of the eras: mass production, global, and cyber.

Working Lifestyle

Caption Answer

Possible answers may include: Not only is biological research finding cures to disease and cancer, but it's helping industries, environmental cleanup, and agriculture. Biology tomorrow is what information technology is today. Genetic engineering could yield better crops, which would help the economy. More research to invent new products means more manufacturing, producing, marketing, selling, distributing, and buying.

3 ASSESS

Reteaching

BUSINESS CYCLE. To reteach the concept of the business cycle, make sure students understand that the intensity of each phase in the business cycle varies. For example, a recession might be very severe or very mild. Ask students what factors might help gauge the severity of a recession and list them on the board. (Possible answers include unemployment and closing businesses.)

Enrichment Strategy

WRITE. Ask students to write 250 words about how the global era affects one business industry.
LS

to work to transporting goods to market. As a result, the price of everything went up and led to a major recession.

Depression

A deep recession that affects the entire economy and lasts for several years is called a **depression**. During a depression there is high unemployment and low productivity. It can be limited to one country but usually spreads to related countries. The state of the economy is affected by large numbers of people out of work, acute shortages, and excess capacity in manufacturing plants.

Working Lifestyle

What are you doing at 10 A.M.?

A Heritage of Life

From spring planting through autumn harvest, Tom Wall's days start at 6:30 A.M. and might not end until 11:00 P.M. It's barely 10:00 A.M. and Wall has already been at work for two-and-a-half hours. He's fed the livestock, cared for newborn pigs, and set the computerized feed mill for the babies.

Wall is a farmer. He and his father farm the land he grew up on near Morse, Iowa. Wall and his family grow corn and soybeans on 900 acres. His 2,100-hog operation is "farrow to finish," which means he raises the animals from babies until they're big enough for market.

The Wall farm isn't just a small business—the family manages several million dollars worth of assets in equipment, buildings, and inventory. He and his father provide most of the labor. In addition to farming, Wall also runs a thriving seed business from a machine-shed/warehouse/office he built on the property. He sells corn, soybean, and alfalfa seed produced by Monsanto and Garst seed companies.

"To succeed as a farmer, you have to wear a lot of different hats," Wall says. "And you have to be willing to commit the time and effort to make things work."

Salary

Full-time farmers earn between $15,704 and $32,188.

Outlook for This Career

The increasing world population will increase the demand for food. Thus the employment outlook for farmers is expected to remain steady.

Connecting Careers Activity

Research how biological career paths might influence dairy, crop growing, and livestock farmers. Write a small paragraph on the influences.

CAREER PATH — Agriculture & Natural Resources

How to Use a Portfolio Activity

The portfolio projects are designed to lead students to develop a collection of their best work to submit to you for assessment. You and each of your students should decide which projects to include in their business portfolio. Refer students to the specific rubric(s) from the *Alternative Assessment Strategies*. These rubrics will alert students to the criteria you'll use to assess their projects.

Fortunately, depressions are rare. The stock market crash on October 29, 1929, or "Black Tuesday," marks the beginning of the Great Depression. Between 1929 and 1933, GDP fell from approximately $103 to $55 billion—a decline of nearly 50 percent. At the same time, the number of people out of work rose nearly 800 percent—from 1.6 to 12.8 million. During the worst years of the Depression, one out of every four workers was jobless. Even workers who had jobs suffered. The average manufacturing wage, which had reached fifty-five cents an hour by 1929, plunged to five cents an hour by 1933.

Many banks across the country failed. The FDIC didn't exist at the time, so depositors were not protected. To prevent panic withdrawals, the federal government declared a "bank holiday" in March of 1933. Every bank in the country closed for several days, and many never reopened.

The money supply fell by one-third. Currency was in such short supply that towns, counties, chambers of commerce, and other civic bodies resorted to printing their own money. This was used to pay teachers, firefighters, police officers, and other municipal employees.

Recovery

A rise in business activity after a recession or depression is called a **recovery**. During a recovery, production starts to increase. People start going back to work and have money to spend again. The new demand for goods and services stimulates more production and the GDP grows. Recovery leads back to prosperity as new businesses open.

A recovery can take a long time or it can happen quickly. In 1939 the United States was only beginning to recover from the depression when World War II began. During the war, the United States recovered much faster because of the demand for war production.

During a recovery businesses might start to innovate a new product or a new way of performing a task. When a business innovates, it often gains an edge on its competition, because its costs go down or its sales go up. Profits increase, business grows, and economic activity soars.

✔ Fast Review

1. What are the four phases of the business cycle?
2. How does the ripple effect impact the economy?

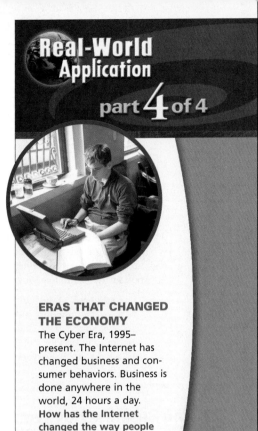

ERAS THAT CHANGED THE ECONOMY
The Cyber Era, 1995–present. The Internet has changed business and consumer behaviors. Business is done anywhere in the world, 24 hours a day. **How has the Internet changed the way people do business?**

ERAS THAT CHANGED THE ECONOMY:
PART 4 OF 4

Consumers can shop online. Businesses can complete work 24 hours a day. Technology allows employees to do their jobs from remote locations.

Technology Resource

GO TO **PUZZLEMAKER CD-ROM.** Check your students' understanding of the chapter's key terms by using the *Puzzlemaker* CD-ROM.

Evaluation

Assign and review the Fast Review sections.

Fast Review Answers ✔

1. Prosperity, recession, depression, and recovery.
2. A recession in one industry spreads to related industries.

Meeting Individual Needs

Gifted. Have students who would benefit from the additional work of an independent project read the following paragraph and complete the assignment: Is your future dinner growing in a scientist's petri dish? The similar chemical makeup of genes in plants and animals has led bioengineers to experiment with the both of them together.

A genetically altered fish gene has been placed in a tomato plant and the plant is now more resistant to disease. Welcome to the bioengineering era.

Your assignment: Interview a bioengineer by phone or e-mail and write a summary of the interview. **CL**, LS

4 CLOSE

Chapter Wrap-Up

Ask students to summarize the top three things they learned in this chapter.

Using Business Key Words

1. standard of living
2. business cycle
3. inflation
4. depression
5. gross domestic product
6. deflation
7. budget deficit
8. recession
9. national debt
10. prosperity
11. recovery
12. budget surplus

Review What You Learned

13. How much a country is producing, whether its economy is growing, and how it compares with other countries.
14. Level of productivity.
15. Work in seasonal industries or be laid off.
16. Whether an economy is picking up or slowing down.
17. Inflation that spirals out of control; when an economy is too productive.
18. Taxes.
19. Prosperity, recession, depression, and recovery.
20. Recession—economic activity slows down and short lasting. Depression—high unemployment and little productivity.
21. From 1861–1914. Invention of heavy machines and a time of rapid industrialization.
22. Led to the growth of other industries.

Summary

1. Gross domestic product, the unemployment rate, and the rate of inflation are types of economic measurements. The GDP is the total value of goods and services produced in a country in a given year. When a country produces much more than other countries it has a higher standard of living. The worst kind of unemployment occurs when the entire economy slows down. People in every industry can lose their jobs because there isn't enough work.

2. Inflation occurs when the costs of goods and services rise. When the supply of goods is greater than the demand it can result in deflation. If wages go up, producers raise prices again to pay for the higher wages then this situation might lead to hyperinflation.

3. The four phases of the business cycle are prosperity, recession, depression, and recovery. Prosperity is the peak of economic activity. During a recession, economic activity slows down. A deep recession that affects the entire economy and lasts for several years is called a depression. The rise in business activity after a recession or depression is called a recovery.

● Using Business Key Words

When talking about the business cycle and economic activity, people use the following terms. See how well you know them by matching each term to its definition.

- **gross domestic product (GDP)**
- **standard of living**
- **budget deficit**
- **budget surplus**
- **national debt**
- **inflation**
- **deflation**
- **business cycle**
- **depression**
- **prosperity**
- **recovery**
- **recession**

1. The amount of goods and services the average citizen can buy.
2. Repeated rise and fall of economic activity over time.
3. A general rise in the prices of goods and services.
4. Period of severe economic decline.
5. The monetary value of all the goods and services produced in a country in a given year.
6. A general decrease in the costs of goods and services.
7. When the government spends more than it collects in taxes.
8. A time when economic activity slows down.
9. The total amount of money a government owes.
10. The peak of economic activity.
11. A rise in business activity after a recession or depression.
12. A situation when a government's revenue exceeds its expenditures during one year.

Quick Quiz

1. List three economic indicators. (Gross domestic product, inflation, and unemployment.)
2. Explain what standard of living measures. (How well the people in a country live.)
3. The four phases of the business cycle are _____. (Prosperity, recession, depression, recovery.)
4. Name the six economic eras the U.S. economy has experienced. (Colonial, Expansion, Industrial Revolution, Mass Production, Global, and Cyber.)

Review What You Learned

13. What do economic indicators measure?
14. What is one very important measure of a country's economic health?
15. Name three reasons people become unemployed.
16. What do changes in the unemployment rate indicate?
17. Describe hyperinflation.
18. What is the main source of income for the U.S. government?
19. What are the four phases of the business cycle?
20. What is the difference between a recession and a depression?
21. Describe the Industrial Revolution.
22. What was the impact of mass production of cars on other industries?

Understanding Business Concepts

23. Explain why you think the gross domestic product (GDP) in the United States is very high compared to other countries.
24. If many people in a country were able to afford a few food items and there was a severe housing shortage, would that country have a high or low standard of living? Explain.
25. Suppose you go to the grocery store to buy toothpaste, canned soup, and a loaf of bread. You also consider buying a can of soda, but notice the price is 20 cents higher than it was last week. The prices of the other items seem to be the same as always. Is the soda price increase an example of inflation? Why or why not?
26. Why do you think inflation would be especially difficult for retired people?

Critical Thinking

27. Do you think it's a good idea for the government to control economic growth when the inflation rate begins to increase? Why or why not?
28. The Internet has revolutionized how people do business. How has it revolutionized school and the teaching and learning process?
29. How would you rate the standard of living for a country in which all the residents have adequate housing, ample food to eat, good medical care, but in which few people have expensive cars, boats, and jewelry?
30. How might knowledge of nationwide economic statistics help you?

Viewing and Representing

Examining the Image. In a group of three, examine the photo and ask one another journalistic questions beginning with the words who, what, where, when, why, and how. Whose point of view is expressed here? How relevant and reliable is this picture? Discuss your reactions to the photograph.

Chapter 3 Economic Activity in a Changing World **45**

Critical Thinking

27. Answers will vary. Some students might say that it is a good idea since inflation affects almost everyone, and that the government should use its power to attack a problem that affects everyone.
28. Answers will vary. Some possible answers might include research over the Internet, teachers using multimedia in their classroom presentations, and distance learning.
29. Answers will vary. The country probably has a fairly high standard of living since all residents' basic needs seem well provided for. The fact that few people can afford luxuries does not indicate a low standard of living.
30. Answers will vary. Possible student response: Such knowledge can be useful in determining if it is a good time to change jobs, make a major investment, or take on debt.

Viewing and Representing

Visual documents can act as catalysts to student thinking, writing, and discussion. Encourage students to listen carefully, without judging others' opinions, and to show respect for others' diverse reactions. Answers and discussion will vary.

Understanding Business Concepts

23. The United States is a very rich country and produces large numbers of goods and services.
24. Food and shelter are basic needs. If people can't afford basic needs, the standard of living is not high.
25. No. Inflation is a prolonged rise in price levels of most goods and services. If the other items were the same price, the circumstances would not indicate inflation.
26. Because they're on fixed incomes. Their income does not go up when the prices of products and services they use do.

4 CLOSE (Cont.)

Building Academic Skills

LANGUAGE ARTS. Encourage the students to really use their imagination. Remind them that there are no right or wrong answers when trying to predict the future. Rubric: Poster.

HISTORY. Students will find information in the library or on the Internet. There are several examples in the chapter, but encourage students to look for others to research. Rubrics: Two-page paper, oral presentation.

MATH. Students will find information in the library or on the Internet. Students might have problems calculating the percentages of increase or decrease. Rubrics: Graphs, math calculations.

COMPUTER/TECHNOLOGY. Make sure all students participate in the group project. Rubrics: Charts, paragraphs.

Linking School to Home

Answers will vary. Rubric: Essay.

Linking School to Work

Answers will vary. If students have trouble locating someone to interview, encourage them to read a biography about someone who lived during the Depression. Rubric: Essay.

Building Academic Skills

 Creating a Poster

In a group of three or four, create the next economic era after the Cyber Era. Describe the inventions, how people will work and go to school, and the impact on the economy. Create a poster that illustrates your new era.

 A Historic Figure

Research an American who had an impact on the U.S. economy during the Colonial Era or the Industrial Revolution. Write a two-page paper and share your findings with the class.

 A Graphic Illustration

Choose five products that you purchase frequently. Find out how prices for these products have changed since you were born. Determine if the rise in price is the result of inflation or other factors. Calculate the percentage of increase or decrease for each product. Present the data graphically.

 Government Databases

The federal government uses many economic indicators to measure how well the economy is doing. Among these indicators are the following: the number of building permits issued, the average workweek for production workers in manufacturing, the number of unfilled orders for durable goods, consumer installment debt, common stock prices, and unemployment claims.

Work in a group of three or four to conduct online research to retrieve government databases of three of these indicators from 1980 to the present. Present the data in chart form and analyze in a brief paragraph what the numbers indicate about the economy.

Linking School to Home

Tracking News Stories. During a two-week period, read the newspaper or watch the national news each day. Be sure to take notes if you're watching television. Write down the news story's crucial points including any key words that you just learned in this chapter. You could also clip and save any newspaper or periodical articles that apply to this assignment. Count how many articles or stories relate to the economy in the United States and in other countries around the world. Select one news story and write a 200-word essay about it.

Linking School to Work

Oral History. Interview a relative or someone in your community who lived through the Great Depression from 1929 to 1939. Find out what he or she remembers about this period in history and how it impacted life. Ask questions about the standard of living at this time. How does it compare to today's economic state? What goods and services weren't available then but are widely used today? Create an oral presentation to share your interview findings with the class. If possible, invite the person you interviewed to attend your presentation.

Chapter **3** Review

E-Homework

Applying Technology

Finding Trends. Using the Internet, find the dollar amount of the current national debt. What was it ten years ago? The year you were born? Fifty years ago? Has it gone up or down?

Web Pages. Imagine you would like to do business on the Internet. You know what kind of business you want to open. You know how to create a Web page. Using the Internet, research several virtual businesses that might be considered your competition. Evaluate their sites for the following:
- Is the price of the product clearly defined?
- What process is used to place orders?
- Is the site easy to use and user friendly?

Connecting Academics

Math. Find unemployment statistics for the following years: 1933, 1944, 1955, 1966, 1977, 1988, 1999, and the most recent year for which statistics are available. Present the information in a bar graph. Use computer software if possible. Discuss the reasons for the differences shown in the graph.

History. Did economists accurately predict the economic boom in the early '90s? Study economic forecasts one year before March 1991. Did all economists agree on the direction the economy would take? What indicators did economists use to base their predictions? Present a scorecard-type summary of economic forecasters, March 1990 to March 1991.

BusinessWeek — Analyzing the Feature Story

You read the first part of "Moving up the Ladder: From Cheap Labor to Skilled Workers" at the beginning of this chapter. Below are a few questions for you to answer about the article. You'll find the answers to these questions when you're reading the entire article. First, here are the questions:

31. What economic era is affecting workers in underdeveloped countries? How has it affected them?
32. What helps underdeveloped countries succeed in the global era?

CREATIVE JOURNAL ACTIVITY

Research another country's economic system. Write a report discussing which economic eras have influenced it in the past. Predict its future.

BUSINESS Online

The Full Story

To learn more about globalization, visit the *Introduction to Business* Web site at www.introbus.glencoe.com, and click on *BusinessWeek* Feature Story, Chapter 3.

E-Homework

FINDING TRENDS. Students might find different figures depending on the site they use for their research. Rubrics: Research, note taking.

WEB PAGES. Students' answers will vary. Rubrics: Note taking, essay, oral presentation.

Connecting Academics

MATH. Answers are in the form of a bar graph.

HISTORY. Students' findings will show discrepancies in the economic forecasts. Encourage creativity and use of real-world examples.

BusinessWeek — *Analyzing the Feature Story*

31. The global era has given workers in Third World countries the opportunity to work in factories and support their families.
32. Governments that make good use of foreign investment and manufacturing expertise are the most successful at improving the standard of living for their workers.

Creative Journal Activity

Encourage students to be creative with their presentation of reports in theme with different eras. Reports could be in the form of a scroll, stone tablet, or some futuristic format. Reports should include discussion of the influence of at least three eras. Predictions will vary. **CL**, **LS**, **P**

SCANS Correlation Chart*

Foundation Skills

Basic Skills	Reading	Writing	Math	Listening	Speaking	
Thinking Skills	Creative Thinking	Decision Making	Problem Solving	Seeing Things in the Mind's Eye	Knowing How to Learn	Reasoning
Personal Qualities	Responsibility	Self-Esteem	Sociability	Self-Management	Integrity/ Honesty	

Workplace Competencies

Resources	Allocating Time	Allocating Money	Allocating Material and Facility Resources	Allocating Human Resources		
Information	Acquiring and Evaluating Information	Organizing and Maintaining Information	Interpreting and Communicating Information	Using Computers to Process Information		
Interpersonal Skills	Participating as a Member of a Team	Teaching Others	Serving Clients/ Customers	Exercising Leadership	Negotiating to Arrive at a Decision	Working With Cultural Diversity
Systems	Understanding Systems	Monitoring and Correcting Performance	Improving and Designing Systems			
Technology	Selecting Technology	Applying Technology to Task	Maintaining and Troubleshooting Technology			

*This chart's highlighted blocks indicate the chapter's content coverage in the Student Edition and the Teacher Wraparound Edition.

Resource Manager

Teaching Transparencies

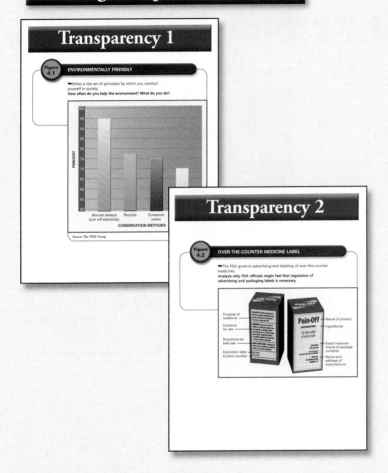

Transparency 1

Figure 4.1 ENVIRONMENTALLY FRIENDLY

Ethics is the set of principles by which you conduct yourself in society.
How often do you help the environment? What do you do?

PERCENT

Almost always turn off electricity | Recycle | Conserve water
CONSERVATION METHODS

Source: The NPD Group

Transparency 2

Figure 4.2 OVER-THE-COUNTER MEDICINE LABEL

The FDA governs advertising and labeling of over-the-counter medicines.
Analyze why FDA officials might feel that regulation of advertising and packaging labels is necessary.

Purpose of medicine
Cautions on use
Directions for safe use
Expiration date
Control number

Pain-Off

Name of product
Ingredients
Exact measurements of package contents
Name and address of manufacturer

Application and Enrichment

- Lesson Plans
- *BusinessWeek* Poster Package
- Teaching Transparencies
- Integrated Software Simulation
- Glencoe Business Video Package

Review and Reinforcement

- *PuzzleMaker*
- Internet Resources
- Student Activity Workbook
- Strat. and Work. for Teaching Transparencies

Assessment and Evaluation

- Reproducible Tests
- Alternative Assessment Strategies
- ExamView® Pro Test Generator

Technology

- *PuzzleMaker*
- ExamView® Pro Test Generator
- Glencoe Business Video Package
- PowerPoint® Presentation
- Integrated Software Simulation
- Interactive Lesson Planner
- *Virtual Business*®

KEY	Printed	Software	Videocassette	Poster
	Transparency	CD-ROM	Internet	

BUSINESS Online

Visit www.introbus.glencoe.com, the Web site companion to *Introduction to Business*. The student's page includes:

- interactive tutor
- additional *BusinessWeek* articles and activities
- business Web links
- homework hints
- real-world application activities
- additional career path activities

Information on how to prepare your students for the high school exit exam and special projects are also included.

Use the Glencoe Web site for additional resources. All essential content is covered in the Student Edition.

Chapter ④

1 FOCUS

Introducing the Chapter

This chapter examines business ethics—what it is and how it affects business. It describes the social responsibility of business. The photo essay, "Off the Beaten Path," explores Patagonia's social responsibility as a clothing outfitter.

Connecting the Objectives

What is a code of ethics? Ask students for examples from their own life as a customer or as a worker of both good and bad ethical business practices.

BusinessWeek
Feature Story

Story's Summary

Corporations in the twenty-first century set social action as a strategic plan. Marian Salzman, director of Intelligence Factory, predicts that by around 2020 corporate sponsorship will pervade education, housing, health care, and the arts.

Find the entire article at www.introbus.glencoe.com, or in the Teacher Resource Binder.

Business Ethics and Social Responsibility

● Learning Objectives

After completing this chapter, you'll be able to:
1. **Explain** business ethics.
2. **Give** reasons why ethical behavior is good for business.
3. **Define** social responsibility.
4. **Describe** the social responsibilities of businesses.

● Why It's Important

Understanding business ethics and social responsibility informs you of your rights as a consumer, employee, and citizen.

● Key Words

ethics
business ethics
sweatshops
Occupational Safety and
    Health Administration
code of ethics
social responsibility
conflict of interest
Food and Drug
    Administration
Equal Pay Act
Environmental Protection
    Agency

48

BusinessWeek Feature Story

Commerce Reweaves the Social Fabric

Companies Apply Money and Expertise to Social Issues. It's Futuretown, USA, circa 2020. The kids attend for-profit schools; the teachers get their technology training from computer specialists dispatched by IBM. Young teachers and other budding professionals seeking affordable housing flock to the Wal-Mart Riverview apartment complex. Elderly residents get their hearing checked at EarCare clinics funded by Abbott Laboratories, makers of the Ensure nutritional supplement for seniors. Culture vultures gawk at contemporary sculpture at the local American Express Museum of Modern Art.

Source: Excerpted with permission from "Commerce Reweaves the Social Fabric," *BusinessWeek Online*, **August 28, 2000.**

An Extension Activity

Some corporations offer employees the opportunity to join volunteer programs during the workweek. Find a company that encourages its employees to volunteer as an alternative to the workplace during the year.

The Full Story

To learn more about corporate citizenship, visit the *Introduction to Business* Web site at www.introbus.glencoe.com, and click on *BusinessWeek* Feature Story, Chapter 4.

Classroom Resources

For the Teacher
- 📁 Student Activity Work. TAE
- 📓 ⊙ Assessment Binder
- ⊙ PowerPoint® Presentation
- ⊙ Interactive Lesson Planner
- 📁 Lesson Plans
- 📓 🖥 Internet Resources
- 🕹 Teaching Transparencies
- 🖥 *Introduction to Business* Web Site

- ⊙ Integrated Soft. Sim. TM
- 📘 *BusinessWeek* Poster Package

For the Student
- 📓 Student Activity Workbook
- ⊙ *Virtual Business®*
- 🖥 *Introduction to Business* Web Site
- ⊙ Integrated Soft. Sim.
- ⊙ *PuzzleMaker*
- 📓 Strategies and Worksheets for Teaching Transparencies

🔔 Bell Ringer Activity

INTEGRITY AND HONESTY.
Write this scenario on the board: "You're stranded on a small island with three other people. What personal traits would you want the others to have?" List the traits students choose. How does this scenario relate to the workplace?

Preteaching Business Key Words

SELF-MANAGEMENT. First, ask students to use the glossary and write the meanings of the key words in their journal. Second, instruct the students to ask themselves two questions: What is the most important thing I learned? and What question(s) do I still have? Inform students that this two-question technique is a quick and simple learning self-evaluation tool. Students can apply this simple technique to find out how well they understood what they have just learned in a paragraph, a chapter, or a lesson.

An Extension Activity

PRESENT. Ask students to give an oral presentation, including examples, to summarize their findings. **CL**, **LS**

Making Connections

Language Arts. Give students two examples of the Occupational Safety and Health Administration's (OSHA's) rulings and their effect: The removal of asbestos in the workplace and schools lessens risk of health hazards; ergonomic regulations and programs to prevent repetitive stress injuries result in a healthier workforce.

Ask students to think of other examples and their effects. Give them three or four minutes to think of an example. Toss a softball to students. When they catch the ball, they tell their example before tossing the ball back to you. **LS**

2 TEACH

Business Connection

BUSINESS ETHICS. In the rapidly changing global business, ethics is taking on new importance. The number of worldwide companies with ethics officers grew from 200 in 1992 to more than 500 in 1998, and the number is still growing. To avoid bad press, lawsuits, and scandal, some companies go to the extent of providing phone hot lines for employees. To comply with laws concerning safety and sexual harassment in the workplace, companies are providing extensive training for their employees.

Develop Concepts

EXPLAIN. In any organization, peer pressure can cause people to behave in ways they normally would not. Ask students how peer pressure in school affects their behavior. How might coworkers' attitudes cause someone to behave unethically? (Answers will vary. One answer is taking company supplies because "everyone does it.") How can companies influence their employees' behavior, and what is the effect? (Answers will vary and may include ethical leadership, strong company mission, and statement of values. Higher employee morale and dedication to the company.)

Figure 4.1 Caption Answer

Answers will vary.

Who Benefits From Business?

Maybe you've heard about auto mechanics that cheat customers by making unnecessary repairs. If they get caught they might be sued, lose their business license, or even go to jail. Even if they don't face legal action, they stand to lose customers and their reputation. Businesses are active and involved in a responsible and fair way in the lives of individual employees and their communities. Their responsibility goes beyond producing goods and services, paying taxes, and providing jobs. Figure 4.1 illustrates conservation methods that help the community and environment.

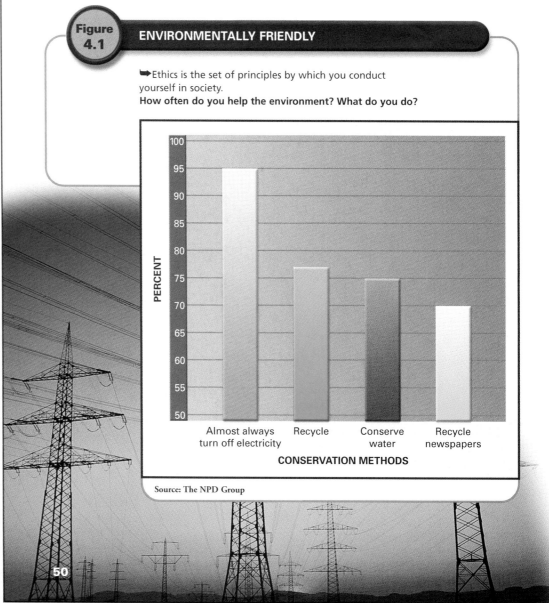

Figure 4.1

ENVIRONMENTALLY FRIENDLY

➡ Ethics is the set of principles by which you conduct yourself in society.
How often do you help the environment? What do you do?

Source: The NPD Group

Cooperative Learning

Highlight. Ask groups to choose one of the following companies: Sun Microsystems, General Motors, American Airlines, Coca-Cola U.S.A., Sunoco, Boeing, Levi Strauss, or Nike. Have groups find the corporate ethics policy, or code of conduct, for the company. Suggest groups print their findings, highlight important points, and share them with the class.

What Is Ethics?

Mom complains about all of the mail order catalogs and e-mail advertisements she receives. She didn't ask for them. Somehow or another her name was part of a mailing list, which was sold to these other firms. She is concerned about her privacy. Then Dad is concerned that one of his colleagues at work spends too much time writing personal e-mails instead of completing work on time. What do all of these things have in common? All of these deal with business ethics.

Ethics is the set of moral principles by which people conduct themselves personally, socially, or professionally. For example, you don't cheat on a test or steal clothing because of your personal honor and integrity. For the good of society, for example, you recycle to take care of the environment. In business, people create a code of business ethics. **Business ethics** is a set of laws about how a business should conduct itself. In general, for any business to be successful, it must operate legally and humanely.

Legal Responsibility

On March 26, 1911, 146 workers—mostly young Eastern European women—died in a fire at the Triangle Shirtwaist Factory Company in New York City. This disaster is one of the worst industrial tragedies in U.S. history. The business's inadequate exit doors and fire escapes and overcrowded factory led to the deaths of the Triangle workers, who jumped ten stories to their death or burned in the fire. This calamity sparked the nation's attention to examine **sweatshops**. Sweatshops are factories that have unsafe working conditions, treat workers badly, and pay poorly.

The U.S. government sets up independent agencies to protect society. The **Occupational Safety and Health Administration** (OSHA) is a division of the Department of Labor that sets and enforces work-related health and safety rules. Other independent agencies protect consumers, monitor broadcast communications, and address discrimination in the workplace.

Businesses that fail to follow laws are subject to fines, lawsuits, and new regulations. Most businesses police themselves by distributing codes of ethics. A **code of ethics** is a set of strict guidelines for maintaining ethics in the workplace. Professional groups such as doctors, lawyers, journalists, and teachers have their own code of ethics. Individual companies usually have their own codes as well. A code of ethics can cover everything from employee behavior to environmental safety. Businesses that regulate themselves are able to operate more freely.

Chapter 4 Business Ethics and Social Responsibility **51**

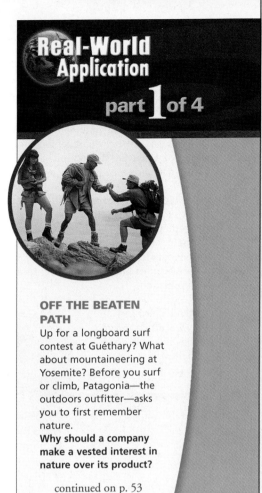

OFF THE BEATEN PATH
Up for a longboard surf contest at Guéthary? What about mountaineering at Yosemite? Before you surf or climb, Patagonia—the outdoors outfitter—asks you to first remember nature.
Why should a company make a vested interest in nature over its product?

continued on p. 53

Technology Resource

GO TO **POWERPOINT.** The *Introduction to Business* PowerPoint® CD-ROM provides visual lecture aids for this chapter.

Independent Practice

REASONING. Explain that many companies are actively involved with ethical manufacturing practices. An example is Kodak's new five-year operational goals. In the goals, Kodak is committed to reducing emissions, cutting waste, and preserving natural resources. Ask students what kind of natural resources Kodak might need, and why they think the company is careful about environmental management. (Answers will include energy usage, water usage, and chemicals such as mercury and lead. Kodak wants to protect the health and safety of employees and communities near their plants, and for future generations.) **LS**

Meeting Individual Needs

Slow and Fast Readers. The simple technique of skimming can be applied to reading textbooks and periodicals. Both slow readers and fast readers alike can benefit by using the skimming technique.

To skim an article, read the title and the heads and subheads, then look at visuals and their captions. Then read the first two paragraphs and the last paragraph. Make a note of important points.

Technology Toolkit

Caption Answer

Some artists believe that if people hear their work over the Internet and like the music, they'll be more inclined to actually buy CDs. People like to play CDs in their car and other places where they don't have access to a computer.

Thinking Critically

SELF-QUESTIONING. You're an accounting clerk for Olive Tree, an Italian restaurant. Lisa, a friend of yours, is planning to open her own restaurant and she's assured you that she'll hire you as the accountant. Lisa asks you to share information about Olive Tree's expenses and sales. What are the ethical issues? Is it against the law? What will you do?

Technology Toolkit

Web-Spun Tunes

Millions of people use their computer's hard drive as a database of personal music selections. Using file-sharing software on the Web downloads a copy of a song. The key to this trend is "player" software. The software allows users to transform the bulky music files on their CDs into a compressed file format called MP3—a process known as "ripping." Music sharing operates on the idea of peer-to-peer computing. Every computer becomes both a sender and receiver of information.

Critical Thinking
How will artists make money if people download music?

Ethics as Good Business

Unethical business practices might affect your business in more ways than one. If you violate government regulations you can be fined or go to jail. If you violate a company code of ethics, you might be fired or lose your license. However, not all unethical practices are covered by the law and, even if they are, you may not get caught for violating the law. Even so, unethical business practices might affect your business indirectly.

Suppose you own an auto body paint shop. To increase your profits you charge top price and use the cheapest paint. One of your customers complains but you don't care because she has already paid. What's one customer, right? The fact is most businesses (especially small businesses) rely on repeat customers and word-of-mouth to get new customers. The amount you make in profits from one unhappy customer translates into a lot more in lost business.

Treating employees unethically can also backfire. Suppose you manage a small film distribution company. You hire Jaime fresh out of business school to run the office. You teach him how to use the computer system, how to deal with customers, and how the business works. You also pay him poorly, make him do all your work for you, and treat him like a doormat. The first chance Jaime gets, he quits and ends up being hired by one of your competitors. You now have to retrain a new employee to take his place. Meanwhile, your competition now has a well-trained employee, who is much more efficient.

Important Ethical Questions

Ethics involves an endless series of relationships—between buyer and seller, employer and employee, business and government, and business and society. When considering a questionable course of action, you have to ask yourself these important questions:
- Is it against the law? Does it violate company or professional policies?
- What if everyone did this? How would I feel if someone did this to me?
- Am I sacrificing long-term benefits for short-term gains?

Ethical decision making leads to more business activity and more efficient production of goods and services. Business works best when there is mutual trust between buyers and sellers.

52 Unit 1 The Economy and You

LANGUAGE ARTS — *Curriculum Connection*

Communication. Tell students to imagine that they work in a large organization. Have pairs of students perform these role-plays:

- Refusing to gossip about another coworker.

- Telling a coworker you've seen another coworker take office supplies home.

- Telling a coworker to say she's "away from her desk" if her boss calls.

- Being asked by a friend who has moved to Atlanta for the company 800 number so he can use it to call you.

- Reporting a substantial error in company financial data made by a coworker.

Making Decisions on Ethical Issues

Making ethical decisions is not a quick task. It takes some real hard thinking. A derivation of the problem-solving process works well for ethical decision making. Here are some steps if you find yourself in an ethical dilemma:

1. Identify the ethical dilemma.
2. Discover alternative actions.
3. Decide who might be affected.
4. List the probable effects of the alternatives.
5. Select the best alternative.

Using this process will enable you to make a more informed ethical choice. Making an ethical decision involves more people than just you.

✓ Fast Review

1. How do companies benefit by enforcing their own codes of ethics?
2. Why does it pay to treat customers ethically?
3. What are some important ethical questions to ask?

Social Responsibility

Social responsibility is the duty to do what is best for the good of society. Business ethics focuses on decisions considered good or bad, correct or incorrect. The social responsibility of business takes into consideration all that business does or does not do to solve problems of society.

The goal of business is to make a profit. Business, however, also involves the interaction of many different people. For a business to prosper it has to offer goods and services that other people want. If you manage a supermarket you rely on your employees to do a good job. When you go to a restaurant you expect to get good service. As a member of society, you're both a consumer and a producer.

Businesses have an ethical obligation to provide safe products, create jobs, protect the environment, and contribute to the overall standard of living in society. An ethical question in business occurs whenever there's a conflict of interest. A **conflict of interest** is when a business is tempted to put profits before social welfare.

The effect of unethical behavior is not always obvious. For example, pocketing a few CDs from the store you work at might not seem like a big deal. After all, you might think, no one will miss them and they're overpriced anyway. One of the reasons CDs cost as much as they do is because people steal them. Consumer and employee theft costs businesses billions of dollars each year. To make up for their losses, businesses have to charge more for their products. As a result, everyone has to pay more.

Chapter 4 Business Ethics and Social Responsibility **53**

OFF THE BEATEN PATH

As the designers of a fleece jacket made from a 2-liter soda bottle, Patagonia distributes clothing and equipment that's environmentally responsible. **How does the consumer pay for a company's inventions?**

continued on p. 55

Real-World Application
Caption Answer

OFF THE BEATEN PATH: PART 2 OF 4

Answers will vary but might include reference to the increased costs of the products. Consumers' increased environmental awareness may make other big businesses suffer if they don't purchase their products anymore.

Fast Review Answers ✓

1. They have less government intrusion and can operate more freely.
2. Most businesses rely on repeat business and word of mouth to get new business.
3. Is it against the law? Does it violate company or professional policies? What if everyone did this? How would I feel if someone did this to me? Am I sacrificing long-term benefits for short-term gains?

Business Connection

SOCIAL RESPONSIBILITY.
The Coalition for Environmentally Responsible Economies (CERES) has a code of environmental conduct, called the CERES Principles. The CERES Principles cover issues such as informing the public, reducing risk, restoring the environment, and manufacturing safe products and services. The CERES Principles are adopted by more than 50 companies including American Airlines, Coca-Cola U.S.A., General Motors, Sunoco, and Nike.

Great Ideas From the Classroom of...

Bill Paden
Cleveland High School
Reseda, Calif.

Risk Takers. You have to take a risk. Who fails more often, risk takers or non-risk takers? Of course risk takers. Who succeeds more often, risk takers or non-risk takers?

Of course risk takers. If you're willing to take the risk to try, members of your peer group and family feel threatened by your risk taking. They'll hold you back by saying, "You can't do that," or mock you saying, "You think you're better than us?" That's something you have to deal with. The great basketball player Dr. Julius Erving said, "You have to dare to be great."

Develop Concepts

SPECIFY. Many businesses feel that ethical business practices are of great importance. For example, General Motors (GM) has a sustainable development policy that addresses the concern of meeting today's needs—without taking from future generations the ability to meet their needs. GM strives to improve operations and products with environmental, economic, and social objectives in mind. GM received an award for an innovative program that reduced the company's solid waste by 30 percent. Ask students to specify examples of ethical business practices of other companies.

Discussion Starter

BUSINESS ETHICS. Ask students to write two short paragraphs starting with the sentence: "I feel business ethics is important because _____." Have volunteers share their paragraphs.

Figure 4.2 Caption Answer

For precautionary reasons—list ingredients, explain the purpose of the medication, and list harmful side effects.

Responsibility to Customers

Customers are a business's first responsibility. Businesses should offer a good, safe product or service at a reasonable price. The **Food and Drug Administration** (FDA), a government agency, protects consumers from dangerous or falsely advertised products. Most companies obey the government's rules. Figure 4.2 asks you to analyze an over-the-counter medicine label.

For example, in 1982 Johnson & Johnson coped with a public health crisis. When people died from poisoned Tylenol capsules the company quickly responded. It alerted the public to the danger and recalled all bottles of its product at a cost of $100 million. The company put Tylenol back on the market in new tamper-proof bottles. Today, Tylenol is one of the best-selling pain medicines.

Fair competition between businesses is healthy for the marketplace, but some companies don't always play reasonably. Some companies use

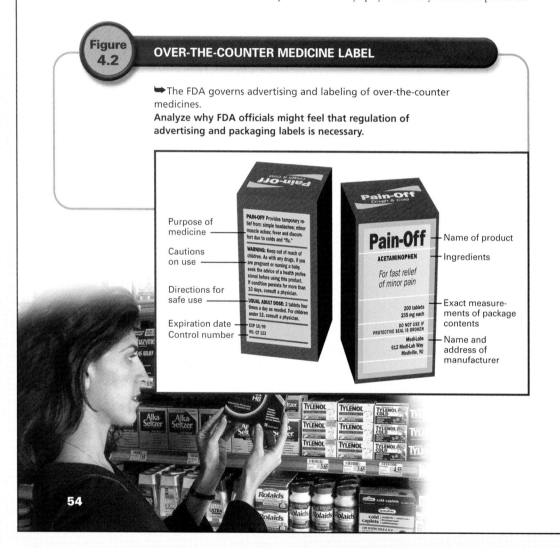

Figure 4.2 OVER-THE-COUNTER MEDICINE LABEL

➡ The FDA governs advertising and labeling of over-the-counter medicines.
Analyze why FDA officials might feel that regulation of advertising and packaging labels is necessary.

Purpose of medicine
Cautions on use
Directions for safe use
Expiration date
Control number
Name of product
Ingredients
Exact measurements of package contents
Name and address of manufacturer

PAIN-OFF Provides temporary relief from: simple headaches; minor muscle aches; fever and discomfort due to colds and "flu."

WARNING: Keep out of reach of children. As with any drugs, if you are pregnant or nursing a baby, seek the advice of a health professional before using this product. If condition persists for more than 10 days, consult a physician.

USUAL ADULT DOSE: 2 tablets four times a day as needed. For children under 12, consult a physician.

EXP 10/99
NO. QT 123

Pain-Off
ACETAMINOPHEN
For fast relief of minor pain
200 tablets
235 mg each
DO NOT USE IF PROTECTIVE SEAL IS BROKEN
Medi-Labs
612 Medi-Lab Way
Mediville, NJ

54

Global Perspective

Social Responsibilities. Levi Strauss was one of the first American companies to take on social responsibilities. In the 1920s, this company offered English and citizenship classes to its immigrant factory workers. During the 1940s and 1950s, it was among the first companies to integrate workers in its factories in the South. Levi Strauss carries on that tradition today with its policy of responsible commercial success. It instituted a Diversity Council, which represents African-American, Asian, Latino, gay, and female employees' interests and sees that they have a voice in management decisions. Have students speculate on the kinds of benefits Levi Strauss receives from around the world from encouraging diversity and empowerment of its workforce.

unethical means to eliminate competition. One of the most common means is to conspire with other companies to control the market for a product. Together, the companies can control the supply of a product and determine the prices.

When companies overpower competition, consumers are affected. Consumers have less choice in what they can buy and how much they have to pay. When a company doesn't have to compete, its productivity decreases. This can backfire on a business. When the market changes or new markets open up, a company can find itself unprepared to compete.

For example, in the 1940s, a handful of entertainment studios controlled the film industry. They controlled the industry by owning most of the theaters. Smaller studios could make movies, but they couldn't get them shown anywhere. The government sued the big studios and forced them to sell their theaters. As a result, small studios were able to compete in the marketplace.

Responsibility to Employees

Businesses have provided work experience for those who haven't been successful in the workplace. Many of these people are public assistance recipients. The purpose of the program is to develop their skills and confidence levels necessary to continue success in the working world.

Many employees take one or more days off during the year to work on a project in the local community while still being paid. Key Bank in upstate New York has implemented this type of program. Volunteerism is another way businesses tackle societal problems.

Businesses have a social responsibility to create jobs. They are also expected to provide employees with safe working conditions, equal treatment, and fair pay. Less than one hundred years ago, however, workers had few rights.

Over the years the government has passed laws to protect workers from a range of issues, from child labor abuses to the rights of workers to organize. As the workplace has changed, the government has passed new laws. The **Equal Pay Act** (passed in 1964) requires that men and women be paid the same wages for doing equal work. More than 40 years later, however, the closing of the wage gap between men and women has been at a rate of less than half a penny a year. The Americans with Disabilities Act bans discrimination against persons with physical or mental disability. More than 50 million current or potential workers are likely to be covered by this law.

Chapter 4 Business Ethics and Social Responsibility **55**

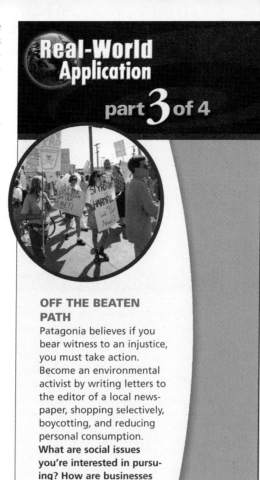

Real-World Application

part 3 of 4

OFF THE BEATEN PATH
Patagonia believes if you bear witness to an injustice, you must take action. Become an environmental activist by writing letters to the editor of a local newspaper, shopping selectively, boycotting, and reducing personal consumption. **What are social issues you're interested in pursuing? How are businesses involved?**

continued on p. 57

Individualized Practice

Together read the following scenario, and then instruct students to ask the important ethical questions outlined in the text.

SCENARIO. Hans and Win are talking in the hallway of XYZ Company. Win says in a hushed voice, "Can you believe this? I've been told it's mandatory to do 25 hours overtime every week. I missed Back-to-School Night last week." Hans says, "I know what you mean, lately I only get to see my kids on the weekend!" Is XYZ Company acting ethically?

L1 Have pairs of students discuss the question: "Is XYZ Company acting ethically?"

L2 Tell students to write their answers to the ethical questions outlined in the text in their notebooks.

L3 Divide the class into two groups—one pro and the other con. Debate the statement: "XYZ Company's actions are ethical."

MATH

Curriculum Connection

Incentives. You're a human resources professional in a company called Fashion Invasion. The company sets aside 15 percent of its annual profits for its profit-sharing program. Last year, the company's total profits were $227,740. Each of the 40 employees receives an equal share of the amount set aside for the profit-sharing program. How much money went into Fashion Invasion's profit-sharing program? How much money did each employee receive? (Answer: $227,740 x 0.15 = $34,161; $34,161 ÷ 40 = $854). As a Fashion Invasion employee, would you find this profit sharing an incentive to put more effort into your work? What other things can the company do to increase employee retention, morale, and productivity?

CAPTION ANSWER

After the students have completed one path, ask them to write in their journal the reason(s) why they chose that path.

3 ASSESS

Reteaching

IMPORTANT ETHICAL QUESTIONS. To reteach the concept of important ethical questions, give the students the following scenario: Imagine that you work in the purchasing department of a large food manufacturer like Nestle. Ordering materials for chocolate making, such as milk and vegetable oil is your responsibility. One supplier has prices slightly higher than others, but if you order through her, she mentioned she would send you free tickets to a big-name concert. What are the ethical issues? Is it against the law? What would you do? What would an ethical company do?

Enrichment Strategy

REPORT. Ask students to research insider trading and find the penalties for being found guilty of such practices. Tell students to make notes about their findings ready to give a short oral presentation. **LS**

Writing for Business

Portfolio Activity

Building on a Sacred Site

This activity gives you the chance to add to your portfolio. Communicate, interview, research, and write your way into a story. Choose one imaginary path, Avid Activist or Determined Developer. Follow your path's steps to complete your own story.

pick a path

Avid Activist

The Setting. A real-estate developer from Insti-House Inc., believes there is a lack of housing for retired people in town.

Rising Action. You discover the site contains historic relics from a Native American village dating back to around 1050 A.D. Additionally, an important nineteenth-century poet built a house on the site. Although the house burned down long ago, the poet's original garden still thrives. You decide to organize a committee to preserve the site's heritage.

Step 1. Present a list of various ways to preserve the site, which will be presented to the committee.

Step 2. After the meeting, you hone and tackle the first item on your list—write a letter to the editor of the local newspaper.

Determined Developer

The Setting. You're the public relations director for Insti-House, Inc. Your boss, the developer, reads the newspaper and sees all the letters to the editor protesting her real-estate development. Citizens of the community are angry. Insti-House wants to develop property on a historic site.

Rising Action. Delaying the development will cost Insti-House thousands of dollars. Its reputation is being damaged by bad publicity.

Step 1. Hoping to sway public opinion, your boss asks you to write a one-page press release outlining the Insti-House position on the development.

Step 2. Find out how you submit press releases to the local media.

Conclusion

Now it's time to reflect on your choice in the last section. Did you face a conflict of interest on any level? Take a few minutes to write in your journal about the business ethics and social responsibility of your situation.

How to Use a Portfolio Activity

The portfolio projects are designed to lead students to develop a collection of their best work to submit to you for assessment. You and each of your students should decide which projects to include in their business portfolio. Refer students to the specific rubric(s) from the *Alternative Assessment Strategies.* These rubrics will alert students to the criteria you'll use to assess their projects.

Most companies have realized the value of treating workers fairly and have adopted codes of ethics in the workplace. For example, United Airlines has a strict policy against sexual harassment on the job. It's in a company's best interest to treat its workers fairly otherwise low morale, poor productivity, and a high turnover rate are its troubles.

Responsibility to Society

In the nineteenth and even into the twentieth century, many polluted and destructed the environment in order to profit. The lapse of judgment to keep the land, water, and air clean hurt many because the tradeoff for a higher standard of living only benefited a few. Around the middle of the twentieth century, many people were questioning whether this was a wise tradeoff. Polluting the environment became an ethical issue.

Businesses have responsibilities not only to customers and to employees but also to society as a whole. One of the biggest social issues facing businesses today is environmental responsibility. In 1970, the U. S. government created the **Environmental Protection Agency** (EPA), a federal agency that enforces rules that protect the environment and control pollution.

Some firms are very concerned about limiting the damage that they do to the environment. Companies obey the pollution standards set by the government for air, water, or land. The Body Shop places environmental concerns as an integral part of its mission. Biodegradable materials are contained in its products. An increasing number of businesses are buying recycled paper to use in their businesses.

The *Los Angeles Times*, a daily newspaper with over one million dedicated readers, uses recyclable paper and environmentally friendly soy-based ink. Car manufacturers like Honda and Toyota offer eco-cars, which reduce air pollution. Businesses that hold fast to environmental policies have better public relations.

An increasing number of businesses, especially corporations, consider social responsibility to be more important than ever. Many of them plan for their social responsibilities just like planning for production and sale of their products.

✓ Fast Review

1. Define social responsibility.
2. What is a conflict of interest?
3. What do companies adopt in the workplace to treat their workers fairly?

Real-World Application

part 4 of 4

OFF THE BEATEN PATH
Patagonia responsibly takes a stand against genetically modified organisms (GMO). Its position states that companies must be held accountable if any GMO released into the environment causes damage. **What government agency has a responsibility to society?**

Real-World Application
Caption Answer

OFF THE BEATEN PATH: PART 4 OF 4
Environmental Protection Agency (EPA).

Technology Resource

GO TO

PUZZLEMAKER CD-ROM. Check your students' understanding of the chapter's key terms by using the *PuzzleMaker* CD-ROM.

Evaluation

Assign and review the Fast Review sections.

Fast Review Answers ✓

1. Doing what's best for the good of society.
2. A choice between the good of society and personal gain.
3. A code of ethics.

Chapter 4 Business Ethics and Social Responsibility **57**

Meeting Individual Needs

Slow and Fast Readers. Using technology to skim read. You don't have to read the whole article to find points that are important to you. When researching information in an article online, highlight a word or two in the text, then click on "Edit" on the menu bar. Click on "Find." Type in the key word or phrase you are looking for and, if it's in the text, the browser will find it for you. Don't forget to click "Find Next" to find the word or phrase if it appears again in the article.

4 CLOSE

Chapter Wrap-Up

Ask students to develop a mnemonic device to help them remember the three areas of business social responsibility—customers, employees, and society.

Using Business Key Words

1. ethics
2. code of ethics
3. sweatshops
4. business ethics
5. social responsibility
6. conflict of interest
7. Occupational Safety and Health Administration (OSHA)
8. Equal Pay Act
9. Food and Drug Administration (FDA)
10. Environmental Protection Agency (EPA)

Review What You Learned

11. The principles you live by and conduct yourself.
12. To protect the health of employees in the workplace.
13. A code of ethics.
14. Fined or jailed. Lose business. Experience higher turnover and spend extra money on retraining.
15. Is it against the law? Does it violate company or professional policies? Am I sacrificing long-term benefits for short-term gains?
16. Conflict between social well-being and personal gain.
17. Protect consumers.
18. Provide safe working conditions, equal treatment, and fair pay.
19. Environmental responsibility.

58

Summary

1. Ethics is the set of moral principles by which people conduct themselves personally, socially, or professionally. Businesses have a legal responsibility to do what is right for society's welfare.

2. Unethical business practices aren't only illegal but they are also bad for business. Good ethics affects a business's profits, customer base, and employee loyalty.

3. Social responsibility is the duty to do what is best for the good of society. Businesses have a responsibility to consumers, workers, and society as a whole. The FDA, Equal Pay Act, and the EPA are examples of government actions that were passed to improve societal concerns.

4. A conflict of interest is when a business puts profits before social welfare.

Using Business Key Words

Companies are expected to run their businesses responsibly. Find out if you understand what it means for companies to be both socially and ethically responsible. Fill each blank with the term that best completes the sentence.

- ethics
- social responsibility
- business ethics
- Equal Pay Act
- conflict of interest
- Food and Drug Administration (FDA)
- sweatshops
- code of ethics
- Occupational Safety and Health Administration (OSHA)
- Environmental Protection Agency (EPA)

1. The principles you live by, like honor and integrity, are called your _____.
2. Most businesses police themselves by distributing a _____.
3. _____ are factories that have unsafe working conditions, treat workers badly, and pay poorly.
4. _____ is a set of laws about how a business should behave.
5. The obligation a business has to do what is best for society is called _____.
6. An ethical question in business will occur when there is a _____ between social well-being and profits.
7. A division of the Department of Labor that sets and enforces work-related health and safety rules is called the _____.
8. The _____ (passed in 1964) requires that men and women be paid the same wages for doing equal work.
9. The _____ is a government agency that protects consumers from dangerous or falsely advertised products.
10. The federal agency that enforces rules that protect the environment and control pollution is called the _____.

Quick Quiz

1. Give a statement defining business ethics. (A set of rules about how a business should conduct itself.)
2. Factories that pay and treat workers poorly are called _____. (Sweatshops.)
3. How does a socially responsible business behave? (It is responsible and fair to its employees and customers and to society as a whole.)

Review What You Learned

11. Describe ethics.
12. Why was the Occupational Safety and Health Administration created?
13. How do most businesses police themselves?
14. Describe some of the ways unethical business practices can affect a business.
15. What are three questions you could ask yourself when considering a questionable course of action?
16. When does a conflict of interest occur?
17. What is the mission of the Food and Drug Administration?
18. What responsibilities do businesses have to their employees?
19. Name the biggest social issue facing businesses today.

Understanding Business Concepts

20. What is the difference between social responsibility and business ethics?
21. Why is it important for a business to treat its employees in an ethical manner?
22. Give an example of a conflict of interest that a business might face.
23. Why is competition important to the consumer?
24. What has the government done to protect workers?
25. How do socially responsible firms improve the quality of life for everyone in society?
26. Do you think the United States should trade with China or other countries with a poor human rights record? Why or why not?

Critical Thinking

27. Do you think most businesses act responsibly towards consumers? Can you think of a company that hasn't? Describe the company's behavior and the consequences of its actions.
28. Do you think a country has the right to impose its ethical standards on another country? Why or why not?
29. What do you think is a manager's role in setting ethical standards?
30. How do you think a business's social responsibility is measured?

Viewing and Representing

Examining the Image. What's going on in this picture? What interests or motivations are behind what's happening in this picture—both for the students and for the company? Compare what's represented in this photograph with the experience of your school and with company volunteer programs; what ways are they similar or different? Write a paragraph answering the questions.

Chapter 4 Business Ethics and Social Responsibility **59**

Critical Thinking

27. Answers may vary. Accept those answers that show a student understands responsible behavior toward consumers.
28. Answers may vary. Students should provide a reasonable explanation for their answers.
29. Answers may vary. Managers are the mouthpieces of corporate rules and standards. It is important for a manager to send a message through his or her actions. A manager's response to breaking ethical codes is more important than a written code. Often, actions speak louder than words.
30. Answers may vary. A company's commitment to the environment and human rights may positively affect its corporate image.

Viewing and Representing

Advertisements and other visual media are intentionally prepared to influence people. It's important for students to become aware of visual media's subtle influence—one way is for students to gain practice in questioning the picture presented. Paragraphs will vary. Students should include a comparison of similarities and differences.

Understanding Business Concepts

20. Social responsibility is the obligation to do what is best for the welfare of society; business ethics governs how business is done.
21. Answers may vary. Employees treated ethically are loyal, work hard, and conduct themselves in an ethical manner.
22. Answers will vary.
23. Choices and prices.
24. Passed child labor laws, the Equal Pay Act, and the Americans with Disabilities Act.
25. Create wealth in society, reduce pollution, and replenish resources.
26. Answers will vary. Students should provide a reasonable explanation for their answers.

4 CLOSE (Cont.)

Building Academic Skills

MATH. $5,500 ÷ 9 = $611.11 per team. Percentage of goal: ($300 ÷ 611.11) × 100 = 49 percent.

LANGUAGE ARTS. Students can use the library or Internet to locate information about the business. Rubric: Oral presentations, note taking.

COMPUTER/TECHNOLOGY. Make sure all students participate in the group project. Rubrics: Note taking, brochures.

HISTORY. Students can use the library or Internet to locate the laws. If there is a law library in your town, encourage the students to use it. Rubric: Essay.

Linking School to Home

Answers will vary. Since some of the ethical issues might be sensitive, do not require the students to share with the class unless they want to do so. Rubrics: Note taking, oral presentation.

Linking School to Work

Make sure all students participate in the creation of the code. Then, make sure all students participate in their groups. Rubrics: Role-plays, note taking.

● Building Academic Skills

 Raising Money

The president of Walker Computer Company wants her company to raise $5,500 for Habitat for Humanity. She divided the employees into teams and asked each team to raise money towards the goal. There are nine teams.
- How much money should each team raise to meet the goal?
- If each group raises $300, what percentage of the goal did each collect?

 Presenting a Company

Research a business (past or present) that has demonstrated social responsibility. Describe the activities that took place and present your findings to the class.

 Desktop Publishing

Promote the idea of social responsibility. Work in groups to create a brochure outlining the service projects and activities that are available in your community. Projects could include feeding the homeless, building projects, raising money for cancer research, and so on. Use word processing or desktop publishing software to create the brochure. If possible, make copies of the brochure and distribute them in school.

 Selecting a Law

Select a law that the U.S. government passed to protect workers. Research the events leading up to the law being passed. Find out what impact the law has had on workers. Write a two-page paper with your findings.

● Linking School to Home

Dealing With a Dilemma. At school you may have been involved in a situation that called your ethics into question. You're not alone—parents deal with dilemmas at work too. Ask your parents or other family members if they have ever been faced with an ethical issue at work. If so, find out what happened and how it was resolved. Discuss with them how they answered the important ethical questions you learned earlier in this chapter. Ask them to walk you through their steps of making an ethical decision.

● Linking School to Work

Creating a Code. As a class, create a formal code of ethics for the classroom. Be sure to include the following:
- purpose of the code
- rules for classroom behavior
- rules for making ethical decisions
- consequences for breaking the code

Then, in teams of three or four, create two different ethical situations that could occur in the classroom. Role-play the situation and the resolution.

E-Homework

Applying Technology

Online Research. Using the Internet, research the code of ethics for a profession (doctor, lawyer, teacher) or a business. Read the code and choose two or three policies to share with the class.

Computer Usage. Imagine you have been hired by a small business to write a code of ethics to cover computer/technology usage. Write four or five rules that the employees of the company must follow.

Connecting Academics

Math. Rhonda, administrator for a non-profit group in Texas, has gathered data on company volunteer programs. She has tracked the number of volunteers working with schools in the area:

Year	Company Volunteers
1996	1500
1997	1530
1998	1570
1999	1600
2000	1660
2001	1740

Present the information in a line graph. Use the graph to make a prediction about how many volunteers there will be in 2010.

Language Arts. Making ethical decisions is part of being a strong leader both in everyday life and in the business world. Think of two examples when you had to make an ethical decision. Walk back through the five steps to making an ethical decision that you learned earlier. Do this for each example you come up with. For both examples, write two paragraphs detailing the situation, the possible choices, the resulting decision, and the effects of the decision.

BusinessWeek — Analyzing the Feature Story

You read the first part of "Commerce Reweaves the Social Fabric" at the beginning of this chapter. Below are a few questions for you to answer about corporate citizenship. You'll find the answers to these questions when you're reading the entire article. First, here are the questions:

31. What is the main motivation for the good corporate citizenship of companies such as Prudential Insurance Co. and Merck & Co.?

32. What are some potential disadvantages for the companies that practice good corporate citizenship?

CREATIVE JOURNAL ACTIVITY

Create your own Futuretown, USA. Using poster board and magic markers, design Main Street and match corporate sponsors with the following public projects: a library, housing for seniors, a city park, and an outdoor concert arena. Explain how each company would benefit from being associated with a specific public work.

BUSINESS Online

The Full Story

To learn more about corporate citizenship, visit the *Introduction to Business* Web site at **www.introbus.glencoe.com**, and click on *BusinessWeek* Feature Story, Chapter 4.

E-Homework

ONLINE RESEARCH. Answers will vary. Some of the codes may be difficult to interpret, but encourage students to read them thoroughly. Rubrics: Essay, oral presentation, note taking.

COMPUTER USAGE. Students might find some information on the Internet. Rubrics: Note taking, written rules.

Connecting Academics

MATH. Answers will vary in the range 2,600 to 2,900 and will be predicted by extending the line graph to the year 2010. The line graph should have years (time is the independent variable) as the x-axis.

SOCIAL SCIENCE. Let students know that their examples will be treated with confidentiality. Reassure students that they will not be called upon to share their stories. Trust is important here. This type of self-analysis may lead to a growth experience. Encourage an honest expression of details.

BusinessWeek — Analyzing the Feature Story

31. The tight labor market may be the most important motivation. Good corporate citizenship is a factor contributing to employee retention. Employees who are spending more time at work would like a more meaningful on-the-job experience.

32. Consumers may begin to take corporate involvement for granted. Consumers will also be more inclined to punish companies that they perceive as socially irresponsible.

Creative Journal Activity

Students might use their knowledge of local sponsors or nationally known sponsors to create a match. Students may invent new corporations or include a future corporation of their own founding. Posters and explanations will vary. **CL**, **LS**, **P**

1 FOCUS

Unit Seminar Overview

In this seminar on China, students analyze a real-life situation using their knowledge of economics and business. Students interpret facts and make inferences about the migration of Chinese workers.

Bell Ringer Activity

WHAT DO YOU KNOW? Ask students what they know about China's labor force. Write responses on the board under these categories: geography, natural resources, climate, population, cities, industries, and crops.

Discussion Starter

CHANGES IN CHINA. Discuss recent changes in China. (Answers may include rapid population increase, increase in tourism, increased privatization, shift to a free market economy, increased prosperity, increase in technology-related industries, and expansion of global trade.)

BusinessWeek Seminar

Unit **1** Global Business

What Is Today's Chinese Business Trend?

In Chapter 3, you read about the Industrial Revolution. Many workers during this historical period worked in the factories and on the railroads. China, with its 1.2 billion people and abundance of natural resources, is facing its own economic revolution. This seminar asks you to investigate China's contemporary business trend.

62

GLOBAL BUSINESS

Newsworthy Trends

Connecting China. After investing more than $1 billion, Nokia's operation in China grew to a colossal 5,000 employees in 1999. Nokia, the supplier of wireless phones, started an office in Beijing six years earlier. The office began in an old movie theater with a staff of about 250. Nokia has more than 70 million wireless subscribers in the Middle Kingdom. New users are signing up at the rate of two million a month.

Factoids

Population. In 1200, Hangchow, China, was the fourth city in the world that had over a million people. (Nearly 700 years later, New York City's population reached a million people.)

Climate. The country has an extreme range of climates from its tropical south to its subarctic north.

Natural Hazards. Typhoons strike along the southern and eastern coasts about five times a year.

Geography. China is the world's fourth-largest country (after Russia, Canada, and the United States).

Downtown. China has half of the world's tallest buildings.

Greetings. A Chinese group applauds anyone introduced to the group. Applaud back.

Investigate the Images

Look at the photographic collage on the left page. What do you see? What do you think? What do you feel? The power of reading visuals is in analyzing and dissecting your observations. On a separate piece of paper, reconstruct the worksheet below in order to complete your investigation. The questions may help shape and focus your analysis.

Your Observations

1. How many photographs do you see?

2. Examine each photograph. How is each assembled in relation to the others?

3. What is the subject of each photograph?

4. Does color signify a message?

5. What issues do you take from these images?

Information

6. Summarize what you know about the photographs from your observations.

Exploring Culture

7. What do you know about China's culture— business, education, politics, and so on?

8. Where do you learn this information (for example, newspapers, TV, magazines, textbooks, films, etc.)?

2 TEACH

Thinking Critically

1. What resources does a city need to support an influx of people? (Answers will include water supply, waste treatment, roads, transportation, and apartments/housing.)

2. What disadvantages might there be as a result of many people moving to the city? (Answers will include overcrowding, spread of disease, and insufficient resources.)

Cooperative Learning

MAPPING A COUNTRY'S TRENDS.   Assign students to groups of four. Groups will draw a map of China on posterboard. Instruct groups to select two industrial cities, find the adjacent rural cities, and then mark all those cities on the map. Encourage students to use creative symbols. Ask groups to give a short oral presentation, with their poster as a visual aid, which details Chinese workers' migration patterns to the industrial cities. **CL**, LS

GLOBAL BUSINESS — *Newsworthy Trends*

Profit in China.   Health-industry entrepreneurs in China are making a good profit as a result of reforms in health care and the nation's economic boom. The expensive health care cost is forcing China to focus on preventative illness therapies and strategies. Sales of vitamins and other health-care products rose to more than six billion dollars in 2000. The average annual income in Shanghai in 1995 was $865. With the economic boom this rose to $1,014 in 2000, giving Chinese consumers more disposable income to spend on health-care products.

2 TEACH (Cont.)

Independent Practice

L1 SUMMARIZE IDEAS

Ask students to find a recent article on ways technology is used in business in China. Have them prepare a summary of the article to share with the class. Lead the class in a discussion of the latest developments in the ways businesses use technology.

L2 E-INTERVIEW

Ask students to find the name of a business owner in China, and send that person an e-mail. Questions could include: What city are you based in? What good or service do you provide? How many employees do you have? How long has the company been in business? How does your business use computers? Have students share the responses. Write important phrases and terms used on the board.

L3 RESEARCH AND REPORT

Ask students to research two modern companies in China, and then write a one-page report. For each company, have students include details about the good or service, the form of business operation, the type of business, the number of employees, the length of time the company has been in business, and ways technology is used in the business.

BusinessWeek Seminar

Taking Aim at Global Business

● Preparation

Find out why Chinese workers are migrating from farming villages to industrial cities, and how their moves affect business trends in China.

Objective

In this *BusinessWeek* Seminar, you will:
- **Research** the media to find articles on Chinese workers' migration patterns.
- **Investigate** the topic by using a journalist's arsenal of key questions—who, what, where, when, why, and how.
- **Interview** a classmate who poses as a migrant worker.

Materials Needed

- ✓ Recent copies of *BusinessWeek*, the *Wall Street Journal*, or Internet access
- ✓ Paper
- ✓ Pencil
- ✓ Small tape recorder (if it's available)
- ✓ Poster board
- ✓ Markers

● Procedures

1. Choose a research partner.

2. Find and read a recent article written about the migration of Chinese workers. If possible, use the Internet to access the Web site of a business publication. For example, access the *BusinessWeek* Web site at **www.businessweek.com**. Click on the tab labeled "Global Business" or use the internal search engine to locate the topic.

3. Consider the following issues:
   - Why are people migrating to the cities?
   - What problems do they encounter?
   - Are the benefits worth the risks?
   - How does this affect China's economy?

4. Create a role-play in which one partner plays a newspaper reporter interviewing a migrant worker, and the other plays the worker. In your role-play, you should describe why the worker left his or her village and what his or her feelings are about living and working in a big city. Make sure to discuss living conditions in the village versus working conditions in the city. The role-play should last two to three minutes. Perform the role-play for the class.

64 Unit 1 The Economy and You

Reteaching Strategy

Draw five circles on the board, with the headings: Wants and Needs, Scarcity, Economic Systems, Economic Measurement, and Social Responsibility. Ask students for important points under each heading and write them in the circle. Then ask students if the knowledge they gained in this unit helped them better understand the economic changes in China.

Chart It

With your partner make two lists: "Advantages of Migrating to the City" and "Disadvantages of Migrating to the City," and list what you think are the three most important of each. As a class, reproduce the table that is below and create a comprehensive list on the board.

Migrating to the City

Advantages	Disadvantages

Analyze and Conclude

After studying the comprehensive list on the board, answer the questions below:

1. **Making Inference.** What is the most important reason a worker has for migrating to a city in China?
2. **Recognizing Cause and Effect.** What are the dangers of migrating?
3. **Interpreting the Facts.** How will the migration of workers influence the economy of China and, therefore, business in China?

Becoming an Informed Citizen

Congratulations, you finished the seminar. Now it's time to reflect on the decisions you made.

Critical Thinking. Why did you choose to report certain aspects of your research and not other parts of the information? Did an article's images play any part in your decision making? Or did you pick an article based on its title?

Analyzing Your Future. How will China's migration patterns affect you as a citizen of the world?

BUSINESS Online

Further Exploration

To find out more about workers' migration patterns in other countries, visit the Glencoe *Introduction to Business* Web site **www.introbus.glencoe.com**.

3 ASSESS

Enrichment

RESEARCH, COMPARE, AND CONTRAST. Ask students to use library resources or the Internet to research economic conditions and trends in another country. How do they compare with China? Ask students to make a diagram to compare and contrast their findings.

Evaluation

RUBRICS. The rubrics for evaluation of written reports and oral presentations are included in *Alternative Assessment Strategies*.

4 CLOSE

Seminar Wrap-Up

IMAGINE YOU LIVE IN CHINA... What would you do if you lived in China? Would you stay in the village or go to work in the city? What changes would there be in your life in the next five years? (Answers will vary and could include increase in income, more goods and services, more career choices, telecommuting for a global company, and more entrepreneurial opportunities.)

Analyze and Conclude Answers

1. To make more money.
2. Unsafe, unhealthy working conditions.
3. With workers earning more money, they may send some of it back to the villages, providing income to the farming communities. Demand for more goods and services among the Chinese improves business opportunities.

Unit ②

Owning and Operating a Business

Unit Objectives

After completing this unit, students will be able to achieve the following outcomes:

- List ways that entrepreneurs and small business owners organize their businesses for success.
- List the three types of business ownership and alternative ways of doing business, and five types of businesses in our economy.
- Explain how managers lead their organizations, and list the responsibilities of a leader.
- Identify a leader's characteristics, the styles of leadership, and leadership in teams.
- Give examples of how the Internet has changed business communications, commerce, and consumerism.

BusinessWeek Connections

In this unit, students will read the following articles from *BusinessWeek*:

Chapter 5 "Paint By Numbers"—Meet the Gamblins, entrepreneurs that turned their love for art into a business

Chapter 6 "Selling Out, Staying One"—Growing your own business might mean not being the CEO anymore

Chapter 7 "A Fruitful Relationship"—A cutting-edge technology firm is tapped by a billion-dollar company to get them wired for the New Economy

Chapter 8 "The Boss in the Web Age"—A look into the future of office space, communication, and compromise

Chapter 9 "Zen and the Art of Net Startups"—Fashion founders use the Internet to expand their company's vision

Key to Descriptive Icons

The following designations will help you decide which activities are appropriate for your students.

L1 Level 1 activities should be within the ability range of all students.

L2 Level 2 activities should be within the ability range of the average to above-average students.

L3 Level 3 activities are designed for the ability range of above-average students.

ELL English Language Learner activities should be within the ability range of the English Language Learner.

LS Learning Styles designation represents activities designed to address different learning styles.

CL Cooperative learning activities are designed for small group work.

P Portfolio designation represents student products that can be placed into a best-work portfolio.

Teacher Classroom Resources*

Program Resources	Chapter 5	Chapter 6	Chapter 7	Chapter 8	Chapter 9
Student Activity Workbook	p. 29	p. 35	p. 43	p. 49	p. 57
Lesson Plans	p. 12	p. 14	p. 16	p. 18	p. 20
Internet Resources	p. 29	p. 31	p. 33	p. 35	p. 37
Reproducible Tests	p. 9	p. 11	p. 13	p. 15	p. 17
Teaching Transparencies	5.1, 5.2	6.1	7.1, 7.2	8.1, 8.2	9.1, 9.2
Strategies and Worksheets for Teaching Transparencies	pp. 3, 27	pp. 3, 29	pp. 3, 30	pp. 4, 32	pp. 4, 34

* Each of these resources is available in print and on the Interactive Lesson Planner CD-ROM.

Technology Resources

- Interactive Lesson Planner CD-ROM
- PowerPoint® Presentation CD-ROM
- ExamView® Pro CD-ROM
- Integrated Software Simulation, Teacher Manual
- Glencoe Business Video Package
- *PuzzleMaker* CD-ROM
- *Introduction to Business* Web site
- *Virtual Business*®
  Virtual Business is a business simulation that introduces students to the principles of business by letting them start and run their own virtual business. In *Virtual Business,* students have the power to control all aspects of a retail convenience store. Students strategize business decisions using a powerful learning tool in the guise of a video game.

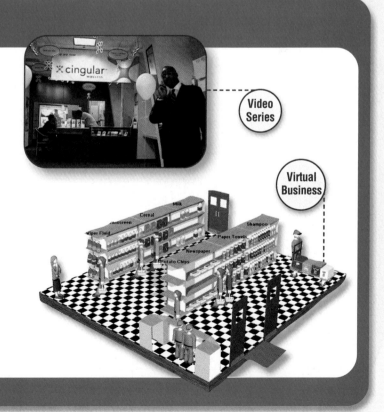

Video Series

Virtual Business

Unit 2

Scope and Sequence

Academic Standards of Learning

	LANGUAGE ARTS	MATH	HISTORY	COMPUTER/ TECHNOLOGY	SOCIAL SCIENCE	
CHAPTER 5	pp. 68, 69, 71, 72, 77, 82, 83	pp. 82, 83	pp. 73, 75, 82	pp. 71, 72, 73, 77, 78, 79, 82, 83	pp. 69, 70, 74, 75	
CHAPTER 6	pp. 84, 85, 87, 88, 90, 92, 93, 96, 97	pp. 87, 96, 97	p. 91	pp. 87, 93, 96, 97	pp. 85, 86, 90, 91, 96	
CHAPTER 7	pp. 98, 99, 100, 101, 102, 104, 105, 106, 107, 110	pp. 103, 105, 110, 111	pp. 104, 110	pp. 101, 107, 110, 111	pp. 98, 99, 100, 103, 104, 107	
CHAPTER 8	pp. 112, 113, 114, 115, 116, 117, 118, 119, 120, 121, 122, 123	pp. 122, 123	pp. 116, 119, 122	pp. 115, 118, 120, 121, 122, 123	pp. 112, 113, 114, 115, 116, 177, 118, 119	
CHAPTER 9	pp. 126, 127, 129, 133, 135, 138	pp. 138, 139	pp. 127, 128, 129, 130, 131, 134, 138	pp. 126, 127, 128, 129, 130, 131, 132, 133, 134, 135, 138, 139	pp. 127, 128, 130, 131, 132, 133, 134, 135	

Scope and Sequence

Themes and Concepts

Business Core	Accounting and Finance	Business Management	Computer/ Technology	Marketing	Entrepreneurship
Methods of Communication Ethics Business Ownership Entrepreneurial Concepts Environmental Issues Business Operations	Decision Making Financial Analysis Budgeting	Competitive Environment Decision Making Basic Management Functions Technology	Computer Applications Supervision Time Management Technological Innovations Telecommunications Bussiness Model	E-commerce Market Research Purchasing Electronic Marketing Risk Management Merchandising—Color Theory	Entrepreneurial Potential Management Marketing Analysis Research and Development Technology
Effectiveness Methods of Comm. Business Ownership Competitive Envir. Goal Setting Retention Money Management Adapting to Change	Cash Management Decision Making Financial Responsibility	Competition Consumers Business Organizations Basic Management Functions Research and Development	Business Environment Business Management Supervision Business Models Customer Service Resource Management	Profitability Distribution Strategy Risk Management	Business Image Management Production Research and Development
Business Ownership Entrepreneurial Concepts Goal Setting Business Relationships Conflict Resolution Teamwork Decision Making	Decision Making	Business Organizations Basic Management Functions Research and Development	Project Management Business Environment Business Management Change Management Business Models	Culture Infra Structure	Risk Management Research and Development
Business Ethics Competitive Environment Business Operations Goal Setting Interest Assessment Teamwork Motivation Personal Qualities	Ethics	Competition Decision Making Opportunity Costs Business Organization	Basic Management Functions Time Management Business Decisions	Culture Risk Management	Entrepreneurial Potential Research and Development
Environmental Factors Employment Transitions Interest Assessment Adapting to Change Planning	Decision Making Computer Accounting Systems Budgeting	Competition Opportunity Costs Research and Development	Project Management Business Management Computer Applications Time Management Business Decisions Emerging Technology and Trends Resource Management	E-Commerce Culture	Business Image Entrepreneurial Potential Management Research and Development

Unit Overview

Unit 2 discusses the fundamental knowledge of owning and operating a business.

CHAPTER 5 explains entrepreneurship and small business, and describes their advantages and disadvantages.

CHAPTER 6 describes forms of business ownership and the types of businesses.

CHAPTER 7 explains managerial organization and its function.

CHAPTER 8 examines the styles and qualities of leaders as well as advantages of working in teams.

CHAPTER 9 explains how technology impacts business, especially e-workforce and e-commerce.

Introducing the Unit

Ask students to list benefits and risks when starting and operating a business. Ask why they think entrepreneurs start businesses. Then have students speculate about how important leadership is to the success of a business organization. Tell students that answering these questions begins their journey into the world of entrepreneurship and business organizations.

Unit 2

Owning and Operating a Business

Go Under the Hybrid's Hood

Disappointed that it's the twenty-first century and cars still can't fly? Well, don't be. There's a new car on the block, and it's called the hybrid model. This machine is a high-tech composite of old and new technology. Honda leads eco-cars on the roadways. Learn more about this car by reading the five important Ps.

● **Pounds**
It takes about 1,000 pounds of batteries to store as much energy as one gallon of gasoline.

● **Power**
The gasoline-electric hybrid car is a cross between a gasoline-powered car and a battery-operated car.

● **Pollutants**
Hybrid cars have been traveling on Japan's roads since the late nineties.

● **Parity**
The hybrid car was created to minimize tailpipe emissions and improve mileage.

● **Passage**
An electric car can go between 50 and 100 miles between charges. A gas-powered car can go 300 miles before refueling. A hybrid car can go 720 miles before refueling!

Technology Resource

 GO TO **INTRODUCTION TO BUSINESS WEB SITE.** To find out more about content in Unit 2, visit the Glencoe *Introduction to Business* Web site. **www.introbus.glencoe.com**

Field Trip Suggestion

A Trip to a Local Manufacturer.
Have students find answers to the following questions about a company:

• What raw materials or processed goods does it use?

• What is its finished product?

• What service providers does this manufacturer use?

• How is the company management organized?

• What type(s) of leadership is or are there in the company?

• Does the company use self-leadership teams?

On the next day of class, ask each pair to give an oral report with specific examples.
LS, CL

Glencoe Poster Teaching Tip

Before introducing the poster, ask student how they think business knowledge will help them in their future and whether or not they plan a career in business. Then ask the students to take the quiz on the poster. Suggest to those students who are considering business careers to spend some time with one or more local businesspeople. They will learn more about what those people do in their daily work.

BUSINESS *Online*
Idea Factory

To learn more about hybrid cars, visit the *Introduction to Business* Web site at **www.introbus.glencoe.com**, and click on Unit 2 Owning and Operating a Business.

⏰ Out of Time?

If time doesn't permit teaching each chapter in this unit, you may use the *Puzzle-Maker* CD-ROM to focus on the business vocabulary.

Portfolio Activity

Question Cards. Write the following categories on the board: entrepreneurs, small businesses, forms of business leadership, and technology. Ask students to write questions on a 3- by 5-inch card about each category. Explain to students that they'll find the answers to their questions as they work through Unit 2, and they can write the answers on the back of the cards.

Short Paper. Ask students to write about the characteristics of two of the following types of businesses: producers, processors, manufacturers, retailers, distributors, and service providers. Lead a discussion about how they are related to one another.

SCANS Correlation Chart*

Foundation Skills

Basic Skills	Reading	Writing	Math	Listening	Speaking	
Thinking Skills	Creative Thinking	Decision Making	Problem Solving	Seeing Things in the Mind's Eye	Knowing How to Learn	Reasoning
Personal Qualities	Responsibility	Self-Esteem	Sociability	Self-Management	Integrity/ Honesty	

Workplace Competencies

Resources	Allocating Time	Allocating Money	Allocating Material and Facility Resources	Allocating Human Resources		
Information	Acquiring and Evaluating Information	Organizing and Maintaining Information	Interpreting and Communicating Information	Using Computers to Process Information		
Interpersonal Skills	Participating as a Member of a Team	Teaching Others	Serving Clients/ Customers	Exercising Leadership	Negotiating to Arrive at a Decision	Working With Cultural Diversity
Systems	Understanding Systems	Monitoring and Correcting Performance	Improving and Designing Systems			
Technology	Selecting Technology	Applying Technology to Task	Maintaining and Troubleshooting Technology			

*This chart's highlighted blocks indicate the chapter's content coverage in the Student Edition and the Teacher Wraparound Edition.

Resource Manager

Teaching Transparencies

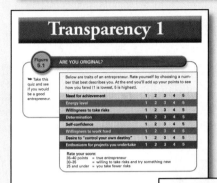

Transparency 1

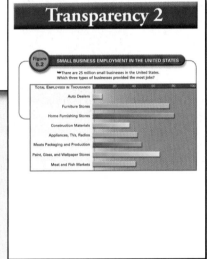

Transparency 2

Application and Enrichment

- Lesson Plans
- *BusinessWeek* Poster Package
- Teaching Transparencies
- Integrated Software Simulation
- Glencoe Business Video Package

Review and Reinforcement

- *PuzzleMaker*
- Internet Resources
- Student Activity Workbook
- Strat. and Work. for Teaching Transparencies

Assessment and Evaluation

- Reproducible Tests
- Alternative Assessment Strategies
- ExamView® Pro Test Generator

Technology

- *PuzzleMaker*
- ExamView® Pro Test Generator
- Glencoe Business Video Package
- PowerPoint® Presentation
- Integrated Software Simulation
- Interactive Lesson Planner
- *Virtual Business*®

KEY	Printed	Software	Videocassette	Poster
	Transparency	CD-ROM	Internet	

BUSINESS Online

Visit www.introbus.glencoe.com, the Web site companion to *Introduction to Business.* The student's page includes:

- interactive tutor
- additional *BusinessWeek* articles and activities
- business Web links
- homework hints
- real-world application activities
- additional career path activities

Information on how to prepare your students for the high school exit exam and special projects are also included.

Use the Glencoe Web site for additional resources. All essential content is covered in the Student Edition.

1 FOCUS

Introducing the Chapter

This chapter introduces entrepreneurship and small business—what they are and their advantages and disadvantages. A photo essay, "The Biz Behind Bozart," about a small business owned by an entrepreneur, enhances the concepts.

Connecting the Objectives

What characteristics does an entrepreneur have? Why might someone become an entrepreneur?

BusinessWeek
Feature Story

Story's Summary

Martha and Robert Gamblin are small business owners. They manufacture artists' colors in their factory in Portland, Oreg. Leading artists worldwide use their paints. Gamblin turned his love of art into a three million dollar company.

Find the entire article at **www.introbus.glencoe.com**, or in the Teacher Resource Binder.

Entrepreneurship and Small Business

● Learning Objectives

After completing this chapter, you'll be able to:

1. **Describe** an entrepreneurship and a small business.
2. **List** the advantages and disadvantages of an entrepreneurship.
3. **Recognize** the advantages and disadvantages of a small business.
4. **Explain** why small businesses may fail.

● Why It's Important

Entrepreneurships and small businesses bring vital energy and innovation to the economy. The risks involved energize entrepreneurs and small business owners to become successful.

● Key Words

entrepreneurship
virtual business
   or dot-com company
entrepreneur
risk taker
profit
small business

68

BusinessWeek Feature Story
Paint by Numbers

Gamblin Artists Colors Paints in Popular Hues. Martha and Robert Gamblin's work hangs in some of the world's top art museums. But don't bother looking for their names on gallery walls.

The Gamblins toil behind the scenes, manufacturing some of the world's finest oil paints. Each year, Gamblin Artists Colors in Portland, Oreg., ships more than 500,000 tubes and cans of paint in some 150 colors to artists and supply stores worldwide. Leading painters such as David Hockney and Chuck Close swear by them. "They make colors other companies just don't," says Wolf Kahn, a West Brattleboro (Vt.) landscape painter whose work is on display in museums nationwide.

Source: Excerpted with permission from "Paint by Numbers," *Frontier*, November 6, 2000.

An Extension Activity

Color is a science. Researchers have studied everything from how color affects brain activity to energy consumption. Study your classroom. Find out if the colors are "brain compatible."

The Full Story

To learn more about Gamblin Artists Colors, visit the *Introduction to Business* Web site at www.introbus.glencoe.com, and click on *BusinessWeek* Feature Story, Chapter 5.

Classroom Resources

For the Teacher

- Student Activity Work. TAE
- Assessment Binder
- PowerPoint® Presentation
- Interactive Lesson Planner
- Lesson Plans
- Internet Resources
- Teaching Transparencies
- *Introduction to Business* Web Site

- Integrated Soft. Sim. TM
- *BusinessWeek* Poster Package

For the Student

- Student Activity Workbook
- *Virtual Business*®
- *Introduction to Business* Web Site
- Integrated Soft. Sim.
- *PuzzleMaker*
- Strategies and Worksheets for Teaching Transparencies

🔔 Bell Ringer Activity

BRAINSTORM. Ask students to describe a student-run business. List the advantages and disadvantages on the board.

Preteaching Business Key Words

TEAMWORK. Appoint students to participate in a Vocabulary Bee. Teams take turns defining a key word given to them. Team members consult one another before giving a definition. **CL**

An Extension Activity

RESEARCH. What does color say about a workplace or classroom? After students have observed the classroom, ask them to research color theory and its effect on the brain. Good sources include: *The Owner's Manual for the Brain* by Pierce J. Howard, Ph.D., and the Web site **www.colormatters.com**. How does color affect performance? Attitude? Behavior?

Making Connections

Daily Living. Have students list several inconveniences they experience over the course of a single school day. Have a volunteer collect the lists and record them on the board. Then ask students to invent goods or services to help eliminate or lessen the inconvenience. Have students write the product and services section of a business plan for their product. Remind students that the product and service portion of their plan should include the following:

- Description of similar products on the market.
- Examples of possible uses for the product.
- Prototype of the item to be produced.

2 TEACH

Business Connection

A reversible camouflage handbag? Well, twenty-something, art-school dropout Monique Moizel thought, why not. Moizel combined her entrepreneurial spirit and creativity and started the Topsy Turvy brand—a handbag fashion line. On Moizel's first day of meeting with Los Angeles retail stores, she went home with $3,500 worth of orders. Her handbags made out of electric fabrics like Astroturf, plush, and fake fur are hitting a few stores in L. A. and Tokyo. Moizel expects the brand's line to gross $1 million this year.

Develop Concepts

WEBBING AND MAPPING.
Create a web or diagram on the board of an entrepreneur's characteristics. (Answers may include desire for independence, self-confidence, self-motivation, self-discipline, and calculated risks.) Then discuss characteristics that an entrepreneur probably wouldn't exhibit. (Answers may include dependent on others, low self-image, lazy, and a procrastinator.) **LS**

Figure 5.1 Caption Answer

Answers will vary. What entrepreneurial ventures might students want to take? **CL**

The Visionaries Behind New Businesses

Imagine you inherit $2,000 and want to start a graphic design business. With the money, you purchase QuarkXpress® and Adobe Illustrator®. Next you design a business card and work hard to bring in business. Three years later a local business magazine awards you Young Entrepreneur of the Year. The award is for creating fantastic designs for the breast cancer awareness campaign. The public responded to its attractive and effective message. Your dream, hard work, and financial investment are paying off.

The Ins and Outs of an Entrepreneurship

An **entrepreneurship** is a business started by someone who notices a need for a product or service. Entrepreneurship soared in the late 1990s as entrepreneurs took their business ideas online. The Internet became the arena to sell products and services.

A **virtual business** or a **dot-com company** is a business that operates on the Internet. A dot-com company may exist only online or it may be in addition to a company's actual storefront.

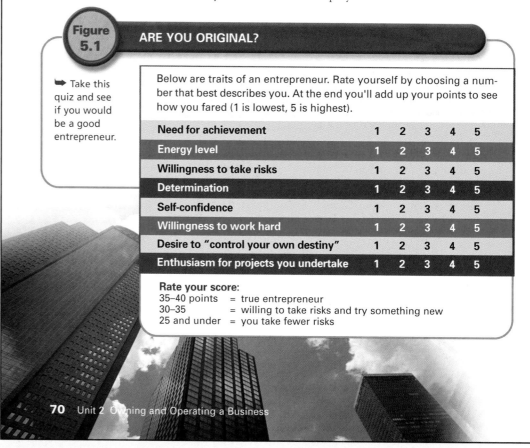

Figure 5.1

➡ Take this quiz and see if you would be a good entrepreneur.

ARE YOU ORIGINAL?

Below are traits of an entrepreneur. Rate yourself by choosing a number that best describes you. At the end you'll add up your points to see how you fared (1 is lowest, 5 is highest).

Need for achievement	1	2	3	4	5
Energy level	1	2	3	4	5
Willingness to take risks	1	2	3	4	5
Determination	1	2	3	4	5
Self-confidence	1	2	3	4	5
Willingness to work hard	1	2	3	4	5
Desire to "control your own destiny"	1	2	3	4	5
Enthusiasm for projects you undertake	1	2	3	4	5

Rate your score:
35–40 points = true entrepreneur
30–35 = willing to take risks and try something new
25 and under = you take fewer risks

70 Unit 2 Owning and Operating a Business

Cooperative Learning

Showing Expertise. Everyone is an expert on something. Ask students to think about what they know a lot about. Once each student discovers what he or she is an expert on, pair up students. Each pair uses its expert knowledge to find an entrepreneurial venture. Once a business is agreed upon, each pair will prepare for the mock press conference in which the business idea is launched. The class acts as a pack of reporters who ask each pair probing questions about the risk involved of starting a business. How will the company handle success; will it give away any of its profits to charity; will they work from home or in an office building, and so on.

In July 1995 Amazon.com opened its virtual doors to the world. The company wanted to change book buying over the Internet. Nearly 29 million customers later, the online e-tailer forges ahead in high-tech shopping.

It may take Amazon.com ten years before it turns a profit but the company's lead man, Jeff Bezos, accepts the challenge. What would you expect from an entrepreneur? An **entrepreneur** is a person who recognizes a business opportunity and organizes, manages, and assumes the risks of a business enterprise, with the intent of increasing the market value of the business. Every year thousands of entrepreneurs start businesses. Many entrepreneurs establish very successful companies that remain small. Many of these businesses will fail within a few years of opening. Others will go on to become giant companies. Figure 5.1 is a quiz you can take to see if you would be a good entrepreneur. You'll rate yourself based upon traits that best describe you.

Advantages of an Entrepreneurship

Entrepreneurs are take-charge, self-directed people. They want to work for themselves. Often an entrepreneur is a **risk taker**, or someone who likes to take risks.

Satisfaction From Taking a Risk and Becoming a Success. Miranda wasn't the kind of person who could sit at a desk all day. She decided this last summer when she was an administrative assistant at a news organization. Every day couriers came into her office with packages for pick up and delivery. They were constantly on the move and she liked that. She decided to leave her position and take the risk of making enough money with her own courier service. Miranda found satisfaction in taking a risk and becoming a success.

Showing Expertise and Skills. Raphael worked as an assistant restaurant manager for three years. He decided it was time to leave that restaurant and open his own establishment. One year later he opened a charming bistro in the hip, arty part of the city. The restaurant's quick success labeled him the hottest entrepreneur in the city. Starting his own business gave Raphael a way to demonstrate his expertise, skills, and self-determination. His experiences as an assistant manager gave him the skills to start his own business.

Working From Home. Briana is among the 20 percent of small business owners running a home-based business. She loves needlework. Instead of working for a large company, she started Briana's Gifts. She sells her homemade gifts at trade shows and conferences. Briana, like many entrepreneurs,

Real-World Application
part 1 of 4

THE BIZ BEHIND BOZART
In the early '90s, the art market slowed down. Larry Mangel, an art dealer, decided to change his career focus and open his own business, Bozart Toys.
What makes Larry Mangel an entrepreneur?

continued on p. 73

THE BIZ BEHIND BOZART: PART 1 OF 4
Mangel demonstrates creativity, willingness to take risks, enthusiasm for business and art, determination, and self-confidence.

Technology Resource

GO TO **POWERPOINT.** The *Introduction to Business* PowerPoint® CD-ROM provides visual lecture aids for this chapter.

Independent Practice

INVENT. Ask students if they ever think soda straws or tape dispensers could be used for different purposes. Students are to imagine and invent a new use for a soda straw, tape dispenser, or any ordinary object. (Encourage students to be creative and have fun.) **LS**

Chapter 5 Entrepreneurship and Small Business **71**

Meeting Individual Needs

Reading Comprehension Disabilities. Students with reading comprehension disabilities often don't practice good self-appraisal and self-management skills while reading. Point out to students that they need to be aware of the processes they use to help them understand reading material. Explain that re-reading is very important for understanding. Another idea is to use a mini recorder to record a first reading and then listen over for review. Encourage students to share other techniques they have used.

Technology Toolkit

Caption Answer

Lane Wyrich uses digital video for its truest color images and its best quality sound. Desktop editing allows Wyrich to edit quickly.

Thinking Critically

TELECOMMUTING NIGHTMARE. The state you live in just declared a state of emergency: No one can use any power appliances for three days; individuals who disobey this crackdown will be heavily fined. Your business is run out of your house, and the Internet is your main lifeline to your customers. What will you do? How will you cope with this power crisis? (Answers will vary. Possible answers include writing letters to your customers, calling customers, waiting for time to pass, sending complimentary gifts (during the crisis), and so on.)

✓ Fast Review Answers

1. Take-charge, self-directed people who want to work for themselves. Risk takers.
2. Satisfaction of having taken a risk uses entrepreneurial skills and is profitable.
3. Total responsibility for the business, irregular hours, and financial risks.
4. The need for money.

Technology Toolkit

It's a Digital World

Entrepreneur Lane Wyrich started a multimedia production company, Xap Interactive. His company uses digital video and computer technology to create videos and movies. Digital recording marries image and sound into single pieces of data. Each piece of data is a complete image or a specific sound. Wyrich uses a computer to edit the digital data (or movie footage) to create the finished product.

Critical Thinking

Why do you think Wyrich uses digital video and computer technology?

prefers to set her own flexible schedule instead of keeping a big company's mandatory workweek.

Gaining Profit. Joseph started his own network consulting company. It was important to him that he received all the profits from his hard work. **Profit** is the money left over after a business has paid all costs of producing its goods or services. In fact, profit is one reason that many entrepreneurs start a business.

Disadvantages of an Entrepreneurship

Entrepreneurs know they are taking a risk when starting a business, and are aware that risk may result in failure. Success means working hard. A successful venture doesn't come easy to an entrepreneur.

Total Responsibility for the Business. Do you remember Miranda, the new owner of a courier service who was introduced a few paragraphs ago? She knows her business's success depends on her managerial skills. She is responsible for her employees, customer service, vendor relations, the finances, and the facility. She has a tough job. A business owner is responsible for everything.

Long Hours. Raphael works longer hours now that he owns his own restaurant. He has been working 80 to 100 hours a week to get his restaurant started. Time and effort are important pieces to making a company successful.

Financial Risks. Money is a worry for entrepreneurs. Joseph's consulting business was profitable but it struggled for the first year. Before his business became profitable he financed all costs. He was in charge of paying his employees, producing his service, and meeting his customers' needs. The main reason why entrepreneurships fail is because they run out of money.

✓ Fast Review

1. What are some characteristics of entrepreneurs?
2. What are three advantages of an entrepreneurship?
3. What are some disadvantages of an entrepreneurship?
4. What is the main reason that entrepreneurships fail?

72 Unit 2 Owning and Operating a Business

LANGUAGE ARTS — *Curriculum Connection*

Advertisement. Have students work in small groups to develop print advertising, radio, or a television spots designed to persuade people to become entrepreneurs. Remind students that while they may want to emphasize the advantages of being an entrepreneur, they'll need to be truthful about the disadvantages. Encourage students to display or broadcast their advertisements.

Small Business: What You Need to Know

The Small Business Administration (SBA) defines a **small business** as an independently owned business that usually has the owner as its manager. A small business serves a limited geographic area, employs fewer than 500 people, and is not dominant in its industry. Figure 5.2 shows the different types of businesses that provide employment.

Most businesses in the United States are small businesses. There are about 25 million small businesses, and they are a vital part of our economy. Small businesses employ more than 50 percent of the total workforce in the United States. They generate more than half the nation's income. They are the principal source of new jobs. Small businesses account for about 38 percent of jobs in high technology.

Advantages of Small Business

Small businesses offer many opportunities and are easier to form than large businesses. As a small business owner you would enjoy meeting the challenges of running a business.

Being the Boss. Michelle owns Paint Your Own Pots, a small business. She said, "I want to provide a high-quality service, so I enjoy managing the store myself." Small business owners like being their own boss. An important advantage of being a small business owner is the ability to be in charge. Small business owners make their own decisions. They usually are the managers as well as the owners. Many small businesses, in fact, have no employees.

Opportunity to Offer Services Large Companies Cannot Offer. Paco saw opportunities that large companies didn't offer. His business was small so he could respond quickly to his customers' needs. For example, Paco knows his customers so well that he can suggest products to meet their individual needs. A large company may not take the time to know its customers on a personal level.

Ease of Formation. Zach noticed how easy it was to form his own hair-cutting salon. He had worked for large businesses before and noticed how hard they were to form. Small businesses require licenses for operation. Their buildings must meet local zoning requirements. Zach found that taking the steps to start his small business took a short time.

Real-World Application

part 2 of 4

THE BIZ BEHIND BOZART
Bozart Toys started with a business plan in '95. One year later Mangel acquired the money and produced the first toy, Marco the Magnificent.
Why do you think Mangel's company became a success?

continued on p. 75

Real-World Application
Caption Answer

THE BIZ BEHIND BOZART: PART 2 OF 4
Mangel took his knowledge of art and business and blended the two into a business plan. He recognized no other toy company blends truly renowned artists and toy-making into one business. He typically works 80 hours a week to manage and organize Bozart Toys.

Business Connection

Doug Ross, small business owner of Evolution Film & Tape Inc., allows workplace freedom. His employees can dress casually, bring their kids to work, and set their own schedules. The freedom to control the workweek is empowering.

Develop Concepts

SUCCESS. Have students research the success story of a dot-com company. Ask them to retell the story in their own words. **LS**

Great Ideas From the Classroom of...

Beth Patzke
Baldwin-Woodville High School
Baldwin, Wis.

SBA Quiz. An exploratory quiz is always a good way to start a unit and to pique students' interests. Ask your students to visit the Small Business Administration (SBA) Web site www.sba.gov, and click on "Starting Your Own Business." Then choose "Success Series." While this quiz is actually for business owners, it gives students an idea of their business-owning potential.

Discussion Starter

SMALL BUSINESSES. Have students list all the people they know who work for small businesses. Then discuss the types of jobs people hold at small businesses. These people work in what industries?

Individualized Practice

Tell the students that the market for small businesses is getting better.

L1 Divide students into pairs to discuss how the economy affects small business owners.

L2 Have students prepare a graph to show how small business ownership will look over the next 40 years.

L3 Have students research how big companies are teaming up with small companies to better serve the marketplace.

Figure 5.2 Caption Answer

Home furnishing stores, furniture stores, and paint, glass, and wallpaper stores. **CL**

Disadvantages of Small Business

When you're a small business owner, you're responsible for decisions. At times, life as a small business owner can create a feeling of loneliness if you're used to a workplace where people foster friendships and collaboration. Working long hours, making hard financial choices, and accepting responsibility don't always beget success.

Successful business practices are key to keeping your small business alive. About four out of five small businesses fail in their first five years. Business closings may result from many factors. Small business owners may mistake the freedom of being in business for oneself for the liberty of working or not. Other times a small business may underprice or overprice goods or services. Going into business with little or no experience and without first learning something about it may result in the business closing.

Normally, the most successful businesses are the ones that require advanced training, like dentists' offices and physicians' offices. Yet one of the businesses with the highest odds of monetary growth is manufacturing. Below are two specific causes of why a small business might not work.

Effect of Change. Styles and trends change. Consumers' tastes change. The economic system goes through ups and downs. All of these factors influence the small business. A small business owner must be aware of change and quickly adapt. If flexibility and change are not part

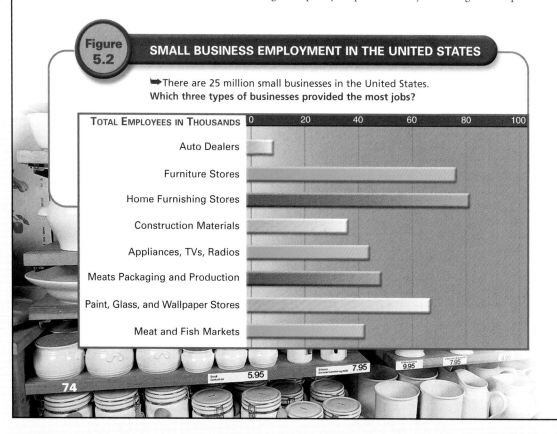

Figure 5.2

SMALL BUSINESS EMPLOYMENT IN THE UNITED STATES

➡There are 25 million small businesses in the United States. **Which three types of businesses provided the most jobs?**

TOTAL EMPLOYEES IN THOUSANDS

- Auto Dealers
- Furniture Stores
- Home Furnishing Stores
- Construction Materials
- Appliances, TVs, Radios
- Meats Packaging and Production
- Paint, Glass, and Wallpaper Stores
- Meat and Fish Markets

(scale: 0, 20, 40, 60, 80, 100)

74

Global Perspective

Investment in Small Business. Many individuals in countries around the world get their start as business owners through the assistance of private investment companies in the United States and Europe. Individuals in these investment companies work directly with individuals in towns, villages, and urban neighborhoods. Businesses established through this type of cooperative effort include anything from craft shops to small power companies. Ask students to discuss the benefits these new small businesses offer the individuals and their communities. (Individuals get pride of ownership; communities get goods, services, and improved local economies.)

of the business then it's likely to fail. Not being market savvy can push a small business down as its smart competitors take advantage of opportunities.

Managerial Skills Needed. A small business owner must have multiple skills. For example, Michele must handle financing, employee relations, production, customer relations, and any other area needing a decision.

Inadequate Financial Planning. To keep the business alive, owners must be financially smart. Starting with little money, spending carelessly, borrowing money without planning how to use it, and forgetting about taxes, insurance, and other business costs may result in closure. Money management helps keep a small business successfully afloat.

 **Fast Review**

1. How does the Small Business Administration define a small business?
2. Give an example of a service that a small business may offer that a large company cannot offer.
3. Which is more difficult to form: a large business or a small business?
4. Give examples of special skills that a small business owner needs.
5. List two financial reasons that small businesses fail.

Preparing for Your Own Business

Once you've decided that you want to start a business, the next step is to analyze what you want to do and find a way to do it. When you begin to plan, you start turning your daydream into reality. Careful planning from the beginning is one way to ensure the success of starting a business.

Whether you're starting up a butterfly-breeding business or a picture-hanging business, it is a good idea to develop a business plan. A *business plan* is a written description of a new business venture that describes all aspects of the business. It helps you focus on exactly what you want to do, how you'll do it, and what you expect to accomplish. The business plan is essential for potential investors and financing agencies you'll go to for start-up funds.

Checklist for Starting a Venture

A checklist is a good way to organize your thinking when you begin planning your own business. Entrepreneurs and small business owners

Chapter 5 Entrepreneurship and Small Business **75**

Real-World Application part 3 of 4

THE BIZ BEHIND BOZART
Mangel manages all aspects of Bozart. He travels to China a few times a year to ensure quality control in the manufacturing of the toys. **Identify some reasons why a small business might be hard to manage.**

continued on p. 77

Chapter 5

Real-World Application Caption Answer

THE BIZ BEHIND BOZART: PART 3 OF 4
Mangel has to oversee all facets of the company. If an entrepreneur isn't tenacious and ready for change, a company can fail. Fortunately, Mangel knows how to manage all the aspects in order to keep his company profitable.

Fast Review Answers

1. As an independently owned business that usually has the owner as its manager, serves a limited geographic area, employs fewer than 500 people, and isn't dominant in its industry.
2. May be able to suggest products or services that meet customers' special needs; restaurant owner may be able to offer menu choices requested by customers.
3. A small business.
4. Skills in handling financing, employee relations, production, customer relations, and every other area about which decisions must be made.
5. Starting with too little money and extending credit too freely.

Social Science **Curriculum Connection**

Inventors. Entrepreneurs improve or enhance an existing process. Ask students to research an inventor's background. Students should present their findings as a bulletin board or poster.

- Automatic traffic light (Garrett A. Morgan)
- Gas mask (Garrett A. Morgan)

- Portable refrigeration units (Frederick McKinley Jones)
- Automatic shoe-lacing machine (Jan Matzeliger)
- Filament for electric light bulbs (Lewis H. Lattimer)
- Process for making refined, white, granulated sugar (Norbert Rillieux)

CAPTION ANSWER

After the students have completed one path, ask them to freewrite for ten minutes in their journal about the process of finding out the information.

3 ASSESS

Reteaching

ENTREPRENEURSHIP. To reteach the concept of entrepreneurship, ask students what characteristics an entrepreneur exhibits. (High energy, willingness to achieve, risk taker, self-confident, hard worker, passion, and enthusiasm.) Ask them to list the pros and cons of starting an entrepreneurship or small business. (Advantages: enjoying risk taking, showing expertise, working from home, and gaining profit. Disadvantages: total responsibility for the business, long hours, and financial risks.) **LS**

Enrichment Strategy

IDENTIFY. Ask students to identify an entrepreneur who owns a small business. What is its impact on the community?

Evaluation

Assign and review the Fast Review sections.

Writing for Business

Portfolio Activity

On Being Your Own Boss

This activity gives you the chance to add to your portfolio. Communicate, interview, research, and write your way into a story. Choose one imaginary path, Designed for Life or Cold Comfort. Follow your path's steps to complete your own story.

pick a path

Designed for Life

The Setting. You're interested in designing attractive spaces where people live and work. The places will be inexpensive and environmentally friendly.

Rising Action. You'll design a living space or work space, organize the whole project, and supervise the actual builders.

Step 1. Draw up a business plan to present to your bank for financial backing.
Step 2. Investigate the local and state regulations about the licensing requirements for starting a contracting business.

Cold Comfort

The Setting. One winter day you were scraping the ice off your car when you came up with a terrific idea for a foolproof ice scraper. Your scraper would touch along the entire edge of the glass regardless of the curvature of the windshield.

Rising Action. Now you want to launch a company to develop, test, produce, and market your ice scraper.

Step 1. Write a business plan for the company. Include a name for your ice scraper.
Step 2. Interview a local attorney, law school professor, or experienced inventor about whether or not you should patent your invention.

Conclusion

Now it's time to write your own story and reflect on your path. Explain your business venture to a group of students. Write a few expository paragraphs that will serve as the basis of your talk. Remember, an effective expository paragraph has appropriate organization and specific details that make sense to your audience.

76

How to Use a Portfolio Activity

The portfolio projects are designed to lead students to develop a collection of their best work to submit to you for assessment. You and each of your students should decide which projects to include in their business portfolio. Refer students to the specific rubric(s) from the *Alternative Assessment Strategies.* These rubrics will alert students to the criteria you'll use to assess their projects.

should keep these questions and their answers in mind as they develop and write their business plan.

Here are some questions to consider: What will I produce? Who are my main competitors? Why is my product needed? How much will my product cost to produce? How many people will I need to run the business? What physical facilities will I need? What licenses, permits, or other legal documents do I need? How much money will I need to get started?

Parts of a Business Plan

The Center for Entrepreneurial Management in New York reports that most business plans take more than five months to prepare. Yet it takes most readers, such as bank officers, fewer than five minutes to decide whether or not to read the entire document. Therefore, a business plan must be well-organized, easy to read, and follow a logical format. The essential parts of a business plan are as follows:

- The *summary* is a one- to three-page overview of the plan. Place it at the beginning of the finished proposal but write it after you complete the rest of the sections. Make sure it intrigues readers so they want to read more.
- The *company description* explains the type of company you plan to start. Will it be a manufacturing plant? A retail business? Will it provide a service?
- Expand on the company description in the *products and services* section. Describe the kinds of products you will sell or the services you will provide.
- The *marketing plan* describes your likely customers and details your competition. Indicate the marketing strategies that you plan to put into place. Include types and location of advertising.
- A good business plan also needs to include a *legal plan* that points out how you will organize your company. Will it be a sole proprietorship, a partnership, or a corporation? (See Chapter 6 for types of business organizations.)
- The *management plan and operating plan* detail the company's key personnel as well as their expertise and experience. Specify the company's daily operations, facilities, overall personnel, materials, and processing requirements.
- Of course, no business plan is complete without a *financial plan*. You should discuss the company's financial needs and financing as well as your projections for revenues, costs, and profits.

 Fast Review _____

1. What is a business plan?
2. Name the essential elements of a business plan.

THE BIZ BEHIND BOZART
The Bozart Toys Web site shows consumers its products, but other online sites and toy stores sell the toys. **What are some benefits of selling toys online?**

Real-World Application
Caption Answer

THE BIZ BEHIND BOZART: PART 4 OF 4
Selling online gives companies a wider customer base. The Bozart Toys Web site doesn't sell its toys, although the company's toys are available for sale on other e-tailers. Mangel is carefully considering his Web site to sell the toys, but no decision is made.

Technology Resource

GO TO **VIRTUAL BUSINESS.** Introduce entrepreneurship and starting a small business using Knowledge Matters' *Virtual Business* interactive simulation. Go to the *Introduction to Business* Web site **www.introbus.glencoe.com** to download the *Virtual Business* activity. Run the *Virtual Business* tutorial before beginning this activity.

Fast Review Answers

1. A written description of a new business venture that describes all aspects of the business.
2. There are seven parts to a business plan: summary, company description, description of products or services, marketing plan, legal plan, management and operating plan, and financial plan.

Meeting Individual Needs

Students With Hearing Impairments. When you talk to a student with a hearing impairment, look directly at the student. It also helps to enunciate clearly. When you are writing on the board, turn toward the class before you speak. When you're referring to a textbook, look up before you talk. When other students speak, students with hearing impairments will probably not hear them. When other students ask questions, or give input, repeat the information while looking toward the class.

What Happens When You Type a URL?

1 FOCUS

More than 145 million Web surfers logged on to the Internet in just one month at the beginning of the twenty-first century. The United States leads the world with 98 million people logged on, and Japan followed with 15 million users. Germany ranked third with 13 million, followed by the United Kingdom with 10 million, and Canada with 9 million Web surfers. Every Web surfer will have used a Universal Resource Locator (URL) to find information.

2 TEACH

A Universal Resource Locator (URL) is the address of a file, or resource, stored in a computer. The resource you want in the Picture This… example is the file that gives the home page of *Business-Week* online. Notice that the URL starts with http://—the Web browser uses the hypertext transfer protocol (HTTP) to access the file. The protocol is a set of rules the computer systems use to communicate with one another. For example, your browser sends the HTTP "get" request to the server asking for the file. Ask them to give examples of other business URLs.

? Did You Know?

Each machine on the Internet is assigned a unique address—the Internet point (IP) address. An IP address is a "dotted-decimal number" such as 175.30.22.200.

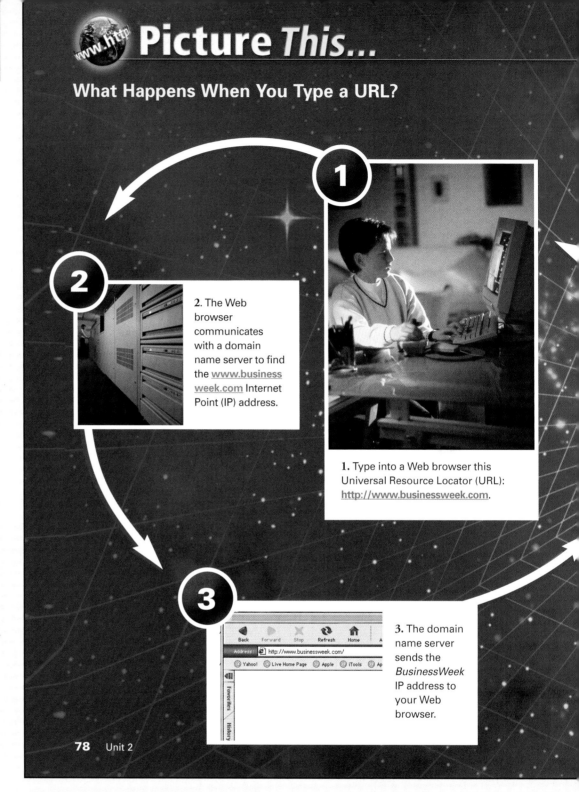

Picture This...

What Happens When You Type a URL?

2. The Web browser communicates with a domain name server to find the www.business week.com Internet Point (IP) address.

1. Type into a Web browser this Universal Resource Locator (URL): http://www.businessweek.com.

3. The domain name server sends the *BusinessWeek* IP address to your Web browser.

78 Unit 2

Extending the Content

The Internet and Business. Can you imagine over $2 million changing hands every minute? That's the expected rate of business-to-business (B2B) e-commerce in the twenty-first century. An example of B2B e-commerce is a corporation registering online with Office Depot to order and pay for printing services.

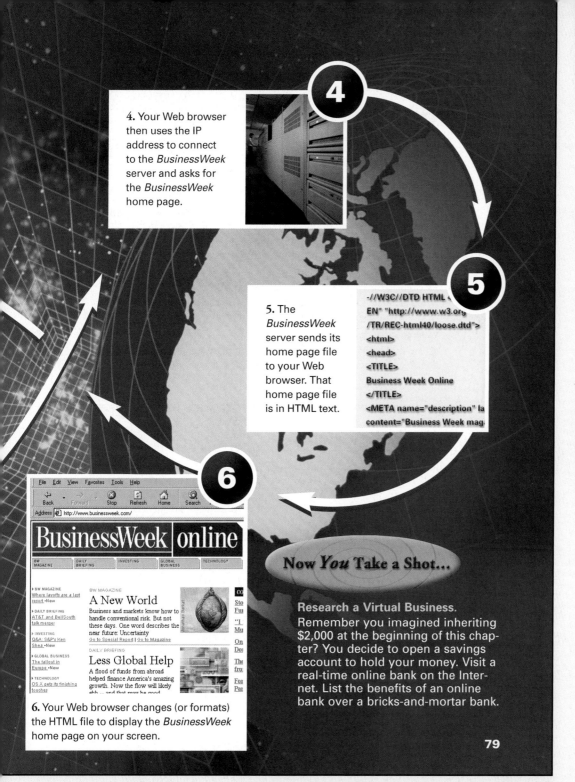

4. Your Web browser then uses the IP address to connect to the *BusinessWeek* server and asks for the *BusinessWeek* home page.

5. The *BusinessWeek* server sends its home page file to your Web browser. That home page file is in HTML text.

```
-//W3C//DTD HTML
EN" "http://www.w3.org
/TR/REC-html40/loose.dtd">
<html>
<head>
<TITLE>
Business Week Online
</TITLE>
<META name="description" la
content="Business Week mag
```

6. Your Web browser changes (or formats) the HTML file to display the *BusinessWeek* home page on your screen.

Now *You* Take a Shot...

Research a Virtual Business.
Remember you imagined inheriting $2,000 at the beginning of this chapter? You decide to open a savings account to hold your money. Visit a real-time online bank on the Internet. List the benefits of an online bank over a bricks-and-mortar bank.

79

3 ASSESS

Ask students to do the activity in Now You Take a Shot...

4 CLOSE

Ask students to use library resources or the Internet to gather information about businesses' impression of the Internet. List these on the board.

? *Did You Know?*

Clicking on a hyperlink accesses a URL—it's the same process as when you type in a URL in the Web browser's field locator.

Now *You* Take a Shot...   *Caption Answer*

Answers will vary and may include that you can get detailed account information from the comfort of your own home, search for specific activity, get up-to-date insurance and financial information, activate a high-interest checking account, and pay bills online.

4 CLOSE

Chapter Wrap-Up

Ask students to explain the significant pros and cons of an entrepreneurship and small business.

Using Business Key Words

1. entrepreneur
2. risk taker
3. virtual business or dot-com company
4. profit
5. small business
6. entrepreneurship

Review What You Learned

7. Identify an opportunity, produce a product or service, and work for a profit.
8. Business started by someone who accepted the risk.
9. Dot-com.
10. Independently owned, owner as its manager, limited geographic area, employs less than 500 people, and isn't dominant in its industry.
11. Money left over after a business has paid all costs of producing its goods or services.
12. Advantages: risk taking and success, use of skills, and profit. Disadvantages: total responsibility, long hours, and financial risks.
13. Because they ran out of money before the business was established.
14. Employ more than 50 percent of the total U.S. workforce and generate more than half of the nation's income.
15. If they aren't aware of the economic impact of trends, they may fail.

Summary

1. An entrepreneur recognizes a business opportunity and organizes, manages, and assumes the risks of a business venture. Small businesses are vital to our economy. They employ more than half of all workers in the United States, and they're the main source of new jobs.

2. Entrepreneurs show expertise, may work from home, and gain the profit from their own work. On the other hand, entrepreneurs have to take total responsibility for the business, work long hours, and endure financial risks when they decide to start the business.

3. The advantages of running a small business include being your own boss, providing great personal service, and easy formation. A small business owner faces potential problems if he or she doesn't adapt to change and possibly lacks the managerial skills needed to successfully run the business.

4. Small businesses often fail because the owners start with little money, freely extend credit, have little business experience, don't keep adequate records, don't plan for the ups and downs of business, and haven't mastered time management.

● Using Business Key Words

Use these business terms correctly in the following sentences.

- **entrepreneurship**
- **entrepreneur**
- **virtual business or dot-com company**
- **risk taker**
- **small business**
- **profit**

1. A(n) _____ is a person who recognizes an opportunity and who organizes, manages, and assumes the risks of a business enterprise, with the intent of increasing the value of the business.
2. A person who likes to take chances is a(n) _____.
3. A(n) _____ is a business that operates on the Internet.
4. The money that is left over after a business has paid all the costs of producing its goods and services is called _____.
5. An independently owned business serving a limited geographic area is called a(n) _____.
6. A business started by someone who accepted the risk of starting and running a business is a(n) _____.

Quick Quiz

1. What is profit? (Profit is the money left over after a business has paid all costs of producing its goods or services.)
2. Name three advantages of small business. (Being the boss, the opportunity to offer services large companies cannot offer, and ease of formation.)
3. What are the two main disadvantages of small business? (The effect of change, and managerial skills are needed.)

Review What You Learned

7. What do all people who start a new business do?
8. What is an entrepreneurship?
9. What is a virtual business sometimes called?
10. How does the Small Business Association (SBA) define a small business?
11. What is profit?
12. Name the advantages and disadvantages of entrepreneurships.
13. Why may an entrepreneurship fail?
14. How do small businesses help the U.S. economy?
15. Why is it important for a small business owner to be aware of consumer trends?

Understanding Business Concepts

16. Why do you think it is important that entrepreneurs be take-charge, self-directed people?
17. Why are so many people starting home-based businesses?
18. Why might it be more satisfying to run your own company than work for someone else?
19. Why does the owner of a business usually put in more hours at work than an employee?
20. Why is the need for money considered to be the most serious problem an entrepreneur faces?
21. Why do you think small businesses are able to offer services that larger companies cannot?
22. Why is it so important for small business owners to be able to keep adequate financial records?

Critical Thinking

23. Why do you think some virtual businesses or dot-com companies fail?
24. What skills and attributes do you think a successful entrepreneur needs? Why?
25. Explain the difference between being self-disciplined and self-motivated.
26. A checklist is a good way to organize an entrepreneur's thinking when beginning to plan a business. What questions might be on the entrepreneur's checklist?

Viewing and Representing

Examining the Image. With a partner, examine this picture. What kinds of questions does this image seem to answer? Are the questions personal, creative, analytical, or informational? How effective is the image itself for drawing viewers or readers into the issue? Write a brief story based upon your perceptions of this image. Share your story with the class.

Chapter 5 Entrepreneurship and Small Business **81**

Critical Thinking

23. Inadequate management skills. Start with too little money, extend credit too freely, too little experience, poor recordkeeping, lack of business knowledge, and mistake the freedom of being in business for oneself for the freedom to work or not to work.
24. Answers will vary.
25. Self-disciplined—person controls his or her own actions without outside direction; self-motivated—person doesn't need the orders of someone else to work.
26. What will I produce? Who are my main competitors? Why is my product needed? How much will my product cost to produce? How many people will I need to run the business? What physical facilities will I need? What licenses, permits, or other legal documents do I need? How much money will I need to get started? How much profit do I expect to make?

Viewing and Representing

EXAMINING THE IMAGE.
Questions might include:
When you start a business,
- what do you need to do?
- what does it look like?
- what equipment do you need?

These questions are personal, analytical, and informational. Student's opinions will vary.

Understanding Business Concepts

16. Does everything that needs to be done without someone else's direction.
17. Computers increase communication and gives people opportunities not available in other companies.
18. Takes advantage of your own skills.
19. Takes care of all business responsibilities.
20. Takes money to start a business and then time to turn a profit. Must have enough financing to cover all costs, pay employees, produce products or services, and meet customer needs.
21. Quick responses to customers' needs.
22. Spot potential problems.

4 CLOSE (Cont.)

Building Academic Skills

HISTORY. Students' communication skills are crucial to understanding and interpreting someone else's story. Rubrics: Oral presentation, note taking.

LANGUAGE ARTS. Be certain each student participates in the group project. Creative sources for this may include other business newsletters, e-newsletters, and e-zines. Rubrics: Oral presentation, note taking.

COMPUTER/TECHNOLOGY. Answers will vary.

MATH. Businesses still open in 2000:
187 − (187 x 0.15) =
187 − 28.05 = 158.95 or 159.

Businesses still open in 2001:

159 − (159 x 0.12) =
159 − 19.08 = 139.92 or 140.
(Answers are rounded up.)
Rubrics: Spreadsheet, diagram, math calculations.

Linking School to Home

Answers will vary. If possible, compile the results as a class and find out if there are any common reasons (like good customer service, unique products or services offered, and so on) for purchasing from a small business or entrepreneur. Rubric: Note taking.

Linking School to Work

Reports will vary. Rubric: Report.

Building Academic Skills

 Oral History

Brainstorm and write questions in order to conduct an interview with someone who is an entrepreneur or a small business owner. Prepare questions that will get the interviewee to tell how his or her life changed as the result of being an entrepreneur or small business owner. Present the interview to the class. Discuss how the interviewees' stories compare with the information in the text.

 Journalism

Pick a partner to produce a newsletter that describes the successes and failures of the small businesses in your community. Some topics might include funding, laws, economic trends, consumer wants and needs, time management, risk management, help wanted ads, technology, and so on.

 Charting Growth

The hottest market for small businesses isn't across a great ocean. It's right here in the United States. Currently, the combined buying power of U.S. minority groups totals $1.3 trillion, or some 20 percent of the country's purchasing power. The Commerce Department estimates that the spending power of non-whites will reach $4.3 trillion, or 32 percent by 2045. In a database program, create a chart or graph to show this likely purchasing power.

 Calculating Closings

In the city of Orange, 187 new businesses opened in 2000. By 2001, 15 percent of businesses were no longer in operation. How many were open in 2001? One year later, another 12 percent were considered discontinued. How many businesses were still open in 2001?

Linking School to Home

Investigate Product Loyalties. Create an inventory of the products and services you and your family use that are produced by small businesses or entrepreneurs. Categorize them by family member. Then interview each family member, and find out why he or she purchases the products and services from the small business or entrepreneur. Compile your results and share them with the class.

Linking School to Work

Portfolio Project. Research the requirements for setting up a small business in your community. Investigate areas such as government regulations, financing, and the costs of leasing space and buying equipment. The local chamber of commerce might direct you in your research. Write a report with your findings.

E-Homework

Applying Technology

Electronic Survey. Use word processing software to create a survey that can be sent to local small business owners and entrepreneurs in your community. Through the survey, find out what technology skills they currently possess and what type of skills they think they'll need in the future. If possible, send out the surveys using e-mail. As a class, compile the results using a spreadsheet or database software.

High-Tech Callings. Research the technology classes that are available in high schools, technical centers, and colleges in your community. As a class, brainstorm a list of businesses that could be started by someone who has technology skills.

Connecting Academics

Math. Joaquin wants to start his own business for renting bikes at the park. He begins researching the age of his hometown's residents. He learns the following:

0–5 years of age	960 residents
6–11	1,840
12–18	4,500
19–35	8,225
36–60	2,960
Over 60	2,960

Construct a bar graph to present this information. Use computer software if possible.

Language Arts. You want to strengthen your entrepreneurial qualities. Complete the following steps to learn more about other entrepreneurs and yourself:

- **Reading.** Go online or to the library to read articles and books about entrepreneurs and entrepreneurial activities.
- **Writing.** Write about individuals you know who are entrepreneurs. Did this person overcome obstacles to achieve success?

- **Watching.** Find films about athletes, businesspeople, or others who achieved success.
- **Practice.** Find case studies that involve goals, creativity, and risk taking.

BusinessWeek Analyzing the Feature Story

You read the first part of "Paint by Numbers" at the beginning of this chapter. Below are a few questions for you to answer about the Gamblins. You'll find the answers to these questions when you're reading the entire article. First, here are the questions:

27. What motivated the Gamblins to take the risk of starting a new business?

28. How does Gamblin Artists Colors use technology in its small business?

29. What's the purpose of the special line of paints the company recently introduced?

CREATIVE JOURNAL ACTIVITY

What are your hobbies or interests? List business ideas related to your hobbies. How can you reap the benefits of your talents?

BUSINESS Online
The Full Story

To learn more about Gamblin Artists Colors, visit the *Introduction to Business* Web site at **www.introbus.glencoe.com**, and click on *BusinessWeek* Feature Story, Chapter 5.

83

E-Homework

ELECTRONIC SURVEY. If students don't have access to computers in the classroom, use those found in the media center, school labs, or the public library. Rubric: Survey and results.

HIGH-TECH CALLINGS. Students can find this information in the school's career center or guidance department. The Internet and local newspapers might have information as well. Rubrics: Note taking, paragraph.

Connecting Academics

MATH. Bar graph showing number of residents in each age range.

LANGUAGE ARTS. Reports should include specific examples of obstacles overcome, ways to achieve success, and behavior that involves risk taking, and creativity. Ask students to compare their own characteristics with those of the entrepreneurs. Rubrics: Note taking, paragraph, oral presentation.

BusinessWeek Analyzing the Feature Story

27. Gamblin started with an interest in and love of art. He was struggling as an oil painter but he was determined to make a living in the art world. He began mixing paints that he liked.

28. Use a computerized system to run the just-in-time inventory system.

29. Designed for restoring old paintings. Used by the National Gallery in London and by the Metropolitan Museum of Art in New York.

Creative Journal Activity

Answers will vary but encourage a fun and creative discussion. **P**, **CL**, **LS**

SCANS Correlation Chart*

Foundation Skills

Basic Skills	Reading	Writing	Math	Listening	Speaking	
Thinking Skills	Creative Thinking	Decision Making	Problem Solving	Seeing Things in the Mind's Eye	Knowing How to Learn	Reasoning
Personal Qualities	Responsibility	Self-Esteem	Sociability	Self-Management	Integrity/ Honesty	

Workplace Competencies

Resources	Allocating Time	Allocating Money	Allocating Material and Facility Resources	Allocating Human Resources		
Information	Acquiring and Evaluating Information	Organizing and Maintaining Information	Interpreting and Communicating Information	Using Computers to Process Information		
Interpersonal Skills	Participating as a Member of a Team	Teaching Others	Serving Clients/ Customers	Exercising Leadership	Negotiating to Arrive at a Decision	Working With Cultural Diversity
Systems	Understanding Systems	Monitoring and Correcting Performance	Improving and Designing Systems			
Technology	Selecting Technology	Applying Technology to Task	Maintaining and Troubleshooting Technology			

*This chart's highlighted blocks indicate the chapter's content coverage in the Student Edition and the Teacher Wraparound Edition.

Resource Manager

Teaching Transparencies

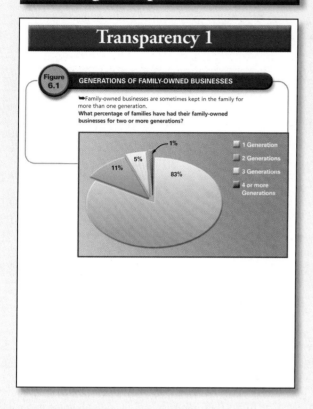

Transparency 1

Figure 6.1 — GENERATIONS OF FAMILY-OWNED BUSINESSES

Family-owned businesses are sometimes kept in the family for more than one generation.

What percentage of families have had their family-owned businesses for two or more generations?

- 1 Generation — 83%
- 2 Generations — 11%
- 3 Generations — 5%
- 4 or more Generations — 1%

Application and Enrichment

- 🖋 Lesson Plans
- 📙 *BusinessWeek* Poster Package
- 📑 Teaching Transparencies
- 💿🖋 Integrated Software Simulation
- 📼🖋 Glencoe Business Video Package

Review and Reinforcement

- 💿 *PuzzleMaker*
- 🖥🖋 Internet Resources
- 🖋 Student Activity Workbook
- 🖋 Strat. and Work. for Teaching Transparencies

Assessment and Evaluation

- 🖋 Reproducible Tests
- 🖋 Alternative Assessment Strategies
- 💿 ExamView® Pro Test Generator

Technology

- 💿 *PuzzleMaker*
- 💿 ExamView® Pro Test Generator
- 📼 Glencoe Business Video Package
- 💿 PowerPoint® Presentation
- 💿🖋 Integrated Software Simulation
- 💿 Interactive Lesson Planner
- 💿 *Virtual Business*®

KEY	🖋 Printed	💾 Software	📼 Videocassette	📙 Poster
	🖉 Transparency	💿 CD-ROM	🖥 Internet	

BUSINESS Online

Visit **www.introbus.glencoe.com**, the Web site companion to *Introduction to Business.* The student's page includes:

- interactive tutor
- additional *BusinessWeek* articles and activities
- business Web links
- homework hints
- real-world application activities
- additional career path activities

Information on how to prepare your students for the high school exit exam and special projects are also included.

Use the Glencoe Web site for additional resources. All essential content is covered in the Student Edition.

1 FOCUS

Introducing the Chapter

This chapter introduces the different forms of business ownership. It identifies the five main types of businesses. A photo essay, "Caution: Low-Flying Fish," enhances the concepts.

Connecting the Objectives

What are three forms of business ownership? Identify some different types of businesses, such as those producing raw goods, and so on.

BusinessWeek
Feature Story

Story's Summary

Instead of looking for capital or going public to grow small start-up companies, some business owners are taking the long view on expansion. To solve capital and technological limitations, entrepreneurs are selling their businesses to large companies. Negotiating positions for themselves high in the corporate ladder is integral to their strategy. This way they assure a future for both their companies and themselves.

Find the entire article at www.introbus.glencoe.com, or in the Teacher Resource Binder.

Business Ownership and Operations

Learning Objectives

After completing this chapter, you'll be able to:
1. **Name** business ownerships.
2. **Compare** the ownerships.
3. **Describe** alternative ways to do business.
4. **Identify** types of businesses.

Why It's Important

You need to understand business ownerships and operations before starting a business.

Key Words

sole proprietorship
unlimited liability
partnership
corporation
stock
limited liability
franchise
nonprofit organization
cooperative
producer
processors
manufacturers
intermediary
wholesaler
retailer

84

BusinessWeek Feature Story

Selling Out, Staying On

Grow Your Business by Selling It. Like any other mountain biker at a crossroads, Steve Christini, 28, relies on experience to choose the best path. In deciding which way to go in selling his mountain bike company, he relied on something else: a cold calculation of the chances Christini Technologies Inc. could ever, on its own, become the big, successful bike manufacturer he dreamed of.

Source: Excerpted with permission from "Selling Out, Staying On," *BusinessWeek Online*, November 6, 2000.

An Extension Activity

After a few teenagers saw your skateboard, they wanted to know where you got it. Fortunately, you and your friends made it. You all decide to manufacture a few of the new skateboards. One friend is the designer, and the other is going to handle marketing. They've asked (and you've agreed) to find investors. How do you go about finding financial investors?

BUSINESS Online
The Full Story
To learn more about Christini's business, visit the *Introduction to Business* Web site at www.introbus.glencoe.com, and click on *BusinessWeek* Feature Story, Chapter 6.

Classroom Resources

For the Teacher
- Student Activity Work. TAE
- Assessment Binder
- PowerPoint® Presentation
- Interactive Lesson Planner
- Lesson Plans
- Internet Resources
- Teaching Transparencies
- *Introduction to Business* Web Site
- Integrated Soft. Sim. TM
- *BusinessWeek* Poster Package

For the Student
- Student Activity Workbook
- *Virtual Business®*
- *Introduction to Business* Web Site
- Integrated Soft. Sim.
- *PuzzleMaker*
- Strategies and Worksheets for Teaching Transparencies

Bell Ringer Activity

REASONING. Write the types of businesses on the board as column headings—producers, processors, manufacturers, intermediaries, and services. Ask students to categorize local businesses according to type. Which businesses might be organized as sole proprietorships?

Preteaching Business Key Words

SPEAKING. Write the key words on the board. Ask for volunteers to explain where they have heard or seen the terms used. **LS**

An Extension Activity

PRESENT. Ask groups to give an oral presentation outlining their plan to find investors. **LS**, **CL**, **P**

Making Connections

Business World. Give students the following scenario and have them make inferences based on the observations. Observation: Doron noticed that a new shop called Bart's Bagels opened up two months ago. The shop is a block away from Doron's donut shop. Ever since Bart's Bagels opened, fewer customers have been coming into Doron's Donut shop. (Possible inference: Some of Doron's health-conscious customers may have started going to Bart's; however, students should mention that more information is needed.)

Business Connection

America is a land of solo entrepreneurs. In 1997, almost three-quarters of the nation's businesses had no paid employees. The nation's non-employers were mostly sole proprietorships but also included corporations and partnerships. According to the U.S. Census, California led solo businesses followed closely by the fishing states of Alaska and Maine.

Develop Concepts

ELEMENTS OF BUSINESS.
After years of working as an editor for a big city newspaper, Susan wants to start a community newspaper in her hometown. She has a little capital from savings and a business loan, but would like to raise more. She is also concerned about protecting herself from lawsuits because of the public and sometimes the controversial nature of newspapers. What type of business should Susan begin and why? (Forming a corporation would allow Susan to raise capital as well as limited liability.)

Figure 6.1 Caption Answer

Eleven percent have had the business for two or more generations.

Organizing a Business

Suppose you're a whiz at computer graphics or car repair and want to go into business. How do you want to set it up? Do you want to own and operate it yourself or go into business with a friend? Do you want to run your own multinational corporation? Starting a business is a real challenge. However, it's possible to lower the risk. Careful planning and analysis might help you bring your business right into focus. Consider your own skills, abilities, and potential market for your product or service. Describing your choice and the reasons for it is an important part of your business plan.

Types of Business Ownership

As your business expands, you might want to change the form of ownership. You have three different ways you can own a business: sole proprietorship, partnership, and incorporation.

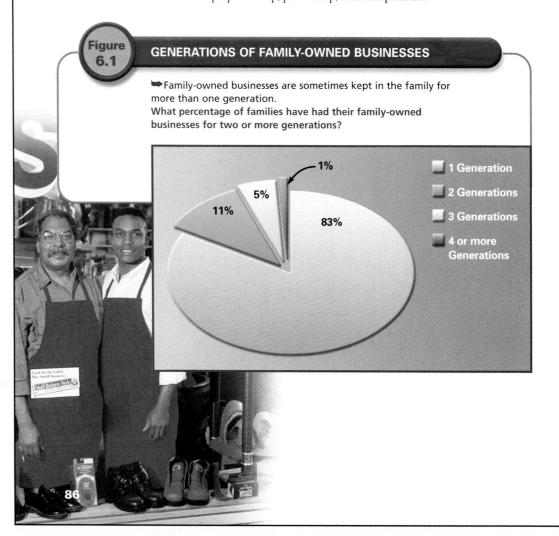

Figure 6.1

GENERATIONS OF FAMILY-OWNED BUSINESSES

➡ Family-owned businesses are sometimes kept in the family for more than one generation.
What percentage of families have had their family-owned businesses for two or more generations?

- 1% —
- 5%
- 11%
- 83%

- 1 Generation
- 2 Generations
- 3 Generations
- 4 or more Generations

86

Cooperative Learning

Types of Business. Have students work in groups to consider the business activities that occur prior to the purchasing of ingredients needed for baking chocolate chip cookies. (Agricultural producers would produce the wheat, eggs, dairy products, sugar, cocoa, and so on. Wheat, dairy products, cocoa, and sugar would all need to be processed. Manufacturers would package the goods, and a wholesaler or other intermediary would distribute the goods to a retail store where students could purchase the necessary ingredients.) Have groups make a poster showing the relationship between the different types of businesses. **CL**

Sole Proprietorship

A **sole proprietorship** is a business owned by only one person. It's especially suitable if you want to start a business that offers a specific product or service, like a car repair shop. Most bookstores and floral shops are sole proprietorships. So are most farms and home-based businesses. About three-quarters of all businesses in the United States are sole proprietorships. Figure 6.1 shows how many generations of family-owned businesses have been passed on.

Owning your own business is great. First of all, it's easy to start. Depending on the local laws, you might need only a license or permit to start a sole proprietorship. Second, you get to be your own boss. You can come and go as you please and run the business as you see fit. Third, you get to keep all the profits from the business yourself. Finally, the taxes are usually low because you only have to pay them on your personal profits.

On the other hand, there are disadvantages to running your own business. First, you have to pay for everything yourself. You have to buy your own supplies, pay for advertising, rent office space, and pay taxes. You might have to use your personal savings or borrow money from the bank to start your business or keep it going. A lot of sole proprietorships fail because they run out of capital.

You might also lack business skills. You might know everything about car repair but nothing about record keeping or tax preparation. You might need to hire an office manager or accountant to help you run your business.

A serious disadvantage to owning a sole proprietorship is that you have **unlimited liability**, or full responsibility for your company's debts. If you lose more money than you make, you have to make up the difference. You could lose your personal savings, your property, and even your car if your business has debts it cannot repay.

Partnership

Starting a sole proprietorship may sound risky to you. It might seem to be too much work for one person. If you don't have enough money to start a sole proprietorship, you could go into business with a partner. You could bring the idea and your partner could find the money. A **partnership** is a business owned by two or more persons who share the risks and rewards. More owners can contribute to the business. All partners who share in the business have good reason to work hard for its success, since they share the rewards. Like the income of a sole proprietorship, the income of a partnership is taxed only once.

To start a partnership you need to draw up a partnership agreement, which is a contract that outlines the rights and responsibilities of each

Chapter 6 Business Ownership and Operations **87**

Real-World Application

part 1 of 4

CAUTION: LOW-FLYING FISH
Nestled between the Waterfront on First and Pike, you'll find Seattle's famous Pike Place Market. Merchants, travelers, and regulars have frequented this open-air market since 1907. In 1973 the Pike Place Merchants Association (PPMA) became officially incorporated as a nonprofit membership organization. **What's the aim of joining forces and starting an organization?**

continued on p. 89

Chapter 6

Real-World Application
Caption Answer

CAUTION: LOW-FLYING FISH: PART 1 OF 4
To further the interests of its members, to represent the opinions and interests of its members, and to plan and implement activities in the interests of its members and the Market.

Technology Resource

GO TO **POWERPOINT.** The *Introduction to Business* PowerPoint® CD-ROM provides visual lecture aids for this chapter.

Independent Practice

WRITE. Sara and Charlie have decided to open a bed and breakfast. Sara is providing three-quarters of the capital. The other quarter is coming from Charlie, who will also be using his marketing prowess and equity to put the bed and breakfast on the map. List four issues that need to be included in their agreement. (How much money will each invest? How will they split profits? They also need to be clear about work schedules and finally, in the event of problems between them, how to end the partnership.) **LS**

Meeting Individual Needs

Students With Behavior Disorders. Students with behavior disorders can at times struggle to maintain the level of attention needed to deal with challenging material. To assist these students and encourage them to persist, you may wish to speak with them on an individual basis about their strengths and weaknesses. It might also be helpful at this time to outline chapter objectives with an eye toward helping them feel successful. This may require a flexible assessment program and enrichment material that capitalizes on their interests.

Thinking Critically

STRENGTH IN NUMBERS. An independent bookstore that has been in your town for 50 years is having difficulty making ends meet. The store is run as a sole proprietorship, so it's not a great candidate for a bank loan. The proprietor has come to you for help. Your job is to convince the proprietor *not* to start a corporation. What should he or she do instead? (A partner might be able to contribute capital and would enable the bookstore to get a loan. A partnership entails only a license, and taxes are required only on personal profits. Setting up a corporation is a little more complicated. The corporation has to pay taxes on its profits and the owners of the corporation have to pay income taxes.)

You Make the Call

Caption Answer

1. Advantages: keeping the profits and a great sense of achievement. Disadvantages: very hard work and a great responsibility.
2. Bring expertise and/or cash. Drawbacks include you're legally responsible if your partner makes a mistake.
3. No, you don't have an obligation to invite him to be a partner. No contract.

partner. If you decide to start a car repair business with your friends, Thelma and Ray, you need to agree on certain things. For example, how much money will each of you invest, and how will you share the profits? You also need to specify how to share the work and how to end the partnership. If Ray decides to leave the business, the partnership legally ends. Your partnership agreement should provide a way to buy Ray's share of the business so the business can continue.

There are several advantages to a partnership. Like a sole proprietorship, you might need only a license to start and have to pay taxes only on your personal profits. Unlike a sole proprietorship, it's easier to obtain capital. Each of your partners can contribute money to start the business. Banks are often more willing to lend money to partnerships than sole proprietorships.

Your partners can also bring different skills to the business. You might be best at fixing cars, Thelma at running the office, and Ray at getting new customers. The business can run more efficiently and each partner has an incentive to do a good job.

There are several disadvantages to a partnership. You not only share the risks with your partners, you also share the profits. You might not get along with Ray or Ray might decide to leave the business. In that case, you have to end the partnership and reorganize the business.

You also share unlimited legal and financial liability with your partners. If one partner makes a bad decision, all partners are equally responsible. A bad decision by one partner can result in the business losing money. All partners are responsible for debts that result from the person's bad decision. If Ray loses the company money by buying bad equipment, you have to share the debt. If Ray does something really

You Make the Call

Going Solo or Partnering Up?

It was raining one Thursday last November, so you and your best friend, Jeremiah, decided to try an experiment. You cooked up some packaging "peanuts" on your mother's stove and discovered they turn into a gummy matter that works wonders to cure a leaky faucet. You decide you'd like to sell some of this caulking material, which you'll call "Peanut Better." Jeremiah hears you talking to your business teacher about the new business and says he wants to be a partner.

Making an Ethical Decision

1. What are the advantages and disadvantages of "going solo" in a business venture?
2. How can having a partner help launch and grow a business? Are there any drawbacks?
3. Since Jeremiah was involved in the initial experiment, do you have an obligation to invite him to be a partner? What if he had been the one who decided to start the business without you?

88 Unit 2 Owning and Operating a Business

LANGUAGE ARTS

Curriculum Connection

Communication. Suggest that students look through recent issues of the *Business-Week* supplement, *Frontier*. Ask students to locate articles about sole proprietorships, partnerships, or corporations.

Ask students to write three paragraphs summarizing their findings, using business terms such as sole proprietorship, license, partnership, limited liability, stock, stockholder, and corporate charter.

stupid, like buying stolen equipment, you could end up sharing a jail cell with him.

Corporation

Suppose your car repair business has grown and you want to add more shops or buy new equipment. You need more capital but you don't want to borrow more money or bring on new partners. What you can do is form a corporation.

A **corporation** is a business owned by many people but treated by law as one person. It can own property, pay taxes, make contracts, and be sued just like a person. However, it exists separate from its owners.

To form a corporation, you need to get a corporate charter from the state your headquarters is in. A corporate charter is a license to run a corporation.

To raise money, you can sell **stock**, or shares of ownership in your corporation. The new owners (or stockholders) pay a set price for each share. For each share of common stock, the stockholder gets a share of the profits and a vote on how the business is run.

You also must have a board of directors who control the corporation. They don't actually run the day-to-day business operations of the company but they hire officers to do it. You get to pick the first board of directors, but each year the stockholders get to vote on them.

A major advantage of a corporation is its **limited liability**. If your company loses money, the stockholders lose only what they invested. Since your corporation exists separately from you, if it goes out of business you can't have your personal property or savings taken away from you.

Another advantage is that the corporation doesn't end if the owners sell their shares. As long as your business makes money, you can continue the company by reselling the shares. You can also raise more capital at any time by selling new shares.

A disadvantage of a corporation is that you often have to pay more taxes. The federal government and some state governments tax corporate profits. The owners are taxed on their income from the corporation. The corporation itself has to pay taxes. The government also closely regulates corporations. It's more difficult to start a corporation than a sole proprietorship or a partnership and running it can be much more complicated.

 Fast Review _____

1. What are some of the advantages of a sole proprietorship?
2. What is the difference between a sole proprietorship and a partnership?
3. If a partner makes a bad business decision, what responsibility do the other partners have?
4. What are the disadvantages of a corporation?

Real-World Application

CAUTION: LOW-FLYING FISH
At 86 Pike Place, you'll find the world-famous fish-flingers at Pike Place Fish. In 1965 John Yokoyama purchased it because he needed the money to make his car payments. **What's the benefit of going into business for yourself?**

continued on p. 91

Real-World Application
Caption Answer

CAUTION: LOW-FLYING FISH: PART 2 OF 4
Easy to start, can be your own boss, and you can keep all the profits of the business for yourself.

Fast Review Answers ✓

1. It's easy to start, you can be your own boss, you keep all the profits, and you pay taxes only once on the income from the business.
2. A sole proprietorship is owned by one person and a partnership is owned by two or more persons.
3. All other partners share responsibility of a bad decision.
4. It's more complex to start, it's more closely regulated by the government, it's more complicated to run, and you pay more in taxes.

Great Ideas From the Classroom of...

Angel Gonzalez
A. B. Miller High School
Fontana, Calif.

Hands-On Learning. The students prepare posters of the unit the teacher is working on. I provide supplies: giant Post-Its™, markers, rulers, etc. First, the teacher covers every topic in the unit. Next, students work in the classroom using instructional time to make a poster for one or two topics at a time. Then the posters are displayed in the classroom and the students can use them for reference. This creates a physical environment that engages students, promotes students' interest in learning goals, and connects prior knowledge and life experiences.

Business Connection

Wheat is grown in many areas of the world. China is the biggest producer of the crop, with the United States only producing 20 percent of the world's wheat export market. Over 40 of our 50 states produce wheat with most of the crop coming from producers in North Dakota. In contrast, the United States produces the largest corn crop in the world at 231 million tons. Most corn producers are located in Iowa, Illinois, and Nebraska.

Develop Concepts

ECONOMIC DRIVERS. Part of our economy relies on the production of products to export to other countries. Give one example of the following: producer, processor, and manufacturer. (Producer—agriculture or mining; Processor—paper mills or refineries; Manufacturer—makes bread out of flour.)

Discussion Starter

NAMING. Ask students to name a franchise. (Taco Bell, Holiday Inn, McDonald's, Burger King, Baskin-Robbins, Wendy's.) Ask students to name two examples of cooperatives. (Ocean Spray, Welches, Ace Hardware.) Ask students to identify a nonprofit organization in their community.

90

Alternative Ways to Do Business

You might find it easier to start a business with the help of an established company. You could also start a business by pooling your resources with other businesses. Maybe you're more interested in providing a service to your community than you're into making a profit. Franchises, cooperatives, and nonprofit organizations offer you other ways to do business.

Franchise

A **franchise** is a contractual agreement to sell a company's products or services in a designated geographic area. You probably have several franchises in your neighborhood, such as Taco Bell. If you decide to open a Blockbuster video store, you're the franchisee. Blockbuster, the existing or parent company, is the franchisor.

To run a franchise you have to invest money and pay the franchisor an annual fee or a share of the profits. In return, the franchisor offers a well-known name and a business plan. It provides management training, advertising, and a system of operation. You can operate a franchise yourself, as a sole proprietor, as a partnership with someone else, or even as a corporation.

An advantage of opening a franchise is that it's easy to start. You can rely on the proven methods and product of the parent company. The name of the parent company can be a big draw for customers. When someone wants to rent a video, they often go to the nearest Blockbuster store.

The disadvantage of running a franchise is that the franchisor is often very strict about how the business is run. Your business must operate like every other franchise. You might be limited in what products or services you can offer your customers. If you want to start a business but lack business know-how, however, you might want to choose a franchise.

Nonprofit Organization

Not everyone goes into business just to make a profit. You might want to start a business whose main purpose is to help children, the poor, local artists, or animals. A **nonprofit organization** is a type of business that focuses on providing a service rather than making a profit. The Children's Television Workshop, the American Red Cross, and Meals on Wheels are nonprofit organizations. Private hospitals, schools, and museums can also be set up that way.

Like a corporation, a nonprofit organization has to register with the government and might be run by a board of directors. Because it doesn't make a profit, however, it doesn't have to pay taxes. Instead of investors, nonprofit organizations rely on government grants and on donations from businesses and individuals. Donors don't receive dividends like investors, but they can deduct their donations from their taxes.

Consider This...

Manufacturing Products
Compaq Computers and Cisco Systems don't build their own products anymore. These companies rely on Flextonics, a company that specializes in manufacturing electronics, to build their equipment. This allows Compaq and Cisco to focus on creating new products. Flextonics has grown into a global contractor that produces $10.5 billion a year in electronic gizmos.
ANALYZE
What do Compaq Computers and Cisco Systems give up when they rely on an outside manufacturer?

90 Unit 2 Owning and Operating a Business

Global Perspective

Types of Ownership. McDonald's, one of the world's largest multinational companies, chooses from several structuring options for its overseas operations. In Europe, the company enters the European market with a wholly owned subsidiary, a company owned by McDonald's but with its own management and board of directors.

In Asia, the burger giant prefers partnerships. In some Middle-Eastern markets, the company uses no equity capital but licenses its name with strict restrictions. Ask students to discuss the advantages the different management options McDonald's offers.

Cooperative

A **cooperative** is an organization owned and operated by its members for the purpose of saving money on the purchase of certain goods and services. For example, Ocean Spray is a cooperative of cranberry growers. A cooperative is like a corporation in that it exists as a separate entity from the individual businesses. You also need a government charter to start one. Like a corporation, a cooperative can also sell stock and choose a board of directors to run it.

With a cooperative, small farmers, book dealers, or antique merchants can pool their resources. They can save money by buying insurance, supplies, and advertising as a group. They can share factory facilities and warehouse space. Cooperatives also pay less in taxes than regular corporations do. Other examples of cooperatives are Ace Hardware and Welch's.

 Fast Review _____

1. What are some examples of franchise businesses?
2. What types of assistance does the franchisor give a franchisee?
3. How is a nonprofit organization like and unlike a corporation?
4. What are some advantages of a cooperative?

Types of Businesses

After school you go to a fast-food restaurant with some friends to get a hamburger. Before you take a bite out of that burger you might stop to consider how much work it took to get it to you. Selling it over the counter is the tip of the iceberg. Before that the food had to be grown, processed, manufactured, refined, transported, and stored by different types of businesses.

There are many different types of businesses and different ways to classify them. One way is to group them by the kind of products they provide:

- producing raw goods
- processing raw goods
- manufacturing goods from raw or processed goods
- distributing goods
- providing services

Producers

A **producer** is a business that gathers raw products in their natural state. Raw goods are materials gathered in their original state from natural

CAUTION: LOW-FLYING FISH

Pike Place Fish didn't become world famous by advertising. (Instead a Spike Lee Levi's commercial, NBC's *Frasier*, and MTV's *Real World* helped expose the market.) Pike Place prides itself on interacting with the people. The staff wants to give each person a memorable experience. **Can a business have a contractual agreement with its customers?**

continued on p. 93

Real-World Application
Caption Answer

CAUTION: LOW-FLYING FISH: PART 3 OF 4

Yes. Its service is designed to intrigue customers and sell products.

Individualized Practice

Ask students to identify two national nonprofit organizations.

L1 Divide students in pairs and ask them to come up with some ideas on what service one of the national nonprofits provides.

L2 Ask students in pairs to conceptualize a new nonprofit organization in their community. What are the tenets of their organization?

L3 Name three ways their organization's services would benefit the community.

Fast Review Answers

1. Fast-food restaurants, video stores, photocopy services, and ice cream stores.
2. Management training, advertising, and a system of operation.
3. Alike: needs to register with the government and might be run by a board of directors. Unlike: doesn't pay taxes and gets money through grants and donations.
4. Pool resources and save money as a group.

HISTORY | *Curriculum Connection*

Two Proprietorships. Two of the original thirteen colonies established in colonial America were proprietorships. Have students research the Pennsylvania colony or the Maryland colony to find out why these two states were originally established as proprietorships, who granted the proprietorships, and who was the primary beneficiary of the arrangements.

3 ASSESS

Reteaching

DEFINE. To reteach the three forms of business ownership, ask students to define the following: sole proprietorship, partnership, and corporation. (Sole proprietorship is a business owned by only one person. A partnership is owned by two or more persons. A corporation is owned by many but treated by law as one person.)

Enrichment Strategy

IDENTIFY. Ask students to recall two disadvantages of the different types of business ownership. (Sole proprietorship—expenses, unlimited liability; partnership—shared profits, unlimited liability; corporation—pay more taxes, government regulations.) **LS**

Working Lifestyle

Caption Answer

Journalist, photojournalist, mechanic, teacher, designer, TV producer, actor, etc.

---

resources such as land or water. A farmer who grows wheat in Kansas is a producer. So is a miner who digs for iron ore in Minnesota and a petroleum worker who drills for crude oil in Alaska. Industries that are producers include agriculture, mining, fishing, and forestry. Business firms that perform activities of this sort are producers of raw goods.

Processors

Most of the time we don't use raw goods in the same form they're found in nature. **Processors** change raw materials into more finished products. They're involved in the processing of raw goods. Processing goods are made from raw goods that may require further processing. For example, wheat is turned into flour, crude oil into gasoline, and iron ore into steel. Paper mills, oil refineries, and smelting plants are types of businesses that process raw goods. Their products, processed goods, are made from raw materials that may require further processing.

Working Lifestyle

What are you doing at 10 A.M.?

The Fast-Paced Circle

"Just when you become an expert on a system, everything changes again and you start learning all over again," says Sunny Kim. This applications specialist for 21st Century Insurance tries to balance a fast-paced career, her family, and attending continuing education courses.

"It's a vicious cycle of knowledge," Kim says. "There's always a challenge to learn a new system and to be aware of how things might change." That's why it's especially important to specialize in one area. Then together with a team of other technology specialists, they interact and contribute to the company's information network.

At 10 A.M. Kim and the other system experts discuss the tasks for the week. Today it's about data storage—they're the ones who will continue creating the "paperless processing" environment. Information never stops. She makes it seamlessly arrive on time for the company to utilize.

Salary

The median income for an applications specialist is $40,000, with a range between $38,000 and $50,000.

Outlook for This Career

This job group is expecting rapid growth among all computer-related occupations.

Connecting Careers Activity

What other occupations require working in a fast-paced environment?

CAREER PATH   *Information Technology*

How to Use a Portfolio Activity

The portfolio projects are designed to lead students to develop a collection of their best work to submit to you for assessment. You and each of your students should decide which projects to include in their business portfolio. Refer students to the specific rubric(s) from the *Alternative Assessment Strategies.* These rubrics will alert students to the criteria you'll use to assess their projects.

Manufacturers

Manufacturers are businesses that make finished products out of processed goods. They turn raw or processed goods into finished goods that require no further processing and that are ready for the market. A bakery makes bread out of flour. An automotive plant makes cars out of steel, glass, and plastic. A furniture factory makes tables out of lumber. Many of the leading businesses in the United States are manufacturers; others are producers and processors. Boeing, Pepsi Co, General Electric, Procter & Gamble, and Eastman Kodak are examples of leading manufacturers in their industry.

Intermediaries

An **intermediary** is a business that moves goods from one business to another. It buys goods, stores them, and then resells them. A **wholesaler**, also known as a distributor, distributes goods. Wholesalers buy goods from manufacturers in huge quantities and resell them in smaller quantities to their customers, usually other companies. The clothing wholesaler, for example, may buy thousands of jackets from several manufacturers. The wholesaler then divides the large quantities into smaller quantities and sells them to retailers. A **retailer** purchases goods from a wholesaler and resells them to the consumer, or the final buyer of the goods. It's another type of business that moves goods. Service stations, record stores, and auto dealers are examples of retailers.

Service Businesses

Service businesses provide services rather than goods. Goods are material products such as cars, CDs, and computers. Services are the products of a skill or an activity such as hairstyling and car repair. Some service businesses meet needs, such as medical clinics and law firms. Some provide conveniences, such as taxi companies and copy shops. Newspapers and Internet services, such as Yahoo!, give us access to information. Service businesses employ about three-quarters of the workforce and are rapidly increasing in numbers.

✔ Fast Review

1. What is the difference between a producer and a processor?
2. What does a manufacturer do with raw or processed goods?
3. What does an intermediary do?
4. Give examples of service businesses.

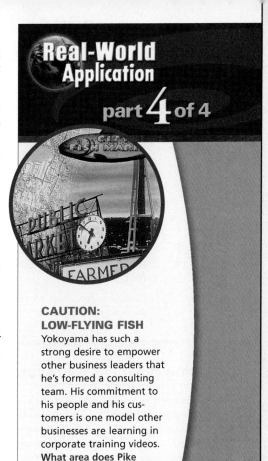

Real-World Application

part 4 of 4

CAUTION: LOW-FLYING FISH
Yokoyama has such a strong desire to empower other business leaders that he's formed a consulting team. His commitment to his people and his customers is one model other businesses are learning in corporate training videos. What area does Pike Place Fish focus on other than fish?

Real-World Application Caption Answer

CAUTION: LOW-FLYING FISH: PART 4 OF 4
Its staff and customers.

Technology Resource

GO TO **VIRTUAL BUSINESS.** Introduce business ownership by using Knowledge Matters' *Virtual Business* interactive simulation. Go to the *Introduction to Business* Web site **www.introbus.glencoe.com** to download the *Virtual Business* activity. Run the *Virtual Business* tutorial before beginning this activity.

Evaluation

Assign and review the Fast Review sections.

Fast Review Answers ✔

1. Producer—gathers or creates raw products. Processor—changes raw products into more finished products.
2. Turns raw or processed goods into finished products.
3. Moves products between businesses or between businesses and the public.
4. Hairstylists, car repair shops, copy shops, law firms, newspapers, Internet services, and taxi companies.

Meeting Individual Needs

Gifted. For students who would benefit from the additional work of an independent project, have them research a successful business in the area. What decision was made about the form of ownership? Did the form of ownership change? What were the advantages and disadvantages of this form of ownership? Students will conduct interviews in order to write a report on their findings.

4 CLOSE

Chapter Wrap-Up

Ask questions for a class bingo activity with the answers being key words and other concepts in this chapter.

Using Business Key Words

1. partnership
2. stock
3. intermediary
4. sole proprietorship
5. corporation
6. processors
7. manufacturers
8. unlimited liability
9. limited liability
10. franchise
11. nonprofit organization
12. cooperative
13. producer
14. wholesaler
15. retailer

Review What You Learned

16. It's simple to start; owner makes decisions; profits aren't divided; the owner pays taxes only once on the profit.
17. At least two; no.
18. The owners are responsible for debt.
19. Legally ended.
20. Its limited liability.
21. Producer—gathers or creates raw products in their natural state. Processors change the raw material into more finished products. Manufacturers—finish products out of the processed goods. Intermediaries move the products.
22. A middleman.
23. 75 percent.

Summary

1. Three types of business ownership are sole proprietorship, partnership, and corporation.

2. Each type of business ownership has its advantages and disadvantages. A sole proprietorship is easier to start than a partnership or corporation. On the other hand, it's easier to obtain capital if you're in a partnership rather than a sole proprietorship. Corporations are more difficult to start than sole proprietorship and partnership.

3. A franchise, nonprofit organization, and cooperative are alternative ways of doing business.

4. Producers, processors, manufacturers, intermediaries and service businesses are types of businesses that treat products differently.

Using Business Key Words

Complete each sentence with the correct term.

- **sole proprietorship**
- **partnership**
- **corporation**
- **intermediary**
- **cooperative**
- **unlimited liability**
- **limited liability**
- **nonprofit organization**
- **wholesaler**
- **processors**
- **manufacturers**
- **franchise**
- **producer**
- **retailer**
- **stock**

1. A _____ is a business organization with two or more owners who share the risks and rewards.
2. Shares of ownership in a corporation are called _____.
3. A _____ buys and resells goods.
4. A business owned by one person is called a _____.
5. A business that is treated by law as a separate entity is a _____.
6. Businesses that change raw goods into more finished products are called _____.
7. _____ turn raw or processed goods into finished products.
8. _____ is full legal and financial responsibility for a business.
9. _____ is financial responsibility only for what the owners of a corporation have invested.
10. A contractual agreement to sell a company's products or services in a designated geographic area is a _____.
11. A business whose main purpose is to provide a service rather than to earn a profit is called a _____.
12. _____ is a group of small businesses banded together into a type of corporation.
13. A _____ is a business that gathers raw products in their natural state.
14. A type of business that buys goods in large amounts and resells them to other businesses in smaller lots is called a _____.
15. A type of business that buys goods from wholesalers or manufacturers and sells them directly to the public is called a _____.

Quick Quiz

1. Name three advantages of starting a corporation. (The corporation can own property, pay taxes, and make contracts but exists separate from its owners. The ability to raise capital. Limited liability.)

2. In what ways are nonprofit organizations and corporations similar? (They both are required to register with government. They can be run by a board of directors.)

3. What does an intermediary do? (It moves products between businesses and the public. It also buys, stores, and resells goods.)

Review What You Learned

16. List four advantages of a business organized as a sole proprietorship.
17. How many people must be involved in a partnership? Is there a limit on the number of partners a business can have?
18. Sole proprietorships and partnerships both have unlimited liability for their business debts. What does that mean to the owners?
19. What happens when a partner leaves the business or dies?
20. What is the major advantage of a corporation? Explain your answer.
21. Describe the differences between producers, processors, manufacturers, and intermediaries.
22. What is another name for an intermediary?
23. Currently, service businesses employ what percentage of the workforce?

Understanding Business Concepts

24. What do you consider to be the biggest disadvantage of a sole proprietorship?
25. Why would two or more people decide to form a partnership instead of forming a sole proprietorship with one of them as the owner?
26. There are more sole proprietorships than partnerships or corporations in the United States. Why do you think so many businesses are organized this way?
27. What is the major way a corporation is different from a sole proprietorship or partnership?
28. Give three examples each of raw goods and processed goods.
29. Think of one of your favorite food products. Describe the raw materials that make up the food, how it might have been processed and then manufactured into the food you enjoy.

Critical Thinking

30. Which of the types of businesses described in this chapter would have the easiest time obtaining money to expand their business? Why?
31. Why do many people believe that profits on sales of finished goods are much higher than they actually are?
32. Describe the steps involved in making a hamburger.
33. Have you ever purchased a defective product? Did you exchange or return the product? Do you think the defective product cost the producer money? Why or why not?

Viewing and Representing

Examining the Image. Describe the contents of this photograph. What does the photographer want the viewer to think or feel? If you and your family ran a wholesale bait business, would you run it as a sole proprietorship or as a corporation? Why? What kind of wholesale business would you be interested in running?

Chapter 6 Business Ownership and Operations **95**

4 CLOSE (Cont.)

Building Academic Skills

LANGUAGE ARTS. If a student doesn't know a sole proprietor, help him or her locate one. If potential interviewees are limited, have the students work in groups. Rubric: Essay.

COMPUTER/TECHNOLOGY. If students don't have experience reading the stock listings, you'll have to provide instruction. Let students choose the method they use to share their results. Rubrics: Charts, oral presentations, note taking.

MATH. Bread: 3.49 × .25 = 0.87; Chocolate cake: 6.99 × .25 = 1.75; Sugar cookies: 3.99 × .25 = 1.00; Apple pie: 4.75 × .25 = 1.19.

SOCIAL SCIENCE. Make sure all students participate in the group project. Students will need to use the library or the Internet to find out what countries were part of the process. Rubrics: Bulletin board, chart, note taking.

Linking School to Home

Answers will vary. Instead of a family member, student could ask a friend to work on the project with him or her. Let students choose the method they use to share their results. Rubrics: Note taking, essay, oral presentation.

Linking School to Work

Make sure all students have questions ready for the panel. Rubrics: Note taking, essay.

Building Academic Skills

 Profiling an Owner

Interview a local sole proprietor about what he or she enjoys and finds difficult in running his or her own business. Discuss the advantages and disadvantages of a sole proprietorship with the owner, then write a profile of the business owner.

 Charting and Comparing

Suppose you have $1,000 to invest. Check the stock listings in your newspaper and choose one or more corporations in which to invest your money. Follow the daily progress of your own stock in the newspaper for one week. Then use graphing software to create a graph showing whether your stock went up or down in value. Compare your stock selection with others in your class.

 Percentage

The neighborhood bakery makes bread, cakes, cookies, and pies. At the end of the day, all the leftover products are reduced by 75 percent. What will the reduced prices be for the following:

Bread	$3.49
Chocolate cake	$6.99
One dozen sugar cookies	$3.99
Apple pie	$4.75

 Research

In a group, prepare a bulletin board or a large chart tracking the route of an item from raw material to the consumer product. On the display, showcase the country or countries that have been a part of the process.

Linking School to Home

Inventory and Interview. Create an inventory of the products and services you and your family use that are produced by small businesses or entrepreneurs. Categorize them by family member. Then, interview each family member and find out why he or she purchases the products and services from the small business or entrepreneur. Compile your results and share them with the class.

Linking School to Work

Guest Speakers. Invite local businesspersons representing sole proprietorships, partnerships, and corporations to serve on a panel discussion in your class. Ask them to share:
- advantages and disadvantages of each type of business ownership
- how they got their start
- qualities they feel are important to the success of the particular type of business ownership they represent

Have questions ready when the panel members arrive. Be sure to thank them for their time.

E-Homework

Applying Technology

Convenient Technology. Computers, personal digital assistants, pagers, and cell phones are tools routinely used in the business world today. Explain whether this technology is as critical to the sole proprietor as it's to a corporation with many stockholders.

Creating a Database. Compile a database of local businesses in which you include fields for the name, address, the telephone number, and the category of business—producer, processor, manufacturer, or intermediary. Use the local Yellow Pages to locate the information. Try to find at least one business in each category and include a minimum of ten businesses. Print out your database. If you can't find a local business in one of the categories, explain why you think this might be so.

Connecting Academics

Math. Draw a circle graph to give a visual representation comparing percentages of the forms of ownership of small businesses. Use the following statistics: corporations 22 percent, partnerships 7 percent, and sole proprietorships 71 percent. Color your graph. What is the most popular form of business ownership? What might be the reason for this?

Language Arts. What interests you most? Choose a form of business ownership or a type of business—from producers to service businesses—to research important details. Create a visual display connected to your chosen topic. Present an oral report to your class.

BusinessWeek — Analyzing the Feature Story

You read the first part of "Selling Out, Staying On" at the beginning of this chapter. Below are a few questions for you to answer about Christini's business. You'll find the answers to these questions when you're reading the entire article. First, here are the questions:

34. What made Christini's business idea suitable for a sole proprietorship?
35. What disadvantage of sole proprietorships was behind Christini and other sole proprietors' decisions to sell their company?

CREATIVE JOURNAL ACTIVITY

An alternative form of business to a sole proprietorship or corporation is a franchise. What questions do you have about how a franchise is run?

BUSINESS Online

The Full Story

To learn more about Christini's business, visit the *Introduction to Business* Web site at **www.introbus.glencoe.com**, and click on *BusinessWeek* Feature Story, Chapter 6.

E-Homework

CONVENIENT TECHNOLOGY. Answers will vary. Encourage students to think about the issue thoroughly. Rubrics: Essay, oral presentation.

CREATING A DATABASE. Databases will vary. Rubrics: Database, charts/tables.

Connecting Academics

MATH. Sole proprietorships, with 71 percent this form of business ownership is the largest segment of the circle. They are simple to start.

LANGUAGE ARTS. Answers will vary. Visual displays can be made up of free-form drawings, photographs, and magazine pictures. Encourage enthusiasm in the oral report. After students pre-sent their topic, ask them why they chose this topic.

BusinessWeek — Analyzing the Feature Story

34. Christini was starting a business that offered a unique product that he knew how to make.
35. Christini and other sole proprietors sometimes sell their businesses to larger corporations because it is difficult to raise enough capital to grow their businesses on their own.

Creative Journal Activity

Questions will vary. Have the class form small groups to conduct an in-depth interview of a franchise owner in the community. Encourage students to ask the owners what advantages and disadvantages they face owning their franchises. **CL**, LS

SCANS Correlation Chart*

Foundation Skills

Basic Skills	Reading	Writing	Math	Listening	Speaking	
Thinking Skills	Creative Thinking	Decision Making	Problem Solving	Seeing Things in the Mind's Eye	Knowing How to Learn	Reasoning
Personal Qualities	Responsibility	Self-Esteem	Sociability	Self-Management	Integrity/Honesty	

Workplace Competencies

Resources	Allocating Time	Allocating Money	Allocating Material and Facility Resources	Allocating Human Resources		
Information	Acquiring and Evaluating Information	Organizing and Maintaining Information	Interpreting and Communicating Information	Using Computers to Process Information		
Interpersonal Skills	Participating as a Member of a Team	Teaching Others	Serving Clients/Customers	Exercising Leadership	Negotiating to Arrive at a Decision	Working With Cultural Diversity
Systems	Understanding Systems	Monitoring and Correcting Performance	Improving and Designing Systems			
Technology	Selecting Technology	Applying Technology to Task	Maintaining and Troubleshooting Technology			

*This chart's highlighted blocks indicate the chapter's content coverage in the Student Edition and the Teacher Wraparound Edition.

Resource Manager

Teaching Transparencies

Transparency 1

Transparency 2

Application and Enrichment

- Lesson Plans
- *BusinessWeek* Poster Package
- Teaching Transparencies
- Integrated Software Simulation
- Glencoe Business Video Package

Review and Reinforcement

- *PuzzleMaker*
- Internet Resources
- Student Activity Workbook
- Strat. and Work. for Teaching Transparencies

Assessment and Evaluation

- Reproducible Tests
- Alternative Assessment Strategies
- ExamView® Pro Test Generator

Technology

- *PuzzleMaker*
- ExamView® Pro Test Generator
- Glencoe Business Video Package
- PowerPoint® Presentation
- Integrated Software Simulation
- Interactive Lesson Planner
- *Virtual Business*®

KEY	Printed	Software	Videocassette	Poster
	Transparency	CD-ROM	Internet	

BUSINESS Online

Visit www.introbus.glencoe.com, the Web site companion to *Introduction to Business.* The student's page includes:

- interactive tutor
- additional *BusinessWeek* articles and activities
- business Web links
- homework hints
- real-world application activities
- additional career path activities

Information on how to prepare your students for the high school exit exam and special projects are also included.

Use the Glencoe Web site for additional resources. All essential content is covered in the Student Edition.

1 FOCUS

Introducing the Chapter

This chapter discusses managerial structures, as well as levels and functions of management. A photo essay, "The Unmanagement Style of Gore," enhances the concepts.

Connecting the Objectives

Have students explain what they know about different roles managers play in different business organizations. Does management mean the same as leadership?

BusinessWeek
Feature Story

Story's Summary

Comparing the management structure of industrial giant Proctor & Gamble Co. to tiny Plumtree Software Inc., is like comparing an elephant to a gazelle. One-hundred-sixty-year-old P&G has a "slow and heavy" corporate culture governed by rules. Brash young management at four-year-old Plumtree quickly deals with any problems.

Find the entire article at **www.introbus.glencoe.com**, or in the Teacher Resource Binder.

Chapter 7

Organizational Structures

● Learning Objectives

After completing this chapter, you'll be able to:
1. **Explain** how businesses organize for management.
2. **List** three levels of management and compare their responsibilities.
3. **Name** the four functions of management.
4. **Analyze** if a managerial position is for you.

● Why It's Important

Understanding business organization and management is key to knowing how a company is run.

● Key Words

management plan
organizational chart
line authority
centralized organization
decentralized organization
departmentalization
top-level managers
middle managers
operational managers

98

BusinessWeek Feature Story

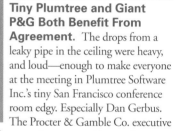

A Fruitful Relationship

Tiny Plumtree and Giant P&G Both Benefit From Agreement. The drops from a leaky pipe in the ceiling were heavy, and loud—enough to make everyone at the meeting in Plumtree Software Inc.'s tiny San Francisco conference room edgy. Especially Dan Gerbus. The Procter & Gamble Co. executive flew into San Francisco that morning to meet Plumtree's managers for the first time. He wondered if P&G, with an annual revenue of $38 billion, was crazy to trust a multimillion-dollar software project to a company with only ten customers, and led by executives who just three years before had been hashing out a business plan in a Berkeley (Calif.) boarding house.

Source: Excerpted with permission from "A Fruitful Relationship," *BusinessWeek Online*, November 20, 2000.

An Extension Activity

Why do you think Procter & Gamble hired an outside firm to get it "wired" as opposed to keeping the project in-house?

The Full Story

To learn more about business organizations, visit the *Introduction to Business* Web site at **www.introbus.glencoe.com**, and click on *BusinessWeek* Feature Story, Chapter 7.

Classroom Resources

For the Teacher
- 📁 Student Activity Work. TAE
- 📓💿 Assessment Binder
- 💿 PowerPoint® Presentation
- 💿 Interactive Lesson Planner
- 📁 Lesson Plans
- 📓💻 Internet Resources
- Teaching Transparencies
- *Introduction to Business* Web Site

- 💿 Integrated Soft. Sim. TM
- 📘 *BusinessWeek* Poster Package

For the Student
- 📓 Student Activity Workbook
- 💿 *Virtual Business®*
- *Introduction to Business* Web Site
- 💿 Integrated Soft. Sim.
- 💿 *PuzzleMaker*
- 📓 Strategies and Worksheets for Teaching Transparencies

UNDERSTANDING SYSTEMS. What is the organizational structure of your school? With student input, create an organization chart on the board. Start with a box representing the principal, or district. Include all aspects of the school, such as the cafeteria, security, and plant maintenance. (An example of an organization chart is shown in Figure 7.2. Refer to this chart during exploration of this chapter.)

Preteaching Business Key Words

SERVING CLIENTS/ CUSTOMERS. Assign half the class to be customer service representatives and half the class to be customers. Have the customers go to a service representative. The representative should smile and say, "How can I help you?" The customers need to find out the meaning of a key word and take notes. The customer service representative looks up the definition of the key word in the glossary and helps the customer understand the key word. The customer should smile, say "Thank you," and move on to a different representative for each key word.

An Extension Activity

Cost efficiency, opportunity cost, expertise, etc.

Making Connections

World of Work. Have students practice the function of organizing—coordinating activities and resources—by giving them the following scenario: You are a manager in charge of demonstrating your company's new telephone system to small groups of employees. Break down the task into steps and indicate what resources you will need to get the job done. (Possible answer: Reserve a time and meeting room for the demonstration; enlist an assistant to help; notify group members of the time, place, and nature of the demonstration; prepare and make copies of an instruction sheet to hand out.)

2 TEACH

Business Connection

United Parcel Service (UPS) management believed that on-time delivery was its first concern. It studied every move. It even sawed off the corners of the drivers' van seats so delivery people could hit the pavement faster. These factors were taken into account to expedite deliveries and make on-time schedules. Surveys, however, showed that customers often had questions for drivers and felt frustrated by UPS's rigid schedule. Top-level management listened to its customers and now allows its drivers time to answer questions or talk with customers.

Develop Concepts

MANAGEMENT ORGANIZATION. George Roberts Architecture made the decision to streamline business and foster creativity. They hired a junior architect and five other associates to handle administrative, graphic support, and marketing. It organized the company around projects and worked in teams. Define its organizational style. (Informal, decentralized.)

Figure 7.1 · Caption Answer

Joint venture actions include protecting, restoring, and enhancing the wetland habitats. Individuals, corporations, conservation organizations, local, state, and federal agencies can help.

Organizing for Management

Suppose you've created your own comic book and want to start a comic book company. Do you want to produce comic books or market and distribute them as well? Do you also want to produce cartoons, video games, and action figures based on your comic books? Either way, you'll need some type of organization.

As a successful business owner, you'll want to accomplish your goals. Your business needs some form of organization that identifies who is responsible for which tasks. Usually a manager directs and coordinates the activities of the workers and deals with any problems that might arise.

Managerial Structures

Any business that employs more than one person needs a management plan. A **management plan** divides a company into different departments run by different managers. Managers direct workers, coordinate activities, and solve problems that might occur. Figure 7.1 asks you to examine how a management plan helps nature. Companies use an **organizational chart** to show how the business is structured

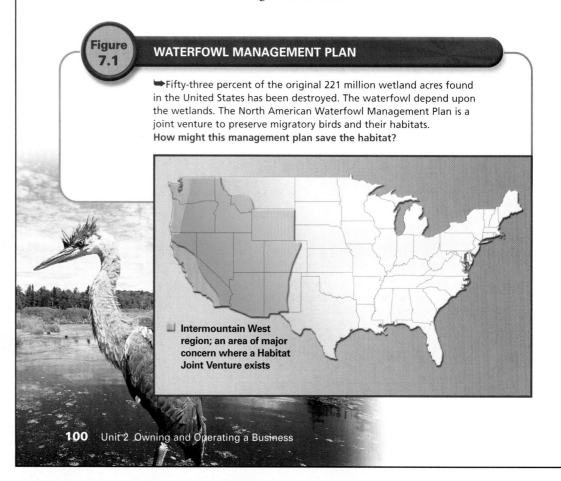

Figure 7.1

WATERFOWL MANAGEMENT PLAN

➡Fifty-three percent of the original 221 million wetland acres found in the United States has been destroyed. The waterfowl depend upon the wetlands. The North American Waterfowl Management Plan is a joint venture to preserve migratory birds and their habitats. **How might this management plan save the habitat?**

◻ Intermountain West region; an area of major concern where a Habitat Joint Venture exists

100 Unit 2 Owning and Operating a Business

Cooperative Learning

Regroup Management. You read about George Roberts Architecture's management decisions to streamline business and foster creativity. Ask students to form pairs to reorganize the firm into a formal, centralized system. Have students draw the new organizational structure. (Robert and George are top managers, the other architect is middle manager, computer and business department personnel are operational managers, and administrative personnel are workers.) **CL**, LS

and who is in charge of whom. In some companies, one person is in charge, and in others, several people might be in charge.

One way to organize management is called **line authority**. The managers at the top of the line are in charge of those beneath them, and so on. **Centralized organization** puts authority in one place, with top management.

Pretend you'd like to run all aspects of your comic book company yourself but it's too much for one person. **Decentralized organization** gives authority to a number of different managers to run their own departments. For example, you might have one person run the production department and another person in charge of marketing.

Formal Structure

Formal structures are usually departmentalized. **Departmentalization** divides responsibility among specific units, or departments. Departments can be organized by what they do, what they make, or by region.

Your comic book's distribution department, for example, is responsible for shipping your product. If your company also produces cartoons and advertisements, you might have a separate department for each. Suppose your company markets comic books nationwide. You'll need managers to run offices in different parts of the country. The Coca-Cola Company markets Coca-Cola® not only in the country but also throughout the world. In each country they have a regional manager who knows his or her market best.

Informal Structure

Smaller businesses can be run more informally. If a business doesn't need a big marketing or distribution network, it doesn't need a lot of managers. The employees can be more flexible and share the duties.

Suppose you decide to publish comic books over the Internet with a couple of partners. One partner is better at computer graphics and the other is better at writing. You can work on projects alone or collaborate on each other's projects. Each week you meet with your partners to plan work on your projects. The informal structure works better for you than having one person in charge.

 Fast Review _____

1. How does a centralized organization differ from a decentralized organization?
2. Give an example of departmentalization.

Chapter 7 Organizational Structures **101**

Real-World Application

part 1 of 4

Creative Technologies Worldwide

THE UNMANAGEMENT STYLE OF GORE
W. L. Gore & Associates, Inc., makers of GORE-TEX®, breaks all the corporate rules with its organizational structure. Bill and Vieve Gore created the lattice organization.
How do you suppose a lattice organization is run?

continued on p. 103

Real-World Application
Caption Answer

THE UNMANAGEMENT STYLE OF GORE: PART 1 OF 4

There is no fixed or assigned authority.

Technology Resource

GO TO **POWERPOINT.** The *Introduction to Business* PowerPoint® CD-ROM provides visual lecture aids for this chapter.

Independent Practice

DIAGRAM. Ask students to diagram possible scenarios for the architecture firm's informal organization. Three architects have three support personnel—administrative, marketing, and graphic. Two other employees operate the company's computer system and business department. Identify top management—who is responsible for setting goals and planning the future? Who are middle and operational managers? **LS**

Fast Review Answers

1. Centralized organization places authority in one place. Decentralized gives authority to many.
2. Sales, marketing, inventory, production, etc.

Meeting Individual Needs

Second Language Learners. If your class includes second language learners, provide outlines of lecture notes or planned classroom discussion topics in advance. Written materials help reinforce what you say. They also make it possible for the student to review materials later on their own time. Keep in mind how you would feel if you suddenly found yourself as a student in another country whose language was only marginally familiar to you. Lecture notes help you comprehend the discussions going on in class. **ELL**

2 TEACH (Cont.)

Thinking Critically

PROBLEM SOLVING. You're a management specialist. A company hired you to solve a problem of disgruntled employees missing deadlines. What level of managers would you talk to first and why? (Answers will vary. One possible answer: Operational managers who are in charge of overseeing workers and meeting deadlines.)

Business Building Blocks

CAPTION ANSWER

After the post-improv discussion, ask students the question: In business, what might be some constraints? (Money, time, talent, resources, and resistance to change.)

Levels of Management

Every aspect of business has to be managed from setting goals to meeting them. Your long-range goal is not only to produce comic books. You also want to produce cartoons, video games, and action figures. You'll need managers to run each division and oversee the day-to-day operations of each division. Most businesses have three levels of managers: top-level managers, middle managers, and operational managers.

Top-level managers are responsible for setting goals and planning for the future. They have titles like president, vice president, and chief executive officer (CEO). Top management usually consists of a small group of people, or even one person. Lucasfilm Ltd., which produced the *Star Wars* movies, has several different divisions. However, George Lucas alone runs the company.

Middle managers carry out the decisions of top management. They include plant managers, regional managers, and department heads. They're responsible for planning and controlling an operation. The person in charge of development for your video game department is a middle manager.

Operational managers are responsible for the daily operations of the business. Supervisors, office managers, and crew leaders are types of operational managers. Their duties include overseeing workers and meeting

Business Building Blocks

Communication

Developing Teamwork

In business, collaboration is key. Working in a team requires flexibility, creativity, good communication, and shared goals. In fact, those characteristics also describe *improvisation*—to arrange something offhand. To accomplish a goal in a company, people must work together.

Practice

1. You and three others are "actors" in an improvisational skit.
2. You can only communicate by asking questions. You and other actors are trying to decide whether or not to check into a sleazy hotel for your vacation.
3. Two actors will communicate at a

time. If one makes a statement rather than asking questions, he or she must step aside and the next person takes over immediately.
4. After five minutes, analyze how you and your fellow actors developed communication skills.

Tips on "*Improv*ing" Your Teamwork

- Working as a team is better than working separately.
- Listen to each other as you brainstorm for solutions.
- Engage in problem solving while creating and offering solutions within constraints.

LANGUAGE ARTS

Curriculum Connection

Communication. Michiko Owada, a manager at Rossville Telecommunications, consults his electronic "to do" list (see the bulleted list). Give students Owada's list and have them rank the tasks according to priority. Students should explain why they set the priorities as they did.

- Get figures and statistics from accounting so budget can be finished. Due Friday!
- Start planning script for presentation to management in two weeks.
- Interview candidate for job at 11:00— review candidate's qualifications beforehand.
- Check e-mail.
- Sift through 60 résumés and set up two interviews for next week.

deadlines. The supervisor of your accounting department is an operational manager.

1. What are three levels of management?
2. Which of the three levels is most involved in the day-to-day supervision of employees?

Managerial Functions

To meet the goals of your company you need good management. A good manager doesn't just pass on orders. A good manager has four different functions: planning, organizing, leading, and controlling.

Some decisions are routine, such as setting deadlines. Some are risky, such as marketing a new product. Sometimes long-term goals have to be changed because of short-term problems. Managers need to make decisions at all four levels.

Planning

Good planning requires setting realistic goals. Suppose your comic books are a big success and you want to branch off into cartoons, video games, and toys. You can't expect to produce them overnight and have them sell well. First, you need to see if there's a big enough market for them. You have to find out what kind of technology to use, and how long it will take to produce them.

Long-range planning involves top-level management deciding how the company should perform. As part of the planning process, management must answer the following key questions:
- What must be done?
- Who will do it?
- How will the work be grouped?
- Who supervises whom?
- Who makes decisions about the work to be done?

These questions are applied and answered when you get together with your management team. The team decides your plan to market a variety of products is too ambitious. You decide on a more realistic plan of only producing a cartoon show. If the show is a big success, then you can consider producing video games and action figures.

Organizing

To organize a business plan you need to assign managers different tasks and coordinate their activities. One manager is in charge of video production and one is in charge of marketing. Another manager is in charge

Chapter 7 Organizational Structures **103**

Real-World Application

part **2** of 4

THE UNMANAGEMENT STYLE OF GORE
The Gore corporate culture has no chain of command, no pre-determined channels of communication. Instead, the staff communicates directly with each other. There is no hierarchy. **What are the benefits of such a management style?**

continued on p. 105

 Real-World Application
Caption Answer

THE UNMANAGEMENT STYLE OF GORE: PART 2 OF 4
Each person gets to interact directly with each person, with no intermediary.

Fast Review Answers ✔

1. Top-level, middle-level, and operational.
2. Operational managers.

Business Connection

Corporate America's top-level managers are some of the most powerful people in the world—and the richest. In a recent year, America's 800 top chief executive officers (CEOs) made more than $5.8 billion combined. Fifty-five-year-old Charles Wang topped the list at $650 million. Next up was Foundry Networks' Bobby R. Johnson, who at the age of 43 made $230 million.

Great Ideas From the Classroom of...

Susan Case
South Beloit High School
South Beloit, Ill.

Department Managers. I teach students how managers must understand costs allocated to their department and how to fill out purchase orders. Break the class into groups of three to four students. Give each group catalogs and purchase order forms. I give groups a budget of $5,000 with which they must furnish an office for their new department. They must purchase appropriate furniture, equipment, and supplies while staying within budget. I grade based on accuracy, appropriate spending, and neatness.

2 TEACH (Cont.)

Develop Concepts

MANAGERIAL FUNCTIONS.
Ask students what they think are the major responsibilities of the cafeteria manager at your school. List their responses on the board. Ask students to categorize the responsibilities listed into planning, organizing, leading, and controlling. **LS**

Discussion Starter

BRAINSTORMING. What are important qualities of strong leaders in business? (Creative vision and the ability to set standards, provide guidance, resolve conflicts, train employees, offer incentives, and help each individual work to his or her potential.)

Figure 7.2 Caption Answer

Organizing.

---

of the budget. Each manager needs to organize his or her department and know what the other managers are doing. Your production manager has to decide whether to set up a small studio or hire an existing one overseas. Your marketing director has to do some research to decide whether your cartoons will sell well in the United States or Japan. Both managers need to know how much money they have in the budget to carry out their tasks.

You also need to determine who makes decisions and who answers to whom. Can some managers make decisions for themselves or do they have to report to you? Figure 7.2 demonstrates the managerial functions in a graphic organizer.

Leading

Good management also requires good leadership. There's more to leading than just giving orders. You have to create a vision of your company to inspire your employees. You need to set standards, such as deadlines and sales quotas, so your managers know their goals. You need to communicate with them to provide guidance and resolve conflicts. Some employees might need training. Others might be self-motivated and work better on their own.

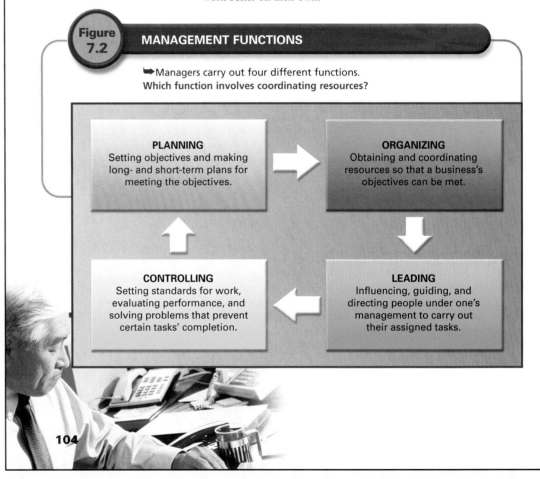

Figure 7.2 MANAGEMENT FUNCTIONS

➡ Managers carry out four different functions. Which function involves coordinating resources?

PLANNING
Setting objectives and making long- and short-term plans for meeting the objectives.

ORGANIZING
Obtaining and coordinating resources so that a business's objectives can be met.

CONTROLLING
Setting standards for work, evaluating performance, and solving problems that prevent certain tasks' completion.

LEADING
Influencing, guiding, and directing people under one's management to carry out their assigned tasks.

104

Global Perspective

Cause-and-Effect Diagram. Since World War II, Japanese managers have focused on improving the quality of products by identifying and solving problems in each phase of production. One tool Japanese managers have developed is a cause-and-effect diagram, in which they identify a problem and list all of the probable causes of that problem. Invite students to create their own cause-and-effect diagrams. Encourage creative diagram design. Have them identify a problem (for example, failure to complete an assignment on time). They should list all possible causes and think of one or more ways to eliminate each cause of the problem. Have them identify possible solutions, select the best solution, and evaluate the solution.

You especially want to encourage your employees. Most companies offer incentives such as pay raises and promotions. Some companies, like Intel and Wal-Mart, offer stock options and profit sharing to their employees so they feel like they have a stake in the company. The primary objective of a good manager is to help each person in the company work to his or her potential.

Controlling

Controlling means keeping the company on track and making sure all goals are met. You have to keep track of the budget, the schedule, and the quality of the product. You also have to monitor your employees and review their performance. Suppose your first cartoon comes in ahead of schedule and it looks great. You might want to reward your production manager with a pay raise or a day off.

On the other hand, sometimes things don't go according to plan. Your first cartoon just came in over-budget and it looks awful. You need to find out what went wrong and fix it. You might have to fire your production manager or find a new studio.

Controlling also involves monitoring customer satisfaction. Your marketing manager can measure the success of your cartoon by studying sales charts and ratings. You might find out your show did well on television but did poorly on video. If your show was more popular with adults than children you might want to come up with a new marketing plan.

 Fast Review

1. What are the four functions of management?
2. What is a manager's objective in leading?

Is Being a Manager for You?

Most managers begin their career as a company employee and are promoted after they have gained experience and have shown certain qualities.
- *Ability to perform varied activities.* Managers usually have many tasks to perform at one time. Managers have to plan their time and decide which tasks are the most important at any one time.
- *Ability to work under pressure.* A manager often has to solve many small problems in a fairly short time. For example, a supervisor may have to organize next week's work schedule, solve a production problem, and train two new employees—all in the same workday. Also included might be attending one meeting, writing seven letters, and skimming four industry periodicals.

Chapter 7 Organizational Structures **105**

THE UNMANAGEMENT STYLE OF GORE
Gore hires associates (not employees) to work on general projects. Within the guidance of sponsors (not bosses) a team is formed. **What are some challenges a Gore team might encounter?**

continued on p. 107

Real-World Application
Caption Answer

THE UNMANAGEMENT STYLE OF GORE: PART 3 OF 4
Objectives need to be well defined, decisions must be made, people must know each other, and compensation must be fair in order for everyone to work equally hard.

Individualized Practice

Have students set up a hypothetical college or high school using the three levels of management as a guide.

L1 Students identify the three levels of management and their responsibilities. Ask students to name one goal of the school. (High-quality education.)

L2 Students explain the goals of the school.

L3 Students describe in detail the operational managers' responsibilities, who they report to, and how they interface with the rest of educational management (e.g., the school). (Teachers usually report to a department chairman or operate under the umbrella of the administration in a decentralized manner.)

Curriculum Connection

 MATH

Budget. A budget is one of the plans a manager makes. A manager at a bicycle manufacturer needs to hire new employees because of an increase in orders. The budget for employees' wages each week will be $4,000. Currently, four employees work 40 hours/week and earn $18/hour. New employees will be hired at $13/hour.

How many employees can be hired without going over budget? (Current wages are $18 \times 40 = \$720 \times 4$ employees $= \$2,880$. Money left for wages for new employees is $\$4,000 - \$2,880 = \$1,120$. Wage for one new employee is $\$13 \times 40 = \$520$. Wages for two new employees are $\$520 \times 2 = \$1,040$. Two new employees can be hired.)

Fast Review Answers

1. Planning, organizing, leading, and controlling.
2. Maximize potential.

2 TEACH (Cont.)

Writing for Business

CAPTION ANSWER

After the students have completed one path, ask them to imagine a career as the person they chose—either the hired consultant or the personnel director. Would they like to do that job? Why or why not?

3 ASSESS

Reteaching

FUNCTIONS OF MANAGEMENT. To reteach the concept of the four functions of management, have students create a chart outlining the four levels of management and the major responsibilities for each.
(Planning: setting realistic goals. Organizing: who and how to implement change. Leadership: setting standards, providing training, inspiration, and guidance. Controlling: keeping budget and quality control on track.)

Writing for Business

Portfolio Activity

Assess and Reorganize

This activity gives you the chance to add to your portfolio. Communicate, interview, research, and write your way into a story. Choose one imaginary path, Hired Consultant or Personnel Director. Follow your path's steps to complete your own story.

pick a path

Hired Consultant

The Setting. The vice president of operations at a tractor-manufacturing company has called you, a consultant. She needs your help in reorganizing the company's managerial positions.

Rising Action. You've never consulted on this type of job before, but you need the money so you cannot turn it down.

Step 1. Call or write to the personnel department of a large corporation. Ask for information about the company's organizational structure.

Step 2. Create a graphic illustration of how the different managerial levels relate.

Step 3. Using this graphic as a model, write brief job descriptions for each managerial position as it relates specifically to the tractor-manufacturing company.

Personnel Director

The Setting. You're the personnel director at a tractor-manufacturing corporation. The company wants to open a manufacturing plant in northern Mexico.

Rising Action. You know the company needs to address issues about global growth. You need to consider the company's organization, wages, and working conditions as they relate to Mexico.

Step 1. Read recent articles about the globalization of American corporations.

Step 2. Prepare a memo to your boss, the vice president of operations. The memo outlines your recommendations about offering fair wages and working conditions abroad.

Step 3. Lastly, explain in the memo how your recommendations benefit the corporation as well as its employees.

Conclusion

Now it's time to reflect on your choice. Take a few minutes to write a note to your teacher about the path. Briefly explain why you chose it and what you learned from researching and writing it. Attach this note to your assignment.

How to Use a Portfolio Activity

The portfolio projects are designed to lead students to develop a collection of their best work to submit to you for assessment. You and each of your students should decide which projects to include in their business portfolio. Refer students to the specific rubric(s) from the *Alternative Assessment Strategies*. These rubrics will alert students to the criteria you'll use to assess their projects.

- *Effective communication.* Every manager has to communicate well. Communicating might be done on the telephone, by fax, or e-mail, in individual or group meetings, or in a written report or a letter. Listening is also an important part of communication. Most of a manager's day is spent interacting with other people.
- *Interpersonal skills.* Managers work with people and need human relations skills, or skills in dealing with people. For example, a manager may be asked to resolve conflicts among employees.
- *Ability to gather and use information.* Managers must be aware of the events and forces in the global market that affect their business. For example, some managers read local and national newspapers daily. They may also use online services to access international news relating to their company's various markets or products.

If you were offered a job with management responsibilities, would you take it? To help you decide, consider some of the advantages and disadvantages.

Advantages

Managers usually earn more money than employees in non-management jobs. People become managers because they're leaders, and good leaders are respected. So, being a manager has prestige. Because managers are leaders, they have more influence than other employees on how the company is run. That is, managers have more authority than other employees do in planning, organizing, directing, controlling, and evaluating company resources. Managers have varied duties and make decisions about many kinds of things. Managers also have greater control over their time and how they'll spend it.

Disadvantages

Managers get the blame when things go wrong, even if another employee caused the problem. Managers are also often targets for criticism. When managers do make mistakes, they can be more costly than other employees' mistakes because their decisions affect many workers. Managers get a lot of pressure to do things right the first time. Finally, some managers feel their relationship with lower-level employees is different than their relationship with fellow managers. Employees are often careful of what they say or do when their manager is around for fear of jeopardizing their jobs.

 Fast Review

1. What are five qualities or skills a manager should have?
2. What are the advantages and disadvantages of being a manager?

THE UNMANAGEMENT STYLE OF GORE
At Gore, everyone will try to be fair, committed, and encourage freedom. Associates are to consult with one another before taking action that might be "below the waterline" and cause serious damage to the company.
What does this saying mean?

Meeting Individual Needs

Students With Visual Impairments.
Coping with the volume of printed material in class can be a challenge for students with visual impairments. To meet this challenge, these students often use a combination of resources, such as readers, books in braille, recorded books, and class lectures. To make lectures more helpful to students with visual impairments, think carefully about what you say in class. Use examples that are clear and specific. Sensitivity to student needs is the key.

4 CLOSE

Chapter Wrap-Up

To close, ask students to complete the following statement: The three most important things I learned during this chapter are (1) _____, (2) _____, and (3) _____.

Using Business Key Words

1. middle managers
2. management plan
3. centralized organization
4. decentralized organization
5. operational managers
6. top-level managers
7. departmentalization
8. organizational chart
9. line authority

Review What You Learned

10. It can be traced in a line from the top of an organization to the bottom.
11. Lower-level managers.
12. By function, by product, or by location.
13. They set goals and plan for the future.
14. Middle managers carry out the decisions of top management. Operational managers are responsible for the daily operations of the business.
15. Planning, organizing, leading, and controlling.
16. Setting realistic goals.
17. It involves creating a vision of your company to inspire employees, setting goals for your managers, communicating, providing guidance and resolving conflicts, teaching, encouraging, and helping each employee reach his or her potential.

Summary

1. Businesses may be organized with authority focused in one place (centralized) or with authority in a number of units (decentralized).

2.
LEVEL OF MANAGEMENT	RESPONSIBILITIES
Top-Level Manager	Set goals and plan for the future.
Middle Manager	Carry out decisions of top management. Planning and controlling an operation.
Operational Manager	Oversee daily operations of business. Manage staff. Meet deadlines.

3. Managers plan, organize, lead, and control.

4. Successful managers are able to carry out varied tasks, perform under pressure, communicate effectively, relate to people, and grasp and use information. Managers have prestige, influence, and power; however, they usually experience a lot of pressure too.

Using Business Key Words

When discussing management and how businesses are organized, it's helpful to know the following terms. Match each term with its definition.

- **centralized organization**
- **middle managers**
- **decentralized organization**
- **management plan**
- **operational managers**
- **organizational chart**
- **line authority**
- **departmentalization**
- **top-level managers**

1. Managers who carry out the decisions of top management.
2. A business plan that divides a company into different departments run by different managers.
3. Authority lies in one place.
4. Authority lies with several different managers.
5. Supervisors, office managers, and crew leaders are examples of this type of manager.
6. Plant managers, regional managers, and department heads are examples of this type of manager.
7. A way of organization that subdivides responsibilities by specific units.
8. A chart that shows how a business is structured and who is in charge of whom.
9. An organizational structure in which managers at the top of the line are in charge of those beneath them.

Quick Quiz

1. What is the primary goal of departmentalization? (To divide responsibility.)
2. What level of management is responsible for setting goals and planning for the future? (Top-level management.)
3. What are the four functions of good management? (Planning, organizing, leading, and controlling.)

Review What You Learned

10. What is line authority, and how does it look on an organizational chart?

11. Who has the decision-making authority in a decentralized organization?

12. Describe the three different ways in which departments are organized.

13. What are the primary responsibilities of top-level managers?

14. What is the difference between middle managers and operational managers?

15. Name the four managerial functions.

16. What does good planning require?

17. Describe the function of leading and how it affects a manager's job.

Understanding Business Concepts

18. What are some of the differences between a business that has a formal organization and one that is informally organized?

19. Why do managers at all levels need to communicate well?

20. Describe the management function of organizing.

21. What is the primary objective of a good manager?

Critical Thinking

22. Would you choose to work in a formally or informally structured organization? Explain why.

23. Describe the ideal manager that you would like to work for someday.

24. Amazon.com and Toys "Я" Us decided to work together to sell toys over the Internet. What decisions would executives from each company have to consider in order to successfully complete this alliance?

25. Business organizations that are run by women are more likely to:
  a. Grow quickly.
  b. Take financial risks.
  c. Place less emphasis on who is in charge.
  d. Or all of the above.

Viewing and Representing

Examining the Image. Team up with a partner. What details do you see in this photograph? What people and objects are shown? Decide whether the organization shown is centralized or decentralized. Explain your reason. Do you feel you would enjoy working in this organization? Why?

Chapter 7 Organizational Structures **109**

Critical Thinking

22. Answers will vary depending on the students' analysis of formal and informal structures.

23. Answers will vary.

24. Executives from both companies first met and created a chart of the strengths, weaknesses, and challenges of an alliance. Then the companies had to agree on how much Amazon.com would be paid for each time a customer went to the Toys "Я" Us Web site. After the deal was signed, the two companies had to teach employees about how the alliance worked.

25. Answer: C. Researchers say women are less focused on hierarchy. They are more inclined to describe themselves as the center of a hub rather than the top of a ladder.

Viewing and Representing

This short activity, with its visual component, can stimulate students' interest and promote practice in results-oriented teamwork. Answers will vary. Invite pairs of students to share their answers with the class.

Understanding Business Concepts

18. In a formal organization, it's very clear how each part of the business should function. In an informal organization, the structure is flexible; people don't always do the same work.

19. Because they interact with people all day.

20. Organizing involves assigning managers different tasks and coordinating their activities.

21. To help each person in the company work to his or her potential.

Chapter **7** Review

4 CLOSE (Cont.)

Building Academic Skills

LANGUAGE ARTS. Make sure both partners get a chance to play each role. Rubric: Note taking.

COMPUTER/TECHNOLOGY. If your school is very large, make a school handbook or directory available to the students. Rubrics: Charts/tables.

HISTORY. Remind students that both large and small companies have top-level management. They may bring in articles about decisions made by the management of smaller, local businesses. Rubrics: Paragraph, oral presentation.

MATH. Make sure all group members participate. Rubrics: Lists, note taking.

Linking School to Home

Projects will vary. Allow students to use pictures of the logos or draw their own. Rubric: Poster.

Linking School to Work

Students' answers will vary. Rubric: Essay.

● Building Academic Skills

 Brainstorming

Work with a partner and imagine that one of you is the manager and the other is an employee. Choose two business situations that a manager must be able to deal with. Each of you should take the role of the manager in one of the situations you chose. After you have acted out the situation, discuss the skills you used. Draw up a list of the management responsibilities and skills that you and your partner think are important for handling the situations you examined.

 Creating a Graphic

Using computer software, create an organizational chart of the administration of your school. Explain what type of organization it has.

 Decision Making

Top-level managers make major decisions and establish company objectives. For example, top-level managers at Coca-Cola® decided several years ago to introduce a "new Coke" with a slightly different recipe. It was a disaster. Consumers didn't like it. So top management decided to bring back the original, calling it "Coca-Cola® Classic." Research a similar top-level management decision. In a short paragraph, summarize the management decision and its effect(s) on the company.

 Exploring Math Skills

Working in groups of three or four, create a list of all the math skills that are needed by managers at each level. Give a detailed explanation of how each skill would be used on the job. As a class, combine the lists.

● Linking School to Home

Family Members' Workplace. Ask a family member how his or her workplace is organized. How is the management structured? Create a poster summarizing your findings.

● Linking School to Work

Functions of Management. Interview a manager from a local business to find out how he or she uses leadership skills to manage people and resources on the job. Use the following questions as a guide when you interview the manager:

- What must be done?
- Who will do it?
- How will the work be grouped?
- Who supervises whom?
- Who makes decisions about the work to be done?

Also, ask the manager what percentage of his or her time is spent on each of the four functions of management (i.e., planning, organizing, leading, and controlling). Then, using the information you have obtained, write a 250-word report.

E-Homework

Applying Technology

Pie Chart. Using the information you obtained from the Linking School to Work activity, create a pie chart demonstrating the percentage breakdown of the four management functions for the manager you interviewed. Title the chart and include the company name, product, and manager's title. Also, carefully label the sections of the chart. Write a short caption for the chart explaining the percentage breakdown. Print out the finished product.

Organization Chart. Work in small groups. Imagine you start a greeting card company. Decide what functions your team members will perform, taking into account the talents and interests of individuals. Will your company be structured formally or informally? Make a chart using presentation software to show how you organized your company. Present your chart to the class.

Connecting Academics

Math. You're a delivery manager at Blue Bag Bakery, a wholesale bakery. The bakery employs two drivers and owns two trucks. Each truck can deliver up to 175 crates of bread a day. The bakery usually has orders for 340 crates a day from local supermarkets, schools, and hospitals. A new supermarket is opening soon and you expect orders to increase 225 percent. How many trucks and drivers will you need to cover your new deliveries?

Math. Fran, merchandise manager for Blue Bag, is planning her department's yearly budget. Fran is in charge of three employees, each earning $350 a week. Fran earns $500 a week. The business pays social security taxes of 8.15 percent on employee earnings for social security taxes.

How much money does Fran need to enter in her department's budget to cover salaries and taxes for the year?

BusinessWeek Analyzing the Feature Story

You read the first part of "A Fruitful Relationship" at the beginning of this chapter. Below are a few questions for you to answer about Plumtree and Proctor & Gamble's business organizations. You'll find the answers to these questions when you're reading the entire article. First, here are the questions:

26. How do Plumtree and Proctor & Gamble's business organizations differ?
27. What management skills did Gerbus of P & G use to make the alliance with Plumtree a success?

CREATIVE JOURNAL ACTIVITY

What kind of organization would you like to work in? Should it have a formal or informal structure? Write a short description of the ideal business environment for you.

BUSINESS Online
The Full Story

To learn more about Plumtree and Proctor & Gamble's business organizations, visit the *Introduction to Business* Web site at **www.introbus.glencoe.com**, and click on *BusinessWeek* Feature Story, Chapter 7.

E-Homework

PIE CHART. Students may want to use a color printer if one is available to color code the sections of their graph. Rubrics: Essay, graphs.

ORGANIZATION CHART. Answers will vary. Allow the students to share their findings with the class. Rubrics: Note taking, oral presentation, essay.

Connecting Academics

MATH. $340 \times 2.25 = 765$ crates. $765 \div 175$ crates $= 4.37$. That is five trucks and five drivers in all are needed.

MATH. $(\$350 \times 3) + \$500 = \$1550$. $\$1550 \times 0.0815 = \$126.33$. Salaries and taxes for the week: $\$1550 + \$126.33 = \$1676.33$. Salaries and taxes for the year: $\$1676.33 \times 52 = \$87,169.16$.

BusinessWeek *Analyzing the Feature Story*

26. Differ in structure and culture. P&G is a large company with a formal, departmentalized structure. Plumtree has an informal structure.
27. Provided them with a private office and took them out to dinner.

Creative Journal Activity

Find out if students have strong feelings about the type of organizational structure they want to work in. Let students know that when they interview for a job, they might ask the interviewer: "Is this a formal or informal business environment?" **LS**

SCANS Correlation Chart*

Foundation Skills

Basic Skills	Reading	Writing	Math	Listening	Speaking	
Thinking Skills	Creative Thinking	Decision Making	Problem Solving	Seeing Things in the Mind's Eye	Knowing How to Learn	Reasoning
Personal Qualities	Responsibility	Self-Esteem	Sociability	Self-Management	Integrity/ Honesty	

Workplace Competencies

Resources	Allocating Time	Allocating Money	Allocating Material and Facility Resources	Allocating Human Resources		
Information	Acquiring and Evaluating Information	Organizing and Maintaining Information	Interpreting and Communicating Information	Using Computers to Process Information		
Interpersonal Skills	Participating as a Member of a Team	Teaching Others	Serving Clients/ Customers	Exercising Leadership	Negotiating to Arrive at a Decision	Working With Cultural Diversity
Systems	Understanding Systems	Monitoring and Correcting Performance	Improving and Designing Systems			
Technology	Selecting Technology	Applying Technology to Task	Maintaining and Troubleshooting Technology			

*This chart's highlighted blocks indicate the chapter's content coverage in the Student Edition and the Teacher Wraparound Edition.

Resource Manager

Teaching Transparencies

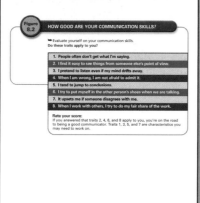

Application and Enrichment

- Lesson Plans
- *BusinessWeek* Poster Package
- Teaching Transparencies
- Integrated Software Simulation
- Glencoe Business Video Package

Review and Reinforcement

- *PuzzleMaker*
- Internet Resources
- Student Activity Workbook
- Strat. and Work. for Teaching Transparencies

Assessment and Evaluation

- Reproducible Tests
- Alternative Assessment Strategies
- ExamView® Pro Test Generator

Technology

- *PuzzleMaker*
- ExamView® Pro Test Generator
- Glencoe Business Video Package
- PowerPoint® Presentation
- Integrated Software Simulation
- Interactive Lesson Planner
- *Virtual Business*®

KEY	✍ Printed	💾 Software	📼 Videocassette	📕 Poster
	🕹 Transparency	💿 CD-ROM	💻 Internet	

Visit **www.introbus.glencoe.com**, the Web site companion to *Introduction to Business.* The student's page includes:

- interactive tutor
- additional *BusinessWeek* articles and activities
- business Web links
- homework hints
- real-world application activities
- additional career path activities

Information on how to prepare your students for the high school exit exam and special projects are also included.

Use the Glencoe Web site for additional resources. All essential content is covered in the Student Edition.

1 FOCUS

Introducing the Chapter

This chapter describes leadership qualities and styles of leadership. A photo essay, "Leading the Pack," enhances the concepts.

Connecting the Objectives

What are the qualities of a good leader? What different styles of leadership are there?

BusinessWeek
Feature Story

Story's Summary

Chief executive officers (CEOs) of the future will need to be able to communicate globally, be Web savvy, and address social issues. For their companies to succeed in the fast-paced business world, CEOs will need the efforts of everyone in their company. CEOs will need to model themselves after directors of symphony orchestras—set a vision and then allow each individual artist to contribute to the performance.

Find the entire article at www.introbus.glencoe.com, or in the Teacher Resource Binder.

Chapter 8

Leadership in Management

Learning Objectives

After completing this chapter, you'll be able to:
1. **Describe** the difference between a manager and a leader.
2. **Name** the qualities needed to be a leader.
3. **Identify** the three styles of leadership.
4. **Illustrate** the advantages of working in teams.

Why It's Important

Managers need to recognize leadership qualities and leadership styles that motivate employees to be creative and productive.

Key Words

leadership
initiative
human relations
integrity
autocratic leadership
democratic leadership
free-rein leadership
delegating
self-managed teams

112

BusinessWeek Feature Story
The Boss in the Web Age

Communicate, Comprise, Think Globally—And Do It Fast. Ask a chief executive officer what the job will be like in the year 2020, and the CEO is apt to give the reply, "Who knows?" With the drop-dead pace of technological upheaval, it's hard enough to scope out the business landscape three months from now, let alone two decades. But by the time today's ambitious, twenty something dot-com entrepreneurs reach middle age and settle into the role of running multibillion-dollar operations, the corner office will hardly be recognizable.

Source: Excerpted with permission from "The Boss in the Web Age," *BusinessWeek Online*, August 28, 2000.

An Extension Activity

Vision motivates people by providing them a direction toward goals. Give an example from your life when a leader inspired you. How did this person's inspiration influence you?

BUSINESS Online
The Full Story
To learn more about business leadership, visit the *Introduction to Business* Web site at www.introbus.glencoe.com, and click on *BusinessWeek* Feature Story, Chapter 8.

Classroom Resources

For the Teacher
- Student Activity Work. TAE
- Assessment Binder
- PowerPoint® Presentation
- Interactive Lesson Planner
- Lesson Plans
- Internet Resources
- Teaching Transparencies
- *Introduction to Business* Web Site
- Integrated Soft. Sim. TM
- *BusinessWeek* Poster Package

For the Student
- Student Activity Workbook
- *Virtual Business®*
- *Introduction to Business* Web Site
- Integrated Soft. Sim.
- *PuzzleMaker*
- Strategies and Worksheets for Teaching Transparencies

Bell Ringer Activity

EXERCISING LEADERSHIP.
Write this assignment on the board: Write a list of experiences you have had when you were the leader. Write a sentence that mentions three qualities you're proud of that you used as a leader. Ask students to read their statements and make a list on the board of the leadership qualities they mention.

Preteaching Business Key Words

INTERPRETING AND COMMUNICATING INFORMATION.
Imagine you've been asked by your supervisor at work to present a three to five minute speech on leadership. Decide what main points you want the audience to know. Use all of this chapter's key words in your talk. Emphasize the differences between an autocratic, democratic, and free-rein leader. Write a paragraph or have notes ready to make your presentation on leadership. **LS, CL**

An Extension Activity

SHARE. Ask students to share their stories.

Making Connections

Learning Techniques. Remind students that many people are visual learners. To aid their learning on leadership, announce to students that they will draw a poster-size graphic organizer. Suggest students use the main headings of this chapter to prepare the diagram or chart to use as a tool to organize the information they will encounter in the chapter. **LS, ELL**

2 TEACH

Business Connection

SUPPORT THE ARTS. Experts predict the new generation of business leaders will need eclectic skills like speed, flexibility, and charm as well as humor, spontaneity, and a genuine concern for employee well being. The old pillars of marketing and finance will always remain, but a new emphasis on the importance of a diverse background like a liberal arts education may help encourage compassion.

Develop Concepts

SEEK LEADERSHIP. Have students identify real-world examples of a leader. (Martin Luther King, former President John Kennedy, and so on.) What qualities do these leaders share? (Displayed integrity, great communicators, intellectually quick and inspired confidence, passion, and motivation.) Ask students to discuss the differences they see between leaders and managers. (Managing is a job; leading is a skill. Managers focus on tasks. Leaders have vision.)

Figure 8.1 Caption Answer

All three statements are false. People can be trained in leadership skills. Leaders are found at all levels of management and within all ranks of employees. If a "boss" is a person who orders people around, a boss isn't a true leader.

The Future of Leadership

You've probably been in a group situation where one person wants to take charge. That person might want to lead for the wrong reasons—to order everyone else around or for personal gain. Others often play "follow the leader" because they just want to be told what to do. There's more to leadership than just being in charge. The business world is faced with many challenges in the twenty-first century. The expanding vision of global business and technology affects organizations, people, and production. Management is focusing on turning individuals into cooperative team members to create and follow through with the company's vision.

Leadership Qualities

In management, **leadership** means providing direction and vision for a company. Test your leadership knowledge in Figure 8.1. Being a manager isn't the same thing as being a leader. Managing is a job. Leading is a skill. Managers focus on specific tasks and make sure the work gets done. They give orders and carry out orders. Leaders have vision. They see the big picture and never lose sight of their goal. They manage others by inspiring them rather than ordering them.

It's possible to be a good manager but not a good leader. Sometimes a good leader isn't even the person in charge. For example, Warren Sapp of the Tampa Bay Buccaneers football team is a defensive lineman and not the

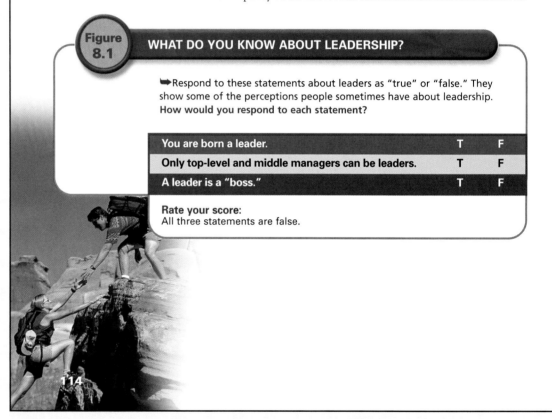

Figure 8.1 WHAT DO YOU KNOW ABOUT LEADERSHIP?

➡ Respond to these statements about leaders as "true" or "false." They show some of the perceptions people sometimes have about leadership. How would you respond to each statement?

You are born a leader.	T	F
Only top-level and middle managers can be leaders.	T	F
A leader is a "boss."	T	F

Rate your score:
All three statements are false.

114

Cooperative Learning

Ready? Go! Assign students to teams of four. Start each team with two sheets of paper, one with the heading "Characteristics of Leadership" and the other with the heading "Characteristics of Management." When you say "Go!" two students in each team start by writing a relevant characteristic on one sheet, then passing that sheet to the student on the left. Continue in this manner for three minutes. At the end of three minutes, stop the race. Make a "T" on the board with the same headings as the sheets of paper. Ask each team to share the characteristics they listed. Write valid characteristics on the board.

quarterback. He is often considered the team's leader because of his energy, experience, and commitment to the team. Ideally, the person in charge is also a leader. To be both a good manager and a good leader takes several qualities.

Motivation

Motivation means three different things. It means having **initiative**, or the desire to take action and get things done. Someone with initiative doesn't wait to be told what to do but takes action. In business, initiative is the main quality of an entrepreneur. Good leaders also motivate others to get things done. They often do this by inspiring others with their energy, enthusiasm, and charisma, or charm.

Most importantly, motivation means having a goal, whether it's to create the best video game or to make the best skateboard ever. A true leader is motivated by a vision and inspires others with it. Civil rights activist and theologian Martin Luther King, Jr. delivered powerful speeches like "I Have a Dream," which built a vivid picture of the future with his language. One year later Congress passed the Civil Rights Act of 1964. The same year King received the Nobel Peace Prize, an outstanding award for his peace efforts.

Confidence

To lead others you also need to inspire their confidence. The best way to do this is by having self-confidence. Self-confidence means more than acting sure of yourself. It means actually knowing what you're doing. To lead you not only need a goal, but some idea of how to reach it. The more others are convinced that you know what to do, the more confidence they'll have in you.

A confident leader is also a decisive leader. Suppose you run a student magazine and it comes back from the printer with a big mistake on the cover. You could put it out as is, remove the covers, or send it back to the printer. The longer you take to decide, the more you'll look like you have no confidence in your judgement. You can get advice from your workers, but then you need to make a decision. If your decision turns out to be wrong, you take responsibility for it. People have more confidence in a leader who is willing to make mistakes and learn from them.

Communication

A leader must be good at **human relations**, or the ability to communicate with people. Even if you have a vision and the confidence to carry it out, you can't lead others if you can't communicate with them. To motivate others, you need to be able to explain what your goals are

LEADING THE PACK

Ancella Livers is a confirmed people-watcher. As a manager for the nonprofit Center for Creative Leadership in Greensboro, North Carolina, she trains managers and executives. **What do you think her role is as a corporate trainer?**

continued on p. 117

Chapter 8

Real-World Application
Caption Answer

**LEADING THE PACK:
PART 1 OF 4**

To guide and teach people leadership skills.

Technology Resource

GO TO **POWERPOINT.** The *Introduction to Business* PowerPoint® CD-ROM provides visual lecture aids for this chapter.

Independent Practice

ORAL REPORT. Emphasize that everyone can develop leadership skills. Ask students to prepare a brief oral report about their own experience and knowledge. Students can choose to give a report on: (1) books, videos, and courses on leadership, (2) working with a leader, (3) being part of a team or organization, or (4) volunteer experience. **LS**

Meeting Individual Needs

Students With Orthopedic Impairments. If you have students with orthopedic impairments, make sure they have clear access to the classroom. Be aware that a barrier might be a stair, a curb, a narrow walkway, a heavy door, or an elevator door that doesn't allow time for a wheelchair to exit. Classroom tables need at least 27½ inches of clearance for a student in a wheelchair.

Thinking Critically

PROBLEM SOLVING. Polluted roadways have become a serious problem in your community. How might you organize workers into teams? What skills would you need to be successful in leading this project? (The teams could be organized by region to be cleaned or by skills set. Each team might consist of a driver and two helpers. You would need communication and motivational skills.)

You Make the Call

Caption Answer

1. Yes, as long as you're an employee and getting compensation for your time.
2. Yes. This is a business decision. Another example would be a designer of an aircraft. The company makes money and the designer's name is not on the aircraft.
3. It would be nice to profit from the success, but it's part of your job. Intellectual property belongs to the company.

---

to them. Many leaders use gestures, draw pictures, or tell stories to communicate their ideas. President Ronald Reagan relied a lot on body language and described scenes from movies to inspire people.

To communicate with people, a leader also needs to be a good listener. By listening to people you can understand them better and get them more involved. You need to listen to people to be informed about what they're doing, what their strengths and weaknesses are, and what they need to do a better job. You can often benefit by listening to other people's ideas and getting their advice. When Bill Clinton ran for president the first time, he traveled the country by bus and held town council meetings to find out what people wanted.

Integrity

Integrity is the most highly valued quality in a leader. **Integrity** means holding to principles like honesty, loyalty, and fairness. In order to lead, you need to set a good example. If you're willing to sacrifice the quality of your product to make a bigger profit, people aren't going to have much faith in your vision. You can't expect your employees to have good work habits if you show up late for work, leave early, and miss deadlines. A leader who tries to cover up mistakes or blame them on employees isn't going to inspire loyalty or confidence.

President Harry Truman had a sign on his desk that said, "The Buck Stops Here." That meant that he took full responsibility for whatever

You Make the Call

Ghostwrite

Ms. Fernandez is the chief executive officer (CEO) of a sunglass manufacturer. She is scheduled to speak at a national trade show. You know Ms. Fernandez isn't a very good public speaker. You're an employee in the communications department of the company, so she asks you to *ghostwrite* a speech for her. (Ghostwriting means to write anonymously for another person who is then recognized as the author of a speech or book.)

The speech is so good, however, that a major publisher asks Ms. Fernandez to expand it and publish it as a how-to book. She asks you to ghostwrite the book. Only her name will be on the cover.

Making an Ethical Decision

1. Is it appropriate for Ms. Fernandez to ask you to write the book without being at least a co-author?
2. Is it appropriate for you to write a book without informing readers about who wrote it?
3. What if the book became an international bestseller—would that change your answers? If so, why?

LANGUAGE ARTS — Curriculum Connection

Communication. Often business leaders use current data, projected data, trend information, and intuition to predict their future customers. Avon Products once heavily relied on door-to-door sales of cosmetics. Company leadership, however, failed to anticipate the impact of the increased number of women working outside of the home. Door-to-door sales declined, and Avon leaders had to create a new plan to sell cosmetics. Avon now sells products in the workplace and these sales provide about 25 percent of the company's revenues. Imagine you are a leader of a global retailer that sells casual apparel. Write a business memo listing the leaders that need to be aware of for the future of your business.

happened, rather than "passing the buck" to someone else. President Truman might be considered an inspiring leader. He evoked confidence, though, because everyone knew they could trust him. If you lose the confidence and respect of people, you can't lead them.

Developing Leadership Skills

Some people say leaders are born and not made. The exact opposite is true. A person with charisma, like the star athlete or coolest kid in class, is often mistaken for a natural born leader. Charisma, however, doesn't make somebody a good leader. President Truman and President Richard Nixon had little charisma but were effective leaders.

Even the shiest person can become a leader. You're not born with self-confidence, vision, and the ability to communicate. These qualities are learned through knowledge and experience. You can learn leadership skills in a number of ways:

- There are many books, videos, and courses on leadership. Some colleges even offer a degree in leadership.
- Work with someone who has leadership ability and study what he or she does. It could be a teacher, a coach, or a relative.
- Join a club, a team, a drama group, or a community organization to develop communications skills.
- Take the initiative at school, at work, or in club activities. Volunteer for projects or activities that give you an opportunity to lead.

 Fast Review _____

1. What is the difference between being a manager and being a leader?
2. Why is integrity an important trait for a leader?

Styles of Leadership

Different leaders have different styles. Some rule with strict discipline and watch your every move. Some are easy going and leave you alone to do your work. Figure 8.2 asks you to test your communication skills. Many leaders use more than one style depending on whom they're managing. There are three basic styles of leadership: autocratic, democratic, and free rein.

Autocratic Leadership

Autocratic means self-ruling. An **autocratic leadership** is when you like to run everything yourself and answer to no one. You make all the

Chapter 8 Leadership in Management **117**

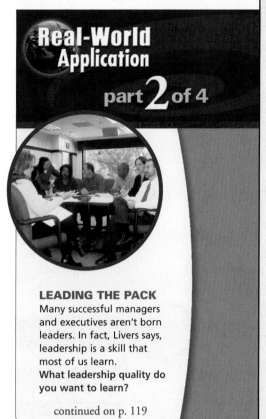

Real-World Application
part **2** of 4

LEADING THE PACK
Many successful managers and executives aren't born leaders. In fact, Livers says, leadership is a skill that most of us learn.
What leadership quality do you want to learn?

continued on p. 119

 **Chapter 8**

Real-World Application
Caption Answer

LEADING THE PACK: PART 2 OF 4
Answers will vary but might include motivation, confidence, communication, or integrity.

 Fast Review Answers

1. Managing is a job and leading is a skill.
2. Sets an example for workers.

Business Connection

Enter "leadership" in an Amazon.com's book search, and you'll get more than 8,700 items! Leadership is a crucial factor in all businesses. Leadership trends are changing from the old autocratic model to shared leadership in a team approach. At Gap Inc., for example, representatives from many departments join together on the environmental affairs team. The team is responsible for guiding company decisions on purchasing, energy efficiency, recycling, transportation, and store construction.

Great Ideas From the Classroom of...

Joe Ree, Ph.D.
Florida State University.
Tallahassee, Fla.

The Businessperson and Other Cultures. Engage students early on in cross-cultural awareness. How do other cultures negotiate, bargain, respond to a business proposition, express uncertainty, satisfaction, displeasure, refusal, etc.? What are the differences in nonverbal communication—gestures, facial expressions, etc.? Send students to visit local stores owned by people of different cultural backgrounds. Have students draft a manual of "Do's and Don'ts for the American Businessperson in Other Cultures."

Develop Concepts

LEADERSHIP IN TEAMS. Many companies are successful when they use self-managed teams. For example, Kinko's is proud of its culture dedicated to—and created by—its coworkers. Kinko's, one of *Fortune's* "100 Best Companies to Work For," feels that its coworkers are the foundation of its success. Kinko's says that its coworkers are energetic, motivated, communicative, creative, and caring people. Ask students to suggest ways that self-managed teams contribute to the success of companies.

Discussion Starter

DIFFERENTIATING. Ask students to describe three styles of leadership and differences between the three styles. (Autocratic, democratic, and free rein. Autocratic leaders make decisions without consulting anyone. Democratic means managers and employees work together to make decisions. Free-rein leadership requires leaders to set goals and allow managers and employees to get the job done.)

Figure 8.2 Caption Answer

Answers will vary.

---

decisions without consulting anyone. When you give orders you expect them to be obeyed without question. Autocratic leaders assume people don't like to work, that they avoid responsibility, and that they have to be watched all the time. They usually control their workers through fear and intimidation. Henry Ford was a classic autocratic leader. He went so far as to hire secret police to spy on his managers to make sure they were doing what he told them.

The biggest problem with autocratic leaders is that people don't like to work for them. The leader's lack of trust in his or her employees doesn't inspire them to be creative. These leaders rarely give credit to their employees so there is little room for initiative. They get people to work hard as long as they're around, but once they leave workers are less productive. If something happens to an autocratic leader, there is usually no one in a position to take over the business.

An autocratic leader is useful in situations where it's important to obey orders without question. Fire fighters, combat troops, and police often have to deal with emergencies where there's no time to consult. Such people are specially trained to work that way, however, and to work as a team. An autocratic style rarely works in a business setting.

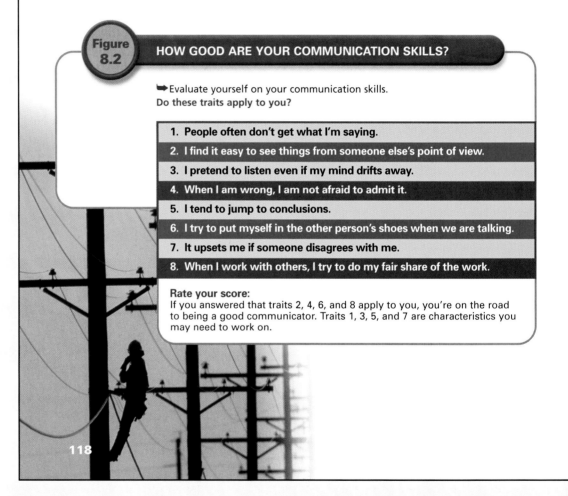

Figure 8.2

HOW GOOD ARE YOUR COMMUNICATION SKILLS?

➡ Evaluate yourself on your communication skills.
Do these traits apply to you?

1. **People often don't get what I'm saying.**
2. **I find it easy to see things from someone else's point of view.**
3. **I pretend to listen even if my mind drifts away.**
4. **When I am wrong, I am not afraid to admit it.**
5. **I tend to jump to conclusions.**
6. **I try to put myself in the other person's shoes when we are talking.**
7. **It upsets me if someone disagrees with me.**
8. **When I work with others, I try to do my fair share of the work.**

Rate your score:
If you answered that traits 2, 4, 6, and 8 apply to you, you're on the road to being a good communicator. Traits 1, 3, 5, and 7 are characteristics you may need to work on.

118

Global Perspective

International Newspapers. Access information on leaders or leadership in international newspapers. To start, enter the URL: **www.all-links.com/newscentral**. Over 3,500 international newspapers are listed. Some leading newspapers, for example Japan's *Asahi Shimbun,* are available in English. Summarize your findings in a short report or table using word processing, presentation, or spreadsheet software.

Democratic Leadership

Democratic leadership means that managers and employees work together to make decisions. Everyone meets, discusses a situation, and listens to everyone's opinion. New ideas are encouraged in this workplace environment. As a democratic leader you still make the final decisions, but you explain your reasons to everyone.

A democratic leader assumes that people aren't lazy and want to work. By giving them more responsibility, workers will be more productive and creative. If they don't have someone looking over their shoulders all the time they will take initiative in their work. By showing your workers you have confidence in them, they're more likely to have confidence in you.

Henry Ford's autocratic style almost ruined his company. General Motors, on the other hand, chose a more democratic style. Alfred Sloan, the chairman of GM, broke the company up into divisions and gave his managers the power to make decisions. As a result, GM started selling more cars than Ford.

Free-Rein Leadership

Free-rein leadership requires the leader to set goals for your managers and employees and then leave them alone to get the job done. This style shows the most trust and confidence in workers. Another name for this type of leadership style is *hands-off leadership*. That doesn't mean you just put other people in charge and leave them alone. You have to deal with the big decisions and keep your managers informed. You also have to be available to them if they have questions or if any problems occur.

Giving managers and employees the power to run things and make decisions is called **delegating**. There are several reasons for a leader to delegate:

- You don't have the time to run everything yourself.
- You can focus on more important work.
- It gets your employees more involved.
- It gives your employees a chance to develop their own potential.

There are also reasons not to delegate. You shouldn't delegate if you're doing it because you're lazy, don't have confidence, or don't want the responsibility. That is not leadership. You also don't want to delegate power to managers who are irresponsible. Who you choose to delegate power to is a test of your leadership skill. Hiring employees who are experienced, reliable, and knowledgeable about the goals leads to success.

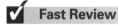 **Fast Review**

1. In what situations is an autocratic style of leadership useful?
2. Give reasons for a manager to delegate authority.

Chapter 8 Leadership in Management **119**

Real-World Application

part 3 of 4

LEADING THE PACK
Today is the second day of training 20 top executives, several of whom are from Fortune 500 companies. Livers asks her students to think of a lesson from childhood that has played out in their adult lives. Livers leads her class in a discussion of how such a childhood role might affect leadership as an adult. **Executives in this workshop are investing time into what resource?**

continued on p. 121

Chapter 8

Real-World Application
Caption Answer

LEADING THE PACK:
PART 3 OF 4
Human resource.

Individualized Practice

Have students break into pairs to evaluate the style of the educational leaders in their school.

L1 What style of leadership is used? Is it only one or a combination of more than one? (Most high schools are a combination of autocratic, democratic, and free rein.)

L2 If teachers are considered leaders and students employees, evaluate the style of leadership in the classroom. (A little bit of each: autocratic, democratic, and free rein.)

L3 What would be an example of democratic leadership in an educational setting. (All-school meetings to discuss goals of the school.)

Fast Review Answers

1. In dealing with new or unmotivated employees and in emergencies.
2. If a job is too big or time-consuming to do alone, a job is too routine to focus on, or a job requires special skills the manager doesn't have.

Curriculum Connection

HISTORY

Leadership Trends. Assign students to groups of three or four. Ask each group to find information using the library or the Internet on styles of leadership in one of the following decades: 1920s, 1930s, 1940s, 1950s, 1960s, 1970s, 1980s, or 1990s. Explain to students that they may need to search or look in the index under the category of management to find any information. Ask each team to create a collage of pictures and words representing the main points of their research, and then share this with the class. Summarize by asking students what trend (or trends) they notice. **CL** , **LS**

Business Building Blocks

CAPTION ANSWER

In business, the most successful teams view diversity as an asset. In Get-to-Know Bingo, students gain first-hand experience in teamwork, communication, respect, and encouraging others.

3 ASSESS

Reteaching

SELF-MANAGED TEAMS. To reteach the concept of self-managed teams, have students list six advantages of self-managed teams. (Self-managed teams are more goal-oriented, faster, and more efficient. Decision-making is simplified and problem solving streamlined. Teams also foster a cooperative team spirit. Team members are more likely to share information and their skills.)

Enrichment Strategy

INTERNET SEARCH. Suggest that students use a search engine to find information on shared leadership and self-managed teams. Ask students to create a list of useful sites they find and summarize the main points of their findings. **LS**

Evaluation

Assign and review the Fast Review sections.

Business Building Blocks

Making a Group Succeed

Building a workable team isn't always an easy task, because everyone is different. Here is an exercise on creative teamwork:

Practice

Get-to-Know Bingo requires that each student takes an active part.

1. Each person takes a piece of paper and creates a 4 x 5 bingo card with 20 enclosed boxes.
2. Inside each box, write a different characteristic. (Examples: Grew up in another state, is fluent in another language, sang in a choir, is afraid of spiders, and so on.)

Communication

3. Ask each student questions. When you discover a characteristic about another player, mark that box on your card with a "X."
4. You must finish the game with a bingo on your card.

Tips for Teamwork

- Make the team's goals your top priority.
- Continue to communicate with team members outside of meetings.
- Respect the other members of your team.
- Try to inspire others to get involved.

Leadership in Teams

Only 20 or 30 years ago autocratic leadership was the main style used in most American companies. As companies learned the value of giving workers more power they started using a more democratic or free-rein style. Today, the trend is to go even further. Many companies have been putting workers on **self-managed teams**, or work groups that supervise themselves. The role of the manager is being replaced by the role of the team leader.

Self-Managed Teams

The use of self-managed teams started in Japan and came to the United States later. American companies had emphasized people working as individuals on separate jobs. Decisions were left up to managers. Japanese companies had stressed people working in teams and making decisions as a group. The Japanese method was such a success that American companies started copying them.

American companies also had too many managers running things. Every decision had to go through several managers before anything could get done. It slowed things down and was very costly. By letting teams manage

---

How to Use a Portfolio Activity

The portfolio projects are designed to lead students to develop a collection of their best work to submit to you for assessment. You and each of your students should decide which projects to include in their business portfolio. Refer students to the specific rubric(s) from the *Alternative Assessment Strategies*. These rubrics will alert students to the criteria you'll use to assess their projects.

themselves, companies were able to get rid of many managing jobs and replace them with a team leader.

In a self-managed team, the leader is a team player rather than a boss. The leader doesn't have to answer to an upper management so the team is freer to get the job done.

A team leader makes decisions with the team rather than alone. This person learns a range of jobs rather than just one. The team usually works on a single project, like designing a video game. This way the project is more goal-oriented rather than task-oriented.

The Organization of Self-Managed Teams

Self-managed teams are organized in two ways: (1) each team member has a special skill or (2) the team selects one team leader. Let's examine the first type of team. Each member of the team might have special skills. For example, Dexter might be an expert in game theory, Pablo a whiz at computer graphics, and Allison skilled at storytelling. The members of your team might also be from different departments. For example, Pablo actually designs the game while Dexter deals with the budget, and Allison handles the marketing. Self-managed teams get to work on their own, but everyone is expected to produce results.

The second type of self-managed team appoints a team leader. The team leader might be appointed by a top manager or selected by the team. At W. L. Gore & Associates, Inc. (creator of GORE-TEX® fabric), there are no hierarchies, bosses, and titles. Its team approach encourages and fosters creativity and opportunity.

A team leader isn't always a manager as much as a team captain. If you're a team leader, your job isn't to give orders but to motivate your team and get the members to work together toward a shared goal.

The idea behind self-managed teams is that the whole is greater than the sum of its parts. Self-managed teams have many advantages:
- They're more goal-oriented than task-oriented.
- They're faster and more efficient.
- Team members have a chance to learn each other's jobs and obtain new skills.
- It simplifies the decision-making process.
- Team members learn to participate and cooperate with each other.
- Self-managed teams learn to solve their own problems.

 Fast Review _____

1. What effect are self-managed teams having on management?
2. What are some advantages of self-managed teams?

Chapter 8 Leadership in Management **121**

Real-World Application
part 4 of 4

LEADING THE PACK
In addition to teaching managers leadership skills, Livers also coaches executives on an individual basis over a period of time. After observing an individual in a variety of settings and under various conditions, Livers presents her observations and offers suggestions for improvement.
Why is it important to seek self-improvement?

Chapter 8

Real-World Application
Caption Answer

LEADING THE PACK: PART 4 OF 4

To give you an advantage in today's fast-paced, high-pressure environment.

Technology Resource

PUZZLEMAKER CD-ROM. Check your students' understanding of the chapter's key terms by using the _Puzzlemaker_ CD-ROM.

Fast Review Answers ✓

1. The main affect is that the role of team leader is replacing the role of manager.
2. Self-managed teams simplify the decision-making process, solve their own problems, are goal-oriented rather than task-oriented, and are faster and more efficient. Team members learn how to do each other's jobs and learn to cooperate and participate.

Meeting Individual Needs

Communication Skills. Many working adults say that oral presentations in class helped them learn presentation techniques and to overcome a fear of public speaking. This _Introduction to Business_ course includes a great variety of opportunities for students to make presentations using props (prepared posters), role-playing, and practicing interview techniques. The many opportunities for students to give oral presentations both as individuals and in groups, leads to increased comfort later on when they must speak in front of coworkers or business clients.

4 CLOSE

Chapter Wrap-Up

Ask students to draw a diagram of the qualities of good leadership and the styles of leadership.

Using Business Key Words

1. autocratic leadership
2. democratic leadership
3. initiative
4. delegating
5. free-rein leadership
6. leadership
7. human relations
8. integrity
9. self-managed teams

Review What You Learned

10. No one style is considered the best.
11. Teamwork.
12. A team approach sometimes makes it difficult to set up a fair evaluation and pay system for employees.
13. Nonverbal actions sometimes say things that words don't. You communicate with your posture and body movements. People form a first impression of you by your dress and appearance. You communicate with your facial expressions. Sometimes the amount of space you put between you and another person communicates a feeling.
14. Projects could be delayed and mistakes might be made. Productivity will go down.

Summary

1. Being a manager isn't the same thing as being a leader. A manager manages projects, people, and situations in a company. A leader has a vision, which inspires others.

2. Leaders need vision, motivation, confidence, integrity, and the ability to communicate.

3. The three basic styles of leadership are autocratic, democratic, and free rein. An autocratic leader likes to rule everything and answer to no one. One person at the top makes decisions. Firefighters, combat troops, and police often work with an autocratic leader when time is of the essence. A democratic leader means managers and employees work together to make decisions. Equal responsibility instills creativity and productivity in the people involved. Lastly, free-rein leadership, or hands-off leadership, allows the leader to set goals and let people work alone to get the job done.

4. Today's leadership trend is toward self-managed teams. The team-oriented approach allows workers to be more goal-oriented, efficient, analytical, creative, productive, and self-reliant.

Using Business Key Words

To be a successful manager, you must be a leader, an effective communicator, and a team player. Fill each blank in the following sentences with the term that best completes each sentence.

- **initiative**
- **free-rein leadership**
- **autocratic leadership**
- **democratic leadership**
- **delegating**
- **human relations**
- **self-managed teams**
- **integrity**
- **leadership**

1. Some managers make decisions without consulting their employees. This type of leadership is called _____.

2. Some managers ask employees for suggestions and discuss alternatives with them. This type of leadership is called _____.

3. A leader shows great _____ if she or he has the desire to take action and get things done.

4. Leaders often engage in _____ if they don't have time to run everything themselves or to get employees more involved.

5. A leadership style in which managers allow employees the freedom to decide how to do their work is called _____.

6. Providing direction and vision is called _____.

7. The ability to communicate with others is called _____.

8. Holding to the principles like honesty, loyalty, and fairness is called _____.

9. _____ is when work groups supervise themselves.

Quick Quiz

1. Name the three different styles of leadership. (Autocratic, democratic, and free rein.)

2. What circumstances may require a leader to delegate responsibility. (Lack of time, inability to focus on more important work, the desire to involve employees and allow them to develop their potential.)

3. Why did American companies begin to adopt the concept of self-managed teams? (The Japanese used teams with great success.)

Review What You Learned

10. Which leadership style is considered the best?
11. What is the key to the modern workplace?
12. Name two disadvantages of working in teams.
13. Explain how nonverbal actions are considered a form of communication.
14. What happens if managers and employees don't communicate well?

Understanding Business Concepts

15. Compare the three leadership styles.
16. Why do you think most managers use a mixture of leadership styles? Do you think it might be confusing to employees? Why or why not?
17. Have you ever worked as part of a team on a class project? What were the advantages and disadvantages of working this way?
18. Explain the flow of communication.
19. How has technology, especially the Internet, changed the way people communicate? Has it made a difference for you? Explain.

Critical Thinking

20. Imagine you're the manager of an ice cream store near your high school. You have five employees—a bookkeeper with ten years of experience, two college students who have worked with you for six months, and two high school students who just started last week. What leadership style(s) do you think you'll use with your employees? Explain your answer.
21. Keep a log of the number and kinds of communication skills used during one day at your school.

22. More companies are adding a new type of executive to its hierarchy: the chief knowledge officer (CKO). How do you think a CKO would benefit a company?
23. Between now and the year 2020, chief executive officers (CEOs) are more likely to:
    a. Be women and minorities.
    b. Stay in their jobs for shorter periods of time.
    c. Place greater emphasis on teams and consensus.
    d. All of the above.

Viewing and Representing

Examining the Image. Draw a sketch of this photograph. Include every detail. What's the main idea? What messages and emotions are team members expressing? Invent names for the members of this self-managed team. Write a brief story on your perceptions of the image. Share your story with the class.

Chapter 8 Leadership in Management **123**

Critical Thinking

20. Answers will vary depending on the students' experiences and understanding of the various leadership styles.
21. Logs will vary.
22. A chief knowledge officer (CKO) is in charge of knowledge management. This position focuses on human skills and relationships as the most precious resource of the company.
23. Answer: D. All of the above. Although nearly all CEOs in 2000 are white and male, by 2020 more of them will be women and minorities. While the average tenure of CEOs is now nine years, it will be shorter in the future. Finally, today's CEOs often lead by command and control; they will be more likely to lead by consensus twenty years from now.

Viewing and Representing

This activity reinforces the students' understanding of the instant power of visual images. How long did it take for students to sketch all the details? The act of having to take the time to physically sketch the picture will emphasize the fact that the eye and mind can rapidly assimilate a great deal of information from images. Sketches and stories will vary. Encourage creativity. CL, LS, ELL

Understanding Business Concepts

15. Autocratic leaders give instructions and make decisions. Democratic leaders ask employees for their suggestions and hold discussions. Free-rein leaders help employees set goals and give them freedom to achieve those goals.
16. Situations vary. Some employees need different styles.
17. Answers will vary.
18. Communication flows in all directions. Managers communicate with each other by sharing ideas, suggestions, and progress.
19. The Internet and e-mail are instant forms of communication. People expect information quick.

4 CLOSE (Cont.)

Building Academic Skills

HISTORY. Make sure all group members participate. The library and the Internet will be good resources. Rubrics: Essay, oral presentations, note taking.

COMPUTER/TECHNOLOGY. Rules will vary. If time permits, combine all the students' rules to create one master list. Rubric: Posters.

MATH. (325 ÷ 350) × 100 = 93 percent of goal. (400 ÷ 350) × 100 = 114 percent of goal.

LANGUAGE ARTS. Current business magazines and the Internet are the best resources for this project. Rubrics: Oral presentation, note taking.

Linking School to Home

Answers will vary. Allow students the opportunity to use their creative imagination for this activity. Rubric: Oral presentation.

Linking School to Work

Students' answers will vary. Rubric: Oral presentation.

● Building Academic Skills

Historic Leadership Styles

In a group of three or four, research the way business was conducted 100 years ago. Examine a variety of issues including leadership styles, employee rights, methods of communication, advertising techniques, and products and services available. Write a two-page paper with your findings and share with the class.

Netiquette

E-mail is a very popular form of communication. Netiquette is network etiquette, or the "dos and don'ts" of online communication. Research netiquette on the Internet and create your own list of ten rules you should follow when communicating in this way. Create a poster of your rules and display in your class.

Percentage of Sales Goal

Your manager at the Burger Barn wants each employee to sell $350 worth of hamburgers and fries during his or her shift. Yesterday your sales totaled $325. Today your sales totaled $400. Determine the percentage you achieved above or below the goal for yesterday and today.

Oral Presentation

Locate and read an article on one of the following topics: effective leadership styles, teamwork, skills needed for management, or effective communication skills. Prepare a summary and present it orally to the class.

● Linking School to Home

Analyzing Big Business. Think about the U.S. government as the manager of a very large corporation. Brainstorm examples of the leadership style(s) the government uses, whether or not teamwork is utilized, and the way information is communicated to the masses. Consult your parents and family members for their thoughts. Share your opinions with the class.

● Linking School to Work

Observations. If you're employed, observe the activities of your manager for a one-week period. Answer the following questions:
- What type of leadership style does your manager use with you? With others in the organization?
- Does your manager organize his or her employees into teams? If so, how effective do you think they are?

Present your findings to the class. (Note: If you aren't employed, observe the activities of a particular teacher or friend for one week.)

E-Homework

Applying Technology

Emoting Emoticons. *Emoticons* are type-written pictures of facial expressions used in e-mail to communicate emotions, like happy, sad, mad, and so on. Using the Internet and other resources, create a list of emoticons.

Leadership Assessment. Use the Internet to research the three leadership styles. If possible, locate an online leadership assessment and try to determine your own leadership style.

Connecting Academics

Math. You're the CEO of Tropic Aquaria, a rapidly expanding company. You've been managing purchasing but you need to spend more time planning company goals. Purchasing takes 10½ hours a week during a five-day workweek. The employee needs to concentrate on purchasing two days a week. Before you delegate the purchasing workload to an employee, you must look at your staff's schedule. Their work hours are:

Maya	6:30 A.M. to 12 noon
Susan	8:15 A.M. to 3:00 P.M., with an hour lunch
Kele	11:45 A.M. to 5:30 P.M., with a half-hour lunch

Which employee would you assign to purchasing? How many hours a week does this person have left to work on other tasks?

Language Arts. You work at Tropic Aquaria. Tropic Aquaria runs many self-managed teams. You're on a team assigned to plan and make a pamphlet describing how to run a successful work team. Work with a small group and create a pamphlet with helpful tips and guidelines.

BusinessWeek — Analyzing the Feature Story

You read the first part of "The Boss in the Web Age" at the beginning of this chapter. Below are a few questions for you to answer about Sylvia Chen and Xcelerent Software Inc. You'll find the answers to these questions when you're reading the entire article. First, here are the questions:

24. What leadership style is best demonstrated by Chen's actions? Give examples to support your argument.
25. How important is communication in regard to one of Xcelerent's new programs?

CREATIVE JOURNAL ACTIVITY

Interview a business or civic leader in your community. Find out how communication and teamwork affect his or her work. What are other keys to success? Report back to the class.

BUSINESS Online
The Full Story

To learn more about business leadership, visit the *Introduction to Business* Web site at www.introbus.glencoe.com, and click on *BusinessWeek* Feature Story, Chapter 8.

E-Homework

EMOTING EMOTICONS.
Emoticon lists will vary. Rubrics: Lists, e-mail messages.

LEADERSHIP ASSESSMENT.
Answers will vary. Allow the students to share their findings with the class. Rubrics: Note taking, oral presentation, essay.

Connecting Academics

MATH. Kele works 5¼ hours a day. 5¼ × 2 = 10½ hours. Kele would be assigned to purchasing. The work hours left a week for Kele are: 5¼ × 3 = 15¾ hours.

LANGUAGE ARTS. Student groups might use the information presented in this chapter and this chapter's "Business Building Blocks" feature as a basis for their pamphlets' tips and guidelines. Groups may research on the Internet or in business magazines for current trends in running work teams. Encourage creative presentation of topics. Pamphlets will vary. **CL**, LS, ELL

BusinessWeek — *Analyzing the Feature Story*

24. Free-rein leadership. Helps coworkers when they have a problem. She lets managers propose solutions and she only challenges them.
25. Chen knows it's crucial to explain Xcelernet's Latin American literacy alliance to employees before Internet news services broadcast the information.

Creative Journal Activity

Ask for three volunteers. As students are reporting the results of their interviews to the class, the volunteers will take turns writing the keys to success on the board. Follow with a discussion of the keys to success. Do students have more keys to success to add to the list?

SCANS Correlation Chart*

Foundation Skills

Basic Skills	Reading	Writing	Math	Listening	Speaking	
Thinking Skills	Creative Thinking	Decision Making	Problem Solving	Seeing Things in the Mind's Eye	Knowing How to Learn	Reasoning
Personal Qualities	Responsibility	Self-Esteem	Sociability	Self-Management	Integrity/ Honesty	

Workplace Competencies

Resources	Allocating Time	Allocating Money	Allocating Material and Facility Resources	Allocating Human Resources		
Information	Acquiring and Evaluating Information	Organizing and Maintaining Information	Interpreting and Communicating Information	Using Computers to Process Information		
Interpersonal Skills	Participating as a Member of a Team	Teaching Others	Serving Clients/ Customers	Exercising Leadership	Negotiating to Arrive at a Decision	Working With Cultural Diversity
Systems	Understanding Systems	Monitoring and Correcting Performance	Improving and Designing Systems			
Technology	Selecting Technology	Applying Technology to Task	Maintaining and Troubleshooting Technology			

*This chart's highlighted blocks indicate the chapter's content coverage in the Student Edition and the Teacher Wraparound Edition.

Resource Manager

Teaching Transparencies

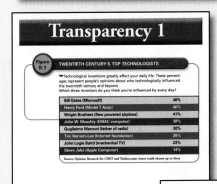

Transparency 1

Figure 9.1 TWENTIETH CENTURY'S TOP TECHNOLOGISTS

Technological inventions greatly affect your daily life. These percentages represent people's opinions about who technologically influenced the twentieth century and beyond.
Which three inventors do you think you're influenced by every day?

Bill Gates (Microsoft)	48%
Henry Ford (Model T Auto)	46%
Wright Brothers (flew powered airplane)	41%
John W. Mauchly (ENIAC computer)	38%
Guglielmo Marconi (father of radio)	30%
Tim Berners-Lee (Internet foundation)	25%
John Logie Baird (mechanical TV)	23%
Steve Jobs (Apple Computer)	14%

Source: Opinion Research for CNET and Techies.com; voters could choose up to three

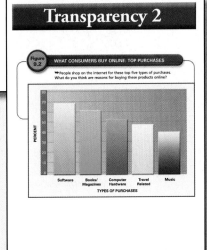

Transparency 2

Figure 9.2 WHAT CONSUMERS BUY ONLINE: TOP PURCHASES

People shop on the Internet for these top five types of purchases. What do you think are reasons for buying these products online?

Application and Enrichment

- Lesson Plans
- *BusinessWeek* Poster Package
- Teaching Transparencies
- Integrated Software Simulation
- Glencoe Business Video Package

Review and Reinforcement

- *PuzzleMaker*
- Internet Resources
- Student Activity Workbook
- Strat. and Work. for Teaching Transparencies

Assessment and Evaluation

- Reproducible Tests
- Alternative Assessment Strategies
- ExamView® Pro Test Generator

Technology

- *PuzzleMaker*
- ExamView® Pro Test Generator
- Glencoe Business Video Package
- PowerPoint® Presentation
- Integrated Software Simulation
- Interactive Lesson Planner
- *Virtual Business*®

KEY				
	Printed	Software	Videocassette	Poster
	Transparency	CD-ROM	Internet	

BUSINESS Online

Visit www.introbus.glencoe.com, the Web site companion to *Introduction to Business.* The student's page includes:

- interactive tutor
- additional *BusinessWeek* articles and activities
- business Web links
- homework hints
- real-world application activities
- additional career path activities

Information on how to prepare your students for the high school exit exam and special projects are also included.

Use the Glencoe Web site for additional resources. All essential content is covered in the Student Edition.

Introducing the Chapter

This chapter discusses how technology has influenced business. It describes the e-workforce and virtual business. A photo essay, "A Stake in a Steak," enhances the concepts.

Connecting the Objectives

What are some examples from the past of how technology has influenced business? What is e-commerce? E-tail?

BusinessWeek
Feature Story

Story's Summary

ZoZa.com plans to sell an exclusive line of clothing on the Web. There are problems though—technology is so slow and rigid it's ruining the planned shopping experience. Mel and Patricia Ziegler wanted to use virtual-reality technology for customers to "try on" clothes, but downloading took too long. The poor color match displayed on a computer monitor and the complexity of pulling discontinued items were also issues. Despite the problems, the Zieglers predict that within seven years, ZoZa.com will be making $1 billion in sales.

Find the entire article at www.introbus.glencoe.com, or in the Teacher Resource Binder.

Chapter 9

Technology's Impact on Business

Learning Objectives

After completing this chapter, you'll be able to:

1. **Explain** how technology influenced business industries.
2. **Describe** the three aspects of the e-workforce.
3. **List** specific examples of e-commerce.
4. **Analyze** the advantages and disadvantages of e-commerce.

Why It's Important

Knowing how technology has influenced business sheds light on new and future industries.

Key Words

e-workforce
digital workflow
start-ups
e-commerce
e-tail
multi-channel retailer
bricks-and-mortar
clicks-and-mortar
e-tickets

126

BusinessWeek Feature Story

Zen and the Art of Net Start-ups

Banana Republic's Founders Try to Work Their Magic Online. Mel Ziegler remembers the exact moment he figured out the Web. It was 18 months ago when his doctor recommended he take fresh ginseng. Unsure of where to get the stuff, the 55-year-old Zen enthusiast turned to the Web. A quick search led him to a small ginseng farmer in Wisconsin. Ziegler marveled at how he could instantaneously communicate with the farmer in Wisconsin while sitting at his computer in Mill Valley, Calif. He also began to wonder how he and his wife, Patricia, co-founders of Banana Republic and the Republic of Tea, might use the medium for business themselves.

Source: Excerpted with permission from "Zen and the Art of Net Start-ups," *BusinessWeek Online*, October 16, 2000.

An Extension Activity

What challenges do businesses face today as they go to the Internet to extend their markets?

BUSINESS Online
The Full Story
To learn more about online start-ups, visit the *Introduction to Business* Web site at www.introbus.glencoe.com, and click on *BusinessWeek* Feature Story, Chapter 9.

Classroom Resources

For the Teacher
📁 Student Activity Work. TAE
📑 Assessment Binder
💿 PowerPoint® Presentation
💿 Interactive Lesson Planner
📁 Lesson Plans
💻 Internet Resources
📠 Teaching Transparencies
💻 *Introduction to Business* Web Site

💿 Integrated Soft. Sim. TM
📖 *BusinessWeek* Poster Package
For the Student
📑 Student Activity Workbook
💿 *Virtual Business*®
💻 *Introduction to Business* Web Site
💿 Integrated Soft. Sim.
💿 *PuzzleMaker*
📑 Strategies and Worksheets for Teaching Transparencies

Bell Ringer Activity

SELECTING TECHNOLOGY.
Write on the board: How is technology used in the community and in the schools? List the name of the technology and its use. (Examples: Computer rooms/ student learning, ATM machines/ get or deposit money, cellular phones/communication, Fax machines/communication, and the Internet/communication, buying and selling.) **CL**, **LS**

Preteaching Business Key Words

SPEAKING. Ask a student to read aloud the chapter's key words from the glossary. Have volunteers repeat in their own words the definition of each word. **LS**

An Extension Activity

ORAL REPORT. Have groups of four students brainstorm a list of challenges and give a brief oral report including examples. **CL**, **LS**, **P**

Making Connections

The Business World. A far-reaching change in business has taken place in the area of financial statements. Information technology has changed the way financial statements are prepared, audited, and used. In the early 1900s, financial statements provided a large part to the information available about a business to its investors. Today, however, investors can get up-to-the-minute data about companies through public and proprietary databases without waiting for quarterly or annual reports. Using information technology, certified public accountants (CPAs) can provide financial statements in a more timely manner.

2 TEACH

Business Connection

THE DAWN OF COMPUTERS.
It's hard to believe that the beginning of computing may have roots as far back as the seventeenth century. That's when someone had the bright idea to use machines to solve mathematical problems. Mathematicians of the day designed and implemented calculators that were capable of addition, subtraction, multiplication, and division. Although there were several pioneers in this area, including Wilhem Schickhard, Blaise Pascal, and Gottfried Leibnitz, the first multi-purpose programmable device was developed by Charles Babbage in 1823. Babbage was ahead of his time and didn't quite succeed in developing what we now know as the computer, but his hard work paid off. He pioneered programming techniques that helped the roots of computing take shape based on his early work and design.

Develop Concepts

TECHNOLOGICAL SAVVY.
Have students identify a technological advance developed in the last five years. (Answers are endless and might include technology and software for personal computers, personal data assistants, and digital cameras.)

Figure 9.1 — Caption Answer

Answers will vary.

The Cyber Age

Michael Furdyk and his partners sold MyDesktop.com for more than $1 million. Their Web site began just for fun as a help line to explain how the Internet works. What's unusual about this story? Furdyk is only 17 years old and hasn't yet graduated from high school. Furdyk is no fluke. A small but growing number of teenagers are starting online businesses. Eight percent of all teens, about 1.6 million in the United States are making at least some money on the Internet.

Technology's Influence on Business

Thomas Edison said his greatest discovery was discovering what people could use. His inventions include the light bulb, the phonograph, and the movie camera. These made the power, music, and film industries possible. Figure 9.1 rates the top technologists over the past century.

Technology refers to the tools and machines people have invented to make life easier. Inventions like the radio and the television entertain and inform us. The telegraph and then the telephone made it easier to communicate with each other. Trains, cars, and airplanes made it easier to get around.

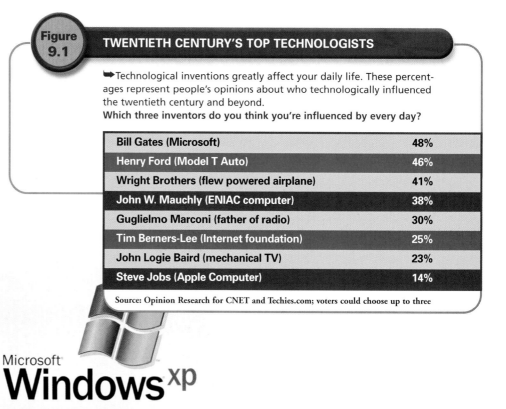

Figure 9.1 — TWENTIETH CENTURY'S TOP TECHNOLOGISTS

➡ Technological inventions greatly affect your daily life. These percentages represent people's opinions about who technologically influenced the twentieth century and beyond.
Which three inventors do you think you're influenced by every day?

Bill Gates (Microsoft)	48%
Henry Ford (Model T Auto)	46%
Wright Brothers (flew powered airplane)	41%
John W. Mauchly (ENIAC computer)	38%
Guglielmo Marconi (father of radio)	30%
Tim Berners-Lee (Internet foundation)	25%
John Logie Baird (mechanical TV)	23%
Steve Jobs (Apple Computer)	14%

Source: Opinion Research for CNET and Techies.com; voters could choose up to three

Microsoft Windows XP

128   Unit 2 Owning and Operating a Business

Cooperative Learning

Web Resource. Keeping up with new technological developments is a challenge for many people. Have students keep portfolios where they can place newspaper clippings, notes, articles, and advertisements of the newest products and trends in the computer industry. As students gather information, have them identify how the new products and developments impact new jobs. Ask groups of students to list ways that people can keep up with the new developments in technology. Have groups design a Web page to present their list of ways. Suggest that groups submit their Web page to be included on your school site or to an online job board, such as Monster.com. **LS**, **CL**

Perhaps the most common technology staple today in businesses is the computer. They electronically store thousands of files, which saves time, labor, and office space. Scanners read the prices of products and record sales instantly, making business move much faster. Accounting and bookkeeping computer software programs help organize, plan, and control businesses operations. The film industry uses digital technology to edit film as well as enhance the colorful images and create animated scenes.

Technology in the Past

Even the simplest invention, like the plow, had a huge impact on business. Before the plow was invented, people had to dig in the earth with hand tools. It took forever to plant a field of corn or wheat. The plow made it possible for one person to do the work of 50 in the same amount of time. More corn could be planted which meant more corn could be produced. This meant hiring more people to harvest the corn, selling more corn in the market, and building a corn-selling business.

Plows were so useful that making them became a big business. Companies specialized in making plows and other farm tools. Woodworkers and metalworkers were needed to make parts for them. General stores could make money selling them. There was a constant demand to produce new and more efficient tools. John Deere invented a better plow in 1838 and started his own business. Today, Deere & Company is one of the leading makers of farm tools in the world.

Since the plow, countless new inventions have changed the way we live, work, and do business. Steam engines, blast furnaces, and boilers provided ways to produce greater power and made factories possible. The automobile made it possible to transport goods faster. Auto making became a major industry and created new demands in other industries like steel, rubber, glass, and oil. New roads needed to be built, creating a boom in construction. The construction industry created new jobs in trucking, mechanics, and engineering.

Modern Technology

In the past 50 years electronics revolutionized business and society. Today, the economies of many countries such as Japan and Taiwan are based on manufacturing electronics. There is a never-ending demand to make electronic goods smaller, faster, cheaper, and more powerful.

Around 1945 a computer took up an entire room and could barely do a math problem. Now a microchip stores billions of bits of information.

Chapter 9 Technology's Impact on Business **129**

Real-World Application

part 1 of 4

A STAKE IN A STEAK
Is it elegant and tender? Firm and hearty? Or what about light and joyous? A cut of meat has more flavor and character than you'd think. Just ask someone at Omaha Steaks, a fifth-generation owned and managed company in Omaha, Nebr. Its new e-commerce site gives you direction your local meat market might not. **Why is it important to take chances in business, particularly when launching a Web site?**

continued on p. 131

2 TEACH (Cont.)

Thinking Critically

BRAINSTORMING. A friend comes to you with an idea for an e-tail clothing business and wants your honest opinion about the disadvantages of selling clothes on the Internet. What do you tell her? (Unless she has plans for a bricks-and-mortar business back up, clothing e-tail is a tough sell. The disadvantages for customers outweigh the advantages. For many, shopping is connected with immediate gratification. With e-tail, you have to wait for delivery. Also, shoppers like to touch, feel, and try on clothing.) What other multichannel retailers would you recommend she look at? (JCPenney and Lands' End.)

✔ Fast Review Answers

1. By saving labor, increasing production, creating new jobs, and creating new industries.
2. By storing thousands of files on disk, saving time, and saving office space.

Working Lifestyle

Caption Answer
graphic designer, painter, visual artist, interior designer, Web designer, photographer, etc.

Computers were first used only by the military. Now, the computer is an important business tool. It can electronically store thousands of files, saving time and office space. The computer also created a boom in nearly all business industries.

 Fast Review _____

1. Explain how the plow changed business.
2. How does the computer help businesses?

E-Workforce

A desk jockey with dry, red eyes is sitting in front of a computer at work. Other workers in the office are in front of computers wearing eyestrain eyeglasses. Down a few more cubicle rows another worker rubs the back of her neck. This is a portrait of today's electronic workforce, or e-workforce.

Working Lifestyle

What are you doing at 10 A.M.?

Piecing Together Footage

"I created a career out of skateboarding by filming and editing local skateboarders' 'sponsor me' tapes," says Wing Ko. The homemade videotapes helped the local skateboarders become pros and got Ko's foot in the door of the industry. Today Ko makes money by skate shops selling his videos.

As a self-employed, skater guru, Ko enjoys the life of being his own boss. That requires pounding the pavement all the time to find projects and understand the relationship between art and business. "This is the hardest skill because they're a lethal combination," says Ko, who studied filmmaking at Columbia College in Chicago.

At 10:00 A.M., Ko is either driving to the editing studio or trying to wake up skateboarders to coordinate video shoots. He recommends, "Love what you do because it makes life easier."

Salary
The median income of a photographer and video editor is $20,940, with a range between $15,250 and $30,820.

Outlook for This Career
This highly competitive and creative field is expected to experience steady growth.

Connecting Careers Activity
What other careers do you need a "good eye" for creativity and imagination? Do these appeal to you?

CAREER PATH   Arts, A/V Technology & Communications

Social Science   *Curriculum Connection*

Spin-off Industries. Have students break into groups to identify some industries that developed as a result of the personal computer. Have groups create a poster collage representing the industries they identified. (Ideas will vary and include industries making products that store information—disks and CD-ROMs. Industries making products that transmit information—printers, faxes, scanners, and modems. Industries producing new computer software that organizes information.)
LS, CL, P

E-workforce is when people work with computers while doing business. According to the Bureau of Labor Statistics more than 70 million people use computers daily.

Employment

Technology created a boom in many industries. It created new markets for products like printers, fax machines, video games, cellular telephones, and modems. New products are constantly being invented, developed, and manufactured by various companies. Innovation means more jobs and more people learning new skills. In every office environment, coworkers like to know they have one technology whiz in their company in case something malfunctions. Technology makes people work easier and faster. Its speed saves time and creates new jobs.

Digital Workflow. Placing hard copies of documents on a digital platform, like CD-ROMs or a database has greatly influenced time efficiency. People have access to a broad range of information more quickly than ever before. A library's catalog and sets of encyclopedias are available in digital format. This places information at your fingertips in an instant.

By switching information to a digital format, there is less paper involved. A **digital workflow** links all the steps in a process digitally. For example, digital workflow has greatly influenced the publishing and printing industry. Authors, editors, marketing, manufacturing, and archiving can work together in a seamless electronic pace. Each department's step in the process of creating a book, journal, or newspaper is linked electronically.

Technology Centers. The high-tech industry can be found in practically any city, but it's heavily populated in various technology centers, like California's Silicon Valley, New York's Silicon Alley, Oregon's Silicon Forest, and Austin's Silicon Hill. Next in line is New Mexico. Computer chip manufacturer Intel Corp. already built a facility in Rio Rancho, New Mexico.

New Jobs. One fraction of the high-tech industry is the Internet. It has created a demand for new jobs such as software writers, online writers, and Web page designers. Companies are now able to post job opportunities on their home page, on a newspaper's online classified section, and partner with an Internet job service, like Monster.com.

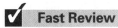 **Fast Review** _____

1. How has the computer created demands for related products?
2. Name an industry that manages a digital workflow?

Real-World Application
part **2** of 4

A STAKE IN A STEAK
Not sure how to properly thaw the filet mignon before Sunday dinner? Omaha Steaks takes pride in its customer service, which is available seven days a week by e-mail or by telephone. More than 1,800 Omaha Steaks employees work to achieve 100-percent-guaranteed service and quality of its products. **Name two things that make Omaha Steaks a success.**

continued on p. 133

Real-World Application
Caption Answer

A STAKE IN A STEAK: PART 2 OF 4

Great customer service and consistently offering a quality product for over 80 years.

Business Connection

BABY E-BUSINESS. The roots of the Internet began as far back as 1957 with the formation of the Advanced Research Projects Agency, the group that first set up a "Cooperative Network of Time Sharing Computers." Although this was the most significant early advance, there was other work going on that resulted in an important paper in the early sixties that discussed "Information Flow in Large Networks." Three decades later, the Internet began to gather steam. In the early nineties, the U.S. president and the World Bank came online. In 1994, communities like Cambridge, Mass., were linked and Web users were able to order pizza online. Soon banks and radio stations joined ranks and the Internet began to resemble the network you know today.

Fast Review Answers

1. The computer created new markets for products like printers, fax machines, video games, cellular phones, and modems.
2. Publishing and printing are industries that manage a digital workflow.

Great Ideas From the Classroom of...

Michelle Walker, Ph.D.
Assistant Professor, Education
University of North Texas
Denton, Tex.

Capstone Activity. Have students plan and implement one activity that promotes teamwork and demonstrates effective human relations and business activities for your program audience (training station employers, business education students, parents, and school personnel). Students can decide upon date, time, location, and components. They will then organize into subcommittees, with specific tasks, and estimate the cost for their portion of the activity. Have subcommittees present and exchange ideas as well as promote the activity. **CL**, **LS**

Develop Concepts

FACTORS OF THE E-WORKFORCE. Have students discuss new companies in their community that are a direct result of new technologies. (Computer stores, wireless telephone companies, and software manufacturers are a few examples.)

Discussion Starter

DIFFERENTIATING. Ask students to identify a technology center in the United States and describe what it is most known for manufacturing. (Silicon Valley, integrated circuits. Silicon Forest, microprocessors and software.)

Figure 9.2 Caption Answer

Convenience, location, time, savings, etc.

Virtual Business

The ease of doing business online has created a boom in new businesses, or **start-ups**. This type of business is called a virtual business. (Virtual business was introduced in Chapter 5.) Vocational schools, universities, colleges, and community centers offer technology training or degrees for people interested in expanding their job skills. These skills will make you very attractive to an employer.

Technology transports your mind to new places in the world. While it would be nice to order a fresh, glazed donut and hot chocolate over the Internet and receive it in five minutes, well, technology isn't there. However, if you don't have a donut shop in your town but still want to purchase donut mix and hot chocolate powder, then you just might be able to purchase these over the Internet.

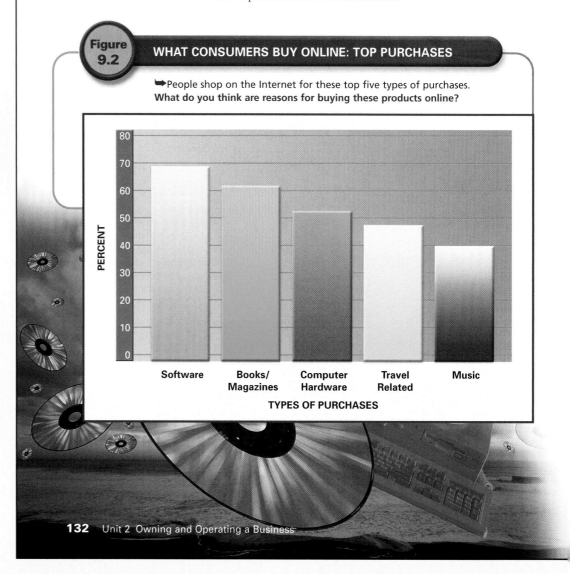

Figure 9.2

WHAT CONSUMERS BUY ONLINE: TOP PURCHASES

➡ People shop on the Internet for these top five types of purchases. **What do you think are reasons for buying these products online?**

Global Perspective

The Web's Borderless Commerce. General Electric purchases its commodities by Web-based reverse auctions. When GE first launched its reverse-auction for the supply of safety glasses, the company with the lowest bid was a Chinese manufacturer. That bid saved GE $200,000 on the price they expected to pay. Suppliers compete in real-time for contracts with most businesses. Trust is the key to international trade. Once a supplier is seen as trustworthy, and the customs process is smoothed over, the actual shipping needs to be done in a cost-effective way.

E-Commerce

Electronic commerce, or **e-commerce**, has made it possible for businesses to directly reach customers anywhere in the world. Everyone hooked up to the Internet is a potential customer. This hasn't only changed the way products are sold, it has changed the way all business activities are conducted. E-tail and e-ticket are two specific examples of e-commerce.

E-Tail. In Chapter 5 you read about dot-com entrepreneurs. Remember Jeff Bezos? He's the entrepreneur of Amazon.com, a clicks-and-mortar company. As a matter of fact, Amazon.com is a well-known and trusted e-tailer. **E-tail** is electronic retail. The business sells products over the Internet. The main activity of e-commerce is buying and selling goods and services. Figure 9.2 shows you what consumers buy most online. Any company can go online to sell any product.

JCPenney, a major department store, sells products in stores, by mail, and online. This type of company is called a **multi-channel retailer**. It uses several means to sell products. Businesses often call their stores and warehouses **bricks-and-mortar**, referring to building materials. Businesses that also use the Internet are called **clicks-and-mortar** operations.

E-commerce makes it easier to send catalogs of e-tailers' products to consumers. This is especially useful for companies that do a lot of mail-order business, like Land's End. Putting catalogs on the Internet rather than shipping them by mail saves a lot of money in printing and mailing costs.

How does e-tail benefit you as a consumer? Here are the advantages:

- *Convenience.* You can shop at home without going to the store. The Internet is never closed, so you can shop 24 hours a day, 7 days a week. If you don't have access to transportation and you need or want an item, you can buy it online, because it's convenient.
- *Choices.* The number of companies selling products online gives you more choice and lets you compare prices easier. Some online companies allow you to download music, computer games, or preview movies trailers. Look for Web sites that compare and contrast goods, like ZDNet.com. Before buying a new or used car, the Internet has many useful sites to explore all elements of the transaction.

Real-World Application
part 3 of 4

A STAKE IN A STEAK
Poultry, gourmet foods, seafood, veal, and lamb aren't typically online consumers' top purchases. Originally, the Web site was another avenue to sell its products just as it did with mail-order catalogs, direct marketing, and retail stores. Omaha Steaks attributes increased sales over the past two years to the Web site. **Why do you think sales increased?**

continued on p. 135

Chapter 9

Real-World Application
Caption Answer

A STAKE IN A STEAK: PART 3 OF 4

The company increased its audience. Buying online is easy, convenient, and saves time.

Individualized Practice

INVENTING TECHNOLOGY. Have students brainstorm to create a new product or research products that are in development. What does world need? How might technology help industries?

L1 Have students work in pairs to discuss new products and new industries.

L2 Ask students to brainstorm in pairs then write two paragraphs summarizing their discussion.

L3 Ask students to work in groups to brainstorm and then prepare a skit to demonstrate their main points to the class.

LANGUAGE ARTS — Curriculum Connection

Differentiating. Ask students to compare their online shopping experience with real-world shopping. What are the different steps involved in each activity? Illustrate the different steps and benefits for each venue. What do they prefer? Why? Have students break into pairs to discuss their own experience with e-commerce. What are the advantages of e-commerce to the consumer? (Convenience and choice.) What are the disadvantages? (Too much buying power, extra charges, lack of immediacy, not relying on direct observation.) **LS**

Writing for Business

CAPTION ANSWER

A thesis statement can also be called a topic sentence. A topic sentence is important because it controls the content of the story. All details in the story support the topic sentence making it possible for the reader to understand what is said.

3 ASSESS

Reteaching

HOW TECHNOLOGY INFLUENCES BUSINESS. To reteach the concept of how technology influences business, have students describe new businesses that resulted from the invention of the automobile. (Businesses include gas stations, manufacturing car parts, car repair shops, auto parts stores, and dealerships.)

Enrichment Strategy

READ. Have students read an article that discusses the future of the e-workforce. How has technology influenced the creation of technology centers and contributed to a changing workforce? **LS**

Evaluation

Assign and review the Fast Review sections.

Writing for Business

Designing Function or Form

This activity gives you the chance to add to your portfolio. Communicate, interview, research, and write your way into a story. Choose one imaginary path, A University's Home Page or Bricks vs. Clicks. Follow your path's steps to complete your own story.

pick a path

A University's Home Page

The Setting. You finally decided to quit your job as a telemarketer and become a freelance Web designer.

Rising Action. The University of Texas has asked you to submit ideas for the design of its new Web site.

Step 1. Using a computer design program or paper, design UT's home page. Look at the Web sites of several colleges and universities for ideas of useful subcategories you could turn into links, including admissions, programs of study, and student life.

Step 2. Use the school colors in your design. Write UT's brief mission statement. Use at least one photograph and other design elements.

Bricks vs. Clicks

The Setting. You support Bookwell, a local independent bookstore, by volunteering to organize its public poetry readings and live acoustic music night on Wednesdays. You work during the day as a Web designer for a design firm.

Rising Action. Your boss has asked you to design a Web page for the firm's new account, Super Books, an online bookstore.

Step 1. You're worried the Super Books e-commerce site will decline the sales at Bookwell. Research how independent bookstores are coping with the advent of mega-online stores.

Step 2. After you've taken a position on whether or not you want to design the Web site, write a letter to your boss, which outlines your position.

Conclusion

Now it's time to write your own story, and reflect on your path. Create and revise a thesis statement for your path. A successful statement does several things: In one sentence it presents the main idea that you'll develop in your paper; it explains your perspective on the topic; and it prepares readers to see how you arrived at your perspective.

134

How to Use a Portfolio Activity

The portfolio projects are designed to lead students to develop a collection of their best work to submit to you for assessment. You and each of your students should decide which projects to include in their business portfolio. Refer students to the specific rubric(s) from the *Alternative Assessment Strategies.* These rubrics will alert students to the criteria you'll use to assess their projects. **P**

On the other hand, there are disadvantages to e-tail. These include:

- *Buying power.* It's easy to overspend. If you're not careful you can order things by mistake.
- *Other charges.* Since most products bought online are delivered by mail, you have to pay shipping charges and usually tax. The exchange and return policies may be pricier than in a store.
- *Immediacy.* While shopping online is convenient, you still have to wait for most products to be delivered. (Unless, of course, you live in New York City. Barnes & Noble online will deliver a book you ordered on the same day.)
- *Relying on observation.* It's hard to know for sure whether you like a sofa unless you sit down and try it. The same can be said for clothes, CDs, or books. Online buying requires you to rely on pictures and descriptions instead of actually touching things yourself.

E-Ticket. With more than 70 million people signed onto the Internet in the United States alone, businesses are finding that customers want to buy services online as well goods. Using their computers, people can now purchase **e-tickets**, or electronic tickets. E-tickets are available for concerts, museums, airlines, movies, and amusement parks.

Some people find purchasing an e-ticket is easier and cheaper than visiting an actual store. For example, a travel agency may charge you a $8 to $25 fee for handling your airline ticket. If you buy a ticket from an online virtual business travel agency you may only be charged $1.

On the other hand, if an airline lost your e-ticket in its system you might be required to buy another ticket. An e-ticket makes it more difficult to transfer to another airline if your flight is cancelled. Due to this, it's often better to have paper tickets. The do-it-yourself attitude to making travel arrangements isn't great news for travel agents. Jupiter Communications estimates that online travel sites will account for 62 percent of online bookings, where as travel agencies will sell 20 percent of conventional ticket sales. E-business in travel is nearly a $70 billion a year industry. There are always precautions you should take when purchasing a ticket online. Always write down the amount of the ticket and the date when you purchased it.

 Fast Review _____

1. How does e-commerce differ from e-workforce?
2. What is a multi-channel retailer?

 **Real-World Application**

part **4** of 4

A STAKE IN A STEAK
Omaha Steaks felt its Web site had to be fluid, easy to use, and navigable otherwise customers might lose patience. Shopping online is a convenient, time-saving activity that's complete with a click of a mouse. What have been your experiences with online shopping?

Real-World Application
Caption Answer

A STAKE IN A STEAK: PART 4 OF 4
Answers will vary.

Technology Resource

GO TO **PUZZLEMAKER CD-ROM.** Check your students' understanding of the chapter's key terms by using the *Puzzlemaker* CD-ROM.

Fast Review Answers

1. E-commerce is business done using the Internet. E-workforce consists of people who use computers to do business.
2. A multi-channel retailer is a company that sells products in stores, by mail, and on the Internet.

Chapter 9 Technology's Impact on Business **135**

Meeting Individual Needs

Students With Behavior Disorders.
Students with behavior disorders of any type require a class environment that provides both support and structure so that they know what to expect and what will be expected of them. Experiment to determine the best learning modality for each student, and structure activities accordingly. For example, a visual learner would benefit from having material presented in the form of photographs or computer graphics. When students are required to give a written response to an activity, using computer software engages them. Allow students who act out in class time on the computer to build their enthusiasm in completing assignments. **LS**

4 CLOSE

Chapter Wrap-Up

Ask students to read this chapter's learning objectives, then write in their journal notes on the four summary points listed in this chapter's review section.

Using Business Key Words

1. e-ticket
2. clicks-and-mortar
3. e-commerce
4. multi-channel retailer
5. start-ups
6. e-workforce
7. digital workflow
8. e-tail
9. bricks-and-mortar

Review What You Learned

10. Businesses that sell both in traditional retail buildings (bricks-and-mortar) and on Web sites.
11. Convenience.
12. Quick and easy to compare prices and shopping can be done anytime.
13. Overbuying, paying extra shipping and handling charges, cannot touch or try out the products, wait for delivery, customer profiles may be sold to other companies.
14. The digital workflow, technology centers, and new jobs.
15. E-tail or e-tickets.
16. Reach customers worldwide, cheaper to send catalogs, it saves labor.
17. Plow, light bulb, phonograph, movie camera, telephone, automobiles, trains, blast furnaces, airplanes.

Summary

1. Technology refers to the tools and machines people have invented to make life easier. Often they inform us and are entertaining. Technology affects business by saving labor, increasing production, and creating new industries.

2. The e-workforce involves people using technology and learning new skills to work it. Part of this includes working with a digital workflow. People have access to a broad range of information more quickly then ever. The growth of technology centers attracts droves of people trying to jump aboard the tech industry's workforce. The new tech jobs might be anything computer related from graphics to database management to quality control. High-tech jobs on the Internet are only a fraction of the entire e-workforce.

3. E-commerce, or electronic commerce, is business done using the Internet. E-tail and e-tickets are two specific examples of e-commerce. People buy many goods online. Consumers buy software, books/magazines, computer hardware, travel tickets, and music the most often online.

4. E-tail has its advantages and disadvantages. On the one hand, buying online is convenient and offers you many choices. On the other hand, it's easy to overspend, you might have to pay for additional charges, products aren't always immediately delivered, and you must rely on observation.

● Using Business Key Words

Technology has dramatically changed the way industry and consumers do business. Match each term below with the correct statement.

- **e-commerce**
- **e-tickets**
- **multi-channel retailer**
- **clicks-and-mortar**
- **bricks-and-mortar**
- **e-tail**
- **start-ups**
- **digital workflow**
- **e-workforce**

1. Short for electronic tickets.
2. The use of both the Internet and buildings, such as stores and warehouses, to do business.
3. Business conducted on the Internet, or electronic commerce.
4. A company that uses several means to sell products, such as retail stores, mail-order catalogs, and the Internet.
5. Businesses that are starting up.
6. People who work with computers while doing business.
7. Linking all the steps in a process digitally.
8. Electronic retailing, or selling, on the Internet.
9. The stores and warehouses that businesses use; referring to the building materials.

Quick Quiz

1. Name three aspects of the e-workforce. (Digital workflow, technology centers, and new jobs.)
2. Name specific examples of e-commerce. (E-tail and e-tickets.)
3. What is digital workflow and why is it important? (It links all steps in many work processes, digitally places information at your fingertips, and eliminates the use of paper.)

Review What You Learned

10. What does the term clicks-and-mortar mean?
11. What is the major reason e-commerce is so popular with consumers?
12. Why is it so convenient to shop online?
13. Describe the disadvantages of e-commerce to consumers.
14. How has e-workforce shaped employment?
15. Give an example of e-commerce.
16. What are three advantages of e-commerce to business?
17. Give two examples of technology that changed business before the invention of computers.

Understanding Business Concepts

18. How does technology change the world of business?
19. Have you ever purchased something online? If so, describe the experience, any problems that occurred, and whether or not you would do it again.
20. Describe how an online company might function as an intermediary.
21. Name two companies that could be described as multi-channel retailers.
22. How can consumers create financial problems for themselves by shopping online?
23. Explain why e-commerce sellers build customer profiles.
24. Do you, as a consumer, feel more loyalty to online companies than bricks-and-mortar businesses or the other way around? Give examples.
25. What trends do you see happening in the e-workforce in the upcoming years?
26. Give an example of digital workflow in your school or work.

Critical Thinking

27. Do you think it's possible for a retailer to be successful as a bricks-and-mortar business but unsuccessful in the online world? Explain why or why not.
28. Are there any products you would never buy online? Explain your answer.
29. Why do you think small business owners are likely to use e-mail, banner ads, and other online tactics to get their message out?
30. Eight percent of all teens, about 1.6 million in the United States, are making money on the Internet. Why are more teens than ever becoming online entrepreneurs?

Viewing and Representing

Examining the Image. Looking at the photograph, list at least ten things that come to mind. How will the technology influence businesses and consumers in the next three years?

Critical Thinking

27. Answers will vary.
28. Answers will vary.
29. Small businesses have limited marketing budgets so it's cheaper to send e-mail; they're also more likely to experiment with distributing information.
30. They're the first generation to grow up in front of a computer screen; interacting online is what teens like.

Viewing and Representing

This visual image is meant to catch your eye and make you think. What does it mean? When you see a road sign, it means that something is ahead. What's ahead in the world of the Internet? Students' predictions will vary for how the Internet will influence business and consumers in the next few years. As in brainstorming, encourage creative thinking by accepting every suggestion without judgment or evaluation. **LS**

Understanding Business Concepts

18. Sparked a new way of doing business.
19. Answers will vary.
20. One dot-com company might develop a relationship with several retailers in a city. The dot-com then handles orders from online customers and coordinates the shipment of goods from those retailers. The dot-com needs no warehouses or plants. It is the connection between customers and retailers.
21. Answers will vary.
22. Easy to overbuy.
23. To target market.
24. Answers will vary.
25. Ideas of trends will vary.
26. The recording of attendance on laptops, or directly by bar code strips.

4 CLOSE (Cont.)

Building Academic Skills

LANGUAGE ARTS. Make sure all students participate in the project. Encourage them to edit each other's brochures to ensure an error-free brochure. Rubrics: Brochure, note taking.

COMPUTER/TECHNOLOGY. Answers will vary. Rubrics: Oral presentations, note taking.

HISTORY. The library and the Internet are good resources for this activity. Rubric: Posters.

MATH. Results will vary depending on the resources used. Rubric: Graphs.

Linking School to Home

Answers will vary. Instead of a family member, student could ask a friend to work on the project with him or her. Let students choose the method they use to share their results. Rubrics: Note taking, essay, oral presentation.

Linking School to Work

Make sure all students find someone to interview. If this is a difficult task, have the students work in groups. Rubrics: Note taking, oral presentation.

● Building Academic Skills

 Creating a Pamphlet

Work with a partner to create a pamphlet for consumers to use when planning to shop online. Include the advantages and disadvantages of shopping online and suggestions for how consumers can protect themselves from potential problems. Also include a list of reputable Web sites for the beginner. If possible, use the computer to make the pamphlet and distribute to students in your school.

 Online Merchant

Select an online merchant and evaluate the Web site for the following information:
- user friendliness
- type of product or service
- payment procedures
- return policy

 Illustrating History

Choose a type of technology, other than the computer, and research its history. Describe when it was invented, who invented it, how it is used, and its prospects for the future. Create a poster illustrating the technology's history and display it in your classroom.

 Graphing Growth

Recent reports estimate that over 16 million people logged onto the Internet for the first time last year. Conduct research to determine the growth of the Internet over the last ten years. Graph your results.

● Linking School to Home

Online Shopping. Research the e-commerce sites that allow consumers to grocery shop online. Although this service is not available in all communities, it's a fast-growing service. Find out how the prices compare on ten products that you and your family purchase frequently. Then ask your parents or other family members if they would ever grocery shop online. Have them explain why or why not.

● Linking School to Work

Local E-Commerce. Interview a manager from a local business to find out how e-commerce has impacted his or her business. Ask the following questions:
- Has e-commerce helped or hurt the business?
- How is business conducted differently now that e-commerce is a viable option for consumers?
- Are there any plans to add e-commerce as another channel of distribution?

Report your findings to the class.

E-Homework

Applying Technology

Distance Learning. Using the Internet, research online high schools and universities such as the Florida Online High School or the University of Phoenix. Write a two-page paper describing online education. Do you think there is a future for online learning? Is it for you? Why or why not?

Online Survey. Conduct a survey of the online service providers used by the students in your class. Find out which provider they use, their level of satisfaction, any problems that occur, and the monthly cost. Create a chart showing the results. If possible, conduct the survey with all the students in your school and compare your results.

Connecting Academics

Math. In a year, half of Dell Computer's sales, $16 billion, came from e-commerce. Overall, corporate and government customers account for 75 percent of its sales. The rest of Dell's sales are to consumers. For the year, what is the total dollar figure of Dell's sales to consumers?

Computer/Technology. Tomorrow, you're in charge of a power meeting to plan your company's use of CD-ROMs, databases, and the latest storage technology to place information quickly and easily at the fingertips of employees. You know that an agenda is a powerful tool for successful meetings. Use the Internet to research current ideas on agendas for successful meetings. Create the agenda for your meeting tomorrow using software suitable for this task.

BusinessWeek | Analyzing the Feature Story

You read the first part of "Zen and the Art of Net Startups" at the beginning of this chapter. Below are a few questions for you to answer about online start-ups. You'll find the answers to these questions when you're reading the entire article. First, here are the questions:

31. Are the founders of ZoZa.com planning to sell exclusively online or as a multi-channel retailer?

32. Why is this strategy important?

CREATIVE JOURNAL ACTIVITY

Research an online e-tailer of your choice. How many different products is it offering through its site? Is it selling exclusively online or through multiple channels? Summarize your findings in a one-page report.

BUSINESS
Online
The Full Story

To learn more about online start-ups, visit the *Introduction to Business* Web site at **www.introbus.glencoe.com**, and click on *BusinessWeek* Feature Story, Chapter 9.

E-Homework

DISTANCE LEARNING. Answers will vary. Encourage students to think about the issue thoroughly. Rubrics: Essay, oral presentation.

ONLINE SURVEY. Answers will vary. Rubric: Tables/charts.

Connecting Academics

MATH. Total sales = 2 × $16 billion = $32 billion in one year. 25 percent of sales are to consumers. Dell's sales to consumers in one year $32 billion × 0.25 = $8 million.

COMPUTER/TECHNOLOGY. Answers will vary. The agenda should include each agenda point, for example, the use of CD-ROMs and so on.

BusinessWeek | *Analyzing the Feature Story*

31. The Zieglers plan to launch ZoZa as a multichannel retailer. While they hope most shoppers will buy online, they're also sending out catalogs and building small kiosks where customers can sample clothing. Finally, they will open 50 flagship stores.

32. Clothing is one of those products that many consumers prefer to see, feel and touch. By offering potential customers access to their apparel at kiosks and through retail stores, ZoZa gives customers an ability to sample their products.

Creative Journal Activity

Have students include a chart or diagram summarizing their findings. What suggestions do students have for online e-tailers?

1 FOCUS

Unit Seminar Overview

In this seminar on entrepreneur-ship and small business, stu-dents analyze a real-life situation using their knowledge of the entrepreneurial spirit and busi-ness organization. Students investigate images, interpret facts, and deduce what makes a small business successful.

Bell Ringer Activity

PREDICT. Write this sentence on the board: "Given the impact of technology on business today, what changes do you think there will be in business and business leadership in the next three years?"

Discussion Starter

RATE THE IMPORTANCE. On a scale of one to ten, have students rate the importance of small business to: the nation, society, and your local commu-nity. Lead a discussion, encour-aging students to back up their statements with specific exam-ples or reasons. **CL**, **LS**

BusinessWeek Seminar

Unit **2**
Small Business

Discovering Small Business

In Chapter 5 you read about the advantages and disadvantages of entrepreneur-ship. An entrepreneur is a person who recognizes a business opportunity and organ-izes, manages, and assumes the risks of a business enterprise. Many of the topics in other chapters of this unit are also important for an entrepreneur to know. For exam-ple, an entrepreneur needs to know how to organize a new business and how to cre-ate a management plan (Chapter 7). Knowing how technology will affect a new business is another important consideration of the entrepreneur.

140

GLOBAL BUSINESS

Newsworthy Trends

And the Winner Is... Each year the Aus-tralian Chamber of Commerce and Indus-try gives out its National Work and Family Awards to the most family-friendly busi-nesses. One of the winners in the Small Business Category was given to Gavin Macleod Concrete Plumbing. The construc-tion company offers paid leave for parents to care for children during the first weeks after birth, care for sick children and spouses, and attend their children's special events, such as the first day of school. The concern for childcare in such a male-dominated industry shows that in the new millennium work and family are no longer just women's issues.

Investigate the Images

Look at the collage on the left page. What do you see? What do you think? What do think the images represent? The power of reading visuals is in analyzing and dissecting your observations. On a separate piece of paper reconstruct the worksheet below in order to complete your investigation. The questions may help shape and focus your analysis.

Your Observations

1. How many photographs do you see?

2. Examine each image. How is each assembled in relation to one another?

3. What is the subject of each photograph?

4. Does color signify a message?

5. What issues do you take from these images?

Information

6. Summarize what you know about the photographs from your observations.

Exploring Culture

7. How does the emphasis on individual achievement in U.S. culture contribute to the success of entrepreneurs in this country? Can you think of activities offered at your school that may foster individuality or an entrepreneurial spirit?

8. How do television shows affect your view about entrepreneurship and small business ownership? What messages do these shows give you about having or starting a small business?

Unit 2 *BusinessWeek* Seminar **141**

Factoids

What Qualifies as Small?
BusinessWeek classifies public, small companies with sales between $25 million and $1.5 billion.

Employee Loyalty. Almost 80 percent of employees working for small companies say that they're very loyal to their companies. In contrast, only 48 percent of those who work for companies with more than 1,000 employees say they're very loyal.

Path for Retiring Entrepreneurs. When they retire, older entrepreneurs may close down full-scale operations. However, many plan to stay in business. Some will work as consultants and others will start part-time businesses with only themselves to manage.

Employment Opportunities. Twenty-two percent of small businesses plan to expand their workforce in the near future.

Capital Expenditures. Two-thirds of small businesses reported recently spending money on new buildings or upgrading current buildings.

2 TEACH

Thinking Critically

1. Picture what a small business means to you. What's your definition of a small business? (Answers will include the students' own measures of number of employees, sales in dollars, and the area covered.)

2. What can company leadership do to promote employee loyalty? (Answers will include making it a priority that the employees feel their work is valued.)

Cooperative Learning

TAKE TWO—ACTION! After discussing "Exploring Culture" (seminar questions 7 and 8), write on the board examples of activities offered at school and messages that television shows give about small business. Have students work in pairs or small groups. Have teams choose two examples or messages. Teams are to think of a situation to exemplify each example or message, and then create a role-play or short scene to perform for their classmates. **LS**, **P**, **CL**

COMPUTER TECHNOLOGY
Newsworthy Trends

Building Community Connections. A recent study by the U.S. Small Business Administration identified San Diego, Calif., as a model of community support for small businesses. To fill the huge need for technology workers, the University of California at San Diego built an engineering school and created new technology programs. It also set up a program called CONNECT that brings together the university, business community, and local politicians to create better business conditions. Networking groups, consisting of CEOs, investors, and business advisers, have come together to help people start new businesses. As a result of these programs, small businesses in San Diego have thrived.

Independent Practice

L1 COMPARE

Ask students to find a recent article on ways technology is used in one of the five types of business. Ask them to explain the type of business and the main points of the article to the class. Follow student presentations with a closing discussion to compare the relative impact of technology on the five types of business.

L2 E-INTERVIEW

Have students search on the Web and choose a small business that interests them. Ask them to send a company executive an e-mail asking questions about the business, such as: Did you start with a business plan? How often do you revise your business goals? How many employees do you have? Does your business give leadership training? Has technology changed your business in the past six months? Year? Two years? Have students write a two-paragraph report. **LS**

L3 RESEARCH AND REPORT

Ask students to research two small businesses either locally or anywhere in the world, and then write a one-page report. For each company, have students focus on finding information on the organizational structure and the style of leadership. Are there self-directed teams? Encourage students to include specific examples in their report. Ask students to close their report with a critique of differences between the two businesses. **CL**

BusinessWeek Seminar

Taking Aim at Small Business

● Preparation

Research an idea for a new business, test market it, and decide how to structure your new company.

Objective

In this *BusinessWeek* Seminar, you'll:
- **Research** a new business idea.
- **Create** a business plan for your idea.
- **Present** your ideas to a group of potential investors.
- **Analyze** the potential of your business and make changes based on feedback from your classmates.

Materials Needed
✓ Notebook paper
✓ Flip chart paper
✓ Construction paper
✓ Pencils
✓ Pens
✓ Markers

● Procedures

1. Brainstorm about products or services that your classmates or community may want or need. Here are a few ideas:
   - Sell a product that is labeled with the school mascot (for example, pencils, plastic cups, or pennants).
   - Offer a tutoring service to students in a specific subject before midterms and final exams.
   - Offer a car wash.

2. Research your idea using one of the following techniques.

- Investigate the competition. How does the competition differ from what you plan to do? What would you do similarly? How are they pricing their product or service? How do they get it to their customer?
- Survey your intended customer. Write a one-page questionnaire to find out more about your customer.

3. Write a two-page business plan. See Chapter 5 for the elements of a business plan.

4. Summarize your business plan on four sheets of flip chart paper. Be creative in how you illustrate your idea.

5. Present your business idea to your classmates. Make sure to include what you would like them to do. Are you looking for financial investment? Employees? Customers?

Reteaching Strategy

Have students work in groups to create a bulletin board display on entrepreneurship and small business, with these elements: a definition or description of entrepreneurship, a definition of small business, traits needed for business success, business structure, leadership in business, and the names of famous entrepreneurs (along with their photos from magazines and newspapers). **LS**, **CL**

Chart It

Find out what your classmates think of your business idea by asking them the following questions.

Strengths	What do they like about your plan? What are its best elements?
Weaknesses	What about the business idea seems unrealistic or difficult?
Opportunities	What changes do they recommend to increase the potential of the business? What opportunities did your plan miss?
Threats	Who do they see as your competition? What other obstacles will you need to overcome to make your business a success?

Create a SWOT analysis. SWOT is an acronym that stands for **s**trengths, **w**eaknesses, **o**pportunities, and **t**hreats. Companies use the SWOT analysis as a technique that evaluates a company's internal strengths and weaknesses and its external opportunities and threats. Together as a class, use your SWOT table to discuss the information.

Analyze and Conclude

After creating the SWOT table, answer the questions below:

1. **Decision Making.** What new things did you learn that would help make your business idea more successful? What changes do you need to make to your plan based on the discussion with your classmates? Were there any suggestions that you won't add to your plan?

2. **Negotiating to Arrive at a Decision.** Share your revised plan with the classmates, who made suggestions that you plan to implement. Do they support your plan more?

3. **Reasoning.** If you were to move forward, would you start over with a new idea or move forward with what you have created?

Becoming an Informed Citizen

Congratulations, you finished the *Business-Week* Seminar. Now it's time to reflect on the decisions you made.

Critical Thinking. What are the essential skills and talents you need to be an entrepreneur? How is entrepreneurship different from what you expected? How is it similar?

Analyzing Your Future. Do you think you would prefer starting your own business or working for someone else?

BUSINESS
Online

Further Exploration

To find out more about an entrepreneurship and small business, visit the Glencoe *Introduction to Business* Web site, **www.introbus.glencoe.com**.

Analyze and Conclude Answers

1. Answers will vary and might be presented in note form or complete sentences.
2. Encourage students to point out the changes to their plan as they share the revised plan.
3. Students' opinions will vary and may depend on the originality of their initial idea. Students will base their opinions on the feedback from their classmates and from their own analysis. Ask students how important intuition, or gut feeling, is to them in making decisions about important topics, such as a business plan.

Groups Affecting Business

Unit Objectives

After completing this unit, students will be able to achieve the following outcomes:

- Explain why nations trade with each other, and describe currency exchange, trade barriers, and trade alliances.
- Name ways government protects and promotes business.
- Describe the functions of money and the Federal Reserve System, and explain the types of banks and the services they provide.

BusinessWeek Connections

In this unit, students will read the following articles from *BusinessWeek*:

Chapter 10 "The Bumpy Road to Global Trade": Trade trips bring opportunities, but they also bring problems.

Chapter 11 "Should Europe Be More Like America?": Economists at the World Economic Forum discuss Europe's productivity, efficiency, and attitude.

Chapter 12 "The Euro: Back From the Depths": The euro needs a boost against not just the dollar, but also the yen in Japan, and several factors make a difference.

Key to Descriptive Icons

The following designations will help you decide which activities are appropriate for your students.

L1 Level 1 activities should be within the ability range of all students.

L2 Level 2 activities should be within the ability range of the average to above-average students.

L3 Level 3 activities are designed for the ability range of above-average students.

ELL Activities should be within the ability range of the English Language Learner.

LS Learning Styles designation represents activities designed to address different learning styles.

CL Cooperative learning activities are designed for small group work.

P Portfolio designation represents student products that can be placed into a best-work portfolio.

Teacher Classroom Resources*

Program Resources	Chapter 10	Chapter 11	Chapter 12
Student Activity Workbook	p. 65	p. 71	p. 79
Lesson Plans	p. 24	p. 26	p. 28
Internet Resources	p. 39	p. 41	p. 43
Reproducible Tests	p. 19	p. 21	p. 23
Teaching Transparencies	10.1, 10.2	11.1, 11.2	12.1, 12.2
Strategies and Worksheets for Teaching Transparencies	pp. 5, 36	pp. 5, 38	pp. 6, 40

* Each of these resources is available in print and on the Interactive Lesson Planner CD-ROM.

Technology Resources

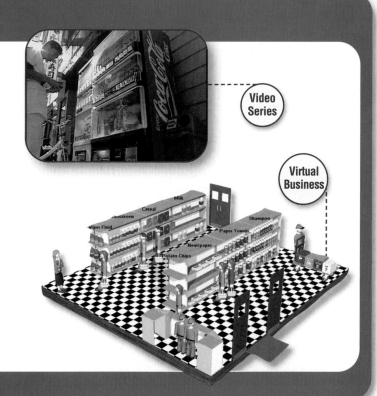

Video Series

Virtual Business

- Interactive Lesson Planner CD-ROM
- PowerPoint® Presentation CD-ROM
- ExamView® Pro Test Generator CD-ROM
- Integrated Software Simulation, Teacher Manual
- Glencoe Business Video Package
- *PuzzleMaker* CD-ROM
- *Introduction to Business* Web Site
- *Virtual Business*®
  Virtual Business is a business simulation that introduces students to the principles of business by letting them start and run their own virtual business. In *Virtual Business,* students have the power to control all aspects of a retail convenience store. Students strategize business decisions using a powerful learning tool in the guise of a video game.

Scope and Sequence

Academic Standards of Learning

	LANGUAGE ARTS	MATH	HISTORY	COMPUTER/ TECHNOLOGY	SOCIAL SCIENCE	
CHAPTER 10	pp. 146, 147, 148, 150, 158	pp. 158, 159	pp. 147, 149, 152, 154, 158, 159	pp. 155, 158, 159	pp. 147, 148, 150, 152, 153, 158	
CHAPTER 11	pp. 160, 161, 162, 164, 167, 168, 172, 173	pp. 165, 172, 173	pp. 166, 172, 173	pp. 163, 169, 172, 173	pp. 162, 163, 164, 168, 172	
CHAPTER 12	pp. 174, 175, 177, 178, 181, 188, 189	pp. 176, 178, 180, 181, 188, 189	pp. 174, 179, 185, 188	pp. 177, 183, 188, 189	pp. 176, 177, 188	

Scope and Sequence

Themes and Concepts

Business Core	Accounting and Finance	Business Management	Computer/Technology	Marketing	Entrepreneurship
Competitive Environment International Trade Economic Culture Exchange Rates Global Business Adapting to Change Global Communications Planning	Decision Making International Finance Financial Markets Trade Finance	Competition Economic Incentives Exchange and Money Productivity Trade Concepts International Regulations	Business Environment Emerging Technology and Trends	Global Alliances Trade Barriers Distribution Strategy Sales in a Global Economy Regulation	International Business Financial Resources
Business Law Interrelations of Business Operations Adapting to Change	Governing Agencies Financial Responsibility Intellectual Property	Economic Institutions Economic System Ethics Government Regulations Sources of Law Legal Rights	Project Management Security Productivity Supervision Business Decisions	Risk Management Information Technology Industry Ethics Regulation	Government Regulations Management Risk Management
Business Law Business/Finance Relationships Investments	Financial Services Investment Analysis	Economic Institutions and Incentives Government Regulations Source of Law	Safety and Security Technical Resources Business Environment Records Management Monitoring and Investigation	Customer Service Infra Structure Financial Institutions Regulation	Collections Government Regulations Legal Considerations and Control

Unit Overview

Unit 3 explains how business is affected by the global economy and by government, and gives details about money and financial institutions.

CHAPTER 10 introduces the global marketplace and global competition.

CHAPTER 11 describes government as a regulator of business and as a provider for business.

CHAPTER 12 examines the history of money, banking, and the Federal Reserve.

Introducing the Unit

Ask students what they have seen in the news recently about trade agreements, global trade, or the Federal Reserve Bank (the Fed). Write students' responses on the board and discuss possible trends that are shown.

Technology Resource

 GO TO **INTRODUCTION TO BUSINESS WEB SITE.** To find out more about content in Unit 3, visit the Glencoe *Introduction to Business* Web site. **www.introbus.glencoe.com**

Unit ③

Groups Affecting Business

Chapter 10
Business in a Global Economy

Chapter 11
The Role of Government in Business

Chapter 12
Money and Financial Institutions

A Model Material

It's early morning on a California boardwalk. You see a surfer riding the leftover wind swell. You also notice someone managing a small radio-controlled plane. What do the surfboard and this plane have in common? Balsa wood. Grown internationally and imported, it's a raw material used for boat and raft building, surfboards, and model airplanes.

● **The Raw Material**
Deep in a Costa Rican jungle grow a few balsa trees, which are valued for their strength and buoyancy.

● **Before Harvesting**
Balsa, a common name for a tropical tree or corkwood, grows to the height of about 70 feet. They grow for at least four years.

● **Free-Market Competition**
The Costa Rican government has begun business transactions with the U.S. government to ensure its share in the global market.

● **Imported to the United States**
The United States imports nearly $96 million worth of tropical wood from Latin America.

● **U.S. Exports to Costa Rica**
The best prospects for U.S. agricultural exports to Costa Rica include: (1) soybeans, (2) corn, (3) wheat, (4) rough rice, (5) fresh fruit, (6) processed fruit/vegetables, and (7) snack foods.

Field Trip Suggestion

Class Choice Trip. As a class, decide on a destination for a field trip. Start by selecting a chairperson and creating an agenda. Run the meeting according to a democratic approach. Final decisions may be reached by a majority vote or by consensus. (Ideas for some trip choices include: a bank, a Federal Reserve bank, Chamber of Commerce, the Small Business Association, or an International Trade Association.) **CL**

Bulletin Board

Glencoe Poster Teaching Tip

Before introducing the poster,
ask students about the economy's current issues. Then focus
students' attention on the covers
of *BusinessWeek* on the left-
hand side of the poster. Briefly
discuss each cover, linking the
cover topic to topics in this unit,
for example, $7.40 an hour links
to Chapter 12, where students
will learn about money.

Remind students they
learned a five-step, decision-
making process in Chapter 1.
Tell them they'll look at a different problem-solving process, the
Meyers model, on this poster.
Then have the students take the
quiz on the poster. Compare the
two decision-making processes.

Portfolio Activity

Great Ideas From the Desk Of... In this
activity, students will produce a teaching
strategy similar to the feature "Great Ideas
From the Classroom Of…" in the Teacher
Wraparound Edition. Have each student
choose one concept presented in this unit
and teach it to someone outside the class—
perhaps a friend or family member. Ask students to also teach the concept to the class.
If possible, take a photograph of each student as he or she presents the lesson. Have
students type an account of their teaching
strategy, including their name and their photograph to place in their portfolio. **P**

⏱Out of Time?

If time doesn't permit teaching each chapter in this unit,
you may use the PowerPoint®
Presentation CD-ROM to
review the chapters.

SCANS Correlation Chart*

Foundation Skills

Basic Skills	Reading	Writing	Math	Listening	Speaking	
Thinking Skills	Creative Thinking	Decision Making	Problem Solving	Seeing Things in the Mind's Eye	Knowing How to Learn	Reasoning
Personal Qualities	Responsibility	Self-Esteem	Sociability	Self-Management	Integrity/ Honesty	

Workplace Competencies

Resources	Allocating Time	Allocating Money	Allocating Material and Facility Resources	Allocating Human Resources		
Information	Acquiring and Evaluating Information	Organizing and Maintaining Information	Interpreting and Communicating Information	Using Computers to Process Information		
Interpersonal Skills	Participating as a Member of a Team	Teaching Others	Serving Clients/ Customers	Exercising Leadership	Negotiating to Arrive at a Decision	Working With Cultural Diversity
Systems	Understanding Systems	Monitoring and Correcting Performance	Improving and Designing Systems			
Technology	Selecting Technology	Applying Technology to Task	Maintaining and Troubleshooting Technology			

*This chart's highlighted blocks indicate the chapter's content coverage in the Student Edition and the Teacher Wraparound Edition.

Resource Manager

Teaching Transparencies

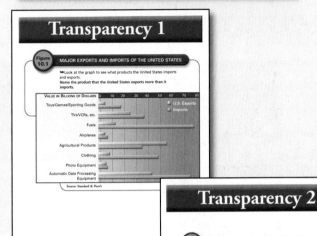

Transparency 1

Figure 10.1 MAJOR EXPORTS AND IMPORTS OF THE UNITED STATES

Look at the graph to see what products the United States imports and exports.
Name the product that the United States exports more than it imports.

Transparency 2

Figure 10.2 MAP OF TRADE ALLIANCES IN THE WORLD

The European Union (EU) is the oldest and best-known economic community formed to promote free trade among the members of the community and to foster common economic policies.
What nations make up the European Union?

Application and Enrichment

- Lesson Plans
- *BusinessWeek* Poster Package
- Teaching Transparencies
- Integrated Software Simulation
- Glencoe Business Video Package

Review and Reinforcement

- *PuzzleMaker*
- Internet Resources
- Student Activity Workbook
- Strat. and Work. for Teaching Transparencies

Assessment and Evaluation

- Reproducible Tests
- Alternative Assessment Strategies
- ExamView® Pro Test Generator

Technology

- *PuzzleMaker*
- ExamView® Pro Test Generator
- Glencoe Business Video Package
- PowerPoint® Presentation
- Integrated Software Simulation
- Interactive Lesson Planner
- *Virtual Business®*

KEY	Printed	Software	Videocassette	Poster
	Transparency	CD-ROM	Internet	

BUSINESS Online

Visit www.introbus.glencoe.com, the Web site companion to *Introduction to Business.* The student's page includes:

- interactive tutor
- additional *BusinessWeek* articles and activities
- business Web links
- homework hints
- real-world application activities
- additional career path activities

Information on how to prepare your students for the high school exit exam and special projects are also included.

Use the Glencoe Web site for additional resources. All essential content is covered in the Student Edition.

1 FOCUS

Introducing the Chapter

This chapter describes the global marketplace and global competition. It explains how currency exchange works. It names the types of trade barriers and major trade alliances in the world today. A photo essay, "Houses That Help The World," enhances the concepts.

Connecting the Objectives

Why does the U.S. import and export some goods and services? How do changes in the value of the Japanese yen or Mexican peso affect your life? Which policy is best—free trade or protectionism?

BusinessWeek
Feature Story

Story's Summary

Access to the world market is easier now than it used to be. There are many trade missions organized by state and commerce groups. The trade trips bring opportunities, but they also bring problems. Mary Ellen Mooney's trip was all but a disaster. Another entrepreneur, Helena Callas, went on a trade mission to Mexico but it took her a full 12 months of hard work negotiating government regulations, obtaining licensing, and finding a distributor to close a $150,000 sale.

Find the entire article at **www.introbus.glencoe.com**, or in the Teacher Resource Binder.

Business in a Global Economy

Learning Objectives

After completing this chapter, you'll be able to:

1. **Explain** why nations need to trade with each other.
2. **Describe** how currency exchange works.
3. **State** the advantages of protectionism and free trade.
4. **Name** types of trade barriers.
5. **Identify** some of the major trade alliances in the world today.

Why It's Important

Global trade doesn't just influence business, it also affects all the countries and people of the world.

Key Words

multinational corporation
imports
exports
exchange rate
balance of trade
protectionism
tariff
quota
embargo
free trade

146

BusinessWeek Feature Story
The Bumpy Road to Global Trade

A Trade Mission Can Put Your Company on the Map. Mary Ellen Mooney, co-owner of $15 million Mooney Farms, was a woman with a mission. She had joined "Baja 2000," a trade tour to Mexico, with one overriding goal: to sell her sun-dried tomato products up and down the coastline they call the Mexican Riviera.

There were problems from the start. First, the bus carrying about 20 California entrepreneurs in food-related businesses spent 45 minutes waiting in Tijuana for one of the organizers. As the bus edged southward along the coastal road, the group was dismayed to see the rugged seascape marred by haphazard lean-tos, ancient trailers, and windblown trash.

Source: Excerpted with permission from "The Bumpy Road to Global Trade," *BusinessWeek Online,* October 9, 2000.

An Extension Activity

What are some problems businesses may face if they try selling their goods or services to another country?

The Full Story

To learn more about global trade, visit the *Introduction to Business* Web site at **www.introbus.glencoe.com**, and click on *BusinessWeek* Feature Story, Chapter 10.

Classroom Resources

For the Teacher
- 📁 Student Activity Work. TAE
- 📖 Assessment Binder
- 💿 PowerPoint® Presentation
- 💿 Interactive Lesson Planner
- 📁 Lesson Plans
- 📖💻 Internet Resources
- 🕹 Teaching Transparencies
- 💻 *Introduction to Business* Web Site

- 💿 Integrated Soft. Sim. TM
- 📘 *BusinessWeek* Poster Package

For the Student
- 📖 Student Activity Workbook
- 💿 *Virtual Business®*
- 💻 *Introduction to Business* Web Site
- 💿 Integrated Soft. Sim.
- 💿 *PuzzleMaker*
- 📖 Strategies and Worksheets for Teaching Transparencies

Bell Ringer Activity

READING.   Write the following assignment on the board: Read the chapter introductory paragraph beginning, "You may not know it but…" Ask students how they would identify an item made in America and one made in another country. Ask students for examples of items they know are made in other countries. Indicate that Chapter 10 presents information about trade between countries around the world.

Preteaching Business Key Words

SPEAKING.   Ask teams of four students at a time to take turns on a mock panel. A student from the "audience" reads aloud one of this chapter's key words from the glossary. A panel member earns a point by defining it in his or her own words. **CL**, LS

An Extension Activity

ROLE-PLAY.   Ask students to role-play possible problems. (Problems might include, language differences, differences in social customs, government regulations, handling shipping, obtaining licensing, and so on.) **CL**, LS

Making Connections

Everyday Living.   Point out to students that ethnic communities throughout the United States often have unique imports for sale. Organize students into groups to research and develop lists of specialty items in their area imported by China, the Middle East, Southeast Asia, India, Pakistan, Puerto Rico, Haiti, or others. Students might include natural and prepared foods and various manufactured items such as saris and chadors. Have students stage an "international bazaar" in which a member of each group tells about the items discovered. **CL**, LS, **ELL**

147

2 TEACH

Business Connection

THE BALANCE OF TRADE.
In January 2001, the U.S. trade deficit grew to $33.3 billion as imports increased over exports, fanning one of the oldest debates in economics. Can a nation be strong with a trade deficit? In the old days, the answer would be no. During the seventeenth and eighteenth centuries, nations accumulated gold. By exporting more than they were importing, they could hoard the extra money—almost always gold or silver—generated by the trade surplus. A treasury bulging with precious metals was considered the true sign of a nation's wealth and strength. Today, it's a different story. In the nineteenth century, the U.S. trade deficit reflected a period of great expansion, and for many, the growing trade deficit of the latter part of twentieth century reflects a time of enormous growth and opportunity in one of the strongest economies in the world.

Develop Concepts

INTERNATIONAL BUYING.
Have students identify services that comprise international trade. (Investments like building factories; exchange of human resources like doctors, managers, and engineers; tourism; military aid; loans; movies and music.)

Figure 10.1 Caption Answer

Agricultural products.

Global Producers and Consumers

You may not know it but you're a part of the global marketplace. You might buy clothes made in Taiwan. Turnover your alarm clock, is there a sticker that reads, "Made in Indonesia"? In the future, you might work for a French company in the United States or for an American company in Paris. During the last 20 years, the United States and other nations have greatly relied on one another's goods and services to stay prosperous. The global marketplace exists anywhere business crosses national borders. Most countries don't produce everything their citizens want. A country might not have the necessary resources, it might not have the technology, or perhaps it's not interested in making the product. However, countries can satisfy their citizens' wants and needs by buying goods in the global market. A consumer, citizen, employee, and business leader of the twenty-first century must have an understanding of international trade and business in order to be an informed decision maker.

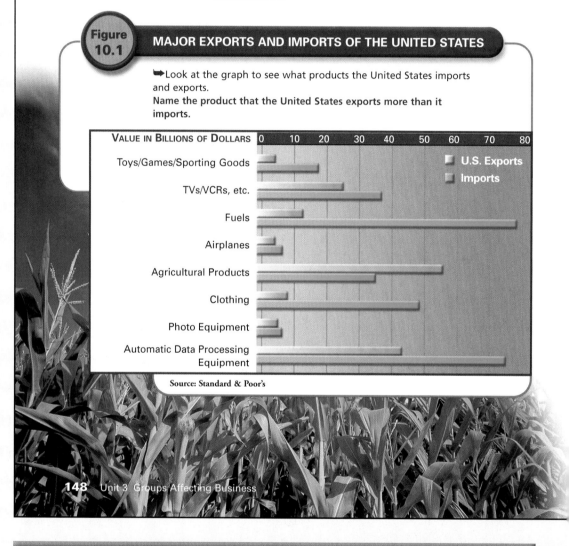

Figure 10.1

MAJOR EXPORTS AND IMPORTS OF THE UNITED STATES

➡ Look at the graph to see what products the United States imports and exports.
Name the product that the United States exports more than it imports.

VALUE IN BILLIONS OF DOLLARS — 0 10 20 30 40 50 60 70 80

- Toys/Games/Sporting Goods
- TVs/VCRs, etc.
- Fuels
- Airplanes
- Agricultural Products
- Clothing
- Photo Equipment
- Automatic Data Processing Equipment

■ U.S. Exports
□ Imports

Source: Standard & Poor's

Cooperative Learning

Class Study Aid. Have students work in teams of four. Ask each team to generate five questions about imports, exports, multinational companies, exchange rates, and balance of trade. Once the questions are complete, have each team send their questions to another team. Direct the second team to answer each of the questions they receive. Finally, have teams pass the questions, along with their answers, to a third team. The third team should evaluate the questions and answers, choosing the best three. Suggest that the class pool the best questions and use them as a study aid.
CL, LS, **ELL**

The Global Marketplace

A company that does business in many countries and has facilities and offices in many countries around the world is a **multinational corporation**. The global marketplace works much like a shopping mall or a supermarket. You go to the store to buy things you need that you can't make yourself, like bread or jeans. In Figure 10.1, notice what products the United States imports and exports. More than likely, you've purchased more than one of these products before.

No matter how much a country produces, it can't make everything itself. The United States is rich in resources—human, natural, and production—but it still needs things from other countries.

Specialization

Specialization builds and sustains a market economy. Few people produce all of the goods and services that they need. Instead, individuals concentrate their activities in a particular area or field, such as being a carpenter, a doctor, or an administrative assistant. Each worker's money buys goods and services that others have specialized in producing. With specialization, everyone is dependent on each other for goods and services.

Countries also specialize and trade some of the items that they produce, in order to gain other countries' goods and services. For example, the United States, Japan, and Germany are the world's top automobile producers. They have the resources—materials, technology, factories, and labor force—needed to produce a large volume of cars. Actually, these countries have a comparative advantage in producing cars—meaning that this is a strong area of production compared to other ways they could use their resources. Other countries could become major producers of cars. Many of them have decided that they have a comparative advantage in producing something else, leaving auto production to such countries as the United States, Japan, and Germany. Money gained from the sales of the cars to other countries is then used to buy items that those other countries produce.

The kinds of resources available to a country often influence what it specializes in producing. For example, a major industry for Colombia is the production of coffee. The climate, soil, and environmental conditions are right for it to produce coffee. Few nations in the world have a climate suitable for raising large amounts of coffee. The United States could raise coffee, but would require a costly controlled environment.

Real-World Application
part 1 of 4

CULTURAL CUISINE
What's for dinner you ask? If Peggy and Andrew Cherng have their way, they'll make sure Chinese food is on your weekly dinner menu. The owners of Panda Restaurant Group are among other business owners interested in serving ethnic food from across the world to your grumbling stomach. The Cherng's founded and built Panda Express, the largest Chinese restaurant chain in history. **In the global marketplace, what is the importance of specialization?**

continued on p. 151

Real-World Application
Caption Answer

HOUSES THAT HELP THE WORLD: PART 1 OF 4

Builds and sustains a market economy. Concentration on an area of interest makes others dependent on you.

Technology Resource

GO TO **POWERPOINT.** The *Introduction to Business* PowerPoint® CD-ROM provides visual lecture aids for this chapter.

Independent Practice

LIST. Ask students to list the main exports of the United States. (Cars, wheat, movies, music, corn syrup.) For what services are countries like Kuwait, Israel, and Ireland known? (Kuwait, oil. Ireland and Israel: tourism.) **LS**

Meeting Individual Needs

Students With Learning Disabilities. Processing information in written or verbal form can be difficult for students with learning disabilities. Visual representations such as graphs, charts, tables, and headings help the students process the information.

Students who have problems with verbal processing are advised to read materials before class discussion. They should also read notes taken in class by other students to ensure that they are not missing any valuable information. **LS**

2 TEACH (Cont.)

Thinking Critically

BALANCING TRADE. Imagine your town as a country in the world marketplace. Your town makes cars but its residents are buying cars from another part of the state because they are cheaper. What might even the playing field? What types of trade barriers might you erect? (A tariff that would make out-of-town cars more expensive.) What types of trade barriers might you erect in the case that a company in another town was exploiting labor and being environmentally irresponsible?

You Make the Call

Caption Answer

1. Opens up competition in resources and knowledge. It's beneficial because it leads to efficiency and innovation. Closed systems are inefficient. The U.S. relies on underdeveloped countries for manufacturing.
2. Employment. Drawbacks: pollution and might destroy the social structure.
3. Compete where they are strong—by providing needed raw materials.
4. Answers will vary.

Therefore, Columbia has a comparative advantage in producing coffee. The United States doesn't have that comparative advantage.

A country with little money or advanced technology but a large population might specialize in manual labor. This means the wages are probably low. In a number of highly populated countries in Asia, such as South Korea and Taiwan, one of their specializations is the assembling of color televisions, videocassette recorders, and computer components sold around the world. Without trade each nation would try to produce the items that it needs and wants, some of which wouldn't be very natural or efficient for them to produce. Similarly, you couldn't specialize in doing one type of job, such as teaching, fixing cars, and building houses unless you had the opportunity to get other things that you need and want from others.

Countries specialize in producing certain goods and services. By specializing, countries can sell what they produce best so they can buy the products they need from other countries. Many countries don't have the capital resources to manufacture goods but have valuable natural resources. Kuwait specializes in producing oil. Some countries like Israel and Ireland rely a lot on their culture to attract tourism. The United States has a wide range of resources so it can specialize in many products such as wheat, cars, and movies.

Types of Trade

The United States buys pepper from India, bananas from Honduras, and coffee from Columbia. These products are called imports. **Imports** are goods and services that a country buys from another country. The

You Make the Call

Global Ethics

You're the buyer for a large department store chain that sells clothing at reasonable prices. Many underdeveloped countries manufacture clothing that the company sells. These manufacturers pay their employees low wages and they work in hot warehouses.

Making an Ethical Decision

1. What are the benefits and drawbacks of a global economy for the United States?
2. What are the benefits and drawbacks of globalization for people living in underdeveloped countries?
3. How can underdeveloped countries break into world markets?
4. Should prosperous, industrialized nations monitor labor issues in other countries? If so, how? If not, who should monitor these issues?

LANGUAGE ARTS — Curriculum Connection

Class Debate.   Ask students to name articles of clothing, watches, shoes, and other items they have with them that are made in other countries. Ask those students who responded why they purchased an article made in another country rather than one made in the United States. Have a class discussion about the reasons. Conclude by holding a class debate. Ask students whether they agree or disagree with the statement: Americans depend too much on other counties. **CL**, LS

United States also sells wheat and corn syrup to places like Mexico and Australia. These products are exports. **Exports** are goods and services that one country sells to another country. One country's exports are another country's imports.

Imports and exports aren't the only types of trade between countries. Countries can invest in other countries by building factories there. Nations also exchange human resources, like doctors, managers, and engineers. Tourism, military aid, and loans are other types of trade. Countries also export cultural products like movies and music. A movie can involve several types of trade. It can be produced by an American company, filmed in Mexico with a Mexican crew, and shown in theaters all over Europe.

Currency

Countries don't directly trade with each other as if swapping clothes for computers. They have to pay for each other's products with *currency.* Currency is another name for money. Just as different countries use different languages they also use different currencies. Americans use dollars, Mexicans use pesos, and the Japanese use yen.

If a tourist from Japan wants to buy something from you, you expect to get paid in dollars, not yen. This means the tourist exchanges his or her yen for dollars at a bank first. The same goes for companies that do business with other countries. If an American company wants to import cheese from a French producer it has to pay for it in euros. To do that, the company has to change dollars into euros on the *foreign exchange market.* The foreign exchange market is made up of banks where different currencies are exchanged.

Exchange Rates. Different currencies have different values compared to each other. The price at which one currency can buy another currency is called its **exchange rate**. For example, one American dollar is worth a certain number of Mexican pesos or Japanese yen. Exchange rates change from day to day and from country to country. One day the value of the American dollar might go up compared to the Mexican peso, but down compared to the Japanese yen. How much the currency of a country is worth depends on how many other countries want to buy its products. If every country wants TVs and VCRs from Japan they'll need Japanese yen to buy them. The increased demand for the yen makes its value increase. If no one wants products from Japan, the value of the yen decreases.

Real-World Application
part 2 of 4

CULTURAL CUISINE
Cherng created the Panda Express concept in 1983 when he modified his cuisine to fit into the shopping mall's food court atmosphere in Glendale, Calif. Instead of rice and egg rolls, he adapted the recipes of his late father, Ming-Tsai, an international chef. Tender orange-flavored chicken and tofu dishes topped off the menu. Now, the fast-food chain is in Japan and Puerto Rico, as well as the United States.
As a restaurant owner, what kinds of things might you import and export?

continued on p. 153

Chapter 10

Real-World Application
Caption Answer

HOUSES THAT HELP THE WORLD: PART 2 OF 4
Suppliers, business plan, ingredients, etc.

Chapter 10 Business in a Global Economy **151**

Great Ideas From the Classroom of...

Jay S. Brown
Pleasant Valley High School
Brodheadsville, Penn.

International Trip. Students plan a vacation with stops in five countries. While on the trip, they will purchase five items (tooth brush, shampoo, T-shirt, coffee mug, and CD) in each country. Students start by setting a reasonable estimate of the cost of each item. Next, they search for an Internet site that will provide the exchange rates for the countries they plan to visit. The Universal Currency Converter or World Currency Exchange can help. Calculate the total cost of the items in the currency of each of the countries students plan to visit.

Consider This...

Caption Answer

Sole proprietorships and partnerships.

✔ **Fast Review Answers**

1. South Africa (diamonds); Japan and Taiwan (labor and equipment); Israel and Ireland (tourism).
2. Investments; human resources; military aid; loans; tourism; and entertainment.
3. To attract business by lowering the costs.

Business Connection

TRICKS OF THE TRADE. The World Trade Organization is the only global international organization that deals with the rules of trade between nations. At its core are the agreements negotiated and signed by the majority of the world's trading nations and ratified in their parliaments. The WTO's goal has been to aid producers of goods and services, exporters, and importers to conduct their business.

Develop Concepts

WORLD MARKETPLACE. Discuss the competition between domestic and foreign car companies. What are a few examples of American versus foreign cars?

Discussion Starter

DIFFERENTIATING. How does protectionism differ from free trade?

Prices. A company follows the change in exchange rates to find the best prices for products. When the value of a country's currency goes up compared to another country's, it has a *favorable exchange rate*. When it goes down, it has an *unfavorable exchange rate*. A country with a favorable exchange rate can buy more of the other country's products. If American dollars go up compared to French euros, it will take fewer dollars to buy French cheese. It also means that American products will cost more for the French to buy. The United States might import more French cheese, but the French might import fewer American TVs. Some countries choose to lower the value of their currency to bring in more business. (It's like putting everything in a store on sale.) When this happens it costs less to buy products from that country. Other countries can build factories and hire labor more cheaply there.

Balance of Trade

A country wants to have more money coming in than going out. The difference in the value between how much a country imports and how much it exports is called its **balance of trade**. When a country exports more than it imports, it has a *trade surplus*. That means it has money left over to buy more products. When a country imports more than it exports, it has a *trade deficit*. That means it is in debt.

A country can have an unfavorable balance of trade with one country and a favorable balance with another. For instance, the United States has a favorable balance with Brazil but an unfavorable balance with France. Overall the United States imports far more than it exports so it has a large trade deficit. Until the 1980s, the United States had a trade surplus. By the year 2000, it had run up a trade deficit of about $330 billion. This changed mostly because of competition from other countries.

Consider This...

The Friendly Asian Markets

Many Asian markets are friendlier to smaller American companies. Consultant Robert Azar works with U.S. businesses that want to plant roots in Asia. According to Azar, Asian businesses may perceive a large company as a threat. In contrast, they often see smaller ones as someone they can join up with.

ANALYZE

This is good news for what type of business ownership?

✔ **Fast Review**

1. Give examples of how countries specialize based on the types of resources they have.
2. Name types of trade between countries other than imports and exports.
3. Why would a country want to devalue its currency?

Global Competition

In the global marketplace, countries benefit from buying one another's products. Countries compete to make the same products. The United States, Japan, and Germany all specialize in making cars. China and the Ukraine both produce steel.

Global competition often leads to *trade disputes* between countries. At the heart of most trade disputes is whether there should be limits on trade or whether trade should be unrestricted. There are two opposing points of view: free trade and protectionism.

Global Perspective

Japan's Keiretsu. Most Japanese firms belong to a *keiretsu* (ky reht soo), a tightly knit group of firms governed by an external board of directors. The keirestsu are often made up of firms that compete with one another. The governing board works to ensure that competition does not force individual firms out of business. In the United States, a similar arrangement among competing firms would be illegal under the antitrust laws. Have students suggest remedies that business or the U.S. government can take to counter the advantages of the *keiretsu*.

Protectionism

Protectionism is the practice of putting limits on foreign trade to protect businesses at home. Most countries sell what they produce at home so they often want to keep out foreign competitors. They also have reasons not to share what they produce with other countries. Here are some of the reasons in favor of protectionism:

- Foreign competition can lower the demand for products made at home.
- Companies at home need to be protected from unfair foreign competition.
- Industries that make products related to national defense, like satellites, aircraft, and weapons, need to be protected.
- The use of cheap labor in other countries can lower wages or threaten jobs at home.
- A country can become too dependent on another country for important products like oil, steel, or grain.
- Other countries might not have the same environmental or human rights standards.

Trade Barriers. To limit competition from other countries, governments put up *trade barriers* to keep foreign products out. For example, the United States and Brazil both produce sugar, but Brazil can sell it in the United States for less. The U.S. government can protect sugar producers at home in three different ways—with a tariff, a quota, or an embargo.

A **tariff** is a tax placed on imports to increase their price in the domestic market. By adding a tax on Brazilian sugar, the United States can make it more expensive than American sugar. A **quota** is a limit placed on the quantities of a product that can be imported. If the United States allows only a small amount of Brazilian sugar into the United States, Americans still have to buy American sugar. An **embargo** is when the government decides to stop an import or export of a product. Embargoes are rare and usually used against another country for political or military reasons.

Free Trade

Economic or foreign policy often determines which countries trade with other countries. Globalization stirs up the controversy about what kind of foreign trade policy to uphold. Supporters of **free trade** believe there should be no limits on trade. All countries should be free to

Chapter 10 Business in a Global Economy **153**

Real-World Application

part **3** of 4

CULTURAL CUISINE
Beside the Cherng's, investors also estimate that the next big thing in dining is Chinese food. With a hot marketplace comes competition. Panda Express competitor P.F. Chang's China Bistro chain is launching Pei Wei, a similar fast-food service. The pressure to remain successful has the Cherng's looking at business expansion plans. **By expanding operations domestically and internationally, how does this affect the economies involved?**

continued on p. 155

Chapter 10

Chapter 10

2 TEACH (Cont.)

Figure 10.2 Caption Answer

Austria, Belgium, Denmark, Finland, France, Germany, Great Britain, Greece, Ireland, Italy, Luxembourg, the Netherlands, Portugal, Spain, and Sweden.

3 ASSESS

Reteaching

DEFINE. To reteach the concept of the global marketplace, ask students to define it. (A global marketplace exists anywhere business crosses borders.) Name the type of corporation that it is located in and that does business in different countries. (Multinational corporation.)

Enrichment Strategy

IDENTIFY. Have students describe the circumstances that might lead a country to specialize in a certain trade. (Some countries, such as Kuwait and China, have abundant natural resources. Other countries like Ireland and Israel have rich cultures that attract tourism.) **LS**

compete anywhere in the world without restrictions. Free trade offers several benefits:

- It opens up new markets in other countries. There are 250 million potential customers in the United States but 6 billion worldwide.
- It creates new jobs, especially in areas related to global trade like shipping, banking, and communications.
- Competition forces businesses to be more efficient and productive.
- Consumers have more choice in the variety, price, and quality of products.
- It promotes cultural understanding and cooperation between countries.
- It helps all countries raise their standard of living.

Trade Alliances. As the economy becomes more global, the trend among countries is toward more free trade. To reduce limits on trade more countries are forming *trade alliances* with each other. In a trade alliance, several countries merge their economies into one huge market. (See Figure 10.2.) For example, NAFTA (North American Free Trade Agreement) combined the economies of the United States, Canada, and

Figure 10.2

MAP OF TRADE ALLIANCES IN THE WORLD

➡ The European Union (EU) is the oldest and best-known economic community formed to promote free trade among the members of the community and to foster common economic policies.
What nations make up the European Union?

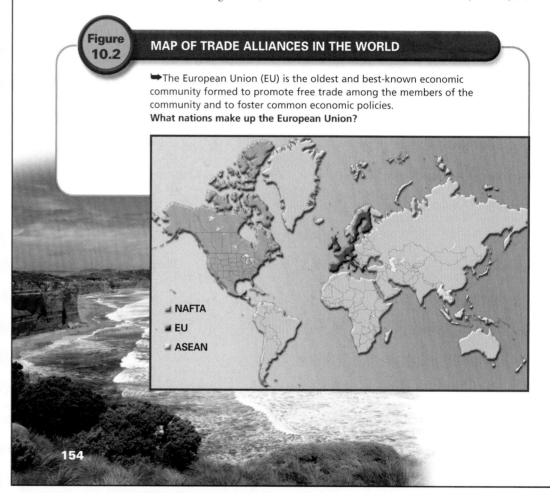

- NAFTA
- EU
- ASEAN

154

How to Use a Portfolio Activity

The portfolio projects are designed to lead students to develop a collection of their best work to submit to you for assessment. You and each of your students should decide which projects to include in their business portfolio. Refer students to the specific rubric(s) from the *Alternative Assessment Strategies*. These rubrics will alert students to the criteria you'll use to assess their projects. **P**

154

Mexico. As a result, it is easier for the United States to buy oil from Mexico and to sell its cars there. Free trade is good in general, but it's not painless. NAFTA was controversial specifically because some workers would be displaced when trade barriers were lowered. Opponents predicted that some high-paid American jobs would be lost to Mexico. Proponents predicted that trade among all three nations would increase dramatically, stimulating growth and bringing a wider variety of lower-cost goods to everyone, protectionists and free traders alike.

With trade alliances, instead of countries competing against other countries, whole areas of the world compete against each other. Some of the major trade alliances in the world today are:

- NAFTA (includes the United States, Canada, and Mexico)
- European Union (EU) (Austria, Belgium, Denmark, Finland, France, Germany, Great Britain, Greece, Ireland, Italy, Luxembourg, the Netherlands, Portugal, Spain, and Sweden)
- Association of Southeast Asian Nations (ASEAN) (Indonesia, Malaysia, Philippines, Singapore, Thailand, Brunei, Vietnam, Laos, Myanmar, and Cambodia)

International Business and Finance Affects Everyone

Understanding international business and finance has become increasingly important for the consumer, wage earner, investor, citizen, and business leader. Citizens should understand international trade in order to make decisions in the polling booth: Does a candidate support or oppose free trade? Investors need to understand international trade when investing in companies both here and in other countries. Which firms will be successful in generating international business and which will not? What will the exchange rate be for the dollar in six months if you decide to sell a particular foreign stock?

An understanding of international business helps you understand why goods and services are at particular prices. You'll also be able to understand why you can buy more goods in some countries than in others. The business leader of tomorrow will have a good grasp of international business and finance.

 Fast Review _____

1. What is a trade war?
2. What are some of the major trade alliances in the world today?

CULTURAL CUISINE
The Cherng's have their eyes set on expanding the business instead of selling out to a mega company. They want to keep it in the family. Their business vision includes opening 10,000 stores. Currently there are 423 Panda Express outlets, employing over 5,000 people. Outlets are franchised, owned by financial investors, and owned by the Cherngs.
How might Panda Express change domestic culture?

Chapter 10

Real-World Application
Caption Answer

HOUSES THAT HELP THE WORLD: PART 4 OF 4
By making Chinese food a staple of the dining experience.

Technology Resource

 PUZZLEMAKER CD-ROM. Check your students' understanding of the chapter's key terms by using the *Puzzlemaker* CD-ROM.

Evaluation

Assign and review the Fast Review sections.

Fast Review Answers

1. A trade war is when two countries impose trade barriers on each other.
2. NAFTA, the European Union, and ASEAN are major trade alliances in the world today.

Meeting Individual Needs

Today's Students. Keeping up on international trade is a challenge for those not directly working in the field. The "rules" can change overnight. To help your students keep up with such changes, encourage them to find at least one business periodical and read it on a regular basis. Also, suggest watching television news coverage of international affairs. **LS**

4 CLOSE

Chapter Wrap-Up

Ask students to draw a diagram of the summary points in this chapter and sketch symbols as a memory aid to represent the points.

Using Business Key Words

1. exports
2. quota
3. embargo
4. protectionism
5. imports
6. tariff
7. exchange rate
8. balance of trade
9. free trade
10. multinational corporation

Review What You Learned

11. Anywhere business crosses national borders.
12. Goods and services that a country buys from another country. Exports are goods and services that one country sells to another country.
13. Banks where different currencies are exchanged.
14. Depends on other countries' demand.
15. To have more money coming in than going out.
16. Competing unfairly by using cheap labor, disputes over fishing rights, environmental laws, and stealing each other's technology.
17. Limits on foreign trade to protect businesses at home; places no limits on trade.
18. Tax or fee on imports; a limit on the amount another country can import; complete ban on a product or all the products from a foreign country.
19. NAFTA.

Summary

1. Countries need to trade with each other because they cannot produce everything themselves.
2. The currency exchange market is made up of different currencies from around the world. To trade with one another countries have to convert their currency into foreign currency.
3. Countries use trade barriers to protect businesses at home from foreign competition. Free trade opens up new markets, creates jobs, gives consumers more choice, and promotes cooperation between countries.
4. Three types of trade barriers are tariffs, quotas, and embargoes.
5. Major trade alliances include NAFTA, EU, and ASEAN.

● Using Business Key Words

Technological advances, trade alliances, and changes in trade barriers have created a global economy. Match the following terms with their definitions to find out how much you know about the global marketplace.

- **imports**
- **protectionism**
- **exports**
- **tariff**
- **exchange rate**
- **quota**
- **balance of trade**
- **embargo**
- **free trade**
- **multinational corporation**

1. Products made in one country and sold in another.
2. A fixed limit, set by the government, on the import of a product.
3. A complete ban on a product or all the products from another country.
4. A view that there should be limits on foreign trade in order to protect business at home.
5. Products one country buys from another country.
6. A special tax on goods made in one country and sold in the United States.
7. The price at which one currency can buy another currency.
8. The difference in value between how much a country imports and how much it exports.
9. A view that all countries should be free to compete anywhere in the world without restrictions.
10. A company that does business in many countries and has facilities and offices in many countries.

Quick Quiz

1. Identify different types of trade. (Imports, exports, business factories, human resources, tourism, military aid.)
2. Give two examples of different currencies. (Mexican pesos and Japanese yen.)
3. What makes a currency strong? (A demand for a country's product drives up the value of their currency.)
4. Why do countries impose trade barriers? (Unfair competition or as a political sanction.) Ask students to name one real-world example. (Cuba, Iraq.)

Review What You Learned

11. Where is the global marketplace?
12. What are imports? What are exports?
13. Define the foreign exchange market.
14. How is the value of a country's currency determined?
15. Why does a country want to export more than it imports?
16. Why does global competition often lead to trade disputes?
17. What is the difference between protectionism and free trade?
18. Define a tariff, a quota, and an embargo.
19. Which trade alliance does the United States belong to?

Understanding Business Concepts

20. How are consumers and producers dependent on other countries?
21. The United States specializes in wheat, cars, and movies. Name some other goods and services that you think the United States specializes in producing.
22. Is it possible for one country to have a favorable balance of trade with one country and an unfavorable balance of trade with another? Explain.
23. Do you think companies in the United States need to be protected from unfair foreign competition? Why or why not?
24. Give an argument for and against having tariffs on imports.
25. Trade barriers can work both ways. Describe why this can be a problem.
26. How does free trade provide consumers with more choices?
27. Name three products you have purchased recently that were imported into the United States.

Critical Thinking

28. Should the United States trade with any country that produces the goods and services that we need and want, regardless of that country's political beliefs? Why or why not?
29. Suppose a country can produce everything its people need at less than it would cost to import these items from other countries. Should that country trade with other countries? Explain.
30. If a product shipped from the United States to Japan is considered a U.S. export, then what is it considered in Japan?
31. Protectionism in Japan may help certain segments of the economy, such as rice farmers or autoworkers, but it doesn't help Japanese consumers. Why would this be?

Viewing and Representing

Examining the Image. With a partner, look closely at this picture. Compare this scene in Bangkok with a typical business district you'd expect to see in a city near you. What's the same, and what's different?

Chapter 10 Business in a Global Economy **157**

4 CLOSE (Cont.)

Building Academic Skills

SOCIAL SCIENCE. Encourage each student to choose a different country to research. Rubrics: Chart/tables, note taking, poster.

COMPUTER/TECHNOLOGY. Students might need additional help when figuring percentages. Rubrics: Charts/graphs, mathematical calculations.

MATH. If students have difficulty creating the graph, have them work in groups and help each other. Rubric: Graph.

LANGUAGE ARTS. Encourage all students in the group to participate. If the students have trouble finding someone to interview, have them choose a large corporation and use the library as a source for the answers. Rubrics: Charts, oral presentations.

Linking School to Home

Answers will vary. Instead of family members, a student could ask a friend to work on the project with him or her. If students have trouble locating a world map, remind them to use the library or the Internet as a resource. Rubrics: Note taking, essay, oral presentation.

Linking School to Work

Answers will vary. Encourage students to choose different countries. Rubrics: Note taking, oral presentation, questions for interview.

Building Academic Skills

 International Business

Understanding how other countries conduct business is important in the global marketplace. Choose a country and research the business and social etiquette that you would need to know and understand before doing business in that country. If possible, include the following:
- Non-verbal communication and gestures
- Verbal communication
- Cultural do's and don'ts
- Dining out
- Business attire
- Gifts and greetings
- Business negotiations

Create a poster of your findings and display in your classroom.

 Graphics Software

Conduct online research to determine how and to what extent your state participates in global trade. Use graphing software to create pie charts that show (1) the percentage breakdown of the products exported to other countries and (2) the percentage breakdown of export income as a portion of state resources.

 Graph It

NAFTA created a total market of nearly 374 million people: 27 million live in Canada, 255 million live in the United States, and 92 million live in Mexico. Graph this data in a format that would best explain it.

 Interview and Report

Use the local telephone directory to locate a business in your community that imports products. Interview the person directly involved with purchasing the products. Compare your findings with the others in your class.

Linking School to Home

Locating International Products. Create a list of international products that you and your family enjoy. Using a world map, locate the countries where the products were produced. Then, determine whether or not a similar product is made in the United States. If it is, what makes the international product more attractive to purchase?

Linking School to Work

Charting Exchange Rates. Choose one of the countries from the list you developed in the

Linking School to Home activity. Research the country's currency and the current rate of exchange. As a class, create a chart that combines all the countries, their currency, and exchange rates. Then, invite someone from a local bank that deals with currency exchange to speak to the class. Prepare questions ahead of time and include the following:
- Is there a cost involved when exchanging currency? If so, what is that cost?
- When traveling to another country, is it better to exchange currency before going to the country? If not, why not?
- How are imported and exported products affected by the exchange rates?

E-Homework

Applying Technology

Internet Search on Trade Alliances. Use the Internet to research one of the trade alliances discussed in this chapter. Find out which countries are involved, when the alliance began, why it was formed, and the impact of the alliance on the rest of the world.

Creating an Advertisement. Imagine you work for a business that exports their products to customers all over the world. Select one of the countries your company markets to and use the computer to create an advertisement for a product your company produces. Research the language, design, and colors that would be appropriate in the advertisement.

Connecting Academics

Math. Next week you'll take an exciting biking trip in Thailand. You have $850 for your trip. When your plane arrives in Bangkok, you'll convert your U.S. dollars to Thai baht. The service charge for exchanging currency is a flat rate of 185 baht. Using the exchange rate below, how many baht will the clerk give you?

1 U.S. dollar = 45.3 Thai baht

History. Research trade barriers and find facts that interest you. Visualize a picture representing global trade barriers. Draw the picture you see. Include at least three types of trade barriers in your picture. Use pencil, markers, watercolors, or collage techniques. Make the picture realistic or abstract, but be prepared to explain your artwork.

BusinessWeek — Analyzing the Feature Story

You read the first part of "The Bumpy Road to Global Trade" at the beginning of this chapter. Below are a few questions for you to answer about trade alliances and Mooney Farms. You'll find the answers to these questions when you're reading the entire article. First, here are the questions:

32. Which trade alliances make it possible for Mooney Farms to sell its sun-dried tomatoes on the Mexican Riviera?
33. What benefit of free trade is Mooney Farms trying to take advantage of by attending the "Baja 2000" trade tour?

CREATIVE JOURNAL ACTIVITY

Mooney improvised and set out on her own. Take a few minutes and think of a situation in your life when you had to improvise. How did you cope? What did you learn? Write it down in your journal.

BUSINESS Online
The Full Story
To learn more about global trade, visit the *Introduction to Business* Web site at **www.introbus.glencoe.com**, and click on *BusinessWeek* Feature Story, Chapter 10.

E-Homework

INTERNET SEARCH ON TRADE ALLIANCES. Research will vary depending on the alliance selected. Rubrics: Note taking, essay, oral presentation.

CREATING AN ADVERTISEMENT. Encourage students to be creative. Rubric: Advertisement, note taking.

Connecting Academics

MATH. ($850 × 45.3) − 185 = 38,320 Thai baht.

HISTORY. The pictures students create will probably be based on a world map (or part of a world map) and show graphic representations of barriers between certain countries. Types of trade barriers to represent might be tariffs, quotas, or embargoes.

BusinessWeek — Analyzing the Feature Story

32. NAFTA
33. Mooney Farms is trying to take advantage of new markets in Mexico.

Creative Journal Activity

This is a good opportunity for students to reflect on and share methods of self-management. Students' actual situations might be personal and private. While respecting students' privacy for exact details, promote a class discussion on coping mechanisms.

Chapter 11

SCANS Correlation Chart*

Foundation Skills

Basic Skills	Reading	Writing	Math	Listening	Speaking	
Thinking Skills	Creative Thinking	Decision Making	Problem Solving	Seeing Things in the Mind's Eye	Knowing How to Learn	Reasoning
Personal Qualities	Responsibility	Self-Esteem	Sociability	Self-Management	Integrity/ Honesty	

Workplace Competencies

Resources	Allocating Time	Allocating Money	Allocating Material and Facility Resources	Allocating Human Resources		
Information	Acquiring and Evaluating Information	Organizing and Maintaining Information	Interpreting and Communicating Information	Using Computers to Process Information		
Interpersonal Skills	Participating as a Member of a Team	Teaching Others	Serving Clients/ Customers	Exercising Leadership	Negotiating to Arrive at a Decision	Working With Cultural Diversity
Systems	Understanding Systems	Monitoring and Correcting Performance	Improving and Designing Systems			
Technology	Selecting Technology	Applying Technology to Task	Maintaining and Troubleshooting Technology			

*This chart's highlighted blocks indicate the chapter's content coverage in the Student Edition and the Teacher Wraparound Edition.

160A

Resource Manager

Teaching Transparencies

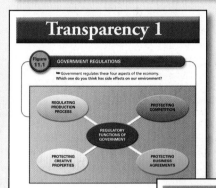

Transparency 1

GOVERNMENT REGULATIONS

Government regulates these four aspects of the economy. Which one do you think has side effects on our environment?

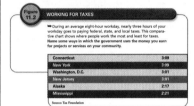

Transparency 2

WORKING FOR TAXES

During an average eight-hour workday, nearly three hours of your workday goes to paying federal, state, and local taxes. This comparative chart shows where people work the most and least for taxes. Name some ways in which the government uses the money you earn for projects or services on your community.

Connecticut	3:09
New York	3:09
Washington, D.C.	3:01
New Jersey	3:01
Alaska	2:17
Mississippi	2:21

Source: Tax Foundation

Application and Enrichment

- Lesson Plans
- *BusinessWeek* Poster Package
- Teaching Transparencies
- Integrated Software Simulation
- Glencoe Business Video Package

Review and Reinforcement

- *PuzzleMaker*
- Internet Resources
- Student Activity Workbook
- Strat. and Work. for Teaching Transparencies

Assessment and Evaluation

- Reproducible Tests
- Alternative Assessment Strategies
- ExamView® Pro Test Generator

Technology

- *PuzzleMaker*
- ExamView® Pro Test Generator
- Glencoe Business Video Package
- PowerPoint® Presentation
- Integrated Software Simulation
- Interactive Lesson Planner
- *Virtual Business*®

KEY

Printed	Software	Videocassette	Poster
Transparency	CD-ROM	Internet	

BUSINESS Online

Visit www.introbus.glencoe.com, the Web site companion to *Introduction to Business.* The student's page includes:

- interactive tutor
- additional *BusinessWeek* articles and activities
- business Web links
- homework hints
- real-world application activities
- additional career path activities

Information on how to prepare your students for the high school exit exam and special projects are also included.

Use the Glencoe Web site for additional resources. All essential content is covered in the Student Edition.

Chapter 11

1 FOCUS

Introducing the Chapter

This chapter presents how government protects and regulates business competition, agreements, and creative rights. A photo essay titled, "Government in Our Daily Lives," enhances the concepts.

Connecting the Objectives

What do students know about how government protects businesses? What services do you and your family use that are provided by local, state, or federal governments?

The Role of Government in Business

Learning Objectives

After reading this chapter, you'll be able to:

1. **Describe** ways government protects business.
2. **Name** some of the services the government provides.
3. **Explain** why the government collects taxes.
4. **State** the ways the government promotes business.

Why It's Important

Government rules promote and regulate the actions of business. The laws influence the production, selling, and pricing of goods and services.

Key Words

interstate commerce	breach of contract
intrastate commerce	copyright
oligopoly	patent
monopoly	trademark
trust	revenue
antitrust laws	subsidies
contract	tax incentives

160

BusinessWeek Feature Story

Should Europe Be More Like America?

The Right Economic Model for the Old World Is the Subject of Great Debate. Economists gathered in Davos, Switzerland, for the World Economic Forum say Europe won't achieve American-style growth rates of 5 percent-plus until governments speed up deregulation, liberalize labor markets, and make deep structural reforms. Only then will Europe be more like the United States. "We're already more flexible and less regulated than many observers think," says Ferdinand Piëch, CEO of Volkswagen, the German automaker. "What we need isn't more liberal labor laws but lower taxes to boost our competitiveness. We should also improve the way the [European Union's] single market functions."

Source: Excerpted with permission from "Should Europe Be More Like America?" *BusinessWeek Online*, January 29, 2001.

An Extension Activity

When a nation experiences an economic slowdown, what does this mean?

BUSINESS *Online*

The Full Story

To learn more about the European economy, visit the *Introduction to Business* Web site at www.introbus.glencoe.com, and click on *BusinessWeek* Feature Story, Chapter 11.

Classroom Resources

For the Teacher

📁 Student Activity Work. TAE
📓 Assessment Binder
💿 PowerPoint® Presentation
💿 Interactive Lesson Planner
📁 Lesson Plans
💻 Internet Resources
🖱️ Teaching Transparencies
💻 *Introduction to Business* Web Site

💿 Integrated Soft. Sim. TM
📘 *BusinessWeek* Poster Package

For the Student

📓 Student Activity Workbook
💿 *Virtual Business®*
💻 *Introduction to Business* Web Site
💿 Integrated Soft. Sim.
💿 *PuzzleMaker*
📓 Strategies and Worksheets for Teaching Transparencies

Bell Ringer Activity

CREATIVE THINKING. Write on the board: "You've just been elected mayor. You decide you need to become familiar with regulations government imposes on businesses. You also need to understand the services government provides businesses." Ask different students to take the role of mayor in order to answer questions about government regulations and services. **LS, CL**

Preteaching Business Key Words

ORGANIZING AND MAINTAINING INFORMATION. First, ask students to make a chart with the following headings: Protecting Competition, Protecting Business Agreements, Protecting Creative Properties, and Government as Provider. Then, ask volunteers to define each key word. Lastly, ask students to write each key word in the appropriate section of the chart. **LS**

An Extension Activity

DISCUSS. Ask students what needs to happen to reverse an economic slowdown. Discuss some solutions. Solutions will include that the federal and state government will take measures to boost business and the economy. **CL**

Making Connections

The Business World. Ask students to prepare a short, informal business presentation in which they explain clearly to a client from another country the workings of interstate commerce and intrastate commerce, oligopoly and monopoly, and trust and antitrust laws. Remind students that visuals in a presentation help both the presenter and the listener organize information. Suggest that students design a chart, diagram, or other visual to support their presentation. **LS, CL**

2 TEACH

Business Connection

GOVERNMENT DEREGULATION. Utilities are changing with states deregulating electricity markets. Now utility companies are looking for revenue not just from the traditional source of business—delivering electricity in the United States—but from other ventures such as meeting the demand for natural gas, trading commodities (such as coal and chemicals), and even selling power in deregulated world markets. For example, TXU Corporation provides many customers not only electricity, but also cable, telephone, and even home security services. TXU is also providing power to customers in Europe and Australia.

Develop Concepts

INTERPRET. What role does a referee have in a wrestling match? (Regulator.) What aspects of being a referee in a wrestling match are like the role of government in business? (Protect the players. Ensure the competition is fair.) What are the three different levels of government, and what are their jurisdictions? (Federal—country, state—individual states, and local—counties and cities.)

Figure 11.1 Caption Answer

Regulating the production process.

How Government Affects Business

Suppose there were no traffic laws or you had to pay the fire department to put out the fire burning in your house. The roads would be chaos and your house would burn down by the time your credit card cleared. That's why government is needed. If you're looking for a street address in an unfamiliar city, you might go to a police officer for directions. If you're looking at a product's label, you might check for FDA approval. In each case, a government agency has helped make your life a little easier.

The government created traffic laws to protect drivers and courts to protect the rights of individuals. It has also created laws to regulate

Figure 11.1

GOVERNMENT REGULATIONS

➡ Government regulates these four aspects of the economy. Which one do you think has side effects on our environment?

- REGULATING PRODUCTION PROCESS
- PROTECTING COMPETITION
- REGULATORY FUNCTIONS OF GOVERNMENT
- PROTECTING CREATIVE PROPERTIES
- PROTECTING BUSINESS AGREEMENTS

162 Unit 3 Groups Affecting Business

Cooperative Learning

Government Regulations. Have student groups work together to decide what kind of small business they wish to operate, for example, auto repair shop, hair salon, or recording studio. Suggest that they research what kinds of government regulations they will encounter as they open and maintain the business: license or permit, zoning permit or other requirement, labor or environmental restrictions. Have groups prepare a four-page illustrated booklet indicating what regulations are associated with the business they chose. **CL**, **LS**, **P**

business. Government agencies regulate everything from the quality of the food you eat to how products are advertised. Their job is to protect both business and the public from unfair, unsafe, and unethical business practices.

One of the government's roles is to foster economic success. The economic health of a nation depends on the success of individual businesses. To promote this economic growth, local, state, and national government pass laws to both promote and regulate business.

Government as Regulator

There are three different levels of government—federal, state, and local. The federal government runs the country, state governments run individual states, and local governments run cities and counties. Each level of government oversees a different level of business. The federal government focuses on business that takes place across all states, or **interstate commerce**. State governments focus on **intrastate commerce**, or business within each state.

The government regulates these four aspects of the economy: (1) protecting competition, (2) protecting business agreements, (3) protecting creative properties, and (4) regulating the production process. Figure 11.1 illustrates these four ways in which the government intervenes in economic activity.

Protecting Competition

When a small number of companies control the market without actually forming a trust, this is called an **oligopoly**. In the 1800s a few large companies took over major industries and wiped out the competition. A company that controls an entire industry is called a **monopoly**, which means "one seller." Since a monopoly doesn't have to compete with other companies it can charge anything it wants for a product. It would be like one shoe company owning all the stores in the country. You would have no choice of what to buy or how much to pay.

Rival companies can also form a monopoly by banding together into a **trust** and agree not to compete with each other. In the 1800s, John D. Rockefeller gained a monopoly on oil. By 1890 there was a sugar trust, a steel trust, a bank trust, and even a tin can trust.

To prevent monopolies and promote competition, the U.S. government passed a series of antitrust laws. **Antitrust laws** allow the government to break up monopolies, regulate them, or take them over. This hasn't always stopped companies from competing unfairly. In the 1940s

Real-World Application

part 1 of 4

GOVERNMENT IN YOUR DAILY LIFE
When you travel on a highway, you're using a resource financed by federal and state money. **List some roadways or highways in your community that need work. Does the city have any plans to repair them?**

continued on p. 165

Real-World Application
Caption Answer

GOVERNMENT IN YOUR DAILY LIFE: PART 1 OF 4
Answers will vary.

Technology Resource

GO TO **POWERPOINT.** The *Introduction to Business* PowerPoint® CD-ROM provides visual lecture aids for this chapter.

Independent Practice

INVESTIGATE. To meet cleaner environmental standards, many manufacturers have spent millions of dollars to install filters and other equipment to lessen their production of air pollutants. Some manufacturers needed to redesign their entire manufacturing process to reduce the amount of solid waste they produce. Large manufacturers can receive tax breaks for reducing pollution or waste. Investigate and write a paragraph on such a manufacturer, including details on the incentive. **LS**

Chapter 11 The Role of Government in Business **163**

Meeting Individual Needs

Students With Language Difficulties.
One of the most common problems for students with language difficulties is an inability to ask questions about concepts or material they don't understand. Divide the class into groups to practice developing questions about the information presented in the section, "Government as a Regulator." Encourage groups to think of as many questions

as possible that could be generated by the material on these pages. Have groups write their questions on posters to display around the room. As you go through this chapter have students find the answers to the questions. For fun, have students write the answer on the appropriate poster, then ring a bell to bring the answer to everyone's attention.

Caption Answer

The advantage to AOL and Time Warner is that the merger puts the company into a leading position to control the set-top box behind the multimillion-dollar market interactive-TV platform. The advantage to the industry as a whole is that the FTC ruling opens the cable broadband pipes to competing Internet-service providers.

Thinking Critically

GOVERNMENT REGULATION. If a local company employed you to organize projects ensuring the company stays within the law in its business practices, under what major headings would you choose to categorize the laws? (Competition, business agreements, creative properties, and if it's a producer, production regulations.)

Consider This...

Limits on Competition
The merger between America Online (AOL) and Time Warner is the largest media merger in history. The new company is worth $110 billion. The Federal Trade Commission was concerned that the new AOL-Time Warner would limit competition. To avoid this, they required Time Warner to open its broadband pipes to competing Internet service providers.
ANALYZE
What are the advantages of the AOL and Time Warner merger?

the government sued a group of studios for trying to take over the film industry. In the 1990s the government sued Microsoft for trying to wipe out its competition.

The government created the Federal Trade Commission (FTC) to regulate interstate trade. Its job includes setting standards for honest advertising. For example, if a company makes false claims about its product or another company's product, it can be sued.

Protecting Business Agreements

One of the most basic ways the government protects business is by enforcing contracts. A **contract** is a legal agreement between two or more parties to conduct business. It can be written, verbal, or even done with a handshake. A rental agreement, a car insurance policy, and even the warranty on a CD player are all types of contracts.

A contract protects all the parties that agree to it. If you take out a student loan and refuse to pay it back later, the lender can take you to court. If your CD player breaks down before the warranty has expired and the company refuses to fix or replace it, you can sue them. When one party fails to live up to the terms of a contract it is called a **breach of contract**. It's important to make a contract and read the terms of it before you do business. For example, suppose you're in a band that plays at a coffeehouse and the manager refuses to pay you. If you didn't have a contract with the manager, there's nothing you can do about it.

Protecting Creative Properties

The government has laws protecting the right to own creative properties. Creative properties are things like inventions and artwork. If you write a great story or invent a time machine and don't legally register it, someone can steal your idea from you. You can protect your property by getting a copyright, patent, or trademark.

A **copyright** gives artists the sole right to own their creations, such as plays, photos, music, paintings, and books. If you own the copyright to a story you wrote, anyone who wants to print it, make a movie out of it, or use it in any way has to get your permission. A copyright usually last until 70 years after the artist has died. That means if a studio wants to use a song by Moby in a movie, it has to pay him for it.

A **patent** gives you the sole right to own an invention. Even the simplest inventions need to be patented. George de Mestral patented his invention, Velcro, in 1955 and made millions of dollars. Thomas Edison owned over 1,000 patents. A **trademark** is a brand name, trade name, trade characteristic, or a combination of these that is given legal protection by the federal government. Familiar trademarks include Frito-Lay's *Doritos®*, Kellogg's *Rice Krispies Treats®* cereal, and *VISA®*.

LANGUAGE ARTS · **Curriculum Connection**

Government as Provider. Form students into three groups. Group one is to investigate public services provided by government; group two is work provided by government; and group three is subsidies provided by government. Each group is to find one interesting aspect of its topic and present this in a two-minute news story. **LS, CL**

Regulating the Production Process

The fourth way the government intervenes with economic activity is by regulating the production process. The government tries to stop industrial pollutants with regulations. These regulations limit the amount of waste that factories can discharge into the environment. As a result of federal budget cutbacks, environmental regulations are often not enforced. Then it is up to the state and local communities to take responsibility for regulating pollution to the water and air.

 Fast Review _____

1. What is the difference between interstate and intrastate commerce?
2. What are the ways the government can deal with a monopoly?
3. What kinds of properties are protected by copyrights?

Government as Provider

In many cases, when you want something you can save your money and then buy it. However, you can't buy some things. For example, you can't buy highways, bridges, or water treatment plants. The government provides these along with a large number of other goods and services. Who decides which goods and services the government should provide? Where does the money to pay for them come from? Who decides how much the government should spend?

The role of government in business isn't limited to passing and enforcing laws. It also takes an active role. It provides important services, conducts business itself, and acts as a partner to business. These activities are carried on at every level of government.

In a democratic system, people make their collective wants known through their elected officials. These officials try to satisfy as many of the people's wants as possible. However, the officials must also consider public welfare. Satisfying the wants of many different groups of people as well as providing for the public welfare can be difficult, because the government's funds are limited. Most government funds come from taxes that people and businesses pay. Government officials, including those you elect to office, determine how much money will be spent.

GOVERNMENT IN YOUR DAILY LIFE
Your school probably receives some form of aid from the local, state, or federal government. **List the issues your local board of education recently passed. What did it want to spend money on?**

continued on p. 167

Chapter 11 The Role of Government in Business **165**

Chapter 11

 Real-World Application
Caption Answer

GOVERNMENT IN YOUR DAILY LIFE: PART 2 OF 4
Answers will vary.

Fast Review Answers ✓

1. Interstate commerce is business between states and is overseen by the federal government. Intrastate commerce is business within a state and is overseen by the state government.
2. Break it up, regulate it, or take it over.
3. Artistic creations like books, movies, music, plays, and photos.

Business Connection

PATENT. Joshua Coates had an idea to give companies quickly accessible, much-needed data storage. His idea uses the Internet and readily available disk drives linked with his specialized software. Coates applied to patent his specialized software so his idea would be protected. Based on this patent-pending idea, Coates started a company called Scale Eight. Viacom's MTVi uses Scale Eight's storage system; it is predicting success in the $20 billion storage-device market.

Great Ideas From the Classroom of...

Phillip Schwenk
Grover Cleveland High School
Reseda, Calif.

Mirror Exercise. Students need to know the "whys" behind the subject matter and examine their own beliefs. It's important that students interact with the information they're studying. I conduct discussions—not lectures—and I'm constantly reminding the students to "Look in the Mirror." I tell them to ask, "What do I have to do with it? What does this have to do with me?" Critical thinking is a very marketable skill. I tell students, "When you go for a job interview, employers are looking for what you can do for them, and they know with critical thinking you can do more."

2 TEACH (Cont.)

Develop Concepts

SPECIFY. Ask students to research and provide one example for each of the following: government services, subsidies, and tax incentives.

Discussion Starter

IDENTIFYING. Ask students to identify some of their own privileges and responsibilities with respect to siblings and peers, agreements, and their own ideas and creations. Then ask students if any privilege has been taken away because they did not meet their responsibilities. How are business laws similar? (Laws are often enacted to ensure that businesses meet their responsibilities in business agreements, regarding competition and in protecting new products.)

Figure 11.2 Caption Answer

Answers will vary but might include paying for streets, libraries, and parks.

People pay for government-provided goods and services through taxes. You probably pay sales tax when you buy a book, video game, or CD. For some goods, such as gasoline, taxes are included in the purchase price. If you have a job, taxes are deducted from your wages.

The idea behind taxes is to pay for public goods and services and to share the cost among many people. (Figure 11.2 illustrates the average workday that goes to paying taxes.) Some people may not receive direct benefits from their tax money. For instance, some people may never need to call on the fire department, but the fire department has value for everyone in the community. Families without children don't directly use the community's schools, but the entire community benefits from having better-educated children and adults.

People who use public goods and services generally don't directly pay the full cost. For example, those who use city parks and libraries usually pay little to no entrance or membership fee. The admission charge for a public museum is rarely enough to cover the museum's costs. The charges people pay for public health services generally are far below the costs. Government uses the taxes it collects from all the people to make up the difference between the actual costs of such goods and services and the amount of those goods and services used.

Government spending decisions directly affect how resources are allocated. If the government spends its revenues on projects such as

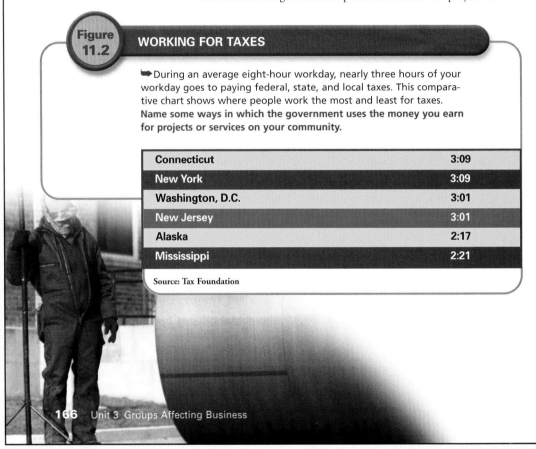

Figure 11.2 — WORKING FOR TAXES

➡ During an average eight-hour workday, nearly three hours of your workday goes to paying federal, state, and local taxes. This comparative chart shows where people work the most and least for taxes. **Name some ways in which the government uses the money you earn for projects or services on your community.**

Connecticut	3:09
New York	3:09
Washington, D.C.	3:01
New Jersey	3:01
Alaska	2:17
Mississippi	2:21

Source: Tax Foundation

166 Unit 3 Groups Affecting Business

Global Perspective

International Copyright Laws. Most countries have their own versions of copyright and patent laws. In addition, many nations subscribe to international copyright protection laws. Even so, sales of pirated tapes and software for perhaps one-tenth of the normal price cost the industries millions of dollars in lost revenue a year.

Concerned nations have indicated that countries who don't enforce protection of creative property may not be welcome in the global marketplace. Suggest students research the annual cost to U.S. businesses of pirated goods made in other countries. Have them present their findings. **LS, CL**

missile systems in rural areas rather than on social welfare programs in urban areas, economic activity is stimulated in rural areas as resources are shifted there. The allocation of resources can be affected indirectly as well. In agriculture, the decision to support the prices of milk, grains, or peanuts keeps the factors of production working in those industries.

Government spending also influences the distribution of income, or the way in which income is allocated among families, individuals, or other designated groups in the economy. The incomes of needy families, for example, can be directly affected by increasing or decreasing transfer payments.

Incomes are affected indirectly when the government decides where to make expenditures. The decision to buy fighter planes from one factory rather than from another has an impact on the communities near both factories. Many businesses not linked to either company will feel the effects when workers are laid off or get new jobs and alter their spending habits. These situations are not merely hypothetical. The military base closings of the 1990s had a devastating impact on incomes in local communities that had come to depend on the military installations.

On the positive side, government can provide temporary income support for selective groups. In 1999, for example, the Department of Agriculture purchased millions of pounds of pork in an attempt to support low pork prices for farmers.

Providing Public Services

The government is the single largest provider of services in the country. Business offers goods and services to individuals on demand to make a profit. The government provides services to the public as a whole for the good of society. It spends the most on transfer payments, like welfare and unemployment compensation.

Many of the services the government provides are necessary for the protection of the public, such as the military, police, and fire department. Other services promote social welfare, like parks, and libraries. The government also provides public education, roads, courts, post offices, and countless other services. Every time you go to a park, take a bus, or mail a letter, you're using a government service.

The cost of providing all these services is enormous. To pay for them, the government has to raise money. The money the government takes in is called **revenue**. The government's main source of revenue is taxes, which is money collected from businesses and the public. Each level of government collects different kinds of taxes for different kinds of services. Federal income tax is used to pay for national highways, defense, and social security.

Real-World Application
part 3 of 4

GOVERNMENT IN YOUR DAILY LIFE
Many goods that you buy are produced in accordance with local, state, and federal regulations.
Has your family ever bought a product that was recalled by the manufacturer because it didn't meet government regulations? What was it?

continued on p. 169

Real-World Application
Caption Answer

GOVERNMENT IN YOUR DAILY LIFE: PART 3 OF 4
Answers might include cars, food, appliances, and so on.

Individualized Practice

SURVEY. Ask students to conduct a survey of family members, students, friends, or teachers on the government's role in the economy. Suggest they ask questions such as: Do you think there is too much, just enough, or too little government regulation? Which regulatory agencies, if any, should be abolished? Which regulatory agencies, if any, should have their powers expanded?

L1 Have pairs of students pool their data and share the answers with the class.

L2 Tell students to make a chart and record the responses to their survey.

L3 Have students ask the following additional survey questions: Which government activity do you feel plays the most important role in maintaining competition in the marketplace? Why? Group students to pool the responses to their surveys, chart the data, and present a summary of the main viewpoints to the class.

LANGUAGE ARTS
Curriculum Connection

Cartoon Drawing. You're a popular cartoonist specializing in illustrating the relationship between government and business. Draw a single-incident or three-stage cartoon, which depicts the relationship of government as a regulator or as a provider. **LS**

3 ASSESS

Reteaching

PROTECTING COMPETITION.
To reteach the concept of protecting competition, ask students to tell what led to the government passing antitrust laws. (Monopolies could charge anything and there was limited choice of products. Rival companies banded together to form trusts.)

Enrichment Strategy

WRITE. Ask students to write a paragraph starting with the sentence, "I feel government regulation is important because . . ." **LS**

Evaluation

Assign and review the Fast Review sections.

Working Lifestyle

Caption Answer

Answers will vary, but might include community, education, health, technology, and a sense of place.

Local taxes are used to pay for streets, libraries, and parks in your community. All three levels (local, state, and federal) of government fund public education.

Providing Work

The government is the single largest employer in the country. The federal government alone employs over three million people. Employees are needed to run the daily operations of government from courthouse clerks to mail carriers. Public officials from your local mayor to the President of the Unites States are public employees. The government pays all members of the army, navy, and air force. Other public employees include teachers, bus drivers, police, trash collectors, and fire fighters.

Working Lifestyle

What are you doing at 10 A.M.?

A Celebration of Urban Design

Walt Disney Corporation launched the successful town called Celebration, Fla. Creating and designing this central Florida town was no Mickey-Mouse project. Just ask Brian Shea.

Shea is a partner in the New York City architectural planning and urban design firm, Cooper, Robertson, & Partners. As part of the team of creative minds that designed Celebration, Shea focused on fitting the 5,000-acre planned community into its natural surroundings.

He asks his receptionist to hold a ten o'clock call as he fine tunes a drawing. Shea's professional tools are rather simple: tracing paper, soft pencils, ink pens, and Magic Markers. He uses hard-line tools, such as a T-square and triangle if transferring a drawing to a computer. As a designer, he endlessly manipulates paper and pencil and thinks analytically about a project.

Salary

A typical urban planner is expected to earn a median base salary of $39,137.

Outlook for This Career

Employment of urban and regional planners is expected to grow about as fast as the average for all occupations. Non-governmental initiatives dealing with historic preservation and redevelopment will provide additional openings.

Connecting Careers Activity

Imagine you've been asked to consult on the design of an urban community. What would be the four major cornerstones (i.e., what services, businesses, or activities might be needed)?

CAREER PATH — Architecture & Construction

How to Use a Portfolio Activity

The portfolio projects are designed to lead students to develop a collection of their best work to submit to you for assessment. You and each of your students should decide which projects to include in their business portfolio. Refer students to the specific rubric(s) from the *Alternative Assessment Strategies*. These rubrics will alert students to the criteria you'll use to assess their projects.

For people temporarily out of work, the government provides unemployment insurance. It offers welfare benefits and job training programs for people who have trouble finding work. Social Security provides insurance by taking certain amount of money out of your paycheck and setting it aside for your future retirement.

Assisting Business

The government is also the single largest consumer of goods and services. It has to buy computers, furniture, and supplies for schools and government offices. To maintain the military it has to buy uniforms, food, ships, aircraft, and weapons. The government buys most of its equipment directly from businesses or has it specially made, such as military aircraft and fire trucks. The government also hires businesses to build courthouses, schools, and roads.

The government promotes and assists business in a number of ways. The Small Business Administration (SBA) offers different kinds of loans to aspiring small-business owners. The government also lends money to big businesses that are in financial trouble. For example, when Chrysler Corporation was on the verge of bankruptcy in 1980, the government lent it $400 million to bail it out. The government even lends money to help foreign countries build up their economies in order to create new markets for American goods.

To protect American businesses from unfair foreign competition, the government sets up trade barriers (as discussed in Chapter 10). In same cases, important businesses like corn or steel have to lower the cost of their products to compete with foreign companies. The government helps them out by giving them subsidies. **Subsidies** are payments the government gives to businesses to make up for their losses.

To encourage socially responsible behavior, government offers businesses reductions in taxes, or **tax incentives**. For example, oil companies that lower the amount of pollution they cause are rewarded with lower taxes. Tax breaks are also given to companies that conserve energy or use alternate sources of fuel. Both loans and tax breaks are offered to businesses that do community development. Community development can consist of donating profits to local schools or setting up a business in a poor area to create jobs.

Real-World Application
part **4** of **4**

GOVERNMENT IN YOUR DAILY LIFE
If you own property, buy goods, or earn an income, you probably pay taxes that help pay for many government activities.
What is the amount of state tax you pay for clothing or food?

✔ **Fast Review** _____

1. What are some services the government provides for the public?
2. Name different types of government workers.
3. What kinds of goods does the government buy from businesses?

Chapter 11 The Role of Government in Business **169**

Meeting Individual Needs

Students With Problems Reading. Students with problems reading or organizing material can benefit from recognizing the kinds of organization used in their textbooks. Have students rewrite the main headings in the chapter as questions—each on a separate page. Ask students to list the subheads for each section beneath their questions. Tell students to use the subheads as a guide to find the answers to their questions by reading the paragraphs. Ask students to explain how the subheads helped them find the answers to their questions.

4 CLOSE

Chapter Wrap-Up

Ask students to list the significant factors of government as a regulator and provider.

Using Business Key Words

1. interstate commerce
2. intrastate commerce
3. patent
4. antitrust laws
5. monopoly
6. copyright
7. trust
8. oligopoly
9. contract
10. breach of contract
11. trademark
12. revenue
13. tax incentives
14. revenue

Review What You Learned

15. To establish the rules so that all competitors have equal opportunities.
16. To regulate interstate commerce.
17. To keep business competition fair.
18. Patent—right that prevents the reproduction of the same thing. Copyright—protects creative property. Trademark—registered name, brand, or symbol that a business lists with the government.
19. Highways, national defense, Social Security, streets, etc.
20. Court systems, schools, libraries, police and fire protection, civic maintenance, and water and sewage treatment.
21. Needs are different.
22. Transfer payments.
23. Big businesses impact the workforce and consumers.

Summary

1. Government protects business competition, agreements, and creative rights.
2. Public protection, public education, roads, courts, and social welfare are examples of government services.
3. The government collects taxes to pay for the services it provides.
4. Government assists businesses with loans, subsidies, and tax breaks.

● Using Business Key Words

The government has a major impact on business in the United States. Find out how much you understand the impact by completing the sentences below.

- **antitrust laws**
- **intrastate commerce**
- **copyright**
- **oligopoly**
- **monopoly**
- **breach of contract**
- **interstate commerce**
- **patent**
- **trademark**
- **subsidies**
- **tax incentives**
- **trust**
- **contract**
- **revenue**

1. The federal government focuses primarily on _____, or business activities that cross state boundaries.
2. Business activities within the state are called _____.
3. A legal "right" that prevents copying or use of an invention is called a _____.
4. _____ control a market and prevent unfair competition.
5. If a large company controls a market's prices, then it has a _____ on the market.
6. A _____ provides protection for authors of books, plays, software, movies, and for other kinds of artists.
7. When a group of companies band together to form a monopoly and eliminate competition, they create a _____.
8. A _____ controls an industry by a small group of companies.
9. A _____ is upheld between two parties. It can be written, verbal, or even done with a handshake.
10. If a party fails to live up to the terms of a contract, this is a _____.
11. Kleenex® is an example of a _____.
12. _____ is government or business income.
13. The government gives businesses _____ to encourage certain activities.
14. The government gives a business _____ to make up for the business's losses.

Quick Quiz

1. How do government regulations foster competition? (By controlling monopolies and oligopolies and ensuring that all competitors have an equal chance of producing a product, entering a market, and making a profit.)

2. Why do government regulations strive to foster competition? (Competition encourages business to work to produce the highest quality goods or services at the lowest price.)

3. How can a business protect its creative property? (By getting a copyright, patent, or trademark.)

Review What You Learned

15. Explain the government's role as regulator.
16. Why was the Federal Trade Commission established?
17. Explain the government's role as protector of individuals.
18. Define a patent, a copyright, and a trademark.
19. For what purpose does the government use the taxes it collects from the public?
20. What types of products and services are provided by the local government?
21. Why might each state government spend its money differently?
22. What is the number-one expenditure for the federal government?
23. Why would the government lend businesses money?

Understanding Business Concepts

24. Why do you think our government wants businesses to succeed?
25. Does competition improve the quality of products or services that consumers purchase? How?
26. If the only two businesses that sell television sets in a small town agree to sell their products at the same price, does that action create a monopoly? Why or why not?
27. List five trademarks you see used in your community.
28. For what purposes do you think your state uses the money it collects through sales tax?
29. Do you agree with the federal government's spending priorities? Explain your answer.

Critical Thinking

30. Do you believe the U.S. government looks out for the common welfare of all the people in the country? Why or why not?
31. When a business is required by U.S. law to install pollution control equipment, who ultimately pays for the cost of the equipment?
32. Make a list of people in your community who help pay for the cost of public goods and services but don't directly use them.
33. How do people in a democracy acknowledge their social wants so that the government can help satisfy these?

Viewing and Representing

Examining the Image. Find every last detail in this photograph. Ask yourself these questions: What do you think's important here? Which taxes are being used? Can you give examples of government-funded work that's going on in your area?

Chapter 11 The Role of Government in Business **171**

Critical Thinking

30. Answers will vary. Students should justify their answers.
31. Answers will vary. Students should justify their answers.
32. Answers will vary but might include people without children who do not directly use schools. Not everyone uses the services of the fire and police department, and not everyone uses the parks that they help support.
33. People make their wants known through their elected officials.

Viewing and Representing

As a variation for this activity, pair students to challenge each other to find every detail in this picture. Have them ask each other the questions listed. Ask pairs to share examples with the class.

Understanding Business Concepts

24. Because businesses provide goods and services to satisfy the wants and needs of the people and provide jobs.
25. Yes. When several businesses produce the same item, they try to outdo each other or make the product better. This benefits the consumer.
26. Yes. If the businesses agree on a price, customers have no choice but to pay the price if they want the product. Since they do not compete, the businesses have a monopoly.
27. Answers will vary. Make sure students understand the definition of a trademark.
28. Answers will vary.
29. Answers will vary. Make sure students justify their answers.

4 CLOSE (Cont.)

Building Academic Skills

LANGUAGE ARTS. Make sure all the students participate in the group project. Allow the students to choose the way they will share their results. Rubrics: Charts/tables, diagrams, oral presentations, posters.

HISTORY. Students will find information in the library or on the Internet. Rubric: Two-page paper.

MATH. If the students have trouble securing the information, encourage them to try locating it in the library or on the Internet. All the students choose the way they will evaluate the expenses. Rubrics: Math calculations, charts/tables, essay, oral presentation.

COMPUTER/TECHNOLOGY. Encourage the students to be creative. If students need help with the computer software, allow other students to provide that help. Rubric: Trademark or logo.

Linking School to Home

Answers will vary. Rubrics: Essay, oral presentation.

Linking School to Work

It might be helpful to invite the student government officers to the class in order for the students to answer the questions. Rubrics: Note taking, essay, oral presentation.

Building Academic Skills

 Compare and Contrast

In a group of three or four, make a list of ways to increase competition among businesses. Make a second list of ways to decrease competition. Compare your lists with those of the other groups in your class. Circle the items that are regulated by the government. Use your lists as the basis for a class display showing the advantages and disadvantages of government regulation of business.

 Researching Antitrust Laws

Research the antitrust laws of a market-driven country (other than the United States). Write a two-page paper comparing the similarities and differences to the antitrust laws in the United States.

 Determine Percentage

In groups of three or four, contact your local city or county government. Ask for a copy of the budget from last year and this year. Determine the percentage increase or decrease of the income and expenses for the city or county government. Evaluate the expenses and decide if there are any services that could be eliminated if necessary. Justify your decisions.

 Graphic Design

Using the computer, design a trademark or logo for a business in your community that you frequent. When creating the design, consider the fact that the trademark or logo could be used on billboards, signs, letterhead, business cards and packaging. Display your completed work in the classroom.

Linking School to Home

Local Businesses. Make a list of all the businesses within a two-mile radius of your home. Use the phone book and newspaper ads to determine the following:
- Which businesses sell products made outside the United States?
- Are there more businesses selling imported products than products made in the United States?

Linking School to Work

Analyzing Student Government. Compare your school's student government to the federal, state, and local government. Then, answer the following questions:
- How does your school's student government look out for the common welfare of all the students within the school?
- What is the role of the student government?
- Has the student government created any rules or regulations that all students must follow? If so, how are they enforced?
- Does the student government have any money to spend? If so, where do they get it? What do they spend it on?

E-Homework

Applying Technology

Government Laws. Using the Internet, research four laws that the government has created to protect individuals. Research one in each of the following categories: (1) environmental protection, (2) consumer protection, (3) employee protection, and (4) general welfare protection.

Copyrighting Music. Imagine a friend has just written a piece of music that will be performed at the next California Music Festival. You suggest she publish the piece. Using the Internet, help her find information about copyrighting music. Research the following:
• What is the procedure for copyrighting music?
• How should your friend register her music with the copyright office?
• What specific laws protect the original works of musicians?

Connecting Academics

Math. You're an event coordinator for A to Z National Conventions. You work from 8:30 A.M. to 5:00 P.M. Tomorrow you're calling: an acrobatic team in New York, a specialty caterer in California, a display designer in Hawaii, a master magician in Colorado, and a video producer in Texas. You assume the companies you're calling are open between 9:00 A.M. and 5:00 P.M. Taking into account time zone differences, make a list of the times you might call each vendor.

History. Choose a local manufacturer. Complete the following steps to learn more about government services and government regulations in business:
• **Investigate.** Find at least five services provided by government.

• **Explore.** Research and then list three activities regulated by government to protect workers, consumers, and the company.

BusinessWeek Analyzing the Feature Story

You read the first part of "Should Europe Be More Like America?" at the beginning of this chapter. Below are a few questions for you to answer about the European economy. You'll find the answers to these questions when you're reading the entire article. First, here are the questions:

34. How do the economists who gathered in Davos, Switzerland, view deregulation in Europe?

35. What type of government reform are European business leaders interested in?

CREATIVE JOURNAL ACTIVITY

Research *BusinessWeek Online* for one of the major regulatory agencies listed in the chapter. What information is available on the site?

The Full Story

To learn more about the European economy, visit the *Introduction to Business* Web site at **www.introbus.glencoe.com**, and click on *BusinessWeek* Feature Story, Chapter 11.

SCANS Correlation Chart*

Foundation Skills

Basic Skills	Reading	Writing	Math	Listening	Speaking	
Thinking Skills	Creative Thinking	Decision Making	Problem Solving	Seeing Things in the Mind's Eye	Knowing How to Learn	Reasoning
Personal Qualities	Responsibility	Self-Esteem	Sociability	Self-Management	Integrity/ Honesty	

Workplace Competencies

Resources	Allocating Time	Allocating Money	Allocating Material and Facility Resources	Allocating Human Resources		
Information	Acquiring and Evaluating Information	Organizing and Maintaining Information	Interpreting and Communicating Information	Using Computers to Process Information		
Interpersonal Skills	Participating as a Member of a Team	Teaching Others	Serving Clients/ Customers	Exercising Leadership	Negotiating to Arrive at a Decision	Working With Cultural Diversity
Systems	Understanding Systems	Monitoring and Correcting Performance	Improving and Designing Systems			
Technology	Selecting Technology	Applying Technology to Task	Maintaining and Troubleshooting Technology			

*This chart's highlighted blocks indicate the chapter's content coverage in the Student Edition and the Teacher Wraparound Edition.

Resource Manager

Teaching Transparencies

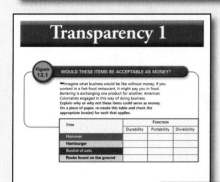

Transparency 1

WOULD THESE ITEMS BE ACCEPTABLE AS MONEY?

Imagine what business would be like without money. If you worked in a fast-food restaurant, it might pay you in food. *Bartering* is exchanging one product for another. American Colonialists engaged in this way of doing business. Explain why or why not these items could serve as money. On a piece of paper, re-create this table and check the appropriate box(es) for each that applies.

ITEM	FUNCTION		
	Durability	Portability	Divisibility
Hammer			
Hamburger			
Bushel of oats			
Rocks found on the ground			

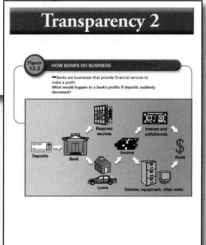

Transparency 2

HOW BANKS DO BUSINESS

Banks are businesses that provide financial services to make a profit. What would happen to a bank's profits if deposits suddenly decreased?

Application and Enrichment

- Lesson Plans
- *BusinessWeek* Poster Package
- Teaching Transparencies
- Integrated Software Simulation
- Glencoe Business Video Package

Review and Reinforcement

- *PuzzleMaker*
- Internet Resources
- Student Activity Workbook
- Strat. and Work. for Teaching Transparencies

Assessment and Evaluation

- Reproducible Tests
- Alternative Assessment Strategies
- ExamView® Pro Test Generator

Technology

- *PuzzleMaker*
- ExamView® Pro Test Generator
- Glencoe Business Video Package
- PowerPoint® Presentation
- Integrated Software Simulation
- Interactive Lesson Planner
- *Virtual Business*®

KEY	Printed	Software	Videocassette	Poster
	Transparency	CD-ROM	Internet	

BUSINESS Online

Visit www.introbus.glencoe.com, the Web site companion to *Introduction to Business.* The student's page includes:

- interactive tutor
- additional *BusinessWeek* articles and activities
- business Web links
- homework hints
- real-world application activities
- additional career path activities

Information on how to prepare your students for the high school exit exam and special projects are also included.

Use the Glencoe Web site for additional resources. All essential content is covered in the Student Edition.

1 FOCUS

Introducing the Chapter

This chapter describes the functions and characteristics of money. It explains the bank services and types of banks. A photo essay titled, "How Banks Create Money," enhances the concepts.

Connecting the Objectives

What are three uses of money? Ask students to tell what they know about banks.

BusinessWeek
Feature Story

Story's Summary

The euro (the European Union's currency) was falling, but then the level began to climb compared with the U.S. dollar. The euro needed a boost against not just the dollar, but also the yen. There's the state of the U.S. economy, European interest rates, the gloomy news of Japan's economy, euro-zone tax cuts, oil prices, global purchases of euro-zone bonds, and corporate spending, among other factors.

Find the entire article at **www.introbus.glencoe.com**, or in the Teacher Resource Binder.

Chapter 12

Money and Financial Institutions

Learning Objectives

After completing this chapter, you'll be able to:
1. **Describe** the functions and characteristics of money.
2. **Explain** the services that banks offer.
3. **Name** the types of banks.
4. **Identify** the functions of the Federal Reserve System.

Why It's Important

Understanding the way money and financial institutions work is crucial to understanding the economy.

Key Words

monetary system
money
financial institution
bank account
deposit
withdrawal
interest
electronic funds transfer (EFT)
collateral
mortgage
safety-deposit box
Federal Reserve System

174

BusinessWeek Feature Story

The Euro: Back From the Depths

The Ups and Downs of the Euro. The chilly December markets were merciful to at least one person—Wim Duisenberg. As late as October, the European Central Bank chief's days seemed numbered as the euro fell against the U.S. dollar. Then, in late November, the currency began climbing. On Christmas Day, it hit 93 cents in thin Tokyo trading. The level stuck. As of December 28, it was holding around 93.10 cents. That's 13 percent above its low of 82.25 cents reached on October 26.

Source: Excerpted with permission from "The Euro: Back From the Depths," *BusinessWeek Online*, January 8, 2001.

An Extension Activity

The Federal Reserve System is the centralized banking organization in the United States. Who is its chairperson, and what do you think he or she does?

BUSINESS *Online*
The Full Story
To learn more about the euro, visit the *Introduction to Business* Web site at **www.introbus.glencoe.com**, and click on *BusinessWeek* Feature Story, Chapter 12.

Classroom Resources

For the Teacher
- Student Activity Work. TAE
- Assessment Binder
- PowerPoint® Presentation
- Interactive Lesson Planner
- Lesson Plans
- Internet Resources
- Teaching Transparencies
- *Introduction to Business* Web Site

- Integrated Soft. Sim. TM
- *BusinessWeek* Poster Package

For the Student
- Student Activity Workbook
- *Virtual Business*®
- *Introduction to Business* Web Site
- Integrated Soft. Sim.
- *PuzzleMaker*
- Strategies and Worksheets for Teaching Transparencies

Bell Ringer Activity

LISTENING. List all the things you paid for over the past week. If money didn't exist, how would you pay for them? How do you compare the costs of different products? How would you define money? Ask students to listen and think carefully as they share their definitions of money, and then to come to a consensus on the definition for money.

Preteaching Business Key Words

SPEAKING. Ask students to take turns using each of the vocabulary words in a sentence. Ask students to discuss their sentences and revise any whose meaning does not match the definition of the term. **LS**

An Extension Activity

SHARE. The answer is the current chairman of the Federal Reserve Board. He or she monitors the development in the U.S. economy.

Making Connections

Everyday Living. Ask students to write a paragraph starting with the sentence, "Yes, I do have a Federal Reserve Note in my possession . . ." (Students will examine and describe the money in their wallets.) Ask students to read an article mentioning the Fed and any recent Fed decisions affecting the economy. Ask students to summarize the implications and effects of the decision. **LS**

Business Connection

BANKING SERVICES. In North Carolina, BB&T is not well known compared with First Union and Bank of America, but the small-town based bank is a huge success. Banks are in business to make a profit, and the average return on assets (ROA) of the nation's banking industry is around 1.1, while BB&T's ROA is around 1.7. Why such a success? One reason is that BB&T is careful about making low-risk loans, and loan making is the meat and potatoes of the banking industry. Another reason is that BB&T keeps small local banks that are able to offer the community a broad range of services such as insurance services, debit cards, and automatic lines of credit.

Develop Concepts

ANALYZE. Call on students to name objects that might be used as money today if there were no dollar bills or coins. Ask the class to select the object that would best serve as money based on their analysis of how well the characteristics of money apply to the object. (Stable in value/scarce, accepted, able to be divided into parts, portable, and durable.) **LS**

Figure 12.1 Caption Answer

Hammer: problem with portability and divisibility. Hamburger: problem with durability. Bushel of oats: problem with durability, portability, and stability. Rocks: divisible, durable.

Money and Banking

Although there are places in the world where money and banks play only a small role in the local economy, it's hard for us to imagine life without them. Money enables people and businesses to buy and sell goods and services around the world with easy efficiency. Banks and the banking system play an extremely important role in managing money and controlling and simulating the economy.

The History of Money

The monetary system makes business much easier. In the **monetary system** goods and services are indirectly exchanged using money, which can then be exchanged for other goods and services. **Money** can be anything that people accept as a standard for payment. Modern society uses coin, currency, checks, and credit cards. In other times and places people have used shells, stones, corn, parrot feathers, and even gopher tails for money. Figure 12.1 illustrates why items might or might not be good sources for money.

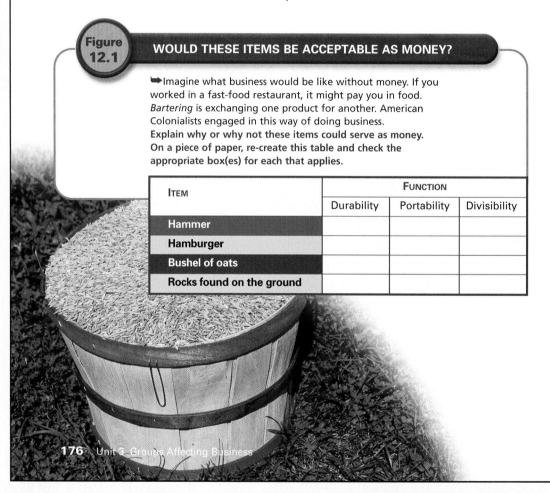

Figure 12.1

WOULD THESE ITEMS BE ACCEPTABLE AS MONEY?

➡️Imagine what business would be like without money. If you worked in a fast-food restaurant, it might pay you in food. *Bartering* is exchanging one product for another. American Colonialists engaged in this way of doing business.
Explain why or why not these items could serve as money. On a piece of paper, re-create this table and check the appropriate box(es) for each that applies.

ITEM	FUNCTION		
	Durability	Portability	Divisibility
Hammer			
Hamburger			
Bushel of oats			
Rocks found on the ground			

Cooperative Learning

Online Banking. Ask groups of students to gather information on online services provided by commercial banks, savings and loan associations, or credit unions. Information should include: services provided, costs, ease of access, possibility of outside tampering, special regulations, confidentiality, and the number of new customers over the past year. Ask groups to give a short report. As a variation, have groups develop a short presentation to teach other students in ninth-, tenth-, and eleventh-grade classes about online services provided by different banking organizations. **LS, CL**

Functions of Money

Money has three basic functions. First of all, it's a *medium of exchange*. Whether you buy a soda or sell a corporation, money changes hands. Without money, people would be forced to *barter*—trade goods or services directly for other goods or services. Barter is a clumsy method of exchange. Suppose you've grown an extra bushel of tomatoes. You'd like to use tomatoes to get new CDs. In the barter system, you'd have to find someone willing to accept tomatoes for CDs. If you have particular CDs in mind, you might have to make several trades to acquire something the CD owner would accept. You could spend a lot of time bartering for things you need. With money, however, the exchange becomes easy—you sell your extra tomatoes for money. You then exchange the money for the CDs you want. In a system that uses money, both buyers and sellers agree on exchanging money. Money itself is not a good or a service but a means of exchanging goods and services. It's a medium in that it's used between people to make business easier, just as radio is a medium that makes communication easier.

Money also functions as a *standard of value*. A standard is a fixed means for measuring the weight, amount, size, or value of something, like a yardstick or a scale. Money provides a means for measuring the value of goods and services. As a standard of value, money makes it possible to set a fixed value on a product and to compare the costs of different products. In the United States, the standard used is the dollar.

Finally, money functions as a *store of value*. That means it holds its value over time and can be stored or saved. You can also accumulate money over time to increase your wealth.

Characteristics of Money

Practically all over the world, paper money and coins are common forms of money. For money to carry out its functions, it must have several characteristics. No matter what form it takes, all money shares these characteristics.

Money must be stable in value. To be used as money, an item must be *scarce*. If the supply of an item is overly plentiful, it loses its value and cannot serve very well as money or a store of value since it would have little worth. People would lose faith in its value as a medium of exchange.

Money must be *accepted*. People have to be willing to take money in exchange for goods and services. Before accepting it, people must have

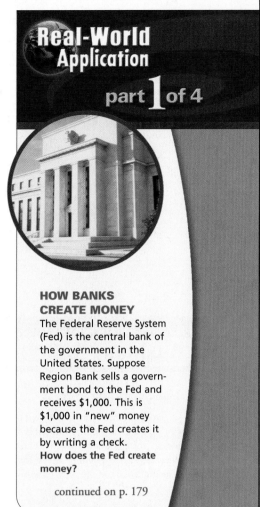

HOW BANKS CREATE MONEY
The Federal Reserve System (Fed) is the central bank of the government in the United States. Suppose Region Bank sells a government bond to the Fed and receives $1,000. This is $1,000 in "new" money because the Fed creates it by writing a check. **How does the Fed create money?**

continued on p. 179

Chapter 12 Money and Financial Institutions **177**

Real-World Application Caption Answer

HOW BANKS CREATE MONEY: PART 1 OF 4
Any time the central bank writes a check it creates money.

Technology Resource

GO TO **POWERPOINT.** The *Introduction to Business* PowerPoint® CD-ROM provides visual lecture aids for this chapter.

Independent Practice

INVESTIGATE. Ask students to research an established bank in the local area. Suggest they contact the bank to find how the bank stores money, transfers money, and lends money. Have students present their findings as a three-minute news feature. **LS**

Meeting Individual Needs

Students Who Have Difficulty With Recall. Some students are unable to recall words they have heard. To reinforce the chapter terms, create some sentence completion exercises on a tape recorder. Record the definition for each word in a partial sentence. Leave a pause where the student is to complete the sentence. The student can record the answer on the tape recorder for independent practice, review responses with a partner, or write the answers.

2 TEACH (Cont.)

✔ Fast Review Answers

1. Goods and services are exchanged indirectly using money, which can then be exchanged for other goods and services.

2. It is used as a fixed means of measuring and comparing the values of different goods and services.

3. Acceptability, portability, durability, divisibility, stability, difficult to counterfeit.

Thinking Critically

PRESENTATION. You're attending the annual Bank & Financial Analysts Association Conference in Key Biscayne, Fla. Your boss asks you to make a presentation about trends in the banking industry for next week's meeting of your department. She recommends that you highlight three main trends and make the presentation colorful and simple. Develop and give a short, lively presentation. **LS**

Business Building Blocks

CAPTION ANSWER

Have students exchange their responses to the question, allowing them to check one another's calculation. Using the formula, the simple interest is $1,200 ($2,000 × 0.12 × 5 = $1,200).

---

faith that the item used as money has value and will continue to hold its value. If people don't have faith in the value of their money, they may use something else like gold or diamonds. To be valuable, money must be acceptable.

Money should be *divisible* into parts. Suppose you have $20 but spend only $4.50 on a sandwich. Since money is divisible, the cashier can give you $15.50 in return. A money system using coins and bills of different values makes that possible.

Finally, money has to be *portable* and *durable*. Coins made of metal and bills made of strong paper can last a long time, can be used over and over again, and are easy to replace.

✔ Fast Review

1. What is the monetary system?
2. How is money a standard of value?
3. What are some of the characteristics money must have to be useful?

Business Building Blocks

Understanding Interest

Math

Simple interest, compounded annually, is a percentage of the amount borrowed. The amount borrowed is called the *principal*. Compound interest may be computed daily, monthly, or yearly.

How to Compute Interest

Simple Interest. Imagine you borrow $1,000 for 3 years at a rate of 10 percent per year. Here's how to find out the amount you owe at the end of three years.

Step 1. Convert the interest rate percent to its decimal equivalent. (10% = $^{10}/_{100}$ = .10)

Step 2. Use this formula: interest = principal x interest rate x time

Principal	x	Decimal Interest Rate	x	Time	=	Interest
$1,000	x	.10	x	3	=	$300

At the end of 3 years, the cost of the loan would be $300. Since you also must pay back the principal, you owe the lender $1,300.

Practice

Find the simple interest on a $2,000 loan at 12 percent interest for 5 years.

LANGUAGE ARTS   Curriculum Connection

Communication. Ask groups of students to collect bank advertisements and brochures and to use them as a base to list the services provided. Have them distinguish between commercial and individual services. Ask each group to present its analysis. **LS, CL**

Banking

Banks manage money, move it around, and maintain a supply of it. A system of banks makes it possible to keep your money in a safe place and get access to it wherever you go. The banking system is the main type of **financial institution**, or organization for managing money, in our economy. Banks offer people a variety of financial services.

Storing Money

One of the primary services banks provide is storing money for customers in bank accounts. A **bank account** is a record of how much money a customer has put in to or taken out of a bank. The money put in a bank is called a **deposit**, and the money taken out is called a **withdrawal**. Keeping your money in a bank prevents you from losing, spending, or having your money stolen too easily.

The two main types of accounts are *checking accounts* and *savings accounts*. Checking accounts are used for storing money in the short term so you can draw on it easily if you want to go shopping or pay a bill. Banks usually charge a fee for checking accounts to pay for the cost of maintaining them. Savings accounts are used for storing money over a long period of time. An advantage of a savings account is that it earns more interest than most checking accounts. **Interest** is a rate the bank pays you for keeping your money there. For example, if a bank pays you 5 percent interest per year on a $1,000 savings account, you'll have earned $50 after one year.

Transferring Money

Every single business transaction involves the transfer of money. Banks make it easy to transfer money from one person or business to another. For example, suppose you have a paycheck for $85 from the store where you work. You take the check to your bank, and they give you $85 cash for it. The bank then transfers the money from the store's bank account to the bank's cash account. You could also deposit the check into your bank account, in which case the store will transfer the amount from the store's account into your account.

Today more banks are using **electronic funds transfer (EFT)** to move money around. With EFT, money is transferred from one account to another through a network of computers. Instead of writing a check, your employer can use EFT to deposit your paycheck into your account

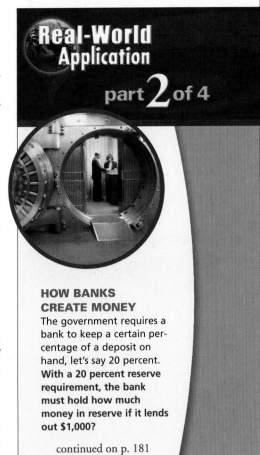

Real-World Application
part 2 of 4

HOW BANKS CREATE MONEY

The government requires a bank to keep a certain percentage of a deposit on hand, let's say 20 percent. With a 20 percent reserve requirement, the bank must hold how much money in reserve if it lends out $1,000?

continued on p. 181

Real-World Application
Caption Answer

HOW BANKS CREATE MONEY: PART 2 OF 4

The bank is free to lend the remaining $800.

Business Connection

THE FED AND BANKS. At a time when the Fed cut interest rates, bank shares climbed. Standard & Poor's index of savings and loan associations rose 19.4 percent and regional banks climbed 22.4 percent. Lower interest rates mean cash is cheaper to get, and banks' loan officers can effectively put credit on sale, bringing in new revenue. Bank stocks then become more in demand.

Chapter 12 Money and Financial Institutions **179**

Great Ideas From the Classroom of...

Vincent Tesi
Colts Neck High School
Colts Neck, N.J.

Money. Use a scale to weigh a dime, quarter, and half dollar. U.S. currency and coins were once backed by silver. In the 1960s silver prices rose steadily. At that time U.S. dimes, quarters and half dollars contained approximately 94 percent pure silver. Using a value of $7 for an ounce of silver, students can calculate that the actual silver content needed to make a dime, quarter, or half dollar exceeds the value of the coin itself. After 1967, the U.S. mint produced dimes, quarters, and half dollars containing no silver at all.

Develop Concepts

CLASSIFY. Ask students to use the local telephone book to make a list of commercial banks, savings and loan associations, and credit unions in your community. Ask students what they know about the differences between these three types of banks.

Discussion Starter

COMPARING. Ask students: How is the amount of money available to you regulated by the adults central to your life? How is this like the way regulations are enforced by the Fed?

Figure 12.2 Caption Answer

Profits would go down because the banks would not have as much to loan out. Loans make the banks money.

electronically. You can also use EFT to pay your phone bill, withdraw money from your account, or buy movie tickets.

Lending Money

The money you deposit in a bank makes it possible for the bank to lend money to other customers. Just as the bank pays you interest on your savings, customers have to pay the interest on the money they borrow from the bank. The interest earned by the bank is then used to pay the interest on savings accounts and to cover the bank's expenses.

Most bank loans require some form of collateral. **Collateral** is something valuable you put up for a loan, such as a car or a coin collection, so that the bank can take it if you fail to pay back the loan. There are four main types of loans banks offer to businesses and individuals:

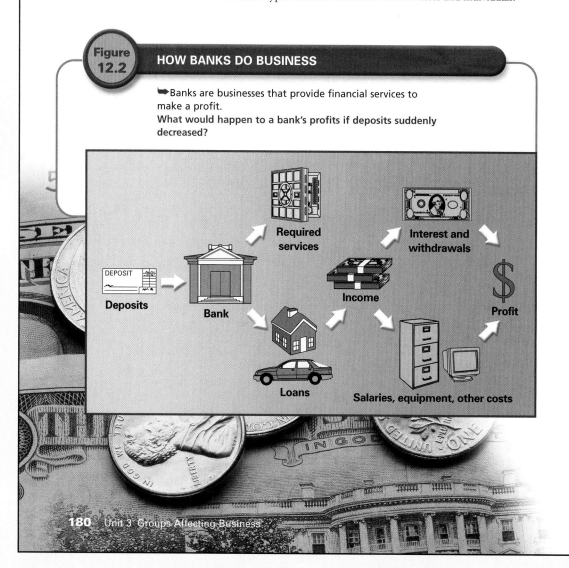

Figure 12.2 HOW BANKS DO BUSINESS

➡Banks are businesses that provide financial services to make a profit.
What would happen to a bank's profits if deposits suddenly decreased?

Deposits — Bank — Required services — Income — Interest and withdrawals — Profit — Loans — Salaries, equipment, other costs

Global Perspective

Other Countries' Central Banks. Encourage students to find information about the central banks of European, Asian, African, and South American nations, with individuals choosing the central bank of one nation to research in depth. Suggest they make a chart comparing and contrasting the central bank's organization and responsibilities with that of the Fed. Students may find researching the German central bank after reunification or the Russian central bank after the disintegration of the Soviet Union particularly interesting. **LS**

- A *mortgage loan* is a loan used to buy real estate, such as a house or an office building. A **mortgage** is a deed to give the lender the property if the loan is not paid back.
- A *commercial loan* is a loan made to businesses to buy supplies and equipment.
- An *individual loan* is a loan made to an individual to pay for personal items like a car, home repairs, or a vacation.
- A *line of credit* is an amount set aside by a bank for preferred customers that is available on demand. For example, a bank can issue a customer a $15,000 line of credit that can be used any time for any purpose.

Other Financial Services

Banks offer a variety of other services. Many of them provide financial advice on managing and investing your money. Not only can you store your money in a bank but you can also store valuable items, such as jewelry and certificates in **safety-deposit boxes**. Many banks offer credit cards such as MasterCard or Visa. Banks also manage *trust funds* such as an inheritance.

 Fast Review

1. What are the three main functions of a bank?
2. How does an EFT work?
3. What are the types of loans a bank offers?

Types of Banks

Banks operate on a state, national, and international level. There are strict rules for starting one because banks handle so much money. To open a federal or a state bank, you have to meet special requirements and apply for a charter from the federal or state government. You must also prove you have enough capital to start a bank. In the United States there are three main types of banks. Figure 12.2 illustrates how banks do business in order to make a profit.

Commercial Banks

Most of the banks in the United States are commercial banks. Commercial banks offer the entire range of services discussed such as checking and savings accounts, loans, and financial advice. They are often called *full-service banks*. They are like businesses in that they operate to make a profit. To make a profit they usually charge much more interest on the money they lend than the interest they pay on savings accounts.

Chapter 12 Money and Financial Institutions **181**

Real-World Application
part 3 of 4

HOW BANKS CREATE MONEY

Suppose you want to buy a new mountain bike. The bank loans you $800. The bank must keep in its reserve 20 percent of a new deposit.
How much money does the bank need to keep in the bank? How much can the bank lend?

continued on p. 183

Chapter 12

 Fast Review Answers

1. To store money, transfer money, and lend money.
2. Money is transferred from one account to another electronically using computers.
3. Mortgage loan, commercial loan, individual loan, and line of credit.

Individualized Practice

EVALUATE. Ask students to contact their district Federal Reserve Bank and the Federal Reserve Bank of New York to obtain their "Public Information Materials," a catalog of free materials.

L1 Have pairs of students discuss the effectiveness of the materials.

L2 Tell students to give a written evaluation of the materials using criteria such as (1) easy to read and understand and (2) technical terms defined clearly.

L3 Form the class into groups to evaluate the tables, charts, and diagrams. Ask groups to present an oral report of their evaluation.

LANGUAGE ARTS *Curriculum Connection*

Advising. Your uncle, who lives on the other side of the country, will soon be moving to your area and wants to change his bank. He knows you've been researching different types of banks and he asks you for advice. You don't know what your uncle does, so you need to ask some questions.

What questions will you ask your uncle and what advice will you give him? (Questions can include: Do you own a company? If you do you'll need a commercial bank. Do you work for a large, established company, or are you a member of a union or professional group? You might consider a credit union.)

Reteaching

LIST. Ask students to list the three main services banks offer. (Storing money, transferring money, and lending money.)

Enrichment

IDENTIFY. Ask students to identify two trends in the banking industry. (Answers may include: Increase in online services, bank mergers.) **LS**

You Make the Call

Caption Answer

1. Money to cover mortgage payments, property taxes, utility bills, and property insurance.
2. Gives people insight into the lives of people who may not be exactly like them.

Savings and Loan Associations

Savings and loan associations were originally set up to offer savings accounts and home mortgage loans. Their purpose was to encourage people to save money and make it easier to buy a home or start a business. To do this they charged lower interest on loans and paid higher interest on savings. In the 1980s about 20 percent of savings and loans failed. The government passed new regulations allowing them to charge higher interest rates and offer more services like credit cards. As a result, most savings and loans today are more like commercial banks.

Credit Unions

Credit unions are nonprofit banks set up by organizations for their members to use. Many companies, labor unions, and professional groups have their own credit unions. Credit unions offer members a full range of services, including credit cards, checking accounts, and loans. They offer low-interest loans and pay high interest rates on savings accounts. Many of them also pay interest on checking accounts.

Other Financial Institutions

There are types of financial institutions other than banks that offer some of the same services. *Mortgage companies* provide loans specifically for buying a home or business. *Finance companies* offer short-term loans to businesses, but at much higher interest rates than banks charge. *Insurance companies* not only provide protection against things like fire and theft, but also offer loans to businesses. *Brokerage firms* that sell stocks and bonds, may also offer a wide range of financial services to its customers.

You Make the Call

Home Equity

You and your family are moving to a new town and you're looking for a house to buy. There's one house everyone likes that's by a creek and on a wooded lot. The realtor mentions that next year a multiplex housing complex for low-income families will be built down the road.

Making an Ethical Decision

1. What are the most important financial issues that people should consider when buying a home?
2. What are the advantages of living in neighborhoods that are economically mixed?

How to Use a Portfolio Activity

The portfolio projects are designed to lead students to develop a collection of their best work to submit to you for assessment. You and each of your students should decide which projects to include in their business portfolio. Refer students to the specific rubric(s) from the *Alternative Assessment Strategies*. These rubrics will alert students to the criteria you'll use to assess their projects. **P**

1. What are the types of banks?
2. How is a credit union different from a commercial bank?
3. Name some financial institutions other than banks that offer similar services.

The Federal Reserve System

The **Federal Reserve System** (or Fed) is the central banking organization in the United States. Congress set up the Fed in 1913 to end the periodic financial panics during the 1800s and early 1900s. It consists of 12 Federal Reserve district banks, 25 branch banks, and about 5,000 member banks. The Fed is run by the Board of Governors, which is headed by a chairperson. It supervises the Federal Reserve district banks and regulates activity of the member banks.

Functions of the Fed

The Fed has six functions. These functions are as follows:

- *Clearing checks.* This transfers funds from one bank to another when you write or deposit a check.
- *Acting as the federal government's fiscal agent.* The Fed spends and distributes money to Federal Reserve member banks and commercial banks. It also tracks the deposits and holds a checking account for the U. S. Treasury.
- *Supervising member banks.* It regulates state banks that are members of the Federal Reserve System.
- *Regulating the money supply.* The primary responsibility of the Fed is to determine the amount of money in circulation. This affects the amount of credit and business activity in the economy.
- *Setting reserve requirements.* Regulating the money supply is the most important function of the Fed. By law, banks are required to keep a certain percentage of their deposits in reserve. This percentage determines the amount of money in circulation.
- *Supplying paper currency.* The Fed is responsible for printing and maintaining the nation's paper currency.

Fast Review _____

1. What is the Fed?
2. Name the six functions of the Fed.

Real-World Application
part 4 of 4

HOW BANKS CREATE MONEY
The bank treats the $640 as a new deposit. Eighty percent of $640 (or $512) might be lent again. The process continues, with each new deposit giving the bank new funds to continue lending.
How does the money supply expand?

Real-World Application
Caption Answer

HOW BANKS CREATE MONEY: PART 4 OF 4
Since banks only keep a fraction of deposits in reserve, they are able to lend.

Fast Review Answers

1. Commercial banks, savings and loans, credit unions.
2. Commercial banks— profit; credit unions— nonprofit.
3. Mortgage, finance, insurance, and brokerage companies.

Technology Resource

GO TO **VIRTUAL BUSINESS.** Introduce the financial aspects of starting a business by using Knowledge Matters' *Virtual Business* interactive simulation. Go to the *Introduction to Business* Web site **www.introbus.glencoe.com** to download the *Virtual Business* activity.

Evaluation

Assign and review the Fast Review sections.

Fast Review Answers

1. Nation's central banking organization.
2. See bulleted list on SE p. 183 under "Functions of the Fed."

Meeting Individual Needs

Students With Weak Study Skills.
Students with weak study skills might benefit from making a time budget for longer assignments. Suggest that students choose an assignment due in two or more weeks. Then suggest that they make a list of the steps—and time—needed to complete the project. Have students make a chart, or mark a calendar or planner, showing which steps should be completed by which date so that the entire assignment can be completed on time. If students are marking a planner, have them block out the time slots needed for each step of the assignment.

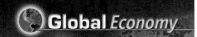

Global *Economy*

A Brief History of Money

1 FOCUS

Ask students if they would be willing to sell an item—for example, a baseball cap or a CD—for a few dollars. Although they might argue about the number of dollars, most students would be willing to make the sale. Then ask them if they would be willing to part with that item for shells, or a block of salt, or a string of beads. When students respond in the negative, point out that in the past, these three commodities—and many others—were readily accepted as money. Conclude by informing students that this feature provides a brief review of the major developments in the history of money.

2 TEACH

Have students read trough the information in the boxes. Then have them arrange the information in a chart, categorizing by content or time period. Suggest that they refer to their charts as they answer the "Thinking Globally" questions.

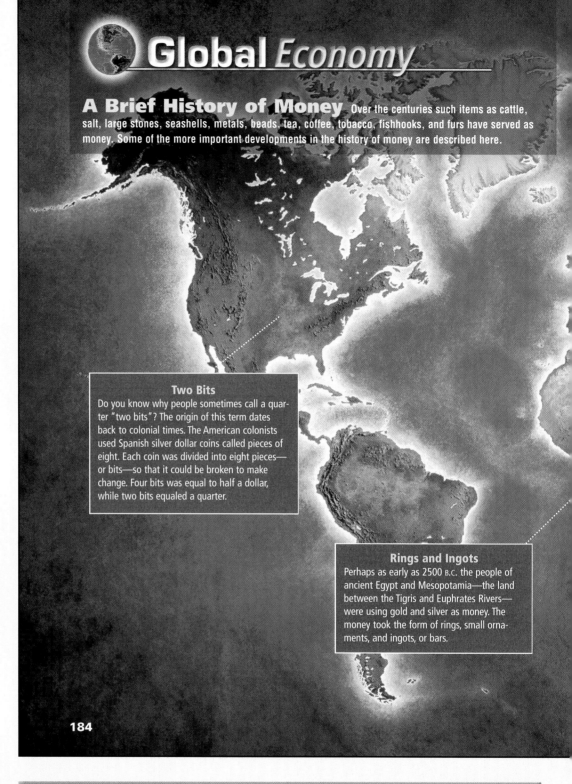

Global *Economy*

A Brief History of Money Over the centuries such items as cattle, salt, large stones, seashells, metals, beads, tea, coffee, tobacco, fishhooks, and furs have served as money. Some of the more important developments in the history of money are described here.

Two Bits
Do you know why people sometimes call a quarter "two bits"? The origin of this term dates back to colonial times. The American colonists used Spanish silver dollar coins called pieces of eight. Each coin was divided into eight pieces—or bits—so that it could be broken to make change. Four bits was equal to half a dollar, while two bits equaled a quarter.

Rings and Ingots
Perhaps as early as 2500 B.C. the people of ancient Egypt and Mesopotamia—the land between the Tigris and Euphrates Rivers—were using gold and silver as money. The money took the form of rings, small ornaments, and ingots, or bars.

184

Extending the Content

Commodity Money. Throughout history people have used commodities—everything from salt to dried fish to coconuts to cattle—as money. Several words with connections to money derive from the commodities once used as a medium of exchange. The English word *salary*, or a fixed income that is paid at regular intervals, comes from the Latin word *salarius*, which means "of salt." Another Latin word, *pecuniarius*—meaning "wealth in cattle"—is the basis for the English word *pecuniary*, which means "related to money."

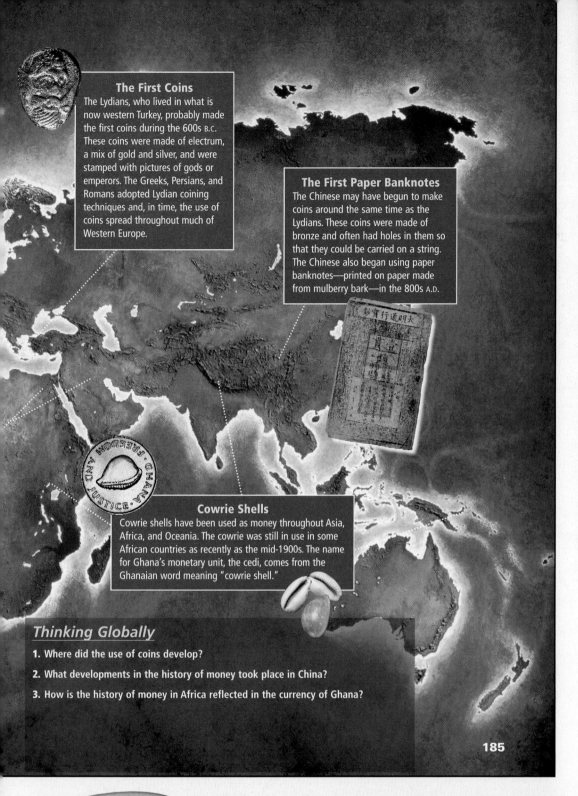

The First Coins
The Lydians, who lived in what is now western Turkey, probably made the first coins during the 600s B.C. These coins were made of electrum, a mix of gold and silver, and were stamped with pictures of gods or emperors. The Greeks, Persians, and Romans adopted Lydian coining techniques and, in time, the use of coins spread throughout much of Western Europe.

The First Paper Banknotes
The Chinese may have begun to make coins around the same time as the Lydians. These coins were made of bronze and often had holes in them so that they could be carried on a string. The Chinese also began using paper banknotes—printed on paper made from mulberry bark—in the 800s A.D.

Cowrie Shells
Cowrie shells have been used as money throughout Asia, Africa, and Oceania. The cowrie was still in use in some African countries as recently as the mid-1900s. The name for Ghana's monetary unit, the cedi, comes from the Ghanaian word meaning "cowrie shell."

Thinking Globally

1. Where did the use of coins develop?

2. What developments in the history of money took place in China?

3. How is the history of money in Africa reflected in the currency of Ghana?

185

3 ASSESS

Have students answer the "Thinking Globally" questions.

4 CLOSE

To conclude, ask students to discuss why they think the various items once used as money fell out of favor and were replaced by coins and paper currency.

? *Did You Know?*

Native Americans probably used wampum—strings of beads made from clamshells—as money long before the arrival of the Europeans. It was among the most popular mediums of exchange when early European settlers and Native Americans traded.

Thinking Globally   **Caption Answer**

1. The use of coins probably developed during the 600s B.C. in what is now western Turkey. Coins may have developed around the same time in China.

2. The Chinese may have begun to make coins around the same time as the Lydians. The Chinese began using paper banknotes in the 800s A.D.

3. Cowrie shells have been used as money throughout Africa, and the name for Ghana's monetary unit, the cedi, means "cowrie."

4 CLOSE

Chapter Wrap-Up

Ask students to list three things they learned in this chapter.

Using Business Key Words

1. safety-deposit box
2. interest
3. deposit
4. Federal Reserve System
5. EFT
6. monetary system
7. money
8. withdrawal
9. financial institution
10. bank account
11. collateral
12. mortgage

Review What You Learned

13. A medium of exchange, standard of value, and store of value.
14. Scarcity and value.
15. Needs to be portable.
16. Transfer via computer from one account to another.
17. Loans.
18. To satisfy depositors who make withdrawals.
19. Mortgage loans buy homes, office buildings, manufacturing facilities, etc. Commercial loans made to businesses for various lengths of time. Individual loans buy a variety of goods.
20. Deposit or take money out of the economy by selling bonds to individuals or groups.
21. Nonprofit associations. Provide savings plans and loans for their members. Offers high-interest payments.
22. The Federal Reserve.
23. Increase in competition.

Summary

1. Money functions as a medium of exchange, a standard of value, and a store of value. The characteristics of money include scarcity, acceptability, divisibility, portability, and durability.
2. Banks offer a variety of financial services including storing money, transferring money, and lending money.
3. The three main types of banks are commercial banks, savings and loan associations, and credit unions.
4. The Fed has six basic functions. Its most important function is regulating the money supply.

Using Business Key Words

Understanding these business terms will help you understand the banking institution. Match the terms below with their definitions.

- **monetary system**
- **deposit**
- **Federal Reserve System**
- **bank account**
- **mortgage**
- **interest**
- **electronic funds transfer (EFT)**
- **money**
- **withdrawal**
- **safety-deposit box**
- **financial institution**
- **collateral**

1. Something to place valuables in at the bank.
2. The money banks pay to depositors for use of their funds.
3. Sums of money placed in accounts in the bank.
4. Responsible for controlling the amount of money in circulation.
5. The process of moving money from one account to another through the use of computers.
6. Goods and services are indirectly exchanged through this medium.
7. Anything accepted as a standard form of payment.
8. Taking money out of the bank.
9. An organization for managing money.
10. Records how much money a customer has put in or taken out of his or her bank.
11. Something of value you put up for a loan.
12. A deed that states if you can't pay back your loan, the lender has right to certain things.

Quick Quiz

1. Name three functions and four characteristics of money. (Medium of exchange, standard of value and store of value; stable, accepted, divisible, portable and durable.)
2. Name three kinds of banks. (Commercial banks, savings and loan associations, credit unions.)
3. What are the six functions of the Fed? (Clearing checks, acting as the federal government's fiscal agent, supervising member banks, regulating the money supply, setting reserve requirements, supplying paper currency.)

Review What You Learned

13. Describe the three functions of money.
14. What are the two characteristics that dollars must have to be accepted as money in our society?
15. Why must money be portable?
16. How does a debit card work?
17. What is the bank's primary source of income?
18. Why does the government require banks to keep a certain percentage of their deposits on hand?
19. Compare the three different types of loans—mortgage, commercial, and individual.
20. How does the Federal Reserve control the amount of money in circulation?
21. Describe the characteristics of a credit union.
22. What is the central banking organization of the United States?
23. What happened when the government deregulated the banking industry?

Understanding Business Concepts

24. Why does money need to be divisible? Give an example.
25. Banks pay depositors for leaving their money in savings accounts. Why?
26. Explain how a bank makes a profit by providing loans to its customers.
27. Compare an individual loan with a line of credit. What are the similarities and differences?
28. Describe how banks help to eliminate money.
29. What other financial institutions, besides banks, savings and loans, and credit unions offer financial services?

Critical Thinking

30. What do you think would happen if all the depositors of a bank requested their deposits at the same time?
31. How can the Federal Reserve use the reserve requirement to slow the economy's growth?
32. Find out how currency is printed and what security measures are taken to avoid counterfeiting. What steps would you take to suggest minimizing counterfeiting?
33. Why do you think coins have been a more desirable form of money than paper currency throughout U.S. history?

Viewing and Representing

Examining the Image. Get ready. For 15 seconds, look closely at the photograph. Then cover it up with a piece of paper. List everything you remember. What did you remember first? Are you surprised at how much information your mind captures in a short time? Do you think that images are powerful? Write a paragraph on your findings and answers.

Chapter 12 Money and Financial Institutions   **187**

Critical Thinking

30. Banks would not have enough currency to cover all the withdrawals.
31. By increasing the reserve requirement. An increased requirement leaves less money for banks to loan and so less money circulates in the economy.
32. Encourage studies to present their findings in an illustrated report.
33. Answers may vary. People believed coins made of gold and silver held their worth longer than paper currency. Also, coins are more durable.

Viewing and Representing

What do you feel is the relationship between the people in the picture? What do you think is going to happen next? What events do you think just happened? With this exercise, students experience first hand the power of the visual image. **LS**

Understanding Business Concepts

24. A buyer spends part of the money.
25. Encourage savings accounts so that the banks can loan part of that money to others.
26. By charging more interest for the money they loan, banks make a profit.
27. A line of credit is a preset amount, arranged ahead of time, with a customer. An individual loan is made to a customer to buy a particular item.
28. When the Federal Reserve offers bonds for sale to the public, individuals buy the bonds through drawing on their checking accounts. This in turn, draws money out of the system so that there is less money on which to make loans.
29. Stock brokerage houses, mortgage companies, and insurance companies.

4 CLOSE (Cont.)

Building Academic Skills

MATH. Make sure all students participate in the group project. Rubrics: Table/chart, oral discussion, note taking.

LANGUAGE ARTS. Make sure all students participate in the group project. Rubrics: Oral discussion, note taking, essay.

COMPUTER/TECHNOLOGY. Allow the students to decide how they want to share their findings. Rubrics: Note taking, e-mails, essay, posters, oral presentation, and bulletin board displays.

HISTORY. Students can use the library or Internet for their research. Rubric: Oral presentation.

Linking School to Home

INTERVIEWING AND CHARTING. Answers will vary. Rubrics: Note taking, chart.

Linking School to Work

LOCAL ADVERTISEMENTS. Make sure all students participate in the class project. Allow the students to decide how to combine the various charts. Rubrics: Note taking, chart.

Building Academic Skills

 Showing Interest

In groups of three or four, call three banks, credit unions, or other financial institutions and find out how much interest they pay on a regular savings account. Create a table to show the results of your research. If possible, use computer software to create the table. Then, as a class, combine your results. Determine which savings institution in your community provides the best interest rate.

 Personal Essay

Team up with three classmates to form a bank. Open your bank with a deposit of $20,000 in pretend game money. Invite classmates to play the role of business and individual customers in your bank. Determine the interest rate you will charge on loans and pay on deposits. Decide what you need to do to place $200,000 into the classroom economy. Remember the following may affect your decisions:

- Your bank must keep 10 percent of each deposit on reserve.
- You'll need to pay salaries, rent, and other costs.
- You'll compete for customers with other banks in your classroom.

Write a 300-word report that explains how your bank works.

 Researching the Fed

Use e-mail to contact the nearest Federal Reserve System branch bank. Request general information about the Federal Reserve System and particular information about the Federal Reserve System branch. Share the information you receive with your classmates.

 Other Nations' Banking

The Bank of England was used as the model for forming and organizing our Federal Reserve System. Choose the central bank of two other nations to research. Identify their main functions and responsibilities and compare them to the Federal Reserve. Prepare a three-minute oral report to share your findings with the class.

Linking School to Home

Interviewing and Charting. Interview your parents or other family members to find out why they chose the financial institution(s) they currently use. Ask them about the services offered, location, quality of customer service provided, and interest rates. Create a chart showing the features that helped make their decision.

Linking School to Work

Local Advertisements. Collect various financial institutions' advertisements from local newspapers. Using the advertisements, list the services provided by each one of the institutions. Create a chart showing the services. Then, as a class, combine the charts. Evaluate the financial institutions based on the services provided and select one that you think is the best. Invite someone from that institution to speak to your class about their institution and the services they provide.

E-Homework

Applying Technology

Banking Decisions. Discuss how technology has affected where people do their banking. Include online banking in your discussion.

Digital Cash. Although cash and checks are still very common methods of paying for goods and services, various access cards are becoming more and more popular. Use the Internet to research stored value cards and digital cash. Write a two-page paper sharing your findings. Present your opinion on whether or not you think cash and checks will soon be an outdated way of doing business.

Connecting Academics

Math. Assume you live in a country where a silver coin is the currency. The weight of one silver dollar is 0.94 ounces. Compute the total weight of the silver dollars you would have to carry to purchase the following: a television set, a round trip plane ticket to Tokyo, and a new sports car.

Computer/Technology. Diagrams often help clarify information in a textbook. Create a diagram indicating the relationship between banks, bank accounts, deposits, withdrawals, interest, electronic fund transfer (EFT), and safety-deposit boxes.

BusinessWeek — Analyzing the Feature Story

You read the first part of "The Euro: Back From the Depths" at the beginning of this chapter. Below are a few questions for you to answer about money. You'll find the answers to these questions when you're reading the entire article. First, here are the questions:

34. What characteristic of money is the main concern of this article?

35. How does globalization affect currency in different countries?

CREATIVE JOURNAL ACTIVITY

Research the current value of the dollar against the currencies of three different countries. See if you can find out what these currencies were worth in dollars last week. How about last year? Create a chart with your results. Which country's economy has the most potential?

BUSINESS Online
The Full Story

To learn more about the euro, visit the *Introduction to Business* Web site at **www.introbus.glencoe.com**, and click on *BusinessWeek* Feature Story, Chapter 12.

E-Homework

BANKING DECISIONS. Answers will vary. Encourage the students to research online banks on the Internet. Possible rubrics: Oral presentation, note taking.

DIGITAL CASH. Answers will vary. Rubric: Note taking, essay.

Connecting Academics

MATH. Answers will vary depending on the prices of the items.

COMPUTER/TECHNOLOGY. Diagrams will vary but should show an understanding of the relationships between the entities listed.

BusinessWeek — *Analyzing the Feature Story*

34. This article is concerned with how *stable in value* the euro is. This reflects the general health of the European economy.

35. The value of currencies can now be compared more easily. Investors can now make decisions about what countries to invest in based on the value of their currency.

Creative Journal Activity

Compare three different currencies. Students might use current news concerning the three countries' economies to make their final decision as to which country's economy is the strongest.

1 FOCUS

Unit Seminar Overview

In this Seminar students analyze three different careers and predict how the state of the economy will affect careers. Students investigate images, interpret facts, and decide the best job to withstand an economic downturn.

Bell Ringer Activity

LIST. Ask the students to think of different careers or jobs they'd like to pursue or learn more about. Tell them to imagine they can do anything they want to do. Have them choose any career or job they're interested in and list at least three.

Discussion Starter

THREE PERSPECTIVES.
Divide the class into three sections X, Y, and Z. Students in each section will look at one-third of the Unit 3 photograph collage on this page. Have section X cover the top two-thirds of the photograph collage and look at the bottom third. Have section Y cover the top and the lower third, so that they see the middle third. Have section Z cover the lower two-thirds and look at the top third. Ask each section in turn: What do you see? From your perspective, what would you say this unit seminar is about?

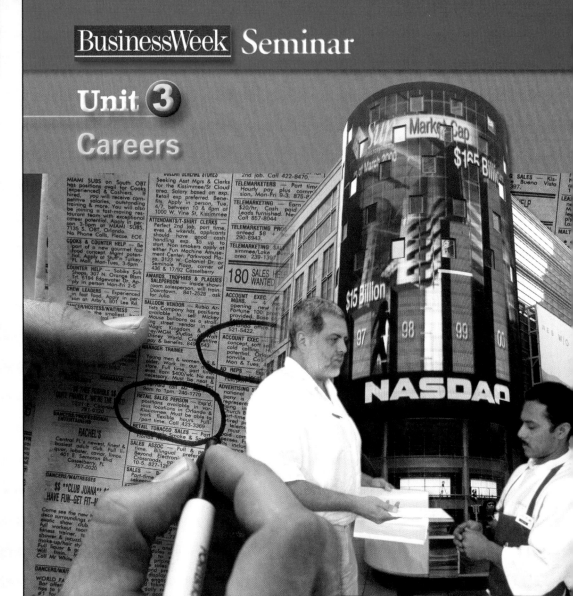

BusinessWeek Seminar

Unit **3**
Careers

Discovering Business Careers

In Chapter 11 you read about the impact of government on a business. One of the ways government affects business is by influencing the economy through policies established by the Federal Reserve, the central banking system of the United States. The Federal Reserve cuts the interest rates that banks charge one another in an effort to strengthen the economy by making borrowing money more affordable for businesses. When businesses can't afford to borrow money, businesses can't grow and workers lose their jobs.

190

LANGUAGE ARTS
Newsworthy Trends

Parlez-vous Français? In the global economy, one of the skills in demand is the ability to speak a foreign language, especially French. French is the only international language other than English. It's the official language of the United Nations, NATO, the European Community, the International Red Cross, and the International Olympic Committee. Of recent job listings by the U.S. State Department, 4 required the ability to speak German, 6 to speak Russian, 38 to speak Spanish, and 92 to speak French. France also has one of the strongest economies in the world and frequently does business with the United States.

2 TEACH

Investigate the Images

Look at the collage on the left page. What do you see? What do you think? What do think the images represent? The power of reading visuals is in analyzing and dissecting your observations. On a separate piece of paper reconstruct the worksheet below in order to complete your investigation. The questions may help shape and focus your analysis.

Your Observations

1. How many photographs do you see?

2. Examine each image. How is each assembled in relation to the other?

3. What is the subject of each photograph?

4. Does color signify a message?

5. What issues do you take from these images?

Information

6. Summarize what you know about the photographs from your observations.

Exploring Culture

7. What do you know about unemployment in this country? How does it affect your community? What about your family?

8. Do you think the media objectively reports why businesses layoff employees? Why or why not? Is the news the source of all truths?

Factoids

Mandatory Vacation. When the economy weakens, some businesses shave dollars off the payroll by forcing people to take unpaid vacation.

Keeping Your Options Open. Cisco Systems lays off 6,000 employees. This San Jose, Calif., company is allowing those terminated the chance to collect one-third of their severance package, plus benefits and stocks if they work for a local nonprofit organization. These individuals are first in line for Cicso's rehire once the economy recovers.

Looking for Opportunities. Users visited Monster.com over two million times in a month.

Job Stability. Seventy-four percent of working adults express some kind of concern about job security.

Employee Development. U.S. companies spend an average of $700 per eligible worker on employee training.

Thinking Critically

1. Do you know someone who is (or who has been) out of work? How did it affect him or her? In the future, will he or she be affected by being out of work? (Answers will vary.)

2. What role has the government played in influencing business and the economy in the last six months? (Answers will vary, depending on the recent economic climate.)

Cooperative Learning

NEWS REPORT. After discussing Exploring Culture (seminar questions 7 and 8), and referring to the Factoid, "Keeping Your Options Open," write these questions on the board: What nonprofit organizations are local to this area? What would you say are the major differences between working for a nonprofit and working for a for-profit company? Would you work for a nonprofit? What's your opinion of Cisco Systems' rehire policy? Have students work in pairs or small groups. Teams are to prepare a short news report, which may be in the form of an interview, including the answers to the questions. Encourage creativity. **CL**, **LS**, **ELL**

MATH *Newsworthy Trends*

Bank on It. According to a recent survey by *Money* magazine, the job that came in second as most satisfying was…a banker. Although up to 450,000 jobs have been lost in the banking industry as a result of the technology revolution and bank mergers, new jobs are taking their place. Traditional banks have branched off into other financial services, such as investment banking and credit cards. Federal Reserve banks are actively recruiting college students with degrees in public policy and computer science for jobs as bank regulators and security experts. There's even a shortage of good managers in the banking industry now. Loan officers, auditors, and technology specialists are also in demand.

2 TEACH (Cont.)

Independent Practice

L1 COMPARE

Ask students to find a recent article about government subsidies or incentives. Ask them to explain the main points of the article to the class. Follow student presentations with a closing discussion where students predict the effect of the subsidies or incentives on business in the current economy. **LS, CL**

L2 E-INTERVIEW

Have students send an e-mail to a company executive of a business in another state. Suggest students include questions such as: How is the current economy affecting your business? Do you feel your business is better off, or worse off, than businesses in my home state? How is local or national government helping your business? Do trade barriers or trade agreements affect your business? If so, how? When students get a reply, have them report to the class. **LS**

L3 INTERVIEW AND REPORT

Arrange for a local business owner who has immigrated to this country to speak to your class about how the free enterprise marketplace in this country differs from the economic system in his or her native country. Have students prepare questions focusing on how some points from this unit may be different in each country. After the interview, have students write a one-page report. **CL, LS**

BusinessWeek Seminar

Taking Aim at Careers

● **Preparation**

In this seminar, you'll research three different jobs and decide which job, if any, would withstand slower economic times.

Objective

In this *BusinessWeek* Seminar, you'll:
- **Research** three different career opportunities available.
- **Participate** in a job fair, in which each member of your class will set up a display of the jobs he or she has researched.
- **Discuss** with your classmates which three jobs are most likely to withstand an economic downturn.

Materials Needed

✓ Recent business news publications, such as the *New York Times* and *BusinessWeek*
✓ The business and classified advertisement sections of your local newspaper
✓ Notebook paper
✓ Posterboard
✓ Construction paper
✓ Pencils
✓ Pens
✓ Markers

● **Procedures**

1. Identify three jobs that interest you.

2. Research these three jobs. Consult the *Occupational Outlook Handbook*, which should be available in your school or local library.

3. Research business and economic trends. Use the Internet to access *BusinessWeek Online* at **www.businessweek.com**.

4. Write a brief report for each of the three jobs you have identified. Each report should describe the job, the training and education required, and the future outlook for that job.

5. Create a poster or brochure that promotes the positive aspects of each job. You'll use them to create interest in the jobs you've researched.

6. As a class, stage a job fair. Set up a display for the jobs you have researched. Visit others students' displays. Write down any concerns you have about a particular job.

Reteaching Strategy

Have students work in groups to prepare a bulletin-board display of important points from this unit. Ask students to display materials and captions that present a picture of the following concepts: the global marketplace, global competition and regulation, the role of government as regulator, government as provider, money, banking, and the Federal Reserve System. **LS, CL**

Chart It

Discuss with the class which jobs seem both interesting and secure during economic downturns. Were many of the same jobs presented by different classmates? Make sure you understand what makes one job more secure than another.

As a class, vote for the three jobs most likely to withstand an economic downturn. As a class reproduce the table that is below and create a comprehensive list on the board.

Jobs to Withstand an Economic Downturn		
Most Interesting Jobs	Most Secure Jobs	Jobs Both Interesting and Secure (Explain)
1.	1.	1.
2.	2.	2.
3.	3.	3.
4.	4.	4.
5.	5.	5.

Analyze and Conclude

After voting for the top three jobs, answer the questions below:

1. **Decision Making.** What were the top three jobs? Of those three, which job is most interesting to you? Why? What makes one job more secure than another?

2. **Negotiating to Arrive at a Decision.** Do you have to choose between interest and security in a job?

3. **Reasoning.** From all the jobs you have learned about, through your own research and the job fair, which job are you most likely to pursue? Why?

Becoming an Informed Citizen

Congratulations, you finished the *Business-Week* Seminar. Now it's time to reflect on the decisions you made.

Critical Thinking. What are the essential elements you look for in career? Is it straightforward? Or creative? What are some ways you can start to pursue your interests in this career?

Analyzing Your Future. How will the state of the economy affect your career?

BUSINESS *Online*

Further Exploration

To find out more about job trends during economic downturns, visit the Glencoe *Introduction to Business* Web site, **www.introbus.glencoe.com**.

Analyze and Conclude Answers

1. Answers will vary but could include careers in technology and in fields where needs are constant, such as health care, education, and housing.
2. Answers will vary, but help students recognize that you don't *have* to choose between an interesting job and a secure one. Sometimes a job can be both.
3. Answers will vary. Encourage students to back up their statements with reasons.

Marketing to the Customer

Chapter 13
Marketing in Today's World

Chapter 14
Advertising: The Art of Attracting an Audience

Unit Objectives

After completing this unit, students will be able to achieve the following outcomes:

- List the functions of marketing, and identify the importance of market research.
- Identify the different types of media businesses can use to advertise their products.
- List advantages and disadvantages for each type of advertising media.
- Name factors in the cost of advertising.

BusinessWeek Connections

In this unit, students will read the following articles from *BusinessWeek*:

Chapter 13 "Can Marvel's Heroes Save the Day?": A look at how the marketing plan is changing at Marvel Enterprises.

Chapter 14 "Yahoo! and Pepsi: 'Fusion Marketing' in Prime Time": Yahoo! attracts new users and Pepsi gets brand recognition.

Key to Descriptive Icons

The following designations will help you decide which activities are appropriate for your students.

L1 Level 1 activities should be within the ability range of all students.

L2 Level 2 activities should be within the ability range of the average to above-average students.

L3 Level 3 activities are designed for the ability range of above-average students.

ELL Activities should be within the ability range of the English Language Learner.

LS Learning Styles designation represents activities designed to address different learning styles.

CL Cooperative learning activities are designed for small group work.

P Portfolio designation represents student products that can be placed into a best-work portfolio.

Teacher Classroom Resources*

Program Resources	Chapter 13	Chapter 14
Student Activity Workbook	p. 85	p. 93
Lesson Plans	p. 32	p. 34
Internet Resources	p. 45	p. 47
Reproducible Tests	p. 25	p. 27
Teaching Transparencies	13.1, 13.2	14.1, 14.2
Strategies and Worksheets for Teaching Transparencies	pp. 6, 42	pp. 7, 44

* Each of these resources is available in print and on the Interactive Lesson Planner CD-ROM.

Technology Resources

- Interactive Lesson Planner CD-ROM
- PowerPoint® Presentation CD-ROM
- ExamView® Pro Test Generator CD-ROM
- Integrated Software Simulation, Teacher Manual
- Glencoe Business Video Package
- *PuzzleMaker* CD-ROM
- *Introduction to Business* Web Site
- *Virtual Business*®
  Virtual Business is a business simulation that introduces students to the principles of business by letting them start and run their own virtual business. In *Virtual Business,* students have the power to control all aspects of a retail convenience store. Students strategize business decisions using a powerful learning tool in the guise of a video game.

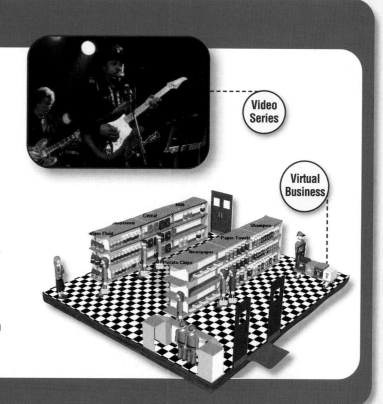

Video Series

Virtual Business

Scope and Sequence

Academic Standards of Learning

	LANGUAGE ARTS	MATH	HISTORY	COMPUTER/ TECHNOLOGY	SOCIAL SCIENCE	
CHAPTER 13	pp. 196, 197, 199, 200, 202, 203, 208, 209	pp. 198, 201, 202, 208, 209	p. 208	pp. 197, 199, 200, 204, 205, 208, 209	pp. 197, 198, 202, 208	
CHAPTER 14	pp. 210, 211, 214, 216, 217, 218, 224, 225	pp. 222, 224, 225	pp. 213, 216, 224	pp. 213, 214, 219, 224, 225	pp. 217, 224	

Scope and Sequence

Themes and Concepts

Business Core	Accounting and Finance	Business Management	Computer/ Technology	Marketing	Entrepreneurship
Competitive Environment Entrepreneurial Concepts Demographics Global Business Teamwork Presentation Communications	Decision Making Economic Factors Budgeting Cost Behavior	Consumers Competition Decision Making Opportunity Costs Policy and Strategy Formulation	Project Management Computer Applications Systems Selection	Customer Service Profitability Culture Marketing Mix Markets Market Analysis Research and Development	Business Image Capital Budgeting Entrepreneurial Concepts Marketing Plan Pricing Strategies Production Promotion
Competitive Environment Interest Assessment Demographics Culture Diversity Adapting to Change Communication	Decision Making Ethics Costing Methods	Competition Consumers Decision Making Technology	Program Design Social Issues Business Decisions Media Types	Cultural Diversity Markets Branding Packaging Positioning Advertising Public Relations/ Publicity Promotion	Business Image Location and Property Analysis Research and Development Technology

Unit Overview

Unit 4 introduces marketing and advertising in the business world of today.

CHAPTER 13 explains the basics of marketing, and describes market research, product development, and channels of distribution.

CHAPTER 14 examines advertising mediums and advertising rates.

Introducing the Unit

To introduce this unit, poll students by asking if they are persuaded to buy products that are advertised in each of the following: magazines, newspapers, on the TV, direct-mail, billboards, transit (buses), radio, cyber-ads, and personalized advertising. Take a blind poll, (i.e., have students close their eyes before raising their hands). After the "vote" you announce the count. After the poll, ask students what are the reasons behind advertising. Tell students that in this unit, they'll be exploring marketing and advertising.

Technology Resource

 INTRODUCTION TO BUSINESS WEB SITE. To find out more about content in Unit 4, visit the Glencoe *Introduction to Business* Web site. **www.introbus.glencoe.com**

Unit 4

Marketing to the Consumer

Chapter 13
Marketing in Today's World

Chapter 14
Advertising: The Art of Attracting an Audience

A Hunting They Will Go

Don't look now, but the Cool Hunters are watching you. Cool Hunters are market researchers who try to spot the next big trend in teen culture, whether it's mood rings, skater slang, or pocket TVs. They hang out at malls, parks, schoolyards, dance clubs, and basketball courts, studying teens and taking notes. They sell their information to big corporations that use it to design products, logos, and ad campaigns for teens.

- **It's the Real Thing**
  During its first year in business, the Coca-Cola Company sold 25 bottles of coke.

- **It's That One Commercial Again, With That Cool Music**
  According to one survey, the average American sees more than 20,000 television commercials each year.

- **Synchronized Watches**
  In ads that show a watch or a clock, the time displayed is usually 10:10.

- **Have a Nice Day**
  The Smiley Face, which has been used in countless ad campaigns, sold more than 50 million buttons at the height of its popularity, and was even issued as a postage stamp. It was designed in 1963 by Harvey Ball, who was paid $45 for it.

- **Soap Box**
  Daytime TV's soap operas got their name from soap companies, who originally sponsored them.

194 Unit 4

Field Trip Suggestion

Trips to Stores. Arrange for your students to visit a store or stores that cater to specific ethnic groups to observe the merchandising techniques they employ as well as the types of products they carry. Have students ask questions of storeowners about product distribution and about marketing techniques that have worked and those that haven't worked. A second part of this trip would be to visit a local mall during a mall-wide promotion. Students should observe the theme of the promotion and how the stores in the mall carry out the promotion. You could make this an ongoing project throughout this course. **CL**

BUSINESS Online
Idea Factory
To learn more about marketing and advertising, visit the *Introduction to Business* Web site at **www.introbus.glencoe.com**, and click on Unit 4 Marketing to the Consumer.

Bulletin Board

Glencoe Poster Teaching Tip

Ask students to make a list of products that come in different varieties, models, or styles. Ask why there are so many versions of one type of product. Then have students speculate about the people a product is targeted to, and how a manufacturer discerns their needs.

Then focus students' attention on the five characters listed in questions one to five of the poster. Tell students to think of a product and say how they would market it to each of the characters. For example, would the same marketing approach work for Sergio and Sophia?

Portfolio Activity

Chart. Have students set up a chart to record their observations and findings from their trips to stores. Lead a class discussion to decide what points to observe and report on, and therefore what to write as column headings. If you assign this as an ongoing project, ask students to include the date of their visit on the chart. Encourage students to mount their completed chart on a collage background decorated with pictures from catalogs, promotional material, and printed ads. **P**, **LS**

🕐 Out of Time?

If time doesn't permit teaching each chapter in this unit, you may use *Virtual Business* to give students experience in making marketing decisions.

SCANS Correlation Chart*

Foundation Skills

Basic Skills	Reading	Writing	Math	Listening	Speaking	
Thinking Skills	Creative Thinking	Decision Making	Problem Solving	Seeing Things in the Mind's Eye	Knowing How to Learn	Reasoning
Personal Qualities	Responsibility	Self-Esteem	Sociability	Self-Management	Integrity/ Honesty	

Workplace Competencies

Resources	Allocating Time	Allocating Money	Allocating Material and Facility Resources	Allocating Human Resources		
Information	Acquiring and Evaluating Information	Organizing and Maintaining Information	Interpreting and Communicating Information	Using Computers to Process Information		
Interpersonal Skills	Participating as a Member of a Team	Teaching Others	Serving Clients/ Customers	Exercising Leadership	Negotiating to Arrive at a Decision	Working With Cultural Diversity
Systems	Understanding Systems	Monitoring and Correcting Performance	Improving and Designing Systems			
Technology	Selecting Technology	Applying Technology to Task	Maintaining and Troubleshooting Technology			

*This chart's highlighted blocks indicate the chapter's content coverage in the Student Edition and the Teacher Wraparound Edition.

Resource Manager

Teaching Transparencies

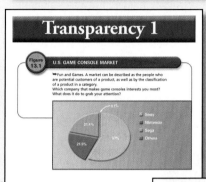

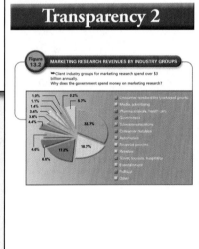

Application and Enrichment

- Lesson Plans
- *BusinessWeek* Poster Package
- Teaching Transparencies
- Integrated Software Simulation
- Glencoe Business Video Package

Review and Reinforcement

- *PuzzleMaker*
- Internet Resources
- Student Activity Workbook
- Strat. and Work. for Teaching Transparencies

Assessment and Evaluation

- Reproducible Tests
- Alternative Assessment Strategies
- ExamView® Pro Test Generator

Technology

- *PuzzleMaker*
- ExamView® Pro Test Generator
- Glencoe Business Video Package
- PowerPoint® Presentation
- Integrated Software Simulation
- Interactive Lesson Planner
- *Virtual Business*®

KEY

| Printed | Software | Videocassette | Poster |
| Transparency | CD-ROM | Internet | |

Visit www.introbus.glencoe.com, the Web site companion to *Introduction to Business.* The student's page includes:

- interactive tutor
- additional *BusinessWeek* articles and activities
- business Web links
- homework hints
- real-world application activities
- additional career path activities

Information on how to prepare your students for the high school exit exam and special projects are also included.

Use the Glencoe Web site for additional resources. All essential content is covered in the Student Edition.

Chapter 13

1 FOCUS

Introducing the Chapter

This chapter discusses the functions of marketing. It also discusses details of market research, product development, and channels of distribution. A photo essay, "Beyond Street-Skaters," enhances the concepts.

Connecting the Objectives

What's important about market research? Ask students for examples from their own life when they've thought about making improvements to a product.

BusinessWeek
Feature Story

Story's Summary

New CEO Peter Cuneo is changing the focus of marketing at Marvel Enterprises. It used to be the money-losing super-hero comic and toy seller. Today it's the entertainment giant, making major movie deals with Marvel action heroes as stars, like the superhuman Daredevil and the cursed green Incredible Hulk. The change in the marketing plan is designed to bring in consistent future revenues for Marvel.

Find the entire article at www.introbus.glencoe.com, or in the Teacher Resource Binder.

Marketing in Today's World

Learning Objectives

After completing this chapter, you'll be able to:
1. **List** the functions of marketing.
2. **Identify** the importance of market research.
3. **Explain** how channels of distribution work.

Why It's Important

Effective marketing puts the products in the hands of its targeted customers.

Key Words

market
marketing
marketing concept
target marketing
relationship marketing
marketing mix
break-even point
market research
demographics
channel of distribution
direct distribution
indirect distribution
wholesaler
retailer

196

BusinessWeek Feature Story

Can Marvel's Heroes Save the Day?

Marvel Treats Its Characters Like Brands to Maximize Profits With Savvy Deals. For a few days in June, Marvel Enterprises saw its lethargic share price jump from $4 to $7, then tumble back to $4. It's easy to see what caused the brief excitement. Marvel owns the fantasy comic-book property *The X-Men* and anticipation of the major motion picture's premier was building. In fact, *The X-Men* film—from 20th Century Fox—was a pretty big summer hit, raking in $150 million at the box office. Too bad Marvel hasn't been able to capitalize on the runaway success of its cool mutant X-Men characters.

Source: Excerpted with permission from "Can Marvel's Heroes Save the Day?" *BusinessWeek Online,* **September 6, 2000.**

An Extension Activity

In Chapter 6 you were part of a start-up company manufacturing new skateboards. You found financial investors. Now your friends ask you to plan the company's channel of distribution. What is your plan?

BUSINESS *Online*
The Full Story

To learn more about Marvel's marketing plan, visit the *Introduction to Business* Web site at www.introbus.glencoe.com, and click on *BusinessWeek* Feature Story, Chapter 13.

Classroom Resources

For the Teacher
- Student Activity Work. TAE
- Assessment Binder
- PowerPoint® Presentation
- Interactive Lesson Planner
- Lesson Plans
- Internet Resources
- Teaching Transparencies
- *Introduction to Business* Web Site
- Integrated Soft. Sim. TM
- *BusinessWeek* Poster Package

For the Student
- Student Activity Workbook
- *Virtual Business*®
- *Introduction to Business* Web Site
- Integrated Soft. Sim.
- *PuzzleMaker*
- Strategies and Worksheets for Teaching Transparencies

Bell Ringer Activity

IMPROVING AND DESIGNING SYSTEMS.   Present this scenario to the students: You regularly take inventory at Ground Swell since you're the manager. You notice that some drinks are more popular in certain seasons. For example, Café Cinnamön sells well only in the winter. You plan to gather a small team of your staff for a marketing meeting to design new products and change your sales system. What ideas do you and your team come up with to increase sales?

Preteaching Business Key Words

ACQUIRING AND EVALUATING INFORMATION.   Divide students into four groups to write the meaning of words assigned to them. Split the key word list in two halves. Give the top half of the list to groups one and two and the bottom half to groups three and four. Ask groups one and three to use the glossary to acquire the meaning of their words. Ask groups two and four to use a dictionary. Ask each group to share the meaning of each of their words and evaluate the accuracy of the meaning. **CL**, **LS**

An Extension Activity

SHARE.   Ask students to share their plan in a short oral presentation. Encourage students to use presentation software or a poster graphic to support their presentation. **CL**, **LS**, **P**

Making Connections

Social Awareness.   Have students choose a product that is potentially harmful and research the issues involved in marketing the product. Remind students that they must show an awareness of the harm from using the product and then must discuss why they think restrictions on marketing the product are or are not necessary. Have students share their findings in an oral presentation to the class. Encourage members of the class to react to the presentations.

2 TEACH

Business Connection

RELATIONSHIP MARKETING. Lands' End has always had a marketing concept based on one-on-one relationships with its customers. The apparel retailer has extended this relationship marketing to a new marketing channel—customer-friendly service on the Internet. For example, Lands' End provides "Lands' End Live," a live chat feature, and "Your Personal Model," where customers can try new clothes on their own body type and see which look best.

Develop Concepts

INVESTIGATE. The market for motorcycles is shrinking. Ask students to research and find out whether this statement is true or false, and why.

Figure 13.1 Caption Answer

If you don't purchase, you are not part of the market and vice-versa.

Marketing Essentials

Marketing a skateboard requires a different strategy than marketing diamond earrings. Each item appeals to people of different ages, genders, and income ranges. Every holiday season more gadgets, toys, and clothes hit the stores. Behind a product is a company's intense research, development, and marketing. To successfully market a product, a company has to understand what people want to buy and why they want to buy it.

Basics of Marketing

It all comes down to knowing your market. **Market** is a group of customers who share common wants and needs, and who have the ability to purchase the product. There's more to marketing than just selling a product. **Marketing** is the process of creating, promoting, and presenting a product to meet the wants and needs of consumers. Marketing involves

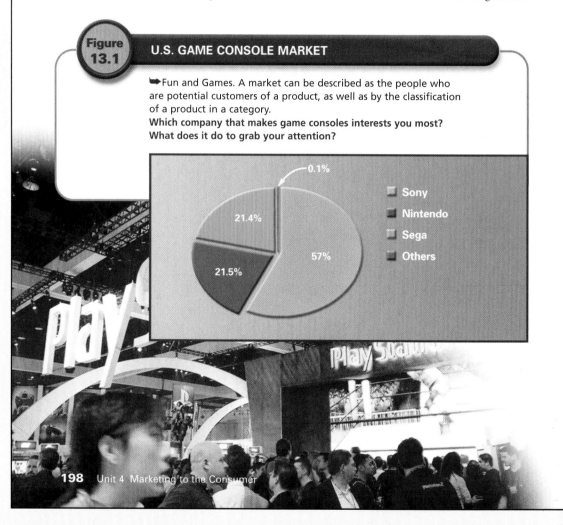

Figure 13.1

U.S. GAME CONSOLE MARKET

➡ Fun and Games. A market can be described as the people who are potential customers of a product, as well as by the classification of a product in a category.
Which company that makes game consoles interests you most? What does it do to grab your attention?

- Sony
- Nintendo
- Sega
- Others

0.1%
21.4%
21.5%
57%

Cooperative Learning

Marketing Mix. XYZ Company wants to introduce a new product. Pair students to be the marketing team of XYZ. Ask pairs to decide on a new product then answer the four questions: (1) Who will the product appeal to and how will it be presented? (2) Where will the product sell best? (3) What should the price be? and (4) What's the best way to let people know about the product? (The four Ps.) Members of the XYZ Marketing Team are excited about their product idea and make an enthusiastic presentation to XYZ management (the class) covering the four Ps of the marketing mix.

a number of stages from studying what people want to buy to designing a product's package. For example, you might be part of the $7 billion market who buys video game consoles (see Figure 13.1). Businesses need to know their customers' wants and needs in order to make a profit. This is known as the **marketing concept**.

Businesses want you to buy their product so they perform detailed research on markets (like teenagers) to find and analyze potential customers in their market. This is called **target marketing**. Later on in this chapter, you'll read how marketing decisions are made based upon target marketing.

Functions of Marketing

There are seven functions of marketing. Each aspect is important to the entire function.

Distribution. This involves moving goods and services from one place to the end user. Trucks, trains, airplanes, and ships are possible transportation methods.

Financing. Money is necessary to keep any business afloat. Businesses decide if customers can pay with credit or other payment options.

Marketing Information Management. Making an informed decision requires good research and development. Companies conduct market research to learn more about their market. (Market research is discussed in more detail later on in this chapter.)

Pricing. Marketers have to figure out what price to charge for a product so the company makes a profit. Marketing needs to consider the impact of distribution, because each time a product goes through another channel of distribution the price goes up. (You'll read more about channels of distribution later in the chapter.)

Product/Service Management. Obtaining information, developing, and maintaining products helps marketers decide how to respond to market opportunities.

Promotion. Communication through any type of media gets a business's product out and into the hands of the public.

Selling. Retailers or the business-to-business market provides customers or industrial users with goods and services. A popular trend in today's marketing world is **relationship marketing**. Companies use

Real-World Application
part 1 of 4

BEYOND STREET-SKATERS
Vans Inc., the maker of slip-on sneakers for maverick teens who like to skateboard, is about being market smart. The last thing its audience wants is to be beaten over the head with slick advertisements. That would be the fastest way to losing loyalty.
Name some qualities about the teen market. What do you want and need?

continued on p. 201

Real-World Application
Caption Answer

BEYOND STREET-SKATERS: PART 1 OF 4
Answers will vary.

Technology Resource

GO TO **POWERPOINT.** The *Introduction to Business* PowerPoint® CD-ROM provides visual lecture aids for this chapter.

Independent Practice

DIAGRAM. Be creative and draw a diagram depicting and labeling the seven functions of marketing. (Distribution, financing, marketing information management, pricing, product/service management, promotion, and selling.) **LS**

Meeting Individual Needs

Students Who Are Gifted. Have gifted students work in small groups to complete an analysis of the promotional mix (going into the specifics) of a company of their choice. Encourage each group to employ a variety of research techniques to put together a profile of the company's use of advertising, publicity, sales promotion, and personal selling techniques. The company may be large or small, national or local, but must have addressed each portion of the promotional mix during the last year. The type of sales promotion will depend on whether the business is a manufacturer/distributor or a retail operation.

2 TEACH (Cont.)

Caption Answer

Smells trigger memories. Aromas influence people to buy immediately. Grocery stores sell more baked goods when there's a smell of fresh-baked cookies. For example, smelling the ocean gives people the desire to sign up for vacation cruises.

Thinking Critically

WHAT'S YOUR OPINION?

Take a trip to a supermarket or bookstore. Notice how products are placed, priced, and promoted. Could the store sell more, in your opinion, if they changed any one of these elements? If the manager of the store asked for your opinions, what advice would you give?

Online Whiffs of Wonder

Is that scent coming from…your computer? Well, DigiScents, Inc., is developing a digital scent device called the iSmell. DigiScents has indexed thousands of odors based on their chemical structure. Each scent is a digitized file, which can be embedded in Web content or an e-mail message. The computer user hooks up iSmell to a computer and requests a scent with the click of a mouse.

Critical Thinking

How might online odors help businesses sell their products?

this strategy to build customer relations. In a competitive world, this keeps a company aware of how it's meeting its customers' wants and needs.

Marketing Mix

Even before a product appears on the market, marketing specialists have to consider a number of questions. Who will the product appeal to? How much should it cost? Where should it be sold? What's the best way to tell people about it? The four elements of marketing—product, place, price, and promotion—are called the **marketing mix**, or the *four Ps*.

Product. Marketing is used first to find out if there is a demand for a product. Then it is concerned with how to present a product to the customer to make it as appealing as possible. How to package a product is a major element of marketing. Packaging includes the design, color, size, and even brand name of a product. Books and CDs rely a lot on cover designs to attract buyers.

Place. Marketers have to figure out where to sell a product to get it to the right customers. One of the first things they have to consider is *where to sell* a product. For example, a company is much more likely to sell snowshoes in Maine than in Texas.

Then marketers have to consider in *what kind of location* to sell their product. Does the product need to be at a fast-food restaurant or gas station? Does the product need to be in a large department store or a boutique?

The *placement* of the product in a store is equally as important. When you first enter a store you'll see featured products on display stands. At checkout counters, you'll find key chains, candy bars, and other small items you might want to buy at the last second.

Price. To determine the price of a product a marketer considers three questions: (1) how much are customers willing to pay, (2) is the price competitive with other products, and (3) can the company make a profit? The amount of money a company has to make on a product to pay for its costs is called the **break-even point**.

Promotion. Promotion consists of making customers aware of a product. The most familiar form of promotion is advertising, which will be covered in the next chapter. There are, however, many other

LANGUAGE ARTS — *Curriculum Connection*

Creating. You've been asked by your company, Scents-Alive, to help it develop a new perfume or cologne. You can suggest anything you think that could help develop and then sell the product, including using consumer surveys, offering special promotions, and finding methods to test and market the product. You're at a coffee shop one evening when suddenly lots of ideas come to mind and you jot them down on a paper napkin.

What are five of your ideas? List them and share them with a partner.

means companies use to promote a product. One way is to offer discounts in the form of coupons, rebates, and sales. Fast-food restaurants offer package deals with free toys.

Another way companies promote their products is through public relations, or *publicity*. Publicity is a kind of free advertising. It consists mostly of news stories on TV, in newspapers, or in magazines. For example, companies like Sony and Microsoft benefit from news articles about the latest in high-tech products. Celebrities go on talk shows and appear on magazine covers to promote their new movie or CD. Big companies sometimes stage *media events*, like a big party or an awards show, to promote the company or one of its products.

Fast Review

1. What is marketing?
2. What are a few functions of marketing?
3. Name the marketing mix, or the four Ps.

Market Research

Have you ever been approached by a marketing researcher while you were shopping at the mall? Market researchers commonly ask shoppers to take a few minutes to answer questions, taste a new food, or watch a new commercial.

Companies do **market research** to gather and study information about consumers to determine what kinds of goods and services to produce. Figure 13.2 (see the next page) breaks down who uses market research the most. Marketing experts keep track of consumers using surveys, sales figures, databases, and the census. Marketers analyze and categorize their markets by demographics. **Demographics** are facts about the population in terms of age, gender, location, income, and education. Once marketers know the demographics of a market, companies can start developing products to fit that particular group.

Real-World Application part 2 of 4

BEYOND STREET-SKATERS

It's no longer just about the shoes. Instead of mass advertisements, Vans integrates its products into lifestyles. The company built skateboard parks from West Orange, Calif., to Houston, Tex., for skateboarders.

Describe the marketing mix of these skateboard parks.

continued on p. 203

Product Development

The demand for products changes constantly. Fads and fashions go in and out of style. New technology replaces old technology. A company's ability to create a new product or a slight variation of an already successful one is important to increasing sales.

There are seven steps in developing a new product. You could use these to develop a car, dish soap, a book, or even clothing. New products invigorate the marketplace. Let's look at the seven important steps.

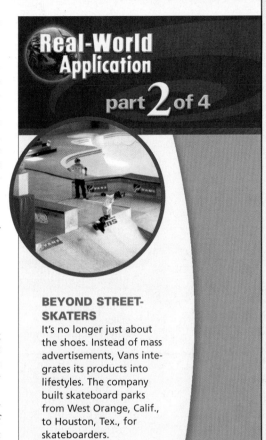

Great Ideas From the Classroom of...

Greg Gregoriou
Parkside High School
Dundas, Ontario, Canada

Marketing Research. Introduce marketing research by having the class name everyday items (gum, chocolate bars, toothbrush, etc.). Then write each item on pieces of paper and put them in a hat or a box. Divide the class into pairs. Each pair selects an item out of the box. Have each pair randomly interview 50 people, noting gender and brand preference for each person surveyed. Have them tabulate their findings. (Percentages work the best.) Have students use a spreadsheet program to graphically display their data.

Real-World Application Caption Answer

BEYOND STREET-SKATERS: PART 2 OF 4

Answers might vary. Product: Vans Inc. Place: Skateboard park. Price: Entrance fee to park. Promotion: Vans Inc. and its apparel.

Fast Review Answers

1. Marketing is the process of researching and then creating, promoting, and presenting a product to meet the wants and needs of consumers.
2. Distribution, financing, marketing information management, pricing, product or service management, promotion, and selling.
3. Product, place, price, and promotion.

Business Connection

DEMOGRAPHIC TREND. Marketing executives are taking note of one demographic trend: Very soon one-quarter of the nation's consumers will be Spanish-speaking. Some big food or beverage companies, such as Kraft, Pepsi, and Proctor & Gamble, each budgeted more than $30 million in one year to market to the Spanish market. Other types of companies, such as those in financial services or technology, are racing to launch Spanish marketing strategies.

Develop Concepts

RESEARCH. Ask students to research and chart local demographic data, such as population, population distribution, and traffic volume by area.

Discussion Starter

GIVING EXAMPLES. Ask students, "How are the products and services you and your family use marketed to you?"

Figure 13.2 Caption Answer

Many governmental agencies have regulatory or legislative mandates to conduct research on matters such as the safety of products, transportation issues, the operation of the postal service, and the services of the Internal Revenue Service. Other agencies need research support to improve their service for the good of the general public.

Generating Ideas. Soda cans and leftover sandwich wrappers litter a conference table. A group of coworkers brainstorm for creative ideas for the company's new product line. One writes down the group's creative ideas on an interactive SMART Board™. People from the company's development department, the market research staff, and even outside market researchers are generating ideas for a new creative product. Collaboration is key to this step.

Screening Ideas. Once the team puts together a final list of creative ideas for the product, they're evaluated. How do these ideas fit the company's mission and the company's strategy? Does the new product compete with one of the company's existing products? If the product's concept is risky, the company might ask consumers about the creative concept. Consumers would identify what they liked or disliked about

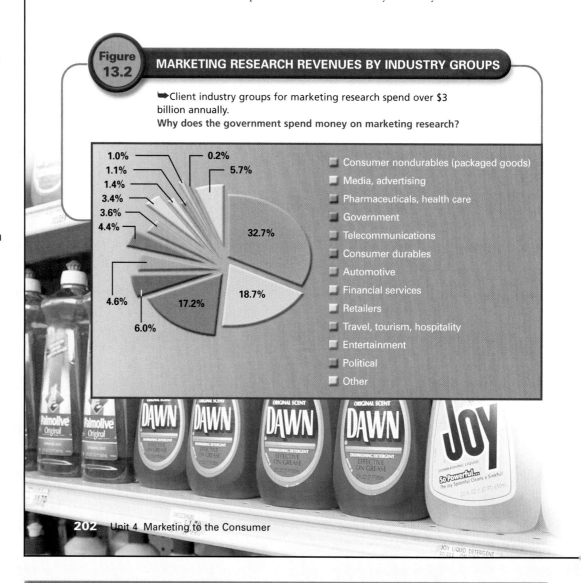

Figure 13.2 MARKETING RESEARCH REVENUES BY INDUSTRY GROUPS

➡Client industry groups for marketing research spend over $3 billion annually.
Why does the government spend money on marketing research?

- 1.0%
- 1.1%
- 1.4%
- 3.4%
- 3.6%
- 4.4%
- 0.2%
- 5.7%
- 32.7%
- 18.7%
- 17.2%
- 4.6%
- 6.0%

- ◻ Consumer nondurables (packaged goods)
- ◼ Media, advertising
- ◼ Pharmaceuticals, health care
- ◼ Government
- ◼ Telecommunications
- ◼ Consumer durables
- ◼ Automotive
- ◼ Financial services
- ◼ Retailers
- ◼ Travel, tourism, hospitality
- ◼ Entertainment
- ◼ Political
- ◼ Other

Global Perspective

Distribution Channels. Challenge students to work on an independent or group project related to distribution channels. Ask students to research channels of distribution in foreign markets, such as Russia or China. Ask students to imagine that they are a U.S manufacturer, who is considering a new market for one or more products. Have students give an oral report on their findings. When presenting their reports, students might imagine they are on a trip to another country and role-play a possible meeting that discusses trade. Encourage creativity.

the concepts. Their responses are crucial as to whether or not the company continues with a proposed product.

Developing a Business Proposal. Once the creative idea passes the screening process, one or two of the ideas are developed into a business plan. (This business plan has many of the same parts and pieces as the business proposal you read about in Chapter 5.) The written proposal provides answers about the market, potential sales, costs, profit potential, market trends, the competition's products, and the level of risk.

Developing the Product. Now that the company's appropriate managers and decision makers are in favor of the product, a prototype is made. This is a model of the actual product. It's used to test ideas. If any aspects of the prototype need to be changed this is the stage to make those changes. A company might experience delays in finalizing the product as it is tested. The government requires extensive testing during various stages of product development. Any one of the testing stages may delay the product.

Test Marketing the Product. Once the product is fully developed, the product might be test marketed. The goal is to collect customers' responses. Sometimes, though, the cost of test marketing a product isn't in the budget. Also, testing may leave time for the competitor to produce a similar product. Then both products may enter the market at the same time.

Introducing the Product. The product passed the market test. Now it's ready for the marketplace. Publicity is used to introduce the product. The costs of doing this are often high. The company has a small amount of time in the market before competition produces a similar product.

Evaluating Customer Acceptance. Once the product is introduced, marketers track customers' responses. The reports answer key questions which inform companies' research and development. Who are their best customers? What new products are they buying? How often do customers buy the new product?

 Fast Review

1. What's the purpose of market research?
2. Name the seven steps in developing a new product.

Real-World Application
part 3 of 4

BEYOND STREET-SKATERS
Innovating shoes has made Vans a reputable business pioneer. The latest is its snowboard boots but it decided against designing inline skates. For its hard-core skateboarders, inline skating isn't in their interest. Why do you think Vans didn't try marketing inline skates?

continued on p. 205

Chapter 13

Real-World Application
Caption Answer

BEYOND STREET-SKATERS: PART 3 OF 4
It wanted to keep the faith of its loyal buyers.

Individualized Practice

IDENTIFYING. Ask students to find the names of companies in the local area that are part of a channel of distribution and the types of products the companies deal with.

L1 Have pairs of students make a list of the companies and the products.

L2 Have pairs of students categorize the companies as distributors, wholesalers, or retailers. Then make a chart including information about the companies and the products.

L3 Tell pairs of students to make a fast-facts booklet, (preferably using a computer), which lists the companies in alphabetical order, along with relevant distribution details.

Fast Review Answers

1. Study consumers who purchase goods and services.
2. Generating ideas, screening ideas, developing a business plan, developing the product, testing the product, introducing the product, and evaluating customer acceptance.

Curriculum Connection

Product Development Collage. Ask groups of students to make a creative collage titled, "Product Development." Have groups choose a product and place the actual product (or a representation made from magazine cuttings, fabric, or any suitable item) in the center of a poster. Make sure seven spokes radiate from the product. Students label each spoke creatively to represent one of the seven steps in developing a new product. (Generating ideas, screening ideas, developing a business proposal, developing the product, testing the product, introducing the product.)

Reteaching

BREAK-EVEN POINT. To reteach the concept of the break-even point, ask students to think of products that cost around $50. Have students give examples of products that are "reasonable" for that price, pointing out that the price of a product should cover the costs of producing, shipping, promoting, and distributing it.

Enrichment Strategy

IDENTIFY TRENDS. Ask students to identify an aspect of marketing and tell ways it has changed in the last five years. **LS**

Working Lifestyle

Caption Answer

Send messages quicker to buyers. Fax, phone, e-mail, or use a pager to get in contact with individuals. Houses can be advertised online.

Channels of Distribution

Marketers have to decide how and where customers will buy their goods and services. (This is the *place* step of the marketing mix that you learned about earlier.) A good marketing strategy includes a distribution plan.

To make this decision, marketers must decide on their channel of distribution. A **channel of distribution** is a particular way to direct products to consumers. Producers use a specific channel to move goods

Working Lifestyle

What are you doing at 10 A.M.?

Reaching Goals

To be a successful real estate broker, Gerardo Villalobos has learned to manage his time, set goals, and determine what steps are necessary to achieve them. "You always have to be prospecting. It's a 24-hour job," he says.

At 10 A.M. Villalobos starts off each morning at the office, where he attends meetings, returns phone calls, and makes a to-do list. It's critical for him to be organized and flexible because he handles many clients at once and each client's case may be in a different stage. Because the real estate market is extremely volatile, he must make long-term adjustments as well: "You see the industry go up and down, and when the hard times come you have to start all over again."

For a real estate broker to succeed, clients must trust him to help them make one of the most important purchases of their lives. As a result, Villalobos must sell more than property; he must also sell personal credibility and individual attention.

The most important qualification, Villalobos says, is to care for your clients. He stresses, "You have to care for people. If you have that quality, people will work with you and you'll get referrals."

Salary

The median income of a real estate broker is $45,640, with a range between $28,680 and $80,070 a year.

Outlook for This Career

This occupation is expected to have steady, average growth.

Connecting Careers Activity

How might technology make a real estate broker's job easier? Does their use of technology affect buyers?

CAREER PATH Retail/Wholesale Sales & Services

How to Use a Portfolio Activity

The portfolio projects are designed to lead students to develop a collection of their best work to submit to you for assessment. You and each of your students should decide which projects to include in their business portfolio. Refer students to the specific rubric(s) from the *Alternative Assessment Strategies*. These rubrics will alert students to the criteria you'll use to assess their projects.

to their final user. **Direct distribution** occurs when the goods or services are sold from the producer directly to the customer; an intermediary isn't involved. **Indirect distribution** involves one or more intermediaries.

The biggest impact distribution has on marketing is how it affects the price of products. Each time a product goes through another channel the cost of marketing it increases. Wholesalers, retailers, truck companies, and warehouses all have to cover their own expenses and make a profit. Therefore, the cost of distributing a product has to be added to its price, which makes it hard for some companies to compete. Let's take a closer look at the channel members of distribution.

Channel Members

Moving the product from manufacturer to the final user is an intermediary, or a go-between. Intermediaries can include distributors, wholesalers, retailers, and today, even the Internet.

Distributors. This kind of intermediary represents a single manufacturer in a geographic area. Cosmetics, cars, furniture, and shoes are sold through distributors.

Wholesalers. A **wholesaler** receives large shipments of products from many different producers. They break the shipments into smaller batches for resale. A company that makes canned peas may sell a truckload of its peas to a wholesaler. The wholesaler, in turn, will sell a few cases of peas to several local supermarkets.

Retailers. A **retailer** sells goods directly to the customer. This is the final stop in the channel of distribution. When you buy something in the supermarket, drugstore, or department store, you're dealing with a retailer.

Some manufacturers or service providers go directly to the customer. The Internet encourages producers to distribute their products themselves. A virtual business (as you learned in Chapter 5) allows customers to order online. This cuts down on the role of intermediaries, and can cut costs and increase profits to the producer.

 Fast Review _____

1. Channels of distribution are classified in which two ways?
2. How does distribution affect the prices of products?
3. What are the major types of intermediaries?

Chapter 13 Marketing in Today's World **205**

Real-World Application
part **4** of 4

BEYOND STREET-SKATERS
The founders of Vans wanted to manufacture shoes and sell them directly to its customers. Over 30 years later, Vans has sold its products through its own retail stores as well as independents.
Do you show product loyalty? If so, what are these brands? Why?

Real-World Application
Caption Answer

BEYOND STREET-SKATERS: PART 4 OF 4
Answers will vary.

Technology Resource

GO TO **VIRTUAL BUSINESS.** Introduce marketing using Knowledge Matters' *Virtual Business* interactive simulation. Go to the *Introduction to Business* Web site **www.introbus.glencoe.com** to download the *Virtual Business* activity. Run the *Virtual Business* tutorial before beginning this activity.

Evaluation

Assign and review the Fast Review sections.

Fast Review Answers ✓

1. Direct or indirect.
2. Wholesalers, retailers, truck companies, and other channels of distribution increase the cost of marketing a product.
3. Wholesalers, retailers, and distributors. Facilities such as stores and warehouses. Means of transportation such as trucks, ships, planes, and trains.

Meeting Individual Needs

Students With Attention Difficulties. Students who have difficulty paying attention in class can benefit from being given a time limit for a task. Ask students to read the section *Channels of Distribution,* which is approximately 400 words. Give students five and a half minutes to read the section. Discuss with students the effect of a time limit on their ability to stay on task.

4 CLOSE

Chapter Wrap-Up

Announce: "Here's a wrap-up race as we come to the end of this chapter. Write for three minutes on marketing today. Go!"

Using Business Key Words

1. demographics
2. marketing
3. channel of distribution
4. marketing mix
5. market research
6. market
7. marketing concept
8. relationship marketing
9. target marketing
10. break-even point
11. direct distribution
12. indirect distribution
13. wholesaler
14. retailer

Review What You Learned

15. Selling
16. Distribution, financing, marketing information management, pricing, product/service management, promotion, and selling.
17. Product, price, promotion, and place.
18. Goods or services you can expect to sell.
19. Demographics
20. Generating ideas, screening ideas, developing a business proposal, developing the product, testing the product, introducing the product, and evaluating customer acceptance.
21. Get product to the user.
22. Distributors are intermediaries. Wholesalers receive shipments from many different producers.

Summary

1. The functions of marketing include distribution, financing, marketing information management, pricing, product and service management, promotion, and selling. The four elements of the marketing mix are product, place, price, and promotion.

2. Market research is important to study the customers' wants and needs and buying behavior. A product goes through seven developmental steps. These include: generating ideas, screening ideas, developing a business proposal, developing the product, test marketing the product, introducing the product, and evaluating customer acceptance.

3. A product has to go through channels of distribution to get from producers to consumers.

● Using Business Key Words

People who market goods and services use the following terms. See how well you know them. Match the word to its definition.

- **target marketing**
- **market**
- **marketing**
- **break-even point**
- **wholesaler**
- **demographics**
- **marketing mix**
- **direct distribution**
- **indirect distribution**
- **retailer**
- **marketing concept**
- **channel of distribution**
- **market research**
- **relationship marketing**

1. The study of population.
2. Analyzing consumer wants and providing goods and services to meet those wants.
3. A way to direct products to consumers.
4. Product, price, promotion, and place—the activities that go into selling a product to consumers.
5. The gathering of information that businesses can use to determine what kinds of goods and services to produce.
6. A group of customers who share common needs and wants.
7. Businesses need to know their customers' wants and needs in order to make a profit.
8. A popular trend in today's marketing world.
9. Detailed research on a particular segment of the population.
10. The amount of money a company has to make on a product to pay for its costs.
11. Goods and services are sold from producer directly to the customer.
12. Delivering goods and services with one or more intermediaries.
13. Receives large shipment of products from many different producers.
14. Sells goods directly to the customer.

Quick Quiz

1. Name the four elements of the marketing mix. (Product, place, price, promotion.)
2. Define demographics. (Facts about the population in terms of age, gender, location, income, and education.)
3. What is a channel of distribution? (A particular way to direct products to consumers.)

Review What You Learned

15. During what marketing function is relationship marketing a consideration?
16. Describe each function of marketing.
17. What are the four Ps?
18. What's the purpose of market research?
19. Marketers analyze and categorize their markets by this.
20. Describe the seven important steps in developing a new product.
21. Why are channels of distribution important?
22. Describe the difference between distributors and wholesalers.

Understanding Business Concepts

23. Which of the four marketing factors do you think is the most important? Explain why.
24. Describe a situation when low pricing does not mean low quality. Give an example that you have personally experienced.
25. List a product that you think might not have been sold for a long time because of the marketplace's lack of interest.
26. Have you ever purchased something based on an interesting marketing campaign? Explain.
27. What information do you like to have included with a product that you buy?
28. What could market researchers learn about a group of people by studying the foods they bought in the last year?
29. Explain how the Internet is a channel of distribution.
30. Why do you think companies try to design easily recognizable logos?

Critical Thinking

31. How might products and services designed to meet customers' wants and needs vary between countries?
32. Some companies plan special events to draw publicity for a new product. What kind of event could a shoe company hold to attract publicity for a new line of athletic shoes?
33. Collect several magazines. Based upon the advertisements, describe which demographic the magazines cater to?

Viewing and Representing

Examining the Image. Carefully observe the photograph and write what you see. What do you already know about the time period and the people shown in the picture? What can you conclude about what is happening in the photograph? What is being promoted here? Is more than one thing being promoted? What picture of the world is being presented? Are the people or other things here being depicted with accuracy, with bias, or with exaggeration? Write your answers.

Chapter 13 Marketing in Today's World   **207**

4 CLOSE (Cont.)

Building Academic Skills

HISTORY. If the students do not have access to many magazines or newspapers, bring some in for them to use. Rubrics: Poster, paragraph.

MATH. $129.99 × 0.115 = $14.94; $129.99 − $14.94 = $115.05.

LANGUAGE ARTS. Encourage all students to participate in the project. It might be necessary to assign different groups (other students, teachers, family members, community members) to the students in order to get a good cross section of results. Rubrics: Survey, chart.

COMPUTER/TECHNOLOGY. Encourage students to be creative. Rubrics: Essay, flyer.

Linking School to Home

Answers will vary. Let students choose the method they use to share their results. Rubrics: Note taking, essay, oral presentation.

Linking School to Work

Answers will vary. Let students choose the method they use to share their results. Rubrics: Note taking, essay, oral presentation.

Building Academic Skills

 Sociological Decisions

In a group, conduct a survey of other students, teachers, family members, and people in the community to find out what factors are most important in their buying decisions. Use the survey to determine:

- Which stores they shop in most frequently.
- What types of advertising they pay the most attention to.
- What factors are most important to them when making decisions about convenience goods and services, shopping goods and services, and specialty goods and services.

Tabulate your results and create a chart to display your findings.

 Pricing

Your boss has asked that you price the new shipment of leather jackets that have just arrived. She wants the jackets to be priced 11.5 percent lower than the store across town. If the jackets sell for $129.99 at the other store, what price will you sell the jackets for at your store?

 Analyzing and Creating

Using magazines or newspapers, find advertisements that appeal to different demographic categories. Mount the ads on poster board and write a paragraph explaining how each ad appeals to the particular demographic category.

 Designing a Flier

Imagine you've been hired to create a publicity event for a shoe store that plans to introduce a new line of athletic shoes. Using a word processor, write a one-page paper about the event you'll create. Using publishing software, create a flier that you could use to promote your event. Display the flier in your class.

Linking School to Home

Mini Survey. During the next two weeks, save all the advertising and promotional material that comes in the mail for you and your family. Categorize each one based on the type of product being advertised. Conduct a mini-survey among your family and friends. Find out whether or not they would buy the products based on the advertising material that has been sent to your home.

Linking School to Work

Promoting a Product. If you're employed, choose a product sold by your company and determine the following:

- The pricing strategy utilized by your company.
- The marketing approach used to sell the product.
- The channel(s) of distribution used to direct the product to the consumer.

If you're not employed, choose a product sold at school.

E-Homework

Applying Technology

Online Want Ads. Use the Internet to research the entry-level advertising positions available online. Find out where the job is located, the starting salary, duties and responsibilities, and education required. Write a paragraph summarizing your findings.

Surveying E-tailers. Select three stores that you shop in regularly that also have a presence on the Internet. Log on to their Web sites and evaluate their Web pages in order to answer these questions:

- Is the site attractive and user friendly?
- What types of products are sold online? Are they different from the products sold in the stores? How?
- What security measures are in place to protect online buyers?

Write a one-page paper describing the site you liked the best and why.

Connecting Academics

Math. You're manager of the sweatshirt department at Trends, a clothing manufacturer. Trends plans to produce 25,000 sweatshirts. The sweatshirts will be sold to stores for $16 each. The cost of manufacturing and marketing each sweatshirt is $10. How many sweatshirts must your department sell at $16 to reach the break-even point?

Language Arts. Working in a team of three, find and read several articles on marketing, market research, or relationship marketing. Together, create a one-minute news report titled, "Marketing Fast Facts" on topics from the articles.

BusinessWeek Analyzing the Feature Story

You read the first part of "Can Marvel's Heroes Save the Day?" at the beginning of this chapter. Below are a few questions for you to answer about Marvel Enterprises. You'll find the answers to these questions when you're reading the entire article. First, here are the questions:

34. What product does Marvel Enterprises plan to use to become the leading entertainment company in the world?
35. How is Marvel planning to change its pricing strategy with movie studios?

CREATIVE JOURNAL ACTIVITY

Break into small groups. You're a product team for Marvel Enterprises. Using one of its characters, come up with a new product to sell. How will you price it? How will you promote it? Where will you sell it? Write your ideas in a marketing plan and then present your ideas to the Marvel Board of Directors (i.e., your class).

The Full Story

To learn more about Marvel's marketing plan, visit the *Introduction to Business* Web site at **www.introbus.glencoe.com**, and click on *BusinessWeek* Feature Story, Chapter 13.

209

E-Homework

ONLINE WANT ADS. Answers will vary depending on the entry-level position selected. Rubrics: Essay, note taking.

SURVEYING E-TAILERS. Answers will vary depending on the Web site selected. Rubrics: Essay, note taking.

Connecting Academics

MATH. 15,625 sweatshirts. (25,000 × 10 = 250,000; 250,000 ÷ 16 = 15,625)

LANGUAGE ARTS. As a variation, ask teams to videotape their one-minute news report to be aired on the TV in class.

BusinessWeek *Analyzing the Feature Story*

34. Marvel Enterprises views its characters as brands. They are going to place them in as many mediums and entertainment venues as possible to build their business.
35. Rather than accepting a licensing fee and the right to make the toys for movies, Marvel plans to ask for more money and participation in the profits for the movie.

Creative Journal Activity

Before the presentations, have students decide on an imagined or real character trait to exaggerate as part of the presentation to the board of directors. Remind students they are imagining a professional product team marketing presentation. If possible, videotape the presentation.

SCANS Correlation Chart*

Foundation Skills

Basic Skills	Reading	Writing	Math	Listening	Speaking	
Thinking Skills	Creative Thinking	Decision Making	Problem Solving	Seeing Things in the Mind's Eye	Knowing How to Learn	Reasoning
Personal Qualities	Responsibility	Self-Esteem	Sociability	Self-Management	Integrity/Honesty	

Workplace Competencies

Resources	Allocating Time	Allocating Money	Allocating Material and Facility Resources	Allocating Human Resources		
Information	Acquiring and Evaluating Information	Organizing and Maintaining Information	Interpreting and Communicating Information	Using Computers to Process Information		
Interpersonal Skills	Participating as a Member of a Team	Teaching Others	Serving Clients/Customers	Exercising Leadership	Negotiating to Arrive at a Decision	Working With Cultural Diversity
Systems	Understanding Systems	Monitoring and Correcting Performance	Improving and Designing Systems			
Technology	Selecting Technology	Applying Technology to Task	Maintaining and Troubleshooting Technology			

*This chart's highlighted blocks indicate the chapter's content coverage in the Student Edition and the Teacher Wraparound Edition.

Resource Manager

Teaching Transparencies

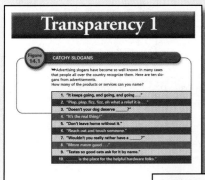

Transparency 1

CATCHY SLOGANS

Figure 14.1

Advertising slogans have become so well known in many cases that people all over the country recognize them. Here are ten slogans from advertisements.
How many of the products or services can you name?

1. "It keeps going, and going, and going . . ."
2. "Plop, plop, fizz, fizz, oh what a relief it is . . ."
3. "Doesn't your dog deserve _____?"
4. "It's the real thing!"
5. "Don't leave home without it."
6. "Reach out and touch someone."
7. "Wouldn't you really rather have a _____?"
8. "Mmm mmm good . . ."
9. "Tastes so good cats ask for it by name."
10. _____ is the place for the helpful hardware folks."

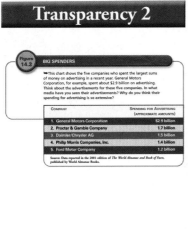

Transparency 2

BIG SPENDERS

Figure 14.2

This chart shows the five companies who spent the largest sums of money on advertising in a recent year. General Motors Corporation, for example, spent about $2.9 billion on advertising. Think about the advertisements for these five companies. In what media have you seen their advertisements? Why do you think their spending for advertising is so extensive?

COMPANY	SPENDING FOR ADVERTISING (APPROXIMATE AMOUNTS)
1. General Motors Corporation	$2.9 billion
2. Procter & Gamble Company	1.7 billion
3. Daimler/Chrysler AG	1.5 billion
4. Philip Morris Companies, Inc.	1.4 billion
5. Ford Motor Company	1.2 billion

Source: Data reported in the 2001 edition of *The World Almanac and Book of Facts*, published by World Almanac Books.

Application and Enrichment

- Lesson Plans
- *BusinessWeek* Poster Package
- Teaching Transparencies
- Integrated Software Simulation
- Glencoe Business Video Package

Review and Reinforcement

- *PuzzleMaker*
- Internet Resources
- Student Activity Workbook
- Strat. and Work. for Teaching Transparencies

Assessment and Evaluation

- Reproducible Tests
- Alternative Assessment Strategies
- ExamView® Pro Test Generator

Technology

- *PuzzleMaker*
- ExamView® Pro Test Generator
- Glencoe Business Video Package
- PowerPoint® Presentation
- Integrated Software Simulation
- Interactive Lesson Planner
- *Virtual Business*®

KEY	Printed	Software	Videocassette	Poster
	Transparency	CD-ROM	Internet	

BUSINESS Online

Visit www.introbus.glencoe.com, the Web site companion to *Introduction to Business*. The student's page includes:

- interactive tutor
- additional *BusinessWeek* articles and activities
- business Web links
- homework hints
- real-world application activities
- additional career path activities

Information on how to prepare your students for the high school exit exam and special projects are also included.

Use the Glencoe Web site for additional resources. All essential content is covered in the Student Edition.

1 FOCUS

Introducing the Chapter

This chapter describes advertising media—the different media and their advantages and disadvantages. It also discusses advertising rates. A photo essay titled, "Bathed in Blue," enhances the concepts.

Connecting the Objectives

Ask students to name different types of advertising and what they know about the relative costs of advertising. Ask students for examples from their own and their families' lives of how advertising affects them.

Advertising: The Art of Attracting an Audience

Learning Objectives

After completing this chapter, you'll be able to:
1. **Identify** the different types of media that can be used to advertise products.
2. **List** advantages and disadvantages for each type of advertising media.
3. **Name** factors in the cost of advertising.

Why It's Important

Businesses rely on advertising to get your attention and to promote their products. Advertising pays for many of the costs of TV, radio, newspapers, and magazines.

Key Words

advertising
mass media
direct-mail advertising
transit advertising
infomercial
webcast
cyber ads
pop-up ads
banner ads
screen ads

210

BusinessWeek Feature Story

Yahoo! and Pepsi: "Fusion Marketing" in Prime Time

The Portal's Approach to Advertising. The slot most coveted by advertisers on Super Bowl Sunday isn't during the pregame show, or right before the start of the celebrity-studded half-time extravaganza. It won't be during the game at all. This year, the crème-de-la-crème of TV commercial positioning will be those precious three minutes between the end of the National Football League's championship game on CBS and the beginning of the network's second *Survivor* series: "The Australian Outback."

Source: Excerpted with permission from "Yahoo! and Pepsi: "Fusion Marketing" in Prime Time," *BusinessWeek Online*, January 26, 2001.

An Extension Activity

Why do companies hire models, actors, or other celebrities to sell products?

BUSINESS Online
The Full Story

To learn more about "fusion marketing," visit the *Introduction to Business* Web site at **www.introbus.glencoe.com**, and click on *BusinessWeek* Feature Story, Chapter 14.

Classroom Resources

For the Teacher
- Student Activity Work. TAE
- Assessment Binder
- PowerPoint® Presentation
- Interactive Lesson Planner
- Lesson Plans
- Internet Resources
- Teaching Transparencies
- *Introduction to Business* Web Site
- Integrated Soft. Sim. TM
- *BusinessWeek* Poster Package

For the Student
- Student Activity Workbook
- *Virtual Business*®
- *Introduction to Business* Web Site
- Integrated Soft. Sim.
- *PuzzleMaker*
- Strategies and Worksheets for Teaching Transparencies

Bell Ringer Activity

KNOWING HOW TO LEARN. Studies show that one of the best ways to learn is to ask questions. Give a dozen 3" by 5" cards to each student. Have students write a question about advertising on one side of each card. Instruct students to keep the cards handy throughout this chapter and to write the answer on the back of the card. **LS**

Preteaching Business Key Words

WRITING. Ask students to create a fill-in-the-blank test for each key word. Randomly pass the tests around the class. Have students complete the vocabulary tests. **LS**, **CL**

An Extension Activity

ROLE-PLAY. Ask students questions to examine their own reactions to the use of celebrities in advertising. Have pairs of students role-play an advertiser in a business meeting with a celebrity. What does the celebrity want? What needs and conditions does the advertiser have?

Making Connections

Humor in Advertising. Many advertisers use humor as a selling technique. Have students check some newspapers and magazines at home and bring in ads that use humor. As a class, analyze the ads to decide how often the ads give useful information versus how often they appeal strictly to the consumer's sense of humor. Discuss the effectiveness of humor in persuading people to buy. Students can keep up with trends in advertising by reading a variety of publications including *Adweek*, *Advertising Age*, *Marketing News*, and other general interest publications.

2 TEACH

Business Connection

ADS. When TV ads seem so popular, it's meaningful that when you go on trips, you still see billboards—roadside billboards are still effective. With new Internet advertising, flashy banner ads have not brought the expected revenues. Traditional approaches to banner ads by companies such as Volkswagen and McDonald's have brought minimal click-through statistics. Advertisers need to have a new approach, for example using increasingly popular pop-up ads. Will banner ads disappear from the Net?

Develop Concepts

IDENTIFY. Have students identify three trends in advertising over the past three years. (Answers will vary, and may include new broadcast media and Internet advertising.)

Figure 14.1 Caption Answer

1. Energizer batteries
2. Alka Seltzer
3. Alpo
4. Coca-Cola
5. American Express card
6. American Telephone and Telegraph (AT&T)
7. Buick
8. Campbell's soup
9. Meow Mix cat food
10. Ace

Confronting Issues With Images

A corporation just might be watching you. What you buy. How you act. Anything that pushes your buttons is of interest to corporations that have something to sell. What they sell you is a product through an image. Buying a product when there's an image attached—that somehow it'll make you better looking or cooler—is exactly what the company wants you to do. This way you help their profits.

Advertising Media

Advertisements are everywhere you look. You see them on TV, in movie theaters, on the streets, at checkout counters, in magazines, on the Internet, and on T-shirts. The average person sees hundreds of ads each week. In a world with so many choices for essentially the same product, advertisers use their wit, wisdom, and originality to get consumer's attention. Often companies with deep pockets gobble up the market share by spending the most on advertising campaigns. **Advertising** is the paid, nonpersonal form of communication that businesses use to

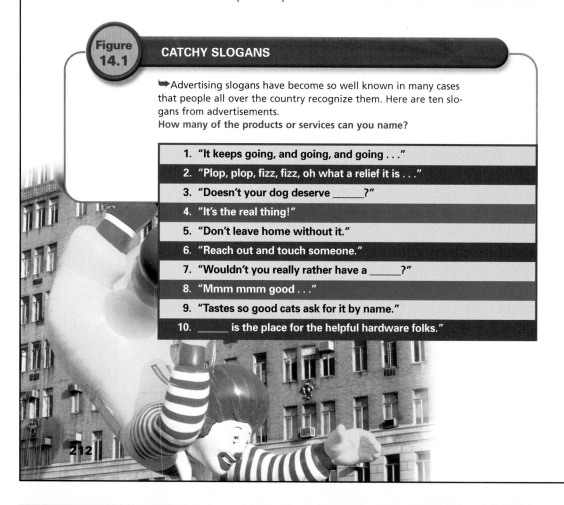

Figure 14.1

CATCHY SLOGANS

➡Advertising slogans have become so well known in many cases that people all over the country recognize them. Here are ten slogans from advertisements.
How many of the products or services can you name?

1. "It keeps going, and going, and going . . ."
2. "Plop, plop, fizz, fizz, oh what a relief it is . . ."
3. "Doesn't your dog deserve _____?"
4. "It's the real thing!"
5. "Don't leave home without it."
6. "Reach out and touch someone."
7. "Wouldn't you really rather have a _____?"
8. "Mmm mmm good . . ."
9. "Tastes so good cats ask for it by name."
10. _____ is the place for the helpful hardware folks."

212

Cooperative Learning

Three-Minute Television Segment. A news broadcast company asks the students to make a three-minute television segment comparing advertising rates. Each minute focuses on print media, broadcast media, and the Internet. Split the class into groups to compete for the best television script. Allow groups to be as creative as they like, to present their scripts, and then to vote on the winning segment.

promote their products. Creating and using a catchy advertising slogan over and over again is one way a company sells a product (see Figure 14.1).

Most ads consist of short messages designed to attract your attention, identify a product, and tell you something about it. They are sent using one or more types of mass media. **Mass media** are means of communication such as TV, radio, and newspapers. The type of medium an advertiser uses depends on the market it wants to reach.

Print Media

Print media uses writing and pictures to communicate. It includes newspapers, magazines, signs, and billboards. In fact, the age of advertising began with the invention of the printing press in the fifteenth century. Fliers could be mass produced and put in newspapers or posted in public places. It's still one of the most popular means of advertising.

Newspapers. Newspapers are the main advertising medium in the United States. More than 50 percent of adults in the United States read newspapers. Advertisers can target people within a certain area. This is especially useful for neighborhood businesses like hair salons and restaurants. Newspapers usually come out daily, which allows businesses to run an ad several days at a time or once a week. Advertisers can also place ads quickly and update them easily.

The cost of printing an ad is fairly cheap. Newspaper ads often include coupons that can be clipped out, so the ads can have a life beyond the newspaper. On the other hand, most people throw their newspapers away after they read them, so an ad's lifespan is usually short. Ads have to compete with news, sports, comics, editorials, and other features for attention. Many readers simply ignore the ads. Since most newspapers are printed in black and white and use recycled paper and soy-based ink, the actual ad design is less intricate than in glossy magazines.

Magazines. Most magazines are national in scope and appear every week (such as *Time*) or every month (such as *Vanity Fair*). People from around the country can see the same ad in an issue of the magazine. Many magazines also offer regional editions for different parts of the country. Special-interest magazines like *Teen* and *Sports Illustrated* make it possible to reach target markets on a large scale. For example, makers of computer software can reach the right market by placing ads in magazines like *PC*.

Real-World Application

part **1** of 4

BATHED IN BLUE
Who doesn't love a sale? The ad promises 40 percent off for that beach towel. "Excellent," you think. And you throw two into your cart as a blue police light flashes.
What store are you in?

continued on p. 215

Chapter 14

Real-World Application
Caption Answer

BATHED IN BLUE:
PART 1 OF 4
Kmart.

Technology Resource

GO TO **POWERPOINT.** The *Introduction to Business* PowerPoint® CD-ROM provides visual lecture aids for this chapter.

Independent Practice

COMPARE AND CONTRAST. Ask students to choose a product or a company. Have students research advertising for that product or company from 20 years ago to present. Ask students to make a presentation comparing and contrasting techniques. **LS**

Chapter 14 Advertising: The Art of Attracting an Audience **213**

Meeting Individual Needs

Second Language Learners. If your class consists of students with differing levels of English fluency, the advertising material can present several challenges—especially in the area of role-plays.

Encourage active participation of all students in these activities, but keep in mind varying ability levels. Pair non-native with native speakers for verbal exercises, when appropriate. **ELL**, **CL**

Thinking Critically

INFORMATION INTERVIEWING. You're considering a career in advertising, but before going ahead with training you want to find out about the typical day of someone in advertising. Your friend's cousin, Dieter, works for Disney, and you have a telephone interview set up for tomorrow at 9:30 A.M. Dieter has 25 minutes to talk with you. Write down your list of questions about Dieter's typical workday, and what training Dieter recommends to be successful on the job.

Technology Toolkit

Pushing the Limits

Advertisers reach people with push technology (also known as webcasting, channeling, niche casting, and narrowcasting). The Massachusetts Institute of Technology (MIT) students called their push product fishWrap®, which refers to the old expression, "Yesterday's news wraps today's fish." This personalized news service is tailor-made for its users, who fill out a personal profile when they subscribe.

Critical Thinking

How might push technology work against companies that try pushing their products to the marketplace?

People take their time to read magazines and often save them, so magazine ads have a much longer lifespan than newspaper ads. Since people tend to look at magazines more than once, they might see the same ad several times. Most magazines are printed in color with much higher quality ink and paper than newspapers. For these reasons the ads often look more attractive.

Magazines are so broadly circulated they're of little use to local advertisers. Another disadvantage is that magazines take longer to prepare so ads are placed weeks or even months in advance. They can't be easily changed or used to promote a limited offer.

Direct-Mail Advertising. **Direct-mail advertising** consists of ads sent by mail to people's homes. It's the biggest advertising medium after TV and newspapers. Direct mail allows advertisers to reach a specific target market. A business can put together a mailing list of customers who live within a certain area, belong to a certain age group, or buy certain kinds of products. It can then mail ads only to people who might be interested. For example, a college student might receive ads in the mail for backpacks, credit cards, or "spring break" specials.

Direct-mail advertisers can use a variety of formats—letters, fliers, postcards, and catalogs—and include coupons or free samples. Internet servers such as America Online (AOL) send out free trial CDs through the mail. Direct mail can also be used to make sales by including order forms.

The cost of sending ads through the mail can be very high. Mailing lists have to be constantly maintained and updated. Only 1 percent of people who receive ads in the mail actually respond. Direct mail is often referred to as "junk mail" because people who receive direct-mail advertising often throw it out without ever looking at it.

Directory Advertising. Directory advertising, which consists mostly of phone books, is especially useful for local advertisers. They can list their number and display an ad under a heading for the type of product or service they offer.

The cost of a directory is usually very cheap. Phone books are used in almost every home, in all areas, and kept for at least a year. They help local businesses by making it easy for consumers to find them on demand.

A disadvantage of directory ads is that they have to compete with numerous similar ads. Directory ads are so brief—often consisting of

214 Unit 4 Marketing to the Consumer

LANGUAGE ARTS — Curriculum Connection

Creative Writing. Resort International is famous for attracting families traveling with teens. The hotel chain offers social events, tours, sports clinics, and a discount on the first room with the booking of a second room. You're newly hired on R.I.'s advertising team. The team's goal is to increase next year's patronage 25 percent by rolling out a new program. What are your ideas to include in the program? **CL**, **LS**

little more than a name, address, and phone number—that they have no way to stand out. Which business a person calls is often randomly picked. Most ads run can't be used to advertise prices, sales, and they can't be easily updated.

Outdoor Advertising. The most common form of outdoor advertising is a billboard. Most billboards are very large and placed near highways where they're highly visible. They can be seen many times by thousands of drivers. A billboard is usually placed for several months. They're useful for local businesses and businesses that cater to travelers, such as fast-food stands, motels, and radio stations.

The main disadvantage of billboards is that people often drive by them too quickly to notice. If you see the same billboard often enough you also begin to ignore it. Billboards are banned in some states, such as Maine and Alaska, because they detract from the scenery. In many urban areas like Los Angeles, billboards are restricted along freeways because they distract drivers too much.

Transit Advertising. Transit advertising uses public transportation, such as buses and trains to display ads. **Transit advertising** usually consists of posters placed on the sides of buses, in subway stations, inside trains, and at airports. They're most common in urban areas where public transportation is used more often. For this reason, they're useful for advertising things like concerts, public events, and local TV.

Broadcast Media

Broadcast media (primarily TV and radio) are the most effective means of advertising. Over 98 percent of all homes in the United States have at least one TV and almost every American owns a radio. The popularity of broadcast media makes it possible for advertisers to reach a mass audience. Figure 14.2 illustrates the amount of money corporations will spend to get their product out there.

Television. Television has an advantage over any other media because it combines sounds, images, and motion. Advertisers can be more informative, entertaining, or creative with TV ads. Some ads are so effective that they become part of our everyday language.

TV ads can be shown on national, local, or cable stations to reach any kind of market. Advertisers can also reach target markets by showing ads during certain types of shows. Ads for an animated movie are shown during Saturday morning cartoons and ads for an action movie are aired during *Monday Night Football*.

Chapter 14 Advertising: The Art of Attracting an Audience **215**

Real-World Application

part 2 of 4

BATHED IN BLUE
Kmart is known for its Blue Light Special. That infamous voice over any one of its store's P.A. systems that calls, "Attention Kmart shoppers!," was started in 1965 by a store manager in Fort Wayne, Ind. **What do you think was the impetus behind this creation?**

continued on p. 217

Real-World Application
Caption Answer

BATHED IN BLUE: PART 2 OF 4

Customers couldn't find the wrapping paper on sale after Christmas. So the store manager attached a light on a long pole and stuck it next to the aisle.

Business Connection

AD COSTS. The Internet may seem to be a threat to print advertising, but William L. Davis, CEO of R.R. Donnelley & Sons Co., the nation's largest commercial printer, believes that the Internet is not an immediate threat. He believes this, in part, because of the cost efficiency of print advertising. In advertising, cost efficiency is measured by the amount spent on advertising for each dollar of sales. For comparison, yellow page directories cost about 4 cents for each dollar of sales, where online the cost is about 11 cents. For further comparison, radio ads are about 15 cents and TV a whopping 19 cents.

Develop Concepts

NAMING. Ask students for names of companies advertising in print media, in broadcast media, and on the Internet. What is the size of these companies? Where do local companies and businesses advertise?

Great Ideas From the Classroom of...

Keith A. Schneider
Cambridge High School
Cambridge, Wis.

Advertise a Local Business. Divide the class into groups and have each develop a radio spot (30 seconds minimum). Each group picks out a business that needs to advertise more. They determine the advertising route that currently exists and either expand upon it or develop a new path. Rough draft of the radio spot is submitted to me. Feedback is given at all times. Why does or doesn't the ad copy work? Was the message sent clearly?

2 TEACH (Cont.)

Discussion Starter

EVALUATING. Ask students which form of advertising they feel was most effective five years ago, is now, and will be in the future.

Individualized Practice

SCENARIO. Roberta and Raul publish a monthly teen-fashion magazine. You're invited as a consultant to a strategic planning meeting. Roberta bangs her fist on the table in frustration saying, "I find many clients only run a single one-quarter-page ad, but I'm convinced they will sell more with repetitive advertising." Raul says, "What do you suggest?" You think fast. "The cost of print advertising is relatively cheap, so here's a win–win solution," you say.

L1 Have pairs of students discuss the solution they will give.

L 2 Tell students to write a paragraph giving their solution.

L 3 Divide the class into groups to role-play the strategic planning meeting and the solution.

Figure 14.2 Caption Answer

They advertise in many mediums in order to reach consumers worldwide.

Most TV ads are 30- or 60-second "spots." Another type of TV ad is the infomercial. An **infomercial** is a TV program, usually 30 minutes long, made to advertise a product. It is often set up like a talk show with a live studio audience and a celebrity guest who demonstrates the product.

The biggest disadvantage of TV ads is that they can be very expensive to produce. Advertisers also have to pay to broadcast an ad during a TV show. The more popular a show is, the more it costs to air an ad during it.

Radio. Like TV ads, radio ads can reach a very wide audience. Radio ads may not be as effective as TV or even magazine ads, because they can't use images. They can, however, use music, dialogue, and sound effects creatively to get an audience's attention.

Radio stations broadcast within certain areas so they're a good medium for local advertising. They also specialize in certain types of programs: talk

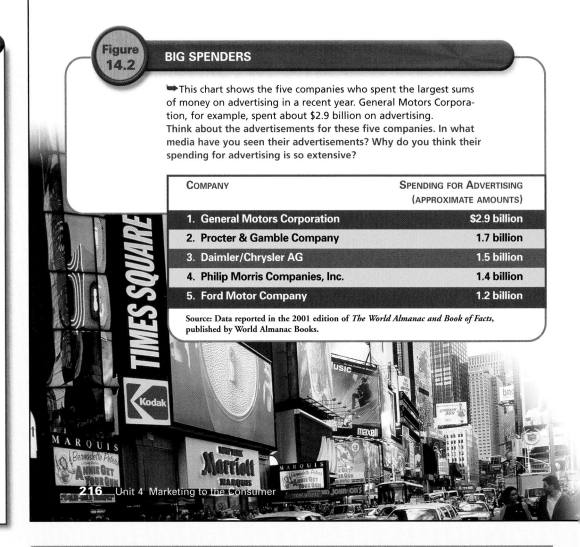

Figure 14.2 — BIG SPENDERS

➡ This chart shows the five companies who spent the largest sums of money on advertising in a recent year. General Motors Corporation, for example, spent about $2.9 billion on advertising.
Think about the advertisements for these five companies. In what media have you seen their advertisements? Why do you think their spending for advertising is so extensive?

COMPANY	SPENDING FOR ADVERTISING (APPROXIMATE AMOUNTS)
1. General Motors Corporation	$2.9 billion
2. Procter & Gamble Company	1.7 billion
3. Daimler/Chrysler AG	1.5 billion
4. Philip Morris Companies, Inc.	1.4 billion
5. Ford Motor Company	1.2 billion

Source: Data reported in the 2001 edition of *The World Almanac and Book of Facts*, published by World Almanac Books.

Global Perspective

Brand Names. Brand names that are successful in one country may not be when translated into another language. Here are some examples of original meanings being lost in translation. The Japanese once tried to sell a baby soap called Skinababe and a hair product called Blow Up. In Spanish-speaking countries, Ford's Fiera meant "ugly old woman" and General Motors' Nova meant "it doesn't go," if pronounced *no va*. Ask students if they have encountered any other such brand name blunders.

shows, news, classical music, rock, or country-western music. Advertisers can reach people on the move—when driving or even jogging with a Walkman®.

Webcasting. Webcasting is a new broadcast medium made possible by the Internet. A **webcast** is like a TV or radio broadcast but it's sent and received over the Web. A webcast usually consists of a live broadcast made by a Web camera (or "cam") crew hired to film a specific location or event. For example, many radio stations now use Web cams so audiences can both see and hear the station. To promote its products, a clothing company can broadcast a live fashion show on the Internet. Marketers can also use webcasting to promote concerts, sports, or other events by broadcasting them live over the Internet.

Cyber Ads

Cyber ads are ads on that appear on the Internet. They're different from webcasts in that they're displayed like magazine ads rather than broadcast like TV ads. The three main types of cyber ads are pop-up ads, banner ads, and screen ads. **Pop-up ads** appear for a few seconds when you first log onto the Internet or when you click on a site. **Banner ads** are displayed across the top or bottom of the screen and remain there. **Screen ads** appear at the left or right of the screen and can be printed for future reference. To get to the advertiser's Web site you simply click on the ad.

Cyber ads have many of the advantages of different types of print media. They can be sent directly to people on mailing lists and can include order forms like direct-mail ads. Like directory ads, consumers can look up a business easily by logging onto the Internet. Cyber ads can even be displayed in public (like billboards) on large computer screens. They have an added advantage in that they can use sound effects and animation.

 Fast Review _____

1. What are some of the differences between newspaper and magazine ads?
2. What are some disadvantages of outdoor ads such as billboards?
3. Name places where you would see transit ads.
4. What are some advantages of advertising on the radio rather than on TV?
5. What are the three biggest media for advertisers?
6. What advantages do print and cyber ads share?

Chapter 14 Advertising: The Art of Attracting an Audience **217**

part **3** of **4**

BATHED IN BLUE
Recently Kmart developed a $30 million campaign to modify the Blue Light Special tradition. The idea is that every hour on the hour, Kmart will select one item and drastically reduce its price for 20 minutes. The blue light will go off and a song like Johnny Cash's "Blue Train" will play. **Why does Kmart go to such creative lengths?**

 Real-World Application
Caption Answer

BATHED IN BLUE: PART 3 OF 4
To sell products and move merchandise out the door.

Fast Review Answers ✓

1. Newspaper ads are one-color, distributed locally, inexpensive, have a shorter life span. Magazine ads are full color, distributed nationally, expensive, have a longer life span.
2. People drive by them quickly, are ignored, and have restricted placement.
3. Anywhere or anything people use for transportation.
4. Cost less, can change frequently, and are transportable.
5. Newspaper, direct mail, and TV.
6. Full color and high quality. Sent directly to customers.

Science **Curriculum Connection**

Storage. To store goods for a long period, many warehouses must be temperature controlled. Have students select several different products and then research how those products would have to be stored to maintain their product quality. Ask students to present their findings in a 250-word report and include diagrams if possible.

3 ASSESS

Reteaching

INFOMERCIAL. To reteach the concept of infomercial, ask students to name examples and discuss the possible effects on an audience unaware that these programs are infomercials.

Enrichment Strategy

WRITE. Ask students to write two paragraphs starting with the sentence, "I feel the Internet is the way of the future in advertising because. . . ." **LS**

Business Building Blocks

CAPTION ANSWER

What do you need to know? You need to know about an inexpensive CD player with an anti-roll feature. Information that's relevant: The CD players with the anti-roll feature are in the corner.

Additional information needed: You still need to know the price.

Advertising Rates

The amount of money it costs to display or broadcast an ad is separate from the amount it costs to actually produce an ad. News and entertainment media pay for much of their costs by selling advertising space. The advertising rates are determined by several factors: the size of the ad, the number of people it reaches, how often it appears, when it appears, and where it's placed.

Print Media

Newspaper and magazine rates are based on circulation, or the number of people who read them. An advertiser usually pays a rate for every

Business Building Blocks

Distinguishing Between Relevant and Irrelevant Information

Information bombards you. On the job, you'll have to figure out what information is necessary, or *relevant*. Other information is *irrelevant*. Irrelevant information may be very interesting, but has no significant connection to your work. To be successful in the business world, you need to know how to distinguish relevant from irrelevant information.

Relevant information will define, explain, illustrate, or offer cause-and-effect relationships concerning the main topic you're exploring. Before gathering information, write down what you need to know. If someone gives you irrelevant information, ask questions that will redirect his or her focus to what's important. If you're reading, learn to sort out irrelevant information from that which is important and useful.

Analysis

Practice

Read the following case study. Decide what information is necessary for the main character to know, and write that information on a piece of paper.

Case Study: Examine the Information

You go to a local store to buy an inexpensive CD player so you can listen to music on the bus. You're especially interested in a feature you saw advertised in the morning newspaper. You're looking for one with the anti-roll feature. The clerk grabs off the shelf a model that's on sale. He says all the cool color CD players are on sale. These also come with three free CDs that are in the bin over there. You ask him how the anti-roll feature works on the model in your hand. He says it doesn't have it. The clerk says that the CD players in the corner have that mechanism, but they're not on sale.

218 Unit 4 Marketing to the Consumer

How to Use a Portfolio Activity

The portfolio projects are designed to lead students to develop a collection of their best work to submit to you for assessment. You and each of your students should decide which projects to include in their business portfolio. Refer students to the specific rubric(s) from the *Alternative Assessment Strategies*. These rubrics will alert students to the criteria you'll use to assess their projects.

1,000 people a newspaper or magazine reaches. Advertising in a local weekly newspaper costs a fraction of an ad in a large daily newspaper. An ad in a national magazine can cost thousands of dollars.

Newspaper and magazine ads are sold by the inch on the page. Ads can be small display ads, half-page ads, or full-page ads. Ads that appear on the front or back cover of a magazine cost more than ads inside the magazine. Whether an ad is in black and white or color also affects the cost.

Broadcast Media

The cost of radio and TV ads depends on the size of the audience. The cost to advertise on a national network is much more expensive than on a local station. The cost also depends on what time of day an ad is broadcast. An ad in *prime time* costs more than an ad aired at midnight. For radio, prime time on weekdays is during the morning or afternoon hours when most people are driving. TV prime time on weekdays is between 8:00 and 11:00 P.M. when most people are home. Advertisers also pay more for special events like the Oscar® Awards or the Super Bowl. During the Super Bowl, a single 30-second ad costs about $2 million.

Radio and TV advertisers usually pay for ads that are 10, 30, or 60 seconds long. They also pay more to show an ad several times a day. Sometimes an advertiser buys ads on different stations to be broadcast at the same time or buys a combination of radio and TV ads. Advertisers often hire media consultants and ad agencies to put together advertising packages for them.

The Internet

The cost of Internet advertising is based on the size and format of ads. Advertisers can buy pop-up ads, banner ads, screen ads, or ads in other formats. Ads can be large, medium, or small. The length of time an ad runs also affects the price. Like newspaper and magazine ads, Internet advertisers pay a certain amount for every 1,000 people that receive the ad. The number of people who click on a Web site determines this.

 Fast Review _____

1. What factors determine media costs?
2. On what day and what time might a film studio advertise an adult, action movie?

Real-World Application
part 4 of 4

BATHED IN BLUE
In the discount store arena, competition is fierce. Kmart is vying for customers just like its main competitors Target and Wal-Mart. Each needs its own image. Kmart has an alliance with Martha Stewart to help distinguish itself from the crowd. **How will Martha Stewart Everyday® help Kmart?**

Real-World Application
Caption Answer

BATHED IN BLUE: PART 4 OF 4

To lure a broader customer base who like Martha Stewart and entice them to shop for items in the store other than just her line of household goods.

Technology Resource

GO TO **VIRTUAL BUSINESS.** Introduce advertising using Knowledge Matters' *Virtual Business* interactive simulation. Go to the *Introduction to Business* Web site **www.introbus.glencoe.com** to download the *Virtual Business* activity. Run the *Virtual Business* tutorial before beginning this activity.

Evaluation

Assign and review the Fast Review sections.

Fast Review Answers

1. The circulation, whether it's national or local, the size of the ad, how often it's run, where it appears, number of colors.
2. During a prime-time action show or a weekend sporting event.

Meeting Individual Needs

Second Language Learners. In regular classroom activities, allow sufficient time for non-native speakers to answer questions. This will help them gain confidence in their communication skills. Also, note that there will be a big difference in students' English skills depending on how long they have been in the United States. **ELL**, **CL**

Demand for Oil

1 FOCUS

Companies around the world spend well over a trillion dollars to market their goods and services. Fewer than 30 countries—most of them in Europe, the Pacific Rim, and North America—account for 90 percent of this spending. About one-third of all advertising dollars are spent by American companies.

2 TEACH

Point out that each of the countries featured represents a particular level of exposure to advertising spending. Vietnam represents the lowest level, Kenya the next-to-lowest level, Egypt the intermediate level, Russia the next-to-highest level. (Mention that countries are graded on a per capita spending basis, not total spending.) Then have students compare spending categories among the countries. Ask them to explain why particular categories might be more widely used in some countries than in others.

? *Did You Know?*

About one-third of all marketing dollars are spent on promotions—cents-off coupons, sweepstakes, giveaways, and so on—rather than regular advertising.

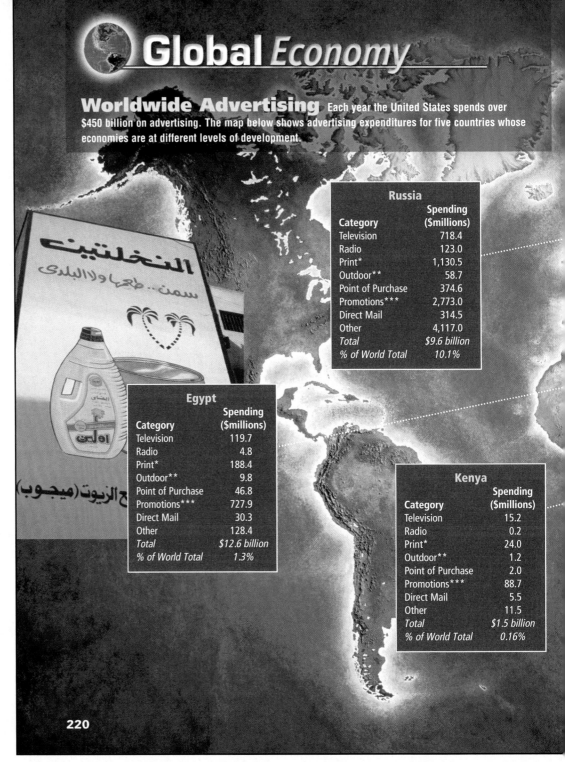

Global *Economy*

Worldwide Advertising Each year the United States spends over $450 billion on advertising. The map below shows advertising expenditures for five countries whose economies are at different levels of development.

Russia

Category	Spending ($millions)
Television	718.4
Radio	123.0
Print*	1,130.5
Outdoor**	58.7
Point of Purchase	374.6
Promotions***	2,773.0
Direct Mail	314.5
Other	4,117.0
Total	$9.6 billion
% of World Total	10.1%

Egypt

Category	Spending ($millions)
Television	119.7
Radio	4.8
Print*	188.4
Outdoor**	9.8
Point of Purchase	46.8
Promotions***	727.9
Direct Mail	30.3
Other	128.4
Total	$12.6 billion
% of World Total	1.3%

Kenya

Category	Spending ($millions)
Television	15.2
Radio	0.2
Print*	24.0
Outdoor**	1.2
Point of Purchase	2.0
Promotions***	88.7
Direct Mail	5.5
Other	11.5
Total	$1.5 billion
% of World Total	0.16%

220

Extending the Content

The Cost to Target a Market. Per capita spending on advertising varies widely between developed and less developed countries. In many of the less developed countries of Africa, Asia, and Latin America, less than $5 per person is spent on advertising. However, in Western Europe, the United States, Canada, Japan, and the stronger economies of the Pacific Rim, per capita spending on advertising stands at nearly $1,400. Japan spends the most per capita—$2,137—on advertising. Another Asian country, Laos, spends the least—just 41 cents.

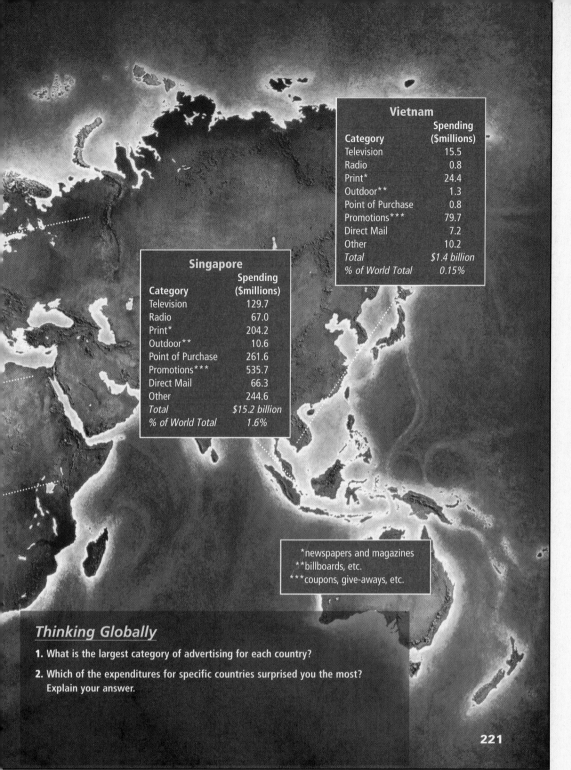

Vietnam

Category	Spending ($millions)
Television	15.5
Radio	0.8
Print*	24.4
Outdoor**	1.3
Point of Purchase	0.8
Promotions***	79.7
Direct Mail	7.2
Other	10.2
Total	*$1.4 billion*
% of World Total	*0.15%*

Singapore

Category	Spending ($millions)
Television	129.7
Radio	67.0
Print*	204.2
Outdoor**	10.6
Point of Purchase	261.6
Promotions***	535.7
Direct Mail	66.3
Other	244.6
Total	*$15.2 billion*
% of World Total	*1.6%*

*newspapers and magazines
**billboards, etc.
***coupons, give-aways, etc.

Thinking Globally

1. What is the largest category of advertising for each country?

2. Which of the expenditures for specific countries surprised you the most? Explain your answer.

221

3 ASSESS

Have students answer the "Thinking Globally" questions.

4 CLOSE

Have students use library resources and the Internet to gather similar statistics for the United States. Suggest that they present these statistics in table form.

? Did You Know?

About two-thirds of the advertising dollars spent around the world are used to market consumer goods and services. The other third is used by businesses to promote their products to other businesses.

Thinking Globally — **Caption Answer**

1. Promotions.

2. Answers may vary. Ensure that students offer reasons for their answers.

4 CLOSE

Chapter Wrap-Up

Discuss questions students asked during the "Bell Ringer Activity."

Using Business Key Words

1. advertising
2. cyber ads
3. mass media
4. webcast
5. infomercial
6. screen ads
7. transit advertising
8. direct-mail advertising
9. banner ads
10. pop-up ads

Review What You Learned

11. Newspapers, magazines, radio, TV, billboards, transit sites, directory pages, Web sites, catalogs, mailings.
12. Pays the production costs.
13. Advantages: place ads quickly, clip and save ads. Disadvantages: disposable, poor print quality.
14. Personalize items to target potential customers.
15. Relatively inexpensive and repeated exposure.
16. Thirty minutes and cost less than a regular 30-second network TV commercial.
17. 50 percent.
18. Banner ads display at the top of the screen. Screen ads appear at the left or right of the screen when a user conducts a search. Pop-up ads appear when a user clicks on a banner ad or screen ad.
19. Circulation, size, type, color, and placement.
20. Transmitting live broadcasts over the Internet.

222

Summary

1. Advertising is a paid, nonpersonal form of communication that businesses use to promote their products. Advertising media include print, broadcast, and the Internet.

2. Print media like newspapers, magazines, direct-mail advertising, directory advertising, outdoors advertising, and transit advertising are all highly visible in today's culture. Constant advertising makes consumers almost immune to its effect. Companies spend millions of dollars hoping you pay attention to their ad. You can find them on newsstands, sent to your home, on the side of buses, or on billboards. Broadcast media like TV, radio, and webcasting offer many advantages and disadvantages as well. While TV is highly visual and reaches national markets, it's also very expensive to produce. Radio reaches a wide audience and is good for local advertising. Lastly, people find cyber ads helpful or annoying. The use of sound effects and animation might capture your attention while surfing the Internet.

3. Advertising rates depend on the length of an ad, when it appears, where it appears, how often it appears, and the number of people it reaches.

● Using Business Key Words

There are many ways to attract an audience in order to sell a product. See how well you understand the terms that businesses use when they want to pass along information about their products. Match each term with its definition.

- **advertising**
- **cyber ads**
- **transit advertising**
- **infomercial**
- **webcast**
- **screen ads**
- **mass media**
- **direct-mail advertising**
- **pop-up ads**
- **banner ads**

1. A nonpersonal way of communicating with the public, using a mass medium.
2. Ads on the Internet.
3. Means of mass communication such as TV, radio, and newspapers.
4. A Web site that uses the Internet to broadcast information.
5. A television program that sells a product.
6. Internet ads displayed on the right or left of the computer screen and that can be printed.
7. Advertising that uses public transportation to display ads.
8. Advertising sent to people's homes by mail.
9. Internet ads that are displayed across the screen like billboards.
10. Internet ads that appear briefly when a user logs on or clicks on a site.

Quick Quiz

1. Name the six forms of print media. (Newspapers, magazines, direct-mail ads, directory ads, outdoor ads, and transit ads.)
2. Define infomercial. (A TV program made to advertise a product.)
3. Name the three types of broadcast media. (Television, radio, webcast.)
4. Name the three types of cyber ads. (Pop-up, banner, screen.)

Review What You Learned

11. What does mass media include?
12. How does advertising serve you as a consumer?
13. What are the advantages and disadvantages of using newspapers as an advertising medium?
14. How can direct mail be personalized?
15. Explain how outdoor advertising and transit advertising are similar.
16. How is an infomercial different from a television commercial?
17. What percentage of adults read the newspaper?
18. Describe the difference between a banner ad, pop-up ads, and screen ads.
19. How are advertising rates determined for newspapers and magazines?
20. Describe how webcasting works.

Understanding Business Concepts

21. Are you more likely to read ads in newspapers or magazines? Explain your answer.
22. Name a special purpose magazine that you or one of your friends enjoys reading. What products are advertised in that magazine? Do you purchase any of those products?
23. How often do you use the yellow pages? Explain your answer.
24. Why do you think television ads are expensive compared to other media?
25. Describe your favorite television ad and your favorite radio ad. Explain why you like them.
26. Why does the future for advertising on the Internet look very promising?

Critical Thinking

27. Choose a product that is marketed specifically to teenagers. What type(s) of media is used to advertise this product?
28. How do you think cable television has changed television advertising?
29. If response rates are very low with online advertising, why do some advertisers continue to use it?
30. Will a prime-time television slot always guarantee an advertiser the best results in selling a product? Why or why not?

Viewing and Representing

Examining the Image. Glance at this ad. Write down your immediate impressions in your journal. Ads are meant to elicit emotion. How do you feel? Does the ad make you feel jealous, angry, cool, good, bad, etc? Take a longer look. When you study the ad do you feel any different? Do you want to buy the product? What background knowledge do you bring to this ad?

Chapter 14 Advertising: The Art of Attracting an Audience **223**

Critical Thinking

27. Answers will vary depending on the product chosen.
28. Local businesses can now advertise in 15-second or 30-second commercial spots on their local cable stations at a more affordable price. The ads can be targeted locally.
29. Even though users may not automatically respond to the online ad, it may subliminally affect them. They may act on it later.
30. Answers will vary, but probably not. The ad may not be effective.

Viewing and Representing

Have students share their answers, and then facilitate further discussion. Point out that ads are designed to make you feel good, so you'll buy the product. What molds these feelings and attitudes? Are any stereotypes evident in this ad or popular current ads?

Understanding Business Concepts

21. Answers will vary. Many students read magazines more than newspapers, so this answer may be the most common.
22. Answers will vary depending on the magazine the student reads.
23. Answers will vary. Make sure the student offers an explanation of their use of the yellow pages.
24. Production (sound, motion, and video) costs are expensive; they do not reach a targeted audience, but can reach large numbers of consumers at one time.
25. Answers will vary.
26. More and more people have access to and are using the Internet.

4 CLOSE (Cont.)

Building Academic Skills

LANGUAGE ARTS. Make sure both partners participate. If possible, include your school's TV or radio production class in the project. Rubric: Radio commercial.

COMPUTER/TECHNOLOGY. Encourage the students to use their creativity. If your school has a Web design class or an art design class, include it in the project. Rubric: Banner ad.

HISTORY. Students can use the library or the Internet as references for their research. Rubric: Essay.

MATH. $595 × 0.15 = $89.25 savings. The $100 rebate would be a better deal.

Linking School to Home

Answers will vary depending on the infomercial watched. Rubrics: Essay, note taking.

Linking School to Work

Students' advertisements will vary. Encourage students to be creative when they redesign their ads. Rubrics: Essay, advertisement.

Building Academic Skills

 Producing a Radio Ad

Work with a partner to create a radio ad for one of your favorite products. Write a 30-second script and use music or other sound effects to enhance the ad. If possible, tape record the ad and play it for your class. Ask your classmates how effective they think the ad would be.

 Design a Banner Ad

Design a banner ad to promote a product on your favorite Web site. Consider the audience who will see the ad when you plan your design. Use the text, color, and graphic elements you think will make your banner ad the most effective.

 Historical Perspective

Choose one of the mass media that is described in the textbook. Research the history of the medium to find out:
- When it first started.
- How it has changed over time.
- The future of the medium.

Report your findings in a one- or two-page paper.

 Calculating Discounts

You receive a coupon in the mail for a 15 percent discount on a digital camera. You receive another coupon that offers a rebate of $100 on the same camera. If the camera costs $595, would you use the coupon or take the rebate?

Linking School to Home

Analyzing an Infomercial. With your family or group of friends, watch an infomercial. Answer the following questions:
- How long was the infomercial?
- Did a celebrity talk and demonstrate the product? If so, did the celebrity make you want to buy the product?
- Was there a toll-free number for customers to call in when ready to buy?
- What day and time did the infomercial air?
- Who in your family liked the infomercial? Who did not? Explain why.

Linking School to Work

Analyzing Ads. Collect a print advertisement from your place of employment. Evaluate the headline, text, illustrations, and design for its effectiveness. Describe the audience the ad is attempting to reach. Then, redesign the advertisement for a different market. If you're not working, choose an advertisement from a place you would like to work.

E-Homework

Applying Technology

Tracking Ads. Keep a log of all the advertisements for computer technology you see during a one-week period. Include all forms of mass media. Which media is used most frequently? Which advertisement did you like the best? Share your findings with your class.

Searching for Bot. Use the Internet to research "bots" or Internet robots. What are their uses? Do you think they could change the way we shop on the Internet? Why or why not? Explore a bot site and describe its function.

Connecting Academics

Math. A local candy company spent $45,000 on advertising last quarter. Radio ads comprised 7 percent of the total ads. How much money did it spend on radio ads?

The company sells a product for $3.10, but marketing costs are 48 percent of the selling price. How much is the actual marketing cost for this product?

Language Arts. Earlier in this chapter you learned about webcasting, also known as channeling, niche casting, or narrowcasting. Think of it as a personalized audio-visual clipping service. Give examples of specific webcasts. Find information about the effectiveness of webcasts. Do you feel webcasts are an effective method of advertising? Why or why not? Justify your conclusion using the information you found.

BusinessWeek Analyzing the Feature Story

You read the first part of "Yahoo! and Pepsi: "Fusion Marketing" in Prime Time" at the beginning of this chapter. Below are a few questions for you to answer about Pepsi's advertising strategy. You'll find the answers to these questions when you're reading the entire article. First, here are the questions:

31. What are the advantages to Pepsi in its Super Bowl advertising strategy?
32. What is a disadvantage of spending money on TV advertising during the Super Bowl?

CREATIVE JOURNAL ACTIVITY

Pay attention to the ads you see on television, hear on the radio, or see on billboards. What kinds of businesses advertise with each? Which medium do large, multinational companies use? Which medium is used by smaller businesses? Write a one-page report describing what you have learned.

BUSINESS *Online*
The Full Story

To learn more about "fusion marketing," visit the *Introduction to Business* Web site at **www.introbus.glencoe.com**, and click on *BusinessWeek* Feature Story, Chapter 14.

225

TRACKING ADS. Answers will vary. Allow the students to choose the way they wish to share their findings with the class. Rubrics: Log, essay, oral presentation, poster/chart.

SEARCHING FOR BOT. Students may wish to help each other with this activity. Allow the students to choose the way they wish to share their findings with the class. Rubrics: Note taking, oral presentation, poster.

Connecting Academics

MATH. $45,000 × 0.07 = $3,150. 3.10 × 0.48 = 1.488. Rounded up this is $1.49.

LANGUAGE ARTS. Answers will vary. Students should include justification for their answers.

BusinessWeek — *Analyzing the Feature Story*

31. By encouraging consumers to think about their product a week before the Super Bowl, Pepsi will boost brand awareness. The company also saves money by recycling old ads. They are also able to build the perception that they are Web-savvy.
32. Television ads are expensive compared to several other media. Pepsi also may not reach a targeted audience with their Super Bowl ads.

Creative Journal Activity

Ask students to monitor ads for one week. Suggest students create a chart to record their findings and include it with their report.

1 FOCUS

Unit Seminar Overview

In this seminar on marketing a product using technology, students research how a company succeeds or fails when using technology to market its products. Students investigate images, interpret facts, and decide their opinion on the question: What's best—marketing and advertising using traditional methods or technology?

Bell Ringer Activity

BRAINSTORM. Pose this scenario: You have three to eight seconds to attract attention in a nonverbal way. How would you do it? **LS**

Discussion Starter

ANALYZE. Post several print ads around the classroom. Have students look at the ads, then close their eyes and say which ads they remember best. Ask them what attracted their attention. In a class discussion, emphasize the point that the purpose of advertising is to attract people's attention and their interest so they will buy a product or service. Ask: You've been looking at print ads—how are Internet ads different? (They may be interactive and include video.) **LS**

BusinessWeek Seminar

Unit 4
Technology

Discovering Technology in Marketing

In this unit, you learned marketing's four Ps: product, price, promotion, and place. You also learned that advertising is one form of promotion. So, how does a product become a household name on the Internet? In the late 1990s the dot-com companies boomed, but just a matter of years later they went bust. While Internet traffic has an ebb and flow, it's here to stay. Companies still look to technology as a pertinent avenue to get their product out in front of consumers. This seminar explores marketing a product using technology.

226

COMPUTER TECHNOLOGY | *Newsworthy Trends*

All's Fair in Love and Advertising. Many in the advertising industry are crying foul over a new e-marketing strategy. An Internet company has created software that makes it possible to place its own advertisers' pop-ups directly over the pop-up ads of other advertisers on the Web. For example, instead of an ad for Toyota a user might see an ad for Ford.

The ads are designed to fit exactly over the original ads and scroll up and down with them, so the user never knows the difference. Critics have questioned the ethics of this kind of "guerilla" marketing. When the CEO of the Internet company was asked if it would be okay for other companies to do this to him, he said they already had.

Factoids

High Speed. BMW commissioned film directors John Frankenheimer, Ang Lee, and Guy Ritchie to each create five-minute films for its advertising campaign. The edited 30-second versions were available as TV spots, but the entire films were only available at **www.BMWfilms.com**. It did this because most Net surfers are men, whose income is $75,000 a year; this is its target audience.

Big Budgets. According to PricewaterhouseCoopers, U.S. advertisers spent $8.2 billion online, $1.8 billion on outdoor advertising, and $11.2 on cable-TV ads.

Online Hours. The average Web user spends 16.5 hours online a week at home and at work.

A Developing Medium. The top U.S. advertising companies spend less than 1 percent of their budget on the Web.

Bang for Your Buck. The average banner ad costs $10,000 to make compared to a TV spot's cost of $340,000.

Investigate the Images

Look at the photographic collage on the left page. What grabs your attention at first? Is it the color or the words? The power in reading visuals is in analyzing and dissecting your observations. On a separate piece of paper, respond to the questions listed below. These questions might help sharpen the focus of your visual mind.

Your Observations

1. How many photographs do you see?

2. Examine each photograph. How is each assembled in relation to one another?

3. What is the subject of each photograph? Is place or location the subject?

4. Does color signify a message?

5. What issues do you take from these images?

Information

6. Summarize what you know about the photographs from your observations.

Exploring Culture

7. Does a product's advertising create a mood or place that persuades you into buying the product?

8. Do you feel a company has ever knowingly targeted you as a consumer? Which company and what was your reaction (i.e., did you purchase something, act differently, change your beliefs, etc.)?

2 TEACH

Thinking Critically

Looking at the "Factoids"

1. What conclusions can you come to? Do the facts seem to make sense? Is this what you expected? What further questions do you have? (Answers will vary and may include: The proportion of expenditure on online ads seems high compared with cable-TV ads. How many viewers see Internet ads, as opposed to TV ads?)

2. If only 1 percent of the budget of top U.S. advertising companies is spent on the Web, what does this indicate? (Answers will vary, and may include: Change away from traditional methods of advertising is slow. The rate of return on Internet advertising is yet to be proven by statistics.)

Cooperative Learning

PANEL PRESENTATION. Have students work in pairs or small groups. After discussing "Exploring Culture" (seminar questions 7 and 8), and referring to the factoid, "Bang for Your Buck," assign the following task: Each student thinks of an example of when they, or someone they know, has been targeted by advertising. In teams, students form a panel. The class asks each team member questions about their example, such as: When did this happen? Were you surprised? How did you feel? Was this on the Internet? Did you buy the product or service? Close with a class discussion on the topic: Do you think the cost of banner advertising is likely to bring in a profit for the companies? **CL**, LS

Newsworthy Trends

COMPUTER TECHNOLOGY

Attention Shoppers. One of the latest developments in advertising technology is a device that projects commercials in mid-air. The device is about the size of a vending machine and projects either still or moving high-definition images about 16 inches in size. The technology combines American-made hardware and Hungarian-made software. The joint company plans to sell advertising space on the device rather than sell the device itself. The company's long-term plan is to install thousands of terminals, controlled by central servers, in shopping centers throughout Europe.

2 TEACH (Cont.)

Independent Practice

L1 SUMMARIZE

Ask students to find a recent article on ways technology is used in advertising or marketing. Ask them to prepare a summary of the article to share with the class. Follow student presentations with a closing discussion on the latest developments in the ways companies advertise using technology. **LS**

L2 E-INTERVIEW

Ask students to find an interesting Internet ad. Ask students to send the company an e-mail to ask questions such as: Have Internet ads increased your volume of business? What other methods of advertising does your company use? What do you think is in the future for Internet ads? Have students chart the responses on a poster and display the poster in class. **LS, CL**

L3 RESEARCH AND REPORT

Arrange for a local owner or manager of a mid-size business to visit your class and explain how he or she uses demographics and relationship marketing in the operation of the business. Have students prepare questions ahead of time, especially questions focusing on the use of technology. After the interview, have students write a one-page report. Encourage students to include specific details in their report. **LS**

BusinessWeek Seminar

Taking Aim at Technology

Preparation

Research how a company succeeds or fails when using technology to market its products. Then discover if other advertising methods might be more suitable for a product.

Objective

In this *BusinessWeek* Seminar, you'll:
- **Research** the media to find articles about a business that used the Internet to market and advertise its product.
- **Select** a product to study.
- **Create** a new Web page for this product.
- **Evaluate** the product's success story.

Materials Needed

✓ Copies of recent business news publications, such as the *Wall Street Journal* and *BusinessWeek* or Internet access
✓ Paper
✓ Posterboard and markers
✓ Copies of publications you can cut up
✓ Audiotape recorder or video camera (optional)
✓ Web page designing software (optional)
✓ Graphic design software (optional)

Procedures

1. With three other students, find and read articles about online businesses' successes and failures.

2. Choose a product to study. This might be an existing product or one you create.

3. Submit a one-page typed paper summarizing the story.

4. Create a new Web site for your product.
   - Each member is responsible for one Web page. Study the basic set up of Web pages. At least have a home page and three other linking pages.
   - Create the Web page with design software or create the design and place it on posterboard. The posterboard will show each page on your Web page. What is the function of each page, and how will it look?

5. Present your Web site to the class. Describe your product, and why you chose to market it the way you did.

Reteaching Strategy

Ask students to collect together their notes on all the important phrases and terms used in this unit seminar. Make a comprehensive list on the board and choose "20 Top Words." Divide students into groups of four. Give each group the 20 words or phrases. Ask individual members of each group to pick five words or phrases, taking turns to pick. Have students write a one-sentence statement for each of their phrases or words. Ask students to sit in a circle and hand their statements in a clockwise direction for each team member to read. **CL, LS, ELL**

Chart It

How do even small companies without big advertising budgets stay alive amid giant corporations? What keeps a company afloat in a competitive marketplace? Create a graphic organizer to brainstorm the answers to this question. As a class, reproduce something like this graphic below.

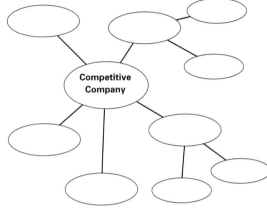

Competitive Company

Analyze and Conclude

After creating the graph, answer the following questions:

1. **Acquiring and Evaluating Information.** What are some common traits companies adhere to when marketing and advertising a product?

2. **Selecting Technology.** Is the Internet considered the end line for reaching out to a new marketplace? Why or why not?

3. **Maintaining and Troubleshooting.** In your opinion, what is the most effective way to market and advertise a product? Is it using the Internet, other technologies, print ads, etc.? State your reasons.

Becoming an Informed Citizen

Congratulations, you finished the seminar. Now it's time to reflect on the decisions you made.

Decision Making. Why did you choose your particular product? What interested you about it and why?

Analyzing Your Future. It's a competitive world and in time you're going to be vying for a job you really want. In order to impress future employers, you want to create a personal Web page. What personal qualities will you highlight on your Web page? How will you market yourself to differentiate yourself from the other applicants?

BUSINESS Online

Further Exploration

To find out more about using technology to market and advertise products, visit the *Introduction to Business* Web site at **www.introbus.glencoe.com**.

White Flower Farm Home Page

White Flower Farm

PLANTSMEN SINCE 1950

□ About Us □ Garden Wisdom □ Customer Service □ Shipping Info

Garden Search
Enter product name or number:

September 26, 2000
Hemerocallis 'Red Rum' (Fall shipped)
Great new Daylily, and a Web exclusive!
See Details

Quantity 1
$15.95 Each
ADD TO CART

Garden Catalogue
Plants ►

Analyze and Conclude Answers

1. Carve out a niche in their marketplace, stick to brand recognition, farm out manufacturing or other traits that aren't central to their business, partner with larger distributors to boost their name, hire a savvy advertising firm, etc.

2. Not necessarily, because it depends on your market. Receiving good press might be the key, or keeping brand loyalty, or affecting a segment part of the culture, or perhaps modernizing in other ways, etc.

3. Answers will vary. Using the Internet is just another avenue for companies to consider when marketing and advertising a product. Still the majority of people see TV and print ads before online ads.

3 ASSESS

Enrichment

COMPARE AND CONTRAST. Have each student interview two people involved in different aspects of marketing, for example, a marketing manager, an artist, or an advertising copywriter. Ask students to write a report comparing and contrasting a typical workday, the career path, and job satisfaction of each. Students should include a statement as to whether or not they would consider doing any of these jobs. **CL**, LS

Evaluation

RUBRICS. The rubrics for evaluation of written reports and oral presentations are included in the supplement, *Alternative Assessment Strategies.* **P**

4 CLOSE

Seminar Wrap-Up

PREDICTING TRENDS. With all the experience and knowledge you've gained through this seminar on discovering technology in marketing, what trends and innovations do you feel are in the future of marketing and advertising? Write important phrases and terms used on the board and have students write them in their notebook. **P**

The Human Resources Advantage

Chapter 15
Human Resources Management

Chapter 16
Culture and Diversity in Business

● Unit Objectives

After completing this unit, students will be able to achieve the following outcomes:

- Give examples of how businesses find new employees, then orient, train, and evaluate them.
- Explain how doing business internationally is affected by cultural differences.
- Identify ways government and business manage diversity.

BusinessWeek Connections

In this unit, students will read the following articles from *BusinessWeek*:

Chapter 15 "Online Benefits": A look at the benefits and the costs of application service providers (ASPs)—software systems that manage human resources.

Chapter 16 "Anthropologists in the Corporate Jungle": When two opposing company cultures join, see how an anthropologist can help.

Key to Descriptive Icons

The following designations will help you decide which activities are appropriate for your students.

L1 Level 1 activities should be within the ability range of all students.

L2 Level 2 activities should be within the ability range of the average to above-average students.

L3 Level 3 activities are designed for the ability range of above-average students.

ELL Activities should be within the ability range of the English Language Learner.

LS Learning Styles designation represents activities designed to address different learning styles.

CL Cooperative learning activities are designed for small group work.

P Portfolio designation represents student products that can be placed into a best-work portfolio.

Teacher Classroom Resources*

Program Resources	Chapter 15	Chapter 16
Student Activity Workbook	p. 101	p. 109
Lesson Plans	p. 38	p. 40
Internet Resources	p. 49	p. 51
Reproducible Tests	p. 29	p. 31
Teaching Transparencies	15.1, 15.2	16.1, 16.2
Strategies and Worksheets for Teaching Transparencies	pp. 7, 46	pp. 8, 48

* Each of these resources is available in print and on the Interactive Lesson Planner CD-ROM.

Technology Resources

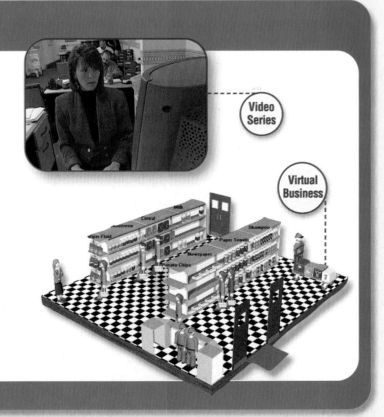

- Interactive Lesson Planner CD-ROM
- PowerPoint® Presentation CD-ROM
- ExamView® Pro Test Generator CD-ROM
- Integrated Software Simulation, Teacher Manual
- Glencoe Business Video Package
- *PuzzleMaker* CD-ROM
- *Introduction to Business* Web Site
- *Virtual Business*®
  Virtual Business is a business simulation that introduces students to the principles of business by letting them start and run their own virtual business. In *Virtual Business,* students have the power to control all aspects of a retail convenience store. Students strategize business decisions using a powerful learning tool in the guise of a video game.

Scope and Sequence

Academic Standards of Learning

	LANGUAGE ARTS	MATH	HISTORY	COMPUTER/ TECHNOLOGY	SOCIAL SCIENCE	
CHAPTER 15	pp. 232, 233, 234, 235, 236, 238, 239, 240, 241, 244	pp. 234, 244, 245	p. 244	pp. 235, 241, 244, 245	pp. 233, 234, 237, 238, 239, 245	
CHAPTER 16	pp. 247, 248, 249, 250, 252, 253, 254, 255, 260	pp. 260, 261	pp. 251, 260	pp. 249, 255, 260, 261	pp. 246, 247, 248, 249, 251, 252, 253, 254, 261	

Scope and Sequence

Themes and Concepts

Business Core	Accounting and Finance	Business Management	Computer/ Technology	Marketing	Entrepreneurship

Career Exploration
Employment
  Transitions
Interest Assessment
Job Acquisition
Job Retention
Adapting to Change
	Technological
	  Applications
	Internal Control
		Decision Making
		Unemployment
		Business
		  Organizations
		Communication
			Business Environment
			Supervision
			Operating Systems
			Human–Computer
			  Interfaces
			Training
				Cultural Diversity
				Logistics
				Technology
					Business Image
					Human Resources
					  Management
					Research and
					  Development

Employee Transitions
Retention
Demographics
Economic Culture
Adapting to Change
Diversity
Teamwork
Work Ethics
Social Issues
	Decision Making
	Ethics
	Economic Factors
	Technology
		Competition
		Ethics
		Human Resource
		  Development and
		  Management
		International
		  Relationships
		Technology
			Business and
			  Technology Ethics
			Business Environment
			Emerging Technology
			  and Trends
				Cultural Diversity
				Customer Relations
				Culture
				Public Relations
					International Business
					Research and
					  Development

Unit Overview

Unit 5 gives information about how businesses manage human resources and how diversity affects business.

CHAPTER 15 explains about finding and training employees, and about employee turnover.

CHAPTER 16 examines the importance of business culture and diversity in the workplace.

Introducing the Unit

Tell students to imagine they own and run a small business. Encourage them to choose the nature of the business. Let them know that they employ between 10 and 50 workers. Ask students how they would get the most out of their workforce.

Technology Resource

GO TO **INTRODUCTION TO BUSINESS WEB SITE.** To find out more about content in Unit 5, visit the Glencoe *Introduction to Business* Web site. **www.introbus.glencoe.com**

Unit 5

The Human Resources Advantage

Chapter 15
Human Resources Management

Chapter 16
Culture and Diversity in Business

When in Rome...

In a global business environment, international diplomacy is no longer just for diplomats. If you're doing business in China, for instance, there are things you need to know just about exchanging business cards. When someone hands you a business card, you should accept it with both hands. Never put it away without looking at it first and never put it in your back pocket.

● **You Just Volunteered for What?!**
In Bulgaria, nodding your head up and down means NO and shaking it back and forth means YES.

● **Put to Rest That Power Grip**
It's customary in France to exchange a quick, light handshake rather than a long, firm one.

● **Keep Your Feet on the Ground**
Be careful about crossing your legs when you sit down in Turkey. It's considered very insulting to expose the bottoms of your feet to someone.

● **Be Sure to Wear Clean Socks**
You might take off your shoes when entering Japanese homes and restaurants.

● **The Right Rules**
Since the left hand is considered unclean in Egypt, use your right hand when eating and touching things.

● **Care for More Warthog?**
Don't be surprised if at a South African home or restaurant, you're served ostrich, hippo, giraffe, or warthog.

230 Unit 5

Field Trip Suggestion

Trip Notebook. Arrange a trip to a large, local corporation that has a diverse workforce. Before the trip, have students prepare a notebook with the following categories as headings on separate pages: "Finding Employees," "Employee Orientation," "Training," "Evaluation," "Turnover," "Transfer," "Business Culture," "Workplace Diversity," "Managing Diversity," and "Benefits of Diversity." Under each category, have students list one or two questions they are interested in finding out about on the trip. Tell students that by the end of the trip they should have written the answer to at least one question for every category. **ELL**, LS

BUSINESS
Online
Idea Factory
To learn more about business cultures, visit the *Introduction to Business* Web site at www.introbus.glencoe.com, and click on Unit 5 The Human Resources Advantage.

Unit 5

Bulletin Board

Glencoe Poster Teaching Tip

Before introducing the poster, ask students what family members, coworkers, or friends say about changes in the demographics of the workforce. Then have the students take the quiz on the poster. Ask students: What factors have influenced changes in the workforce over the past ten years? Have students work in groups to create a ten-year timeline recording major events and trends that might have influenced the workforce in the past ten years. Display the timeline in the classroom.

Portfolio Activity

Interview. Research the system of values in another culture. Interview someone who grew up in a different culture or research using the Internet or an encyclopedia. Name and describe three values. How do these values affect the workplace in that culture? How is the workplace different in the U.S.? Write a two-page account detailing your findings in the form of an interview—either real or imagined. Illustrate your account. **CL**, **LS**, **P**

⏱ Out of Time?

If time doesn't permit teaching each chapter in this unit, you may use the *PuzzleMaker* CD-ROM to focus on the business vocabulary.

SCANS Correlation Chart*

Foundation Skills

Basic Skills	Reading	Writing	Math	Listening	Speaking	
Thinking Skills	Creative Thinking	Decision Making	Problem Solving	Seeing Things in the Mind's Eye	Knowing How to Learn	Reasoning
Personal Qualities	Responsibility	Self-Esteem	Sociability	Self-Management	Integrity/ Honesty	

Workplace Competencies

Resources	Allocating Time	Allocating Money	Allocating Material and Facility Resources	Allocating Human Resources		
Information	Acquiring and Evaluating Information	Organizing and Maintaining Information	Interpreting and Communicating Information	Using Computers to Process Information		
Interpersonal Skills	Participating as a Member of a Team	Teaching Others	Serving Clients/ Customers	Exercising Leadership	Negotiating to Arrive at a Decision	Working With Cultural Diversity
Systems	Understanding Systems	Monitoring and Correcting Performance	Improving and Designing Systems			
Technology	Selecting Technology	Applying Technology to Task	Maintaining and Troubleshooting Technology			

*This chart's highlighted blocks indicate the chapter's content coverage in the Student Edition and the Teacher Wraparound Edition.

Resource Manager

Teaching Transparencies

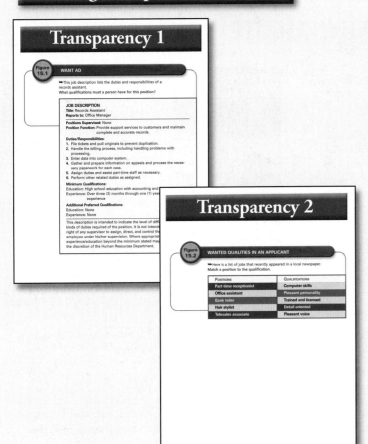

Transparency 1

WANT AD

Figure 15.1

➡This job description lists the duties and responsibilities of a records assistant.
What qualifications must a person have for this position?

JOB DESCRIPTION
Title: Records Assistant
Reports to: Office Manager

Positions Supervised: None
Position Function: Provide support services to customers and maintain complete and accurate records.

Duties/Responsibilities:
1. File tickets and pull originals to prevent duplication.
2. Handle the billing process, including handling problems with processing.
3. Enter data into computer system.
4. Gather and prepare information on appeals and process the necessary paperwork for each case.
5. Assign duties and assist part-time staff as necessary.
6. Perform other related duties as assigned.

Minimum Qualifications:
Education: High school education with accounting and
Experience: Over three (3) months through one (1) year experience

Additional Preferred Qualifications:
Education: None
Experience: None

This description is intended to indicate the level of different kinds of duties required of the position. It is not intended right of any supervisor to assign, direct, and control the employee under his/her supervision. Where appropriate experience/education beyond the minimum stated may be at the discretion of the Human Resources Department.

Transparency 2

WANTED QUALITIES IN AN APPLICANT

Figure 15.2

➡Here is a list of jobs that recently appeared in a local newspaper. Match a position to the qualification.

POSITIONS	QUALIFICATIONS
Part-time receptionist	Computer skills
Office assistant	Pleasant personality
Bank teller	Trained and licensed
Hair stylist	Detail oriented
Telesales associate	Pleasant voice

Application and Enrichment

- Lesson Plans
- *BusinessWeek* Poster Package
- Teaching Transparencies
- Integrated Software Simulation
- Glencoe Business Video Package

Review and Reinforcement

- *PuzzleMaker*
- Internet Resources
- Student Activity Workbook
- Strat. and Work. for Teaching Transparencies

Assessment and Evaluation

- Reproducible Tests
- Alternative Assessment Strategies
- ExamView® Pro Test Generator

Technology

- *PuzzleMaker*
- ExamView® Pro Test Generator
- Glencoe Business Video Package
- PowerPoint® Presentation
- Integrated Software Simulation
- Interactive Lesson Planner
- *Virtual Business*®

KEY

Printed	Software	Videocassette	Poster
Transparency	CD-ROM	Internet	

Business Online

Visit www.introbus.glencoe.com, the Web site companion to *Introduction to Business*. The student's page includes:

- interactive tutor
- additional *BusinessWeek* articles and activities
- business Web links
- homework hints
- real-world application activities
- additional career path activities

Information on how to prepare your students for the high school exit exam and special projects are also included.

Use the Glencoe Web site for additional resources. All essential content is covered in the Student Edition.

Introducing the Chapter

This chapter introduces human resources management—the process of finding, selecting, training, and evaluating employees. A photo essay, "Hunter Heads Headhunters," enhances the concepts.

Connecting the Objectives

What is a business's most important resource? Ask students to give examples of how businesses find employees and train them. Ask students what causes employee turnover.

BusinessWeek
Feature Story

Story's Summary

Rhonda Mae Botello is the human resources manager at CardStore.com, based in Emeryville, Calif. When Botello hires new employees, many forms have to be filled out. She simply goes to eBenefits.com. eBenefits is an application service provider (ASP), a system that manages human resources. Though ASPs range in cost from $0 installed and $30 to $100,000 per month, the prediction is that more companies from entrepreneurships to large organizations will be using ASPs. ASPs handle the paperwork. This frees up the manager to handle the "human" side of human resources.

Find the entire article at **www.introbus.glencoe.com**, or in the Teacher Resource Binder.

232

Chapter 15

Human Resources Management

Learning Objectives

After completing this chapter, you'll be able to:

1. **Give** examples of how businesses find new employees.
2. **Name** ways employees are oriented, trained, and evaluated.
3. **List** the ways an employee's status might change.

Why It's Important

To get the most out of its workforce, a business has to find the right employees, properly train them, and evaluate their performances.

Key Words

human resources management
job description
compensation
recruitment
orientation
on-the-job training
group training
performance appraisal
promotion
transfer
separation

232

BusinessWeek Feature Story
Online Benefits

New Application Service Helps Businesses Manage Human Resources Online. CardStore.com, an Emeryville (Calif.) online retailer with about 35 employees, is in a hiring frenzy. So you might expect to find the company's human resources manager, Rhonda Mae Botello, buried in forms for payroll, health coverage, taxes, and the like. She's busy all right, but not with paperwork. When a new worker comes on board, Botello simply logs onto the Web, surfs over to eBenefits.com, and enters the new name and start date.

Source: Excerpted with permission from "New Application Service Helps Businesses Manage Human Resources Online," *BusinessWeek Online,* April 24, 2000.

An Extension Activity

CardStore.com wants to be the industry leader in personalized communication like postcards and posters. Even before it satisfies its customers, whom must it satisfy first? How?

BUSINESS *Online*
The Full Story

To learn more about online human resources, visit the *Introduction to Business* Web site at **www.introbus.glencoe.com**, and click on *BusinessWeek* Feature Story, Chapter 15.

Classroom Resources

For the Teacher
- 📁 Student Activity Work. TAE
- 📓 💿 Assessment Binder
- 💿 PowerPoint® Presentation
- 💿 Interactive Lesson Planner
- 📁 Lesson Plans
- 📓 💻 Internet Resources
- 📱 Teaching Transparencies
- 💻 *Introduction to Business* Web Site

- 💿 Integrated Soft. Sim. TM
- 📘 *BusinessWeek* Poster Package

For the Student
- 📓 Student Activity Workbook
- 💿 *Virtual Business*®
- 💻 *Introduction to Business* Web Site
- 💿 Integrated Soft. Sim.
- 💿 *PuzzleMaker*
- 📓 Strategies and Worksheets for Teaching Transparencies

Bell Ringer Activity

INTERPRETING AND COMMU-NICATING INFORMATION. You're a manager for a sportswear store and need to hire a sales assistant. Write the job description, including the job title, location, and skills required. Write a description of duties starting with: "Assists the store manager in the daily _____, _____, and _____. Also responsible for _____, _____, and _____."

Preteaching Business Key Words

READING. Ask students to read the definition of this chapter's vocabulary words in the glossary and look for one or two key words to describe them. For example, "detailed duties" for job description. **LS, CL**

An Extension Activity

ANSWER. It must satisfy its employees first. One way is to offer them a nice benefits package.

Making Connections

Business Ethics. The federal government has banned the use of lie detector tests as a screening device for most employment situations. As a substitute for these tests, many businesses employ psychological exams. These exams attempt to predict an individual's tendency to steal by matching their test results with those of known thieves. Questions may be obvious: "How often do you tell the truth?" or obscure—"How often do you make your bed?" Ask students to discuss whether they feel this type of testing is appropriate in a business environment. How about if you were a small business owner and wanted someone to work at the front register? **CL**

2 TEACH

Business Connection

HUMAN RESOURCES. The Americans with Disabilities Act (ADA) prohibits pre-job-offer medical testing or questions about medical conditions. Employers may ask only if the applicant can perform the functions of the job. Additionally, employers are required to provide reasonable provisions to help people with disabilities do the job.

Develop Concepts

JOB RECRUITMENT. Surveys of recruiters from more than 50 companies indicate that the most important skills for personnel are interpersonal and communication skills—true or false? (True.) Have students discuss the steps they think a company needs to take to recruit people. **CL**, LS

Figure 15.1 Caption Answer

Minimum qualifications are a high school education with accounting and computer classes, and three months to one year of office experience.

Employees: The Key to Success

A business's human resource is the people who work for it. These employees provide the skills, knowledge, labor, and experience needed to make a business productive. According to Henry Ford, "You can take my factories, burn up my building, but give me my people and I'll build the business right back up again."

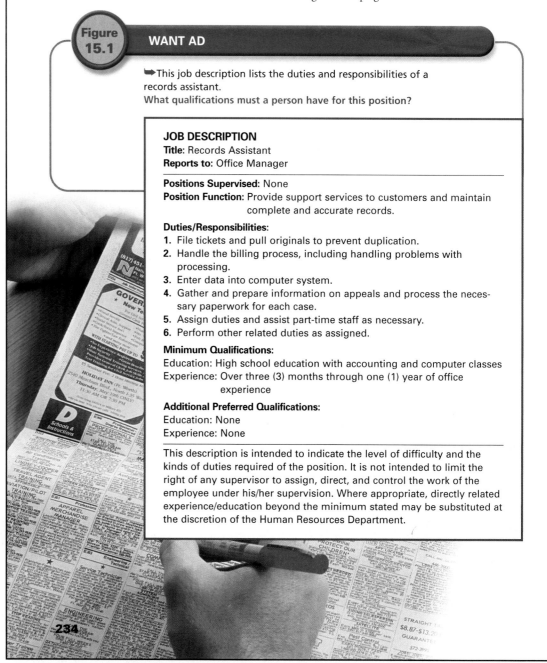

Figure 15.1 WANT AD

➡ This job description lists the duties and responsibilities of a records assistant.
What qualifications must a person have for this position?

JOB DESCRIPTION
Title: Records Assistant
Reports to: Office Manager

Positions Supervised: None
Position Function: Provide support services to customers and maintain complete and accurate records.

Duties/Responsibilities:
1. File tickets and pull originals to prevent duplication.
2. Handle the billing process, including handling problems with processing.
3. Enter data into computer system.
4. Gather and prepare information on appeals and process the necessary paperwork for each case.
5. Assign duties and assist part-time staff as necessary.
6. Perform other related duties as assigned.

Minimum Qualifications:
Education: High school education with accounting and computer classes
Experience: Over three (3) months through one (1) year of office experience

Additional Preferred Qualifications:
Education: None
Experience: None

This description is intended to indicate the level of difficulty and the kinds of duties required of the position. It is not intended to limit the right of any supervisor to assign, direct, and control the work of the employee under his/her supervision. Where appropriate, directly related experience/education beyond the minimum stated may be substituted at the discretion of the Human Resources Department.

Cooperative Learning

Collecting. Ask students to work in groups to collect job applications from local businesses. Suggest they try to gather applications from fast-food restaurants, local banks, and nationwide retail stores as well as smaller local businesses. Each group should gather at least six applications. Have students take note of the kinds of information requested on all applications. Using the sample applications as a base, have students develop an application for a position at school such as bandleader, football coach, or school receptionist. **CL**, LS

Finding Employees

Managing human resources isn't the same thing as supervising workers. **Human resources management** is the process of finding, selecting, training, and evaluating employees. The first step in this process is finding the right person for the job.

Job Description

If you're a human resources manager trying to fill a job you have to begin by writing a job description. A **job description** is a detailed outline of the duties, qualifications, and conditions required to do a specific job (see Figure 15.1). For example, if the job is for a graphic artist you need to say if it involves working with a supervisor, meeting deadlines, creativity, or using a computer. The job might also require someone with a certain amount of experience or education.

You also need to say if the job is part-time, full-time, permanent, or temporary. The job might need someone for only 20 hours a week or full-time for only a few months. Anyone who might be interested in the job will want to know what kind of compensation it offers. **Compensation** is how much the job pays and the benefits offered. Does the job pay minimum wage or $25 an hour? Does the company offer health insurance, sick leave, and paid holidays? Can a part-time position turn into a full-time position? A good compensation package is important to attract the most qualified people.

Employee Benefits. Employers need to meet your needs as an employee. You might evaluate a job opportunity based on the benefits package. Pay attention to the health care, retirement benefits, and specific needs of your family. Remember, it's important to look out for your own present and future needs. Let's take a closer look at different types of benefits.

People are living longer than ever before. Retirement programs are important to consider. A company's *pension plan*, a retirement plan that is funded at least in part by an employer, is important. Some plans provide you with a fixed amount of money. If you work for a business with a profit-sharing plan, it makes an annual contribution to your retirement fund each year. The third type of plan is a 401(k). You decide what portion of your check is set aside from each paycheck to go into your 401(k) fund. Your employer will often match a percentage of your contribution.

Real-World Application

part 1 of 4

HUNTER HEADS HEADHUNTERS

From her third-floor corner office with a mountain view, Sharon Hunter helps connect corporations with top-level professionals and executives looking for new jobs.
Has anyone ever helped you get a job before?

continued on p. 237

Real-World Application
Caption Answer

HUNTER HEADS HEADHUNTERS: PART 1 OF 4
Answers will vary.

Technology Resource

GO TO **POWERPOINT.** The *Introduction to Business* PowerPoint® CD-ROM provides visual lecture aids for this chapter.

Independent Practice

INTERVIEW. Ask students to find examples of job advertisements from a local large- or medium-sized company. Have students call the human resources department and ask how the company recruits people, how the company selects the right people, what the company's hiring process involves, and what benefits the company offers. Ask students to give a written or oral report. **LS**

Meeting Individual Needs

Gifted. Gifted students may find that the material in this chapter offers them a first look at real-world organizational behavior. Encourage these students to take on a wide variety of enrichment and independent activities that will put them in contact with people in the business world and allow them to observe the daily practices that lead to success. Be sure they have the opportunity to present written summaries of their findings and let them share what they observed with the group.

Thinking Critically

CRITICAL DECISION MAKING. You're office manager in your school's main office. There's far too much for you to handle—things like answering the phone, filing papers, typing short letters, ordering supplies, and so on—and this week's been particularly bad. You grab a cold soda, scribble a "DO NOT DISTURB" note, shut your office door, pull out a sheet of paper, and give yourself 20 minutes to think. You want to hire a student to work after school. To choose the right person for the job, you decide to make a list of information you need about the potential employee. (Possible notes: attitude, interpersonal skills, experience, interests, and desire to succeed.)

Figure 15.2 Caption Answer

Part-time receptionist—pleasant personality
Office assistant—computer skills
Bank teller—detail oriented
Hair stylist—trained and licensed
Telesales associate—pleasant phone voice

Job Recruitment

To find the best people for a job a human resources manager has to recruit them. **Recruitment** means actively looking for qualified people to fill a job. Figure 15.2 illustrates qualities that certain positions might want you to exhibit. If you work for a large enough company, you start by looking for people who already work there. If no one is qualified, interested, or available, then you look outside the company.

One way to recruit people is by placing ads in newspapers, in magazines, at schools, or on the Internet. For example, to find a graphic artist you can post an ad for the job at an art school. You can also put an ad in an art magazine or trade paper. There are many Internet sites such as Monster.com that match people with certain skills to businesses looking for people with those skills. Employment agencies, employees' recommendations, or conventions are also ways to find qualified people.

The Selection Process

Companies want the best-qualified person for the job, the one most likely to succeed. Population trends are changing the pool of applicants. For example, the workforce is getting older. In relation to other age groups, fewer young people are entering the workplace. "Baby Boomers," workers aged 40 to 55, now are a larger share of the population. Workers are staying on the job longer. Retirement is no longer expected of all people who reach a certain age.

In the past, more men than women were in the paid workplace, but that has changed, too. An increase in the number of women in the workplace brought about a change in business practices. Childcare is a critical issue. As more men and women work, they must have care for their

Figure 15.2 WANTED QUALITIES IN AN APPLICANT

➡ Here is a list of jobs that recently appeared in a local newspaper. Match a position to the qualification.

POSITIONS	QUALIFICATIONS
Part-time receptionist	Computer skills
Office assistant	Pleasant personality
Bank teller	Trained and licensed
Hair stylist	Detail oriented
Telesales associate	Pleasant voice

236

LANGUAGE ARTS — Curriculum Connection

Communication. Ask students to work in groups to plan, write, and illustrate a student handbook for new students entering their school. Have groups decide what information a new student would need about the physical layout of the school (drinking fountains, stairways, bathrooms, classrooms); behavior expectations (dress code, class attendance); and other useful information (sports teams, extracurricular activities). Post the completed handbooks. **LS, CL**

children. Family issues receive more attention as the percentage of women in the workplace increases.

What can you do to increase your chances of getting the job you want in the future? You must convince the employer that you're the best person for the job. Early in this course, you learned that a first impression is very important. What will impress a prospective employer? You must look like a person who's exactly what the employer is looking for. A neat appearance, poise, and confidence will help. You must have the skills needed for the job. The job description gives a clear picture of what the job requires. It will be your task to convince an employer that you can do everything in that job description well.

Human resources managers often say that prospective employees' lack communication skills. They want employees who can communicate well in writing and orally. You can begin to build your communication skills now. Inevitably, you'll have to give a presentation in front of a group. Learning how to give speeches is an excellent skill to possess. Accept opportunities to speak and learn how to perform in front of others in order to meet that requirement for selection by a business.

You live in a global economy. Business firms of all sizes do business around the world. Employees must know how to do business in other countries. What if you were to find a job with a company that does business in Brazil? How could you find out what are acceptable business practices in Brazil? Get acquainted with what other countries do. Read about international business customs (see the Unit 5 opening content and Chapter 16). Check the Internet for information about international business. You may find knowledge about other countries to be a selling point for you someday.

After recruiting enough people, you have to decide which one to hire. There are four steps to selecting the right person or *candidate* for the job. First, each candidate has to fill out an *application* listing his or her job experience, education, skills, and references. Then you *interview* the candidates to get more detailed information about them and see how they communicate. The next step is *testing* the candidates to make sure they have the right skills. Finally, you check out their *references* to make sure they went to school or worked where they claimed.

 Fast Review

1. What are some of the ways a human resources manager can recruit people for a job?
2. What kind of information does a job description contain?
3. What are the four steps in selecting a candidate for a job?

Real-World Application
part 2 of 4

HUNTER HEADS HEADHUNTERS

Hunter is president of Management Recruiters of Boulder, a "head-hunting" company that scouts talented professionals in the fields of radio frequency engineering, information technology, and construction. **What is the purpose of a headhunter?**

continued on p. 239

Real-World Application
Caption Answer

HUNTER HEADS HEADHUNTERS: PART 2 OF 4

To identify and interview people that its client companies might be interested in hiring.

Fast Review Answers

1. From inside the company; ads in newspapers, in magazines, at schools, or on the Internet; employment agencies; recommendations from employees or other companies.
2. The duties, qualifications, and conditions needed to do the job. Whether the job is full-time, part-time, temporary, or permanent. The pay and benefits the job offers.
3. Reading applications, interviewing, testing, and checking references.

Great Ideas From the Classroom of...

Linda R. Burkett
South Vermillion High School
Clinton, Ind.

Technology Idea.   As a class, students plan a small business that will operate within our school. Each chapter helps us along our path of business development.

By the time this chapter is introduced my students have developed their business plan and are preparing to open for business. I introduce a publishing software—Microsoft Publisher. The students create business cards, advertising brochures, signs to post at the store site, and a Web page. The Web page is linked to my home page for easy access to the whole school.

Business Connection

CROSS-TRAINING. Rohm & Haas, the developer of Plexiglas, practices job rotation at a plant in Connecticut. Workers are cross-trained and work as self-managers. Machinists work on loading docks when needed, and line personnel inspect finished products during peak periods.

Develop Concepts

PERFORMANCE APPRAISALS. Ask students to compare their performance appraisals, grades, and parent–teacher conferences with job performance appraisals. Ask students to explain how their grades and portfolio assessments are similar to a performance appraisal and how the two kinds of evaluation are different. **LS**, **CL**

Discussion Starter

QUESTIONING. Ask students: What does compensation mean? What might be part of a benefits package?

Caption Answer

1. It is illegal to discriminate or make a hiring decision on the basis of many factors including gender, race, sexual orientation, and age.
2. Answer No. 1 applies.
3. To uphold the law, hire the person best qualified for the position.

238

Developing Employees

Suppose you decided to hire Gayle for the graphic artist job. Even if she has lots of experience working for other companies she needs to adjust to her new job and might have to learn some new skills. You also need to keep track of how she's doing her job. To develop Gayle as an employee she needs to be oriented, trained, and evaluated.

Orientation

Orientation is the process of helping new employees adjust to a company. The first step in orienting Gayle is taking her on a tour of the building and introducing her to other employees. She might go to a group orientation session and watch a video about the company. She'll receive a manual that explains everything from how the company is organized to the office's safety rules. She'll also need to read the company's code of ethics describing the company's goals and appropriate behavior.

Training

New employees usually need some training to learn the specific job they were hired to do. For example, Gayle might have to learn how to use a new computer graphics program, like Adobe Illustrator®. She can get either group training or on-the-job training. **On-the-job training** involves learning a new job by actually doing it. This is usually done under the guidance of a supervisor. Gayle's supervisor might demonstrate the program for Gayle, watch her use it, and give her feedback.

In small businesses, employees often must be able to do several jobs. In larger companies, too, a worker may have to fill in for a coworker who is absent. To be sure employees can fill in for each other,

You Make the Call

A Great Balancing Act

Thirty years ago, most law students and lawyers were men. Today, many law schools enroll more women than men. The law firm you work for needs another attorney on its staff. You're on the hiring committee.

Making an Ethical Decision

1. Do you try to hire a woman because women were discriminated against until fairly recently?
2. Do you try to hire a man because today fewer men are being trained as lawyers?
3. Do you ignore gender as an issue in hiring?

Global Perspective

Trained Outside the U.S. Nearly half the computer industry's revenue is generated from markets outside the United States. As a result, individuals who can compete in the international market are in demand. To meet this demand, many hardware and software companies have appointed managers and executives born or trained outside the United States. Ask students to discuss what advantages the companies gain by appointing such individuals to positions in the international market. **CL**, **LS**

managers use job rotation. In job rotation, employees move from job to job—or rotate—for several hours, days, or weeks at a time until they learn the various tasks. Job rotation is also used to prevent boredom and keep morale high. If an employee has a variety of work experiences, the work is more interesting. Job rotation helps managers make more effective use of the company's human resources. If someone is absent or leaves, others know how to handle the tasks.

With **group training** an instructor or manager teaches Gayle how to use the program with a group of other employees like a class. This allows Gayle to learn the program in a more relaxed way and to share ideas with other employees. The company might also provide her with a course on videotape or CD. In recent years, many companies have begun using courses available on the Internet to train employees. Companies also send employees to institutes and conferences to learn new skills for the job.

Evaluating Employees

After Gayle is oriented and trained her performance needs to be monitored. This is usually done every three or six months with a performance appraisal. A **performance appraisal** is an evaluation of how well she's doing her job. This might consist of Gayle sitting down with her manager to go over her strengths and weaknesses, listen to any complaints, and suggest improvements. The appraisal is used to determine whether Gayle should get a raise, a promotion, or new training.

✓ Fast Review

1. How might a new employee be oriented at a company?
2. What are some of the ways a company can train a new employee?

Employee Turnover

A human resources manager needs to keep track of changes in the status of employees, or employee turnover. For example, Gayle might be promoted to a better position, transferred to another department, or fired. As a result, she might need to be reoriented, retrained, or replaced.

Promotion

A **promotion** is a move to a higher-level job with more authority, responsibility, and pay. Promotions are merit-based and encourage performance. If Gayle is doing a great job, she might be promoted to a

Chapter 15 Human Resources Management **239**

Real-World Application

part **3** of 4

HUNTER HEADS HEADHUNTERS
Management Recruiters tries to link corporations to people. It's a fun but challenging job. Yesterday, for instance, one of its clients—a satellite subscriber company—rejected a candidate that Hunter felt was right for the job. Why might a company pass over a qualified applicant for a job?

continued on p. 241

Real-World Application Caption Answer

HUNTER HEADS HEADHUNTERS: PART 3 OF 4
The candidate might not interview well or the reference might not check out.

Individualized Practice

LAYOFFS. Ask students to browse through the business section of local newspapers looking for reports of layoffs and downsizing. Have students record their findings, listing the company, whether they are service- or goods-producing, and the reason given for the layoffs.

L1 Have pairs of students discuss the companies and the reasons for the layoffs.

L2 Have students make a chart of the information.

L3 Have students pool their findings and decide what economic causes they can find in the reports.

Fast Review Answers ✓

1. Given a tour, introduced to others, attend orientation, read company literature.
2. On-the-job training, group training, extension courses.

LANGUAGE ARTS   *Curriculum Connection*

Focusing.   You're a photographer freelancing for a local newspaper's business section. Your assignment is to get some eye-catching shots that show people in a variety of training situations—orientation, group training, and on-the-job training. You visit companies and industries you're interested in, take some pictures, and develop them. Write a description of one picture from each type of training situation, including the setting, subject, focus, and point of view. **LS**

Reteaching

JOB DESCRIPTION. To reteach the concept of a job description, ask students what types of information are included in a job description. (Answers will include: qualifications required, duties, conditions, full-time/part-time, temporary/permanent.)

Enrichment Strategy

WRITE. Ask students to write one paragraph starting with the sentence, "I know someone who moved jobs because . . ." **LS**

Working Lifestyle

Caption Answer

Psychologists, attorneys, doctors, photojournalists, artists, police officers, etc.

---

managing position. She might also be promoted on the basis of *seniority* after working for the company for a certain length of time.

In promotions, it is important to consider not only how an employee performs in the current job, but also how he or she will adapt to the new one. An organization that does not consider this becomes subject to the Peter Principle. The Peter Principle states that it is possible for employees to be promoted until they reach a level at which they can no longer perform.

Suppose a management position opens up in the Quarkville Advanced Physics Laboratory. Michelle Grayson is selected for the job based on her performance as a senior scientist. When she becomes lab chief, it is clear that she has poor management skills.

The laboratory has gained a mediocre supervisor and lost an excellent

Working Lifestyle

What are you doing at 10 A.M.?

Helping Patients Cope

Maya Bhaumik is a psychiatric social worker at a large hospital. Her department helps nearly 100 patients whose afflictions include anxiety, stress, eating disorders, schizophrenia, Alzheimer's, and senility. "You see people come in the depths of depression or abuse," says Bhaumik. "You try to help them feel better and go on with their lives."

Typically at 10:00 A.M., Bhaumik facilitates group therapy for 10 to 15 in-patients. In the sessions, she talks with patients about what brought them to the hospital. They assist other patients and help themselves find new coping skills. In addition to excellent communication skills, Bhaumik's duties require strong organizational skills, deductive reasoning, and the ability to keep calm in the face of stress.

Bhaumik's position requires considerable education and experience. Bhaumik, who

specialized in child psychology in India, has earned numerous degrees in the United States, including a masters in social work and a Ph.D. in psychiatric social work. She works hard to follow the latest trends, treatments, and theories in psychology.

The unique challenges of Bhaumik's profession might be overwhelming if not for her positive attitude. "You have to keep perspective and not lose hope—especially in the face of tremendous problems," she says. "You need to keep your optimism and believe in the goodness of people."

Salary

Median annual earnings of social workers are $30,590, with a range between $24,160 and $39,240.

Outlook for Career

This profession is expected to grow faster than average due to a growing and aging population, which drives the overall growth of health care services.

Connecting Careers Activity

Name career occupations that might seek a psychologist to discuss job-related issues.

CAREER PATH Human Services

How to Use a Portfolio Activity

The portfolio projects are designed to lead students to develop a collection of their best work to submit to you for assessment. You and each of your students should decide which projects to include in their business portfolio. Refer students to the specific rubric(s) from the *Alternative Assessment Strategies*. These rubrics will alert students to the criteria you'll use to assess their projects. **P**

working scientist. It is unlikely that Michelle will be considered for further promotions, based on her performance. She has "risen to her level of incompetence." This can be avoided by considering the aptitudes and interest of candidates for promotion, in addition to performance in their current job.

Transfer

A **transfer** is a move to another job within a company at the same level and pay. Gayle might be transferred because another department needs her, her job has been eliminated, or she needs new training. An employee is usually transferred because the company moves or opens a new office. If Gayle works for a company that has offices around the world, she might be transferred to a foreign country if she speaks the language.

Separation

The final way in which an employee leaves a position is through separation. **Separation** means leaving a company for any reason. Gayle might quit, resign, or retire.

Separation may be voluntary or involuntary. A voluntary separation occurs when an employee resigns. This separation process usually involves an exit interview. An exit interview pinpoints why an employee is leaving, such as a noncompetitive pay structure.

Involuntary separations include layoffs and terminations. If the company is losing money and needs to *downsize*, or reduce the number of employees, Gayle might be *laid off*. Layoffs occur when there isn't enough work for all employees. For example, factory layoffs may follow a cut in production. Layoffs are often temporary and Gayle could be brought back if conditions improve. If the layoff is permanent, the company might help her find another job.

Gayle could be fired, or *terminated*, for being late all the time, doing a poor job, or breaking company rules. This is the last resort. Training, counseling, and disciplinary action are all solutions to personnel problems. However, if these fail, termination is necessary. In addition to upsetting employees, it wastes company resources and time invested in hiring and training that individual. Instead of terminating an unproductive employee, the company L.L. Bean will reassign the worker to a less stressful work site, with a lower volume of sales.

 Fast Review

1. What is the difference between a promotion and a transfer?
2. What are the reasons an employee might separate from a company?

HUNTER HEADS HEADHUNTERS
Executive recruiters need to stay ahead of the game. They need to know trends in the field, whether a company is struggling, is laying off employees, or is looking to expand.
What kind of qualities do you think an executive recruiter needs to exhibit when working with clients and candidates?

**Real-World Application
Caption Answer**

HUNTER HEADS HEADHUNTERS: PART 4 OF 4
Tact, diplomacy, and good listening skills.

Technology Resource

 GO TO **PUZZLEMAKER CD-ROM.** Check your students' understanding of the chapter's key terms by using the *Puzzlemaker* CD-ROM.

Evaluation

Assign and review the Fast Review sections.

Fast Review Answers

1. A promotion is a move to a higher-level job with more authority, responsibility, and pay. A transfer is a move to another job within the company at the same level and pay.
2. Quit, retire, resign, fired, or laid off.

Meeting Individual Needs

Students With Comprehension Difficulties. Introduce a focused reading exercise to assist students experiencing comprehension difficulties. Direct students to read the paragraph "Training" on page 238. Have them write in their journals what they remember of the subsection. Let students know there's a simple self-help tool to aid comprehension: Make up questions to ask yourself as you read the material. Suggest that they read the paragraph again, this time asking themselves questions such as, "Why do new employees need training?" "What two types of training can Gayle get?"

4 CLOSE

Chapter Wrap-Up

Have students develop a mnemonic jingle to help them remember the four steps of the selection process—application, interview, testing, and references.

Using Business Key Words

1. job description
2. orientation
3. on-the-job training
4. performance appraisals
5. compensation
6. human resources management
7. group training sessions
8. recruitment
9. separation
10. transfer
11. promotion

Review What You Learned

12. Show interest. Visit businesses. Read employment section of the newspaper.
13. Internal promotions. Advertise, recommendations. Employment agencies.
14. The workforce is getting older.
15. Childcare and family issues.
16. Help them learn their job and workplace rules.
17. Supervisor, orientation, or employee manuals.
18. On-the-job training prepares new employees for their responsibilities. In job rotation, employees move from job to job to learn the various tasks.
19. Monitor and evaluate employees' performance.

Summary

1. Human resources management is the process of finding, selecting, training, and evaluating employees. Human resources managers recruit employees from within the company and through ads, employment agencies, and recommendations.

2. Employees are often oriented to a new workplace by touring the building, attending group orientation sessions, and reading a company manual and code of ethics. Employees receive training on-the job or in group training. Periodic monitoring and performance appraisals are ways to evaluate employees.

3. The status of an employee changes as a result of promotion, transfer, or separation.

Using Business Key Words

Understanding these terms will help you become a better employee and one day, maybe a better employer. Fill each blank in the following sentences with the term that best completes the sentence.

- **compensation**
- **human resources management**
- **on-the-job training**
- **job description**
- **separation**
- **recruitment**
- **transfer**
- **group training**
- **orientation**
- **performance appraisal**
- **promotion**

1. A(n) _____ lists the duties and responsibilities of a job.
2. _____ is the process of helping new employees learn about and adjust to the company.
3. _____ occurs when a new employee works with a supervisor who demonstrates the job.
4. A(n) _____ is an evaluation method in which a manager shares information with the employee about how he or she is doing on the job.
5. Companies offer _____, which is pay and benefits.
6. The process of organizing all the aspects of recruiting, selecting, orienting, training, and developing employees is called _____.
7. Instead of training employees individually, many companies hold _____.
8. When an employer is actively looking for qualified people it is a form of _____.
9. A _____ occurs when an employee retires or resigns.
10. Moving to another job within a company at the same level and pay is called a _____.
11. When you receive a _____ it means more authority, responsibility, and pay.

Quick Quiz

1. Some ways a human resources manager can recruit people for a job are _____. (People inside the company; ads in newspapers, in magazines, at schools, or on the Internet; employment agencies; recommendations from employees.)

2. What are three types of training? (Orientation, on-the-job, group.)

3. When might layoffs occur? (When demand for a company's products or services goes down and the company has to reduce production.)

Chapter **15** Review

Review What You Learned

12. What are some of the ways you can obtain information about job openings?
13. What are some of the ways human resources managers seek new employees?
14. What population trends have led to a change in the pool of job applicants?
15. How has an increase in the number of women in the workforce brought about a change in business practices?
16. Why is orientation important for new employees?
17. What are some of the different ways employees are oriented to their new workplace?
18. Describe the difference between on-the-job training and job rotation.
19. What do managers do after their workers are oriented and trained?

Understanding Business Concepts

20. Why is a job description important when a company is looking for a new employee?
21. Who would you use as a reference when you apply for a job? Explain why.
22. How does the global economy affect employees in the United States?
23. On your first day of this class, did your teacher conduct an orientation? Explain what he or she did to help you learn about and adjust to the class.
24. Why is job rotation so important?
25. What skills and attitudes do you think you have that human resources managers would want? What skills and attitudes do you need to build in order to get and keep a job? Explain your answers.

Critical Thinking

26. What are the advantages of recruiting applicants for new positions from within the company?
27. Read the local classified ads. Which jobs seem to have the most openings? Can you find any clues about what businesses want and how you can prepare for the workplace through those advertisements? Explain.
28. List two questions to be asked if you were applying for a job at a fast-food restaurant.
29. What are five leadership traits that a human resources manager might have?

Viewing and Representing

Examining the Image. In a group of three, examine the photograph and ask each other journalistic questions beginning with the words who, what, where, when, why, and how. What's important in this picture? How do you think the new employees are feeling? Discuss your reactions to the photograph.

Chapter 15 Human Resources Management **243**

Critical Thinking

26. Answers will vary. Employee's work habits are already known; recruiting costs are kept down; minimizes the disruption of the business operation; can motivate other employees to work harder for future promotions; employee already understands the rules and regulations of the company.
27. Answers will vary.
28. Answers will vary.
29. Answers will vary, but may include adaptability, human relation skills, emotional and social maturity, insight, and motivation.

Viewing and Representing

Ask groups to role-play the parts of a manager giving orientation to employees on the first day of their new jobs. Have students switch roles.

Understanding Business Concepts

20. It lists the duties and responsibilities of the job, education required, and the skills needed.
21. A reference is someone who can supply information about them and their qualifications for employment.
22. Since business firms do business around the world, employees must know how to do business around the world.
23. Answers will vary.
24. It prevents boredom and helps keep morale high among employees. It helps managers make more effective use of the company's human resources.
25. Answers will vary.

4 CLOSE (Cont.)

Building Academic Skills

COMPUTER/TECHNOLOGY. If students struggle with the selection of a job, allow them to use the newspaper ads or the Internet for examples. Rubrics: Want ad and job description.

MATH. $565 \times 136 = 76,840$.

HISTORY. If youth apprenticeship programs exist at your school or in your community, encourage the students to include information from them in their research. Rubric: Essay.

LANGUAGE ARTS. Encourage all students in the group to participate in the project. Current business magazines and the Internet are the best resources for this project. Rubrics: Note taking, debate.

Linking School to Home

Answers will vary. Rubrics: Note taking, tables/charts, oral presentation.

Linking School to Work

Role-plays will vary. Rubric: Role-play.

• Building Academic Skills

 Keyboarding

Select a job, research its requirements, and write a job description for it. Then write a newspaper want ad for the job. Use word processing software to attractively format both items and print out the results.

 Calculating Benefits

If the new employee orientation workshop costs the company $565 per employee, how much will the company spend during a 12-month period if they train 136 new employees?

 Writing About Apprenticeship

One form of on-the-job training that has existed for hundreds of years is called apprenticeship. Write a 250-word paper on the history of the apprenticeship program. Include information about the current status of these programs.

 Preparing for an Interview

Human resources managers struggle with issues such as drug use, theft in the workplace, sexual harassment, and cultural diversity. In groups of five or six, choose one of the issues and research it using the library and the Internet. If possible, interview local business managers about the ways they deal with the issue.

• Linking School to Home

Researching Jobs. Survey your family members and friends about their current jobs. Ask them the following questions:
- How did you hear about the job?
- Did you have to fill out a job application?
- Did you have to interview for the job?
- Do you have a written job description?
- How is your performance evaluated?
- What types of training programs are available for employees?

Compile your results and share the information with your class.

• Linking School to Work

Role-play. In teams of two, role-play the following situation that might occur at an employee's performance appraisal. One student will play the part of the manager and the other student will play the part of the employee.

Situation: When Joan first started working at the company, she worked faster and more accurately than any other employee. During the last few months however, she has frequently been late to work and her work isn't as accurate as it should be. Her manager Helen, discusses the situation with Joan during her performance appraisal.

In the role-play, attempt to resolve this problem.

E-Homework

Applying Technology

Online Job Search. Create a list of ten Web sites that are dedicated to career and job searches.

Exchange Rates. Since companies of all sizes conduct business around the world, employees often have to understand how to figure exchange rates. Locate an Internet exchange-rate calculator online and convert a US $1 to Japanese, Canadian, German, and English currency.

Connecting Academics

Math. You're a human resources representative for a local biomedical company. To hire and keep good research workers, your company wants to offer a competitive salary compared with other companies in your area. You research other companies' salaries and find the following:

Company A	$60,100 (Annual Salary)
Company B	$45,900
Company C	$64,000
Company D	$58,500

What is the average salary (rounded to the nearest one hundred dollars)?

Social Science. Working in a team of three, choose one of the following topics related to human resources management: candidate selection, recruitment, developing employees, employee orientation, training, performance appraisal, or employee turnover. Together, find and read several articles on your chosen topic. Members of your team become the experts on this topic. Form an ask-the-experts panel. The rest of the class asks questions on your topic and listens attentively to the answers.

BusinessWeek — Analyzing the Feature Story

You read the first part of "Online Benefits" at the beginning of this chapter. Below are a few questions for you to answer about online application service providers (ASPs). You'll find the answers to these questions when you're reading the entire article. First, here are the questions:

30. What are some of the advantages of using online application service providers?
31. What are some of the disadvantages?

CREATIVE JOURNAL ACTIVITY

Visit the Web sites for eBenefits.com, **www.ebenefits.com** or Employease Inc., **www.employease.com**. Write in your journal about surprising findings.

BUSINESS Online
The Full Story

To learn more about human resources, visit the *Introduction to Business* Web site at **www.introbus.glencoe.com**, and click on *BusinessWeek* Feature Story, Chapter 15.

E-Homework

ONLINE JOB SEARCH. Web sites will vary. Rubric: Lists.

EXCHANGE RATES. Since exchange rates change daily, answers will vary depending on the day the student completes the assignment. Allow the students to choose the way they wish to share their findings with the class. Rubrics: Note taking, math calculation, oral presentation, essay.

Connecting Academics

MATH. (60,100 + 45,900 + 64,000 + 58,500) ÷ 4 = $57,100 (Rounded to the nearest 100 dollars.)

SOCIAL SCIENCE. Answers will vary. Activity is in the form of an "Ask the Experts" panel.

BusinessWeek — *Analyzing the Feature Story*

30. It frees HR managers to focus on hiring. It also gives offsite employees access to HR systems.
31. ASPs, like other technology tools, do not replace the human touch that is so important in human resources. ASPs are also less flexible than a system that is customized to individual companies.

Creative Journal Activity

After students have completed the activity, facilitate a class discussion of surprising findings. As a variation, ask students to identify an aspect of human resources and discuss ways it impacts companies. **LS**, **CL**

SCANS Correlation Chart*

Foundation Skills

Basic Skills	Reading	Writing	Math	Listening	Speaking
Thinking Skills	Creative Thinking	Decision Making	Problem Solving	Seeing Things in the Mind's Eye	Knowing How to Learn	Reasoning
Personal Qualities	Responsibility	Self-Esteem	Sociability	Self-Management	Integrity/Honesty	

Workplace Competencies

Resources	Allocating Time	Allocating Money	Allocating Material and Facility Resources	Allocating Human Resources		
Information	Acquiring and Evaluating Information	Organizing and Maintaining Information	Interpreting and Communicating Information	Using Computers to Process Information		
Interpersonal Skills	Participating as a Member of a Team	Teaching Others	Serving Clients/Customers	Exercising Leadership	Negotiating to Arrive at a Decision	Working With Cultural Diversity
Systems	Understanding Systems	Monitoring and Correcting Performance	Improving and Designing Systems			
Technology	Selecting Technology	Applying Technology to Task	Maintaining and Troubleshooting Technology			

*This chart's highlighted blocks indicate the chapter's content coverage in the Student Edition and the Teacher Wraparound Edition.

Resource Manager

Teaching Transparencies

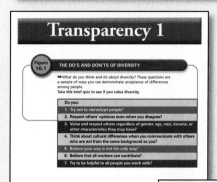

Transparency 1

Figure 16.1 THE DO'S AND DON'TS OF DIVERSITY

➤ What do you think and do about diversity? These questions are a sample of ways you can demonstrate acceptance of differences among people.
Take this brief quiz to see if you value diversity.

Do you:

1. Try not to stereotype people?
2. Respect others' opinions even when you disagree?
3. Value and respect others regardless of gender, age, race, income, or other characteristics they may have?
4. Think about cultural differences when you communicate with others who are not from the same background as you?
5. Believe your way is not the only way?
6. Believe that all workers can contribute?
7. Try to be helpful to all people you work with?

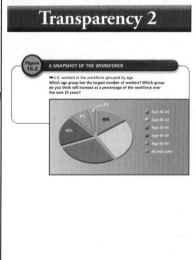

Transparency 2

Figure 16.2 A SNAPSHOT OF THE WORKFORCE

➤ U.S. workers in the workforce grouped by age. Which age group has the largest number of workers? Which group do you think will increase as a percentage of the workforce over the next 25 years?

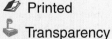

- Age 16-24
- Age 25-34
- Age 35-44
- Age 45-54
- Age 55-64
- 65 and older

Application and Enrichment

- *Lesson Plans*
- *BusinessWeek* Poster Package
- Teaching Transparencies
- Integrated Software Simulation
- Glencoe Business Video Package

Review and Reinforcement

- *PuzzleMaker*
- Internet Resources
- Student Activity Workbook
- Strat. and Work. for Teaching Transparencies

Assessment and Evaluation

- Reproducible Tests
- Alternative Assessment Strategies
- ExamView® Pro Test Generator

Technology

- *PuzzleMaker*
- ExamView® Pro Test Generator
- Glencoe Business Video Package
- PowerPoint® Presentation
- Integrated Software Simulation
- Interactive Lesson Planner
- *Virtual Business*®

KEY	✐ Printed	💾 Software	📼 Videocassette	📕 Poster
	🕹 Transparency	💿 CD-ROM	💻 Internet	

BUSINESS Online

Visit **www.introbus.glencoe.com**, the Web site companion to *Introduction to Business.* The student's page includes:

- interactive tutor
- additional *BusinessWeek* articles and activities
- business Web links
- homework hints
- real-world application activities
- additional career path activities

Information on how to prepare your students for the high school exit exam and special projects are also included.

Use the Glencoe Web site for additional resources. All essential content is covered in the Student Edition.

1 FOCUS

Introducing the Chapter

This chapter discusses the importance of business culture both globally and within a company. It also discusses diversity in the workplace. A photo essay, "Digging for Knowledge," enhances the concepts.

Connecting the Objectives

What makes up a corporate business culture? Ask students to give examples of the effects culture has on global business. What can students tell about diversity in the workplace?

BusinessWeek
Feature Story

Story's Summary

Kath Fell is an anthropologist observing human behavior in the Motorola Corporation. Motorola's company culture was in turmoil after fast acquisitions a few years ago showed problems with combining opposing cultures: cooperative versus competitive, diverse versus homogeneous, and marketing-focused versus engineering-focused. Fell's work to improve company culture is important. With a good company culture, good people stay, efficiency is maximized, communication within the company improves, and employee morale increases.

Find the entire article at www.introbus.glencoe.com, or in the Teacher Resource Binder.

Culture and Diversity in Business

Learning Objectives

After completing this chapter, you'll be able to:
1. **Explain** how cultural differences affect doing business internationally.
2. **Define** the characteristics of a corporate culture.
3. **Describe** the effect of population changes on business.
4. **Identify** ways in which government and business deal with diversity.

Why It's Important

To succeed in the workplace, know a company's corporate culture and diversity issues.

Key Words

culture
business etiquette
corporate culture
hierarchy
bureaucracy
diversity
stereotype
baby boom generation
discrimination
ageism
Equal Employment Opportunity Act
Americans with Disabilities Act (ADA)

246

BusinessWeek Feature Story

Anthropologists in the Corporate Jungle

Their Special Skills of Observation Figure Out How Humans Work Together.
When your company's culture is famously dysfunctional because of warring tribes, what can you do but call in an anthropologist? The idea sounded good to Motorola, which hired one of these professional observers of human behavior two years ago, during what's now regarded as a remarkable turnaround period for the company.

Source: Excerpted with permission from "Anthropologists in the Corporate Jungle," *BusinessWeek Online*, September 20, 2000.

An Extension Activity

No one lives or works the exact same life. Hence we're all individuals. When you think about it, there are a lot of codes of conduct that need to be upheld in order to get along with people. Give examples of rules you need to follow in order to get along with all kinds of people.

BUSINESS
Online
The Full Story
To learn more about corporate culture, visit the *Introduction to Business* Web site at www.introbus.glencoe.com, and click on *BusinessWeek* Feature Story, Chapter 16.

Classroom Resources

For the Teacher
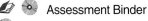 Student Activity Work. TAE
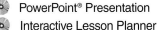 Assessment Binder
PowerPoint® Presentation
Interactive Lesson Planner
 Lesson Plans
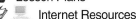 Internet Resources
Teaching Transparencies
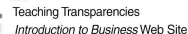 *Introduction to Business* Web Site

Integrated Soft. Sim. TM
BusinessWeek Poster Package

For the Student
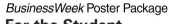 Student Activity Workbook
Virtual Business®
Introduction to Business Web Site
Integrated Soft. Sim.
PuzzleMaker
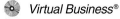 Strategies and Worksheets for Teaching Transparencies

Bell Ringer Activity

WORKING WITH CULTURAL DIVERSITY. You're the owner of Ice Edge, a manufacturer of ice skates, snowboards, and skis. You're committed to hiring employees from diverse backgrounds and cultures. You're launching a series of workshops on cultural acceptance and diversity. Develop a list of 12 items to discuss in the workshops—items dealing with ethnicity, gender, age, and other diversity issues in the workplace.

Preteaching Business Key Words

SOCIABILITY. Divide the class into teams to play "Quiz Bowl." Each team writes questions about the key words on the front of index cards. Possible questions include, "Supply the correct word for [insert a given glossary definition]"; "Give an example of [insert vocabulary word]." Include key words from three or four other chapters. **CL**, **LS**

An Extension Activity

SHARE. Ask students to share their ideas of rules to follow and behaviors to exhibit. **CL**

Making Connections

Workplace Trends. Have students read an article mentioning corporate culture or diversity in the workplace. Ask students to summarize the article and draw attention to any trends mentioned. Ask students to identify two trends in corporate culture. (Answers may include an increased awareness of diversity issues and more informal corporate cultures.) As an additional activity, ask students to write a paragraph starting with the sentence, "The Baby Boom generation is affecting the workforce in these ways . . ." **LS**, **P**

2 TEACH

Business Connection

CORPORATE CULTURE. Cisco Systems' CEO has initiated a corporate culture actively seeking to employ workers with disabilities. One example is that Cisco trains its recruiters to better communicate with job applicants who have disabilities. Another example is that the company carefully tailors its Web site to be accessible to people with visual impairments. One reason for this approach is that it's good for business.

Develop Concepts

ANALYZE. Distribute an article concerning culture in business to the students. Ask students to analyze the article for important points. **LS**

Figure 16.1 Caption Answer

All seven questions will be answered with "yes" if a person values diversity and accepts differences in others.

The Importance of Culture in Business

When you think of the word culture, you might think of fine art, pop culture, or even subculture. The word can have several different meanings. In general, culture is the beliefs, customs, and attitudes of a distinct group of people. A group's **culture** is often defined in terms of its dress, food, language, and art. On a deeper level it can be defined in terms of a group's history, geography, and religious beliefs. It can refer to an entire country or ethnic group, but it can also refer to a specific social group or institution. How comfortable are you with diversity? Take the brief quiz in Figure 16.1 to find out.

The global economy creates a diverse culture for business. As companies trade globally, they must be aware of different cultural and business practices. Otherwise, they will not win customers. Rules for etiquette, business customs, and personal interaction are different in other cultures. In some countries, business people get acquainted before they discuss business. In other countries, it's all right to get to the point immediately. Knowing how to properly approach people from different cultures makes you smarter and more considerate.

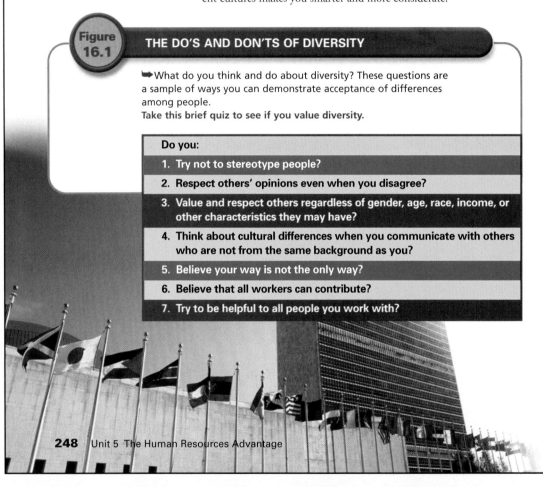

Figure 16.1 THE DO'S AND DON'TS OF DIVERSITY

➡ What do you think and do about diversity? These questions are a sample of ways you can demonstrate acceptance of differences among people.
Take this brief quiz to see if you value diversity.

Do you:
1. Try not to stereotype people?
2. Respect others' opinions even when you disagree?
3. Value and respect others regardless of gender, age, race, income, or other characteristics they may have?
4. Think about cultural differences when you communicate with others who are not from the same background as you?
5. Believe your way is not the only way?
6. Believe that all workers can contribute?
7. Try to be helpful to all people you work with?

Cooperative Learning

The Importance of Culture in Business. Ask students to work in teams of four to play "Send-a-Question." Have each team generate five questions (based on this chapter material) about business customs, marketing abroad, cultural differences in the global workplace, ways companies avoid cultural problems, factors that influence company culture, and formal and informal company cultures. Each team then sends their questions to another team. Direct the second team to answer each of the questions they receive. Finally, teams pass the questions, along with their answers, to a third team for them to evaluate the questions and answers, choosing the best three. Suggest the class pool the best questions to use as a study aid. **CL**, **LS**

Cultural Mores

In business, culture has two important meanings. In the broad sense, it refers to the culture of other countries with which companies have to do business. Specifically, it refers to the standards of a particular company.

Culture in a Global Economy

Companies that trade with other countries must be aware of differences in language, currencies, laws, and even systems of measurement. They must also be aware of differences in eating habits, customs, and the way people do business. In the United States it's common to point at or touch someone to make a point. In some countries pointing at or touching another person is considered rude. Americans like to eat quickly and whenever they feel like it. In other cultures, people eat only at certain hours and like to take their time. Failure to understand the culture of a country where you're doing business can ruin a deal or lead to a marketing disaster.

Marketing Abroad. To successfully market products in another country, you need to be aware of differences in language and customs. For example, when Pillsbury translated "Jolly Green Giant" into Arabic, the phrase became "Intimidating Green Ogre." Coca-Cola changes the amount of carbonation and sugar in its products to suit the tastes of different countries.

Workers Abroad. Companies doing business in other countries need to be aware of cultural differences in the workplace. When the Walt Disney Co. opened Euro Disney, French workers objected to greeting everyone with a smile, shaving, and other conditions. As a result, 3,000 workers quit.

American managers have had to adjust to working in Islamic countries, where it's customary to stop work five times a day to pray. In some cultures, workers are used to managers making all the decisions. If an American manager asks them for their opinions, they think the manager doesn't know what to do. This may be a sign of weakness on the manager's part.

Business Etiquette. What is considered acceptable social behavior and manners in business, or **business etiquette**, differs from country to country. In the United States, receiving a gift from a business partner could be seen as a bribe. In Japan, it's a custom and there are many rituals involved. For example, it's polite to refuse the gift once or twice

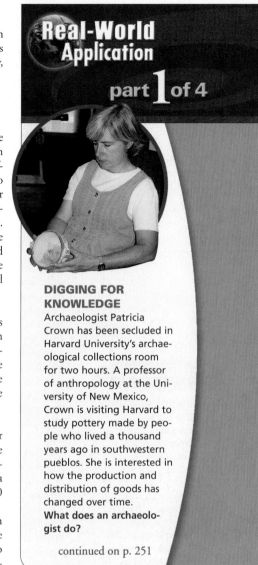

Real-World Application

part 1 of 4

DIGGING FOR KNOWLEDGE

Archaeologist Patricia Crown has been secluded in Harvard University's archaeological collections room for two hours. A professor of anthropology at the University of New Mexico, Crown is visiting Harvard to study pottery made by people who lived a thousand years ago in southwestern pueblos. She is interested in how the production and distribution of goods has changed over time. **What does an archaeologist do?**

continued on p. 251

Chapter 16 Culture and Diversity in Business **249**

Real-World Application
Caption Answer

DIGGING FOR KNOWLEDGE: PART 1 OF 4

Study the remains of a culture.

Technology Resource

GO TO **POWERPOINT.** The *Introduction to Business* PowerPoint® CD-ROM provides visual lecture aids for this chapter.

Independent Practice

COMMUNICATE. Ask students to research a company that has a formal or informal corporate culture. (Some suggestions: IBM, Jack in the Box, Gap Inc., Levi Strauss, Southwest Airlines, Cisco Systems, Office Depot.) Have students decide whether the company culture is formal or informal and find examples from their research to support their decision. Ask students to discuss their examples in a presentation. **LS**

Meeting Individual Needs

Second Language Learners. One of the most difficult parts of learning a second language can be navigating cultural differences. In some cultures, asking personal questions related to income, preferences, etc., could be considered an invasion of privacy. Some activities in this course require students to conduct surveys. If they have arrived in this country recently, students may need additional practice and examples of real research questionnaires to get a sense of the types of questions asked and the range of personal questions included. Likewise, those who have grown up in the United States with these survey tools as a way of life need to be aware of the cultural issues regarding the use of surveys.

2 TEACH (Cont.)

Thinking Critically

PHONE CALL ROLE-PLAY.
The company you work for places emphasis on high morale. Everyone in the company has a responsibility to keep the workplace environment inclusive. You're part of an exciting team where everyone has a unique background, perspective, and experience-base—the Diversity Inclusion Group (D.I.G.). The team's planning a diversity-awareness event. You call one of your D.I.G. teammates to give her your ideas for the event. Present your ideas in a role-play. **LS, CL**

Consider This...

Caption Answer

Technology that provides text-enlargement, navigators, voice synthesizers, special software, bar-code readers, Braille output devices, and adaptive devices make it possible for workers with an impairment to be a productive part of the workforce. This increases the diversity within a company.

Consider This...

Columbia Lighthouse for the Blind

The Columbia Lighthouse for the Blind (CLB) in Washington, D.C. trains thousands of people for jobs as technical specialists. Tools such as voice software and braille output devices let people with visual impairments function efficiently in an office environment. The key is to educate business leaders about the extent and availability of assistive devices.

ANALYZE
How can assistive technology enhance company diversity?

---

before accepting it. Before getting down to business in India it's customary to have tea. In Mexico, throwing documents on a table during a meeting is an insult. To convince partners in other countries you can do business in their country, you first need to show them you know and respect their customs.

Many companies avoid cultural problems by hiring local managers in countries where they do business. Companies also train their own managers to live and work in other countries. As more companies trade globally, there is an increasing demand for people who have studied other languages and cultures.

Corporate Culture

A business must be aware of diversity in its own company, too. Workers come from different backgrounds, cultures, and experiences that affect the company's culture. A company's **corporate culture** is its shared values, beliefs, and goals. It can be defined formally through a company code of ethics, a written manual, and the orientation process. It can also be defined informally through dress codes, work habits, and social activities. The cultures at McDonald's and Disney, for example, stress customer service and family values. Employees are expected to be clean-cut and greet each customer with a smile. Kinko's and Ben & Jerry's, on the other hand, stress worker satisfaction and concern for the environment.

A founder, such as William Hewlett of Hewlett-Packard, who stressed a people-first culture, can influence a company's culture. Region and tradition can also play big parts. A banker at an old Wall Street firm in New York is expected to wear a suit and tie. At a high-tech company on the West Coast, like a dot-com company in San Jose, a worker might wear a T-shirt and shorts to work.

Formal Culture. A company's culture affects the way it's organized and does business. In a formal culture, there might be a strict **hierarchy**, or chain of command, with one person at the top who makes all the decisions. There might be several levels of management, or **bureaucracy**, below. To make changes or pass down decisions can be very complicated and time consuming. Job titles are very important as indicators of power and status within a company. Dress codes and work hours are strictly enforced.

Informal Culture. At a company with an informal culture, employees are encouraged to make decisions on their own rather than going through layers of management. They're allowed to dress casually and have more flexible work hours. In some cases they can even work at home. Job titles aren't as important as creativity and teamwork. At Kingston Technology the founders of the company sit in cubicles so they can interact with employees and be available to them. At Southwest Airlines, the head of the company has all his employees call him by his first name.

250 Unit 5 The Human Resources Advantage

LANGUAGE ARTS — Curriculum Connection

Artwork. The company you work for places a high value on diversity. The CEO asks you to create a piece of artwork that must represent diversity and a feeling of inclusion. Choose any aspect of diversity in your company and any medium you wish—sculpture, model, painting, sketch, collage, etc. Since the artwork will be placed in a prominent place in the lobby, you're proud to do your best work. **LS, CL**

Few companies have a culture that is entirely formal or informal. Within the same company there are often different cultures. In the entertainment industry, for example, executives and artists have their own cultures. Executives are called "suits" and artists are called "creatives."

 Fast Review _____

1. What are two ways companies can avoid cultural problems with another country?
2. Name ways a company defines its corporate culture.
3. What are some characteristics of a formal corporate culture?

Diversity in the Workplace

Why change? Global trade isn't the only place where companies must be aware of diversity. Diversity is a feature of people in the workforce. You know that no two people are alike. Your friends have a variety of backgrounds, skills, and viewpoints. In the workplace, you'll find your coworkers are a diverse group. Your success on the job will depend on how well you work with and for people who are different from you.

Diversity in the workplace also means differences in skills, work habits, and approaches to tasks. People with the same assignments will carry them out in different ways. There is often more than one way to do a job. How are people different now, and what will the workplace be like in the future?

Companies not only have to deal with the cultural differences of people in other countries. They also have to deal with a variety of people with different backgrounds and identities, or **diversity**, in the workplace. People are diverse in terms of age, gender, ethnicity, and individual needs. People also differ in terms of education, marital and parental status, income, and religious beliefs.

There is a tendency to stereotype people who are different in some way. To **stereotype** people is to identify them by a single trait or as a member of a certain group rather than as individuals. In fact, no two people are alike. Everybody has special skills, knowledge, and experience. Dealing with diversity doesn't mean ignoring the differences between people. It means understanding and appreciating those differences.

The Impact of Diversity on Business

The population of the United States has become more ethnically diverse. For example, the fastest growing groups in the country are

Chapter 16 Culture and Diversity in Business **251**

Real-World Application part 2 of 4

DIGGING FOR KNOWLEDGE
Harvard's collection of ancient pottery is stored in floor-to-ceiling drawers. Crown examines crudely made pottery. She is studying how people in different societies learn a skill and produce goods.
Does society rank people based upon their job titles?

continued on p. 253

Chapter 16

Real-World Application Caption Answer

DIGGING FOR KNOWLEDGE: PART 2 OF 4
More often than not, yes it does.

Fast Review Answers ✔

1. By hiring local managers from the country where they do business. Diversity training.
2. A code of ethics, the company manual, and their orientation process.
3. Strict hierarchy, bureaucracy, importance of job titles, and strict dress codes and work hours.

Business Connection

DIVERSITY IN THE WORK-FORCE. Levi Strauss took on social responsibilitiy. In the 1920s, this company offered English and citizenship classes to its immigrant factory workers. Today it continues to be "responsible commercial success." It instituted the Diversity Council, which represents African-American, Asian, Latino, gay, and women's interests.

Great Ideas From the Classroom of...

Janet Fisher
Beavercreek High School
Beavercreek, Ohio

Let's Discover! Learning the differences in world cultures is always an eye opener for students. One excellent resource for information is the school's foreign exchange students. To allow the students to discover cultures on their own, I have them generate an international poster or booklet. Using the Internet and textbooks, each student is to choose six foreign countries. Each country's page can include a map, the flag, its currency, and customs. Pages glued to poster board can be displayed in class.

2 TEACH (Cont.)

Develop Concepts

SPECULATE. Have students speculate on the kinds of benefits Levi Strauss (see Business Connection page 251) receives from encouraging diversity and empowerment of its workforce. (Studies show that companies that value diversity have increased productivity and efficiency, lower turnover rates, less absenteeism, and fewer legal costs from employee grievances.)

Discussion Starter

LISTING. Ask students to make a list of differences that affect companies trading globally. (Answers may include different laws, systems of measurement, customs, language, and currencies.)

Figure 16.2 Caption Answer

The largest group of workers is the age group of 35 to 44. The age groups of 55 to 65, and 65 and older will increase in percentage as people now 35 to 44 years old reach those ages, since they are now the largest group.

Hispanics and Asians. Between 1990 and 2000, the Hispanic population grew by almost 60 percent. In California and Texas, Hispanics are no longer classified as a minority. Ten percent of Americans were born in other countries.

The population is also getting older and living longer. The 76 million babies born in the United States between 1946 and 1964 are called the **baby boom generation**. They control $2.6 trillion and have about 51 percent of the wealth in the country. The older baby boomers will turn 65 in 2011 and the number of Americans over 65 will nearly double in 2030.

Other population changes are taking place. The number of families with single parents is now around 30 percent. Changes like these have a far-reaching effect on business.

Changes in the Workplace. As the population has become more diverse, so has the workplace. (See Figure 16.2.) In the last few years about 85 percent of the people who entered the workforce were women and members of ethnic minorities. There are greater numbers of women,

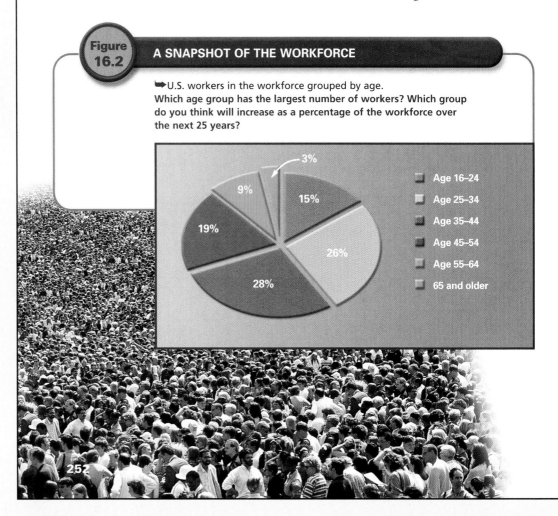

Figure 16.2

A SNAPSHOT OF THE WORKFORCE

➡️ U.S. workers in the workforce grouped by age.
Which age group has the largest number of workers? Which group do you think will increase as a percentage of the workforce over the next 25 years?

- Age 16–24 — 15%
- Age 25–34 — 26%
- Age 35–44 — 28%
- Age 45–54 — 19%
- Age 55–64 — 9%
- 65 and older — 3%

252

Global Perspective

Cross-Cultural Training. Cross-cultural training is becoming increasingly important to today's managers. When doing business with individuals from other countries, managers must respect cultural differences and be careful not to offend clients or employees, which could jeopardize business activities. Have students research some specifics about cross-cultural training, using business periodicals and the Internet. Suggest that students present their findings as part of a cross-cultural training bulletin board. **CL**, **LS**

Asians, Hispanics, and African Americans in management positions.

The youth labor force (ages 16 to 24) is expected to grow more rapidly than the overall labor force for the first time in 25 years. Meanwhile, people are working more years than ever before. In the workplace, many people are coming into contact for the first time with people of different ages, ethnic backgrounds, and abilities. Within the next 50 years, groups now considered ethnic minorities will make up half the population. As a result, the workplace will become even more diverse.

Changes in the Marketplace. A more diverse population also means a more diverse marketplace. With more jobs, women and ethnic groups have more spending power and a larger share of the market. Companies that used to target only white males now target many groups. For example, sportswear companies will run ads in both English and Spanish and separate ads for women, African-Americans, and Asians. Baby boomers aren't only one of the largest groups, they also spend more than any other group. As they get older, the market for health and recreational products will increase to suit their changing needs.

Managing Diversity

Human resources managers manage diversity. They seek to find ways to make the company an inclusive organization. This leads to greater productivity and a competitive advantage. Workers know that a good diversity management program is a mark of a company that's good to work for. It's a good recruiting tool for new workers.

Diversity management programs have a broad objective. Their goal is to help all employees find a place in the company and help the company achieve its objectives. The workplace includes people with all kinds of backgrounds. Companies with diversity management programs recognize that people with different characteristics are good employees. Their goal is to create an inclusive, respectful environment. They want to draw on the strength of the diversity of their workers. What unique contributions can each worker bring to the company? How will they use their abilities, backgrounds, and skills? Diversity programs try to answer these questions. Up until the 1970s, white males dominated business in the United States. In general, people tend to hire other people most like themselves. Excluding someone on the basis of age, gender, or ethnicity is called **discrimination**. Changes in the laws and in company policies have done much toward correcting the problem.

Real-World Application
part 3 of 4

DIGGING FOR KNOWLEDGE
In modern industrial society, most children learn in school from a teacher who tells them information and answers questions. In historic Pueblo societies, however, children learned from family members. **How will elders influence the future of the U.S. workforce?**

continued on p. 255

DIGGING FOR KNOWLEDGE: PART 3 OF 4

The number of baby boomers retiring will allow for more people of all ages to enter the workforce.

Individualized Practice

ANALYZE. Ask students to find articles on cultural diversity. Complete activity L1, L2, or L3, then hold a classroom discussion on the question: Did you learn anything new, and if so, did it change your way of thinking?

L1 Have pairs of students discuss points raised in the articles.

L2 Ask students to write a one-page summary of what they learned.

L3 Form the class into groups to discuss points raised in the articles, then discuss the following questions: Is the local community experiencing a demographic change as a result of cultural diversity? How does that affect the workforce?

Chapter 16 Culture and Diversity in Business **253**

Curriculum Connection

Working With Cultural Diversity. Post eight blank posters at the side of the classroom and ask students to gather in small groups at the posters. Write this list on the board: doctor, company president, person with a disability, lawyer, firefighter, teacher, pilot, engineer, secretary, and health-care worker. Ask each group to list on its poster at least four words that describe each person. Discuss any stereotypes that arise and how they affect people's perceptions (for example, describing a doctor as "male"). Ask students what companies do to overcome stereotypes. **LS, CL**

Chapter 16

3 ASSESS

Reteaching

NAME. To reteach the concept of benefits of diversity, ask students to name the benefits. (Reduces conflict, offers a range of ideas, helps the company serve the needs of the diverse marketplace, increases morale, and increases recruitment of qualified workers.)

Enrichment Strategy

ORAL REPORT. Ask students to give an oral report answering the questions: How would you feel about working for a company that does not seem to honor diversity? How would it make you feel to be a mentor for a coworker with a different background than you? **LS**

Business Building Blocks

CAPTION ANSWER

The parents in the new markets make the decisions. Instead of advertising to the teenagers in the new market, the new advertising will be aimed at the parents. The advertising will stress qualities the parents want such as the durability and ease of laundering of the jeans.

Laws Against Discrimination. It might surprise you that workers over the age of 40 were often fired or denied jobs in the past in favor of younger workers. This form of discrimination is called **ageism**. To protect older workers, the U.S. government passed the *Age Discrimination in Employment Act*. A few years later, the **Equal Employment Opportunity Act** was passed to strengthen laws protecting workers from discrimination on the basis of gender, ethnicity, or other aspects of identity. People with individual needs, such as people with physical disabilities, often couldn't work simply because buildings lacked proper access or equipment. In 1990, the **Americans with Disabilities Act (ADA)** was passed requiring businesses to provide facilities such as wheelchair ramps.

Diversity Programs. Most company codes of ethics have rules against discrimination. This, however, isn't always enough. Many employees still have trouble working with people who are different. To deal with diversity in the workplace, most companies now offer diversity training programs. American Express, for example, uses employee

Business Building Blocks

Interpreting Points of View

You have your own point of view. If you hope to succeed in business, you'll have to recognize and be sensitive to the points of view of your coworkers, suppliers, and customers. A company that is active in the global marketplace must carefully consider whether its products will appeal to people in countries with different cultural and social viewpoints.

Practice

The following case study describes the marketing of products in a country whose cultural or social points of view differ from those in the United States. Explain how you would change

Analysis

the marketing strategy to take into account the potential customers' point of view.

Case Study

2-B-Me sells blue jeans by suggesting that its denim designs bring teenagers freedom, power, and popularity. The company hopes to expand its market to several countries that emphasize respect and obedience to elders. Teenagers in these countries spend most of their time outside of school with their families. Parents in this country chaperone and monitor the lives of their teenage children.

How to Use a Portfolio Activity

The portfolio projects are designed to lead students to develop a collection of their best work to submit to you for assessment. You and each of your students should decide which projects to include in their business portfolio. Refer students to the specific rubric(s) from the *Alternative Assessment Strategies*. These rubrics will alert students to the criteria you'll use to assess their projects. **P**

networking to bring together people from different groups. Corning and IBM have seminars on diversity. Other companies hire consultants or use diversity-training manuals. The goal of these programs is to promote trust and cooperation among workers of different backgrounds so they work more effectively together.

Diversity training increases acceptance of diversity by breaking down stereotypes, which reflect ignorance. People who have never worked with people with physical disabilities, for example, may assume that these workers are less capable. People who have never worked with people from other countries often make incorrect assumptions about the way foreigners think and act.

To bring together all of the people who work for them, managers must avoid stereotyping. They must create a work environment in which prejudice is not tolerated and diversity is welcomed and respected. Employees need to feel that they are valued and respected for who they are. Managers should always be sensitive to the backgrounds of their workers, and should foster a diverse and understanding corporate culture.

Benefits of Diversity. Why is diversity important? Instead of banishing people based upon diversity, differences are celebrated. Now, companies have programs to provide opportunities to employees. They recruit, develop, and retain more diverse employees. In turn, those employees are an asset in dealing with diverse clients and customers. Businesses that promote diversity in the workplace have discovered many benefits:

- Diversity reduces possible conflicts between workers.
- A diverse workforce offers a broader range of ideas and ways of looking at things.
- Greater diversity in the workplace helps a company better understand and serve the needs of a more diverse marketplace.
- It creates a greater sense of morale among employees and commitment to company goals.

Studies show that companies that value diversity have increased productivity and efficiency, lower turnover rates, less absenteeism, and fewer legal costs from employee grievances.

✓ Fast Review

1. In what ways are people diverse?
2. How have changes in the population affected business?
3. Name some of the laws against discrimination.
4. What is the goal of diversity training programs?

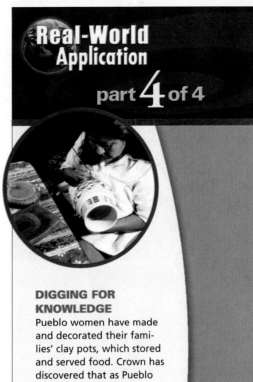

Real-World Application
part 4 of 4

DIGGING FOR KNOWLEDGE
Pueblo women have made and decorated their families' clay pots, which stored and served food. Crown has discovered that as Pueblo pottery started to become a trade item a thousand years ago, the method of producing it also began to change. To increase output, women often made and completed most of the decoration on pots and then allowed their children to finish the decoration. **Understanding other cultures gives you a greater appreciation for what?**

Chapter 16

Real-World Application
Caption Answer

DIGGING FOR KNOWLEDGE: PART 4 OF 4
Answers will vary but might include diversity, customs, and culture.

Technology Resource

GO TO INTEGRATED SOFTWARE SIMULATION.
Use the Integrated Software Simulation to apply this unit's concepts.

Evaluation
Assign and review the Fast Review sections.

Fast Review Answers ✓

1. Age, gender, ethnicity, individual needs, education, marital and parental status, income, and religious beliefs.
2. Becoming more diverse.
3. The Age Discrimination in Employment Act, the Equal Employment Opportunity Act, and the Americans with Disabilities Act.
4. Promote trust and cooperation among workers.

Meeting Individual Needs

Students With Visual Impairments.
Students with visual impairments face special risks and require special tools in order to participate in academic and workplace environments. The specific tools can vary from reading machines to Braille texts to the use of guide dogs. Some students benefit from working with a peer "visual translator" who is able to verbally describe visual images, such as the photos in the textbook. If you have students with visual impairments in your class, you may wish to implement this cooperative learning technique.

 **Picture** *This...*

How Passports Work

1 FOCUS

Students who want to work, study, or travel abroad have to go through a formal process before they can travel. They have to obtain a passport, visa, and/or work permit. Students who want to study abroad can apply through a full-time undergraduate program at many U.S. colleges and universities. They can also apply through many organizations, such as the American Institute of Foreign Studies, or apply directly to a foreign university. Students who want to work abroad may or may not be required to have a job already lined up before they can obtain a work visa.

2 TEACH

Describe some of the resources available to students who want to go abroad. The U.S. government, for example, issues Consular Information Sheets, Public Announcements, and Travel Warnings for Americans traveling to other countries. Information on study and job opportunities abroad can be found at libraries, colleges and universities, and the Internet.

? Did You Know?

Some countries require International Certificates of Vaccination for diseases like yellow fever before you can enter.

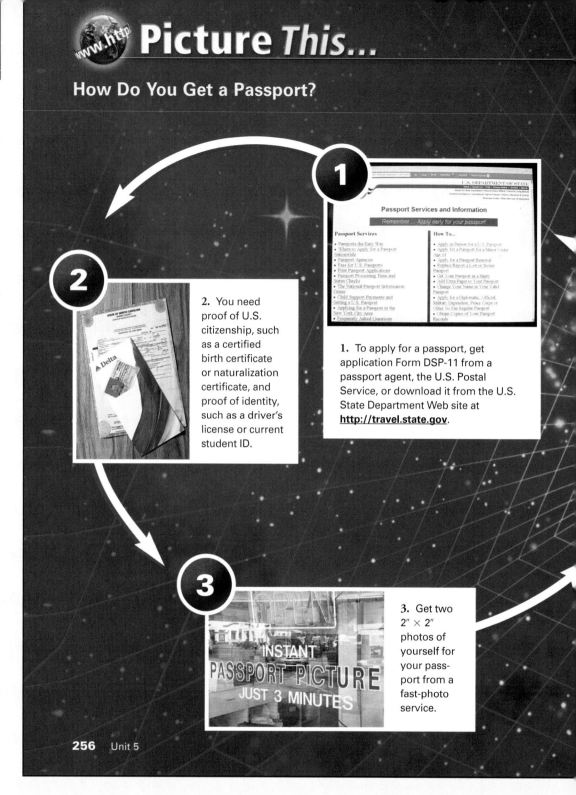

Picture *This...*

How Do You Get a Passport?

1. To apply for a passport, get application Form DSP-11 from a passport agent, the U.S. Postal Service, or download it from the U.S. State Department Web site at **http://travel.state.gov**.

2. You need proof of U.S. citizenship, such as a certified birth certificate or naturalization certificate, and proof of identity, such as a driver's license or current student ID.

3. Get two 2″ × 2″ photos of yourself for your passport from a fast-photo service.

256   Unit 5

Extending the Content

Pertinent Documents.   To work or study abroad, you not only need a passport, you need a student or work visa. To apply for a visa, you need to apply through the embassy or consulate in the United States for the country where you want to work or study. You can also obtain a visa through a service such as Visa Advisors.

256

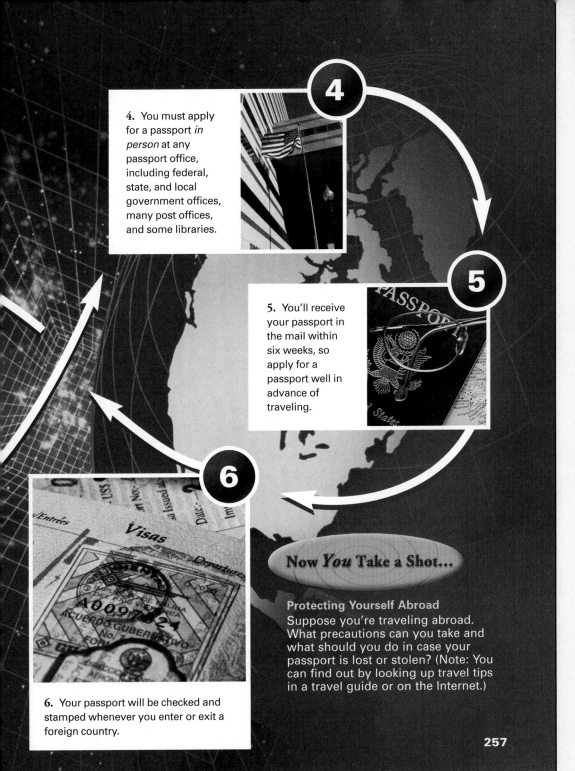

4. You must apply for a passport *in person* at any passport office, including federal, state, and local government offices, many post offices, and some libraries.

5. You'll receive your passport in the mail within six weeks, so apply for a passport well in advance of traveling.

6. Your passport will be checked and stamped whenever you enter or exit a foreign country.

Now *You* Take a Shot...

Protecting Yourself Abroad
Suppose you're traveling abroad. What precautions can you take and what should you do in case your passport is lost or stolen? (Note: You can find out by looking up travel tips in a travel guide or on the Internet.)

257

Picture This...

3 ASSESS

Have students answer the question in "Now You Take a Shot…"

4 CLOSE

Have students use a newspaper or the Internet to look up travel information in a country of their choice, e.g., the weather, currency exchange rate, time difference, and travel fares. Have students compare their findings.

? *Did You Know?*

It's not necessary to have travel experience, know a foreign language, or study a foreign country to find an international job. Many jobs are more skill oriented and someone with a degree in business, engineering, or computer science might be more in demand than someone who speaks a foreign language.

Now *You* Take a Shot...   *Caption Answer*

Answers may vary. Most travel guides recommend that you make two copies of the identification page in your passport. Leave one copy at home with relatives or friends. Keep the other copy in a safe place separate from your passport. If you lose your passport, you should report it to the local American consulate or to a travel service such as American Express.

4 CLOSE

Chapter Wrap-Up

To close, ask students to complete the following statement: "During this chapter I discovered that _____."

Using Business Key Words

1. business etiquette
2. corporate culture
3. Equal Employment Opportunity Act
4. hierarchy
5. culture
6. stereotype
7. diversity
8. ageism
9. baby boom generation
10. Americans with Disabilities Act (ADA)
11. discrimination
12. bureaucracy

Review What You Learned

13. Formally—code of ethics. Informally—dress codes, work habits, and activities.
14. Answers could vary. Coca-Cola makes its products sweeter or less carbonated for some countries. Ford cars have been adapted for left-handed drive in England and Australia. McDonald's sells chili sauce in Mexico for its sandwiches.
15. Hispanics and Asians.
16. About 85 percent of the growth in the labor force in the United States was people of color, women, and immigrants.
17. Different groups spend money on different products and services.
18. Including individual and group differences of all kinds.

Summary

1. To do business in another country successfully, a company must be aware of differences in cultural customs as well as differences in language, laws, and currencies.

2. A company's corporate culture can be formally defined by a code of ethics, a manual, and the orientation process or informally defined by dress codes, work habits, and social activities.

3. As a result of changes in the population, the workplace and the marketplace are becoming increasingly more diverse.

4. Laws, company codes of ethics, and diversity training programs protect and encourage diversity in the workplace.

● Using Business Key Words

Understanding the diverse business cultures that exist in the world is essential for success in business. See how many terms you know by matching each term with the correct statement below.

- **culture**
- **business etiquette**
- **corporate culture**
- **hierarchy**
- **bureaucracy**
- **diversity**
- **stereotype**
- **baby boom generation**
- **discrimination**
- **ageism**
- **Equal Employment Opportunity Act**
- **Americans with Disabilities Act (ADA)**

1. The acceptable social behavior and manner in business.
2. A company's shared values, beliefs, and goals.
3. A law protecting against discrimination of workers on the basis of gender, ethnicity, or other differences.
4. A formal chain of command.
5. The beliefs, customs, and attitudes of a distinct group of people.
6. Identifying someone by a single trait or as a member of a certain group rather than as an individual.
7. A variety of people with different backgrounds and identities.
8. Discrimination on the basis of age.
9. People born between 1946 and 1964.
10. A law requiring businesses to provide facilities for people with special needs.
11. Excluding someone on the basis of age, gender, ethnicity, or other aspect of identity.
12. A formal organization consisting of many levels of management.

Quick Quiz

1. A company's shared values, beliefs, and goals a1re its _____? (Corporate culture.)
2. How can managers foster cooperation in a diverse workplace? (Answers may include: by providing strong leadership honoring diversity, and providing diversity-awareness training and orientation.)
3. To identify people by a single trait or as a member of a certain group rather than as individuals is to _____ them. (Stereotype.)

Review What You Learned

13. Describe how a company defines its culture formally and informally.
14. Provide an example of how a U.S. product has been adapted for sale in another country.
15. What are the fastest growing segments of the United States population?
16. Describe how the labor force in the United States has changed over the last several years.
17. Explain how changes in demographics can mean changes for businesses.
18. How do companies define diversity?

Understanding Business Concepts

19. Explain why it's important for companies, especially those who trade globally, to be aware of different cultures and business practices.
20. How do human resources managers manage diversity?
21. Describe what you think you'll be doing in 15 years. How will your consumer needs be different than today?
22. Name an industry in your community that might be affected by a population that's living longer.
23. Describe your own workplace diversity. What talents, skills, and characteristics do you have that might be seen as valuable to an employer?

Critical Thinking

24. The corporate culture is the setting in which workers operate. Describe your classroom culture. What classroom rules, work habits, and activities help shape how you work, act, and deal with problems?

25. If you had the opportunity to become an exchange student in another country, what would you do to learn about the culture of that country?
26. Would you feel comfortable in a formal or informal company culture? Compare the advantages of each organizational model.
27. How could a manager's openness to suggestions influence coworkers' loyalty? Would this vary in other cultures?

Viewing and Representing

Examining the Image. Study this photograph. What does the photographer want you to think and feel? What do you consider others would think and feel looking at this photograph—a baby boomer, a grade-school student, a person with a physical disability, a person with a different ethnic background, and so on? How do you think diversity benefits the workplace?

Chapter 16 Culture and Diversity in Business **259**

Critical Thinking

24. Answers will vary.
25. Answers will vary.
26. Answers will vary. Each person's personality might dictate what environment he or she will feel more comfortable in.
27. Answers will vary. Employee may feel more respected and a part of the decision-making process.

Viewing and Representing

Have a class discussion centered on the students' responses to the questions in this activity. What do students think the photographer wants them to think and feel? Remind students that companies producing media campaigns and ads have a specific focus intended to influence their audience. What's the motivation behind this? How does the photographer or producer want you to react? How will the photographer, producer, or company benefit from your actions after viewing this? Continue discussion of the other questions in the activity. **LS**, **CL**

Understanding Business Concepts

19. If they don't, they might not win customers or be able to conduct business in that country.
20. They seek to find ways to make the company an inclusive organization. They offer diversity management programs.
21. Answers will vary.
22. Answers will vary.
23. Answers will vary.

4 CLOSE (Cont.)

Building Academic Skills

HISTORY. Current business magazines and the Internet are good resources for this project. Rubric: Oral presentation.

COMPUTER/TECHNOLOGY. If students have trouble finding someone to interview, allow the students to read articles about people who telecommute. Let the students choose how they wish to present their findings to the class. Rubrics: Oral presentations, essay, poster.

LANGUAGE ARTS. Encourage students to be very creative in this project. Rubric: Poster.

MATH. The library and the Internet are good resources for this activity. Rubric: Graphs.

Linking School to Home

Answers will vary. Rubrics: Note taking, essay.

Linking School to Work

Make sure all students find a human resources department to contact. If this is a difficult task, have the students work in groups. Allow the students to choose the way they wish to share their findings. Rubrics: Note taking, oral presentation, essay.

Building Academic Skills

 Adapting to Customs

Research a major U.S. corporation that conducts business in another country. Find out how the corporation had to adapt to the customs and cultures of the other country. What adaptations to the products had to take place before the product could be sold? How is the product marketed? Are there local managers in the other country? Present your findings orally to your class.

 Influences on the Workplace

Interview someone who works in a formal corporate culture. Find out the following information:

- How long has he or she been working in this environment?
- What are the advantages and disadvantages?
- What technology is essential in order to perform his or her job?
- How often does communication with a supervisor occur?

- Would he or she recommend this culture type to others?

Use a word processing program to write about your findings. Share this with the class.

 Visualizing Your Future

Think ahead to when you'll be 60 years old. Create a poster that visually describes what you will be doing. Will you be working? Will you be retired? What activities will you be involved in? What products and services will you buy? How will you financially provide for yourself? Display your poster in your classroom.

 Creating a Chart

Using the statistics from the latest U.S. census, create a pie chart that shows the diverse segments of our population. Then, create another graph that shows the diverse segments of your state's population.

Linking School to Home

Examining Diversity. Religious beliefs, geographic location, parental status, marital status, work background, and income are considered elements of diversity. Acknowledging diversity and treating everyone fairly are assets in dealing with clients, coworkers, and customers. Diversity is a description of variety. Determine the diversity in your own family or group of friends. What differences in gender, age, race, abilities, skills, and education are there? Write a one-page paper explaining how these differences are an asset to your family or friends.

Linking School to Work

Diversity Training. Businesses have defined diversity. They promote nondiscrimination in the workplace. Their programs are intended to assist all workers to collaborate, trust, and work together in the workplace. Contact the human resources department of a business in your community. Ask about the diversity training and programs that are offered at their company. Find out when they began, who participates, what type of information is included, and how the training has improved their business.

E-Homework

Applying Technology

Online Research. Using the Internet, research the Web sites of several major corporations. See if you can find one with an informal corporate culture and one with a formal corporate culture. Then write a paragraph explaining why you chose each site.

Creating a Model. Using your imagination, create a three-dimensional model of a piece of technology that would be beneficial to a telecommuter. (Create something that hasn't yet been invented.) Write a paragraph explaining how it works and present your project to your class.

Connecting Academics

Math. In 1988 Shoshana founded Workplace Solutions, a training company specializing in diversity awareness in the workplace. Shoshana immigrated to the United States 24 years prior to founding her company. In the year 2002, Shoshana celebrated her fifty-fourth birthday. What year was Shoshana born? How old was she when she immigrated? Is Shoshana part of the baby boom generation?

Social Science. Watch three or four TV shows showing people of different ethnic backgrounds in work situations. How did the different characters behave? Did their actions follow an ethnic stereotype? What cultural differences did you see? Did you see any evidence of discrimination? Did you see people using special skills to work better together? What were they?

BusinessWeek — Analyzing the Feature Story

You read the first part of "Anthropologists in the Corporate Jungle" at the beginning of this chapter. Below are a few questions for you to answer about Kath Fell. You'll find the answers to these questions when you're reading the entire article. First, here are the questions:

28. Why did Motorola hire anthropologist Kath Fell?

29. What role did diversity play in the strategies Kath Fell asked Motorola to implement?

CREATIVE JOURNAL ACTIVITY

You're an anthropologist who observes nonverbal behavior. The assignment is to observe others at a distance—across the ball field, the other side of the cafeteria, the other end of a corridor, and so on.

- What repeated rituals, such as saying goodbye, do you see?
- Can you interpret people's feelings by their body language?

Write your observations in your journal.

BUSINESS Online
The Full Story

To learn more about corporate culture, visit the *Introduction to Business* Web site at **www.introbus.glencoe.com**, and click on *BusinessWeek* Feature Story, Chapter 16.

261

E-Homework

ONLINE RESEARCH. Answers will vary. Students will have to make their own judgments regarding whether or not the corporate culture is formal or informal. As long as the students can justify their findings, accept their answers. Rubric: Essay.

CREATING A MODEL. Encourage fun and creativity with this activity. Rubric: Three-dimensional model, essay.

Connecting Academics

MATH. Shoshana was born in 1948 (2002 − 54 = 1948). She immigrated when she was 16 years old (1988 − 24 = 1964, 1964 − 1948 = 16 years old). Yes, she was born between 1946 and 1964.

SOCIAL SCIENCE. Encourage students to take notes as they watch the TV shows. Ask for specific, brief accounts of examples of behavior and differences. This gives students practice in a valuable business skill—to be able to decide the most important point and then communicate this point concisely.

BusinessWeek — Analyzing the Feature Story

28. Motorola had recently acquired several small Internet start-ups. Kath Fell's job was to help merge the corporate cultures.

29. Fell recognized that people from different disciplines such as marketing and engineering were talking different languages. Fell also persuaded executives to reinstate a set of employee councils for women, African Americans and other groups.

Creative Journal Activity

Begin a class discussion by asking volunteers to share their observations. Ask volunteers to describe the body language and rituals they observed, and their interpretations of the behavior. **LS, CL**

1 FOCUS

Unit Seminar Overview

In this seminar students work in pairs to gain first-hand experience in finding the right people for the job. Students investigate images, interpret facts, and develop their own business simulation to search for employees. Students will chart ways that employers look for employees and decide which methods might work best for their imagined business.

Bell Ringer Activity

FINISH THE SENTENCE. Write on the board: "If you don't work, imagine working in a job. Think about your work ethics. Write and complete this sentences in your journal: At work, I'm proud of the way I _____. Imagine being someone else and complete the sentence again."

Discussion Starter

DIFFERENTIATE. A smile is universal. Is it? Have you ever seen a person smile when they're confused or uncomfortable in a situation? In many cultures, in Japan and in India for example, people do just that. Is there any trait in business that's universal? (Perhaps looking into people's eyes to interpret the meaning of a smile might make the smile a universal trait.)

BusinessWeek Seminar

Unit 5 Careers

Using Resources of Find the Right People

In Chapter 15, you read about how businesses find employees. A business isn't successful without the right people. In order to find the right people for the job, businesses have to be resourceful to seek out candidates. In this seminar you and a partner will develop a business and research different ways to look for employees.

262

Social Science — Newsworthy Trends

Diversity Recruitment. Eighty-five percent of all workers entering the workplace are women and members of ethnic minorities. At the same time, the total number of new workers is declining. Because of this, diversity recruitment and training has become a priority for most employers. More companies are hiring workers based on their training rather than their experience. They're establishing relationships with schools that have a diverse student body and offering more internships to people from diverse backgrounds. Job opportunities for women and minorities have dramatically increased to keep up with dramatic changes in the population.

Factoids

A Non-Question. An employer should never consider your economic status part of a decision whether or not to extend a job offer.

Those Who Lie. Twenty-four percent of job applicants misrepresent work or personal experience.

Proper Questions. The federal Equal Employment Opportunity Commission publishes guidelines listing proper and improper questions for employers to ask prospective candidates.

An Agreement. A job application is considered a legal document.

Necessary Training. More than 52 percent of companies utilize diversity training. By 2010, women and minorities will comprise 70 percent of the new candidates in the workforce.

Investigate the Images

Look at the photographic collage on the left page. What grabs your attention at first? Is it the color or the words? The power in reading visuals is in analyzing and dissecting your observations. On a separate piece of paper, respond to the questions listed below. These questions might help sharpen the focus of your visual mind.

Your Observations

1. How many photographs do you see?

2. Examine each photograph. How is each assembled in relation to one another?

3. What is the subject of each photograph? Is place or location the subject?

4. Does color signify a message?

5. What issues do you take from these images?

Information

6. Summarize what you know about the photographs from your observations.

Exploring Culture

7. You want to work for a particular company, but it's in a hiring freeze. Does this deter you or do you still pursue the company?

8. A good photograph will hold you captive as you interpret what you see. Think of an interview in much the same way. The employer is the viewer and you're the subject. How will you portray yourself? What kind of things will you reveal about yourself to the employer?

Unit 5 *BusinessWeek* Seminar **263**

2 TEACH

Thinking Critically

Imagine you are an employer who needs to find new employees on a regular basis, and then answer the questions below:

1. How would the first four factoids affect you? (Answers will vary and may include: reminder to self to ignore economic status, consider checking the background of applicants, consult the EEOC guidelines or a reliable book on job interviews, and ensure the application is signed and dated.)

2. Looking at the factoid "Necessary Training," how will these statistics affect your business? (Answers will vary, and may include adding the cost of diversity training to your business budget, and making a decision to create in-house training or arrange to hire a training company.)

Cooperative Learning

DIVERSITY TRAINING ONLINE. Have students work in pairs or small groups to investigate online training. Is online diversity training available? If possible, have groups try out a sample online training program and give their opinion on the effectiveness of the training. What improvements could be made? **CL**, **ELL**, LS

Social Science
Newsworthy Trends

Uncle Sam Wants You. Among the most important international issues in the twenty-first century are human rights, foreign intelligence, and the environment. The U.S. Department of State has its own Web site to recruit people for the Foreign and Civil Services at <u>www.usajobs.opm.gov</u>.

Jobs include everything from lawyers to negotiate treaties, to computer experts to design security systems. There are positions for accountants, engineers, architects, and secretaries. To work for the State Department, you must be a U.S. citizen at least 16 years old.

2 TEACH (Cont.)

Independent Practice

L1 DIAGRAM AND REPORT

Ask students to find a recent article on culture or diversity in business. Tell them to start by reading the first and the last paragraph of the article before reading the full article. Have them decide on the main points of the article and enter them in a chart or diagram and then give a brief oral presentation for their classmates. Encourage creativity in the presentation. **LS**

L2 CHECKLIST

Imagine that you are an employee in the human resources department of a large company. Your supervisor wants you to develop a checklist of positive ways to promote good communication between members of the company's diverse workforce. In addition, you make a list of attitudes to avoid and submit both lists. **LS**

L3 INTERVIEW AND REPORT

Choose a company that employs 25 or more people. Set up an information interview with a manager. Ask the manager to explain the diversity of his or her workplace and provide details about how that diversity benefits both the business and the workers. Ask the manager about the ways this particular workplace has encouraged diversity and what procedures are in place for handling problems that may arise. Present a report on your interview to your classmates. **LS**

264

BusinessWeek Seminar

Taking Aim at Careers

● Preparation

Determine two specific jobs needed for your business and the qualifications for those jobs.

Objective

- **Decide** on a business you're interested in starting.
- **Identify** ways to look for employees for job openings at your business.
- **Create** and write job descriptions and application forms.
- **Role-play** a job interview, with a fellow classmate as the job applicant.

Materials Needed

✓ Copies of recent news publications, such as the *Wall Street Journal* and *BusinessWeek* or Internet access
✓ Paper, pencils, pens, markers
✓ Posterboard
✓ Props for a job interview (e.g., file folders, interview attire, table or desk, and chairs)

● Procedures

1. Choose a research partner.

2. Imagine that you're business partners in a start-up. The two of you need to decide on a business. Type a one-page description of your business that includes the name, your product (good or service), location, and reason for starting this particular business.

3. You need to hire a manager and an entry-level employee for the business.

4. Research the different ways employers look for employees.

5. Using your research in No. 4, choose two or three ways to look for a manager and entry-level employee. Consider the following:
   - Describe the qualification of each position.
   - How important is it to find the right person for the job? Or how much money are you willing to spend to find an employee for each position?

6. Write up a formal job description for each.

7. In front of the class, role-play an interview for one of the two positions. Then explain to the class how you found this particular person.

Reteaching Strategy

Ask students to talk with a family member or friend who has worked with a person from a different country. Suggest students ask these questions: What did you each contribute to the job you were doing? In your opinion, how was the quality of the finished product affected? What did you learn about yourself by working with the other person? What did you have in common? What differences were there?

Give each student the choice of conducting a live interview in front of the class (by inviting his or her family member or friend to class) or writing a brief report of their interview. **ELL**, **CL**

Chart It

With your partner, re-create this chart below on a separate piece of paper. List all of the ways you discovered that employers look for employees. Then indicate which methods would work best for the workers your business needs. Lastly, share your chart with other students and, as a class, create a comprehensive chart on the board.

Types of Workers	Methods for Finding Employees		
	Executive Search Firms	Classified Ads	
Executives, VP for Engineering, VP Marketing, etc.	X		
Middle Management, Chief Engineer, Editorial Director, etc.	X		
Engineers, Marketers, Editors, etc.	X	X	
Entry Level, Administrative Assistants, Receptionists, Clerks, etc.		X	

Analyze and Conclude

After considering your research and studying the comprehensive list on the board, answer the questions below:

1. **Allocating Time.** Is there one method that reaches more potential candidates than any other? If so, what is it? If not, why not?

2. **Improving and Designing a System.** Which method(s) would you use to find an employee? Why?

3. **Responsibility.** When it's your chance to find a job, how will you go about finding one?

Becoming an Informed Citizen

Congratulations, you finished the seminar. Now it's time to reflect on the decisions you made.

Participating as a Member of a Team. Discuss the process of deciding on a business to start and the qualifications of each employee. How did you rule out the qualifications your employees shouldn't have? Describe your selection process.

Analyzing Your Future. Before you enter the job market, sit down and take a personal inventory of your skills, qualities, and qualifications. Based upon these factors, what kind of job will you pursue?

BUSINESS Online

Further Exploration

To find out more about employment resources, visit the Glencoe *Introduction to Business* Web site at **www.introbus.glencoe.com**.

Unit 5 Seminar

3 ASSESS

Enrichment

GUIDELINES. In a culturally diverse workplace how might a strong sense of humor be useful? What might be the drawbacks in the use of humor? Develop a set of guidelines for using humor in the workplace of today. Include your reasoning.

Evaluation

RUBRICS. The rubrics for evaluation of written reports, role-plays, and oral presentations are included in *Alternative Assessment Strategies.* **P**

4 CLOSE

Seminar Wrap-Up

RECALL. With all the knowledge and experience you've gained through this seminar, recall one factor about each of the following: business etiquette, corporate culture, benefits of diversity, stereotype, job qualifications, job application, and online training.

Analyze and Conclude Answers

1. Answers might vary, but many will suggest that the Internet reaches the largest number of potential employees because of the wide spectrum of people that post and look for jobs on the Internet.

2. Answers will vary. Accept those that explain how certain employees are most often found using the method(s) they cited.

3. Answers will vary. Accept those that explain how the job they want is most often recruited using the method(s) they cited.

Managing Financial and Technological Resources

Unit Objectives

After completing this unit, students will be able to achieve the following outcomes:

- Explain important aspects of financial planning, and name the responsibilities of a financial manager.
- Describe the types of budgets and financial records businesses use.
- Identify different ways technology has changed the workplace.
- Describe the role of information technology in business, and identify how businesses share information.
- Identify hardware components of a computer system, and describe software programs used by businesses.

BusinessWeek Connections

In this unit, students will read the following articles from *BusinessWeek*:

Chapter 17 "Scrutiny on the Bounty": Can BountySystems.com raise the millions of dollars in capital that it needs?

Chapter 18 "Korea Is Leaving Japan in the Digital-Age Dust": See how South Korea's investment in information technology has helped its economy.

Chapter 19 "A Powerful Shareware Rival to Mighty Microsoft": If it sounds too good to be true, perhaps it is—see what you think.

Key to Descriptive Icons

The following designations will help you decide which activities are appropriate for your students.

L1 Level 1 activities should be within the ability range of all students.

L2 Level 2 activities should be within the ability range of the average to above-average students.

L3 Level 3 activities are designed for the ability range of above-average students.

ELL Activities should be within the ability range of the English Language Learner.

LS Learning Styles designation represents activities designed to address different learning styles.

CL Cooperative learning activities are designed for small group work.

P Portfolio designation represents student products that can be placed into a best-work portfolio.

Teacher Classroom Resources*

Program Resources	Chapter 17	Chapter 18	Chapter 19
Student Activity Workbook	p. 117	p. 125	p. 133
Lesson Plans	p. 44	p. 46	p. 48
Internet Resources	p. 53	p. 55	p. 57
Reproducible Tests	p. 33	p. 35	p. 37
Teaching Transparencies	17.1, 17.2	18.1, 18.2	19.1, 19.2
Strategies and Worksheets for Teaching Transparencies	pp. 8, 50	pp. 9, 52	pp. 9, 54

* Each of these resources is available in print and on the Interactive Lesson Planner CD-ROM.

Technology Resources

- Interactive Lesson Planner CD-ROM
- PowerPoint® Presentation CD-ROM
- ExamView® Pro Test Generator CD-ROM
- Integrated Software Simulation, Teacher Manual
- Glencoe Business Video Package
- *PuzzleMaker* CD-ROM
- *Introduction to Business* Web Site
- *Virtual Business*®

  Virtual Business is a business simulation that introduces students to the principles of business by letting them start and run their own virtual business. In *Virtual Business,* students have the power to control all aspects of a retail convenience store. Students strategize business decisions using a powerful learning tool in the guise of a video game.

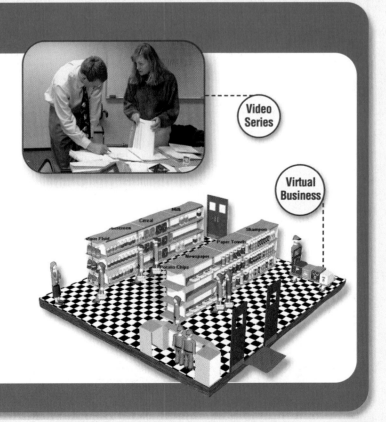

Video Series

Virtual Business

Scope and Sequence

	Academic Standards of Learning				
	LANGUAGE ARTS	**MATH**	**HISTORY**	**COMPUTER/ TECHNOLOGY**	**SOCIAL SCIENCE**
CHAPTER 17	pp. 269, 271, 272, 274, 276, 280	pp. 268, 270, 273, 275, 280, 281	pp. 274, 280	pp. 271, 277, 280, 281	pp. 269, 270, 271, 272, 274, 275, 276, 277, 281
CHAPTER 18	pp. 283, 285, 286, 287, 289, 296, 297	pp. 284, 296, 297	pp. 282, 288, 292, 296	pp. 282, 283, 284, 285, 286, 287, 288, 290, 291, 292, 296, 297	pp. 282, 284, 285, 286, 287, 288, 290, 291, 292
CHAPTER 19	pp. 299, 305, 310, 311	pp. 301, 303, 310, 311	p. 299	pp. 298, 299, 300, 301, 302, 303, 304, 305, 306, 307, 310, 311	pp. 300, 301, 302, 304, 305, 307, 310

Scope and Sequence

Themes and Concepts

Business Core	Accounting and Finance	Business Management	Computer/ Technology	Marketing	Entrepreneurship

Business Law
Interrelationships in
  Business Operations
Financial Statements
Financial Systems
Money Management
	Accounting Principles
	Cash Management
	Financial Analysis
	Payroll
	Financial Responsibility
	Budgeting
	Internal Control
	Revenue and Expense
	  Recognition
		Decision Making
		Opportunity Costs
		Finance
			Records Management
			Systems Analysis
				Profitability
				Industry Ethics
				Policies and
				  Procedures
					Collections
					Contracts
					Inventory Management

Business Ethics
Business Law
Employment
  Transitions
Technological
  Inventions
Telecommunications
	Decision Making
	Technological
	  Applications
		Consumers
		Productivity
			Communications
			Technology
				E-Commerce
				Technology
				Information
				  Technology
				Electronic Marketing
					Management
					Research and
					  Development
					Risk Management

Adapting to Change
Conflict Resolution
Time Management
Applications
Computer Operations
Technology
  Innovations
	Computer Accounting
	  Systems
	Technological
	  Applications
		Opportunity Costs
		Technological
		  Applications
			Ethics
			Information
			  Technology
			Computer
			  Applications
			Computer and
			  Communication
			  Systems
				Security
				Systems Analysis
				  and Design
				Resource Management
					Entrepreneurial
					  Potential
					Legal Considerations
					Management
					Technology

Unit Overview

Unit 6 gives information about business finances, technology and computers, and how they're utilized in business today.

CHAPTER 17 explains financial managers' responsibilities, financial planning, business budgets, and business financial records.

CHAPTER 18 describes the role of information technology in business and discusses different ways technology has changed the workplace.

CHAPTER 19 examines computer hardware and the software programs businesses use.

Introducing the Unit

You will give students three choices. Ask students to rank the choices in order. Ask students: (1) Who would you rather be: a computer technician, a software programmer, or a financial manager? (2) Would you rather live and work in business: fifty years ago, in the present day, twenty years in the future? (3) What would you like most to learn about: technological advancements, computer software used in business, financial forecasts? Have volunteers share their reasons why they chose the way they did.

Technology Resource

 GO TO **INTRODUCTION TO BUSINESS WEB SITE.** To find out more about content in Unit 6, visit the Glencoe *Introduction to Business* Web site. **www.introbus.glencoe.com**

Managing Financial and Technological Resources

Chapter 17
Managing Business Finances

Chapter 18
Technology Advancements in the Workplace

Chapter 19
Basics of Computers

You Ought to Be in Pictures

Today, flying through the air has never looked more real in the movies. Thanks to computer-generated characters, the manipulation of pixels is replacing stunt doubles and actors in movies. Digital tape costs much less than film and provides better sound and image quality; you can edit it using a desktop computer system. With the development of ever more affordable digital movie cameras, it is possible for anyone to make a movie.

● **Careful Where You Step**
The original King Kong was only 18 inches tall and made out of a metal skeleton covered with foam rubber and rabbit fur.

● **What's My Motivation?**
In the 1985 *Young Sherlock Holmes* movie, a knight steps out of a stained-glass window. This first fully computer-generated effect lasted for 30 seconds and took 6 months to complete.

● **And the Best Vactor Oscar for 2050 Goes to…**
"Vactors" or "synthespians" are digitally-generated virtual actors.

● **Hair-Raising**
In the movie *Toy Story*, Sid, the sadistic kid next door, had 15,977 computer-generated hairs.

● **The Cost of a Creation's Tools**
According to Jim Blinn, a pioneer in computer animation, "The cost of the basic tools of my trade—of making images with a computer—has gone from about $500,000 to about $2,000."

Field Trip Suggestion

Technology in Business. Arrange to visit a company that does much of its business overseas or a company that uses specialized technology. Ask a company representative to explain how high-tech communication affects its business. If you visit a company with specialized technology, also ask how the technology works. Have students take notes while on the tour. After the tour, ask students to write a one- to two-page report on interesting aspects of the use of technology. Reports should comment on how the business changed with technology. In addition to the written report, have students choose one main point they took from the visit. Ask students to form small groups to demonstrate the point in a role-play. **P**, **CL**, **LS**, **ELL**

Glencoe Poster Teaching Tip

Ask students: What is an *intranet?* (An intranet is Internet-like technology that allows a company to connect employees, but it's closed to public access.) Let students know that in Chapter 18 of this unit they'll be looking at how technology is used in the workplace. Then have the students take the quiz on the poster. Discuss the need for technology and computer skills for future careers. Poll the students and ask which software packages they know or have used. Have they seen Webcasts? Ask students how they plan to acquire or improve their technology skills. **CL**, **LS**

BUSINESS *Online*

Idea Factory

To learn more about technology's influences, visit the *Introduction to Business* Web site at **www.introbus.glencoe.com**, and click on Unit 6 Managing Financial and Technological Resources.

🕐 Out of Time?

If time doesn't permit teaching each chapter use *Virtual Business* to give students experience in making financial decisions. **CL**, **LS**, **ELL**, **P**

Portfolio Activity

Technology Skills Assessment. Have students use a word processor or spreadsheet program to chart an analysis of their technology skills. Ask students to include an assessment of their current skills, an analysis of the skills they need to acquire, a plan for acquiring needed skills, and a plan for keeping current on the innovations in technology. Throughout this course, or throughout the year, have students record their progress in needed areas. **P**, **LS**

SCANS Correlation Chart*

Foundation Skills

Basic Skills	Reading	Writing	Math	Listening	Speaking	
Thinking Skills	Creative Thinking	Decision Making	Problem Solving	Seeing Things in the Mind's Eye	Knowing How to Learn	Reasoning
Personal Qualities	Responsibility	Self-Esteem	Sociability	Self-Management	Integrity/ Honesty	

Workplace Competencies

Resources	Allocating Time	Allocating Money	Allocating Material and Facility Resources	Allocating Human Resources		
Information	Acquiring and Evaluating Information	Organizing and Maintaining Information	Interpreting and Communicating Information	Using Computers to Process Information		
Interpersonal Skills	Participating as a Member of a Team	Teaching Others	Serving Clients/ Customers	Exercising Leadership	Negotiating to Arrive at a Decision	Working With Cultural Diversity
Systems	Understanding Systems	Monitoring and Correcting Performance	Improving and Designing Systems			
Technology	Selecting Technology	Applying Technology to Task	Maintaining and Troubleshooting Technology			

*This chart's highlighted blocks indicate the chapter's content coverage in the Student Edition and the Teacher Wraparound Edition.

Resource Manager

Teaching Transparencies

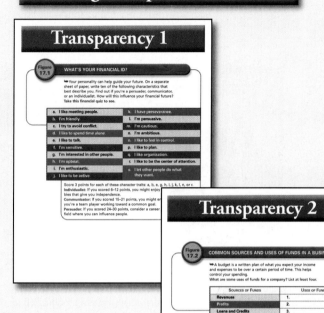

Transparency 1

WHAT'S YOUR FINANCIAL ID?

Transparency 2

COMMON SOURCES AND USES OF FUNDS IN A BUSINESS

Application and Enrichment

- Lesson Plans
- *BusinessWeek* Poster Package
- Teaching Transparencies
- Integrated Software Simulation
- Glencoe Business Video Package

Review and Reinforcement

- *PuzzleMaker*
- Internet Resources
- Student Activity Workbook
- Strat. and Work. for Teaching Transparencies

Assessment and Evaluation

- Reproducible Tests
- Alternative Assessment Strategies
- ExamView® Pro Test Generator

Technology

- *PuzzleMaker*
- ExamView® Pro Test Generator
- Glencoe Business Video Package
- PowerPoint® Presentation
- Integrated Software Simulation
- Interactive Lesson Planner
- *Virtual Business*®

KEY	Printed	Software	Videocassette	Poster
	Transparency	CD-ROM	Internet	

Visit **www.introbus.glencoe.com**, the Web site companion to *Introduction to Business.* The student's page includes:

- interactive tutor
- additional *BusinessWeek* articles and activities
- business Web links
- homework hints
- real-world application activities
- additional career path activities

Information on how to prepare your students for the high school exit exam and special projects are also included.

Use the Glencoe Web site for additional resources. All essential content is covered in the Student Edition.

1 FOCUS

Introducing the Chapter

This chapter presents aspects of managing business finances. It discusses business accounting and financial record keeping. A photo essay, "A Solid Foundation," enhances the concepts.

Connecting the Objectives

What financial aspects does a business need to handle? Ask students to tell what they know about accounting in business. What financial records does a business need to keep?

BusinessWeek
Feature Story

Story's Summary

Look closely for BountySystems Inc. in New York's rag trade district. BountySystems, a young company, hopes to raise $12 million in funding. It's already raised $8 million and has $4 million more to go. Allen Davis, BountySystems' founder, uses the fee-paying or "bounty" system to find venture capital funding. For example, Davis paid a fee to a broker who found Sentinel Capital Partners, which invested about $2 million in BountySystems. The other $6 million already raised came from other investors, including Mass Ventures in Hadley, Mass., and Prospect Street Ventures in New York.

Find the entire article at **www.introbus.glencoe.com**, or in the Teacher Resource Binder.

Chapter 17

Managing Business Finances

● Learning Objectives

After completing this chapter, you'll be able to:
1. **Explain** the three important aspects of financial planning.
2. **Name** the responsibilities of a financial manager.
3. **Identify** different types of budgets for managing business finances.
4. **Describe** the types of financial records businesses use.

● Why It's Important

Every large or small business has to have a financial plan, a budget, and financial records to manage its financial resources.

● Key Words

financial plan
asset
financial forecast
accounting
financial manager
budget
fiscal year
owner's equity
income statement
balance sheet

268

BusinessWeek Feature Story

Scrutiny on the Bounty

BountySystems.com Needs More Capital. "Arm the alarm," reads the white board that hangs inside the front door at Bounty-Systems.com. No, it's not a market warning for the Internet start-up, which creates online sites where individuals or companies offer cash rewards for help in finding anything from a new employee to an apartment in New York to a baby grand for a synagogue. The note is just a reminder to the last employee to lock up the midtown Manhattan headquarters at the end of the day. But as the young company searches for new funding, a visitor can't help but wonder whether the meaning might change.

Source: Excerpted with permission from "Scrutiny on the Bounty," *BusinessWeek Online*, April 17, 2001.

An Extension Activity

What are some major concerns a start-up company might have within its first year of business? Create a table with the pros and cons of a start-up.

The Full Story
To learn more about a company's search for funding, visit the *Introduction to Business* Web site at www.introbus.glencoe.com, and click on *BusinessWeek* Feature Story, Chapter 17.

Classroom Resources

For the Teacher
📁 Student Activity Work. TAE
📒💿 Assessment Binder
💿 PowerPoint® Presentation
💿 Interactive Lesson Planner
📁 Lesson Plans
📒💻 Internet Resources
🖱 Teaching Transparencies
💻 *Introduction to Business* Web Site

💿 Integrated Soft. Sim. TM
📘 *BusinessWeek* Poster Package
For the Student
📒 Student Activity Workbook
💿 *Virtual Business*®
💻 *Introduction to Business* Web Site
💿 Integrated Soft. Sim.
💿 *PuzzleMaker*
📒 Strategies and Worksheets for Teaching Transparencies

Bell Ringer Activity

ALLOCATING MATERIAL AND FACILITY RESOURCES. Bring to class several samples of published annual reports. Have students look at the reports and make a list of the types of financial information presented.

Preteaching Business Key Words

SEEING THINGS IN THE MIND'S EYE. First, ask students to make a diagram with three large circles labeled: Aspects of Financial Management, Accounting, and Financial Records. Second, ask students to find each key word in the chapter and note in which part of the chapter it appears. Third, ask students to write each key word in the appropriate circle, and then write their definitions. **LS**

An Extension Activity

COLLECT. Make one poster with the heading "Pros," and a second with the heading, "Cons." Ask students to share their lists of pros and cons. Have two volunteers collect together the pros and cons by writing them on the posters. Display the posters and add to the pros and cons as the class goes through this chapter. **CL**, **LS**

Making Connections

The World of Business. Adine and Donzel Garcia are fun-loving people and plan to open an amusement park. They're considering buying Fun-for-All. About eight months ago it added a room for birthday parties. The Garcias have been given Fun-for-All's financial statements for the past 12 months. What questions should they be asking the current owner? What should they be paying attention to on the financial statements? (Questions might include: Has income increased, remained the same, or decreased? Have liabilities increased? Has the company earned a net income? How has catering to birthdays affected revenue? Have expenses increased or decreased?)

2 TEACH

Business Connection

PURCHASING ASSETS. Leslie Johnson received a $500 loan from the Woman's Economic Development Corporation (WEDCO) in St. Paul, Minn., to purchase roses to sell on Valentine's Day. The WEDCO loan had to be repaid within five days. Johnson made $2,500 selling the roses and paid off the loan. Johnson had an initial financial plan to use a series of such loans to earn and save enough money to start her own floral business. Johnson now has three locations and her business grosses $740,000 a year.

Develop Concepts

PLAN. Give this scenario to students: your school is going to form a company making decorated T-shirts. What items will be needed, and about how much will be the total cost? How much will student workers be paid and what will be the total cost of payroll each week? How will the start-up money be raised? (Funding.) How much will T-shirts sell for, what are the expected sales, and what is the expected income? Will the company make a profit? Looking ahead over the next six months, how will the company manage its financial needs, expenses, and goals?

Figure 17.1 Caption Answer

Answers will vary.

Aspects of Financial Management

Suppose that some day you want to run your own small business, such as an Italian restaurant. How much money will you need to open it? Are your expenses more than your income? Will you need to borrow money to expand your operation? To run a business successfully you need to manage its finances. This involves putting together a financial plan, budgeting, and keeping track of your income and expenses.

A new business, whether large or small, needs financing. Its owner must manage the company's finances well to avoid failure. Software packages for business plans can help. They guide a person in planning a new business and tracking its finances. Take the personal inventory in Figure 17.1 to assess your career's financial future.

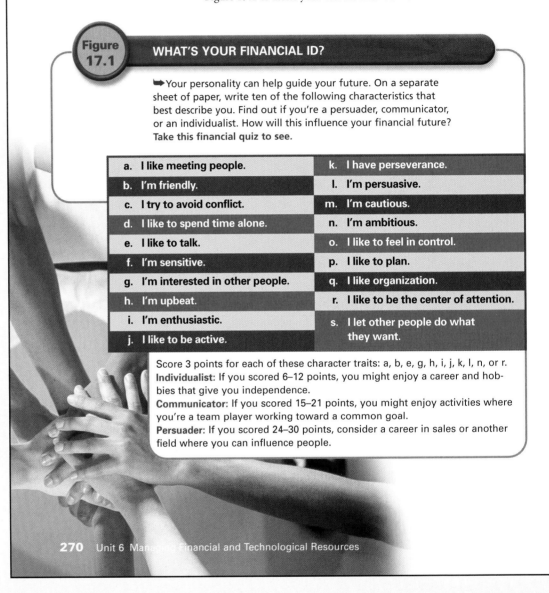

Figure 17.1

WHAT'S YOUR FINANCIAL ID?

➡ Your personality can help guide your future. On a separate sheet of paper, write ten of the following characteristics that best describe you. Find out if you're a persuader, communicator, or an individualist. How will this influence your financial future? **Take this financial quiz to see.**

a.	I like meeting people.	k.	I have perseverance.
b.	I'm friendly.	l.	I'm persuasive.
c.	I try to avoid conflict.	m.	I'm cautious.
d.	I like to spend time alone.	n.	I'm ambitious.
e.	I like to talk.	o.	I like to feel in control.
f.	I'm sensitive.	p.	I like to plan.
g.	I'm interested in other people.	q.	I like organization.
h.	I'm upbeat.	r.	I like to be the center of attention.
i.	I'm enthusiastic.	s.	I let other people do what they want.
j.	I like to be active.		

Score 3 points for each of these character traits: a, b, e, g, h, i, j, k, l, n, or r.
Individualist: If you scored 6–12 points, you might enjoy a career and hobbies that give you independence.
Communicator: If you scored 15–21 points, you might enjoy activities where you're a team player working toward a common goal.
Persuader: If you scored 24–30 points, consider a career in sales or another field where you can influence people.

Cooperative Learning

Business Financial Planning. Have students work in groups of four to plan, secure, and conduct an in-class interview of a small business owner who started his or her business. Encourage students to request the business owner bring copies of his or her financial plan. Ask students to be ready with questions about assets needed, how funding was used to start the business, and changes the business owner foresees will influence his or her business in the future. **CL**, LS

Managing a business requires accurate, up-to-date financial information. Managers use that information to evaluate their company's financial health and to plan for the future. A business may need additional money to grow or expand. It can seek a loan or additional money from investors. Lenders or investors must have accurate financial information to decide whether or not to risk their money with the company.

Financial Planning

The first step in financial management is drawing up a financial plan. A **financial plan** is an outline of your expenses, needs, and goals, and how you expect to meet them. It works like a game plan, a road map, or an outline for a paper. The plan helps you keep your business on track and determine what its financial state is at any given time.

You need a financial plan to tell you how much money you'll need to start out and to operate your restaurant once it's running. This includes all expenses from buying equipment to paying for deliveries. You also need the financial plan to explain how you're going to cover those expenses. Do you plan on borrowing money, using your savings, or making enough profits? A financial plan must include a way of keeping records on income and expenses. The Small Business Administration can help you come up with a financial plan.

An entrepreneur starting a new business must also plan for finances. Your start-up needs how much money? A business needs to make how much money in order to cover its costs? Until it reaches that point, a new business relies on savings or cash reserves to meet its expenses. In order to keep the business running, how much money does it need for expansion? The entrepreneur must find adequate funding. Otherwise, the business risks closure because of a lack of money.

Assets Needed

First, you need to identify your assets. Any property or item of value that your business owns is an **asset**. Cash, equipment, buildings, supplies, inventory, and land are all examples of assets. Researching your options is important before buying any major asset. Analyze and compare the price of each different item. Once your analysis is complete you'll want to purchase the item. You want to know you're getting the best item for your money. Take this careful approach with each asset.

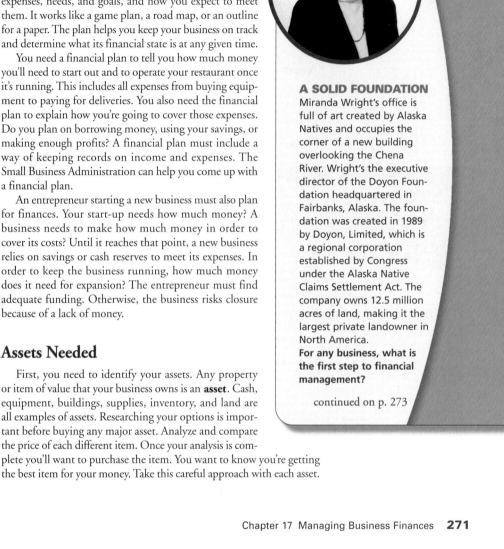

Real-World Application

part 1 of 4

A SOLID FOUNDATION
Miranda Wright's office is full of art created by Alaska Natives and occupies the corner of a new building overlooking the Chena River. Wright's the executive director of the Doyon Foundation headquartered in Fairbanks, Alaska. The foundation was created in 1989 by Doyon, Limited, which is a regional corporation established by Congress under the Alaska Native Claims Settlement Act. The company owns 12.5 million acres of land, making it the largest private landowner in North America.
For any business, what is the first step to financial management?

continued on p. 273

Chapter 17

Technology Resource

GO TO

POWERPOINT.
The *Introduction to Business* PowerPoint® CD-ROM provides visual lecture aids for this chapter.

Independent Practice

INVESTIGATE. Point out to students that in their lifetime they will make a large number of financing decisions to purchase things that will last, such as appliances, cars, and apartments or houses. To manage these purchases they will budget, save, and possibly take out loans. Have them imagine they are business owners who must make decisions about the business finances. Have students generate an outline of the business financial plan including the three main steps of financial planning. (1. Identify your assets. 2. Purchase assets. 3. Address accounting requirements.) **LS**

Meeting Individual Needs

Students With Hearing Impairments. Students with hearing impairments can and do participate in a wide range of classroom activities. To encourage their maximum participation, look toward these students when you speak. Do this even if the student talks with the assistance of an interpreter. Not only is this more courteous, but it also allows the student with hearing impairments the option of viewing you and your lip movements directly. If class materials involve technical terminology, supply a list of these words in advance to the student and his or her interpreter. Unfamiliar words can be difficult to lip-read or sign without prior exposure.

Thinking Critically

BUSINESS ADVISING. You're a columnist for *Building Bricks*, a national construction magazine. A reader writes to you saying, "I started my roofing business six months ago. I've had plenty of customers, some with small repair jobs and some with big jobs to replace the whole roof, but I'm losing money. What should I do?" Write your answer to publish in *Building Bricks* telling the reader about financial planning. It will be concise and to the point—your column only has space for three paragraphs. **LS**

You Make the Call

Caption Answer

1. Employs only a few people and covers a limited area.
2. A professional accountant is certified and insured.
3. A professional accountant is more likely to handle the money honestly.
4. The board of directors will vote on the decision to hire a professional accountant.

Purchasing Assets

Purchasing your assets is the second step in your financial planning. Before you purchase your items, you'll want to determine the method you'll use to purchase the items. You may want to answer a few of the following important questions: Can you purchase the items with available cash? Do you have to borrow money—either through using credit or a loan—for part or all of the purchases?

Before you can answer these questions, once again you'll need to carefully analyze your financial situation. Investigate all sources of credit and loan. This step is important in effective financial management.

When you're a business owner you might want to purchase items that are beyond your means. You may not have enough cash and you might not be able to afford everything you want. It's important, therefore, to look carefully at the needs of your business. If you're working with limited resources, you need to make decisions based upon your needs and how you'll pay for them, whether with cash or credit.

Accounting Requirements

Recognizing the financial records you need to keep is the third important step in financial planning. A **financial forecast** is an estimate of what business conditions will be like in the future. If you're just starting a restaurant business you might not make a profit for a year. To meet

You Make the Call

The Qualified Volunteer

Your daughter plays softball with a local club and you're a member of the club's board of directors. Like you, the treasurer is a volunteer parent. The club has grown recently and now operates with professional coaches and a $100,000 annual budget. You feel it's time to hire an accountant, but the treasurer insists he can do the job just fine. Several club parents have questioned whether a volunteer who isn't an accountant should be handling that much money.

Making an Ethical Decision

1. In what ways is this nonprofit really more like a business than a club?
2. What can an accountant provide that a parent volunteer cannot?
3. In what ways would ethical questions arise under the current system? How would hiring an accountant help address those ethical issues?
4. How would you tactfully convince the treasurer to step down from his role in handling the budget? Are there other roles that a volunteer treasurer could still fulfill within the club?

LANGUAGE ARTS — Curriculum Connection

Communication. Financial professionals are often called upon to state complex financial issues in a simple and straightforward manner. At times they are asked to produce a "one-page memo" describing the strategy, financial health, and future outlook of a company. Suggest that pairs of students choose a multi-page business article from a recent periodical. Have the team condense the article into a one-page memo of 250 words or less. Then encourage the team to condense the article further, producing a summary of 100 words or less. Have teams exchange summaries and discuss whether the summary conveys the main idea of the article. **LS, CL**

any unexpected expenses that might come up, you need to keep cash or savings on hand.

A forecast also includes planning for changes in the economy that might affect your business. For example, if the cost of energy is going up, you can expect to pay more to operate your equipment. To play it safe, it's best to be conservative and estimate your income on the low side and your expenses on the high side.

With current up-to-date financial information, you can make informed, reasonable decisions. This information is used for analyzing financial statements, controlling cash, and paying debts. Remember that thousands of small businesses close each year because of poor financial management.

 Fast Review _____

1. Why is financial planning important to a business?
2. What are examples of assets?
3. Describe the three steps of a financial plan.

Accounting

Accounting is the systematic process of recording and reporting the financial position of a business. Accounting records and reports help a business operate efficiently. To have a profitable business you need to track how much the business earns and spends. Figure 17.2 on page 274 outlines the common sources and uses of funds in a business.

The person in charge of a business's financial planning, funding, and accounting is the **financial manager**. As a financial manager you have three important responsibilities. First, you have to manage the funds and make sure the business is meeting its financial obligations. You need to pay your cook and waiters a weekly salary. *Cash reserves*, or savings, have to be kept on hand to pay for operating expenses like deliveries. If your business borrowed money you need to make sure the loans are paid on time.

Second, you have to find sources for additional funds. For your business to grow you'll need more money. If the restaurant makes a profit, the money can be used to buy new equipment or hire more workers. If the restaurant isn't making money you might have to borrow from investors or from a bank.

The third responsibility is planning long-range financial goals. Where do you want your business to be in five years? Do you want to open a chain of restaurants throughout the country? Do you want to market your own line of frozen dinners in grocery stores? A financial plan outlines the information you need to make decisions for the future.

A SOLID FOUNDATION
The Doyon Foundation promotes the health, education, social, and economic development and well being of Alaska Natives. Wright, who is Athabaskan, guides the foundation's blanket program. **Name some long-range goals the Foundation might have.**

continued on p. 275

Chapter 17

Real-World Application Caption Answer

A SOLID FOUNDATION: PART 2 OF 4
Make sure the financial goals are met and find additional funds.

Fast Review Answers ✔

1. To figure out how much a business needs to get started and to keep it going.
2. Cash, equipment, buildings, supplies, and land.
3. Putting together a financial plan, budgeting, and tracking income and expenses.

Chapter 17 Managing Business Finances **273**

Great Ideas From the Classroom of...

Edward J. Murphy
John Jay High School
Hopewell Junction, N.Y.

Financial Statements. Place the following items in a paper bag: toy money, invoices, magazine photos of trucks, machines, supplies, furniture, and equipment.

Ask the students to prepare a simple balance sheet for the company using the materials from the bag. Arrange the assets on one side and the liabilities on the other side to find out what the business is worth. This activity puts more meaning to the term balance sheet, since an introductory course does not go into great depth, like an accounting course does.

Business Connection

OPERATING BUDGET. Inter-Digital Communications (IDC) has a strong balance sheet and new CEO, Mark Gercenstein, is optimistic. IDC is developing third-generation (3G) wireless technology, and revenues are meeting projections for this year. IDC has already set an operating budget for the year and Gercenstein intends to keep operations costs at or below budget. Over the next few years, with careful planning, IDC forecasts revenues in the hundreds of millions from sales of its 3G technology.

Develop Concepts

SPECIFY. Ask students to research and provide one example for each of the following: start-up budget, cash budget, and operating budget.

Discussion Starter

IDENTIFYING. Ask students to identify some of their own belongings (assets) and estimate their total dollar value. How are business assets similar? How are they different? (Answers will vary. Differences will include a business' possible need for buildings and land.)

Figure 17.2 Caption Answer

Inventories, equipment, rent, taxation and insurance, wages and salaries, utilities, and advertising.

274

Budgeting

A **budget** is a written plan of what you expect your income and expenses to be over a certain period of time. It helps you predict how much money you'll need and helps control your spending. You need to compare it periodically to your actual income and expenses to avoid financial problems. There are three main types of budgets: start-up budget, cash budget, and operating budget. Let's take a closer look at each.

Start-up Budget. A start-up budget is a plan for your income and expenses from the time you start the business to when it makes a profit. To start a restaurant you need to buy equipment and supplies, rent property, and hire workers. To pay for everything you might use your savings or borrow money from a bank. If you need to borrow money, the lender will want to see a detailed start-up budget. Most new businesses don't make a profit during the first year so you also need to plan for covering your own personal expenses.

Cash Budget. A cash budget is a plan for the actual money you expect to spend and earn on a daily, weekly, or monthly basis. This includes paying waiters' salaries, utility bills, and rent regularly. A cash budget tells you how much money is needed on hand at all times for day-to-day transactions.

Operating Budget. An operating budget is a plan for how much you expect to spend and earn over a given period of time, usually six

Figure 17.2 COMMON SOURCES AND USES OF FUNDS IN A BUSINESS

➡ A budget is a written plan of what you expect your income and expenses to be over a certain period of time. This helps control your spending.
What are some uses of funds for a company? List at least four.

SOURCES OF FUNDS	USES OF FUNDS
Revenues	1.
Profits	2.
Loans and Credits	3.
Owner's Equity	4.

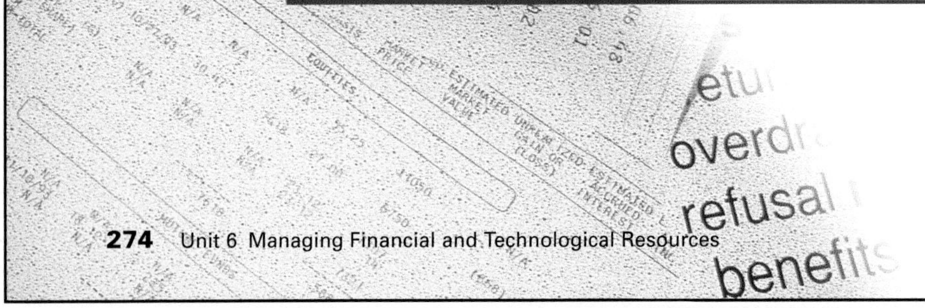

Global Perspective

International Accounting Standards. U.S. businesses entering joint ventures with businesses in the former Soviet Union have had to deal with vast differences between U.S. and Russian accounting standards. As the global market grows, the need for international accounting standards increases. The International Accounting Standards Committee has been charged with the task of developing accounting standards that can be used by businesses having operations in several countries and in various types of economies. Ask students to speculate on why international accounting standards are necessary.

274

months or a year. It covers the total amount of regular transactions as well as other operating expenses such as advertising, taxes, and new equipment. The operating budget tells you how much money you need to keep your business running over the long term. It gives a picture of the finances and becomes a "road map" for the company.

 Fast Review _____

1. What are some of the expenses a start-up budget includes?
2. What is the main difference between a cash budget and an operating budget?

Financial Records

To keep track of how your restaurant is actually doing financially, you need to keep accurate written accounts. Your accounts tell you how well you're sticking to your budget and what your profits or losses are during a certain period. As a result, you might decide to cut costs, borrow more money, or expand your business. Your investors and creditors also want to see your financial accounts now and then.

An accounting period may be one month, three months, or one year. If the reports are for one year, the accounting period is a **fiscal year**. At the close of a fiscal year, you have to prepare reports to show your business's finances. Then you have to summarize the year with an income statement and a balance sheet. There are many business software programs you can buy that not only set up budgets, but also keep financial records.

Financial Statements

Accounting records keep track of money coming into and going out of your business. They provide a system for recording, classifying, summarizing, and interpreting financial data. The records show all daily transactions. Every sale, payment, or purchase is a transaction. Accounting records sort out the transactions to show what your business owns, how much money it takes in, and how much it owes to others.

Any amount your business owes is a *liability*. When you buy anything from a supplier, such as food products, you usually buy it on credit. The amount you owe to the supplier is a liability, or a claim against your restaurant's assets. Any debts you owe banks or investors are also claims against the assets of your restaurant. Their claim is called the **owner's equity**. Owner's equity is equal to the total assets of the business minus

part 3 of 4

A SOLID FOUNDATION
Each year the Doyon Foundation asks Alaska Native artists to submit work that can be adapted for use as a blanket design. Profits from sale of the blankets go to the Doyon Foundation's college-bound student scholarship fund. At the beginning of the year, the Foundation predicts how much money it will need. **What helps it control its spending?**

continued on p. 277

Real-World Application
Caption Answer

A SOLID FOUNDATION: PART 3 OF 4
A set budget.

Individualized Practice

RESEARCH. Investors are sometimes called "angels." Ask students to research the cost of financing a theater production. Suggest that they report their findings separately for musical and nonmusical productions.

L1 Have pairs of students work together and share their findings with the class.

L2 Tell pairs of students to work together and make two graphs to represent the data for musical and nonmusical productions.

L3 Group students to pool their research, graph the data, and present a summary.

Fast Review Answers

1. Buying equipment and supplies, renting property, hiring workers, borrowing money.
2. Cash budget—plan for the actual money you expect to spend. Operating budget— total amount of money you expect to spend in a six-month period or a year.

Reteaching

BUSINESS FINANCIAL MANAGEMENT. To reteach the concept of business financial management, ask students to tell the three important responsibilities of a financial manager. (Manage funds, find additional funds, and planning financial goals.)

Enrichment Strategy

WRITE. Ask students to write a paragraph starting with the sentence, "Financial planning is important to companies because...." **LS**

Working Lifestyle

Caption Answer

Students' hobbies and interests will vary. Most people have many talents. It's important to point out to students that a career or job is not likely to utilize *all* of their talents. Most people use some talents in their work and employ other talents in hobbies and interests that they pursue outside of their work. **LS**

---

the total liabilities. The relationship between a company's assets and the claims against those assets is expressed by an equation:

$$\text{Assets} = \text{Liabilities} + \text{Owner's Equity}$$

Assets should always appear on the left side of the equation. Liabilities and owner's equity always appear on the right side of the equation. The two sides of the accounting equation must always balance. This is only logical since the value of the assets must equal the claims (of owners

Working Lifestyle

What are you doing at 10 A.M.?

A Patient Account

Accounting is like fly-fishing for Jon Louvar. You're working alone in the middle of a swiftly moving current. Sometimes you slip and you end up downstream. Fortunately, if you learn the lesson and remember the mistake, you're more likely to catch the big prize next time. Both accounting and fly-fishing require patience, strategy, and risk.

Louvar uses analytical strategy to help run Trompeter Electronics, Inc., in Westlake Village, Calif. As an accounting supervisor, he uses accounting (the language of business) to track annual sales over $100 million and an inventory of more than 8,000 parts. He analyzes the company's performance and then helps its executives set and achieve corporate goals.

During a ten o'clock meeting this morning, Louvar will meet with Trompeter's controller and chief financial officer to help set the company's monthly goals. "Our overall goal is to increase value," he says, "and we try to accomplish this by identifying technological trends."

Louvar asks questions like a journalist and analyzes the answers like a mathematician. For example, did profit margins change due to an increase in energy or suppliers' costs? The engineers came up with a perfect design, but is the company manufacturing it efficiently and economically?

"You've got to be willing to attack a problem from a lot of different angles and analyze things through comparison. When you're able to understand the whole system and can explain how it all fits together—that's very satisfying," he says as he finishes his mid-morning cup of coffee.

Salary

A typical accounting supervisor earns a median base salary of $76,948, with a range between $64,494 and $91,617.

Outlook for This Career

Employment of accountants and auditors will grow faster than average.

Connecting Careers Activity

Examine your hobbies and interests. What occupations could you pursue that require you to utilize your talents?

CAREER PATH   *Business & Administration*

How to Use a Portfolio Activity

The portfolio projects are designed to lead students to develop a collection of their best work to submit to you for assessment. You and each of your students should decide which projects to include in their business portfolio. Refer students to the specific rubric(s) from the *Alternative Assessment Strategies.* These rubrics will alert students to the criteria you'll use to assess their projects. **P**

and others) against those assets. Every business transaction that takes place in the company affects this basic accounting equation.

Income Statement. The **income statement** is a report of *net income* or *net loss* over an accounting period. If your restaurant's total revenue, or earnings, is greater than its total expenses, it has a net income. If its expenses are greater than its revenue, then it has a net loss. As the owner of the restaurant, you must be sure that the revenue is enough to cover expenses. The income statement, however, isn't a complete picture of the financial health of your restaurant. A balance sheet provides more information.

Balance Sheet. A **balance sheet** is a report of the financial state of your business on a certain date. It includes a report of assets, liabilities, and the owner's equity. The left side of the sheet lists all your assets and the right side lists all your liabilities and equity. When added up, the two sides must be equal, or balanced. A balance sheet is like a photograph of your business's finances at a specific moment.

Business managers use the information in financial statements for decision making. They're responsible for decisions about budgets, ways to cut costs, and tax planning. Stockholders, employees, banks, and investment companies want to know about the financial condition of the business, too. They can compare the most recent statements with earlier statements and evaluate the business.

Whether a business is large or small, one person is usually responsible for financial management. In a small business, the owner may be responsible. Accounting managers have three important financial responsibilities: manage company funds, find sources for additional funds, and determine long-range goals for the company.

The owner or managers must manage the funds and be sure the company meets its financial obligations. Are payments made on time? Does the company have enough money to pay all its operating expenses? Wages and salaries must be paid on time. Cash reserves must be on hand for operating expenses. As a company grows, where will it find additional funds? The owner or managers must find those sources. If the company is profitable, it might use them for expansion. If it must borrow money, the owner or managers are responsible for repaying the loans on time.

 Fast Review _____

1. What's the purpose of financial records?
2. Explain the difference between total assets and total liabilities.

A SOLID FOUNDATION
The blanket project depicts some elements of the three traditional Athabaskan clans: Water, Copper, and Caribou. The Doyon Foundation has already raised $40,000 to support students. **What does the Doyon Foundation use to track the money coming in and going out?**

Meeting Individual Needs

Students With Speech Impairments. Students with speech impairments often do not feel comfortable participating in exercises devoted to interpersonal skills because the physical difficulties they experience can make the exercises uncomfortable for them. Even so, these students can benefit from watching others and participating at a level they select as comfortable.

Enforcing classroom rules regarding non-judgmental behavior and never allowing ridicule of any sort in the classroom can go a long way to encourage participation from all students. Another way to give students with speech impairments an outlet is to allow students to submit written comments and questions about material covered in any exercise that they find challenging.

4 CLOSE

Chapter Wrap-Up

Ask students to refer to the three-circles diagram they made in the "Preteaching Business Key Words" activity and check their understanding of the chapter's key terms.

Using Business Key Words

1. owner's equity
2. financial forecast
3. accounting
4. balance sheet
5. financial plan
6. asset
7. fiscal year
8. income statement
9. financial manager
10. budget

Review What You Learned

11. They evaluate their company's financial health and plan for the future.
12. Predicts how much cash will be needed and spending power.
13. A detailed plan for income and expenses until the business becomes profitable. A cash budget plans for receivables that will be paid out over time.
14. They keep track of money coming in and going out.
15. A balance sheet.
16. The owner.

Summary

1. A financial plan outlines a business's expenses, needs, goals, and how to meet them. Financial planning includes figuring out the assets that are needed, purchasing assets, and being knowledgeable of accounting requirements.

2. A financial manager is responsible for managing a business's funds, finding resources for additional funds, and planning long-range financial goals.

3. The three main types of budgets are start-up budgets, cash budgets, and operating budgets.

4. Businesses keep track of their financial records by using financial statements like income statements and balance sheets.

Using Business Key Words

Keeping accurate financial records is crucial to running a successful business. See how many of the following financial terms you know by filling in the blank with the word that best completes the sentence.

- **financial plan**
- **owner's equity**
- **financial manager**
- **financial forecast**
- **fiscal year**
- **asset**
- **income statement**
- **budget**
- **accounting**
- **balance sheet**

1. _____ is equal to the total assets of the business minus the total liabilities.
2. An estimate of the future business climate for the company is called a(n) _____.
3. The systematic process of recording and reporting the financial position of a business is called _____.
4. A report of the financial state of a company on a certain date is called the _____.
5. The _____ charts incoming and outgoing funds and outlines uses of the funds.
6. Cash, items to sell, equipment, buildings, and land are each an example of a(n) _____.
7. An accounting period for a company is a(n) _____.
8. A report of the net income or loss over an accounting period is the _____.
9. The person in charge of a business's financial planning, funding, and accounting is called a(n) _____.
10. A written plan of what you expect your income and expenses to be over a certain period of time is called a(n) _____.

Quick Quiz

1. What information do you need to provide in a financial plan? (Assets, start-up costs, expected business income, and expected business expenses.)
2. What is a fiscal year? (A one-year accounting period that may not start in January.)
3. What two financial statements give an overview of a company's financial health? (Income statement and balance sheet.)

Review What You Learned

11. What do managers do with the financial information they receive about their businesses?
12. Why is good management of finances critical for a new business?
13. What is a start-up budget? How is it different from a cash budget?
14. What are the purposes of accounting records?
15. Which report furnishes more information—the income statement or the balance sheet? Explain.
16. In a small business, who's usually responsible for the financial management?

Understanding Business Concepts

17. How do banks and other financial institutions use the financial information about a business?
18. What kind of information is included in a forecast?
19. Explain how an operating budget is a "road map" for the company.
20. How are liabilities created?
21. Explain why the income statement is an incomplete picture of the financial health of a company.
22. Why is a financial forecast important to a company?
23. Name the responsibilities of a financial manager. Briefly explain how each responsibility impacts the business.
24. If you tracked your own cash budget, how much do you expect to spend and earn on a weekly basis?
25. Why is it important that both sides of the equation must balance?

Critical Thinking

26. Do you think a business could operate without financial management? Why or why not?
27. What skills, knowledge, and interests do you have that would make you a successful finance or accounting employee?
28. What might happen to a business that only analyzes its finances twice a year?
29. What might happen if a company doesn't have enough cash reserves?

Viewing and Representing

Examining the Image. Team up with a partner. What details do you see in this photograph? What people and objects are shown? Discuss whether or not you have performed this task yet. If not, what do you need to get started?

Chapter 17 Managing Business Finances   **279**

4 CLOSE (Cont.)

Building Academic Skills

HISTORY. Students may use the library, accounting textbooks, and the Internet as resources for their research. Allow the students to choose the way they would like to present their findings. Rubrics: Oral presentation, note taking, essay, poster.

LANGUAGE ARTS. Students can research software at a computer store, in computer or business magazines, and on the Internet. If necessary, remind students about the proper format for a business memo. Rubric: Memo.

MATH. Make sure all students participate in the group project. Students can locate annual reports in the public library or on the Internet. They can also write to companies and request annual reports. Rubrics: Note taking, essay.

COMPUTER/TECHNOLOGY. If students haven't had enough experience to use a spreadsheet program, allow them to help each other. Rubric: Spreadsheet.

Linking School to Home

Encourage students to use a spreadsheet program for this activity. Allow the students to choose the way they would like to present their personal financial information. Since the information could be sensitive, do not require students to share with the class if they don't want to. Rubrics: Spreadsheet, charts/tables, essay.

Linking School to Work

Answers will vary depending on whom the students interview. Rubric: Essay.

280

Building Academic Skills

 History of Accounting

The accounting system provides a common language for all businesses to speak. Research the history of accounting and answer the following questions:

- Where and when did accounting get its start?
- What was the impact of the Industrial Revolution on the system of accounting?
- How did the advent of computers change the accounting process?

 Creating a Spreadsheet

Select a business you would like to open. Using a spreadsheet program, create a 12-month budget for the business. Estimate all the income and expenses you'll have for the first year. Then, choose a partner in your class and review each other's budgets. Offer suggestions and make any necessary corrections.

 Evaluating Financial Conditions

Work in teams to find and review the annual reports for three different companies. In each report, find the following:

- The value of the corporation's assets
- The value of its liabilities
- The value of the owner's equity
- Add the liabilities and the owner's equity. Do they equal the assets?

Evaluate the financial condition of each company. Choose the company you think is in the best financial condition. Write a group report explaining your decision.

 Writing a Memo

Research two or three different financial software programs that a business might use. Compare the features, costs, and the type of computer needed to run the software. Then, write an imaginary memo recommending one of the programs. Be sure to justify your recommendation.

Linking School to Home

Creating a Budget. Managing personal finances is very similar to managing business finances. First, create a personal financial statement and include your assets and liabilities. Second, create a budget for the next six months showing all your income and expenses. Third, set some financial goals for your future.

Linking School to Work

Interviewing a Financial Manager. In groups of three or four, interview a business financial manager or accountant. Ask about:

- The long-range business plans for the company.
- How financial forecasting is used.
- The software used for the financial management of the company.
- The most common financial mistakes businesses make.

Write up the interview as a group.

E-Homework

Applying Technology

Researching Requirements. Use the Internet to research the education and certification requirements for the following careers:
- Bookkeeper
- Accountant
- Certified Public Accountant
- Financial Manager
- Controller

Creditable Web Sites. Create a list of ten Web sites that a financial manager might find valuable.

Connecting Academics

Math. Tran, an entrepreneur, wants to earn $42,000 in profits. His research shows that the average net profit for his type of business is 15 percent. To bring in $42,000 in profits the business will need annual sales of $280,000. Tran used the following formula:

Annual Income Desired ÷
Percentage of Average Annual Net Profit =
Total Yearly Sales Volume
($42,000 ÷ 0.15 = $280,000)

Find the total yearly sales volume for the following examples:

Annual Income	Percentage of Average Annual Net Profit
$30,000	0.08
$55,000	0.20

Computer/Technology. Working in groups of four, choose an extracurricular activity (e.g., the football team, band, debate team, theatre, etc.). Select an appropriate computer program and enter the activity's anticipated expenses and income for the entire school year. You'll maintain records of the income and expenses on a weekly basis, perform calculations, and provide reports.

BusinessWeek — Analyzing the Feature Story

You read the first part of "Scrutiny on the Bounty" at the beginning of this chapter. Below are a few questions for you to answer about Bounty-Systems's search for funding. You'll find the answers to these questions when you're reading the entire article. First, here are the questions:

30. What does BountySystems's CEO Lon Otremba say about the search for funding?

31. How did Allen Davis find venture-capital funding, and what are the names of the three main companies that invested in BountySystems.com?

CREATIVE JOURNAL ACTIVITY

Break into small groups and create a start-up budget for a new company. Consider the different expenses you might incur including rent, utilities, salaries, and office expenses. How much income will you need to meet expenses?

BUSINESS Online
The Full Story
To learn more about BountySystems's search for funding, visit the *Introduction to Business* Web site at **www.introbus.glencoe.com**, and click on *BusinessWeek* Feature Story, Chapter 17.

E-Homework

RESEARCHING REQUIREMENTS. The career center in your school might be a good resource for this activity. Allow students to choose the way they would like to present their findings. Rubrics: Chart/tables, essay, poster, oral presentation.

CREDITABLE WEB SITES. Students' answers will vary. Rubric: List.

Connecting Academics

MATH. $30,000 ÷ 0.08 = $375,000. Total yearly sales volume needed is $375,000. $55,000 ÷ 0.20 = $275,000. Total yearly sales volume needed is $275,000.

COMPUTER/TECHNOLOGY. Liaise with the coach or leader of the extracurricular activity to set up this cross-curricular activity. This is an excellent opportunity for business students to serve as a resource to the school. An appropriate software might be a spreadsheet or database program.

BusinessWeek — Analyzing the Feature Story

30. Otremba says the search for funding is tough.

31. Davis paid a fee to a broker to help find venture-capital funding. The three main investment companies are Sentinel Capital Partners in New York, Prospect Street Ventures in New York and Mass Ventures in Hadley, Mass.

Creative Journal Activity

After groups have completed their budgets, ask students what financial changes they think there will be in the community in the next six months. (What will be the cost of energy/gasoline? Is there a big company closing/opening? Are we coming into a good season for this area?) **CL**, **P**, LS

SCANS Correlation Chart*

Foundation Skills

Basic Skills	Reading	Writing	Math	Listening	Speaking	
Thinking Skills	Creative Thinking	Decision Making	Problem Solving	Seeing Things in the Mind's Eye	Knowing How to Learn	Reasoning
Personal Qualities	Responsibility	Self-Esteem	Sociability	Self-Management	Integrity/ Honesty	

Workplace Competencies

Resources	Allocating Time	Allocating Money	Allocating Material and Facility Resources	Allocating Human Resources		
Information	Acquiring and Evaluating Information	Organizing and Maintaining Information	Interpreting and Communicating Information	Using Computers to Process Information		
Interpersonal Skills	Participating as a Member of a Team	Teaching Others	Serving Clients/ Customers	Exercising Leadership	Negotiating to Arrive at a Decision	Working With Cultural Diversity
Systems	Understanding Systems	Monitoring and Correcting Performance	Improving and Designing Systems			
Technology	Selecting Technology	Applying Technology to Task	Maintaining and Troubleshooting Technology			

*This chart's highlighted blocks indicate the chapter's content coverage in the Student Edition and the Teacher Wraparound Edition.

Resource Manager

Teaching Transparencies

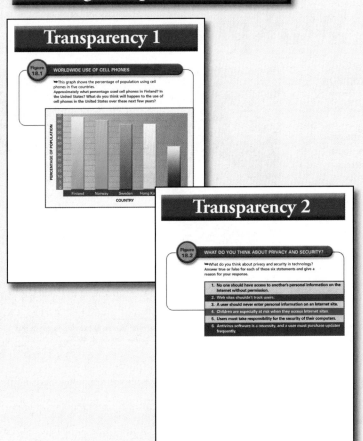

Transparency 1

Figure 18.1 WORLDWIDE USE OF CELL PHONES

➡This graph shows the percentage of population using cell phones in five countries. Approximately what percentage used cell phones in Finland? In the United States? What do you think will happen to the use of cell phones in the United States over these next few years?

PERCENTAGE OF POPULATION

Finland Norway Sweden Hong Ko...

COUNTRY

Transparency 2

Figure 18.2 WHAT DO YOU THINK ABOUT PRIVACY AND SECURITY?

➡What do you think about privacy and security in technology? Answer true or false for each of these six statements and give a reason for your response.

1. No one should have access to another's personal information on the Internet without permission.
2. Web sites shouldn't track users.
3. A user should never enter personal information on an Internet site.
4. Children are especially at risk when they access Internet sites.
5. Users must take responsibility for the security of their computers.
6. Antivirus software is a necessity, and a user must purchase updates frequently.

Application and Enrichment

- Lesson Plans
- *BusinessWeek* Poster Package
- Teaching Transparencies
- Integrated Software Simulation
- Glencoe Business Video Package

Review and Reinforcement

- *PuzzleMaker*
- Internet Resources
- Student Activity Workbook
- Strat. and Work. for Teaching Transparencies

Assessment and Evaluation

- Reproducible Tests
- Alternative Assessment Strategies
- ExamView® Pro Test Generator

Technology

- *PuzzleMaker*
- ExamView® Pro Test Generator
- Glencoe Business Video Package
- PowerPoint® Presentation
- Integrated Software Simulation
- Interactive Lesson Planner
- *Virtual Business*®

KEY	🖊 Printed	💾 Software	📼 Videocassette	📕 Poster
	🕹 Transparency	💿 CD-ROM	🖥 Internet	

BUSINESS Online

Visit www.introbus.glencoe.com, the Web site companion to *Introduction to Business*. The student's page includes:

- interactive tutor
- additional *BusinessWeek* articles and activities
- business Web links
- homework hints
- real-world application activities
- additional career path activities

Information on how to prepare your students for the high school exit exam and special projects are also included.

Use the Glencoe Web site for additional resources. All essential content is covered in the Student Edition.

1 FOCUS

Introducing the Chapter

This chapter describes the use of technological advances in the workplace. A photo essay, "Engineering Solutions," enhances the concepts.

Connecting the Objectives

What is information technology? Ask students to tell what they know about telecommuting, wearable computers, and electronic information transfer. What can students tell about the use of the Internet in the workplace?

BusinessWeek
Feature Story

Story's Summary

South Korea is leaping into digital technologies and its economy is growing. South Korean spending and investment in information technology a few years ago accounted for 40 percent of the country's whopping 10.6 percent economic growth. Japan could learn a couple of lessons. First, leap ahead with a spirit of adventure and change to the latest technology. Japan takes slow steps to change. Second, have widely available, affordable, high-speed Internet access. In Japan, the phone system is expensive—using the Internet daily can result in a $100 phone bill.

Find the entire article at www.introbus.glencoe.com, or in the Teacher Resource Binder.

Chapter 18

Technology Advancements in the Workplace

Learning Objectives

After completing this chapter, you'll be able to:
1. **Describe** the role of information technology in business.
2. **Name** different ways technology has changed the workplace.
3. **Identify** how businesses share knowledge.

Why It's Important

The advent and progression of businesses using technology has changed the workplace in numerous ways, often making it more efficient and productive.

Key Words

information technology (IT)
telecommuting
wearable computers
computer-aided design (CAD)
expert system
Internet
Web browser
intranet
extranet
hacker
cookies

282

BusinessWeek Feature Story

Korea Is Leaving Japan in the Digital-Age Dust

Korea's Big Leap to the Net Has Helped Recharge Its Economy. It's only a two-hour flight from Tokyo, but Seoul seems to be in another universe altogether when it comes to embracing the Digital Age. With South Korea's economy back on the fast track, its information technology sector in overdrive, and its citizenry going online in droves, South Korea is leaving out-to-lunch Japan in the dust.

Source: Excerpted with permission from "Korea Is Leaving Japan in the Digital-Age Dust," *BusinessWeek Online,* **August 8, 2000.**

An Extension Activity

Why might one country embrace technology and another country might not?

BUSINESS
Online
The Full Story
To learn more about information technology in Korea, visit the *Introduction to Business* Web site at www.introbus.glencoe.com, and click on *BusinessWeek* Feature Story, Chapter 18.

Classroom Resources

For the Teacher
- Student Activity Work. TAE
- Assessment Binder
- PowerPoint® Presentation
- Interactive Lesson Planner
- Lesson Plans
- Internet Resources
- Teaching Transparencies
- *Introduction to Business* Web Site

- Integrated Soft. Sim. TM
- *BusinessWeek* Poster Package

For the Student
- Student Activity Workbook
- *Virtual Business®*
- *Introduction to Business* Web Site
- Integrated Soft. Sim.
- *PuzzleMaker*
- Strategies and Worksheets for Teaching Transparencies

Bell Ringer Activity

APPLYING TECHNOLOGY TO TASK. Write the following scenario on the board: "Bob's Market, a pet food and hardware store, is just around the corner from where you live. Bob's has been there forever. When you go in, you like seeing the old phone and old cash register. Yesterday, while you were buying dog food, Bob asked, 'Can you work part-time and bring my store into the 21st century? I want computers to handle inventory, the reports and letters, and taxes. Can you give me a list of what equipment and software I need? It'll save me so much time—I'll pay you well.'" Complete a list with all the items Bob might need.

Preteaching Business Key Words

SPEAKING. Ask students to take turns using each of the vocabulary words in a sentence. Ask students to discuss their sentences and revise any whose meaning does not match the definition of the term. **LS, CL**

An Extension Activity

ANSWER. A number of factors could be at work, such as social norms and technological and financial resources.

Making Connections

Everyday Living. New computer improvements and developments happen monthly and weekly. In order to keep current of changes, students should read at least one computer magazine on a regular basis. Two good general magazines are *PC World* and *PC Magazine*. Both offer industry updates and new information along with the results of consumer and industry surveys of new and existing products. In addition to reading, however, it is most important that students have a regular opportunity to try out new software and other products and to learn to use the most popular programs. This can be achieved by taking classes or by volunteering at work to attend training seminars.

2 TEACH

Business Connection

EXPERT SYSTEM. BizWorks is a new expert system being used by Myers Industries Inc. Myers' Dawson Springs plant has huge injection-molding machines that sometimes produce faulty products. BizWorks, linked by sensors to the big machines, can tell when they are going to malfunction. BizWorks then alerts engineers. The question at Myers Industries now is, "What else can BizWorks do?"

Develop Concepts

INVESTIGATE. Call on students to name as many different technological advances as they can think of that are used in the workplace today. List them on the board. Ask the class to pick one to investigate and find out more details. (Answers will vary and include wearable computers, expert systems, and virtual training.)

Figure 18.1 Caption Answer

In Finland more than 60 percent of the population was using cell phones. In the United States about 35 percent were using cell phones. The number of people using cell phones in the United States will grow very rapidly in the next few years.

Utilizing Technology to Manage Information

The information revolution is here, and data and research are firmly planted in many companies' networks. Data is the raw, unanalyzed, and unsummarized facts and figures. Businesses thrive on collecting, analyzing, and sharing information. In the 1990s businesses started approaching information differently. They shifted to using new technology and new methods of collecting and analyzing information.

The Role of Information Technology

Today, three-quarters of employees work with information on a daily basis. The rest of the workers use information for decision making in their jobs. **Information technology (IT)** is hardware and software for creating, processing, storing, and communicating information.

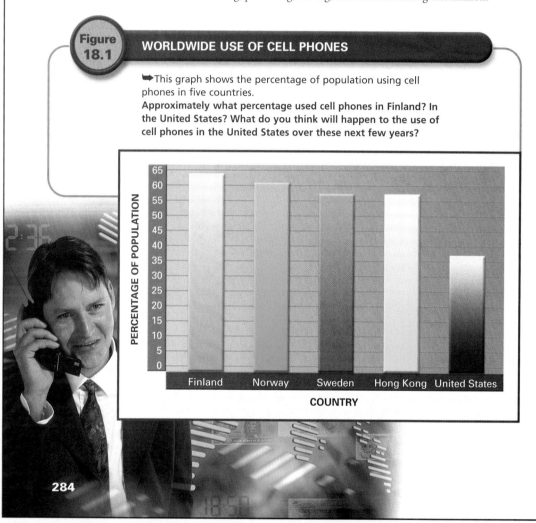

Figure 18.1

WORLDWIDE USE OF CELL PHONES

➡ This graph shows the percentage of population using cell phones in five countries.
Approximately what percentage used cell phones in Finland? In the United States? What do you think will happen to the use of cell phones in the United States over these next few years?

Bar graph — PERCENTAGE OF POPULATION (0–65) vs. COUNTRY: Finland, Norway, Sweden, Hong Kong, United States

284

Cooperative Learning

Technology in Manufacturing. Ask each student to find an article about technology in manufacturing. (CAD, CAM, or any other technology.) To help students focus their work, ask each student to write two sentences about the technology they chose. Team students in pairs to share articles and evaluate each other's statements. **CL**, **LS**

Computers are an important part of information technology. So are other tools. The telephone, for example, has been in use for many years. Faxes send information through the telephone system. Wireless technology has led to cell phones (see Figure 18.1). Wireless technology is used in other devices, too. For example, computers and printers might communicate with each other without cables.

Computers that design and produce products have made a difference in manufacturing. Wearable computers provide on-the-spot information and directions. Millions of employees stay at home and work. Others have their own businesses in their homes. Information technology makes all of these innovations possible.

Even if you don't realize it, computers affect you. Appliances are computerized. You use computers for your schoolwork. You may know people who process information in their jobs.

Changes in the Workplace

When computers were first used in business, employees only used the computer at work. Now mobile computers and communications technology allow workers to work from home. They can stay in touch with their offices through technology.

New technology is changing the workplace. Wearable computers, manufacturing technology, and all kinds of specialized software packages make a difference.

Telecommuting. Does working in your pajamas at home sound inviting? The Gartner Group, a market research firm, estimates that about 29.7 million Americans frequently work from home. (This is about 22 percent of the labor force.)

Telecommuting is a work arrangement that allows employees to work away from the workplace. Employees stay in touch with the workplace using computer and communications technology. Some are full-time telecommuters, and others are part-time. Some telecommuters don't go to the office at all. They work at home instead of traveling to a regular workplace. Others work in a center. Center-based telecommuting uses office space close to home. The employee works at the center without direct supervision.

Telecommuting has advantages. Workers like having less commute time. They like the freedom to schedule their work with flexible hours. Employers often have found that the quality of telecommuters' work improved. Some telecommuters are absent or sick less often than when they worked full-time at the company.

Chapter 18 Technology Advancements in the Workplace **285**

Real-World Application

part 1 of 4

ENGINEERING SOLUTIONS

Barb Sines is a "people person." She is outgoing, likes to work in teams, and she's a good manager and problem solver. Sines is an industrial engineer—someone who works on the "people side" of machines: equipment, production, and business.

How has automation changed the workforce?

continued on p. 287

Real-World Application
Caption Answer

ENGINEERING SOLUTIONS: PART 1 OF 4

More complex computer operations; machines replace human labor.

Technology Resource

GO TO **POWERPOINT.** The *Introduction to Business* PowerPoint® CD-ROM provides visual lecture aids for this chapter.

Independent Practice

ORGANIZE. Ask students to make a simple diagram arranging the technological advances in the workplace in an eye-catching diagram to be used as a study aid. (Technological advances in the workplace include telecommuting, wearable computers, technology in manufacturing, expert systems, electronic information transfer, virtual training.) **LS**

Meeting Individual Needs

Students With Orthopedic Impairments. If your class involves field research or field trips of any kind, encourage students with orthopedic impairments to participate in site selection and transportation planning to ensure access to all sites for all students. Access issues are of major concern for students who use wheelchairs. Barriers such as stairs, curbs, narrow walkways, heavy doors, and so on, must be taken into account when planning an event. By making the fieldwork accessible to all students, you allow a positive rather than an exclusionary situation. Awareness is the key issue, along with a willingness to learn of the daily problems faced by those with physical challenges.

2 TEACH (Cont.)

Caption Answer

Students' opinions will vary. Students should explain their decisions. For the patient, the advantages are that the surgery is safer and more effective, and recovery is quicker. For the doctor, robotic surgery enhances the doctor's precision, decreases fatigue due to the operation, and makes it possible to do more complex operations successfully.

Thinking Critically

TELECOMMUTING. A company in Australia needs your expertise. The company asks you to set up your room at home as an office—all expenses paid. You're due to start telecommuting next week. What equipment and software do you get? (Answers will vary and will include scanner, computer, Internet connection, faxing software, and any other specialized software.)

Dr. R2D2?

Two California companies, Intuitive Surgical, Inc., and Computer Motion, Inc., have designed and tested robotic devices that can perform surgery on the heart, gall bladder, and digestive tract. Doctors using these devises now can perform surgery through incisions no wider than a pencil. The surgeons use handgrips and a foot console to control three robotic arms that carry the camera and instruments. Less pain, faster recovery, and tiny scars are the end results.

Analyze

Who do you think benefits more from robotic surgery: the doctors or the patients? Explain.

A major problem with telecommuting is the lack of contact with other workers. Many telecommuters don't like to be isolated from other workers. Some people have too many distractions at home and can't get their work done. For employers, a major problem is supervising an employee at a remote site. They also have to have more equipment. Offices already have computers and communications equipment. Buying more equipment for the telecommuter at home adds costs for the employer.

Wearable Computers. In many industries you might use **wearable computers**. They're small, lightweight computers that workers carry with them. They use head mounts, with a processor attached by cable. These computers understand and record speech.

A worker can check information on a miniature display screen. They get what they need from the wearable computer while walking or working with their hands. For example, equipment engineers check maintenance manuals stored on the computer. Farmers can collect and record data and search for information while out in the field.

Technology in Manufacturing. Computers have made a difference in design and manufacturing. **Computer-aided design (CAD)** is software for designing products with a computer. CAD is a powerful tool for planning and design.

When CAD and computer-aided manufacturing (CAM) programs are used together, companies can custom design and produce products. With CAD, engineers can design without paper. They can change designs quickly and easily.

Manufacturing plants now are partly or wholly automated. Robots and computer-controlled machine tools do the work. They can do hard jobs that were done in the past by people. In the plants, highly skilled workers with technical training direct these robots and machine tools.

Expert Systems. An **expert system** is computer software that stores and uses knowledge that a human expert would have on the same subject. Expert systems are used in many businesses. For example, software that checks for problems in an automobile analyzes them like an expert would. In the medical field, an expert system compares hundreds of symptoms to help a doctor identify an illness. Airlines use expert systems to find the best use of an airport's terminal gates.

Expert systems protect data and databases. The computer's expert system can identify possible problems. Many credit card companies use

---

LANGUAGE ARTS   ***Curriculum Connection***

Communication. Assign students to groups of four or five persons. Ask each group to research one of the following topics: information technology (IT), telecommuting, wearable computers, or expert systems. Groups are to divide responsibilities and apply a cooperative effort to accomplish their task. If you have access to a software presentation program, ask students to make their class presentation using the software. Have each group present a mini-lesson to the class. **LS**, **CL**, **P**

expert systems to prevent fraud. The software uses pre-stored data to imitate the decisions that a human expert would make.

Electronic Information Transfer. Electronic information transfer gives businesses information quickly and easily. Many companies electronically transfer paychecks to employees' bank accounts. A national sales manager uses electronic mail to transmit sales figures to regional managers. The vice president for development faxes a report to the company's overseas offices. A bank officer in New York City authorizes electronic transfer of funds to a bank branch in London. All of these people use technology to transfer information electronically.

Consumers use electronic information transfer, too. The automated teller machine (ATM) at a bank is a familiar tool. The ATM process uses a terminal, the bank's network, a computer, and transaction processing software. An ATM user has an ATM account, an ATM card, and a personal identification number (PIN).

The Internet makes it possible to transfer information electronically. With Internet access and software, a consumer can transact business online. Banking online is a growing technology. Trading on the stock market electronically from a home computer is commonplace. Paying bills through your home computer is routine. More and more consumers are using electronic transfer services.

Virtual Training. Virtual training allows learners to simulate a real situation through a computer. A computer-run flight simulator allows pilots to learn how to fly aircraft. The simulator includes a room with cockpit controls and a video screen that shows pilots the results of their actions. The entire room is movable, with its motion controlled by a computer.

Schools use computer-based science labs. Students conduct science experiments, complete with mistakes, from a computer keyboard. They use a menu to choose chemicals to combine and in what amounts. They are safe—no danger of explosion if they make a mistake.

Virtual reality is used in training. The computer recreates physical places and actions that seem real to people. A computer with specially designed technology creates the feeling of being in space. The senses of sight, sound, motion, and touch give the illusion of real objects or places.

The user views events from inside a head-mounted display in a helmet. Inside the helmet, two miniature television screens show slightly different images to each eye. These screens imitate human eyes and show the user three-dimensional viewing. A data glove is the input device. The data glove relays the movements of the user's hand to the computer.

Chapter 18 Technology Advancements in the Workplace **287**

ENGINEERING SOLUTIONS
Sines, the vice president and general manager of Rockwell Automation, is in charge of the company's graphical terminals, which control automated production lines in many industries worldwide.
How might Rockwell Automation use an expert system?

continued on p. 289

Chapter 18

Real-World Application
Caption Answer

ENGINEERING SOLUTIONS: PART 2 OF 4
To identify possible problems on the production line.

Business Connection

NETWORK SECURITY. Check-Point Software is expecting high demand for its network security products. CheckPoint sells its intranet and extranet security, firewall, and other security software products to companies around the world. Companies are placing a top priority on protecting their information, so they are willing to invest on security software.

Develop Concepts

QUESTIONING. Ask students to tell the difference between the Internet and an intranet. Ask students to discuss computer viruses, privacy, and security, and to write eight questions they have about the risks of conducting business using computers today.
CL

Great Ideas From the Classroom of...

Miranda Nixon Blocker
Heyward Career and Technology Center
Columbia, S.C.

Let Your Students Do the Ordering.
Give your students a chance to implement inventory control of materials and supplies needed to complete classroom projects. Encourage the use of computer software. Some suggested activities include: submitting a list of supplies and materials needed, updating classroom inventory spreadsheets of available materials and supplies, and developing a plan for receiving, checking, and distributing classroom supplies.

CAPTION ANSWER

After students have completed one path and responded to the conclusion, ask them to free-write in their journal about cause-and-effect and coincidence.

Discussion Starter

LISTING. Ask students to list advantages and disadvantages of telecommuting. Ask students for examples of types of electronic information transfer. (Answers include direct deposit of paychecks, electronic mail, faxes, and ATMs.) **LS**

Individualized Practice

CONTACT. Ask students to contact a variety of local companies and gather information about how they use the Internet and what security measures they take.

L1 Have pairs of students discuss their findings.

L2 Have students write a three-paragraph summary of the information they gather.

L3 Form the class into groups to share the information they gathered. Ask groups to chart the information and present an oral report.

Writing for Business

Portfolio Activity

Analyzing Sci-Fi

This activity gives you a chance to add to your portfolio. Communicate, interview, research, and write your way into a story. Choose one imaginary path, Searching for Sci-Fi Gizmos or Dissecting Technology. Follow your path's steps to complete your own story.

pick a path

Searching for Sci-Fi Gizmos

The Setting. You've just finished reading Jules Verne's famous novel, *Twenty Thousand Leagues Under the Sea*. Verne combined his knowledge of science with his ability to tell a good adventure story. Now you want to write one of your own.

Rising Action. Think about several challenges that technology might solve.

Step 1. Consider what those technological innovations must do and how they can meet the challenge. Using your common sense, your knowledge of technology and mechanics, and your imagination, write a description of two such possible devices.

Step 2. Add a paragraph describing how you would market these devices to people who were skeptical about their potential effectiveness.

Dissecting Technology

The Setting. Writers have presented their ideas about the future. George Orwell's novel, *1984*, described a totalitarian society of the future. In 1938, actor Orson Welles performed a radio version of H.G. Wells's *War of the Worlds* that convinced listeners aliens had landed on earth.

Rising Action. You're interested in how the media portrays technology.

Step 1. Read a science-fiction novel or watch an old science-fiction movie. Is the futuristic technology believable? Has the problem been solved by other technology? Is the technology believable because it was based on an actual scientific principle?

Step 2. Write your arguments and descriptions in a one-page essay.

Conclusion

To determine the precise relationship of events, it's important to look at the connections between events and their causes or consequences. For example, many causes may lead to one effect. In other cases, one event can have several effects. How does a cause-and-effect relationship affect your story? In your journal, explain why certain events are connected to other events.

288

Global Perspective

Sharing Business Knowledge. Ask students to read an article mentioning any recent technology affecting global business. Ask students to summarize the changes. Ask students to use photos, graphics, and words from magazines to create posters showing the use of the Internet in the global workplace and representing security issues. **LS**, **CL**

The information is processed and sent to the headset. As a result, the user can "reach into" the three-dimensional scene. The sensitive data glove allows surgeons to practice medical operations without real patients.

 Fast Review _____

1. Define information technology.
2. List the pros and cons of telecommuting.
3. How might CAD improve a manufacturing plant?
4. The ATM is an example of which type of technological change?

Sharing Business Knowledge

The virtual frontier is about deciphering which information to keep and which to ignore. Knowledge management is the key to time efficiency and production. A company needs to learn how to manage and use the knowledge to stay competitive. New technologies allow a business to communicate with vendors, suppliers, and customers.

The Internet

The Internet is a way businesses are establishing and keeping relationships with their customers. The **Internet** is a collection of tens of thousands of connected computer networks. The Internet isn't owned or controlled by any one person. The closest thing to an Internet manager is the Internet Society (ISOC) in Reston, Va. This professional, nonprofit organization leads the future of the Internet with constructive insight, leadership, and monitoring new technologies. The ISOC runs Internet conferences around the world.

The Internet was made *user friendly* by the creation of the World Wide Web (or the Web). So, what's the difference between the Internet and the Web? The Web is a means of accessing, organizing, and moving through information on the Internet. Therefore, the Web is part of the Internet. The Internet is really a large library full of information except it's not very organized.

Web Browser. A **Web browser** is a program that makes it easier for you to search and retrieve information on the Web. Netscape® and Microsoft Internet Explorer are two of the most widely used Web browsers. The inclusion of design, graphics, and sound on the Web makes it more enjoyable to *surf* for information.

Chapter 18 Technology Advancements in the Workplace **289**

Real-World Application
part 3 of 4

ENGINEERING SOLUTIONS
The plant produces graphic display terminals that perform real-time machine control. "The concept is similar to the touch-screens we use at automatic bank machines," Sines says. Over the noise of production, she talks with several line workers. She is trying to figure out how to improve their work conditions. **Could virtual reality exist in a production environment? Why or why not?**

continued on p. 291

Real-World Application
Caption Answer

ENGINEERING SOLUTIONS: PART 3 OF 4

Yes. Answers might include that virtual reality could be used for people changing the height of a chair when an employee is pulling levers, or to change the angle of a worker's wrist as he or she uses a screwdriver, to learn different jobs, and increase efficiency.

Fast Review Answers ✓

1. Information technology is hardware and software for creating, processing, storing, and communicating information.
2. Pros: Working in comfortable clothing, no direct supervision, less travel time, flexible work hours, quality of work improves, less absence. Cons: Lack of contact with coworkers, distractions at home, problems in supervision, cost of equipment.
3. CAD can be used to custom design products quickly and easily.
4. Electronic information transfer.

LANGUAGE ARTS | *Curriculum Connection*

Advising. The company you work for has grown and Tala King, your manager, has decided to switch from the old system of independent computers to a network linked to the Internet. Tala values your input. Write a point-by-point outline of the benefits of using the Internet and the precautions to take to keep company information secure. **LS**

3 ASSESS

Reteaching

LIST. To reteach the concept of technological advances in the workplace, ask students to list them. (The list will include telecommuting, wearable computers, technology in manufacturing, expert systems, electronic information transfer, and virtual training.) **LS**

Enrichment Strategy

IDENTIFY. Ask students to identify two trends in the use of new technology in the workplace. (Answers will vary and may include: Increase in use of online business-to-business services.) **LS**

Figure 18.2 Caption Answer

1. True. People who enter personal information should have confidence that the company requesting the information will not share it.
2. False. This practice is a part of marketing research by companies who sell products or services.
3. False. For example, unless a user enters personal information, he or she cannot buy online.
4. True. Children may not be as aware of problems they could encounter as older users are.
5. True. Users must protect their systems.
6. True. Thousands of viruses have been developed and a user must protect against them. Antivirus software must be kept up-to-date to protect your system.

Other Types of Links

A company may want to give its employees information but deny the public access to this information. An **intranet** allows a company to connect employees with Internet-like technology, but it's closed to public access. The employee handbook, benefits package, employee directory, code of ethics, and announcements may be included on a company's intranet.

There is another type of link that companies use called the **extranet**. This is a semiprivate network that allows more than one company to access the same information. It allows different companies to share information and to collaborate. A company may also use the extranet to manage and communicate with customers, vendors, suppliers, and other organizations by secure Web sites.

Managing the Threats

With the advent of technology, danger looms. Anyone using a computer or network needs be aware of hackers. Take the quiz on Figure 18.2 to see what you think about privacy and security in technology.

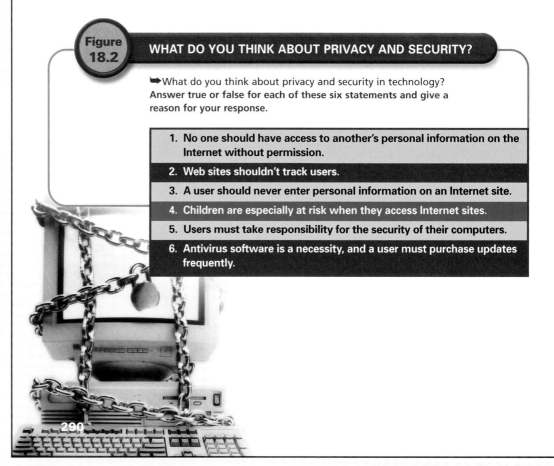

Figure 18.2

WHAT DO YOU THINK ABOUT PRIVACY AND SECURITY?

➡ What do you think about privacy and security in technology? Answer true or false for each of these six statements and give a reason for your response.

1. No one should have access to another's personal information on the Internet without permission.
2. Web sites shouldn't track users.
3. A user should never enter personal information on an Internet site.
4. Children are especially at risk when they access Internet sites.
5. Users must take responsibility for the security of their computers.
6. Antivirus software is a necessity, and a user must purchase updates frequently.

How to Use a Portfolio Activity

The portfolio projects are designed to lead students to develop a collection of their best work to submit to you for assessment. You and each of your students should decide which projects to include in their business portfolio. Refer students to the specific rubric(s) from the *Alternative Assessment Strategies*. These rubrics will alert students to the criteria you'll use to assess their projects. **P**

A **hacker** is a person who breaks into computer systems for illegal purposes and vandalizes Web sites, hard drives, and government agencies. Last year there were over 22,000 hacker attacks against the U.S. Defense Department. Each attempt costs the government $1 million.

Privacy Issues

You probably enter personal information into the computer often and don't think about what could happen to that information. Software tools allow companies to track you online. Web sites often send **cookies** to your computer. Cookies are pieces of information about a computer user, which are stored on your hard drive and accessed by a server when the user connects to a Web site. Every time you visit a Web site, even if you don't buy anything, your personal information can be stored.

You can buy software to protect yourself, and it's a good investment. You can use software to protect your e-mail. The software can code your e-mail messages or automatically destroy them after a given time. You can route your e-mail through a secure site. You can use software to protect information about your Web browsing so it isn't shared with site operators.

Virus. A virus is a big problem for computer users. A computer *virus* is a program that infects computer files by copying itself into those files. A virus may do little harm, or it may destroy your files. Every user needs antivirus software to protect the computer. New viruses are created every day, so the software must be updated regularly.

Firewall. Other software packages can protect computer systems. You can buy personal firewall software for your computer. A *firewall* is a software program that acts as a security wall between your computer and the Internet. It protects your personal information on the Internet.

Real-World Application

part **4** of 4

ENGINEERING SOLUTIONS

"If a machine breaks down or we get a new production unit or we decide to revamp our team approach—I can be called in to help," Sines says. "That's my job—to solve problems, to help other engineers, corporate managers, and employees work as a team, and in the process, to add value to the product."

Time efficiency and quality production are examples of what?

✓ Fast Review

1. What are some ways you can protect personal information on your computer?
2. What is the purpose of antivirus software?
3. Describe the Internet.
4. What are two other types of links a business might use as a form of communication?

Chapter 18 Technology Advancements in the Workplace **291**

How Cell Phones Work

1 FOCUS

Cell phones have made communications much easier and more efficient, but at the same time they have created new problems. Many studies have linked cell phone use while driving to auto accidents. Cell phone use in vehicles has already been banned in some parts of the country. In response, many cell phone manufacturers are now marketing hands-free devices such as voice-activated dialing, earphones, and clip-on microphones. Because they can be used anywhere, cell phones are often a nuisance in public. Web sites have even appeared to instruct people in cell phone etiquette.

2 TEACH

Introduce students to the concept of cell phone etiquette, or when and where it's appropriate to use a cell phone in public. Have students describe places where cell phone use is inappropriate, such as a movie theater, church, restaurant, or business meeting. Have students describe why it's inappropriate in terms of both public and private responsibility. Students could also discuss why using a cell phone while driving is potentially dangerous and what they think should be done about it. **CL**

? Did You Know?

In 1987, there were about 1 million cell phones in the United States. By the year 2000, there were about 50 million.

Picture *This...*

Why Do They Call It a Cell Phone?

1. When you turn on a cell phone, it transmits a signal.

2. The signal is picked up by the Mobile Telephone Switching Office (MTSO), the central office of the phone company, or service carrier, you use.

3. The MTSO identifies which part of the city—or cell—you're in and routes your signal to its transmitter, or base station, within that cell.

292 Unit 6

Extending the Content

Anywhere in the World. The latest stage in mobile phone technology is FOMA, or freedom of mobile multimedia access. FOMA handsets have a built-in video digital camera, videoconference calling, and e-mail messaging. They are already available in Tokyo. Mobile videophones that combine a small video camera, transmitter, and satellite phone are being used by news organizations such as CNN. With a videophone, a news correspondent can broadcast live from anywhere in the world.

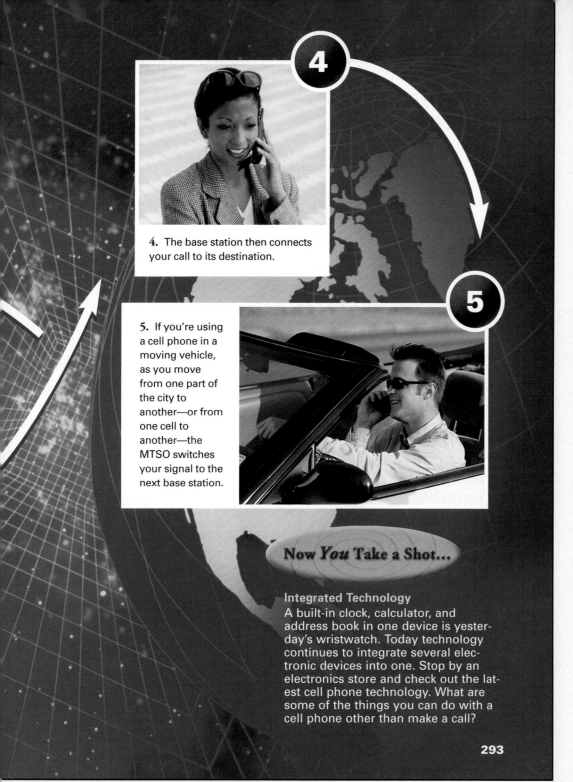

4. The base station then connects your call to its destination.

5. If you're using a cell phone in a moving vehicle, as you move from one part of the city to another—or from one cell to another—the MTSO switches your signal to the next base station.

Now *You* Take a Shot...

Integrated Technology
A built-in clock, calculator, and address book in one device is yesterday's wristwatch. Today technology continues to integrate several electronic devices into one. Stop by an electronics store and check out the latest cell phone technology. What are some of the things you can do with a cell phone other than make a call?

 **Picture** *This...*

3 ASSESS

Have students answer the question in "Now You Take a Shot..."

4 CLOSE

Have students describe and discuss situations where it would be appropriate, and even important, to have a cell phone. A cell phone would be handy to have in a car, for example, if it breaks down, you're in an accident, or you become stranded. Cell phones can be especially useful in an emergency, if there's a power failure, or if you're trapped somewhere. **CL**

Did You Know?
There is hardware available that will jam cell phone transmissions within a small area. It's used primarily in hospital zones, where cell phone signals can disrupt medical equipment.

Now *You* Take a Shot...
Caption Answer

Answers may vary depending on the latest technology available. Features many cell phones have include a built-in clock, calculator, and address book. Some cell phones can also be used to access e-mail, search the Web, and play video games.

Chapter 18 Review

4 CLOSE

Chapter Wrap-Up

To close, ask students to make a "Top 10" list of important facts from this chapter. **LS**

Using Business Key Words

1. telecommuting
2. CAD
3. expert systems
4. Internet
5. information technology
6. Web browser
7. wearable computers
8. intranet
9. extranet
10. cookies
11. hacker

Review What You Learned

12. Advantages: less travel, more freedom, quality of work, sick less often. Disadvantages: Lack of contact with coworkers, distractions at home, harder to supervise, more equipment is needed.
13. Custom design products.
14. Automotive industry, medical field, and airline industry.
15. ATM is connected to the bank's headquarters. The computer has a database of customer information. When a customer uses an ATM, the computer finds the customer's records in the database. Then it presents a menu of choices to that customer.
16. Banking online, paying bills.
17. Simulate a real situation.
18. Personal Identification Number; password.
19. A professional organization that leads the future of the Internet.

294

Summary

1. Information technology allows business employees the capability to create, process, store, and communicate information.
2. Telecommuting, wearable computers, technology in manufacturing, expert systems, electronic information transfer, and virtual training are technological advances that have changed the workplace.
3. The Internet, intranet, and extranet are all ways businesses communicate with one another.

Using Business Key Words

It seems like each day technology dramatically changes the workplace. See how ready you are for the technologically savvy workplace by completing the sentences below, with the following key terms.

- **information technology (IT)**
- **Internet**
- **expert system**
- **Web browser**
- **cookies**
- **telecommuting**
- **wearable computers**
- **intranet**
- **extranet**
- **hacker**
- **computer-aided design (CAD)**

1. A work arrangement called _____ allows employees to work away from the workplace.
2. A powerful tool for planning and design is called _____.
3. Computer software that stores and uses knowledge that a human would have on the same subject is _____.
4. A collection of tens of thousands of connected computer networks is called the _____.
5. Hardware and software for creating, processing, storing, and communicating information is called _____.
6. A program that makes it easier for you to search and retrieve information on the Web is called a(n) _____.
7. Small, lightweight computers that workers carry with them are called _____.
8. A program that allows a company to connect employees with Internet-like technology, but is closed to public access, is called the _____.
9. A program that allows more than one company to access the same information is called the _____.
10. Pieces of information about a computer user, which are stored on your hard drive, and accessed by a server when the user connects to a Web site are called _____.
11. A person who breaks into computer systems for illegal purposes is called a _____.

Quick Quiz

1. What is data? (Raw, unanalyzed, and unsummarized facts and figures.)
2. Name some technological advances that have changed the workplace. (Telecommuting, CAD/CAM, expert systems, wearable computers, electronic information transfer, virtual training.)
3. What are cookies? (Pieces of information about a computer user accessed by a server when the user connects to a Web site.)

Review What You Learned

12. Describe the advantages and disadvantages of telecommuting.
13. What happens when CAD and CAM programs are used together?
14. What types of businesses use expert systems?
15. Explain how an ATM terminal works.
16. How are consumers using the Internet to transact business online?
17. How is virtual reality used to train pilots?
18. What is a PIN and how is it used?
19. What does the Internet Society do?

Understanding Business Concepts

20. Describe a job you think could be done through telecommuting.
21. Can you think of a local business where a robot could be used to complete a job or part of a job? Explain.
22. Why do you think electronic information transfer is becoming so popular?
23. Have you every played a virtual reality game? If so, describe your experience. If not, describe what you think it would be like.
24. Do you think people will be able to replace their keyboarding skills with speech recognition technology? Explain your answer.
25. Explain why technology is just a tool.
26. Name a few industries that use expert systems. What's the purpose of these systems?
27. What's the difference between the Internet and the Web?

Critical Thinking

28. Do you think it's good that people can be in touch with their workplace all day, every day? Explain why or why not.
29. What are some problems with too many people using the Internet?
30. Which office occupations might be downsized with these technological changes?
31. Hypothesize about the fastest-growing occupations that use technology. How do these generate new openings in the information-technology world?

Viewing and Representing

Examining the Image. What's happening in this photograph? Write a product summary based upon your perceptions of each device. Share the summaries with the class.

Critical Thinking

28. Answers will vary. Make sure students justify their answers.
29. Answers will vary. Too many people online may result in retrieving information slowly.
30. Computer operators; billing, posting and calculating machines; telephone operators; typists and word processors; bank tellers.
31. Computer engineers and scientists, systems analysts, physical therapists, special education teachers, and operations research analysts.

Viewing and Representing

Having the ability to dissect the meaning and interpretation of a visual image can be useful to students now, on the job, and in life. Knowing the components of visual images and the resulting emotional overtones can help individuals evaluate images in advertisements and other media throughout the day. This activity gives students practice in critical analysis, allowing them to develop an awareness of analyzing images. **LS**, **CL**

Understanding Business Concepts

20. Answers will vary.
21. Answers will vary. Manufacturing work, filling soft drinks at a fast food restaurant, or washing cars.
22. Quick and easy delivery of information.
23. Answers will vary.
24. Students should have valid justification for their answers.
25. Create, send, and receive information, a tool to acquire the knowledge.
26. Auto industry, the medical field, airlines, and the credit card industry.
27. The Internet is a collection of thousands of connected computer networks. Web—means of accessing, organizing, and moving through information on the Internet.

4 CLOSE (Cont.)

Building Academic Skills

LANGUAGE ARTS. Encourage students to use the library, computer magazines, and the Internet as resources for this project. Rubric: Essay.

HISTORY. Students will find information in the library or on the Internet. Rubric: Oral presentation.

MATH. Make sure all students participate in the group project. Answers will vary depending on the careers selected. Encourage the students to choose careers they might be interested in pursuing. Allow the students to choose the way they would like to share their findings. Rubrics: Spreadsheet, chart/table, essay, oral presentation, poster.

COMPUTER/TECHNOLOGY. Encourage students to prepare questions before the interview and to keep the questions short and to the point. Rubric: Interview.

Linking School to Home

Answers will vary. Rubrics: Guide, brochure, poster.

Linking School to Work

Make sure all students participate in the group project. Answers will vary depending on the business owner interviewed. Allow the students to choose the way they would like to present their information. Rubrics: Essay, oral presentation, poster.

Building Academic Skills

 Research Emerging Technology

Research a piece of emerging technology and write a 250-word paper on the impact it might have on the business world.

 Creating an Oral Presentation

Research virtual reality and find out:
- When it first emerged
- Who was the first to use it
- Equipment needed
- Examples of how it might be used in the future

Create an oral presentation to share your findings with the class.

 Needed Math Skills

In a group of three or four, choose five different information technology related careers. Research the math skills that are needed to be successful in those careers.

 Targeting Technology

Interview someone who uses a computer system in his or her business. Does this person have any problems running the system? Has technology given him or her any problems while trying to run the business? Did technology solve any problems? How? Write your findings in your journal. Be thorough about how the business solved any technological problems.

Linking School to Home

Brainstorm About Managing Information. Never before has there been more information available to you with the click of a mouse. Using your time efficiently means knowing what information to keep or discard. Explain to your family and friends how important it might be to protect your company information from other competitors. Brainstorm with them and come up with several ways to keep your information secure. Create a guide to share with others about how a company can create privacy.

Linking School to Work

Technology Affects Business. As mentioned earlier in this chapter, three-quarters of employees work with information on a daily basis. If not working directly with information, then you might be using it to make decisions. Interview a small business owner in your community to learn about how technology has changed the way his or her business operates. What changes have been made based on information technology? What expenses were incurred? What changes are planned for the future?

E-Homework

Applying Technology

Creating Your Ideal Work Space. Imagine you have the opportunity to work from home. Create a picture of your ideal home office and include the technology tools you'll need in order to do your job.

Researching Wearable Computers. Visit a computer store in your community or online. Research the wearable computers that are described in the text. Select one that you think would help you in school and write a paragraph about it.

Connecting Academics

Math. You're tired of working for other people. Now is your chance to break away and start your own consulting company. In order to find investors in your business idea, you've got to conduct a lot of research. You want your business to be national in scope so it can't be limited to just your local community. Technology has influenced the way business is done around the world. Find statistics about the increased use of a particular type of technology used in business. Draw a graph of your findings.

Language Arts. You work for Ads Etc., which needs to hire six temporary designers. There's no office space so Twyla, your boss, asks you to research the advantages of having these designers telecommute. Write a business memo or e-mail to Twyla outlining the advantages. Include two things Ads Etc. will need to do to protect information when setting up the communication between the off-site designers and the company.

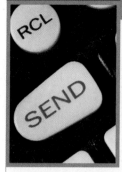

BusinessWeek — Analyzing the Feature Story

You read the first part of "Korea Is Leaving Japan in the Digital-Age Dust" at the beginning of this chapter. Below are a few questions for you to answer about South Korea. You'll find the answers to these questions when you're reading the entire article. First, here are the questions:

32. How much of South Korea's economic growth was based on info-tech spending and investment?
33. What theories do South Koreans have for their success in entering the Digital Age in comparison to Japan's?

CREATIVE JOURNAL ACTIVITY

Write how a country's lack of attention to technology might influence it. How would it differ from a technologically advanced country?

BUSINESS Online

To learn more about information technology in Korea, visit the *Introduction to Business* Web site at www.introbus.glencoe.com, and click on *BusinessWeek* Feature Story, Chapter 18.

297

SCANS Correlation Chart*

Foundation Skills

Basic Skills	Reading	Writing	Math	Listening	Speaking	
Thinking Skills	Creative Thinking	Decision Making	Problem Solving	Seeing Things in the Mind's Eye	Knowing How to Learn	Reasoning
Personal Qualities	Responsibility	Self-Esteem	Sociability	Self-Management	Integrity/ Honesty	

Workplace Competencies

Resources	Allocating Time	Allocating Money	Allocating Material and Facility Resources	Allocating Human Resources		
Information	Acquiring and Evaluating Information	Organizing and Maintaining Information	Interpreting and Communicating Information	Using Computers to Process Information		
Interpersonal Skills	Participating as a Member of a Team	Teaching Others	Serving Clients/ Customers	Exercising Leadership	Negotiating to Arrive at a Decision	Working With Cultural Diversity
Systems	Understanding Systems	Monitoring and Correcting Performance	Improving and Designing Systems			
Technology	Selecting Technology	Applying Technology to Task	Maintaining and Troubleshooting Technology			

*This chart's highlighted blocks indicate the chapter's content coverage in the Student Edition and the Teacher Wraparound Edition.

Resource Manager

Teaching Transparencies

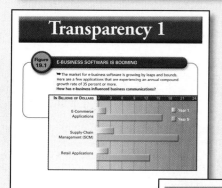

Transparency 1

Figure 19.1 — E-BUSINESS SOFTWARE IS BOOMING

The market for e-business software is growing by leaps and bounds. Here are a few applications that are experiencing an annual compound growth rate of 35 percent or more.
How has e-business influenced business communications?

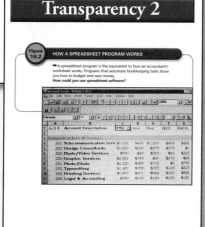

Transparency 2

Figure 19.2 — HOW A SPREADSHEET PROGRAM WORKS

A spreadsheet program is the equivalent to how an accountant's worksheet works. Programs that automate bookkeeping tasks show you how to budget and save money.
How could you use spreadsheet software?

Application and Enrichment

- Lesson Plans
- *BusinessWeek* Poster Package
- Teaching Transparencies
- Integrated Software Simulation
- Glencoe Business Video Package

Review and Reinforcement

- *PuzzleMaker*
- Internet Resources
- Student Activity Workbook
- Strat. and Work. for Teaching Transparencies

Assessment and Evaluation

- Reproducible Tests
- Alternative Assessment Strategies
- ExamView® Pro Test Generator

Technology

- *PuzzleMaker*
- ExamView® Pro Test Generator
- Glencoe Business Video Package
- PowerPoint® Presentation
- Integrated Software Simulation
- Interactive Lesson Planner
- *Virtual Business*®

KEY	📖 Printed	💾 Software	📼 Videocassette	🖼 Poster
	🕹 Transparency	💿 CD-ROM	🖥 Internet	

BUSINESS Online

Visit **www.introbus.glencoe.com**, the Web site companion to *Introduction to Business*. The student's page includes:

- interactive tutor
- additional *BusinessWeek* articles and activities
- business Web links
- homework hints
- real-world application activities
- additional career path activities

Information on how to prepare your students for the high school exit exam and special projects are also included.

Use the Glencoe Web site for additional resources. All essential content is covered in the Student Edition.

1 FOCUS

Introducing the Chapter

This chapter describes the types and parts of computers. It also discusses computer software. A photo essay, "Weaving a Network," enhances the concepts.

Connecting the Objectives

Ask students to name different types of computers. What are the basic parts of a computer system? Ask students for examples of computer software used in business.

BusinessWeek
Feature Story

Story's Summary

Idea Keeper is a software package for the Macintosh that's very much like Microsoft Word. Idea Keeper is rich in word-processing and information-management features and great for gathering separate bits of information in one place. Idea Keeper is shareware and only costs $15. If it sounds too good to be true, perhaps it is. Idea Keeper does lack such essentials as the ability to create headers and footers and spell check.

Find the entire article at www.introbus.glencoe.com, or in the Teacher Resource Binder.

Basics of Computers

● Learning Objectives

After completing this chapter, you'll be able to:
1. **Describe** the parts of a complete computer system.
2. **Name** the different hardware components of a computer.
3. **Identify** measurements for computer memory and storage.
4. **Explain** the various software programs available to businesses.

● Why It's Important

For every kind of business task, from accounting to graphic design, there is a software program available.

● Key Words

personal digital assistant (PDA)
scanner
hardware
random access memory (RAM)
byte
software
desktop publishing
spreadsheet program
database
groupware

298

BusinessWeek Feature Story

A Powerful Shareware Rival to Mighty Microsoft

Idea Keeper Is an Everything-Software Program. Idea Keeper is shareware for the Macintosh at its best. This little, inexpensive program is nearly as powerful as Microsoft Word. It can even do some things that mighty Word can't, such as automatically stripping out the weird formatting of e-mail text. Not a bad trick for a program that costs only $15. For starters, Idea Keeper looks different. You're not greeted with a word processor's traditional blank page at startup.

Source: Excerpted with permission from "A Powerful Shareware Rival to Mighty Microsoft," *BusinessWeek Online*, May 3, 2000.

An Extension Activity

How does technology affect productivity and efficiency? Research ten facts then write a one-page report.

BUSINESS *Online*
The Full Story
To learn more about Idea Keeper, visit the *Introduction to Business* Web site at www.introbus.glencoe.com, and click on *BusinessWeek* Feature Story, Chapter 19.

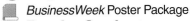
Classroom Resources

For the Teacher
 Student Activity Work. TAE
Assessment Binder
PowerPoint® Presentation
Interactive Lesson Planner
Lesson Plans
Internet Resources
Teaching Transparencies
Introduction to Business Web Site

Integrated Soft. Sim. TM
BusinessWeek Poster Package
For the Student
Student Activity Workbook
Virtual Business®
Introduction to Business Web Site
Integrated Soft. Sim.
PuzzleMaker
Strategies and Worksheets for Teaching Transparencies

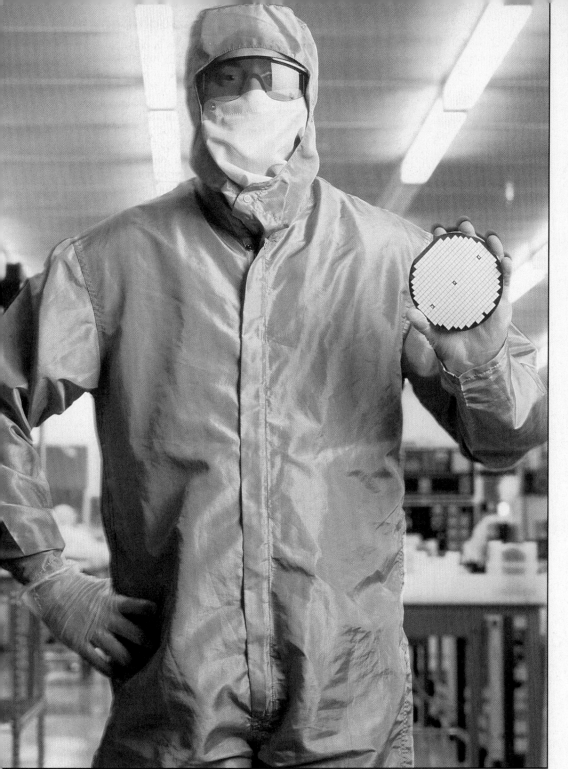

Bell Ringer Activity

DECISION MAKING. Write on the board: "Write a sentence about each of the following: types of computers, the parts of a computer, and computer software. Reread each of your sentences by asking yourself, "How much would a person new to computers learn from this sentence?" Decide if your sentence is clear and make changes if needed." **LS**

Preteaching Business Key Words

PROBLEM SOLVING. Ask students to create a fill-in-the-blank test for each key word. Randomly pass the tests around the class. Have students complete the vocabulary test. **LS**

An Extension Activity

SHARE. Technology highly improves productivity and time management in a business or individual project. Ask students to share their knowledge about the effect of technology. **CL**

Making Connections

The Workplace. Imagine you work currently in an office of a large company. Your manager, Clarissa, is planning what projects to send your way and asks you to write answers to the following questions: What types of computer skills do you have? List the software you can use now and rate your skill as expert, proficient, or fair in each. What computer skills would you like to learn or improve on? Clarissa assures you that no matter where your computer skills are now, she thinks you have the right attitude and potential to succeed on your job. She will arrange training on any skills you need. You write an honest answer to each question.

Figure 19.1 Caption Answer

Answers will vary but might include an increase in productivity and the speed of communication.

Communicating Through Computers

Scouting out aisles filled with software in your neighborhood office-supplies store may be mind-boggling. Whether you're looking for crossword puzzle software to create your own games or you're looking to update your computer software, the choices are endless. Before you buy the best product for your needs it's a good idea to know the basics about computers—both the software and the hardware.

You might take computers for granted. People depend on them to handle work of all kinds. When your parents pay a bill, a computer records the payment. You can use your computer to pay the bill electronically. In that case, your computer communicates with the computer at the business you're paying. Computers of all sizes and types run appliances, cars, calculators, and other devices. They're everywhere.

The Speed of Communication

Computers have increased the speed of communication. While there's the initial expense of the computer equipment you need, you save time and increase productivity down the road. As Benjamin Franklin said,

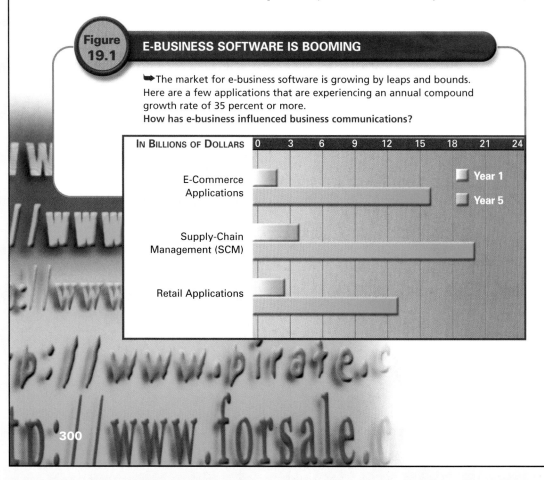

Figure 19.1

E-BUSINESS SOFTWARE IS BOOMING

➡ The market for e-business software is growing by leaps and bounds. Here are a few applications that are experiencing an annual compound growth rate of 35 percent or more.
How has e-business influenced business communications?

300

"Time is money." Businesses can access data, send e-mail, or make bank deposits in the blink of an eye. As technology continues to change, businesses keep finding more and more uses for computers (see Figure 19.1).

In the workplace, computers handle just about every kind of task for businesses. Handheld devices track appointments, telephone numbers, addresses, and other data. The personal computer (PC) is an essential tool for the workplace. Businesses of all sizes use PCs to record information and keep track of those records. Entrepreneurs and small business owners rely on computers as much as large corporations do. In fact, they couldn't get along without them.

Types of Computers

Business and its employees are constantly on the move. With laptop computers, cellular phones, and pagers you can do business anywhere you go. A **personal digital assistant (PDA)** is a hand-held computer you can use as an address book, an appointment book, and a voice recorder. You can even use a PDA to go on the Internet. The Palm™ Pilot and Compaq iPAQ Pocket PC are two different types of PDAs.

In the workplace, the desktop computer can perform countless different tasks. It can be used to type reports, analyze sales records, prepare taxes, deposit checks, store files, and send e-mail. In large companies, computers are linked to each other through either a central computer called a *mainframe* or a *network computing system*. This allows the computers to share files, data, printers, and e-mail within the company.

There are also different types of computers for different types of jobs. In retail stores, computerized cash registers automatically record the prices of items using a scanner. A **scanner** is a device that reads images, such as price codes, and records or transfers the information. Most car repair shops can now tell what's wrong with your car by hooking it up to a diagnostic computer. Film studios use special computers to produce sound and visual effects for movies.

Parts of a Computer System

Regardless of how many parts and pieces make up a computer, it's controlled by programmed instructions. These instructions give the computer guidance. A complete computer system consists of four parts: software, people, data, and hardware.

Software tells the computer what to do. It's a set of electronic information consisting of complex codes to make the computer perform

Chapter 19 Basics of Computers **301**

Real-World Application

part **1** of 4

WEAVING A NETWORK

Amiel Dunn is on the trail of two mysteries. Dunn is a senior network analyst for Howard University in Washington, D.C. Several years ago, he and the rest of a small staff created the school's sophisticated computer network, which links students, faculty members, and staff into one system. **What do you use a computer for?**

continued on p. 303

Chapter 19

Real-World Application
Caption Answer

WEAVING A NETWORK: PART 1 OF 4

Answers may vary but might include saving information, sending e-mail, and purchasing goods online.

Technology Resource

POWERPOINT. The *Introduction to Business* PowerPoint® CD-ROM provides visual lecture aids for this chapter.

Independent Practice

ASSESS.   Ask students to find out all they can about the most popular hand-held computer systems in business use. Have students choose two such systems. Ask students to make a presentation comparing and contrasting the systems. **LS**

Meeting Individual Needs

Students With Visual Impairments.   Students with visual or spatial difficulties may have difficulty working with spreadsheets. You will need to describe spreadsheet operations specifically with these students in mind. Don't assume that they can follow what you are saying while you perform calculations on the board. Take special care to name categories, for example spreadsheet cells, and to explain how figures are calculated. In addition, provide an opportunity for students to ask questions or request assistance with calculations.

2 TEACH (Cont.)

Thinking Critically

COMPUTER TUTORING. You see a want ad posted in your local mini-market: "Computer tutor wanted for sixth grader. Needs to learn word-processing for school reports. One hour lesson per week, $25." You call and set up the first lesson. You think back to what helped you most when you first started learning word-processing. This is exciting—it'll be great to use your skills to help a student new to computers. You take out a piece of paper and write an outline of your first lesson in ten-minute segments. **LS,** **CL**

Technology Toolkit

Reading Your Palm

Pocket-size and smart—this is a hand-held computer, or a personal digital assistant (PDA). This complements (not replaces) your personal computer. If you record an appointment in your PDA, you need to upload it to your laptop. If you write a memo on your desktop computer and want to revise it during a trip, you'll need to transfer it to the PDA. This communication between a PDA and a PC is *data synchronization*, or *syncing*. A cable or infrared light syncs the information.

Critical Thinking
How could competing software companies try to monopolize the hand-held computer market?

tasks. In order to make the computer operational, people need to be the users. Whether you're designing, building, or using a computer, it requires your attention.

As discussed in Chapter 18, computers make sense of all the data. The computer alters and moves the data into comprehensible information. Data may be letters, sound, graphics, or numbers.

The physical components of a computer system are called the **hardware**. It includes a processor, memory, input and output devices, and storage devices. Each computer system uses these main elements. Here's a closer look at each important piece of the whole.

Processors. The *processor* is the brain of a computer. It transforms the data into usable information for the user. The processor interprets and carries out instructions for the user. It performs calculations and logical comparisons at extremely high speeds. One of the advancements in computers over the last several years has been higher and higher processor speed. It's located in the central processing unit (CPU) of personal computers. In a personal computer the processor usually consists of chips. These are small pieces of silicon or other material with electronic circuits. The data passes through these pieces of silicon to other areas to complete the instruction in the computer.

Memory. The computer's *memory* can be thought of as a kind of scratch pad. The computer uses memory to hold all of the data and instructions required during operation. The most common type of memory is called **random access memory**, or RAM. When a computer saves information, the first place it goes is to RAM. As long as your computer is on, the information remains in this temporary memory for the computer to use quickly. As soon as you turn off the computer, RAM loses information. For that reason, storage is a very important part of a computer system.

Memory's capacity is measured in bytes. A **byte** is the amount of memory it takes to store a single character. With the advance of science and technology research and production, the number of bytes per computer can increase. The most common units of measurement for computer memory and storage are as follows:

Kilobyte (KB)	1,000 bytes
Megabyte (MB)	1 million
Gigabyte (GB)	1 billion
Terabyte (TB)	1 trillion

LANGUAGE ARTS — Curriculum Connection

Communication Software. Split the class into groups to research communication software such as Eudora® and Microsoft Outlook®. Ask groups to give a short report on how the software is used in business, including any interesting facts. Have each group compile a list of useful Web sites on this topic. **CL**, **LS**

Input and Output Devices. Without the input and output of information a computer would be useless. Input devices accept data and instructions. Examples of input devices include a keyboard, mouse, touchpad, joystick, digital camera, and microphone. The output device returns the processed data back to the user or to another computer system. Examples of output devices include a computer monitor, printer, fax machine, and speakers.

Storage Devices. *Storage devices*, such as hard drives, floppy disks, and CD-ROMs, all save and hold information. Computer storage devices save all the bits of information you and your computer use. You can think of storage devices as file cabinets in which you can keep information. The hard drive is like a huge filing cabinet. It has space for all the work you want to do and it stores all the data you need to carry out your instructions. The hard drive is sealed inside a box in your computer. As technology advances, hard drives have more and more capacity, too.

Portable storage devices are also popular methods to store information, since the hard drive is sealed inside the computer. You can easily move these from machine to machine. ZIP disks are widely used to store information permanently. Small diskettes (only three-and-a-half inches in diameter) can hold hundreds of files. You can think of a hard drive as a filing cabinet. Think of a diskette as a file folder. It can hold lots of information, but not nearly as much as a hard drive.

Diskettes cannot hold some of the complex software programs needed for the work that powerful computers can do. ZIP disks and CD-ROMs also can store data, and they have much greater capacity. Most software programs sold to consumers now are stored on CD-ROMs.

✓ Fast Review

1. What four parts complete a computer system?
2. The hardware of a computer is comprised of these four categories. Name them.

Computer Software

Computers are just machines. Sometimes people are in awe of them, but they cannot do anything without instruction from human beings. As discussed earlier in this chapter, **software**, or a computer program, is a set of instructions that tell computers what to do. Some software programs tell a computer how to calculate numbers or arrange words.

part 2 of 4

WEAVING A NETWORK
A network is a combination of computer hardware and software that allows people to share resources immediately and across long distances. It's a complex system that occasionally can develop glitches. Dunn's first mystery occurred when some network users received a momentary "error" message. Trying to solve this particular type of mystery can be frustrating because it doesn't last long enough to pinpoint. **How have you handled a computer's error message?**

continued on p. 305

Real-World Application
Caption Answer

WEAVING A NETWORK: PART 2 OF 4
Answers will vary.

Fast Review Answers

1. Software, people, data, and software.
2. Processor, memory, input and output devices, and storage devices.

Business Connection

BUSINESS SOFTWARE. Voice-recognition software, produced by Nuance Communications Inc., based in Menlo Park, Calif., allows humans to talk to computers—and have the computer "understand." Nuance's system has already been used for some years in the customer-service departments of Charles Schwab and American Airlines among others. After dialing the company 800 number, customers need only ask for a stock quote or say a menu option, and the computer handles the request. Growth is expected in the use of voice-recognition software on the Web via voice portals. For example, just say a movie title and the site tells you where the movie's playing in your neighborhood.

Great Ideas From the Classroom of...

Gail Sobel
De Ruyter Central School
De Ruyter, N.Y.

Scheduling Spreadsheet. You're a manager at CDesign in the mall. The store is open 13 hours per day Monday to Saturday and 6 hours on Sunday. Erika is the only other manager. Managers can fill in up to 8 hours per week helping customers. You have eight part-time workers (make up their names). Each worker can work up to 20 hours a week but no more. The store must be staffed with two people at all times. Design a spreadsheet. Prepare a weekly work schedule for the managers and eight part-time workers.

2 TEACH (Cont.)

Develop Concepts

GIVING EXAMPLES. Ask students to give examples of various uses businesses make of the following types of software programs: word-processing, spreadsheet, accounting, database, and graphics presentation. (Answers will vary and may include letters, memos, worksheets, payroll accounts, bills, inventory control, advertising flyers, and newsletters.) What are other specialized business uses of software? (Answers will vary and may include dental records, special effects for movies, scientific simulations.)

Discussion Starter

NAMING. In 45 seconds, have students name as many input devices to computers as they can. (Answers will vary, and will include keyboard, mouse, touch pad, joystick, digital camera, and microphone.)

You Make the Call

Caption Answer

1. The responsibility of the CEO of the competitor is to protect private information.
2. It's your decision what use you will make of the new information.
3. No. The conversation is public information.

Other software programs are custom-made for special uses, such as preparing taxes or designing a house. For every kind of business activity there are software programs available. Without software a computer is just a collection of parts. Since software is so essential, software development is a career field with great opportunity. Anything a computer does must have software instructions.

Word Processing Programs

What if you want to send 30 letters to members of a club? Or you would like to send an announcement about a meeting? Having to write 30 letters is a lot of work. When you have written the letters, you still have to prepare envelopes. Word processing software prepares letters, announcements, and envelopes with ease.

Word processing is one of the most popular types of software for business. Businesses of all sizes and types create documents, and word processing software makes document creation easy. Documents are created and then edited and printed. Users find word processors important in the step of revising documents. The editing features make it possible for a user to make multiple changes easily.

Word processing programs, such as Microsoft® Word, are the most commonly used type of computer software. If you have a computer you've

You Make the Call

Portable Phones, Portable Privacy

As the vice president of production for a biotechnology company, business travel is a weekly occurrence. While waiting for a flight you overhear a woman talking on a cell phone behind you and realize she's the chief executive officer (CEO) of your biggest competitor. She's talking about important information regarding an experiment. Everyone in the biotech industry knows that whoever discovers the answer first will reap millions of dollars worth of profit from the patent. The CEO has just mentioned something that could be the final piece to the research puzzle for your company.

Making an Ethical Decision

1. Are you eavesdropping on privileged information? If so, should you walk away until you're out of earshot?
2. Should you tell the CEO you overheard her conversation?
3. Is someone who uses a cell phone in a public place entitled to the same privacy as someone who uses it in a workplace?

Global Perspective

Web-Based Global Training. Cross your knees, but be sure not to show the bottom of your feet. Bow only after being acknowledged at a meeting. There are books filled with tips and hints for businesspeople doing business overseas. How can one person remember all of these facts? The folks at Globesmart, a global training and consulting company in San Francisco, Calif., wondered the same thing. Globesmart offers Web-based training for individuals who travel on business. Globesmart picks out those facts that are the most vital for business people to know, and makes them easily accessible on the Web. The program includes 30 different countries, and will help you with the most important dos and don'ts of the culture.

probably used a word processing program to write a school paper. It allows you to use your computer like a typewriter but with many added features. For example, you can type over words, rearrange paragraphs, change margins, and check your spelling with ease.

Some programs combine word processing with graphics so you can do desktop publishing. **Desktop publishing** consists of writing, designing, and laying out documents on your computer like a professional publisher. With desktop publishing, you can produce high-quality reports, newsletters, presentations, and magazines.

Spreadsheet Programs

A **spreadsheet program** is a computerized worksheet. Sales figures, quantities, prices, and production costs can be easily listed and compared. With a click of a button, information can be changed instantly. If the dates or costs change, you can enter the new data in one place, press a key, and your spreadsheet will automatically update the list for you. Two of the most popular spreadsheet programs are Lotus® 1-2-3 and Microsoft® Excel. Figure 19.2 on page 306 is an example of a spreadsheet program.

Accounting Programs

All businesses need to keep accurate, up-to-date accounting records. With an accounting software package, you can keep records, prepare reports, and even write checks on the computer. The software handles all financial transactions. You can use it to keep payroll accounts, send out bills, and do your taxes. With a keystroke you can find out what your profits or losses are at any given time. Peachtree® and QuickBooks® are two programs you can use.

Database Programs

A **database** is a collection of information usually kept in a list. It can consist of a list of names, supplies, products, or schedules. With database software, a list can easily be updated, changed, or rearranged. You can print out part of a list or display it any way you like. The same list can be used at different times for different purposes. For example, an employee database can be used to keep track of workers' hours, wages, vacations, or benefits.

Databases are also used to keep track of inventory and sales. Sales records can then be used to make long-range forecasts. The ability to

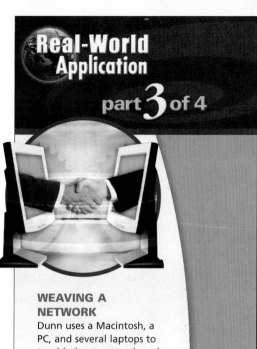

Real-World Application
part 3 of 4

WEAVING A NETWORK
Dunn uses a Macintosh, a PC, and several laptops to troubleshoot network problems at the university. The laptops are especially important because they allow him to "communicate" with the larger machines. "The laptop is like a screwdriver," Dunn says. "I actually take it to the computer on campus where I think the problem has developed, plug in the laptop, and then use it to find and fix the problem."
Explain how you might troubleshoot a computer glitch.

continued on p. 307

Chapter 19 Basics of Computers **305**

Real-World Application
Caption Answer

WEAVING A NETWORK: PART 3 OF 4
Answers will vary.

Individualized Practice

INTERVIEW. Have students conduct an in-class interview of a local manager whose mid- to large-sized company uses groupware or project management software. Ask students to be ready with questions about how the manager uses the software, what effects it has had on business, and how the manager foresees it will influence their business in the future.

L1 Have pairs of students tell each other what they learned from the interview.

L2 Ask students to write a paragraph about the benefits of groupware described by the manager.

L3 Divide the class into groups to chart the uses the manager makes of groupware, its benefits, and trends the manager foresees.

Curriculum Connection
LANGUAGE ARTS

Categorizing Software. Divide students into eight groups and assign each group one of the software categories discussed in this chapter. Using magazines, newspapers, retail stores, or Internet sites that sell software, have each group locate within that category four to six popular software programs currently on the market. Students should identify the titles and publishers and include the cost, features, benefits, and availability of each program. Students should produce the data in either a spreadsheet or database. **CL**, **LS**, **P**

Reteaching

OUTPUT DEVICES. To reteach the concept of output devices, ask students to give examples. Do students themselves prefer one type of output over another? (Answers will include computer monitor, printer, fax machine, speakers.)

Enrichment Strategy

SUMMARIZE. Ask students to read an article about a software program used in business that is of particular interest to them and write a summary of the article. **LS**

Evaluation

Assign and review the Fast Review sections.

Figure 19.2 Caption Answer

Answers will vary but might include to make a personal budget, keep a rosta of team information, and to track baseball scores.

search large amounts of data at great speed to find specific information is an important part of making sound business decisions. Corel Paradox® is an example of a database manager.

Graphics and Presentation Programs

Presentation software is used to produce professional presentations. With it you can take data from spreadsheets and put it in the form of graphs, charts, or figures for visual presentations. You can do layouts for a slide show and arrange them in any order. Special effects such as shadows, backgrounds, and textures can be added to make them more interesting. Sound effects, animation, and video clips can be added to make a presentation even more effective. Among the most popular presentation and graphics programs are Microsoft PowerPoint® and Harvard Graphics.

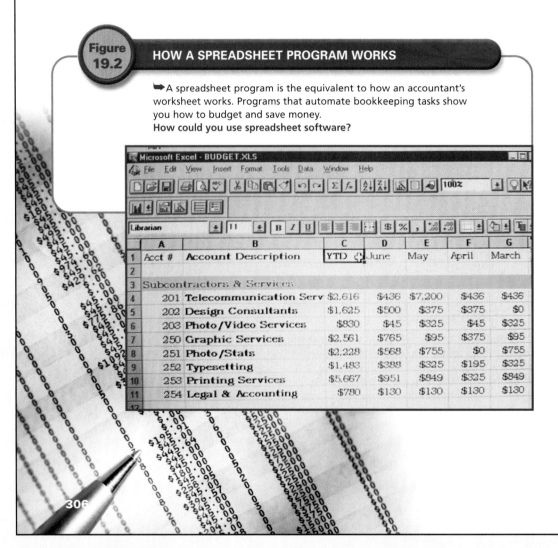

Figure 19.2 HOW A SPREADSHEET PROGRAM WORKS

➡A spreadsheet program is the equivalent to how an accountant's worksheet works. Programs that automate bookkeeping tasks show you how to budget and save money.
How could you use spreadsheet software?

How to Use a Portfolio Activity

The portfolio projects are designed to lead students to develop a collection of their best work to submit to you for assessment. You and each of your students should decide which projects to include in their business portfolio. Refer students to the specific rubric(s) from the *Alternative Assessment Strategies.* These rubrics will alert students to the criteria you'll use to assess their projects. **P**

Communications Software

Communications software makes it possible for computers to communicate with each other. You need it if you want to send a file to another computer. You also need it to send and receive e-mail. Businesses also use communications software to access databases, accounts, and other shared files. With some programs, you can receive faxes and voice mail directly on your computer. Microsoft® Outlook and QUALCOMM® Eudora are two popular communication programs.

Groupware

As discussed in Chapter 8, the trend in business is toward self-managed teams. **Groupware**, or project management software, makes it easier for team members to work together on the same project. The program is run on a network so all members of the team can access it. It can be used to track costs, schedules, resources, and tasks. It can also compute the best way to complete tasks, manage resources, and meet deadlines.

The program can also create graphs and charts to guide workers on a project. A builder, for example, can use the program to plan a construction project. The software can help the builder to complete the project within the estimated budget and schedule. By planning the entire project for the workers, the software makes it possible to complete the project more efficiently. Lotus® Notes is an example of a groupware program available.

Web Page Programs

The World Wide Web is an important part of businesses reaching the world. Web pages make it possible for businesses to market their products. Macromedia® Dreamweaver and SiteRack are the two most popular Web page programs.

 Fast Review _____

1. What can you do with desktop publishing?
2. What kinds of information might be kept in a database?
3. What are some special effects you can produce with presentation software?
4. What kind of software is useful for managing team projects?

Real-World Application

part **4** of 4

WEAVING A NETWORK

Dunn's colleagues tell him that they've located a computer on campus where someone is trying to hack into another PC somewhere in the Midwest. Dunn begins working on the day's second mystery—tracking down a culprit using the computer network he helps keep tied together.

What do you do to manage computer threats?

Chapter 19

Real-World Application Caption Answer

WEAVING A NETWORK: PART 4 OF 4

Answers will vary but might include installing virus protection software.

Technology Resource

GO TO **INTEGRATED SOFTWARE SIMULATION CD-ROM.** Check your students' understanding of the chapter's key terms by using the *Integrated Software Simulation* CD-ROM.

Fast Review Answers

1. Write, design, and lay out documents like a professional publisher.
2. Information on customers and employees, supplies, products, schedules, inventory, and sales records.
3. Shadows, backgrounds, textures, sound effects, animation, video clips.
4. Groupware.

Meeting Individual Needs

Students With Hearing Impairments. Students who wear hearing aids can be easily distracted by background noise, so it is important to restrict unneeded interference. Each hearing aid has its own limited range of use. Therefore, you will need to learn how close to stand so the student can hear you. Keep in mind that comments made in the back of the room may be inaudible. You can repeat questions or comments for the benefit of the hearing-impaired, or include a question in your answer.

4 CLOSE

Chapter Wrap-Up

Ask students to fold a sheet of paper in half, lengthways, and write ten concepts from this chapter on the left-hand side. To the right of the fold line, have students write an explanation of each concept. Students can use this sheet as a study aid by first covering the right-hand side and attempting to explain a concept before checking the written explanation. **LS**

Using Business Key Words

1. hardware
2. spreadsheet
3. software
4. database
5. scanner
6. personal digital assistant
7. random access memory
8. groupware
9. desktop publishing
10. byte

Review What You Learned

11. Software is essential to a computer.
12. The processor.
13. Floppy disks and CD-ROMs.
14. Letters, envelopes, tables.
15. Design and lay out.
16. Labels (names), numbers, dates (or times), and formulas.
17. Accounting functions.
18. Track information, keep records.
19. Electronically communicate.
20. Track project's tasks.

Summary

1. Software, people, data, and hardware are the four parts to a complete computer system.

2. Hardware is comprised of the processor, memory, input and output devices, and storage devices. The processor is the brain of the computer. The memory holds the data and is measured in bytes. Input devices accept data and instructions. Output devices return the processed data back to the user or to another computer system.

3. The following is a list of the most common units of measurement for computer memory and storage:

Kilobyte (KB)	1,000 bytes
Megabyte (MB)	1 million
Gigabyte (GB)	1 billion
Terabyte (TB)	1 trillion

4. Business software programs exist for accounting, spreadsheets, databases, communications, and Web design. Businesses can use desktop publishing and graphics software to produce high-quality reports and presentations.

Using Business Key Words

Match each of the following key words with its definition. Then, using magazines, newspapers, and the Internet, find a picture that represents each word.

- **scanner**
- **software**
- **random access memory (RAM)**
- **spreadsheet program**
- **hardware**
- **byte**
- **desktop publishing**
- **database**
- **personal digital assistant (PDA)**
- **groupware**

1. The physical components of a computer system.
2. Used by accountants to calculate revenue, expenses, net income, etc.
3. Sets of instructions that tell computers what to do.
4. A collection of related records.
5. A small scanning device that allows a printer to read printed product codes.
6. A hand-held computer you can use as a personal organizer.
7. This is the most common form of memory.
8. This is project management software.
9. Software that consists of writing, designing, and laying out documents on your computer.
10. Memory is measured in this.

Quick Quiz

1. Name the four parts of a complete computer system. (Software, people, data, and hardware.)
2. A gigabyte is _____ bytes. (One billion.)
3. Name seven types of software programs commonly used in business. (Word-processing, communication, spreadsheet, graphics, accounting, databases, groupware.)

Review What You Learned

11. Why is software development a career field with great potential?
12. What's the heart of a computer?
13. Name two examples of portable storage devices.
14. What types of documents do businesses create using word processing software?
15. Describe elements of a publication produced with desktop publishing.
16. Name the four types of information that can go into a spreadsheet.
17. How does a business utilize a spreadsheet program?
18. What are some examples of the ways businesses use electronic databases?
19. What does communication software allow us to do?
20. What does project management software allow us to do?

Understanding Business Concepts

21. Explain why storage is such an important part of a computer system.
22. Create a list of ten business tasks that computers can perform.
23. Why do you think word processing software is one of the most-used software programs for business?
24. How do you think your school might use databases?
25. How do you think your school might use presentation software?
26. Explain why you think communication software has become a necessity for businesses and consumers.
27. Imagine you're on the planning team for this year's prom. Describe how project management software might be useful for your team.

Critical Thinking

28. Do you think it's possible to run a successful business today without using a computer? Explain why or why not.
29. Describe how you could use word processing, spreadsheet, database, communication, presentation, and project management software to enhance your schoolwork.
30. How can you avoid losing information you may have saved on a business's network?
31. What steps would you take to share important project information with coworkers?

Viewing and Representing

Examining the Image. Looking at the photograph, list details that you see. Who do you think benefits from handheld computers? What new computer-related inventions have there been in the last few years?

Critical Thinking

28. Answers will vary. Most students will say that it is not possible to run a business without a computer. Make sure students provide reasons for their answers.
29. Answers will vary.
30. Back up information on more than one source (e.g., diskette or CD-ROM).
31. Groupware, save it on the network, and print off hard copies.

Viewing and Representing

Pair students to compare their lists of details. Have student pairs interview each other at the front of the room to find their partner's answers to the questions: Who do you think benefits from handheld computers? What new computer-related inventions have there been in the last two or three years? What ways have they impacted business since they were brought into use. **LS**

Understanding Business Concepts

21. The information has to be stored or you will not be able to access it again.
22. Create form letters, mailing labels, store data, accounting tasks, create presentations, store documents digitally, create graphs, and faxing.
23. Document creation is a common business task.
24. Store student enrollment information.
25. Presentations to educational personnel, parents, students, etc.
26. Quick communication, transportable communication.
27. Answers will vary.

4 CLOSE (Cont.)

Building Academic Skills

COMPUTER/TECHNOLOGY.
Allow the students to choose the way they would like to share their findings. Rubrics: Charts/tables, essay, oral presentation, poster.

MATH. Answers will vary depending on the computer system selected. Rubric: Cost estimate.

SOCIAL SCIENCE. Make sure all students participate in the group project. Encourage creativity. Have the students use the library and the Internet as resources. Rubric: Diagram.

LANGUAGE ARTS. Letters will vary. If students have trouble remembering how to format a business letter, have them use classroom resources as a reference. Rubric: Business letter.

Linking School to Home

Answers will vary. Rubrics: Survey, chart.

Linking School to Work

Answers will vary. Allow students to choose the way they would like to share their findings. Rubrics: Oral presentation, poster, essay.

Building Academic Skills

 Online Bill Pay

Research an electronic bill paying service. Answer the following questions:
- How much does it cost?
- What features are available?
- How is security handled?
- How are problems resolved?
- What are the requirements to enroll?

 Preparing a Cost Estimate

A local business owner has asked you to prepare a cost estimate for a new computer system. The owner will use the computer in every aspect of her business—communication, accounting, marketing, and project management. Using the newspaper, magazines, and the Internet, prepare the estimate. Be sure to include software and a printer.

 Composing a Letter

You work as an administrative assistant for a cookie company. Your boss has asked you to write a form letter to your customers describing the new cookie that will be on the market next week. Compose and word-process the letter.

 Historical Timeline

In a group of three or four, create a timeline that shows how computers have been used in the workplace. Begin with the early 1950s. Add pictures and graphics to add interest to your timeline. Display in your classroom.

Linking School to Home

Creating a Chart. Take a survey of your family and friends. Find out what types of software they use to make their lives easier. Create a chart that shows the name of the software, the tasks it performs, and how often it is used.

Linking School to Work

Researching Handheld Computers. PDAs are becoming more and more popular in the workplace. Research one brand of these handheld devices and find out the following:
- Cost
- Business features
- Personal features
- How it interfaces with a desktop computer
  Share your results with the class.

E-Homework

Applying Technology

Designing a Letterhead. Design is about line, value, shape, color, and texture. There is no precise formula for design, unlike grammar that requires parts of speech to perfectly interlock into meaning. Think about a designer's basic ingredients for this assignment. Create a letterhead logo and business card for an imaginary business. Use clip art and interesting fonts that will make your business appealing.

Creating a Database. Sport occupies a vast majority of people's time. Whether they're watching a little league game, rooting for a major league team, or buying team memorabilia, sport is part of culture. Now, this is your chance to research and calculate a sports team of your interest. Create a database of your favorite sports team. Include players' names, colleges, years in the league, and game statistics.

Connecting Academics

Math. Daily newspapers across the country have special technology sections. The advent of new gadgets always gets attention. Research major newspapers' archives to find information about trends in personal digital assistants (PDAs). Create a bar chart or circle chart representing the trends.

Language Arts. Break into groups. Find photographs and graphics from newspapers and magazines representing computers being used in the workplace to process information. Create a poster.

BusinessWeek — Analyzing the Feature Story

You read the first part of "A Powerful Shareware Rival to Mighty Microsoft" at the beginning of this chapter. Below are a few questions for you to answer about Idea Keeper. You'll find the answers to these questions when you're reading the entire article. First, here are the questions:

32. What are some benefits of Idea Keeper in comparison to traditional word processing software?

33. What are some disadvantages of Idea Keeper compared to word processing software?

CREATIVE JOURNAL ACTIVITY

Go to the Web site for *PC World* or *PC Magazine* and research new business software. How much of it is shareware in relation to software? Did you find any other software that's a hybrid of word processing, spreadsheet, or presentation software? Write a one-page report summarizing your findings.

The Full Story

To learn more about Idea Keeper, visit the *Introduction to Business* Web site at **www.introbus.glencoe.com**, and click on *BusinessWeek* Feature Story, Chapter 19.

E-Homework

DESIGNING A LETTERHEAD. Projects will vary. Encourage creativity. If students are not familiar with the computer software for this project, allow them to help each other. Rubrics: Business letterhead, business card.

CREATING A DATABASE. Databases will vary. Rubric: Database.

Connecting Academics

MATH. Bar charts or circle charts will vary. Have students share trends and point out any surprising statistics. Discuss main trends.

LANGUAGE ARTS. Have groups share their posters with the class.

BusinessWeek — Analyzing the Feature Story

32. The ability to catalog or bookmark ideas across several topics is a powerful way to access information. Links are also easier to create. It links information in layers rather than page by page.

33. Idea Keeper lacks high-powered features such as the ability to create headers and footers, spell-check text, and author-capitalize sentences.

Creative Journal Activity

After students have written their reports, ask students the following question: Which type of computer software do you feel was most used in business five years ago, is now, and will be in the future? **LS**, **P**

1 FOCUS

Unit Seminar Overview

In this seminar students create or enhance a product that uses new technologies. Students investigate images, interpret facts, and decide their opinion on the question: What's the greatest benefit to the quality of life of using new technology?

Bell Ringer Activity

QUESTIONS AND ANSWERS. Ask students these questions: Do you know a "gadget person?" Do you know someone who loves to look around electronics stores? What characteristics do these people have in common? Have you ever wondered, "How does this work or how is this made?" Have you ever thought, "I could make this better and cheaper?" What items were you thinking about? Were any of these items technology items?

Discussion Starter

GIVE EXAMPLES. Ask students to give examples of recent technology that's improved the quality of life, or helped people be healthier. (Answers will vary and will depend on recent news and students' experience.)

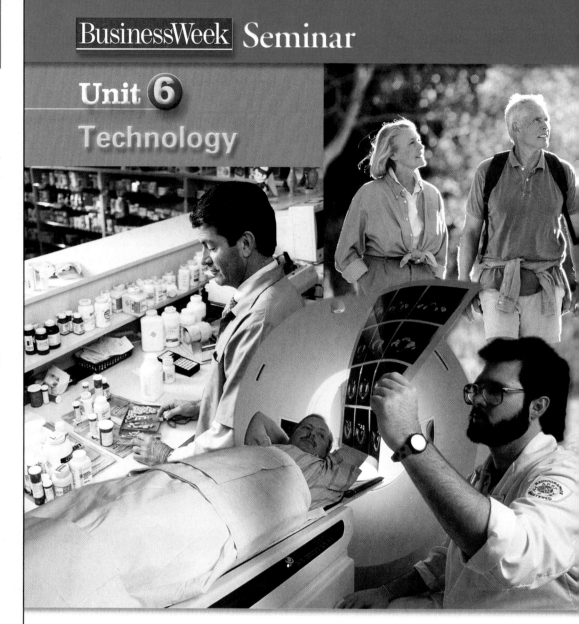

BusinessWeek Seminar

Unit 6
Technology

Applying Technology to New Business Ideas

In Chapter 19 you learned about technology's impact on the way you live. Not only does technology influence the workplace, culture, and business, but it also influences the environment, health, and science. In this seminar you'll work in a group to develop or refine a product that uses technology to improve health or to better a quality of life.

312

COMPUTER TECHNOLOGY
Newsworthy Trends

Ergonomics. Technological changes in the workplace have led to a whole new class of work-related health problems. The widespread use of computers has made eyestrain, back pain, and problems with exotic names like "carpal tunnel syndrome" and "repetitive strain injury" common. It's also produced a new word, "ergonomics" or the science of designing the job to fit the worker. Ergonomic improvements in the workplace include specially designed screens, keyboards, office furniture, wristbands, exercise sessions, and a whole new class of government regulations.

Factoids

Living in a Bubble. A couple builds what is believed to be the nation's first antimicrobial home near Simi Valley, Calif. It's engineered to stop the growth of fungus, mold, and bacteria.

A Slow, Constant Zap. Researchers hope to use low-radio frequency waves instead of chemicals to control zebra mussels in intake pipes at power plants.

Ending a Tragedy. Child malnutrition in Latin America is expected to end by 2010 with agricultural investments of $140 million.

A Promising Pledge. Microsoft promised $58 million over the next five years to help President Vicente Fox's initiative called "e-Mexico" to get 98 percent of the country online. The Internet will help Mexico's education and health sectors.

A Photograph That Stays With You. For $895 you can get a full-body computed tomography (or CT) exam, which is a scan of your internal body. The scan can detect future health problems that might not be diagnosed right away.

Investigate the Images

Look at the photographic collage on the left page. What grabs your attention? Is it the color or the words? The power in reading visuals is in analyzing and dissecting your observations. On a separate piece of paper, respond to the questions listed below. These questions might help sharpen the focus of your visual mind.

Your Observations

1. How many photographs do you see?

2. Examine each photograph. How are they assembled in relation to one another?

3. What is the subject of each photograph? Is place or location the subject?

4. Does color signify a message?

5. What issues do you take from these images?

Information

6. Summarize what you know about the photographs from your observations.

Exploring Culture

7. What aspect of your daily life is influenced by technology? Does it create stress in your life?

8. How, where, and on whom should scientists and doctors perform experimental medical research?

2 TEACH

Thinking Critically

Look at the factoids:

1. Would you like to live in a "bubble?" Why do you think the couple did this? (Answers will vary and may include: The couple feels they'll live healthier lives. They may have a child who needs to be protected from germs.)

2. Which do you think is more worthwhile, "Ending a Tragedy" or "A Promising Pledge?" Why? (Students' answers and reasons for their responses will vary.)

Cooperative Learning

TECH FAIR. Have students work in small groups. After discussing "Exploring Culture" (seminar questions 7 and 8), assign the following task: groups should set up decorated booths in the classroom for a Tech Fair. Each student should bring in an actual technology item or a picture of a technology item to place on his or her group's booth. Students should be prepared to demonstrate or explain their item, and answer questions about what aspects of daily life are affected by this technology and if the item creates or relieves stress. Have half of the groups work their booths, while the other groups visit the booths. **CL**, LS

COMPUTER TECHNOLOGY
Newsworthy Trends

The Doctor Is Online. The Internet has changed the way medicine is practiced in the United States. In 1996, about 8 million Americans went online to get health information on the Internet. By the year 2000, it was over 33 million. The most common medical use of the Internet is to research specific illnesses such as allergies and depression. The next most common use is to research diet and nutrition. As a result, the Internet has changed the relationship between doctors and patients.

2 TEACH (Cont.)

Independent Practice

L1 SUMMARIZE

Ask students to find a recent article on ways technology is used in medicine, the health industry, or agriculture. Ask them to prepare a summary of the article to share with the class. **CL**, LS

L2 SPREAD THE WORD

Have each student take a part in preparing and giving a ten-minute presentation to a PTA group describing recent advances in the use of technology for improving people's lives. If you have access to a presentation program, have students use it to create an electronic presentation. **CL**, LS

L3 TIME LINE

Have students research technological innovations in medicine, the health industry, or agriculture over the past 20 years and create a time line. Students should include at least six technological innovations and include important details of their effect on society. Have students share their time line with their classmates. **CL**, LS

BusinessWeek Seminar

Taking Aim at Technology

● Preparation

Discover how a business uses technology to enhance a product's form and function, and decide the benefits of applying technology to it.

Objective
- **Research** a product that uses technology.
- **Examine** a marketable idea for a product, and explain why it's beneficial or desirable.
- **Create** a marketing plan for your product, and create a model that describes the benefits of using technology.

Materials Needed
- ✓ Copies of recent news and technology publications such as *Yahoo! Internet Life, BusinessWeek,* or a major newspaper.
- ✓ Paper, pencils, pens, markers
- ✓ Posterboard
- ✓ Materials for product mock-up or sketches

● Procedures

1. With two other students, find and read articles about applying new technologies to daily living. Possible topics include home networking, interconnected appliances, and robotics. Use the Internet to access business or technology publications or sections of the newspaper.

2. Brainstorm ideas for products that use new technologies. Either create a new product or refine a product's function that you read about.

3. As a group, submit a one-page, typed paper describing your product and answering these questions:
   - What is your product?
   - What new technology is being used?
   - How would it be used in daily living?
   - Who is your market? Who would buy this product?

4. Review what you learned in Chapter 13 and create a marketing plan. Decide which media—Internet, television, radio, magazines, newspapers, etc.—would advertise your product most effectively. Decide, too, how you would distribute your product.

5. Display a mock-up or drawing of your product and explain how it works. Present your product and marketing plan to the class.

314 Unit 6 Managing Financial and Technological Resources

Reteaching Strategy

In step two of this seminar's "Taking Aim at Technology," student groups created or refined a product. Create a chart on the board to compare and contrast the products. Headings for the chart could include: "New Technology Used," "Use in Daily Living," "Market," and "Customer Demographics." Ask students to point out similarities and differences in the products.

Chart It

With your group compile a list of reasons for using new technology in everyday life. Use the information presented by the class and found during your research. On a separate sheet of paper, draw a pie chart that describes how your group ranks the reasons for using technology in daily living. Compare your pie chart with other groups.

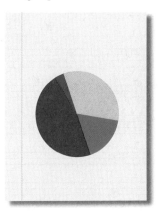

Analyze and Conclude

After considering your research and the other groups' charts, answer the questions below:

1. **Participating as a Group.** Which is the most popular reason (within your entire class) for using new technology?

2. **Teaching Others.** In your group's opinion, which is the most popular reason for using new technology?

3. **Applying Technology to a Task.** Name three other reasons for using new technology in daily living.

4. **Selecting Technology.** What do you think is the greatest benefit for using new technology? Give your reasons.

Becoming an Informed Citizen

Congratulations, you finished the seminar. Now it's time to reflect on the decisions you made.

Knowing How to Learn. Why is it important to think about technology on a larger scale than just how it affects a business and a workplace?

Analyzing Your Future. Knowing the importance of health and technology in your daily life, what are some possible career opportunities that might be available to you in the future?

BUSINESS Online

Further Exploration

To find out more about using technology in daily life, visit *Introduction to Business* Web site at **www.introbus.glencoe.com**.

Analyze and Conclude Answers

1. Answers may vary but should reflect the reason given most frequently in the largest number of charts.
2. Answers may vary from group to group but should reflect the largest portion of that group's pie chart.
3. Answers will vary.
4. Answers will vary and should be supported with clear reasoning.

Career Planning in a Global Economy

Chapter 20
Developing a Career Plan

Chapter 21
Getting a Job

Unit Objectives

After completing this unit, students will be able to achieve the following outcomes:

- Explain the difference between a career and a job and name ways to find career options.
- Describe a personal inventory and list ways to prepare for a career.
- List employability skills and information sources for job openings.
- Describe how to prepare a résumé and explain the job application process.

BusinessWeek Connections

In this unit, students will read the following articles from *BusinessWeek*:

Chapter 20 "Can Your Nerves Take a Dot-Com Job?": Take a look at what it means to work in a start-up tech company—then decide.

Chapter 21 "Asking the Right Questions": Interviewers are coming up with new ways to find the right person for the job and the questions can be tricky for the candidate.

Key to Descriptive Icons

The following designations will help you decide which activities are appropriate for your students.

L1 Level 1 activities should be within the ability range of all students.

L2 Level 2 activities should be within the ability range of the average to above-average students.

L3 Level 3 activities are designed for the ability range of above-average students.

ELL Activities should be within the ability range of the English Language Learner.

LS Learning Styles designation represents activities designed to address different learning styles.

CL Cooperative learning activities are designed for small group work.

P Portfolio designation represents student products that can be placed into a best-work portfolio.

Teacher Classroom Resources*

Program Resources	Chapter 20	Chapter 21
Student Activity Workbook	p. 141	p. 151
Lesson Plans	p. 52	p. 54
Internet Resources	p. 59	p. 61
Reproducible Tests	p. 39	p. 41
Teaching Transparencies	20.1, 20.2	21.1, 21.2, 21.3
Strategies and Worksheets for Teaching Transparencies	pp. 10, 56	pp. 10, 58

* Each of these resources is available in print and on the Interactive Lesson Planner CD-ROM.

Technology Resources

- Interactive Lesson Planner CD-ROM
- PowerPoint® Presentation CD-ROM
- ExamView® Pro Test Generator CD-ROM
- Integrated Software Simulation, Teacher Manual
- Glencoe Business Video Package
- *PuzzleMaker* CD-ROM
- *Introduction to Business* Web Site
- *Virtual Business*®
  Virtual Business is a business simulation that introduces students to the principles of business by letting them start and run their own virtual business. In *Virtual Business,* students have the power to control all aspects of a retail convenience store. Students strategize business decisions using a powerful learning tool in the guise of a video game.

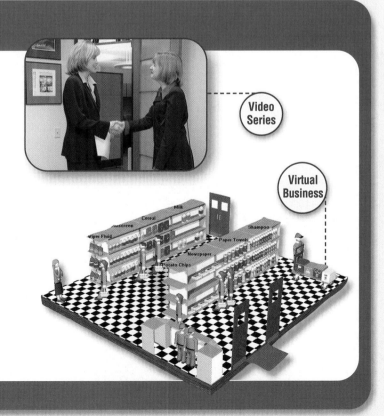

Video Series

Virtual Business

Scope and Sequence

	Academic Standards of Learning				
	LANGUAGE ARTS	MATH	HISTORY	COMPUTER/ TECHNOLOGY	SOCIAL SCIENCE	
CHAPTER 20	pp. 319, 320, 323, 325, 327, 330, 331	pp. 318, 330, 331	pp. 321, 324, 325	pp. 321, 327, 330, 331	pp. 319, 320, 321, 323, 324, 326, 327, 330	
CHAPTER 21	pp. 333, 334, 336, 338, 339, 345, 346, 347	pp. 337, 346, 347	pp. 343, 346	pp. 335, 341, 342, 346, 347	pp. 333, 334, 335, 336, 338, 339, 341, 342	

Scope and Sequence

Themes and Concepts

Business Core	Accounting and Finance	Business Management	Computer/ Technology	Marketing	Entrepreneurship
Competitive Envir. Career Exploration Employ. Transitions Goal Setting Job Acquisition Job Retention Teamwork Motivation Personal Qualities	Decision Making Competition	Unemployment Employment Law Contracts Human Resources Development and Management	Program Design and Development Business Management Business Decisions Culture	Motives and Behavior Policies and Procedures	Business Image Entrepreneurial Potential Human Resources Management Technology
Entrepreneurial Concepts Career Exploration Employment Transitions Goal Setting Interest Assessment Job Acquisition Retention	Decision Making Technology	Competition Consumers Decision Making Productivity Unemployment Employment Law Ethics Environmental Factors	Computer and Communication Systems Program Design Social Issues	Cultural Diversity Risk Management	Entrepreneurial Concepts Management

Unit Overview

In Unit 7 you'll take a look at how to plan for your career and get a job in today's working world.

CHAPTER 20 explains the three steps to planning a career: Decide what you want to do, analyze your job options, and then research a career.

CHAPTER 21 outlines the employability skills and then explains the process of getting a job beginning with your job search and contacting potential employers.

Introducing the Unit

Tell students: "You know you're going to one of your favorite events tomorrow—a ball game or a concert. How do you feel when you wake up in the morning?" Then ask, "Would you like to feel like that on days when you get up to go to work?" Let students know that many people do feel that way, whether they're entrepreneurs or employees in large corporations. It's possible to be passionate about your work, especially when you plan a career goal and go and get it—and this unit is a great place to start.

Technology Resource

GO TO **INTRODUCTION TO BUSINESS WEB SITE.** To find out more about content in Unit 7, visit the Glencoe *Introduction to Business* Web site.
www.introbus.glencoe.com

Unit 7

Career Planning in a Global Economy

Chapter 20
Developing a Career Plan

Chapter 21
Getting a Job

Wanted: A Cool Job

When most people think of a career, they think of something like business, construction, publishing, or law. There are, however, more types of jobs out there than you can imagine. If you want to be an artist, for instance, your only option isn't to move into a loft in New York and slowly starve. You could get a job carving ice sculptures, designing film sets, or doing police sketches. If you like animals, you could start a pet day-care. Find more jobs at **www.cooljobs.com** and **www.jobs.net**.

● **How Is Your English?**
You could live in Thailand, China, or Germany certified as a TEFL (Teaching English as a Foreign Language) instructor. You don't even need to know a foreign language.

● **Shop Till You Drop**
Market research companies hire a mystery shopper to shop at stores and evaluate the quality of goods and services.

● **Paid to Play**
Software companies have game testers, who test new games they're developing for technical glitches and level of difficulty.

● **Watch Out Where You Land**
Smokejumpers, the commandos of firefighting, fly into fire areas and parachute in to control and "mop-up" fires.

Field Trip Suggestion

Focus on Job Skills. Ahead of the trip assign students to groups and ask each group to prepare to bring at least one camera. Arrange to take students to a company known for its job-training program. Ask a company representative ahead of time if students may take photographs. During the tour, ask a representative to explain what is involved in the company job-training program—the skills, education, and attitude it looks for in new employees, and the training and education benefits available. Tell student groups to take photographs to illustrate important employability skills and characteristics. After the trip, have student groups create a photograph collage with labels featuring the important factors. **CL**, **LS**, **ELL**

BUSINESS Online

Idea Factory

To learn more about the jobs and careers, visit the *Introduction to Business* Web site at **www.introbus.glencoe.com**, and click on Unit 7 Career Planning in a Global Economy.

Bulletin Board

Glencoe Poster Teaching Tip

Before introducing the poster, ask students if they admire someone and the work that person does, such as a movie director, a building contractor, or their doctor. Ask students if they want to do work like that and let them know about mentoring programs. Then have the students take a look at the poster. Do any students want to be like Steve Jobs? Ask students what skills and characteristics Steve Jobs has. List the answers on the board. Have students take the test on the poster. Discuss students' answers.

Portfolio Activity

The Right Résumé. Imagine that a car corporation has just opened a new regional headquarters in your area. It's advertising for a payroll clerk, and you're interested in working with numbers. You'd like to get the job but you're afraid that you don't have the right qualifications. A friend suggests that you "change" your résumé to make yourself look better.

Have students write a page about what they would do, and why. After students have completed writing, point out that it's better to avoid stretching the truth. Presenting an accurate picture of yourself is most important. Your résumé should highlight your skills and knowledge that a potential employer would find valuable, but it doesn't need to point out your weaknesses. **P**, **LS**

🕐 Out of Time?

If time doesn't permit teaching each chapter in this unit, you may use the PowerPoint® Presentation CD-ROM to review the chapter's content.

SCANS Correlation Chart*

Foundation Skills

Basic Skills	Reading	Writing	Math	Listening	Speaking	
Thinking Skills	Creative Thinking	Decision Making	Problem Solving	Seeing Things in the Mind's Eye	Knowing How to Learn	Reasoning
Personal Qualities	Responsibility	Self-Esteem	Sociability	Self-Management	Integrity/ Honesty	

Workplace Competencies

Resources	Allocating Time	Allocating Money	Allocating Material and Facility Resources	Allocating Human Resources		
Information	Acquiring and Evaluating Information	Organizing and Maintaining Information	Interpreting and Communicating Information	Using Computers to Process Information		
Interpersonal Skills	Participating as a Member of a Team	Teaching Others	Serving Clients/ Customers	Exercising Leadership	Negotiating to Arrive at a Decision	Working With Cultural Diversity
Systems	Understanding Systems	Monitoring and Correcting Performance	Improving and Designing Systems			
Technology	Selecting Technology	Applying Technology to Task	Maintaining and Troubleshooting Technology			

*This chart's highlighted blocks indicate the chapter's content coverage in the Student Edition and the Teacher Wraparound Edition.

Resource Manager

Teaching Transparencies

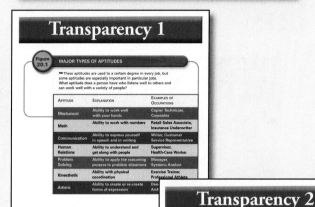

Transparency 1

Figure 20.1 — MAJOR TYPES OF APTITUDES

These aptitudes are used to a certain degree in every job, but some aptitudes are especially important in particular jobs. What aptitude does a person have who listens well to others and can work well with a variety of people?

Aptitude	Explanation	Examples of Occupations
Mechanical	Ability to work well with your hands	Copier Technician, Carpenter
Math	Ability to work with numbers	Retail Sales Associate, Insurance Underwriter
Communication	Ability to express yourself in speech and in writing	Writer, Customer Service Representative
Human Relations	Ability to understand and get along with people	Supervisor, Health-Care Worker
Problem Solving	Ability to apply the reasoning process to problem situations	Manager, Systems Analyst
Kinesthetic	Ability with physical coordination	Exercise Trainer, Professional Athlete
Artistic	Ability to create or re-create forms of expression	Dancer, Architect

Transparency 2

Figure 20.2 — JOB SEARCH METHODS

Most job searchers don't find employment with just traditional search methods. What percentage of people answered want ads?

Source: JIST Works, Inc.

Application and Enrichment

- Lesson Plans
- *BusinessWeek* Poster Package
- Teaching Transparencies
- Integrated Software Simulation
- Glencoe Business Video Package

Review and Reinforcement

- *PuzzleMaker*
- Internet Resources
- Student Activity Workbook
- Strat. and Work. for Teaching Transparencies

Assessment and Evaluation

- Reproducible Tests
- Alternative Assessment Strategies
- ExamView® Pro Test Generator

Technology

- *PuzzleMaker*
- ExamView® Pro Test Generator
- Glencoe Business Video Package
- PowerPoint® Presentation
- Integrated Software Simulation
- Interactive Lesson Planner
- *Virtual Business®*

KEY	
Printed	Software	Videocassette	Poster
Transparency	CD-ROM	Internet	

BUSINESS Online

Visit **www.introbus.glencoe.com**, the Web site companion to *Introduction to Business.* The student's page includes:

- interactive tutor
- additional *BusinessWeek* articles and activities
- business Web links
- homework hints
- real-world application activities
- additional career path activities

Information on how to prepare your students for the high school exit exam and special projects are also included.

Use the Glencoe Web site for additional resources. All essential content is covered in the Student Edition.

Introducing the Chapter

This chapter introduces the three steps of planning a career—deciding what you want to do, analyzing job options, and researching a career. A photo essay, "The Write Business," enhances the concepts.

Connecting the Objectives

What job options have you looked into that might fit your abilities? How might you find out about career options?

BusinessWeek
Feature Story

Story's Summary

Fast-paced tech start-up jobs offer you great responsibility and practice in risk-taking. Going for a job? Now's the time to write down the salary you need, calculate the financial risks, and decide on your career expectations.

Find the entire article at www.introbus.glencoe.com, or in the Teacher Resource Binder.

Chapter 20

Developing a Career Plan

● Learning Objectives

After completing this chapter, you'll be able to:

1. **Explain** the difference between a career and a job.
2. **Describe** a personal inventory.
3. **Name** ways to find out about your career options.
4. **List** the things you can do to get prepared for a career.

● Why It's Important

There's no better time than the present to start planning a career. There are positive steps you can take toward reaching a career goal.

● Key Words

career	profession
career	trade
planning	apprenticeship
aptitudes	journeyworker
skills	internship
career	shadowing
counselor	career ladder
networking	entry-level job

BusinessWeek Feature Story

Can Your Nerves Take a Dot-Com Job?

The New Frontier of Career Opportunities. How much personal risk you can and should tolerate is a very subjective matter. Simply stated, you should not sign up for a tech start-up situation where you would be highly uncomfortable. You may be in a situation where you are outside your normal comfort zone. If you're a first-time tech start-up prospect, then the tech start-up will definitely push your comfort envelope. However, in today's economy, taking calculated risks is becoming more necessary than ever.

Source: Excerpted with permission from "Can Your Nerves Take a Dot-Com Job?" *BusinessWeek Online*, September 8, 2000.

An Extension Activity

Depending on your path in life, money will always be an issue—too little, too late, too much, and so on. Do you equate a career choice with making a lot of money? Or not? What are the advantages and disadvantages of taking career risks?

BUSINESS *Online*

The Full Story

To learn more about taking career risks, visit the *Introduction to Business* Web site at www.introbus.glencoe.com, and click on *BusinessWeek* Feature Story, Chapter 20.

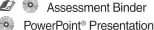

Classroom Resources

For the Teacher

- 📁 Student Activity Work. TAE
- 📓 ⊙   Assessment Binder
- ⊙ PowerPoint® Presentation
- ⊙ Interactive Lesson Planner
- 📁 Lesson Plans
- 📓 💻   Internet Resources
- 📠 Teaching Transparencies
- 💻 *Introduction to Business* Web Site

- ⊙ Integrated Soft. Sim. TM
- 🖥 *BusinessWeek* Poster Package

For the Student

- 📓 Student Activity Workbook
- ⊙ *Virtual Business®*
- 🖥 *Introduction to Business* Web Site
- ⊙ Integrated Soft. Sim.
- ⊙ *PuzzleMaker*
- 📓 Strategies and Worksheets for Teaching Transparencies

Bell Ringer Activity

ORGANIZING AND MAINTAINING INFORMATION. Create a chart to keep track of what you will learn about yourself and your career. Use these headings or add your own: Interests, Abilities, Values, Job Options, Education, Experience, and so on.

Preteaching Business Key Words

CREATIVE THINKING. Write a sentence for each key word but replace each key word with a nonsense word. Volunteers read aloud the sentence while others insert the correct word. **CL**

An Extension Activity

RISK INVENTORY. Take an inventory of times you remember taking a risk. What happened? Draw a line down the middle of a piece of paper. Write the risk on the left. Write the result on the right. Did you grow from the experience? **LS**

Making Connections

Postsecondary Education. Ask a representative from a community college or technical institute to discuss programs offered, entrance requirements, extracurricular activities, and cost. Have students prepare questions ahead of time on 3" by 5" cards. **LS**, **CL**

2 TEACH

Business Connection

Priti Patel is job hunting and finishing her second year as a Master of Business Administration (MBA) student. In her journal, Patel compares her first year at Kellogg to starting a new job—there's the same feeling of having butterflies, the novelty, and the anticipation. The second year brings more responsibility and more challenges, which is good practice for the job she hopes to get soon.

Develop Concepts

COMPARE AND CONTRAST.
What's the difference between a job and a career? How could they be the same? (Answers will vary and may include that a job is something you just do to make money, whereas a career is a field or occupation you plan to work in over a long period of time.)

Figure 20.1 Caption Answer

A human relations aptitude.

Three Steps to Planning a Career

The auditorium is a mass of mortarboards and gowns from your view in the balcony. Your sister is graduating from high school, and this fall she will attend a nearby state university. Your mother keeps encouraging her to study her interests, like painting and writing. As you lean on the balcony's railing, trying to find your sister in the crowd, you start drifting into your own career daydream. You've always liked taking apart circuit boards and dissecting bugs in the summer. Yet you've always been interested in history. As a sophomore in high school, it's never too soon to start planning.

Choosing a career is a very important decision that each person has to make. The decision will affect the rest of your life. But what's a career? How is it different from the job you do after school or on weekends or vacations? Unlike simply getting a part-time job or doing work during a vacation, a career involves preparation, such as education or training, as well as specialized skills or abilities. A wise career choice

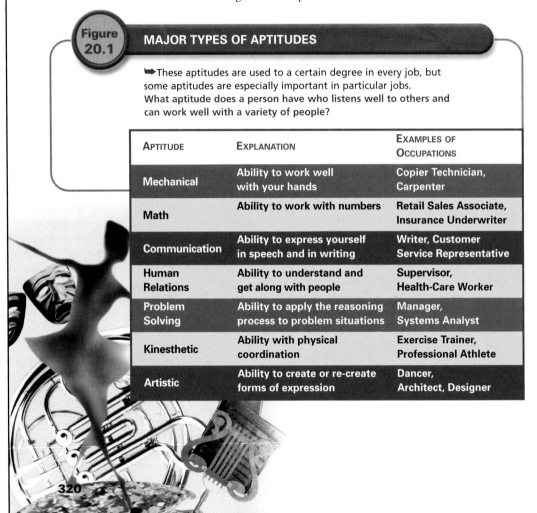

Figure 20.1

MAJOR TYPES OF APTITUDES

➡ These aptitudes are used to a certain degree in every job, but some aptitudes are especially important in particular jobs. What aptitude does a person have who listens well to others and can work well with a variety of people?

APTITUDE	EXPLANATION	EXAMPLES OF OCCUPATIONS
Mechanical	Ability to work well with your hands	Copier Technician, Carpenter
Math	Ability to work with numbers	Retail Sales Associate, Insurance Underwriter
Communication	Ability to express yourself in speech and in writing	Writer, Customer Service Representative
Human Relations	Ability to understand and get along with people	Supervisor, Health-Care Worker
Problem Solving	Ability to apply the reasoning process to problem situations	Manager, Systems Analyst
Kinesthetic	Ability with physical coordination	Exercise Trainer, Professional Athlete
Artistic	Ability to create or re-create forms of expression	Dancer, Architect, Designer

320

Cooperative Learning

Career Day. Set up a committee system in your class to plan and put on a career day for the school. Activities to be planned, scheduled, and executed include: gaining permission from school administration, canvassing parent and community volunteers, contacting career professionals to set up booths, and advertising the career day. **LS, CL**

may require more of you, but will provide more to you in return. Your choice affects the amount of money you will earn but more importantly, it affects the amount of satisfaction that you can gain from your work. It's a good idea to choose work that is satisfying since you'll be spending a lot of time earning a living.

Step 1: Deciding What You Want to Do

When you leave school you'll have to work for a living. You have a choice of whether to get a job or whether to pursue a career. A job is something you do to make money. A **career** is an occupation or field in which you work over a long period of time. To pursue a career takes time, training, experience, and most of all, planning. **Career planning** consists of assessing your potential, analyzing your options, and preparing for the future. The first step in choosing a career is taking inventory of your interests, abilities, goals, and values (see Figure 20.1). The second step is analyzing your job options, and the third step is researching a career.

Interests

What do you enjoy doing? Your answer to this question will tell a lot about your interests. Many people's hobbies are their interests. For example, cooking, writing stories, hiking, and playing musical instruments are all hobbies. Each one might suggest a possible occupation. You might also consider what subjects and activities you enjoy at school. If you like to do science experiments or write articles for the school newspaper, you may find that one of those interests could lead to a career.

As you talk with people, read about jobs, and see workers in action, you'll probably be drawn to a few choices. To narrow your choices, you need detailed information about specific jobs. Keep the following questions in mind when looking at specific occupations or careers:
- What tasks do people in the position typically perform? What are their responsibilities? Do they work with information, people, machines, tools, or a combination of these? Do they perform a variety of tasks, or do they do the same thing over many times?
- What qualifications were necessary to secure the position? These are the requirements for specific jobs, such as education, training, experience, and special skills.
- Which skills do people in the position use? Are these skills learned on the job, or must workers already have these skills to apply for the position?

Real-World Application

part 1 of 4

THE WRITE BUSINESS
As a freelance and newspaper staff reporter for the last ten years, Larisa Brass has written about the world of business in Tennessee. She's a business reporter for the *Knoxville News-Sentinel*, where she specializes in technology and telecommunications reporting. Brass got her start in high school. **What activities do you do now that could turn into a career?**

continued on p. 323

Chapter 20 Developing a Career Plan **321**

Real-World Application
Caption Answer

THE WRITE BUSINESS:
PART 1 OF 4
Answers will vary.

Technology Resource

GO TO **POWERPOINT.** The *Introduction to Business* PowerPoint® CD-ROM provides visual lecture aids for this chapter.

Independent Practice

ILLUSTRATE.   As in all careers, being a chef requires a particular mix of skills, aptitudes, and personal characteristics. Draw an illustration or make a collage representing the skills, aptitudes, and personal characteristics you think a chef has. How do they compare with yours? (Encourage students to be creative and have fun.) **LS**

Meeting Individual Needs

Americans with Disabilities Act of 1990. The Americans with Disabilities Act of 1990 makes it illegal for companies to deny employment opportunities to otherwise qualified individuals who have real or perceived mental or physical disabilities. It also requires employers to make reasonable accommodations to enable disabled workers to perform their work. This includes access to entrances and exits and to the work itself. These factors influence workplace design and personnel space design. You may wish to consider these issues in chapter discussions.

Thinking Critically

DAYDREAM. One warm afternoon you're staring at the ceiling and thinking about what you'll be doing in ten years. You wish you could work on something you'd love to do and make more than enough money to live the lifestyle you want. Just suppose your wishes come true. There are no obstacles. The work you'll be happiest doing is just waiting for you. Describe what you know you'd love to do and know you could do well.

Fast Review Answers

1. A job is something you do to make money. A career is an occupation or field in which you work for a long period of time.
2. An aptitude is a natural talent. A skill is an ability you develop through learning and experience.

Consider This...

Caption Answer

Sclafani turned his enthusiasm for baseball and his knowledge of the major league into a business because he saw a need for personalized recruiting.

- What personal and physical characteristics are necessary? What type of personality is best for the position? Do the tasks require problem-solving skills or good manual dexterity?
- Is any previous work experience required or preferred? If so, what kind?
- What are the wage levels for the position? What are the opportunities for advancement?
- What is the outlook for this occupation? How will technology affect it and will the product or service being produced become less or more in demand? What are the advantages and disadvantages of the occupation?

Abilities

After you have considered what you like to do, ask yourself what you're good at doing. Identifying the things that you do well will help you choose a career. Every person has certain skills and aptitudes. Aptitudes are very different from skills. **Aptitudes** are talents that come naturally. **Skills** are abilities developed through learning and experience.

If you're good at figuring out how to fix things, you probably have mechanical aptitude. You need more than aptitude, however, to repair a personal computer. To fix a computer, you would need to develop skills through the study of electronics. You might want to pursue a career in art if you have an aptitude for it, but you will also need to acquire skills working with different materials.

Goals and Values

When you choose a career, it's important to consider whether it will give you the satisfaction that you want. Most of us have similar values, but we put them in vastly different orders of importance. The occupations that you choose should relate to what you value or think is important for your life. Keep in mind that your values could well change during your life. At this point, though, you should make choices based on the values that you hold right now.

If you place great emphasis on freedom and independence, you might want to become an entrepreneur and start your own business. On the other hand, many people prefer working for others. They value the security of having someone else in charge as well as the steady income and benefits. If you place a high value on helping others, you might consider a career in teaching, social work, or health care. You might want to be an artist and also make a lot of money. Since artists often don't make very much money, you have to decide which goal is more important to you.

Consider This...

A Home Run Career Decision

Steve Sclafani dreamed of a career in major league baseball. As a star second baseman at the University of Pennsylvania, he thought he might have a shot. The pro scouts thought otherwise. Instead, he founded Baseball Factory, which specializes in getting high school players onto college teams. It does it by holding "showcase" games so talented high school players can perform for college coaches.

ANALYZE

How did Sclafani morph his talents into a business?

Fast Review

1. What is the difference between a job and a career?
2. What is the difference between an aptitude and a skill?

LANGUAGE ARTS
Curriculum Connection

Recruiting. Have students work in small groups to develop print advertising, a radio ad, or a television spot designed to recruit applicants with certain aptitudes and skills to a specific position. Encourage groups to display or broadcast their advertisements. **LS,** **CL**

Step 2: Analyzing Your Job Options

The second step in planning a career is figuring out your options. What kinds of jobs will be in demand in the future? What kinds of skills will you need? Where can you get information? Before deciding on a career, you need to find out where the jobs are and how to find them.

The Job Market

The job market changes along with changes in population, technology, and other factors. For example, as a result of the boom in computer technology, there's a great demand for computer experts. In contrast, the demand for typists, bank tellers, and office workers is much less. The popularity of desktop publishing has resulted in little demand for typesetters and paste-up workers. Almost any career you want to pursue will require computer skills.

As the population increases, there will be an increased demand for workers in construction and engineering. More workers will be needed to design and build houses, roads, and bridges. The demand for nurses and teachers will increase. Health care is expected to be one of the biggest areas of growth. There will be a greater demand for physical therapists, speech therapists, and medical assistants.

Sources of Career Information

Investigating the job market can be overwhelming. After all, there are thousands of different occupations from which to choose. However, career information is plentiful and simple to use if you know how to find it.

Asking Career Counselors. One of the best ways to get information is by speaking to a career counselor. A **career counselor** is a person trained to provide information and guidance on choosing a career. A career counselor can also help you learn more about your interests and abilities. For example, if you've done public service or played on a team, a counselor might recognize leadership or organizing skills you've shown. A counselor can inform you about what careers might suit you and advise you on what classes would prepare you best for these careers.

Your school probably has a career or guidance counselor. If you're interested in going to a community college or a university, a counselor there can help you make long-range plans. Your teachers might also be able to suggest careers that would use the abilities and interests you have shown in class.

Networking. Another way to get information is by networking. **Networking** consists of meeting and talking to people in different

Real-World Application
part 2 of 4

THE WRITE BUSINESS
"I revived our high school newspaper," she says, "and discovered that journalism was my thing." After studying journalism in college, Brass worked for one year at a small newspaper in Oak Ridge, Tenn.
Image a career you're interested in. What steps can you take today to learn more about the career?

continued on p. 325

Real-World Application
Caption Answer

THE WRITE BUSINESS: PART 2 OF 4
Answers will vary but might include asking career counselors, networking, and researching careers.

Business Connection

Arnelle Productions, a provider of Web content, based in San Francisco, Calif., employs three staff members. There's more work to be done, though, and it gets done by ten unpaid interns. The interns, all high-school students, gain hands-on work experience so they can make informed career choices.

Develop Concepts

INTERVIEW AND REPORT. Working in pairs, interview each other by asking the question: What are the best sources of career information in the local area, nationally, and on the Internet? The interviewer reports the partner's ideas to the class.

Chapter 20 Developing a Career Plan **323**

Great Ideas From the Classroom of...

Jane Keegan
Franklin County High School
Brookville, Ind.

Profession of Interest. After reading this chapter, students choose an adult they admire who has a profession of interest to them. Students contact that individual and ask them to come to class for 20 to 25 minutes to discuss their career. Speakers are given a questionnaire to follow, including statements such as: describe a typical day, tell why you choose this profession, etc. Students have the task of introducing their speaker and writing a thank you letter as a follow-up. **LS, CL**

occupations to find out what they do and to make connections. By talking to people you can learn about what their job involves, how they got it, what their training was, and whether you'd like it. Most people are happy to talk about what they do. You can start by talking to relatives, family friends, and local business owners. Some companies have open houses and give tours of their facilities. If you're interested in a job someone told you about ask that person for career-planning advice.

Researching Careers. Figure 20.2 illustrates the most widely used job search methods. You can find information about careers at your school library or public library. For example, the *Occupational Outlook Handbook (OOH)* describes more than 300 occupations. It lists the fastest-growing job fields and gives addresses of places to write for more information. The *OOH* is also available on CD-ROM and on the Internet. The *Encyclopedia of Careers and Vocational Guidance* describes over 1,500 jobs including educational requirements, employment outlook, and opportunities for experience.

A simple way to learn what the market is for certain types of occupations is by looking in the want ads of a newspaper. You'll usually find plenty of listings for engineers, teachers, and nurses. Business magazines and journals are a good source of information on changing job trends.

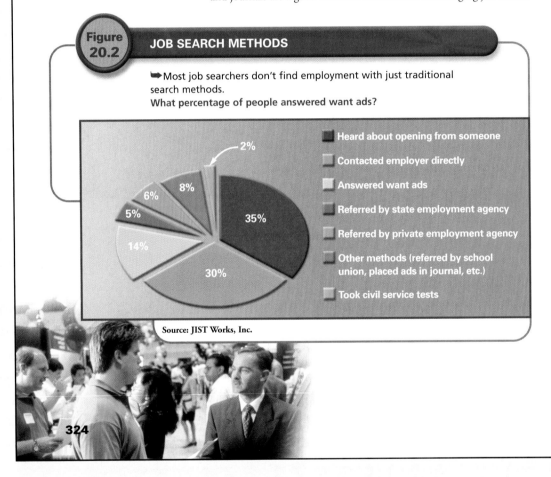

Figure 20.2

JOB SEARCH METHODS

➡ Most job searchers don't find employment with just traditional search methods.
What percentage of people answered want ads?

- Heard about opening from someone — 35%
- Contacted employer directly — 30%
- Answered want ads — 14%
- Referred by state employment agency — 5%
- Referred by private employment agency — 6%
- Other methods (referred by school union, placed ads in journal, etc.) — 8%
- Took civil service tests — 2%

Source: JIST Works, Inc.

324

Global Perspective

Global Challenge. Work in pairs. International trade is big business today. To increase your career choices and success, whether you wish to work abroad or in this country, ask each other these questions: Have you talked with people about the rewards and pitfalls of working in other countries? Are you becoming fluent in a second language?

What trends do you see in international trade? What challenges will businesses in the United States face in the next ten years? How might you help meet those challenges? After the interview, note any specific actions you plan to take to prepare yourself for working in the global marketplace.

You can find a lot of information on the Internet by checking out the Bureau of Labor Statistics or job Web sites such as **www.monster.com**. For other sources of information, you can attend career days and job fairs that might be held at a local school or community center.

 ## Fast Review

1. Name some areas where there's expected to be an increased demand for workers.
2. What are sources you can use to research careers?

Step 3: Researching a Career

At this point in your life you might not be able to decide what kind of career you want to pursue. There are numerous ways to research careers. During the course of your lifetime, you might also change careers more than once. Whether you know what you want to do or not, however, you can increase your options with education and experience. The more skills you acquire, the better your chances of having the career you want and the more money you're likely to make.

Education

Most jobs today require at least a high school education. To pursue a career, you'll probably need some form of advanced education. There are different types of schools to choose from depending on whether you want to go into a profession or a trade. A **profession** is a field that requires a high level of education, such as law, medicine, or architecture. A **trade** is a field that requires a high level of manual or technical skill, such as carpentry, mechanics, or computer programming.

To pursue a profession, you have to study at a college or university for many years and get an advanced degree. If you want to learn a skill, you can go to a trade, technical, or vocational school. These types of schools prepare you for a specific occupation, emphasize hands-on training, and help you find a job afterward. Most schools offer students some form of financial aid, or money to help you pay for your education. Your career counselor or the financial aid officer at a school you'd like to attend can tell you what types of aid you can get.

Experience

In planning for a career, gaining experience is as important as getting an education. If you don't plan on going to college, or you want to

THE WRITE BUSINESS
Brass is trying to meet a deadline for a story about local high-tech start-up companies. "This part of Tennessee is a Silicon Valley wannabe," she says. "With the University of Tennessee and National Laboratories nearby, technology companies should be attracted to the area."
Is your career plan contingent upon living in a particular region?

continued on p. 327

THE WRITE BUSINESS: PART 3 OF 4
Answers will vary.

Fast Review Answers ✓

1. Computers, construction, engineering, teaching, and health care.
2. Manuals, newspapers, business magazines and journals, the Internet, career days, and job fairs.

Individualized Practice

Many companies and organizations can be found on the Internet. They often post job openings. Have each student research job openings at a company they might want to work for in the future.

L1 Have students work in pairs to discuss the job openings listed.

L2 Have students prepare a chart listing the job opportunities and important details of the positions.

L3 Have students send a business e-mail to the company requesting information about the availability of internships, job shadowing, steps in the career ladder, and part-time jobs.

HISTORY — *Curriculum Connection*

Apprenticeships. Apprenticeships date back to about A.D. 1000. A young person would become apprenticed to learn a trade such as metalworking, printing, or weaving. Often the young person lived away from home with a master to learn the trade for about seven years. Research one type of apprenticeship or one apprentice and give a brief oral report. **LS, CL**

3 ASSESS

Reteaching

RESEARCHING A CAREER.
To reteach the concept of researching a career, ask students to give specific examples of ways of gaining work experience. (Specific examples of volunteering, internships, apprenticeships, job shadowing, and so on.)

Enrichment Strategy

IDENTIFY. Ask students to identify trends in the local job market. What is the impact on the community? **LS**

Working Lifestyle

Caption Answer

Occupations in food production and agriculture to produce the raw materials for baking, such as flour, chocolate, raisins, and fruit. In the manufacturing, maintenance, and reparations of large equipment such as ovens to such things as spatulas. In the training of chefs. In service industries, such as laundries (for uniforms) and cleaning.

---

enhance your education, there are a number of ways you can gain work experience.

Apprenticeship. An **apprenticeship** consists of learning a trade by working under the guidance of a skilled worker, such as a chef, a plumber, or an electrician. Many apprenticeship programs are available through labor unions and trade schools. You can also find out about them through your state employment office. An apprenticeship can last from two to five years. During the program, an apprentice might not make very much money. As an apprentice's skills increase, however, so does the pay. An apprentice who completes a program is called a **journeyworker**, or skilled craftsperson, and can make very high wages.

Internship. An **internship** is a program that provides hands-on experience for a beginner in an occupation, usually as a temporary, unpaid trainee. Most internships are offered to students through colleges or on the Internet. Internships are available in almost every type of business and profession, such as marketing, film production, and law. If you're

Working Lifestyle

What are you doing at 10 A.M.?

The Sweet Life

Kate Jansen's mother taught her cooking skills but her passion for fare took her to Italy for 11 months. There she studied the fine art of making pastries and Italian cuisine. In 1993, Jansen decided to open her own business, and she and her partners—a bread baker and a financial expert—launched Firehook Bakery.

Today Jansen is one of the finest pastry chefs in Washington, D.C. By 10:00 A.M. she already has been working for 4 hours, supervising her staff of 15, and checking orders.

Even an embassy order for chocolate raspberry truffle cakes doesn't cause Jansen to overlook her regular customers. She chats with them while folding the cake boxes for a noon delivery.

Salary

In large cities, pastry chefs can earn an average salary between $44,000 and $65,000 per year.

Outlook for This Career

The food service industry is expanding. People increasingly want fine, unprocessed food. The outlook for this occupation is very good.

Connecting Careers Activity

List other occupations that contribute to making a pastry come to life.

CAREER PATH

Hospitality & Tourism

How to Use a Portfolio Activity

The portfolio projects are designed to lead students to develop a collection of their best work to submit to you for assessment. You and each of your students should decide which projects to include in their business portfolio. Refer students to the specific rubric(s) from the *Alternative Assessment Strategies*. These rubrics will alert students to the criteria you'll use to assess their projects. **P**

interested in going into broadcasting, you can start by getting an internship at a TV or radio station. Internships allow you to learn how a business works from the inside and can lead directly to a job.

Other Types of Experience. You can also gain valuable skills and experience by doing volunteer work. If you're interested in learning broadcasting but can't get an internship, you can volunteer to work at a local TV or radio station. By volunteering for community service, you can learn organizing and leadership skills. If you plan on starting your own business some day, you can volunteer to work at a family or local business. Even if you don't intend to go into that particular line of business, you can learn how a business is run.

Your school might have a cooperative work or earn-and-learn program. In this type of program, business and community leaders, teachers, and students work together to plan students' work experiences and educational goals. Studies have shown that students with such work experiences have great success getting their first job. In some cases, you may be able to shadow a person in a certain business or trade. **Shadowing** means following a person throughout a workday to see what a job involves. Some schools provide shadowing experience for students.

The Career Ladder

You can't expect to go from broadcasting school or an internship at a TV station to landing a job as the anchor for the national news. You have to move up the **career ladder**, or through different job levels within an occupation. You might have to start out with an **entry-level job**, or a beginning career job. For example, if you want to become a newspaper reporter, you might have to start out as a fact checker. You climb the ladder to better positions as you gain more skills, knowledge, and experience.

You might not like the idea of borrowing money to pay for college, taking a low-paying entry-level job, or working as an unpaid intern. Building a career, however, takes time and patience. Keep in mind that people who obtain the right skills and education end up earning a lot more money in the long run. The time and money you spend preparing for a career is an investment in your future.

 Fast Review _____

1. What is the difference between a profession and a trade?
2. What are some ways you can gain work experience?
3. Where can you find out about apprenticeship programs?

THE WRITE BUSINESS
Brass says her favorite stories have focused on the impact of venture capital on local technology start-ups. She explores what's happening in the area, why the growth of local technology-based industries hasn't met expectations, and what's needed to change that situation. **How can you take your experiences and apply them to a career plan?**

Real-World Application
Caption Answer

THE WRITE BUSINESS: PART 4 OF 4
Answers will vary.

Technology Resource

 GO TO **INTEGRATED SOFTWARE SIMULATION CD-ROM.**
Check your students' understanding of the chapter's key terms by using the *Integrated Software Simulation* CD-ROM.

Evaluation

Assign and review the Fast Review sections.

Fast Review Answers ✔

1. A profession is a field that requires a high level of education. A trade is a field that requires a high level of manual or technical skill.
2. Apprenticeship, internship, volunteer work, working in a family or local business, cooperative work or earn-and-learn program, shadowing.
3. Labor unions, trade schools, and the state employment office.

Meeting Individual Needs

English Language Learners. The job search process can be a monumental challenge to people whose native language is other than English, especially if they are newcomers. In order for these individuals to attain their goals, extensive practice and role-play dealing with the job search situations described in the chapter can make the difference between employment and despair. Peer partners selected for role-play should include one native speaker and one nonnative speaker, if possible. Give extra attention to telephone situations and dealing with government agencies, both of which can be intimidating situations for those who feel uncertain about using English. Encourage the students to be assertive. **ELL**, **LS**

4 CLOSE

Chapter Wrap-Up

Ask students to elaborate on the three steps of planning a career.

Using Business Key Words

1. career
2. career ladder
3. internship
4. apprenticeship
5. shadowing
6. trade
7. journeyworker
8. networking
9. skills
10. career planning
11. career counselor
12. aptitudes
13. profession
14. entry-level job

Review What You Learned

15. A career involves education or training. A part-time job is less involved.
16. Self-evaluation and studying various occupations.
17. Interests are what you enjoy doing. Abilities are what you are good at doing.
18. Increase production.
19. *Occupational Outlook Handbook; The Encyclopedia of Careers and Vocational Guidance.*
20. Moving from one level to another.
21. Plan the students' work experience and education goals.
22. Someone who earns a wage while learning a trade by working with a master tradesman; mechanical and construction trades.
23. Values and goals as well as interests and abilities.
24. Course work and work.

Summary

1. A job is something you do to make money. A career is a lifetime occupation that takes time, training, experience, and planning to pursue.

2. A personal inventory consists of assessing your interests, abilities, goals, and values.

3. You can find out about your career options by:
   - Studying the job market.
   - Meeting with a career counselor.
   - Networking.
   - Doing research.

4. You can prepare yourself for a career by going to a college or trade school or getting experience through an apprenticeship, internship, volunteer work, or school program.

Using Business Key Words

The following terms will help you understand how to plan and decide on a career plan. Match each term to its definition.

- **career**
- **entry-level job**
- **career ladder**
- **career counselor**
- **aptitudes**
- **networking**
- **profession**
- **shadowing**
- **apprenticeship**
- **career planning**
- **journeyworker**
- **skills**
- **trade**
- **internship**

1. An occupation or field in which a person works over a long period of time.
2. The mobility possibility from an entry-level position to one at the top of the field.
3. A program that provides hands-on experience for a beginner in an occupation, usually as a temporary and unpaid trainee.
4. Learning a trade by working under the guidance of a skilled worker.
5. Accompanying an employee throughout his or her workday to see what the position involves.
6. A field that requires a high level of manual or technical skill, such as carpentry, mechanics, or computer programming.
7. A skilled craftsperson who has completed an apprenticeship.
8. Talking to people about their jobs.
9. Abilities developed through training and experience.
10. Assessing one's potential, analyzing one's options, and preparing to pursue a career.
11. A person who provides career advice.
12. Ability that comes naturally.
13. A field that requires a high level of education, such as law, medicine, or architecture.
14. A beginning career job.

Quick Quiz

1. What is the first step on the career ladder? (An entry-level job.)
2. Explain what networking means. (Talking to other people about their jobs.)
3. What are two things you can do while still in school to prepare for a particular career field? (Answers may include: Take courses to gain needed skills, get an internship or apprenticeship, or get a part-time job related to the field.)

Review What You Learned

15. How is a career different from a part-time job?

16. Name the three steps of a good career plan.

17. Explain the difference between interests and abilities.

18. How does technology play an important role in the workplace?

19. Name three sources of career information.

20. What is a career ladder?

21. Describe a cooperative work program.

22. What is an apprentice? In what occupations are most apprentices found?

23. What should the criteria for evaluating a career be based upon?

24. How can you prepare for a career while still in high school?

Understanding Business Concepts

25. List three of your interests and three of your abilities. Do any suggest a possible occupation? Explain.

26. Why are guidance counselors and teachers especially helpful in matching your aptitudes to possible careers?

27. Review the list of common aptitudes located in the chapter. Choose two and explain why they're important to you.

28. What's the advantage of networking?

29. What's an entry-level position? Give an example of such a position, and describe what types of jobs it might lead to within the same career field.

30. Why is the money you spend on education like investing in yourself?

31. Create a list of criteria that is important to you when you evaluate a career.

Critical Thinking

32. Choose a job you're interested in pursuing. What three qualifications do you think you would need for it?

33. Describe your personal career goals. What steps will you take to ensure you achieve those goals?

34. Describe ways people move up the career ladder.

35. How does the economy affect career choices?

Viewing and Representing

Examining the Image. Look closely at the photograph. Use your five senses to step into the photograph. What do you hear? What else do you see around you? Imagine you're doing this work. Is this the type of job you want? Would this job fit your aptitudes and skills? Would you make the best use of your abilities and skills in this career?

Chapter 20 Developing a Career Plan **329**

Critical Thinking

32. Answers will vary depending on the job chosen.

33. Answers will vary.

34. Answer will vary but might include higher levels of education, experience, and networking.

35. Answer will vary but may include the employment rate, businesses' profits, and a recession or depression.

Viewing and Representing

Point out to students that it's important to like the environment in which you'll work. If you like being outdoors and can't stand being inside all day, you'll need to choose an outdoor occupation, such as a park ranger. The type of people you'll be working with also makes a difference. If you're a pet lover, you'll probably be happy to be around other animal lovers. When students have chosen career fields they are interested in, encourage them to find out about the environment, people, and working conditions, by arranging a visit, a job-shadowing experience, or an internship. **LS**

Understanding Business Concepts

25. Answers will vary.

26. They also might recognize certain aptitudes and skills in you.

27. Answers will vary.

28. Your network of friends, relatives, and acquaintances probably can help you find someone who works in any field in which you might have an interest.

29. The beginning level of the career ladder. Examples will vary.

30. Because additional education usually means a better job which will lead to the ability to earn more money. So, if you invest in your education now, it will pay off in the future when you are able to earn more money.

31. Answers will vary.

Chapter 20 Review

4 CLOSE (Cont.)

Building Academic Skills

LANGUAGE ARTS. Be certain each student participates in the group project. Rubric: Essay.

COMPUTER/TECHNOLOGY. Encourage students to spend time researching the skills necessary in the career cluster. Rubric: Word-processed document.

MATH. Students can use the library or the Internet as references for their research. Answers will vary depending on the careers selected. Encourage students to share their findings with others in the class. Rubric: Chart/tables.

SOCIAL SCIENCE. Students can use the library or the Internet as references for their research. Students might also speak to foreign exchange students in their school about the program. Rubric: Essay.

Linking School to Home

Answers will vary. Rubric: Diagram.

Linking School to Work

If students need help getting started, suggest they contact your school guidance office. Rubrics: Chart/tables, lists.

Building Academic Skills

 Essay Writing

Work in groups of four. Brainstorm a list of ten careers. For each career write the interests, abilities, values, and goals you think would be relevant. Then divide into pairs. Interview your partner about his or her interests, abilities, values, and goals. Suggest one or two careers from your group's list that you think would be suitable for your partner. Then switch roles. Write a brief essay about the career your partner suggested for you and why you think it might or might not be suitable for you.

 Preparing a Plan

Select a career cluster and determine the skills and knowledge necessary for it. Devise a personal plan to achieve competency in that career cluster. Use word processing software to prepare a copy of your plan.

 Average Salaries

Choose two careers that interest you. Research the average salaries for those careers. Research the education requirements and costs to obtain the skills necessary to be successful in the careers. Prepare a chart of your findings.

 Studying Abroad

Understanding the world outside the borders of the United States is becoming a very marketable skill for many career fields. Student exchange programs and overseas internships are two ways to gain experience abroad. Research opportunities to live and work overseas. Write a two-page paper with your findings and explain whether or not you would like to take advantage of an overseas experience.

Linking School to Home

Diagraming Career Paths. Interview a family member about his or her career ladder. Create a diagram that shows the jobs your family member has had. Then connect the skills, experience, education, and leadership roles that led to advanced positions on the ladder. If you prefer, interview a teacher, neighbor, or mentor instead.

Linking School to Work

Finding Programs. Compile a chart of the programs in your school and community that link school to work. Be sure to ask the guidance counselors and teachers to help you. Include names, addresses, telephone numbers, and contact people. Then, as a class, compile all the charts. Prepare a document that can be shared with other students in your school.

E-Homework

Applying Technology

Career Sites. Use the Internet to research the various career planning Web sites available. Create a list of the ten best sites and explain why you think they would be a valuable resource to someone who is planning and making career decisions.

Jobs in Technology. Research the entry-level jobs in the field of technology. Choose two you might be interested in finding out more about. What are the educational requirements of the two jobs selected? Do you have an interest in either one? Why or why not?

Connecting Academics

Math. The *Occupational Outlook Handbook (OOH)* contains descriptions of more than 300 broad categories of occupations in 11 occupational grouping. It lists the fastest-growing job fields and provides addresses of places to write for more information. The *OOH* is also available on CD-ROM and on the Internet. The *Occupational Outlook Handbook* puts the average weekly salary range for a career at $750 to $900. Laticia earns the minimum of this range and then receives a 5 percent raise. What is her new weekly salary?

Language Arts. Send an e-mail or letter introducing yourself to someone working in a career that interests you. Describe why you're interested in the career and request an information interview. Include a list of six questions for the person.

BusinessWeek Analyzing the Feature Story

You read the first part of "Can Your Nerves Take a Dot-Com Job?" at the beginning of this chapter. Below are a few questions for you to answer about working at a tech start-up. You'll find the answers to these questions when you're reading the entire article. First, here are the questions:

36. What values or goals would you need to take a job with a tech start-up?
37. What is one way to minimize the risk of working for a tech start-up?

Creative Journal Activity

List three skills you currently have. Now list three more that you would like to have. Choose three jobs you might consider as a career. Do any of these jobs match the six skills?

BUSINESS Online
The Full Story
To learn more about taking career risks, visit the *Introduction to Business* Web site at **www.introbus.glencoe.com**, and click on *BusinessWeek* Feature Story, Chapter 20.

331

E-Homework

CAREER SITES. Web sites will vary. Allow the students to choose the way they wish to share their findings with the class. Rubrics: Lists, essay, oral presentation, poster/chart.

JOBS IN TECHNOLOGY. Students may wish to help each other with this activity. Rubrics: Note taking, oral presentation.

Connecting Academics

MATH. Yearly: $13,000 to $15,000. Weekly, after raise: $262.50.

LANGUAGE ARTS. Letters or e-mails will vary and should include a list of six questions.

BusinessWeek Analyzing the Feature Story

36. The values of adventure or a willingness to take risks would be important in working for a tech start-up.
37. Make sure you understand the responsibilities of the job and be sure it will provide you with the experience you are looking for.

Creative Journal Activity
Often others can see strengths in a person that the person himself or herself doesn't recognize. Ask students to pair up with another student they know fairly well. Ask each partner to write a list of five strengths of his or her partner. After partners have exchanged and discussed their lists, ask students if they learned anything new. **LS, CL**

SCANS Correlation Chart*

Foundation Skills

Basic Skills	Reading	Writing	Math	Listening	Speaking	
Thinking Skills	Creative Thinking	Decision Making	Problem Solving	Seeing Things in the Mind's Eye	Knowing How to Learn	Reasoning
Personal Qualities	Responsibility	Self-Esteem	Sociability	Self-Management	Integrity/ Honesty	

Workplace Competencies

Resources	Allocating Time	Allocating Money	Allocating Material and Facility Resources	Allocating Human Resources		
Information	Acquiring and Evaluating Information	Organizing and Maintaining Information	Interpreting and Communicating Information	Using Computers to Process Information		
Interpersonal Skills	Participating as a Member of a Team	Teaching Others	Serving Clients/ Customers	Exercising Leadership	Negotiating to Arrive at a Decision	Working With Cultural Diversity
Systems	Understanding Systems	Monitoring and Correcting Performance	Improving and Designing Systems			
Technology	Selecting Technology	Applying Technology to Task	Maintaining and Troubleshooting Technology			

*This chart's highlighted blocks indicate the chapter's content coverage in the Student Edition and the Teacher Wraparound Edition.

Resource Manager

Teaching Transparencies

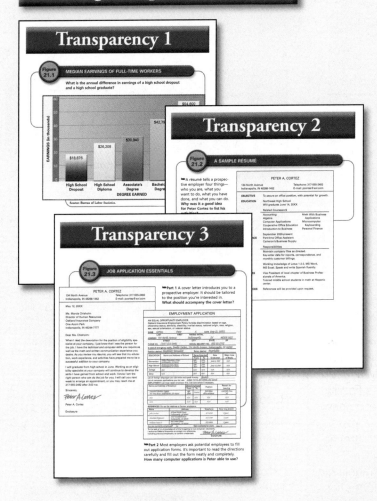

Application and Enrichment

- 🖋 Lesson Plans
- 📕 *BusinessWeek* Poster Package
- 🕹 Teaching Transparencies
- 💿🖋 Integrated Software Simulation
- 📼🖋 Glencoe Business Video Package

Review and Reinforcement

- 💿 *PuzzleMaker*
- 🖥🖋 Internet Resources
- 🖋 Student Activity Workbook
- 🖋 Strat. and Work. for Teaching Transparencies

Assessment and Evaluation

- 🖋 Reproducible Tests
- 🖋 Alternative Assessment Strategies
- 💿 ExamView® Pro Test Generator

Technology

- 💿 *PuzzleMaker*
- 💿 ExamView® Pro Test Generator
- 📼 Glencoe Business Video Package
- 💿 PowerPoint® Presentation
- 💿🖋 Integrated Software Simulation
- 💿 Interactive Lesson Planner
- 💿 *Virtual Business*®

KEY	🖋 Printed	🖴 Software	📼 Videocassette	📕 Poster
	🕹 Transparency	💿 CD-ROM	🖥 Internet	

Visit **www.introbus.glencoe.com**, the Web site companion to *Introduction to Business*. The student's page includes:

- interactive tutor
- additional *BusinessWeek* articles and activities
- business Web links
- homework hints
- real-world application activities
- additional career path activities

Information on how to prepare your students for the high school exit exam and special projects are also included.

Use the Glencoe Web site for additional resources. All essential content is covered in the Student Edition.

1 FOCUS

Introducing the Chapter

This chapter outlines employability skills. It describes how to prepare a résumé and how to apply and interview for a job. A photo essay, "An Illustrative Visionary," enhances the concepts.

Connecting the Objectives

What things would you look for in a person you were going to employ to help you organize your room? What ways can you look for a job? Apply for a job?

BusinessWeek
Feature Story

Story's Summary

Roopa Foley's quick thinking in a job interview got her the job. Interviewers might ask candidates difficult questions, like brainteasers, puzzles, or real-world problems. Sometimes it doesn't even matter if your answer's wrong—it may be your thinking process that the interviewer's studying.

Find the entire article at **www.introbus.glencoe.com**, or in the Teacher Resource Binder.

Getting a Job

● Learning Objectives

After completing this chapter, you'll be able to:
1. **Name** the employability skills.
2. **Describe** how to prepare a résumé.
3. **List** sources of information about job openings.
4. **Explain** the job application process.

● Why It's Important

Most employers follow similar procedures when they have job openings to fill. Once you know the procedures you can move through the steps with confidence.

● Key Words

qualifications
employability skills
body language
résumé
reference
employment objective
job lead
referral
employment agencies
cover letter
job interview

332

BusinessWeek Feature Story
Asking the Right Questions

Companies Rely on a Variety of Techniques to Interview Candidates. During a job interview six months ago, Roopea Mehendale Foley came up with a well-reasoned analysis. That's one reason why she's now vice president for product development in the New York City based e-commerce outfit, Dash. The company didn't hire a consultant or use a formal personality test, however. It turned to the time-honored approach of using probing questions, getting Foley to solve puzzles, and react to real-world situations.

Source: Excerpted with permission from "Asking the Right Questions," *BusinessWeek Online*, October 13, 2000.

An Extension Activity

How can you prepare for brainteasers an interviewer may ask you to solve? Ask any of your family members or friends who have been at a job interview some of the difficult questions the interviewer asked.

BUSINESS *Online*
The Full Story
To learn more about job interviews, visit the *Introduction to Business* Web site at www.introbus.glencoe.com, and click on *BusinessWeek* Feature Story, Chapter 21.

Classroom Resources

For the Teacher
- 📁 Student Activity Work. TAE
- 📓 💿 Assessment Binder
- 💿 PowerPoint® Presentation
- 💿 Interactive Lesson Planner
- 📁 Lesson Plans
- 📓 💻 Internet Resources
- 🎞 Teaching Transparencies
- 💻 *Introduction to Business* Web Site

- 💿 Integrated Soft. Sim. TM
- 💻 *BusinessWeek* Poster Package
For the Student
- 📓 Student Activity Workbook
- 💿 *Virtual Business®*
- 💻 *Introduction to Business* Web Site
- 💿 Integrated Soft. Sim.
- 💿 *PuzzleMaker*
- 📓 Strategies and Worksheets for Teaching Transparencies

Bell Ringer Activity

SOCIABILITY. You're at a job interview. "How will you get along with your coworkers?" the interviewer asks. Think of what you will say and give two examples from your own school or community experience to back up your answer.

Preteaching Business Key Words

DECISION MAKING. Attempt to write your own definition for each key word. Decide which are most difficult to define. Copy the glossary definition for these words. **LS**

An Extension Activity

PRACTICE. After students interview family and friends, ask them to chart the questions and answers. Ask students to record how they would respond to similar questions.

Making Connections

Being an Entrepreneur. Students who believe they have entrepreneurial potential need to continue their education to gain the skills needed to run their own successful businesses. Many high schools, colleges, and adult education programs offer courses specific to entrepreneurship and small business management. Other helpful courses include accounting, computer classes, as well as additional business and marketing classes for entrepreneurs. Joining a nonprofit organization that provides information to individuals, such as the National Business Association, can also be helpful.

Business Connection

Which skills and abilities do employers consider most important for employees in today's workplace? Smeal College of Business Administration at Penn State recently surveyed Fortune 500 companies to find out. The top five skills and abilities identified by the survey are:

- Oral and written communication
- Leadership
- Analytical skills
- Ability to work in teams
- Ability to manage rapid change

Develop Concepts

SCENARIO. You're a manager at Xtreme, a store that sells athletic goods. Today you're interviewing a candidate for a sales representative position. The representative will be working the cash register and answering customers' questions. What's your profile of the ideal candidate? (Answers will vary and should include education, skills, previous experience, and personality.)

Figure 21.1 Caption Answer

$7,332. ($26,208 − $18,876.)

On Becoming a Producer in Society

Club sports and student government never really interested you. You're bored after school and tired of not having any money to buy the latest CD, jeans, or tennis shoes. One day on your way home from school you see a want ad in the local pizzeria's window. You look past the sign into the shop and see a cook gracefully tossing dough in the air. You walk inside, ask the manager for an application, and take it home to fill it out.

Employability Skills

You need to know what employers look for when they hire a new employee. Different jobs require different **qualifications**, or education, skills, and work experience to do a particular job. What's important for one job might be less important for another. Employers look for

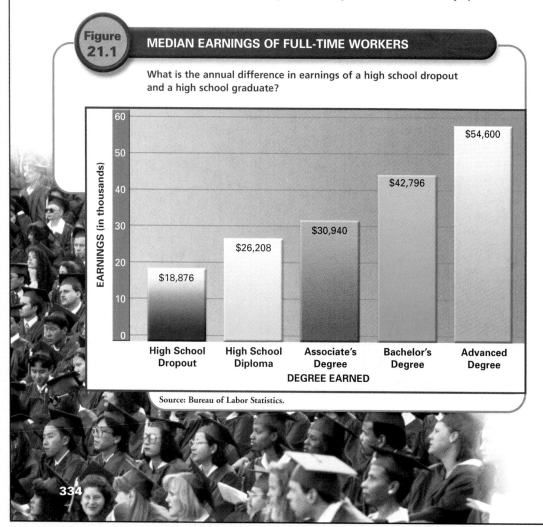

Figure 21.1

MEDIAN EARNINGS OF FULL-TIME WORKERS

What is the annual difference in earnings of a high school dropout and a high school graduate?

Source: Bureau of Labor Statistics.

334

Cooperative Learning

Job Interview. Work with a partner. Choose the job for which you will interview. Take turns being the interviewer and the job applicant. Act as if this is a real job interview. The interviewer asks the following questions.

- Why are you interested in this position?
- What school classes do you do well in and how do they relate to this job?
- Describe three of your strengths that would be useful in this job.
- Describe a weakness you might need to address in this job.
- What questions do you have about the job? **CL**

more than just job qualifications, however. They also consider a person's character, personality, and ability to work with others. All these factors combined are called **employability skills**.

Level of Education

For most jobs, employers want applicants to have at least a high school diploma. High school dropouts have fewer job opportunities, especially if they have no previous work experience. On the whole, the level of education of workers in our country has risen. The more skills and education you have, the wider the job market will be for you. Figure 21.1 illustrates the average income gap between high school dropout and earning an advanced degree.

Required Skills

Employers expect workers to have certain basic skills for practically any job. Employees must be able to read well enough to function in their jobs. They must be able to communicate with others and do simple math problems. Basic computer skills, such as entering or accessing data on a computer, are also necessary. An employee must be able to follow instructions and be able to work well with others.

Work Experience

Many employers look for people with some work experience. Sometimes employers even require that potential employees have a certain number of years of experience. Experienced workers have proven skills and a familiarity with the job. They need less training to take over a new job. This, of course, can be a problem if you're looking for your first job. That's why it's important to get some kind of experience either through a school program, volunteer work, or even helping out at a family business. Some jobs require little or no experience. The more skill and experience a job requires, however, the better it pays.

Character and Personality

Though skills are important, employers also look for employees who have certain character traits. Employers value honesty, dependability, and hard work. They also want employees who have a good attitude toward work, a desire to do the job well, and the ability to get along

Real-World Application

part 1 of 4

AN ILLUSTRATIVE VISIONARY

"Find something you love to do and do it. If you work hard at a career you really like, the money will take care of itself," says Gary Kelley, a graphic artist. "Freelance graphic art is a life without structure. I go to my studio six days a week, and more often than not, four of those days will be very different from one another." **What kind of skills would you need to be a freelancer?**

continued on p. 337

Chapter 21 Getting a Job **335**

Chapter 21

Meeting Individual Needs

Students With Visual Impairments. Students with visual impairments may not be able to maintain good eye contact. Depending on the type of impairment, they may in fact have no control over eye movement. This can put them at a disadvantage in some parts of the interview process. However, these students may excel at giving tasks undivided attention because they are not distracted by visual images. In some work situations, they may actually be at an advantage. Often, listening skills are enhanced when visual impairment is present. A challenge in one area can result in strength in another area. Encourage students with visual impairments to emphasize their strengths in their résumé and in an interview.

2 TEACH (Cont.)

Thinking Critically

VISIONING. You're nervous and excited at the same time. You've found just the right part-time job. You want to do well in the interview so you're imagining a possible question the interviewer might ask: "Describe a situation, in your volunteer work or in school, where you were challenged in using your communication skills. Tell me about it in detail." You think over some possible challenging times. Then you use the STAR (Situation, Task, Action, Result) technique to frame your answer. First you describe the situation and the task, or problem, that needed action. Then you describe the action you took and the results. (Answers will vary.)

Caption Answer

Look at classified ads and see what words other people applying for similar positions use to describe their skills.

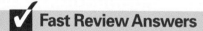

✔ Fast Review Answers

1. Education, job skills, work experience, character, personality, and ability to work with others.
2. Your body language, school records, and extracurricular activities.

E-Résumés

E-mailing your résumé through the Internet presents special challenges. Send your résumé as a text-only document on a PC and then paste it into a message. Don't send it as an attachment—the company you're sending it to may not be able to open it. After you've e-mailed your résumé, send a hard copy through the mail. E-mailed documents sometimes lose their formatting, such as boldface and italics. Companies now use computers to scan résumés so fancy typefaces and graphics don't scan well.

Critical Thinking

Companies often use computer programs to look for key words in résumés. How can you find out what those key words are?

with other workers. Research shows that the main reason people lose their jobs is because of a poor attitude and difficulty working with others. An employer can learn about these traits in several ways.

Body Language. Your **body language**, or nonverbal communication, often says more about you than your spoken or written words. Posture, eye contact, facial expression, and gestures can either add to or take away from the impression you make. For instance, if you seem fidgety or bored during an interview it looks like you have a short attention span or aren't really interested in the job.

School Records. Employers might check school records for information. Good grades show motivation and a willingness to apply yourself to a task. Employers usually check attendance records. Even if you don't have the best grades, good attendance and punctuality indicate that you're reliable and will show up for work on time.

Extracurricular Activities. Extracurricular activities are social activities that you take part in outside of school. They indicate extra effort on your part, as well as possible leadership ability. For example, taking part in team sports shows an ability to work with a group. Any volunteer work you do shows a sense of commitment and responsibility. What you're doing now, in and out of school, is creating a record that your future employers will want to see.

✔ Fast Review

1. What are the employability skills employers look for when considering a job applicant?
2. What are things an employer can look at to learn about your character?

Beginning Your Job Search

Before you begin looking for a job, you need to discover which jobs you would like most and which you would be able to do best. You should avoid limiting your search to one type of job. Some jobs require little or no experience. Other jobs require work experience. Still others might require certain skills.

LANGUAGE ARTS · Curriculum Connection

Evaluation. Think about your experience being interviewed and answer the following questions. Think about the partner you interviewed and comment on how well they interviewed and point out one possible area for improvement.

- Did you use good eye contact, speak clearly, and have an enthusiastic attitude?
- Which questions did you answer easily?
- Which were more difficult to answer?
- What relevant positive qualities about yourself were you able to point out?
- List areas you would need to improve for a real job interview. **LS**, **CL**

Preparing Your Résumé

One of the first steps in finding a job is preparing a résumé. A **résumé** is a summary of your skills, education, and work experience (see Figure 21.2). Its purpose is to persuade potential employers to grant you an interview. The beginning of a résumé includes personal information such as your name, address, and telephone number. Some people also include a fax number or an e-mail address.

Your education and work history tell an employer about your abilities and work ethic. Be sure to include volunteer work you've done, such as working on a school fundraiser. If you have a good school record as well as experience related to the job, an employer is more likely to be interested in hiring you.

The appearance of your résumé makes the first impression on an employer. If it's disorganized and chock-full of grammatical errors, your chances of getting an interview are slim. Therefore, be sure the résumé is neatly formatted and that the information is presented clearly. Check your grammar and spelling before sending it.

Reference. A **reference** is a person an employer can contact to find out about your experience, education, and character. A reference could be a teacher, former employer, or other adult. Job and school references are used to verify that you worked and went to school where you claimed. Personal references are used to testify to your character. Before using people as references, be sure to get their permission.

Employment Objective. Résumés might vary in content, but usually include an **employment objective**. This is a statement of your career goals or interest in a business. You might state that you're interested in a career in the field, are working your way through school, or think you can learn a lot from the job. Your statement should be brief and to the point.

Looking for Openings

You're not aware of all of life's opportunities until you start looking for them. How do you go about finding a job? You need to get a **job lead**, or information about a job opening. Job leads can come from several sources.

Your Network. Your network consists of people you know, such as friends, relatives, neighbors, and members of groups to which you belong. They're often the best source of job leads. They might be able to tell you about better job openings or openings that aren't advertised.

Chapter 21 Getting a Job **337**

Real-World Application

part 2 of 4

AN ILLUSTRATIVE VISIONARY

Today he is at the top of his profession, a world-renowned graphic artist whose illustrations grace magazine, book covers, posters, and postcards. How might your extracurricular activities turn into something more, like a job?

continued on p. 339

Chapter 21

Real-World Application
Caption Answer

AN ILLUSTRATIVE VISIONARY: PART 2 OF 4
Answers will vary.

Business Connection

Southwest Airlines finds that an informal approach to job interviewing pays off. Southwest interviews a small group of candidates together to see how the candidates work together and to gauge each individual's ability to work in a team. The airline considers teamwork one of the cornerstones of its success.

Develop Concepts

ORGANIZE. As a job hunter, you'll need to keep track of companies and organizations you're interested in. Make a check sheet for each company including the name of the company, address, phone, fax, e-mail, type of industry, product or service, and name of the person you contacted. Develop a filing system for your job search. **LS**

Great Ideas From the Classroom of...

Luis F. Varela
Oconee County High School
Watkinsville, Ga.

Present Your Portfolio. In the portfolio, students keep a collection of work representing their best efforts throughout the course. Students are motivated because it's a hands-on activity since they'll be making a presentation to their classmates. It's not only a fun activity, but it also teaches the students organizational skills and responsibility. At the completion of the course, students leave with tangible evidence of skills mastered, which can be used in college interviews, job interviews, and other presentations.

Discussion Starter

INVENT. Invent an imaginary character who's searching for a job. Give your character a name and a personality. List the steps your character needs to go through in a job search. Start by preparing the résumé. **LS**

Individualized Practice

Look in the classified employment section and choose a job you'd consider applying for.

L1 Have students work in pairs to discuss the relevant things to include in a cover letter for this classified ad.

L2 Ask students to write a cover letter using the guidelines in this chapter to apply for this job. The letter should be properly formatted.

L3 Ask students to write a cover letter. Have students exchange cover letters with a partner for proofreading and critiquing. Have students rework their cover letters incorporating the changes suggested by their partners.

Figure 21.2 Caption Answer

Yes. It's a good idea because Peter Cortez's activities are relevant to the position for which he's applying. They show he's capable of taking leadership roles, getting on with a diverse group of people, and is interested in business.

If you're interested, they can also give you a **referral**, a personal recommendation to an employer or other job lead.

Your School. Your school might have a work placement office. Someone there can help you look for job leads. Employers frequently post job openings there. Your school might also have a cooperative education or work experience program. Besides helping you plan your career, these programs can help you find a job. You can talk with your guidance counselor and teachers about the kind of job you'd like to have.

Want Ads. Recruitment advertisements in newspapers can be useful in several ways. First, you can find out quickly if any jobs are listed in which you might be interested. You can also get a good idea about how much certain jobs pay and what skills or education are required. You can search local and national databases on the Internet for jobs. The databases

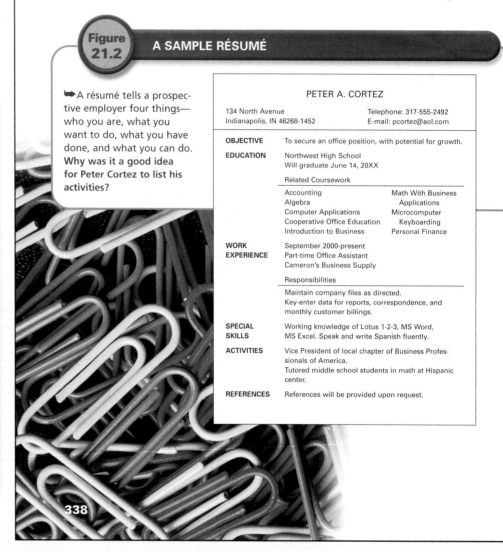

Figure 21.2

A SAMPLE RÉSUMÉ

➥A résumé tells a prospective employer four things—who you are, what you want to do, what you have done, and what you can do. **Why was it a good idea for Peter Cortez to list his activities?**

PETER A. CORTEZ

134 North Avenue
Indianapolis, IN 46268-1452

Telephone: 317-555-2492
E-mail: pcortez@aol.com

OBJECTIVE To secure an office position, with potential for growth.

EDUCATION Northwest High School
Will graduate June 14, 20XX

Related Coursework

Accounting	Math With Business
Algebra	Applications
Computer Applications	Microcomputer
Cooperative Office Education	Keyboarding
Introduction to Business	Personal Finance

WORK EXPERIENCE September 2000-present
Part-time Office Assistant
Cameron's Business Supply

Responsibilities

Maintain company files as directed.
Key-enter data for reports, correspondence, and monthly customer billings.

SPECIAL SKILLS Working knowledge of Lotus 1-2-3, MS Word, MS Excel. Speak and write Spanish fluently.

ACTIVITIES Vice President of local chapter of Business Professionals of America.
Tutored middle school students in math at Hispanic center.

REFERENCES References will be provided upon request.

338

Global Perspective

Bilingual Workers Are in Demand. Many U.S. companies are expanding into Spanish-speaking and other countries. Corporate America is hiring people who speak two languages, especially in their marketing and sales departments. Another needed area is in operations, where companies need supervisors and managers who understand the workforce, which is often Hispanic. Who's hiring bilingual professionals? Most of the Fortune 1000 companies and some of the big-name companies like IBM, Texaco, Target, and American Express. **ELL**

are updated often and usually provide detailed descriptions of jobs.

Local Businesses. Some businesses post job notices on bulletin boards in supermarkets or in shopping malls. You can also call a company's personnel office to see if they have jobs open. You might find help-wanted signs in businesses' windows. Sometimes you can find a job by walking around your local business district and asking business owners if they're hiring.

Employment Agencies. Services that help people find jobs are called **employment agencies**. These can be public or private. Public agencies are usually run by the state or local government and might be connected with the unemployment office. They often offer tests to help you identify what kind of job you'd like and for which you'd be qualified. The Federal Job Information Center has regional agencies that can give you information about government job openings. Private employment agencies, such as temp services, charge for their services. If you contact an agency, be sure to find out if they charge a fee.

 Fast Review _____

1. What is the purpose of a résumé?
2. What is the difference between a job or school reference and a personal reference?
3. Name four ways you can look for jobs at local businesses.

Contacting Potential Employers

You've prepared a résumé and found several interesting job openings. How do you go about applying for the jobs? The process includes several steps: the cover letter, job application, employment testing, and the interview.

Cover Letter

You should always include a cover letter with your résumé. A **cover letter** is a one-page letter that tells the employer about you and why you're applying for the job. It should be specifically addressed to the employer. For example, if you're applying for a job at a video store, your cover letter should include the name and address of the store, and the title and name of the manager. Like your résumé, the cover letter also needs to make a good impression. Your cover letter should be properly formatted and free from errors (see Figure 21.3).

Real-World Application

part 3 of 4

AN ILLUSTRATIVE VISIONARY
Kelley is waiting for a phone call from one of his clients, *Rolling Stone* magazine. He began the day by doodling. "I often start by doing a thumbnail sketch of my ideas using pencil and tracing paper," says Kelley from his studio. "As a graphic artist, you can think until you're blue in the face, but until you actually put something on paper, you're not making progress." **How can you use your free time to research job opportunities?**

continued on p. 341

Chapter 21 Getting a Job **339**

Chapter 21

 Real-World Application
Caption Answer

AN ILLUSTRATIVE VISIONARY: PART 3 OF 4
Answers might vary but include working with a counselor to define your career goals, volunteering, finding an internship, etc.

Fast Review Answers

1. To persuade potential employers to grant you an interview.
2. Job and school references are used to verify that you worked and went to school where you claimed. Personal references are used to testify to your character.
3. Check bulletin boards in supermarkets and shopping malls, call a company's personnel office, look for help-wanted signs in windows, and walk around the local business district and ask business owners.

LANGUAGE ARTS   *Curriculum Connection*

Communication. Have students suppose that they found out the level of competition is very high for jobs in the field they wanted to go into. Would they still pursue jobs in that field or would they look for a field with less job competition? Allow students 15 minutes to write a paragraph explaining what they would do and why. The paragraph should be organized and concise.

If your school has a work-based learning program, ask the coordinator of the program to speak about the requirements for the program, the types of experiences offered, and the advantages of the program for career exploration. Encourage students to prepare questions ahead of the presentation. **CL**, **LS**, **P**

Reteaching

JOB LEADS. To reteach the concept of job leads, ask students to tell ways of finding job openings. (Answers should include your network, your school, want ads, local businesses, and employment agencies.)

Enrichment Strategies

EVALUATE. Work in pairs to role-play the parts of an applicant for a position at a local bank or retail store and the manager looking for a prospective employee. Applicants compose their own résumés and submit them to the manager. Managers evaluate the résumés based on the information they would need to hire the right applicant. Switch roles. **LS**

Evaluation

Assign and review the Fast Review sections.

Figure 21.3 Caption Answer

PART 1. Your résumé.
PART 2. Three.

Job Application

Most employers ask a job applicant to fill out an application form (see Figure 21.3). Like your résumé, this form presents you to a potential employer so you should carefully follow the directions. Provide the information requested and write neatly. The process will be easier if you have your résumé and list of references with you since you often have to include this information on the application. Begin by answering each question. Don't leave any blanks. If a question doesn't apply to you, write "not applicable," or N/A as the shorthand.

Figure 21.3 JOB APPLICATION ESSENTIALS

➡ **Part 1** A cover letter introduces you to a prospective employer. It should be tailored to the position you're interested in. **What should accompany the cover letter?**

➡ **Part 2** Most employers ask potential employees to fill out application forms. It's important to read the directions carefully and fill out the form neatly and completely. **How many computer applications is Peter able to use?**

How to Use a Portfolio Activity

The portfolio projects are designed to lead students to develop a collection of their best work to submit to you for assessment. You and each of your students should decide which projects to include in their business portfolio. Refer students to the specific rubric(s) from the *Alternative Assessment Strategies.* These rubrics will alert students to the criteria you'll use to assess their projects. **P**

Employment Testing

When you apply for a job you might be asked to take a test to see if you have the proper skills. For example, if you apply for a job as an office assistant your computer skills might be tested. If you apply for a job where you have to make deliveries, you might have to take a driving test. If you want to work for a bank, you'll probably have to take a math test. Jobs for the government or in law enforcement often require drug tests and lie-detector tests.

Job Interview

A **job interview** is a formal face-to-face discussion between an employer and a potential employee. It's an exchange of information about the nature of the job and your qualifications for it. Keep in mind these few things about the interview:

- *Do some homework about the job.* Find out as much as you can about the company in advance.
- *Be on time.* If you're late, an employer will think you're careless about being on time for work and meeting deadlines. If you can't be on time, call and inform the interviewer.
- *Wear appropriate clothes.* Dress neatly and in a style appropriate for the job you're seeking.
- *Put your best foot forward.* Be courteous and cooperative during the interview. Make eye contact and beware of your body language.
- *Ask questions about the job.* You need to learn if the job is right for you. Ask about the pay and benefits. Asking questions also suggests that you're interested in the job.
- *Don't expect an answer right away.* The employer might have other people to interview and need time to make a decision.

You should also follow up after the interview. Call or write a letter thanking the interviewer. This shows you're still interested in the job and allows you to add anything you forgot to mention in the interview. If you don't hear from the interviewer, call back in a few days.

 Fast Review

1. What's the purpose of a cover letter?
2. Name different kinds of tests you might have to take for different kind of jobs.
3. Why should you follow up after a job interview?

AN ILLUSTRATIVE VISIONARY

Kelley is trying to capture *The Great White Hope* on paper. It's going to be presented by the famous Washington, D.C. theater, Arena Stage. He goes to the library to look for images from around 1915. He wants to get the design's details—boxing rings, clothing, ropes, and boxing shoes—right. In order to impress the client, his art must connect the whole story from beginning to end. **What are some things you need to do in order to impress a potential employer?**

Chapter 21

Real-World Application Caption Answer

AN ILLUSTRATIVE VISIONARY: PART 4 OF 4

Do some homework about the job, be on time, wear appropriate clothing, have a great attitude, ask questions about the job, and don't expect an answer right away.

Technology Resource

 GO TO **PUZZLEMAKER CD-ROM.** Check your students' understanding of the chapter's key terms by using the *Puzzlemaker* CD-ROM.

Fast Review Answers

1. To tell an employer about you and why you're applying for the job.
2. Computer skills test for an office job, driving test for a job where you have to make deliveries, math test for a bank job, drug and lie-detector tests for jobs in government or law enforcement.
3. To let the interviewer know you are still interested in the job and to allow you to add anything you forgot to mention in the interview.

Meeting Individual Needs

Students With Orthopedic Impairments. Career choices for students with orthopedic impairments need not be limited in any way other than by the interests and talents of the individual student. In order to help all students overcome preconceived notions about existing career choices, invite a marketer, entrepreneur, or other successful person with physical impairments to class to speak about his or her career. Invite him or her to discuss any obstacles that could have hindered his or her success and how they were overcome. Allow time for questions and encourage students to ask questions about physical barriers to entering buildings as well as biased treatment.

How a Laser Printer Works

1 FOCUS

A printer that can produce high-quality résumés, term papers, and other documents is only one element of a home workstation. Today, a home workstation is practically a necessity for both school and business. A workstation enables the user to produce and communicate with greater speed, quality, and efficiency. The basic elements of a workstation include a computer, a printer, and a modem for Internet access. Other elements can include a fax machine, telephone, and business or other specialized software.

2 TEACH

Discuss with students the various ways a home workstation can make it easier to find a job. Internet access, for example, makes it easier to research careers and job opportunities. A printer makes it easier not only to produce high-quality résumés, but business stationary such as business cards, letterheads, and envelopes. A demonstrable ability to work with computers, business software, and the Internet increases one's chances for employment.

❓ Did You Know?

Most employers don't look at résumés to select the best-qualified candidates but to screen out applicants. Employers spend about 15–30 seconds reading a résumé. An employer will reject a résumé if it's poorly formatted or has a misspelled word.

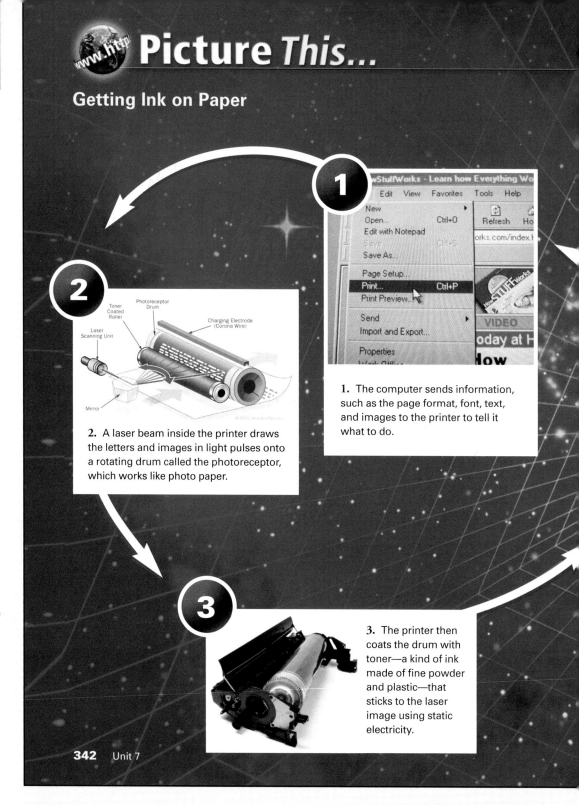

Picture *This...*

Getting Ink on Paper

1. The computer sends information, such as the page format, font, text, and images to the printer to tell it what to do.

2. A laser beam inside the printer draws the letters and images in light pulses onto a rotating drum called the photoreceptor, which works like photo paper.

3. The printer then coats the drum with toner—a kind of ink made of fine powder and plastic—that sticks to the laser image using static electricity.

342 Unit 7

Extending the Content

Braille Printers. There are not only printers that can print in a variety of colors and typefaces, there are printers available that can also print in Braille. To meet the needs of the visually impaired, Braille printers or "embossers" are now found in many schools, businesses, and government offices. All it takes to adapt a Braille printer to an ordinary computer is translation software. The printer itself simply connects to one of the computer's printer ports.

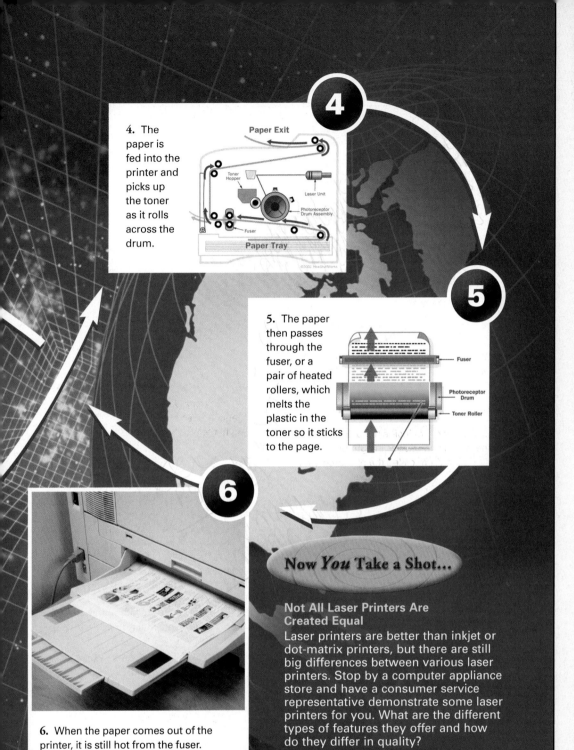

4. The paper is fed into the printer and picks up the toner as it rolls across the drum.

Paper Exit

Toner Hopper

Laser Unit

Photoreceptor Drum Assembly

Fuser

Paper Tray

©2002 HowStuffWorks

5. The paper then passes through the fuser, or a pair of heated rollers, which melts the plastic in the toner so it sticks to the page.

Fuser

Photoreceptor Drum

Toner Roller

©2002 HowStuffWorks

6. When the paper comes out of the printer, it is still hot from the fuser.

Now *You* Take a Shot...

Not All Laser Printers Are Created Equal

Laser printers are better than inkjet or dot-matrix printers, but there are still big differences between various laser printers. Stop by a computer appliance store and have a consumer service representative demonstrate some laser printers for you. What are the different types of features they offer and how do they differ in quality?

343

3 ASSESS

Have students do the activity and answer the question in "Now You Take a Shot..."

4 CLOSE

Students can increase their chances of finding a job by putting out their résumés in as many ways as possible. Have students name different methods they can use to send out or post a résumé and list them on the board. Some of the methods include sending a résumé through the regular mail, e-mailing it, faxing it, posting it on a Web page or a Web site, and scanning it.

? *Did You Know?*

Before the advent of the home computer and desktop publishing, designing and printing even the simplest document was an expensive and time-consuming task. Just putting together a flyer required physically typing, cutting, laying out, and pasting each element. To produce a flyer often required the services of a professional typesetter and printer.

Now *You* Take a Shot... *Caption Answer*

Answers may vary depending on the printers demonstrated and the current technology available. Differences between printers should include the speed, image quality, range of colors, graphics capability, and number of fonts or typefaces.

4 CLOSE

Chapter Wrap-Up

Ask students to give five main points for each part of getting a job—employability skills, beginning your job search, and contacting potential employers.

Using Business Key Words

1. employment agencies
2. reference
3. cover letter
4. employment objective
5. employability skills
6. résumé
7. body language
8. job lead
9. qualifications
10. referral
11. job interview

Review What You Learned

12. Communication, mathematical skills, basic computer skills.
13. Needs less training.
14. Poor attitude.
15. Enthusiasm.
16. Inform them of your abilities or qualifications.
17. Get their permission.
18. Mentors, teachers, professionals, neighbors, etc.
19. Help people find jobs.
20. Shows interest and discipline.

Summary

1. Employability skills include education, job skills, work experience, character, personality, and ability to work with others.

2. A résumé is a summary of your skills, education, and work experience. It includes references and an employment objective. Make sure you proofread your résumé very carefully before sending it to an employer.

3. You can find out about job openings through your personal network, your school, want ads, local businesses, and employment agencies.

4. The job application process includes writing a cover letter, filling out an application, taking a test, and interviewing for a job.

● Using Business Key Words

Are you ready for the world of work? There are many employability skills that will help you succeed in a job. See how ready you are by choosing the term below that best completes each of the following sentences.

- **body language**
- **qualifications**
- **employability skills**
- **referral**
- **résumé**
- **job lead**
- **employment agencies**
- **reference**
- **cover letter**
- **employment objective**
- **job interview**

1. Organizations set up to help people find jobs are called _____.
2. A(n) _____ may be a teacher, former employer, or other adult who can assess your personal and work habits.

3. When you send your résumé to a prospective employer, you should also send a _____.
4. A(n) _____ is a statement that tells the prospective employer about your motivation and interest in their business.
5. Qualities that employers look for in a person they want to work for them and the techniques for letting an employer know you have the qualities are called _____.
6. A document that highlights your job qualifications is called a(n) _____.
7. Nonverbal communication, such as posture, eye contact, facial expression, and gestures is called _____.
8. Information about a job opening is called _____.
9. _____ is (are) the education, skills, and experience required for doing a particular job.
10. A personal recommendation to an employer or other job lead is a _____.
11. A formal face-to-face discussion between an employer and a potential employee is a(n) _____.

Quick Quiz

1. What body language should you use in an interview? (Answers should include good posture, eye contact, a smile, and a firm handshake.)
2. Services that help people find jobs are called _____? (Employment agencies.)
3. What factors make up your employability skills? (Answers may include level of education, extracurricular activities, basic skills, work experience, and your character.)

Review What You Learned

12. What are the basic skills many employers expect workers to have?
13. Why do many employers look for people with work experience?
14. What is the No. 1 reason why people lose their jobs?
15. What do your extracurricular activities indicate to a potential employer?
16. What is the purpose of a résumé?
17. Before you use someone as a reference, what should you do?
18. What people could you use as a reference?
19. What services do public employment agencies provide?
20. Why is it important to be on time for a job interview?

Understanding Business Concepts

21. Which character traits do employers want their employees to have? Which one do you think is the most important? Explain your answer.
22. What might be a disadvantage of using a private employment agency?
23. Why might you be asked to take job-related tests when applying for a job?
24. When you're interviewing for a position, why is it important to ask questions about the job or the company itself?
25. Should you expect to be offered a job immediately following an interview? Why or why not?
26. Why is it important to write a thank-you letter after the interview?

Critical Thinking

27. Do you have a good attitude? Explain. Then, name three things you could do to improve your attitude at home, school, and work.
28. Why is it important to find out as much as possible about a position before you're offered the job?
29. How much does your personality play in working with other coworkers?
30. What are some ways to ensure that your résumé is correct before sending it to an employer?

Viewing and Representing

Examining the Image. Working with a partner, challenge each other to find important details in this photograph. Ask each other these questions: If you were doing this, what skills would you be using? Could you use these skills in a job? In an interview, you could be asked to give examples of your skills. If you were working as a volunteer like this, what examples could you give to demonstrate your skills?

Chapter 21 Getting a Job **345**

Critical Thinking

27. Answers will vary.
28. Students should mention that it is important to find out whether they will like and be able to do the job before they accept an offer. They might miss an opportunity elsewhere or have a very bad experience if they make a poor choice.
29. A lot. Not getting along with others can cost you your job.
30. Allow an English teacher, guidance counselor, or adult to proofread your résumé.

Viewing and Representing

Point out to students that skills they gain in volunteer positions, extracurricular activities, and part-time jobs are often transferable to the job they're seeking. These are called transferable skills. Also point out to students that in an interview a short story to show a skill or ability will stick in the mind of the interviewer and might just get them the job. For example, if the interviewer asks: "If you're in the middle of a task and your boss brings you a new project to work on, what will you do?" Students might reply with an example giving the steps they took in a similar situation from their volunteer or part-time positions. **LS**

Understanding Business Concepts

21. Honesty, dependability, hard work, positive attitude, and get along with others.
22. You might have to pay a fee.
23. Test your skills.
24. To show interest.
25. No. Most interviewers need time to think about your qualifications in relation to the job.
26. It shows you are still interested in the job and allows you to clarify something you said in the interview or mention something that occurred to you after the interview.

4 CLOSE (Cont.)

Building Academic Skills

COMPUTER/TECHNOLOGY. Answers will vary somewhat. If students are having difficulty, they may want to contact the guidance department for additional help. Rubric: Spreadsheet.

LANGUAGE ARTS. Students' role-plays will vary, but might include: Pat and his or her friend listing job pluses; finding new ways to do the job; planning how Pat could advance to a supervisory position; and suggesting to management that cleaners work in pairs. Rubric: Role-play.

HISTORY. Students can use the library or the Internet as references. Allow the students to choose the way they would like to share their findings. Rubrics: Essay, oral presentation, poster, chart.

MATH. Make sure all students in the group participate in the project. Encourage groups to contact different employers. Rubric: Math worksheet and answer key.

Linking School to Home

Suggest the students create a list of questions to ask the interviewees. Rubric: Oral presentation.

Linking School to Work

Documents will vary but should contain all the information necessary to complete a job application. Rubric: Small document for wallet.

● Building Academic Skills

 Researching and Graphing

Conduct online research to gather data on the annual and lifetime earnings for workers with varying levels of education. Create a spreadsheet of the information you find. Then, use software to graph the information. Print your spreadsheet and graphs.

 Role-Playing

Read the following scenario about Pat (see below). With a partner, develop a role-play in which a friend helps Pat maintain a positive attitude at work. Feel free to add details about Pat and the work situation. Present your role-play to the class.

Scenario: Pat works in a hotel cleaning rooms and making beds. The wages for this job are low, but sometimes guests leave tips. The hours of the job are 8 A.M. until 4 P.M. or until all the rooms are clean. Pat can walk to work and the hotel provides free lunches for its workers. The job takes hard work, cleaning and organizational skills, and could lead to a cleaning supervisor's job. Although other workers do the same tasks, they work alone. Pat seldom talks to fellow workers, because everyone is busy. Pat is frequently bored and lonely at work.

 Labor Laws

Research the child labor laws in your state. Write a two-page paper and include the following information:

- When and why the laws were passed.
- The number of hours per week a child is allowed to work.
- Activities that can't be performed by minors on the job.
- Allowable exceptions (students who are enrolled in work experience programs, youth apprenticeships, and so on).

 Writing a Survey

In a group of four or five, survey several local retail and fast-food businesses in your community. Find out what kind of math skills they're looking for when hiring employees. Then, create a handout of workplace math problems. Create an answer key as well. Provide copies of the handouts for classmates who want to practice their math skills before they apply for a job.

● Linking School to Home

Interviewing and Presenting. Interview two relatives or friends who are working. Find out what kind of training they had when they began working. Have they received training on the job and what new skills have they developed? How have their job responsibilities and opportunities changed since they first started their jobs? Have they changed jobs? Make an oral presentation to your class with your findings.

● Linking School to Work

Creating an Information Card. Create a small document you can carry in your wallet with all the pertinent information necessary to complete a job application. Obtain sample job applications to use as a resource for this activity.

E-Homework

Applying Technology

Reading the Want Ads. For a period of two weeks, study the jobs that are advertised on the Internet and the local newspaper. What conclusions can you draw about the kinds of jobs offered in your area, the salary range for various jobs, the benefits available, and the qualifications or work experience required? Are there any differences between the jobs advertised on the Internet and those advertised in the newspaper? Write a 250-word summary of your findings.

Résumé Software. Use the Internet to research the résumé writing software available. Locate at least three different products and compare them for the following:
- Cost
- Features offered
- Minimum computer specifications
- Technical support provided
Based on your research, which product would you purchase? Why?

Connecting Academics

Math. You have two job offers. Job A salary is $2,400 a month and requires a daily 48-mile round-trip commute. Job B is closer to home and the salary is $1,920 a month. You'll be working five days a week. Taking into account the current price of gas and your car's gas mileage, how much will the commute to Job A cost you each month? Which job will benefit you most?

Language Arts. Break into groups of three. Select an interviewer, a job candidate, and an observer. Conduct a mock job interview for one of the following positions: grocery store clerk, lifeguard, or newspaper delivery person. After ten minutes, the observer provides feedback to the interviewer and interviewee. What questions were most relevant? What answer gave the best information? Now switch roles and conduct the next interview. Repeat until everyone has been in each role.

BusinessWeek | **Analyzing the Feature Story**

You read the first part of "Asking the Right Questions" at the beginning of this chapter. Below are a few questions for you to answer about job interviews. You'll find the answers to these questions when you're reading the entire article online. First, here are the questions:

31. What characteristics are these employers looking for in job applicants?

32. Are interviewers looking for one correct answer?

CREATIVE JOURNAL ACTIVITY

In a group of four, create a job interview checklist. Include insights your classmates have gained from their own interview experiences.

The Full Story

To learn more about job interviews, visit the *Introduction to Business* Web site at **www.introbus.glencoe.com**, and click on *BusinessWeek* Feature Story, Chapter 21.

E-Homework

READING THE WANT ADS. Students may also want to include the want ads in newspapers that serve surrounding counties. Rubric: Essay.

RÉSUMÉ SOFTWARE. If students are having difficulty, allow them to help each other. Allow the students to choose the way they wish to share their findings with the class. Rubrics: Note taking, oral presentation, essay.

Connecting Academics

MATH. Answer depends on the price of gas used to calculate the cost of the commute for Job A. Job B may give a better monthly return.

LANGUAGE ARTS. Role-plays will vary.

BusinessWeek | *Analyzing the Feature Story*

31. If candidates are capable of quickly understanding the goals and mission of their employers. GoRefer is interested in the intelligence of job applicants.

32. Interviewers are not necessarily looking for one right answer so much as a glimpse into how candidate thinks and reacts to challenges under pressure.

Creative Journal Activity

Poll the class to see what careers are most interesting. Ask students to invite workers in those fields to talk to the class about their work. Students should prepare questions ahead of time. Topics could include ways to prepare for an interview, qualities that a person needs to be successful in the field, and the projected employment outlook for the field.

1 FOCUS

Unit Seminar Overview

In this seminar on career opportunities in other countries, students investigate images, make decisions, and analyze classmates' responses. Students find out if there's any relationship between particular career goals and international locations.

Bell Ringer Activity

TIME TO DREAM. Write this scenario on the board: You've got your passport, you've had the necessary medical shots. You're actually on your way to work in another country, right now. Where do you land? Assuming you can use a language you know, what job will you do?

Discussion Starter

SCENARIO. Imagine you've been working in Brazil or Japan for three years and you're having a great time. You want one of your close friends from the United States to come and join you. What do you say to try and convince him or her to come? (Answers might include the type of lifestyle, the adventure, the exotic country, the people, the climate, the opportunities in your company, and so on.)

BusinessWeek Seminar

Unit **7**
Global Business

Career Options in a Global Economy

In this unit you learned about how to develop a career plan and gain skills that will help you reach your career goals. Getting the job you really want takes careful research, detailed planning, and smart follow-up. In this seminar, you'll investigate career opportunities in other parts of the world.

348

GLOBAL BUSINESS

Newsworthy Trends

Deskchair Traveler. Do you want to work in the world of international business but don't want to be separated from your family and friends? Thanks to global communications you can do business with other countries without ever leaving home. Multinational companies exist in almost every city in the United States. If you know Spanish, for example, many companies based in Texas and Florida do business with Latin America. State governments have offices that deal with overseas trade. If you decide you do want to travel, you can start your international business career at home and then transfer to another country later.

2 TEACH

Thinking Critically

Look at the factoids, then answer the questions:

1. Do you think communication is important in international business? What are the benefits of being a member of an international organization, such as Toastmasters International? (Answers will vary and may include the positives and negatives of different cultures, and the use of English or another language. Being a member of an international organization would immediately give you connections and networking opportunities.)

2. How many corporate American employees work overseas? Is that number a surprise to you? Is it larger or smaller than you would think? Do you think the trend is for more people to work in other countries, or less? (Three hundred thousand. Students' answers and opinions will vary.)

Cooperative Learning

COMPARE AND CONTRAST. Have students work in small groups. After discussing "Exploring Culture" (seminar questions 7 and 8), and referring to the factoid, "Worldly Vision," assign the following task: For five minutes, each student is to imagine that he or she is working in another country and is blind. Ask students to record their experiences in these circumstances. After students have written their experiences, ask them to share their insights with their group. What were the major differences in this experience from the imagined experience in the Discussion Starter? **CL**, **LS**

Factoids

Communicating Around the World. English is the language for international business, finance, and technology.

Worldly Vision. Marriott selects trainees from the Braille Institute in Anaheim, Calif., to attend its Pathways program, which trains persons with visual impairments for a career in its international reservation center.

Speak Up. Toastmasters International is a nonprofit organization that helps members become better public speakers.

Know Your Culture. Prove you've got credentials and keen insight into the U.S. psyche if you're looking at a company overseas. This may make you more qualified than the country's natives.

Overseas Opportunities. There are more than 300,000 corporate American employees working overseas. The international assignments usually last between two and four years.

Investigate the Images

Look at the photographic collage on the left page. What grabs your attention first? Is it the color or the words? The power in reading visuals is in analyzing and dissecting your observations. On a separate piece of paper, respond to the questions listed below. These questions might help sharpen the focus of your visual mind.

Your Observations

1. How many photographs do you see?

2. Examine each photograph. How are they assembled in relation to one another?

3. What is the subject of each photograph? Is place or location the subject?

4. Does color signify a message?

5. What issues do you take from these images?

Information

6. Summarize what you think about the photographs from your observations.

Exploring Culture

7. Imagine you're in an interview for an international position. The interviewer asks you to describe U.S. culture. What is your response?

8. Give an example of a company that has changed U.S. culture. How were people influenced by this company or its products?

Newsworthy Trends

GLOBAL BUSINESS

Leave the Moving to Us. If you get a job in another country and need help moving, Directmoving.com offers international relocation services over the Internet. The company will find you a house or apartment, open a bank account for you, and help you select a school if you have children. It will help you move in, have your utilities turned on for you, and find you a housekeeper or plumber if you need one. The company will even fix you up with a work permit, car, insurance, and driver's license.

2 TEACH (Cont.)

Independent Practice

L1 SUMMARIZE

Ask students to find a recent article on careers in other countries. Ask them to prepare a summary of the article to share with the class. Ask students to close their presentations with a comment on the latest opportunities for working in other countries. **LS**

L2 INTERNET RESEARCH

Ask students to research online to find interesting facts about Toastmasters International, or another international not-for-profit organization. Have students find out about the costs of membership, when meetings are held, the procedure to contact member groups in other countries, and the cost of transfer of membership. Ask students to report their findings to their classmates. **LS**

L3 INTERVIEW AND REPORT

How do companies manage to communicate efficiently with their employees overseas? Arrange for a local owner or manager of a business operating globally to visit your class. Conduct a question-and-answer session. Have students prepare questions ahead of time, especially questions focusing on how the company promotes efficient communication. After the interview, have students write a one-page report including specific details and examples. **LS**

BusinessWeek Seminar

Taking Aim at Global Business

● Preparation

Research international employment opportunities that sound interesting based upon your own career interests.

Objective

- **Investigate** jobs in countries outside the United States.
- **Decide** on an international career, and create a plan for achieving that career goal.
- **Analyze** classmates' responses and create a final document.

Materials Needed

✓ Copies of recent business news publications such as the *Wall Street Journal* or *BusinessWeek*, or business sections of international news publications, such as the *New York Times*.

✓ Access to the Internet and your local or school library.

✓ Paper, pens, pencils

● Procedures

1. Research international job opportunities. First, you might want to look into various business opportunities in different countries. Try *BusinessWeek Online*, **www.monsterboard.com**, or **www.coolworks.com** as references.

2. Select an international career. Recall your career interests. Try to match your career interests and your knowledge about the jobs you're interested in with international businesses or consumers in other countries.

3. Create a plan for achieving that career goal. Develop two or three short- and medium-term goals that you'll need to reach to achieve your long-term international career goal.

4. Submit a written or typed report that describes your international career goal. List the steps you need to take to achieve that goal. Be specific.

5. Present your international career goal to the class. Describe your career goal and explain your plan to achieve that goal. Using a world map, identify your international career location.

Reteaching Strategy

Tell students that they are being interviewed for a job as a travel guide in another country. The job involves taking a group of tourists to historic and cultural sights, keeping track of luggage, keeping the group on schedule to catch buses and trains, and overcoming any obstacles or problems. Have students give responses to possible interview questions that would help them get this job. **LS**, **CL**, **ELL**

Chart It

After the presentations have been given, as a class re-create on the board a chart like the one below. It lists career paths and countries to live in. Use X's to show which places students want to go for certain careers. Then, make a separate list of the different reasons classmembers gave for wanting to go to a particular area.

Examples of Countries With Opportunities					
Career Goals	England	Japan	Brazil	South Africa	Pakistan
Nurse		X		X	X
Engineer		XXX		X	
Import/ Export Entre- preneur					X
Teacher	X	X	X	X	X
Minister				X	

Analyze and Conclude

After considering the chart, identify the classes' international career goals and locations, and then answer the questions below:

1. **Interpreting and Communicating Information.** What's the most popular choice of country among classmembers? Why is that country more popular than any other?
2. **Organizing and Maintaining Information.** Is there any special relationship between particular career goals and places? If so, please explain.
3. **Reasoning.** Were you influenced by the choices of other classmates when choosing an international location? Why or why not?

Becoming an Informed Citizen

Congratulations, you finished the seminar. Now it's time to reflect on the decisions you made.

Seeing Things in the Mind's Eye. What does working internationally teach you?

Analyzing Your Future. As the U.S. economy motions for more free trade among industries, how might this influence your career options and moves?

BUSINESS Online

Further Exploration
To find out more about international employment opportunities, visit the *Introduction to Business* Web site at **www.introbus.glencoe.com**.

Analyze and Conclude Answers

1. Answers will vary depending on current business, cultural trends, and students' aptitudes.
2. Help students interpret the chart, "Examples of Countries With Opportunities."
3. Answers will vary. Encourage a discussion which is open and non judgmental.

Buying Goods and Services

● Unit Objectives

After completing this unit, students will be able to achieve the following outcomes:

- Describe choices consumers make and list ways to be a smart consumer.
- Name the seven rights of consumers and list consumers' responsibilities and ways you can learn consumer skills.
- Describe actions consumers can take when they have problems with products.
- Identify consumer advocate groups, how government protects consumers, and ways businesses help consumers.

BusinessWeek Connections

In this unit, students will read the following articles from *BusinessWeek*:

Chapter 22 "Dead Letter?": Take a look at what consumers want when they buy stamps online.

Chapter 23 "A Dogfight Over Net Travel Info?": Consumers have a right to know about cheap travel—see if you agree.

Chapter 24 "He's Raring to Fight for Fund Investors' Rights": One person thinks that fund investors and the mutual-fund industry both need protection.

Key to Descriptive Icons

The following designations will help you decide which activities are appropriate for your students.

L1 Level 1 activities should be within the ability range of all students.

L2 Level 2 activities should be within the ability range of the average to above-average students.

L3 Level 3 activities are designed for the ability range of above-average students.

ELL Activities should be within the ability range of the English Language Learner.

LS Learning Styles designation represents activities designed to address different learning styles.

CL Cooperative learning activities are designed for small group work.

P Portfolio designation represents student products that can be placed into a best-work portfolio.

Teacher Classroom Resources*

Program Resources	Chapter 22	Chapter 23	Chapter 24
Student Activity Workbook	p. 161	p. 169	p. 177
Lesson Plans	p. 58	p. 60	p. 62
Internet Resources	p. 63	p. 65	p. 67
Reproducible Tests	p. 43	p. 45	p. 47
Teaching Transparencies	22.1, 22.2	23.1, 23.2	24.1, 24.2
Strategies and Worksheets for Teaching Transparencies	pp. 11, 61	pp. 11, 63	pp. 12, 65

* Each of these resources is available in print and on the Interactive Lesson Planner CD-ROM.

Technology Resources

- Interactive Lesson Planner CD-ROM
- PowerPoint® Presentation CD-ROM
- ExamView® Pro Test Generator CD-ROM
- Integrated Software Simulation, Teacher Manual
- Glencoe Business Video Package
- *PuzzleMaker* CD-ROM
- *Introduction to Business* Web Site
- *Virtual Business*®
  Virtual Business is a business simulation that introduces students to the principles of business by letting them start and run their own virtual business. In *Virtual Business,* students have the power to control all aspects of a retail convenience store. Students strategize business decisions using a powerful learning tool in the guise of a video game.

Video Series

Virtual Business

Scope and Sequence

Academic Standards of Learning

	LANGUAGE ARTS	MATH	HISTORY	COMPUTER/ TECHNOLOGY	SOCIAL SCIENCE	
CHAPTER 22	pp. 355, 361, 363, 368	pp. 359, 361, 365, 368, 369	pp. 356, 358, 368	pp. 354, 357, 363, 364, 368, 369	pp. 356, 357, 358, 360, 362, 367	
CHAPTER 23	pp. 371, 375, 377, 382, 383	pp. 378, 382, 383	pp. 371, 374, 377	pp. 370, 371, 373, 379, 382, 383	pp. 370, 371, 372, 373, 375, 376, 378, 379, 382	
CHAPTER 24	pp. 385, 387, 388, 391, 392, 393, 396, 397	pp. 396, 397	pp. 385, 386, 390, 396	pp. 387, 389, 393, 396, 397	pp. 385, 386, 387, 388, 390, 391, 393, 396	

Scope and Sequence

Themes and Concepts

Business Core	Accounting and Finance	Business Management	Computer/ Technology	Marketing	Entrepreneurship
Business Law Competitive Environment Interrelations of Business Operations Economic Culture Demographics Adapting to Change Communications	Decision Making Accounting Principles	Competition Consumers Decision Making Opportunity Costs Productivity Communication	Knowledge Management Business Procedures Social Issues Business Decisions Customer Support	Customer Relations Customer Service E-Commerce Culture Marketing Strategy and Planning Buying Motives and Behaviors Customer Transactions	Business Image Contracts Pricing Strategies Production Promotion
Business Law Business Ethics Competitive Environment Adapting to Change Information Resources	Decision Making Ethics	Competition Consumers Decision Making Change Research Communications	Knowledge Management Change Management Needs Analysis	Customer Relations Customer Service Pricing Strategy Buying Motives and Behaviors	Management Product Pricing Strategies
Business Law Business Ownership Problem Solving Communications Decision Making Governing Agencies	Revenue and Expense Recognition	Competition Consumers Decision Making Government Regulations Legal Rights Sources of Law	Security Technical Resources Business Environment Business Management Safety	Customer Relations Customer Service Regulation Policies and Procedures	Contracts Government Regulations Management Purchasing and Inventory Management

Unit Overview

Unit 8 outlines important aspects of being a consumer and consumer protection.

CHAPTER 22 explains consumer choices and how to be a smart consumer.

CHAPTER 23 explains the consumer bill of rights and details your responsibilities as a consumer.

CHAPTER 24 describes how consumers can handle problems and how consumers are protected.

Introducing the Unit

Have students rank on a scale of one to ten, the amount of power they think consumers have on the economy. Ask students to justify why they assigned the rank they did. Ask students if they've heard of the Consumer's Bill of Rights and what it might include.

Technology Resource

 INTRODUCTION TO BUSINESS WEB SITE. To find out more about content in Unit 8, visit the Glencoe *Introduction to Business* Web site. **www.introbus.glencoe.com**

Unit 8

Buying Goods and Services

Recycling in the Cyber Era

Where do old computers go when they die? About 500 million computers will become obsolete within the next few years. Ninety-seven percent of the materials in a computer are recyclable. While 70 percent of all major appliances are recycled, only 6 percent of computers are. Many computer companies will recycle old computers. Contact Electronics Industries Alliance at **www.eiae.org** for more information about recycling computers.

● **...And It Makes a Nice Paperweight**
French and British companies have come up with a way to make nuclear waste easier to transport and store—by turning it into glass.

● **Save a Tree**
China throws out 45 billion pairs of chopsticks each year, which is equal to about 25 million trees.

● **Go Shower**
The average bath uses up about 20 gallons of water. The average shower uses up about 13 gallons.

● **Where Wildlife Thrives**
Rainforests take up only 7 percent of the world's dry land, but are home to 50 percent of the world's plants and animals.

● **When Tossing the Soda Can**
It takes the same amount of energy to make 20 cans out of recycled aluminum as it does to make 1 new aluminum can.

Field Trip Suggestion

Discuss Deception. Take students to a shopping mall. Arrange to visit several types of retail stores, such as clothing, music, food, books, and so on. Have students look for deceptive packaging or labeling, and compare prices for name brands and store or generic brands. After the trip, have students give an oral presentation of their "Top Eight Deceptions." Allow students to choose to pair up, form small groups, or act as an individual to give their presentations. After the presentations, have students vote on the "Class Top Three Deceptions" and list them on the board. Lead a class discussion of their findings. **CL**, **LS**, **ELL**

BUSINESS
Online
Idea Factory
To learn more about conservation, visit the *Introduction to Business* Web site at **www.introbus.glencoe.com**, and click on Unit 8 Buying Goods and Services.

Bulletin Board

Glencoe Poster Teaching Tip

Let students know that in Chapters 23 and 24 of this unit they'll be discussing consumer rights, the consumer movement, and consumer advocates. Then have students read the paragraph on the poster starting, "The women's movement, civil-rights movement…" and so on. What are the similarities between the women's movement and the consumer movement? The civil-rights movement? Then point out the changes in the workforce detailed on the poster and ask students: What changes do you think the consumer rights movement brought about? Will bring about?

⏱ Out of Time?

If time doesn't permit teaching each chapter, use the chapter's Preteaching Business Key Words activity and the summary.

Portfolio Activity

Consumer Affairs Report. Contact a local newspaper, or radio or TV station, and invite the consumer affairs reporter to your class. Ask the guest to discuss the most common kinds of fraud and ways to avoid fraud. Have students prepare for the visit by researching consumer fraud.

After the guest visit, have students choose one example of consumer fraud and write a newspaper article. Students should give their article a headline and be creative in developing a story line. Students may sketch a picture, or include a magazine cut out to accompany their article. **P**, **CL**, **LS**

SCANS Correlation Chart*

Foundation Skills

Basic Skills	Reading	Writing	Math	Listening	Speaking	
Thinking Skills	Creative Thinking	Decision Making	Problem Solving	Seeing Things in the Mind's Eye	Knowing How to Learn	Reasoning
Personal Qualities	Responsibility	Self-Esteem	Sociability	Self-Management	Integrity/ Honesty	

Workplace Competencies

Resources	Allocating Time	Allocating Money	Allocating Material and Facility Resources	Allocating Human Resources		
Information	Acquiring and Evaluating Information	Organizing and Maintaining Information	Interpreting and Communicating Information	Using Computers to Process Information		
Interpersonal Skills	Participating as a Member of a Team	Teaching Others	Serving Clients/ Customers	Exercising Leadership	Negotiating to Arrive at a Decision	Working With Cultural Diversity
Systems	Understanding Systems	Monitoring and Correcting Performance	Improving and Designing Systems			
Technology	Selecting Technology	Applying Technology to Task	Maintaining and Troubleshooting Technology			

*This chart's highlighted blocks indicate the chapter's content coverage in the Student Edition and the Teacher Wraparound Edition.

Resource Manager

Teaching Transparencies

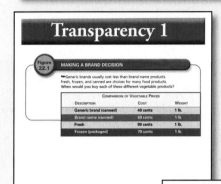

Transparency 1

MAKING A BRAND DECISION

Generic brands usually cost less than brand-name products. Fresh, frozen, and canned are choices for many food products. When would you buy each of these different vegetable products?

COMPARISON OF VEGETABLE PRICES

DESCRIPTION	COST	WEIGHT
Generic brand (canned)	49 cents	1 lb.
Brand name (canned)	69 cents	1 lb.
Fresh	99 cents	1 lb.
Frozen (packaged)	79 cents	1 lb.

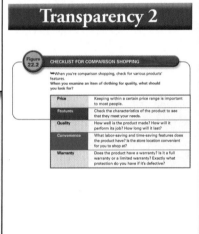

Transparency 2

CHECKLIST FOR COMPARISON SHOPPING

When you're comparison shopping, check for various products' features.
When you examine an item of clothing for quality, what should you look for?

Price	Keeping within a certain price range is important to most people.
Features	Check the characteristics of the product to see that they meet your needs.
Quality	How well is the product made? How will it perform its job? How long will it last?
Convenience	What labor-saving and time-saving features does the product have? Is the store location convenient for you to shop at?
Warranty	Does the product have a warranty? Is it a full warranty or a limited warranty? Exactly what protection do you have if it's defective?

Application and Enrichment

- Lesson Plans
- *BusinessWeek* Poster Package
- Teaching Transparencies
- Integrated Software Simulation
- Glencoe Business Video Package

Review and Reinforcement

- *PuzzleMaker*
- Internet Resources
- Student Activity Workbook
- Strat. and Work. for Teaching Transparencies

Assessment and Evaluation

- Reproducible Tests
- Alternative Assessment Strategies
- ExamView® Pro Test Generator

Technology

- *PuzzleMaker*
- ExamView® Pro Test Generator
- Glencoe Business Video Package
- PowerPoint® Presentation
- Integrated Software Simulation
- Interactive Lesson Planner
- *Virtual Business*®

KEY	Printed	Software	Videocassette	Poster
	Transparency	CD-ROM	Internet	

BUSINESS Online

Visit **www.introbus.glencoe.com**, the Web site companion to *Introduction to Business*. The student's page includes:

- interactive tutor
- additional *BusinessWeek* articles and activities
- business Web links
- homework hints
- real-world application activities
- additional career path activities

Information on how to prepare your students for the high school exit exam and special projects are also included.

Use the Glencoe Web site for additional resources. All essential content is covered in the Student Edition.

Chapter 22

1 FOCUS

Introducing the Chapter

This chapter explains the choices consumers have and how to be a smart consumer. A photo essay, "How Are You Swayed?," enhances the concepts.

Connecting the Objectives

What are the different ways that you buy products or services? What things do you do to be a smart consumer?

BusinessWeek Feature Story

Story's Summary

Consumers are resisting buying stamps online. Stamps.com and E-Stamp are finding that their intended customers—home-based small businesses—want systems that are easier to use. Consumers want a service that's more reliable, more convenient, and a better value.

Find the entire article at www.introbus.glencoe.com, or in the Teacher Resource Binder.

Making Consumer Decisions

Learning Objectives

After completing this chapter, you'll be able to:

1. **Describe** choices consumers make when buying goods and services.
2. **Identify** types of stores where consumers can make purchases.
3. **List** ways to be a smart consumer.

Why It's Important

As a consumer you have the issue of making your money go as far as possible. If you want to get the most for your money, you have to learn how to make good consumer decisions.

Key Words

brand name
generic products
comparison shopping
unit price
promotional sale
clearance sale
loss leaders
impulse buying
warranty

BusinessWeek Feature Story

Dead Letter?

Stamps.com and E-Stamp Struggling for Online Buyers. A little over a year ago, two California start-ups thought they had an irresistible sales pitch: Buy stamps on the Web and you'll never have to stand in line at the post office again. Investors loved the idea. After going public in June 1999, Stamps.com's stock soared fourfold to $48 a share—even before it had sold its first stamp.

Today, Stamps.com and E-Stamp are taking an unexpected licking. Both set out to sell their products to small and home-office customers that don't use postage meters—a potential market of nearly $22 billion in annual sales.

Source: Excerpted with permission from "Dead Letter?" *BusinessWeek Online*, October 23, 2001.

An Extension Activity

When you want to buy a product and more than one company offers similar versions of the same product, how do you decide which one to buy? What factors influence your decision?

BUSINESS Online

The Full Story

To learn more about online buyers, visit the *Introduction to Business* Web site at www.introbus.glencoe.com, and click on *BusinessWeek* Feature Story, Chapter 22.

Classroom Resources

For the Teacher

- Student Activity Work. TAE
- Assessment Binder
- PowerPoint® Presentation
- Interactive Lesson Planner
- Lesson Plans
- Internet Resources
- Teaching Transparencies
- *Introduction to Business* Web Site
- Integrated Soft. Sim. TM
- *BusinessWeek* Poster Package

For the Student

- Student Activity Workbook
- *Virtual Business*®
- *Introduction to Business* Web Site
- Integrated Soft. Sim.
- *PuzzleMaker*
- Strategies and Worksheets for Teaching Transparencies

🔔 Bell Ringer Activity

PROBLEM SOLVING. Write on the board: "Your friend has to decide whether to buy generic or brand-name products. What do you tell your friend about the pros and cons of buying different types of generic items?"

Preteaching Business Key Words

IMPROVING AND DESIGNING SYSTEMS. With a partner, create a "Do's and Don'ts" poster to advise students in your school about ways to be a smart shopper and to avoid getting "taken in." Use all of this chapter's key words in your poster. **CL**

An Extension Activity

An online company's sales force might try different segments of the marketplace or team up with bigger, more powerful companies to achieve sales and recognition.

Making Connections

Marketing. Ask students to contrast the marketing process for a brand name bar of soap with that of a generic bar. Ask students if they have ever seen a commercial for a generic product. Why do they think this is so? Note that producers of generic products save money on promotion and package design.

Business Connection

Consumers need to trust they're getting a good deal. Would you buy any large-ticket item without a "money-back guarantee?" Probably not, but the idea is not a new one. Customers of Wedgwood, the pottery company, were able to take advantage of money-back guarantees as early as the 1760s. Now every successful business works to earn consumers' trust, including companies that ensure quality products such as Starbucks, Estée Lauder, and Dell Computers.

Develop Concepts

CHOOSING. Tell students to imagine they want to buy a new bicycle. On the board write: "What to Buy," "When to Buy," "Where to Buy," and "What to Pay." Ask students to think of as many considerations as they can for each category. (Answers should mention generic products, outlet stores, online shopping, comparison shopping, and so on.)

Figure 22.1 Caption Answer

Buy the generic brand canned vegetables for cooking in soup, stew, or other combination dishes. Buy fresh vegetables in season for the best-tasting product. Buy frozen, packaged vegetables as the best alternative to fresh vegetables.

Buying Goods and Services

When you shop, making choices isn't always easy, especially when you have so many options. Tennis shoes. Jeans. Shirts. Skirts. Sweaters. The malls are filled with tantalizing trends. Even at the grocery store you have thousands of options of different products on sale. Even small neighborhood stores have several hundred different products from which you can choose. In addition, there are many places to look for the best buy.

Consumer Choices

Being a consumer—a person who selects, purchases, uses, and disposes of goods and services—is difficult when you have many choices. If you had unlimited money, you could buy whatever you wanted. People can't do that, though. They have to stretch their dollars to meet their wants and needs.

What to Buy

The first problem of being a consumer is deciding what to buy. Usually you must decide which item has the highest priority for you at any one time, such as a CD or new shoes. After you decide what goods or

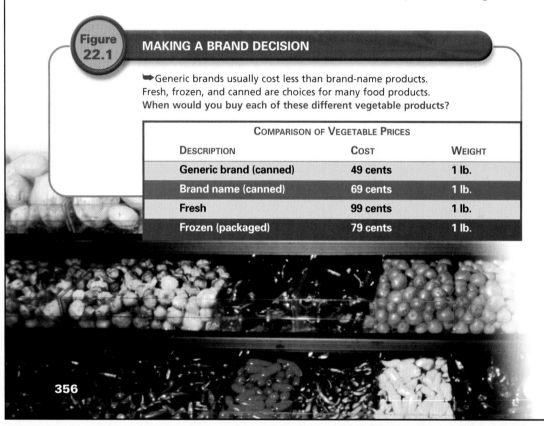

Figure 22.1

MAKING A BRAND DECISION

➡ Generic brands usually cost less than brand-name products. Fresh, frozen, and canned are choices for many food products. When would you buy each of these different vegetable products?

COMPARISON OF VEGETABLE PRICES		
DESCRIPTION	COST	WEIGHT
Generic brand (canned)	49 cents	1 lb.
Brand name (canned)	69 cents	1 lb.
Fresh	99 cents	1 lb.
Frozen (packaged)	79 cents	1 lb.

356

services you want, you must then select from various choices. You can choose to buy either a brand-name product or a generic product. A **brand name** is a word or name on a product that helps consumers distinguish it from other products. Familiar brand names include Nike, Reebok, Healthy Choice, Campbell's, Coke and Pepsi.

On the other hand, **generic products** are plainly labeled, unadvertised, and sold at lower prices. Most generic products are either medicines or grocery items, such as aspirin, paper towels, and peanut butter. On the average, generic products cost 40 percent less than name-brand products. The main reason they cost less is because the producers spend so little on marketing and advertising. Despite the difference in cost, they are often the same quality as brand-name products. Figure 22.1 illustrates a comparative chart on making a brand decision.

When to Buy

Prices for many items change during different times of the year. Postponing a purchase or planning a purchase in advance can save you a lot of money. For example, if you plan on buying a car or a computer, the prices usually go way down shortly before the new models are released. If you want to own a nice raincoat or wool sweater, you can get one for much less during the summer when it's out of season. You might be tempted to buy yourself a few things while shopping for others during the holidays. If you wait until after the holidays, however, you can usually get the same items for less when the stores have big sales to clear out their remaining stock.

Where to Buy

Along with choosing what to buy, you also have to decide where to shop. Do you want to go to a well-known department store, an outlet mall, or a warehouse store? Do you want to stay home and shop online? There are three reasons consumers choose where they shop: the kinds of goods and services sold, the prices, and the convenience.

Department Stores. Department stores sell a wide variety of goods, such as clothing, furniture, appliances, and sporting goods. Because department stores offer name brands and customer services, their prices are often higher than other types of stores. Macy's and Marshall Field's are examples of department stores.

Discount Stores. Discount stores sell a wide variety of goods like department stores but at lower prices. They can sell for less because they

Real-World Application
part 1 of 4

HOW ARE YOU SWAYED?
Has a catchy advertisement ever lured you into a store? Businesses want your business so they'll use advertisements to hook you. Here's a test: You see a sign that reads "CD Bargain Bin. Regular $7.95, on sale for $5.95."
Is this statement rational or emotional?

continued on p. 359

Chapter 22 Making Consumer Decisions **357**

Real-World Application
Caption Answer

HOW ARE YOU SWAYED?: PART 1 OF 4
Rational.

Technology Resource

 POWERPOINT.
The *Introduction to Business* PowerPoint® CD-ROM provides visual lecture aids for this chapter.

Independent Practice

COMPARE AND CONTRAST. List products that you would buy at a store that was convenient to you. Then list products for which you would shop around at several stores, even if you had to travel to them. Write a paragraph to compare and contrast the two types of products. (Answers will vary and may include products in two different price ranges.) **LS**

Meeting Individual Needs

Students With Speech Impairments. Students with speech impairments may have impediments ranging from problems with articulation or voice strength. These impairments can include stuttering, chronic hoarseness, or difficulty in expressing an appropriate word or phrase. Typically, such students refrain as much as possible from class participation. When speaking with a student with speech impairments, use normal communication patterns and refrain from completing words or phrases for the student. Some students use electronic speaking machines or are adept at using body language to communicate. Your role as teacher is to create an environment in which all students can participate to the best of their abilities.

Thinking Critically

You're chatting with friends over the phone one day and one friend mentions how the price of cell phone service has dropped because of the increased competition in the marketplace. That starts you thinking—first, you start listing other products whose prices have dropped significantly over the years. Second, you choose something you'd like to buy soon because the price has now become affordable.

(Answers will vary and may include cameras, stereo equipment, flat-screen computer monitors, software, and home exercise equipment.)

Working Lifestyle

Caption Answer

New jobs, more opportunities, new career paths, etc.

---

offer few services and stock merchandise in large quantities. Kmart is an example of a discount store.

Off-Price and Outlet Stores. These types of stores carry well-known brand names at bargain prices. They're able to offer large discounts because the items they sell have minor flaws, are out of season, or have been discontinued. T.J. Maxx, Stein Mart, and Loehmann's are examples.

Limited-Line Retailers. Limited-line retailers, or specialty stores, sell a large assortment of goods in one product line or a few related lines. They often sell clothes, sporting goods, or home appliances. Foot Locker and Ace Hardware are two examples.

Superstores and Hypermarkets. These stores are like supermarkets but sell items such as books, hardware, and clothing as well as

Working Lifestyle

What are you doing at 10 A.M.?

Houses That Help the World

Lilia Abron and her 130 employees at PEER Africa apply scientific knowledge and business know-how to help black South Africans build houses that are affordable, energy-efficient, and environmentally friendly. At 10 A.M., these three factors keep this environmental engineer's mind busy.

Poor housing and inefficient energy use created severe environmental problems in parts of Africa, including dangerous air pollution, deforestation, and water shortages. PEER Africa's designs tackle both the human and the environmental problems.

Abron's Washington-D.C.-based company has grown to include offices in ten cities and projects in four African countries. Although Abron's company isn't in the construction business, it helps builders apply good engineering and scientific principles to the building process.

Salary

The median income for environmental engineers is $57,262.

Outlook for This Career

The overall employment for engineers is expected to increase as fast as the rest of other occupations.

Connecting Careers Activity

You're entering the century of advanced scientific research. How will new technologies and research benefit the economy and your career path?

CAREER PATH   Scientific Research & Engineering

HISTORY   *Curriculum Connection*

Interview.   The emergence of superstores, warehouse stores, and Internet shopping have all contributed to a shift in the way Americans buy things. Mom-and-Pop corner groceries and five-and-dime variety stores are quickly becoming relics of the past. Have students interview relatives or acquaintances to find out how consumer buying habits have changed over the years. Some questions they could ask include: How often did people shop? Where did they shop? What kind of variety of goods was available? Have students write a 150-word summary of their interviews. **LS**

groceries. Like supermarkets, they're also self-serve. Kroger, Meijer, and Safeway operate superstores.

Warehouse Stores. Warehouse stores typically are about the size of a football field. They carry a huge selection of food and nonfood items at low prices and in bulk quantities. They sometimes require customers to become members of the store by paying a membership fee. Costco and Wal-Mart's Sam's Wholesale Club are examples of warehouse clubs.

Showroom Retailers. These stores sell from showrooms where they display samples of their products. Customers visit the showroom and select from the samples. They fill out an order form and the orders are filled from a backroom warehouse. Best Products and Service Merchandise are examples.

Shopping at Home. You can also shop without ever leaving your home by ordering products through home shopping channels, through mail-order catalogs, or on the Internet. Some retail stores, such as Crate & Barrel and Eddie Bauer, also send out catalogs. Many companies sell items only through the mail or on the Internet. Because money doesn't change hands directly, you usually have to buy products by filling out an order form and providing a credit card number.

What to Pay

The number of choices in any store gives you a wide range of prices. Some people think the most expensive item is always the best quality. In fact, the least expensive item or the one in the middle might be the best buy for you. On the other hand, it's often worth paying more for higher quality. If you want to buy a new TV, it might be worth paying more for one that lasts five years instead of paying less for one that could burn out in two years.

Checking the price and quality of a product in more than one store is called **comparison shopping**. Comparison shopping is most important when you're making a major purchase, such as a car or a computer, because the difference in cost can be so much. (See Figure 22.2 on page 360, which illustrates comparison shopping.) For smaller purchases, you need to consider the cost of the time and energy you spend comparison shopping in contrast to the money you might save. If you spend $2.35 on transportation to save $1.50 on an item, you're losing money.

Some products come in so many different sizes it can be hard to determine which is the best buy. That's why it's important to look at the unit price of an item. The **unit price** is the cost of an item for a

HOW ARE YOU SWAYED?
You've saved up enough money from your part-time job to buy a scooter. At a sporting goods store, an advertisement next to the $50 scooter you want says, "We match prices." You remember a friend talking about a superstore that carried one style.
What do you do next?

continued on p. 361

Chapter 22

Real-World Application
Caption Answer

HOW ARE YOU SWAYED?: PART 2 OF 4
Visit the competing store to check on its price for scooters.

Business Connection

Mark J. Zeabin, a 25-year-old Canadian entrepreneur, designs and sells coffin furniture. On a customer's eventual death, the furniture—a book shelf, couch, entertainment center, or coffee table—can be converted into a casket. Zeabin does not offer loss leaders such as two-for-one specials, but a competing company attracts customers with promotional sales.

Develop Concepts

GIVING EXAMPLES. Ask students to give examples of situations in which information saved them money or helped them purchase a better product or service. What was the source of the information about the product or service?

Great Ideas From the Classroom of...

Tej Bhatia, Ph.D.
Syracuse University
Syracuse, N.Y.

Presentations: Answering Tricky Questions. When you're the presenter, you might be asked tricky questions. First, the long question. It's hard to understand the meaning of a long question. Ask the person to rephrase the question. Second, the negative question. It takes a presenter more time to make sense of a negative question. Repeat the question to check the meaning. Third, beware of jargon. Communication is more effective when everyone understands the meaning of jargon or acronyms.

2 TEACH (Cont.)

Discussion Starter

BUYING. Sita is waiting in the grocery checkout line. She looks at the attractive display and puts a king-sized candy bar into her shopping cart, even though it wasn't on her list. What is this type of buying behavior called? How did the store contribute to Sita's buying behavior? (Impulse buying. The store contributed by purposely placing tempting items in an area where customers are waiting.)

✔ Fast Review Answers

1. Producers spend less on marketing and advertising.
2. Before a new model is released, when it's out of season, or after holidays.
3. Through home-shopping channels on TV, through mail-order catalogs, and on the Internet.
4. Divide the total price by its weight, volume, or number of items.

Figure 22.2 Caption Answer

Check the clothing for general appearance: Are the seams well sewn? Do stripes or plaids line up correctly? Are buttons and trim sewn on tightly? Does the material seem to be of good quality? Does the tag tell you how to care for it?

standard unit of measurement, such as an ounce. Peanut butter, for example, often comes in three or four different-sized containers. If you're looking for the best buy, it helps to know that Brand A costs 17.3 cents per ounce and Brand B costs 19.9 cents per ounce. Many stores list the unit price under the posted cost of an item. If not, you can calculate the unit price of an item yourself by dividing the total price by its weight, volume, or number. For example, if a 12-pack of soda costs $3.60, dividing $3.60 by 12 tells you that each costs 30 cents.

✔ Fast Review

1. Why do generic products cost less than brand-name products?
2. When is a good time to shop for a product like a car, a computer, or an item of clothing?
3. What are ways you can shop at home?
4. How can you calculate the unit price of an item?

How to Be a Smart Consumer

As a consumer, you have to decide what's really a bargain for you. You can become a smart consumer by planning in advance. Start by checking

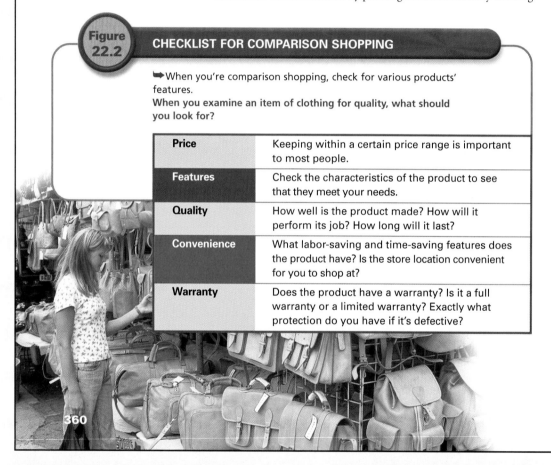

Figure 22.2

CHECKLIST FOR COMPARISON SHOPPING

➡ When you're comparison shopping, check for various products' features.
When you examine an item of clothing for quality, what should you look for?

Price	Keeping within a certain price range is important to most people.
Features	Check the characteristics of the product to see that they meet your needs.
Quality	How well is the product made? How will it perform its job? How long will it last?
Convenience	What labor-saving and time-saving features does the product have? Is the store location convenient for you to shop at?
Warranty	Does the product have a warranty? Is it a full warranty or a limited warranty? Exactly what protection do you have if it's defective?

360

Global Perspective

Check the Tag. Have students check the tags or labels of items such as backpacks, calculators, shoes, clothing, and other things in the classroom. Record the names of the items on the board and the countries in which they were manufactured. How many of the goods are imported? What's the percentage of the total recorded? Are similar items manufactured in both the United States and in other countries? Discuss with students their impressions of imported goods. Are they more expensive? Less expensive? How do the goods compare in quality? **CL**

to see what the good buys are. Newspapers and magazines include advertising that can help. Big stores often send out their own advertisements.

Study Advertisements

U.S. companies spend about $135 billion a year on advertising. To be a wise consumer, you should learn how to read advertisements. Most advertisements are one of two types. *Rational advertising* attempts to convince you with facts and information. It tries to persuade you that you should choose a specific product because it's the best one for your purpose. On the other hand, *emotional advertising* appeals to your feelings. Emotional advertising might suggest, for example, that if you buy something, you'll be the most popular person in town.

When you look at advertising, decide whether it gives you useful information. An ad that simply says "The best buy in town!" won't necessarily help you become a smarter consumer. On the other hand, an ad that says "9 oz. Sparkle-Plenty Toothpaste, $1.99" might be very helpful. If you know that Sparkle-Plenty Toothpaste is good, and that it usually sells for $2.79 for 9 ounces, you know the sale is a good buy.

Read Consumer Publications

Magazines such as *Consumer Reports* and *Consumers Research Magazine* give detailed information about goods that have been tested and rated by them. If you're considering buying an expensive item, such as a used car, you can learn about any car's gas mileage, brake system, and repair record.

Consumer magazines examine and rate everything from bottled iced-tea beverages to travel agencies. Many specialty magazines, such as those for photographers or hikers, rate equipment like cameras or hiking boots. Libraries and online services are good places to find these sources of consumer information.

Shop at Sales

Some shopping experts say that the average consumer can save up to 15 percent by taking advantage of sales. Stores might use two different kinds of sales. A **promotional sale** is one that gives you a special buy on a new product or a product that's in season. It's usually held at a time when consumer buying is down, such as in January after the holidays. A store might also have a **clearance sale** to clear out goods that are going out of season or are no longer profitable in order to make room for new merchandise. Clearance sales often mark the end of a season.

HOW ARE YOU SWAYED?

Sunday morning after you read the comics you turn to the newspaper's pull out advertisement section. You're looking to buy a new DVD player. A few stores have them on sale. One ad reads: "The best buy in town. Sale ends today!"

Is this statement rational or emotional?

continued on p. 363

Real-World Application Caption Answer

HOW ARE YOU SWAYED?: PART 3 OF 4

Emotional.

Individualized Practice

Find the unit price of an item by dividing the price by the weight or volume. The unit price helps you decide which product is the best buy. Which size jar of peanut butter is the best buy?

12 oz	28 oz	64 oz.
$1.72	$3.25	$7.97

L1 Draw on the board three jars of peanut butter and label the weight of each jar. Calculate the unit price of each jar. Have students share reasons why prices may vary with the size of the item. (The 28 oz. jar is the best buy.

$1.72/12 oz = 14.3 cents/oz
$3.25/28 oz = 11.6 cents/oz
$7.97/64 oz = 12.5 cents/oz)

L2 Divide students into pairs to work together to draw three jars of peanut butter and label the weight and unit price of each jar. Then ask students to give other examples of unit price and the influence of item size and demand.

L3 Ask students to draw three jars of peanut butter, label the weight and unit price of each jar, and then write a paragraph discussing the relationships between unit price and demand, and item size and unit price.

Curriculum Connection

LANGUAGE ARTS

Communication. Have teams participate in "Trade-a-Question." First, teams write questions on key points from this chapter on 3" by 5" cards. Second, teams trade their questions with another team and write the answers on the reverse side of the cards. Third, teams trade again for the teams to get exposure to more questions and attempt the answers before looking at the answers written on the cards. Finally, teams should continue trading questions to gain more practice, until all teams have attempted all questions on the cards. **LS**

3 ASSESS

Reteaching

HOW TO BE A SMART CONSUMER. To reteach the concept of how to be a smart consumer, ask students to list six ways of being a smart consumer and to give examples of each. (Studying advertisements, reading consumer publications, shopping at sales, using shopping lists, resisting pressure and gimmicks, reading labels and warranties.)

Enrichment Strategy

READ. Have students read an article that mentions how to be a smart consumer. Ask them to share information about the article. **LS**

Business Building Blocks

CAPTION ANSWER

Direct students to make an eight-column chart with the skills they should practice in the first column. In the second column, ask students to write situations in which they could best practice the needed skills. Use the next six columns to track their progress over a six-week period.

During sales, look for products that are advertised as selling at a loss or below cost. These advertised specials are called **loss leaders**. Even though a store doesn't make any money on these products, the low prices bring customers into the store in hope that they'll buy other things.

Use Shopping Lists

It's fairly easy to fall into the trap of impulse buying when you don't have a firm idea about what you want before you enter a store. Have you heard of impulse buying? **Impulse buying** is purchasing things on the spur of the moment. It can ruin your budget and result in buying things you really don't need.

To cut down on unplanned buying, use a shopping list. It might keep you from making unnecessary shopping trips because you forgot

Business Building Blocks

Communication

Developing Listening Skills

In business, good communication spells success. Active listening is an important part of good communication. You can learn and improve active listening.

Practice

Use the following checklist to become an active listener. On a separate sheet of paper, answer each question in the box with these ratings: **A** (Always), **F** (Frequently), **S** (Sometimes), or **N** (Never).

Rate your score:

Answered mostly A and F = great listening skills

Answered mostly S and N = listening needs improvement

Each week choose two of these questions. Practice the skills indicated in the questions. Keep notes about your active listening.

Checklist for Active Listening

When you're listening, do you:
- ☐ Fidget?
- ☐ Ignore distracting things?
- ☐ Keep your eyes on the speaker?
- ☐ Concentrate on what the person is saying?
- ☐ Pick out the important ideas and think about how they're related?
- ☐ Summarize the ideas in your head?
- ☐ Take notes to help you focus and remember?
- ☐ Ask the person to repeat or explain something that isn't clear to you?
- ☐ Avoid interrupting before the speaker is finished talking?
- ☐ Avoid thinking of what you'll say next?
- ☐ Pay attention even if the person doesn't interest you?

How to Use a Portfolio Activity

The portfolio projects are designed to lead students to develop a collection of their best work to submit to you for assessment. You and each of your students should decide which projects to include in their business portfolio. Refer students to the specific rubric(s) from the *Alternative Assessment Strategies*. These rubrics will alert students to the criteria you'll use to assess their projects. **P**

something you need. A shopping list might save you money as well, because you have decided ahead of time what to buy and you resist buying on the spur of the moment.

Resist Pressure and Gimmicks

Some salespersons use high-pressure tactics to try to get you to buy what they're selling. They can be very persuasive. You should always ask yourself if what the salesperson is saying is true, if you need the product or service, and whether you can afford it.

Sales gimmicks, such as "free prizes" or "super low prices" are meant to grab your attention and get you into the store or draw you into buying something. For example, you might get a notice in the mail that says you've won a "free" prize. However, after reading carefully, you realize you won't receive the prize unless you buy something else. You should always closely examine any deal or bargain that seems too good to be true.

Read Labels and Warranties

Before buying a product, read the label. You might find information on the label that will make you decide not to buy the product. For example, a sweater that needs to be dry-cleaned presents you with the problems of extra expense and inconvenience. You might want to look around for a machine-washable sweater. If you're in the market for fruit juice, you should read the food label for the contents. You might discover that what you thought was 100 percent fruit juice consists mostly of corn syrup.

Many items, such as cars and CD players, come with warranties. A **warranty** is a legal document that states the rights and responsibilities agreed to by the consumer and the store or the manufacturer. Full warranties state that the seller will repair a product that doesn't work, usually free of charge. It could also offer to replace the product or refund your money. Full warranties are usually good for a stated time period, such as 90 days or one year. Limited warranties cover only certain parts of a product.

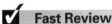 **Fast Review** _____

1. What is the difference between rational advertising and emotional advertising?
2. What two consumer magazines are good sources of information about products?
3. Why do stores have clearance sales?
4. What is the difference between a full warranty and a limited warranty?

HOW ARE YOU SWAYED?
The last item on your family's grocery list is orange juice. There are oodles of choices. One label reads: 100 percent fruit juice; 8 ounces gives you 75 percent of your daily requirement of Vitamin C.
Is this statement rational or emotional?

Chapter 22

Real-World Application
Caption Answer

HOW ARE YOU SWAYED?: PART 4 OF 4
Rational—provides good information to the consumer.

Technology Resource

GO TO **VIRTUAL BUSINESS.** Introduce merchandising or pricing using Knowledge Matters' *Virtual Business* interactive simulation. Go to the *Introduction to Business* Web site **www.introbus.glencoe.com** to download the *Virtual Business* activity. Run the *Virtual Business* tutorial before beginning this activity.

Evaluation

Assign and review the Fast Review sections.

Fast Review Answers

1. Rational advertising tries to convince you to buy with facts and information. Emotional advertising appeals to your feelings.
2. *Consumer Reports* and *Consumers Research Magazine.*
3. To clear out goods.
4. A full warranty covers an entire product. A limited warranty covers only certain parts of a product.

Meeting Individual Needs

Second Language Learners. Students whose native language is other than English may find the legal terminology used in extended warranty features or in credit applications overwhelming. Because these topics are important to students and consumers alike, you may wish to spend extra time going over this vocabulary and provide real-life examples for students to read. Allow time for students to ask questions and receive clarification of any unfamiliar terminology. **ELL**

How Coupons Work

1 FOCUS

Coupons are a basic promotional tool. They're designed to lure customers into a store by offering them discounts on individual products only at the store that issued the coupons. Coupons come in a variety of forms, such as clip-out coupons, e-coupons, and "couponless" supermarket checkout cards. Many stores accept coupons from rival stores or offer "double coupons," in which they'll double the value of coupons.

2 TEACH

Ask students to identify the different ways coupons add to the cost of marketing. Stores and manufacturers, for example, not only lose money on the value of the coupon, but also had to pay printing, advertising, and mailing costs. Manufacturers also have to pay the costs of processing coupons through a clearinghouse. Ask students to identify ways stores and manufacturers have reduced the marketing costs of coupons. E-coupons, as described below, help cut the costs of printing and distribution. Couponless checkout cards help cut the costs of clearinghouses.

? Did You Know?

Manufacturers distribute over $380 billion worth of grocery store coupons each year but only about $3.6 billion worth, or less than 1 percent, are actually used.

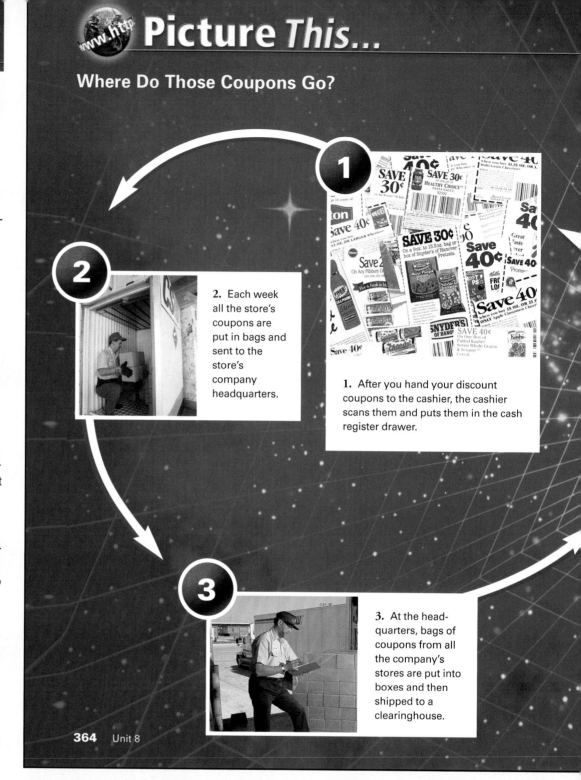

Where Do Those Coupons Go?

1. After you hand your discount coupons to the cashier, the cashier scans them and puts them in the cash register drawer.

2. Each week all the store's coupons are put in bags and sent to the store's company headquarters.

3. At the headquarters, bags of coupons from all the company's stores are put into boxes and then shipped to a clearinghouse.

364 Unit 8

Extending the Content

E-coupons. There are e-tickets, e-mail, and e-tail, and now there are e-coupons. E-coupons are coupons available online. Rather than search through newspapers and junk mail for coupons, consumers can print out coupons off the Internet for the specific products they want to buy. E-coupons benefit businesses because they save on the cost of printing and distribution. It also enables businesses to identify and target the customers who actually use their coupons.

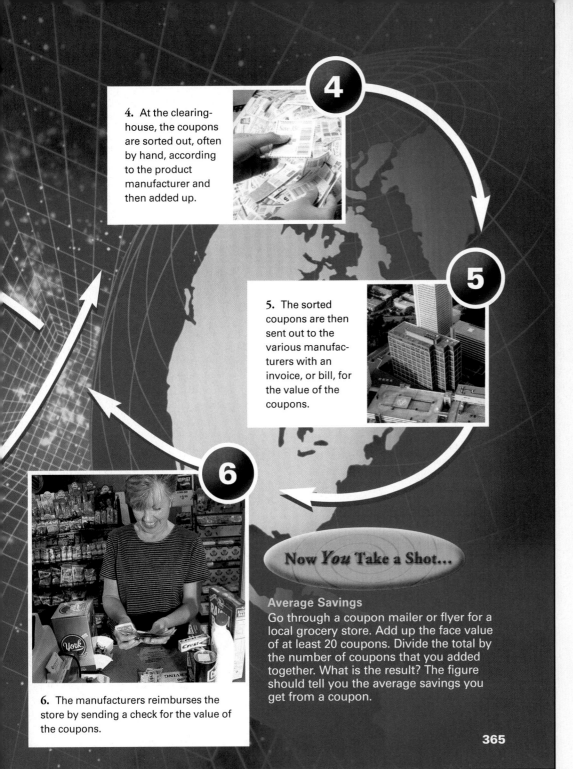

4. At the clearing-house, the coupons are sorted out, often by hand, according to the product manufacturer and then added up.

5. The sorted coupons are then sent out to the various manufacturers with an invoice, or bill, for the value of the coupons.

6. The manufacturers reimburses the store by sending a check for the value of the coupons.

Now *You* Take a Shot...

Average Savings

Go through a coupon mailer or flyer for a local grocery store. Add up the face value of at least 20 coupons. Divide the total by the number of coupons that you added together. What is the result? The figure should tell you the average savings you get from a coupon.

365

3 ASSESS

Ask students to do the activity in "Now You Take a Shot…"

4 CLOSE

Have students pick a common grocery store item, such as potato chips or soda, and search for coupons in the newspaper, in direct-mail ads, and on the Internet. Students should also look for special deals such as double coupons. Have students compare notes to see who came up with the biggest savings.

? *Did You Know?*

The manufacturing and distribution of coupons is considered a recession-proof business. During a recession, people are more worried about their finances so they tend to use coupons more.

Now *You* Take a Shot... **Caption Answer**

Answers will vary. According to different marketing and promotional services, the average face value of a coupon is anywhere from 86 cents to $1.08. This exercise could be extended by having students get together in groups of five, add their figures together, and then divide by five to come up with a new average. The different groups can then compare their averages with each other.

4 CLOSE

Chapter Wrap-Up

Ask students to complete the following statement: "The three things I learned during this chapter that are most useful to me in my life are...."

Using Business Key Words

1. unit pricing
2. clearance sale
3. impulse buying
4. comparison shopping
5. promotional sale
6. generic products
7. loss leaders
8. warranty
9. brand name

Review What You Learned

10. Plain labels and lower prices.
11. Department stores sell moderately priced to expensive products. Discount stores sell items at reasonable prices. They usually offer fewer services than department stores.
12. Because they buy merchandise from producers who have surpluses.
13. For the convenience.
14. About $135 billion per year.
15. Convince you with facts and other information.
16. Detailed information about goods that have been tested and rated by their organization.
17. A promotional sale attracts buyers to merchandise that is in season or that is new in the store. A clearance sale clears out old merchandise to make room for new items.
18. Ruin your budget.
19. Pertinent information.

Summary

1. When you shop, you have choices about what to buy, when to buy, where to buy, and what to pay.

2. You can buy from a number of different types of stores, order from a catalog, or buy online. Your choice of store depends on the type of product, the price, and the convenience.

3. Smart consumers study advertisements, shop at sales, use shopping lists, read consumer publications, resist gimmicks and pressure from salespeople, and read labels and warranties.

Using Business Key Words

Part of being a good consumer means understanding the terms connected with buying goods and services. See how well you know them. Match each term to its definition.

- **brand name**
- **clearance sale**
- **generic products**
- **loss leaders**
- **comparison shopping**
- **impulse buying**
- **unit price**
- **warranty**
- **promotional sale**

1. A price expressed in a standard measurement, such as per ounce, for the same product.
2. A sale to move goods that are going out of season or that are no longer profitable.
3. Purchasing things on the spur of the moment.
4. Activity in which a consumer checks the price and quality of a product in more than one store.
5. A sale that gives you a special buy on a new product or a product that is in season.
6. Products that have plain labels, lower prices, and no brand name.
7. Products that are sold below cost in order to bring customers into the store.
8. A legal document that states the rights and responsibilities agreed to by the consumer and the store or manufacturer.
9. A word, picture, or logo on a product that helps consumers distinguish it from other products.

Quick Quiz

1. When you figure out unit prices for different sized products, what does that tell you? (Which product is the best buy.)
2. Name two kinds of advertising. (Rational and emotional.)
3. What is a warranty? (Legal document that states the rights and responsibilities agreed to by the consumer and the store or manufacturer.)

Review What You Learned

10. How do generic products differ from brand-name products?
11. Describe the differences between department stores and discount stores?
12. Why are off-price and outlet stores able to offer large discounts?
13. Why are consumers willing to pay higher prices at stores like White Hen Pantry Inc. and 7-Eleven?
14. How much money do U.S. advertisers spend per year on advertising?
15. Describe rational advertising.
16. What kind of information will you find in consumer publications?
17. Compare a promotional sale with a clearance sale.
18. What problems can occur if you fall into the trap of impulse buying?
19. Why is it important to read the label before you buy a piece of clothing?

Understanding Business Concepts

20. Of all the places where consumers can buy goods and services, which do you think will have a bright future? Do you think any will become less popular in the next ten years? Explain your answers.
21. List some advantages and disadvantages of shopping online.
22. Why is unit pricing important in getting the best buy?
23. In many grocery stores, racks in front of the checkout lanes have a wide range of "convenience" goods on display. Why do you think those products such as candy, magazines, razor blades, and chewing gum are displayed in that way?
24. When does it make sense to buy certain products in large quantities?

Critical Thinking

25. Bring some labels, tags, seals, or packaging from various products to class. List the information you find on those items. Which type of information is helpful? Which is not?
26. Using newspapers and magazines, find two examples of rational advertising and two examples of emotional advertising. Mount them on a poster and display in your class.
27. What useful information could you find in an advertisement other than price and quality?

Viewing and Representing

Examining the Image. Choose one small area of this photograph and imagine you can zoom in on that area. Write a short description of the area. Read your description to a partner. Can your partner find the area in the actual photograph? What's the overall message of the photograph to consumers? Discuss possible messages with your partner.

Chapter 22 Making Consumer Decisions **367**

4 CLOSE (Cont.)

Building Academic Skills

COMPUTER/TECHNOLOGY. Answers will vary. Rubric: Database.

HISTORY. The library and the Internet are good resources for this activity. Rubric: Essay.

MATH. Students must determine the unit price by dividing the number of ounces into the price. The 9 oz package costs the least per ounce, so it is the best buy. Rubric: Calculation.

LANGUAGE ARTS. Make sure all students participate in the group project. Rubrics: Survey, essay.

Linking School to Home

Provide a conversion chart (pounds to ounces, pints to quarts, etc.) for students to use when calculating unit prices. Rubric: Chart.

Linking School to Work

If your community is a large one, divide the community into smaller segments and assign a segment to a student or group of students. Rubric: Chart.

Building Academic Skills

 ### Creating a Database for Comparative Shopping

Select a big-ticket item that you're interested in purchasing. Use database software to create a database of stores in your area that stock the item you're interested in purchasing. Include names, addresses, telephone numbers, prices, and any other information you determine to be relevant to the purchasing decision. Print out the database and use the information to analyze the best place to purchase the item you want.

 ### Writing a Research Paper

Before the advent of department stores, convenience stores, and online shopping networks, there were trading posts and general stores. Conduct research on the ways people in the United States shopped in the 1800s and the early 1900s. Write a 250-word paper with your findings.

 ### Analyzing the Cost Savings

Five ounces of toothpaste cost $2.09. Eight ounces cost $2.69, and 9 ounces cost $2.88. Which is the best buy?

 ### Devising a Survey

In groups of three or four, devise a shoppers' survey. Include questions such as these in your survey:
- Do you use a shopping list?
- Do you compare unit prices?
- Do you buy large, economy-sized products?
- Do you wait for sales?
- Do you read consumer publications?

Each group member can survey shoppers at a different store. Tally your survey results and then write a profile of typical consumer behavior in your community.

Linking School to Home

Smart Shopping. Visit a grocery store and choose five items that are available as generic products. Record their prices. Find brand-name versions of the same items and record their prices. Calculate the unit prices of the brand-name items and the generic items. Make a chart showing how much money your family might be able to save by buying generic products.

Linking School to Work

Categorizing Your Community. Using the yellow pages and local newspapers, create a chart of the types of places to shop in your community. Use the categories found in this chapter. If possible, list at least three examples of each type of store. Include the address of each store in your chart.

E-Homework

Applying Technology

Membership Fees. Using the Internet, research the cost of joining a warehouse club like Costco or Sam's Club. Find out the membership terms, cost, and whether or not you can purchase items online.

Product Research. Choose a product you are thinking about purchasing in the next few months. Using the Internet, find as much information as possible about the product that would help you make an informed decision about purchasing. Use online consumer publications as resource sites.

Connecting Academics

Math. Shantha is shopping for two pounds of basmati rice. Annapurna Grocery sells basmati rice for $1.39 a pound. Foodstuffs sells 8-ounce packages for 99 cents. Grocerola sells a 32-ounce package for $2.89. Calculate the unit price in ounces for each choice so you can advise Shantha which store offers the best price.

Language Arts. Adar, your boss at the consumer protection agency, comes to your desk and says, "Here's your project for this week. Make an eye-catching poster which gives ten tips on how to make good consumer decisions. Illustrate each tip with drawings, magazine cut-outs, or photos."

Math. At Super-Market, Maria found milk on sale for $2.99 a gallon. Other stores were selling milk from $3.09 to $3.39 a gallon. Why might Super-Market have a lower price?

BusinessWeek — Analyzing the Feature Story

You read the first part of "Dead Letter?" at the beginning of this chapter. Below are a few questions for you to answer about E-Stamps. You'll find the answers to these questions when you're reading the entire article. First, here are the questions:

28. Why have the sales of online stamps been so much lower than expected?

29. What strategies are E-Stamps and Stamps.com planning to try to appeal to consumers?

CREATIVE JOURNAL ACTIVITY

Research a product or service that you buy on a regular basis. Where can you buy it? How do you predict what most people pay (cash or credit) for it? How often is this product or service offered at a discount? Why do you think this is the case? Write a one-page report of your results.

BUSINESS Online — The Full Story

To learn more about online buyers, visit the *Introduction to Business* Web site at www.introbus.glencoe.com, and click on *BusinessWeek* Feature Story, Chapter 22.

369

E-Homework

MEMBERSHIP FEES. Answers may vary. Allow the students to choose the way they share their findings with the class. Rubrics: Essay, poster, chart/table, oral presentation.

PRODUCT RESEARCH. If students are having difficulty with this activity, allow them to help each other. Rubrics: Essay, oral presentation, chart/table.

Connecting Academics

MATH. Annapurna Grocery has the best price: $1.39 ÷ 16 = 8.7 cents per ounce. Foodstuffs: 0.99 ÷ 8 = 12.4 cents per ounce. Grocerola: $2.89 ÷ 32 = 9 cents per ounce.

LANGUAGE ARTS. Posters should include ten informative tips presented creatively.

MATH. Generic brand, too much inventory, more customers, etc.

BusinessWeek — Analyzing the Feature Story

28. Consumers will buy stamps online if it is more convenient to do so.

29. Both companies plan to use their technology for online printing of labels and for concert and movie tickets.

Creative Journal Activity

Tell students that one advantage of shopping by mail or on the Internet is that out-of-state customers don't have to pay a state's sales tax. Have students list what types of purchases they would make by mail or on the Web. The sales tax savings on larger purchases often more than makes up for the cost of delivery.

SCANS Correlation Chart*

Foundation Skills

Basic Skills	Reading	Writing	Math	Listening	Speaking	
Thinking Skills	Creative Thinking	Decision Making	Problem Solving	Seeing Things in the Mind's Eye	Knowing How to Learn	Reasoning
Personal Qualities	Responsibility	Self-Esteem	Sociability	Self-Management	Integrity/ Honesty	

Workplace Competencies

Resources	Allocating Time	Allocating Money	Allocating Material and Facility Resources	Allocating Human Resources		
Information	Acquiring and Evaluating Information	Organizing and Maintaining Information	Interpreting and Communicating Information	Using Computers to Process Information		
Interpersonal Skills	Participating as a Member of a Team	Teaching Others	Serving Clients/ Customers	Exercising Leadership	Negotiating to Arrive at a Decision	Working With Cultural Diversity
Systems	Understanding Systems	Monitoring and Correcting Performance	Improving and Designing Systems			
Technology	Selecting Technology	Applying Technology to Task	Maintaining and Troubleshooting Technology			

*This chart's highlighted blocks indicate the chapter's content coverage in the Student Edition and the Teacher Wraparound Edition.

Resource Manager

Teaching Transparencies

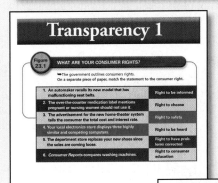

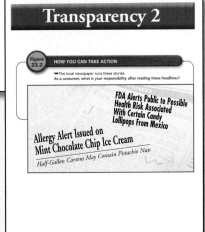

Application and Enrichment

- Lesson Plans
- *BusinessWeek* Poster Package
- Teaching Transparencies
- Integrated Software Simulation
- Glencoe Business Video Package

Review and Reinforcement

- *PuzzleMaker*
- Internet Resources
- Student Activity Workbook
- Strat. and Work. for Teaching Transparencies

Assessment and Evaluation

- Reproducible Tests
- Alternative Assessment Strategies
- ExamView® Pro Test Generator

Technology

- *PuzzleMaker*
- ExamView® Pro Test Generator
- Glencoe Business Video Package
- PowerPoint® Presentation
- Integrated Software Simulation
- Interactive Lesson Planner
- *Virtual Business*®

KEY

- Printed
- Transparency
- Software
- CD-ROM
- Videocassette
- Internet
- Poster

BUSINESS Online

Visit www.introbus.glencoe.com, the Web site companion to *Introduction to Business.* The student's page includes:

- interactive tutor
- additional *BusinessWeek* articles and activities
- business Web links
- homework hints
- real-world application activities
- additional career path activities

Information on how to prepare your students for the high school exit exam and special projects are also included.

Use the Glencoe Web site for additional resources. All essential content is covered in the Student Edition.

1 FOCUS

Introducing the Chapter

This chapter describes the seven rights of consumers. It also explains your responsibilities as a consumer. A photo essay, "Guide to Better Living," enhances the concepts.

Connecting the Objectives

Consumers have the right to choose. What other rights do consumers have? What responsibilities do consumers have?

BusinessWeek

Feature Story

Story's Summary

Qixo, a mega Web search engine for cheap travel, provides two things to which consumers have a right—the right to be informed and the right to choose. This is big business. Overall, consumers are expected to spend billions of dollars on travel in the coming years. Consumers have a responsibility to be informed, and are happy about the convenience of using so-called fare-scraper Internet travel sites, such as Qixo and FareChase.

Find the entire article at www.introbus.glencoe.com, or in the Teacher Resource Binder.

Consumer Rights and Responsibilities

● Learning Objectives

After completing this chapter, you'll be able to:
1. **Name** the seven rights of consumers.
2. **List** the basic responsibilities of a consumer.
3. **Explain** how you can conserve resources.
4. **Describe** ways you can learn consumer skills.

● Why It's Important

As a consumer, you have rights about the safety and the quality of the products you buy. Along with those rights, you also have responsibilities to choose and use products wisely.

● Key Words

consumer rights
consumer movement
product liability
bait and switch
fraud
pollution
conservation
recycling
boycott

370

BusinessWeek Feature Story

A Dogfight Over Net Travel Info?

Airlines and Online Travel Giants Aren't Happy With the Small Dot-Coms Gathering Airfare Info. When Web surfers hunt for cheap travel deals at search engine Qixo, they get a wealth of airfare information from 19 separate travel sites. That helps customers find cheaper fares with less effort. Just one problem: Qixo never bothered to ask Travelocity or Expedia for permission to mine their sites. In fact, Qixo CEO Daniel S. Ko has partnership deals with only seven of the sites his company scours, most of them hotel resellers.

Source: Excerpted with permission from "A Dogfight Over Net Travel Info?" *BusinessWeek Online*, November 30, 2000.

An Extension Activity

Before the advent of booking travel arrangements online, consumers continually approached travel agencies. To date, Web surfers have spent more than $12 billion on online travel purchases. How might this affect travel agencies?

BUSINESS *Online*

The Full Story

To learn more about online airfare information, visit the *Introduction to Business* Web site at www.introbus.glencoe.com, and click on *BusinessWeek* Feature Story, Chapter 23.

Classroom Resources

For the Teacher
- 📁 Student Activity Work. TAE
- 📀 Assessment Binder
- 📀 PowerPoint® Presentation
- 📀 Interactive Lesson Planner
- 📁 Lesson Plans
- 📝💻 Internet Resources
- 🖥 Teaching Transparencies
- 🖥 *Introduction to Business* Web Site

- 📀 Integrated Soft. Sim. TM
- 📕 *BusinessWeek* Poster Package

For the Student
- 📝 Student Activity Workbook
- 📀 *Virtual Business*®
- 🖥 *Introduction to Business* Web Site
- 📀 Integrated Soft. Sim.
- 📀 *PuzzleMaker*
- 📝 Strategies and Worksheets for Teaching Transparencies

🔔 Bell Ringer Activity

SERVING CLIENTS AND CUS-TOMERS.   Write on the board this scenario: "You're training as a sales representative and your boss asks, 'How will you treat your prospective customers, and why will you treat them this way?' Write down your answer."

Preteaching Business Key Words

ALLOCATING TIME.   Allow students two minutes to make a presentation describing a recent shopping experience, an historical event, or a time they remember that centers around one of the key words. **CL**

An Extension Activity

Online ticket sites and airlines that book tickets online are replacing travel agents as intermediaries.

Making Connections

The World of Business.   Have groups of students collect newspaper and magazine articles from consumer publications that illustrate how consumers influenced businesses to change their policies or improve

their products. Have groups make a "Consumers Speak Out!" bulletin board to display their articles. Students may also conduct online research and include printed materials in their display. **CL**, LS

2 TEACH

Business Connection

Xerox Corporation is one of the most progressive companies when it comes to environmental consciousness. Consumers like to know they're contributing toward recycling, so Xerox's goal of zero waste disposal is good for business. Among other things, Xerox provides a program for consumers to recycle used copier cartridges.

Develop Concepts

GIVING EXAMPLES. Consumer rights issues have a major impact on business. Ask students to skim read the first few pages of this chapter to find the seven rights listed. Invite students to give examples of what they think each right could refer to.
(Answers will vary.)

Figure 23.1 Caption Answer

1. Right to have problems corrected
2. Right to safety
3. Right to be informed
4. Right to choose
5. Right to be heard
6. Right to consumer education

Being a Smart Consumer

Your new boss just handed you a paycheck for two week's worth of work. It's Friday night and you're ready to go shopping with your friends. All of the new summer clothes are in the stores and there's one item you've had your eye on. When you get to the mall, you talk your friends into going to the clothing store so you can buy the shirt. The store's got your size. You plan on wearing it tomorrow when you and your friends go to the movies. Saturday arrives and you put it on, look in the mirror, and notice a hole in the shoulder. The good news is that as the owner of the new shirt, you've got rights.

The Consumer Bill of Rights

In 1962, President John F. Kennedy outlined what he called the Consumer Bill of Rights. The bill said that every person has these four basic **consumer rights**—the right to be informed, the right to choose, the right to safety, and the right to be heard. These rights received a lot of attention from the **consumer movement**, a movement to pass laws protecting consumers from unfair and unsafe business practices. Over the years, three more rights were added—the right to have problems corrected, the right to consumer education, and the right to service. Figure 23.1 asks you to match the scenarios to the appropriate consumer right.

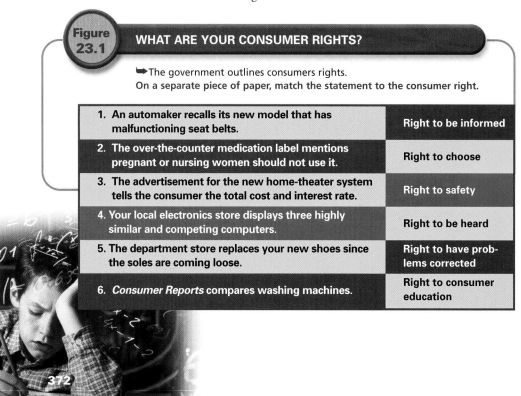

Figure 23.1

WHAT ARE YOUR CONSUMER RIGHTS?

➡ The government outlines consumers rights.
On a separate piece of paper, match the statement to the consumer right.

1. An automaker recalls its new model that has malfunctioning seat belts.	Right to be informed
2. The over-the-counter medication label mentions pregnant or nursing women should not use it.	Right to choose
3. The advertisement for the new home-theater system tells the consumer the total cost and interest rate.	Right to safety
4. Your local electronics store displays three highly similar and competing computers.	Right to be heard
5. The department store replaces your new shoes since the soles are coming loose.	Right to have problems corrected
6. *Consumer Reports* compares washing machines.	Right to consumer education

372

Cooperative Learning

Planning a Lesson. Have teams of students draw up a lesson plan for teaching a group of younger students how to develop good consumer skills. Encourage teams to think of examples and visual aids they could use to help teach some of the concepts. If possible, have teams actually prepare lessons and arrange to present the lessons to students in a lower grade. **CL**, **LS**, **P**

The Right to Be Informed

Consumers can make wise decisions only if they have the information they need. As a consumer, you have a right to accurate information. For example, customers weren't always told in the past how much interest charges would add to the cost of an item, such as a car or house bought over time. Some businesses hid the interest charges in long, complicated agreements. According to consumer laws, companies must clearly list interest charges.

Businesses are also required to give you certain information about their products. Drug companies must list the minerals and vitamins in vitamin pills. Clothing manufacturers must list the fibers used in materials. Packaged foods must list all ingredients starting with what they contain the most. For example, if you buy a bran muffin that lists sugar, flour, and vegetable oil before bran, that means it contains more of those ingredients than it does bran.

The Right to Choose

Consumers can choose from a wide variety of goods and services, because the United States has a market economy. Businesses compete with each other to sell their products to consumers. They try to offer new products, the lowest prices, the highest quality, or the best service to get you to choose their products. Competition means choice. When one company controls the market, it has a monopoly. If only one company produces television sets, you could buy only the models it sells and only at the prices it sets. Lack of competition hurts the consumer.

The federal government has the power to keep markets competitive. It can use antitrust laws to stop monopolies from forming or to break up them. Sometimes the government will prevent a large company from buying a smaller company if it might lead to control of the market.

The Right to Safety

You have a right to products that are safe to use. Federal laws ensure that clothing, food, toys, and other items won't harm consumers. The legal responsibility that manufacturers have to make a safe product is called **product liability**. Before new drugs are sold to the public they must be tested extensively and proven safe. Tools and appliances must have safety devices for your protection. Products that might be dangerous if used improperly must have instructions for correct and safe operation.

Real-World Application

part 1 of 4

GUIDE TO BETTER LIVING

Americans *waste* as much energy as two-thirds of the world's population consumes. When buying household appliances, ask your family to purchase them with the highest-energy efficiency stickers. Look for a yellow and black Energy Guide label on the product. This could save your family about $400 per year in energy bills.
How much money could your family save in five years if you used energy-efficient appliances?

continued on p. 375

Real-World Application
Caption Answer

GUIDE TO BETTER LIVING: PART 1 OF 4
$2,000.

Technology Resource

GO TO **POWERPOINT.** The *Introduction to Business* PowerPoint® CD-ROM provides visual lecture aids for this chapter.

Independent Practice

REPORT. Regulations for automobile safety belts, air bags, antilock brakes, food and drug labels, and unleaded gasoline are responsible for the prevention of injury, illness, and the loss of life. Ask students to choose one of the topics mentioned above or another of their own choosing, and research what effects the regulation has had on consumer safety. Ask students to present their research in a 250-word report. (Answers will vary.) **LS**

Meeting Individual Needs

Students With Hearing Impairments. Many students with hearing impairments, ranging from complete loss to moderate loss, communicate mainly by sign language. When it comes to written English, they are actually using it as a second language, much like students who are non-native speakers.

Many factors affect the comfort level of students with hearing impairments. These include personality, intelligence, degree of deafness, residual hearing, age of onset of deafness, and family environment. This does not mean, however, that you should overlook errors in spoken or written English. Improvement can occur with increased use, correction, and exposure.

Thinking Critically

SOUND SYSTEM. It's a hot day. You're looking forward to a relaxing day at home listening to your new sound system. You grab an ice-cold soda, collapse on the couch, and turn up the volume but nothing happens. All you get is static. You jiggle the connections, try everything, but the sound system's defective. You bought it from a small online outlet that's gone out of business, so you write to the manufacturer to ask for a replacement. In your letter you include all relevant information and documents, and give the time allowed for the problem to be fixed.

Working Lifestyle

Caption Answer

Answers might vary but possibly include air safety investigator, environmental protection agent, park ranger, agricultural commodity grader, or public health quarantine inspector.

The Right to Be Heard

Consumers who have complaints about products or services have a right to be heard. Suppose you buy a bike helmet from a sporting goods store. After wearing the helmet a few times, you find that the strap under your chin keeps coming loose. If you let the store know you're not happy with the helmet, it might be able to fix or replace the helmet. Businesses rely on satisfying their customers in order to stay in business. If you're not happy, they generally want to hear about it so they can fix the problem and keep you as a customer.

There are always some businesses that don't operate in the best interests of the consumer. They might place a high price tag on an item and then mark it down to make it look like the item is discounted. They might also try a tactic known as **bait and switch**. This consists of advertising an item at a low price to lure you into the store. Once you're there, the salespeople tell you they're out of the item and try to get you to switch to a more expensive item.

There are a number of laws to protect consumers from **fraud**, or deliberately misleading business practices. You can turn to various government

Working Lifestyle

What are you doing at 10 A.M.?

Searching for Blight

From tree to table, walnuts from Summers' Farms in California are among the finest quality in the world. The farm foreman, Paul Stanfield, has supervised the raising of walnuts on the farm for 16 years.

"We're delivering a crop of walnuts to the co-op at 10:00 A.M. today," Stanfield says. "We can't deliver walnuts in the shell that are more than eight percent moisture, so we dry them in a bin."

Stanfield can determine certain other qualities about the crop, including the presence of walnut blight. "We're looking to produce the biggest, prettiest walnut inside the shell," he says. "Blight can affect the meat, but to the trained eye, blight is apparent on the hull even in the disease's early stages."

Salary

A typical quality inspector earns $36,820, with a range between $28,540 and $48,670.

Outlook for This Career

Employment of inspectors and compliance officers will grow as the public continues to demand for a safe environment and quality products.

Connecting Careers Activity

Name other industries that need inspection officers. Do any of these industries interest you?

CAREER PATH Manufacturing

HISTORY — *Curriculum Connection*

Consumer Movement. The consumer movement began in the 1960s. Most of the rights consumers enjoy today are the results of consumer advocacy during that time. Have students research the history of the consumer movement and prepare an oral report on one of the aspects of the consumer movement. Have students share their reports with the class. **CL**, LS

or consumer organizations for help if you have a problem. You will learn about those organizations in the next chapter.

The Right to Have Problems Corrected

Sometimes products don't work properly after you buy them. Usually if you take a defective item back to the store with your receipt, the business will replace the item or refund your money. Many large businesses have customer service departments to handle consumer problems. If a business refuses to correct a problem, you can write to the manufacturer to find out how to get the problem resolved. Communicating your problem clearly, concisely, and courteously will speed up the solution.

The Right to Consumer Education

Consumers have the right to learn how a market system works. You should be able to get the best value and the greatest satisfaction for your money. When you decide to buy an item, you should know that different stores might charge different prices. You can comparison shop to find the best buy. Check the information required by law on labels and fact sheets about the products you buy. Schools and colleges offer consumer education classes. Magazines such as *Consumer Reports* and consumer organizations provide consumers with information so they can make educated choices.

The Right to Service

Customers have a right to be treated in a respectful and courteous manner. This is the case whether you're being served in a restaurant, by a salesperson, or by a repair department. You have the right to expect fast delivery of goods or services and that they meet the standard of quality a business claims. You also have the right to be served without discrimination on the basis of your race, gender, income, or age. If you ever feel you're not being treated fairly by a salesperson, you should complain to the person's manager. Sometimes just asking to speak to the manager changes the person's attitude right away.

 Fast Review _____

1. How are the ingredients in packaged foods listed?
2. What is a manufacturer's legal responsibility to make a safe product called?
3. What is bait and switch?
4. Name some sources of consumer education.

 **Real-World Application**

part 2 of 4

GUIDE TO BETTER LIVING

Cars are responsible for 25 percent of the greenhouse effect. Avoid using the car whenever possible. Instead use public transportation, walk, or bike. Encourage your local government to construct bike lanes for bikers and sidewalks for pedestrians. **How will this help everyone?**

continued on p. 377

 Real-World Application Caption Answer

GUIDE TO BETTER LIVING: PART 2 OF 4

Less consumption, less pollution, and less street congestion.

Fast Review Answers ✓

1. In order of what they contain the most.
2. Product liability.
3. A business advertises an item at a low price to lure customers into the store, and then the salespeople try to get customers to switch to a more expensive item.
4. Labels and fact sheets on products, school and college classes, magazines, and consumer organizations.

Great Ideas From the Classroom of...

Paul Richmond
Thomas Edison High School
Elmira Heights, N.Y.

Buying Goods and Services. I have my class choose a product they enjoy (soda, clothing, candy, etc.) and write a letter to the company, explaining how they use or enjoy the product. The company always responds and will thank them with a catalog, gift certificate, or some other type of surprise.

This interaction with the company (usually their public relations or marketing manager) teaches the students that companies take them seriously, value their input, and like to hear about choices they make as consumers. They also enjoy *positive* feedback.

Business Connection

Today about two-thirds of American consumers say that they're willing to pay ten percent more to buy environmentally friendly products. Areas of the country with the largest concentrations of buyers of environmentally friendly products are: Alaska, California, New England, and the Chicago metropolitan area.

Develop Concepts

IDENTIFY. To comply with consumer safety laws, manufacturers provide purchasers of hair dryers with instruction booklets for the safe operation of the units. Ask students to identify the consumer's responsibility. (To read and follow the instructions for the safe operation of the units.)

Discussion Starter

CHOOSING CAREFULLY. Until recently, only a small number of food products were low in fat. Today, food companies produce a wide variety of goods containing reduced fat, low fat, or no fat. What do you think caused food companies to change?

Figure 23.2 Caption Answer

Answer might vary and might include taking responsibility to educate yourself with information and apply your knowledge.

Your Responsibilities as a Consumer

Along with rights come responsibilities. As a consumer, you have the responsibility to educate yourself. If information about a product is available, you have the responsibility to read that information and to use the product the way it is intended. Figure 23.2 asks you how a newspaper's headlines should make you a responsible consumer.

The Responsibility to Be Informed

Responsible consumers know what they're buying. Whenever you shop for food, read the labels for nutritional facts. They can tell you how much salt, sugar, fat, and protein a product contains. When you shop for clothes, read the labels to find out what materials they contain and how they should be washed. If you toss your new wool sweater into the dryer because you didn't read the label and it comes out the size of a dog sweater, you have only yourself to blame.

Before making a major purchase you should always do some homework. Read the Fact Sheets from the *Consumer Product Safety Commission*. The Fact Sheets tell how a product is rated on safety, performance, and value. You can

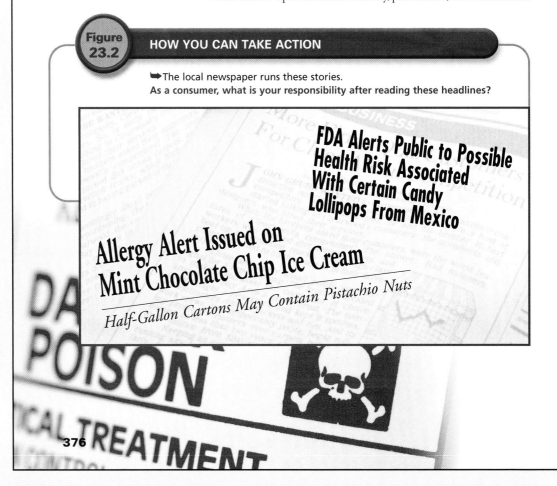

Figure 23.2

HOW YOU CAN TAKE ACTION

➡ The local newspaper runs these stories.
As a consumer, what is your responsibility after reading these headlines?

FDA Alerts Public to Possible Health Risk Associated With Certain Candy Lollipops From Mexico

Allergy Alert Issued on Mint Chocolate Chip Ice Cream
Half-Gallon Cartons May Contain Pistachio Nuts

376

Global Perspective

Conservation of Water. Some 40 percent of world food production depends on irrigation. The supply of groundwater is diminishing. For example, the water table beneath most of India is falling at around six feet annually, and Mexico City is sinking because of the amount of groundwater being used. In Texas, farmers use efficient sprinklers to improve their water efficiency to more than 90 percent. In Malaysia, rice farmers cut water wastage almost in half by new methods. Anywhere drip irrigation systems are used to deliver water to the plant's roots, water usage can be cut 30 to 70 percent. Have students research organizations which monitor water quality and usage.

also find out information on the Internet. Consumer organizations and most manufacturers have sites for consumers.

The Responsibility to Choose Carefully

Responsible consumers make comparisons to find the best product or service at the best price. Which electronics company offers the best guarantee? Which cars have the best record for reliability? Which computer will best fit your budget and your needs? Taking time to make comparisons pays. You can examine the options and prices and then make an educated choice.

Pollution. One of the most serious concerns facing consumers is the effect that buying patterns have on the environment. Individuals have a right to drink pure water, breathe clean air, and live in a healthful place. However, the environment is threatened with all kinds of **pollution**, or contamination of air, water, and land. Pollution is caused by waste from products as well as the ways we use those products. A large share of air pollution comes from exhaust fumes from vehicles. Consumers (and producers) must do their part to cut down on pollution.

Conserving Resources. At one time, it seemed that the United States had boundless resources. Over the years, however, the population has grown and people have increased their demands for all kinds of resources. Now people and businesses have learned that they must conserve resources. **Conservation** is the process of preserving, protecting, and planning the management of resources. Every consumer should be aware of the limited supplies of resources and adjust their consumption accordingly.

Recycling. Part of conservation is learning to avoid waste. You can help by reducing, reusing, and recycling materials in your daily life. Why not recycle! **Recycling** involves collecting products for processing so that they can be used again. Many cities have programs to collect products made of paper, plastic, metal, and glass for recycling. Unfortunately, many cities have a hard time persuading consumers to recycle. It's the responsibility of all consumers to reduce the use of disposable materials, reuse products when they can, and recycle materials to reduce waste.

The Responsibility to Use Products Safely

The government has passed many laws to make products safe. However, consumers must follow the instructions given by the manufacturer for the

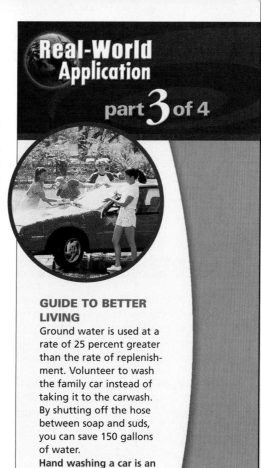

GUIDE TO BETTER LIVING
Ground water is used at a rate of 25 percent greater than the rate of replenishment. Volunteer to wash the family car instead of taking it to the carwash. By shutting off the hose between soap and suds, you can save 150 gallons of water.
Hand washing a car is an example of which consumer responsibility?

continued on p. 379

Chapter 23

Real-World Application
Caption Answer

GUIDE TO BETTER LIVING: PART 3 OF 4
The responsibility to choose carefully.

Individualized Practice

In Ireland, in the 1800s, a landlord named Charles C. Boycott would not lower rents. His tenants refused to have anything to do with him. Activities like theirs bear his name to this day when people *boycott* a product, service, or company they disapprove of. Research boycotts of the last several years and choose one to research more thoroughly.

L1 Ask students to work in pairs to discuss the boycotts they researched.

L2 Ask students to work in groups to make a creative poster depicting the boycott.

L3 Ask groups of students to give a brief oral report on the boycott including when the boycott started and how the business being boycotted responded.

LANGUAGE ARTS *Curriculum Connection*

Communication. Manufacturers sometimes recall products that have been discovered to be unsafe. Have students check consumer magazines or a consumer-information site on the Internet for recall notices. Have them describe for the class the product being recalled, the problem with the product, and the procedure for getting the problem resolved. **LS**, **CL**

3 ASSESS

Reteaching

YOUR RESPONSIBILITIES AS A CONSUMER. To reteach the concept of your responsibilities as a consumer, ask students to sketch a study aid of the six responsibilities. (Responsibility to: be informed, choose carefully, use products safely, speak out, seek remedy, and learn consumer skills.) **LS**

Enrichment Strategies

IDENTIFY. Bring in nutritional labels from boxes of different types of cereal. Pass them around and then discuss how nutritional labels can help consumers choose carefully. Ask: Which product would be the best choice for someone on a low-salt (sodium) diet? Which would be best for someone who wants to avoid sugar? Avoid fat? **LS**

Writing for Business

CAPTION ANSWER

Before this activity, remind students to take note of the sources of information they use for their timelines. At the time students share their timelines, note any discrepancies in the types of turning points and their dates. After students share their timelines, facilitate a discussion on any discrepancies in the information, the sources of information and their reliability. **LS, P**

Writing for Business

Seeing the Big Environmental Picture

This activity gives you the chance to add to your portfolio. Communicate, interview, research, and write your way into a story. Choose one imaginary path, The Recyclable Plan or The Science of Garbage. Follow your path's steps to complete your own story.

pick a path

A Recyclable Plan

The Setting. During the Great Depression many people lost their jobs and often struggled to obtain necessities, including food. Almost everyone was forced to live with fewer consumer goods such as new clothing and cars.

Rising Action. Research the various ways recycling is done in your community. Call your local government offices to find out how organizations help recycle materials in your town.

Step 1. Make a chart that shows what items are recycled by various local organizations. Do they throw away items that could be recycled? Make a list of these items.

Step 2. Now brainstorm ideas about how you could develop a business to recycle these items and materials. Also write several sentences about how you would convince local residents to pay you to recycle these things.

The Science of Garbage

The Setting. The University of Arizona Bureau of Applied Research in Anthropology has conducted research on garbage. The researchers interview people about what they believe they throw away and then compare those beliefs to what is actually thrown away in certain communities.

Rising Action. Research the various ways your family recycles.

Step 1. Write down everything you think your family throws away during a week. Include numbers of items (for example, one empty box of tissues and two broken lightbulbs).

Step 2. Then keep a log and record what actually is thrown away, including food, packaging materials, and items that could be reused or recycled. Talk to your family about what you have discovered.

Conclusion

Now it's time to write your own story, and reflect on your path. Reducing waste, reusing consumer goods, and recycling materials are part of daily life and your future. One way to understand the overall direction of environmental conservation is to construct a timeline. Start with the beginning dates of recycling. Identify the major turning points. Then insert details and look at the big picture. Share your timeline.

378

How to Use a Portfolio Activity

The portfolio projects are designed to lead students to develop a collection of their best work to submit to you for assessment. You and each of your students should decide which projects to include in their business portfolio. Refer students to the specific rubric(s) from the *Alternative Assessment Strategies.* These rubrics will alert students to the criteria you'll use to assess their projects. **P**

safe use of products. You must read the label of a cold remedy to find out the recommended dosage. You should use common sense when handling or storing chemicals or electrical devices. You can have safety problems if you buy products from an unreliable source. If you know it's unsafe, contact a consumer protection agency about the product.

The Responsibility to Speak Out

A responsible consumer can help improve the policies and products of the businesses where they shop. Most of all, you can let the company know if you don't approve of its products or policies. You also have a responsibility to report unfair, unsafe, and illegal business practices. Reporting those practices helps protect other consumers from problems. There are actions you can take as a consumer. If you object to a company's policies or products, you can **boycott**, or refuse to buy, a company's goods or services.

The Responsibility to Seek Remedy

Part of being a good consumer is getting the best value for your money. You have a responsibility to seek remedy for a defective product. If you plan to exchange an item or get a refund, it's your responsibility to bring with you the item, the receipt, and any warranties or guarantees that came with the item. If the store can't solve the problem to your satisfaction, you should write to the manufacturer or contact a consumer organization for help.

The Responsibility to Learn Consumer Skills

Find information to help you make consumer decisions. It's a bit overwhelming to think of researching every purchase you make. However, you can follow a few simple tips:
- Read information on labels and packages.
- Compare prices at different stores and look for sales.
- Pay attention to the media to become aware of illegal practices.
- Read consumer information publications.
- Attend classes or workshops on consumer issues and problems.

 Fast Review _____

1. Why is it important to read product labels?
2. Would you choose not to buy a manufacturer's products for ethical reasons?
3. What are three things you can do to conserve resources?
4. Do you have a responsibility to report illegal business practices?

GUIDE TO BETTER LIVING
Next time you're done with lunch don't just throw everything into the garbage: Recycle it. If your school doesn't have recycling bins for plastic, glass, and aluminum in the lunchroom, ask your teachers or write a letter to the editor about starting a recycling program. What consumer responsibility are you demonstrating by trying to improve the environment?

Real-World Application
Caption Answer

GUIDE TO BETTER LIVING: PART 4 OF 4
Responsibility to speak out.

Technology Resource

GO TO **PUZZLEMAKER CD-ROM.** Check your students' understanding of the chapter's key terms by using the *Puzzlemaker* CD-ROM.

Evaluation

Assign and review the Fast Review sections.

Fast Review Answers ✓

1. To find out nutritional facts about food, what fabrics clothes contain and how to wash them, and how to use a product safely.
2. Students' opinions will vary. Reasons might be the manufacturer adds to the pollution problem or has an unfair hiring policy.
3. Reduce the use of disposable materials, reuse products, and recycle materials.
4. Yes, to help protect other consumers.

Meeting Individual Needs

Students With Orthopedic Impairments. One of the special situations brought up by having students with orthopedic impairments in your class is that you have the opportunity to educate other students and adults about people with physical impairments. Speak with your students who have orthopedic impairments ahead of time, discuss any issues you feel uncertain about,

and read the various educational journals about ways in which students with physical impairments are succeeding in the world. You can learn a great deal and overcome any doubts you may have about the capabilities of these individuals. Be aware that the way you treat students with physical impairments will be imitated. Use the opportunity to increase student awareness.

4 CLOSE

Chapter Wrap-Up

Ask students to write for three minutes on the most important topics of this chapter.

Using Business Key Words

1. boycott
2. bait and switch
3. pollution
4. recycling
5. conservation
6. consumer rights
7. consumer movement
8. product liability
9. fraud

Review What You Learned

10. The right to be informed, to choose, to safety, to be heard, to have problems corrected, to consumer education, and to service.
11. Concerns of starting a monopoly.
12. To the store where you purchased the item.
13. Contact the manufacturer.
14. They use it to make educated choices about the products and services they wish to purchase.
15. The responsibility to be informed, to choose carefully, to use products safely, to speak out, to seek remedy, and to learn consumer skills.
16. Limited supply of many resources.
17. Speaking out and writing letters. Boycott.

Summary

1. Consumers have seven basic rights—the right to choose, the right to be heard, the right to be informed, the right to safety, the right to have problems corrected, the right to consumer education, and the right to service.

2. Consumers have a responsibility to be informed, to choose carefully, to use products safely, to speak out, to seek remedy, and to learn consumer skills.

3. Consumers can conserve resources by saving energy, avoiding waste, and recycling.

4. Consumers can learn consumer skills by reading labels, comparing prices, listening to and reading local media, reading consumer publications, and attending classes or workshops.

Using Business Key Words

When dealing with consumer rights and responsibilities, it's important to know the following terms. See how well you know them. Complete each sentence with the correct term.

- **bait and switch**
- **recycling**
- **pollution**
- **boycott**
- **conservation**
- **consumer rights**
- **consumer movement**
- **product liability**
- **fraud**

1. The consumer group decided to _____ the food-processing company because of its policy towards workers.
2. The practice of advertising a lower-priced item to lure customers to the store and then attempt to get the customers to buy a higher-priced item is called _____.
3. A large share of air _____ comes from exhaust fumes from cars.
4. _____ involves collecting products for processing so that they can be used again.
5. The process of preserving, protecting, and planning the management of resources is called _____.
6. The right to choose, the right to be heard, and the right to be informed are three examples of _____.
7. The _____ protects consumers from unfair and unsafe business practices.
8. Manufacturers have a legal responsibility to make a safe product and this is called _____.
9. A deliberately misleading business practice is called _____.

Quick Quiz

1. Name the seven basic consumer rights. (Right to be informed, to choose, to safety, to be heard, to have problems corrected, to consumer education, and to service.)
2. What is a boycott, and what can it do? (Consumers refuse to buy a company's products or services because they disagree with the company's policies; it can cause a company to change its policies.)
3. What three things can consumers do to help conserve resources? (Reduce, reuse, and recycle.)

Review What You Learned

10. What are your basic consumer rights?

11. Why might the government try and prevent a large company from buying a smaller company?

12. Where would you go first if you had a problem with an item you purchased?

13. If a business refuses to correct a problem for you as a consumer, what should you do next?

14. What do consumers do with the information they receive from magazines like *Consumer Reports?*

15. What responsibilities do you have as a consumer?

16. Why is the conservation of resources so important?

17. How can responsible consumers help improve the policies and products of the businesses where they shop?

Understanding Business Concepts

18. What is the difference between consumer rights and consumer responsibilities?

19. How does a market economy affect the consumer?

20. Describe an environmental problem around your community. List your responsibilities to help solve the problem. What actions could be taken?

21. Why is safely using products a consumer responsibility?

22. As a consumer, how can you make sure you get the best value for your money when you make a purchase?

Critical Thinking

23. Compile a list of sources for consumer information in your city or local area.

Then describe how a person could use each of the sources.

24. What measures could your community take to conserve resources?

25. Imagine a company is dumping hazardous waste into a reservoir just outside of the city limits near a state park. What are some actions you can take to stop this company from its behavior?

26. A growing number of organizations are aimed at teaching kids the virtues of giving. KidCredits is a Web site that allows 8- to 13-year-olds to donate up to $10 to charity. The donation is based on pre-approved amounts charged to a parent's credit card. What might be the goal of this site?

Viewing and Representing

Examining the Image. Can you think of public persons who represent consumer rights and responsibilities? What are the benefits of a celebrity being the voice and face of an issue? Would a celebrity or public person persuade you to take action for his or her cause just because of fame or status?

Chapter 23 Consumer Rights and Responsibilities **381**

Critical Thinking

23. Answers will vary depending on the area.

24. Answers will vary depending on the community.

25. Write a letter to the newspaper's editor, boycott the company, talk to local conservation officials, and so on.

26. The goal is for kids to pick up the habit of philanthropy.

Viewing and Representing

This activity reinforces the students' understanding of the subtle power of visual images and how important it is not to go by first impressions but to analyze what you see. Encourage discussion of other pictures or advertisements students have seen that influence consumers' decisions.

Understanding Business Concepts

18. Consumer rights are what people are entitled to; responsibilities are the actions people must take to deserve those rights.

19. Competition means choice. Consumers can choose from a wide variety of goods and services. Businesses compete with each other to sell their products to consumers.

20. Answers will vary depending on the community.

21. Consumers are responsible for following the safety recommendations given by the manufacturer of the products they purchase.

22. You have a responsibility to seek remedies for defective products.

4 CLOSE (Cont.)

Building Academic Skills

SOCIAL SCIENCE. Make sure all team members participate in the project. Rubrics: Survey, essay.

COMPUTER/TECHNOLOGY. Encourage the students to use a professional style when creating the table. Rubric: Table.

LANGUAGE ARTS. If students are not sure of the appropriate letter format, have them research this using a keyboarding textbook or the Internet. Rubric: Business letter.

MATH. Allow the students to choose the method they will use to share their findings. Rubrics: Oral presentation, essay, poster, chart/table.

Linking School to Home

Answers will vary depending on your family and friends' experience and knowledge. Rubrics: Essay, lists.

Linking School to Work

Answers will vary. Rubric: Essay.

● Building Academic Skills

 Developing a Survey

As a team, develop and then conduct a survey to determine the awareness of environmental issues by local businesses and community members. Your survey could include some of the following information:

- What conservation methods are used?
- Do you recycle? What items?
- Did consumers' wishes influence your conservation measures?

Compile your team's findings in a written report and share it with the class.

 Building a Table

Survey five different local stores (department, hardware, computer, clothing, books, shoes, and so on) regarding their returns policy. Then use word processing software to compile the information in an attractive table. Print out the results of the survey and share it with the class.

 Writing a Letter of Complaint

Suppose you bought a defective DVD player from the local electronics store. You spoke with the manager and asked for a replacement. She refused to replace your player. Write a letter to the manufacturer asking for a replacement and expressing your concern about the store's return policy.

 Studying a Product Label

Bring a food label to class. Read the label and answer the following questions:

- What is the serving size?
- How many servings per container?
- How many calories per serving?
- How many grams of fat per serving? How many milligrams of sodium per serving?
- What percentage of your daily value of vitamin A does the product contain? Vitamin C? Calcium?

● Linking School to Home

Sharing Consumer Tips. Ask your family and friends to share their consumer tips with you. Find out how they make wise decisions about the products and services they purchase. Compile their tips and share them with your class.

● Linking School to Work

Interview and Report. Interview a local businessperson to find out how he or she ensures the business caters to the rights of consumers. Prepare your questions in advance, and include questions similar to these:

- How does your business inform consumers?
- What choices does your business offer?
- How does your business ensure safe products?
- Describe the customer service.
- How does your business correct problems?

Write a report of the businessperson's responses.

E-Homework

Applying Technology

Comparison Shopping. Using the Internet, select a product you plan to purchase soon. Find several different online sites that sell the product and then comparison shop. Which site offers the best value for the money?

Presenting Your Consumer Rights. Do you think other students at your school know about their rights as consumers? Why is it important to know your rights? How can knowledge help you? Inform others with your arsenal of consumer rights and responsibilities material. Using presentation software, create a presentation outlining your consumer rights. Then, give the presentation to other classes in your school.

Connecting Academics

Math. Miguel saw an ad for Mundane biking shorts for $19.99. He went to Ibex Cycle Shop to buy a pair. Kristin, the salesperson, told Miguel that Ibex was out of Mundane shorts but that Mountain King biking shorts were priced at $27.99 and were on sale for 30 percent off. Kristin also said, "Mountain King shorts are really a much better product." Calculate the sale price of Mountain King shorts. Was Ibex trying to use the bait-and-switch tactic on Miguel?

Language Arts. Give three examples of times you or a member of your family has taken responsibility as a consumer—that is the responsibility to report unfair, unsafe, or illegal business practices, or the responsibility to seek remedy for a defective product. Give a short presentation of your examples. What was the outcome? Would this person take action again?

BusinessWeek — Analyzing the Feature Story

You read the first part of "A Dogfight Over Net Travel Info?" at the beginning of this chapter. Below are a few questions for you to answer about Qixo and Orbitz. You'll find the answers to these questions when you're reading the entire article. First, here are the questions:

27. Qixo's business model depends upon what consumer rights?
28. Why is the justice department investigating Orbitz, the big airlines, and travel companies' competing sites?

CREATIVE JOURNAL ACTIVITY

Divide into groups. One team represents the airline companies and travel sites and the other team represents Qixo. Prepare your arguments showing how your side benefits consumers. Conduct a short debate.

BUSINESS Online

The Full Story

To learn more about Qixo, visit the *Introduction to Business* Web site at **www.introbus.glencoe.com**, and click on *BusinessWeek* Feature Story, Chapter 23.

E-Homework

COMPARISON SHOPPING. Answers will vary. Allow the students to choose the way they wish to share their findings with the class. Rubrics: List, essay, oral presentation, poster, chart.

PRESENTING YOUR CONSUMER RIGHTS. Students may wish to help each other with this activity. Rubrics: Computerized presentation, oral presentation.

Connecting Academics

MATH. No. On sale, Mountain King shorts are actually slightly cheaper than Mundane shorts. $27.99 × 0.30 = $8.40. $27.99 − $8.40 = $19.59.

LANGUAGE ARTS. Examples and presentations will vary. Ask students what they've learned from the presentations.

BusinessWeek — Analyzing the Feature Story

27. Qixo depends upon consumers' rights to be informed about and choose the cheapest airfares.
28. The Justice Department is concerned that these big companies might be colluding. Bonus: This could lead to less competition and higher prices.

Creative Journal Activity

After groups have presented arguments, have them decide the outcome of the debate. Take an informal poll to find out whether anyone changed his or her mind as a result of the debate. **CL**, LS

SCANS Correlation Chart*

Foundation Skills

Basic Skills	Reading	Writing	Math	Listening	Speaking	
Thinking Skills	Creative Thinking	Decision Making	Problem Solving	Seeing Things in the Mind's Eye	Knowing How to Learn	Reasoning
Personal Qualities	Responsibility	Self-Esteem	Sociability	Self-Management	Integrity/ Honesty	

Workplace Competencies

Resources	Allocating Time	Allocating Money	Allocating Material and Facility Resources	Allocating Human Resources		
Information	Acquiring and Evaluating Information	Organizing and Maintaining Information	Interpreting and Communicating Information	Using Computers to Process Information		
Interpersonal Skills	Participating as a Member of a Team	Teaching Others	Serving Clients/ Customers	Exercising Leadership	Negotiating to Arrive at a Decision	Working With Cultural Diversity
Systems	Understanding Systems	Monitoring and Correcting Performance	Improving and Designing Systems			
Technology	Selecting Technology	Applying Technology to Task	Maintaining and Troubleshooting Technology			

*This chart's highlighted blocks indicate the chapter's content coverage in the Student Edition and the Teacher Wraparound Edition.

Resource Manager

Teaching Transparencies

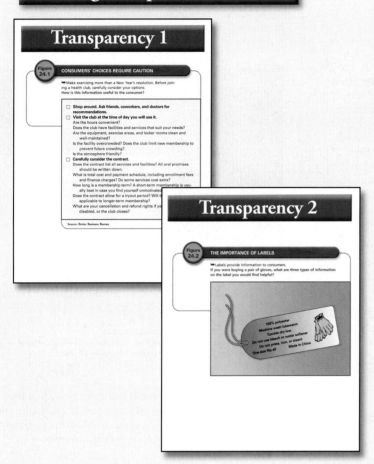

Transparency 1

Figure 24.1 — CONSUMERS' CHOICES REQUIRE CAUTION

Make exercising more than a New Year's resolution. Before joining a health club, carefully consider your options. How is this information useful to the consumer?

- Shop around. Ask friends, coworkers, and doctors for recommendations.
- Visit the club at the time of day you will use it.
  Are the hours convenient?
  Does the club have facilities and services that suit your needs?
  Are the equipment, exercise areas, and locker rooms clean and well-maintained?
  Is the facility overcrowded? Does the club limit new membership to prevent future crowding?
  Is the atmosphere friendly?
- Carefully consider the contract.
  Does the contract list all services and facilities? All oral promises should be written down.
  What is total cost and payment schedule, including enrollment fees and finance charges? Do some services cost extra?
  How long is a membership term? A short-term membership is usually best in case you find yourself unmotivated.
  Does the contract allow for a tryout period? Will the applicable to longer-term membership?
  What are your cancellation and refund rights if you disabled, or the club closes?

Source: Better Business Bureau

Transparency 2

Figure 24.2 — THE IMPORTANCE OF LABELS

Labels provide information to consumers. If you were buying a pair of gloves, what are three types of information on the label you would find helpful?

100% polyester
Machine wash lukewarm
Tumble dry low
Do not use bleach or water softener
Do not press, iron, or steam
One size fits all   Made in China

Application and Enrichment

- Lesson Plans
- *BusinessWeek* Poster Package
- Teaching Transparencies
- Integrated Software Simulation
- Glencoe Business Video Package

Review and Reinforcement

- *PuzzleMaker*
- Internet Resources
- Student Activity Workbook
- Strat. and Work. for Teaching Transparencies

Assessment and Evaluation

- Reproducible Tests
- Alternative Assessment Strategies
- ExamView® Pro Test Generator

Technology

- *PuzzleMaker*
- ExamView® Pro Test Generator
- Glencoe Business Video Package
- PowerPoint® Presentation
- Integrated Software Simulation
- Interactive Lesson Planner
- *Virtual Business*®

KEY	Printed	Software	Videocassette	Poster
	Transparency	CD-ROM	Internet	

BUSINESS Online

Visit www.introbus.glencoe.com, the Web site companion to *Introduction to Business.* The student's page includes:

- interactive tutor
- additional *BusinessWeek* articles and activities
- business Web links
- homework hints
- real-world application activities
- additional career path activities

Information on how to prepare your students for the high school exit exam and special projects are also included.

Use the Glencoe Web site for additional resources. All essential content is covered in the Student Edition.

Introducing the Chapter

This chapter describes your power as a consumer. It explains how government and private organizations protect and help consumers. A photo essay, "The Truth About French Fries," enhances the concepts.

Connecting the Objectives

When you have a problem with a product, what can you do? Name some organizations and some resources that help consumers.

BusinessWeek
Feature Story

Story's Summary

Mutual-fund investors have an independent organization to protect their rights—Fund Democracy. Fund Democracy's CEO, Mercer Bullard, thinks his organization provides two benefits: Investors gain protection from exorbitant fees or major losses, and the mutual-fund industry will continue to keep its clean reputation.

Find the entire article at www.introbus.glencoe.com, or in the Teacher Resource Binder.

Chapter 24

Protecting Consumers

Learning Objectives

After completing this chapter, you'll be able to:

1. **Describe** what consumers can do when they have problems with products.
2. **Identify** groups and individuals that act as consumer advocates.
3. **Explain** how government protects consumers.
4. **Name** ways in which businesses help and inform consumers.

Why It's Important

As a consumer, you're empowered by the establishment of resources and organizations.

Key Words

refund
small claims court
consumer advocates
consumer reporter
grade labels
recall
legal monopolies
licenses
Better Business Bureau (BBB)

384

BusinessWeek Feature Story

He's Raring to Fight for Fund Investors' Rights

An Industry's Clean Reputation. Do mutual fund investors need a consumer advocate? Mercer Bullard thinks so. And just who is Mercer Bullard? A 39-year-old former Securities and Exchange Commission attorney, Bullard is the founder and CEO—and still the only employee—of Fund Democracy. He hopes to make Fund Democracy a force for change in the mutual fund world. He has already ruffled feathers in the industry and among his former colleagues at the SEC.

Source: Excerpted with permission from "He's Raring to Fight for Fund Investors' Rights," *BusinessWeek Online*, November 17, 2000.

An Extension Activity

List some TV programs you've seen that revealed businesses' shaky professional practices. Which businesses do you think need an objective watchdog to make sure they're not engaging in any misguided practices? How did the businesses change?

BUSINESS
Online

The Full Story

To learn more about consumer advocate Mercer Bullard, visit the *Introduction to Business* Web site at www.introbus.glencoe.com, and click on *BusinessWeek* Feature Story, Chapter 24.

Classroom Resources

For the Teacher
- Student Activity Work. TAE
- Assessment Binder
- PowerPoint® Presentation
- Interactive Lesson Planner
- Lesson Plans
- Internet Resources
- Teaching Transparencies
- *Introduction to Business* Web Site

- Integrated Soft. Sim. TM
- *BusinessWeek* Poster Package

For the Student
- Student Activity Workbook
- *Virtual Business*®
- *Introduction to Business* Web Site
- Integrated Soft. Sim.
- *PuzzleMaker*
- Strategies and Worksheets for Teaching Transparencies

🔔 *Bell Ringer Activity*

TEACHING OTHERS. You're going to produce a user-friendly handbook called *Survival Kit for Consumers.* To start, list some useful tips and strategies to help consumers who say: How do I have an effect on business? How do I know if a hairdresser's qualified? What's a recall?

Preteaching Business Key Words

REASONING. List the key words and their definitions in your journal. What conclusions can you draw about how each key word might be used in this chapter? **LS**

An Extension Activity

CHART. After students have individually compiled their lists, ask groups of students to pool their findings in a chart. **CL**

Making Connections

Consumers and Business. Ask students to name some products that were available a few years ago and have been discontinued. Have students hypothesize about why the items might no longer be available. (Consumers lost interest in the product, the product never sold as well as expected.) Interested students may want to research the history of the products mentioned and report the reasons for the product's demise to the class. **CL**, **LS**

Business Connection

ADVOCACY. Ralph Nader is an advocate of consumer rights. His book *Unsafe at Any Speed* focused attention on the auto industry's need to emphasize car safety features. Nader formed the consumer organization Public Citizen, which today continues to investigate consumer issues. You can see how it educates people about consumer issues online at www.citizen.org.

Develop Concepts

CONSUMERS HAVE INFLUENCE. Ask students: What kinds of choices do you make right now as consumers that will affect businesses? What are the possible effects? (Answers will vary and may include: When you buy, you send a message to a company that you like the product. A business might fail if you don't like their product or service.)

Figure 24.1 Caption Answer

Alerts the consumer to the important questions to ask.

Protecting Consumers From Unsafe Products

You'll probably have trouble with a product at some point. There are things you can do yourself. There are many agencies, organizations, and individuals who work to promote the health, safety, and honest treatment of the public. Legislators at the local, state, and national levels have passed laws that establish rules and regulations to protect and inform customers. In addition to government agencies, there are many nongovernmental organizations that work on behalf of consumers. Even businesses themselves offer avenues for consumer complaints and concerns.

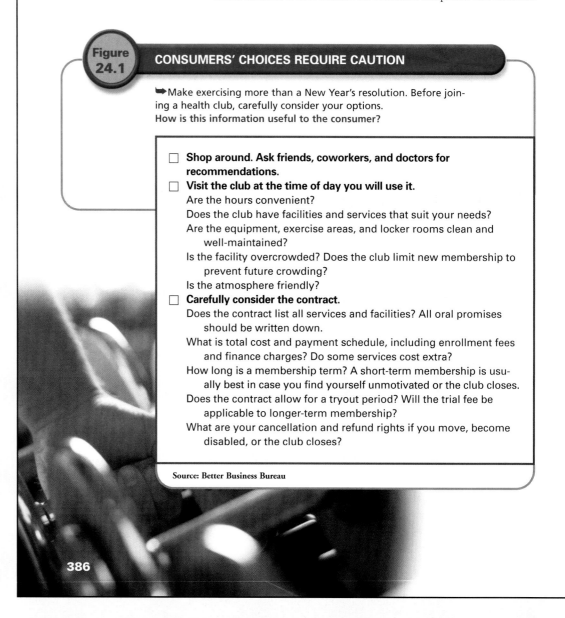

Figure 24.1

CONSUMERS' CHOICES REQUIRE CAUTION

➡ Make exercising more than a New Year's resolution. Before joining a health club, carefully consider your options.
How is this information useful to the consumer?

- ☐ **Shop around. Ask friends, coworkers, and doctors for recommendations.**
- ☐ **Visit the club at the time of day you will use it.**
  Are the hours convenient?
  Does the club have facilities and services that suit your needs?
  Are the equipment, exercise areas, and locker rooms clean and well-maintained?
  Is the facility overcrowded? Does the club limit new membership to prevent future crowding?
  Is the atmosphere friendly?
- ☐ **Carefully consider the contract.**
  Does the contract list all services and facilities? All oral promises should be written down.
  What is total cost and payment schedule, including enrollment fees and finance charges? Do some services cost extra?
  How long is a membership term? A short-term membership is usually best in case you find yourself unmotivated or the club closes.
  Does the contract allow for a tryout period? Will the trial fee be applicable to longer-term membership?
  What are your cancellation and refund rights if you move, become disabled, or the club closes?

Source: Better Business Bureau

386

Cooperative Learning

Debate. Through bioengineering, scientists can manipulate a plant's DNA in order to alter some of the plant's traits. Some results of bioengineering include the development of virus- and drought-resistant varieties of plants. The FDA approved selling these bioengineered plants in 1994. Some ecologists and consumer groups, however, claim that a more thorough examination of the potential risks of the technology should be conducted. Many people feel that food products, which are a result of bioengineering should be clearly labeled, so that people can make their own decisions on consumption. Have groups of students choose a side of the issue, gather evidence, present arguments, and evaluate the outcome of the debate. **CL**, LS

Your Power as a Consumer

You have a role as a consumer. You also have power as a consumer (see Figure 24.1). Every time you buy a good or service, you send a message to the company that you like its product. If enough people support the product, the company will continue to produce it. You and other consumers are responsible for the company's success or failure.

On the other hand, suppose that few consumers buy an item. Eventually, the company will discontinue the item because it isn't profitable. The business's choice to discontinue the item affects your choices. You have fewer items from which to choose. Whenever you visit a store, you send a message that the location is convenient for you. If a business finds its location doesn't attract customers, it might move to a more convenient location. You have a voice in what's sold and where stores are located.

Customer Satisfaction

Although an informed consumer can usually avoid problems, they sometimes do occur. Suppose you buy a printer that turns out to be defective. The first thing you should do is take it back to the store. In most cases, the problem is simply a bad part that an inspector missed and isn't the fault of the store or the salesperson. The store will usually give you a **refund** (return the cost of a product to you), fix the item, or replace it. Businesses are generally willing to offer refunds or replacements to satisfy an unhappy customer.

Legal Action

Sometimes a business might refuse to satisfy a customer. For example, you take your faulty printer back to the store and they refuse to refund your money, or you pay someone to fix your bike and they don't do the job right. In that case, you can take them to small claims court. **Small claims court** settles cases involving relatively small amounts of money. In most states, a consumer can go to small claims court with little cost and without a lawyer. The size of claims varies from state to state but can be as low as $25 or as high as $5,000.

✓ Fast Review

1. If you return a faulty product to a store, what are the three things the store might do to satisfy you?
2. What is the range of claims in small claims court?

Real-World Application

part **1** of 4

THE TRUTH ABOUT FRENCH FRIES
Idaho Spuds. Depending on your favorite grease-to-salt ratio, these thinly cut potatoes, with crispy outer edges and meaty middles, are a craving for many. Nearly a decade ago, a few fast food restaurants listened to the public's concern about fries' impact on cholesterol.
Name one way restaurants made this favorite fast-food side order healthier?

continued on p. 389

Real-World Application
Caption Answer

THE TRUTH ABOUT FRENCH FRIES: PART 1 OF 4

The restaurant stopped cooking fries in animal-based cooking oil and switched to vegetable oil.

Technology Resource

POWERPOINT. The *Introduction to Business* PowerPoint® CD-ROM provides visual lecture aids for this chapter.

Independent Practice

INTERVIEW. Find out about one consumer organization in your community. Prepare five or six questions about the organization. Conduct a phone interview with a representative of the organization to get answers to your questions. Share your findings with the class. (Encourage students to be creative.) **CL**, LS

Fast Review Answers ✓

1. Refund your money, exchange the product, or fix it.
2. As low as $25 or as high as $5,000.

Meeting Individual Needs

Students With Speech Impairments.
Students with speech impairments benefit by having an opportunity to make a contribution in ways other than by contributing to class discussion. For example, students might prepare a bulletin board display, a study-aid chart, or a report on a topic that could be distributed to all students. Make assignments in accordance with students' interests and talents. The opportunity to participate is the key, and involvement can take root if students are given regular opportunities. Keep in mind, these students do benefit from listening to class discussion even if they are not comfortable contributing.

Thinking Critically

TESTING. You're watching TV and there's a short spot featuring testing by the Federal Drug Administration (FDA). You learn that the testing of a new medicial drug can take up to ten years. First, a drug is used on animals. Then drug companies must pay for three phases of clinical tests on humans. The first phase involves testing on volunteers. Second, sick people take the drug to check its side effects. Third, sick people take the drug for three or four years to judge possible long-term effects. Some people think the testing takes too long and argue that lives are lost while extremely ill patients wait for FDA approval. Others think the testing is necessary so that the drug can be safely used to treat illness. What do you think?
(Answers will vary.)

Working Lifestyle

Caption Answer

Answers will vary. Flexible work hours, workplace environment, coworkers, and so on may contribute to finding a meaningful and favorable work schedule.

Consumer Organizations

Groups and individuals that work to protect, inform, and defend consumers are called **consumer advocates**. Many groups are private, nonprofit organizations. Some test products and report their findings. Their information is usually available in magazines. Most of these organizations also have their own Web sites. They help consumers become better informed.

Consumer Federation of America

There are a number of national consumer organizations. The Consumer Federation of America (CFA) is one of the largest. Since 1968 it has worked to inform the public and government about consumer issues. It has more than 50 million members in over 260 groups. The members study federal laws that affect consumers. When Congress considers consumer bills, the Federation lets its members know. It works to promote laws that help consumers. Its six major areas are financial services, utilities, product safety, transportation, health care, and food safety.

Working Lifestyle

What are you doing at 10 A.M.?

Four-Car Carrier

"I drive what they call a four-car carrier," says José Guzman. "Usually by 10:00 A.M., I'm picking up my third car from a body shop and getting ready for my fourth."

Guzman drives for a national auto salvage business that works mostly with insurance companies. He explains, "We take a car, check to see if it's totaled, then sell it. Most of our sales are for recycling."

Before Guzman began driving trucks, he worked at his employer's impound yard as a forklift operator and shipping manager. He applied for a Class B driver's license and transferred to a driving position in order to make more money. "My dad used to be a truck driver and he taught me," explains Guzman. "All my life I've been driving big trucks."

Patience and safety, Guzman says, are key to good driving. "It's tiring after a while, especially dealing with traffic. I have to be patient."

Salary

The median hourly earnings of truck drivers is $11.67, with a range between $8.80 and $15.57 an hour.

Outlook for This Career

The occupation is expected to grow at a steady rate.

Connecting Careers Activity

Competition is high for good wages and favorable work schedules. What constitutes a favorable work schedule to you? Does that matter when choosing a career?

CAREER PATH

Transportation, Distribution & Logistics

LANGUAGE ARTS · *Curriculum Connection*

Communication. As you learned in Chapter 13, before a company introduces a new product to the general market, it does market research to find out what consumers would be likely to buy. Even so, products frequently fail. Consumers failed to buy NutraSweet's Simple Pleasure ice cream, which was made with a fat substitute. It seemed like a sure bet. Ask students to research a product that did not sell as expected, and write a paragraph summarizing their findings. **LS, P**

National Consumers League

The National Consumers League also works on behalf of consumers' rights. It's the nation's oldest nonprofit consumer group. Membership is open to anyone. It provides government, businesses, and other agencies with the consumer's point of view. One of its services is a national fraud information center. It also monitors the Internet to prevent consumer fraud.

Consumers Union

Consumers Union is the nonprofit publisher of the magazine *Consumer Reports*. Consumers can subscribe to the magazine, which reports on consumer products. Consumers Union tests products in its laboratories and reports the findings in its magazine. The magazine doesn't advertise products or allow its findings to be used in advertisements. Consumers Union also testifies before government agencies on consumer concerns.

Major Appliance Consumer Action Program

Some industries have consumer assistance panels. The Major Appliance Consumer Action Program (MACAP) is an active panel. MACAP helps consumers solve problems with large appliances such as washers, stoves, and freezers. Most major appliance dealers are members of MACAP. If a company doesn't respond to a consumer's problem with an appliance, MACAP will help.

Radio and Television

Local radio and TV stations in many cities use the power of the press to help consumers with problems. They often have a **consumer reporter**, who reports on issues important to consumers, such as product safety, testing, and shopping. The reporter might feature one consumer's problem with a local business and visit the business to try to resolve the problem. The chance that the problem will be featured on radio or TV is often enough to get a company to settle the conflict.

 Fast Review _____

1. What is *Consumer Reports'* policy about advertising?
2. If you have problems with a new stove or washer, what organization can help you?

Real-World Application

part **2** of 4

THE TRUTH ABOUT FRENCH FRIES

Give just the fry facts folks. McDonald's U.S.A. believes in sharing its nutritional and ingredient information. In any one of its stores you'll find posters, wallet-sized cards, and brochures offering the facts. A description of its french fries is in compliance with the U.S. Food and Drug Administration.

What's the purpose of providing nutritional facts?

continued on p. 391

Chapter 24

Real-World Application
Caption Answer

THE TRUTH ABOUT FRENCH FRIES: PART 2 OF 4

To let consumers know the nutritional contents of the food that's available for consumption.

Fast Review Answers ✔

1. It doesn't advertise products or allow its findings to be used in advertisements.
2. The Major Appliance Consumer Action Program (MACAP).

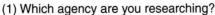

Great Ideas From the Classroom of...

Sharon Larson
Praire Ridge High School
Crystal Lake, Ill.

Consumer Protection Agencies.
Choose a consumer protection agency to research on the Internet. From your research, answer these questions:
(1) Which agency are you researching?
(2) What does this agency do to protect or help consumers? (3) What information is the same as the textbook? (4) What new information did you discover? (You must have at least one new point.)

2 TEACH (Cont.)

Business Connection

One way government protects consumers is by requiring people practicing certain professions to be licensed. Hair stylists, for example, must have a license that ensures proper training. Hairdressers use potentially dangerous chemicals in coloring, permanent waving, bleaching, and straightening hair. The training teaches them how to handle these chemicals so they won't hurt themselves or their customers.

Develop Concepts

STATES PROTECT CONSUMERS. States issue licenses to make sure workers in some occupations are qualified. What are some examples of professions, other than hair stylists, require a license? (Answers will include doctors, teachers, roofers, architects, plumbers, and so on.)

Discussion Starter

ASKING WHY. Ask students: Why do you think businesses are willing to organize and support organizations such as the Better Business Bureau (BBB)?

Figure 24.2 Caption Answer

Answers might vary.

Government Organizations

Many federal, state, and local governments provide consumer information. They publish materials to help consumers with their buying decisions and problems. They also pass laws to protect consumers.

Federal Agencies

Consumers can order publications from government agencies. The Consumer Information Center in Pueblo, Colorado is a good source for those materials. Some of the booklets are free and others have a small fee. Consumers can order by mail, phone, or the Internet. These booklets give advice to help consumers decide what and where to buy.

Many federal agencies have been set up to protect consumers. The Federal Trade Commission (FTC) enforces laws about business practices. The U.S. Department of Agriculture (USDA) inspects foods such as meat and gives them **grade labels** that indicate the level of quality. Meat, for example, might be graded as "prime" or "choice." You can use the

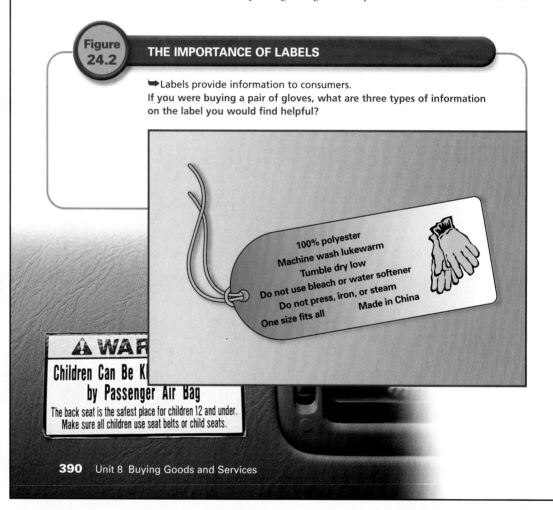

Figure 24.2 THE IMPORTANCE OF LABELS

➡ Labels provide information to consumers.
If you were buying a pair of gloves, what are three types of information on the label you would find helpful?

100% polyester
Machine wash lukewarm
Tumble dry low
Do not use bleach or water softener
Do not press, iron, or steam
One size fits all   Made in China

⚠ WAR[NING]
Children Can Be K[illed]
by Passenger Air Bag
The back seat is the safest place for children 12 and under.
Make sure all children use seat belts or child seats.

390 Unit 8 Buying Goods and Services

Global Perspective

Consumer Rights in Africa. Although consumer movements gained ground in some African countries in the 1990s, in general, African consumers suffer from a lack of goods and services, a lack of funds to do something about it, and an unfamiliarity with consumer rights. In 1994, the International Organization of Consumers Unions opened its first African office in Harare, Zimbabwe. Have students choose a country in Africa and research the state of consumer rights and consumer protection in that country. How could the country benefit from the efforts of a consumers' union that unifies the whole continent? Have students share their findings with the class. **CL**, LS

grade labels as a guide in choosing what to buy. (Figure 24.2 illustrates how labels on products inform consumers of what they're getting.) The Food and Drug Administration (FDA) tests and approves all drugs before they can be offered to consumers. The National Highway Traffic Safety Administration can order automakers to **recall**, or take back and repair or replace cars with defective parts.

State Agencies

Each state has a consumer affairs division. In some states, the attorney general's office handles consumer affairs. These offices help consumers with their problems and enforce consumer laws. State governments work to prevent unfair practices such as false advertising. States have laws about credit card interest rates, health care businesses, banking and mortgage rates, and other consumer services. Each state agency provides consumer information for the areas they regulate.

Public Utilities. Public utilities are **legal monopolies**, or companies that are allowed to operate without competition. A state public utilities commission regulates the rates charged by electric, gas, and water companies. In some areas, they also regulate local telephone services. The commission protects consumers from unfair prices for their gas, electricity, or water.

If a utility plans a rate increase, the commission usually holds a public meeting where consumers and consumer groups can speak out. The commission listens to all sides before ruling on a rate increase. A state insurance commission controls and approves insurance rates in the same way.

Licenses. If you need someone to fix your plumbing or do your taxes, how do you know if they're qualified? To prevent people from practicing occupations they're not qualified to do, states issue **licenses**, or legal permits to conduct business. Doctors, teachers, roofers, hair stylists, architects, and even professional wrestlers are required to have a license. To get a license, a person usually needs special training and has to pass a test. When you hire someone to provide a special service, you should first check to see if that person has a license.

 Fast Review

1. What does the U.S. Department of Agriculture do to protect consumers?
2. How does a state public utilities commission protect consumers?
3. What are some occupations that require a license?

part **3** of 4

THE TRUTH ABOUT FRENCH FRIES
A recent study shows that teenagers consume almost a third of the total vegetable intake required through two high-fat, low-nutrition foods: french fries and potato chips. Do you know what's exactly in that food you're eating? To find out more about fast-food restaurants' nutritional offerings, visit their Web site.
As a consumer, how often do you study nutritional labels? Why or why not?

continued on p. 393

Real-World Application
Caption Answer

THE TRUTH ABOUT FRENCH FRIES: PART 3 OF 4
Answers will vary. May include personal dietary habits, health risks, ingredient knowledge, etc.

Individualized Practice

Develop a handbook with this chapter's main headings.

L1 Ask students to work in pairs to discuss the titles.

L2 Have students write an outline of the main headings, ideas, and strategies to include in the handbook.

L3 Ask students to create a handbook that may be duplicated and distributed in the school. The handbook will include main headings, subheadings, and useful facts, tips, and strategies.

Fast Review Answers

1. It inspects and grades food such as meat.
2. It regulates the rates charged by public utilities for electricity, gas, water, and some local telephone services.
3. Doctors, teachers, roofers, hair stylists, architects.

Social Science   **Curriculum Connection**

Continuing Education. Continuing education is part of the licensing requirements for many occupations. Ask students why states would require people such as physicians, architects, teachers, and building contractors to periodically return to school. (To make sure they learn the newest techniques and keep up with current information on how to best do their jobs.)

3 ASSESS

Reteaching

LEGAL MONOPOLIES. To reteach the concept of legal monopolies, ask students to give specific examples of legal monopolies and tell how they are regulated to protect consumers. (Public utilities, such as electric, gas, and water companies. State public utilities commissions regulate the prices the utilities can charge.)

Enrichment Strategy

REQUESTING INFORMATION. Ask students to check the labels of shampoo, conditioner, and packaged food products to find consumer-relations 800 numbers, then call and request consumer information pamphlets from the manufacturers. Display the information on a bulletin board and have students analyze if the information is genuinely helpful to consumers. **LS**

Business Building Blocks

CAPTION ANSWER

1. Body language, appearance, age, and gender affect how people interact with each other.

2. Some ideas might be to keep lines of communication open by asking questions, listening to the answers, and clearly stating whom you'll take next.

The Business Community

The business community also provides consumers with information. For example, most products come with product labels, which you can read. Often they tell you about the product in detail. If you shop for clothing, the label tells you about the fabric, how to care for the item, and where the product was made. Food labels tell you about nutrition and how to use the product.

Customer Service Representatives

Customer service representatives can answer questions or help you with problems. Most businesses have a customer service representative. When you buy a product, the package often lists the address, telephone number, or Web site for a customer relations representative. If you have a question or a problem, you can contact the representative. The company might also provide you with consumer booklets about its products at little or no cost.

Business Building Blocks

Customer Service

Have you ever wanted to buy something in a store and the salesperson wasn't around? Or maybe you have worked as a salesperson and had to deal with cranky customers. For a business to succeed, everyone involved needs to be treated with respect.

Practice

Look at the tips in the box and write down how you would respond in the following situations:

1. You sell cars. A man comes in to buy a used car. After he introduces himself, do you address him by his first name?

2. You're the only person working behind the counter at a

Analysis

convenience store. Two lines form and one customer complains that you served someone else before her.

Tips for Good Customer Service

- Pay attention to what's happening around you.
- Look for clues. How are people interacting?
- When someone is acting inappropriately, ask yourself what might be motivating such behavior.
- Keep lines of communication open.
- Everyone deserves respect.

392 Unit 8 Buying Goods and Services

How to Use a Portfolio Activity

The portfolio projects are designed to lead students to develop a collection of their best work to submit to you for assessment. You and each of your students should decide which projects to include in their business portfolio. Refer students to the specific rubric(s) from the *Alternative Assessment Strategies.* These rubrics will alert students to the criteria you'll use to assess their projects. **P**

Some companies have specialists to help you select the best product for your needs. For example, if you want to buy a new furnace, a specialist will help you select the right one. The specialist plans the installation and checks to be sure that your furnace works properly after it's installed.

The Better Business Bureau

Local businesses support the **Better Business Bureau (BBB)**, a well-known organization that helps consumers. The BBB is a nonprofit organization that collects information on local businesses and handles complaints. If a consumer has a complaint about a local business, the BBB will try to help. It also shares information about problems that consumers have had and distributes consumer publications. The BBB doesn't enforce laws and it won't recommend one local business over another.

Advertising

Advertising can be a good source of consumer information. Although businesses use ads to promote their products, they also use them to tell consumers as much about their products as possible. Ads tell you not only how much a product costs, but also what kinds of features it offers. For example, an ad for a computer will tell you how much memory it has, what type of processor it uses, and what kinds of drives come with it. You can use the information in ads to compare products and decide which one best suits your needs.

Magazines

Some commercial magazines are good sources for consumer information. They include articles or guides to help you choose products. If you want to buy a household appliance, for example, you can compare different brands featured in the guides. *Good Housekeeping* features consumer information and endorses products with a "seal of approval." Specialty magazines on cars, computers, sports, and travel can give you information about certain types of products.

 Fast Review _____

1. What is the Better Business Bureau (BBB)?
2. How can advertising be used as a source of consumer information?

Real-World Application
part 4 of 4

THE TRUTH ABOUT FRENCH FRIES
Are you one of the average Americans who eats 30 pounds of french fries in one year? No matter what restaurants deep fat fry fries in, there is still medical evidence that the fatty cooking substance increases consumers' risk of heart disease. One company, Proctor & Gamble, developed a calorie-free fat replacer called Olestra.
How might this affect the consumer? What if Olestra caused unpleasant side effects?

Chapter 24

Real-World Application
Caption Answer

THE TRUTH ABOUT FRENCH FRIES: PART 4 OF 4
Better health, longer life. Might cause unpleasant temporary ailments.

Technology Resource

 EXAMVIEW® PRO CD-ROM.
Check your students' understanding of the chapter's key concepts and terms by using the ExamView® Pro CD-ROM.

Evaluation
Assign and review the Fast Review sections.

Fast Review Answers ✔

1. A nonprofit organization that collects information on local businesses, handles complaints, shares information about problems that consumers have had, and distributes consumer publications.
2. Ads can tell you not only how much a product costs but also what kinds of features it offers.

Meeting Individual Needs

Students With Hearing Impairments.
You may find it helpful to pair students who have hearing impairments with hearing partners to work on the activities and questions presented in this chapter. Hearing students can assist students with hearing impairments by writing a summary of all oral directions given in class. In addition to the benefits gained by students with hearing impairments, the hearing student will also benefit from the enhanced knowledge they gain about how students with hearing impairments compensate for their challenge.

4 CLOSE

Chapter Wrap-Up

Ask students to create a chart or diagram showcasing this chapter's four summary points.

Using Business Key Words

1. consumer advocates
2. grade labels
3. legal monopolies
4. consumer reporter
5. refund
6. small claims court
7. recall
8. licenses
9. Better Business Bureau (BBB)

Review What You Learned

10. Government at all levels, consumer organizations, businesses, and magazines.
11. Responsible for the company's success or failure.
12. The Consumer Federation of America—promotes laws that help consumers.
13. The quality of the food.
14. State governments work to prevent unfair practices such as false advertising. States have laws about credit card interest rates, health care businesses, banking and mortgage rates, and other consumer services. Each state agency provides consumer information for the area it regulates.
15. It collects information on local businesses, handles complaints, and distributes consumer publications. It shares information about problems that consumers have had with businesses.

Summary

1. Consumers who have problems with a product can return products, go to small claims court, or seek help from consumer groups.

2. Consumer advocates, organizations, and reporters protect, inform, and defend consumers. The Consumer Federation of America (CFA), National Consumers League, Consumers Union, Major Appliance Consumer Action Program (MACAP), and the Better Business Bureau (BBB) are examples of consumer organizations.

3. Federal and state government agencies protect consumers by regulating business, enforcing laws, inspecting food, testing drugs, requiring licenses, and informing consumers.

4. Businesses help and inform consumers through customer service representatives, advertising, and magazines.

Using Business Key Words

An informed consumer is a smart consumer. See how smart you are by matching the following terms with their definitions.

- **consumer advocates**
- **grade labels**
- **consumer reporter**
- **legal monopolies**
- **refund**
- **small claims court**
- **recall**
- **licenses**
- **Better Business Bureau (BBB)**

1. Champions on the side of consumers' rights.
2. Labels that indicate the quality of a food.
3. Companies that are allowed to operate without competition.
4. Someone who provides information on consumer problems and then tries to resolve them.
5. To return the cost of a product.
6. A court that settles cases involving relatively small amounts of money.
7. An order to take back or repair defective products.
8. A legal permit to conduct business, usually issued by states.
9. A nonprofit organization that collects information on local businesses, handles complaints, shares information about problems that consumers have had, and distributes consumer publications.

Quick Quiz

1. What are three consumer problems that might be resolved in small claims court? (Tenant/landlord disputes, warranty disputes, and unsatisfactory products purchased from a business.)

2. Name three consumer organizations. (Consumer Federation of America (CFA), National Consumers League, Consumers Union, or Major Appliance Consumer Action Program (MACAP).)

3. What does the Federal Trade Commission (FTC) do to protect consumers? (Enforces laws about business practices.)

Review What You Learned

10. Name four sources of help for consumers who have experienced problems with products they have purchased.

11. What is your role as a consumer?

12. Which consumer organization is one of the largest? Describe its main function.

13. What do grade labels indicate?

14. How do state governments protect consumers?

15. What services does the Better Business Bureau (BBB) provide?

Understanding Business Concepts

16. The new CD you purchased skips two of your favorite tracks each time it plays. What should you do?

17. Which consumer organization monitors the Internet to prevent consumer fraud?

18. Why do you think large companies have entire departments devoted to customer service?

19. Why do you think the need for consumer protection has grown over time?

20. Some people believe that the government should not be so involved in consumer protection. What do you think? Explain your answer.

Critical Thinking

21. Some people argue that consumers are intelligent enough to make wise choices when buying goods and services and don't need all the protection that's provided. Others say that consumer affairs offices and government agencies are necessary. Choose a partner and debate the topic.

22. Why do you think manufacturers of food, drugs, and cosmetics are required to have their products checked by the Food and Drug Administration?

23. One way government protects consumers is by requiring people practicing certain professions to be licensed. What kinds of professions need licenses in your state?

24. Name a few types of complaints that might be taken to small claims court.

Viewing and Representing

Examining the Image. Write down your impressions of this picture in your journal. How do you feel? Does the picture make you feel tense, angry, good, bad, etc? Have you, or anyone in your family, been to small claims court? If not, use your background knowledge. How are your judgements formed based upon events you've never experienced? What is your thought process? Write about the experience.

Critical Thinking

21. Debates will vary depending on the students' point of view.

22. Answers should focus on the need to protect consumers from potentially harmful products.

23. Answers will vary but may include teachers, doctors, lawyers, cosmetologists, accountants, etc.

24. Tenant/landlord disputes, unsatisfactory products purchased from a business, and warranty disputes.

Viewing and Representing

This activity reinforces students' critical viewing skills. It strengthens students' reasoning and critical thinking skills to analyze the impact of the visual information they receive. Suggest to students that they help members of their family also develop these skills. Suggest students show this picture, and others they choose from the newspaper or magazines, to members of their family and ask their family similar questions to those in this activity. **LS**

Understanding Business Concepts

16. First, go to the store where you purchased the CD and explain the problem. If the store clerk or managers do not help, take your complaint to the district or national sales managers. If that does not help, write to the CD manufacturer explaining the problem.

17. The National Consumers League.

18. Good for public relations for providing information about the quality of the goods or services being sold.

19. More and more goods and services are being offered in the marketplace and it is getting more difficult for individual consumers to know about all areas of product safety and performance.

20. Answers will vary.

4 CLOSE (Cont.)

Building Academic Skills

HISTORY. The library and the Internet are good resources for this project. Rubric: Oral presentation.

COMPUTER/TECHNOLOGY. Encourage students to choose different advertisements. Rubric: Oral presentation.

MATH. If the students have trouble figuring percentage increase or decrease, have them work with another student. Rubrics: Math calculation, chart, note taking.

LANGUAGE ARTS. Suggest that the students consider how the graphics are used to present the information. Rubric: Paragraph.

Linking School to Home

Answers will vary. Rubric: Paragraph.

Linking School to Work

Make sure all students participate in the group project. Rubric: Oral presentation.

Building Academic Skills

 Oral Presentation

Select one of the national consumer information organizations discussed in the text. Research how, when, and why it got started. Prepare a two-minute oral presentation and share your findings with the class.

 Writing a Critique

Choose an advertisement for a product or service from your local newspaper. Note any special claims, incentives, or time limits. Contact the seller/supplier/vendor to verify the information in the advertisement. Using word-processing software, write and print out a one-paragraph critique of the advertisement from the point of view of the consumer.

 Calculating a Rate Increase

Contact one of the public utilities in your community. Find out what the rates are for the utility service. Also, find out the last time the rates were changed. Determine the percentage increase (or decrease) of the rate change.

 Researching Products

Study an issue of *Consumer Reports* or *Consumers' Research Magazine.* List the types of products that are reported. Write a summary of the kinds of information provided about each product and indicate how you might find more information about the products.

Linking School to Home

Watching Consumer News. With your family, watch or listen to a consumer news program. Write a paragraph about the specific complaint, how it was resolved, and whether or not you would purchase the product. After seeing or hearing the report, do you make a decision right away? If not, why? Also discuss with your family how the media influences your decisions to purchase something or not. Where else do you get your information in order to make an informed, educated decision?

Linking School to Work

Choosing a Product. Work in teams of four or five students. Choose a product that a team member or family member has found unsatisfactory. Prepare a short presentation showing how to file a complaint about the product or service. Be sure your presentation includes:
- A description of how to approach the business where the goods or services were purchased.
- A sample letter describing the problem and a possible solution.
- A private, state, local, or federal consumer advocate or agency that might handle the complaint.

E-Homework

Applying Technology

Online Ordering. Using the Internet, locate the Consumer Information Center. Order one of the free publications that interests you. If it's impossible to order one, then choose one you would like to order.

Creating a Database. Create a database of the various ways consumers can obtain information. Include company or agency names, addresses, phone numbers, and any other pertinent information. Print out the database and share the information with your classmates.

Connecting Academics

Math. As you read earlier, the Better Business Bureau is a nonprofit organization that helps consumers collect information on local businesses and handles complaints. The 150 Better Business Bureaus in the United States handle ten million consumer questions a year. One third of these questions is about retail businesses, one third is about home improvement companies, and one quarter is about service firms. The remaining portion is about other types of businesses. Draw a pie chart of this data. Include the actual number of consumer questions in each category.

Math. The display failed on your one-month old camera so you exchanged it for a new one at the electronics store. After just six weeks the flash on your new replacement camera stopped working. Now what action could you take to solve your problem? If that failed, what further action could you take?

BusinessWeek — Analyzing the Feature Story

You read the first part of "He's Raring to Fight for Fund Investors' Rights" at the beginning of this chapter. Below are a few questions for you to answer about consumer advocate Mercer Bullard. You'll find the answers to these questions when you're reading the entire article. First, here are the questions:

25. What are the main goals of Fund Democracy?
26. In Bullard's opinion, how is government's ability to advocate for mutual fund investors limited?

CREATIVE JOURNAL ACTIVITY

Select a product that you or your family may want to buy in the near future. Go ahead and research different brands of this product on the *Consumer Reports* Web site or by reading back issues of the periodical at your local library. Decide which brand is best for you based on price and features.

BUSINESS Online
The Full Story

To learn more about consumer advocates, visit the *Introduction to Business* Web site at www.introbus.glencoe.com, and click on *BusinessWeek* Feature Story, Chapter 24.

397

E-Homework

ONLINE ORDERING. If students don't have access to computers in the classroom, use those found in the media center, school labs, or the public library. Ask students to write a paragraph summarizing the information in the free publication. Rubric: Paragraph.

CREATING A DATABASE. Databases will vary. If students struggle with this activity, have them work in groups. Rubric: Database.

Connecting Academics

MATH. Number of questions about: Retail businesses = 3.33 million; home improvement companies = 3.33 million; service firms = 2.5 million; other types of business = 0.44 million. Rubric: Calculation.

MATH. Take the camera to the store and ask for another replacement camera or ask to exchange the camera for a different brand. Further action could be to write to the manufacturer explaining the problem and asking for a new model.

BusinessWeek — *Analyzing the Feature Story*

25. Fund Democracy would like to see more information made available to investors to make investments decisions. Bullard would also like to see lower fees.
26. He believes that the SEC does not have the resources to provide a strong voice to the mutual-fund shareholder.

Creative Journal Activity

Have students work in groups to create their own study aid for the main points from this chapter's last two sections: "Government Organizations" and "The Business Community." Groups should find at least ten main points and make a chart, diagram, or list with easy-to-remember icons.

1 FOCUS

Unit Seminar Overview

In this seminar on investigating OPEC, students will choose a petroleum-based product to research. Students examine images, interpret facts, and create a model of the relationship between the price of a petroleum-based product and the price of crude oil.

Bell Ringer Activity

OBSERVATION. Ask students to look around the classroom, look at each other, even look at their own clothes and name as many petroleum-based products as they can see. (Plastics and some synthetic fibers are petroleum-based products.) **LS**

Discussion Starter

QUESTION AND ANSWERS. Ask students what they know about the Organization of Petroleum Exporting Countries (OPEC). (Answers may include that it controls the price of crude oil, is a group of oil-exporting developing countries, Saudi Arabia, Iraq, Kuwait, Iran, and Venezuela were founder members, and that changing prices and supply greatly affect the global economy.)

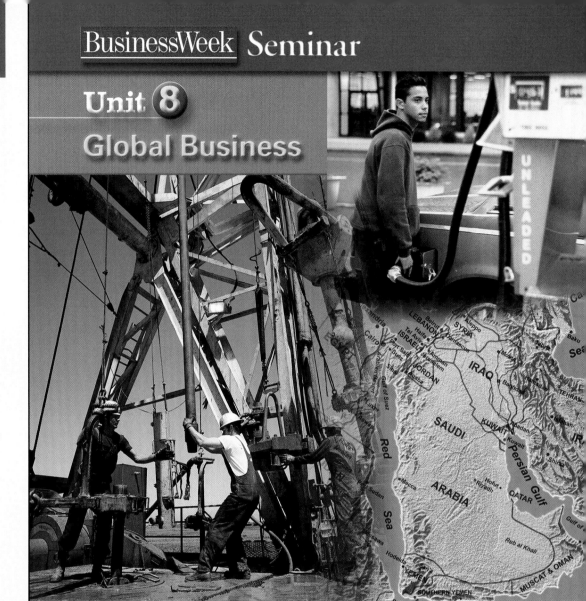

BusinessWeek Seminar

Unit 8
Global Business

Understanding OPEC

In this unit you learned about making wise consumer decisions. You learned that a smart consumer needs plenty of information in order to buy a product or service. Take, for example, crude petroleum oil. It affects the prices of many other consumer products, like gasoline, heating oil, plastics, and synthetic fabrics. In this seminar you'll discover how the Organization of Petroleum Exporting Countries (OPEC) helps you as a consumer.

398

GLOBAL BUSINESS

Newsworthy Trends

X-raying the Earth. To meet the increasing worldwide demand for oil, energy companies have developed new technology to find new sources of oil. The problem isn't just finding out where the oil is but how deep down it is. This is possible with 3-D seismic technology software. The specially designed software can map out 3-D images of the depths of the earth using sound waves. It works like sonar, or an earth x-ray machine. The technology enables companies to locate oil with much greater accuracy and to drill fewer wells.

2 TEACH

Thinking Critically

Read "Factoids," and then answer the questions below:

1. Do you forecast that OPEC's production will increase, decrease, or stay the same? (Answers will vary. OPEC forecasts its production will grow to more than 50 percent in the next 20 years.)

2. When exports of oil account for as much as 90 percent of a country's income, what might be the concerns of that country? (Answers will vary, and may include: issues threatening the security of world oil supplies, such as taxation on oil in consumer countries, issues ensuring future supplies of oil, and issues that might affect oil prices.)

Cooperative Learning

UNDER INVESTIGATION.
Have students work as detectives in small groups. After discussing "Exploring Culture" (seminar questions 7 and 8), assign the following task: First, decide on a question relating to oil or petroleum-based products to which you'd like to find the answer. (Questions such as: What happens to used engine oil, anyway? How are oil spills cleaned up in the ocean? Why does oil clog drains?) Second, investigate to find the answer. Third, take the part of detectives and present the group's findings to the class. Be creative. **CL**, LS

Factoids

Barrels of Money. OPEC pumps about 40 percent of the world's oil. Its average crude basket price per barrel is about $23.

Piece of the Income. Oil accounts for less than 10 percent of Mexico's exports, whereas in OPEC countries, it can account for 90 percent of a government's income.

Market Maneuver. In 1911, the U.S. courts broke up the Pacific Coast and John D. Rockefeller's Standard Oil Company monopoly.

Buy and Sell. The oil exploration industry has the most publicly traded companies on the stock market.

Clogged Drains. Restaurants improper disposal of cooking grease harms a city's sewers as it coagulates, blocks, and hardens leading to spills.

Investigate the Images

Look at the photographic collage on the left page. What grabs your attention? Is it the color or the words? The power in reading visuals is in analyzing and dissecting your observations. On a separate piece of paper, respond to the questions listed below. These questions might help sharpen the focus of your visual mind.

Your Observations

1. How many photographs do you see?

2. Examine each photograph. How are they each assembled in relation to one another?

3. What is the subject of each photograph? Is place or location the subject?

4. Does color signify a message?

5. What issues do you take from these images?

Information

6. Summarize what you know about the photographs from your observations.

Exploring Culture

7. How might the increased cost of crude oil affect automakers? If the price of gas became too high, how would they lure consumers' into buying their product?

8. In your daily life, how often and how much oil and gas does your family consume? Can you think of conservation methods to use less?

Unit 8 *BusinessWeek* Seminar **399**

Newsworthy Trends

GLOBAL BUSINESS

Cleaning Up the Mess. One of the biggest environmental hazards posed by oil companies is spilling oil into the ocean. Cleaning up ocean oil spills has become an industry in itself. Companies that specialize in cleaning up oil have developed various new technologies to absorb it, collect it, pump it, disperse it, or vacuum it up.

One research laboratory is developing a way to make water oil spills, thought to be nonflammable, easier to burn. Burning oil might sound especially toxic, but it's actually the fastest, most efficient, most inexpensive, and most environmentally friendly method of cleanup.

2 TEACH (Cont.)

Independent Practice

L1 SUMMARIZE

Ask students to find a recent article on OPEC or a petroleum-based product. Ask them to prepare a summary of the article to share with the class. Have students organize their summary starting with the source of the article, the name of the article, and the name of the author. **LS**

L2 LIST

Ask students to make four separate lists of all the ways an increase in oil prices could affect them, their family, the community, and the nation. **LS**

L3 MAP MEMBER COUNTRIES

Have students create a simple map of the world, locate OPEC's member countries, and mark them on the map. Ask students to find details about each member country. A useful Internet site is www.opec.org. Details should include information on each country's production, and oil and gas reserves. Have students describe their map to their classmates in a short oral presentation. **LS**, **CL**

Taking Aim at Global Business

● Preparation

In this seminar, you'll research OPEC and the current price of crude oil.

Objective

- **Choose** a petroleum-based product to research.
- **Explain** how knowing about this product affects consumer decisions.
- **Create** a model of the relationship between the price of your chosen product and the price of oil.

Materials Needed

✓ Copies of recent business news publications, such as the *Wall Street Journal,* the *New York Times,* and *BusinessWeek*
✓ Access to the Internet and your local or school library
✓ Paper, pens, and pencils
✓ Posterboard and markers

● Procedures

1. With a partner, research OPEC. Use the *Reader's Guide to Periodical Literature,* your local or school library's CD-ROM database, or the Internet to find out the basics about OPEC.

2. Write a brief report about OPEC that answers the following questions:
   - Which countries started OPEC?
   - When was it started?

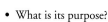

- What is its purpose?
- What countries make up OPEC today?
- What have crude oil prices been for the past two to five years?

3. Choose a product made from oil and research this product. (Suggestions include gasoline, automotive oil, heating oil, and plastics.)
   - Find out how your chosen product is made, and what part oil plays in its production.
   - Research the prices for your product. If possible, find prices for the past two to five years.

4. Present your report to the class.

Reteaching Strategy

Be prepared to time for 30 seconds in a team game called "Can You Explain _____?" Ask students to collect together their notes used in this unit seminar. Have two volunteers write the key terms and phrases on the board as students call them out. After the list on the board is complete, split the class into two teams—Team OP and Team EC. Ask for two new volunteers. Have the first volunteer randomly choose a term or phrase on the board, circle it, say "Can you explain (the term)," and call on a member of Team OP to give an explanation. An answer earns a point if it's correct. In rapid succession, the second volunteer does the same, choosing from terms that have not been circled, and this time calling on a member of Team EC. Continue until all terms are circled. **CL**, **LS**

Chart It

Using the price information obtained from your research, create a graph that shows the relationship between the price of crude oil and your product. Draw your graph on poster board to use in your presentation to the class.

EXAMPLE:

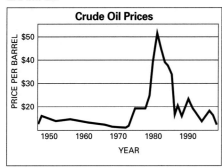

Crude Oil Prices

Analyze and Conclude

Study the graph that you created in Chart It. Then answer the questions below.

1. **Acquiring and Evaluating Information.** What is the relationship between crude oil prices and the price of your product?
2. **Interpreting and Communicating Information.** Does understanding this relationship affect any consumer choices you make or will make? If so, how? If not, why not?
3. **Reasoning.** How does understanding OPEC help you make wiser consumer purchases?

Becoming an Informed Citizen

Congratulations, you finished the seminar. Now it's time to reflect on the decisions you made.

Interpreting and Communicating Information. If you were standing at the pump to buy gas for your family car, what factors would you consider when choosing a kind of gasoline?

Critical Thinking. What do you think would happen if OPEC disbanded?

BUSINESS Online

Further Exploration
To find out more about consumerism, visit the *Introduction to Business* Web site at **www.introbus.glencoe.com**.

3 ASSESS

Enrichment

REASONING. Ask students, what is the main reason that OPEC's member countries want stable oil prices? How do they keep or attempt to keep prices stable? Does this benefit consumer nations? Why or why not?

Evaluation

RUBRICS. The rubrics for evaluation of written reports, oral presentations, and charts are included in *Alternative Assessment Strategies.* **P**

4 CLOSE

Seminar Wrap-Up

DISCUSS TRENDS. You've gained experience and knowledge throughout this seminar; now discuss any recent trends or changes in the U.S. economy due to crude oil prices.

Analyze and Conclude Answers

1. Students' answers will vary depending on the chosen product, however, it's likely that there is a correlation in price changes, with a delay in the price change of the chosen product.
2. Answers will vary and might include future purchases of items such as stoves, automobiles, or types of home-heating will be influenced by the possibility of price increases in crude oil.
3. Answers will vary and might include taking into account pollution, conservation, recycling, and other environmental and economic factors when considering purchases.

Credit

Unit Objectives

After completing this unit, students will be able to achieve the following outcomes:

- Explain credit, the advantages and disadvantages of using credit, and the three main types of charge accounts.
- Identify the places to get credit and the types of credit cards.
- Describe factors determining credit worthiness and how to maintain a good credit rating.
- Explain the types of credit you can use and the costs involved in paying for credit.
- Name federal laws that protect consumers and identify consumers' credit rights.

BusinessWeek Connections

In this unit, students will read the following articles from *BusinessWeek*:

Chapter 25 "Tapping Teens' Plastic Potential": Find out the advantages and disadvantages of teen credit cards.

Chapter 26 "Majoring in Debt": Take a look at the statistics—more college students are getting into thousands of dollars of debt.

Chapter 27 "Credit Cards: Entrepreneurs Are Tapping Them More Than Ever": See what a national survey shows about small-business owners using credit cards to finance their business and see why there's reason for concern.

Key to Descriptive Icons

The following designations will help you decide which activities are appropriate for your students.

L1 Level 1 activities should be within the ability range of all students.

L2 Level 2 activities should be within the ability range of the average to above-average students.

L3 Level 3 activities are designed for the ability range of above-average students.

ELL Activities should be within the ability range of the English Language Learner.

LS Learning Styles designation represents activities designed to address different learning styles.

CL Cooperative learning activities are designed for small group work.

P Portfolio designation represents student products that can be placed into a best-work portfolio.

Teacher Classroom Resources*

Program Resources	Chapter 25	Chapter 26	Chapter 27
Student Activity Workbook	p. 183	p. 191	p. 199
Lesson Plans	p. 66	p. 68	p. 70
Internet Resources	p. 69	p. 71	p. 73
Reproducible Tests	p. 49	p. 51	p. 53
Teaching Transparencies	25.1, 25.2	26.1, 26.2	27.1, 27.2
Strategies and Worksheets for Teaching Transparencies	pp. 12, 67	pp. 13, 69	pp. 13, 71

* Each of these resources is available in print and on the Interactive Lesson Planner CD-ROM.

Technology Resources

- Interactive Lesson Planner CD-ROM
- PowerPoint® Presentation CD-ROM
- ExamView® Pro Test Generator CD-ROM
- Integrated Software Simulation, Teacher Manual
- Glencoe Business Video Package
- *PuzzleMaker* CD-ROM
- *Introduction to Business* Web Site
- *Virtual Business*®

  Virtual Business is a business simulation that introduces students to the principles of business by letting them start and run their own virtual business. In *Virtual Business,* students have the power to control all aspects of a retail convenience store. Students strategize business decisions using a powerful learning tool in the guise of a video game.

Video Series

Virtual Business

Scope and Sequence

Academic Standards of Learning

	LANGUAGE ARTS	MATH	HISTORY	COMPUTER/ TECHNOLOGY	SOCIAL SCIENCE
CHAPTER 25	pp. 405, 408, 410, 412, 413, 416	pp. 410, 416, 417	p. 409	pp. 405, 406, 413, 416, 417	pp. 405, 406, 407, 409, 415, 416, 417
CHAPTER 26	pp. 419, 421, 422, 423, 425, 426, 432	pp. 420, 421, 423, 424, 425, 426, 432, 433	pp. 424, 432	pp. 421, 426, 432	pp. 418, 419, 420, 424, 425, 426, 427, 433
CHAPTER 27	pp. 435, 436, 437, 438, 439, 440, 441, 442, 443, 446, 447	pp. 446, 447	pp. 436, 438, 441, 446	pp. 435, 437, 439, 443, 446, 447	pp. 436, 437, 438, 440, 441, 443

Scope and Sequence

Themes and Concepts

Business Core	Accounting and Finance	Business Management	Computer/ Technology	Marketing	Entrepreneurship

Business Ethics
Business Law
Financial Statements
Decision Making
Planning
	Decision Making
	Payroll
	Credit Analysis
	Financial Services
	Risk Analysis
		Consumers
		Decision Making
		Opportunity Costs
		Policy & Strategy
		  Formulation
			Business and
			  Technology Ethics
			Safety and Security
			Risk Analysis
				Risk Management
				New Product/Service
				Purchasing
					Contracts
					Collections

Competitive
  Environment
Financial Statements
Money Management
Adapting to Change
Decision Making
	Financial Systems
	Money Management
	Adapting to Change
	Document
	  Processing
	Information
	  Resources
	Decision Making
		Technological
		  Applications
		Credit Analysis
		Financial Services
		Consumers
		Exchange and Money
		Management
			Security
			Change Management
			Risk Analysis
			Business Decisions
				Purchasing
				Product/Service Mix
				Buying Motives and
				  Behaviors
					Collections
					Contracts
					Research and
					  Development
					Sales

Business Law
Business/Financial
  Relationships
Planning
Personal Qualities
	Ethics
	Financial Analysis
	Governing Agencies
	Credit Analysis
	Revenue and Expense
	  Recognition
		Consumers
		Decision Making
		Contracts
		Government
		  Regulations
		Sources of Law
			Business Environment
			Safety and Security
			Social Issues
			Needs Analysis
				Customer Relations
				Risk Management
				Products and Service
				  Knowledge
				Credit Review
				Financial Institutions
				Regulation
					Contracts
					Collections
					Financial Resources
					Government
					  Regulations
					Human Resources
					  Management

Unit Overview

Unit 9 gives information about credit that affects everyday life.

CHAPTER 25 describes what credit is, who uses credit, and types of credit.

CHAPTER 26 explains picking a credit card, and using, paying for, and keeping credit.

CHAPTER 27 describes how federal and state governments protect your credit rights and how to handle credit problems.

Introducing the Unit

Ask students: How does a credit card company make a profit? If no one comes up with the concept of interest, introduce it. Ask students' opinions on: Is it a good idea to open more than one or two charge cards? Charge more than you can quickly pay off? Check your credit rating at least once a year?

Technology Resource

GO TO **INTRODUCTION TO BUSINESS WEB SITE.** To find out more about content in Unit 9, visit the Glencoe *Introduction to Business* Web site. **www.introbus.glencoe.com**

Unit 9

Credit

402 Unit 9

The Price of Debt

Not good on your word to pay back money? In the good old days, if you couldn't pay back your debts you were thrown into debtor's prison. The cells were generally small, overcrowded, unheated, filthy, and disease-ridden. A debt as little as 50 cents could put you in prison. To get out, you not only had to pay back your debt, but the cost of your imprisonment as well. When debtor's prisons became too overcrowded, the government enacted bankruptcy laws.

● **That's the Way the Money Goes**
The children's song *Pop Goes the Weasel* is about borrowing money from a pawnshop. "Pop" is slang for pawn, and "weasel" is slang for coat.

● **I Owe U**
The major credit card companies pay some universities millions of dollars for the right to market their credit cards on campus. They often offer free gifts, such as T-shirts and flashlights, to students who apply for a card.

● **Check Please**
The first credit card appeared in 1951 in the United States. Twenty-seven restaurants in New York accepted the Diners Club credit card.

● **Don't Leave Home Without It**
Financier Eli Broad, who charged a Roy Lichtenstein painting for $2.5 million to his American Express platinum card, was the biggest credit card purchase ever made.

Field Trip Suggestion

Visit a Financial Institution. Visit a local bank, credit union, or other financial institution. Arrange for an employee to give the students advice about obtaining and using credit. Ahead of the visit, ask students to prepare questions and take a notebook to record the answers. Have students ask questions about special suggestions the institution offers concerning credit management. After the trip, have students prepare a brief written report on their findings using two headings: "Obtaining Credit" and "Using Credit." **LS**, **CL**, **ELL**

Glencoe Poster Teaching Tip

Poll students to see if they or any of their family members use credit cards to purchase items online. Ask students what advantages or disadvantages they see to using credit online. Remind students that they already took the quiz on this poster in Unit 6. Lead a class discussion by asking students: Do you think consumers are confident using credit cards to pay for items purchased online? Why or why not? Encourage students to back up their opinions with reasons. **LS**

BUSINESS
Online
Idea Factory

To learn more about credit cards, visit the *Introduction to Business* Web site at **www.introbus.glencoe.com**, and click on Unit 9 Credit.

⏱ Out of Time?

If time doesn't permit teaching each chapter in this unit, you may use the *Puzzle-Maker* CD-ROM to focus on the business vocabulary. **LS**

Portfolio Activity

Wise Buying on Credit. Using credit wisely takes experience and self-discipline. Have students work with their family members to identify different types of credit purchases their families have made in the past year (for example, buying groceries, or gas for the family car, or a loan for college tuition, or to buy a car). Have students write at least three examples of how using credit wisely has affected their families. Require that students write about each example with the following four section headings: "What the Family Bought," "How the Family Used Credit," "How the Family Was Affected," and "How This Was a Wise Credit Purchase." **P**

SCANS Correlation Chart*

Foundation Skills

Basic Skills	Reading	Writing	Math	Listening	Speaking	
Thinking Skills	Creative Thinking	Decision Making	Problem Solving	Seeing Things in the Mind's Eye	Knowing How to Learn	Reasoning
Personal Qualities	Responsibility	Self-Esteem	Sociability	Self-Management	Integrity/ Honesty	

Workplace Competencies

Resources	Allocating Time	Allocating Money	Allocating Material and Facility Resources	Allocating Human Resources		
Information	Acquiring and Evaluating Information	Organizing and Maintaining Information	Interpreting and Communicating Information	Using Computers to Process Information		
Interpersonal Skills	Participating as a Member of a Team	Teaching Others	Serving Clients/ Customers	Exercising Leadership	Negotiating to Arrive at a Decision	Working with Cultural Diversity
Systems	Understanding Systems	Monitoring and Correcting Performance	Improving and Designing Systems			
Technology	Selecting Technology	Applying Technology to Task	Maintaining and Troubleshooting Technology			

*This chart's highlighted blocks indicate the chapter's content coverage in the Student Edition and the Teacher Wraparound Edition.

Resource Manager

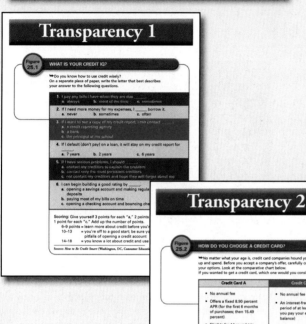

Application and Enrichment

- Lesson Plans
- *BusinessWeek* Poster Package
- Teaching Transparencies
- Integrated Software Simulation
- Glencoe Business Video Package

Review and Reinforcement

- *PuzzleMaker*
- Internet Resources
- Student Activity Workbook
- Strat. and Work. for Teaching Transparencies

Assessment and Evaluation

- Reproducible Tests
- Alternative Assessment Strategies
- ExamView® Pro Test Generator

Technology

- *PuzzleMaker*
- ExamView® Pro Test Generator
- Glencoe Business Video Package
- PowerPoint® Presentation
- Integrated Software Simulation
- Interactive Lesson Planner
- *Virtual Business*®

KEY	Printed	Software	Videocassette	Poster
	Transparency	CD-ROM	Internet	

Business Online

Visit www.introbus.glencoe.com, the Web site companion to *Introduction to Business.* The student's page includes:

- interactive tutor
- additional *BusinessWeek* articles and activities
- business Web links
- homework hints
- real-world application activities
- additional career path activities

Information on how to prepare your students for the high school exit exam and special projects are also included.

Use the Glencoe Web site for additional resources. All essential content is covered in the Student Edition.

Introducing the Chapter

This chapter describes what credit is and the types of credit. A photo essay, "Before You Say Yes, Compute It!," enhances the concepts.

Connecting the Objectives

What would you say are the advantages and disadvantages of using credit? Where is credit available?

BusinessWeek
Feature Story

Story's Summary

Teen credit cards, like VisaBuxx and Cobaltcard, aren't really credit cards. They're actually more like pre-paid telephone cards—where they're first loaded or reloaded with money, or stored value. An advantage is that teen credit cards are smaller, simpler, and safer to carry than cash. A disadvantage, as with any credit card, is the temptation to over spend.

Find the entire article at www.introbus.glencoe.com, or in the Teacher Resource Binder.

What Is Credit?

Learning Objectives

After completing this chapter, you'll be able to:
1. **Describe** the nature of credit.
2. **Explain** the advantages and disadvantages of using credit.
3. **Name** the places where you can get credit.
4. **List** the three main types of charge accounts.
5. **Identify** the different types of credit cards.

Why It's Important

You'll probably use credit some day. When you do, it will be helpful to know what credit is and the types of credit you can use.

Key Words

credit
creditor
debtor
interest
consumer credit
commercial credit
credit rating
charge account
revolving account
installment loans

404

BusinessWeek Feature Story

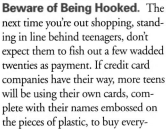

Tapping Teens' Plastic Potential

Beware of Being Hooked. The next time you're out shopping, standing in line behind teenagers, don't expect them to fish out a few wadded twenties as payment. If credit card companies have their way, more teens will be using their own cards, complete with their names embossed on the pieces of plastic, to buy everything from the latest must-have pair of jeans to movie tickets.

Credit card company representatives have been signing up card members on college campuses for years. But in a new twist on the concept of plastic and young people, several credit card giants, including American Express and Visa International, have developed cards specifically for the high school set and younger.

Source: Excerpted with permission from "Tapping Teens' Plastic Potential," *BusinessWeek Online*, January 11, 2001.

An Extension Activity

Have you ever been approached by a company to sign up for a credit card? How did you handle the offer? Was it a tempting offer? Or did you leave it behind? Explain your situation.

The Full Story

To learn more about teen credit cards, visit the *Introduction to Business* Web site at www.introbus.glencoe.com, and click on *BusinessWeek* Feature Story, Chapter 25.

Classroom Resources

For the Teacher
- 📁 Student Activity Work. TAE
- 📓 💿 Assessment Binder
- 💿 PowerPoint® Presentation
- 💿 Interactive Lesson Planner
- 📁 Lesson Plans
- 📓 💻 Internet Resources
- 🖥 Teaching Transparencies
- 💻 *Introduction to Business* Web Site

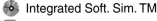

- 💿 Integrated Soft. Sim. TM
- 📕 *BusinessWeek* Poster Package

For the Student
- 📓 Student Activity Workbook
- 💿 *Virtual Business*®
- 💻 *Introduction to Business* Web Site
- 💿 Integrated Soft. Sim.
- 💿 *PuzzleMaker*
- 📓 Strategies and Worksheets for Teaching Transparencies

Bell Ringer Activity

SELF-MANAGEMENT. Part of self-management is setting realistic and specific personal learning goals. Write in your journal your personal learning plan for this chapter. List different parts of this chapter and the deadline by which you plan to learn each part. **LS**, **P**

Preteaching Business Key Words

SELECTING TECHNOLOGY. Choose a word processor with a thesaurus and type this chapter's key words. Use the thesaurus to look up alternative meanings for each word. Where the key term has two words, look up each word separately. **LS**

An Extension Activity

PRESENTATION. Instruct students: After creating your poster, give a two-minute presentation describing and explaining your points. **LS**, **P**

Making Connections

Advertising. Tell students that there is a great deal of competition among credit card issuers and that advertising plays a large role. Some cards use direct mail to offer special introductory rates or credit protection services. Others use glossy ads in magazines intended to promote the prestige of using their card. Over a few weeks have students bring in credit card ads or offers. Have students evaluate the way cards are advertised. Are some of the offers actually good deals? How often do the ads and offers seem less appealing once students read the small print? **CL**, **LS**, **P**

2 TEACH

Business Connection

Entrepreneurs, like Sheryl Woodhouse-Keese, borrow against their credit cards to develop their businesses. Woodhouse-Keese recently charged $4,000 to her credit card to attend a trade show in Philadelphia. Woodhouse-Keese makes handmade invitation cards. With the profit from sales of her cards at the trade show, she plans to hire help and hopes to eventually double her profits and pay off the credit card bill.

Develop Concepts

COMMERCIAL CREDIT. Ask students to think of reasons why a small business, such as a restaurant, video store, or doctor's office, might choose to obtain credit. (Answers will vary and may include to buy materials, new equipment, or office space, or to pay salaries.)

Figure 25.1 Caption Answer

As a follow-up discussion, ask students what their attitude is toward using credit. What's the attitude of other members in their family? Is there a correlation between their attitude and their family's attitude?

The Nature of Credit

Buying an item now and paying for it later can be an easy and convenient way to make a purchase. Consumers use credit to buy everything from a tank of gasoline to a new car. How does buying on credit work? What are the advantages and disadvantages of using credit?

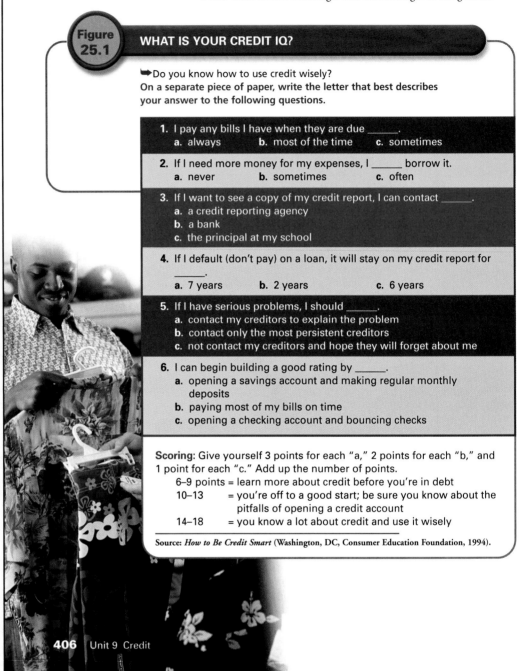

Figure 25.1

WHAT IS YOUR CREDIT IQ?

➡ Do you know how to use credit wisely?
On a separate piece of paper, write the letter that best describes your answer to the following questions.

1. I pay any bills I have when they are due _____.
   a. always   b. most of the time   c. sometimes

2. If I need more money for my expenses, I _____ borrow it.
   a. never   b. sometimes   c. often

3. If I want to see a copy of my credit report, I can contact _____.
   a. a credit reporting agency
   b. a bank
   c. the principal at my school

4. If I default (don't pay) on a loan, it will stay on my credit report for _____.
   a. 7 years   b. 2 years   c. 6 years

5. If I have serious problems, I should _____.
   a. contact my creditors to explain the problem
   b. contact only the most persistent creditors
   c. not contact my creditors and hope they will forget about me

6. I can begin building a good rating by _____.
   a. opening a savings account and making regular monthly deposits
   b. paying most of my bills on time
   c. opening a checking account and bouncing checks

Scoring: Give yourself 3 points for each "a," 2 points for each "b," and 1 point for each "c." Add up the number of points.
- 6–9 points = learn more about credit before you're in debt
- 10–13 = you're off to a good start; be sure you know about the pitfalls of opening a credit account
- 14–18 = you know a lot about credit and use it wisely

Source: *How to Be Credit Smart* (Washington, DC, Consumer Education Foundation, 1994).

Cooperative Learning

Imagine. Help students see the positive uses of credit by asking them to imagine our economy without credit. Divide the class into groups and have them think about how people would purchase large appliances, cars, and houses, or pay for a college education if they did not have the option of using credit. Have groups come up with several ideas. Bring the class back together and have a member of each group share the group's ideas with the class. **CL**, LS

Credit: The Promise to Pay

Credit is an agreement to get money, goods, or services now in exchange for a promise to pay in the future. When buying on credit, you're delaying the payment for the item. (Learn to see if you might use credit wisely by taking the quiz in Figure 25.1.)

The one who lends money or provides credit is called the **creditor**. The one who borrows money or uses credit is called the **debtor**. Credit is based on the creditor's confidence that the debtor can and will make the payments. In other words, credit is a matter of trust.

Creditors charge a fee for using their money, which is called **interest**. The amount of interest is based on three factors. One of them is the interest rate, which is a percentage of the total amount borrowed. A second factor is the length of the loan. The longer you take to pay off a loan, the more interest you have to pay. The third factor is the amount of the loan. The larger the amount, the more the interest. The amount of interest varies from one provider to the next. It's important to shop around for credit because creditors may charge different rates.

Who Uses Credit?

Many people use credit today. To a great extent it has replaced money as a means of making purchases. Credit is used practically everywhere. You'll probably use credit in the future to buy CDs, eat at restaurants, or take out a student loan. The type of credit used by people for personal reasons is called **consumer credit**.

Businesses often use credit for the same reasons that consumers do. They might need to borrow money to buy goods or pay salaries. Manufacturers borrow money to buy raw materials, new machinery, factories, or trucks. Credit used by business is called **commercial credit**. When businesses borrow money, however, they often pass along the cost of interest to consumers by charging higher prices on their products.

The federal government uses credit to pay for many of the services and programs it provides to its citizens. For example, during World War II, the federal government used credit to finance military spending. State and local governments use credit to pay for such things as highways, public housing, stadiums, and water systems.

Advantages of Credit

The main advantage of credit is that it's convenient. You can shop and travel without carrying large amounts of cash. You don't have to worry

Real-World Application

part 1 of 4

BEFORE YOU SAY YES, COMPUTE IT!
You may be eligible for credit as soon as you begin working at a job. You may think it's a great idea to open charge accounts—after all, you can get things you want right away. There is an important drawback, however: finance charges. How does credit work?

continued on p. 409

Real-World Application
Caption Answer

BEFORE YOU SAY YES, COMPUTE IT!:
PART 1 OF 4
Agreement to get money, goods, or services now in exchange for a promise to pay in the future.

Technology Resource

GO TO POWERPOINT.
The *Introduction to Business* PowerPoint® CD-ROM provides visual lecture aids for this chapter.

Independent Practice

COMPARE.   Make a chart to compare the pros and cons of using both cash and credit. Add to your chart all through the discussion of this chapter. (Encourage creativity.) **LS**

Chapter 25 What Is Credit?   **407**

Meeting Individual Needs

Students With Learning Disabilities. Students with difficulty categorizing information will find it helpful to draw a chart comparing the different types of credit discussed in this chapter. Suggest that students include one to three distinguishing characteristics of the credit included in each category. Remind students that drawing simple freehand or funny sketches might help them remember each category.

2 TEACH (Cont.)

Thinking Critically

AT THE GAME. You're with your friends in the crowd before the Friday night game at school. One of your friends asks you if she can borrow $25 because it's her dad's birthday next Friday. You don't have $25 to loan to her, so you throw out the idea that she might somehow get credit. She's interested, so you tell her all you know about credit. Things like what it is, who can use it, and the advantages and disadvantages. Write a story of your conversation. (Encourage creativity. Answers will vary.) **LS, CL, P**

Consider This...

Caption Answer

You could check your spending and the balance remaining on your account.

✔ Fast Review Answers

1. A creditor lends money or provides credit. A debtor borrows money or uses credit.
2. Credit used by businesses.
3. It easy to buy things you can't afford, buy too much, or buy things you don't need; it costs more; it's possible to lower your credit rating.

---

about getting cash before you go to the store or having it lost or stolen. Instead of saving for an expensive item, like a car or computer, you can get it and use it right away. Credit is especially useful in an emergency. If you lose your job, you can use credit to pay for food and rent. If your car breaks down and you don't have the cash to fix it, you can use credit. Without credit, you couldn't buy some things. To order airline tickets over the phone or shop on the Internet, you need a credit card.

Buying on credit enables you to establish a credit rating. A **credit rating** is a measure of a person's ability and willingness to pay debts on time. A good credit rating tells other lenders that you're a responsible borrower and a good credit risk. Credit also helps you keep track of your spending. Whenever you buy something on credit, it goes on your credit card bill so you have a record of your expenses.

Finally, credit contributes to the growth of our economy. If you use credit, you can buy more goods and services. Since so many consumers make credit purchases, businesses must hire more workers and produce more goods to keep up with the demand.

Disadvantages of Credit

Since credit is so convenient to use, it can also be easy to misuse. With credit, it's tempting to buy things you can't afford, buy too much, or buy things you don't need. Advertising and salespersons constantly urge you to buy more things. You might find it hard to resist a clothes sale or splurging on a new DVD player.

Items also cost more when you use credit instead of cash because of the interest. The more items you charge and the longer you take to pay off your credit cards, the more you pay in interest.

As credit card bills pile up, you might have trouble paying them. After awhile, you may reach your credit limit, the point where you can't charge any more. Late or missed payments lower your credit rating, which will make it difficult for you to get credit in the future. According to a recent report, half of all people with credit problems are between the ages of 18 and 32. Always remember when you use credit that it's not money you own, it's money you owe!

✔ Fast Review

1. What is the difference between a creditor and a debtor?
2. What is commercial credit?
3. Name the disadvantages of using credit.

Types of Credit

Credit is available from many different sources. These sources provide different types of loans for varying lengths of time. Loans can be short-term (one year or less), medium-term (one to five years), or long-term (more than five years). The risk a creditor takes in lending money

Consider This...

Credit on Your eWallet

People may soon be able to use their personal digital assistant (PDA) like a credit card. Purchasers will beam their payment to the cash register with infrared technology using their handheld computer. Later users can sync their PDA with their desktop PCs to update expense records. Palm™ Pilot is testing eWallet technology.

ANALYZE
What would be the benefits of having your current credit card statement with you at all times?

LANGUAGE ARTS   *Curriculum Connection*

Communication. Explain that businesses usually benefit by offering credit. Give students the following scenario: Tina was shopping for a winter coat in Lemmon's department store. Tina saw only one coat she liked, but it cost $20 more than she had. Since she didn't have any credit cards, Tina decided she wouldn't be able to buy the coat and started to leave the store.

As she neared the exit, a customer service representative offered her instant credit with a Lemmon's charge card. Tina signed up for the card and charged the coat. Have students analyze the situation and explain how the store benefited from offering credit and whether they think Tina benefited from obtaining credit to buy the coat.

or selling on credit is the most important factor in determining the cost of credit. Businesses and banks lose up to $1.5 billion per year in credit card fraud alone. Consumers who have a good credit rating will usually pay less interest than those who have a poor rating. In general, the lower the risk, the lower the costs of obtaining credit.

Charge Accounts

One of the most common types of short-term and medium-term credit is the **charge account**. Dealers or stores generally offer these. Customers who have charge accounts at a store can use their credit to buy now and pay later. When the bill arrives in the mail, the customer can pay some of the total amount owed or the entire amount. There are three main types of charge accounts: regular, revolving, and budget.

Regular Charge Accounts. These accounts require that you pay for purchases in full within a certain period, usually 25 or 30 days. If the bill is paid on time, you don't have to pay interest. If you don't pay the entire bill, interest is charged on the amount that hasn't been paid.

Revolving Charge Accounts. A **revolving account** allows you to borrow or charge up to a certain amount of money, such as $3,000, and pay back a part of the total or the entire balance for each month. Interest is charged on the unpaid amount.

Budget Charge Accounts. These accounts let you pay for costly items in equal payments spread out over a period of time. Many of these are medium-term loans for up to five years. Each payment includes part of the total due on the item plus interest. Large home appliances, cars, and furniture are often bought this way.

Credit Cards

Credit cards are like charge accounts but some can be used in many different places. Those issued by banks, for example, can be used in different stores, including companies that sell on the Internet. Some of the cards have annual fees, which might range from $25 to $80. Credit card companies earn money from the interest they charge. Interest rates vary a lot. You can find credit card rates on the Internet at various Web sites. There are three basic types of credit cards: single-purpose, multipurpose, and travel and entertainment. Figure 25.2 illustrates two credit card companies that are vying for your business. Which would you choose?

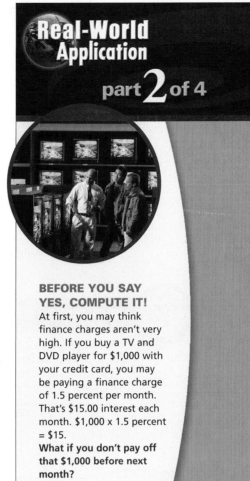

BEFORE YOU SAY YES, COMPUTE IT!
At first, you may think finance charges aren't very high. If you buy a TV and DVD player for $1,000 with your credit card, you may be paying a finance charge of 1.5 percent per month. That's $15.00 interest each month. $1,000 x 1.5 percent = $15.
What if you don't pay off that $1,000 before next month?

continued on p. 411

Chapter 25 What Is Credit? **409**

BEFORE YOU SAY YES, COMPUTE IT!:
PART 2 OF 4
Charged three percent in finance charges.

Business Connection

Installment credit jumped $13.9 billion in one month recently, according to an economic survey by Standard & Poor's. Revolving debt—made up mostly of credit-card debt—accounted for two-thirds of that new debt.

Develop Concepts

WHERE TO GO FOR CREDIT. Ask students: If you need money quickly and the only way to get the amount you need is to borrow it, where would you go to borrow money? Name all the places people could go to borrow money. Record students' ideas on the board and ask them for their opinions on the various options. (Answers will vary and may include banks, credit card companies, furniture stores, and pawnshops.) **CL**, LS

Great Ideas From the Classroom of...

Larry Condra
Abilene High School
Abilene, Tex.

Credit Simulations. Students complete credit applications using as much of their own information as possible (and inventing any other needed information). A bank processes them just as if they were live credit applications. The bank rates the students just as if they were adults. Then a guest speaker from the bank comes to explain why the ratings were such. This personalized credit simulation internalizes the learning that your credit reputation is the most valuable asset you'll ever own.

2 TEACH (Cont.)

Discussion Starter

FIRST CREDIT CARDS. The first credit cards came into use in the 1920s. They were single-purpose cards issued by businesses, such as hotel chains and oil companies. In 1950 Diners Club introduced the first card that could be used at a variety of businesses. In 1958 American Express introduced its card. What kind of cards are the Diners Club and American Express? (Travel and entertainment.)

Figure 25.2 Caption Answer

Choices will vary. Make sure students back up their answers with reasons.

Single-Purpose Cards. These cards can only be used to buy goods or services at the business that issued the card. Single-purpose cards operate like revolving charge accounts. Each month you receive a statement listing all the purchases you made in the past 30 days. You can pay part or the entire amount you owe. Credit cards issued by oil companies are examples of single-purpose credit cards. There is no annual fee for single-purpose cards.

Multipurpose Cards. These cards are also called bank credit cards because banks issue them. Multipurpose cards work like a revolving charge account. These cards may be used at many different stores, restaurants, and other businesses all over the world. MasterCard® and VISA® are examples of multipurpose cards.

Travel and Entertainment Cards. These cards usually work like regular charge accounts. You must pay the full amount due each month. Cards such as American Express® and Diners Club® are examples. They are accepted worldwide for purchases connected with travel, business,

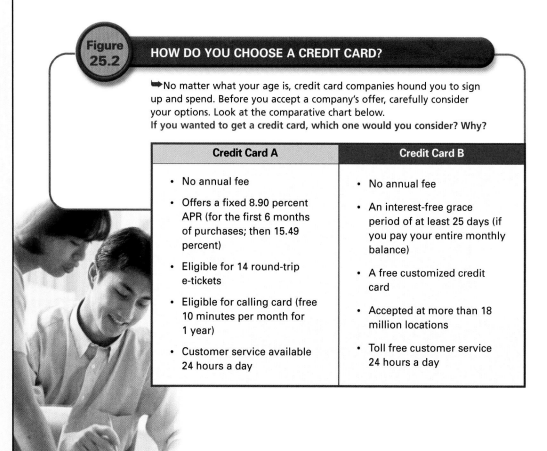

Figure 25.2

HOW DO YOU CHOOSE A CREDIT CARD?

➡ No matter what your age is, credit card companies hound you to sign up and spend. Before you accept a company's offer, carefully consider your options. Look at the comparative chart below.
If you wanted to get a credit card, which one would you consider? Why?

Credit Card A	Credit Card B
• No annual fee	• No annual fee
• Offers a fixed 8.90 percent APR (for the first 6 months of purchases; then 15.49 percent)	• An interest-free grace period of at least 25 days (if you pay your entire monthly balance)
• Eligible for 14 round-trip e-tickets	• A free customized credit card
• Eligible for calling card (free 10 minutes per month for 1 year)	• Accepted at more than 18 million locations
• Customer service available 24 hours a day	• Toll free customer service 24 hours a day

410

Global Perspective

Credit Around the World. Have students work in groups of four to research the kinds of consumer credit used in various countries in the Eastern Hemisphere (Europe, Asia, Africa, and Australia) and Western Hemisphere (North, Central, and South America). See that each group chooses a different country. Suggest that groups include information about restrictions on the use of personal consumer credit and also the effect of credit use on savings. After each group presents its information, have the class discuss whether Americans could learn some credit lessons from other nations. **CL**, LS, **P**

and entertainment such as restaurant and hotel bills, car rentals, and airline tickets. Often they have an annual fee, which is higher than a multipurpose card.

Banks and Other Financial Institutions

Financial institutions, such as banks, savings and loans, and credit unions offer many types of loans. They usually have the lowest rates on their loans. They do place more demands on the borrower, however, which can make it more difficult to get a loan. For example, these financial institutions only want to lend money to people with good credit ratings. Many credit unions only lend money to credit union members and employees in a certain business or field (such as a teachers' credit union).

Single Payment Loan. As the name suggests, the debtor pays back this type of loan in one payment, including interest (at the end of the loan period). Many farmers secure single payment loans in the spring to pay for their seed and fertilizer. They then pay back the loan in the fall after they have harvested their crops.

Installment Loan. Student loans, personal loans, and home improvement loans are types of **installment loans**, or loans repaid in regular payments over a period of time. The debtor receives the loan money for a certain period, such as two years. Over that period, the debtor makes equal monthly payments, which cover the amount of the loan and the interest.

Mortgage Loan. A mortgage loan is a form of an installment loan only it's written for a long period, such as 15 to 30 years. Over the period of the loan, the debtor makes regular payments (usually monthly). Some loans require *collateral*, which is something of value the bank can take if you don't make the required loan payments. Cars, houses, and boats are used as collateral when you borrow money to finance them.

Seller-Provided Credit

Many stores provide credit for their customers. Clothing, furniture, appliance, boat, hardware, and car dealers are among those who offer credit for customers. Generally, seller-provided credit is extended for less than one year, up to five years. One of the reasons they provide such credit is to make it easier for consumers to buy their products and to not go elsewhere.

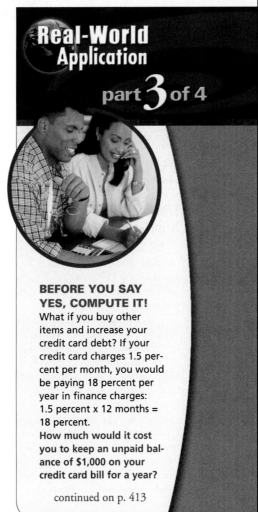

Real-World Application

part **3** of 4

BEFORE YOU SAY YES, COMPUTE IT!
What if you buy other items and increase your credit card debt? If your credit card charges 1.5 percent per month, you would be paying 18 percent per year in finance charges: 1.5 percent x 12 months = 18 percent.
How much would it cost you to keep an unpaid balance of $1,000 on your credit card bill for a year?

continued on p. 413

Chapter 25 What Is Credit? **411**

Individualized Practice

Have students visit businesses such as clothing stores, department stores, and gas stations to collect charge account applications. Ask students to work in small groups to make a display of the applications.

L1 Have pairs of students study their display then compare the applications, discussing the similarities and differences.

L2 Ask students to study the applications and chart similarities and differences.

L3 Ask students to write a paragraph telling what they think the creditors are trying to determine by asking for certain kinds of information.

LANGUAGE ARTS   *Curriculum Connection*

Type of Credit Account. Horace Porter's charge account bill at Bryson's department store records last month's payment of $10.00 and interest charges of $3.74 on his unpaid balance of $117.00 from last month. The bill requests that he make a minimum payment of $10.00 this month. Have students review the information about the account and draw conclusions about whether Horace's account is revolving or regular. (The account is a revolving account, because Horace paid only a portion of the bill, has been charged interest on the unpaid balance, and may continue to pay off only a portion of his bill.)

Reteaching

CHARGE ACCOUNTS. To reteach the concept of charge accounts, ask students to name the three types of charge accounts and describe the differences. (Answers should include regular, revolving, and budget.)

Enrichment Strategy

INTERVIEW. Ask students to interview a manager or officer in a credit union or savings and loan about the services offered. Topics they could explore in their interview include the advantages and disadvantages there are to using the services of a credit union or savings and loan compared with using those of a commercial bank. Have students summarize their interviews in a written report. **LS**

Business Building Blocks

CAPTION ANSWER

Arrange to have the class visit the school library. Make sure students know where to find reference sources and how to use them. Have students find the answers to the three questions, making sure to note the source of the information, page number (if appropriate), and the publication or copyright date of the source.

Consumer Finance Companies

You can have trouble borrowing from banks or other financial institutions if you don't have a steady job or if you have a poor credit rating. Consumer finance companies specialize in loans to people who might not be able to get credit elsewhere. Their loans usually range from less than one year, up to five years. The cost of a loan from a consumer

---

Business Building Blocks

Communication

Locating and Verifying Information

When you work, you rely on your colleagues and others for many different reasons. This is especially true when you need information to complete your own projects.

You can find or verify information in many ways. Some information, like last year's sales figures, will be available from your own company. To obtain other information you may have to rely on reference books, interviews, and the Internet.

Make sure the sources you use are reliable and up-to-date. Check the copyright date of books or the issue date of periodicals. Verify your information whenever possible by cross-checking with another source.

Practice

How can you be certain you're getting accurate, up-to-date information? Read the Information Source Guide in the box for recommendations. Use it to figure out how to find the following information:
1. Population of your town or city.
2. Number of cars your favorite car manufacturer sold last year.

3. Names and addresses of two companies that manufacture a product or provide a service in a career field that interests you.

Information Source Guide

Newspapers. The *New York Times* and *Wall Street Journal.*

Magazines. Consult the *Reader's Guide to Periodical Literature* for general interest magazines. Search specialized indexes, such as the *Business Periodicals Index*, too.

Directories. Specialized directories may have exactly the information you need. The *Thomas Register of American Manufacturers*, for example, is published annually.

Atlases. An atlas can be a great source for certain kinds of facts and figures. Even old editions can be useful if you're doing historical research.

Internet. The amount and type of information can change daily, so keep up-to-date by consulting the "last time modified" clause on a Web page.

The U.S. Government. The Government Printing Office publishes free or inexpensive information about many subjects.

How to Use a Portfolio Activity

The portfolio projects are designed to lead students to develop a collection of their best work to submit to you for assessment. You and each of your students should decide which projects to include in their business portfolio. Refer students to the specific rubric(s) from the *Alternative Assessment Strategies.* These rubrics will alert students to the criteria you'll use to assess their projects. **P**

finance company is higher than the cost of a loan from other sources since this loan involves a greater risk.

The interest rate a consumer finance company charges varies from state to state and can be more than 20 percent, which is quite high. Before securing a loan from a consumer finance company, check to see if you can secure a comparable loan from a bank, savings and loan, savings bank, or credit union. Also, check out whether you can get a better deal on a credit card where you're eligible.

Payroll Advance Services

Many people have difficulty making their paychecks stretch from one payday to the next. If you don't have any savings and an unexpected expense occurs, you might look for a short-term loan until payday.

Pawnshop Loan. This type of loan is based on the value of something you own. For example, you could pawn your bicycle for an amount of money that's less than the bike is worth. You receive a ticket for the item and can redeem, or buy back, your bike within a certain period of time for the loan amount plus a service charge. The service charge is like interest. If you don't redeem it, the pawnshop sells your bike. Generally, the cost of this type of loan is very high.

"Borrow Until Payday" Loan. Some businesses provide very short-term loans, usually for 5 to 14 days. The cost of this kind of loan is especially high. In some cases, it could be 1,000 percent when you calculate it on an annual basis. This kind of loan isn't permitted in some states and limited in others by a maximum fee or loan amount allowed.

A payday loan is made without a credit check, but you must have proof of a checking account and employment. It's strongly recommended that you don't use this source of credit. People with poor credit ratings are most likely to use this service because they can't get a loan anywhere else.

✓ **Fast Review** _____

1. What is the most important factor for a creditor in determining the cost of credit?
2. What are the three types of charge accounts?
3. What is the difference between a single payment loan and an installment loan?
4. What three types of loans usually cost the most?

Chapter 25 What Is Credit? **413**

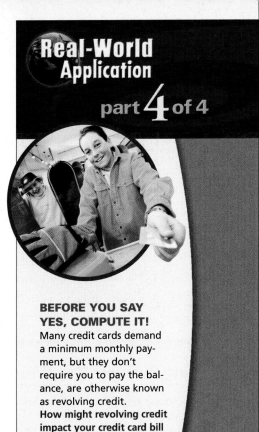

Real-World Application
Caption Answer

BEFORE YOU SAY YES, COMPUTE IT!: PART 4 OF 4
Can result in a rapid buildup.

Technology Resource

GO TO **PUZZLEMAKER CD-ROM.** Check your students' understanding of the chapter's key terms by using the *Puzzlemaker* CD-ROM.

Evaluation

Assign and review the Fast Review sections.

✓ **Fast Review Answers** ✓

1. The risk involved in lending money or selling on credit.
2. Regular, revolving, and budget.
3. A single-payment loan is paid back in one payment. An installment load is repaid in regular payments over a period of time.
4. Loans from consumer finance companies, pawnshop loans, and "Borrow Until Payday" loans.

4 CLOSE

Chapter Wrap-Up

Ask students to draw a cartoon representing one key concept.

Using Business Key Words

1. creditor
2. revolving credit
3. installment loans
4. commercial credit
5. debtor
6. consumer credit
7. credit
8. interest
9. credit rating
10. charge account

Review What You Learned

11. Opportunity cost.
12. Income, current debt, information about a person's personal life, and repaid debts.
13. Your ability to buy goods and services increases.
14. Interest.
15. Short-term—less than one year; medium-term—one to five years; long-term—over five years.
16. Can't get credit elsewhere.
17. A regular charge account requires that people pay for purchases in full within a certain period. Revolving charge accounts allow people to pay a portion of the amount owed each month. Budget charge accounts permit payment with equal installment payments spread over a period of time.
18. Multipurpose cards.
19. Very high interest.
20. Business must pay a percentage of each credit purchase to the credit card company or bank that issued the card.

Summary

1. Credit is an agreement to get money, goods, or services now by promising to pay later. Creditors charge a fee (interest) for using their services.
2. Using credit is convenient, useful in an emergency, helps you establish a credit rating, helps you keep track of your spending, and contributes to the growth of the economy. It also costs more, can lead to overspending, and, if handled improperly, may lower your credit rating.
3. Credit is available through charge accounts, credit cards, banks, businesses, consumer finance companies, and pawnshops.
4. The three main types of charge accounts are regular, revolving, and budget.
5. The three basic types of credit cards are single-purpose, multipurpose, and travel and entertainment.

● Using Business Key Words

Consumers use credit to make purchases every day. It's a convenient way to buy something, but it's something you need to learn to use wisely. See how well you know these credit terms. Complete each sentence with the correct term.

- **credit**
- **charge account**
- **creditor**
- **revolving account**
- **debtor**
- **consumer credit**
- **installment loans**
- **interest**
- **commercial credit**
- **credit rating**

1. A (n) _____ lends money or provides credit.
2. A form of credit account, which allows one to borrow or charge up to a certain amount of money and pay back a part of the total each month, is called a(n) _____.

3. Loans repaid in regular payments over a period of time are called _____.
4. Credit used by businesses to buy goods, pay salaries, or buy property is called _____.
5. The _____ is the one who borrows the money or uses the credit.
6. Credit used by consumers for personal purchases is called _____.
7. _____ is the opportunity to obtain money, goods, or services now in exchange for a promise to pay in the future.
8. Creditors usually charge _____, or a fee for using their money.
9. Some factors that determine a person's _____ are income, current debt, and debt history.
10. A short-term credit arrangement provided by a store or company to purchase their product is called a _____.

Quick Quiz

1. How do businesses use credit? (To purchase raw materials, new machinery, trucks, and other expensive equipment.)
2. What are three disadvantages of credit? (Easy to spend too much, items cost more when you pay interest, can cause problems with your credit rating.)
3. Name the three main types of credit cards. (Single-purpose, multipurpose, and travel and entertainment.)

Review What You Learned

11. What is the cost of using credit?
12. What are the factors that determine a person's credit rating?
13. How does credit contribute to the growth of the economy?
14. Why does it often cost more to purchase an item on credit than it does when you purchase the item with cash?
15. What is the difference between a short-term, medium-term, and long-term loan?
16. Who usually borrows money from consumer finance companies?
17. Explain the differences between a regular charge account, a revolving charge account, and a budget charge account.
18. MasterCard® and Visa® are examples of what type of credit cards?
19. Why is it strongly recommended that you not use a "borrow until payday" loan as a source of credit?
20. How can offering credit become a disadvantage to a business?

Understanding Business Concepts

21. Why do people like to buy on credit?
22. Describe two situations in which cash is more convenient. Next, describe two situations in which credit is the better choice.
23. Why is it important to take care of your credit rating?
24. Why do consumer finance companies have higher finance charges than other places?
25. Why do credit card companies try so hard to persuade you to use their card?
26. If people use credit, does that mean they have money problems? Explain.
27. How do businesses use credit to help sell their products?

Critical Thinking

28. "Everyone would gain if there were no consumer credit. Consumers would benefit because goods and services could be sold at a lower price. The lower price means the businesses would sell more goods and services." Do you agree or disagree with these statements? Explain.
29. What types of consumers would benefit from a travel and entertainment credit card? Explain.
30. What are your thoughts on the pros and cons of credit?
31. What trends in credit have you noticed?

Viewing and Representing

Examining the Image. In a group of three, examine the photograph and ask one another questions about the content. What's important in this photograph? Discuss your ideas about using credit.

Chapter 25 What Is Credit? **415**

Critical Thinking

28. Answers will vary. Disagree with this statement. Curtailing credit could cause an increase in prices because demand would fall off. Agree with this statement. People would not have to pay interest on their purchases, thus keeping prices lower. Also, they would not have to pay their share of the bad debts.
29. People who travel worldwide, who entertain, or who have many business expenses.
30. Answers will vary and depend on the students' opinions.
31. Answers will depend upon current trends.

Viewing and Representing

This activity is a springboard to open discussion in the groups of three. This is an opportunity to practice good sociability skills. Before starting this activity, remind students of the importance of listening to one other and respecting, not judging, others' opinions and ideas. This is an opportunity for students to practice relating well to others by building their understanding, empathy, and politeness, and by the appropriateness of their responses. This activity involves not only sociability skills but also self-management skills. **LS, CL**

Understanding Business Concepts

21. Convenience.
22. Cash pays cab, bus, subway fares, or tips. Use credit to order items online, and when making expensive purchases.
23. Plays a major role as to where you can secure credit and what you will pay for it.
24. Lend money to people who cannot get credit elsewhere.
25. They earn money from the interest.
26. Not necessarily. Many people use credit wisely and efficiently.
27. Easier for consumers to buy and make money from interest on their own store credit card.

Chapter 25 Review

Chapter 25 Review

4 CLOSE (Cont.)

Building Academic Skills

LANGUAGE ARTS. Save newspapers and magazines for those students who do not have access to any. Rubric: Paragraph.

MATH. Make sure all of the students in the group participate in the project. Point out to students that interest rates may vary according to the circumstances of the loan. Rubric: Charts/tables.

COMPUTER/TECHNOLOGY. Rubrics: Surveys, spreadsheet.

SOCIAL SCIENCE. Make sure all of the students in the group participate in the project. Rubric: Note taking.

Linking School to Home

Answers will vary depending on the promotional items collected. Rubrics: Lists, survey.

Linking School to Work

Answers will vary depending on the applications that were obtained. Allow the students to choose the way they wish to share their findings with the class. Rubrics: Essay, note taking, charts/tables.

Building Academic Skills

LANGUAGE ARTS — Writing About Credit

Keeping a business financially stable is a requirement in order to stay open. As you've learned in this chapter, a business relies on lenders for credit to help continue expanding its company. The media continually reports on businesses' financial situations. Bring in several newspaper articles and advertisements that show uses of credit by consumers, businesses, and the government. Write a paragraph for each explaining who benefits the most from these examples of credit.

MATH — Analyzing the Cost of Credit

In a group, research the cost of credit from each of the sources listed below. Use newspaper and radio advertisements or make phone calls to local creditors to gather the information. Then rank them in order, from the lowest interest rates to the highest interest rates.

- Consumer finance company
- Revolving charge account
- Travel and entertainment credit card
- Credit union
- Commercial bank

COMPUTER/TECHNOLOGY — Surveying Students

Create a survey to find out what the students in your school know about credit. Ask questions like (1) what is credit?, (2) do you have a credit card?, and (3) if so, what do you use it for?

Add at least five other questions to the survey. Compile the results using a spreadsheet program. Print your results.

Social Science — A Collective Discussion

In a group, discuss whether you agree or disagree with the following statements. Try to come to consensus. Record the reasons for the group's opinions. Share your opinions with other groups.

- The use of credit is usually justified for necessities but not for luxuries.
- The best way to minimize the cost of credit is to borrow at the lowest available interest rate and repay the loan in the shortest possible time.
- A good credit rating is a valuable thing to have, so a consumer should protect that rating.
- It's best to shop for credit just as you would shop for any major purchase.

Linking School to Home

Analyzing Advertisements. During the next two weeks, save all the advertisements and junk mail that come to your home, which try to persuade you and your family to become a user of their credit cards. Log the promotional offers that are advertised. Conduct a mini-survey among your family and friends and find out whether or not they would choose one of the cards based on the advertising material that has been sent to your home.

Linking School to Work

Comparing Credit Cards. Obtain a credit card application from two different retail stores or gas stations. As a group, compare the applications and list the similarities and differences. Be sure to examine the interest rates and repayment procedures. Create a table in a word processor or a spreadsheet. Discuss your findings with the class.

E-Homework

Applying Technology

Comparing Credit Cards. Use the Internet to research interest rates and credit lines of multi-purpose credit cards. Find examples of at least four and compare their rates, repayment terms, and the application process.

Flexible Credit. Some small business owners only need small loans. Banks, however, usually prefer to make loans of $50,000 or more. Heather McCartney needed $5,000 to give her ethnic-themed cookie cutter business a boost. She got the cash from a nonprofit micro-lender called Count Me In for Women's Economic Independence. Go to the Internet to find out more about this nonprofit organization.

Connecting Academics

Math. A generally accepted consumer credit scoring scale, The Fair Isaac Company (FICO) score, ranges from about 350 to 900 points. A good score is often considered 600 or greater. Banks and other companies may not give credit to people with scores below 600. List whether or not the following people are likely to receive credit:

Sam	300 credit score
Jill	590
Tina	480
Guillermo	600

Social Science. Working in a team of three, choose one of the following topics: what is credit, advantages and disadvantages of credit, types of charge accounts, types of credit cards, or types of loans. Together, research your chosen topic. Imagine members of your team are customer service representatives at a local credit information organization. Now you're ready to take client calls (i.e., classmates voicing issues and asking customer-oriented questions).

You read the first part of "Tapping Teens' Plastic Potential" at the beginning of this chapter. Below are a few questions for you to answer about teen credit cards. You'll find the answers to these questions when you're reading the entire article. First, here are the questions:

32. How do teen credit cards differ from normal credit cards?
33. According to marketing experts, what are the credit card companies' motives for promoting the cards to teens?

CREATIVE JOURNAL ACTIVITY

Consider the consumer advantages and disadvantages of having a teen card. Create a poster illustrating your points.

BUSINESS
Online
The Full Story

To learn more about teen credit cards, visit the *Introduction to Business* Web site at www.introbus.glencoe.com, and click on *BusinessWeek* Feature Story, Chapter 25.

COMPARING CREDIT CARDS. Answers will vary depending on the cards selected. Allow the students to choose the way they wish to share their findings with the class. Rubrics: List, essay, oral presentation, poster/chart.

FLEXIBLE CREDIT. Allow the students to choose the way they wish to share their findings with the class. Rubrics: Note taking, oral presentation, poster.

Connecting Academics

MATH. No for Sam, Jill, and Tina. Yes for Guillermo.

SOCIAL SCIENCE. Answers will vary.

---

32. They are actually reloadable stored-value cards. The teen or the teen's parent adds money to the card. The biggest difference is the card can't accumulate debt.
33. The new cards attract new customers early in life. The company is interested in cementing a new consumer relationship.

Creative Journal Activity

Ask students to find out about any trends in the use of teen cards over the past few years and report to the class. Have students research statistics for the number of credit cardholders in the U.S. and the number of teen credit cardholders. **LS, CL**

SCANS Correlation Chart*

Foundation Skills

Basic Skills	Reading	Writing	Math	Listening	Speaking	
Thinking Skills	Creative Thinking	Decision Making	Problem Solving	Seeing Things in the Mind's Eye	Knowing How to Learn	Reasoning
Personal Qualities	Responsibility	Self-Esteem	Sociability	Self-Management	Integrity/Honesty	

Workplace Competencies

Resources	Allocating Time	Allocating Money	Allocating Material and Facility Resources	Allocating Human Resources		
Information	Acquiring and Evaluating Information	Organizing and Maintaining Information	Interpreting and Communicating Information	Using Computers to Process Information		
Interpersonal Skills	Participating as a Member of a Team	Teaching Others	Serving Clients/Customers	Exercising Leadership	Negotiating to Arrive at a Decision	Working With Cultural Diversity
Systems	Understanding Systems	Monitoring and Correcting Performance	Improving and Designing Systems			
Technology	Selecting Technology	Applying Technology to Task	Maintaining and Troubleshooting Technology			

*This chart's highlighted blocks indicate the chapter's content coverage in the Student Edition and the Teacher Wraparound Edition.

Resource Manager

Teaching Transparencies

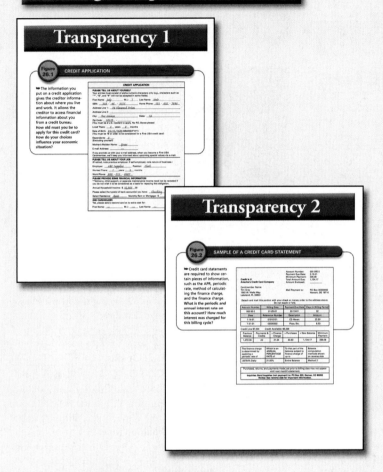

Application and Enrichment

- 📖 Lesson Plans
- 📖 *BusinessWeek* Poster Package
- 🖨 Teaching Transparencies
- 💿📖 Integrated Software Simulation
- 📼📖 Glencoe Business Video Package

Review and Reinforcement

- 💿 *PuzzleMaker*
- 💻📖 Internet Resources
- 📖 Student Activity Workbook
- 📖 Strat. and Work. for Teaching Transparencies

Assessment and Evaluation

- 📖 Reproducible Tests
- 📖 Alternative Assessment Strategies
- 💿 ExamView® Pro Test Generator

Technology

- 💿 *PuzzleMaker* CD-ROM
- 💿 ExamView® Pro Test Generator
- 📼 Glencoe Business Video Package
- 💿 PowerPoint® Presentation
- 💿📖 Integrated Software Simulation
- 💿 Interactive Lesson Planner
- 💿 *Virtual Business*®

KEY	📖 Printed	💾 Software	📼 Videocassette	📕 Poster
	🖨 Transparency	💿 CD-ROM	💻 Internet	

BUSINESS Online

Visit **www.introbus.glencoe.com**, the Web site companion to *Introduction to Business*. The student's page includes:

- interactive tutor
- additional *BusinessWeek* articles and activities
- business Web links
- homework hints
- real-world application activities
- additional career path activities

Information on how to prepare your students for the high school exit exam and special projects are also included.

Use the Glencoe Web site for additional resources. All essential content is covered in the Student Edition.

1 FOCUS

Introducing the Chapter

This chapter explains about choosing a credit card and using credit. It describes the costs of credit and keeping good credit. A photo essay, "Road Trip to Marfa," enhances the concepts.

Connecting the Objectives

What is credit worthiness? What problems are there with credit? What can happen if a person can't keep up with their payments?

BusinessWeek
Feature Story

Story's Summary

College students are bombarded by credit-card issuers and by tricky promotions that can lead them into problems. A study shows that 56 percent of college students have credit cards, and the number is rising. Many are getting into thousands of dollars of debt. One example is Daniel Pena, age 24, who has $10,000 in credit card debt as well as his bachelor's degree in biology. Pena regrets that he's going to spend years living frugally and working to pay off his debt.

Find the entire article at **www.introbus.glencoe.com**, or in the Teacher Resource Binder.

How to Get and Keep Credit

● Learning Objectives

After completing this chapter, you'll be able to:
1. **Name** the five factors creditors use to consider credit worthiness.
2. **Identify** the types of credit you can use.
3. **Explain** some of the costs involved in paying for credit.
4. **Describe** how to maintain a good credit rating.

● Why It's Important

Credit can enhance your life if used properly, or it can cause major problems if used improperly.

● Key Words

credit bureau	finance
credit limit	charge
cosigner	variable rate
down payment	cash
principal	advance
secured loan	grace period
unsecured loan	garnishment
annual percent-	of wages
age rate	repossess

418

BusinessWeek *Feature Story*
Majoring in Debt

Many College Students Aren't Ready for Plastic.
Daniel Peña graduated from the University of California at Riverside last year with a degree in biology—and almost $10,000 in credit-card debt. He had used his three Visas, two MasterCards, and one Discover card to charge books, a computer, video and stereo gear, restaurant meals, and clothing. "I couldn't even make the minimum payment each month," says Peña, 24, who abandoned plans to go to medical school to take a job in computers. "It's going to take me a few years of living frugally before I'm debt-free."

Source: Excerpted with permission from "Majoring in Debt," *BusinessWeek Online*, September 25, 2000.

An Extension Activity

It takes time to build a good credit history. You can begin by applying for a department store or gas station credit card. These are easier to qualify for. Why do you think it's important to pay your credit card bills on time?

The Full Story
To learn more about credit cards, visit the *Introduction to Business* Web site at **www.introbus.glencoe.com**, and click on *BusinessWeek* Feature Story, Chapter 26.

Classroom Resources

For the Teacher
- 📁 Student Activity Work. TAE
- 💿✴ Assessment Binder
- ✴ PowerPoint® Presentation
- ✴ Interactive Lesson Planner
- 📁 Lesson Plans
- ✍💻 Internet Resources
- Teaching Transparencies
- Introduction to Business Web Site

- 💿 Integrated Soft. Sim. TM
- 📕 BusinessWeek Poster Package

For the Student
- ✍ Student Activity Workbook
- ✴ Virtual Business®
- 💻 Introduction to Business Web Site
- ✴ Integrated Soft. Sim.
- ✴ PuzzleMaker
- ✍ Strategies and Worksheets for Teaching Transparencies

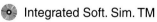
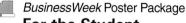

Bell Ringer Activity

RESPONSIBILITY. What can you do to make sure you manage credit responsibly? Write a paragraph in your journal. **LS**

Preteaching Business Key Words

EXERCISING LEADERSHIP. Part of being a leader is to motivate others. Working in pairs, take turns to motivate your partner in learning and understanding the key words for this chapter. **CL**, **LS**

An Extension Activity

ANSWER. It affects your credit rating. A credit rating might influence your chances of renting an apartment or buying a home—future lenders may charge you a higher interest rate.

Making Connections

Everyday Living. As many as 15 million Americans may be compulsive shoppers who go shopping when they are under stress. Researchers at the University of Minnesota classified compulsive shoppers into three categories: binge buyers, daily shoppers, and multiple buyers. One thing all compulsive shoppers had in common was that they invariably charged large amounts of goods to credit cards without having the funds available to pay their debts. Ask students: Do you think this knowledge will help you analyze and possibly modify your own shopping behavior?

2 TEACH

Business Connection

Having good credit matters. That's the message from experienced credit counselors at www.mycounsel.com. You'll probably need to use credit in the future for major purchases such as a car, vacation, house, or home improvement. You might need to borrow money for major changes in your life, such as losing your job or a divorce. You should plan to establish a good credit history because lenders review this history before allowing you to open a credit card account.

Develop Concepts

ESTABLISHING CREDIT. If someone asks you for a loan, what factors make you decide to say yes or no? How and when would you expect the person to repay the loan? Creditors, or lending institutions, use similar criteria to determine whether they should give someone a loan. (Answers will vary and should include the five "Cs of credit"—capacity to pay back, character, credit history, capital, and collateral.)

Figure 26.1 Caption Answer

You must be 18 years of age to be considered for this credit card.

Getting Credit

Credit card applications bombard just about everyone's mailbox weekly. The average college student has about three credit cards and is $1,843 in debt. You should try not to use credit if you can, but sometimes it's unavoidable. You might need to get a student loan or finance a car. You might want to keep a credit card around for convenience or for emergencies. If you do decide to get a credit card, there are several things you need to know.

Figure 26.1 CREDIT APPLICATION

➡ The information you put on a credit application gives the creditor information about where you live and work. It allows the creditor to access financial information about you from a credit bureau. **How old must you be to apply for this credit card? How do your choices influence your economic situation?**

CREDIT APPLICATION

PLEASE TELL US ABOUT YOURSELF
Your entries must consist of alpha-numeric characters only (e.g., characters such as "*", "$", and "#" will not be accepted in some fields).

First Name: _Jody_   M.I.: _S_   Last Name: _Meir_
SSN: _320_ - _46_ - _3555_   Home Phone: _123_ - _456_ - _7890_
Address Line 1: _26 Elmwood Drive_
Address Line 2:
City: _Des Moines_   State: _IA_
Zip Code: _50313_ -
(You must be a U.S. resident to apply. No P.O. Boxes please)
Lived There: _2_ years _0_ months
Date of Birth: _03/12/1989_ (MM/DD/YYYY)
(You must be 18 or older to be considered for a First USA credit card)
Dependents: _0_
(Excluding yourself)
Mother's Maiden Name: _Greer_
E-mail Address:
If you provide us with your e-mail address, when you become a First USA Cardmember, we'll keep you informed about upcoming special values via e-mail.

PLEASE TELL US ABOUT YOUR JOB
(If retired, note previous employer. If self-employed, note nature of business.)
Employer: _ABC Supplies_   Position: _Clerk_
Worked There: _1_ years _3_ months
Work Phone: _800_ - _555_ - _0987_

PLEASE PROVIDE SOME FINANCIAL INFORMATION
**Alimony, child support, or separate maintenance income need not be revealed if you do not wish it to be considered as a basis for repaying this obligation.
Annual Household Income: $ _16,000_ .00
Please select the type(s) of bank account(s) you have: _Checking_
Select Residence: _Rent_   Monthly Rent or Mortgage: $ _600_ .00

2ND CARDHOLDER
Yes, please send a second card at no extra cost for:
First Name: __   M.I.: __   Last Name: __

Cooperative Learning

Consumer Credit Analysis. Reva Alhusen bought new living room furniture on credit from Belair's Furniture Store. Reva's total purchase came to $1,036.29, and she qualified for interest free financing for one year. Reva made a down payment of $36.29 and agreed to pay $50 twice a month until the $1,000 balance due was paid. The security agreement she signed said in part, "No finance fee if amount financed is paid in 12 months." Belair's told Reva that Triangle Financial Services, a finance company that handled the store's credit sales, would service her account. When her payment book arrived from Triangle Financial Services, Reva found 24 monthly payment coupons each in the amount of $49.92. What should Reva do? (See Curriculum Connection, p. 422.)

Picking a Credit Card

The main consideration in choosing a credit card is the cost of credit, which will be discussed later. Besides costs there are other features to consider. Who accepts the card? What is the amount you can charge to meet your needs? Can you use the card to get cash? Some cards offer benefits such as rebates or refunds on a percentage of how much you charge. Other cards offer free travel or contributions to a charity after you charge a certain amount.

Applying for Credit

To open a credit or charge account, you'll have to fill out an application form. Figure 26.1 is a sample of a credit application you might fill out. The form asks for information about where you live, where you work, and what other credit you've received. It'll also ask questions about your income and how much savings you have. If a company accepts your application, you'll receive a security agreement. The agreement explains how interest will be charged on the account. When you sign your name on it, you agree to follow the rules described in the agreement.

Your Credit Worthiness: The Five Cs

Before creditors give you a charge or credit account, they want to make sure you're worth the risk. There are several factors they consider, which are usually referred to as the "five Cs of credit."

Capacity. One of the first things creditors consider is your capacity to pay. If you already have a large amount of debt, creditors will be unlikely to give you more credit. To determine your ability to pay, they'll check to see whether you have a job, how much you make, and how long you've been employed.

Character. Creditors want to know what kind of person you're before they lend money to you. They might ask for *credit references* from businesses or people you've borrowed from in the past who can testify to your reliability.

Credit History. The creditor then checks with a **credit bureau**, an agency that collects information about you and other credit consumers. Your credit bureau report tells whether you pay your bills on time or have failed to pay debts. It also indicates the amount of debt that you have.

Real-World Application
part **1** of 4

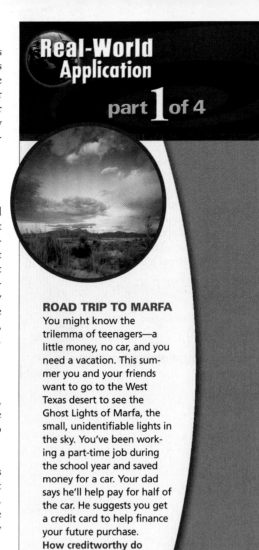

ROAD TRIP TO MARFA
You might know the trilemma of teenagers—a little money, no car, and you need a vacation. This summer you and your friends want to go to the West Texas desert to see the Ghost Lights of Marfa, the small, unidentifiable lights in the sky. You've been working a part-time job during the school year and saved money for a car. Your dad says he'll help pay for half of the car. He suggests you get a credit card to help finance your future purchase. **How creditworthy do you think you are?**

continued on p. 423

Chapter 26 How to Get and Keep Credit **421**

Real-World Application
Caption Answer

ROAD TRIP TO MARFA: PART 1 OF 4

Answers will vary. Take into consideration the five Cs of credit worthiness.

Technology Resource

GO TO **POWERPOINT.** The *Introduction to Business* PowerPoint® CD-ROM provides visual lecture aids for this chapter.

Independent Practice

IMAGINE. Imagine that someone has asked you to cosign a loan. Find out about what is involved in being a cosigner on a loan. Make a chart of the reasons why you would or would not be willing to cosign. (Display the charts.) **LS**

Thinking Critically

CHOICES. Your family's washing machine broke. A new machine will cost $390, but it will take eight months for the family to save the money. You could buy a new machine on credit now for $498, including the finance charges. For each of the three choices below list the advantages and disadvantages.

a. Repair the broken one.
b. Buy a new washing machine on credit.
c. Save to buy a new washing machine for cash.

Which choice do you suggest?

Meeting Individual Needs

Students With Difficulties in Math. Calculating interest and finance charges can be confusing to students whose math skills are below average. Make sure they know how to use the formulas for determining the cost of credit. Have them go through an exercise in which they make an imaginary credit purchase and must calculate and compare the costs using different interest rates. Explain that knowing how to find the best credit bargain can save them hundreds of dollars.

✓ Fast Review Answers

1. Cash, savings, investments, and possessions.
2. The maximum amount you can spend or charge on a credit account.
3. A cosigner has to pay back a loan if the borrower fails to pay.
4. Capacity, character, credit history, capital, collateral.

Technology Toolkit

Caption Answer

A credit card is associated with an account that has a spending limit, for example $5,000, and payments can be made on a regular basis. A smart card is pre-paid, and often more expensive to use than a credit card.

Technology Toolkit

How Smart Is Your Card?

A smart card is a small plastic card that contains a computer. It carries information on an imbedded chip. People can use smart cards to buy items online, to enter a theater, or even to buy their school lunches. You decide to add an account to your card, like your favorite clothing store. You can get rid of any account whenever you want. After graduating from high school you won't want that school lunch account anymore.

Thinking Critically
How is a credit card different from a smart card?

Capital. Your capital is how much you have beyond what you owe. It includes cash, savings, investments, and possessions. Creditors want to know if you have enough capital so that if you lose your job, you can still pay them back with savings or by selling something.

Collateral. Collateral is like capital in that it consists of property or valuables. Unlike capital, collateral is used as security for a loan. If you fail to pay back a loan, the creditor can take whatever you put up as security, such as a house, car, or boat.

Your Credit Limit

The creditor will take into account all these factors to decide how much you can borrow. The maximum amount you can spend or charge on a credit account is your **credit limit**. If you have a $1,000 credit limit, you won't be able to charge more than that amount. If you pay your bills regularly, the creditor will often increase your credit limit.

Cosigners

If you have no credit history, a poor credit rating, or no collateral, you can still get a credit card or loan by having someone cosign it for you. This person, a **cosigner**, is responsible for a loan if you don't make the payments. A cosigner might be a relative or a close friend who not only knows you, but also knows you can be relied on to pay your debts.

✓ Fast Review

1. What kinds of things can be used as collateral for a loan?
2. What is a credit limit?
3. What is the responsibility of a cosigner?
4. List the five Cs of credit.

Using Credit

Credit cards and charge accounts are convenient ways to make inexpensive purchases. For expensive items, such as cars, furniture, and appliances, many consumers spread out the cost over a period of months or even years by taking out a loan. Loans from banks usually cost less in interest than credit cards or other sources of credit.

LANGUAGE ARTS · Curriculum Connection

Communication. First, allow groups about five minutes to discuss and analyze the scenario in the Cooperative Learning activity, page 420. Have a representative from each group give a brief oral report to summarize the group's answer. (The answer to "What should Reva do?" is that she should make her $50 payments as planned, using the finance company coupons to assure accurate recording of her name, address, account number, and payment and to save finance charges. She can write in the amount she's paying. The finance company has given her the option of stretching her payments over two years instead of one, but will charge $198.08 for this option.) **CL**, **LS**

Installment Loans

If you buy a car or large appliance in an installment plan, you might have to make a down payment. The **down payment** is a portion of the total cost that you pay when you purchase a product. The **principal** is the amount of money you still owe and on which the interest is based. For example, if you buy a used car for $5,000 you might be required to pay $1,000 up front and pay the rest in installments. The $1,000 is the down payment and the remaining $4,000 is the principal.

Cash Loans

Cash loans can be obtained from banks, credit unions, savings and loans, and finance companies. A cash loan can be used to purchase an item anywhere and is paid back like an installment loan. Bank credit cards, such as VISA®, are another source of cash loans. In this case, the payments are billed on a monthly credit card statement. The interest charged for cash loans varies widely. Some people get cash loans from their credit cards because they're unable to get a cash loan from the other sources.

Secured and Unsecured Loans

When you receive an installment loan or a cash loan, you must sign a written agreement to repay the loan within a certain period of time. If the loan is backed by collateral, it's called a **secured loan**. If not, then it's called an **unsecured loan**. Because of the increased risk, the interest charges on an unsecured loan are often higher than on a secured loan.

 Fast Review _____

1. If you make a $500 down payment on furniture that costs $2,000, what is the $1,500 that you still owe called?
2. What is the difference between a secured loan and an unsecured loan?

Paying for Credit

Before you take out a loan or apply for a credit card, you should figure out the costs to see if you can afford it. Different cards have different interest rates. There are also different types of fees and other charges you might not have realized.

ROAD TRIP TO MARFA
Lately you've been doing more chores around the house even before your dad asks you. While this shows responsibility it's not going to convince a credit card company you're worth its risk. You have no credit history and the credit card company needs evidence that you're good on your promise to pay.
What can you do to get that credit card?

continued on p. 425

Real-World Application
Caption Answer

ROAD TRIP TO MARFA: PART 2 OF 4
Find a cosigner.

Fast Review Answers ✔

1. The principal.
2. A secured loan is backed by collateral. An unsecured loan has no collateral.

Great Ideas From the Classroom of...

Cheryl A. Moore
Ellison High School
Killeen, Tex.

Shopping for a Credit Card. Have students go to different banks and obtain five bank credit card applications. Divide the class into groups of four or five students. Look at the type of questions and information required on the application. Next have each group locate the fees required by the company. Have them put this information on graph paper or posterboard and display posters around the room. When all groups are finished, have students go around and look at each poster and determine the three best bankcards.

2 TEACH (Cont.)

Business Connection

According to a survey conducted by Princeton Survey Research Associates, some 40 percent of credit cardholders have no idea how much interest they are paying. There's danger in this ignorance. For example, Tom carried an average balance of $850. With an interest rate of 19 percent, he paid a whopping $161.50 in finance charges! ($850 × 0.19) With an interest rate of 8 percent, the finance charges for the year would have only been $68. ($850 × 0.08)

Develop Concepts

PAYING FOR CREDIT. When you buy things with a credit card or a charge card, you receive a monthly statement detailing the purchases. The statement also details any of your payments that have been posted to the account. You'll want to check your monthly statement against your own records. Why? (To make sure no mistakes have been made and that there is no fraudulent use of your card.)

Figure 26.2 Caption Answer

The periodic rate is 0.05754 percent daily, and the APR is 21.00 percent. There was a charge of $21.24 for this billing cycle.

Annual Percentage Rate

What's the best way to gauge the cost of credit? Look at the **annual percentage rate (APR)**. This percentage rate determines the cost of your credit on a yearly basis. For example, an APR of 18 percent means that for each $100 you owe, you pay $18 per year or $1.50 per month. The amount of interest you pay in a year depends on the interest rate, the total length of the loan, and the amount of the loan.

Finance Charges

According to law, each lender must indicate the APR and the finance charge of a loan. The **finance charge** is the total amount it costs you to finance the loan stated in dollars and cents. It includes the interest and any other charges, such as an application fee. This law was passed so consumers would have a way to compare prices for credit. Figure 26.2 illustrates how these charges might appear on your credit card statement each month.

Figure 26.2 — SAMPLE OF A CREDIT CARD STATEMENT

➡ Credit card statements are required to show certain pieces of information, such as the APR, periodic rate, method of calculating the finance charge, and the finance charge. What is the periodic and annual interest rate on this account? How much interest was charged for this billing cycle?

Credit Is U
America's Credit Card Company

Account Number:	000 000 0
Payment Due Date:	2-19-01
Minimum Payment:	236.08
Total Amount Due:	1,124.17
Amount Enclosed:	_____

Cardmember Name:
Tim Gray
1562 W. Wells Way
Lakeland, FL 33803

Mail Payment to: PO Box 00000000 Newark, DE 19716

Detach and mail this portion with your check or money order to the address above. Do not staple or fold.

Account Number	Billing Date	Payment Due Date	Days in Billing Period
000 00 0	01-25-01	02-19-01	32

Date	Reference Number	Description	Amount
1-14-01	01010101	CD Haven	22.30
1-21-01	02020202	Pizza, Etc.	8.33

Credit Line $7,500   Credit Available: $6,336

Previous Balance	- Payments & Credits	+ Finance Charge	+ Purchases	= New Balance	Minimum Payment
1,072.30	.00	21.24	30.63	1,124.17	236.08

The finance charge is determined by applying a periodic rate of	Which is an ANNUAL PERCENTAGE RATE of	To that part of the balance subject to finance charge of up to	Balance computation methods shown on reverse side
.05754% Daily	21.00%	Entire Balance	Method 2

Purchases, returns, and payments made just prior to billing date may not appear until next month's statement.

Inquiries: Send inquiries (not payment) to: PO Box 222, Denver, CO 80202
Notice: See reverse side for important information.

424

Global Perspective

International Monetary Fund (IMF). The International Monetary Fund (IMF) is an agency of the United Nations that works to help developing countries achieve economic growth, a high level of employment, and an improved standard of living. Have students find articles about recent IMF loans and explain the reason for the loan, the terms of the loan, and what criteria the IMF used in deciding to make the loan. Have students summarize their findings in a paragraph. **CL**, LS

For example, the used car you want costs $5,000. You don't have enough money, so you make a $1,000 down payment and pay the other $4,000 in installments. The installments cost you $160 a month for 36 months. Your total cost on the car comes to $6,760. The extra $1,760 you pay ($6,760–$5,000) is the finance charge, or the amount you pay in interest.

Changes in Interest Rates

It's important to note whether or not the interest rate will change on a credit card or loan. With a **variable rate**, the rate changes as interest rates in the banking system change. For example, banks might change the rate they charge for home loans to adjust for inflation. With a *fixed rate*, the interest rate always remains the same.

You should beware of introductory rates creditors offer. In many cases, a credit card might offer a low introductory rate like 3 percent. After a few months, however, the rate might jump up to 20 percent. If you charged some big items and didn't pay off your card before the rate changed, you're stuck with a much higher interest rate than you expected.

Fees

In some cases, you have to pay an application fee for a card to cover the cost of a credit check. Some companies charge an annual fee to use their card that can range from $20 to $80 or more per year. There is often a separate fee for a cash advance. With a **cash advance** you borrow money on a credit card rather than use it to make a purchase. A late or missed payment fee is charged when you miss a payment or don't make a payment on time. This fee can be a lot and is added to the balance you owe. Fees are charged in addition to interest and added to the total amount interest is calculated on.

Grace Period

The **grace period** is amount of time you get to pay off a debt without having to pay interest charges. If you pay the total amount you owe by the due date, you won't be charged any interest. This is the one case where credit doesn't cost money. Cards also have a grace period for making a late payment before extra interest is charged or the card is cancelled.

 Fast Review

1. Why should you beware of low introductory interest rates?
2. What are some types of fees credit cards charge?

Chapter 26 How to Get and Keep Credit **425**

 **Real-World Application**

part **3** of **4**

ROAD TRIP TO MARFA
After the credit card application process and the company's approval, you're ready to go car shopping with dad. Two test drives and a mechanic's assessment later, you've found your first car. The car costs $4,000. You've got a $3,000 down payment between you and your dad.
When using credit to pay for the balance, what types of fees do you need to remember?

continued on p. 427

Chapter 26

Real-World Application
Caption Answer

ROAD TRIP TO MARFA:
PART 3 OF 4
APR, finance charge, and interest rate.

Discussion Starter

PAYING FOR CREDIT. Give seven 3" by 5" cards to each student and ask them to write the following terms on one side of the card: APR, finance charge, interest rate, variable rate, fees, cash advance, grace period. Ask students to fill in information about each term on the reverse side of the card.

Individualized Practice

As a class, collect credit card information.

L1 Ask students work in pairs to choose one credit card company and answer the following question: What is the interest rate, late payment fee, minimum payment, and advantages offered?

L2 Ask students to work individually and choose two companies, then answer the question in L1 above.

L3 Ask the group to fill in the chart to compare four or five different companies.

Fast Review Answers

1. Jump to a higher rate over time.
2. Application fee, annual fee, cash advance fee, and late or missed payment fee.

Curriculum Connection

Social Science

Trust. The word credit comes from the Latin word *credo*, meaning, "I trust." Banks and other lending institutions trust borrowers to pay them back. Merchants give credit to buyers because they trust that they will be paid back. Ask students to list loans they've received from relatives or friends, and when they repaid them or plan to repay them. Have students evaluate their own creditworthiness by making a chart using the five Cs of credit. Have them evaluate their own capacity and determination to repay a loan. Suggest they assign up to ten points to each item in each category and have students add up their scores. Higher scores indicate a better risk. **LS, CL**

Reteaching

PRINCIPAL AND INTEREST.
To reteach the concept of principal and interest, ask students to calculate the following: Ludmilla put a $795 down payment on a computer system that cost $2,795. What is the principal of the loan? ($2,000.) The interest rate of her loan is 12 percent and the length of the loan is one year. What will Ludmilla's monthly payment be? ($2,000 × 0.12 = $240 + (interest) $2,000 (principal) = $2,240 ÷ 12 months = $186.65.)

Enrichment Strategy

RESEARCH AND PRESENT.
Work in pairs to research information on responsible use of credit. Prepare a three-minute oral presentation. **LS**

Evaluation

Assign and review the Fast Review sections.

You Make the Call

Caption Answer

1. Sophia Rocca.
2. Re-negotiate the loan or obtain a loan from another institution.
3. Due to seasonal work, there's a risk she'll be late with a payment. To avoid the car being repossessed, she might re-negotiate the loan or get a loan from another institution.

Keeping Credit

Someday you might want to get a loan for a major expense, such as a house or a business. You also might want to increase your credit limit or apply for another credit card. To continue using credit or to get new credit, you need to maintain a good credit rating. If you always make your payments on time, you'll probably have an excellent credit rating. If not, your credit rating will be poor. Creditors are happy to extend credit to people with a good rating, but refuse those with a poor rating.

Your Credit Burden

You need to consider how much credit you can afford. Experts in personal finance say that you shouldn't use more than 20 percent of your income for credit payments. Suppose you get your first full-time job for $2,000 a month. After taxes are taken out, you bring home $1,500. You already have two monthly loan payments—$120 for a student loan and $160 for a car payment. You see a new entertainment system you just can't resist and could get it by paying $50 a month over three years. Can you afford it? No. Twenty percent of your income is $300. Your total payments each month would be $330, which is more than 20 percent.

You Make the Call

A Little Garnishment on That?

You're a financial advisor in Springville. One of your clients, Sophia Rocca, has two young children and works at the local ice cream shop. She has a fairly high credit card debt, has bounced several checks, and her work is seasonal. With your help, she is trying to reorganize her finances and start saving money to go to a two-year technical college.

Rocca wants to buy a used car. She brings you a contract for a loan to look over. The used car salesman is also one of your clients. You notice clauses in the contract that indicate if she is late with one repayment of the loan, the lender/car salesman can either repossess the car, demand full payment of the loan, or garnish Rocca's wages. You have faith that Rocca will pay despite her past financial problems.

Making an Ethical Decision

1. Who is your client in this situation?
2. What choices does Rocca have?
3. What advice would you give her? What explanation would you provide for that advice?

How to Use a Portfolio Activity

The portfolio projects are designed to lead students to develop a collection of their best work to submit to you for assessment. You and each of your students should decide which projects to include in their business portfolio. Refer students to the specific rubric(s) from the *Alternative Assessment Strategies*. These rubrics will alert students to the criteria you'll use to assess their projects. **P**

Making the Minimum Payment

Each credit card statement always includes a *minimum payment* you have to make on a bill. For example, if you owe $2,000 on a credit card, you might have to make a minimum payment of $50 each month. Many people think they can get by just making the minimum payment. To pay off a credit card debt of $2,500 at 18.9 percent interest, however, it would take over 30 years if you only make the minimum required payment. The total interest would be more than $7,800. You should always pay more than the minimum payment and pay off a debt as soon as possible.

Overextending Your Credit

One problem that could occur is that once you reach your credit limit on a card, you might be tempted to use another credit card. The more credit cards you have, the more you might be tempted to make impulse purchases. You can quickly reach the credit limit on several cards. If this happens, eventually you can't charge any more on your cards and it becomes a struggle just to make the minimum payments on them each month. Additionally, you wouldn't have credit available for emergencies.

Credit Problems

Do you have trouble making even the minimum monthly payment on your credit card bills? Do you receive second or third payment due notices from creditors? If so, these are two warning signs that you might be in financial trouble. Late payments, missed payments, too much credit, and other problems can give you a bad credit rating. If you want to borrow money to buy a house or a car, you might have a hard time because creditors consider you too much of a risk.

Misusing credit can also lead to more immediate problems. Some credit contracts allow the creditor to take all or part of your paycheck if you miss a payment. This is called **garnishment of wages**. If you put up something valuable as collateral on a loan, such as a car, a creditor has the legal right to **repossess** it, or take back the collateral. The creditor then sells the car to someone else to obtain the money you still owe.

 Fast Review _____

1. What is the highest percentage of your income that personal finance experts say you should spend on credit payments?
2. What is garnishment of wages?

DINER

ROAD TRIP TO MARFA
You and your friends are heading south on Highway 17 to Marfa. The gas gauge points ever closer to empty and you're all hungry. There's not much around in the vast flat landscape, so you decide to stop at this one roadside gas station and diner. You pay for your bill with a credit card. The waitress processes your card and it comes through as rejected.
What are the keys to keeping your credit intact?

Real-World Application
Caption Answer

ROAD TRIP TO MARFA: PART 4 OF 4
Spend less than 20 percent of your income on credit payments, make more than minimum payment, and avoid overextending your credit.

 Technology Resource

GO TO **PUZZLEMAKER CD-ROM.** Check your students' understanding of the chapter's key terms by using the *Puzzlemaker* CD-ROM.

Fast Review Answers

1. Twenty percent of your income.
2. When a creditor takes all or part of your paycheck if you miss a payment.

Meeting Individual Needs

Students With Learning Disabilities. Students with learning disabilities may have trouble with symbols, such as numbers, therefore learning some of the material in this chapter could present challenges. Some students can more easily access the information when it is read aloud, either by a person or on tape. Students who have difficulty communicating effectively through printing or cursive writing may prefer to use a computer to perform calculations or to dictate their work to another person. In general, students with learning disabilities benefit from a classroom that incorporates a wide variety of learning modalities (e.g., visual, auditory, tactile, and kinesthetic).

Picture This...

How a Magnetic Stripe Works

1 FOCUS

A smart card has a microprocessor imbedded it. This enables it to store vast amounts of information and perform a variety of functions. One smart card can be used as a credit card, bank card, phone card, driver's license, and passport, as well as to access your car, computer, and workplace. Smart cards are designed so they can only be used by the cardholder and can't be easily counterfeited. Smart cards are expected to become the internationally accepted standard of identification.

2 TEACH

Explain to students what a smart card is and discuss some of the advantages and disadvantages. Smart cards are more convenient, for example, because they make it unnecessary to carry around several different types of cards. On the other hand, people who lose their smart card or can't get one could have trouble identifying themselves or making transactions. For smart cards to be practical, all computers would have to be equipped with smart card readers, which involves a lot of time and expense.

Did You Know?

Eighty percent of the credit card industry is controlled by ten companies.

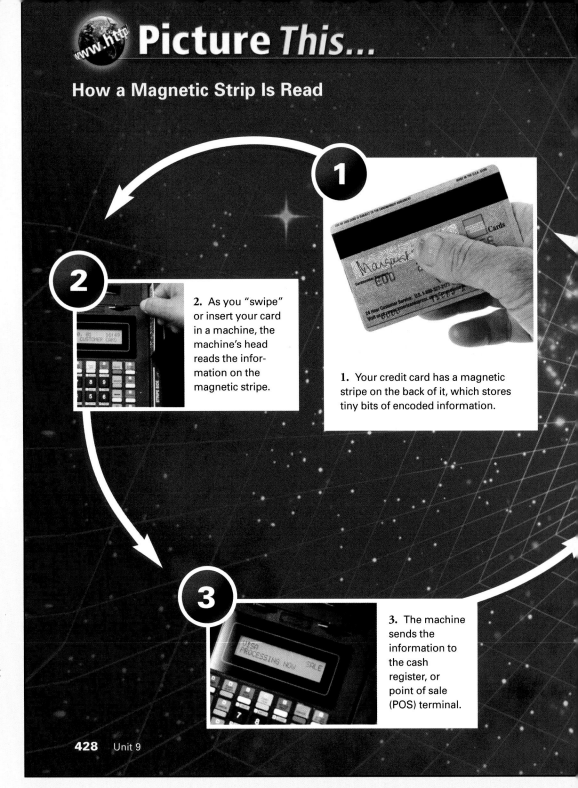

Picture This...

How a Magnetic Strip Is Read

1. Your credit card has a magnetic stripe on the back of it, which stores tiny bits of encoded information.

2. As you "swipe" or insert your card in a machine, the machine's head reads the information on the magnetic stripe.

3. The machine sends the information to the cash register, or point of sale (POS) terminal.

428 Unit 9

Extending the Content

Credit Card Code Numbers. The digits in a credit card number all have a particular meaning. The first two digits indicate what type of card it is, such as American Express or Visa. The next four or five digits identify the bank that issued the card. The next several digits are the actual account number of the cardholder. The last digit is the "check number." The check number is produced by applying a special mathematical formula to the other numbers and is used to check their validity.

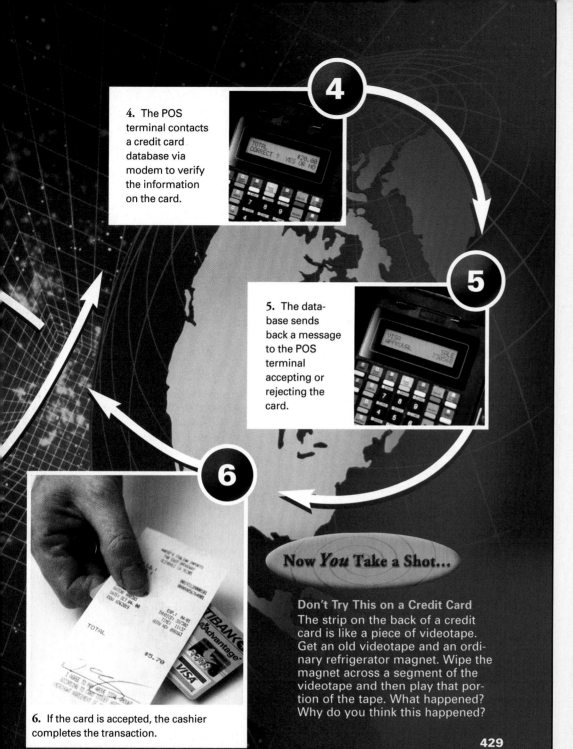

4. The POS terminal contacts a credit card database via modem to verify the information on the card.

5. The database sends back a message to the POS terminal accepting or rejecting the card.

6. If the card is accepted, the cashier completes the transaction.

Now *You* Take a Shot...

Don't Try This on a Credit Card
The strip on the back of a credit card is like a piece of videotape. Get an old videotape and an ordinary refrigerator magnet. Wipe the magnet across a segment of the videotape and then play that portion of the tape. What happened? Why do you think this happened?

429

3 ASSESS

Have students do the experiment and answer the questions in "Now You Take a Shot..."

4 CLOSE

Have students discuss the issues of privacy and security raised by smart cards. Smart cards, for example, can be used to improve security at airports, on the Internet, and in the workplace. On the other hand, there is the threat that someone will learn how to "hack" or counterfeit smart cards and gain much greater access to secure sites or cardholders' information. There is also concern that smart cards can be used by businesses, employers, and the government to track and collect information on ordinary citizens.

? *Did You Know?*

Bankruptcy filings have reached an all-time high in the United States. The leading contributor to the increased filings is credit card debt. According to a financial planner recently quoted by the Federal Deposit Insurance Corporation, "I've never seen anyone come in with a financial problem that wasn't related to credit cards."

Now *You* Take a Shot...   *Caption Answer*

The segment of the videotape that the magnet was rubbed against will be blank. Credit card stripes, videotapes, cassette tapes, and computer disks all store information using magnetized iron-based particles. Rubbing a magnet against the magnetized particles essentially "erases" the information on them.

4 CLOSE

Chapter Wrap-Up

Ask students to complete the following statement: "The three things I learned during this chapter that will be most useful to me are...."

Using Business Key Words

1. secured loan
2. unsecured loan
3. credit bureau
4. annual percentage rate (APR)
5. principal
6. grace period
7. down payment
8. cosigner
9. finance charge
10. variable rate
11. credit limit
12. repossess
13. cash advance
14. garnishment of wages

Review What You Learned

15. Convenient, instant gratification.
16. Plan meets your budget.
17. Good on your promise to repay.
18. To decide how much you can borrow.
19. Because of the increased risk on an unsecured loan.
20. The APR and finance charge.
21. APR, interest rate, annual fees, cash advance fees, and missed payment fees.
22. Requires you to open and maintain a savings account as security. For people with a poor credit history.
23. Average daily balance, adjusted balance, and balance.
24. Misuse of credit cards.

Summary

1. The "five Cs" creditors use to consider a borrower's credit worthiness are capacity to pay, character, credit history, capital, and collateral.

2. The types of credit you can use include installment loans, cash loans, secured loans, and unsecured loans.

3. The costs of credit include an annual percentage rate (APR) and different types of fees. The total cost of credit for a purchase is called the finance charge.

4. To maintain a good credit rating, you should spend less than 20 percent of your income on credit payments, make more than the minimum payment each month, and avoid overextending your credit.

● Using Business Key Words

When establishing and using a credit card, it's important to know the following terms. Match each term to its definition.

- **credit bureau**
- **credit limit**
- **cosigner**
- **down payment**
- **finance charge**
- **principal**
- **annual percentage rate (APR)**
- **secured loan**
- **grace period**
- **unsecured loan**
- **repossess**
- **garnishment of wages**
- **variable rate**
- **cash advance**

1. A loan that is backed by collateral.
2. A loan that is not backed by collateral.
3. An agency that collects information about you and other credit consumers.

4. This determines the cost of your credit on a yearly basis.
5. The amount of money owed and upon which the interest is calculated.
6. The number of days available to pay a credit card balance without having any interest charged.
7. An initial portion of the total cost paid with cash or with a check.
8. Someone who agrees to make payments on a loan if you fail to do so.
9. The cost of credit stated in dollars and cents.
10. A type of loan where the rate changes as interest rates in the banking system change.
11. The maximum amount you can spend or charge on a credit account.
12. The legal right to take back collateral.
13. Something you get when you borrow money on a credit card rather than use it to make a purchase.
14. When a creditor takes all or part of your paycheck if you miss credit card payments.

Quick Quiz

1. What five factors do creditors consider when determining whether to extend credit? (Capacity to pay, character, credit history, capital, collateral.)
2. What is a finance charge? (The total amount it costs you to finance the loan stated in dollars and cents.)

3. Name two actions a creditor could take if a borrower failed to make payments on a loan. (A creditor could repossess the item purchased on credit or could garnish the debtor's wages.)

Review What You Learned

15. How can credit make your life easier?
16. Why is it important to comparison shop when you enter the credit market?
17. Why do creditors look at the amount of collateral you have before deciding whether or not to loan you money?
18. What do creditors use your credit rating for when deciding whether or not to loan you money?
19. Why is the interest rate charged on an unsecured loan often higher than that charged on a secured loan?
20. What does the law require a lender to provide to a consumer when he or she is considering borrowing money?
21. What should you consider when looking at the cost of a credit card?
22. What is a secured credit loan? Who are they marketed to?
23. Explain the three ways finance charges are calculated on unpaid credit card balances.
24. What is one of the primary causes of debt problems?

Understanding Business Concepts

25. When a person uses credit, is he or she really borrowing money? Explain your answer.
26. "The real benefit of credit cards comes when a consumer pays his or her bill in full each month." What does this mean?
27. Would you be willing to cosign on a loan for your best friend? Why or why not?
28. What is the best way for consumers to compare interest rates?
29. Why is making the minimum payment on credit card bills a bad idea?

Critical Thinking

30. Survey a number of adults on their opinions about buying expensive items. Do they favor using credit for such purchases? For what types of items would they pay cash only? Write a summary of your survey.
31. What criteria would you use in choosing a credit card?
32. Do you agree that you should always pay off a debt as soon as possible? Why or why not?

Viewing and Representing

Examining the Image. Make a list of everything you see in this photograph. Describe what you think is happening in this picture. Has anyone ever asked you for a loan? What factors made you decide to say yes or no? If you loaned money, how and when would you expect the person to repay the loan?

Critical Thinking

30. Summaries will vary depending on the adults surveyed.
31. Answers will vary and may include considering the cost of credit, and considering where the card is accepted.
32. Answers will vary and may be yes, to cut down the high cost of finance charges.

Viewing and Representing

This activity promotes students' powers of observation, description, interpretation, and critical thinking. After students have made their lists, have volunteers give their interpretation of what is happening in the picture. At this time, remind students to respect each other's viewpoints. This is also a time to listen to all volunteers' thoughts without evaluation, judgment, or asking for supporting reasoning. Any evaluation will stop the flow of creative thought. After all volunteers have spoken, have students respond to the remaining Viewing and Representing questions in their journal.
LS, P, CL

Understanding Business Concepts

25. Yes. A person is really borrowing money when using credit. The money is to buy the goods or services and must be repaid.
26. If the bill is paid in full each month, the user pays no finance charge. The user gets to use someone else's money for a period of time, often 30 days, with no additional charge.
27. Answers will vary.
28. Consumers should compare the APR of various forms of credit.
29. Very little is being paid on the principal and added interest; most goes to the interest payment.

4 CLOSE (Cont.)

Building Academic Skills

LANGUAGE ARTS. Make sure all students participate in this group project. Rubrics: Charts/tables, paragraph.

MATH. Tables will vary depending on the credit card applications selected. Rubrics: Charts/tables, paragraph.

COMPUTER TECHNOLOGY. Make sure the students use the computer formulas for their spreadsheet. Rubric: Chart.

HISTORY. Presentations will vary. Rubric: Oral presentation.

Linking School to Home

Answers will vary. Rubric: Business letter.

Linking School to Work

The local library or consumer credit counseling agency are good sources of information. Rubric: Essay.

Building Academic Skills

 Investigating Credit

As a group, choose a high-priced item such as a used car, a sound system, or a computer system that would probably be purchased on credit. Each team member should investigate the terms of credit from a different credit source, such as commercial banks, credit unions, or savings and loans. Consider these questions:
- Is credit available from the seller?
- Is a down payment required?
- What is the annual percentage rate?
- What would the monthly payments be?

Make a chart of the information that you and your team have gathered. Use the chart to decide which source offers the best credit terms. Write a paragraph describing your group's decision.

 Determining Finance Charges

Select two different credit card applications in local stores or banks. Check their monthly finance charges and their annual percentage rates. Using the information from each of the applications, determine for each of the cards how long it would take to pay off $700 if you made a $75 payment each month. What would you pay in finance charges for each of the cards? Create a table to compare the numbers and write a short paragraph explaining which card you would choose and why.

 Creating a Spreadsheet

Many installment loans require a percentage of the total price as a down payment. Use spreadsheet software to set up a spreadsheet to compute the down payment for each of the items in the table below.

Item	Price	Required Down Payment	Amount of Down Payment
CD Player	$ 295	10%	$
Color TV	298	10%	
Electric Stove	489	20%	
Desk and Chair	263	15%	
Used Car	5,495	25%	
Sofa	995	17%	

HISTORY Oral Presentation

Research the history of consumer credit in the United States. Find out when and why it started. Then, give an oral presentation with at least one visual aid.

Linking School to Home

Composing a Letter. Imagine a family member or a friend received his or her credit card statement and it contained an error. Help write a letter to the credit card company requesting a correction. Compose the letter using a word processor.

Linking School to Work

Write About a Credit Counselor. Research the career of a credit counselor. Find out what the job entails, the skills the counselor should have, what education is required, and the salary range for an entry-level counselor. Investigate the certification offered by the National Foundation for Consumer Credit. Write a one-page paper with your findings.

E-Homework

Applying Technology

Multimedia Presentation. Unfortunately, a majority of young people are in debt. There are plenty of professionals out there with books and advice on debt management. Use the Internet to research information about debt or debt management. Create a computerized presentation of your findings.

Searching for Consumer Credit. Use the Internet to locate Web sites that provide consumer credit information. Select five sites you think are the best and explain why.

Connecting Academics

Math. The safe debt load—the debt a person can take on after accounting for all necessary expenses—is often estimated by subtracting total expenses from after-tax income and dividing the difference by three. Devon's annual take-home pay is $23,980. This year he estimates $4,800 for housing, $4,900 for food, $1,280 for transportation, and $950 for clothes. What is Devon's safe debt load?

Math. Imagine you've charged a lot on your credit cards. You're earning a good salary and you feel it's up to you to become more financially responsible. What is your plan of action to become debt free?

Social Science. Many items can be bought with cash, with installment payments, or with a credit card. Decide what you think is the best way to purchase each of the following items: a swimming pool, a bag of groceries, a car, a pair of shoes, a refrigerator, books for school, a sofa and chair, and a CD player. Give reasons for each option that you choose.

BusinessWeek — Analyzing the Feature Story

You read the first part of "Majoring in Debt" at the beginning of this chapter. Below are a few questions for you to answer about credit cards. You'll find the answers to these questions when you're reading the entire article. First, here are the questions:

33. Why are consumer advocates concerned about college kids having and using credit cards?
34. What is one common trick that credit card companies use?

CREATIVE JOURNAL ACTIVITY

Visit the financial center of the *BusinessWeek* Web site. Explore different credit card types, and compare the features of each. Interview an adult to learn more about what credit card he or she uses and why.

BUSINESS Online
The Full Story

To learn more about credit cards, visit the *Introduction to Business* Web site at **www.introbus.glencoe.com**, and click on *BusinessWeek* Feature Story, Chapter 26.

E-Homework

MULTIMEDIA PRESENTATION. Presentations will vary. If students struggle with the technology, allow other students to help. Rubric: Computerized presentation.

SEARCHING FOR CONSUMER CREDIT. Web sites will vary. Allow the students to choose the way they would like to present their findings. Rubrics: Lists, paragraphs, oral presentation, posters.

Connecting Academics

MATH. $4,800 + $4,900 + $1,280 + $950 = $11,930. $23,980 − $11,930 = $12,050 ÷ 3 = $4,016.

MATH. Answers will vary and may include stop using credit cards and talk with a credit counselor.

SOCIAL SCIENCE. Answers will vary depending on the students' values. Generally however, the most expensive items are most likely to be purchased on credit.

BusinessWeek — Analyzing the Feature Story

33. Consumer advocates worry that kids will misuse credit because they lack the financial knowledge to use cards sensibly.
34. Cards often advertise low interest rates that only last a few months. Then the rates shoot up to around 20 percent.

Creative Journal Activity

Create a chart to summarize your comparisons. Make a visual aid to show the results of your interview. Use these visual aids in a short oral presentation to your class. **LS**, **CL**, **P**

SCANS Correlation Chart*

Foundation Skills

Basic Skills	Reading	Writing	Math	Listening	Speaking	
Thinking Skills	Creative Thinking	Decision Making	Problem Solving	Seeing Things in the Mind's Eye	Knowing How to Learn	Reasoning
Personal Qualities	Responsibility	Self-Esteem	Sociability	Self-Management	Integrity/ Honesty	

Workplace Competencies

Resources	Allocating Time	Allocating Money	Allocating Material and Facility Resources	Allocating Human Resources		
Information	Acquiring and Evaluating Information	Organizing and Maintaining Information	Interpreting and Communicating Information	Using Computers to Process Information		
Interpersonal Skills	Participating as a Member of a Team	Teaching Others	Serving Clients/ Customers	Exercising Leadership	Negotiating to Arrive at a Decision	Working With Cultural Diversity
Systems	Understanding Systems	Monitoring and Correcting Performance	Improving and Designing Systems			
Technology	Selecting Technology	Applying Technology to Task	Maintaining and Troubleshooting Technology			

*This chart's highlighted blocks indicate the chapter's content coverage in the Student Edition and the Teacher Wraparound Edition.

Resource Manager

Teaching Transparencies

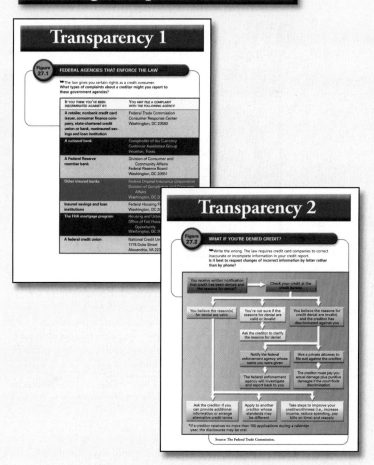

Application and Enrichment

- 🖉 Lesson Plans
- 📖 *BusinessWeek* Poster Package
- 🕹 Teaching Transparencies
- ◉ 🖉 Integrated Software Simulation
- 📼 🖉 Glencoe Business Video Package

Review and Reinforcement

- ◉ *PuzzleMaker*
- 🖥 🖉 Internet Resources
- 🖉 Student Activity Workbook
- 🖉 Strat. and Work. for Teaching Transparencies

Assessment and Evaluation

- 🖉 Reproducible Tests
- 🖉 Alternative Assessment Strategies
- ◉ ExamView® Pro Test Generator

Technology

- ◉ *PuzzleMaker*
- ◉ ExamView® Pro Test Generator
- 📼 Glencoe Business Video Package
- ◉ PowerPoint® Presentation
- ◉ 🖉 Integrated Software Simulation
- ◉ Interactive Lesson Planner
- ◉ *Virtual Business®*

KEY	🖉 Printed	💾 Software	📼 Videocassette	📖 Poster
	🕹 Transparency	◉ CD-ROM	🖥 Internet	

Visit www.introbus.glencoe.com, the Web site companion to *Introduction to Business.* The student's page includes:

- interactive tutor
- additional *BusinessWeek* articles and activities
- business Web links
- homework hints
- real-world application activities
- additional career path activities

Information on how to prepare your students for the high school exit exam and special projects are also included.

Use the Glencoe Web site for additional resources. All essential content is covered in the Student Edition.

1 FOCUS

Introducing the Chapter

This chapter describes your credit rights protection and explains how to handle credit problems. A photo essay, "Identity Crisis: Protect Yourself," enhances the concepts.

Connecting the Objectives

What protection do consumers have when using credit? What can you do if you have credit problems?

BusinessWeek
Feature Story

Story's Summary

New entrepreneurs are using credit cards more than ever for financing. A national survey showed that the percentage of small-business owners using credit cards to finance their business all but doubled in two years. According to the American Bankruptcy Institute, more than 1.4 million consumers and businesses filed bankruptcy in one year alone, so there's reason for concern.

Find the entire article at www.introbus.glencoe.com, or in the Teacher Resource Binder.

Chapter 27

Your Credit and the Law

Learning Objectives

After completing this chapter, you'll be able to:
1. **Explain** how government protects credit rights.
2. **Name** federal laws that protect consumers.
3. **Identify** consumers' credit rights.
4. **Describe** credit problems.

Why It's Important

To maintain a good credit rating you have specific rights and protections under the law.

Key Words

usury law
Consumer Credit
    Protection Act
truth-in-lending disclosure
Equal Credit Opportunity Act
Fair Credit Reporting Act
Fair Credit Billing Act
collection agent
Fair Debt Collection
    Practices Act (FDCPA)
credit counselor
consolidation loan
bankruptcy

434

BusinessWeek Feature Story

Credit Cards: Entrepreneurs Are Tapping Them More Than Ever

Small Businesses to Qualify for Credit. When Paul Baum started his computer hardware company in 1991, he did what new entrepreneurs have long done: He whipped out his credit cards for instant financing.

Seven years later, he's still plunking down plastic—4 cards now, down from a high of 15, with credit lines totaling more than $2 million. Says Baum, CEO of Rumarson Technologies Inc. in Kenilworth, N.J.: "I've never had a bank loan." He has a $1.8 million bank credit line, which charges ¼-percentage point over the prime rate the moment he taps it. Still, he prefers his cards because by paying the balance every month, the financing is free.

Source: Excerpted with permission from "Credit Cards: Entrepreneurs Are Tapping Them More Than Ever," *BusinessWeek Online*, December 14, 1998.

An Extension Activity

What concerns might you have in using credit as opposed to cash? Create a table with the pros and cons of using credit.

BUSINESS Online
The Full Story

To learn more about the use of credit cards, visit the *Introduction to Business* Web site at www.introbus.glencoe.com, and click on *BusinessWeek* Feature Story, Chapter 27.

Classroom Resources

For the Teacher
📁 Student Activity Work. TAE
📓💿   Assessment Binder
💿 PowerPoint® Presentation
💿 Interactive Lesson Planner
📁 Lesson Plans
📓💻   Internet Resources
🔦 Teaching Transparencies
💻 *Introduction to Business* Web Site

💿 Integrated Soft. Sim. TM
📋 *BusinessWeek* Poster Package
For the Student
📓 Student Activity Workbook
💿 *Virtual Business*®
💻 *Introduction to Business* Web Site
💿 Integrated Soft. Sim.
💿 *PuzzleMaker*
📓 Strategies and Worksheets for Teaching Transparencies

Bell Ringer Activity

USING COMPUTERS TO PROCESS INFORMATION. Imagine you work for a credit counseling agency. There are four parts to your job. You research information about credit, provide information to clients, help clients budget, and help clients find other sources of income. List how you might use a computer for each part of your job. **LS**

Preteaching Business Key Words

RESPONSIBILITY. Part of taking responsibility on-the-job is paying attention to detail and concentrating on completing a task. To practice taking responsibility in this chapter, here's your task: First, select the five acts relating to credit and write the definition for each act on a separate page. Second, write each of the remaining key words and their definitions on a separate page. **LS**

An Extension Activity

DISCUSS. Discuss the pros and cons of small businesses using credit.

Making Connections

Everyday Life. Give students the following scenario: A few years ago, Ralph Weiss withheld a portion of his rent because his landlord refused to make necessary repairs to his apartment. Last month Ralph was denied a loan. He checked his credit report and found a statement saying he hadn't paid his rent. According to the landlord-tenant laws in Ralph's city, withholding rent was the correct action to take in his situation.

Have students draft a letter explaining Ralph's side of the issue. Students may use their imaginations to fill in reasonable details. **LS, P**

2 TEACH

Business Connection

Congress passed a revision to the Fair Credit Reporting Act in 1994. The revision made it easier for consumers to correct errors in their credit reports. The revision was necessary because consumer advocates found that 61 percent of the people denied credit, jobs, or housing were turned down because of errors in their credit reports.

Develop Concepts

CREDIT RIGHTS. Ask students if they think that laws alone will ensure that a person's credit rights aren't abused. (No. Lending institutions and other creditors might not follow the laws. It's also up to consumers to know their rights and take the proper action to make sure they are treated fairly.)

Figure 27.1 Caption Answer

Answers will vary but should reflect an understanding of consumer credit laws.

Continuing Your Creditworthiness

If you have more than one credit card, it's important not to accumulate more debt after you pay off your cards. It's not advisable to have more than one credit card open with no balance. Before you get into trouble you may want to close the accounts.

While credit is widely used, relying on credit has created certain problems. Billing mistakes, unfair credit charges, and misleading claims are just a few problems that consumers face. The government has passed laws to protect consumers from credit abuses. See Figure 27.1 to see where consumers can go if they have a complaint.

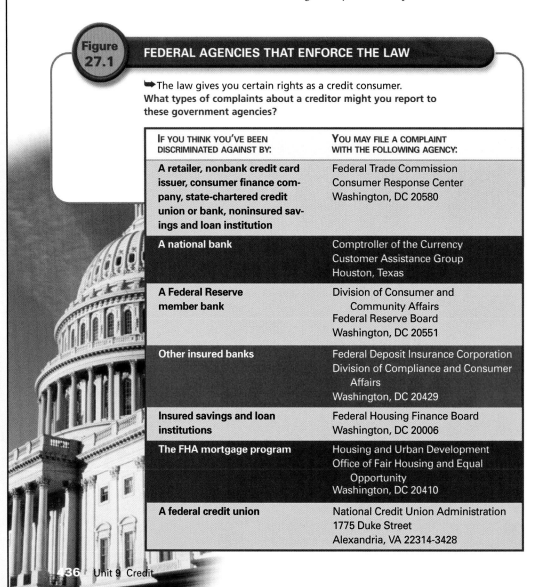

Figure 27.1

FEDERAL AGENCIES THAT ENFORCE THE LAW

➡ The law gives you certain rights as a credit consumer. What types of complaints about a creditor might you report to these government agencies?

IF YOU THINK YOU'VE BEEN DISCRIMINATED AGAINST BY:	YOU MAY FILE A COMPLAINT WITH THE FOLLOWING AGENCY:
A retailer, nonbank credit card issuer, consumer finance company, state-chartered credit union or bank, noninsured savings and loan institution	Federal Trade Commission Consumer Response Center Washington, DC 20580
A national bank	Comptroller of the Currency Customer Assistance Group Houston, Texas
A Federal Reserve member bank	Division of Consumer and Community Affairs Federal Reserve Board Washington, DC 20551
Other insured banks	Federal Deposit Insurance Corporation Division of Compliance and Consumer Affairs Washington, DC 20429
Insured savings and loan institutions	Federal Housing Finance Board Washington, DC 20006
The FHA mortgage program	Housing and Urban Development Office of Fair Housing and Equal Opportunity Washington, DC 20410
A federal credit union	National Credit Union Administration 1775 Duke Street Alexandria, VA 22314-3428

436 Unit 9 Credit

Cooperative Learning

"Team Teaching." Have students do this activity part way through this chapter, or at the end of the chapter. Divide the class into teams and have individual members each write a note explaining what they understand about the chapter so far. They should also write a question about a concept that is not clear to them. Team members should trade notes with each other and write answers to other team members' questions. **CL**, LS

Protecting Your Credit Rights

To protect consumers, both the federal and state governments control and regulate the credit industry. Most states, for example, have set a maximum on the interest rates that may be charged for certain types of credit. A law restricting the amount of interest that can be charged for credit is called a **usury law**.

Concern about consumer problems has also resulted in the passage of a series of federal laws. Among other things, these laws help inform consumers about the costs of credit. They also set rules and regulations concerning the credit application process, credit history information, privacy, and debt collection.

Consumer Credit Protection Act

At one time, consumers who bought with credit didn't know how much the credit would cost. To make comparing credit costs easier, Congress passed the **Consumer Credit Protection Act**, also known as the Truth in Lending Law. It requires creditors to inform consumers about the costs and terms of credit and it protects consumers if their credit cards are lost or stolen.

Truth-in-Lending Disclosure. The most important part of the Consumer Credit Protection Act is the requirement that all costs of borrowing be made known to the consumer. **Truth-in-lending disclosure** provides the costs that a creditor gives to a borrower. Costs must be expressed in two ways. One is the dollar cost of credit, or the total finance charge. The other is the annual percentage rate (APR). A truth-in-lending disclosure shows the total finance charge so the borrower can determine whether buying on credit is worth the extra cost.

In addition, the disclosure shows the APR so the borrower can compare it with interest rates at various banks, credit unions, and finance companies. The truth-in-lending disclosure also states the credit terms and conditions. For instance, what happens if a payment is late? Is the finance charge reduced if the loan is paid off earlier than agreed? If so, how much is the finance charged reduced? Is there a penalty for paying off the loan ahead of time?

Advertising Credit. Another important condition in the Truth in Lending Law involves the advertising of credit. An advertisement must

Real-World Application
part 1 of 4

IDENTITY CRISIS: PROTECT YOURSELF
Experts say that nearly half-a-million people are victims of identity theft each year. Identity theft is the fastest growing type of robbery. Thieves steal your identity and then they start opening credit cards and charging away. Federal law limits consumer liability to $50 for credit card fraud. **How might this affect your credit history?**

continued on p. 439

Chapter 27

Real-World Application
Caption Answer

IDENTITY CRISIS: PROTECT YOURSELF: PART 1 OF 4

Could potentially ruin it; important to take exhaustive measures to clear your charges.

Technology Resource

POWERPOINT. The *Introduction to Business* PowerPoint® CD-ROM provides visual lecture aids for this chapter.

Independent Practice

COLLECT. Ask students to collect newspaper ads or direct-mail offers that demonstrate compliance with the Truth in Lending Law. This law is a part of which act? (Consumer Credit Protection Act. Encourage discussion of costs of borrowing disclosed in the ads.) **LS**

Meeting Individual Needs

Second Language Learners. Students with limited proficiency in English may have trouble distinguishing among the different federal acts. Have them write the name of the act, write the acronym, and copy the main points of each act onto different colored paper to "color code" the information. They will then be able to associate the different colors with the information for different acts. **ELL**, **LS**

2 TEACH (Cont.)

Thinking Critically

ADVISING. While you're spending time at a friend's house, you overhear a conversation. Your friend's older brother is on the phone with his credit card company explaining a problem with his bill. You're concerned. You know that to get the protection of the Fair Credit Billing Act, you must notify the credit card company in writing within 60 days of receiving the bill. A phone call will not give you protection under the law. Also, you know to always keep a copy of the letter. You want to make sure your friend's brother knows all this but at the same time be tactful. What do you say? (Answers will vary.)

Consider This...

Caption Answer

Competitive pressures increase the technology market volatility.

Consider This...

Financial Flexibility

Corporations also get credit ratings. Standard & Poor's assigns ratings to corporations based on several factors. A company's market position and how much it will grow in the near future are considerations. The financial situation of a corporation is also important. Finally, Standard & Poor's considers the risk associated with the company's industry. Technology, for example, has a high degree of risk.

ANALYZE

Why do you think technology companies are considered risky corporations?

---

tell the number of payments, the amount, and the period of payments if the amount of the down payment is given. In other words, if an advertisement offers credit at $10 down and $2 a week payment, the number of weeks must also be given.

Protecting Card Owners. Finally, the Truth in Lending Law protects credit card customers. If your card is lost or stolen and is used by someone else, your payment for any unauthorized purchases is limited to $50. Some credit card companies don't make you pay the $50 if you report the loss immediately. Also, credit card companies aren't allowed to send cards to consumers who didn't request a credit card.

Equal Credit Opportunity Act

When you apply for a loan or a credit card, you must provide certain information. This information is used to determine whether you're a good credit risk. The **Equal Credit Opportunity Act** says that the application can be judged only on the basis of financial responsibility. No person can be denied credit on the basis of gender, age, ethnicity, or religion. It allows only three reasons for denying credit: (1) low income, (2) large current debts, and (3) a poor record of making payments in the past.

The Equal Credit Opportunity Act also requires that all credit applicants be informed of whether their application has been accepted or rejected within 30 days. Any person who is denied credit must be given a written statement listing the reasons why.

Fair Credit Reporting Act

When you apply for and use credit, the information goes into a file at one or more credit bureaus. As you learned in Chapter 26, a credit bureau is an agency that collects and maintains information about the paying habits of consumers. Figure 27.2 on page 440 provides a checklist for building and protecting your credit history. Lenders rely heavily on credit reports when they consider loan applications.

A credit file includes personal, employment, and financial information. In the past, there was concern about the accuracy of credit file information. Inaccurate or false information was often included in a file. For these and other reasons, the **Fair Credit Reporting Act** was passed.

Right to Know. The Fair Credit Reporting Act gives you the right to know what's in your credit file. If incorrect information is found, it must be removed from your file after the situation is examined. If there's disagreement between you and the business that made the statement, you have the right to have your version of the situation placed in your file.

HISTORY — Curriculum Connection

Usury Law. In Europe there were no real laws about charging interest on loans until the 1500s. Up until that time, most people thought that interest should not be charged. In 1545, King Henry VIII of England passed laws that allowed some forms of interest. The laws also set a maximum rate for the amount of interest—the first usury law. Ask students: What is the reason that interest is charged on loans?

For example, suppose you stopped payments on a stereo system because you believed it was defective and you informed the store of your concerns. The store where you bought the system might report that you missed a payment. Both your version and the store's version must be included in your credit file if no agreement is reached.

Right to Be Notified. The Fair Credit Reporting Act also states that you must be notified when an investigation is being conducted on your credit record. If you're denied credit, insurance, or a job because of a credit report, you must be given the name and address of the credit bureau that provided the report.

Right to Privacy. The privacy of the information in your credit file is important. According to the law, only authorized persons can see a copy of your credit report. People can legally obtain your credit report when you apply for additional credit, a job, or insurance.

Fair Credit Billing Act

Every month millions of credit card and charge account customers receive their monthly statements. Most of the time these bills are correct, but sometimes a billing error can occur. An error might be due to a computer problem. There might be an incorrect amount for a charge. The **Fair Credit Billing Act** requires creditors to correct billing mistakes brought to their attention. The law also requires that consumers be informed of the steps they need to take to get an error corrected.

Notify the Creditor. The first step in correcting errors is to notify the creditor in writing. In the letter, you must give your name, account number, an explanation of the error, and the amount of the error. The creditor must either correct the error or explain in writing why the account is correct. If the creditor made the mistake, you don't have to pay any finance charge on the amount in error. If there was no error, you might have to pay a fee for any late payments.

Stop Payment. The Fair Credit Billing Act permits consumers to stop a credit card payment for items that are damaged or defective. Before stopping payment, however, you must attempt to return the item to the place where you bought it. A creditor that fails to follow the rules that apply to correcting any billing errors will automatically give up the amount owed on the item in question and any finance charge on it, up to a combined total of $50. This is true even if the bill is correct.

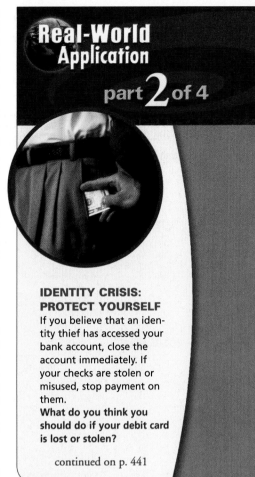

Real-World Application
part 2 of 4

IDENTITY CRISIS: PROTECT YOURSELF
If you believe that an identity thief has accessed your bank account, close the account immediately. If your checks are stolen or misused, stop payment on them.
What do you think you should do if your debit card is lost or stolen?

continued on p. 441

Chapter 27

Real-World Application
Caption Answer

IDENTITY CRISIS: PROTECT YOURSELF: PART 2 OF 4
Cancel it and get another with a new Personal Identification Number (PIN).

Business Connection

If you ever need a credit counselor, keep in mind that counselors should not charge more than 12 percent of your debt as a fee. You might want to check out one of the nonprofit credit counseling agencies. For a list of agencies in the United States, look at the National Foundation for Consumer Credit Web site at **www.nfcc.org**.

Develop Concepts

OPTIONS. What options are available for someone who has gone too far in using credit? (Answers may include credit counseling, consolidating debts, bankruptcy, and credit services.)

Chapter 27 Your Credit and the Law **439**

Great Ideas From the Classroom of...

Therese Velasquez
Patrick Henry High School
San Diego, Calif.

Note Taking. Divide your paper into two sides, with the right side wider than the left. On the top of the left side, write "Thoughts, Cues, or Topics." On the top of the right side write, "Notes From Book/Lecture." Fill in the right side using the text or discussion. Line up notes with the topics on the left side. When you're taking notes from a textbook, use bold titles or subtitles as the cues of important information. Use the topics on the left to guide you, and you can write down reflective questions or comments on the left side that pertain to the notes.

Discussion Starter

CONSOLIDATE. What does consolidate mean? Where have you heard the words consolidate, consolidation, or consolidating used? (To join together. Answers will vary and may include construction sites, political debate, corporate businesses, loans, and so on.)

Figure 27.2 Caption Answer

A letter provides written documentation of your request. Moreover, it's impossible to verify supporting documents related to your claim over the phone.

Fair Debt Collection Practices Act

A **collection agent** is a person or business that has the job of collecting overdue bills. This agent might contact consumers who get behind in their credit payments. At one time, collection agents could use almost any method they chose to collect overdue bills. They could call

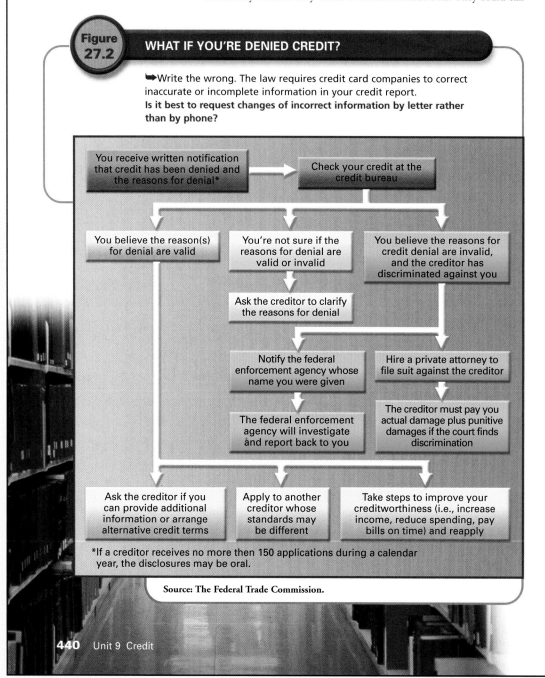

Figure 27.2

WHAT IF YOU'RE DENIED CREDIT?

➡ Write the wrong. The law requires credit card companies to correct inaccurate or incomplete information in your credit report.

Is it best to request changes of incorrect information by letter rather than by phone?

You receive written notification that credit has been denied and the reasons for denial* → Check your credit at the credit bureau

You believe the reason(s) for denial are valid

You're not sure if the reasons for denial are valid or invalid

You believe the reasons for credit denial are invalid, and the creditor has discriminated against you

Ask the creditor to clarify the reasons for denial

Notify the federal enforcement agency whose name you were given

Hire a private attorney to file suit against the creditor

The federal enforcement agency will investigate and report back to you

The creditor must pay you actual damage plus punitive damages if the court finds discrimination

Ask the creditor if you can provide additional information or arrange alternative credit terms

Apply to another creditor whose standards may be different

Take steps to improve your creditworthiness (i.e., increase income, reduce spending, pay bills on time) and reapply

*If a creditor receives no more then 150 applications during a calendar year, the disclosures may be oral.

Source: The Federal Trade Commission.

Global Perspective

World Bank. Many developing nations borrow money for economic development from the World Bank and the International Monetary Fund (IMF). Sometimes, for a variety of reasons (war, economic instability, natural disaster, other debt), a country falls behind in payments or is unable to pay the loan back in time. Have students find out what measures the World Bank and the IMF take when a country has trouble repaying a loan. Suggest that students find specific examples and explain the reason the country had trouble repaying its loan and the action taken by the lending agency.

late at night, use threats of jail or seizing property, and even try to collect more than was owed. They could show up at your workplace and harass you for the money. The **Fair Debt Collection Practices Act (FDCPA)** made all of these practices illegal.

The FDCPA protects consumers from collection agents in several ways. First, collection agents must identify themselves to the people whose bills they're trying to collect. They can't tell others about the debt. This is considered a violation of privacy and is forbidden by the law. They can't contact a person at work if the employer doesn't permit it. If they use the phone, they can't keep calling all the time or pretend to be someone else. Finally, they can't state the amount of a debt on a postcard that a neighbor or someone else might see.

Enforcing the Laws

The federal government has established numerous agencies to regulate business activities. One agency is the *Federal Trade Commission (FTC)*. In addition to protecting competition, the FTC is responsible for enforcing the laws on credit. The FTC also helps consumers with credit problems. It handles complaints about being denied credit unfairly, being overcharged on a bill, or being bothered by collection agents. Several other federal government agencies deal with specific credit matters.

On the state level, you can contact your state banking department about credit problems. A consumer protection division of your state attorney general's office deals with complaints that other government agencies might not handle. Many city and local governments also have consumer credit protection agencies.

 Fast Review _____

1. What does the usury law do?
2. In what two ways must the costs of credit be expressed in a truth-in-lending disclosure?
3. What are the only three reasons a person can be denied credit according to the Equal Credit Opportunity Act?
4. Name the three rights the Fair Credit Reporting Act guarantees.
5. What does the Fair Debt Collection Practices Act prevent collection agents from doing?

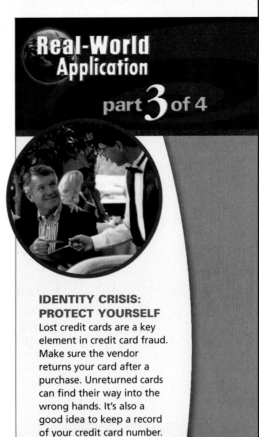

Real-World Application

part **3** of 4

IDENTITY CRISIS: PROTECT YOURSELF
Lost credit cards are a key element in credit card fraud. Make sure the vendor returns your card after a purchase. Unreturned cards can find their way into the wrong hands. It's also a good idea to keep a record of your credit card number. You should keep this record separate from your card. **If someone does steal your credit card, by federal law, how much are you responsible to pay?**

continued on p. 443

Real-World Application
Caption Answer

IDENTITY CRISIS: PROTECT YOURSELF: PART 3 OF 4
Fifty dollars.

Individualized Practice

Invite a credit counselor to speak to the class. Ask the counselor to provide students with methods of staying out of credit trouble.

L1 Ask students to work in pairs to discuss the points made by the speaker.

L2 Ask students to take notes during the presentation then discuss the presentation.

L3 After the presentation, form students into groups. Have half of the groups prepare a skit about how people get into credit trouble.

Fast Review Answers

1. Restricts interest charged.
2. The dollar cost and APR.
3. Low income, debts, and late payments.
4. Your credit file, notification if your credit is investigated, and privacy.
5. Divulging a person's debt, contacting a person at work, calling on the phone repeatedly, and stating a debt on a postcard.

HISTORY **Curriculum Connection**

Equal Credit Opportunity Act. Tell students that the Equal Credit Opportunity Act was passed in 1974. Have groups of students research the origins of the act and find out why such a law became necessary. Have them report their findings to the class.

Encourage creativity in their method of presentation—since this is an investigation the presentation could be made in the form of a detective-style theme, a trial theme, or a western-style theme, and so on. **CL**, **LS**

3 ASSESS

Reteaching

LAWS PROTECTING CREDIT RIGHTS. To reteach credit and the law, refer students to this chapter's Preteaching Key Words. Write a summary of each act. (Encourage thoroughness.) **LS**

Enrichment Strategy

IDENTIFY. Ask students what law offers protection in each situation: **LS**

- A debt collector calls you several times a day. (Fair Debt Collection Practices Act.)
- Discover a mistake on your credit card bill. (Fair Credit Billing Act.)
- Refused a loan but given no reason. (Equal Credit Opportunity Act.)
- Interest on your loan is not what you were told. (Consumer Credit Protection Act, also called Truth in Lending Law.)
- Credit report has incorrect information. (Fair Credit Reporting Act.)

Caption Answer

1. Yes.
2. Collection agents must identify themselves, not tell others about the debt, seal mailed notices, not contact a person at work, and allow reasonable time period between calls.
3. No. The law requires the company to use live callers during the daytime.

Handling Your Credit Problems

What can you do when you have a credit problem or when you've gone too far in your use of credit? Of course, it's best to avoid a credit problem in the first place. If you're already in trouble, however, there are ways to deal with your problem.

Credit Counseling

If you can't meet your payments, the first thing you should do is contact the creditor. Talk to the credit manager and try to work out a plan that will make your payments easier. Consumers who are unable to work out their own credit problems or who repeatedly have problems with credit should talk to a **credit counselor**. Credit counselors help consumers with their credit problems. They can help you revise your budget, contact creditors to arrange new payment plans, or help you find other sources of income.

Consolidating Debts

Another possible solution is to get a consolidation loan. A **consolidation loan** combines all your debts into one loan with lower payments. For example, suppose you have to make monthly payments on several credit cards, student loans, and a car. You can consolidate all your debts into one monthly payment. There are two problems with a consolidation loan, however. First, it usually has a high interest rate because people

 **Collection Protection**

A year ago, you launched a very successful catalog sales business that offers specialty children's clothing, Bubble Bee Knees. It even has its own credit card. Lately, however, you've gotten complaints from credit card customers. It seems the credit card company uses a recorded message to repeatedly call customers who don't pay their monthly bills.

Making an Ethical Decision

1. Does the credit card company have the right to call customers whose payment is overdue?
2. How does the Fair Debt Collection Practices Act protect customers?
3. Is a credit card company that uses recorded messages rather than live callers to collect late payments following the spirit of the law? Why or why not?

 ### How to Use a Portfolio Activity

The portfolio projects are designed to lead students to develop a collection of their best work to submit to you for assessment. You and each of your students should decide which projects to include in their business portfolio. Refer students to the specific rubric(s) from the *Alternative Assessment Strategies*. These rubrics will alert students to the criteria you'll use to assess their projects. **P**

who get such loans are considered poor credit risks. Second, because there is only one monthly payment, you might feel that the credit problem is under control and start charging new purchases.

Bankruptcy

The last resort is to declare **bankruptcy**. This is a legal process in which you're relieved of your debts, but your creditors can take some or all of your assets, such as a car, savings, or business. Individuals or businesses can declare bankruptcy. When bankruptcy is declared, the debtor, the creditor, and a court-appointed trustee come up with a plan to repay the debt on an installment basis. You should avoid bankruptcy because it gives you a bad credit record. Recent changes in the law have also made it harder to declare bankruptcy.

Credit Services

Some companies will provide credit even if your credit rating is poor or if you have been denied credit in the past. Their interest rates or fees are much higher than banks, credit unions, or even finance companies. They might also require some form of collateral. Loans that offer a credit line for the value of a house require the house as collateral. The cost of the loan is often so high that borrowers end up losing their homes.

Others charge a fee to "clean up" your credit rating but they're seldom able to restore a bad credit rating. Accurate reports of missed payments or bankruptcy can't legally be removed from your credit report. If your credit rating has been unfairly damaged by inaccurate information, you can work with a credit agency or bureau to correct the errors.

There are also some very good credit companies that provide quality services for consumers. The Better Business Bureau will give you a complaint history if it already has a name. Also, the Chamber of Commerce will give you names of businesses, but it doesn't recommend one over another. Many reputable credit counselors offer their services at a very low fee.

✓ **Fast Review** _____

1. What are two problems with a consolidation loan?
2. What effect does declaring bankruptcy have?

Real-World Application
part 4 of 4

IDENTITY CRISIS: PROTECT YOURSELF

Surfing the Internet is as typical as watching television and talking on the telephone. Increasing numbers of consumers shop, invest, and bank online. Before shopping online, sharpen your "fraud sensors."

How can you make sure all online transactions are secure?

Chapter 27

Real-World Application
Caption Answer

IDENTITY CRISIS: PROTECT YOURSELF: PART 4 OF 4

Use a secure browser, keep records of your online transactions, review your monthly bank and credit card statements, read privacy and security policies on Web sites, keep personal information private, and don't download files that strangers have sent you.

Technology Resource

 EXAMVIEW PRO CD-ROM. Check your students' understanding of this chapter using the *ExamView Pro®* CD-ROM.

Evaluation

Assign and review the Fast Review sections.

Fast Review Answers ✓

1. High interest rate; false impression of charging control.
2. Creditors can take your assets, and it gives you a bad credit record.

Meeting Individual Needs

Students With Learning Disabilities.
Students with learning disabilities may require additional assistance completing some of the activities in this chapter. The scope of distinguishing the acts and disclosure can be complex and requires analytical ability and methodical work. Break the required tasks up into self-contained steps and provide additional assistance as needed. A variety of resources can come into play, including peer assistance or adult mentors. Students with learning disabilities require more support and structure. Clearly specify the scope of the assignments and review their work on a regular basis throughout the course of this chapter.

4 CLOSE

Chapter Wrap-Up

Have students re-read the definitions of the key words that are not acts. Ask students to add something they can remember from this chapter about each of the six concepts.

Using Business Key Words

1. collection agent
2. usury law
3. truth-in-lending disclosure
4. credit counselor
5. consolidation loan
6. bankruptcy
7. Consumer Credit Protection Act
8. Equal Credit Opportunity Act
9. Fair Credit Reporting Act
10. Fair Credit Billing Act
11. Fair Debt Collection Practices Act

Review What You Learned

12. Problems repaying, billing mistakes, unfair credit charges, misleading claims, hidden costs, and difficulty getting credit approval.
13. Write a letter to the card issuer to resolve the error.
14. $50.
15. Curb excessive interest rates.
16. Reveal the total finance charge and APR.
17. The Fair Credit Reporting Act.
18. Ensure competition and enforce the laws on credit.
19. Revise clients' budgets, arrange new payment plans, and help clients find extra sources of income.
20. Bad effect on a consumer's credit rating.

444

Summary

1. Federal and state governments have passed laws to help consumers with credit problems. Federal agencies, including the Federal Trade Commission, enforce federal credit laws.

2. Federal laws that protect consumers include the Consumer Credit Protection Act, the Equal Credit Opportunity Act, the Fair Credit Reporting Act, the Fair Credit Billing Act, and the Fair Debt Collection Practices Act.

3. Consumers have the right to be informed of the terms and costs of credit, to know what's in their credit files, to have billing mistakes resolved, and to be protected from collection agents.

4. If you have credit problems, you can get credit counseling, get a consolidation loan, or declare bankruptcy.

● Using Business Key Words

Credit is used every day in the United States. Laws have been written to protect consumers who use credit. Understanding the legal aspects of credit is important. See how many of these terms you know by matching each one with the correct statement below.

- usury law
- Consumer Credit Protection Act
- truth-in-lending disclosure
- credit counselor
- collection agent
- consolidation loan
- Equal Credit Opportunity Act
- Fair Credit Reporting Act
- bankruptcy
- Fair Debt Collection Practices Act (FDCPA)
- Fair Credit Billing Act

1. Person who has the job of collecting debts that are overdue.
2. Law designed to limit rates consumers can be charged for credit.

3. A document that informs consumers about all the costs of borrowing money.
4. A person who helps people with credit problems.
5. A loan that combines all of a person's debt.
6. A legal process in which some or all of the assets of the debtor are distributed among the creditors.
7. A law, also known as the Truth in Lending Law, that requires creditors to provide information about credit to consumers and protects consumers if their credit cards are lost or stolen.
8. A law against denying credit on the basis of gender, age, ethnicity, or religion.
9. A law giving people the right to know what is in their credit file at credit bureaus.
10. A law requiring creditors to correct billing mistakes brought to their attention.
11. A law that protects debtors from unfair methods or practices used by collection agents.

Quick Quiz

1. How does a truth-in-lending disclosure allow consumers to compare the cost of credit? (It requires businesses to reveal the total finance charge and annual percentage rate for any loan, so consumers can calculate credit costs.)

2. Name four examples of credit discrimination. (Refusal to offer credit on the basis of age, gender, ethnicity, or religion.)

3. What happens to a person's credit rating if he or she declares bankruptcy? (That person will be rated as a very poor credit risk and will have great difficulty obtaining credit.)

Review What You Learned

12. What problems do some people face because of their reliance on credit?
13. What should you do if you suspect there is an error on your credit card statement?
14. If your credit card is stolen and you report the loss immediately, what is the dollar amount of unauthorized charges that you'll be responsible for?
15. What is the purpose of a usury law?
16. How does a truth-in-lending disclosure help consumers compare credit costs?
17. Which act gives you the "right to know" what is in your credit file?
18. What is the responsibility of the FTC?
19. How does a credit counselor help people with their credit problems?
20. Why is bankruptcy a last resort for a consumer with debt problems?

Understanding Business Concepts

21. A person may be denied credit only if he or she has a low income, owes large sums of money, or has a poor credit record. Why do you think the Equal Credit Opportunity Act allows credit to be denied for these reasons? In what other ways does the act protect consumers?
22. You have applied for credit at a department store. The store has denied you credit because of your credit rating. Since you know that you have always paid your bills on time, what action should you take?
23. For a fee, you can receive a copy of the information in your credit file at the credit bureau. Why would you want to check your credit record?
24. How can the truth-in-lending disclosure help protect consumers from credit problems?

Critical Thinking

25. The Truth in Lending Law requires that consumers be given complete credit cost information in advertisements that mention credit sales. Decide whether each of the following credit information blurbs is complete. Explain your answers.
    • $20 down, $43 a month
    • Finance charge is $10 a month, 18.15 APR
    • $35 down, $14 a month for 2 years
    • Payments for 52 weeks and only $15 down payment
26. Do you think the federal government should have to pass so many credit protection laws? Shouldn't people take responsibility for themselves?

Viewing and Representing

Examining the Image. Team up with a partner. What details do you see in this photograph? What do you think these people are discussing? Discuss how life would be without credit protection under the law. What would be the effect on individuals? On businesses?

Chapter 27 Your Credit and the Law **445**

---

25. Students' answers should contain the following information for each of the bulleted items:
    • Incomplete information; number of monthly payments is not given.
    • Complete information; for advertisements, the law does not require that the APR be given.
    • Incomplete information; monthly payment is not given.
26. Answers will vary.

Viewing and Representing

This activity promotes meaningful discussion with the open-ended question, "What would life be like without credit protection?" Students need to feel safe that their opinions, reasoning, and contributions are taken seriously and respected. As a teacher, you can set up the guidelines for discussions ahead of time to help students feel safe in sharing. After student pairs have had time to discuss the question, facilitate a class discussion on the topic. **LS**

Understanding Business Concepts

21. Poor chance of repaying their debts. From further problems with credit and credit discrimination.
22. Request the written report that gives the reason for the denial. Decide if it's a valid mistake or not. Request a copy of your record from the credit bureau and have the incorrect information removed.
23. To check information and accuracy.
24. Know how much using credit will cost.

4 CLOSE (Cont.)

Building Academic Skills

HISTORY. Make sure all students participate in this group project. Allow the students to choose the way they wish to present their findings. Rubrics: Oral presentation, essay, poster.

COMPUTER/TECHNOLOGY. Students with no access to a computer may team with someone who does. Rubrics: Charts/tables.

LANGUAGE ARTS. Students' lists will vary. Rubrics: List, table.

MATH. 1,460,000 ÷ 180,000 = 8.11 × 100 = 811 percent. Rubrics: Calculation.

Linking School to Home

Answers will vary. Rubric: Note taking.

Linking School to Work

Role-plays will vary. Make sure the students are prepared on the day the credit counselor comes to your class. Rubrics: Role-play.

Building Academic Skills

 Contacting a Local Credit Counselor

As a team, contact a consumer credit counseling service in your area. Find out when it first began providing services. How have the requests for services changed over the years? Are there more requests or fewer requests? Then, find out if the service has copies of any educational materials about using credit wisely. If possible, obtain a copy.

 Research and Chart the Law

Use e-mail to contact your state consumer protection agency. Retrieve information regarding the consumer protection laws in your state. Then use word processing software to create a chart summarizing the laws and their provisions. Print out the chart and post it in your classroom.

 Organized List of Agencies

Using the local telephone book, compile a list of all the agencies that provide consumer credit protection for people in your community. Organize the list according to local, state, and federal agencies.

MATH **Percentage Increase**

Unfortunately, many people view bankruptcy as an easy way to solve their money problems. The total number of personal bankruptcies has risen over the past 40 years. Records indicate that there were approximately 180,000 bankruptcies filed in 1960 and 1,460,000 filed in 1999. What was the percentage of increase in bankruptcies during that time?

Linking School to Home

Stories Behind the Laws. Interview your family members and find out what they know about the credit protection laws. Ask them specifically about the Truth in Lending Law, the Equal Credit Opportunity Act, and the Fair Debt Collection Practices Act. If your family members' knowledge is limited, educate them. Ask them if they think the three reasons for denying credit under the Equal Credit Opportunity Act are fair. Would they add any others? Why or why not?

Linking School to Work

Role-Playing. You're a small business owner and some customers are behind in their payments. How might the Fair Debt Collection Practices Act affect your business attempts to collect the payments? Work with a partner to role-play a situation where a consumer with credit problems is confronted by you, the business owner.

E-Homework

Applying Technology

Internet Puzzle. Create an Internet scavenger hunt about managing credit, avoiding credit problems, and the laws designed to protect consumers. Locate Web sites that would be appropriate and provide clues for the players of your game.

FTC Web Site. Explore the Federal Trade Commission's Web site. Is the site user-friendly? What major topics are found on the site? Are there any links for children or students?

Connecting Academics

Math. States regulate the maximum annual interest rate that may be charged for credit cards. In Connecticut the maximum is 19.8 percent. In New Jersey it's 30 percent. Marika maintained a credit card balance of $750 for a year. If she lived in Connecticut, what is the amount of finance charge owed? What about in New Jersey?

Language Arts. You applied for a charge account at Rogers and Hall Department Store. The store turned down your application. You ask for an appointment with its credit department manager. Describe what preparation you'll make for the meeting. What documents will you take with you? How will you convince the manager that you're a good credit risk?

Language Arts. You're a credit counselor and your friend is seeking advice on a credit problem. After your friend explains the problem, you outline several strategies for dealing with it based on your education and experience. Explain some basic approaches on how your friend can handle the problems.

BusinessWeek Analyzing the Feature Story

You read the first part of "Credit Cards: Entrepreneurs Are Tapping Them More Than Ever" at the beginning of this chapter. Below are a few questions for you to answer about the use of credit cards.

You'll find the answers to these questions when you're reading the entire article. First, here are the questions:

27. Why are entrepreneurs using credit cards rather than more conventional funding options?

28. What is one of the risks of using credit cards to fund a business idea?

CREATIVE JOURNAL ACTIVITY

Break into groups with two other students. You're the product team for a credit card company that's launching a new card specifically aimed at small business owners. Create an advertisement for the card using the medium of print, video, or radio. What message will be most compelling to your target market? What are the advantages of using a credit card for entrepreneurial funding? Present your ad to the class.

BUSINESS
Online
The Full Story

To learn more about the use of credit cards, visit the *Introduction to Business* Web site at www.introbus.glencoe.com, and click on *BusinessWeek* Feature Story, Chapter 27.

447

1 FOCUS

Unit Seminar Overview

In this seminar, students research how small businesses raise money through credit. Students investigate images, research loan information, chart results, and decide their opinion on the question: Which loan would you choose if you were starting a new business?

Bell Ringer Activity

IDENTIFY. Ask students to identify things that businesses might buy on credit.

Discussion Starter

CLASS DISCUSSION. Write this statement on the board: "Business credit is essential to the economy." Have students debate this issue. (Without credit businesses might not be able to obtain materials, equipment, or facilities when they need them.)
LS, CL, ELL

BusinessWeek Seminar

Unit 9
Small Business

Using Credit to Start a Small Business

In Chapter 25 you learned about credit and the different places to get credit. Many, if not most, new businesses need credit to get started, and they need credit to keep their businesses growing. In this seminar you'll research how a person might use credit to start up a business.

448

Social Science

Newsworthy Trends

Rolodex Financing. Rolodex or family-and-friends financing refers to borrowing from friends, relatives, or supporters to finance a new business. It's an alternative to commercial credit that has gained in popularity. In 1990, an estimated 30 percent of start-up businesses relied on personal contacts for financing. In 1996, it was up to 43 percent. Today, according to *Inc.* magazine, it's about 75 percent. Borrowing from friends and relatives can damage a relationship, so financial experts advise following the same rules as commercial credit. The borrower should provide a complete business plan and sign a written agreement with all the terms laid out just like a bank loan.

2 TEACH

Thinking Critically

Look at the "Factoids," then answer these questions:

1. If Wahoo's called you in as a business consultant, what advice would you give it on how to best use the $1.5 million in its expansion? (Answers will vary and may include: researching demographics, developing restaurant sites, training skilled personnel, and advertising.)

2. Imagine you were starting up a business in another country. Assume you are fairly fluent in the language. What hurdles do you imagine you might come across? Where might you go for help? (Answers will vary and may include: Being able to understand national and local taxes and business laws. Organizations similar to the Small Business Administration, Chamber of Commerce, or local groups of small business owners.)

Cooperative Learning

ROLE-PLAY. Have students work in pairs or small groups. After discussing "Exploring Culture" (seminar questions 7 and 8), have groups plan, produce, and then present a role-play where a first-generation immigrant entrepreneur goes to a bank to ask for a loan. Assign groups to approach the scenario from different perspectives. **CL**, **LS**, **ELL**

Factoids

Bigger Fish to Fry. Owners of Wahoo's Fish Taco received a $1.5-million line of credit from Merrill Lynch in order to expand its market in Southern California. It's competing for market share in fresh Mexican food, the fastest growing segment in the restaurant business.

Caller, You're on the Air. Due to dwindling federal funds, public radio broadcasting depends on corporate underwriting and fund-drive pledges to keep them thriving with news and entertaining programs. Have you supported your local public radio station today?

Learn the Language. It's tough to get a business loan if you don't know English or if you aren't familiar with American business practices. Anyone interested in starting a company must put together a business plan, tax returns, and personal financial statements, which can be a daunting task.

Investigate the Images

Look at the photographic collage on the left page. What grabs your attention first? Is it the color or the words? The power in reading visuals is in analyzing and dissecting your observations. On a separate piece of paper, respond to the questions listed below. These questions might help sharpen the focus of your visual mind.

Your Observations

1. How many photographs do you see?

2. Examine each photograph. How are they assembled in relation to one another?

3. What is the subject of each photograph? Is place or location the subject?

4. Does color signify a message?

5. What issues do you take from these images?

Information

6. Summarize what you know about the photographs from your observations.

Exploring Culture

7. Federal and state laws prohibit banks or lending institutions from discriminating against clients based on ethnicity or gender. What options do you have if you've been discriminated against?

8. Minority-owned banks often focus on relationship building. Why might a first-generation immigrant entrepreneur choose to use this particular bank over another one when seeking start-up funds?

Unit 9 *BusinessWeek* Seminar **449**

Social Science

Newsworthy Trends

Angel Investors. Angel investors are taking over the role of venture capitalists in financing businesses. In theater slang, an "angel" is a wealthy investor willing to put up money to produce a play. A business angel is a wealthy investor willing to put up money to fund a new start-up company.

The usual angel investment is between $25,000 and $50,000. The Small Business Administration has a database of angel investors called the Angel Capital Electronic Investor. As with commercial credit, business angels expect a return on its investments.

2 TEACH (Cont.)

Independent Practice

L1 SUMMARIZE

Ask students to find a recent article on how small businesses use credit. Ask them to prepare a summary of the article to share it with the class. Lead a closing discussion on the latest trends in usage of credit by small business. **LS**

L2 GUEST VISIT

Arrange for the owner of a successful local start-up company to visit your class. Ask the owner to give a short presentation about the company and how credit or loans impacted the company. Ask students to take notes during the visit, and then write two paragraphs. In the first paragraph, students should describe the company and how it is successful. In the second paragraph students should summarize the part credit or loans played in the company's success. **LS**

L3 RESEARCH AND REPORT

Ask students to research two start-up companies. The research may be indirect on the Internet or direct by interviewing managers of local companies. Have students write a one-page report. For each company, have students include specifics about the company and include details of what use the company has made of credit or loans. **LS**

Taking Aim at Small Business

● Preparation

Research how people use credit and other types of funding to start up a small business.

Objective

In this *BusinessWeek* Seminar, you'll:
- **Research** how small businesses raise money through credit.
- **Contact** the Small Business Administration (SBA) for information.
- **Create** a chart that describes some of the different SBA loans.

Materials Needed
- ✓ Copies of recent business news publications such as *BusinessWeek* or *Frontier*
- ✓ Access to the Internet and your local or school library
- ✓ Paper, pens, pencils
- ✓ Posterboard and markers

● Procedures

1. With one or two partners, find and read articles about how small businesses raise money through credit. One resource is the "Small Business Guide" accessible at the *BusinessWeek* Web site on the Internet at **www.businessweek.com**.

2. Write a one-page report on your research.

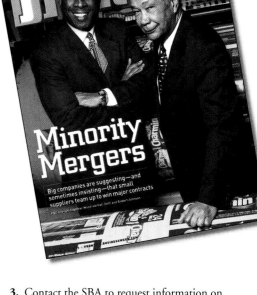

3. Contact the SBA to request information on loans available to small businesses. You can access SBA information on the Internet at **www.sba.gov**. Then click on the link "Financing Your Business." You can also find the SBA office nearest you by calling 1-800-U-ASK-SBA or by looking in your local telephone directory under "United States Government."

4. After you've compiled information from the SBA, write a report that answers these questions:
   - What is the SBA?
   - How does the SBA help small businesses acquire loans?
   - What are three different SBA loan programs? How do they compare to one another?

450 Unit 9 Credit

Reteaching Strategy

Ask students to take part in a speedy summary. To prepare, ask students to write down three or four main points they learned as part of this unit and this unit seminar. These main points may include definitions, memorized facts, or points the student felt were most meaningful to his or her own life. As you rapidly and randomly call on students in the class, each student tells a point. No point may be repeated. When called on, each student must give a new main point. **LS, ELL**

Chart It

Using the information about loan programs from the SBA, create a chart that compares them. The chart should include the name of the program, purpose of the program, collateral required, maturity, interest rates, maximum loan amount, and eligibility.

Name of Loan Program	Program No. 1	Program No. 2	Program No. 3
Purpose of Loan Program			
Collateral			
Maturity			
Interest Rates			
Maximum Loan Amount			
Small Business Eligibility			

Analyze and Conclude

After studying your research and your chart, answer the questions below:

1. **Interpreting and Communicating Information.** What is the biggest difference between the three loan programs?

2. **Decision Making.** How are the three programs similar?

3. **Creative Thinking.** Which loan would you choose if you were starting a new business and why?

Becoming an Informed Citizen

Congratulations, you finished the seminar. Now it's time to reflect on the decisions you made.

Critical Thinking. Why do you think there are so many loan programs available?

Exercising Leadership. Imagine a group of your friends want to start a business, but they know nothing about starting up a company. They look to you for guidance since you're the only one who has taken this business course. Where do you tell them to start with their plan? What kinds of advice do you give them?

BUSINESS Online

Further Exploration
To find out more about small businesses and finding funding, visit the Glencoe *Introduction to Business* Web site at **www.introbus.glencoe.com**.

3 ASSESS

Enrichment

DEMONSTRATE. Have groups of students imagine they are starting a small business and demonstrate the process that they would take to apply for credit or a loan.

Evaluation

RUBRICS. The rubrics for evaluation of written reports, charts, and oral presentations are included in *Alternative Assessment Strategies.* **P**

4 CLOSE

Seminar Wrap-Up

QUICK QUIZ. In groups of four, have students write eight questions on topics covered in class discussions and presentations during this seminar. Ask groups to pass their test sheet to the next group. Members of the next group decide together on the answers then write their answers. Finally the groups pass their answered test to the next group to check. **CL**, **LS**, **ELL**

Analyze and Conclude Answers

1. The biggest difference will vary depending on the three loan programs charted.
2. Similarities between the loan programs will vary depending on the three loan programs charted.
3. Answers will vary. Require students to back up their decisions with reasoned arguments.

Money Management

Unit Objectives

After completing this unit, students will be able to achieve the following outcomes:

- Explain how a budget is helpful, and list the five steps in planning a budget.
- Identify types of checking accounts, and explain ways transactions are recorded and how to reconcile a checking account.
- Identify types of savings accounts, and explain reasons for saving money.
- Explain how stock is bought and sold, and identify the indexes used to track stock prices.
- Describe the different types of bonds and their characteristics, and list reasons for buying real estate.

BusinessWeek Connections

In this unit, students will read the following articles from *BusinessWeek*:

Chapter 28 "Why Higher Rates Aren't Denting Consumers' Spirits": Personal budgeting changes depending on the economy.

Chapter 29 "The Dynamo of E-Banking": What's the reason for the big difference when it comes to Nordea?

Chapter 30 "How to Cash Out Your College Fund": Saving for college is just one part of the big juggling act involved.

Chapter 31 "Where Kids Can Log On to Learn Their Investing ABCs": Compare sites for yourself.

Chapter 32 "Will Refis Help Refloat the Economy?": Take a look at the choices homeowners are taking.

Key to Descriptive Icons

The following designations will help you decide which activities are appropriate for your students.

L1 Level 1 activities should be within the ability range of all students.

L2 Level 2 activities should be within the ability range of the average to above-average students.

L3 Level 3 activities are designed for the ability range of above-average students.

ELL Activities should be within the ability range of the English Language Learner.

LS Learning Styles designation represents activities designed to address different learning styles.

CL Cooperative learning activities are designed for small group work.

P Portfolio designation represents student products that can be placed into a best-work portfolio.

Teacher Classroom Resources*

Program Resources	Chapter 28	Chapter 29	Chapter 30	Chapter 31	Chapter 32
Student Activity Workbook	p. 209	p. 217	p. 225	p. 233	p. 239
Lesson Plans	p. 74	p. 76	p. 78	p. 80	p. 82
Internet Resources	p. 75	p. 77	p. 79	p. 81	p. 83
Reproducible Tests	p. 55	p. 57	p. 59	p. 61	p. 63
Teaching Transparencies	28.1, 28.2	29.1, 29.2	30.1, 30.2	31.1, 31.2	32.1, 32.2
Strategies and Worksheets for Teaching Transparencies	pp. 14, 75	pp. 14, 75	pp. 15, 77	pp. 15, 79	pp. 16, 81

* Each of these resources is available in print and on the Interactive Lesson Planner CD-ROM.

Technology Resources

- Interactive Lesson Planner CD-ROM
- PowerPoint® Presentation CD-ROM
- ExamView® Pro Test Generator CD-ROM
- Integrated Software Simulation, Teacher Manual
- Glencoe Business Video Package
- *PuzzleMaker* CD-ROM
- *Introduction to Business* Web Site
- *Virtual Business*®
  Virtual Business is a business simulation that introduces students to the principles of business by letting them start and run their own virtual business. In *Virtual Business,* students have the power to control all aspects of a retail convenience store. Students strategize business decisions using a powerful learning tool in the guise of a video game.

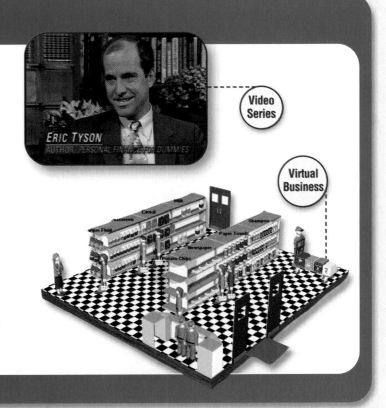

ERIC TYSON
AUTHOR, PERSONAL FINANCE FOR DUMMIES

Video Series

Virtual Business

Scope and Sequence

Academic Standards of Learning

	LANGUAGE ARTS	MATH	HISTORY	COMPUTER/ TECHNOLOGY	SOCIAL SCIENCE	
CHAPTER 28	pp. 455, 457, 459, 461, 462, 463, 468, 469	pp. 455, 458, 459, 460, 462, 468	p. 468	pp. 457, 461, 463, 468, 469	pp. 454, 460, 463, 464, 465, 469	
CHAPTER 29	pp. 471, 473, 474, 476, 477, 479, 482, 483	pp. 472, 477, 482, 483	p. 470	pp. 473, 479, 482, 483	pp. 470, 471, 474, 476, 482	
CHAPTER 30	pp. 485, 486, 487, 488, 489, 490, 491, 492, 493, 496, 497	pp. 485, 487, 488, 489, 496, 497	p. 496	pp. 487, 493, 496, 497	pp. 486, 488, 490	
CHAPTER 31	pp. 499, 501, 503, 505, 506, 507, 510, 511	pp. 502, 503, 504, 510, 511	pp. 502, 510	pp. 498, 501, 507, 510, 511	pp. 499, 503, 504, 506, 509	
CHAPTER 32	pp. 513, 514, 515, 516, 519, 520, 521, 524	pp. 513, 516, 518, 524, 525	pp. 513, 520, 524	pp. 515, 521, 524, 525	pp. 513, 514, 516, 518, 519	

Scope and Sequence

Themes and Concepts

Business Core	Accounting and Finance	Business Management	Computer/ Technology	Marketing	Entrepreneurship

Goal Setting
Interest Assessment
Communication
Decision Making
Personal Qualities
Planning
	Cash Management
	Decision Making
	Financial Analysis
	Revenue and Expense
	  Recognition
	Taxation
		Consumers
		Decision Making
		Communication
		Time Management
		Needs Analysis
			Records Management
			Business Decisions
				Profitability
				Risk Management
				Purchasing
				Buys Motives and
				  Behaviors
				Credit Review
					Contracts
					Entrepreneurial
					  Potential
					Financial Resources
					Management

Environmental Issues
Goal Setting
Business/Financial
  Relationship
Financial Statement
Financial System
Money Management
	Cash Management
	Decision Making
	Technological
	  Applications
	Financial Statements
	Budgeting
	Cost Behavior
		Consumers
		Decision Making
			Computer Applications
			Security
			Records Management
			Needs Analysis
				Risk Management
				Security and Loss
				  Prevention
					Financial Planning
					Management

Business Law
Competitive
  Environment
Financial Statements
Money Management
Document Processing
Decision Making
Planning
	Cash Management
	Decision Making
	Industry/Market
	  Analysis
	Risk Analysis
	Budgeting
		Decision Making
		Competition
		Economic Indicators
		Research and
		  Development
		Policy and Strategies
		  Formulation
		Comparative
		  Advantages
			Security
			Time Management
			Risk Analysis
				Market Analysis
				Risk Management
				Products and Service
				  Knowledge
				Financial Institutions
					Collections
					Contracts
					Financial Resources
					Financial Planning
					Government
					  Regulations
					Pricing Strategies
					Management

Business Ethics
Business Law
Business Ownership
Business/Financial
  Relationships
Economic Culture
Economic System
Investments
	Decision Making
	Financial Analysis
	International Finance
	Governing Agencies
	International Finance
	Economic Factors
	Investment Analysis
		Economic Indicators
		Decision Making
		Ethics
		Research and
		  Development
		Comparative
		  Advantage
			Needs Analysis
			Resource
			  Management
			Risk Analysis
				Risk Management
				Branding
				Positioning
				Purchasing
				Product/Service
				  Classification
				Policies and
				  Procedures
					Management
					Property Analysis
					Risk Management

Business Law
Entrepreneurial
  Concepts
Economic Culture
Investment
Money Management
	Cash Management
	Decision Making
	Financial Analysis
		Decision Making
		Contracts
		Finance
			Records Management
			Needs Analysis
			Risk Analysis
				Buying Motives and
				  Behaviors
				Customer
				  Transactions
				Financial Institutions
				Risk Management
				Policies and
				  Procedures
				Regulation
					Contracts
					Entrepreneurial
					  Potential
					Financial Resources
					Financial Planning
					Location and Property
					  Analysis

Unit Overview

Unit 10 gives information about budgeting, saving, and investing that affects everyday life now and in the future.

CHAPTER 28 describes lifestyle costs and introduces a sample budget.

CHAPTER 29 explains opening a checking account, services on accounts, account records, and reconciling a checking account.

CHAPTER 30 names reasons to save, and the types, and advantages and disadvantages of savings accounts.

CHAPTER 31 introduces investing in stocks and the advantages and disadvantages of stocks.

CHAPTER 32 describes bonds, and examines investing in real estate.

Introducing the Unit

Ask students to play a word association game. When you say the word *budget*, ask students to identify the first word that comes to mind. List the words on the board. Point out that the purpose of a budget is to help achieve financial goals. Play again with the words *savings,* then *investment.* Discuss the students' responses and point out that they'll be looking at budgeting, checking accounts, savings, and investment in this unit. **CL** , **LS**

Technology Resource

GO TO **INTRODUCTION TO BUSINESS WEB SITE.** To find out more about content in Unit 10, visit the Glencoe *Introduction to Business* Web site.
www.introbus.glencoe.com

Unit 10

Money Management

Tiptoe Through the Tulips

Tulips are closely associated with Holland, but in 1550 they were unknown in Europe. A Dutch botanist brought home a tulip bulb from Turkey and the flower caught on like wildfire. People overvalued tulips bulbs and started investing in them like stocks. At the height of the tulip frenzy, a single bulb sold for as much as $10,000. People borrowed large sums of money or mortgaged their homes and businesses to buy them. In 1637 when the tulip market crashed, tulip investors felt that financial crunch.

● **The British Are Coming**
Wall Street, home of the New York Stock Exchange, gets its name from a wall built in 1653 by Dutch colonists to protect themselves from English invaders.

● **How Do Your Future Finances Look?**
The Psychic Investor and The Wall Street Psychic use methods such as tarot cards, astrology, numerology, clairvoyance, and candle magic to predict the stock market.

● **The Day the Value Dropped**
The biggest drop in stock market history wasn't "Black Monday," October 28, 1929, when the Dow Jones fell 13 percent and the Great Depression began, but October 19, 1987, when the Dow Jones fell 519 points in one day, or 22.6 percent.

Field Trip Suggestion

Stock Brokerage Firm. Take students to a stock brokerage firm. Before going on the trip, tell students to imagine they have unlimited funds and to write in their journals goals they have when they're 20, 25, 30, 35, and so on. Share one goal and together assign an approximate value. For example, goals might be traveling (3 trips $10,000), sky diving ($400), climbing Mount Everest ($5,000), learning to paint ($4,000), going to a concert ($300), putting a down payment on a home ($5,000), and so on.

Show students how the stock market works and explain the risks and returns of buying stocks. **P** , **LS**

Glencoe Poster Teaching Tip

Before introducing the poster, ask students if they schedule time every week or every month to manage their budget. Let students know that the quiz on the poster is directed to managers at work, but some tips might be handy to apply to personal time management. Then have the students take the quiz on the poster. Lead a class discussion by asking students: Do you think it's important to make a regular time to plan for the future? Why or why not? Encourage students to give examples. **LS**, **CL**

BUSINESS
Online
Idea Factory
To learn more about trading stocks, visit the *Introduction to Business* Web site at **www.introbus.glencoe.com**, and click on Unit 10 Money Management.

Portfolio Activity

Word Association Insights. Assign students to play the word association game (outlined in "Introducing the Unit" on the previous page) with their family and friends. Ask students to make notes on first responses to words or phrases such as: budget, savings, checking account, investment, stocks, home ownership, and your life goals. Did they have any insights as a result of this exercise? Have students chart the responses and give a written explanation of any insights they had. **P**

Out of Time?

If time doesn't permit teaching each chapter in this unit, you may use the PowerPoint® Presentation CD-ROM to review the chapter's content.

SCANS Correlation Chart*

Foundation Skills

Basic Skills	Reading	Writing	Math	Listening	Speaking	
Thinking Skills	Creative Thinking	Decision Making	Problem Solving	Seeing Things in the Mind's Eye	Knowing How to Learn	Reasoning
Personal Qualities	Responsibility	Self-Esteem	Sociability	Self-Management	Integrity/ Honesty	

Workplace Competencies

Resources	Allocating Time	Allocating Money	Allocating Material and Facility Resources	Allocating Human Resources		
Information	Acquiring and Evaluating Information	Organizing and Maintaining Information	Interpreting and Communicating Information	Using Computers to Process Information		
Interpersonal Skills	Participating as a Member of a Team	Teaching Others	Serving Clients/ Customers	Exercising Leadership	Negotiating to Arrive at a Decision	Working With Cultural Diversity
Systems	Understanding Systems	Monitoring and Correcting Performance	Improving and Designing Systems			
Technology	Selecting Technology	Applying Technology to Task	Maintaining and Troubleshooting Technology			

*This chart's highlighted blocks indicate the chapter's content coverage in the Student Edition and the Teacher Wraparound Edition.

Resource Manager

Teaching Transparencies

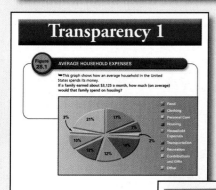

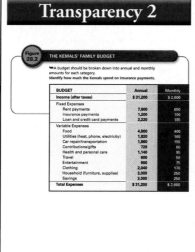

Application and Enrichment

- Lesson Plans
- *BusinessWeek* Poster Package
- Teaching Transparencies
- Integrated Software Simulation
- Glencoe Business Video Package

Review and Reinforcement

- *PuzzleMaker*
- Internet Resources
- Student Activity Workbook
- Strat. and Work. for Teaching Transparencies

Assessment and Evaluation

- Reproducible Tests
- Alternative Assessment Strategies
- ExamView® Pro Test Generator

Technology

- *PuzzleMaker*
- ExamView® Pro Test Generator
- Glencoe Business Video Package
- PowerPoint® Presentation
- Integrated Software Simulation
- Interactive Lesson Planner
- *Virtual Business*®

KEY

- Printed
- Transparency
- Software
- CD-ROM
- Videocassette
- Internet
- Poster

BUSINESS Online

Visit www.introbus.glencoe.com, the Web site companion to *Introduction to Business.* The student's page includes:

- interactive tutor
- additional *BusinessWeek* articles and activities
- business Web links
- homework hints
- real-world application activities
- additional career path activities

Information on how to prepare your students for the high school exit exam and special projects are also included.

Use the Glencoe Web site for additional resources. All essential content is covered in the Student Edition.

1 FOCUS

Introducing the Chapter

This chapter describes how to budget and presents a sample budget. A photo essay, "The Striving Artists," enhances the concepts.

Connecting the Objectives

How can you develop a budget? What are some examples of different types of income? Expenses?

BusinessWeek
Feature Story

Story's Summary

Personal budgeting characteristics change depending on factors in the economy. One major factor is the labor market. Other factors include the conditions of the housing sector and the stock market. When these three conditions are good, and there is a sense of well being, personal budgeting actually tends to be personal spending. When there is an element of uncertainty or a downturn, especially in the labor market, personal budgeting tends more toward personal saving.

Find the entire article at **www.introbus.glencoe.com**, or in the Teacher Resource Binder.

Planning a Budget

● Learning Objectives

After completing this chapter, you'll be able to:
1. **Explain** how budgeting is helpful.
2. **List** the five steps in planning a budget.
3. **Name** different types of income and expenses.
4. **Describe** how a computer is used in budgeting.

● Why It's Important

Budgeting techniques help you keep track of where your money goes so that you can make it go further.

● Key Words

money management
budget
income
gross pay
deductions
net pay
withholding
expenditures
fixed expenses
variable expenses
budget variance

454

BusinessWeek Feature Story

Why Higher Rates Aren't Denting Consumers' Spirits

Tight Job Market Keeps Households Right on Spending. You would think that consumers might have become more wary of financial conditions by now. After all, the Dow Jones Industrial Average is off 8 percent this year, and the tech-oriented Nasdaq has plunged by nearly a third since mid-March. Moreover, mortgage rates have risen by a full point in the past six months. But so far, consumers have just shrugged, as if to say, "So what?"

With consumer confidence through May as high as ever, it's clear that the labor markets are the major force shaping overall household attitudes and buying behavior.

Source: Excerpted with permission from "Why Higher Rates Aren't Denting Consumers' Spirits," *BusinessWeek Online*, June 12, 2000.

An Extension Activity

How does the job market affect your household? Ask a parent how the outlook for the economy affects how your family spends its money.

BUSINESS Online
The Full Story

To learn more about personal budgeting, visit the *Introduction to Business* Web site at **www.introbus.glencoe.com**, and click on *BusinessWeek* Feature Story, Chapter 28.

Classroom Resources

For the Teacher
📁 Student Activity Work. TAE
📗 💿 Assessment Binder
💿 PowerPoint® Presentation
💿 Interactive Lesson Planner
📁 Lesson Plans
📗 💻 Internet Resources
🕹 Teaching Transparencies
💻 *Introduction to Business* Web Site

💿 Integrated Soft. Sim. TM
📘 *BusinessWeek* Poster Package
For the Student
📗 Student Activity Workbook
💿 *Virtual Business®*
💻 *Introduction to Business* Web Site
💿 Integrated Soft. Sim.
💿 *PuzzleMaker*
📗 Strategies and Worksheets for Teaching Transparencies

Bell Ringer Activity

PARTICIPATING AS A MEMBER OF A TEAM. Working in a team of three students, come up with nine questions about planning a budget. You'll use these questions in this chapter's "Individualized Practice" activity on page 459.

Preteaching Business Key Words

DECISION MAKING. Attempt to write your own definition for each key word. Decide which are most difficult to define. Copy the glossary definition for these words.

An Extension Activity

PRESENT. After students have interviewed their families, ask volunteers to present the results of their interviews. **CL**, LS

Making Connections

Everyday Life. Suggest student investigate what costs they would incur if their current lifestyle included a car. Have them choose a late-model used car to "purchase." Then have them find out the average monthly cost of owning the car, not counting the cost of the car itself. Research items by consulting the Internet, consumer magazines, or automobile periodicals.

- Insurance costs for make and model year of the car, as well as gender and age of driver.
- City sticker, state license.
- Cost of gasoline based on average 12,000 miles a year.
- Regular maintenance costs: oil changes, coolant, etc.

2 TEACH

Business Connection

BUDGETING. Would you like to have an income of $165,000 a year or $240,000 a year? A recent survey showed that when you write a budget, you're more likely to have a higher income. When you prepare a budget, you're acting as a manager of your own business. The survey showed that of small-business entrepreneurs, the two-thirds with a written financial plan were the ones making an average of $240,000 a year. It's important that you put your financial plan in writing.

Develop Concepts

EXPENSES. Ask students to list some of the activities they enjoy, and how much the activities cost—watching sports, playing sports, going to concerts, and so on. Ask students: What kind of expenses are these? (Variable expenses.)

Figure 28.1 Caption Answer

About $500.

Money Management

Andre Becker is a 22-year-old single man who works as a radiology technician. He shares an apartment with two other roommates. When Andre decided to make up a budget, he thought carefully about his lifestyle. He doesn't spend much money on clothes for work. There is little transportation expense because the bus is just down the street from his apartment. On the weekends he likes to go out with his friends to restaurants, otherwise he eats meals at home. How would your lifestyle description be different from Andre's? How would it be the same?

Lifestyle Costs

Money is a limited resource. Most people want more goods and services than they can buy with their money. **Money management** is the process of planning how to get the most from your money. With planning, you can figure out how to use the money you have to buy the things you really want or need. Figure 28.1 illustrates how the average household spends its money.

A **budget** is a plan for using your money in a way that best meets your wants and needs. It's like a road map or guide that you set up and

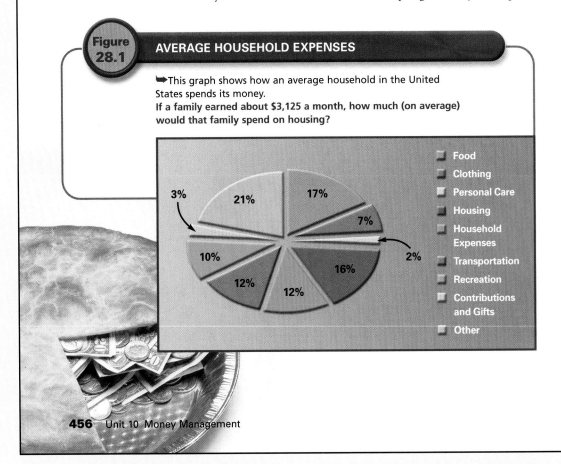

Figure 28.1

AVERAGE HOUSEHOLD EXPENSES

➡ This graph shows how an average household in the United States spends its money.
If a family earned about $3,125 a month, how much (on average) would that family spend on housing?

- Food
- Clothing
- Personal Care
- Housing
- Household Expenses
- Transportation
- Recreation
- Contributions and Gifts
- Other

3% · 21% · 17% · 7% · 10% · 16% · 12% · 12% · 2%

How to Use a Portfolio Activity

The portfolio projects are designed to lead students to develop a collection of their best work to submit to you for assessment. You and each of your students should decide which projects to include in their business portfolio. Refer students to the specific rubric(s) from the *Alternative Assessment Strategies*. These rubrics will alert students to the criteria you'll use to assess their projects. **P**

try to follow. A budget includes a record of your expected income, your planned expenses, and your planned savings over a certain period of time. You avoid wasting money on things that aren't very important to you, because you decide in advance how you'll use your money. A good budget helps you set priorities for spending and saving and keeps track of how you're managing your money.

Planning a budget is easier if you divide the process into five steps: Set your goals, estimate your income, estimate your expenses, plan for savings, and balance and adjust your budget as needed.

Set Goals

As you prepare to set your monetary goals, you have to consider several questions: What do I want to accomplish in the next month? The next year? The next five years? What is important to me? Are my goals practical? It's useless to set a goal of buying a new computer in one year if your total income for the year is less than the cost of the computer. A budget should help you decide which goals you can meet with the amount of money you have.

Estimate Income

Knowing how much money you have available is an important step in the budgeting process. Your **income** is the actual amount of money you earn or receive during a given time period. If you get a weekly allowance, that's income. Wages you earn as a stock clerk at a supermarket or tips you get waiting tables are income. Any interest you earn on a savings account or money from investments is also part of your income.

Gross Pay. If you have a job, you may remember your surprise when you got your first paycheck. Your **gross pay**, the total amount of money you earned for a specific time, may have seemed like a lot of money. For example, if you worked 20 hours a week at $6.50 an hour, your gross pay was $130 for the week.

Net Pay. You don't get to keep all of your gross pay, however. Your gross pay is reduced by various **deductions**, or amounts that are taken out of your pay before you receive your paycheck. Deductions include things like taxes, health insurance, retirement, and union dues. Your take-home pay, or **net pay**, is your gross pay minus deductions. For example, if your gross pay is $200 a week and 20 percent is taken out in deductions, your net pay is $160 a week.

Real-World Application
part 1 of 4

THE STRIVING ARTISTS

Austin, Tex. In a bare-bones, big room at Audio Arts Studio, musicians Barry Whittaker, Jason Lee, Will Tabanou, and Mark David get ready for their recording session. Their band, The Agency, is recording a demo CD. Before they stepped foot into the studio, they negotiated a fee to use the space.
In order to negotiate a fee, what did they have to know first?

continued on p. 459

Chapter 28 Planning a Budget **457**

Technology Resource

GO TO **POWERPOINT.** The *Introduction to Business* PowerPoint® CD-ROM provides visual lecture aids for this chapter.

Independent Practice

ASKING QUESTIONS. Arrange for a school's budget officer or sports department budget officer to come to be interviewed as a class guest. Before the guest's visit, have students prepare questions such as these: What goals drive the budget? How often is the budget changed or revised? What are the advantages of budgeting? What are the challenges associated with budgeting? What advice do you have for personal budgeting? (Encourage discussion.) **LS**

Meeting Individual Needs

Students With Difficulty Differentiating. Some students have difficulty mastering the skill of differentiation. Present students with the following general reasons for saving: (1) for a purchase, (2) for emergencies, or (3) for financial security. Then provide the list of goals below. Have the students provide the general reason for saving associated with each of the goals.

a. Unexpected medical bills (2)
b. Vacation trip (1)
c. College education (1)
d. Retirement home (1 or 3)
e. Unplanned repairs of water pipes (2)

Thinking Critically

VISIONING. The crowd around you is deafening. The feeling's electric. You're at a concert with friends. This is one of the happiest days of your life. It didn't come easy. You saved for six months for the ticket. When you get home, you can't sleep. You keep thinking of more fun things and great things you'd like to do in your life. You take a roll of gift-wrap and make a long scroll. You sketch a time line for the next ten years. You mark five short-term goals for the next six months, and then you mark a few long-term goals at five years and at ten years. (Answers will vary.)

Business Building Blocks

CAPTION ANSWER

Suggest that students work in pairs to complete the practice item. Then direct students to make up three problems that require finding the average. Have them exchange problems with their partner, work their partner's problems, and turn the answers back to their partner for evaluation. The average price is $26.45. ($25.95 + 24.50 + 27.95 + 24.36 + 26.00 + 29.95) ÷ 6.

Other Income. If your net pay is the only income you have to consider, it's easy to figure your total income. If you're budgeting for a family and other members contribute to the total income, include their take-home pay in the budget. Don't count on gifts or unusual income, however. If part of your income is from tips, don't overestimate how much you expect to receive in tips. To stay within your budget, use a figure that's lower than what you think you'll receive. Think conservatively.

Taxes. Full-time workers pay several kinds of taxes, which are deducted from their paychecks. **Withholding**, or subtracting taxes from a paycheck to be forwarded to the government, may include federal, state, and local income taxes. In addition, the worker's contribution to social security is withheld. These taxes reduce the amount of take-home pay. Employers are responsible for forwarding the taxes that are withheld to the government units that assessed them.

Workers who don't have all taxes withheld from their paychecks must budget for payment of those taxes. Self-employed persons, for example, pay their taxes directly to the government. They must budget for those payments on a regular basis.

Business Building Blocks

Math

Determining Averages

If you've ever figured out your average grade for a series of math tests, you're familiar with an *average*, or mean. An average is a single number used to represent a group of numbers. The average, or mean, of two or more numbers is the sum of the numbers divided by the number of items added.

Practice

First, review the rules and examples for computing an average (mean) in the box. Then complete this problem: You want to buy a new pair of jeans before visiting your friend in Chicago. At the local mall you visit six different clothing stores. Each store charges a different price for a pair of jeans: $25.95, $24.50, $27.95, $24.36, $26, and $29.95. What is the average price?

Review on Computing an Average

Over the years, Sam has earned the following hourly wages: $4.75, $6.68, $7.36, and $10.19. What is Sam's average hourly wage?

Step 1. Add up the different wages.
$4.75 + 6.68 + 7.36 + 10.19 = $28.98

Step 2. Divide the total by the number of different wages.
$28.98 ÷ 4 = $7.24.

MATH — *Curriculum Connection*

Graph. Remind students that often a graph or diagram helps you to understand numerical information. In the "Great Ideas from the Classroom of…" activity on page 459, the class will collect pay stubs. Suggest that groups of students use the information at the bottom of a pay stub to make a circle chart. If feasible, suggest that students construct their circle chart using graphing software. Ask groups to explain how the diagram can help them better understand the relationship between total pay, deductions, and take-home pay. **CL**, **LS**

Estimate Expenses

Money you make is called income. You have to plan for a variety of expenses. Food, rent, and clothing are called **expenditures**. You must plan for rent, food, transportation, and any unexpected expenses, such as medical visits. You also have to take into account the rising costs of some expenses, such as gas. If a budget doesn't include all estimated expenses, real problems might arise. There are two basic types of expenses you have to consider: fixed and variable.

Fixed Expenses. **Fixed expenses** are expenses that occur regularly and that are regularly paid. They include such things as rent, insurance, and car payments. The amount of a fixed expense might change from time to time, but it's usually about the same over long periods. You can't reduce or avoid fixed expenses without creating problems.

Variable Expenses. **Variable expenses** are expenses that fluctuate. They include expenses such as food, long-distance phone charges, entertainment, and gifts. The amounts for these expenses usually vary from month to month. A good way to begin estimating your expenses is to look at how much you paid for similar items in the past. The more expenses you track, the easier it's to estimate expenses for your budget.

Plan for Savings

A budget isn't complete without a regular plan for savings. Not only will savings make it possible for you to meet future wants, but they're also a protection. Savings protect you against expenses that you didn't budget for, that are higher than you expected, or that are completely unexpected. You also need a savings plan if your long-term goal is to buy a new computer or take a vacation.

Balance and Adjust the Budget

The most difficult step in the budgeting process is balancing and adjusting the budget. The total estimated income for a period—usually a month or a year—should equal the total estimated expenses. The difference between how much you planned to spend and how much you actually spent is the **budget variance**. If total expenses are greater than total income, you have to make some changes in the budget. You must either decrease your expenses or increase your income. You might need

THE STRIVING ARTISTS
After recording six songs they run out of money. Whittaker takes out more student loans and continues balancing art school and work. The rest of the guys continue working full time. Each spends his monthly income on food, clothing, rent, and entertainment. These things are examples of what?

continued on p. 461

Chapter 28

Real-World Application
Caption Answer

THE STRIVING ARTISTS:
PART 2 OF 4
Expenditures.

Individualized Practice

You worked in a group of three in this chapter's Bell Ringer Activity. Working with the same group, compare each of your nine questions with the kinds of questions Michael and Nora Kemal answered when they prepared their budget (see page 462 or Figure 28.2).

L1 Have groups compare their questions with the Kemal's budget process.

L2 Ask groups to make a chart comparing the questions, and then present their chart to the class.

L3 Ask groups to prepare and present a one-act play depicting the steps the Kemals took in preparing their budget.

Great Ideas From the Classroom of...

Gloria Farris
Seneca High School
Louisville, Ky.

Analyzing Paycheck Stubs. Although many teenagers have jobs, they don't always understand the information provided on their pay stubs. Present a display of sample paycheck stubs to show the similarities and differences in payroll deductions. Discuss both the required and optional deductions represented on the pay stubs. Perform calculations to determine the percentage subtracted for each deduction.

✓ Fast Review Answers

1. Gross pay is the total amount you earn. Net pay is the amount you take home after deductions.
2. Taxes, health insurance, retirement, and union dues.
3. Federal, state, and local income taxes and social security.
4. Food, long-distance phone charges, entertainment, and gifts.
5. The difference between planned spending and actual spending.

Working Lifestyle

Caption Answer

What are the advantages and disadvantages to you of this occupation? Have students add their answer to this question to the presentation of their findings. **CL**, **LS**, **P**

Business Connection

SAVINGS. Ferrell McDonald increased her personal savings rate from 5 percent to 15 percent after one crash course with Financial Finesse, a financial education firm. Financial Finesse, based in San Francisco, runs seminars around the U.S. teaching people that small savings add up. The best thing is when you're saving and managing your money you don't have to depend on anyone else—you're an independent person.

---

to move into an apartment with lower rent or cut down on your phone or electricity usage. You might need to add a part-time job or try to find a higher-paying job to meet your expenses.

✓ Fast Review

1. What is the difference between gross pay and net pay?
2. Give some examples of deductions.
3. What types of taxes are often withheld from a paycheck?
4. Give examples of variable expenses.
5. What is a budget variance?

Working Lifestyle

What are you doing at 10 A.M.?

An English Teacher Sets the Stage

At 6:45 A.M. Susanna Barkataki grabs a toasted bagel on her way out the door and drives to her old high school. Though she hasn't grown any taller since she was a student, she now walks the halls as an English teacher. Now, she's on the other side of the desk, with the grade book and a tattered copy of *Catcher in the Rye* at her side.

By 10 A.M. Barkataki sets the stage by asking the students to open their journals and respond to some wacky question like "Will the sun rise tomorrow? How do you know? What would you do if it didn't?" Students laugh, occasionally roll their eyes, and then start writing. Barkataki uses the students' responses as a starting point for the theme of the day's class. Other times she sets up a day's theme by asking critical thinking questions, which require them to use their interpretive skills.

Barkataki has a passion for books, ideas, and language. "I'm doing what I love," she says, even at the end of a day of teaching. "My students discuss great ideas and bring a fresh perspective. I'm constantly asking them to look deeper into literature by connecting these universal themes to their lives and our world."

Salary

A typical high school teacher earns a median income of $43,761, with a range between $37,519 and $54,571.

Outlook for This Career

Employment of teachers is expected to grow faster than other occupations. Teaching positions in rural and urban locations are especially plentiful.

Connecting Careers Activity

Imagine you are a high-school teacher six years from now. What one value, or one book, would you teach? List at least ten good questions you would ask the students.

CAREER PATH — Education & Training

Global Perspective

Percentage Savings. Americans save about 5 percent of their income. Individuals in many other countries save a larger percentage of their income. Other countries with a notably higher percentage of savings include Belgium 22 percent, Denmark 16.2 percent, Japan 15.7 percent, and Canada 8 percent. Have students research the average per capita savings in several other nations and display their findings in a bar graph. **P**, **CL**, **LS**

A Sample Budget

Let's follow the steps that a young couple, Michael and Nora Kemal, used to set up a budget. They want to plan their spending so they can get the most for their money. They decided to set up a monthly budget and an annual budget.

Step 1: Setting Goals

First, they drew up a list of their goals, both short-term and long-term. They decided which of their wants were most important to them. Setting goals is the first step in developing a spending plan that will meet as many of their goals as possible.

Step 2: Estimating Income

Next, the Kemals estimated their income for the year. They wanted to know how much money they would have available during the planning period. Michael, a salesperson, earns a gross annual income of $19,000. Nora is a management trainee and earns $21,500 a year. Michael and Nora included only their take-home pay as income. Although they earn a total of $40,500, their take-home pay is only about $31,200. They used that amount in their planning, since that's the amount they actually have to spend.

If the Kemals had an income from investments or rental properties, they would include this income in their budget. They don't have a large savings account. Most of their savings have gone to rent a new apartment. They don't, therefore, include interest from their savings account in their budget. When they have built up their savings again, they may be able to add interest income to their estimated total income.

Step 3: Estimating Expenses

Next, the Kemals estimated their expenses for the planning period. They kept a record of actual expenses for the past several months. Then they made a list of planned expenses and savings for the year. The list included their fixed expenses like rent, variable expenses like food and clothing, and money to put in their savings account.

Step 4: Planning for Savings

When Michael and Nora prepared their budget, they took their goals into consideration. Their savings budget reflects their goals. To begin saving for a vacation, they're cutting their entertainment expenses.

Real-World Application
part 3 of 4

THE STRIVING ARTISTS
Five months later and armed with greener pockets, they head back into the studio to finish recording their demo. Tabanou uses his sound engineering skills to finalize each track's mix. Whittaker applies his talents to the CD artwork. Between the prepress shop and manufacturing costs, The Agency forks over another $1,700 for production costs.
Name some of their estimated expenses in order to finish the CD.

continued on p. 463

Real-World Application
Caption Answer

THE STRIVING ARTISTS: PART 3 OF 4
Studio space, artwork, and manufacturing costs.

Develop Concepts

STEPS.   Ask students to choose two short-term goals from the time line they made in this chapter's "Critical Thinking" activity. For each goal, have students write steps they plan to take to achieve the goal. (Steps will include estimating the cost, planning for savings, and estimating expenses.)

Discussion Starter

WHAT HAPPENS?   Imagine you've got a written budget. What happens when you have an unexpected expense, such as buying a gift? Imagine you've set your budget up using a computer. Now what happens when you have unexpected expenses or new income?

COMPUTER TECHNOLOGY   *Curriculum Connection*

Budget Software.   Point out that computerized budget programs work along the same principles as business accounting programs and spreadsheets. When an entry in one classification is changed, other categories are automatically adjusted. Ask students to give two specific examples of changes that a computerized budget would handle. Ask students whether they think they would be more or less likely to stick to a budget developed on the computer. Have them explain their answers. (If income goes up, the computer can show how savings could be increased. If an expense goes up, the computer can show what changes will be needed.) **CL**, LS

3 ASSESS

Reteaching

NET PAY. To reteach the concept of net pay, ask students to create a sketch that shows the relationship between gross pay, deductions, and net or take-home pay. Students should write a mathematical sentence or equation that defines the relationship. (Gross pay – deductions = net pay.)

Enrichment Strategy

DIAGRAM. Work in pairs to create and illustrate a poster graphically representing the five steps in setting up a budget. Show details in each step. **LS**

Evaluation

Assign and review the Fast Review sections.

Figure 28.2 Caption Answer

$1,200 (annual) or $100 (monthly).

Michael and Nora know that to save money, they need to have a regular, systematic plan. The Kemals' budget is shown in Figure 28.2.

When they developed their budget, Michael and Nora had to be sure that the total income figure was the same as the total for planned expenses and savings. If their planned expenses and savings had been more than their income, they would have had to cut some expenses or find some other source of income.

Step 5: Balancing and Adjusting the Budget

After their budget was prepared, the Kemals kept records of their actual expenses. They organized their expenses into various categories, such as car expenses, rent, and entertainment. After they had estimated annual expenses and income, the Kemals developed a monthly budget. They divided the yearly figures by 12 to estimate how to manage their money from one month to the next. At the end of each month, Michael

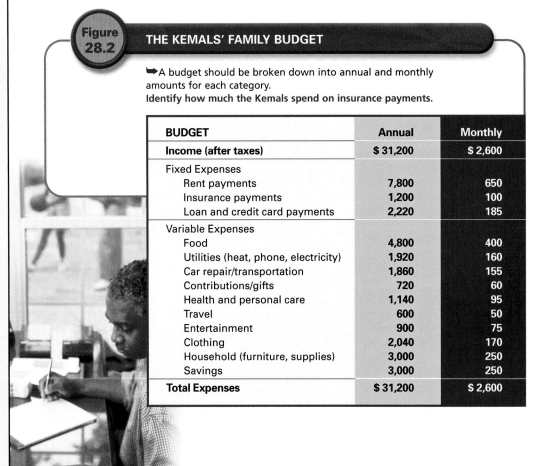

Figure 28.2

THE KEMALS' FAMILY BUDGET

➡A budget should be broken down into annual and monthly amounts for each category.
Identify how much the Kemals spend on insurance payments.

BUDGET	Annual	Monthly
Income (after taxes)	**$ 31,200**	**$ 2,600**
Fixed Expenses		
Rent payments	7,800	650
Insurance payments	1,200	100
Loan and credit card payments	2,220	185
Variable Expenses		
Food	4,800	400
Utilities (heat, phone, electricity)	1,920	160
Car repair/transportation	1,860	155
Contributions/gifts	720	60
Health and personal care	1,140	95
Travel	600	50
Entertainment	900	75
Clothing	2,040	170
Household (furniture, supplies)	3,000	250
Savings	3,000	250
Total Expenses	**$ 31,200**	**$ 2,600**

462

Cooperative Learning

Group Discussion. Organize students into groups to conduct a panel discussion on issues related to the sample budget in Figure 28.2. Topics might include how the Kemals might change the amounts they budget for food and rent, how to keep the budget balanced even with increasing health care, or how to control over spending (depending on loans and credit cards for purchases). In addition, prepare slips of paper and write on them changes to items in the Kemal's budget. Have groups select one or more slips and determine how the family's budget will change. **CL**, **LS**

and Nora totaled their actual expenses for each item. They then compared these totals with their budgeted amounts to see if they were keeping within their budget.

Balancing the Budget. When they compared their monthly budgeted amounts with their actual expenses, the Kemals found that they spent less than they had budgeted for food, utilities, car expenses, and entertainment. On the other hand, they spent more than their budgeted amounts for health care, clothing, and household expenses. Even with these differences, Michael and Nora had money left at the end of the month. Their total expenses were close to their total income for the month. They were living within their budget.

Adjusting the Budget. After looking at their actual expenses, the Kemals decided to make some changes in their budget. They chose to reduce the amount budgeted for food. They decided not to decrease the other budgeted amounts, since their utility bills or car expenses may be higher in the future. They increased the budget for clothing and household expenses, the two main areas in which their expenses were more than the budgeted amounts. They increased those two items by the amount they reduced the food budget. The Kemals have adjusted their budget according to their needs.

Using a Computer for Budgeting

Many people have computers in their homes. Several kinds of software programs are available for setting up and maintaining a household budget. With a computerized budgeting program, you can store your budgeted amounts and enter your expenses as they occur or at the end of the month. The computer can give you a quick analysis of total expenses, including amounts that are over and under the budget.

In addition, the computer can help with "what if" situations. For example, what if Nora Kemal's income increased by ten percent? With their computer, the Kemals can easily find out how much more they could save each month. What if their rent went up by $50 a month? What if they also wanted to save for a new computer? How much more would they have to cut their entertainment and travel expenses to buy the computer in one year? By using a computer, the Kemals could quickly see how such changes would affect their budget.

 Fast Review _____

1. What is the Kemals' gross income and net income?
2. How did the Kemals use their annual figures to come up with a monthly budget?

Chapter 28 Planning a Budget   **463**

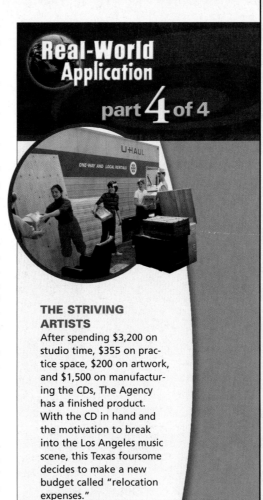

THE STRIVING ARTISTS
After spending $3,200 on studio time, $355 on practice space, $200 on artwork, and $1,500 on manufacturing the CDs, The Agency has a finished product. With the CD in hand and the motivation to break into the Los Angeles music scene, this Texas foursome decides to make a new budget called "relocation expenses."
How might they have to adjust their budget in order to move to a bigger city?

Chapter 28

Real-World Application
Caption Answer

THE STRIVING ARTISTS: PART 4 OF 4

Account for higher living expenses (i.e., food, housing, utilities, health care, transportation, entertainment, etc.).

Technology Resource

GO TO **VIRTUAL BUSINESS.** Introduce budget planning using Knowledge Matters' *Virtual Business* interactive simulation. Go to the *Introduction to Business* Web site **www.introbus.glencoe.com** to download the *Virtual Business* activity. Run the *Virtual Business* tutorial before beginning this activity.

Fast Review Answers

1. Gross income $40,500. Net income $31,200.
2. They divided the yearly figures by 12.

Meeting Individual Needs

Students With Writing Difficulties. Students with writing difficulties often copy answers directly from the book and have problems when they encounter questions that require some interpretation. Help them practice "reading between the lines" in the text, not only to have students make interpretation but also to help them recognize when information is implied.

A Day on the Town

1 FOCUS

Direct students' attention to the prices listed under the various cities. Point out that these are average prices, based on surveys of many stores, restaurants, gasoline stations, and movie theaters.

2 TEACH

Have students note the varying prices of lunch from city to city. Then point out that there are many reasons for these differences. First, the type of food might be of varying qualities. Second, the costs of production vary greatly from country to country. For instance, labor tends to be cheaper in less developed countries, such as India.

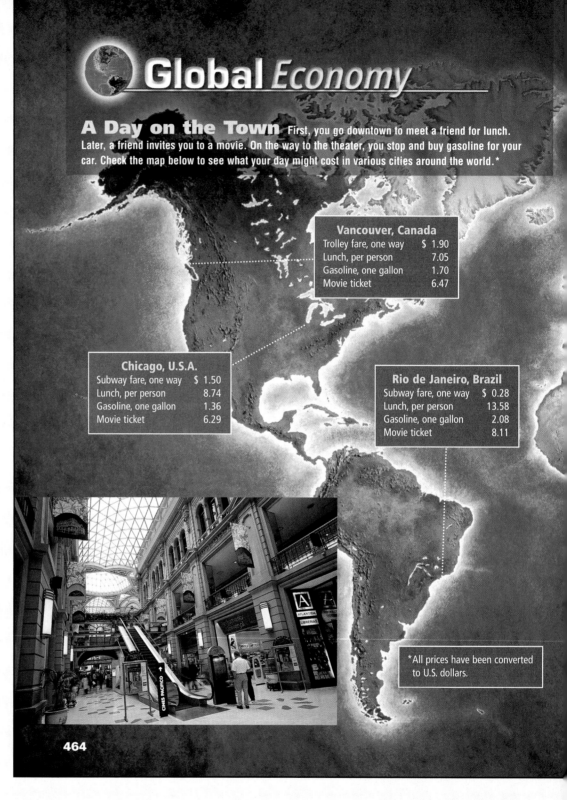

Global *Economy*

A Day on the Town First, you go downtown to meet a friend for lunch. Later, a friend invites you to a movie. On the way to the theater, you stop and buy gasoline for your car. Check the map below to see what your day might cost in various cities around the world.*

Vancouver, Canada

Trolley fare, one way	$ 1.90
Lunch, per person	7.05
Gasoline, one gallon	1.70
Movie ticket	6.47

Chicago, U.S.A.

Subway fare, one way	$ 1.50
Lunch, per person	8.74
Gasoline, one gallon	1.36
Movie ticket	6.29

Rio de Janeiro, Brazil

Subway fare, one way	$ 0.28
Lunch, per person	13.58
Gasoline, one gallon	2.08
Movie ticket	8.11

*All prices have been converted to U.S. dollars.

464

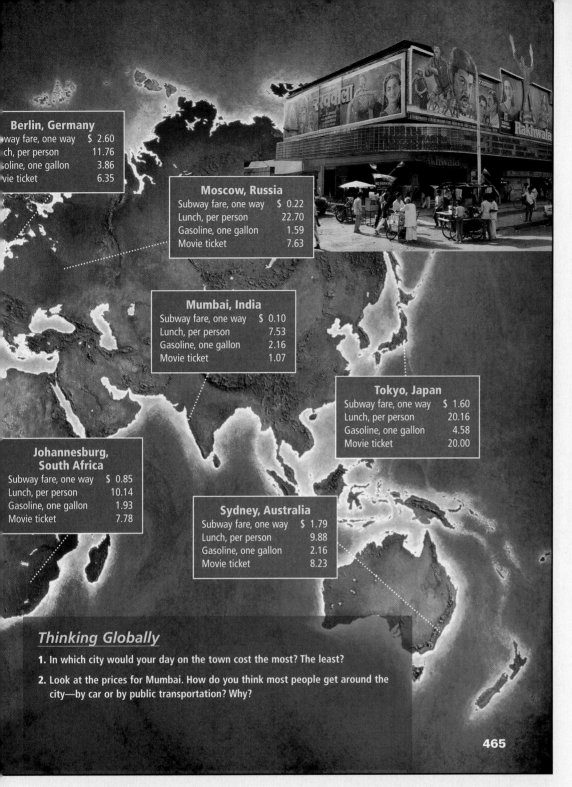

Berlin, Germany

way fare, one way	$ 2.60
ch, per person	11.76
soline, one gallon	3.86
vie ticket	6.35

Moscow, Russia

Subway fare, one way	$ 0.22
Lunch, per person	22.70
Gasoline, one gallon	1.59
Movie ticket	7.63

Mumbai, India

Subway fare, one way	$ 0.10
Lunch, per person	7.53
Gasoline, one gallon	2.16
Movie ticket	1.07

Tokyo, Japan

Subway fare, one way	$ 1.60
Lunch, per person	20.16
Gasoline, one gallon	4.58
Movie ticket	20.00

Johannesburg, South Africa

Subway fare, one way	$ 0.85
Lunch, per person	10.14
Gasoline, one gallon	1.93
Movie ticket	7.78

Sydney, Australia

Subway fare, one way	$ 1.79
Lunch, per person	9.88
Gasoline, one gallon	2.16
Movie ticket	8.23

Thinking Globally

1. In which city would your day on the town cost the most? The least?

2. Look at the prices for Mumbai. How do you think most people get around the city—by car or by public transportation? Why?

465

3 ASSESS

Have students answer the "Thinking Globally" questions.

4 CLOSE

You might close this feature by asking students the following question: Which of the prices did you find the most surprising? Why?

? Did You Know?

Which is the most expensive city in the world? According to a study conducted by the European Union (EU) the most expensive city in the world for business travelers is Moscow, closely followed by Tokyo, Buenos Aires, and Hong Kong. Another study by the EU found that the most expensive EU city to live in was Copenhagen, followed by Paris and Berlin.

Thinking Globally — *Caption Answer*

1. The day on the town would cost the most in Tokyo. It would cost the least in Mumbai.

2. By public transportation, because the subway fare is only 10¢, while a gallon of gasoline is over $2.

4 CLOSE

Chapter Wrap-Up

To close, ask students to complete the following statement: "The three things I learned during this chapter that I will use in my life are (1) _____, (2) _____, and (3) _____."

Using Business Key Words

1. variable expenses
2. net pay
3. budget
4. gross pay
5. fixed expenses
6. deductions
7. money management
8. income
9. withholding
10. expenditures
11. budget variance

Review What You Learned

12. A monetary plan.
13. Guide your spending.
14. Expected income, planned expenses, and long-term spending.
15. Yes.
16. Fixed expenses occur regularly (e.g., rent, car payment). The amount can change from time to time, but it usually stays about the same over long periods. Variable expenses fluctuate (e.g., food, gifts).
17. Protect you against unexpected expenses.
18. Track expenses, quick analysis, etc.

Summary

1. A good budget helps you set priorities for spending and saving and keeps track of how you're managing your money.

2. The five steps in planning a budget are setting goals, estimating income, estimating expenses, planning for savings, and adjusting the budget as needed.

3. Gross pay is the total amount of money you earn; net pay is the amount you take home after deductions. Fixed expenses are expenses that must be paid regularly; variable expenses are expenses that change and you have some control over.

4. Computer software can help you set up, maintain a budget, and predict how changes will affect your budget.

Using Business Key Words

When you're trying to manage your money, it's important to know the following terms. See how well you know them by completing each sentence with the correct term.

- **budget**
- **net pay**
- **gross pay**
- **budget variance**
- **fixed expenses**
- **income**
- **money management**
- **deductions**
- **withholding**
- **variable expenses**
- **expenditures**

1. _____ are expenses that fluctuate and over which you have no control.
2. Your _____ is your gross pay minus deductions.
3. An important part of managing money is making a plan, or a _____.
4. Your _____ is the total amount of money you earn for a specific time.
5. _____ are expenses that occur regularly and that must be paid regularly.
6. Taxes, insurance payments, retirement contributions, and union dues are examples of _____.
7. The process of planning how to get the most from your money is called _____.
8. Your _____ is the actual amount of money you earn or receive during a given time period.
9. Money subtracted from a paycheck for taxes is called your _____.
10. Clothing, food, and rent are examples of spending money on _____.
11. The difference between planned, or budgeted spending, and actual spending is called _____.

Quick Quiz

1. What's the most important factor in setting your budget? (Your goals.)
2. What part does saving play in a budget? (Allows you to do things you like to do. Helps protect against unplanned expenses.)
3. Subtracting taxes from a paycheck is called _____. (Withholding.)

Review What You Learned

12. What is money management?
13. What is the purpose of a budget?
14. What are the three categories of items that should be included in a budget?
15. Should a budget ever be changed? Why or why not?
16. What is the difference between fixed expenses and variable expenses? Give an example of each.
17. Why is it important to save part of your income on a regular basis?
18. How can using a computer help in budgeting?

Understanding Business Concepts

19. Your friends spend money like water. Sometimes you wonder how they afford to buy nice clothes and shoes. Has it ever occurred to you they might be living above their means? Perhaps they're living off credit? What do people's spending habits say about them? How should a budget relate to your values and goals?
20. When you make a budget, why is it best not to include gifts or unusual income?
21. What is a good way to estimate your expenses from month to month when you are preparing a budget?
22. What is the most difficult step in the budgeting process? Explain why.
23. Did the Kemals follow the five steps as they prepared their budget? Explain.

Critical Thinking

24. In planning a budget, why is it important that the figure for take-home pay (not gross pay) be used for income?
25. Examine your own fixed and variable expenses. Which are higher? Explain why.
26. Kareen, a friend who started working full-time, got her first paycheck last week. Explain Kareen's withholding.
27. Do you think a computer is useful in keeping a budget? Explain why or why not.

Viewing and Representing

Examining the Image. Look at the picture. How does it make you feel? Imagine you have a million dollars. What would you do to manage a million dollars? Make a list of how you would allocate the money to yourself, your family, and any other purposes.

Critical Thinking

24. The difference between gross pay and take-home pay is not yours to spend. It is the money deducted from your check for taxes, insurance, etc. If you used it for income you would be utilizing an inaccurate figure in your budget.
25. Answers will vary.
26. Withholding is when social security and federal, state, and income taxes are deducted from a paycheck. These deductions mean the amount of take-home pay is usually about one-third less than the gross pay.
27. Answers will vary and may include a computer program is useful because of the automatic calculations and recalculations.

Viewing and Representing

Survey students' reactions in answer to the questions in this activity. To keep the answers confidential, tell students to close their eyes when they answer. Immediately report to the class the count of "yes" and "no" votes. Ask questions such as: Did the idea of having so much money make you scared? To manage the million dollars, did you first write down your goals in life? To manage the million dollars, did you first write down your values? Did you include any charitable contributions on your list? **LS**

Understanding Business Concepts

19. Reflect your own goals and values.
20. Answers may vary. Budget based on steady income.
21. Estimate your expenses based on personal history.
22. Balancing and adjusting the budget.
23. Yes. They set their goals, estimated their income ($37,500 take-home pay), estimated expenses, planned for savings, and balanced and adjusted as necessary.

4 CLOSE (Cont.)

Building Academic Skills

LANGUAGE ARTS. Rubrics: Note taking, essay.

MATH. Remind students to be specific about all expenditures. There should be no miscellaneous categories! Rubric: Budget.

COMPUTER/TECHNOLOGY. Rubric: Spreadsheet.

HISTORY. Make sure all group members participate in this project. If possible, encourage different groups to obtain budgets from different entities. If the students are having trouble obtaining the budgets, acquire one for them and distribute. Allow the students to choose the way they wish to share their findings. Rubrics: Charts/tables, oral presentation, essay.

Linking School to Home

Papers will vary depending on the person interviewed. Encourage students to develop their questions before the interview begins. Rubric: Essay.

Linking School to Work

Students' workshops will vary. Rubrics: Oral presentation.

Building Academic Skills

 Writing Down Goals

What are your goals for the future? Write a description of where you see yourself living and what you see yourself doing in ten years. Then, write a short plan describing the money management techniques you'll use in order to meet your goals.

Preparing a Personal Budget

Select a postsecondary institution (e.g., technical school, community college, or university) that you would like to attend after high school. Obtain information on tuition and other fees. Add to these amounts the costs of food, shelter, clothing, books and supplies, transportation, and any other items you believe are part of the cost of the education you would like to receive. Estimate the total cost of the education. Then, estimate how you'll pay for the education. Include income from parents or relatives, loans, scholarships, personal savings, and part-time employment. Prepare a budget for the length of time that will be needed to finance and complete your education.

 Spreadsheet Software Application

Prepare a personal budget with your information above and present it in spreadsheet form.

 Comparing Budgets

In groups, obtain a copy of the budget for your school, school district, local government agency, or other public entity from ten years ago. Then, obtain a current copy. Compare the budgets. Has income increased or decreased? Have the expenses increased or decreased?

Linking School to Home

Interviewing. The accessibility to personal finance software makes it easier for everyone to become personally empowered by controlling his or her own finances. Interview someone who uses technology to record and organize his or her budgets and other financial records. Ask for an explanation of how the technology has affected the way he or she handles money and budgets for expenditures. How much does this person estimate he or she saved by adhering to a budget? Write a one-page paper with your findings.

Linking School to Work

Creating a Workshop. Unfortunately many people are working to just pay their bills instead of learning how to reevaluate their personal financial situation. Become an investor in your future by learning how to budget, which is one step closer to financial freedom. In groups of four or five, create a workshop based on the five steps in this chapter. Present the workshop in class and ask your fellow students to critique it. Make any changes that are necessary and offer the workshop to other students, faculty, and community members.

E-Homework

Applying Technology

Personal Finance Software. Using the Internet, locate examples of free software that can be used for budgeting and/or money management. Choose the best one you can find and share the Web site with your class.

Researching Social Security. One of the deductions from your paycheck is to the Social Security Administration. Log onto the Web site for the Social Security Administration (**www.ssa.gov**). Find out what benefits are paid for through this fund.

Connecting Academics

Math. Collect from magazines pictures and prices of three big-ticket items you'd like. For each item, figure out the equivalent cost in movies (at $7 per movie) and the equivalent cost in eating out (at $9 per meal). For example, if a stereo costs $350, its cost-equivalent is 50 movies. If you gave up one movie a week, how long would it take to save enough money to purchase each item? If you gave up eating out twice a month, how long would it take to save enough money to purchase each item?

Social Science. To become wealthy and self-reliant, you must be a savvy investor. You need to decide if purchasing the latest gadget or an expensive meal is more important than a larger goal like buying a car, going to college, or investing in your retirement plan. A big boost to your self-worth comes from managing your money. Make a realistic spending plan for this week and stick to it. By keeping to your plan and knowing you're in control of your money, you'll build your self-esteem. It's evidence that you can set and achieve a goal.

BusinessWeek | Analyzing the Feature Story

You read the first part of "Why Higher Rates Aren't Denting Consumers' Spirits" at the beginning of this chapter. Below are a few questions for you to answer about personal budgeting. You'll find the answers to these questions when you're reading the entire article. First, here are the questions:

28. Why does the Federal Reserve care about household spending?

29. How would personal budgeting help consumers who spend at a faster rate than their incomes grow?

CREATIVE JOURNAL ACTIVITY

Create a budget based on your weekly allowance or earnings from part-time work. How much money do you want to spend on entertainment or eating out? What percentage would you like to save for a special purchase?

BUSINESS Online
The Full Story

To learn more about personal budgeting, visit the *Introduction to Business* Web site at **www.introbus.glencoe.com**, and click on *BusinessWeek* Feature Story, Chapter 28.

E-Homework

PERSONAL FINANCE SOFTWARE. Answers will vary depending on the Web site selected. Rubric: Oral presentation.

RESEARCHING SOCIAL SECURITY. Allow the students to share their findings with the class. Rubrics: Note taking, oral presentation, essay.

Connecting Academics

MATH. Answers will depend on the prices of the items chosen.

SOCIAL SCIENCE. Spending plans will vary. Let students know you expect them to give a follow-up report in a week. Have students report their successes, failures, and ideas for changes to incorporate in their next budget.

BusinessWeek | Analyzing the Feature Story

28. Consumer spending can be a predictor of how the economy is doing overall.

29. A budget would show individual consumers that their incomes would not be able to keep up with their spending indefinitely. Budgeting makes you set goals and priorities for your spending.

Creative Journal Activity

The most common errors in planning a budget include failure to plan for predictable expenses, unrealistic expense estimates, and failure to be specific in setting up budget categories (such as "extras.") Have students discuss how to avoid these errors when planning their budget. **LS, CL**

SCANS Correlation Chart*

Foundation Skills

Basic Skills	Reading	Writing	Math	Listening	Speaking	
Thinking Skills	Creative Thinking	Decision Making	Problem Solving	Seeing Things in the Mind's Eye	Knowing How to Learn	Reasoning
Personal Qualities	Responsibility	Self-Esteem	Sociability	Self-Management	Integrity/Honesty	

Workplace Competencies

Resources	Allocating Time	Allocating Money	Allocating Material and Facility Resources	Allocating Human Resources		
Information	Acquiring and Evaluating Information	Organizing and Maintaining Information	Interpreting and Communicating Information	Using Computers to Process Information		
Interpersonal Skills	Participating as a Member of a Team	Teaching Others	Serving Clients/Customers	Exercising Leadership	Negotiating to Arrive at a Decision	Working With Cultural Diversity
Systems	Understanding Systems	Monitoring and Correcting Performance	Improving and Designing Systems			
Technology	Selecting Technology	Applying Technology to Task	Maintaining and Troubleshooting Technology			

*This chart's highlighted blocks indicate the chapter's content coverage in the Student Edition and the Teacher Wraparound Edition.

Resource Manager

Teaching Transparencies

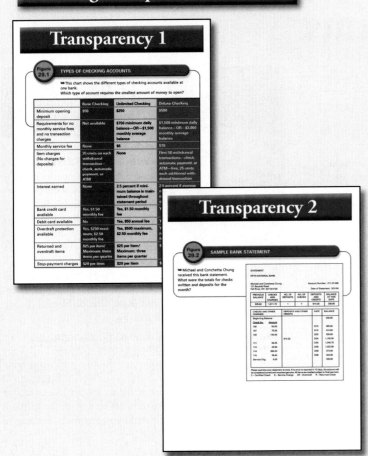

Transparency 1

Figure 29.1 — TYPES OF CHECKING ACCOUNTS

Transparency 2

Figure 29.2 — SAMPLE BANK STATEMENT

Application and Enrichment

- Lesson Plans
- *BusinessWeek* Poster Package
- Teaching Transparencies
- Integrated Software Simulation
- Glencoe Business Video Package

Review and Reinforcement

- *PuzzleMaker*
- Internet Resources
- Student Activity Workbook
- Strat. and Work. for Teaching Transparencies

Assessment and Evaluation

- Reproducible Tests
- Alternative Assessment Strategies
- ExamView® Pro Test Generator

Technology

- *PuzzleMaker*
- ExamView® Pro Test Generator
- Glencoe Business Video Package
- PowerPoint® Presentation
- Integrated Software Simulation
- Interactive Lesson Planner
- *Virtual Business*®

KEY	Printed	Software	Videocassette	Poster
	Transparency	CD-ROM	Internet	

BUSINESS Online

Visit www.introbus.glencoe.com, the Web site companion to *Introduction to Business*. The student's page includes:

- interactive tutor
- additional *BusinessWeek* articles and activities
- business Web links
- homework hints
- real-world application activities
- additional career path activities

Information on how to prepare your students for the high school exit exam and special projects are also included.

Use the Glencoe Web site for additional resources. All essential content is covered in the Student Edition.

1 FOCUS

Introducing the Chapter

This chapter explains the basics of checking accounts. It also describes the major services that banks offer. A photo essay, "Where Does That Check Go?," enhances the concepts.

Connecting the Objectives

What are checking accounts used for? How can you make sure that the bank and you agree about the amount of money in your account?

BusinessWeek
Feature Story

Story's Summary

Nordea, based in Finland, is the world's most successful online bank. Nordea has branches throughout Scandinavia and it handles 6.9 million online transactions each month. The largest online-only bank, Egg, handles only one-fourteenth that many transactions. Why the big difference? It comes down to Nordea having an existing customer base and good customer relationships. Nordea has spent only $18 million over five years on its online bank. Egg needed to invest $650 million just to attract customers.

Find the entire article at www.introbus.glencoe.com, or in the Teacher Resource Binder.

Checking Accounts

Learning Objectives

After completing this chapter, you'll be able to:
1. **Identify** types of checking accounts.
2. **Describe** some of the major services that banks provide.
3. **Name** the ways checking transactions are recorded.
4. **Explain** how to reconcile a checking account.

Why It's Important

Paying with checks is the most common medium of exchange.

Key Words

demand deposits
interest-bearing account
signature card
overdrawing
overdraft protection
stop payment
debit card
check register
endorsement
bank statement
canceled checks
bank reconciliation
outstanding checks

470

BusinessWeek Feature Story

The Dynamo of E-Banking

Inside Scandinavia's Successful Internet Bank. Five years ago, lunchtime queues at the dozen teller windows of the Nordea bank branch in Helsinki's financial district would have stretched to a half-hour. But shortly after noon on a recent Monday, only four tellers serve customers—and even then, no lines. The reason for the change? Simple: Nearly two-thirds of Nordea's Finnish clients bank on the Internet. "There's nothing more natural than banking with your computer," says Bo Harald, Nordea's director of electronic banking.

Source: Excerpted with permission from "The Dynamo of E-Banking," *BusinessWeek Online,* **April 16, 2001.**

An Extension Activity

What might be a big hurdle for an upstart like an online bank? Visit an online bank to see what kind of transactions can be made online. What would make you become a customer of an online bank?

BUSINESS
Online
The Full Story
To learn more about e-banking, visit the *Introduction to Business* Web site at www.introbus.glencoe.com, and click on *BusinessWeek* Feature Story, Chapter 29.

Classroom Resources

For the Teacher
- Student Activity Work. TAE
- Assessment Binder
- PowerPoint® Presentation
- Interactive Lesson Planner
- Lesson Plans
- Internet Resources
- Teaching Transparencies
- *Introduction to Business* Web Site

- Integrated Soft. Sim. TM
- *BusinessWeek* Poster Package

For the Student
- Student Activity Workbook
- *Virtual Business*®
- *Introduction to Business* Web Site
- Integrated Soft. Sim.
- *PuzzleMaker*
- Strategies and Worksheets for Teaching Transparencies

Bell Ringer Activity

SELF-ESTEEM. You can build your self-esteem by knowing that you will remember important information. Here's a memory aid you can adapt to many situations— "Carry Connection." Simply draw four different backpacks, cases, or totes, to "carry" the main ideas from each of the four parts of this chapter: Opening a Checking Account, Account Services, Account Records, and Bank Reconciliation. Fill the "totes" with important points as you go through this chapter. **LS**

Preteaching Business Key Words

WRITING. Ask students to create a fill-in-the-blank test for each key word. The tests will be used in the "Chapter Wrap-Up" activity. **LS**

An Extension Activity

ANSWER. Credibility and customer confidence. Lead students in a discussion of the pros and cons of online banking.

Making Connections

Everyday Life. Very often people have joint checking accounts. Many married couples have joint checking accounts. A parent can be on a joint account with a son or daughter. This is especially useful when a son or daughter is in college, living away from home, and regularly needing funds. Another example is when a parent has a joint account with a son or daughter who is a single adult. This ensures that in case of an accident, the parent can access the son or daughter's account. Ask students: If Anita and Raj have a joint checking account, but only Anita's name is printed on the check, who can write checks on the account? (Anita and Raj.)

2 TEACH

Business Connection

CHECKING ACCOUNTS. Peoples Heritage Bank, based in Portland, Maine, provides what people want—checking accounts that are simple and easy to use. Peoples offers three choices: SimplyFree Checking, Interest Checking, and High Rate Checking. With the High Rate Checking account, a high minimum balance is required but the account earns interest.

Develop Concepts

BANKING SERVICES. Ask students to generate a list of the banking services a person might require for their checking account. (Answers will include overdraft protection, stop payment, debit cards, and online checking.) **LS**, **CL**

Figure 29.1 Caption Answer

The Basic Checking Account requires only $50 to open.

The Basics of a Checking Account

You've learned about money, banking, and the Federal Reserve. This information should help you get the "big picture" of banking and banking services. As part of the federal government, the Fed oversees and establishes financial policy for banks that serve the public. Now it's your

Figure 29.1

TYPES OF CHECKING ACCOUNTS

➡ This chart shows the different types of checking accounts available at one bank.

Which type of account requires the smallest amount of money to open?

	Basic Checking	Unlimited Checking	Deluxe Checking
Minimum opening deposit	$50	$250	$500
Requirements for no monthly service fees and no transaction charges	Not available	$750 minimum daily balance—OR—$1,500 monthly average balance	$1,500 minimum daily balance—OR—$3,000 monthly average balance
Monthly service fee	None	$6	$10
Item charges (No charges for deposits)	35 cents on each withdrawal transaction—check, automatic payment, or ATM	None	First 50 withdrawal transactions—check, automatic payment, or ATM—free; 25 cents each additional withdrawal transaction
Interest earned	None	2.5 percent if minimum balance is maintained throughout statement period	2.5 percent if average minimum balance is maintained throughout statement period
Bank credit card available	Yes, $1.50 monthly fee	Yes, $1.50 monthly fee	Yes, no charge
Debit card available	No	Yes, $50 annual fee	Yes, no annual fee
Overdraft protection available	Yes, $250 maximum, $2.50 monthly fee	Yes, $500 maximum, $2.50 monthly fee	Yes, $1,000 maximum, no monthly fee
Returned and overdraft items	$25 per item/ Maximum: three items per quarter	$25 per item/ Maximum: three items per quarter	$25 per item
Stop-payment charges	$20 per item	$20 per item	$20 per item

Cooperative Learning

Math Pairs. Ask pairs of students to use the information in Figure 29.1 above to answer the following questions: Vinita Kumar has an unlimited checking account. If Vinita keeps a $1,500 average balance for one month, how much interest does she earn? Last month, Vinita's account had an average balance of $2,150. How much interest did she earn last month? ($1,500 × 0.025 = $37.50. Last month: $2,150 × 0.025 = $53.75.)

chance to find out the basics about checking accounts, whether or not you have one now or in the near future.

You may already know that banks offer savings and checking accounts. However, banks also offer other services such as credit cards, loans, financial planning services, and investments. The Federal Reserve System, the central banking authority in the United States, regulates many of these services. As part of federal government, the Fed oversees and establishes financial policy for banks that serve the public. In this chapter you'll learn how you, as a consumer, can use checking account services offered by banks and other financial institutions.

Opening an Account

One of the most important services banks provide is the convenience of checking accounts. It's hard to imagine how businesses would function without the convenience of checks. About 85 percent of all U.S. households have checking accounts. Figure 29.1 illustrates the types of accounts often available. With a checking account, a customer deposits money in an account and receives a book of checks. The checks can then be used to pay for purchases anywhere. Checking accounts are sometimes called **demand deposits** because each check a customer writes is an order to the bank to release money from the account on demand. The check is paid to the payee, the person or business indicated on the check. Checks are the most common medium of exchange. They're more widely used than cash or credit cards.

Types of Accounts

Most banks offer several types of checking accounts. Before opening a checking account, a wise consumer investigates all the kinds of accounts available, as well as their advantages and costs. The customer service representatives at banks can answer questions about account services, fees, and charges. You might also want to ask other people about their experience with different banks and different types of accounts. Shop around and compare financial institutions and what they have to offer.

Regular Account. A regular checking account is designed for customers who write a few checks each month and don't keep a minimum amount of money in the account. If a customer can afford to keep a minimum balance—ranging from $50 to $500—other options are available. Withdrawals from a checking account include checks the customer

Real-World Application

part 1 of 4

WHERE DOES THAT CHECK GO?
Just in the United States, an estimated 70 billion checks are written each year. Every day people write and hand over 270 million checks for some kind of transaction. As you stand in line at the grocery store perusing a glossy magazine and gazing at the tabloids' headlines, you notice your mom writing a check for the groceries.
What do you think the grocery store does with her check?

continued on p. 475

Chapter 29 Checking Accounts **473**

Chapter 29

Technology Resource

GO TO POWERPOINT. The *Introduction to Business* PowerPoint® CD-ROM provides visual lecture aids for this chapter.

Independent Practice

CHART. Create a chart or freeform diagram summarizing the characteristics of the three main types of checking accounts. Which type would you choose to use? (Regular, interest-bearing, joint.) **LS**

Meeting Individual Needs

Students With Learning Disorders.
For students who have difficulties with attention, presenting the steps required for reconciling a checking account in the Individualized Practice activity on page 477. Attention difficulties can cause sequencing disturbances. Thus, any material involving sequence of events can take longer for students to process and may even require visual reinforcement. Role-play once the students have the concepts firmly in mind, and allow them to determine the best way to remember the steps in the correct order.

2 TEACH (Cont.)

Thinking Critically

ADVISING. Apparently, some members of your friend's family work part-time jobs for cash. They keep the cash hidden around the house. Your friend knows you're learning about handling money and comes to you for help. Your job is to convince them *not* to keep cash in the house. Tell your friend about the convenience of checking accounts and the services banks provide. (Answers will vary.)

Consider This...

Caption Answer

CheckFree is also successful because it has relationships with hundreds of billers, from utilities to credit card companies.

Fast Review Answers

1. It earns interest on the balance but requires a high minimum balance.
2. To verify your identity.

---

has written, automatic deductions (such as car payments), and automated teller machine (ATM) withdrawals.

Some accounts do require a minimum balance. If the balance falls below the minimum, a service charge is deducted from the account. A $7 or $8 charge every month can take quite a bite out of your funds. Usually this can be reduced or eliminated by having your pay directly deposited. A service charge is a fee for the paperwork the bank does to maintain the account. This charge might be a flat fee, such as $5 or $10 a month. In addition, the bank might charge an individual fee for each check paid from the account.

Interest-Bearing Account. In addition to regular checking accounts, most banks offer interesting-bearing accounts. An **interest-bearing account** is a checking account that earns interest on your account's balance. It usually has a minimum balance requirement with an unlimited number of checks allowed each month. The minimum balance might be much higher than for a regular checking account, and could run from $1,000 to $10,000.

Joint Account. You might also open a joint account, an account shared by two people who are equally responsible for the account. They are often used by married couples or for businesses with more than one owner. With a joint checking account, either person can write checks on the account.

Signature Card

Once you decide what type of account you want, you have to fill out a signature card. A **signature card** is a record of your signature used by the bank to verify your identity. The bank can check your signature card when one of your checks is presented for payment. If the signature matches, the check will be cashed. If it doesn't match, the bank won't cash the check. This helps prevent other people from cashing your checks.

The signature you put on your card is the same one you have to use when you sign your checks. For example, if you sign your card with your middle initial rather than with your full name, you have to sign your checks the same way. If you're opening a joint account, both owners of the account have to sign the signature card. You also have to provide your address, phone number, and the name and address of your employer on the card. The bank then assigns you a checking account number and issues you a book of checks.

Fast Review

1. What is an advantage and a disadvantage of an interest-bearing checking account?
2. What is the main purpose of a signature card?

Consider This...

Online Bill-Paying
CheckFree provides the online bill-paying functionality for the majority of the United States' largest banks. It works with the banks that want to provide online bill paying for their customers. CheckFree has little competition since others don't want to build the required complex computer system.
ANALYZE
What other vendors could CheckFree build relationships with in order to be successful?

LANGUAGE ARTS — *Curriculum Connection*

"Crime Stoppers." The banking industry loses about $85 million a year through consumer fraud and forgeries. This may translate into higher fees for regular customers. Suggest that students interview local bank officials to find out how often the bank receives notice of forged checks and what procedure it follows when dealing with forgery. Have students work in pairs to present their findings as a two-minute "Crime Stoppers" feature for the evening news. **LS, CL**

Account Services

Banks offer various services for checking accounts. Some of these services are offered as protection to the consumer. Other services are designed to make banking more convenient.

Overdraft Protection

One risk of having a checking account is writing checks for more money than you have in your account, or **overdrawing** your account. If you write a check to someone without enough funds to cover it, the bank returns the check to the person. Your account is then charged a returned check fee. Some banks charge $20 or $25 for each returned check. The business you wrote the check to will probably also charge a fee.

Some banks offer a service to protect a customer from this problem. **Overdraft protection** is a line of credit for overdrawn checks. If you write a check for more than you have in the account, the bank will cover the check up to a certain amount. The amount can vary from hundreds to thousands of dollars. You pay a service fee for the overdraft protection and interest on the overdrawn amount until it is repaid.

Stop Payment

There might be a time when you want to stop the payment on a check. A **stop payment** is an order for a bank not to cash a particular check. For example, you might have misplaced a check, sent a check for a wrong amount, or sent a check to the wrong address. If you wish to stop the check, contact the bank immediately. If the check hasn't yet been processed, the bank won't cash the check. As with other services, banks charge a fee to stop payment on a check.

Debit Cards

Many banks also offer check cards, or debit cards. A **debit card** is like a credit card but money is taken directly from your checking account when you use it rather than charging the amount to a credit account. A debit card can be used almost anywhere a credit card can, such as a movie theater or grocery store. You don't pay interest on the purchase because it is used as a kind of check rather than a credit card. Debit cards are often referred to as ATM cards.

WHERE DOES THAT CHECK GO?

Everyone doesn't hold a checking account at the same bank. This means the grocery store's bank probably isn't the same as your family's bank. So the grocery store's bank must verify your mom's check before it can convert her check to cash. This is often when checks go to an intermediary bank.

What do you think an intermediary bank does?

continued on p. 477

Real-World Application
Caption Answer

WHERE DOES THAT CHECK GO?: PART 2 OF 4

Most banks don't communicate directly with each other so there is an intermediary bank (the middleman) that verifies the clearing of your mom's check.

Business Connection

CANCELLED CHECKS. Once you've reconciled your checking account, don't throw those checks away. Experts suggest that you keep canceled checks relating to your tax returns for at least three years, in case your tax return is audited. Canceled checks for major improvements to your home should be kept for as long as you own the house, plus three years.

Develop Concepts

CHECKING PROCESS. Ask students: What happens when you write a check to the phone company? On the board develop a diagram showing the process involved. LS, **CL**

Great Ideas From the Classroom of...

John Bucci
Arvada High School
Arvada, Colo.

Attendance Contest. Improve classroom attendance by rewarding students for perfect attendance. Hold "perfect attendance" contests and watch daily attendance improve with increasing enthusiasm! First, obtain various prizes (i.e., gift certificates and merchandise from local businesses.) For example, all students who maintain perfect attendance will be eligible to win. Draw the name of a student with perfect attendance. Announce the winner. Vary the length of your perfect attendance periods and be sure to thank prize donors.

Chapter 29

2 TEACH (Cont.)

Discussion Starter

CHECK WRITING. Distribute double-sided copies of sample checks for students to fill in the payee and sign as the drawer. Ask students: What is the name of the drawee? (The name of the bank.)

Technology Toolkit

Caption Answer

Cost effective when it comes to maintaining traditional security and password systems.

Your Eyes Say It All

Bank United was the first bank in the United States to use iris recognition at ATMs. Iris recognition technology identifies a user through the appearance of the iris—the colored part of the eye. The iris is a more accurate identity marker than fingerprints. Here's how it works: Your iris is photographed and it's compared with a previously taken image of your eye. The match enables access to your account information. Bank United provided secure financial transactions in the blink of an eye.

Thinking Critically
How might iris recognition benefit large corporations?

Online Checking

Banks and other financial institutions offer a broad range of ways to handle your money. Banking technology offers customers quick and easy handling of their checking accounts through online banking. Online banking allows you to check your accounts, transfer money, or pay bills at any time of the day. With online banking, your checking account information is available to you from your home computer 24 hours a day, 7 days a week. To use online checking, you need access to the Internet, an ID, and a password. Online checking is less expensive for banks, so service fees are often lower than a traditional account.

For online checking, you can use an Internet browser on your computer. With personal finance software, you can store information about your transactions for your records. You can pay your bills online if you choose, saving the cost of mailing your checks. Often banks offer the option of scheduling automatic payment of your bills from the checking account, too.

✓ Fast Review

1. What happens if a customer has insufficient funds in a checking account to pay a check?
2. How is a debit card different from a credit card?

Account Records

An advantage of a checking account is that it enables you to keep records of your financial transactions. There are various types of checking account records that you keep yourself or that your bank provides for you. With these records, you can keep track of your income and expenses.

Writing a Check

There are usually three people, or parties, named on a check. The party to whom the check is written and who is cashing the check is the *payee.* The party who wrote the check and is paying the money, or

476 Unit 10 Money Management

Global Perspective

Swiss Bank Accounts. Swiss bank accounts have earned a reputation for safety and intrigue. The accounts, coupled with other financial, insurance, and real estate services, comprise 13 percent of Switzerland's gross domestic product (GDP). Direct students to prepare an oral report on one of the following topics:

- How to open a numbered Swiss bank account.
- What part international politics plays in the Swiss banking system.
- What part banking services play in the Swiss economy.

drawing it from an account, is called the *drawer*. The third party is the *drawee*, the bank or financial institution where the drawer has an account.

When you write a check, record the check number, the amount of the check, the date, and the name of the payee in your check register. Your **check register** is your checkbook log where you keep track of all your checking transactions. If you don't record the check immediately, you might forget some of the information. Some checks also have a line where you can write the purpose of the check. If you're writing a check to a utility, loan, or insurance company, you should use the line to write your account number with the company.

Depositing a Check

To deposit a check in your account you need to fill out a deposit ticket. The deposit ticket lists the amount of cash and checks as well as the total amount you're depositing. After you make the deposit, record it in your check register. Many ATM machines don't require a deposit ticket and you can use the ATM receipt as a record of your transactions.

To deposit or cash a check requires an **endorsement**, or the signature of the payee on the back of the check. To endorse a check, follow these rules for your protection:

- Endorse the check on the back (on the lines printed for the endorsement). Don't write below those lines.
- Use a black pen so your signature can't be erased.
- Sign your name exactly as it's written on the front of the check.
- If you're depositing a check rather than cashing it, write "For Deposit Only" above your signature. That way, if the check is lost or stolen, it can only be used for depositing in your account.

Bank Statements

Periodically, usually once a month, banks issue a bank statement. A **bank statement** is the bank's record of all the transactions in your checking account (see Figure 29.2). It includes a record of all withdrawals, deposits, interest, and fees. It also includes a record of all **canceled checks**, or checks you've written that have been cashed. Your canceled checks are proof that the money has been paid to the payees.

 Fast Review _____

1. What are the three different parties on a check?
2. Why should you write "For Deposit Only" on the back of a check?

Real-World Application

part **3** of 4

WHERE DOES THAT CHECK GO?
Now the intermediary bank needs to identify the paying bank. It knows this by looking at the routing number on the bottom left-hand corner of your mom's check.
What's the purpose of the routing number?

continued on p. 479

Real-World Application
Caption Answer

WHERE DOES THAT CHECK GO?: PART 3 OF 4
It identifies the bank that issued the check.

Individualized Practice

Classroom activities can bridge to work skills. Employers often provide a set of procedures that provide step-by-step instructions for employees to complete a task. Have students develop a step-by-step guide for reconciling a checking account.

L1 Have students work in pairs to discuss the relevant steps to include and the order in which to do them.

L2 Ask students to create an easy-to-follow step-by-step guide.

L3 Ask students to work in groups to make a step-by-step guide and create a sample reconciliation as an example of using their guide.

Fast Review Answers

1. The check "bounces," or is returned to the person who tried to cash it.
2. A debit card takes money directly from your checking account and you don't pay interest on the purchase.

LANGUAGE ARTS — ***Curriculum Connection***

"A Day in the Life of a Check." Have students work in groups of four to plan and design storyboards for a documentary called "A Day in the Life of a Check" that describes a check's life from writing through canceling and return with the bank statement. Ask groups to present their documentary. If feasible, have students videotape their productions. **CL**, **LS**, **P**

Bank Reconciliation

Bank reconciliation is the process of seeing whether your records agree with the bank's records for your account. To reconcile is to bring into agreement, or balance. You can usually reconcile your account by using a form on the back of your bank statement. If the bank statement shows a different balance than your check register, you should reconcile the two records.

Balancing Your Checkbook

The first step to reconciling your account is to see whether the bank has processed all your checks and deposits. With the bank statement and your check register, you can identify your **outstanding checks**, or checks that have been written but haven't yet been cashed. The total dollar amounts of outstanding checks should be subtracted from the balance shown on the bank statement.

Figure 29.2 SAMPLE BANK STATEMENT

➡ Michael and Conchetta Chung received this bank statement. What were the totals for checks written and deposits for the month?

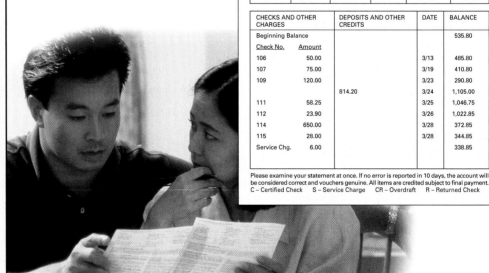

STATEMENT

FIFTH NATIONAL BANK

Michael and Conchetta Chung
121 Bayside Road
Fall River, OH 42119-0120

Account Number: 211-37-065

Date of Statement: 3/31/04

PREVIOUS BALANCE	CHECKS AND CHARGES	NO. OF DEPOSITS	NO. OF CHECKS	DEPOSITS AND CREDITS	BALANCE AT THIS DATE
535.80	1,011.15	1	7	814.20	338.85

CHECKS AND OTHER CHARGES		DEPOSITS AND OTHER CREDITS	DATE	BALANCE
Beginning Balance				535.80
Check No.	Amount			
106	50.00		3/13	485.80
107	75.00		3/19	410.80
109	120.00		3/23	290.80
		814.20	3/24	1,105.00
111	58.25		3/25	1,046.75
112	23.90		3/26	1,022.85
114	650.00		3/28	372.85
115	28.00		3/28	344.85
Service Chg.	6.00			338.85

Please examine your statement at once. If no error is reported in 10 days, the account will be considered correct and vouchers genuine. All items are credited subject to final payment.
C – Certified Check   S – Service Charge   CR – Overdraft   R – Returned Check

How to Use a Portfolio Activity

The portfolio projects are designed to lead students to develop a collection of their best work to submit to you for assessment. You and each of your students should decide which projects to include in their business portfolio. Refer students to the specific rubric(s) from the *Alternative Assessment Strategies*. These rubrics will alert students to the criteria you'll use to assess their projects. **P**

If you have made any deposits that haven't been recorded on the bank statement, those deposits should be added to the bank statement balance. If the bank charged any service fees, you may not have recorded them in your check register. The service fee should be subtracted from the balance in your check register. If your account earns interest, add the interest shown on the bank statement to your check register.

After you have recorded outstanding checks and unrecorded deposits on the bank statement, and service fees and interest earned in your check register, the balance on the bank statement and in your check register should be the same, or should agree. If they agree, you've reconciled (or brought into agreement) your check register balance with the bank statement balance.

Finding Errors

Sometimes bank reconciliation isn't that easy. You may follow all of these steps and still find a difference between your records and the bank statement. If your balance still differs from the bank's balance, you can follow these steps to find the problem.

- Check your own account records to see whether you wrote the correct amount for each check and deposit.
- Check all your additions and subtractions. You may find mistakes in your arithmetic.
- Check to see whether you carried the correct balance forward for each new page of your check register.
- Recheck to see that you have correctly identified all of the outstanding checks and deposits that haven't been processed by the bank.
- Check the bank's additions and subtractions. Are all canceled checks and deposits listed on the bank statement? If you find a mistake in the bank's figures, report it immediately.

 Fast Review

1. What is the difference between a canceled check and an outstanding check?
2. What charges do you need to add and subtract from your check register to reconcile it with your bank statement?

WHERE DOES THAT CHECK GO?
The intermediary bank identifies your mom's paying bank and submits the check and a payment request. Your mom's check is cleared when the bank gives the intermediary bank the go-ahead. It debits your mom's checking account and uses this money to credit the grocery store's bank. How does your mom know that the grocery store's bank cleared her check?

Chapter 29 Checking Accounts **479**

 Chapter 29

Real-World Application Caption Answer

WHERE DOES THAT CHECK GO?: PART 4 OF 4
The bank debits her checking account and it's listed as such on her month's bank statement.

Technology Resource

GO TO **PUZZLEMAKER CD-ROM.** Check your students' understanding of the chapter's key terms by using the *Puzzlemaker* CD-ROM.

Evaluation

Assign and review the Fast Review sections.

Fast Review Answers

1. A canceled check has been cashed by the bank. An outstanding check is a check that's been written but hasn't been cashed yet.
2. You need to add interest and subtract services fees.

Meeting Individual Needs

Gifted. For students who would benefit from the additional work of an independent project, assign the task of researching the trend in the number and kinds of banking services offered online. If possible, have them arrange to visit a bank in their community that offers online banking. Ask students to gather information on costs, ease of access, possibility of outside tampering, special regulations, confidentiality, and the number of customer sign-ups over the past year. Have students plan a brief news report describing trends in online banking. **P**, **LS**, **CL**

4 CLOSE

Chapter Wrap-Up

Students prepared vocabulary tests in this chapter's "Preteaching Key Words" activity. Complete these.

Using Business Key Words

1. signature card
2. bank reconciliation
3. outstanding checks
4. demand deposits
5. endorsement
6. check register
7. overdraft protection
8. interest-bearing account
9. overdrawing
10. stop payment
11. debit card
12. bank statement
13. canceled checks

Review What You Learned

14. Savings and checking accounts, credit cards, loans, financial planning services, and investments.
15. Convenience.
16. 85 percent.
17. When you don't want the bank to cash a particular check.
18. Your signature.
19. Look for errors.
20. (1) Check account records; (2) check all additions and subtractions; (3) check your math; (4) recheck outstanding checks and deposits; and (5) check the bank's additions and subtractions.
21. Contact the bank.
22. Payee—person who gets the money. Drawer—person who signs the check. Drawee—a financial institution holding the drawer's account.

480

Summary

1. Banks offer regular checking accounts, interest-bearing accounts, and joint accounts.
2. Checking account services include overdraft protection, stop payment orders, debit cards, and online checking.
3. Canceled checks, check registers, and bank statements are used to keep track of account transactions.
4. You reconcile an account by matching your check register with your bank statement.

Using Business Key Words

One of the most important services banks provide is the checking account. If you don't have one already, you probably will very soon. Understanding key terms about checking accounts will help you be a more informed user of your account. Write the term that best completes the sentence.

- **demand deposits**
- **bank reconciliation**
- **overdraft protection**
- **outstanding checks**
- **signature card**
- **endorsement**
- **check register**
- **interest-bearing account**
- **overdrawing**
- **stop payment**
- **debit card**
- **bank statement**
- **canceled checks**

1. A(n) _____ is used by the bank to verify your identity.
2. The process of seeing whether your records agree with the bank's records for your account is called _____.
3. Checks that have been written but haven't yet reached the bank are _____.
4. Checking accounts are often called _____ because each check a customer writes and signs is an order to the bank to release the specified amount.
5. The _____ is necessary for cashing a check.
6. The _____ is the section of your checkbook where you keep track of all your transactions.
7. A prearranged line of credit for overdrawn checks is called _____.
8. A(n) _____ earns interest on the balance left in the account.
9. _____ is when you write a check for more money than there is in your checking account.
10. A(n) _____ orders the bank not to cash a particular check.
11. A(n) _____ is like using a credit card but money is deducted directly from a checking account rather than a credit account.
12. A bank's record of all the transactions in a checking account is called a(n) _____.
13. _____ are checks that are written that have been cashed.

Quick Quiz

1. What banking services do members of your family use? (Answers will vary.)
2. When you write a check, you record the details on your _____ _____. (Check register.)
3. Where can a consumer find a list of the checks that cleared in the last month? (Checking account bank statement.)

Review What You Learned

14. What major services do banks provide?
15. Why do most businesses and most people have checking accounts?
16. What percentage of U.S. households have checking accounts?
17. When would you want to use a stop payment order?
18. What is the most important part of the signature card? Why?
19. Why is it important to review your monthly bank statement?
20. When you reconcile your bank statement, you might not be able to balance it. List the steps you can follow to find the problem.
21. What should you do if you absolutely cannot reconcile your balance with the bank statement balance?
22. Define the payee, the drawer, and the drawee.

Understanding Business Concepts

23. Why should you shop around before opening a checking account?
24. Why is overdrawing your checking account poor financial management?
25. How does a debit card differ from a credit card?
26. Do you think the bank could make a mistake on your bank statement? Explain.
27. Why is recording your check in the check register before you actually write the check a good idea?
28. Where should the endorsement be written on a check?

Critical Thinking

29. Banks will not accept a check that has been postdated, that is, dated for a future date. Why do you think banks have this policy?
30. Some people are concerned that banking online is risky. They're worried about security, hackers, and not being able to access their money when needed. How would you answer someone who asks you whether or not he or she should consider banking online?
31. What information might the bank or financial institution need from you when you open a checking account?
32. Would you consider taking overdraft protection? Why or why not?

Viewing and Representing

Examining the Image. Look at the photograph and list details that you see. What bills do you or your family pay by check? What needs or wants of your family are met by paying these bills?

Critical Thinking

29. The account might have insufficient funds if another check is cashed before the date on which the check is to be paid.
30. Answers will vary.
31. Your social security number, age, personal details, the amount you want to put in as the initial deposit, and your signature on a form.
32. Answers will vary but may be yes because an overdraft can cost a lot of money in fees.

Viewing and Representing

Before students do this activity, make them aware they will need to find out the answer to the question, "What bills do you or your family pay by check?" After students have done this activity, lead a discussion to make sure they have correctly categorized items as needs or wants. (Needs and wants are explained in Chapter 1.) Ask students: Which of these bill payments might be better done online? **LS**

Understanding Business Concepts

23. Compare accounts and services, fees and charges.
24. You're charged for each overdrawn check.
25. Debit card withdraws directly from a checking account.
26. Yes.
27. To track payments.
28. On the left end of the back of the check on the lines printed for the endorsement.

4 CLOSE (Cont.)

Building Academic Skills

LANGUAGE ARTS. Make sure all students in the group participate in the project. Suggest they collaborate to get information from several different banks. Rubric: Charts/tables.

COMPUTER/TECHNOLOGY. Answers will vary. Rubrics: Note taking, essay.

SOCIAL SCIENCE. Make sure all students in the group participate in the project. Results will vary depending on the game created. Encourage creativity and remind the students that their audience is middle-school students. Rubric: Teaching tool.

MATH. Subtracting the service fee from the checkbook balance leaves $424.67. Add the outstanding deposits to the bank statement balance ($47.86 + 844.71 = $892.57). Subtract the outstanding checks from the bank statement balance ($435 + $32.90 = $467.90; $892.57 − $467.90 = $424.67). Rubrics: Charts/tables, paragraph.

Linking School to Home

Answers will vary. Let students choose the method they use to share their results. Rubrics: Note taking, essay, oral presentation.

Linking School to Work

Students could work in groups on this activity. Allow the students to choose the method they use to share their findings. Rubrics: Note taking, oral presentation, essay, poster, chart.

Building Academic Skills

 Researching Services

In a team, choose a local bank to research. Each team member should concentrate on a different service offered by the bank. Visit or telephone the bank for information. The Internet may also be a resource that could be used. Create a chart of the bank's services and share this information with the class.

 Comparing and Contrasting

Some banks don't return canceled checks to their customers. Use online research to collect information about the pros and cons of this practice. Write a two-page report about the advantages and disadvantages of this practice for both the banks and their customers.

 Create a Teaching Tool

In a group, create a board game that could be used to teach middle-school students about checking accounts. Emphasize the reasons why someone should have a checking account, how to reconcile a check register with a bank statement, and the trend towards online banking. Test the game by playing it in class; then offer to take the game to a middle-school class and use it as a teaching tool.

 Reconciling an Account

Review the check register, bank statement, and steps for reconciling a checking account presented in this chapter. Then, reconcile the balance on the check register shown below with a bank statement balance of $844.71. The bank has charged a $4 service fee. The statement doesn't include check numbers 578 and 581. Also missing is a deposit in the amount of $47.86. Write an explanation of what you did.

No.	Date	Description	Payment	Deposit	Balance
					624.83
575	6/27	Sam's Good Gifts	22.95		601.88
-	7/1	Paycheck		650.77	1252.65
576	7/1	Finer, Fresher Foods	42.13		1210.52
577	7/10	Cash	100.00		1110.52
578	7/15	Rent	435.00		675.52
579	7/21	Phone Bill	34.67		640.85
580	7/25	World Wide Airlines	227.14		413.71
581	7/29	Electric Bill	32.90		380.81
-	7/31	Al's Check		47.86	428.67

Linking School to Home

Surveying Bank Services. Interview your parents or other family members about their checking accounts. Find out which bank they use, why they chose that particular bank, what type of checking account they have, the service charges they pay, and anything else you think is important.

Linking School to Work

Reporting About Financial Institutions. Call several financial institutions in your area and find out what you would have to do to open a checking account. Ask about the age requirements, initial deposit, service charge, and whether or not they offer interest-bearing accounts. Share your findings with the class.

E-Homework

Applying Technology

Online Banking. Use the Internet to research online banking. Find two different banks that offer the service online and evaluate them based on the following information:

- How is online banking different from doing business at your local bricks-and-mortar bank branch?
- Is online banking suitable for businesses as well as individuals?
- Are there cost savings with online banking? Or is it more expensive?
- What type of security is in place to protect consumers who choose to bank online? Share your findings with the class.

Upcoming Checking Accounts. Checking accounts might look very different in just a few years. Use the Internet to research one of the following topics: digital checks, digital coupons, digital cashier's checks, and divisible cash, e-money, or smart cards. Write a two-page paper with your findings.

Connecting Academics

Math. You and your friend Sal spend Saturday shopping. Sal uses checks to make the purchases, but needs help writing out the dollar amount. Practice writing out the following amounts as you'd write them on a check: $36.45, $152.79, $16.14, and $1,311.35.

Language Arts. Pair up with a partner and create a system to review topics in this chapter. For example, the system could be using questions and answers on 3″ by 5″ cards. Join with another pair and share ideas to improve both study systems.

BusinessWeek — Analyzing the Feature Story

You read the first part of "The Dynamo of E-Banking" at the beginning of this chapter. Below are a few questions for you to answer about Nordea. You'll find the answers to these questions when you're reading the entire article. First, here are the questions:

33. How has online banking helped Nordea's bottom line?
34. What advantage do banks like Nordea have over banks that offer their services exclusively online?

CREATIVE JOURNAL ACTIVITY

Interview three adults to find out if and why they use online banking. Write a short report summarizing the similarities and differences between the three responses.

BUSINESS Online
The Full Story

To learn more about e-banking, visit the *Introduction to Business* Web site at **www.introbus.glencoe.com**, and click on *BusinessWeek* Feature Story, Chapter 29.

E-Homework

ONLINE BANKING. Answers will vary. Allow students to share their findings in any way they choose. Rubrics: Essay, oral presentation, charts/tables.

UPCOMING CHECKING ACCOUNTS. Answers will vary depending on the topic selected. Rubric: Essay.

Connecting Academics

MATH. Thirty-six and $^{45}/_{100}$ dollars, one hundred fifty-two and $^{79}/_{100}$ dollars, sixteen and $^{14}/_{100}$ dollars, one thousand three hundred eleven and $^{35}/_{100}$ dollars.

LANGUAGE ARTS. The design of study systems will vary. When pairs of students group with other pairs to critique the study systems, caution students to avoid negative or demeaning comments about the systems. Encourage positive feedback and suggestions for improvement, explaining that this is the way people learn best and gain confidence.

BusinessWeek — Analyzing the Feature Story

33. Nordea has been able to eliminate half of its branches and 5,000 jobs in Finland, even as the bank has increased its number of transactions by a third.
34. Internet-only banks have to spend as much as $225 in marketing costs to woo each new client.

Creative Journal Activity

After students have written their report, have them write responses to the following questions: What's your opinion of online banking? Do you use it, or do you think you'll use it? Why or why not?

SCANS Correlation Chart*

Foundation Skills

Basic Skills	Reading	Writing	Math	Listening	Speaking	
Thinking Skills	Creative Thinking	Decision Making	Problem Solving	Seeing Things in the Mind's Eye	Knowing How to Learn	Reasoning
Personal Qualities	Responsibility	Self-Esteem	Sociability	Self-Management	Integrity/ Honesty	

Workplace Competencies

Resources	Allocating Time	Allocating Money	Allocating Material and Facility Resources	Allocating Human Resources		
Information	Acquiring and Evaluating Information	Organizing and Maintaining Information	Interpreting and Communicating Information	Using Computers to Process Information		
Interpersonal Skills	Participating as a Member of a Team	Teaching Others	Serving Clients/ Customers	Exercising Leadership	Negotiating to Arrive at a Decision	Working With Cultural Diversity
Systems	Understanding Systems	Monitoring and Correcting Performance	Improving and Designing Systems			
Technology	Selecting Technology	Applying Technology to Task	Maintaining and Troubleshooting Technology			

*This chart's highlighted blocks indicate the chapter's content coverage in the Student Edition and the Teacher Wraparound Edition.

Resource Manager

Teaching Transparencies

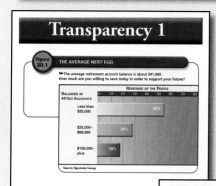

Transparency 1

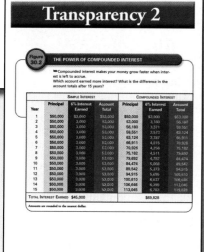

Transparency 2

Application and Enrichment

- 🖋 Lesson Plans
- 📕 *BusinessWeek* Poster Package
- 🖋 Teaching Transparencies
- 💿 🖋 Integrated Software Simulation
- 📼 🖋 Glencoe Business Video Package

Review and Reinforcement

- 💿 *PuzzleMaker*
- 💻 🖋 Internet Resources
- 🖋 Student Activity Workbook
- 🖋 Strat. and Work. for Teaching Transparencies

Assessment and Evaluation

- 🖋 Reproducible Tests
- 🖋 Alternative Assessment Strategies
- 💿 ExamView® Pro Test Generator

Technology

- 💿 *PuzzleMaker*
- 💿 ExamView® Pro Test Generator
- 📼 Glencoe Business Video Package
- 💿 PowerPoint® Presentation
- 💿 🖋 Integrated Software Simulation
- 💿 Interactive Lesson Planner
- 💿 *Virtual Business*®

KEY	🖋 Printed	💾 Software	📼 Videocassette	📕 Poster
	🖋 Transparency	💿 CD-ROM	💻 Internet	

BUSINESS Online

Visit www.introbus.glencoe.com, the Web site companion to *Introduction to Business*. The student's page includes:

- interactive tutor
- additional *BusinessWeek* articles and activities
- business Web links
- homework hints
- real-world application activities
- additional career path activities

Information on how to prepare your students for the high school exit exam and special projects are also included.

Use the Glencoe Web site for additional resources. All essential content is covered in the Student Edition.

1 FOCUS

Introducing the Chapter

This chapter outlines reasons for saving. It describes the types of savings accounts and their advantages and disadvantages. A photo essay, "How Long Is a CD's Life?," enhances the concepts.

Connecting the Objectives

Why save? What are the names of some types of savings accounts?

BusinessWeek
Feature Story

Story's Summary

Saving for college is just one part of the picture. To maximize your family's use of money, imagine juggling four balls: earnings, savings, taxes, and financial aid. On the savings side, by the sophomore year risky investments need to be converted into safe investments. These include money-market funds or certificates of deposit timed to mature when tuition is due.

Find the entire article at www.introbus.glencoe.com, or in the Teacher Resource Binder.

Chapter 30

Savings Accounts

● Learning Objectives

After completing this chapter, you'll be able to:
1. **Name** reasons for saving money.
2. **Explain** how interest is earned.
3. **Identify** types of savings accounts.
4. **Describe** savings accounts.

● Why It's Important

Savings accounts allow you to put money aside and help make your money grow.

● Key Words

savings
opportunity cost
simple interest
compound interest
passbook savings account
statement savings account
certificate of deposit (CD)
maturity date
money market fund
money market deposit account
Federal Deposit Insurance
  Corporation (FDIC)
liquidity
inflation risk

484

BusinessWeek Feature Story

How to Cash Out Your College Fund

The Tricky Part Is Curbing Taxes and Boosting Aid. Congratulations! Your parents have been saving ever since you were a toddler, and now that you're a strapping high schooler, you have a hefty sum stashed away in growth stocks for college. You're among a tiny elite: By some estimates, only 2 percent of families with children have $5,000 or more saved for college expenses.

Now, how are you going to get those funds out of your account and into Wattasmatta U's? College planning focuses so much on the first phase—savings—that few are aware of the hurdles that await during the endgame.

Source: Excerpted with permission from "How to Cash Out Junior's College Fund," *BusinessWeek Online*, March 12, 2001.

An Extension Activity

Find a college, university, or institution that you're interested in attending after high-school graduation. How much money will you need to afford the tuition plus expenses? What steps do you need to take in order to pay for your future?

BUSINESS *Online*

The Full Story

To learn more about savings plans, visit the *Introduction to Business* Web site at www.introbus.glencoe.com, and click on *BusinessWeek* Feature Story, Chapter 30.

Classroom Resources

For the Teacher
📁 Student Activity Work. TAE
📓💿   Assessment Binder
💿 PowerPoint® Presentation
💿 Interactive Lesson Planner
📁 Lesson Plans
📓💻   Internet Resources
📠 Teaching Transparencies
💻 *Introduction to Business* Web Site

💿 Integrated Soft. Sim. TM
📖 *BusinessWeek* Poster Package
For the Student
📓 Student Activity Workbook
💿 *Virtual Business*®
💻 *Introduction to Business* Web Site
💿 Integrated Soft. Sim.
💿 *PuzzleMaker*
📓 Strategies and Worksheets for
  Teaching Transparencies

Bell Ringer Activity

ALLOCATING TIME. Being resourceful on the job includes allocating time to complete tasks. You can practice this skill by dividing this chapter into learning tasks. Mark the tasks in time-slots on your planner.

Preteaching Business Key Words

WRITING. Ask students to work in pairs to look up the definition of each key word then write the definition in their journal. **LS**, **P**

An Extension Activity

WRITE. After students have calculated the monthly savings needed for the future expense, ask them what type of account they would choose in which to save their money. **LS**

Making Connections

Everyday Life. Have students conduct an informal poll among family members, neighbors, and friends to discover how many save and for what reasons. Suggest that students pool their results and present them along with graphs or charts as a poster for classroom display. **LS**, **CL**, **P**

Business Connection

CERTIFICATES OF DEPOSIT. More than 40 percent of Americans put their savings in certificates of deposit (CDs). CDs are popular because they usually pay higher interest rates than traditional savings accounts and money market accounts, yet they're safe. Another plus is that CDs are deposited for a specific length of time and that stops people spending the money sooner than they intended. This low liquidity helps people save for long-term goals.

Develop Concepts

BENEFITS OF SAVING. Ask students to think of times they've heard people talking about saving, or using savings. What do you, your family, or your friends, save for? (Answers will vary and might include major purchases, vacation, wedding, house, unemployment, other emergencies, further training and education, and retirement.)

Figure 30.1 Caption Answer

Answers will vary.

A Guide to Saving

You work part-time as a sales associate at the local department store. Every other week you receive a paycheck. You decide to start setting some financial goals since your checking account is almost empty by the time your next pay period comes around. You also decide to analyze your lifestyle costs. How can you manage your cash to save for your future?

Why You Should Save

A personal budget isn't complete without a plan for regular savings. **Savings** is money put aside for future use. The amount of money you save depends on how much of your income you're willing not to spend. Figure 30.1 illustrates the average account balance. What do you think this says about people's attitude toward lifestyle choices, money, and the future? All savings involve some sacrifice. When you save money, you're putting off spending money now to get something later. This is called the **opportunity cost**, or trade-off; this is what you give up when you make one choice instead of another. The opportunity cost of going to college is working at a full-time job. Choosing between alternatives involves knowing what you gain.

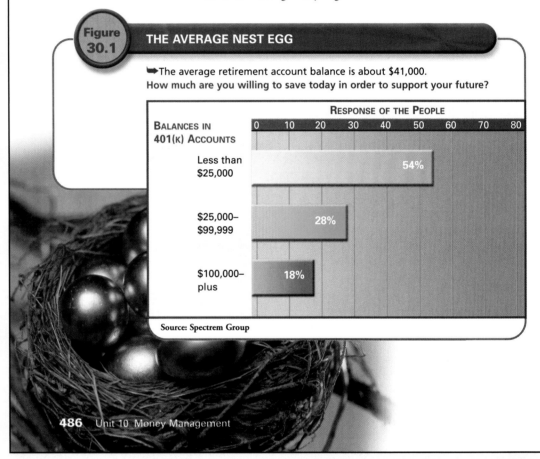

Figure 30.1

THE AVERAGE NEST EGG

➡ The average retirement account balance is about $41,000. How much are you willing to save today in order to support your future?

RESPONSE OF THE PEOPLE

BALANCES IN 401(K) ACCOUNTS

Balance	Response
Less than $25,000	54%
$25,000–$99,999	28%
$100,000–plus	18%

Source: Spectrem Group

Cooperative Learning

Brochure. Have students work in groups of four to design, write, and produce a brochure titled "Savings, the Key to Your Future." Suggest that in the brochure students indicate reasons to save and ways to make saving a regular habit. Encourage them to include examples of how saving helps individuals meet their financial and life goals. If possible, copy and distribute brochures to the school community. **LS, CL**

Why do people save money? People set up and maintain a savings plan for three major reasons: to make major purchases, to provide for emergencies, and to have income for retirement.

Major Purchases

Suppose you would like to have a really nice sound system, a top-of-the-line guitar, a car, or a two-year degree from a technical college. You'll probably need to save money before you can buy these. You might even need to save for an entire year or two before you have enough.

Remember, if you purchase items on credit or borrow money to make purchases, you have to pay finance charges. If you use cash for the purchase, you don't have to pay those charges. Finance charges can average 15 to 18 percent, which adds a lot to the cost of the item.

Emergencies

You might face financial emergencies in your life—your car breaks down, you lose your job, or you develop a health problem. Experts in personal finance strongly recommend that each person have money saved for emergencies. In fact, they recommend that you have at least six months of income set aside in case of an emergency.

Retirement

It might seem too early to think about saving for retirement, but it's best to begin early. Most workers in the United States receive some income from the federal social security program when they retire. Many, but not all, people have some type of retirement plan where they work, which will provide additional income. Individuals with their own businesses can also set up retirement plans.

For most people, though, social security and retirement plans still don't provide enough money to retire comfortably. A third source of income is savings made through the years. If you start early in your life, you can easily accumulate quite a nest egg from which to draw retirement income. For example, if you put away just $20 per week starting now, by the time you retire you would have $50,000. With interest earned on a savings account, it could come to several times more than that.

 Fast Review

1. What is a major advantage of saving to buy an item instead of buying it on credit?
2. What are the three main sources of retirement income?

Real-World Application

part 1 of 4

HOW LONG IS A CD'S LIFE?
You've invested loads of money in audio CDs, CD-ROM multimedia games, and photo CDs. A CD's spiral track of pits stores your favorite data for at least 100 years if you treat them like investments. The opportunity cost of carefully handling your CD collection is what?

continued on p. 489

HOW LONG IS A CD'S LIFE?: PART 1 OF 4

Here CD means compact disc. It applies financial concepts to a typical teen investment, CDs. Spend the time and effort now to protect the CDs so you don't have to replace them in the future.

Technology Resource

GO TO **POWERPOINT.** The *Introduction to Business* PowerPoint® CD-ROM provides visual lecture aids for this chapter.

Independent Practice

SAVING. Imagine that in a year you're planning to buy sound equipment that you estimate will cost $500. How much money per month would you need to save to be able to buy the equipment? How would you save that amount? ($500 ÷ 12 = $41.66 a month, or about the cost of six movies.) **LS**

Fast Review Answers

1. You don't have to pay the added finance charge.
2. Work retirement plan, savings, and Social Security.

Meeting Individual Needs

Students With Reading Difficulties. Many students who are not good readers can still locate information in the text when their attention is directed to it. Without direction, however, they often cannot make distinctions between important facts and elaboration. The notes they take may contain irrelevant information. Have students read the "Why You Should Save" and "Earning Interest on Savings" subsections and find one sentence in each paragraph that best states the main idea. Have them explain their choices.

Thinking Critically

TRENDS.   You're spending time with friends, when one friend says: "It's strange how just three years ago I didn't save a dime. Now I want my own car, so I'm saving like mad." Another friend asks, "Where are you putting your money?" That starts you all talking about how people save and where they put their money. Looking back over the last three years, what trends have you noticed in people's savings? What factors might have influenced those trends? (Answers will vary.)

Writing for Business

CAPTION ANSWER

After students have completed their chosen path and responded to the conclusion, have them silently re-read their own story and list the vivid descriptive words they used. Ask for volunteers to share the words they used and, if they wish, the context for those words. **LS**, **P**, **CL**

Writing for Business

Portfolio Activity

A Specialized Plan

This activity gives you the chance to add to your portfolio. Communicate, interview, research, and write your way into a story. Choose one imaginary path, The Way to Catering or A Bookish Party. Follow your path's steps to complete your own story.

pick a path

The Way to Catering

The Setting. You're a great cook and plan to start a catering business, specializing in Kosher meats.

Rising Action. You continue working at your current job to save enough for a down payment on Kosher cooking equipment. You decide to save $25 per week from your paycheck.

Step 1. Call a bank and ask for interest rates for savings accounts, money market accounts, and certificates of deposit. Also find out the qualifications to open an account. Can you qualify for any? If not, calculate how long you would have to save in order to qualify.

Step 2. Assuming you do qualify, make a chart comparing the different benefits and risks of each savings plan. Decide which you would invest in and write a paragraph explaining why.

A Bookish Party

The Setting. Your book club just finished Myla Goldberg's *Bee Season*, and you're to host the next book party.

Rising Action. You've always wanted to throw a party, with lots of interesting foods. Use your savings to invest in creating a party worth remembering.

Step 1. Find a cookbook of recipes for Kosher food. Select three recipes that seem to call for inexpensive ingredients. Make a list of all the ingredients. Go to a Kosher food store or the Kosher section of your grocery store and write down the price of all the ingredients.

Step 2. Calculate how much it would cost to make enough of each recipe to feed 15 people.

Conclusion

Now it's time to write your own story and write a personal narrative about your path. Be sure to include your insights into the experiences that have shaped your decisions. What details will you keep or discard? Use vivid descriptions to reveal your own character. Specific details draw the reader into your narrative. Be creative.

LANGUAGE ARTS   *Curriculum Connection*

Communication.   Direct students to collect information from local banks concerning the method each uses to compute interest. Have students highlight information in banking brochures that tells the method the bank uses to compute interest.

Have students discuss whether the bank's materials clearly state the method used to compute interest. Allow students to propose revised information for those brochures they feel are unclear. **CL**, **LS**

Earning Interest on Savings

All savings don't necessarily earn income. For those who put their savings into a jar or under the mattress, no income is earned. Remember what you learned about credit in previous chapters. If you get a loan you must pay interest, which is like a rental fee for using someone else's money.

In this case, *your* money is being used to lend money to someone else, so *you* receive the rental fee or interest. Many different financial institutions, such as banks and credit unions, want to use your savings to make loans. If you put money into one of their savings accounts, you're actually lending them your money. They then use your money to make loans to other people. In return for letting them use your money, part of the interest they receive is used to pay interest to you.

Simple Interest

Simple interest is interest earned only on the money you deposited into your savings account, or the principal. The amount of interest you receive depends on three major factors—the amount of savings, the interest rate, and the length of time of the account. Does this sound familiar? A person who starts a savings account is actually a creditor with the same conditions for lending money.

For example, if you have a savings account that pays you 5 percent annual interest and $1,000 is in the account for the entire year, you'll receive $50 in interest. If you had $2,000 in that account during the year with the same interest rate, you would earn $100 in interest. In this case, the interest doubled because of doubling the amount of savings. If the account pays 10 percent interest and you have $1,000 for one year, you would also earn $100. When moving from 5 to 10 percent interest for the same amount of principal and the same time span, the interest doubles from $50 to $100.

Compound Interest

Compound interest is interest earned on both the principal—the money you deposited in your savings account—and any interest you earned on it. In other words, compound interest is interest on interest. For example, suppose you had $50,000 in a savings account at 6 percent annual interest. After one year, you would earn $3,000 in interest. With simple interest, you would continue to earn interest on the $50,000 principal. With compound interest, the $3,000 would be added to the $50,000 and you would start earning interest on $53,000. With simple interest, after 15 years you would earn $45,000. With compound interest, you would earn almost $70,000, or about $25,000 more.

Chapter 30 Savings Accounts **489**

HOW LONG IS A CD'S LIFE?
You wouldn't leave your digitally remastered import CDs in plastic sleeves under the summer's sun; this isn't proper care. Assume you start lending out your CDs to friends at school because they love your eclectic taste in music. Often it's weeks before you get them back, which is just too long. You decide to start charging interest when they return the CDs late.
What can you do with the interest you earn?

continued on p. 491

Chapter 30

Real-World Application
Caption Answer

HOW LONG IS A CD'S LIFE?: PART 2 OF 4
Answers will vary but may include put the money in a savings account or buy more CDs.

Business Connection

When you're looking for the best certificate of deposit (CD) to fit your needs, the Internet is definitely the place to go. It makes your search efficient, because you can take advantage of surveys such as Bankrate.com's "The 100-Highest Yields." Second, you're likely to find the highest CD rates with Internet-only banks. You can choose to pay the initial deposit online, or print an application and mail it in with your deposit.

Develop Concepts

RISK. Imagine you have worked hard to accumulate $5,000 to put in savings. Would you think your money was secure in a savings account with a bank? With a brokerage firm, or other financial institution? What makes a difference? (Bank savings are insured up to $100,000 by the Federal Deposit Insurance Corporation (FDIC), while brokerage firm savings are not. Although most brokerage firms have other forms of insurance on their accounts.)

Great Ideas From the Classroom of...

Barry Danziger
Franklin High School
Somerset, N.J.

The Two-Week Vacation. Students plan a two-week road trip in the continental U.S. Record in their travel journals each town, the route taken, including mileage, the time taken, and any expenses they incur (food, fuel, boarding, tolls, recreation events, souvenirs, postcards, and other assorted items). They can use any reliable resource as their reference except for travel planning agencies (tour books and magazines are fine). They have a set amount of money. Their itinerary should include no less than 25 cities or towns in at least two states.

✓ Fast Review Answers

1. They are paying to use, or borrow, the money to lend to someone else.
2. Simple interest is interest only on the money deposited in an account, or the principal. Compound interest is interest on both the principal and any interest earned.

Discussion Starter

RECOGNIZING. Ask students what comments they're hearing currently in the news about inflation. Ask students: What do you think is the effect of inflation on savings? (Answers will vary and should include discussion of inflation and inflation risk.)

Figure 30.2 Caption Answer

The account in which the interest was left to accrue earned $24,824 more than the account where the interest was withdrawn. After 15 years, the difference is $69,828 more in the accrued interest account.

Compound interest is usually earned daily, monthly, quarterly, or annually. The more often interest is compounded, the more you make in extra interest.

✓ Fast Review

1. Why do financial institutions pay interest on savings accounts?
2. What is the difference between simple interest and compound interest?

Types of Savings Accounts

Banks, savings and loans, savings banks, credit unions, and brokerage firms all offer different types of savings accounts. There are three

Figure 30.2

THE POWER OF COMPOUNDED INTEREST

➥ Compounded interest makes your money grow faster when interest is left to accrue.

Which account earned more interest? What is the difference in the account totals after 15 years?

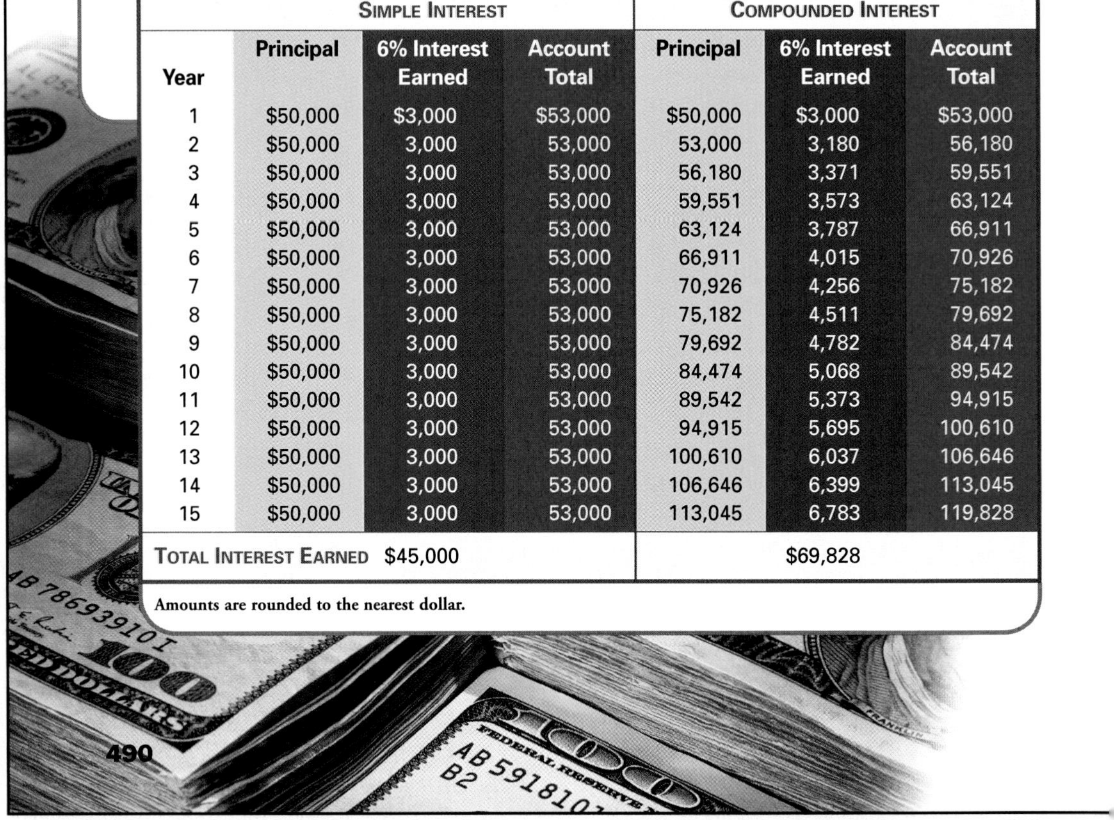

Year	SIMPLE INTEREST			COMPOUNDED INTEREST		
	Principal	6% Interest Earned	Account Total	Principal	6% Interest Earned	Account Total
1	$50,000	$3,000	$53,000	$50,000	$3,000	$53,000
2	$50,000	3,000	53,000	53,000	3,180	56,180
3	$50,000	3,000	53,000	56,180	3,371	59,551
4	$50,000	3,000	53,000	59,551	3,573	63,124
5	$50,000	3,000	53,000	63,124	3,787	66,911
6	$50,000	3,000	53,000	66,911	4,015	70,926
7	$50,000	3,000	53,000	70,926	4,256	75,182
8	$50,000	3,000	53,000	75,182	4,511	79,692
9	$50,000	3,000	53,000	79,692	4,782	84,474
10	$50,000	3,000	53,000	84,474	5,068	89,542
11	$50,000	3,000	53,000	89,542	5,373	94,915
12	$50,000	3,000	53,000	94,915	5,695	100,610
13	$50,000	3,000	53,000	100,610	6,037	106,646
14	$50,000	3,000	53,000	106,646	6,399	113,045
15	$50,000	3,000	53,000	113,045	6,783	119,828
TOTAL INTEREST EARNED	$45,000			$69,828		

Amounts are rounded to the nearest dollar.

Global Perspective

Savings. Explain to students that on average individuals in the United States save about 5 percent of their income. In contrast, individuals in many other countries save a larger percentage of their income. Encourage students to acknowledge that they live in a country where people save very little.

Direct students to discuss the economic problems the country faces because of the low level of savings. Then have them write a letter or e-mail to a friend detailing the advantages of savings for the individual and for the country. **LS**

basic types of savings accounts: traditional, certificates of deposit, and money market accounts.

Traditional Savings Account

This account is offered by all of the institutions named previously except brokerage firms. Generally, a low minimum deposit, such as $100, is required to open a traditional savings account. The interest rate varies from one financial institution to another. The rate can also change over time.

There are two types of traditional savings accounts. One is a **passbook savings account** in which all of the deposits and withdrawals are recorded in a book that the depositor keeps. With the **statement savings account**, all of the activity in the account is recorded on a statement that is sent to the person who has the account. With either account, you can withdraw money from your account at any time without any penalty. The interest rate on the traditional savings accounts is usually quite low. Many banks also charge a service fee if the savings account falls below a certain minimum balance.

The traditional savings account is a place for a small amount of money that you might need in the near future. You won't earn much interest on your savings, but the money is easy to get when you need it.

Certificate of Deposit

Another type of savings account, called a **certificate of deposit (CD)**, requires you to deposit a minimum amount of money in an account for a minimum period of time. The amount is usually at least $500. The length of time might be 6 months, 1 year, or 5 years. A CD has a **maturity date**, which is when the money becomes available to you. The interest rate on a CD is higher than a regular savings account. If you cash in the CD before the maturity date, however, you lose interest and might have to pay a penalty fee.

Money Market Fund

Brokerage firms, financial institutions that buy and sell stocks and bonds, offer a special type of savings account called a money market fund. A **money market fund** is a kind of mutual fund, or pool of money, put into a variety of short-term debt (less than one year) by business and government. In a way, you're lending your money to a business or the government to invest.

The interest rate on a money market fund varies from month-to-month. An advantage is that you can withdraw your money at any time. There are,

Chapter 30 Savings Accounts **491**

Real-World Application
part **3** of 4

HOW LONG IS A CD'S LIFE?

A friend suggests you save some money on CD purchases by joining a music club, where you get 12 CDs free. In the club's brochure the fine print requires that each member order five full-priced CDs *before* choosing the free CDs. What is the maturity date of those free CDs?

continued on p. 493

Chapter 30

Real-World Application
Caption Answer

HOW LONG IS A CD'S LIFE?: PART 3 OF 4

Maturity date is when the free CDs become available to you, or only after buying five full-priced CDs.

Individualized Practice

You will research information on a specific type of savings account. Research to answer the following questions: What is the type of savings account you are assigned? What are the benefits of this savings account? What are the disadvantages of this account? Where can this type of savings account be opened? (Types of savings accounts to be assigned: passbook savings, statement savings, certificates of deposit, money market fund, or money market deposit account.)

L1 Assign a type of account to pairs of students and ask the students to discuss their answers to the questions given above.

L2 Assign a type of account to pairs of students and ask the students to create a chart of their answers to the questions given above.

L3 Assign a type of account to groups of students and ask the groups to create a chart of their answers to the questions given above. Have the groups present their chart to the class.

LANGUAGE ARTS
Curriculum Connection

Communication. Suggest that students find out the current rates offered by local banks on certificates of deposit. Remind students that each bank or savings institution may offer a variety of CDs, each with a different maturity date. Have students pool their information in a chart or table. Ask volunteers to make a generalization about the relationship between the interest rate and the maturity date. Also ask for a generalization about the interest rate and the current rate of inflation. (Longer-term CDs offer higher interest rates. The interest rate is or is not enough to cover inflation.) **LS, CL**

3 ASSESS

Reteaching

ADVANTAGES AND DISAD-VANTAGES. To reteach the concept of advantages and disadvantages of savings accounts, ask students to work in teams of four to develop a quiz for the material. Suggest they include five true-or-false questions and five multiple-choice questions. Randomly distribute the quizzes. (Encourage teamwork.)

Enrichment Strategy

PRESENT. Have students work in small groups to plan and then present a brief news report describing and comparing types of savings accounts. **LS**

 Fast Review Answers

1. You lose the interest on it and you might have to pay a penalty fee.
2. A money market fund is offered by brokerage firms. A money market deposit account is offered by banks, savings and loans, and credit unions.

Caption Answer

1. Make an investment decision.
2. Discuss his options once again.
3. It still means keeping a balanced investment portfolio.

492

---

however, two disadvantages. You usually need to put at least $1,000 into a money market fund, and you can only write a limited number of checks. Each check might have to be above a certain minimum, such as $500.

Money Market Deposit Account

Banks, savings and loans, and credit unions have their own form of money market fund called a **money market deposit account**. It has the same basic requirements and characteristics of a money market fund. One difference between them is that the federal government insures the money in a market deposit account.

 Fast Review

1. What happens if you cash in a CD before the maturity date?
2. What is the difference between a money market fund and a money market deposit account?

Advantages and Disadvantages of Savings Accounts

As with any choice, there are trade-offs to having a savings account. The opportunity cost, in which you give up something in order to get something later, has a trade-off. The main advantage of a savings account, of course, is that you earn interest on it. There are other advantages and disadvantages as well.

 **Risking Someone Else's Future**

As a financial planner, you work hard for your clients. This morning one of your best clients talked with you about his investments. He is 67, retired, and has a moderately strong portfolio. He wants to shift all his money from conservative investments such as savings accounts, CDs, and municipal bonds to high-risk stocks. You know that if he uses your services to buy stocks, you stand to gain more in service charges than if he keeps his investments in bank accounts. On the other hand, you believe at his age, he is better off not risking so much of his secure investments.

Making an Ethical Decision

1. What should you do?
2. What if he insists on transferring his money to high-risk stocks?
3. What if he were 87 years old?

How to Use a Portfolio Activity

The portfolio projects are designed to lead students to develop a collection of their best work to submit to you for assessment. You and each of your students should decide which projects to include in their business portfolio. Refer students to the specific rubric(s) from the *Alternative Assessment Strategies*. These rubrics will alert students to the criteria you'll use to assess their projects. **P**

Insurance Against Loss

Banks, savings and loans, and credit unions all have insurance. For example, the **Federal Deposit Insurance Corporation (FDIC)**, a government agency, insures bank accounts. Even if a bank fails, the FDIC will replace depositors' accounts for up to $100,000. Money market funds offered by brokerage firms aren't federally insured, but most brokerage firms have insurance on their accounts.

Liquidity

Liquidity means the ability to quickly turn an investment into cash. An investment such as a car or a business isn't very liquid because you have to sell it in order to get cash. Savings accounts, on the other hand, are highly liquid because you can easily withdraw cash from them. You can even cash in a CD before it matures. You won't get its full value, though, and you'll have to pay a penalty fee for cashing it in before the maturity date.

Inflation Risk

Inflation is a general increase in the cost of goods and services. **Inflation risk** is the risk that the rate of inflation will increase more than the rate of interest on savings. Suppose you have $1,000 in a savings account that earns 4 percent interest. During the next year, inflation increases by 6 percent. That means it cost $1,060 at the end of the year to buy what you could for $1,000 at the beginning of the year. With interest, your savings only increased to $1,040, so you actually lost money. The interest rates on most savings accounts, however, increase with inflation. The main risk is with CDs, where you're locked into an interest rate over a long period of time.

Costs of Savings Accounts

Savings accounts earn interest but they can also cost money. Some accounts charge a penalty fee for early withdrawal or if the account balance falls below a certain minimum. Other accounts charge a fee for each deposit and withdrawal. The money you earn in interest on a savings account is also considered income. As a result, you have to pay income tax on it.

Fast Review

1. What kinds of savings accounts doesn't the FDIC insure?
2. In what ways can a savings account cost you money?

Real-World Application

part **4** of 4

HOW LONG IS A CD'S LIFE?
Four years or so later, your music tastes have greatly changed. As a matter of fact, you can't believe you bought and listened to some of the things you did. A used audio CD store just opened in your town. You decide to sell your CDs to the store and it gives you cash in return.
Is this an example of liquidity or inflation?

Chapter 30

Real-World Application Caption Answer

HOW LONG IS A CD'S LIFE?: PART 4 OF 4
Liquidity.

Technology Resource

 EXAMVIEW PRO CD-ROM. Check your students' understanding of the chapter's key concepts and terms by using the *ExamView Pro®* CD-ROM.

Evaluation

Assign and review the Fast Review sections.

Fast Review Answers ✔

1. Money market funds.
2. If inflation increases more than the interest rate on an account. Penalty fees for early withdrawal or the balance falling below a certain minimum. Fees for each deposit and withdrawal, and taxes on interest income.

Meeting Individual Needs

Students With Learning Disabilities. Diagrams can help in clarifying information presented in a text. Ask several volunteers to draw on the board diagrams that represent the structure of the two sub sections "Types of Savings Accounts" and "Advantages and Disadvantages of Savings Accounts." Suggest students use word webs illustrated with simple symbols, or any relevant sketch. Have students discuss the diagrams, indicating ways in which a diagram might be revised to be more helpful. Once students are satisfied with the diagrams, suggest they copy the one that seems most useful to them and use it as a study aid.

4 CLOSE

Chapter Wrap-Up

Draw a large sketch of four eggs piled in a nest. Give each part a heading corresponding with the main concepts of this chapter. In each part, write main points to use as a study aid.

Using Business Key Words

1. CD
2. compound interest
3. liquidity
4. inflation risk
5. money market deposit account
6. passbook savings account
7. statement savings account
8. money market fund
9. savings
10. opportunity cost
11. simple interest
12. maturity date
13. FDIC

Review What You Learned

14. Social security and retirement plans do not provide enough money to retire comfortably.
15. Savings, the interest rate you're receiving, and loan period.
16. By not drawing out the interest as it is earned.
17. It figures the total amount of interest earned for the year divided by the amount in the account at the beginning of the year plus deposits.
18. The traditional savings account.
19. Hold on to your money longer.
20. Yes.
21. Money market plan.
22. Opportunity cost of spending.

Summary

1. The three main reasons for saving money are for major purchases, for emergencies, and for retirement.

2. Financial institutions pay interest on savings accounts in return for using (or borrowing) the money. As with a credit account, the amount of interest earned depends on the interest rate, the size of the account, and the length of time you keep the account.

3. Passbook savings, statement savings, certificates of deposit, money market funds, and money market deposit accounts are different types of savings accounts.

4. Savings accounts earn interest, are usually insured, and have high liquidity. They can also cost money in fees, in taxes, and by not keeping up with inflation.

● Using Business Key Words

Saving money is important. More important, however, is making that money you save work for you. See how many of the following terms you know by matching each one with its definition.

- savings
- certificate of deposit (CD)
- compound interest
- money market fund
- money market deposit account
- passbook savings account
- liquidity
- opportunity cost
- statement savings account
- inflation risk
- simple interest
- maturity date
- Federal Deposit Insurance Corporation (FDIC)

1. The depositor keeps money in an account for a higher rate of interest.
2. Interest that is calculated on the principal and previously accumulated interest.
3. The ability to turn your savings into cash.
4. The loss of your savings dollar.
5. A safe mutual fund offered by brokerage houses.
6. An account where all the deposits and withdrawals are recorded in a book the depositor keeps.
7. An account where all of the activity in the account is recorded on a statement that is sent to the person who has the account.
8. A safe mutual fund offered by banks, savings and loan associations, mutual savings banks, and credit unions.
9. Money you put aside for the future.
10. Giving up the opportunity to buy something in order to buy something else.
11. Interest earned only on the principal, or the money deposited into a savings account.
12. The date when money in a certificate of deposit becomes available to the depositor.
13. A government agency that insures commercial bank accounts for up to $100,000.

Quick Quiz

1. Name three main reasons people save money. (Major purchases, emergencies, and retirement.)
2. What is compound interest? (Interest earned on both the principal and any interest earned.)
3. Name the three main types of savings accounts. (Traditional savings accounts, certificates of deposit, and money market accounts.)

Review What You Learned

14. Why is it best to begin saving for retirement early?
15. The amount of interest you receive from your savings depends on three factors. What are they?
16. How do savers benefit from compound interest?
17. Explain what the FDIC is and what it does.
18. What type of savings account would be appropriate for a small amount of money you may need in the near future?
19. Why are banks or other financial institutions willing to pay a higher rate of interest for a CD than for a traditional savings account?
20. Can you withdraw money from a money market fund at any time without penalty?
21. What type of savings account would be appropriate for a large amount of money that you might want to use for something in the near future?
22. Explain why all savings involve some trade-off.

Understanding Business Concepts

23. What three sources of income are people able to rely on when they retire?
24. Explain how your savings account is like a loan to the bank or financial institution.
25. Which earns you more money—interest compounded daily or interest compounded yearly? Explain your answer.
26. If you're planning to go to college next year, what type of savings account should you have? Why?
27. What is the tradeoff for savings accounts that are liquid and safe?

Critical Thinking

28. Are you currently saving money? If so, what are you saving for? If not, why not?
29. Describe a person who would be a good candidate to use CDs as a method of saving money.
30. What do you think would happen if the FDIC didn't exist?
31. How does inflation affect your savings decisions?

Viewing and Representing

Examining the Image. Look closely at the photograph. What's important in this picture? Name something you want to buy that's expensive. What type of account would you choose to hold your money?

Critical Thinking

28. Answers will vary.
29. Answers will vary. Some possible answers might include: someone who is saving for something far into the future; someone who has money to invest but wants a very safe investment; someone who doesn't need his/her money soon.
30. Answers will vary. A possible answer is that people could lose a lot of money and so would be more cautious about putting their money into savings. This would slow down the savings and loan business.
31. Answers will vary. Some answers might include the need to factor the cost of inflation into savings goals.

Viewing and Representing

This activity launches students into applying their newly found knowledge about savings accounts to a personal situation. Ask volunteers to share the type of account they chose and give reasons for their decision. **LS**, **CL**

Understanding Business Concepts

23. Social security, retirement plans, and savings.
24. You are giving the bank your money for a specific period of time, but you expect it back. They pay you interest, which is a return on your savings.
25. Interest compounded daily.
26. Answers could vary. CD and money market.
27. Higher interest rates or the ability to grow the purchasing power of your savings.

4 CLOSE (Cont.)

Building Academic Skills

HISTORY. Answers will vary. The Internet and the library are good sources of information for this project. Rubrics: Note taking, paragraph.

MATH. Annual interest: $1,000 × 0.06 × 1 = $60. Interest compounded daily: Use chart in Figure 30.2. Rubric: Calculation.

LANGUAGE ARTS. Make sure all students participate in the group project. Rubrics: Poster, computer presentation, chart, diagram.

COMPUTER/TECHNOLOGY. Spreadsheets will vary depending on the information gathered. This project could also be done in groups. Rubrics: Spreadsheet, paragraphs.

Linking School to Home

Allow the students to share their results any way they choose. Rubrics: Essay, poster, oral presentation, chart.

Linking School to Work

Answers will vary. Rubric: Brochure.

Building Academic Skills

 Research the Federal Deposit Insurance Corporation (FDIC)

Write a paragraph about how and why the FDIC impacted U.S. history and continues to do so today.

 Calculating Interest

If you have a savings account that pays you 6 percent annual interest and $1,000 is in the account for the entire year, how much interest will you earn? If your savings plan pays 6 percent interest compounded daily, how much will you earn?

Creating a Visual Aid

As a group, choose one type of savings account. Conduct research and prepare a visual display describing the advantages and disadvantages of the selected savings account. Use local banks and the Internet as resources for your research. Share your visual display with the class.

 A Comparative Spreadsheet

Survey banks, savings and loan associations, and credit unions about the interest rates they pay on their savings accounts, certificates of deposit, and money market accounts. Also, compile information on their minimum deposits and balances, allowable number of transactions, minimum balances to earn interest, and limits on withdrawals. Create a spreadsheet with the information you gather that will calculate the return for each kind of savings account you discover. Input varying amounts of money from small to very large and print out the results. Then decide which institutions are best for growth when small amounts are saved and which are best for larger amounts. Write a paragraph with your decision.

Linking School to Home

Money Leftover. Savings is money put aside for future use. The amount of money you save depends on how much of your income you're willing not to spend. Obtain a large jar or other container and ask everyone in your family to "deposit" their change there each night when they come home from work or school. After one month, count the money. How much have you saved? As a family, decide what you would like to do with the money—for example, you could go out to dinner, see a movie, or donate it to a local charity.

Linking School to Work

Rephrasing Documentation. A brokerage firm might insure the money market fund. This is one of the many opportunities made available to you by a financial institution. Financial institutions generally have brochures or other written documentation about their various savings accounts. Obtain one of them and rewrite it in terms that a preteen might understand.

E-Homework

Applying Technology

Calculating Compound Interest. Compound interest is interest earned on both the principal—the money you deposited in your savings account—and any interest you earned on it. Create a spreadsheet and the formulas necessary to calculate interest compounded daily, monthly, and yearly. The spreadsheet should contain at least five different interest rates.

Online Research. Use the Internet to find out if there are any local banks or online banks that offer special savings accounts for students.

Connecting Academics

Math. Use the data below to compute the total savings on a $1,000 deposit at the end of one year. This might be a good opportunity to use spreadsheet software.

a. passbook savings account	3.5 percent simple interest
b. certificate of deposit (CD)	7 percent compounded quarterly
c. certificate of deposit (CD)	3.5 percent compounded monthly

Social Science. Social skills on the job are important for success. You're a member of a news team for a public television program. Together, with several of your coworkers (classmates), develop and present a two-minute segment for the afternoon news called, "Savings Today." Assign one team member to observe the development process and report on how each team member relates to the others.

BusinessWeek — Analyzing the Feature Story

You read the first part of "How to Cash Out Your College Fund" at the beginning of this chapter. Below are a few questions for you to answer about savings plans. You'll find the answers to these questions when you're reading the entire article. First, here are the questions:

32. What is the first step for parents who wish to begin a savings plan for their child's college tuition?

33. Why shouldn't parents keep college savings in their child's name?

CREATIVE JOURNAL ACTIVITY

Consider a family's expenditures. How much needs to be saved to afford them? What is a reasonable savings goal for each item? Estimate how much time the family will need to save for each expenditure.

BUSINESS Online
The Full Story

To learn more about savings plans, visit the *Introduction to Business* Web site at www.introbus.glencoe.com, and click on *BusinessWeek* Feature Story, Chapter 30.

E-Homework

CALCULATING COMPOUND INTEREST. If students struggle with using formulas, ask other students to help. Rubric: Spreadsheet.

ONLINE RESEARCH. Students' answers will vary. Allow the students to share their findings any way they choose. Rubrics: Note taking, essay, oral presentation, poster.

Connecting Academics

MATH. Passbook savings: $1,000 × 0.035 = $35. CD, 7 percent interest compounded quarterly: first quarter $1,087.50; second quarter $1,163.63; third quarter $1,245.08; fourth quarter $1,332.24. CD, 3.5 percent interest compounded monthly, interest at the end of months 2 through 12: $1,071.23, $1,108.72, $1,147.53, $1,187.69, $1,229.26, $1,272.28, $1,316.81, $1,362.90, $1,410.60, $1,459.97, $1,511.07.

SOCIAL SCIENCE. In addition to the "Savings Today" presentation, have the observers in each team report on sociability and how team members relate to others. Encourage the observers to use specific examples to support points in their reports.

BusinessWeek — *Analyzing the Feature Story*

32. Parents should first research what financial aid their child may be eligible for.

33. The formulas used for calculating financial aid eligibility hit students' assets harder than parents. Students are expected to put 35 percent of their assets toward education. Parents are only expected to put 5.6 percent of assets toward their child's education.

Creative Journal Activity
Ask students to consider their own family or an imaginary "typical" family. Suggest students create a chart summarizing the information and estimates. **LS**

SCANS Correlation Chart*

Foundation Skills

Basic Skills	Reading	Writing	Math	Listening	Speaking	
Thinking Skills	Creative Thinking	Decision Making	Problem Solving	Seeing Things in the Mind's Eye	Knowing How to Learn	Reasoning
Personal Qualities	Responsibility	Self-Esteem	Sociability	Self-Management	Integrity/ Honesty	

Workplace Competencies

Resources	Allocating Time	Allocating Money	Allocating Material and Facility Resources	Allocating Human Resources		
Information	Acquiring and Evaluating Information	Organizing and Maintaining Information	Interpreting and Communicating Information	Using Computers to Process Information		
Interpersonal Skills	Participating as a Member of a Team	Teaching Others	Serving Clients/ Customers	Exercising Leadership	Negotiating to Arrive at a Decision	Working With Cultural Diversity
Systems	Understanding Systems	Monitoring and Correcting Performance	Improving and Designing Systems			
Technology	Selecting Technology	Applying Technology to Task	Maintaining and Troubleshooting Technology			

*This chart's highlighted blocks indicate the chapter's content coverage in the Student Edition and the Teacher Wraparound Edition.

Resource Manager

Teaching Transparencies

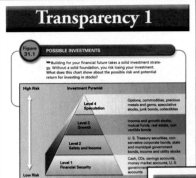

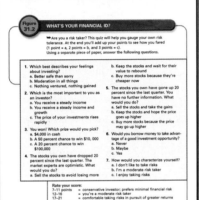

Application and Enrichment

- 🖋 Lesson Plans
- 📕 *BusinessWeek* Poster Package
- 🖋 Teaching Transparencies
- 💿 🖋 Integrated Software Simulation
- 📼 🖋 Glencoe Business Video Package

Review and Reinforcement

- 💿 *PuzzleMaker*
- 💻 🖋 Internet Resources
- 🖋 Student Activity Workbook
- 🖋 Strat. and Work. for Teaching Transparencies

Assessment and Evaluation

- 🖋 Reproducible Tests
- 🖋 Alternative Assessment Strategies
- 💿 ExamView® Pro Test Generator

Technology

- 💿 *PuzzleMaker*
- 💿 ExamView® Pro Test Generator
- 📼 Glencoe Business Video Package
- 💿 PowerPoint® Presentation
- 💿 🖋 Integrated Software Simulation
- 💿 Interactive Lesson Planner
- 💿 *Virtual Business*®

KEY	🖋 Printed	💾 Software	📼 Videocassette	📕 Poster
	🖋 Transparency	💿 CD-ROM	💻 Internet	

BUSINESS Online

Visit www.introbus.glencoe.com, the Web site companion to *Introduction to Business.* The student's page includes:

- interactive tutor
- additional *BusinessWeek* articles and activities
- business Web links
- homework hints
- real-world application activities
- additional career path activities

Information on how to prepare your students for the high school exit exam and special projects are also included.

Use the Glencoe Web site for additional resources. All essential content is covered in the Student Edition.

1 FOCUS

Introducing the Chapter

This chapter explains the fundamentals of investing. It describes the advantages and disadvantages of investing in stocks. A photo essay, "Typical Day on the Floor," enhances the concepts.

Connecting the Objectives

What is stock and how can you buy stock? What information is in the daily stock quotations?

BusinessWeek
Feature Story

Story's Summary

YoungInvestor Web site is one of the best tools to learn about savings and investment. A strong point about YoungInvestor Web site is that it's simple and fun to use, yet it provides solid information and advice. A weak point is that the site needs to be kept up-to-date in some areas. Another top site is the Kids & Money page on www.Kiplinger.com.

Find the entire article at www.introbus.glencoe.com, or in the Teacher Resource Binder.

Chapter 31

Investing in Stocks

● Learning Objectives

After completing this chapter, you'll be able to:
1. **Define** stock.
2. **Explain** how stock is bought and sold.
3. **Identify** the indexes that track stock prices over the long run.

● Why It's Important

Making good investment decisions helps you reach your financial goals.

● Key Words

investing
stock
yield
dividends
capital gain
capital loss
common stock
preferred stock
broker
stock exchange
mutual fund
blue-chip stocks
speculative stocks

498

BusinessWeek Feature Story

Where Kids Can Log On to Learn Their Investing ABCs

Intelligent and Fun Personal Finance Sites for Kids. Kids today seem to spend half their lives surfing the Web and the other half spending money. This year teens will spend $153 billion, including $105 billion of their own, according to Teenage Research Unlimited of Northbrook, Ill. So parents and teachers should be able to use the Internet to find communities that teach youths how to manage finances. But it turns out that learning about dollars and cents online is tougher than spending money there.

Source: Excerpted with permission from "Where Kids Can Log On to Learn Their Investing ABCs," *BusinessWeek Online*, November 12, 1999.

An Extension Activity

How much should your parents pay you? Be reasonable. Who can live on the least amount of money? Who has the greatest wants or needs? How do your wants and needs fit into your family's budget? Create an interactive debate to challenge each other to find a solution.

BUSINESS
Online
The Full Story

To learn more about investing, visit the *Introduction to Business* Web site www.introbus.glencoe.com, and click on *BusinessWeek* Feature Story, Chapter 31.

Classroom Resources

For the Teacher
📁 Student Activity Work. TAE
📓💿 Assessment Binder
💿 PowerPoint® Presentation
💿 Interactive Lesson Planner
📁 Lesson Plans
📓💻 Internet Resources
🖱 Teaching Transparencies
💻 *Introduction to Business* Web Site

💿 Integrated Soft. Sim. TM
📕 *BusinessWeek* Poster Package

For the Student
📓 Student Activity Workbook
💿 *Virtual Business*®
💻 *Introduction to Business* Web Site
💿 Integrated Soft. Sim.
💿 *PuzzleMaker*
📓 Strategies and Worksheets for Teaching Transparencies

Bell Ringer Activity

WRITING. Write a paragraph about the main things you know about investing in stocks. Include a sentence or two about your feelings on investing in stocks. **LS**

Preteaching Business Key Words

READING. Ask a student to read out loud the chapter's key words from the glossary. Have volunteers repeat in their own words the definition of each word. **LS**

An Extension Activity

REVIEW. Encourage active debate, and then review the solutions.

Making Connections

Everyday Life. One inexpensive and informative way to invest in stocks is to join an investment club. For $25 a month, about a dozen club members research stocks, choose purchases, and pool their money to make purchases. Some investment clubs have done remarkably well.

Business Connection

EMPLOYEE BENEFIT.
McDonald's Corporation offers a direct investment service to non-employees. Through McDirect, potential investors can purchase up to $50 or more of McDonald's stock per month. The initial fee is $5. The transactions are free when arranged through a direct payroll deduction.

Develop Concepts

COMPARE. What's the first thing anyone asks when he or she is going to invest? It's likely to be, "How much will this investment make?" A wise investor compares a number of factors. What might they be? (Answers will vary and should include risk, rate of return, availability of the money, resistance to inflation, and tax considerations.)

Figure 31.1 Caption Answer

The greater the risk, the better the potential for monetary return.

Fundamentals of Investing

You won a youth national writing contest, with a cash reward of $3,000. Instead of placing all of the money in your savings account, you decide to invest some of the money so that it can earn a potentially higher return. With money you set aside for long-term goals like college, a house, or retirement, you'll need more than the rates usually paid on a savings account to stay ahead of inflation and taxes.

Investing in Stocks

Investing is putting your money to use in order to make money on it. Putting money in a savings account is a form of investing. Savings are loans made to banks or other financial institutions in return for earning interest. Investing in stocks, however, is quite different. Figure 31.1 illustrates the types of investments with the severity of their risk.

You might remember from Chapter 6 that there are three primary forms of business ownership: sole proprietorships, partnerships, and

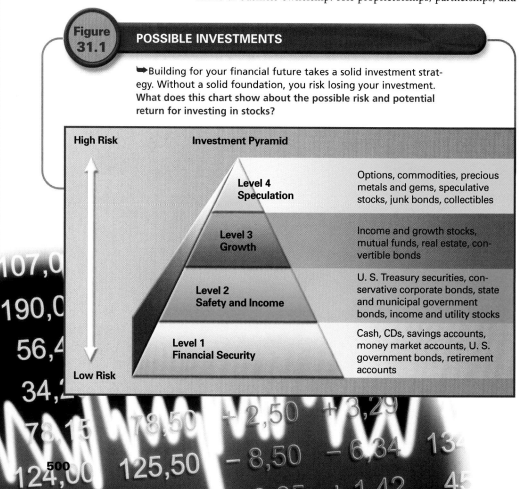

Figure 31.1 POSSIBLE INVESTMENTS

➡Building for your financial future takes a solid investment strategy. Without a solid foundation, you risk losing your investment. What does this chart show about the possible risk and potential return for investing in stocks?

High Risk — Investment Pyramid — Low Risk

Level 4 Speculation — Options, commodities, precious metals and gems, speculative stocks, junk bonds, collectibles

Level 3 Growth — Income and growth stocks, mutual funds, real estate, convertible bonds

Level 2 Safety and Income — U. S. Treasury securities, conservative corporate bonds, state and municipal government bonds, income and utility stocks

Level 1 Financial Security — Cash, CDs, savings accounts, money market accounts, U. S. government bonds, retirement accounts

Cooperative Learning

"Top Ten Investment Tips!" Investment periodicals and advisors point out that successful investors seem to follow two common investment rules: (1) invest regularly and (2) invest for the longer-term. Have students work in groups to research some tips or pointers about investing. Have students use their findings to compose a "Top Ten" list of investment rules. **CL**

corporations. One way a corporation raises money to start or to enlarge its business is by selling stock. **Stock** is a share of ownership in a business. When you buy stock in a company, you aren't lending it money. When you buy stock, you receive a stock certificate indicating that you are now part owner of the company. Sole proprietorships and partnerships, on the other hand, don't sell stock.

Return on Stocks

The return on an investment, or **yield**, is the amount of money the investment earns. The return on a stock investment depends on the type of return and the rate of return.

Types of Return. There are two ways that you can make a return on stocks. One is through the payment of **dividends**, which is a share of profits. If a corporation makes a lot of money over a certain period of time, it distributes the profits among its shareholders in the form of dividends. Dividends are usually paid quarterly.

Stockholders can also earn income on their stocks by selling their stock shares for more than they paid for them. For example, if Juanita buys 100 shares of stock at $25 (total cost = $2,500) and sells it for $35 (total return = $3,500), she will earn additional income of $1,000 ($3,500 − $2,500).

Selling stock for *more than* you paid for it is called a **capital gain**. Juanita might also sell her stock for *less than* she paid for it because she needs the cash or the company is doing badly. In that case, she would be taking a **capital loss**. As with any form of income, the government taxes the amount you make in dividends or in capital gains.

Rate of Return. The rate of return on stocks is always expressed as a percent of the original investment and figured on an annual basis. For example, suppose $1,000 in a savings account earns a $50 interest payment for one year. The rate of return on the investment is 5 percent ($50/$1,000 = 0.05). A single share of stock whose value increases from $50 to $55 in a year and pays a $5 dividend during the year has a 20 percent rate of return ($10 return/$50 original investment = 0.20).

Types of Stocks

When a company sells stock, it usually offers two different types: common stock and preferred stock. **Common stock** is the primary form of ownership in a corporation. All corporations must issue common stock and many issue common stock only. For each share of common

Real-World Application
part 1 of 4

TYPICAL DAY ON THE FLOOR
You made a decision to sell some of your stock. The next morning your account executive receives your order to sell stock and relays the order electronically to the brokerage firm's representative on the stock exchange.
What are some reasons why you might sell your stock?

continued on p. 503

Chapter 31 Investing in Stocks **501**

Chapter 31

Real-World Application
Caption Answer

TYPICAL DAY ON THE FLOOR: PART 1 OF 4
Answers will vary but include the company isn't profitable, reinvest the money somewhere else, etc.

Technology Resource

GO TO **POWERPOINT.** The *Introduction to Business* PowerPoint® CD-ROM provides visual lecture aids for this chapter.

Independent Practice

POSTER. Make a creative poster to showcase the main points of the following: return on stocks, types of stocks, stockbrokers, stock exchanges, over-the-counter markets, and mutual funds. (Encourage creativity.) **LS**

Meeting Individual Needs

Students With Comprehension Difficulties. Introduce a focused reading exercise to assist students experiencing comprehension problems. Direct students to read the subsection "Types of Return." Have them write in their notebooks what they remember of the subsection. Suggest that they read the subsection to find the answers to the questions that follow and add to their written notes any points they missed on the first reading. Questions: How many ways can you make a return on stocks? What are they? What is a capital gain? What is a capital loss? Are capital gains taxed? Why or why not? **LS**

2 TEACH (Cont.)

Thinking Critically

ANALYSIS. Eric and Allison Moser are married and have one child. Their annual income is $38,000. Two years ago they bought a house. The mortgage will be paid up in 28 years. The Mosers have life insurance of $70,000. They've just made the last payment on their three-year-old car. The Mosers' budget shows that they can now save $100 a month. What kind of savings and investment plan would you recommend they begin? Would you recommend investing in stocks now, or in the future? (Answers will vary.)

Business Building Blocks

CAPTION ANSWER

Ask volunteers to explain what the numbers in each column of the example in the box represent. Allow students time to become familiar with the stock market quotations in the box. Then suggest that students work in pairs to complete the numbered practice items.

1. $65.88
2. $45.25
3. 30,124,000
4. $2,063. ($65.88 × 100) − ($45.25 × 100)

---

stock that you own, you get a vote in how to run the corporation. Every year the stockholders have a meeting where they vote on various issues and elect members to the Board of Directors. The Board of Directors is responsible for representing the interests of the stockholders in the running of the corporation.

A company might also issue **preferred stock**. Preferred stock gives its holders certain privileges that common stockholders don't have. If the company pays dividends, dividends on preferred stocks are paid before dividends on common stocks. If a company fails, preferred stockholders get a share of whatever assets are left after the company's debts are paid before the common stockholders do.

Business Building Blocks

Math

Reading Stock Market Quotations

If you're involved in the world of business, or have invested part of your savings in shares of corporate stock, you must be able to understand stock market quotations in newspaper financial pages. During a single day, the price of a stock may go up and down several times.

Practice

Study the examples of the stock quotation in the box and answer these questions:

1. What was the closing price for MCD?
2. What was the lowest price paid for MCD during a 52-week period?
3. How many shares of MCD were traded?
4. If you had bought 100 shares of MCD at the year's lowest price, how much more would they be worth today?

Example of a Stock Quotation Table

COLUMN										
1	2	3	4	5	6	7	8	9	10	11
52-Week Hi Lo	Stock	Sym	Div	Yld %	PE	Vol 100s	Hi	Lo	Close	Net Chg
66½ 45¼	McDonald's	MCD	.33	.5	28	30,124	66	63½	65⅞	+3¹⁄₁₆

Column 1 Highest and lowest selling price of the stock during the preceding 52 weeks.
Column 2 Company's name
Column 3 Ticker symbol
Column 4 Last year's dividend
Column 5 Yield. Last year's dividend divided by current price
Column 6 Price to earnings ratio. Current price divided by earnings per share
Column 7 Number of shares traded this day X 100
Column 8 Highest price the stock traded during this day
Column 9 Lowest price the stock traded during the day
Column 10 Last price the stock traded during this day
Column 11 Change between the closing price yesterday and this day

---

HISTORY *Curriculum Connection*

Dow Jones Industrial Average. As you check the Dow Jones Industrial Average, you might wonder who Dow and Jones were. Charles Henry Dow and Edward D. Jones were financial journalists in New York. In November 1882, they founded Dow Jones & Company, a firm that provided financial news services. Dow Jones & Company delivered bulletins to Wall Street financial firms by messenger. The last delivery of the day consisted of a newssheet that later became the *Wall Street Journal*. Dow was this newspaper's first editor from 1889 to 1902.

Stockbrokers

A **broker** is a person who acts as a go-between for buyers and sellers. Brokers process the purchase and sale of stocks. They charge either a percent of the value of the stock or a set amount for each transaction as a fee for their services, which could be up to $500.

Stock Exchanges

Most stocks are bought and sold through a trading market known as a **stock exchange**. These exchanges provide a central place where traders meet to buy and sell stock. When people sell stocks through their stockbrokers, their wishes are sent to the broker's representative on the stock exchange floor. A process like an auction takes place at a booth where the stock is bought and sold.

Some of the best-known exchanges are the New York Stock Exchange (NYSE) in New York City, regional exchanges—such as the Midwest Stock Exchange in Chicago—as well as the London Stock Exchange and the Tokyo Exchange. Only the stocks listed on an exchange can be traded. For example, if the ABC Corporation isn't listed on the New York Stock Exchange, then its stock isn't traded there. Exchanges have rules about what types of companies they'll list. To be listed on an exchange, a corporation must prove to the exchange that it's in good financial condition.

Over-the-Counter Markets

Many stocks not listed on a major exchange can be bought and sold through the National Association of Securities Dealers Automated Quotations (NASDAQ) market. The NASDAQ is a system that quotes over-the-counter securities—all investments bought and sold. In this case, a brokerage house makes a market in a particular stock, or provides a place where that stock can be bought and sold. For example, if you want to sell a stock that isn't listed on any of the exchanges in the United States, your broker will find out if any brokerage house is making a market in that stock.

Mutual Funds

An investor can participate in the stock market without buying stocks in a specific corporation by buying shares in a stock mutual fund. To determine your financial risk-taking personality, take the quiz in Figure 31.2 (on page 504). A **mutual fund** is a fund created by an investment company that raises money from many shareholders and invests it in a variety of stocks. A mutual fund has much greater buying power because

Chapter 31 Investing in Stocks **503**

Real-World Application

part **2** of 4

TYPICAL DAY ON THE FLOOR
On the stock exchange floor a clerk for the firm signals the transaction to a floor broker on the stock exchange floor.
Name one of the best-known exchanges.

continued on p. 505

Real-World Application
Caption Answer

TYPICAL DAY ON THE FLOOR: PART 2 OF 4

The New York Stock Exchange (NYSE) and Midwest Stock Exchange in Chicago.

Individualized Practice

Ask students to search local television listings to find what, if any, channels in your area broadcast continuous stock quotations throughout the day. From the TV or from the Internet, have students gather information on New York Stock Exchange (NYSE) quotes, Chicago Board of Trade (CBOT) quotes, and commodity prices.

L1 Have students work in pairs to discuss the kinds of information presented.

L2 Ask students to write a one-page report about the kinds of information presented.

L3 Ask students to work in groups to prepare an oral report on what kinds of information are presented. Ask groups to also report on what, if any, analysis the programs or the Internet provided.

Great Ideas From the Classroom of...

Claudia Harris
Delta High School
Clarksburg, Calif.

Students' Stock Portfolio. Students work in pairs and "buy" at least four different stocks worth a combined total of $100,000. Every Friday they check their portfolio. They calculate their profit or loss and what percentage that is of the original value. They can sell or buy during the year, but they can't bank any money. The pair getting the highest profit at the end of the year get PayDay candy bars. The pair with the highest loss get Milk Duds.

2 TEACH (Cont.)

Discussion Starter

DAY TRADING. Ask students: What do you think day trading is? Do you know anyone who is a day trader? What's your feeling about the extent of risk involved?

Figure 31.2 Caption Answer

Answers will vary depending on a student's financial outlook. Discuss what it means to be a conservative investor, moderate risk taker, and a big risk taker. How does it influence who a person is or might become?

Business Connection

You can almost hear the old football cheer, "DEE-fense! DEE-fense!" sometimes when it comes to the stock market. Defensive stocks are popular in a slowing economy because they have a reputation of being resistant to a slowdown. At a time when the NASDAQ and the Dow were seeing big losses, defensive issues such as Boeing and Merck were posting significant gains.

504

it has a greater amount of money available to invest. If the stocks owned by the mutual fund make a profit, then the mutual fund shareholders earn a dividend. Mutual fund shareholders, like stock shareholders, also have capital gains or losses when they sell their shares.

Mutual funds are a way to limit your risk of investing in the stock market. The risk is spread out because a mutual fund consists of stocks

Figure 31.2

WHAT'S YOUR FINANCIAL ID?

➡Are you a risk taker? This quiz will help you gauge your own risk tolerance. At the end you'll add up your points to see how you fared (1 point = a, 2 points = b, and 3 points = c).
Using a separate piece of paper, answer the following questions.

1. Which best describes your feelings about investing?
   a. Better safe than sorry
   b. Moderation in all things
   c. Nothing ventured, nothing gained

2. Which is the most important to you as an investor?
   a. You receive a steady income
   b. You receive a steady income and growth
   c. The price of your investments rises rapidly

3. You won! Which prize would you pick?
   a. $4,000 in cash
   b. A 50 percent chance to win $10, 000
   c. A 20 percent chance to win $100,000

4. The stocks you own have dropped 20 percent since the last quarter. The market experts are optimistic. What would you do?
   a. Sell the stocks to avoid losing more

   b. Keep the stocks and wait for their value to rebound
   c. Buy more stocks because they're cheaper now

5. The stocks you own have gone up 20 percent since the last quarter. You have no further information. What would you do?
   a. Sell the stocks and take the gains
   b. Keep the stocks and hope the price goes up higher
   c. Buy more stocks because the price may go up higher

6. Would you borrow money to take advantage of a good investment opportunity?
   a. Never
   b. Maybe
   c. Yes

7. How would you characterize yourself?
   a. I don't like to take risks
   b. I'm a moderate risk taker
   c. I enjoy taking risks

Rate your score:
7–11 points	= conservative investor; prefers minimal financial risk
12–16	= you're a moderate risk taker
17–21	= comfortable taking risks in pursuit of greater returns

Source: "Five-Minute Quiz" from Standard & Poor's *Your Financial Future*
(© 1996 by The McGraw-Hill Companies)

504

Global Perspective

Stock Markets. Stock markets have national, regional, and even local bases, however, stock market trading routinely crosses national boundaries. United States stock brokers sometimes buy and sell stock in the middle of the night in order to do business as soon as Japanese markets open each day. Suggest that students consult the business section of the local newspapers to find the Japanese and London equivalents of the Dow Jones Industrial Average. (Nikkei 225; FTSE 100, often called "Footsy.") Have students find out the time differences between the three countries.

in many companies. If one stock performs poorly, the loss is limited and can be made up by other, better-performing stocks. Many people also prefer mutual funds because the professional managers of the mutual funds have more experience in selecting stocks than they do.

Stock Indexes. There are many ways to determine the value of your stock at any given time. The various stock exchanges' figures can be found in major newspapers, such as the *Wall Street Journal* or the *New York Times*, as well as on their Web sites.

There are some general indexes, or indicators, which are commonly reported on television and radio. An index is a measuring system that tracks stock prices over the long run. The Dow Jones Industrial Average (DJIA) and Standard & Poor's (S&P) are the two most common indexes.

The DJIA represents the 30 largest U.S. companies to measure the well-being of the stock market as a whole. Have you ever heard a report on a TV broadcast say that "the Dow went down 20 points today?" This doesn't mean that all stocks went down 20 points. A change of 20 points in the Dow means that the average for 30 selected stocks listed on the NYSE that the Dow represents went down 20 points.

The S&P 500 index tracks how the top 500 companies are doing. It's a gauge against which they compare their returns on stocks. Investing in an index fund over the long run is better than investing in individual stocks.

 Fast Review _____

1. What kinds of businesses can sell stock?
2. What privileges do preferred stockholders get?
3. What kinds of fees do brokers charge for their services?
4. Name the advantages of a mutual fund.

Advantages and Disadvantages of Stocks

There is a general principle at work in the world of investing—the greater the risk, the greater the possibility of a larger return. You have much more risk of losing your investment when putting your money into stocks rather than savings accounts, certificates of deposit, or money market funds. Stocks generally carry more risk but they also carry the possibility of a better return. Long-term comparisons of returns on stocks compared to savings show that stocks do better over time.

Chapter 31 Investing in Stocks **505**

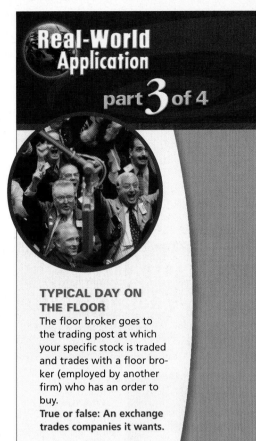

Real-World Application

part **3** of 4

TYPICAL DAY ON THE FLOOR
The floor broker goes to the trading post at which your specific stock is traded and trades with a floor broker (employed by another firm) who has an order to buy.
True or false: An exchange trades companies it wants.

continued on p. 507

Real-World Application
Caption Answer

TYPICAL DAY ON THE FLOOR: PART 3 OF 4
False. Only those listed on an exchange. Exchanges have rules about the types of companies they'll list.

Develop Concepts

RISK. Different kinds of investments have different levels of risk. For example, on any given day General Motors or IBM may lose rather than earn money, but the overall risk for investment in such companies is relatively small. Ask students to name some companies and estimate their level of risk. **LS**

Fast Review Answers

1. Corporations only.
2. They receive dividends if a company makes a profit or get a share of the assets (before common stockholders) if a company fails.
3. Either a percentage of the value of a stock or a set amount for each transaction.
4. It has greater buying power because it has more money to invest. The risk is spread out among a variety of stocks. Professional managers of mutual funds have more experience in selecting stocks for the mutual fund portfolio.

LANGUAGE ARTS   *Curriculum Connection*

Investment Ads. Have students work in groups of four to search local newspapers for advertisements for investments such as stocks, bonds, mutual funds, and so on. Have students collect the ads and highlight or circle the terms rate of return, yield, fixed rate, and variable rate. Have students rewrite the advertising copy, substituting their own words for the highlighted terms. **LS**, **CL**, **P**

3 ASSESS

Reteaching

TYPES OF STOCKS. To reteach the concept of types of stocks, ask students to name and describe the two different types. (Answers should include a description of common stock and preferred stock.)

Enrichment Strategy

THE DOW JONES INDUSTRIAL AVERAGE (DJIA). Work in pairs to research which companies currently make up the 30 largest U.S. companies used in the Dow Jones. **LS**

Working Lifestyle

Caption Answer

Students' opinions will vary. Suggest students write the answer in their journals. Ask students to write in their journals about their own interests. Encourage volunteers to share their answers. Guide a discussion on the topic. **LS**, **CL**

Levels of Risk

The risk of losing your investment varies from stock to stock. There are, however, two basic categories of stocks that offer different levels of risk.

Blue-Chip Stocks. The safest investment is in blue-chip stocks. **Blue-chip stocks** are stocks in large, well-established companies that have a good track record of profitability and success. International Business Machines (IBM) and General Motors (GM) are examples of blue-chip stocks. There is little likelihood that you'll lose your money when you invest in those stocks. However, even the value of blue-chip stocks goes up and down. You could still lose money if you sell them when the value is lower than what you paid for them.

Working Lifestyle

What are you doing at 10 A.M.?

In Stock

When he was a high school student, Thomas Zuttermeister's reading and television viewing habits were very focused. He and his mother watched the Financial News Network together. As he began advising his mother and investing some of his own resources, the financially precocious teenager managed to do very well—and not very well.

Most of Zuttermeister's clients are retired. It's important for him to help them invest their money safely. "I deal mostly in mutual funds, which helps distribute the risk. And when the market experiences fluctuations, I tell my clients, 'Don't *you* worry—that's part of my job.'"

As the Claremont, N.H., financial advisor reads the 10:00 A.M. stock market report, he says the rewards of his job are more than financial. He says, "It's a good feeling when you know you've helped someone. And those clients are very appreciative—they come back."

Salary

A typical stockbroker earns a median base salary of $46,210. Half of the people in this job earn between $40,136 and $50,025.

Outlook for This Career

The need for stockbrokers is strong. People often seek better returns on their investments.

Connecting Careers Activity

Zuttermeister turned his teenage interest into a career. What's more important to you: doing something you're passionate about or making a lot of money?

CAREER PATH *Finance*

How to Use a Portfolio Activity

The portfolio projects are designed to lead students to develop a collection of their best work to submit to you for assessment. You and each of your students should decide which projects to include in their business portfolio. Refer students to the specific rubric(s) from the *Alternative Assessment Strategies*. These rubrics will alert students to the criteria you'll use to assess their projects. **P**

Speculative Stocks. The story is different with speculative stocks. **Speculative stocks** are stocks in relatively new firms that don't have an established track record of success. They're often small firms that are developing new types of goods and services. Many technology stocks offered in the late 1990s and early 2000s were examples of speculative stocks. A few succeeded and made big money for their owners.

Day Trading

Some people have attempted to make quick money in the stock market by *day trading*. This means they're buying and selling stock, usually on the Internet, based on minute-by-minute changes in the price of the stock. This is extremely risky. You not only risk losing your original investment but also risk sustaining great financial losses.

Liquidity

Liquidity refers to how easily an investment can be turned into cash. In general, stocks are very liquid because they can be turned into cash quickly by selling them. You're not guaranteed to get all the money out of your investment, however, because the value of the stock might have gone down since you bought it. If the stock isn't listed on one of the exchanges or on the NASDAQ market, liquidity can be a problem. If it's not listed anywhere, there's no market for it and you won't be able to sell it.

Inflation Risk

Inflation risk is whether a rate of return or an investment keeps up with the rate of inflation. For example, if there is 4 percent inflation over the year, you must have 4 percent more money at the end of the year than at the beginning of the year to buy the same amount of goods and services. That means your stock needs to go up in value more than 4 percent to earn a return on your investment. Stocks have generally done very well in this category.

 Fast Review _____

1. What is the difference between blue-chip stocks and speculative stocks?
2. Why is online trading very risky?

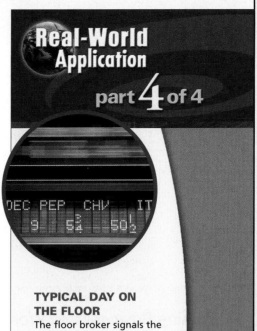

Real-World Application
part 4 of 4

TYPICAL DAY ON THE FLOOR
The floor broker signals the transaction back to the clerk. Then a floor reporter—an employee of the exchange—collects the information about the transaction and inputs it into the ticker system. The sale appears on the price board, and a confirmation is relayed back to your account executive, who then notifies you of the completed transaction. **Are stocks considered to have great liquidity?**

Chapter 31

Technology Resource

GO TO **INTEGRATED SOFTWARE SIMULATION CD-ROM.**
Check your students' understanding of the chapter's concepts by assigning an activity from the *Integrated Software Simulation* CD-ROM.

Evaluation

Assign and review the Fast Review sections.

Fast Review Answers ✓

1. Blue-chip stocks are stocks in large, well-established companies with a track record of success. Speculative stocks are stocks in smaller, newer companies with little or no track record.
2. Because it's easy to buy too much and go heavily into debt.

Meeting Individual Needs

Students With Oral Expression Difficulties. It is common practice to grade students on their oral participation in class. Students with oral expression difficulties find it hard to participate. They need encouragement and, perhaps, special assistance to contribute to class discussions. It may be helpful to ask factual questions such as "What is the basic category of stocks that is safest?" or "What are speculative stocks?" Allow students time to find the answers in the chapter.

4 CLOSE

Chapter Wrap-Up

Ask students to give ten main points from this chapter.

Using Business Key Words

1. mutual fund
2. speculative stocks
3. capital gain
4. preferred stock
5. stock
6. investing
7. yield
8. blue-chip stocks
9. capital loss
10. broker
11. common stock
12. stock exchange
13. dividends

Review What You Learned

14. Savings is putting money aside for future expenditures. Investing is using money to gain a return.
15. By selling stock.
16. Preferred stockholders have the right to receive their share of whatever assets are left after debts are paid before common stockholders.
17. A stockbroker specializes in stock transactions.
18. They consist of stocks of many companies at the same time.
19. Index and indicator of the health of one section of the stock market.
20. More risk.
21. Buying and selling stock, usually over the Internet.
22. Growth stocks—profits of the firm not be distributed. Income stocks—concentrate on trying to always pay a dividend.
23. Yes.

508

Chapter 31 Review

Summary

1. Stocks are shares in ownership of a business. Only corporations sell stock.

2. Brokers buy and sell stock at stock exchanges. Brokers may research, advise, buy, and sell various stocks for you. When you tell a broker to buy or sell a stock, the broker contacts his or her representative on a stock exchange floor. The process is like an auction. Unlike organized exchanges, over-the-counter stocks are not traded in a specific place. Instead, brokerage firms hold these stocks for investors. The NASDAQ lists these over-the-counter stocks.

3. The DJIA and S&P 500 are two indexes that track stock prices over the long run.

● Using Business Key Words

Investors have the ability to choose among many different options. Understanding the terminology is the first step to successful investing. Rewrite the sentences by filling in the blank with the term that best completes the sentence.

- investing
- preferred stock
- stock
- yield
- broker
- stock exchange
- mutual fund
- dividends
- blue-chip stocks
- capital gain
- speculative stocks
- capital loss
- common stock

1. A(n) _____ is created by an investment company, which purchases the securities of many corporations by selling shares in the fund.

2. _____ are generally stocks in relatively new firms, and which don't have a track record for success.

3. A positive return on stock when you sell stock for more than the purchase price is called a(n) _____.

4. Stock that gives its holders certain privileges is called _____.

5. A(n) _____ is a share of ownership in a business.

6. _____ is using money to gain a return.

7. The rate of return on an investment or amount of money an investment earns is the _____.

8. IBM and General Motors are examples of _____.

9. A negative return on stock when you sell the stock for less than the purchase price is called a(n) _____.

10. A dealer who specializes in buying and selling stock is called a(n) _____.

11. _____ is the stock that all corporations must issue.

12. A market where stocks are bought and sold is the _____.

13. A share of the profits of a corporation paid to stockholders is called _____.

Quick Quiz

1. How are saving and investment alike? How are they different? (Each is setting aside money for future use. Money is invested to earn income, saved money does not generally earn income.)

2. How can you become an owner of General Motors? (Purchase stock.)

3. A mutual fund made up of a(n) _____. (Variety of stocks.)

Review What You Learned

14. What is the difference between saving and investing?
15. What is one way that a corporation raises money to start or grow its business?
16. What privileges do preferred stockholders have?
17. What is the function of a stockbroker?
18. Why is the investment risk generally lower for mutual funds?
19. What is the Dow Jones Industrial Average?
20. Do you have more or less risk of losing your investment when you put your money into stocks rather than a savings account? Explain.
21. Describe day trading.
22. What are the differences between growth stocks and income stocks?
23. Are stocks considered liquid investments? Explain.

Understanding Business Concepts

24. How do stockholders earn income?
25. Is it possible for a company to issue only preferred stock?
26. Is it possible to buy stock without going through a stock exchange? If so, give an example.
27. What is the difference between the DJIA and the S&P 500?
28. Do you believe the following general principle? The higher the risk, the higher the possibility of a greater return. Explain your answer.
29. If you had $1,000 to invest, how much investment risk would you feel comfortable with?

Critical Thinking

30. Imagine you own 100 shares of a particular stock. What do you think will happen to your investment if the company goes out of business?
31. If you have only a small amount of money, would you invest it in a high-risk stock or a low-risk stock? Explain why.
32. Given the current business climate, would you invest $5,000 in tech-sector stocks? Explain why or why not.
33. Investing is a very personal decision. Do you agree or disagree with her? Explain your answer.

Viewing and Representing

Examining the Image. Focus on the background of this photograph and list details you see. Pair up with a classmate and discuss the following question: Before investing in stock, what resources would you use to make informed decisions?

Critical Thinking

30. Answers will vary. Accept those answers that show a student understands that they could lose all their money.
31. Answers will vary. Students should provide a reasonable explanation for their answers.
32. Answers will vary.
33. Answers will vary. Some students might agree with Nokomis and include savings goals that depend on the values and lifestyle of the person.

Viewing and Representing

This activity helps students recognize that the background is important in a picture. Your mind picks up background information even though you may feel you're focused on the main subject of the photograph. Ask students: Do you feel that when you're looking at media, it's important to take into account the effect of the background images? Why or why not? **LS**

Understanding Business Concepts

24. Through the payment of dividends and by selling stock for more than you paid for it.
25. No. All corporations must issue common stock.
26. Yes. You can buy stocks that are not available on an exchange. For example, the stock for a small community bank may only be available at the bank itself.
27. The DJIA is an index of an average of 30 well-established, stable companies traded on the New York Stock Exchange. The S&P 500 is based on a broader array of stocks—500 popular stocks listed on the New York Stock Exchange.
28. Answers will vary.
29. Answers will vary.

4 CLOSE (Cont.)

Building Academic Skills

MATH. Answers will vary. Allow the students to choose the way they share their information. Rubrics: Essay, oral presentation, note taking, poster, chart.

HISTORY. Make sure all the students participate in the project. Allow the students to choose the way they share their information. Rubrics: Essay, oral presentation, poster, chart.

COMPUTER/TECHNOLOGY. Answers will vary. Allow the students to choose the way they share their information. Rubrics: Essay, oral presentations, note taking, poster, chart.

LANGUAGE ARTS. Students can use the library or Internet to locate information about the stock exchanges. Rubric: Essay.

Linking School to Home

Answers will vary. Allow the students to choose the way they share their information. Rubrics: Note taking, oral presentation, essay, poster, chart.

Linking School to Work

Answers will vary depending on the brokerage firm researched. Allow the students to choose the way they share their information. Rubrics: Note taking, oral presentation, essay, poster, chart.

Building Academic Skills

 Reading the Financial Section

Locate the financial section of the newspaper. Choose three different stocks and study the stock listings for the following information:
- Which stock traded the most shares on this day? How many shares were traded?
- Which stock lost the most from the day before? How much did it lose?
- If you buy $100 shares of each stock you selected, how much would it cost you?

 Industry's Stock Research

In a group, select an industry in the business world. Each member of the group should collect current information on the stock prices for one company in that industry. Then, use the Internet to check on the stock information from six months ago and one year ago. Use the information to answer the following questions:
- What was the selling price of the stock six months ago? One year ago?
- What rate of return or yield does the company report?
- What was the amount of the most recent dividend the company distributed?

- What were the high and low prices during the year?
- Compare the performance of the companies your group researched. Was one much better than another? Much worse?

Use the information you collect about the companies to make an industry profile. Explain whether you think companies in this industry might be a good investment and why.

 Online Trading

Research e-trading or online trading. Use the Internet to gather information about at least two different companies that offer trading online. Find out what services are offered online and how much it costs per transaction.

 Writing About Stock Exchanges

Research one of the leading stock exchanges in the world. (Examples include the NYSE, the London Stock Exchange, or the Nikkei Exchange in Tokyo.) Write a two-page paper with your findings. Be sure to include how the exchange began, the average amount of trading that occurs each day, and the process used to buy and sell stocks.

Linking School to Home

Financial News. With family members and friends, listen to or watch a radio or television broadcast that focuses on the stock market. (Examples include *MG and the Stock Doctor*, CNBC's *Bloomberg's Market Watch*, and CNN's *Moneyline News Hour*.) Evaluate the experts and the stock advice they offer. Ask your family members and friends for their opinions as well.

Linking School to Work

Local Brokerage Firm. Investigate one of the brokerage firms in your community. Ask about the services they provide, the educational outreach they offer, and the fees they charge. If possible, invite a stockbroker to your classroom to discuss his or her job.

E-Homework

Applying Technology

E-Trading Behavior. The values of stocks or mutual funds go up and down in value over time. There are many Internet sites that provide information about prices and sales as they occur. Many magazines and publications are devoted to studying stocks and mutual funds and are another source of information about investments. Use the Internet to research how the Internet has changed our investment behavior. What resources are available online? How have chat rooms and discussion groups impacted investment decisions?

NASDAQ Research. Stocks represent ownership in a business. There's no promise that the business will succeed. It could fail and you could lose all of your investment. There is no federal agency insuring your investment in stocks as there is with banks, so you won't get your money back if the company goes out of business. Therefore, it's important to make tactical, wise decisions despite all the hype you hear in the media. Most of the technology stocks are traded on the NASDAQ. Find out what the NASDAQ stands for, where it's located, its history, and how many different stocks are traded there.

Connecting Academics

Math. Sarah buys 500 shares of stock at $18 and sells the holding for a capital gain of $3,000. What was the share price at the time of sale?

Language Arts. When faced with making hard decisions, your integrity or honesty might be tested. A debate sharpens your skills of discernment and decision making. As a class, debate the following: Buying stock is a good way to invest money and to promote the entrepreneurial spirit.

BusinessWeek — Analyzing the Feature Story

You read the first part of "Where Kids Can Log On to Learn Their Investing ABC's" at the beginning of this chapter. Below are a few questions for you to answer about managing finances. You'll find the answers to these questions when you're reading the entire article. First, here are the questions:

34. Why is it important for kids to learn how to manage finances?

35. What are some of the strong points of Younginvestor.com?

CREATIVE JOURNAL ACTIVITY

Visit Kiplinger.com's Kids & Money page, **www.kiplinger.com/managing/kids**, Kids-Bank.org, **www.kidsbank.org**, or another financial educational Web site for kids. Surf the site. What do you like about it? What would make it more useful? Write a one-page review of the site.

BUSINESS Online
The Full Story

To learn more about investing, visit the *Introduction to Business* Web site at **www.introbus.glencoe.com**, and click on *BusinessWeek* Feature Story, Chapter 31.

SCANS Correlation Chart*

Foundation Skills

Basic Skills	Reading	Writing	Math	Listening	Speaking	
Thinking Skills	Creative Thinking	Decision Making	Problem Solving	Seeing Things in the Mind's Eye	Knowing How to Learn	Reasoning
Personal Qualities	Responsibility	Self-Esteem	Sociability	Self-Management	Integrity/ Honesty	

Workplace Competencies

Resources	Allocating Time	Allocating Money	Allocating Material and Facility Resources	Allocating Human Resources		
Information	Acquiring and Evaluating Information	Organizing and Maintaining Information	Interpreting and Communicating Information	Using Computers to Process Information		
Interpersonal Skills	Participating as a Member of a Team	Teaching Others	Serving Clients/ Customers	Exercising Leadership	Negotiating to Arrive at a Decision	Working With Cultural Diversity
Systems	Understanding Systems	Monitoring and Correcting Performance	Improving and Designing Systems			
Technology	Selecting Technology	Applying Technology to Task	Maintaining and Troubleshooting Technology			

*This chart's highlighted blocks indicate the chapter's content coverage in the Student Edition and the Teacher Wraparound Edition.

Resource Manager

Teaching Transparencies

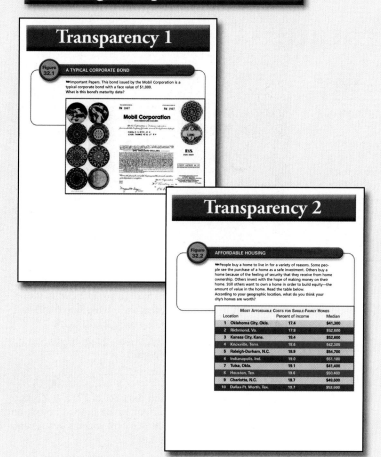

Transparency 1

A TYPICAL CORPORATE BOND

Important Papers. This bond issued by the Mobil Corporation is a typical corporate bond with a face value of $1,000. What is this bond's maturity date?

Transparency 2

AFFORDABLE HOUSING

People buy a home to live in for a variety of reasons. Some people see the purchase of a home as a safe investment. Others buy a home because of the feeling of security that they receive from home ownership. Others invest with the hope of making money on their home. Still others want to own a home in order to build equity—the amount of value in the home. Read the table below. According to your geographic location, what do you think your city's homes are worth?

MOST AFFORDABLE COSTS FOR SINGLE-FAMILY HOMES

	Location	Percent of income	Median
1	Oklahoma City, Okla.	17.4	$41,300
2	Richmond, Va.	17.8	$52,600
3	Kansas City, Kans.	18.4	$52,600
4	Knoxville, Tenn.	18.6	$42,300
5	Raleigh-Durham, N.C.	18.9	$54,700
6	Indianapolis, Ind.	19.0	$51,100
7	Tulsa, Okla.	19.1	$41,400
8	Houston, Tex.	19.6	$50,400
9	Charlotte, N.C.	19.7	$49,600
10	Dallas-Ft. Worth, Tex.	19.7	$53,690

Application and Enrichment

- Lesson Plans
- *BusinessWeek* Poster Package
- Teaching Transparencies
- Integrated Software Simulation
- Glencoe Business Video Package

Review and Reinforcement

- *PuzzleMaker*
- Internet Resources
- Student Activity Workbook
- Strat. and Work. for Teaching Transparencies

Assessment and Evaluation

- Reproducible Tests
- Alternative Assessment Strategies
- ExamView® Pro Test Generator

Technology

- *PuzzleMaker*
- ExamView® Pro Test Generator
- Glencoe Business Video Package
- PowerPoint® Presentation
- Integrated Software Simulation
- Interactive Lesson Planner
- *Virtual Business*®

KEY

Printed	Software	Videocassette	Poster	
Transparency	CD-ROM	Internet		

Visit **www.introbus.glencoe.com**, the Web site companion to *Introduction to Business*. The student's page includes:

- interactive tutor
- additional *BusinessWeek* articles and activities
- business Web links
- homework hints
- real-world application activities
- additional career path activities

Information on how to prepare your students for the high school exit exam and special projects are also included.

Use the Glencoe Web site for additional resources. All essential content is covered in the Student Edition.

Introducing the Chapter

This chapter examines two common investment choices, bonds and real estate. A photo essay, "Hunting for a Home," enhances the concepts.

Connecting the Objectives

What kinds of investments have you heard about in the news? What ways do people invest in real estate?

Feature Story

Story's Summary

Homeowners, like Anton and Audrey Scholl, might choose to refinance their mortgages because they can save hundreds of dollars on their monthly mortgage payments. Other homeowners might choose to cash-out the equity in their homes and take on bigger mortgages.

Find the entire article at www.introbus.glencoe.com, or in the Teacher Resource Binder.

Chapter 32

Bonds and Real Estate

Learning Objectives

After completing this chapter, you'll be able to:
1. **Describe** the characteristics of bonds.
2. **Identify** the different types of bonds.
3. **Name** the main reasons for buying real estate.

Why It's Important

Bonds and real estate are two of the safest financial investments you can make.

Key Words

bonds
coupon rate
bond discount
savings bonds
municipal bonds
corporate bonds
junk bonds
real estate
real estate agent
income property
undeveloped property

Feature Story

Will Refis Help Refloat the Economy?

Equity Into Cash: So Far, Owners Are Spending, Not Paying Down Debt. When Anton and Audrey Scholl bought their $249,000 townhouse in Itasca, Ill., a year ago, they had no idea they'd refinance their mortgage within a year. But when their broker called in January advising they convert their 30-year adjustable rate mortgage to a 30-year fixed mortgage with a lower interest rate and no closing costs, the Scholls bit. The new 7.25 percent rate, a reduction of 1.25 percentage points, cuts their monthly payments by $225.

Source: Excerpted with permission from "Will Refis Help Refloat the Economy?" *BusinessWeek Online*, April 2, 2001.

An Extension Activity

Imagine you receive a cash payment of $20,000 or more. Would you seek professional advice on how to invest your newfound wealth? Explain the details of your decision-making process.

BUSINESS
Online
The Full Story

To learn more about mortgage rates, visit the *Introduction to Business* Web site at www.introbus.glencoe.com, and click on *BusinessWeek* Feature Story, Chapter 32.

512

Classroom Resources

For the Teacher
📁 Student Activity Work. TAE
📓 ⊙ Assessment Binder
⊙ PowerPoint® Presentation
⊙ Interactive Lesson Planner
📁 Lesson Plans
📓 💻 Internet Resources
🖨 Teaching Transparencies
💻 *Introduction to Business* Web Site

⊙ Integrated Soft. Sim. TM
📘 *BusinessWeek* Poster Package
For the Student
📓 Student Activity Workbook
⊙ *Virtual Business*®
💻 *Introduction to Business* Web Site
⊙ Integrated Soft. Sim.
⊙ *PuzzleMaker*
📓 Strategies and Worksheets for Teaching Transparencies

MONITORING AND CORRECT-ING PERFORMANCE. Identifying trends and predicting changes are highly prized skills on the job. List any news or trends you've heard about in bonds and in real estate—including home owner-ship, income property, or undevel-oped property.

Preteaching Business Key Words

UNDERSTANDING SYSTEMS. Which of this chapter's key words is familiar to you? Give an example of the contexts in which they were used—any phrase or words used in connection with the key word. For the terms you're not familiar with, note the definitions from the glossary. **LS**

An Extension Activity

DISCUSS. After students have decided what they will do with their $20,000, have volunteers tell their decision. Encourage discussion related to investments in bonds or real estate. **CL**

Making Connections

Everyday Living. People today have the opportunity to live longer, healthier lives than past generations. Have students research the current life span for males and females in the United States. What has been the trend over the past several decades? Ask students: What factors can you include in your lifestyle to increase your expected life span? You'll expect to enjoy many years of retirement. What advice do financial planners give about starting retire-ment savings?

Common Investment Choices

There are many ways you can invest your money. The type of investment you choose depends on your goals. Do you want a return in the quickest time possible? Or do you want a steady, reasonable, and predictable flow of cash? Selecting a bond or purchasing real estate is an investment option. You can tailor an investment program to meet your individual needs. Choosing an investment program means making and completing your financial plan to make your money grow.

Bonds

Corporations can raise money by selling stock, but they can also raise money by borrowing. When a corporation or the government needs to borrow a large amount of money for a long time, they often issue bonds. **Bonds** are written promises to repay a loan with interest on a specific date (the *maturity date*). (See Figure 32.1 to examine a bond.) The buyer

Figure 32.1

A TYPICAL CORPORATE BOND

➥ Important Papers. This bond issued by the Mobil Corporation is a typical corporate bond with a face value of $1,000.
What is this bond's maturity date?

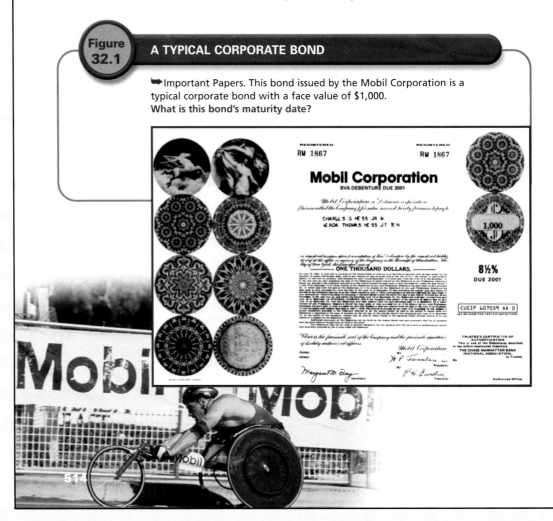

of a bond becomes a creditor (or lender) to the corporation or government that issued the bond.

Characteristics of Bonds

Like savings accounts and other types of investments, bonds earn interest. The rate of interest on a bond is referred to as the **coupon rate**. Interest is usually paid once or twice a year. For example, a $1,000 bond with a 6 percent coupon rate will pay $60 once a year or $30 twice a year. Many bonds are sold at a discount, or below their face value, and gather interest until they reach their full value. The difference between the amount you pay for the bond and its face value is the **bond discount**.

The prices of bonds are listed in the financial section of newspapers and are also found on the Internet. Bonds are rated according to their risks by several agencies, such as Standard & Poor's and Moody's. Bonds are usually rated from *secure* (the highest rating) to *speculative* (the lowest rating). Bonds with more risk carry a higher interest rate than those that are more secure.

Bonds are generally considered a safe place to invest your money. If the corporation or government doesn't pay back the loan or the interest, you can take legal action to collect the amount owed. Even if the corporation that issued you a bond goes bankrupt, you would be repaid before the stockholders. Although the prices of bonds don't go up and down as much as stocks, they do fluctuate. There are three types of bonds you can buy: federal, municipal, and corporate.

Federal Bonds

Bonds that are sold by the federal government are called **savings bonds**. U.S. savings bonds are considered one of the safest kinds of investments and are bought through a bank or a payroll plan at work. There are several types of government-issued bonds.

EE Bonds. A series EE savings bond costs half the amount of its face value to buy. For example, a $100 bond costs $50 and a $1,000 bond costs $500. After a certain number of years the bond becomes worth its full face value. The time it takes to reach its maturity rate depends on the rate of interest. If you cash in an EE bond before its maturity date, you have to pay a penalty. On the other hand, if you keep an EE bond past its maturity, it continues to earn interest for up to 30 years and can become worth more than its face value.

Real-World Application

part 1 of 4

HUNTING FOR A HOME

Just look in the real estate section of a newspaper and the options might make you dizzy. House. Townhouse. Cooperative. Mobile home. Let's break down the differences. For a homeowner, he or she takes on all aspects of ownership. That means the owner is responsible for maintaining the lawn, painting, repairs, and taxes.
What are some other costs that come along with owning a home?

continued on p. 517

Real-World Application
Caption Answer

HUNTING FOR A HOME: PART 1 OF 4

Possible homeowner's association fees, home maintenance, property taxes, driveway maintenance, fencing, and insurance.

Technology Resource

 POWERPOINT. The *Introduction to Business* PowerPoint® CD-ROM provides visual lecture aids for this chapter.

Independent Practice

SUMMARIZE AND REPORT.
Find one or two articles on bonds or mutual funds. Summarize the information in the articles. Who's the intended audience of the article? What's the main point? Give a short oral report. Use a number of this chapter's key words about bonds in your report. (Words to use might also include secure, speculative, or Treasury notes.) **LS**

Meeting Individual Needs

Students With Attention Difficulties. Imposing a time limit for a task for students who have difficulty paying attention can help them stay on task. Ask students to read the section "Federal Bonds" (approximately 380 words). Give students five and a half minutes to read the section—that's enough time for average readers. Ask students if they think they might use this time-limit method themselves to help them learn other parts of this chapter, or even parts of this course. **LS**

2 TEACH (Cont.)

Thinking Critically

SERVICE CLUB. You're a member of your school's service club. At the end of the month, a small service team is going to give a presentation on investments to a group of local retirees. The team's asked you to give a one- to two-minute presentation about junk bonds. They want you to include a caution about buying junk bonds. Write your outline for your presentation. (Answers will vary and should include that junk bonds are very risky, that you can lose everything you've invested, and a caution not to buy.) **CL**, **LS**, **P**

Consider This...

Caption Answer

Students' attitudes will vary. Ask students what their attitude might be in five year's time, and if they have a family of their own to support. Financial advisers suggest if you're newly rich and want to get that shopping spree out of your system, to use no more than 5 percent of the windfall.

Consider This...

Spending Your Windfall Wisely

Smart people who inherit large sums of money don't spend their windfall quickly. Instead, more than half seek financial advice and invest it. If you're newly rich, you might need to pay off high-interest credit cards or other debts. Windfalls starting at $50,000 require a financial plan. This would include your home and retirement account, mutual funds, tax-free bonds, and real estate.

ANALYZE

What is your monetary attitude toward investing versus spending?

I Bonds. Another type of U. S. savings bond is the I bond. This is a bond for which you pay the face value. If you buy a $500 I bond, you would pay $500. The interest rate on this bond fluctuates over time with the rate of inflation. The higher the rate of inflation, the higher the interest rate on the bond. The interest doesn't fall if there is deflation during a period of time. You can lose interest if you cash it in early (much like the EE bond). Like the EE bond, there are certain restrictions on how much you'll receive if you cash it in before its maturity date. For example, if you earn an I bond during the first five years of your investment, you'll forfeit, or lose, three months of interest.

EE bonds and I bonds are attractive to people who want safe, guaranteed long-term investments. There are also tax advantages for the income earned on these bonds. Interest from savings bonds isn't subject to state and local income taxes. You pay reduced taxes or no taxes at all if you're paying for college and your household income is below a certain level.

Other Federal Bonds. The U.S. Treasury issues three kinds of bonds. The main difference between them is the length of time it takes to mature. *Treasury bills* (or *T-bills*) are issued for three months to one year, *Treasury notes* are issued for two to ten years, and *Treasury bonds* are issued for ten or more years. The longer the maturity, the higher the interest rate. The smallest amount of any of these bonds is $1,000 (treasury bonds). T-bills are only available as $10,000 bonds, and T-notes range from $1,000 to $5,000. You can buy (and sell) these bonds through brokerage firms, banks, and other financial institutions, at a Federal Reserve Bank, or over the Internet.

They can be sold just like stocks at any given time before their maturity date. The U. S. government, based on its ability to tax and collect money from its citizens, guarantees treasury bonds. T-bills are sold at a discount like EE bonds.

Municipal Bonds

Local and state governments issue **municipal bonds**. They're sold to finance projects such as schools, highways, and airports. You can buy them from a broker or directly from the government. The main advantage of municipal bonds is that the government doesn't generally tax the interest you earn on them. Like treasury bonds, you don't have to hold on to a municipal bond until it reaches its maturity date. If you sell it before it matures, however, you might receive less than the face value of the bond.

Corporate Bonds

Bonds issued by corporations are called **corporate bonds**. Corporate bonds can be bought and sold through brokerage firms. They're usually used to finance building and equipment. The value of a corporate

LANGUAGE ARTS | Curriculum Connection

Bonds. Unlike stocks, bond prices are generally quoted as a percent of face value. A bond quote of 98 indicates that a bond with a value of $1,000 is being sold for $980. Suggest that students work in pairs to research some of the terms associated with bonds. Have pairs find out the definitions of the terms coupon, maturity, and par value. (Coupon: stated interest on the debt. Maturity: length of time until the debt is repaid. Par value: the amount that will be repaid to the lender at maturity, often called face value.)

bond fluctuates according to the overall interest rates in the economy. If you buy a corporate bond with a high interest rate and interest rates fall, the corporation may be able to *call* your bond, or buy it back before the maturity date. This way the corporation doesn't have to pay off the bonds at the higher interest rate. It then issues new bonds at lower rates.

Junk Bonds. Junk bonds belong to a special category of corporate bonds. **Junk bonds** are bonds that have a low or speculative rating and are issued by companies that don't have successful track records. They offer a high rate of interest and a high rate of risk. Remember risk and return trade off. They are not considered a very safe investment. If a company defaults on its junk bonds, there's little chance you'll be able to get any of your money back. In fact, many junk-bond holders lose their entire investment.

 Fast Review _____

1. How much does an EE bond cost to buy?
2. What is the main difference between a Treasury bill, a Treasury note, and a Treasury bond?
3. What is the main advantage of municipal bonds?

Real Estate

You would think that there couldn't be a safer, surer investment than real estate. **Real estate** is land and anything attached to it, such as buildings or natural resources. Real estate is considered the safest form of investment for one simple reason: As the population continues to increase and the demand for land increases, the supply of desirable land remains the same. According to the law of supply and demand, the more demand exceeds supply, the more the item in demand increases in value. In fact, the value of real estate only seems to increase over time.

People buy real estate for a number of reasons. Most people buy property for the safety and security of owning their own home. Some people buy property to make an income from it, like raising crops or renting office space. Others buy unused property hoping its value will increase. Buying real estate is a major investment.

How then can anyone make a poor real estate investment? There are a number of mistakes that people can make. When demand decreases, the value of real estate goes down. For instance, people can buy in the wrong location—one that is or becomes unpopular or unattractive to others. When the owner wants to sell such property, its value may be less

Chapter 32 Bonds and Real Estate **517**

HUNTING FOR A HOME
From San Francisco to Brooklyn, people also invest in townhouses. The owner owns both the structure and the land, except it isn't free standing. There may be a front yard or back yard, but each townhouse connects to the next. **How does a townhouse differ from a house?**

continued on p. 519

HUNTING FOR A HOME: PART 2 OF 4
Not responsible for maintenance, connected to another townhouse, doesn't own entire plot of land, usually two to three stories tall, and so on.

Fast Review Answers ✓

1. One half of its face value.
2. The length of time it takes them to mature.
3. The interest earned on them is generally not taxed by the government.

Business Connection
One Florida couple, with children ages seven, five, and four, are concerned about whether their financial plan will give them a secure future. Sue Stevens, director of financial planning at Morningstar, did an analysis and found that the couple is in a strong financial position. They have a mortgage on their own home and investments in mutual funds and stock. Their annual income after taxes is $70,000. As extra income they have an investment property that brings in $600 per month, after paying the mortgage, taxes, and insurance.

Great Ideas From the Classroom of...

Jennifer Harrison, Teacher
Cleveland High School
Reseda, Calif.

Connect With a Quote.   Famous quotes spark students' interest. The quote opens the class discussion on many levels. I like the

book, *African American Quotations,* compiled by Richard Newman. It's broken down by topic. For example, I'll choose a quote from an executive I admire. If we have a serious topic, I like to break up the seriousness by adding humor—it wakes everybody up. Humor and quotations help the students open up to hearing and learning more.

2 TEACH (Cont.)

Develop Concepts

HOME OWNERSHIP Do you want to own your own home? Why or why not? Gather a list on the board of advantages and disadvantages of home ownership.

Discussion Starter

UNDEVELOPED LAND. How can undeveloped property be used as an investment?

Figure 32.2 Caption Answer

Answers will vary. Discuss how students might find the information needed to answer this question. Have students compare the median cost of single-family homes in their city with the ten cities in the chart in Figure 32.2.

---

than what the owner has invested in it. People can choose (or need to buy or sell) at a poor time. They can pay too much—either initially or through unexpected hidden costs. Perhaps they might make a poor choice regarding the type of real estate in which they invest.

Home Ownership

Buying a home is the most expensive purchase most people make in their lives. Before buying a home, there are a number of factors to consider.

Types of Homes. There are different types of homes you can buy depending on your income and needs. The most popular is the single-family house. It usually sits on its own lot, with its own yard. It's separate from other buildings and provides privacy. Single-family houses range from modest two-bedroom homes to huge mansions.

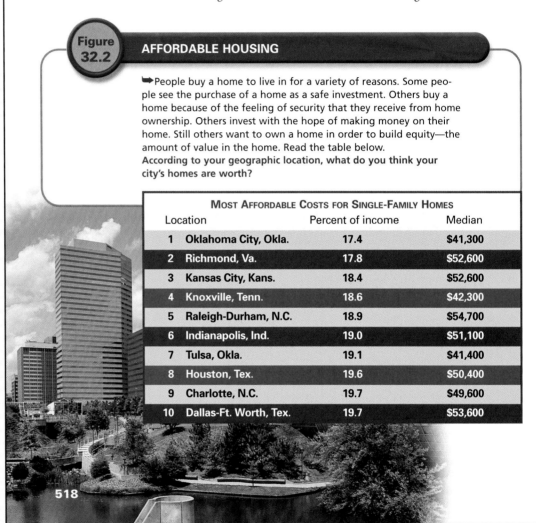

Figure 32.2

AFFORDABLE HOUSING

➡ People buy a home to live in for a variety of reasons. Some people see the purchase of a home as a safe investment. Others buy a home because of the feeling of security that they receive from home ownership. Others invest with the hope of making money on their home. Still others want to own a home in order to build equity—the amount of value in the home. Read the table below.
According to your geographic location, what do you think your city's homes are worth?

MOST AFFORDABLE COSTS FOR SINGLE-FAMILY HOMES		
Location	Percent of income	Median
1 Oklahoma City, Okla.	17.4	$41,300
2 Richmond, Va.	17.8	$52,600
3 Kansas City, Kans.	18.4	$52,600
4 Knoxville, Tenn.	18.6	$42,300
5 Raleigh-Durham, N.C.	18.9	$54,700
6 Indianapolis, Ind.	19.0	$51,100
7 Tulsa, Okla.	19.1	$41,400
8 Houston, Tex.	19.6	$50,400
9 Charlotte, N.C.	19.7	$49,600
10 Dallas-Ft. Worth, Tex.	19.7	$53,600

518

Global Perspective

Land Ownership. Not all cultures of the world have the same concepts about owning land as the concept generally held in the western world. In Australia, groups of indigenous people believe in owning land in common rather than as individuals. Each group of Aborigines lives within a particular geographic area. The group owns the land in common and cannot sell the land to anyone else. Aborigines believe they hold the land in trust and are responsible for taking care of it.

Multi-unit housing includes duplexes, townhouses, and condominiums. Multi-unit houses are usually single buildings divided into various units, with a separate person or family living in each unit. They are like apartment buildings only the people who live in them own rather than rent the space.

Mobile homes are usually produced in parts by a factory and assembled on a building site. They're sometimes referred to as prefabricated houses. The owner often doesn't own any land but rents space for the house in a mobile-home park. Because the parts of these homes can be mass-produced cheaply, they usually cost much less than other types of houses.

Buying a Home. Few people have enough money to pay for a house in full and have to finance it with a *home mortgage loan*, or a long-term property loan. To buy a house also requires a down payment, usually about 20 percent. The down payment is money you have to come up with yourself. That means if you want to buy a house for $100,000, you need $20,000 for the down payment.

Homebuyers often use the services of a real estate agent to help them find a home. A **real estate agent** is a person licensed to arrange the buying and selling of homes as well as other types of real estate. Real estate agents charge a fee for their services, but it is usually charged to the seller and not the buyer.

Once you find a house you're interested in buying, it's a good idea to hire a qualified building inspector. A house that looks good on the surface might have serious plumbing or electrical problems. The cost of a building inspection can be high, but it can save a lot of money in repairs.

Home Values. There are a number of factors that affect the value of a house, such as the size, condition, and location. Location is especially important. A house that seems like a bargain might turn out to be in a bad neighborhood or in the path of a noisy airport. If you buy a house in an area where many businesses are closing, the value of your house will go down as more people move out to find other jobs and the demand for housing decreases.

Home Equity. The amount of equity you have in a home is very important. Your home equity is the amount on the house you actually own as opposed to how much you owe. As you pay off the mortgage on the house, your equity increases. For example, if you make a $20,000 down payment on a $100,000 house and pay off $3,000 over four years, your equity increases from $20,000 to $23,000. Your equity also increases as the value of your home increases. Suppose over those four years, the value of your house increased by $20,000. Your equity would then be $43,000 instead of $23,000.

Chapter 32 Bonds and Real Estate **519**

Real-World Application
part 3 of 4

HUNTING FOR A HOME

Depending on the context, cooperative means either helpful or a company. In the context of real estate, a cooperative (or co-op) is just that—you share ownership in a cooperative corporation. You can live in the co-op, but you don't get complete ownership. As a co-op member you help pay for building maintenance, shared spaces, and management issues.

Do you foresee any problems with being part owner of a co-op?

continued on p. 521

Real-World Application
Caption Answer

HUNTING FOR A HOME: PART 3 OF 4

More difficult to finance than other real estate because only certain banks deal with cooperatives.

Individualized Practice

Arrange to interview a panel of several homeowners to find out how they feel about owning their own home. Prepare questions ahead of time, such as: Knowing what you know now, would you buy a home again? What advice would you give to someone thinking about buying a home? Do you think owning your own home is a good investment?

L1 Have students work in pairs to discuss the answers the panelists gave.

L2 Ask students to write a one-page report summarizing the panelists' answers.

L3 Ask students to work in groups to summarize the panelists' answers and prepare a series of skits to demonstrate the summary points to the class.

LANGUAGE ARTS | *Curriculum Connection*

Communication. Have students find an article on personal investment options such as bonds or real estate. Have them make note of at least three savings suggestions offered in the article and share their findings in class.

Reteaching

UNDEVELOPED PROPERTY.
To reteach the concept of undeveloped property, ask students to scan newspapers and other sources for articles describing land speculation—the purchase of undeveloped property on the hope of development. Discuss students' findings.

Enrichment Strategy

INVESTMENT "BIOGRAPHY."
Write a "biography" of an investment such as bonds or real estate. Include in your biography information such as the investment's history, its major characteristics, and the investment's risks and benefits. **LS**

Evaluation

Assign and review the Fast Review sections.

You Make the Call

Caption Answer

1. The question to ask yourself is, "What would a second-hand shop owner with high ethical standards do in this situation?" The answer would be to contact the individual who brought in the box and give a fair amount in reimbursement.
2. The answer is the same.
3. The answer is the same.

Advantages of Home Ownership. Some of the advantages of owning a home have already been stated. First of all, the value of a home usually increases over time, so it's a good investment. Owning your own home rather than renting provides a sense of security and stability. Homeowners also get tax breaks. You can deduct the interest you pay on your mortgage loans and the taxes you pay on your property from your federal income taxes.

As a homeowner, you will also reap financial benefits. You can deduct the interest charges on your loan payments from your federal income taxes each year. Your property taxes are also deductible. Moreover, the value of many homes rises steadily, so homeowners often can sell their homes for a profit depending on their *equity*—the value of the home less the amount still owed on the money borrowed to purchase it. Finally, once the money they borrowed is paid off, homeowners have no further financial obligation other than property taxes, homeowner's insurance, and maintenance costs.

Disadvantages of Home Ownership. Of course, buying a house doesn't guarantee happiness. Home ownership involves financial risk. Saving money for a down payment is very difficult for many people. Property value doesn't always go up, either; in some cases, they may even decline.

As with any investment, owning a home also has some disadvantages. While owning a home gives you more stability, it also gives you less mobility. If you want to move, you have to sell your house first. Because it can take a long time to sell a house and turn it into cash, it's the least liquid of all investments. In both cases, the process can be slow and may result in a financial loss.

There are also several costs to owning a house besides mortgage payments. You have to buy homeowner's insurance and pay property taxes. You also

You Make the Call

One Person's Junk Is Another Person's...

The second-hand shop you own is a popular spot for antique shoppers in search of reasonably priced furniture and collectibles. You build your inventory from attending auctions and buying objects brought in by individuals. One day, a man brings a box full of odds and ends from his great aunt's attic. He says it's all just junk and asks for $10. You glance through it and agree. After he leaves, you notice a pocket watch that is lodged in the corner. As you lift it out and look at it, you realize it is worth hundreds of dollars.

Making an Ethical Decision

1. What should you do?
2. What if the watch was worth thousands of dollars? Would that change your answer?
3. Let's say you're a pocket-watch collector? Would that change your view of what is ethical behavior?

How to Use a Portfolio Activity

The portfolio projects are designed to lead students to develop a collection of their best work to submit to you for assessment. You and each of your students should decide which projects to include in their business portfolio. Refer students to the specific rubric(s) from the *Alternative Assessment Strategies*. These rubrics will alert students to the criteria you'll use to assess their projects. **P**

need to pay for repairs and maintenance, such as fixing the plumbing, putting on a new roof, or repainting the house. Repairs can be very costly, and if neglected, lower the value of your home. The cost of taking care of a home can be quite high, even if the homeowners do most of the work themselves.

Income Property

Another reason for buying real estate is to obtain **income property**, or property used to generate an income. A common type of income property is farmland for producing and selling crops. Land can also be used for raising sheep or cattle. Natural resources found on land, such as oil, timber, or gas, can be produced and sold.

Stores, factories, and office buildings are other kinds of income property. You could buy an apartment building and rent out the units to earn an income. Some people buy a multi-unit home, move into one unit, and rent out the others. The rental income can then be used to pay the mortgage and taxes on the property. With income property, the owner can produce income in two ways. First, the owner can make money from the rent, crops, or natural resources on the property. Second, the owner can make investment income by selling the property for a profit after its value increases.

Undeveloped Property

Undeveloped property is unused land intended only for investment purposes. Usually the land isn't cleared and has no utility services such as drinking water, sewage, or electricity. Within large tracts of undeveloped land there are usually no public roads. This type of land is often inexpensive to buy.

Investors in undeveloped property hope that its value will increase sharply over the years. The land might be chosen as the site of a shopping center, housing development, or industrial park. In other cases, however, the land's value might stay the same or even decrease. For example, a planned highway might never be built, leaving the land along its proposed route undeveloped. With undeveloped land, there is no return, like rent or the sale of crops. The income earned on undeveloped property comes through the sale of the property after it has gone up in value.

 Fast Review _____

1. Why does the value of real estate generally increase over time?
2. What are the two ways the equity in your home can increase?
3. What are the two ways an owner can produce income with income property?

Real-World Application
part 4 of 4

HUNTING FOR A HOME
A mobile home is also one of the most common types of real estate investments. When you buy this home you're the owner, but its value depreciates unlike other real estate investments. Depending if you hit the open road with your mobile home or decide to settle in a mobile home park, each situation has different taxes and fees involved.
Why isn't buying a mobile home considered a safe investment?

Real-World Application
Caption Answer

HUNTING FOR A HOME: PART 4 OF 4
It depreciates.

Technology Resource

GO TO **PUZZLEMAKER CD-ROM.** Check your students' understanding of the chapter's key terms by using the *Puzzlemaker* CD-ROM.

Fast Review Answers ✔

1. As the demand for land increases, the supply of desirable land remains the same.
2. You pay off more of the mortgage and the value of the home increases.
3. By making money off rent, crops, or natural resources and by selling the property for a profit when its value increases.

Meeting Individual Needs

Second Language Learners. Students whose native language is other than English often have difficulty formulating questions about material they don't understand. Split the class into groups. Have groups write question starters such as, what, where, when, how, why, and who, at the top of separate pieces of paper. Have groups generate as many questions as they can about the information in the section on "Real Estate." Lead a class discussion to answer a sample of the questions. **CL**, LS

4 CLOSE

Chapter Wrap-Up

Ask students to chart main points on home ownership from this chapter.

Using Business Key Words

1. corporate bonds
2. bonds
3. real estate agent
4. coupon rate
5. undeveloped property
6. bond discount
7. savings bonds
8. junk bond
9. municipal bonds
10. real estate
11. income property

Review What You Learned

12. On a certain date it will repay the lender in full.
13. Bondholders are repaid before stockholders.
14. Series EE requires the investor to pay half of its face value. "I" bond is a bond for which you pay face value.
15. Not subject to state and local income taxes.
16. Local or state governments.
17. Bonds are rated by their risks.
18. Wrong location, wrong time, poor investment, etc.
19. Bonds possess less risk than real estate in regard to losing part or all of your investment.
20. Real estate. It generally takes time to find a buyer for real estate.

Summary

1. Bonds are written promises to repay a loan on a specific date. They earn interest like savings accounts and are considered a safe place to invest your money.

2. The federal government sells U.S. savings bonds, state and local governments sell municipal bonds, and corporations sell corporation bonds and junk bonds.

3. The main reasons people buy real estate are to own a home, to generate an income, and to make an investment.

4.

Home Ownership	
Advantages	**Disadvantages**
• A good investment	• Less mobility
• Provides security and stability	• Have to buy insurance and pay property taxes
• Homeowners earn tax breaks	• Have to pay for maintenance and repairs

● Using Business Key Words

Understanding these investment terms will help you when you decide to invest in bonds and real estate. Match each term with its definition.

- **bonds**
- **real estate**
- **coupon rate**
- **bond discount**
- **municipal bonds**
- **savings bonds**
- **corporate bonds**
- **undeveloped property**
- **real estate agent**
- **income property**
- **junk bonds**

1. Bonds that can be bought or sold through brokerage firms.

2. Debt obligations that are written promises to repay not only the loan but also the interest on the loan.

3. A person licensed to arrange the buying and selling of homes.

4. The rate of interest on a bond.

5. Land in its natural state.

6. The difference between the amount paid for a bond and its face value.

7. Bonds sold by the federal government.

8. Bonds that carry a high rate of interest but also carry a high rate of risk.

9. Bonds sold to finance projects by local or state governments and by certain government agencies.

10. Land and anything attached to it, such as buildings or natural resources.

11. Property used to generate an income, such as a farm or apartment building.

Quick Quiz

1. How can you lend money to a city to build a stadium? (Purchase municipal bonds.)

2. What is a bond? (A written promise to repay a loan with interest on a specific date.)

3. What is real estate? (Land and anything attached to it, such as a building or natural resource.)

Review What You Learned

12. The corporation or government issuing the bond makes two promises. What are they?
13. Why are bonds considered a safe place to invest your money?
14. What is the difference between the EE and the I bonds?
15. What is the tax advantage for the income earned on savings bonds?
16. What do municipal bonds finance?
17. How are bonds rated?
18. How are poor real estate investments made?
19. Which possess less risk—bonds or real estate? Explain.
20. Which of the following is the least liquid—CDs, stocks, bonds, or real estate? Explain.

Understanding Business Concepts

21. Why do you think the U.S. government issues bonds?
22. Describe the differences between T-bills, Treasury notes, and Treasury bonds.
23. The costs of home ownership include more than the purchase price, which is most often financed through a long-term mortgage. Property taxes, the cost of utilities, gas, water, and sewage add to the monthly costs. With all these expenses, why do you think people buy a home?
24. Why is the timing of a sale of a home important?
25. How do people earn income by investing in undeveloped property?
26. What criteria should you use to evaluate various types of investments?

Critical Thinking

27. Do you believe bonds are less risky than stocks? Explain your answer.
28. Do you think home ownership is a good investment? Explain why or why not.
29. What proportion of your savings would you consider putting in bonds? In stocks? Explain your answer.
30. What would your advice be to a friend who is considering buying a home?

Viewing and Representing

Examining the Image. Give a written description of this picture. What's the message? To prevent this happening to you, how do you plan to invest in the future? Together with a partner share and discuss your investment plans.

Critical Thinking

27. Most students should say that bonds are less risky than stocks because there is more risk of losing your investment when you own something rather than when you are a creditor.
28. Answers will vary. Students should justify their answers.
29. Answers will vary.
30. Answers will vary and should include a discussion of the advantages and disadvantages of buying a home.

Viewing and Representing

In this activity, the picture is used as a visual cue to stimulate students' critical thinking. The activity also gives students practice in descriptive writing. The message conveyed is that money's going down the drain. Ask students if seeing the picture makes them think more carefully about how to invest their money. Point out the impact of visual media and how it can influence the way you think. Student discussions of their investment plans will vary and might include a balance of risky and more conservative investments. **LS**

Understanding Business Concepts

21. In order to borrow a large amount of money for a long period of time.
22. T-bills are issued for three months to one year. Treasury notes are issued for two to ten years, and treasury bonds are issued for ten or more years. The longer the maturity, the higher the interest rate.
23. Investment, security.
24. Dependent on a loan.
25. When the sale of property is greater than the purchase price.
26. The risk of losing your investment; the risk of losing annual return from investment; the rate of return; the liquidity; and the inflation risk.

4 CLOSE (Cont.)

Building Academic Skills

LANGUAGE ARTS. Allow the students to choose the way they will share their results. Rubrics: Posters, charts/tables, diagrams, oral presentations.

HISTORY. Students will find information in the library or on the Internet. Rubric: Essay.

MATH. If the students have trouble securing the information, encourage them to try and locate it in the library or on the Internet. Allow the students to choose the way they will share their results. Rubrics: Math calculations, charts/tables, essay, oral presentation.

COMPUTER/TECHNOLOGY. Encourage all students to participate in the project. The Internet, classified ads, and local realtors would be good sources of information. Rubric: Spreadsheet.

Linking School to Home

Answers will vary. Allow students to choose the way they would like to share their findings. Rubrics: Essay, oral presentation, chart/ table.

Linking School to Work

Rubric: Essay.

Building Academic Skills

 Planning a Dream House

Create a poster of your dream house. Use magazines, the Internet, or your own drawings to depict what features it will have, where it will be located, and what it will look like. Then, use the newspaper or the Internet to locate a real home that might look like what you designed. Use the real home's price to create a reasonable purchase price for your home.

 Researching Social Responsibility

Habitat for Humanity builds houses for families in need. Its mission is to eliminate homelessness from the world and to make decent shelter a matter of conscience and action. Research the history of Habitat for Humanity and its plans for the future. Write a two-page paper with your findings.

 Tracking Bonds

Imagine you have $5,000 to invest and you decide to buy bonds. Using the newspaper or the Internet, choose two bonds in which to invest your imaginary money. Note today's actual market price for your bonds. In two weeks, check the price again. Do the same in one month. How do they compare?

 Comparative Research

In groups of three or four, research the average price for a home in your area. Include single- and multiple-family housing. Create a spreadsheet with your findings.

Linking School to Home

Conducting a Mini-Survey. Do you own any savings bonds? Many people give savings bonds as gifts for birthdays or to be used for college tuition. You can buy and sell U.S. savings bonds at banks and other financial institutions. The minimum face value of such a bond is $50; the maximum is $10,000. Conduct a mini-survey among your family and friends and find out if they have any bonds, what they plan to do with them, and whether or not they have given any as gifts. Also, ask them what they think of savings bonds as an investment.

Linking School to Work

Profiling a Career. Research the careers associated with the real-estate profession. Choose one of the following: sales agents, brokers, real-estate lawyers, commercial real estate investment counselors, appraisers, urban planners, and real-estate researchers. Interview someone in the profession. What skills does it take to have that job? How do you prepare for that job? Remember to use the journalist questions: who, what, where, when, why, and how. Write a two-page paper with your findings. Be sure to include a description of the career, the education and training necessary to succeed, average earnings, and the opportunities in the field.

E-Homework

Applying Technology

Comparing Municipal Bonds. Municipal bonds are sold to finance projects by local or state governments and by certain government agencies. Municipal bonds finance highway construction, schools, and other government projects. They can be bought and sold like stocks. In other words, like treasury bonds, you don't have to hold on to a municipal bond until it matures. Using the Internet, research the relationship between the current interest rate and the interest earned from the purchase of municipal bonds. Write a paragraph describing the relationship.

Researching the Process. Research the steps necessary to purchase U.S. savings bonds online. Then, find out if there are other types of bonds you can purchase online. Create a flowchart with the steps.

Connecting Academics

Math. Maria is considering a $10,000 corporate bond offering 7 percent or a $10,000 municipal bond paying 5 percent. Maria pays a tax of 31 percent on her income. Which of the investments will result in the greatest gain?

Computer/Technology. You're an employee in a real-estate office that has just acquired new computer equipment. Your coworkers are useless with new technology and look to you as the technology expert. What technical problems might arise, and what steps do you take to solve them?

BusinessWeek Analyzing the Feature Story

You read the first part of "Will Refis Help Refloat the Economy?" at the beginning of this chapter. Below are a few questions for you to answer about mortgage rates. You'll find the answers to these questions when you're reading the entire article. First, here are the questions:

31. What are some of the reasons for lower mortgage rates?

32. Why are homeowners like Anton and Audrey Scholl choosing to refinance their mortgages?

CREATIVE JOURNAL ACTIVITY

You just inherited $300,000 after taxes. Create a financial plan for this windfall. How much of your new wealth would you like to invest in real estate? Stocks? Bonds? Collectibles? Do you plan to borrow money for your real-estate investment? Why or why not? Break into teams and share your financial plan with a partner. How would you improve your partner's plan?

BUSINESS Online
The Full Story

To learn more about mortgage rates, visit the *Introduction to Business* Web site at **www.introbus.glencoe.com**, and click on *BusinessWeek* Feature Story, Chapter 32.

E-Homework

COMPARING MUNICIPAL BONDS. Answers may vary. Rubric: Essay.

RESEARCHING THE PROCESS. Rubric: Diagram.

Connecting Academics

MATH. Municipal bond will pay $10,000 × 0.05 = $500 interest. Corporate bond will pay $10,000 × 0.07 = $700 interest, but the tax will be 0.31 × $700 = $217, leaving $483 return.

COMPUTER/TECHNOLOGY. Answers will vary. Answers may include problems with connections, printers, network, software installation, and solutions to those problems.

BusinessWeek Analyzing the Feature Story

31. Competition among mortgage lenders, falling transaction costs, and a push from the Federal Reserve to trim interest rates has led to lower mortgage rates.

32. In addition to refinancing because of lower mortgage rates, many homeowners are interested in refinancing to have more liquid assets.

Creative Journal Activity

After students have completed the activity, have each student sketch their own investment pyramid and record on the sketch the details of their plan to invest their new wealth. **CL**, LS

1 FOCUS

Unit Seminar Overview

In this seminar students choose and track a stock. Students investigate images and interpret facts. Students graph price changes and decide their opinion on the question: Would you recommend buying your chosen stock?

Bell Ringer Activity

LIST AND NAME. Ask students to list, in three minutes, the names of national or global companies. Then have students tell the names and have a volunteer count how many different companies the class named.

Discussion Starter

WHAT'S HAPPENING LATELY? Ask students what's been happening lately in the stock market. Is there any news of major changes? Do students know any news of company break-ups or mergers? Ask students to bring to class relevant articles from the business section of the newspaper or from the Internet. **LS**

BusinessWeek Seminar

Unit **10** Technology

Tracking Investments on the Internet

Buy in and sell at the right time to make your money grow. Sometimes the stock market is the quickest game of chance. In Chapter 31, you read about investing in stock. The Internet has made information about stocks and investing much more accessible than ever before. Never before has it been easier for you to become your own financial manager. All it takes is lots of research, reading, and analysis. This seminar gives you a chance to discover the information only stockbrokers had in the past. Today this information is available to anyone with Internet access.

526

COMPUTER TECHNOLOGY

Newsworthy Trends

Online Competition. Since the advent of online stock trading, online stockbrokers have become increasingly more competitive. E*Trade, one of the first online brokers, took on traditional Wall Street firms by offering discount stock trading, with little or no advice, for as low as $14.95 per trade. To compete, firms that dismissed online trading at first, such as Merrill Lynch and Schwab, started offering online trading. Then other online brokers started lowering their fees. A trade for 300 shares of Yahoo! stock that cost $29.95 at Schwab cost $19.95 on E*Trade. The same trade cost $9.99 at Datek Online and only $5.00 at George Brown & Company.

Factoids

Paying a Financial Planner. If you need a money makeover, consider consulting a financial planner. Call around for different planners to find out what they charge for their services. Determine whether you can afford a commission-only planner, fee-based planner, or fee-only planner.

Match Your Employer. Assume you sock away $100 a month to your 401(k) and your company matches that amount by 50 percent. In 20 years you'll be sitting on about $184,000.

Fund Tracker. The past performance of a stock is no indicator of its future results.

Risk Taker. Fund managers often fall into two categories of risk takers: popular high-earnings growth and undiscovered bargain stocks.

Choose One. There are about 8,000 mutual funds available. Most people have only heard of 250 of them.

Investigate the Images

Look at the photographic collage on the left page. What grabs your attention first? Is it the color or the words? The power in reading visuals is in analyzing and dissecting your observations. On a separate piece of paper, respond to the questions listed below. These questions might help sharpen the focus of your visual mind.

Your Observations

1. How many photographs do you see?

2. Examine each photograph. How are they assembled in relation to one another?

3. What is the subject of each photograph? Is place or location the subject?

4. Does color signify a message?

5. What issues do you take from these images?

Information

6. Summarize what you know about the photographs from your observations.

Exploring Culture

7. Why do you think investing in stocks or mutual bonds can be a stressful, anxiety-ridden activity?

8. Corporate profits represent an average of 9.2 percent of the GDP. Over long periods of time corporate profits reflect the state of the nation's economy. In today's economy, what can you glean from this?

2 TEACH

Thinking Critically

Read "Factoids," and then answer these questions:

1. Do you think a commission-only financial planner would give you sound advice that's in your best interest? (The planner is likely to advise you to buy funds that return a high commission to him or her. Choose a fee-only planner for unbiased advice.)

2. In the factoid "Choose One," people have heard of about 250 mutual funds. How many large companies did your class name in the Bell Ringer activity? What are some names of mutual funds, and why do you think they're named that way? (Answers will vary. Mutual funds often have the word "growth" in their title.)

Cooperative Learning

MUTUAL FUNDS VS. STOCKS. Have students work in small groups to compare mutual funds with stocks. After discussing "Exploring Culture" (seminar questions 7 and 8), and referring to the Factoid, "Risk Taker," assign three or four groups to research mutual funds and the rest to research stocks. Have groups present their findings on factors such as: definition, relative risk, interesting statistics, important facts, and characteristics of the consumer base. **CL**, **LS**

COMPUTER TECHNOLOGY
Newsworthy Trends

Clicks-and-Mortar. After the dot-com bust at the end of the 1990s and a decline in online trading, online brokers are winning back customers by expanding the types of services they offer. Instead of limiting themselves to stock trading, online brokers are branching out into financial planning, stock-picking advice, and money management. The new model they're using are the clicks-and-mortar companies that operate both online and through more conventional means. E*Trade, for example, is offering customer service both online and over the phone by working with traditional accounting firms such as Ernst & Young.

2 TEACH (Cont.)

Independent Practice

L1 SUMMARIZE

Ask students to find a recent article on stocks or mutual funds. Ask them to take notes as they read, listing at least four points they could follow to improve their investment skills. Have students share the points with the class. Follow student presentations with a question and answer session. **LS**

L2 INTERVIEW

It's often fascinating to find out about the founder or CEO of a successful company and see who's behind the success. Ask students to use the Internet or the business section of the newspaper to choose a company leader to interview. Tell students to decide on their interview questions ahead of time. Students might ask the secret of the company's success and for investment opinions and advice. Have students set up a phone interview, if possible. Ask students to summarize their findings and write a one-page report. **LS**

L3 INVESTIGATE AND REPORT

Ask students to access *BusinessWeek Online* at **www.businessweek.com**, and click on the "Markets" link from the choices on the left. Ask students to describe the trends shown by the indexes. Have students find and click on the link to "Market Snapshot." Ask them to read the article and report on interesting points.

528

BusinessWeek Seminar

Taking Aim at Technology

Preparation

Research, discover, and track a stock as if it were your own investment.

Objective

In this *BusinessWeek* seminar, you'll:

- **Research** companies on the Internet. Discover the stocks you're hypothetically interested in buying.
- **Select** a particular stock and track its progress for one week. Calculate earnings and losses for one year.
- **Create** a chart to display your chosen stock's performance that year.

Materials Needed

✓ Internet access (Note: Internet access is preferable but not necessary. The Internet just makes the information easier to find.)
✓ Copies of recent business news publications such as *BusinessWeek* and the *Wall Street Journal*
✓ Paper, pens, and pencils
✓ Posterboard and markers

Procedures

1. Find and read articles about investing. To use the Internet, access the Web site of a business magazine, such as *BusinessWeek* at **www.businessweek.com**. Click on the tab labeled "Investing" and scan the various articles, columns, and reports available. Read those that interest you until you find a specific company that you would like to research.

528 Unit 10 Money Management

BusinessWeek

MARCH 19, 2007

SPECIAL REPORT
Mighty Mini-Dots
Do It Right

WEB SMART
Siemens'
ShareNet
Pays Off

e.biz

Harsh Lessons From a Dot-com's Travails

How EPO.com's dream of online stock offerings came to grief

EPO founder Ola Lauritzson

2. Research how a company's stock performed over time. To use the Internet, again access *BusinessWeek Online* and find a blank field labeled "Stock Lookup." Enter the name of the company. Write a brief summary of your findings by completing your own stock quotation table. (See a sample of this in Chapter 31 on page 502.)

3. Check these same figures in one week. How do they compare? Write another brief summary like the one in No. 2.

4. Imagine that a year ago you purchased 40 shares of the stock you've been researching. Using the "Historical Quotes" link, calculate whether your stock has increased or decreased in value. If you sold your stock today, how much would you earn or lose?

Reteaching Strategy

Lead. Have six or seven student volunteers lead small discussion groups focusing on important topics learned during this seminar. Ask the volunteer discussion leaders to appoint a secretary to note topics and appoint a spokesperson to report the group's comments to the class at the end of the discussion. **CL**, **LS**

Chart It

On posterboard, draw a graph that shows the changes in price per share of your stock over the past year. Use the price per share for the first day of each month to create the graph. Display your graph in class.

EXAMPLE:

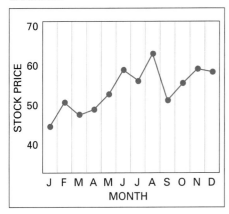

Analyze and Conclude

After considering your research and your chart, answer the questions below.

1. **Interpreting and Communicating Information.** When was the price per share at its highest this past year? When was the price per share at its lowest this past year?

2. **Knowing How to Learn.** Overall, is the price per share of your stock increasing or decreasing in value? Would you recommend buying this stock? Why or why not?

3. **Decision Making.** Why did you choose to research the stock of this company?

Becoming an Informed Citizen

Congratulations, you finished the seminar. Now it's time to reflect on the decisions you made.

Allocating Money. How do you know how much money you'll allocate to stocks in the future? What factors will influence your decisions?

Analyzing Your Future. Why is it important to start investing for your future today?

BUSINESS
Online

Further Exploration
To find out more about investing, visit the *Introduction to Business* Web site at **www.introbus.glencoe.com**.

3 ASSESS

Enrichment

COMPANY MEETING. After completing the "Taking Aim at Technology" section of this seminar, imagine that you are called to report to a meeting of the company you chose. The company wants you to give a report, from your research and opinions, of the position of their stock. You deliver your report at the meeting (your class). **CL**, **LS**

Evaluation

RUBRICS. The rubrics for evaluation of written reports and oral presentations are included in *Alternative Assessment Strategies.* **P**

4 CLOSE

Seminar Wrap-Up

YOUR OPINION. With all the experience and knowledge you've gained through this seminar on investing in stock, what do you feel are the important things for a novice to look into before investing? Ask students to write a paragraph. **LS**

Analyze and Conclude Answers

1. Answers will vary depending on the chosen stock.

2. Answers and recommendations will vary depending on the chosen stock. Require students to back up their statements with clearly defined reasons.

3. Answers will vary.

Risk Management

Chapter 33
Vehicle Insurance

Chapter 34
Property Insurance

Chapter 35
Life and Health Insurance

Unit Objectives

After completing this unit, students will be able to achieve the following outcomes:

- Name the types of vehicle insurance coverage, and explain the laws on vehicle insurance.
- Identify factors affecting the cost of vehicle, property, and life insurance premiums.
- Explain types of property insurance, and name the six kinds of homeowner's policies.
- Describe types of life insurance and health insurance.

BusinessWeek Connections

In this unit, students will read the following articles from *BusinessWeek*:

Chapter 33 "An Insurance Hunter's System of Choice: The Web": It's easier to compare auto insurance prices on the Web, and here are some tips to make your hunt more useful.

Chapter 34 "Containing Your Risk": Find out how businesses need to insure against the basic losses, such as from fire, and newer risks in the global marketplace.

Chapter 35 "Staying Insured When You're on Your Own": Find out how to get the best deals in health insurance coverage.

Key to Descriptive Icons

The following designations will help you decide which activities are appropriate for your students.

L1 Level 1 activities should be within the ability range of all students.

L2 Level 2 activities should be within the ability range of the average to above-average students.

L3 Level 3 activities are designed for the ability range of above-average students.

ELL Activities should be within the ability range of the English Language Learner.

LS Learning Styles designation represents activities designed to address different learning styles.

CL Cooperative learning activities are designed for small group work.

P Portfolio designation represents student products that can be placed into a best-work portfolio.

Teacher Classroom Resources*

Program Resources	Chapter 33	Chapter 34	Chapter 35
Student Activity Workbook	p. 249	p. 257	p. 267
Lesson Plans	p. 86	p. 88	p. 90
Internet Resources	p. 85	p. 87	p. 89
Reproducible Tests	p. 65	p. 67	p. 69
Teaching Transparencies	33.1, 33.2	34.1, 34.2	35.1, 35.2
Strategies and Worksheets for Teaching Transparencies	pp. 16, 83	pp. 16. 85	pp. 17, 87

* Each of these resources is available in print and on the Interactive Lesson Planner CD-ROM.

Technology Resources

- Interactive Lesson Planner CD-ROM
- PowerPoint® Presentation CD-ROM
- ExamView® Pro Test Generator CD-ROM
- Integrated Software Simulation, Teacher Manual
- Glencoe Business Video Package
- *PuzzleMaker* CD-ROM
- *Introduction to Business* Web Site
- *Virtual Business*®
  Virtual Business is a business simulation that introduces students to the principles of business by letting them start and run their own virtual business. In *Virtual Business,* students have the power to control all aspects of a retail convenience store. Students strategize business decisions using a powerful learning tool in the guise of a video game.

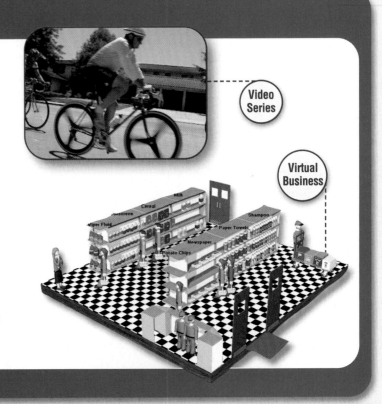

Video Series

Virtual Business

Scope and Sequence

Academic Standards of Learning

	LANGUAGE ARTS	MATH	HISTORY	COMPUTER/ TECHNOLOGY	SOCIAL SCIENCE	
CHAPTER 33	pp. 533, 534, 535, 536, 537, 538, 539, 540, 541, 546	pp. 533, 538, 546, 547	p. 534	pp. 532, 534, 535, 541, 546, 547	pp. 533, 536, 538, 539, 540, 542, 543, 546, 547	
CHAPTER 34	pp. 549, 550, 551, 552, 553, 555, 560	pp. 549, 552, 560, 561	pp. 554, 560	pp. 551, 557, 560, 561	pp. 549, 550, 553, 554, 557, 561	
CHAPTER 35	pp. 563, 564, 566, 567, 568, 569, 570, 574, 575	pp. 564, 566, 570, 574, 575	p. 564	pp. 565, 571, 574, 575	pp. 563, 568, 569, 574	

Scope and Sequence

Themes and Concepts

Business Core	Accounting and Finance	Business Management	Computer/ Technology	Marketing	Entrepreneurship

Business Law
Occupational Safety
Communication
	Decision Making
	Governing Agencies
	Financial Responsibility
	Risk Analysis
	Technology
	Costing Methods
		Consumers
		Decision Making
		Contracts
		Government
		  Regulations
		Legal Rights
		Sources of Law
			Systems Analysis and
			  Design
			Security
			Social Issues
				Customer Relations
				Risk Management
				Technology
				Salesmanship
				Policies and
				  Procedures
				Regulation
					Contracts
					Collections
					Financial Resources
					Government
					  Regulations
					Location and Property
					  Analysis

Business Law
Occupational Safety
Communication
	Decision Making
	Financial
	  Responsibility
	Risk Analysis
	Technology
		Consumers
		Decision Making
		Contracts
		Legal Rights
		Sources of Law
			Security
			Social Issues
				Risk Management
				Technology
				Salesmanship
				Policies and
				  Procedures
				Regulation
					Contracts
					Collections
					Financial Resources
					Location and Property
					  Analysis

Business Ethics
Business Law
Investment
Money Management
Document Processing
Information
  Resources
Communication
	Decision Making
	Financial
	  Responsibility
	Risk Analysis
	Technology
		Decision Making
		Financial
		  Responsibility
		Risk Analysis
		Technology
			Computer and
			  Communication
			  Systems
			Records Management
			Needs Analysis
			Business Decisions
				Customer Relations
				Risk Management
				Technology
				Policies and
				  Procedures
				Regulation
					Contracts
					Collections
					Financial Resources
					Government
					  Regulations
					Location and Property
					  Analysis

Unit Overview

Unit 11 gives information about managing risk and protecting yourself and your loved ones financially.

CHAPTER 33 explains types and costs of vehicle insurance and laws covering vehicle insurance.

CHAPTER 34 describes types of property insurance and the homeowner's policy and explains buying a policy.

CHAPTER 35 introduces life insurance and health insurance.

Introducing the Unit

When you have savings or property, or a business, you want to protect yourself against accidents or disasters. Emergencies such as these could wipe out hard-earned savings or destroy property. Purchasing insurance is one way to lower the financial risk. Ask students to give examples of when insurance is a requirement. (Certain levels of vehicle insurance are required by the state. Homeowner's insurance may be required by the lender.)

Technology Resource

 INTRODUCTION TO BUSINESS WEB SITE. To find out more about content in Unit 11, visit the Glencoe *Introduction to Business* Web site.
www.introbus.glencoe.com

Unit 11

Risk Management

Insurance of the Weird

For every type of risk there is some form of insurance coverage. You can buy insurance for pets, insurance against crocodile attacks, and insurance against employees who quit if they win the lottery. What can you do if aliens abduct you? In fact there are a few companies that provide alien abduction insurance. One company offers coverage not only for alien abductions, but also for injury caused by an asteroid or a piece of falling satellite.

● **Fancy Feet**
Fred Astaire, the famous dancer, had his legs insured for $650,000.

● **Famous Face**
When the *Mona Lisa*, valued at $100 million, was transported from Paris to the United States for an exhibition, the painting wasn't insured because the premiums were too high.

● **For Ransom**
Many U.S. corporations buy kidnap and ransom insurance for their overseas executives, since over 1,000 are kidnapped each year and the average ransom is $10 million.

● **Fore!**
In Japan, many golfers buy "hole-in-one" insurance, since the lucky occasion calls for buying expensive dinners and gifts that can cost as much as $15,000.

Field Trip Suggestion

Major Insurance Company. Arrange a visit to the regional office of a major insurance company or a broker for a major company. Ask a representative to discuss three or four dramatic instances where being insured has helped people's lives or helped a business. Ahead of the trip have students prepare questions to ask the representative about the background work that supports the insurance industry, such as actuarial, underwriting, claims analysis, and payment systems. After the visit, form students into groups of four. Have groups decide on a topic related to this unit and the field trip. Allow five minutes for groups to choose a topic then list each topic on the board. Each topic must be different. Have groups lead a short class discussion on their chosen topic. **CL**, LS, **ELL**

Bulletin Board

Glencoe/McGraw-Hill & Business Week

Glencoe Poster Teaching Tip

Read together the introduction on this poster. Remind students they already took the quiz on this poster in Unit 3. Tell students that the Meyers model is about problem solving. Tell students to sketch a diagram with seven stages and write the heading: Problems. Have students leave the first stage blank and fill in the next six stages with the steps of the Meyers model in the correct sequence. Lead a class discussion. What's this unit about? What might you put in the first stage that you left blank? (Prevention.)

BUSINESS Online

Idea Factory

To learn more about the insurance industry, visit the *Introduction to Business* Web site at www.introbus.glencoe.com, and click on Unit 11 Risk Management.

Out of Time?

If time doesn't permit teaching each chapter in this unit, you may use the *Puzzle-Maker* CD-ROM to focus on the business vocabulary.

Portfolio Activity

Anticipate. Tell students to think for a moment on what they know from their own experience on the topic of insurance. This could be anything from naming types of disasters to the cost of a family member's life insurance. After a few moments, have the students anticipate the information they will be studying in the three chapters in this unit. Have students freewrite or draw a mind map for three minutes to jot down their anticipations. After covering the unit, have students check back and highlight the anticipated topics they learned about. Ask students to evaluate whether taking a few moments to anticipate topics helped their learning in this unit. **P**

SCANS Correlation Chart*

Foundation Skills

Basic Skills	Reading	Writing	Math	Listening	Speaking	
Thinking Skills	Creative Thinking	Decision Making	Problem Solving	Seeing Things in the Mind's Eye	Knowing How to Learn	Reasoning
Personal Qualities	Responsibility	Self-Esteem	Sociability	Self-Management	Integrity/ Honesty	

Workplace Competencies

Resources	Allocating Time	Allocating Money	Allocating Material and Facility Resources	Allocating Human Resources		
Information	Acquiring and Evaluating Information	Organizing and Maintaining Information	Interpreting and Communicating Information	Using Computers to Process Information		
Interpersonal Skills	Participating as a Member of a Team	Teaching Others	Serving Clients/ Customers	Exercising Leadership	Negotiating to Arrive at a Decision	Working With Cultural Diversity
Systems	Understanding Systems	Monitoring and Correcting Performance	Improving and Designing Systems			
Technology	Selecting Technology	Applying Technology to Task	Maintaining and Troubleshooting Technology			

*This chart's highlighted blocks indicate the chapter's content coverage in the Student Edition and the Teacher Wraparound Edition.

Resource Manager

Teaching Transparencies

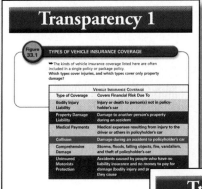

Transparency 1

TYPES OF VEHICLE INSURANCE COVERAGE

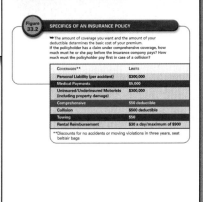

Transparency 2

SPECIFICS OF AN INSURANCE POLICY

Application and Enrichment

- Lesson Plans
- *BusinessWeek* Poster Package
- Teaching Transparencies
- Integrated Software Simulation
- Glencoe Business Video Package

Review and Reinforcement

- *PuzzleMaker*
- Internet Resources
- Student Activity Workbook
- Strat. and Work. for Teaching Transparencies

Assessment and Evaluation

- Reproducible Tests
- Alternative Assessment Strategies
- ExamView® Pro Test Generator

Technology

- *PuzzleMaker*
- ExamView® Pro Test Generator
- Glencoe Business Video Package
- PowerPoint® Presentation
- Integrated Software Simulation
- Interactive Lesson Planner
- *Virtual Business*®

KEY	
Printed	Software	Videocassette	Poster
Transparency	CD-ROM	Internet	

BUSINESS Online

Visit **www.introbus.glencoe.com**, the Web site companion to *Introduction to Business*. The student's page includes:

- interactive tutor
- additional *BusinessWeek* articles and activities
- business Web links
- homework hints
- real-world application activities
- additional career path activities

Information on how to prepare your students for the high school exit exam and special projects are also included.

Use the Glencoe Web site for additional resources. All essential content is covered in the Student Edition.

1 FOCUS

Introducing the Chapter

This chapter explains the types of vehicle insurance coverage, laws on vehicle insurance, and costs of insurance. A photo essay, "Beware of the Combinations," enhances the concepts.

Connecting the Objectives

What might happen if you didn't have vehicle insurance? What factors affect the cost of vehicle insurance?

BusinessWeek
Feature Story

Story's Summary

It's easier to compare auto insurance prices on the Web. Todd Eyler, senior analyst at Forrester Research in Cambridge, Mass., says the more questions sites ask you, the closer the quote will be to the premium you'll pay. Look at a number of sites that gather quotes from insurers. Be prepared to answer questions about your age, home address, and driving record.

Find the entire article at www.introbus.glencoe.com, or in the Teacher Resource Binder.

Vehicle Insurance

Learning Objectives

After completing this chapter, you'll be able to:
1. **Name** the different types of vehicle insurance coverage.
2. **Explain** the laws on vehicle insurance.
3. **Describe** the factors that affect the costs of vehicle insurance.

Why It's Important

Most states require you to have some form of vehicle insurance. To get the best value, you need to know the choices in coverage and the costs of insurance.

Key Words

insurance
policy
liability insurance
actual cash value
depreciation
financial responsibility law
compulsory insurance law
no-fault insurance
claim
premium
deductible

532

BusinessWeek Feature Story

An Insurance Hunter's System of Choice: The Web

The Do's and Don'ts of Finding an Affordable Policy Online. Buying insurance has never been a very consumer-friendly experience. Until recently, scouting out the best deal meant spending hours on the phone with various salespeople to compare policies. Even then, you could never hope to sample more than a fraction of the insurers licensed by your state.

Source: Excerpted with permission from "An Insurance Hunter's System of Choice: The Web," *BusinessWeek Online*, June 11, 2001.

An Extension Activity

Take an industry that you know a little about. What industry is it? How would you change things to make it more consumer oriented, friendly, and efficient?

BUSINESS *Online*
The Full Story

To learn more about vehicle insurance, visit the *Introduction to Business* Web site at www.introbus.glencoe.com, and click on *BusinessWeek* Feature Story, Chapter 33.

Classroom Resources

For the Teacher
- Student Activity Work. TAE
- Assessment Binder
- PowerPoint® Presentation
- Interactive Lesson Planner
- Lesson Plans
- Internet Resources
- Teaching Transparencies
- *Introduction to Business* Web Site

- Integrated Soft. Sim. TM
- *BusinessWeek* Poster Package

For the Student
- Student Activity Workbook
- *Virtual Business®*
- *Introduction to Business* Web Site
- Integrated Soft. Sim.
- *PuzzleMaker*
- Strategies and Worksheets for Teaching Transparencies

Bell Ringer Activity

ALLOCATING MONEY. Imagine you're saving up to buy a car. Make an estimate of the cost of auto insurance to cover the first six months. How long is it before you buy your car? How much do you need to save each month to cover the insurance cost?

Preteaching Business Key Words

MONITORING AND CORRECTING PERFORMANCE. Guess a definition for each key word. Check your definition against the glossary definition. How did you do? Make any needed corrections. **LS**

An Extension Activity

PRESENT. After students have researched vehicle insurance, have them give a short oral presentation explaining their findings. **LS**

Making Connections

Everyday Life. Consumers should evaluate an insurance company as well as the insurance policy. Consumers need to make sure the company is licensed and has adequate financial backing. They should also investigate if the company has a reinsurer and if it has had complaints lodged against it.

2 TEACH

Business Connection

When you have questions about vehicle insurance, going to a Web site, such as **Insurance.com**, may give you all the answers. Vehicle insurance sites often include a tutorial on vehicle insurance basics, and tips on events in your life that can affect your coverage, such as moving or marriage. Just in case you're not sure what questions to ask, sites often include a "Frequently Asked Questions (FAQ)" page.

Develop Concepts

BENEFITS. List things you would want covered in a vehicle insurance policy. Give examples of incidents when vehicle insurance was a benefit to you, your friends, or your family. (Students' suggestions should include bodily injury, property damage, and damage to their own or other people's cars. Examples should show that the major benefit is protection.) **LS**

Figure 33.1 Caption Answer

Bodily injury liability, medical payments, and uninsured motorists protection insurance cover injuries. Property damage liability, collision, and comprehensive damage cover property damage.

Preparing to Drive Safely

No one wants to pay for an accident for the rest of his or her life. Not only is being a smart, careful driver good for everyone on the road, but becoming a vehicle insurance holder will protect you against any number of situations. Even before you start looking at cars in the used or new sales lot at the local auto dealer, remember to carefully consider the expenses of any vehicle's insurance before making a decision to buy a car.

Types of Vehicle Insurance

Headlines like "Icy Roads Cause Fender-Benders" and "Wet Freeways Lead to Accidents" show how accidents might happen. How can drivers reduce the risk of financial losses resulting from accidents? One way is to buy insurance. **Insurance** is paid protection against losses due to injury or property damage. To get insurance, you have to purchase a contract called a **policy** from an insurance company. The policy explains how much and what kinds of protection you have. The company that issues the policy is called the *insurer* and the buyer of the policy is called the *policyholder*. Figure 33.1 covers the types of vehicle insurance.

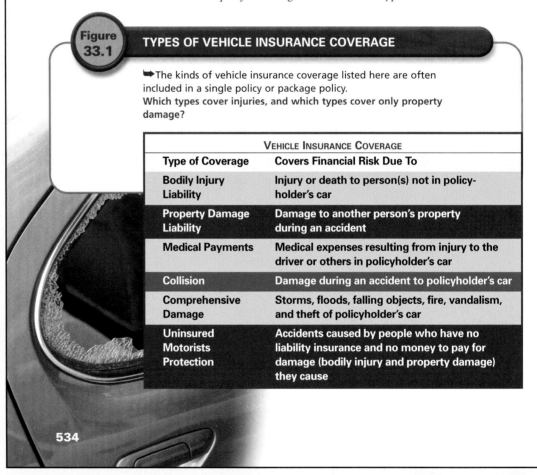

Figure 33.1

TYPES OF VEHICLE INSURANCE COVERAGE

➡ The kinds of vehicle insurance coverage listed here are often included in a single policy or package policy.
Which types cover injuries, and which types cover only property damage?

VEHICLE INSURANCE COVERAGE	
Type of Coverage	**Covers Financial Risk Due To**
Bodily Injury Liability	Injury or death to person(s) not in policyholder's car
Property Damage Liability	Damage to another person's property during an accident
Medical Payments	Medical expenses resulting from injury to the driver or others in policyholder's car
Collision	Damage during an accident to policyholder's car
Comprehensive Damage	Storms, floods, falling objects, fire, vandalism, and theft of policyholder's car
Uninsured Motorists Protection	Accidents caused by people who have no liability insurance and no money to pay for damage (bodily injury and property damage) they cause

534

Cooperative Learning

Go Team! Divide the class into seven teams. Give each team a topic that is one of the six types of coverage, or miscellaneous coverage. Have each team prepare a short lesson on their topic. Their lesson must utilize the four-step teaching plan, modeled in the chapters in this textbook: Focus, Teach, Assess, and Close. In Focus, the group must ask a motivating question and stress the importance of their topic. In Teach, the group must give instruction, and then provide a short class activity. In Assess, the group must give a short evaluation quiz. In Close, the group must give the class a short study-aid activity to wrap up their presentation. In 25 minutes, or less, have each team present their lesson. **CL**, **LS**

The type and amount of protection you have with an insurance policy depends on how much you're willing to pay. Vehicle insurance offers seven types of protection:

- bodily injury liability
- property damage liability
- collision
- medical payments
- comprehensive coverage
- uninsured motorist protection
- miscellaneous coverage

The most basic type of coverage (required by most states) is liability insurance. **Liability insurance** protects you from claims of injury or property damage to others in case you're held responsible for an accident. A policyholder should at least have liability insurance and then add other types of coverage.

Bodily Injury Liability

Bodily injury liability insurance covers injuries to someone else. It is a must for all drivers. The policy states the amount of protection in thousands of dollars. One figure applies to injuries to one person, and the second is a total for one accident. For 100/300 bodily injury coverage, the insurance pays up to $100,000 for injuries to one person. For one accident, it pays up to $300,000 for all claims. How much coverage do you need? A good rule is to buy as much as you can afford. Once you have basic insurance, it doesn't cost that much to increase protection.

Property Damage Liability

Property damage liability insurance covers damage to another person's vehicle or other property. It also covers damage to property, such as telephone poles or street signs. All drivers should have both bodily injury and property damage liability insurance. A policy might quote all liability limits together. The figure 100/300/50 means $100,000 and $300,000 for bodily injury and $50,000 for property damage. Drivers should carry as much coverage as they can afford.

Collision Insurance

Property damage liability insurance covers damages to *someone else's* vehicle. Collision insurance covers damages to your *own vehicle*. The maximum amount covered is based on the **actual cash value** of your vehicle, which is the value of the car when it's new minus depreciation. **Depreciation** is the decline in value of a vehicle because of use. In other words, its actual cash value is how much the car is worth used.

Suppose you get into an accident and the estimate for repairs on your car is $3,000. If the current value of your car, the actual cash value, is only $2,000,

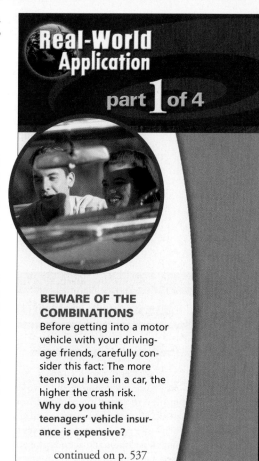

Real-World Application

part 1 of 4

BEWARE OF THE COMBINATIONS
Before getting into a motor vehicle with your driving-age friends, carefully consider this fact: The more teens you have in a car, the higher the crash risk. **Why do you think teenagers' vehicle insurance is expensive?**

continued on p. 537

Chapter 33 Vehicle Insurance **535**

Technology Resource

GO TO **POWERPOINT.** The *Introduction to Business* PowerPoint® CD-ROM provides visual lecture aids for this chapter.

Independent Practice

CREATE. As an aid to understanding the terms used in vehicle insurance, create a multiple-choice quiz of ten questions. Your quiz will be used in this chapter's wrap-up. **LS**

Meeting Individual Needs

Students With Dyslexia. Consider these tips on classroom management when a student has dyslexia:

- Use instructional methods that provide structure, such as using lists to summarize, previews to pre-organize, and repetition to reinforce.

- Use visuals and graphics to clarify the chapter content.
- Provide frequent feedback.
- Provide activities to enable students to put concepts and theory into practice. **LS**

2 TEACH (Cont.)

Thinking Critically

DEMONSTRATE. You're a member of a service club at your school. The service club is dedicated to informing students school-wide about life-skills topics. This month's topic is vehicle insurance. You volunteered to prepare a demonstration and an eye-catching, free-form diagram to describe the six types of vehicle insurance coverage. You use model cars and toy figures as part of your demonstration. (The demonstration should cover bodily injury liability, property damage liability, medical payments, and collision, comprehensive, and uninsured motorist protection.)

Business Building Blocks

CAPTION ANSWER

Discuss the steps for predicting consequences with the class. Ask students to describe various situations in which they already use these steps.

---

the insurance won't pay more than $2,000. If you have an old car that's cheaper to replace than to repair, you might not need collision coverage.

Medical Payments Coverage

Medical payments coverage is also called personal injury protection. It covers injuries to you and anyone else in your car. If you're injured in an accident and have to go to the hospital, this coverage pays your medical bills. Since medical costs are rising, you should have as much medical coverage as you can afford. Drivers often carry coverage of $5,000 or $10,000.

Comprehensive Coverage

Comprehensive insurance covers damage to a policyholder's vehicle caused by things other than a car accident. It covers losses from falling

Business Building Blocks

Analysis

Predicting Consequences

You attend a rock concert. As a result, you enjoy yourself, but have less money to spend on a movie next week. These consequences—good and bad—are easy to predict. However, not all decisions and actions give you clear-cut consequences.

Businesspeople often find their success depends on their ability to predict the consequences of business decisions and actions. Predictions are so important that successful businesspeople try to follow a logical process of predicting outcomes. They first try to learn as much as possible about the decision or action.

the possible results of each action. Write an explanation of this problem: You want to start a business producing all-natural jams. Your savings are small and your start-up costs will be large. You could: (1) ask a local bank for a loan, (2) accept the offer of money from your Uncle José, or (3) talk to an investment firm in your city.

Steps for Predicting Consequences

1. Gather information about the decision or action.
2. Identify as many consequences as possible.
3. Analyze each consequence by asking how likely it is to occur.
4. Figure out ways to ensure favorable consequences and prevent unfavorable ones.

Practice

Using what you've learned about financing a business, follow the "steps for predicting consequences" to clarify

---

LANGUAGE ARTS — Curriculum Connection

Communication. Have students write to your state's commissioner of insurance and ask for information on the state's minimum requirements for automobile insurance. Ask students to share their responses in class. Have students give their opinion on the minimum requirements. What amount of insurance do they feel they need to be fully protected? **LS, CL**

objects, theft, flood damage, vandalism, and other causes. With this type of insurance, you're covered if someone smashes your window and steals your car stereo. Like collision coverage, comprehensive coverage will not cover more than the actual cash value of your car.

Uninsured Motorist Protection

What if you're in an accident caused by someone without insurance? Uninsured motorist coverage protects you from people who can't pay insurance claims. If you have this kind of coverage, anyone riding with you is also protected. It also protects you if you're hit by a vehicle while walking or if you get into an accident caused by a hit-and-run driver. Most states require this coverage.

Miscellaneous Coverage

Besides these basic types of coverage, you can add other types of protection. For example, you can add coverage for a rental car. Insurance might pay the cost of towing. You need to add insurance to cover someone else who uses your car. If you're required to drive a vehicle for your job, you can add that vehicle to your policy. Your insurance agent can help you add the protection you need.

People who ride motorcycles, motor scooters, or snowmobiles need insurance, too. Most policies won't cover any damages caused as a result of racing. They might not cover passengers or anyone who borrows your motorcycle or snowmobile. Some policies don't include medical payments coverage for the owner.

 Fast Review

1. What does liability insurance cover?
2. What do the figures 100/300 mean?
3. What is the maximum amount an insurance company will cover in damages to a vehicle?
4. What types of losses will comprehensive insurance cover?

Laws on Vehicle Insurance

If you drive an old car that's not worth much, consider yourself a safe driver, or just don't have the money, you might think you don't need insurance. States have laws requiring drivers to show proof that they can pay for any injuries or damages they may cause. This not only makes you responsible for any accidents you cause, but protects you from others drivers. Vehicle insurance laws vary from state to state.

Chapter 33 Vehicle Insurance **537**

Real-World Application
part 2 of 4

BEWARE OF THE COMBINATIONS
The Fatality Analysis Reporting System (FARS), a census of fatal motor vehicle crashes on the U.S. public roads, found that 64 percent of the deaths of 13- to 19-year-old passengers occurred when other teenagers were driving.
In case of an accident, how much medical coverage should your vehicle insurance cover?

continued on p. 539

Chapter 33

Real-World Application
Caption Answer

BEWARE OF THE COMBINATIONS: PART 2 OF 4
With the rising costs of medical coverage, you should get as much as you can afford. Drivers often carry coverage for $5,000 to $10,000.

Fast Review Answers

1. Claims of injury or property damage to someone else.
2. Liability coverage of up to $100,000 for injuries to one person and up to $300,000 in total claims for one accident.
3. The actual cash value of the car.
4. Damage to a policyholder's car from things other than a car accident, such as falling objects, theft, flood damage, and vandalism.

Great Ideas From the Classroom of...

Robert D. Madison, Ph.D
Boys & Girls High School
Brooklyn, N.Y.

Risk Management Professionals. Invite local insurance agents into the class. Organize students into groups related to their interest in vehicle, property, life, and health insurance. Match each guest with each group of students. Have guests meet with their individual groups for about 10 minutes and answer students' questions. After 10 minutes, meet as a large group for a panel discussion with the professional guests serving as the panelists. **CL**, LS

2 TEACH (Cont.)

Business Connection

Trends in the insurance industry will have a major impact on consumers. One significant trend is the merger of insurance agencies and carriers. Competition should lead to lower premiums and more choices; it's up to you, the consumer, to be knowledgeable about what you need and the best deal out there.

Develop Concepts

DEDUCTIBLE. To help students understand the cost of insurance ask: What's a deductible? What's a premium? What do you think will happen to the premium if a person chooses a deductible of $200, instead of $500? Why do most insurance policies have a deductible clause? (Higher deductibles generally mean lower premiums. A deductible requires a policyholder to share the risk of loss.)

Discussion Starter

OPINION. What's your opinion—what are the pros and cons of vehicle insurance? After a discussion, what is the consensus of the class?

Writing for Business

CAPTION ANSWER

After the students have completed one path, ask them to write in their journal whether the experience has made them interested in being a civic journalist or investigative reporter. **P**, LS, **CL**

Writing for Business

Portfolio Activity

News Reporting and Writing

This activity gives you a chance to add to your portfolio. Communicate, interview, research, and write your way into a story. Choose one imaginary path, Civic Journalism or Investigative Reporter. Follow your path's steps to complete your own story.

pick a path

Civic Journalism

The Setting. You're a journalist for the local newspaper. Your editor has assigned you to write a story about car accidents involving young drivers.

Rising Action. Take careful notes during your interviews in order to create a final feature article. Arrange a series of quotes from your sources that you would like to include.

Step 1. Interview the crew of a local automobile towing and wrecking company. Prepare questions ahead of time.

Step 2. Interview one of the wrecker drivers and, if possible, the company owner. Try to find out their perspectives on car accidents. Ask if they have any particularly interesting stories about their work. Did their own driving habits change after they began working as wrecker drivers?

Investigative Reporter

The Setting. From what you've heard young drivers' vehicle insurance is expensive.

Rising Action. Investigate and develop an article on why young people pay high insurance rates. Summarize your interview in an outline that you can expand into a feature article.

Step 1. Talk with a local insurance agent about insurance for young drivers. Why are insurance rates for young drivers higher than those for more mature individuals? Why are young men charged more for insurance?

Step 2. Gather compelling statistics about how certain behaviors—underage drinking, loud music, and too many passengers—increase the risk of accidents.

Conclusion

Journalists determine the importance of a news story based upon timeliness, impact (on the reader), conflict, unusual events, and interest in ongoing issues. How newsworthy is your story? Write a one-page query letter, persuading a newspaper editor to publish your story.

538

Global Perspective

Mexican Tourist Card. If you're planning to tour in Mexico, you'll need a Mexican tourist card. U.S. insurance policies aren't recognized as valid in Mexico by the Mexican government. You'll always need to carry with you proof of U.S. citizenship, such as your passport. Mexican immigration officials must validate the card at the border crossing. The card is valid for a set period of time.

Financial Responsibility Law

All states have some form of financial responsibility law. A **financial responsibility law** says you must pay for any damage or injury you cause in an accident either with insurance, with savings, or by selling property. If you can't pay, you can be sued, lose your license, or even lose your car. The best way to demonstrate financial responsibility is to have car insurance.

Compulsory Insurance Law

Most states also have some form of compulsory insurance law. A **compulsory insurance law** legally requires drivers to have a minimum amount of car insurance. This ensures that drivers will be held responsible for any accidents or injuries they cause as a result of bad driving. According to the law, you have to show proof of insurance before you can get a license or register your car. You might also have to show proof of insurance if the police stop you for a moving violation.

No-Fault Insurance

Suppose you get into an accident with another driver where both of you are injured and there's some dispute about whose fault it is. It can lead to costly lawsuits and take a long time to settle the insurance claims. In order to reduce the amount of time and money it takes to settle injury cases, many states have no-fault insurance laws. Under **no-fault insurance**, it doesn't matter who caused the accident. It requires drivers involved in accidents to collect damages from their own insurance companies no matter who is at fault.

✓ Fast Review

1. What is the difference between a financial responsibility law and a compulsory insurance law?
2. What can happen if you can't show proof of financial responsibility or insurance?

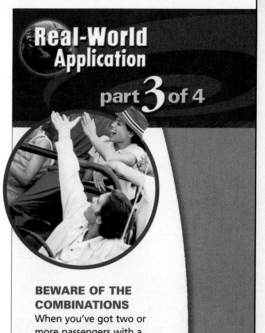

Real-World Application
part 3 of 4

BEWARE OF THE COMBINATIONS
When you've got two or more passengers with a teenage driver the fatal crash risk jumps five times as high as driving alone. Distractions such as music playing, turning to talk with someone in the rear seat, and passengers fooling around are largely the result of the risk-taking factors. Should there be a law to improve the safety of teenage drivers?

continued on p. 541

The Costs of Insurance

Paying for car insurance can take a lot out of your budget. The average person pays about $1,200 in car insurance per year. The costs of insurance are directly affected by the amount of money insurers pay each year in insurance claims. A **claim** is a request for payment from an insurer for any damages covered by a policy. The more money insurance companies have to pay in claims, the more they have to charge for insurance to make up for it.

Real-World Application
Caption Answer

BEWARE OF THE COMBINATIONS: PART 3 OF 4
Answers will vary.

Individualized Practice

Invite a vehicle insurance agent to your class. Prepare questions ahead of time.

L1 Have students work in pairs to discuss the answers given by the insurance agent.

L2 Ask students to generate a list of factors that can help lower auto insurance premiums and those factors that tend to make premiums higher.

L3 Ask students to work in groups to summarize in chart form, all the session's questions and answers.

Fast Review Answers ✓

1. A financial responsibility law requires you to pay for any damages or injuries you cause. A compulsory insurance law requires you to have a minimum amount of insurance.
2. You can be sued, have your license or registration taken away, or lose your vehicle.

LANGUAGE ARTS
Curriculum Connection

Communication. Have students work in groups of four. Ask groups to find out how many states require that motorists have automobile insurance coverage. Suggest that they also find out how states enforce the law and what penalties are associated with breaking the law. Have groups present a two-minute summary. **LS**,

Reteaching

LAWS. To reteach the concept of laws on vehicle insurance, ask students to explain the laws and write important points on the board. (Answers should include financial responsibility law, compulsory insurance law, and no-fault insurance.)

Enrichment Strategy

EVALUATE. Work in pairs to find an article about current trends and issues in the auto insurance industry. Summarize the main points of the article. **LS**

Evaluation

Assign and review the Fast Review sections.

Figure 33.2 Caption Answer

Both comprehensive and collision coverages have deductibles. Under the comprehensive coverage, the policyholder would pay $50. For a collision, the policyholder would pay the first $500 of losses.

Insurance Premiums

The amount an insurance company charges a policyholder for an insurance policy is called the **premium**. The premium covers the policyholder for a limited period of time, usually for a month, six months, or a year. At the end of the period, the policy is renewed. The insurance company can also cancel a policy or refuse coverage for someone with a record of accidents. (See Figure 33.2 for more specifics on an insurance policy.)

Deductible

Most collision insurance has a deductible. A **deductible** is an amount in damages a policyholder must pay before the insurance company pays anything. For example, you get into an accident and it costs $700 to repair the damage to your car. If your deductible is $200, you pay for $200 of the damages and the insurance company pays the other $500. A deductible makes you responsible for small losses and the insurance helps pay for the larger losses.

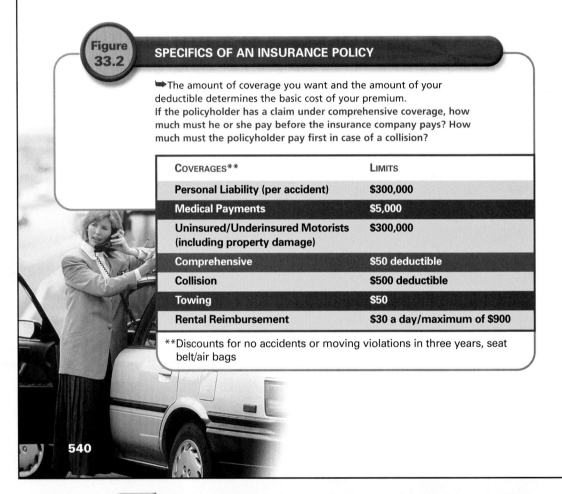

Figure 33.2

SPECIFICS OF AN INSURANCE POLICY

➥The amount of coverage you want and the amount of your deductible determines the basic cost of your premium.
If the policyholder has a claim under comprehensive coverage, how much must he or she pay before the insurance company pays? How much must the policyholder pay first in case of a collision?

COVERAGES**	LIMITS
Personal Liability (per accident)	$300,000
Medical Payments	$5,000
Uninsured/Underinsured Motorists (including property damage)	$300,000
Comprehensive	$50 deductible
Collision	$500 deductible
Towing	$50
Rental Reimbursement	$30 a day/maximum of $900

**Discounts for no accidents or moving violations in three years, seat belt/air bags

540

How to Use a Portfolio Activity

The portfolio projects are designed to lead students to develop a collection of their best work to submit to you for assessment. You and each of your students should decide which projects to include in their business portfolio. Refer students to the specific rubric(s) from the *Alternative Assessment Strategies*. These rubrics will alert students to the criteria you'll use to assess their projects. **P**

Factors Affecting the Costs of Insurance

The costs of paying claims affect the costs of insurance in general. The amount of coverage you want and the amount of your deductible determines the basic cost of your premium. In addition, there are a variety of specific factors that affect the cost of your premium: type of vehicle, vehicle usage, geographic location, and your age.

Type of Vehicle. The amount of your premium will vary according to the make, model, and year of the vehicle you drive. A brand new $30,000 car will cost more to insure than an old car worth about $2,000. That's because if the new car is wrecked, it can cost the insurance company a lot more to replace. Similarly, cars with parts that are expensive to repair will cost more to insure.

Location. The area where you live has an affect on your insurance premium. If you live in an area with a high crime rate where vehicles are vandalized or stolen more often, your premium will be higher than in areas with a lower crime rate. City drivers usually pay more than drivers in rural areas because there is a greater likelihood of accidents in the city.

Driver Classification. Driver classification includes factors like your age, gender, and marital status. Drivers under the age of 25 or over the age of 70 have accidents more often so they pay more in insurance premiums. Young men often have more accidents than young women, so they have to pay more. On the other hand, middle-aged drivers are generally considered less of a risk because they have more driving experience.

Driving Record. Your driving record is a major factor in the cost of your premium. Drivers with a record of accidents or traffic violations pay the most in premiums, because they pose the greatest risk. You can qualify for a lower premium if you complete a driver education course or have good grades. Some companies find that good students have a better safety record, so their rates are lower.

 Fast Review _____

1. How does a deductible affect the cost of a premium?
2. Why do drivers under the age of 25 and over the age of 70 pay more in premiums?
3. How can younger drivers qualify for a lower premium?

Real-World Application

part 4 of 4

BEWARE OF THE COMBINATIONS
An Auto Club of Southern California study found that the Graduated Drivers License Law has improved the safety of teen motorists. Under this law, new drivers under the age of 18 must hold their learner's permit for at least six months before getting a license. During this time, the teen motorist must spend at least 50 hours behind the wheel, with a parent or guardian aboard. The number of passengers killed or injured in crashes involving 16-year-old motorists dropped 40 percent.
Has your state adopted a version of this law?

Chapter 33

Real-World Application Caption Answer

BEWARE OF THE COMBINATIONS: PART 4 OF 4
Answers will vary. Check with the Auto Club, which is campaigning to pass the law in all 50 states.

Technology Resource

GO TO **PUZZLEMAKER CD-ROM.** Check your students' understanding of the chapter's key terms by using the *PuzzleMaker* CD-ROM.

Fast Review Answers ✓

1. The higher the deductible, the lower the premium since the insurance company doesn't have to pay as much for a claim.
2. They have accidents more often.
3. By completing a driver education class or getting high grades.

Meeting Individual Needs

Second Language Learners or Students With Hearing Impairments. If you have second language learners or students with hearing impairments in your class, slow down your speech patterns but do not use an unnatural, choppy, syllable-by-syllable style of pronunciation. Instead, mentally group your sentences into groups of words that make sense together. Then increase the length of pauses between groups of words and between sentences. These longer pauses, along with grouping words by sense, will give students more time to process what they are seeing and hearing. **P**

What Happens During a Crash Test?

1 FOCUS

As emphasized in this chapter, vehicle insurance rates are highest for teenagers because they're involved in more accidents than any other group. One of the main reasons for this is that they have less experience and training. The problem is exacerbated by the fact that, because of budget cuts, only about half of high schools in the United States offer driver training courses. The problem is further compounded because the number of teenagers, and consequently teenage drivers has steadily increased in the past few years.

2 TEACH

Discuss with students the main causes of vehicle accidents among teenagers and what they can do to avoid them.

? *Did You Know?*

Along with radar and speed cameras, lasers are now used to identify speeding drivers. Lasers can identify a speeding vehicle even in heavy traffic and can't be picked up by radar detectors.

542

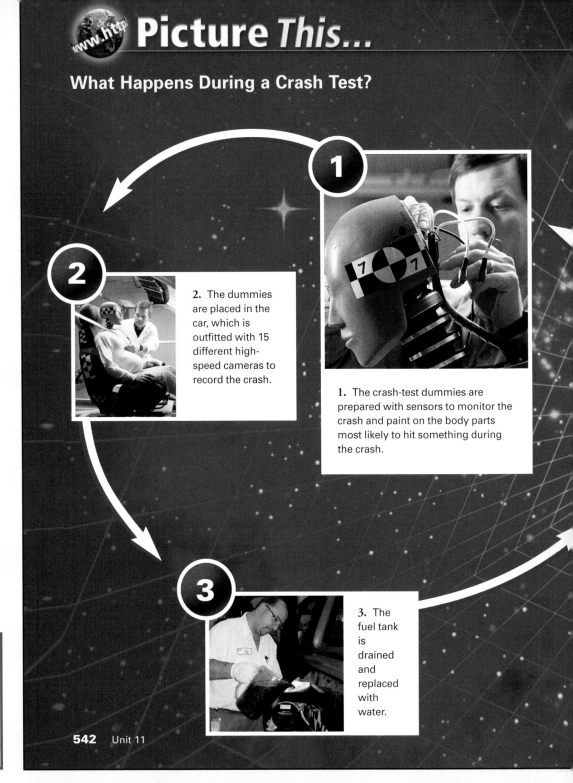

Picture *This...*

What Happens During a Crash Test?

2. The dummies are placed in the car, which is outfitted with 15 different high-speed cameras to record the crash.

1. The crash-test dummies are prepared with sensors to monitor the crash and paint on the body parts most likely to hit something during the crash.

3. The fuel tank is drained and replaced with water.

Extending the Content

The Vehicle Research Center of the National Highway Traffic Safety Administration (NHTSA) doesn't just perform crash tests. It also investigates real-world vehicle collisions. Researchers aren't interested in what caused the crashes, but in what kinds of injuries and damage resulted from them. This helps researchers to design their crash tests so they focus on problems that occur in real crashes.

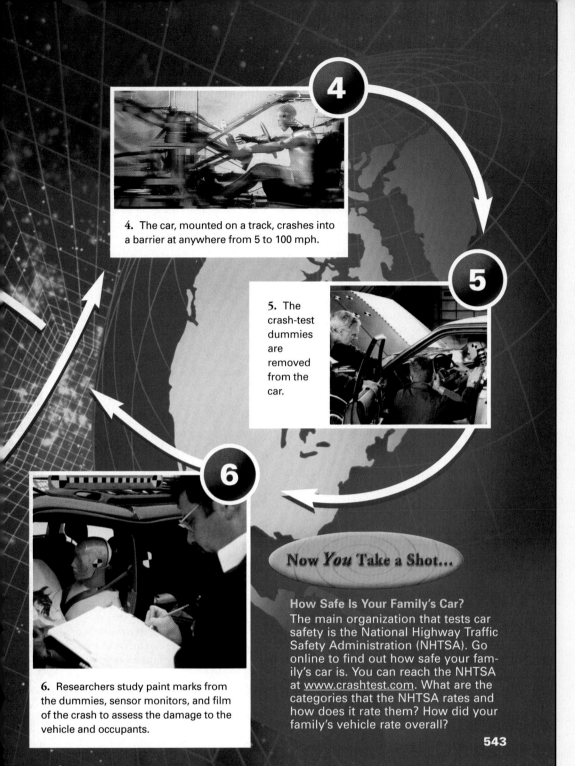

4. The car, mounted on a track, crashes into a barrier at anywhere from 5 to 100 mph.

5. The crash-test dummies are removed from the car.

6. Researchers study paint marks from the dummies, sensor monitors, and film of the crash to assess the damage to the vehicle and occupants.

Now *You* Take a Shot...

How Safe Is Your Family's Car?
The main organization that tests car safety is the National Highway Traffic Safety Administration (NHTSA). Go online to find out how safe your family's car is. You can reach the NHTSA at www.crashtest.com. What are the categories that the NHTSA rates and how does it rate them? How did your family's vehicle rate overall?

543

3 ASSESS

Have students answer the questions in "Now You Take a Shot..."

4 CLOSE

Introduce students to the concept of defensive driving, or looking out for other drivers who might cause an accident. Have students come up with suggestions and write them on the board. Also have students share any experiences they've had with bad drivers.

? *Did You Know?*

Last year, three of the five vehicles with the highest rate of insurance losses for theft were sport utility vehicles, or SUVs. It was the fourth year in a row that SUVs topped the list of stolen vehicles.

Now *You* Take a Shot... **Caption Answer**

Answers will vary depending on the vehicle. The NHTSA rates the safety of vehicles according to their weight, structure, injury rate, death rate, and how they performed in front and side collisions. The ratings in each category range from poor to excellent.

4 CLOSE

Chapter Wrap-Up

Ask students to randomly exchange the quizzes they made in the "Individualized Practice" activity. After they have completed the quiz, have students exchange quizzes to grade them.

Using Business Key Words

1. insurance
2. policy
3. compulsory insurance law
4. deductible
5. premium
6. financial responsibility law
7. liability insurance
8. depreciation
9. no-fault insurance
10. claim
11. actual cash value

Review What You Learned

12. By having large numbers of people share risks and losses.
13. Liability insurance because it protects a driver from claims of others.
14. Buy as much insurance as you can afford.
15. Property damage liability.
16. Comprehensive insurance covers damage to a policyholder's car. It covers losses from glass breakage, falling objects, theft, windstorm, hail, flood damage, and vandalism.
17. If you can afford to replace your wrecked vehicle, then you can drop collision and comprehensive coverage.

Summary

1. Types of vehicle insurance include bodily injury liability, property damage liability, medical payments, collision, comprehensive coverage, uninsured motorist protection and miscellaneous coverage. Liability insurance protects you from claims of bodily injury or property damage to others.

2. State law requires drivers to prove financial responsibility in case of an accident. Most states also require you to carry a minimum amount of insurance. No-fault insurance requires drivers involved in accidents to collect damages from their own insurance companies no matter who is at fault. These laws vary from state to state.

3. The costs of insurance premiums are affected by:
   - The costs insurance companies pay in claims.
   - The amount of coverage and the deductible on a policy.
   - The type of vehicle, the area where the vehicle is used, the driver's age, gender, and marital status, and the driver's driving record.

● Using Business Key Words

Vehicle insurance is something you'll probably purchase during most of your adult lifetime. Knowing the terms surrounding the insurance industry will help you become a better consumer. Match the terms with their definitions.

- **insurance**
- **policy**
- **deductible**
- **liability insurance**
- **compulsory insurance law**
- **depreciation**
- **financial responsibility law**
- **premium**
- **no-fault insurance**
- **claim**
- **actual cash value**

1. Paid protection against losses due to injury or property damage.
2. A contract between an insurance company and policyholder.

3. A law that requires drivers to have a minimum amount of car insurance.
4. The amount of damages that an insurance policyholder must pay before the insurance company pays.
5. Amount of money charged by an insurance company for protection for a given time period.
6. Requires proof that drivers can pay for damages in an accident.
7. Protection against claims of injury or property damage.
8. Decline in value of a vehicle because of age, and wear and tear.
9. A law that requires drivers involved in accidents to collect damages from their own insurance companies no matter who is at fault.
10. A request for payment from an insurer for any damages covered by an insurance policy.
11. How much the used item is worth.

Quick Quiz

1. Explain collision insurance. (Collision insurance covers damages to your own vehicle.)
2. What is a claim? (A request for payment from an insurer for any damages covered by a policy.)

3. Name three factors that affect auto insurance premiums. (Possible answers include driving record, type of car, number of miles you drive, where you live, the amount of the deductible, and your age.)

Review What You Learned

12. How does insurance reduce the risk of financial loss?
13. Which type of insurance is the most important protection? Why?
14. How much insurance should a driver purchase?
15. Which type of insurance covers damage to a telephone pole or street sign?
16. What does comprehensive insurance cover?
17. When would it be possible to drop your collision and comprehensive insurance coverage?

Understanding Business Concepts

18. Why do you think the laws in most states require proof that drivers can pay for damages in an accident?
19. What does 100/300/50 mean?
20. How does a deductible cut the cost of insurance?
21. What does uninsured motorist coverage protect?
22. Why do you think an insurance policy would not cover a driver in a motorcycle-racing contest?
23. Why do you think insurance for a sports utility vehicle would cost more than a mid-size sedan?

Critical Thinking

24. Teenage boys usually pay more for vehicle insurance than teenage girls. Why do you think this is the case? Is it fair?
25. Create a list of ways you can reduce your vehicle insurance premiums.
26. Do you agree that no-fault insurance is a good thing? Explain your answer.
27. How might knowledge of the different types of vehicle insurance coverage help you?

Viewing and Representing

Examining the Image. Draw a sketch of things that stand out in this picture. Do you think the photographer took this picture with a point of view in mind? What does the photographer want you to think or do? Group with three other students. Share your knowledge and experience of vehicle accidents and vehicle insurance.

Chapter 33 Vehicle Insurance **545**

Critical Thinking

24. Answers will vary.
25. Lists will vary.
26. Answers will vary and should include an explanation.
27. Answers will vary and might include that with the knowledge, students can make more informed decisions about the extent of coverage needed and find better deals on the costs of vehicle insurance.

Viewing and Representing

Remind students that images in print and in the media are often designed to affect consumer's perceptions. Ask students: How can you be more aware of the possible hidden message of an image? Discuss student suggestions, which may include self-questions such as: How does this make me feel? Is this a true representation of reality? **LS**

Understanding Business Concepts

18. Show responsibility for damages.
19. The insurance coverage will pay up to $100,000 for injuries to one person, up to $300,000 for all claims, and up to $50,000 for property insurance.
20. Insurance helps with small and larger losses.
21. Cover you if someone doesn't have insurance.
22. High risk of accident and injury.
23. Insurance, parts, repairs, and other factors.

4 CLOSE (Cont.)

Building Academic Skills

LANGUAGE ARTS. Make sure both partners participate in the role-play. Allow the students to make the decision about how they present their role-plays to the class. Rubric: Role-play.

SOCIAL STUDIES. Answers will vary. Students can use the library or Internet as resources. Allow the students to choose the method they will use to share their findings. Rubrics: Essay, note taking, oral presentation, poster, table.

COMPUTER/TECHNOLOGY. Make sure all members of the team participate in the project. Rubric: Spreadsheet.

MATH. (a) 16 year olds; (b) 17–19 year olds; and (c) 20–49 year olds. Rubric: Calculation.

Linking School to Home

Answers will vary depending on your family's insurance coverage. Allow the students to choose the method they will use to share their findings. Rubrics: Essay, computerized presentation, oral presentation, table/chart.

Linking School to Work

Answers will vary. Rubric: Paragraph.

Building Academic Skills

 Role-playing

With a partner, role-play an imaginary meeting with an insurance agent. Use at least eight new terms you learned from this chapter in your role-play and present it to your class.

 Researching State Insurance

Research the laws in your state regarding motor vehicle insurance. Find out if drivers are required to carry insurance, the type of coverage required, and what penalties exist if a driver does not carry vehicle insurance. Then choose another state and compare the same information with what you found out about your own state.

 Brainstorming About Risks

Work in teams of four to create a spreadsheet. The first column of the spreadsheet should be "Driving Risks." The second column should be titled, "Ways to Reduce Risks." The third column should be titled, "Ways to Avoid Risks." As a group, brainstorm risks you might face while driving. Enter those into the spreadsheet and then complete the other two columns. Print your spreadsheet.

 Reading a Chart

Using the chart below, answer the following questions:
- Which age group has the highest number of fatal crashes caused by speeding?
- Which age group has the second-highest number of fatal crashes caused by driver error?
- Which age group has the highest number of fatal crashes caused by drinking and driving?

Percentage of Fatal Crashes by Characteristic			
Driver Age:	16	17–19	20–49
Driver error	80	75	62
Speeding	36	31	22
3+ occupants	33	26	19
Single vehicle	41	37	30
Drivers killed with 0.01+ BAC (blood alcohol content)	8	25	47

Source: Insurance Institute for Highway Safety.

Linking School to Home

Family Vehicle Insurance. Ask your parents about the vehicle insurance coverage they carry. Find out what types of protection they carry, how much coverage they carry, and the cost of the insurance premium. If you're insured under their policy, find out what your coverage costs. Share your findings with the class.

Linking School to Work

Comparing Reasons. Millions of Americans carry vehicle insurance. However, millions of others don't. Write a paragraph explaining the advantages and disadvantages of having car insurance. Address this complaint: "I sure am wasting a lot of money. I'm a careful driver, and I probably will never have an accident."

E-Homework

Applying Technology

Examine Crime. Premiums are also higher for vehicles that are known to break down or get stolen often. You'll pay more for insurance if you live in an area where there is a higher rate of car accidents. Use the Internet to research the type of car that has the highest theft rate in the United States. Write a paragraph explaining why you think this is the case.

Researching Insurance Premiums. Many new vehicles come equipped with safety features like air bags and security systems. How a vehicle is used affects the cost, too. If you drive your vehicle to work every day, your insurance might cost more than if you only use it on weekends. Use the Internet to create a list of those features that are currently available and those that will be in the near future. Then, contact an insurance company and find out how these features can help reduce insurance premiums.

Connecting Academics

Math. Insurance companies rely on the laws of probability. These laws enable an insurance mathematician, called an actuary, to determine the likelihood that an event will actually take place. Find out about actuarial figures and create a poster display of your findings.

Social Science. Imagine you'll get delivery of the car of your dreams in two weeks. You need to research the different types and costs of insurance, but with your busy schedule when will you have the time? If you don't already have a weekly planner or schedule, make one for next week. Estimate how much time you'll need to research insurance, and which times of day are best to be online or to make telephone calls. Mark the time slots on your schedule.

BusinessWeek | Analyzing the Feature Story

You read the first part of "An Insurance Hunter's System of Choice" at the beginning of this chapter. Below are a few questions for you to answer about insurance hunter's choices. You'll find the answers to these questions when you're reading the entire article. First, here are the questions:

28. What percentage of insurance policies is sold online?

29. What kind of insurance is purchased the most online?

CREATIVE JOURNAL ACTIVITY

People who have been driving for years without any accidents or traffic tickets enjoy the lowest premiums. Investigate some other conditions that will lower your car insurance premiums. Interview an auto insurance agent or research rates on the Internet. What did you learn?

BUSINESS *Online*

The Full Story

To learn more about buying insurance, visit the *Introduction to Business* Web site at www.introbus.glencoe.com, and click on *BusinessWeek* Feature Story, Chapter 33.

E-Homework

EXAMINE CRIME. Answers will vary depending on the resources used. Rubric: Paragraph.

RESEARCHING INSURANCE PREMIUMS. Students may wish to help each other with this activity. If you prefer, invite a representative from an insurance company into the class to answer the questions. Allow the students to choose the method they will use to share their findings. Rubrics: Essay, computerized presentation, oral presentation, table/chart.

Connecting Academics

MATH. Poster displays will vary. If students have difficulty finding information, have them enter the keyword, "actuarial" in an Internet search engine.

SOCIAL SCIENCE. Schedules or planners will vary. Have volunteers draw sections of their schedule on the board and have the class tell the length of the time allotted. Usually, time-slots are in increments of at least a quarter hour.

BusinessWeek | *Analyzing the Feature Story*

28. One percent.

29. Auto related.

Creative Journal Activity

After students have researched rates or interviewed an auto insurance agent, have them work in groups to create a poster of "Do's & Don'ts: To Get Value from Auto Insurance." If possible, display posters in the main office or hallway of the school.
CL, LS

SCANS Correlation Chart*

Foundation Skills

Basic Skills	Reading	Writing	Math	Listening	Speaking	
Thinking Skills	Creative Thinking	Decision Making	Problem Solving	Seeing Things in the Mind's Eye	Knowing How to Learn	Reasoning
Personal Qualities	Responsibility	Self-Esteem	Sociability	Self-Management	Integrity/ Honesty	

Workplace Competencies

Resources	Allocating Time	Allocating Money	Allocating Material and Facility Resources	Allocating Human Resources		
Information	Acquiring and Evaluating Information	Organizing and Maintaining Information	Interpreting and Communicating Information	Using Computers to Process Information		
Interpersonal Skills	Participating as a Member of a Team	Teaching Others	Serving Clients/ Customers	Exercising Leadership	Negotiating to Arrive at a Decision	Working With Cultural Diversity
Systems	Understanding Systems	Monitoring and Correcting Performance	Improving and Designing Systems			
Technology	Selecting Technology	Applying Technology to Task	Maintaining and Troubleshooting Technology			

*This chart's highlighted blocks indicate the chapter's content coverage in the Student Edition and the Teacher Wraparound Edition.

Resource Manager

Teaching Transparencies

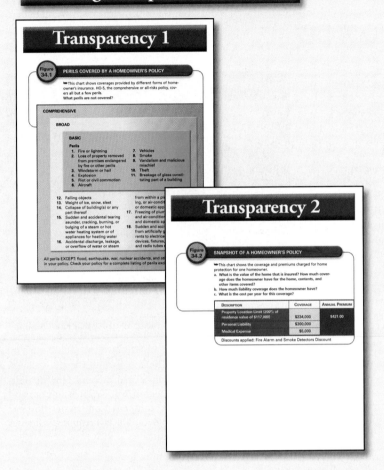

Transparency 1

Figure 34.1 — PERILS COVERED BY A HOMEOWNER'S POLICY

➡ This chart shows coverages provided by different forms of home-owner's insurance. HO-5, the comprehensive or all-risks policy, covers all but a few perils.
What perils are not covered?

COMPREHENSIVE

BROAD

BASIC

Perils
1. Fire or lightning
2. Loss of property removed from premises endangered by fire or other perils
3. Windstorm or hail
4. Explosion
5. Riot or civil commotion
6. Aircraft
7. Vehicles
8. Smoke
9. Vandalism and malicious mischief
10. Theft
11. Breakage of glass constituting part of a building

12. Falling objects
13. Weight of ice, snow, sleet
14. Collapse of building(s) or any part thereof
15. Sudden and accidental tearing asunder, cracking, burning, or bulging of a steam or hot water heating system or of appliances for heating water
16. Accidental discharge, leakage, or overflow of water or steam
17. Freezing of plumbing and air-conditioning and domestic appliances
18. Sudden and accidental damage from artificially generated currents to electrical devices, fixtures, and radio tubes

All perils EXCEPT: flood, earthquake, war, nuclear accidents, and others in your policy. Check your policy for a complete listing of perils excluded.

Transparency 2

Figure 34.2 — SNAPSHOT OF A HOMEOWNER'S POLICY

➡ This chart shows the coverage and premiums charged for home protection for one homeowner.
a. What is the value of the home that is insured? How much coverage does the homeowner have for the home, contents, and other items covered?
b. How much liability coverage does the homeowner have?
c. What is the cost per year for this coverage?

DESCRIPTION	COVERAGE	ANNUAL PREMIUM
Property Location Limit (200% of residence value of $117,000)	$234,000	$421.00
Personal Liability	$300,000	
Medical Expense	$5,000	

Discounts applied: Fire Alarm and Smoke Detectors Discount

Application and Enrichment

- 🖉 Lesson Plans
- 📖 *BusinessWeek* Poster Package
- 📥 Teaching Transparencies
- 💿 🖉 Integrated Software Simulation
- 📼 🖉 Glencoe Business Video Package

Review and Reinforcement

- 💿 *PuzzleMaker*
- 💻 🖉 Internet Resources
- 🖉 Student Activity Workbook
- 🖉 Strat. and Work. for Teaching Transparencies

Assessment and Evaluation

- 🖉 Reproducible Tests
- 🖉 Alternative Assessment Strategies
- 💿 ExamView® Pro Test Generator

Technology

- 💿 *PuzzleMaker*
- 💿 ExamView® Pro Test Generator
- 📼 Glencoe Business Video Package
- 💿 PowerPoint® Presentation
- 💿 🖉 Integrated Software Simulation
- 💿 Interactive Lesson Planner
- 💿 *Virtual Business*®

KEY	🖉 Printed	💾 Software	📼 Videocassette	🖥 Poster
	📥 Transparency	💿 CD-ROM	💻 Internet	

BUSINESS Online

Visit www.introbus.glencoe.com, the Web site companion to *Introduction to Business*. The student's page includes:

- interactive tutor
- additional *BusinessWeek* articles and activities
- business Web links
- homework hints
- real-world application activities
- additional career path activities

Information on how to prepare your students for the high school exit exam and special projects are also included.

Use the Glencoe Web site for additional resources. All essential content is covered in the Student Edition.

1 FOCUS

Introducing the Chapter

This chapter explains real and personal property insurance. It describes the kinds of insurance and their costs. A photo essay, "Tidal Wave in an Apartment," enhances the concepts.

Connecting the Objectives

What is real property? What personal property do people insure? Why would you insure your home and personal property?

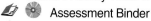

BusinessWeek
Feature Story

Story's Summary

If you currently own your own small business, you need to consider insuring against newer risks in the economy—risks in the global marketplace, risks to intellectual property, and risks of the Internet, such as viruses. As a business owner, though, don't forget the basics. Businesses need to insure against the basic losses, such as losses from fire, accidents, and theft.

Find the entire article at www.introbus.glencoe.com, or in the Teacher Resource Binder.

Property Insurance

Learning Objectives

After completing this chapter, you'll be able to:

1. **Describe** what kinds of property you can insure.
2. **Explain** the different types of property insurance.
3. **Name** the six kinds of homeowner's policies.
4. **Identify** the factors that affect the cost of property insurance premiums.

Why It's Important

Property insurance can protect you financially if your home is destroyed or your possessions are stolen.

Key Words

property insurance
real property
personal property
renter's insurance
standard fire policy
extended coverage
homeowner's policy
eleven perils
rider
replacement value

548

BusinessWeek Feature Story
Containing Your Risk

And You Thought Insurance Was Dull? Flood, fire, death, even clerical errors. Until now, Stefan E. Szyszko, president of United Planet in Novi, Mich., has had the right insurance to cover just about any disaster that could befall his nine-person direct-marketing firm. He's not an insurance junkie. Mostly, Szyszko was motivated by the experience of a friend whose business burned to the ground, but got back up and running again in just three weeks' time using proceeds from his coverage.

Source: Excerpted with permission from "Containing Your Risk," *BusinessWeek Online*, **April 27, 2000.**

An Extension Activity

Are you aware of any work-related lawsuits? How do businesses protect themselves against work-related injuries and illnesses? Research workers' compensation laws to find out about your rights as an employee. The law requires businesses to have workers' compensation.

BUSINESS
Online
The Full Story

To learn more about risks and insurance, visit the *Introduction to Business* Web site at www.introbus.glencoe.com, and click on *BusinessWeek* Feature Story, Chapter 34.

Classroom Resources

For the Teacher
- Student Activity Work. TAE
- Assessment Binder
- PowerPoint® Presentation
- Interactive Lesson Planner
- Lesson Plans
- Internet Resources
- Teaching Transparencies
- *Introduction to Business* Web Site
- Integrated Soft. Sim. TM
- *BusinessWeek* Poster Package

For the Student
- Student Activity Workbook
- *Virtual Business*®
- *Introduction to Business* Web Site
- Integrated Soft. Sim.
- *PuzzleMaker*
- Strategies and Worksheets for Teaching Transparencies

Chapter 34

🔔 Bell Ringer Activity

CREATIVE THINKING. Make an inventory of your personal possessions. Include everything you'd want to replace if your home was struck by a natural disaster. List the name of the item, the approximate cost when new, and the replacement cost. Use your list to decide whether or not you could benefit from some type of insurance. How about ten years from now? **LS**

Preteaching Business Key Words

SEEING THINGS IN THE MIND'S EYE. Have students study the list of key words and conjure up mental images of what they represent. Ask volunteers to describe an image they've created. Ask members of the class to match a key word with the description. **LS, CL**

An Extension Activity

PRESENT. After students research workers' compensation laws, ask them to give a short oral presentation about work-related lawsuits. **LS, CL**

Making Connections

Business Ethics. In an effort to control costs, some insurance companies refuse to offer homeowner's or renter's policies in some urban areas. This practice is called *redlining* and is illegal, however, redlining is often difficult to prove because the areas traditionally have a high percentage of crime and many of the individuals in the neighborhood are poor. Have students discuss what effects redlining has on a neighborhood, an insurance company's reputation, and on the stockholders of the insurance company.

2 TEACH

Business Connection

NATURAL DISASTERS. A catastrophe can hit at any time. The Atlantic hurricane season is June 1 to November 30, while the East Pacific tropical season is May 15 to November 30. Allstate Insurance Company declares a "claims catastrophe" when damage exceeds $1 million to customers' properties in a certain area. Insurance companies, such as Allstate Insurance, have national catastrophe teams ready to assist customers with claims in the case of a disaster.

Develop Concepts

TYPES OF INSURANCE. Renter's insurance is one of the most common types of real and personal property insurance. What are other types of property insurance? (Homeowner's, business insurance, standard fire policy, liability protection, and additional living expenses.)

Caption Answer

1. No. Insurance companies set up their policies based on actuarial decisions and may choose not to insure certain risk situations.
2. It needs to cover the cost of doing business. If the actuarial decision is to cover a higher risk, the company may adopt a policy to charge higher premiums only in the high-risk situations.

Insuring Your Valuable Property

Hurricane Floyd swept through 16 different states on the East Coast, from Maine to Florida, destroying homes and businesses, and causing billions of dollars in property damage. Each year property is destroyed due to earthquakes, fires, floods, and various other disasters. More property is lost or damaged due to lesser causes such as accidents, theft, and vandalism. Almost everyone at some point has his or her property damaged or stolen. You can protect yourself from financial loss on your property with **property insurance**.

Types of Property Insurance

The two kinds of property you can insure are real property and personal property. **Real property** is property attached to land, like a house, business, garage, or other building. **Personal property** consists of possessions that can be moved, like furniture, jewelry, and electronic equipment. Insurance companies offer different kinds of protection for real and personal property. The cost of insurance might seem high, but it's nothing compared to losing everything with no financial backing.

Renter's Insurance

When people first start out on their own, they usually rent an apartment rather than buy a house. Suppose you're living in an apartment and someone breaks in and steals your computer. Is there anything you can do about it? The owner of the building will probably have property

You Make the Call

Risky Business?

A man comes to your insurance agency asking for renter's insurance. After talking to him, you find out that he lives in a high-crime part of town where the number of burglaries is particularly high.

Making an Ethical Decision

1. Do insurance companies have an obligation to insure any potential client? If so, how might insuring high-risk clients affect their business? If not, how might the refusal to sell insurance affect individuals and neighborhoods?
2. Insurance companies can't "redline" clients in certain neighborhoods (i.e., refuse residents insurance simply because of their economic or ethnic backgrounds). On the other hand, they raise rates in high-risk areas. How would you balance these conflicting issues?

Cooperative Learning

Flooding. Indicate to students that financial losses due to flooding are not generally covered by homeowner's policies. Suggest that groups find out what kinds of government programs and insurance are available to people who live in areas that experience frequent flooding. Suggest that they present their findings in a three-minute "Consumer Watch" segment for the evening news. **LS**, **CL**, **P**

insurance, but it won't pay for loss or damage to a renter's personal property.

You might not realize that you can buy **renter's insurance** to cover any loss or damage to your personal possessions. Renter's insurance covers such items as televisions, large appliances, and furniture. It can also include liability protection in case someone is injured in your apartment. The cost of renter's insurance depends on the amount of coverage, the type of building, and the location. It's fairly inexpensive and offers you the same kinds of protection homeowners get.

Standard Fire Policy

Property owners can buy individual insurance policies to protect themselves against specific types of threats, such as floods or earthquakes. The greatest threat to property is fire. Fires account for 85 percent of all property damage in the United States. Whereas earthquakes and floods are rare natural disasters, a fire can start any time because of an electrical short, an overturned candle, or a towel left too close to a heater. For that reason, many people buy a **standard fire policy** to insure against damage due to fire or lightning.

A policyholder can add other types of protection to this basic policy. **Extended coverage** also protects against damage from riots, car or airplane crashes, windstorms, hail, and even explosions. Extended coverage also pays for damages if someone breaks into your house or vandalizes your property.

Liability Protection

What if someone slips on your kitchen floor and breaks an arm? Even if it wasn't your fault, you might be sued. Just as vehicle owners can buy liability insurance to cover injury to others, so can property owners. Liability insurance protects you from the costs of injuries to others on your property. It pays for two things. First, it pays for the actual damages for which you are held liable, such as medical expenses. Second, it pays legal expenses for the accident in case you're sued.

Additional Living Expenses

What if your house or apartment building burns down and you have to live somewhere else while it's being rebuilt? Vehicle insurance often pays for a rental car if you can't use your car while it's being repaired. Additional living expenses insurance provides similar coverage. It pays

Real-World Application
part 1 of 4

TIDAL WAVE IN AN APARTMENT
Tricia Musel heard one of her roommates scream her name followed by a "get down here, now." This stopped Musel writing mid sentence as she neared the end of her screenplay's first draft. Musel raced downstairs where she was stopped by an unusual sound. She put her ear to the wall: Water was rushing behind the wall, like a dishwasher.
An apartment is an example of real or personal property?

continued on p. 553

Chapter 34 Property Insurance   **551**

2 TEACH (Cont.)

Thinking Critically

SCENARIO. In 1993, the Kramer family bought a house for $100,000 and a homeowner's policy to cover that amount. Suppose that the value of the house went up by 15 percent a year. If the house was totally destroyed eight years later, what amount would the Kramers receive? Would it cover the loss? What could they have done? *(They would receive $100,000, which would not cover the loss. There is guaranteed replacement cost on some policies, too. Their house was increasing in value, so they should have increased the insured amount on their homeowner's policy.)*

Figure 34.1 Caption Answer

Flood, earthquake, war, nuclear accidents, and others specified in the homeowner's policy are not covered.

---

for the cost of renting another place to live if your home is damaged.

The amount of coverage might be limited to 10 or 20 percent of the coverage on your home. For example, if the coverage on your home is $150,000, additional living expenses insurance will cover only up to $15,000 or $30,000 of your costs while you live somewhere else. The

Figure 34.1

PERILS COVERED BY A HOMEOWNER'S POLICY

➡ This chart shows coverages provided by different forms of homeowner's insurance. HO-5, the comprehensive or all-risks policy, covers all but a few perils.
What perils are not covered?

COMPREHENSIVE

BROAD

BASIC

Perils
1. Fire or lightning
2. Loss of property removed from premises endangered by fire or other perils
3. Windstorm or hail
4. Explosion
5. Riot or civil commotion
6. Aircraft
7. Vehicles
8. Smoke
9. Vandalism and malicious mischief
10. Theft
11. Breakage of glass constituting part of a building

12. Falling objects
13. Weight of ice, snow, sleet
14. Collapse of building(s) or any part thereof
15. Sudden and accidental tearing asunder, cracking, burning, or bulging of a steam or hot water heating system or of appliances for heating water
16. Accidental discharge, leakage, or overflow of water or steam
from within a plumbing, heating, or air-conditioning system or domestic appliance
17. Freezing of plumbing, heating, and air-conditioning systems and domestic appliances
18. Sudden and accidental injury from artificially generated currents to electrical appliances, devices, fixtures, and wiring (TV and radio tubes not included)

All perils EXCEPT: flood, earthquake, war, nuclear accidents, and others specified in your policy. Check your policy for a complete listing of perils excluded.

552

LANGUAGE ARTS | *Curriculum Connection*

Communication. Have students read a typical homeowner's insurance policy. If possible, obtain copies of sample policies from a local insurance agent. As students read the policies, have them list the types of losses covered. What are the exceptions to the policy coverage? Have students write 150-word summaries of the main points in the policies. **LS**, **CL**, **P**

length of time you're covered might also be limited to six months or a year.

Business Insurance

Business owners need property insurance just like renters and homeowners. Suppose you own a café and a falling tree or vandals destroy your plate-glass window. A large store window can cost thousands of dollars to replace. If your business property isn't insured and you don't have the money to replace it, you could go out of business.

Business owners can get insurance to cover the costs of property. They can also get liability insurance to protect themselves from claims by anyone injured on the premises. It's especially important for business owners to carry insurance because of the potential loss of income if they have to close down for a while.

 Fast Review

1. What is the difference between real property and personal property?
2. What is the main cause of property damage?
3. What does additional living expenses insurance cover?

The Homeowner's Policy

Many insurance companies offer a combination policy with different kinds of home protection called a **homeowner's policy**. Homeowner's policies provide protection against loss from the eleven perils. The **eleven perils** are the most common causes of property damage or loss. They include fire, smoke, windstorms, vehicles, riots, theft, vandalism, and breaking glass. All homeowner's policies cover the eleven perils. Figure 34.1 illustrates the perils covered by a homeowner's policy.

There are six standard homeowner (HO) policies, or forms, for different kinds of risks:

- HO-1 Basic Form
- HO-2 Broad Form
- HO-3 Special Form
- HO-4 Renter's Form
- HO-5 Comprehensive Form, or All-Risks Policy
- HO-6 Condominium Owner's Form

Basic Coverage

HO-1, the basic form, is the least expensive policy, but provides less coverage than some of the other forms. This policy protects a home and

Chapter 34 Property Insurance **553**

TIDAL WAVE IN AN APARTMENT
Musel walked into her college roommate Jamie Caslavaka's bedroom. Caslavaka stood underneath the room's ceiling light with the kitchen trashcan catching the steady stream of water coming from the light. Suddenly, the water started gushing and pouring into the trashcan as it nearly topped off. Musel ran out of the room to the kitchen to get pots and pans. **What basic insurance provides coverage against the eleven perils?**

continued on p. 555

Real-World Application
Caption Answer

TIDAL WAVE IN AN APARTMENT: PART 2 OF 4
HO-1.

Fast Review Answers ✓

1. Real property is property attached to land, such as houses, garages, and other buildings. Personal property is possessions that can be moved, like furniture, jewelry, and electronic equipment.
2. Fire.
3. The cost of renting another place to live while your home is being rebuilt.

Business Connection

HOME-BASED BUSINESS. If you're going to be running a home-based business, don't assume that your homeowner's or renter's insurance policy will pay for losses relating to your business. The rapid growth of home-based businesses is prompting insurance companies to design and offer policies targeted for home-business owners. State Farm has designed its Business in the Home Program to give protection for business property, liability, records, or loss of income.

Great Ideas From the Classroom of...

Mary Valigura
Sandia High School
Albuquerque, N. Mex.

Fun Teaching Strategy. Have individual students teach unit segments to the class. Divide a unit into topics and let the team members create the instruction. Have them wear business attire on their presentation day and introduce themselves in a professional manner. Students in the class should evaluate their peers on eye contact, voice tone, and enthusiasm. Collect the students' evaluations and review them so they have immediate feedback on their presentation.

Develop Concepts

INSURANCE COSTS. As with all other insurance, the costs for renter's and homeowner's insurance depend on a variety of factors. What are some of the factors? (Answers will vary and may include the type of policy, amount of coverage, the deductible, the value of the property, discounts for preventive measures, location, and the type of building.)

Discussion Starter

REPLACEMENT VALUE. Give examples of what happens when you insure property for its replacement value.

Figure 34.2 Caption Answer

a. The value of the home is $117,000. Total coverage is $234,000—200 percent of the home's value.

b. The homeowner has $300,000 in liability protection.

c. The coverage costs $421 per year.

personal property against the eleven perils. It provides liability protection for the homeowner if someone is injured on the insured property. If you break a valuable item while visiting someone else's home, the policy might cover the cost. It also covers additional living expenses if you are temporarily displaced because of damage to your home.

Additional Coverage

HO-2, the broad form, adds more coverage to the HO-1. This policy also covers damage from falling objects, collapse of a building, ice and snow, steam, water, and electrical systems. It's the most popular homeowner's policy. (See Figure 34.2 as a snapshot of a homeowner's policy.)

The second most popular policy is HO-3. It provides maximum protection for the house itself, with less coverage for contents or personal property. The extra protection on the building is worth the extra cost to policyholders.

HO-4 is the policy for renters. It covers the personal property of the renter and includes additional living expenses coverage. The policyholder doesn't own the building, so it's not covered.

HO-5, the all-risks policy, provides the most comprehensive coverage. It insures a building and its contents with maximum coverage. Because it offers the most protection, it's also the most expensive.

HO-6 is a policy for condominium owners. It covers personal property and anything else inside the unit. The building itself is covered under a separate policy.

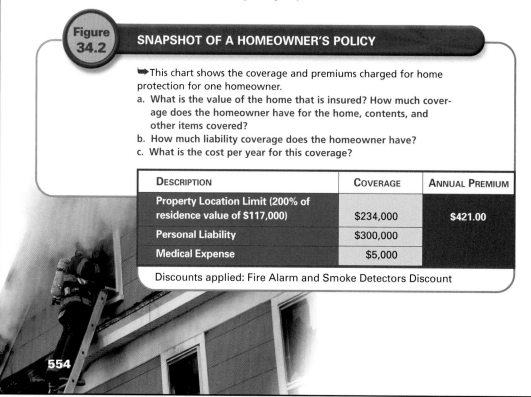

Figure 34.2 SNAPSHOT OF A HOMEOWNER'S POLICY

➡ This chart shows the coverage and premiums charged for home protection for one homeowner.

a. What is the value of the home that is insured? How much coverage does the homeowner have for the home, contents, and other items covered?

b. How much liability coverage does the homeowner have?

c. What is the cost per year for this coverage?

DESCRIPTION	COVERAGE	ANNUAL PREMIUM
Property Location Limit (200% of residence value of $117,000)	$234,000	$421.00
Personal Liability	$300,000	
Medical Expense	$5,000	

Discounts applied: Fire Alarm and Smoke Detectors Discount

554

Global Perspective

Increasing Costs of Global Warming. Global warming is pushing world weather to extremes—so climatologists believe. Sizzling summers, record snowfalls, devastating droughts, and torrential rains are in the long-range forecast. The official scorekeeper for global weather, the National Oceanic & Atmospheric Administration's National Climatic Data Center (NCDC), in Asheville, N.C., has records showing each year in the 1990s as being one of the top warmest of the twentieth century. An NCDC study reported an epidemic of storms from 1990 to 1996 causing property insurance losses in excess of $100 million.

Special Coverage

Most standard homeowner's policies cover special items for limited amounts. For example, a homeowner's policy might cover jewelry for up to $500. A homeowner can buy this extra coverage with a rider. A **rider** is an addition to a policy that covers specific property or damages. The extra cost is usually low. Riders are often used for antiques, art, or silver. Homeowners can also buy extra burglary and robbery protection. The premium depends on the crime rate in the area.

None of the homeowner's policies cover loss from floods, earthquakes, landslides, acts of war, or nuclear hazards. Homeowners, however, can also get riders to cover these conditions. Earthquake insurance is available, but it's more expensive where earthquakes occur often, such as California. The federal government offers low-cost flood insurance through the National Flood Insurance Program. If you live where floods are a problem, such as the Midwest, you might be able to buy flood insurance.

 Fast Review

1. What type of protection is covered by all homeowner's policies?
2. Which homeowner's policy provides the most coverage?

Buying a Policy

The type of policy you buy depends on your particular needs. Most homeowners get either the HO-2 or HO-3 form, but the HO-5 form is better if you can afford the extra cost. If you rent an apartment rather than own a house, the HO-4 renter's form is obviously better suited to your needs. Many people buy only the standard fire policy and add extended coverage. Before you buy insurance, it's important to know how much insurance you'll need and the costs of insurance.

Amount of Insurance

Insurance companies recommend that you insure your home for 80 percent of its market value. That's because even a large fire or flood doesn't destroy a building completely. The land and the building's foundation won't be destroyed and will hold their value. Real estate increases in value, so increase your coverage every few years. If the value of your home increases from $200,000 to $300,000 and you didn't increase your coverage, the insurance company will still only pay $160,000 if it's destroyed.

Chapter 34 Property Insurance **555**

Real-World Application

part 3 of 4

TIDAL WAVE IN AN APARTMENT
By the time Musel returned with pots and pans, Caslavaka stood by the bedroom door just staring at the ceiling's plaster starting to flake onto her bed. After a loud creaking sound, the entire ceiling fell in one large piece followed by a tidal wave bursting through. **What kind of insurance might cover any loss or damage of personal possessions?**

continued on p. 557

Real-World Application Caption Answer

TIDAL WAVE IN AN APARTMENT: PART 3 OF 4
Renter's insurance.

Fast Review Answers ✔

1. Protection against the eleven perils, including fire, smoke, windstorms, vehicles, riots, theft, vandalism, and breaking glass.
2. The HO-5 comprehensive form, or All-Risks Policy.

Individualized Practice

Write an outline indicating what you understand about the eleven perils and the six standard homeowner policies.

L1 Have students work in pairs to discuss their understanding of the questions.

L2 Ask students to work in pairs to trade questions and write answers to the other partner's questions.

L3 Group students to trade questions and write answers to one another's questions. Assign one of the six forms to each group. Ask the group to prepare a presentation to teach their classmates about the form.

LANGUAGE ARTS ***Curriculum Connection***

Decide. Property insurance rates are sometimes lower for those people who live near fire stations or who have homes built of brick or stone rather than wood or siding. Is this fair? Explain your answer. Write a 250-word report including examples from your own or your friends' experience. If necessary, research to find facts and examples to support your answer. **CL**, **LS**

Chapter 34

3 ASSESS

Reteaching

TYPES OF PROPERTY INSURANCE. To reteach the concept of types of property insurance, ask students to list at least five types of property insurance. (Renter's, standard fire policy, liability protection, additional living expenses, business insurance.)

Enrichment Strategies

CREATE A POSTER. In groups, list the important concepts from this chapter. Then use photos and graphics from magazines to create a poster illustrating these important concepts. **LS**

Evaluation

Assign and review the Fast Review sections.

Working Lifestyle

Caption Answer

Careers in information technology (IT), firefighting, the medical field, and electrical contracting are some examples of careers where workers might be required to be "on call." Ask students if they know someone who works this way and can tell how the person feels about being "on call." Ask students to consider whether they would like to live an "on call" lifestyle. **LS**

You can also insure property for either its actual cash value or its replacement value. The actual cash value is the value of the property new minus devaluation from use. For example, suppose you bought a new bike for $300 but it's depreciated in value by $100. If the bike is stolen, the insurance company will only pay you $200. The **replacement value**, on the other hand, is the full cost of repairing or replacing the property, regardless of the depreciation value. If your bike is stolen, the insurance company will pay you the full $300 you paid for it.

Working Lifestyle

What are you doing at 10 A.M.?

Creative Construction

Standing in what will eventually be the kitchen of a new home, Don Otto is surrounded by piles of lumber, an uninstalled dishwasher, half-a-dozen plumbing pipes, two carpenters, an electrician, and a lot of sawdust. It's only 10 A.M. and this general contractor discusses the next step with the skilled builders.

Otto's business, DPO Construction in Iowa City, Iowa, has one employee—him. He doesn't work solo, however, but directs the efforts of dozens of skilled builders, sometimes at several different job sites at once. He's involved in organizing and directing every aspect of building a house, from the design through construction.

"My job," he says, checking his watch, "is to keep things on schedule and know every detail about the house. I always try to make sure this is a team effort—and the customers are a vital part of that team."

He negotiates contracts, schedules production, maintains a dialogue with the owners and crewmembers, inspects the work, and monitors the project's progress. Sometimes he can be found standing on a ladder sealing duct joints or disappearing into an attic to check out the insulation.

A DPO-built house won the first five-star rating from the Energy Rated Homes of Iowa Program. Don's commitment to energy-efficient design and construction spurs him to attend conferences around the country where he learns about the latest products and developments in his field.

Salary

A typical construction manager earns $47,610. Half of the people in this occupation will earn between $36,360 and $70,910.

Outlook for This Career

Employment of construction managers will increase faster than the average occupation. The increasing complexity of construction projects will increase demand for positions at the managerial level.

Connecting Careers Activity

Construction managers must be "on call" 24 hours a day to deal with delays, bad weather, or emergencies at the site. What other careers might require someone to be "on call"?

CAREER PATH — Architecture & Construction

How to Use a Portfolio Activity

The portfolio projects are designed to lead students to develop a collection of their best work to submit to you for assessment. You and each of your students should decide which projects to include in their business portfolio. Refer students to the specific rubric(s) from the *Alternative Assessment Strategies*. These rubrics will alert students to the criteria you'll use to assess their projects. **P**

Costs of Insurance

Property insurance has many of the same costs vehicle insurance does. The number of claims insurance companies have to pay each year affects the overall cost of insurance. Your premium, or the amount you pay for your policy, depends on the amount of coverage and the type of policy you want. It'll cost you less for a standard fire policy than it'll for comprehensive homeowner's insurance. Replacement value coverage costs more than actual cash value coverage. The amount of your premium is also determined by specific factors.

Deductible. The deductible, as you'll recall from the last chapter, is the amount of money you pay out of your own pocket before the insurance company pays for any losses. If your deductible is $250 and damage to your property is $600, you pay $250 and the insurance company pays the other $350. The higher your deductible is, the lower your premium is since it costs the insurance company less to pay your claims.

Location. The location of a home affects the cost of your insurance. If you live in high-crime area or an area with no fire department, your premium will be higher. Insurance will cost you more if you live in an area with frequent brushfires or tornadoes. A fire hydrant near your property, on the other hand, can reduce the cost.

Type of Building. The type of home and building materials used also affect the cost of your insurance. A house made of brick will cost less to insure than a house made of wood. A house that's worth $500,000 will cost more to insure, of course, than a house that's worth $150,000. It might also cost more to insure a house that's 100 years old than a new house.

Preventive Measures. You can get discounts on your insurance rates by taking preventive measures to protect your property. For example, if you install deadbolts and burglar alarms to prevent theft, your insurance will be lower. Similarly, your rates will be lower if you have smoke detectors, fire extinguishers, or sprinklers in your home.

 Fast Review

1. Why does replacement value coverage cost more than actual cash value coverage?
2. What preventive measures might lower your insurance rates?

TIDAL WAVE IN AN APARTMENT

Firefighters came and turned off the building's sprinkling system, which was the culprit of the disaster. Then their landlord walked in and said, "I hope someone has renter's insurance." They didn't have renter's insurance. Instead they were left with sodden insulation and drywall covering furniture, clothes, computers, notebooks, and photo albums.
Why is it important to have renter's insurance?

Real-World Application
Caption Answer

TIDAL WAVE IN AN APARTMENT:
PART 4 OF 4
Protects the renter, much like the protection homeowners get.

Technology Resource

 PUZZLEMAKER CD-ROM. Check your students' understanding of the chapter's key terms by using the *Puzzlemaker* CD-ROM.

Fast Review Answers

1. With actual cash value coverage, the insurance company pays for how much an item is worth used (the value of the item new minus depreciation). With replacement value coverage, the insurance company pays for the current full cost of replacing an item, regardless of depreciation, so the premium is more.
2. Installing deadbolts, burglar alarms, smoke detectors, fire extinguishers, or sprinklers.

Meeting Individual Needs

Students With Visual Impairments.
Students with visual impairments often have difficulty seeing text or images on the screen when using a computer. First, be sure the student's eyes are the correct distance (18 to 26 inches) from the monitor. Increasing the size of the font (type size) may help. Another possibility is using the zoom feature to enlarge text and images. It may also be helpful to change the screen contrast and to customize color combinations, since some color combinations are more distinct than others. **LS**

4 CLOSE

Chapter Wrap-Up

To close, ask students to make a "Top 10" list of facts from this chapter that they feel are most useful to them.

Using Business Key Words

1. personal property
2. real property
3. rider
4. property insurance
5. standard fire policy
6. renter's insurance
7. replacement value
8. eleven perils
9. extended coverage
10. homeowner's policy

Review What You Learned

11. It covers damages to a renter's personal property. Some examples are televisions, large appliances, and furniture.
12. Extended coverage protects against damage from riots, aircraft or vehicles, windstorm and hail, and vandalism or mischief. If someone breaks into your house, extended coverage pays for any damage.
13. HO-1, Basic Form.
14. HO-5, All-Risk Policy.
15. The market value of a home includes the foundation and land. The land and foundation of a building are rarely damaged in a major disaster and will hold their value.

Summary

1. You can insure both real property (for example, a house, business, or other type of building) and personal property (for example, furniture, jewelry, and electronic equipment).

2. There are many different kinds of property insurance, including renter's insurance, standard fire policy, liability, additional living expenses, and business insurance.

3. There are six kinds of homeowner's policies for different needs: basic, broad, special, renter's, comprehensive, and condominium owner's. All of them include protection against the eleven perils, which are the most common causes of property damage or loss.

4. The cost of property insurance premiums is affected by the type of policy, amount of coverage, deductible, location, type of building, and preventive measures you might take.

● Using Business Key Words

Insuring your property, both real and personal, is necessary to protect your investments. Complete the following sentences with these terms to see how well you understand these property insurance concepts.

- **real property**
- **personal property**
- **rider**
- **standard fire policy**
- **property insurance**
- **renter's insurance**
- **extended coverage**
- **homeowner's policy**
- **eleven perils**
- **replacement value**

1. Some examples of _____ are furniture, jewelry, and electronic equipment.
2. Some examples of _____ are houses, barns, garages, and other buildings.

3. A(n) _____ is an addition to a policy that covers specific property.
4. Protection from financial loss on property due to damage or theft is called _____.
5. If smoke and heat from an explosion damages your property, a(n) _____ covers the loss.
6. It's important to obtain _____ when you first move into an apartment.
7. If your insurance company fully pays for the cost of your stolen bike, it's paid you the _____ of the bike.
8. A homeowner's policy provides protection against such things as fire, smoke, windstorms, and riots, or otherwise known as the _____.
9. Insurance coverage added to a standard fire policy that protects against other types of property damage is _____ coverage.
10. A(n) _____ is a combination policy offering different kinds of home protection designed for homeowners.

Quick Quiz

1. Name four types of property insurance. (Renter's, homeowner's, standard fire policy, liability protection, additional living expenses, or business insurance.)
2. What is a rider? (An additional policy that covers specific property or damages.)

3. What preventive measures can you take to get discounts on your property insurance? (Answers may include install a burglar alarm, deadbolt locks, smoke detectors, or fire extinguishers.)

Review What You Learned

11. What does renter's insurance cover?

12. What does extended coverage insurance cover?

13. Name the least expensive form of homeowner's insurance.

14. Which homeowner's policy provides the most comprehensive coverage?

15. Why is insurance for 80 percent of the market value of a home usually enough?

Understanding Business Concepts

16. When you buy a home, why do you think the bank or mortgage company will insist you buy insurance on it?

17. Renter's insurance covers any loss or damage to your personal possessions. Explain how renter's insurance is different from homeowner's insurance.

18. Give an example of an accident that could happen around your house.

19. There are numerous types of coverages in a homeowner's policy: basic, broad, and comprehensive. Each coverage provides more and different coverage than the next step. What type of homeowner's policy would cover damage caused by ice and snow?

20. Why do you think you have to buy a special insurance policy for flood, earthquake, and landslide protection?

21. What is wrong with carrying too much insurance on your home?

22. In Chapter 33 you learned about vehicle insurance. Remember that insurance is paid protection against losses due to injury or property damage. To get insurance, you have to purchase a policy from an insurance company. What is the main point of insurance?

Critical Thinking

23. Property insurance rates are sometimes lower for people who live near fire stations or who have homes built out of brick or stone rather than wood. Is this fair? Explain your answer.

24. Why do you think an insurance company would not want to insure every home in the same neighborhood?

25. Do you think it's a good idea for renters and homeowners to review their insurance coverage every two years? Why or why not?

26. Describe the steps you would take to research property insurance before you purchase a policy.

Viewing and Representing

Examining the Image. Write down your impressions of this picture in your journal. How would you feel if you lived there? What are the eleven perils covered by property insurance? Do you know of someone who suffered property loss? Was the property covered by insurance? Write about the experience.

Chapter 34 Property Insurance **559**

Critical Thinking

23. Answers will vary. Students need to explain their answer.

24. Answers will vary. Students need to explain their answer.

25. Answers will vary and should include an explanation.

26. Steps will vary, but may include preparing a personal inventory, calling insurance companies, asking friends and family, and researching on the Internet.

Viewing and Representing

This image is used as a springboard to give students practice in critical thinking and experiential writing. Experiential writing, because it's written from first-hand experience, gives students the opportunity to convey emotion and have impact. Students should try to include the smallest details as they can make the biggest impact. HO-1, the basic policy, covers the structure of your home and your personal belongings from eleven kinds of perils, such as: theft, fire or lightning, smoke, explosion, hailstorm or wind, aircraft accidents, civil commotion or catastrophe, vehicles, acts of malicious mischief, damage by glass, and volcanoes. **LS**

Understanding Business Concepts

16. Bank or mortgage company has a vested interest in your home since they hold the note.

17. Renter's insurance covers only personal property, while homeowner's insurance protects the home and personal property.

18. Answers will vary.

19. HO-2, Broad Form.

20. Floods, earthquakes, and landslides usually cause more damage than the other 11 perils. Insurance companies charge more to cover damages caused by them.

21. Answers may vary but students should show they understand that the more insurance carried, the higher the cost.

22. To protect against major losses.

4 CLOSE (Cont.)

Building Academic Skills

MATH. Allow each student to choose the method they wish to share their results. Rubrics: Charts/tables, note taking, posters.

LANGUAGE ARTS. Encourage all students in the group to participate. Students could use the computer to make their posters. Rubric: Posters.

HISTORY. The library and the Internet are good sources of information. Rubric: Oral presentation.

COMPUTER/TECHNOLOGY. Rubric: Spreadsheet.

Linking School to Home

Answers will vary. Allow the students to choose the method they wish to use to share their findings. Rubrics: Table/chart, note taking, essay, poster, oral presentation.

Linking School to Work

Answers will vary. Rubrics: Note taking, oral presentation.

Building Academic Skills

 Estimating Replacement Cost

Imagine you were going to buy insurance on the contents in your room. Take an inventory of the items in your room and estimate the total cost to replace each item. Then figure a total replacement cost.

 Promoting Fire Safety

In groups of three or four, create a poster to promote fire safety. The poster should include information about how to protect your home from fire and smoke damage. Display the posters in your school or take them to a local elementary or middle school and display them there.

 Delving Into the Past

Research the historical development of the insurance industry. Find out about bottomry contracts, early commercial and maritime insurance, and fire insurance. Present your findings orally to the class.

 Compiling Information

Before making a decision about insurance policies, it's important to research and compile data. This will help you make an informed decision. Compile and print out a spreadsheet related to the various kinds of property insurance, coverages, and premiums.

Linking School to Home

Inquiring About Insurance. You may take shelter for granted if it's something you've always had. Imagine that your home is damaged and uninhabitable. What will happen to you and your family's belongings? How are you protected against loss or damage? Interview your parents or other family members about the various types of property insurance coverage they carry. Ask them what factors affected their purchasing decisions.

Linking School to Work

Contacting an Agent. The time has come and you've officially entered into adulthood: You're renting an apartment and you're financially independent. It's your responsibility to call around on insurance rates for your new apartment. Using the amount you figured your personal property was worth in the math activity above, contact an insurance agent and find out the cost of renter's insurance.

E-Homework

Applying Technology

Focusing Your Search. Use the Internet to research one insurance trade association. Write a one-page paper explaining the association's mission, how and when it was founded, and the key issues upon which it focuses.

Obtaining a Quote. Imagine that you have approximately $10,000 in property you wish to insure. Using the Internet, obtain a quote for renter's insurance. In addition, evaluate the Web site for ease of use. Share your findings with other classmates.

Connecting Academics

Math. As you learned earlier, there are numerous factors that influence the cost of insurance. Location and type of building are two examples that influence costs. Find out the cost of renter's insurance offered by insurance companies in your area. Get at least five estimates. Draw a bar graph of your findings. Include an analysis of why some insurance companies might vary in prices when your personal property value remains constant.

Social Science. Keeping current, easily-accessible records of your possessions' values and our insurance coverage is essential. Ask family members what record-keeping methods they use. Write two paragraphs outlining your findings and your plan for keeping insurance information.

BusinessWeek — Analyzing the Feature Story

You read the first part of "Containing Your Risk" at the beginning of this chapter. Below are a few questions for you to answer about risks and insurance. You'll find the answers to these questions when you're reading the entire article. First, here are the questions:

27. What is the range of costs for an insurance policy to protect a business online?
28. What are some of the new risks in the global New Economy?

CREATIVE JOURNAL ACTIVITY

It's summertime and you'd like to barbeque with your friends. Your parents' old grill doesn't work anymore so you go shopping for a new one. The local store has a gas grill that bears the mark of an independent testing laboratory. This is reputable, so you buy it and take it home. What are the risks of having a gas grill near your home? Can you think of any preventative measures you should take to insure a safe grilling experience?

BUSINESS Online
The Full Story
To learn more about risks and insurance, visit the *Introduction to Business* Web site at **www.introbus.glencoe.com**, and click on *BusinessWeek* Feature Story, Chapter 34.

561

E-Homework

FOCUSING YOUR SEARCH. Research will vary depending on the association selected. Rubric: Essay.

OBTAINING A QUOTE. If students are having trouble with this activity, allow them to work together. Allow the students to choose the method they wish to use to share their findings. Rubrics: Table/chart, note taking, essay, poster, oral presentation.

Connecting Academics

MATH. Bar graphs will vary. Lead a class discussion to compare the bar graphs and discuss the main points illustrated by the bar graphs.

SOCIAL SCIENCE. Findings and plans will vary. Ask volunteers to share their findings and their plans.

BusinessWeek — *Analyzing the Feature Story*

27. $10,000 to $150,000 a year.
28. Someone may steal a company's intellectual property. If a small business branches out overseas, the policy may need to cover a business that is sued in another country. Or, a worker may get injured while working abroad.

Creative Journal Activity

Chose a gas grill with a testing laboratory mark of approval. The National Fire Protection Association (NFPA) advises to keep grills away from dry vegetation, cars, and your home, and store the gas cylinders outside away from structures.

SCANS Correlation Chart*

Foundation Skills

Basic Skills	Reading	Writing	Math	Listening	Speaking	
Thinking Skills	Creative Thinking	Decision Making	Problem Solving	Seeing Things in the Mind's Eye	Knowing How to Learn	Reasoning
Personal Qualities	Responsibility	Self-Esteem	Sociability	Self-Management	Integrity/ Honesty	

Workplace Competencies

Resources	Allocating Time	Allocating Money	Allocating Material and Facility Resources	Allocating Human Resources		
Information	Acquiring and Evaluating Information	Organizing and Maintaining Information	Interpreting and Communicating Information	Using Computers to Process Information		
Interpersonal Skills	Participating as a Member of a Team	Teaching Others	Serving Clients/ Customers	Exercising Leadership	Negotiating to Arrive at a Decision	Working With Cultural Diversity
Systems	Understanding Systems	Monitoring and Correcting Performance	Improving and Designing Systems			
Technology	Selecting Technology	Applying Technology to Task	Maintaining and Troubleshooting Technology			

*This chart's highlighted blocks indicate the chapter's content coverage in the Student Edition and the Teacher Wraparound Edition.

Resource Manager

Teaching Transparencies

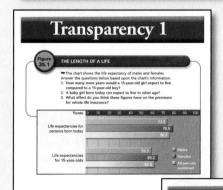

Transparency 1

Figure 35.1 · THE LENGTH OF A LIFE

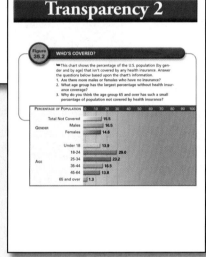

Transparency 2

Figure 35.2 · WHO'S COVERED?

Application and Enrichment

- Lesson Plans
- *BusinessWeek* Poster Package
- Teaching Transparencies
- Integrated Software Simulation
- Glencoe Business Video Package

Review and Reinforcement

- *PuzzleMaker*
- Internet Resources
- Student Activity Workbook
- Strat. and Work. for Teaching Transparencies

Assessment and Evaluation

- Reproducible Tests
- Alternative Assessment Strategies
- ExamView® Pro Test Generator

Technology

- *PuzzleMaker*
- ExamView® Pro Test Generator
- Glencoe Business Video Package
- PowerPoint® Presentation
- Integrated Software Simulation
- Interactive Lesson Planner
- *Virtual Business*®

KEY	
Printed	Software — Videocassette — Poster
Transparency	CD-ROM — Internet

BUSINESS Online

Visit www.introbus.glencoe.com, the Web site companion to *Introduction to Business*. The student's page includes:

- interactive tutor
- additional *BusinessWeek* articles and activities
- business Web links
- homework hints
- real-world application activities
- additional career path activities

Information on how to prepare your students for the high school exit exam and special projects are also included.

Use the Glencoe Web site for additional resources. All essential content is covered in the Student Edition.

1 FOCUS

Introducing the Chapter

This chapter describes the types of life and health insurance, and their costs. A photo essay, "Inside the ER," enhances the concepts.

Connecting the Objectives

Why do you need health insurance? What different types are there? Members of your family probably have life insurance. Why?

BusinessWeek
Feature Story

Story's Summary

If you're self-employed, or if your place of work doesn't cover health insurance, you need to find coverage yourself. Shopping for insurance takes effort, but it's worth it. You can make sure you cover your needs and get the best deal not only by going online, but also by talking with friends, looking at magazines, and contacting associations.

Find the entire article at www.introbus.glencoe.com, or in the Teacher Resource Binder.

Life and Health Insurance

● Learning Objectives

After completing this chapter, you'll be able to:
1. **Define** cash-value and term insurance.
2. **Identify** the factors that affect the cost of life insurance.
3. **Describe** the types of health insurance.
4. **Name** the types of health insurance plans.

● Why It's Important

Life insurance and health insurance protect you and your loved ones financially.

● Key Words

proceeds
beneficiary
cash-value insurance
term insurance
coinsurance
health maintenance
    organization (HMO)
Medicare
Medicaid
copayment
pre-existing condition

562

BusinessWeek Feature Story

Staying Insured When You're on Your Own

How to Sort Out Health-Care Options for the Self-Employed. Obtaining health insurance if you're leaving the corporate fold or already on your own can be a grueling endeavor. Ask Ruth Sheridan, a freelance business writer from New York. When she wanted a change from her health maintenance organization recently, Sheridan turned herself into a one-woman search engine. She scoured the yellow pages, read articles, and grilled friends to find insurance companies with plans for the self-employed.

Source: Excerpted with permission from "Staying Insured When You're on Your Own," *BusinessWeek Online*, September 6, 1999.

An Extension Activity

Think of a situation when you had to shop wisely for a service or product. What was your process? How did you find out where to shop? Share your process with the class.

BUSINESS *Online*
The Full Story

To learn more about health and life insurance, visit the *Introduction to Business* Web site at www.introbus.glencoe.com, and click on *BusinessWeek* Feature Story, Chapter 35.

Classroom Resources

For the Teacher
- 📁 Student Activity Work. TAE
- 💿 Assessment Binder
- 💿 PowerPoint® Presentation
- 💿 Interactive Lesson Planner
- 📁 Lesson Plans
- 💻 Internet Resources
- 🕹 Teaching Transparencies
- 💻 *Introduction to Business* Web Site

- 💿 Integrated Soft. Sim. TM
- 🖼 *BusinessWeek* Poster Package

For the Student
- 💿 Student Activity Workbook
- 💿 *Virtual Business*®
- 💻 *Introduction to Business* Web Site
- 💿 Integrated Soft. Sim.
- 💿 *PuzzleMaker*
- 💿 Strategies and Worksheets for Teaching Transparencies

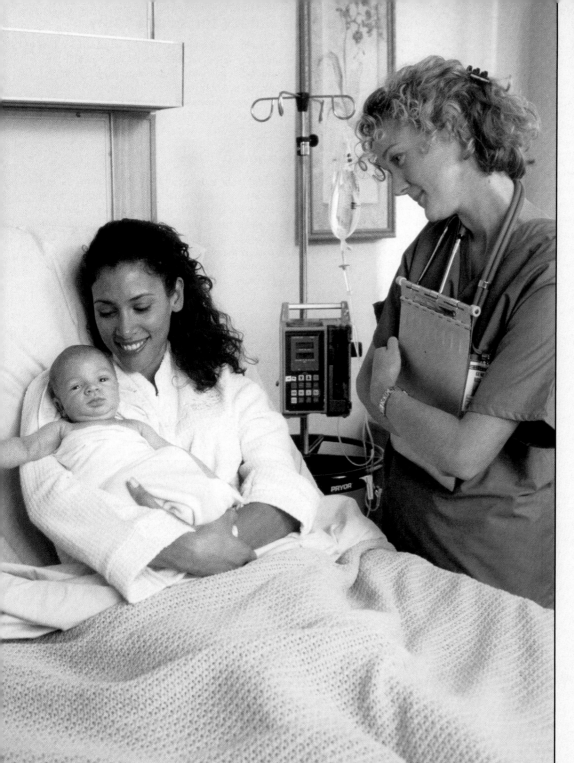

🔔 Bell Ringer Activity

KNOWING HOW TO LEARN. Drawing sketches, diagrams, and charts helps you to learn. To get ready to make learning easy in this chapter, make two charts: (1) "Life Insurance," with the headings "Cash-Value Insurance," "Term Insurance," and "Costs" and (2) "Health Insurance," with headings corresponding to the six headings in the chapter. Add a heading for "Costs of Health Insurance."

Preteaching Business Key Words

SELF-ESTEEM. Part of self-esteem is being confident in your own abilities. You can be more confident about your ability to learn this chapter when you prepare by recording the meaning of the key words. List the definitions in your journal. **LS, P**

An Extension Activity

PRESENT. After students have done their research, have them give a short oral presentation explaining their findings. **CL, LS**

Making Connections

Small Business. Japan's health care system balances universal coverage at reasonable cost. The government acts as insurer and subsidizes health care spending for the employees of small enterprises and the self-employed. Have students investigate what kinds of health care regulations or assistance the U.S. government provides to small enterprises, employees of small enterprises, and self-employed individuals.

2 TEACH

Business Connection

Life insurers predict losses through a table that lists how long people usually live. It's called a mortality table. The astronomer Edmund Halley (of Halley's Comet fame) made up a table based on statistical laws of mortality in 1693. In 1756, Joseph Dodson corrected this table to allow for a person's age. Insurance companies continue to update mortality tables as the life expectancy of the population changes.

Develop Concepts

COST. What factors do you think affect the cost of life insurance? (Answers will vary and should include the amount of coverage, the type of policy, age, health, and occupation.)

Figure 35.1 — Caption Answer

1. Fifteen-year-old males can expect to live 59.7 years. Females, 65.2 years.
2. To the age of 79.5.
3. Females will live longer, on average, so they will pay premiums longer. Their premium payments may be slightly less than for males.

Ensuring Safety for Your Family

What would happen to a family if one of the wage earners dies? How will the survivors support themselves? What would happen if the wage earner was seriously injured and couldn't work for months? You might not think you need life or health insurance, but you might if there are people financially dependent on you or you have a dangerous job.

Life Insurance

Life insurance protects the standard of living of the survivors. Figure 35.1 is a chart on life expectancy to illustrate how life insurance premiums are affected by life spans. At the policyholder's death, the insurance company pays survivors the face value of a life insurance policy. The money paid to the survivors is called the **proceeds**. Each person who receives part of the proceeds is a called a **beneficiary**. The person who buys the policy names the beneficiaries. There are several types of life insurance to fit different needs.

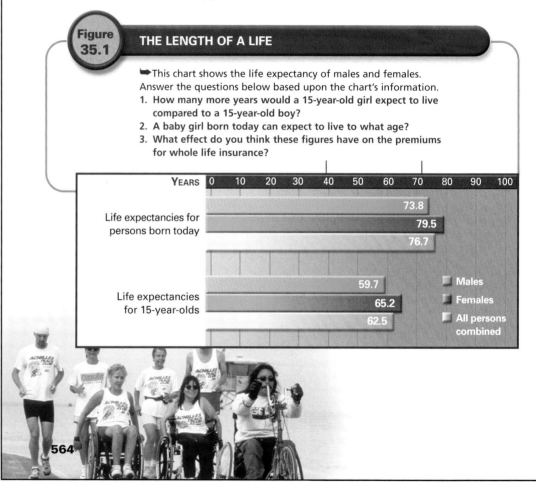

Figure 35.1 — THE LENGTH OF A LIFE

➡ This chart shows the life expectancy of males and females. Answer the questions below based upon the chart's information.

1. How many more years would a 15-year-old girl expect to live compared to a 15-year-old boy?
2. A baby girl born today can expect to live to what age?
3. What effect do you think these figures have on the premiums for whole life insurance?

YEARS: 0 10 20 30 40 50 60 70 80 90 100

Life expectancies for persons born today:
- 73.8
- 79.5
- 76.7

Life expectancies for 15-year-olds:
- 59.7
- 65.2
- 62.5

Legend:
- Males
- Females
- All persons combined

564

Cooperative Learning

Ten Questions. Ask students to work in groups of four to develop a ten-question quiz for the "Life Insurance" section. Direct them to include questions on proceeds, beneficiary, cash-value, whole life, limited-payment life, variable life, endowment, term insurance, and costs of life insurance. **CL**, **LS**

Cash-Value Insurance

Cash-value insurance provides both savings and death benefits. Part of the premium pays for death benefits. The rest builds up cash value like a savings account. The cash value increases throughout the life of the policy. If you cancel the policy, you can collect the amount of the cash value. In an emergency, you can borrow part or all of the cash value, but you have to pay interest on it just as you would on any loan. Policyholders can buy different forms of cash-value insurance.

Whole Life Insurance. With whole life insurance, a policyholder pays a premium that stays the same throughout his or her lifetime. The policy stays the same until the insured dies as long as the premiums are paid. Whole life insurance provides savings during the policyholder's life and pays benefits at death.

Limited-Payment Life Insurance. The policyholder pays premiums for a certain number of years for limited-payment life insurance. For example, if you have a 20-payment life policy, you pay premiums for 20 years. Then your policy is considered paid up and you don't have to pay any more premiums. One popular type of limited-payment life insurance is "paid up at age 65." Since many people retire at age 65, they won't have to pay premiums after their paychecks stop.

Variable Life Insurance. With variable life insurance, the cash value part of the premium is invested in things like stocks, bonds, and mutual funds rather than in savings. Like other types of cash-value insurance, the rest of the premium is used for guaranteed death benefits. The cash value is variable because it can increase or decrease in value depending on how the investments do. For example, if part of the premium is used to invest in stocks and the stocks double in value, the cash value will be worth double.

Endowment Insurance. Endowment insurance is a special type of cash-value insurance. An endowment policy is based more on savings than on death benefits. It provides coverage for a specific period of time, usually 20 to 30 years. The proceeds go to the policyholder if he or she is still alive at the end of that period. If the policyholder dies during the endowment period, the beneficiary receives the proceeds. Policyholders often use endowment insurance to provide retirement income or an education fund. To provide funds for college, parents might buy an 18-year, $15,000 endowment policy when a child is born.

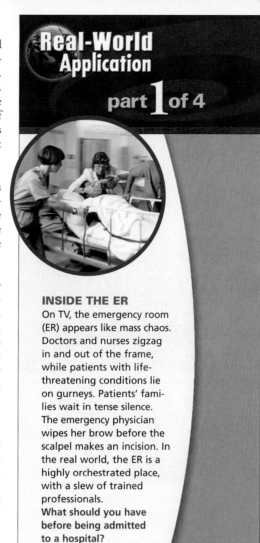

INSIDE THE ER
On TV, the emergency room (ER) appears like mass chaos. Doctors and nurses zigzag in and out of the frame, while patients with life-threatening conditions lie on gurneys. Patients' families wait in tense silence. The emergency physician wipes her brow before the scalpel makes an incision. In the real world, the ER is a highly orchestrated place, with a slew of trained professionals.
What should you have before being admitted to a hospital?

continued on p. 567

2 TEACH (Cont.)

Thinking Critically

LONG-TERM VIEW. Many people use life insurance as a form of long-term investment. The cash value of a life insurance policy increases over time and earns interest. That means that in addition to providing insurance the policy can provide savings. Do you think you would use life insurance to save? Why or why not? (Answers will vary.)

Working Lifestyle

Caption Answer

An example of formal training would be for an attorney, who must complete a four-year college degree, then a three-year law degree, and then pass the bar examination, before he or she can practice law.

Term Insurance

Term insurance covers a person for a specific period of time. The length of the term might be 5, 10, or 20 years. It pays benefits only if the insured dies during the term of the policy. If the insured person lives beyond the term of the policy, the policy has no value. It can be renewed, but usually with a higher premium. Term insurance is sometimes called "pure protection," since it's used only to pay death benefits and doesn't build cash value. The major advantage of term insurance is its low cost.

How does term insurance work? If Gabriel buys a five-year, $10,000 policy, it covers him for five years. If he dies during that five years, his beneficiary will receive $10,000. After five years, his coverage ends. Gabriel can then renew the policy. As he gets older, however, his premium will increase.

Policyholders often have term insurance as a part of group life insurance. An employer or organization might provide term insurance to

Working Lifestyle

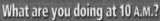

What are you doing at 10 A.M.?

Settling Medical Disputes

Helen Walthier is sitting in the Pima County Courthouse, reading papers she has prepared for a medical malpractice case. Roberts and one of the senior attorneys in her law firm will try to convince a judge to dismiss the case against one of their clients, a local pediatrician.

This Tucson, Ariz., attorney enjoys handling very complex cases.

"In Arizona, a medical malpractice plaintiff must prove two things," Walthier says. "First, a plaintiff must prove that the health care professional did not meet Arizona's standard of reasonable medical care. Next, they must prove that this failure caused damage to the plaintiff." Walthier's clients

can be doctors, nurses, physician's assistants, physical therapists, or hospitals.

"Good legal practice involves adopting the best strategy to help your client," Walthier says. She gathers up her papers, puts them in her leather briefcase, and walks into the courtroom for the 10:00 A.M. hearing.

Salary

A typical lawyer of earns $78,170. Half of the people in this job earn between $51,450 and $114,520.

Outlook for This Career

Employment will grow at roughly the same rate as the average for all occupations. Opportunities in health care law, intellectual property, elder law, sexual harassment issues, and environmental law look promising.

Connecting Careers Activity

Most careers require formal training. Discover the formal training requirements you'll need as you pursue your career. Share your findings with your family.

CAREER PATH Law & Public Safety

LANGUAGE ARTS — *Curriculum Connection*

Communication. Have students survey adult family members and friends to determine if they have health insurance through their employer and whether it is traditional insurance, an HMO, a PPO, or other. Encourage students to ask respondents if they are satisfied with their coverage. Suggest that students pool their results and make graphs or charts to display their findings.

employees or members. One master insurance policy covers everyone in the group. When a member of the group leaves, the coverage ends for that person. For example, if you work for a company that provides term insurance as a benefit, you lose that coverage if you leave the company.

Workers or their companies usually pay less for a group policy than for individual policies. If the company provides coverage as a benefit, the employee often pays nothing for the coverage. The employer pays the entire cost of the insurance.

Costs of Life Insurance

As with any type of insurance, the amount of the premium on a life insurance policy depends on the type of policy and the amount of coverage. Term insurance costs less than cash-value insurance. A policy for $100,000 costs more than a policy for $50,000.

Like other forms of insurance, there are specific factors that also affect the cost of the premium on life insurance, such as age, health, and occupation. Many people have to take a physical before they're sold an insurance policy to ensure they're in good health. The older a person is, the higher the premium will be because of the likelihood the company will have to pay benefits sooner. Life insurance also costs more for people in dangerous occupations, such as a high-rise construction worker or a stunt pilot.

 Fast Review

1. How is variable life insurance different from other types of cash-value insurance?
2. Why is term insurance sometimes called "pure protection?"
3. What are three of the specific factors that affect the cost of a life insurance premium?

Health Insurance

Many people are concerned about their families if they should die, and they also worry about what happens if they become sick or disabled. Health care for a serious illness or accident is very expensive. Few people have enough savings to pay for medical costs on their own. In fact, medical expenses can be financially disastrous. The average cost of a stay in the hospital is $5,000 *per day*. Health insurance provides protection against the costs of illness and accidents. Figure 35.2 shows the percentage of the U.S. population that isn't covered by any health insurance.

Real-World Application
part **2** of 4

INSIDE THE ER
How many of you can afford to spend $5,000 per day? Probably not many of you, but that's how much it costs on average to stay in the hospital. Depending on the severity of your health problem when you check into the ER, a nurse will categorize your condition: life threatening, urgent but not life threatening, or less urgent. The nurse monitoring your vital signs determines your category.
Why is it important to know about your medical history?

continued on p. 569

Real-World Application
Caption Answer

INSIDE THE ER: PART 2 OF 4

Allows nurse to know if you're allergic to medications, have past medical problems, and if you've filed medical complaints in order for the nurse to properly categorize you.

Fast Review Answers ✓

1. The cash value part of the premium is invested in things like stocks, bonds, and mutual funds rather than in savings.
2. It's used only to pay death benefits and doesn't build cash value.
3. Occupation, age, and health.

Great Ideas From the Classroom of...

John J. Trujillo
& Loreli LaFortune, Ph.D
Deer Creek Middle School
Littleton, Col.

Classroom Cohesion. Develop student personality profiles in order to create a comfortable classroom atmosphere. Have students fill out a personal biography sheet in class. Compile the students' answers to create a fill-in-the-blank question sheet. The next day students seek out their classmates in order to fill in the blanks by walking around the room and asking one another different questions. As you proceed through the course, allow the class to monitor their roles.

Business Connection

COMPANY PLAN. Deere and Co., the manufacturer of farm machinery, created its own health maintenance organization. It is popular with employees and has cut the company's health insurance costs. The health plan is growing, with members in Virginia, Illinois, Tennessee, and Iowa. The National Committee for Quality Assurance (NCQA) awarded John Deere Health Plan, Inc., an "Excellent" accreditation status.

Develop Concepts

CONTRAST. How do your health care needs differ from those of a couple in their thirties with two young children?

Discussion Starter

COMPARE. Why do group health insurance policies often offer more benefits for less money than do individual policies?

Figure 35.2 Caption Answer

1. More males than females are lacking health insurance coverage.
2. The age group of 18–24 has the largest percentage without health insurance coverage.
3. Many people age 65 and over have Medicare and Medicaid health insurance coverage.

Major Medical Insurance

Major medical insurance, sometimes called catastrophe insurance, is the most important coverage for a serious illness or accident. Major medical pays for most kinds of care in and out of the hospital. It covers hospital care, doctors' bills, tests and x-rays, and nursing care. Most policies have a deductible, or an amount the policyholder must pay, of several hundred dollars.

With some plans, you also have to pay coinsurance. **Coinsurance** is a percentage of medical expenses a policyholder must pay beyond the deductible. Major medical insurance is intended to cover the health costs not covered by other types of insurance. The insurance company usually pays 75 or 80 percent of the costs and the policyholder pays the other 20 or 25 percent. For example, suppose your insurance has a $1,000 deductible and a coinsurance payment of 20 percent. If you're hospitalized and your medical bills come to $6,000, you have to pay $2,000 ($1,000 deductible plus 20 percent of $5,000).

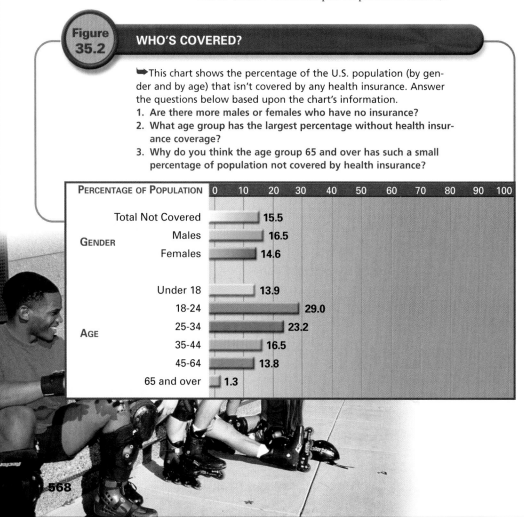

Figure 35.2 WHO'S COVERED?

➡ This chart shows the percentage of the U.S. population (by gender and by age) that isn't covered by any health insurance. Answer the questions below based upon the chart's information.
1. Are there more males or females who have no insurance?
2. What age group has the largest percentage without health insurance coverage?
3. Why do you think the age group 65 and over has such a small percentage of population not covered by health insurance?

PERCENTAGE OF POPULATION

Total Not Covered	15.5
GENDER Males	16.5
Females	14.6
AGE Under 18	13.9
18-24	29.0
25-34	23.2
35-44	16.5
45-64	13.8
65 and over	1.3

568

Global Perspective

AFLAC. Headquartered in Georgia, AFLAC (the American Family Life Assurance Company) is the largest supplemental health insurance company in the world. The company receives 79 percent of its revenues from Japan. The company entered the Japanese market offering only cancer insurance policies. Ask students to research how AFLAC approached the Japanese market. Encourage students to discuss the difference between the Japanese and U.S. insurance markets. **CL**

Hospital Expense Insurance

Hospital expense insurance pays for hospital care for a given period of time. It covers room and board, tests and x-rays, operating room costs, nursing care, and fees for drugs and treatments. Like major medical insurance, it might have a deductible. Some policies set a limit for each specific expense. Others set a maximum amount per day for up to a maximum number of days. Hospital expense is the most popular type of health insurance because hospitalization is so expensive.

Surgical Expense Insurance

Surgical expense insurance pays part of a surgeon's entire fee for an operation. Most policies set a maximum payment for a particular surgical expense. A policy lists the surgical procedures and the costs allowed. In many cases, major medical picks up where this coverage ends. Surgical expense insurance is usually bought with hospital expense insurance. The higher the maximums for each operation, the higher the premium for surgical expense insurance.

Medical Expense Insurance

Medical expense insurance covers the costs of a doctor's care *not* involving surgery. It might cover visits to a doctor's office or a doctor's calls at the hospital. This insurance is usually bought with hospital and surgical expense insurance. An insurance company might combine all three types of insurance into a basic health coverage plan.

Group Health Insurance

A group health insurance plan is the least expensive form of health insurance for most people. A company or organization usually provides group insurance for its employees or members. The company pays for part or all of the cost of the plan and employees can add extra coverage at their own expense.

Most private insurance companies offer group health insurance plans. Under these plans, you choose where and to whom you want to go for health care. A **health maintenance organization (HMO)** provides health care at its own health center for a fixed fee per month.

What's the difference between regular group insurance and an HMO plan? With an HMO, you must go to its own clinic. You must choose a doctor from its network. HMO plans stress preventive health care to keep medical costs down.

Chapter 35 Life and Health Insurance **569**

Real-World Application
part 3 of 4

INSIDE THE ER

The nurse asks to see your insurance information once you're categorized. This might be your Medicare, Medicaid, or your HMO card. This lets you and the hospital know how much you pay versus how much the insurance company pays for tests or procedures. Most health insurance plans have a deductible. **What is a deductible?**

continued on p. 571

Real-World Application
Caption Answer

INSIDE THE ER:
PART 3 OF 4

The amount the policyholder must pay. Sometimes the health insurance plan covers the deductible.

Individualized Practice

Have groups of four students find two articles about managed health care. Tell students to consider the following questions: What is managed care? What are the benefits of managed care? What do consumers think about managed care?

L1 Ask students to choose one article and then work in pairs to discuss the questions above.

L2 Ask students to write answers to the questions above, including any specific examples from the article.

L3 Ask students to work in groups to make a poster giving the answers to the questions above with examples from the article. Have groups pose further questions of their own and include both the questions and the answers on their poster. Have groups share their answers with the class.

Curriculum Connection

LANGUAGE ARTS

Managed Health Care. Have each student find and read an article about managed health care. Tell students to find answers to these questions: What is managed care? What does managed care mean for consumers in terms of accessibility and quality of health care? Have students share their findings in class. Encourage students to think about their own needs as they move from coverage under a parent's policy to their own plan. Ask students to decide what health insurance plan they would choose. **LS**

3 ASSESS

Reteaching

CASH-VALUE INSURANCE.
To reteach the concept of cash value insurance, ask students to tell about the different forms. (Answers should include explanations of whole life, limited payment life, variable life, and endowment insurance.)

Enrichment Strategies

ROLE-PLAY. Work in pairs to role-play the parts of an interviewer and a consumer. The interviewer asks the questions: How important is it to you to have an employer offer and partially pay for a group health insurance plan? Would you turn down a job that didn't include health insurance? The consumer responds. Switch roles. **LS**

Evaluation

Assign and review the Fast Review sections.

Writing for Business

CAPTION ANSWER

Ask students to write in their journals. Write on the board: Why did you choose your path? If you chose "Evaluating Evidence," do you feel more comfortable talking with people than working with your hands? If you chose "Stating Your Case," do you prefer to use your skills of observation and design rather than talking with people? Explain. **P**, **LS**

Writing for Business

Constructing Your Opinion on HMOs

This activity gives you the chance to add to your portfolio. Communicate, interview, research, and write your way into a story. Choose one imaginary path, Evaluating Evidence or Stating Your Case. Follow your path's steps to complete your own story.

pick a path

Evaluating Evidence

The Setting. Health maintenance organizations (HMOs) generally cost less than private practitioners, but patients can't always choose which of the clinic doctors they will see.

Rising Action. You're interested in surveying community members on their experiences and opinions of health care.

Step 1. Survey at least 20 individuals in your community about their health care. Ask at least five questions to find out what kind of health care service they receive, whether they are satisfied with it, and how they think it might be improved.

Step 2. Make a chart to organize the responses.

Stating Your Case

The Setting. A local hospital that operates like an HMO is associated with the state university. The hospital and its clinics, which serve patients from a three-state area, are renowned for its cardiovascular (heart) research.

Rising Action. Hospital administrators have asked your advertising company to draw up a marketing campaign to get the word out about the quality of the hospital and its specialization.

Step 1. Research other hospital marketing campaigns (either nationally or locally). Observe their techniques, messages, and layout.

Step 2. Using a design program on a computer or traditional art materials, design a poster that will help market the hospital.

Conclusion

To make a message persuasive, it needs to be clear, concise, and direct. This focus captures your reader's attention and helps hold his or her interest. Describe the strategy you used to organize your position. How did the evidence you gathered help you conclude your position? How did you know in what order of importance to list them? A strong opinion is also more persuasive when backed with facts, reasons, and examples.

570

How to Use a Portfolio Activity

The portfolio projects are designed to lead students to develop a collection of their best work to submit to you for assessment. You and each of your students should decide which projects to include in their business portfolio. Refer students to the specific rubric(s) from the *Alternative Assessment Strategies*. These rubrics will alert students to the criteria you'll use to assess their projects. **P**, **LS**

Government Health Insurance

Most people who have health insurance receive it through their jobs or buy it from private companies. Many people also receive health insurance through state and federal government programs.

Medicare. **Medicare** is a major health insurance program set up by the federal government. Medicare coverage has two parts. Part A is hospital insurance that covers hospital care. Part B is medical insurance that covers doctors' fees and tests.

People covered by Medicare pay a deductible, coinsurance, and a monthly premium for their medical insurance. For their hospital insurance, they also have to pay a deductible. Many medical services aren't covered by Medicare.

Medicaid. **Medicaid** is another government health care plan for certain groups of citizens. It provides care for those who are unable to pay for insurance or health care. The coverage it provides is much more comprehensive than Medicare.

Costs of Health Insurance

Many policies have a *coinsurance clause* that requires you to pay a certain percentage of medical expenses beyond the deductible. Many policies also require a **copayment**, or a fee paid each time a service is used. For example, you might have to pay between $5 and $15 every time you visit the doctor or fill a prescription. Another factor is the number of people covered by a policy, such as dependent children. The more people covered by the policy, the higher the premium.

Some services, such as dental, vision, or mental health care, might not be covered by a policy. In those cases, you have to pay out of your own pocket and pay for additional insurance. Many policies won't cover a **pre-existing condition**, which is a serious health condition diagnosed before a person obtained health insurance. For example, if someone suffers from a heart condition, an insurance company might refuse to cover it.

 Fast Review _____

1. What is the least expensive form of health insurance for most people?
2. What is the difference between an HMO plan and regular group insurance?

Real-World Application
part 4 of 4

INSIDE THE ER
At any point in the ER, you may encounter an emergency physician, emergency nurse, physician assistant, emergency department technician, unit secretary, or a physician in training. Every one has a specific, important job to do and looks out for you. A physician assistant gives your ailment an educated diagnosis. You don't need surgery.
According to these facts, what kind of health insurance probably covers this visit?

Real-World Application
Caption Answer

INSIDE THE ER:
PART 4 OF 4

Major medical, hospital, surgical, medical, group health, and government health.

Technology Resource

GO TO **EXAMVIEW PRO CD-ROM.** Check your students' understanding of the chapter's key concepts and terms by using the *ExamView Pro®* CD-ROM.

Fast Review Answers

1. Group health insurance, usually provided by a company or organization for employees or members.
2. With an HMO, you must go to its health center and use a doctor who works on staff there. An HMO costs less than regular group insurance.

Meeting Individual Needs

Students With Low Self-Esteem and Confidence. Here are some tips to build self-esteem and confidence:

- Focus on your strengths and positive qualities, and find ways to boost them.
- Be yourself, and don't compare yourself with others.

- Look upon mistakes or limitations as a chance to learn. Don't dwell on them, accept them and move on.
- Replace negative thoughts and images with positive ones.
- Take responsibility for your life instead of blaming others.
- Control your own thoughts, emotions, words, and actions.

4 CLOSE

Chapter Wrap-Up

Ask questions for a class bingo activity with the answers being key words and other concepts in this chapter.

Using Business Key Words

1. term insurance
2. HMO
3. Medicare
4. proceeds
5. cash value insurance
6. coinsurance
7. Medicaid
8. beneficiary
9. copayment
10. pre-existing condition

Review What You Learned

11. Standard of living of the survivors.
12. The person who buys the insurance.
13. Whole life insurance—a policyholder pays a premium that stays the same throughout his or her lifetime. Term life insurance—covers a person for a specific period of time.
14. Care in and out of the hospital.
15. Costs of a doctor's care not involved in surgery.
16. (1) The use of the HMO health care center, and (2) the cost.
17. Hospital insurance and medical insurance.

Summary

1. Cash-value life insurance provides both protection and builds up savings. Term life insurance, or pure protection, provides death benefits only.

2. The cost of life insurance depends on the type of policy, the amount of coverage, and the age, health, and occupation of the insured.

3. Types of health insurance include major medical, hospital expense, surgical expense, medical expense, group health, and government health.

4. Companies and organizations provide group medical insurance to their employees and members. An HMO is a type of group insurance plan that has its own facilities and doctors, costs less than other plans, and stresses preventive health care. Medicare and Medicaid are government health insurance programs for retired persons, low-income families, people with medical needs, dependent children, and people receiving government assistance.

Using Business Key Words

Life and health insurance protect people from the financial risks associated with injury, illness, or death. See how many of the insurance-related terms you can match with the sentences below.

- **proceeds**
- **health maintenance organization (HMO)**
- **cash-value insurance**
- **term insurance**
- **Medicare**
- **beneficiary**
- **copayment**
- **pre-existing condition**
- **coinsurance**
- **Medicaid**

1. Covers a person for a specified period of time.
2. Provides health care at its health-care center for a fixed fee per patient.
3. A major health insurance program set up by the federal government.
4. Money paid from the policy.
5. Provides both savings and protection.
6. Specifies the percentage of costs, after the deductible, which the insurance company will pay.
7. Provides care for those who are unable to pay for other insurance or for health care.
8. Person who receives part or all of the proceeds from a life insurance policy.
9. A fee paid each time a service covered by a health insurance plan is used, such as a doctor's visit or a prescription.
10. A serious health condition diagnosed before a person obtained health insurance and which might not be covered by a policy.

Quick Quiz

1. What type of insurance is term insurance? (Life insurance that covers a person for a specific period of time.)
2. What is the difference between term and cash value life insurance? (Term life insurance, or pure protection, provides death benefits only. Cash value life insurance provides protection and builds up savings.)
3. Name six kinds of health insurance. (Major medical, hospital expense, surgical expense, medical expense, group health, government health.)

Review What You Learned

11. What does life insurance protect?
12. Who names the beneficiary of a life insurance policy?
13. What is the difference between whole life insurance and term insurance?
14. Major medical insurance usually covers what kinds of care?
15. What does medical expense insurance cover?
16. Name two differences between a regular group insurance plan and an HMO.
17. Describe the two parts of Medicare.

Understanding Business Concepts

18. A person who receives part of a life insurance policy's proceeds is called a beneficiary. Why do you think the person who buys the life insurance policy names the beneficiary?
19. Cash-value insurance provides both savings and death benefits. Part of the premium pays for death benefits and the other builds up cash value like a savings account. Limited-payment insurance and endowment insurance are two types of cash-value insurance. What is the difference between limited-payment life insurance and endowment insurance?
20. If you work for a company that provides term insurance as a benefit, why do you think you would lose that insurance coverage if you leave the company?
21. Why do you think companies offer health insurance benefits for their employees?
22. Why do you think the federal government provides health care coverage for retired persons who are 65 and older?

Critical Thinking

23. Do you think a young, single person needs life insurance? Explain your answer.
24. Why do you think HMO plans are generally less expensive than other health care plans?
25. Would you work for a company because it offers good health benefits? Explain your answer.
26. Do you think that providing health care for retired persons should be the role of government? Explain why or why not.

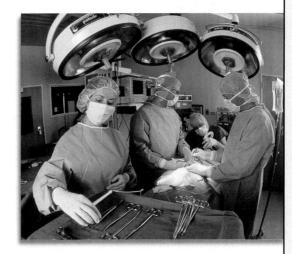

Viewing and Representing

Examining the Image. Examine the picture. If you buy health and life insurance, what coverage would you probably purchase now, in five years, or in ten years? What assumptions are you making? Create a chart summarizing your decisions.

Chapter 35 Life and Health Insurance **573**

Critical Thinking

23. Answers will vary.
24. Answers will vary. Possible answers might include: lack of choice in doctors and doctor's offices, and more people sharing the risk and therefore the cost.
25. Answers will vary and should include an explanation.
26. Answers will vary and should be backed up with reasons.

Viewing and Representing

Ask students to comment on the picture. Ask students how the use of color affects them. Would they like to color-enhance some of their own photographs? For what effect? Ask volunteers to share their charts. Discuss how health care needs are different, depending upon personal situations. **LS**

Understanding Business Concepts

18. You're able to choose who will receive the benefits when the policyholder dies.
19. Limited payment life insurance is a type of cash value insurance. Endowment insurance is a special type of cash value insurance. It emphasizes savings and provides an income for the policyholder at the end of the endowment period.
20. Term insurance provides no accumulation of savings.
21. Attract employees to a particular company.
22. Answers will vary. Make sure the students explain their answers.

4 CLOSE (Cont.)

Building Academic Skills

LANGUAGE ARTS. Encourage both members of the team to participate in the debate. Rubric: Oral presentation.

COMPUTER/TECHNOLOGY. Rubrics: Calculations, spreadsheet.

MATH. $11,000 − $100 = $10,900. $10,900 × 0.25 = $2,725. $2,725 + $100 = $2,825, the total amount the policyholder would pay. Rubric: Calculations.

SOCIAL SCIENCE. Encourage all students to participate in the project. The library and the Internet are good sources of information. Rubric: Oral presentation.

Linking School to Home

Scenarios will vary. Allow the students to share their scenarios using a method they choose. Rubrics: Note taking, essay, oral presentation, poster.

Linking School to Work

Encourage all students in the group to participate in the project. If possible, ask each group to contact a different hospital. Let students choose the method they use to share their results. Rubrics: Note taking, essay, oral presentation.

Building Academic Skills

 A Debatable Issue

Health care is nearly unaffordable without health insurance. Eighteen percent of the population in the United States lack insurance. Why do you think so many don't have insurance? With a partner, debate the ethics issues surrounding a doctor who charges a lower fee when the patient doesn't have health insurance.

 Prefiguring Your Premiums

Use a spreadsheet program to figure your health insurance premiums for the next ten years. Assume they are currently $800 per year and will increase at a rate of 5 percent per year. Calculate the increase at 4 percent and 6 percent as well. Print out your spreadsheet.

 Calculating Percentage

Suppose a policyholder's medical bills come to $11,000. The policyholder has a $100 deductible. The coinsurance clause states that the insurance company will pay 75 percent of the remaining balance and the policyholder will pay the other 25 percent. How much will the policyholder actually pay?

 Covering Controversy

In groups of three or four, research the controversy surrounding national health care coverage in the United States. Include information about the political, social, and economic issues involved. Create an oral presentation with visuals to share your findings with the class.

Linking School to Home

Sharing a Scenario. Consider these facts about the uninsured:
- Sixty-five percent earn less than $26,580 for a family of three.
- Forty percent have no family physician.
- Forty percent go without recommended medical tests or treatments.

Discuss with your parents or other family members the importance of having health insurance. Together, describe a scenario where a high school student would need health insurance. Share your scenario with the class.

Linking School to Work

Inquiring About Local Charges. The uninsured are more likely to be hospitalized than those insured, because of avoiding medical tests or treatments. Do you have any idea how this might financially cripple an uninsured family? In groups of three or four, contact a local hospital and find out how much it costs for room and board during a hospital stay. Find out if there are additional charges for intensive-care rooms. Then research the cost of an average hospital stay today and ten years ago.

Chapter 35 Review

E-Homework

Applying Technology

Explore a Career. Use the Internet to research the variety of careers in the insurance industry. One good resource is the *Occupational Outlook Handbook* by the U. S. Department of Labor. This handbook describes jobs, working conditions, training and education needed, earnings potential, and expected job growth. Choose one and find out the:

- educational requirements
- salary range
- duties and responsibilities

Lifestyle Choices. Use the Internet to obtain a quote for term life insurance for yourself. What are the lifestyle choices that might impact the cost of term life insurance?

Connecting Academics

Math. Nin lost her job. She could continue the group health coverage of her former employer through the COBRA plan, but the monthly payment is 18 percent higher than an ample coverage she can purchase herself. Nin decides to buy independent health coverage, with monthly payments of $143. How much would have the COBRA plan cost Nin?

Language Arts. Working in a team of four, choose one of the following insurance topics: cash-value life, term life, government health, group health, or other health insurance. Together, assess the knowledge and skills of the members of your team then decide on the best person for each task of the team project. Research the team's chosen topic and prepare a visual presentation.

BusinessWeek | Analyzing the Feature Story

You read the first part of "Staying Insured When You're on Your Own" at the beginning of this chapter. Below are a few questions for you to answer about health insurance. You'll find the answers to these questions when you're reading the entire article. First, here are the questions:

27. How long can someone continue the health insurance offered by their former employer under COBRA?
28. What is one of the least expensive ways for a self-employed person to buy coverage?

CREATIVE JOURNAL ACTIVITY

Go to the library or online and research federal laws such as COBRA or HIPAA. What information or programs does your state offer related to one of these acts? Summarize your findings in a short report.

BUSINESS *Online*

The Full Story

To learn more about health or life insurance, visit the *Introduction to Business* Web site at **www.introbus.glencoe.com**, and click on *BusinessWeek* Feature Story, Chapter 35.

E-Homework

EXPLORE A CAREER. Answers will vary depending on the entry-level position selected. Rubrics: Essay, note taking.

LIFESTYLE CHOICES. Answers will vary depending on the Web site selected. Rubrics: Essay, note taking.

Connecting Academics

MATH. $143 × 0.18 = $25.74. $143 + $25.74 = $168.74.

LANGUAGE ARTS. Presentations will vary. As an exercise in allocating human resources (a SCANS workplace skill) each team decided on the best person for each task of the team project. Ask teams to report on the steps in their decision-making process.

BusinessWeek | Analyzing the Feature Story

27. 18 months
28. The least expensive way to buy health insurance is usually as a member of a group rather than as an individual.

Creative Journal Activity

Tell students to answer these questions about their own health care: Do you wait until you're ill to seek health care, or do you get regular checkups? Do you prefer to choose your own health care providers, or would you be willing to let your insurance company choose for you? Would you prefer to go to a clinic and perhaps see a different doctor each time, or would you prefer to see one doctor only? Have students think about these questions and write their responses, explaining their choices. LS, **CL**

1 FOCUS

Unit Seminar Overview

Congratulations to you the teacher. You've led your students through this *Introduction to Business* course. Now it's time for the students to engage in this final seminar. Students investigate business schools, chart students' choices, and decide the answer to the question: What reason do students give most often for their choice of business school?

Bell Ringer Activity

CONCLUDING. Have students write and complete the following sentences: "To me, the most exciting part of this course was _____. I'm glad I learned about _____, it will help me in my life. I'm still confused about _____ and I'd like to understand more about it."

Discussion Starter

SHARING. Ask students this question: What is the most interesting part of business to you? Prompt students, if needed, with questions such as: Is it being an entrepreneur? Is it the financial aspect? Is it studying effects on the economy? Is it being a leader in a large corporation? Is it working with people? Is it developing new technology?

BusinessWeek Seminar

Unit 11
Careers

Investigating Business Schools

Throughout this book, you've read about the different ways businesses are managed—from finances and technical resources to risk. To make informed decisions, it's important to obtain as much information as possible. Education is the best training for this. Therefore, examine both undergraduate and graduate college degrees in business. In this seminar, you'll research a business school and find out about the different programs available.

576

Social Science

Newsworthy Trends

Going Global. The latest trend in business schools is to prepare students for management positions in a global economy. Business schools in the United States are building relationships with business schools in countries overseas by sharing their educational programs and doing joint research. They've set up student and faculty exchange programs so students can gain international experience. Business schools are also recruiting more overseas students so American students can learn in a multinational environment. Meanwhile, the number of business schools in other countries has increased to provide their own pool of trained managers.

Factoids

Not Just Another Degree.
With an MBA (Masters of Business Administration) on your résumé you're guaranteed more money in an industry. Starting salaries of the top graduates start at about $75,000 including stock options and signing bonuses.

Higher Education Near You.
Nearly 700 universities and colleges offer MBA programs.

In Your Future. The typical new business-school grad is 28 years old.

Reap the Benefits. Investing in business school usually pays off in five to eight years, including the two full years you spent in graduate school.

Expanding Your Horizons.
About 75 percent of full-time MBA graduates change the direction of their career after completing the degree. It's an excellent opportunity to broaden your career opportunities.

Investigate the Images

Look at the photographic collage on the left page. What grabs your attention first? Is it the color or the words? The power in reading visuals is in analyzing and dissecting your observations. On a separate piece of paper, respond to the questions listed below. These questions might help sharpen the focus of your visual mind.

Your Observations

1. How many photographs do you see?

2. Examine each photograph. How are they assembled in relation to one another?

3. What is the subject of each photograph? Is place or location the subject?

4. Does color signify a message?

5. What issues do you take from these images?

Information

6. Summarize what you know about the photographs from your observations.

Exploring Culture

7. Reprimand in private, and praise in public is a manager's old adage. As a future employee or employer, why is feedback important to success? How do you gain the respect of an employer?

8. Does an increase in salary indicate your worth to a company? Why or why not?

2 TEACH

Thinking Critically

Read "Factoids," and then answer these questions:

1. Rank how important earning a large salary is to you, on a scale of one to ten. What other factors are important to you in your daily work life? How do you rank these? (Ethical conduct, fun, adventure, helping others, using your talents, constant learning, working independently.)

2. Looking at the factoid "Expanding Your Horizons," who do you know who has changed the direction of his or her career? Think of examples and share them with the class. (Answers will vary, and may include: Change away from traditional gender roles, change due to variations in the economy and in the workforce.)

Cooperative Learning

ANALYSIS OF FEEDBACK.
Have students work in small groups. After discussing "Exploring Culture" (seminar questions 7 and 8), assign the following task: Each student thinks of examples of compliments that meant something special to him or her. Ask students to analyze what made the feedback special: How was the comment or compliment phrased? What made the message so meaningful? Was the message general or specific? Have groups chart their examples of feedback. Write a selection of excellent feedback on the board. **CL**

Social Science — Newsworthy Trends

Joint Education. More schools are offering joint professional and business programs for both students and working professionals. The Stanford Graduate School of Business, the School of Engineering, and Harvard Business School recently created a joint Web site to teach executives in various professions about business management. To prepare future doctors for working in budget-conscious HMOs, 25 of the 125 U.S. medical schools now offer a joint business and medicine program. Along with anatomy and biology, students take classes in health economics and professional liability.

2 TEACH (Cont.)

Independent Practice

L1 SUMMARIZE

Ask students to find a recent article on business schools. Ask them to prepare a summary of the article to share it with the class. Follow student presentations by asking students to form pairs and share their reactions to the presentations. Allow a few minutes for students to exchange their thoughts and questions. **CL**, **LS**, **ELL**

L2 DIAGRAM

Sometimes when research takes many steps, such as that involved in delving into business schools, it's easy to lose track of what you need to do next. Have students draw a poster-size diagram representing a journey or growth, such as a windy road or a tree. Ask students to mark research steps progressively on their diagram, perhaps as road signs, or as parts of a tree. Provide double-sided tape and have students create a moveable graphic, such as a car, to indicate the current stage of their research. **CL**, **LS**

L3 PANEL INTERVIEW

Arrange for three or four students attending a local business school to visit your class and form a panel to answer students' questions. Have students prepare questions ahead of time to find out what it's like to be in business school and what preparations the panel members made before starting business school. After the interview, have students write a one-page report concluding with a comment about what aspect of the panel interview was most helpful to them. **CL**, **LS**

BusinessWeek Seminar

Taking Aim at Careers

Preparation

Learning to manage the different aspects of a business requires training and education.

Objective
In this *BusinessWeek* Seminar, you'll:
- **Research** a business school.
- **Investigate** the school's admissions procedures.
- **Create** a brochure that describes the business school you'd like to attend.

Materials Needed
✓ Copies of recent news publications such as *BusinessWeek*, the *Wall Street Journal*, or *US News and World Report*
✓ Access to the Internet or your local or school library
✓ Paper, pens, pencils, and markers
✓ Copies of magazines you can cut up

Procedures

1. Find and read articles about business schools—colleges and universities that offer degrees in business administration. Business magazines and newspapers publish articles about business schools. At **www.businessweek.com** there is a link to "B-Schools" where you can access information about business schools.

2. Choose a specific school to investigate. Select one that is nearby, one that is highly ranked, or one that interests you.

3. Research your chosen school and a particular business program, such as marketing or business administration. Find information on admissions, tuition and fees, and requirements for graduation. Find out about campus life and extracurricular activities. If you'd like, research scholarships, loans, and other financing arrangements.

4. Create a brochure that describes your chosen business school. Explain why you've chosen this school and include information on the business program that interests you. Cut up old magazines for visuals and be sure to include contact information.

5. As a class, create a display of the brochures. Be sure to review other students' brochures and ask questions about their research to compare your business school to theirs.

Reteaching Strategy

Asking students to summarize material automatically means the students need to think over the whole concept, and then decide on the most significant parts. Ask each student to summarize his or her experience in this seminar in less than 40 words. Have students make a list of the main things they have learned in this seminar. **LS**, **ELL**

Chart It

As a class, make a chart on the board that lists the business schools researched, the programs students are interested in, and why they were chosen.

Business Schools	Business Programs	Why Did You Choose These?

Analyze and Conclude

After reviewing the chart, answer the questions below.

1. **Acquiring and Evaluating Information.** Did more than one student research the same school and/or program? Name the school(s) and program(s).

2. **Building Self-Esteem.** What are the benefits of selecting a business school appropriate for your wants and needs?

3. **Decision Making.** What reason was given most often for the student's choice of school and/or program?

Becoming an Informed Citizen

Congratulations, you finished the seminar. Now it's time to reflect on the decisions you made.

Creative Thinking. Business schools like applicants with a variety of backgrounds and different objectives. How would you sell yourself in a personal statement to a business school? Examine how your different experiences would compliment your classmates.

Analyzing Your Future. What actions can you take today in order to prepare yourself for a future you really want? What is your purpose in life?

BUSINESS Online

Further Exploration
To find out more about business schools, visit the *Introduction to Business* Web site at www.introbus.glencoe.com.

3 ASSESS

Enrichment

WHAT'S THE DIFFERENCE? Have each student note differences between the business schools researched. In a rapid response exercise have students in turn quickly say one difference. Repetition is not allowed. Students may pass if they have no new input.

Evaluation

RUBRICS. The rubrics for evaluation of written reports, diagrams, and oral presentations are included in *Alternative Assessment Strategies.* **P**

4 CLOSE

Seminar Wrap-Up

PROBLEM SOLVING. Ask students two questions: What motivates people to attend business school? What might be a better way of finding out about the right business school for you?

Analyze and Conclude Answers

1. Answers will vary depending on the students' research.
2. Answers will vary and might include, increased engagement, learning, and achievement.
3. The answer will vary depending on the class. Have students explore this question further by ranking the answers in order of popularity.

WRITING NUMBERS AS WORDS AND ROUNDING NUMBERS

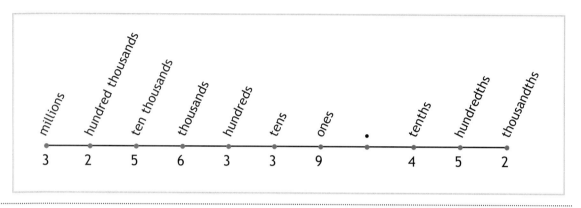

The place-value chart shows the value of each digit in the number 3,256,339.452. The place-value chart can help you write numbers.

EXAMPLE

482
8.557
$39.45

SOLUTION

four hundred eighty-two
eight and five hundred fifty-seven thousandths
thirty-nine and forty-five hundredths dollars
or thirty-nine and $^{45}/_{100}$ dollars

Place value is also used in rounding numbers. If the digit to the right of the place value you want to round is 5 or more, round up by adding 1 to the number in the place value. Then change all the digits to the right of the place value to zeros. If the number is 4 or less, round down by changing all the numbers to the right of the place value to zeros.

EXAMPLE

Round 4765 to the nearest hundred.

SOLUTION

4765   A. Find the digit in the hundred place. It is 7.

4765   B. Is the digit to the right 5 or more? Yes.

4800   C. Add 1 to the hundreds place. Change the digits to the right to zeros.

EXAMPLE

Round 0.843 to the nearest tenth.

SOLUTION

0.843   A. Find the digit in the tenth place. It is 8.

0.843   B. Is the digit to the right 5 or more? No.

0.8   C. Do not change the tenths digit. Drop the digits to the right.

WRITING NUMBERS AS WORDS AND ROUNDING NUMBERS

Dollar and cents amounts are often rounded to the nearest cent, or the hundredths place.

EXAMPLE	$26.7443	**SOLUTION**	$26.74
	$683.1582		$683.16

PROBLEMS

Write as numbers.
1. three thousand four hundred ninety-nine   3499
2. one hundred eleven and $^{32}/_{100}$ dollars $111.32
3. two hundred six and eighty-eight thousandths   206.088

Write in word form.
4. 572   five hundred seventy-two
5. 2.897   two and eight hundred ninety-seven thousandths
6. $325.10   three hundred twenty-five and $^{10}/_{100}$ dollars

Round to the nearest place value shown.

7. ten thousand	327,975	330,000	11. one	28.91	29
8. thousand	816,777	817,000	12. tenth	86.379	86.4
9. hundred	26,312	26,300	13. hundredth	5.5787	5.58
10. ten	6336	6340			

Round 23,793,611 to the place value shown.
14. millions   24,000,000
15. ten millions   20,000,000
16. thousands   23,794,000
17. hundreds   23,793,600
18. ten thousands   23,790,000
19. hundred thousands   23,800,000

Round to the nearest place value shown.

20. cent	$87.2671	$87.27	23. ten dollars	$5,982	$5,980
21. ten cents	$213.432	$213.40	24. hundred dollars	$12,785	$12,800
22. one dollar	$671.98	$672.00			

APPLICATIONS

25. As an accountant for the advertising agency of Phillips & Phillips, Marcia Strasser writes many checks. Write each check amount in words.
    a. $27.83   twenty-seven and $^{83}/_{100}$ dollars
    b. $121.77   one hundred twenty-one and $^{77}/_{100}$ dollars
    c. $569.14   five hundred sixty-nine and $^{14}/_{100}$ dollars
    d. $8,721.65   eight thousand seven hundred twenty-one and $^{65}/_{100}$ dollars

26. Juan Sanchez, an inventory clerk for a lumber yard, often rounds inventory figures for easier handling. Round the number from the inventory list to the nearest ten.
    a. grade 1 oak   519 ft.   520
    b. grade 2 oak   795 ft.   800
    c. grade 1 pine   323 ft.   320
    d. grade 2 pine   477 ft.   480

ADDING AND SUBTRACTING DECIMALS

When adding decimals, write the addition problem in vertical form. Be sure to line up the decimal points. When adding amounts with different numbers of decimal places, write zeros in the empty decimal places.

EXAMPLE $15.27 + 16.39 + 36.19$

SOLUTION

$$
\begin{array}{r}
15.27 \\
16.39 \\
+36.19 \\
\hline
67.85
\end{array}
$$

EXAMPLE $58.2 + 3.97 + 8 + 123.796$

SOLUTION

$$
\begin{array}{r}
58.2 \\
3.97 \\
8. \\
+123.796 \\
\end{array}
\qquad
\begin{array}{r}
58.200 \\
3.970 \\
8.000 \\
+123.796 \\
\hline
193.966
\end{array}
$$

When subtracting decimals, write the subtraction problem in vertical form. Be sure to line up the decimal points. When subtracting amounts with different numbers of decimal places, write zeros in the empty decimal places.

EXAMPLE $78.63 - 42.41$

SOLUTION

$$
\begin{array}{r}
78.63 \\
-42.41 \\
\hline
36.22
\end{array}
$$

EXAMPLE $149.9 - 28.37$

SOLUTION

$$
\begin{array}{r}
149.9 \\
-28.37 \\
\end{array}
\qquad
\begin{array}{r}
149.90 \\
-28.37 \\
\hline
121.53
\end{array}
$$

Adding and subtracting amounts of money is just like adding and subtracting decimals. The decimal point separates the dollars and cents. Remember to put a dollar sign in the total.

EXAMPLE $\$74.99 + \$8.76$

SOLUTION

$$
\begin{array}{r}
\$74.99 \\
+8.76 \\
\hline
\$\ 83.75
\end{array}
$$

EXAMPLE $\$750 - \$43.29$

SOLUTION

$$
\begin{array}{r}
\$750.00 \\
-43.29 \\
\hline
\$706.71
\end{array}
$$

PROBLEMS

1.
$$
\begin{array}{r}
19.87 \\
32.24 \\
+27.55 \\
\hline
79.66
\end{array}
$$

2.
$$
\begin{array}{r}
4.377 \\
6.829 \\
+2.707 \\
\hline
13.913
\end{array}
$$

3.
$$
\begin{array}{r}
8.3 \\
12.78 \\
+322.437 \\
\hline
343.517
\end{array}
$$

4.
$$
\begin{array}{r}
46.65 \\
3.5 \\
+125.397 \\
\hline
175.547
\end{array}
$$

5.
$$
\begin{array}{r}
\$\ 2.77 \\
35.96 \\
+10.37 \\
\hline
\$\ 49.10
\end{array}
$$

6. $22.19 + 47.75 + 13.88 + 19.85$ 103.67

7. $0.78 + 9.82 + 36.242 + 37.4$ 84.242

8. $6.7 + 27.81 + 653.47 + 5.5$ 693.48

9. $54.32 + 0.37 + 2.5 + 0.797$ 57.987

10. $\$6.22 + \$53.19 + \$.33 + \$7.85$ $67.59

11. $\$4.78 + \$12.50 + \$22 + \$17.10$ $56.38

12.
$$
\begin{array}{r}
3.75 \\
-2.18 \\
\hline
1.57
\end{array}
$$

13.
$$
\begin{array}{r}
376.55 \\
-27.42 \\
\hline
349.13
\end{array}
$$

14.
$$
\begin{array}{r}
468.47 \\
-233.55 \\
\hline
234.92
\end{array}
$$

15.
$$
\begin{array}{r}
367.05 \\
-219.87 \\
\hline
147.18
\end{array}
$$

16.
$$
\begin{array}{r}
\$363.27 \\
-79.14 \\
\hline
\$284.13
\end{array}
$$

ADDING AND SUBTRACTING DECIMALS

17.	547.7 − 127.6	420.10	18.	76.99 − 3.87	73.12
19.	695.13 − 428.1	267.03	20.	3076 − 2205.50	870.5
21.	$300 − $5.75	$294.25	22.	$445.19 − $175.76	$269.43

APPLICATIONS Complete the sales receipts by finding the subtotals and the totals.

23. a. 189.95   b. 203.25

Date 6/1/--	Auth. No. 86430	Identification	Clerk DL	Reg./Dept.	☑ Take ☐ Send
Qty	Class	Description	Price	Amount	
1		dress		77	98
1		jacket		85	99
2		hosiery	12.99 ea	25	98

a. Freight charges will be included with your invoice at the time of shipping. You will be billed the published rates from UPS, US Postal Service.

	Subtotal	?
CUSTOMER SIGNATURE X *Shelley Turner*	Tax	13	30

b. Sales Slip | Total | ? |

24. a. 879.83   b. 937.02

Date 3/14/--	Auth. No. 42	Identification	Clerk JR	Reg./Dept.	☑ Take ☐ Send
Qty	Class	Description	Price	Amount	
1		couch		599	95
1 pr		draperies		279	88

a. Freight charges will be included with your invoice at the time of shipping. You will be billed the published rates from UPS, US Postal Service.

	Subtotal	?
CUSTOMER SIGNATURE X *Betty Clark*	Tax	57	19

b. Sales Slip | Total | ? |

Complete the bank deposit slips by finding the subtotals and the total deposits.

25.

		DOLLARS	CENTS
CASH	CURRENCY	72	00
	COINS		
CHECKS	LIST SEPARATELY 95-76	413	12
	98-11	25	00
	95-13	211	10
a.	SUBTOTAL	?	
⟲	LESS CASH RECEIVED	50	00
b.	TOTAL DEPOSIT	?	

a. 721.22
b. 671.22

26.

		DOLLARS	CENTS
CASH	CURRENCY	23	00
	COINS	7	44
CHECKS	LIST SEPARATELY 85-76	175	66
	88-11	23	33
		12	87
a.	SUBTOTAL	?	
⟲	LESS CASH RECEIVED	75	00
b.	TOTAL DEPOSIT	?	

a. 242.30
b. 167.30

27.

		DOLLARS	CENTS
CASH	CURRENCY		
	COINS	4	75
CHECKS	LIST SEPARATELY 57-12	25	95
	57-10	38	11
a.	SUBTOTAL	?	
⟲	LESS CASH RECEIVED	25	00
b.	TOTAL DEPOSIT	?	

a. 68.81
b. 43.81

28. You are a cashier at a coffee shop. Compute the correct change for each of the following orders.

	Customer's Order	Customer Gives You	Change
a.	$8.76	$10.00	$1.24
b.	$12.94	$15.00	$2.06
c.	$9.30	$10.50	$1.20
d.	$16.11	$20.00	$3.89
e.	$5.57	$5.75	$0.18
f.	$22.02	$25.00	$2.98
g.	$7.12	$7.15	$0.03
h.	$3.33	$5.00	$1.67
i.	$28.04	$30.04	$2.00
j.	$6.12	$10.25	$4.13

MULTIPLYING AND DIVIDING DECIMALS

When multiplying decimals, multiply as if the decimal numbers were whole numbers. Then count the total number of decimal places in the factors. This number will be the number of decimal places in the product.

EXAMPLE

18.7 ← factor
× 0.34 ← factor
748
561
6358 ← product

SOLUTION

18.7 ← 1 decimal place
× 0.34 ← + 2 decimal places
748
561
6.358 ← 3 decimal places

If the product does not have enough digits to place the decimal in the correct position, you will need to write zeros. Start at the right of the product in counting the decimal places and write zeros at the left.

EXAMPLE

0.63
× 0.05
315

SOLUTION

0.63 ← 2 decimal places
× 0.05 ← + 2 decimal places
0.0315 ← 4 decimal places

When multiplying amounts of money, round the answer to the nearest cent. Remember to put a dollar sign in the answer.

EXAMPLE

$2.25
× 1.5
3.375

SOLUTION

$ 2.25 ← 2 places
× 1.5 ← + 1 place
$3.375 ← 3 places

$2.25 × 1.5 = $3.375
= $3.38
rounded to the nearest cent

When multiplying by 10, 100, or 1000, count the number of zeros. Then move the decimal point to the right the same number of spaces.

EXAMPLE

8.32 × 100

SOLUTION

8.32 × 100 = 8.32 = 832   100 has 2 zeros; move decimal 2 places.

PROBLEMS

1. 18.3
× 2.5
45.75

2. 27.5
× 8.2
225.50

3. 56.8
× 0.33
18.744

4. 88.1
× 0.23
20.263

5. 0.57
× 0.14
0.0798

6. 0.88
× 0.07
0.0616

7. 0.93
× 0.04
0.0372

8. 0.323
× 0.005
0.001615

9. $17.85 × 15.5 = $276.675 = $276.68
10. $25.24 × 6.3 = $159.012 = $159.01
11. $18.15 × 6.5 = $117.975 = $117.98
12. $14.98 × 8.7 = $130.326 = $130.33

13. 33.8 × 10 = 338
14. 55.399 × 100 = 5539.9
15. 0.518 × 1000 = 518
16. 532.788 × 10,000 = 5,327,880

MULTIPLYING AND DIVIDING DECIMALS

APPLICATION

17. Below are partial payroll records for Fanciful Flowers. Complete the records by calculating gross earnings (hourly rate x hours worked), Social Security tax (gross earnings × 0.062), Medicare tax (gross earnings × 0.0145), federal income tax (gross earnings × 0.15), and state income tax (gross earnings × 0.045). Round each deduction to the nearest cent. Find the total deductions and subtract from gross earnings to find the net pay.

	Employee	Hourly Rate	Number of Hours	Gross Earnings	Social Security Tax	Medicare Tax	Federal Inc. Tax	State Inc. Tax	Total Deductions	Net Pay
a.	M. Smith	$8.25	24	198.00	12.28	2.87	29.70	8.91	53.76	144.24
b.	R. Nash	$9.15	33	301.95	18.72	4.38	45.29	13.59	81.98	219.97
c.	C. Young	$7.75	15	116.25	7.21	1.69	17.44	5.23	31.57	84.68
d.	D. Cha	$9.15	30	274.50	17.02	3.98	41.18	12.35	74.53	199.97

When dividing decimals, if there is a decimal point in the divisor, you must move it to the right to make the divisor a whole number. Move the decimal point in the dividend to the right the same number of places you moved the decimal point in the divisor. Then divide as with whole numbers.

$$\text{divisor} \rightarrow 6\overline{)840} \leftarrow \text{dividend} \qquad \overset{140 \leftarrow \text{quotient}}{}$$

EXAMPLE

$$3.44\overline{)15.5488}$$

SOLUTION

$$3.44\overline{)15.5488}$$

$$
\begin{array}{r}
4.52 \\
344\overline{)1554.88} \\
-1376 \\
\hline
1788 \\
-1720 \\
\hline
688 \\
-688 \\
\hline
\end{array}
$$

Add zeros to the right of the decimal point in the dividend if needed.

EXAMPLE

$$0.42\overline{)0.147}$$

SOLUTION

$$0.42\overline{)0.147}$$

$$
\begin{array}{r}
0.35 \\
42\overline{)14.70} \quad \text{zero added} \\
-126 \\
\hline
210 \\
-210 \\
\hline
\end{array}
$$

When the dividend is an amount of money, remember to place the dollar sign in the quotient and round the answer to the nearest cent.

EXAMPLE

$$48\overline{)\$95.12}$$

SOLUTION

$$
\begin{array}{r}
\$1.981 \\
48\overline{)\$95.120}
\end{array}
$$

$95.12 \div 48 = \$1.98$ rounded to the nearest cent.

Appendix

MULTIPLYING AND DIVIDING DECIMALS

When dividing by 10, 100, or 1000, count the number of zeros in 10, 100, or 1000 and move the decimal point to the left the same number of places.

EXAMPLE

15,213.7 ÷ 1000

SOLUTION

15,213.7 ÷ 1000 = 15213.7   1000 has 3 zeros;
  =15.2137   move decimal 3 places

PROBLEMS

Round to the nearest hundredth or the nearest cent.

18. 4.3
    $2.7\overline{)11.61}$

19. 5.9
    $1.3\overline{)7.67}$

20. 7.1
    $6.2\overline{)44.02}$

21. 5.4
    $0.3\overline{)1.62}$

22. 29.4
    $.05\overline{)1.47}$

23. 710
    $.04\overline{)28.4}$

24. 5.66
    $8.3\overline{)46.99}$

25. 52.44
    $3.4\overline{)178.3}$

26. $\$4.05$
    $88\overline{)\$356.68}$

27. $\$.95$
    $45\overline{)\$42.79}$

28. $\$5.82$
    $15\overline{)\$87.32}$

29. 0.55
    $14.1\overline{)7.823}$

APPLICATIONS

30. Your family is looking into buying a late model, used car. Calculate (to the nearest tenth) the gas mileage for the following types of cars.

	Type of Vehicle	Miles	Gallons of Fuel	Miles per Gallon
a.	Subcompact	631	17.8	35.4
b.	4-door sedan	471.4	16.6	28.4
c.	Minivan	405.1	18.2	22.3
d.	Compact	512.2	15.7	32.6
e.	SUV	298.1	23.2	12.8

FRACTION TO DECIMAL, DECIMAL TO FRACTION

Any fraction can be renamed as a decimal and any decimal can be renamed as a fraction. To rename a fraction as a decimal, use division. Think of the fraction bar in the fraction as meaning "divide by." For example, $5/8$ means "5 divided by 8." After the 5, write a decimal point and as many zeros as are needed. Then divide by 8.

EXAMPLE Change $3/8$ to a decimal.

SOLUTION

$$
3/8 \;\to\; 8\overline{)3.000} \quad
\begin{array}{r}
0.375 \\
\hline
-24 \\
\hline
60 \\
-56 \\
\hline
40 \\
-40 \\
\end{array}
$$

EXAMPLE Change $1/5$ to a decimal.

SOLUTION

$$
1/5 \;\to\; 5\overline{)1.0} \quad
\begin{array}{r}
0.2 \\
\hline
-10 \\
\end{array}
$$

If a fraction does not divide evenly, divide to one more decimal place than you are rounding to.

EXAMPLE Change $5/7$ to a decimal rounded to the nearest hundredth. (Divide to the thousandths place.)

SOLUTION

$$
5/7 \;\to\; 7\overline{)5.000} \quad
\begin{array}{r}
0.714 = 0.71 \\
\hline
-49 \\
\hline
10 \\
-7 \\
\hline
30 \\
-28 \\
\hline
2 \\
\end{array}
$$

EXAMPLE Change $2/7$ to a decimal rounded to the nearest thousandth. (Divide to the ten thousandths place.)

SOLUTION

$$
2/7 \;\to\; 7\overline{)2.0000} \quad
\begin{array}{r}
0.2857 = 0.286 \\
\hline
-14 \\
\hline
60 \\
-56 \\
\hline
40 \\
-35 \\
\hline
50 \\
-49 \\
\hline
1 \\
\end{array}
$$

To rename a decimal as a fraction, name the place value of the digit at the far right. This is the denominator of the fraction.

$$0.83 = 83/100$$

3 is in the hundredths place, so the denominator is 100.

$$0.007 = 7/1000$$

7 is in the thousandths place, so the denominator is 1000.

Note that the number of zeros in the denominator is the same as the number of places to the right of the decimal point. The fraction should always be written in lowest terms.

$$0.25 = 25/100 = 1/4$$

$$3.375 = 3\,375/1000 = 3\,3/8$$

Appendix

FRACTION TO DECIMAL, DECIMAL TO FRACTION

PROBLEMS

Change the fractions to decimals. Round to the nearest thousandth.

1. $^2/_5$ 0.4	2. $^5/_6$ 0.833	3. $^4/_9$ 0.444	4. $^7/_{10}$ 0.7
5. $^9/_{25}$ 0.36	6. $^{115}/_{200}$ 0.575	7. $^1/_7$ 0.143	8. $^{13}/_{40}$ 0.325
9. $^4/_{15}$ 0.267	10. $^5/_{12}$ 0.417	11. $^{11}/_{16}$ 0.688	12. $^1/_4$ 0.25

Change the fractions to decimals. Round to the nearest hundredth.

13. $^1/_8$ 0.13	14. $^5/_9$ 0.56	15. $^{33}/_{35}$ 0.94	16. $^{12}/_{25}$ 0.48
17. $^7/_{20}$ 0.35	18. $^2/_{25}$ 0.08	19. $^{15}/_{16}$ 0.94	20. $^2/_9$ 0.22
21. $^3/_7$ 0.43	22. $^3/_4$ 0.75	23. $^1/_6$ 0.17	24. $^{31}/_{32}$ 0.97

Change the decimals to fractions reduced to lowest terms.

25. 0.275 $^{11}/_{40}$	26. 0.3 $^3/_{10}$	27. 0.15 $^3/_{20}$	28. 0.8 $^4/_5$
29. 1.125 $1^1/_8$	30. 0.117 $^{117}/_{1000}$	31. 0.32 $^8/_{25}$	32. 2.5 $2^1/_2$
33. 44.755 $44^{151}/_{200}$	34. 0.005 $^1/_{200}$	35. 5.545 $5^{109}/_{200}$	36. 0.2 $^1/_5$

APPLICATIONS

37. Stock prices have traditionally been quoted as dollars and fractions of a dollar. Change the stock prices to dollars and cents. Round to the nearest cent.

Stock	Price	
a. AdobeSy	$61^5/_{16}$	$61.31
b. AirTran	$4^{15}/_{32}$	$4.47
c. CNET	$50^3/_4$	$50.75
d. ETrade	$20^1/_4$	$20.25
e. Omnipoint	$112^5/_8$	$112.63
f. Qualcomm	$142^1/_{16}$	$142.06
g. WebLink	$17^{13}/_{16}$	$17.81
h. Winstar	$70^{23}/_{32}$	$70.72

38. Individual bowling averages in the Southern Community League are carried to the nearest hundredth. Convert the decimals to fractions reduced to the lowest terms.

Name	Average	
a. B. Taylor	220.13	$220^{13}/_{100}$
b. J. Scott	217.02	$217^1/_{50}$
c. T. Anfinson	216.97	$216^{97}/_{100}$
d. G. Ingram	212.08	$212^2/_{25}$
e. D. Ingram	210.50	$210^1/_2$
f. B. Jordan	209.25	$209^1/_4$
g. G. Maddux	207.88	$207^{44}/_{50}$
h. A. Jones	205.15	$205^3/_{20}$

PERCENT TO DECIMAL, DECIMAL TO PERCENT

Percent is an abbreviation of the Latin words *per centum*, meaning "by the hundred." So percent means "divide by 100." A percent can be written as a decimal. To change a percent to a decimal, first write the percent as a fraction with a denominator of 100, then divide by 100.

EXAMPLE Change 31% to a decimal.

SOLUTION $31\% = {}^{31}/_{100} = 0.31$

EXAMPLE Change 17.3% to a decimal.

SOLUTION $17.3\% = {}^{17.3}/_{100} = 0.173$

When dividing by 100, you can just move the decimal point two places to the left. When you write a percent as a decimal, you are moving the decimal point two places to the left and dropping the percent sign (%). If necessary, use zero as a placeholder.

EXAMPLE

A. 31%

B. 7%

SOLUTION

A. $31\% = 31. = 0.31$ ← Drop % sign.
— Move decimal 2 places.

B. $7\% = 07. = 0.07$ — Insert a zero as a placeholder.

To write a decimal as a percent, move the decimal point two places to the right and add a percent sign (%).

EXAMPLE

A. 0.31

B. 0.07

C. 2.5

D. 0.008

SOLUTION

A. $0.31 = 0.31 = 31\%$ ← Add % sign.
— Move decimal 2 places.

B. $0.07 = 0.07 = 7\%$

C. $2.5 = 2.50 = 250\%$

D. $0.008 = 0.008 = 0.8\%$

PROBLEMS

Write as decimals.

1. 35%
0.35

2. 22%
0.22

3. 68%
0.68

4. 30%
0.30

5. 49.2%
0.492

6. 88.7%
0.887

7. 11.5%
0.115

8. 92.9%
0.929

9. 322%
3.22

10. 526%
5.26

11. 663%
6.63

12. 275%
2.75

13. 9%
0.09

14. 5%
0.05

15. 4%
0.04

16. 12%
0.12

17. 7.03%
0.0703

18. 9.02%
0.0902

19. 2.0725%
0.020725

20. 3.0843%
0.030843

Write as percents.

21. 0.75
75%

22. 0.17
17%

23. 0.44
44%

24. 0.26
26%

Appendix

PERCENT TO DECIMAL, DECIMAL TO PERCENT

25. 0.06 6%	**26.** 0.07 7%	**27.** 0.01 1%	**28.** 0.02 2%
29. 0.003 0.3%	**30.** 0.009 0.9%	**31.** 0.0045 0.45%	**32.** 0.0029 0.29%
33. 3.12 312%	**34.** 4.14 414%	**35.** 6.007 600.7%	**36.** 5.000 500%
37. 0.1 10%	**38.** 0.5 50%	**39.** 325.5 32,550%	**40.** 0.2015 20.15%

APPLICATIONS

41. The percent changes in retail sales were reported as a decimal in the October issue of *Retail Monthly* magazine. Change the decimals to percents.

Retail Sales

	Month	Change		
a.	February	0.012	a.	1.2%
b.	March	0.006	b.	0.6%
c.	April	0.013	c.	1.3%
d.	May	0.038	d.	3.8%
e.	June	0.043	e.	4.3%
f.	July	0.011	f.	1.1%
g.	August	0.022	g.	2.2%

42. The commission rate schedule for a stockbroker is shown. Change the percents to decimals.

Commission Rate Schedule

	Dollar Amount	% of Dollar Amount		
a.	$0 – $2,499	2.3%, minimum $30	a.	0.023
b.	$2,500 – $4,999	2.0%, minimum $42	b.	0.020
c.	$5,000 – $9,999	1.5%, minimum $65	c.	0.015
d.	$10,000 – $14,999	1.1%, minimum $110	d.	0.011
e.	$15,000 – $24,999	0.9%, minimum $135	e.	0.009
f.	$25,000 – $49,999	0.6%, minimum $175	f.	0.006
	$50,000 and above	negotiated		

PERCENT TO DECIMAL, DECIMAL TO PERCENT

43. During the National Basketball Association season, the teams had these won–lost records. The Pct. column shows the percent of games won, expressed as a decimal. Change the decimals to percents.

EASTERN CONFERENCE
Atlantic Division

		W	L	Pct.	GB	
a.	Miami	28	16	.636	-	63.6%
b.	New York	27	17	.614	1	61.4%
c.	Philadelphia	25	21	.543	4	54.3%
d.	Boston	21	25	.457	8	45.7%
e.	Orlando	21	26	.447	8 $1/2$	44.7%
f.	New Jersey	17	29	.370	12	37.0%
g.	Washington	15	31	.326	14	32.6%

WESTERN CONFERENCE
Midwest Division

		W	L	Pct.	GB	
p.	San Antonio	30	16	.652	-	65.2%
q.	Utah	27	17	.614	2	61.4%
r.	Minnesota	25	18	.581	3 $1/2$	58.1%
s.	Denver	21	22	.488	7 $1/2$	48.8%
t.	Houston	19	27	.413	11	41.3%
u.	Dallas	18	27	.400	11 $1/2$	40.0%
v.	Vancouver	12	32	.273	17	27.3%

Central Division

		W	L	Pct.	GB	
h.	Indiana	29	15	.659	-	65.9%
i.	Milwaukee	26	21	.553	4 $1/2$	55.3%
j.	Charlotte	24	20	.545	5	54.5%
k.	Toronto	24	20	.545	5	54.5%
l.	Detroit	22	23	.489	7 $1/2$	48.9%
m.	Cleveland	19	26	.422	10 $1/2$	42.2%
n.	Atlanta	17	26	.395	11 $1/2$	39.5%
o.	Chicago	9	34	.209	19 $1/2$	20.9%

Pacific Division

		W	L	Pct.	GB	
w.	L.A. Lakers	34	11	.756	-	75.6%
x.	Portland	34	11	.756	-	75.6%
y.	Sacramento	28	16	.636	5 $1/2$	63.6%
z.	Seattle	29	18	.617	6	61.7%
aa.	Phoenix	26	18	.591	7 $1/2$	59.1%
ab.	Golden State	11	32	.256	22	25.6%
ac.	L.A. Clippers	11	34	.244	23	24.4%

44. How many teams have won more than 75% of their games?   2
Who are they?   L.A. Lakers and Portland

45. How many teams have won more than 50% of their games?   15

46. How many have won less than 30% of their games?   4

Appendix

FINDING A PERCENTAGE

Finding a percentage means finding a percent of a number. To find a percent of a number, you change the percent to a decimal, then multiply it by the number.

EXAMPLE 30% of 90 is what number?

SOLUTION $30\% \times 90 = n$ — In mathematics, *of* means "times" and *is* means "equals." Let n stand for the unknown number.

$0.30 \times 90 = n$ Change the percent to a decimal.

$27 = n$ Multiply.

30% of $90 = 27$ Write the answer.

EXAMPLE The delivery charge is 8% of the selling price of $145.00. Find the delivery charge.

SOLUTION
$8\% \times \$145.00 = n$
$0.08 \times \$145.00 = n$
$\$11.60 = n$
$8\% \times \$145.00 = \$11.60$ delivery charge

EXAMPLE The student had 95% correct out of 80 questions. How many answers were correct?

SOLUTION
$95\% \times 80 = n$
$0.95 \times 80 = n$
$76 = n$
$95\% \times 80 = 76$ correct

PROBLEMS

Find the percentage.

1. 25% of 60
15

2. 45% of 80
36

3. 40% of 30
12

4. 33% of 112
36.96

5. 58% of 420
243.6

6. 50% of 422
211

7. 3% of 100
3

8. 2% of 247
4.94

9. 110% of 65
71.5

10. 7% of 785
54.95

11. 1% of 819
8.19

12. 4% of 19.5
0.78

13. 185% of 95
175.75

14. 200% of 720
1440

15. 135% of 860
1161

16. 120% of 3.35
4.02

17. 4.5% of 50
2.25

18. 1.25% of 300
3.75

19. 33.3% of 80
26.64

20. 67.2% of 365
245.28

Round the answer to the nearest cent.

21. 7% of $35.78
$2.50

22. 6.5% of $80
$5.20

23. 10% of $93.20
$9.32

24. 5.5% of $135
$7.43

25. 4.25% of $65.00
$2.76

26. 2.75% of $115
$3.16

27. 125% of $98
$122.50

28. 7.5% of $150
$11.25

29. 0.3% of $450
$1.35

30. 0.15% of $125
$.19

31. 8.2% of $19.89
$1.63

32. 5.25% of $110.15
$5.78

FINDING A PERCENTAGE

APPLICATIONS

33. The following items appeared in a sales flyer for a major department store. Calculate the amount saved from the regular price as well as the sale price for each item. Round to the nearest cent.

		Amount Saved	Sale Price
a.	Save 25% on juniors knit shirts. Reg. $18.	$4.50	$13.50
b.	Save 30% on women's dresses. Reg. $69.99	$21.00	$48.99
c.	Save 20% on men's shoes. Reg. $135.	$27.00	$108.00
d.	Save 25% on all nursery cribs. Reg. $119.99	$30.00	$89.99
e.	Save 25% on all boxed jewelry sets. Reg. $19.99	$5.00	$14.99
f.	Save 30% on family athletic shoes. Reg. $59.99	$18.00	$41.99

34. Student Sean Hu received these test scores. How many answers were correct on each test?

	Subject	Test Score	Number of Items	Correct Answers
a.	Math	90%	80	72
b.	English	70%	90	63
c.	Science	80%	110	88
d.	Spanish	90%	50	45
e.	Government	85%	100	85

35. Sales taxes are found by multiplying the tax rate times the selling price of the item. The total purchase price is the selling price plus the sales tax. Find the sales tax and total purchase price for each selling price. Round to the nearest cent.

	Selling Price	Tax Rate	Sales Tax	Total Purchase Price
a.	$14.78	4%	$0.59	$15.37
b.	$22.50	5%	$1.13	$23.63
c.	$3.88	6%	$0.23	$4.11
d.	$95.85	6.5%	$6.23	$102.08
e.	$212.00	7.25%	$15.37	$227.37
f.	$85.06	8.25%	$7.02	$92.08
g.	$199.99	7.455%	$14.91	$214.90

Appendix

AVERAGE (MEAN)

The average, or mean, is a single number used to represent a group of numbers. The average, or mean, of two or more numbers is the sum of the numbers divided by the number of items added.

EXAMPLE Find the average of 8, 5, 3, 7, and 2.   Add to find the total.

SOLUTION

$$\frac{8 + 5 + 3 + 7 + 2}{5} = \frac{25}{5} = 5$$ Divide by the number of items.

EXAMPLE Find the average of 278, 340, 205, and 235.

SOLUTION

$$\frac{278 + 340 + 205 + 235}{4} = \frac{1058}{4} = 264.5$$

EXAMPLE Find the average of 4.3, 7.1, 1.5, 3.2, and 6.4. Round to the nearest tenth.

SOLUTION

$$\frac{4.3 + 7.1 + 1.5 + 3.2 + 6.4}{5} = \frac{22.5}{5} = 4.5$$

EXAMPLE Find the average of $12, $35, $19, $23, $11, and $21. Round to the nearest dollar.

SOLUTION

$$\frac{\$12 + \$35 + \$19 + \$23 + \$11 + \$21}{6} = \frac{\$121}{6} = \$20.17 = \$20$$

PROBLEMS

Find the average for each group.

1. 3, 5, 7, 9, 11   7
2. 25, 40, 35, 50   37.5
3. 211, 197, 132   180
4. 416, 310, 344, 430   375
5. 4.4, 2.9, 3.7, 1.8, 6.5   3.86
6. 3.6, 7.1, 4.8, 4.7, 6.3, 5.3   5.3
7. $23, $21, $25, $24, $26 $23.80
8. $98, $87, $79, $85, $88, $91 $88

Find the average for each group. Round to the nearest hundredth or cent.

9. 8.1, 8.6, 7.7, 9.2, 5.5, 6.9, 7.3   7.61
10. 3.3, 5.8, 4.6, 2.8, 3.4, 5.2   4.18
11. $31.70, $33.91, $36.17, $33.85 $33.91
12. $4.37, $3.74, $4.90, $5.74, $6.11 $4.97
13. $55.78, $44.20, $43.95, $34.36 $44.57

AVERAGE (MEAN)

14. $121.19, $115.08, $135, $129.05, $111.88 $122.44

15. Ben Agars had bowling scores of 187, 154, and 130. What was his average?   157

16. Kelley O'Reilly's tips from being a waitress were $5.00, $5.50, $4.75, $3.00, $4.50, $2.00, $5.75, and $4.50. What was her average tip? $4.38

17. Last year, Michael Legato's telephone bills averaged $66.12 a month. What was his total bill for the year? $793.44

18. Mark Purdue recorded his math test scores this quarter. What is his average?   83.5

Test Number	1	2	3	4	5	6	7	8
Score	65	77	81	79	90	86	92	98

19. What does he need on the next test to have an average of 85?   97

20. If Mark got a 97 on test 9 and 100 on test 10, what would be his average?   86.5

APPLICATIONS

21. As captain of the school golf team, Erica Samuelson has to complete this form after each game. Help her by computing the total and the average for each golfer. She also computes the total and the team average for each game. Round to the nearest whole number.

	Golfer	Game 1	Game 2	Game 3	Total	Average
a.	Samuelson	86	78	75	239	80
b.	Haas	80	81	70	231	77
c.	Sutherland	82	77	71	230	77
d.	Beck	80	66	73	219	73
e.	McCarron	78	81	82	241	80
f.	Total	406	383	371		
g.	Team average	81	77	74		

ELAPSED TIME

To find elapsed time, subtract the earlier time from the later time.

EXAMPLE Find the elapsed time for Kaitlin Harper who worked from:
  A. 4:30 P.M. to 11:45 P.M.   B. 5:15 A.M. to 10:33 A.M.

SOLUTIONS

$$\begin{array}{r} 11:45 \\ -\ 4:30 \\ \hline 7:15 \end{array} = 7 \text{ hours 15 minutes}$$
written as 7 h: 15 min

$$\begin{array}{r} 10:33 \\ -\ 5:15 \\ \hline 5:18 \end{array} = 5 \text{ hours 18 minutes}$$
written as 5 h: 18 min

You cannot subtract 45 minutes from 30 minutes unless you borrow an hour and add it to the 30 minutes. Remember that 1 hour = 60 minutes.

EXAMPLE Find the elapsed time from 2:50 P.M. to 9:15 P.M.

SOLUTION

$$\begin{array}{r} 9:15 \\ -\ 2:50 \end{array} = \begin{array}{r} 8:15 \\ -\ 2:50 \end{array} + :60 = \begin{array}{r} 8:75 \\ -\ 2:50 \\ \hline 6:25 \end{array} \text{ borrowed 1 hour}$$

6:25 = 6 h: 25 min

To find elapsed time when the time period goes past noon, add 12 hours to the later time before subtracting.

EXAMPLE Find the elapsed time from 6:00 A.M. to 3:15 P.M.

SOLUTION

$$\begin{array}{r} 3:15 \\ -\ 6:00 \end{array} = \begin{array}{r} 3:15 \\ \end{array} + \begin{array}{r} 12:00 \\ -\ 6:00 \end{array} = \begin{array}{r} 15:15 \\ -\ 6:00 \\ \hline 9:15 \end{array}$$

9:15 = 9 h: 15 min

EXAMPLE Find the elapsed time from 10:35 P.M. to 3:12 A.M.

SOLUTION

$$\begin{array}{r} 3:12 \\ -\ 10:35 \end{array} = \begin{array}{r} 15:12 \\ -\ 10:35 \end{array} = \begin{array}{r} 14:12 \\ -\ 10:35 \end{array} + :60 = \begin{array}{r} 14:72 \\ -\ 10:35 \\ \hline 4:37 \end{array}$$

4:37 = 4 h: 37 min

PROBLEMS

Find the elapsed time.

1. From 2:30 P.M. to 6:35 P.M.   4 h: 5 min
2. From 1:18 P.M. to 7:25 P.M.   6 h: 7 min
3. From 4:40 A.M. to 8:57 A.M.   4 h: 17 min
4. From 3:33 a.m. to 10:47 A.M.   7 h: 14 min
5. From 3:15 A.M. to 5:20 A.M.   2 h: 5 min
6. From 1:25 P.M. to 9:05 P.M.   7 h: 40 min
7. From 7:35 P.M. to 11:12 P.M.   3 h: 37 min
8. From 8:43 A.M. to 11:30 A.M.   2 h: 47 min
9. From 6:00 A.M. to 3:30 P.M.   9 h: 30 min
10. From 10:30 A.M. to 6:45 P.M.   8 h: 15 min
11. From 5:45 A.M. to 9:16 A.M.   3 h: 31 min
12. From 1:45 A.M. to 7:05 A.M.   5 h: 20 min
13. From 6:10 P.M. to 8:08 P.M.   1 h: 58 min
14. From 3:28 A.M. to 11:16 A.M.   7 h: 48 min
15. From 2:27 P.M. to 9:11 P.M.   6 h: 44 min
16. From 3:56 P.M. to 10:22 P.M.   6 h: 26 min

ELAPSED TIME

17. From 12:07 A.M. to 7:25 A.M.   7 h: 18 min
18. From 12:35 P.M. to 6:45 P.M.   6 h: 10 min
19. From 8:10 A.M. to 4:45 P.M.   8 h: 35 min
20. From 7:45 A.M. to 5:30 P.M.   9 h: 45 min
21. From 7:00 A.M. to 3:00 P.M.   8 h
22. From 8:30 A.M. to 5:00 P.M.   8 h: 30 min
23. From 7:30 A.M. to 4:10 P.M.   8 h: 40 min
24. From 8:23 A.M. to 5:04 P.M.   8 h: 41 min
25. From 5:45 A.M. to 2:15 P.M.   8 h: 30 min
26. From 7:43 A.M. to 4:21 P.M.   8 h: 38 min
27. From 8:45 P.M. to 1:18 A.M.   4 h: 33 min
28. From 9:47 A.M. to 7:08 P.M.   9 h: 21 min
29. From 11:27 P.M. to 4:11 A.M.   4 h: 44 min
30. From 5:55 P.M. to 1:55 A.M.   8 h

APPLICATIONS

31. Jack Keegan worked from 7:15 A.M. to 5:00 P.M. How long did he work?   9 h: 45 min

32. Elena Diaz took a bus that left Cincinnati at 5:45 P.M. and arrived in Cleveland at 1:10 A.M. How long was the trip?   7 h: 25 min

33. National Delivery Service (N.D.S.) ships hundreds of packages across the United States every day by air freight. Below is an N.D.S. air freight schedule. Calculate the total transit time for each shipment. (Note that all times given are Eastern Standard Time; therefore, time zones do not need to be taken into account.)

	Shipped From	Shipped To	Departure Time	Arrival Time	Total Transit Time
a.	Chattanooga, TN	Atlanta, GA	7:35 A.M.	8:20 A.M.	45 min
b.	Chicago, IL	Houston, TX	8:10 A.M.	12:57 P.M.	4 h: 47 min
c.	Los Angeles, CA	New Orleans, LA	8:35 A.M.	2:17 P.M.	5 h: 42 min
d.	New York, NY	Cleveland, OH	5:25 P.M.	7:25 P.M.	2 h
e.	Boston, MA	Phoenix, AZ	11:45 A.M.	7:28 P.M.	7 h: 43 min
f.	Atlanta, GA	Miami, FL	7:07 A.M.	9:00 A.M.	1 h: 53 min

Appendix

READING TABLES AND CHARTS

To read a table or chart, find the *column* containing one of the pieces of information you have. Look across the *row* containing the other piece of information. Read down the column and across the row. Read the information you need where the column and row intersect.

Shipping Costs

Not Over (lbs)	Zone 2 & 3	Zone 4	Zone 5	Zone 6	Zone 7
1	$4.00	$4.00	$4.00	$4.00	$4.00
2	$4.00	$4.00	$4.00	$4.00	$4.00
3	$5.10	$5.10	$5.10	$5.10	$5.10
4	$6.20	$6.20	$6.20	$6.20	$6.20
5	$7.30	$7.30	$7.30	$7.30	$7.30
6	$8.60	$8.90	$9.10	$9.45	$9.70
7	$8.70	$9.30	$9.70	$10.40	$10.90
8	$8.80	$9.70	$10.30	$11.35	$12.10
9	$8.90	$10.10	$10.90	$12.30	$13.30
10	$9.00	$10.50	$11.50	$13.25	$14.50

EXAMPLE What is the cost to ship a 6-lb package to Zone 5?

SOLUTION
a. Find the Zone 5 column.   b. Find the 6-lb row.
c. Read across the 6-lb row to the Zone 5 column. The cost is $9.10.

To classify an item, find the row that contains the known data. Then read the classification from the head of the column.

Men's Body Measurement

Size	S	M	L	XL	XXL
Neck	14–14 $\frac{1}{2}$	15–15 $\frac{1}{2}$	16–16 $\frac{1}{2}$	17–17 $\frac{1}{2}$	18–18 $\frac{1}{2}$
Chest	34–36	38–40	42–44	46–48	50–52
Waist	28–30	32–34	36–38	40–42	44–46
Reg. Sleeve	32–33	33–34	34–35	35–36	36–37
Tall Sleeve	33–34	34–35	35–36	36–37	37–38
Height	Reg. 5′8″–6′	Tall 6′1″–6′4″			

Talls: Measure 2″ longer overall, 1″ at sleeves

EXAMPLE What size shirt should a man with a 42-inch chest order?

SOLUTION
a. Find the row for the Chest measurements.   b. Read across the row to 42–44.
c. Read the size at the head of the column (L). A man with a 42-inch chest should order a size L, which stands for large.

PROBLEMS

Use the shipping chart above to find the cost to ship each package to the indicated zone.

1. 3 lb, Zone 3 $5.10
2. 4 lb, Zone 7 $6.20
3. 9 lb, Zone 4 $10.10
4. 2 lb, Zone 6 $4.00
5. 6 lb, Zone 2 $8.60
6. 5 lb, Zone 5 $7.30
7. 1.5 lb, Zone 5 $4.00
8. 6.4 lb, Zone 7 $10.90
9. 8.2 lb, Zone 3 $8.90
10. 7.1 lb, Zone 6 $11.35
11. 5.8 lb, Zone 4 $8.90
12. 9.3 lb, Zone 3 $9.00

READING TABLES AND CHARTS

Use the size chart on the previous page to determine what size to order. In-between sizes should order the next size up.

13. Shorts—waist 33   32–34, M
14. Shirt—chest 37   38–40, M
15. Jacket—chest 47   46–48, XL
16. Pants—waist 43   44–46, XXL
17. Sweater—chest 43   42–44, L
18. Shirt—height 6'2", sleeves 36   Tall, L

APPLICATIONS

19. Use the shipping chart on the previous page to determine the maximum amount a package can weigh.

	a.	b.	c.	d.	e.	f.
Shipping Zone	2	5	7	3	6	4
Shipping Cost	$7.30	$4.00	$13.30	$8.90	$7.30	$5.10
Maximum Weight	5 lb	2 lb	9 lb	9 lb	5 lb	3 lb

Use the Federal Income Tax Table to find the amount of tax withheld in questions 20–25 and the amount of wages earned in questions 26–31:

Federal Income Tax Table
MARRIED Persons—WEEKLY Payroll Period

If the wages are—		And the number of withholding allowances claimed is—							
At least	But less than	0	1	2	3	4	5	6	7
		The amount of income tax to be withheld is—							
$480	$490	$63	$56	$50	$44	$38	$32	$25	$19
490	500	64	58	52	45	39	33	27	21
500	510	66	59	53	47	41	35	28	22
510	520	67	61	55	48	42	36	30	24
520	530	69	62	56	50	44	38	31	25
530	540	70	64	58	51	45	39	33	27
540	550	72	65	59	53	47	41	34	28
550	560	73	67	61	54	48	42	36	30
560	570	75	68	62	56	50	44	37	31
570	580	76	70	64	57	51	45	39	33
580	590	78	71	65	59	53	47	40	34
590	600	79	73	67	60	54	48	42	36
600	610	81	74	68	62	56	50	43	37
610	620	82	76	70	63	57	51	45	39
620	630	84	77	71	65	59	53	46	40

	20.	21.	22.	23.	24.	25.
Income	$491.77	$501.07	$617.30	$525.00	$600.00	$531.13
Allowances	2	1	3	0	4	6
Amount Withheld	$52.00	$59.00	$63.00	$69.00	$56.00	$33.00

	Number of Allowances	Tax Withheld	Wages At least	But less than
26.	5	$47	580	590
27.	2	$71	620	630
28.	3	$53	540	550
29.	1	$62	520	530
30.	4	$38	480	490
31.	0	$76	570	580

Appendix

CONSTRUCTING GRAPHS

A **bar graph** is a picture that displays and compares numerical facts in the form of vertical or horizontal bars. To construct a vertical bar graph, follow these steps:

a. Draw the vertical and horizontal axes.
b. Scale the vertical axis to correspond to the given data.
c. Draw one bar to represent each quantity.
d. Label each bar and the vertical and horizontal axes.
e. Title the graph.

Metropolitan Statistical Areas
Population (in millions)

Chicago, IL	8.6
San Francisco, CA	6.6
Philadelphia, PA	6.0
Detroit, MI	5.3

EXAMPLE Construct a vertical bar graph of the given data.

SOLUTION
a. Draw vertical and horizontal axes.
b. Scale the vertical axis.
c. Draw one bar to represent each quantity.
d. Label each bar and the vertical and horizontal axes.
e. Title the graph.

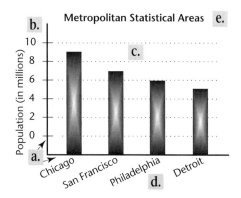

A **line graph** is a picture used to compare data over a period of time. It is an excellent way to show trends (increases or decreases). To construct a line graph, follow these steps:

a. Draw the vertical and horizontal axes.
b. Scale the vertical axis to correspond to the given data.
c. Label the axes.
d. Place a point on the graph to correspond to each item of data.
e. Connect the points from left to right.
f. Title the graph.

Percentage of Women in the Total Workforce

1950	29.6%
1960	33.4%
1970	38.1%
1980	42.5%
1990	45.8%
2000	47.5%

EXAMPLE Construct a line graph of the given data.

SOLUTION
a. Draw the vertical and horizontal axes.
b. Scale the vertical axis.
c. Label the axes.
d. Place a point to correspond to each item of data.
e. Connect the points from left to right.
f. Title the graph.

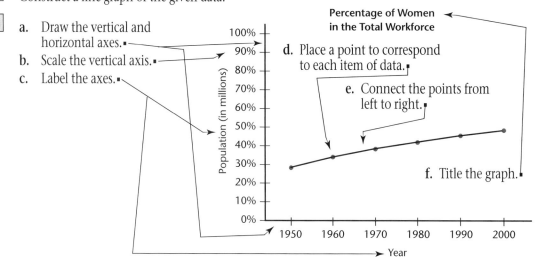

CONSTRUCTING GRAPHS

PROBLEMS

1. Construct a vertical bar graph of the given data.

Wrenn's Department Store
Total Sales by Department (in thousands)

Housewares	122
Men's Clothing	145
Women's Clothing	160
Appliances	183
Electronics	214

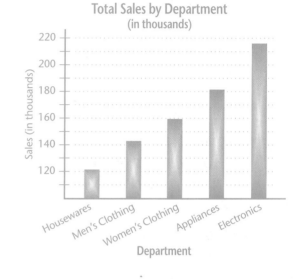

Total Sales by Department
(in thousands)

2. Read the vertical bar graph.

a. Of the metropolitan areas listed, which is projected to have the largest population in 2033? Los Angeles

b. Which of the metropolitan areas listed is projected to have the smallest population in 2033? Washington, DC

c. What is Chicago's projected population for 2033? about 9 million

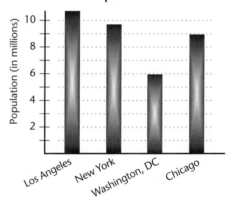

Projected Metropolitan Area Populations for 2033

3. Construct a line graph of the given data.

Tollhouse Industries Stock

Month	Average
Jan.	16.50
Feb.	17
Mar.	16.25
Apr.	15
May	17.50
June	18

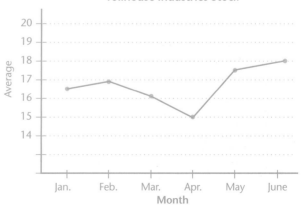

Tollhouse Industries Stock

Appendix

UNITS OF MEASURE

Here are abbreviations and conversions for units of measure in the customary measurement system.

Length	Volume	Weight
12 inches (in) = 1 foot (ft)	2 cups (c) = 1 pint (pt)	16 ounces (oz) = 1 pound (lb)
3 ft = 1 yard (yd)	2 pt = 1 quart (qt)	2000 lb = 1 ton (t)
5280 ft = 1 mile (mi)	4 qt = 1 gallon (gal)	

Here are symbols and conversions for units of measure in the metric system.

Length	Volume
1000 millimeters (mm) = 1 meter (m)	1000 milliliters (mL) = 1 liter (L)
100 centimeters (cm) = 1 m	**Mass**
1000 m = 1 kilometer (km)	1000 grams (g) = 1 kilogram (kg)

To convert from one unit of measure to another, use the conversions lists above.

When converting to a smaller unit, multiply.

EXAMPLE

SOLUTION

Convert 5 feet to inches.

Use 12 in = 1 ft

5 ft: 5 × 12 = 60

5 ft = 60 in

Convert 4 meters to centimeters.

Use 100 cm = 1 m

4 m: 4 × 100 = 400

4 m = 400 cm

When converting to a larger unit, divide.

EXAMPLE

SOLUTION

Convert 6 pints to quarts.

Use 2 pt = 1 qt

6 pt: 6 ÷ 2 = 3

6 pt = 3 qt

Convert 6500 grams to kilograms.

Use 1000 g = 1 kg

6500 g: 6500 ÷ 1000 = 6.5

6500 g = 6.5 kg

PROBLEMS

Make the following conversions.

1. 12 yd to feet — 36 ft
2. 8 gal to quarts — 32 qt
3. 9 lb to ounces — 144 oz
4. 2 ft to inches — 24 in
5. 3 lb to ounces — 48 oz
6. 5 L to milliliters — 5000 mL
7. 2.4 km to meters — 2400 m
8. 24 pt to cups — 48 c
9. 3.6 kg to grams — 3600 g
10. 99 in to yards — 2.75 yd
11. 15 qt to gallons — 3.75 gal
12. 66 oz to pounds — 4.125 lb
13. 18 qt to gallons — 4.5 gal
14. 24 oz to pounds — 1.5 lb
15. 7000 g to kilograms — 7 kg
16. 60 cm to meters — 0.6 m
17. 2200 mL to liters — 2.2 L
18. 350 cm to meters — 3.5 m
19. 29 kg to grams — 29,000 g
20. 17.3 L to milliliters — 17,300 mL
21. 522 g to kilograms — 0.522 kg
22. 10.122 mL to liters — 0.010122 L
23. 72 cm to millimeters — 720 mm
24. 432.2 cm to meters — 4.322 m
25. 1 yd 7 in to inches — 43 in
26. 5 ft 7 in to inches — 67 in
27. 3 qt 1 pt to pints — 7 pt
28. 6 lb 9 oz to ounces — 105 oz
29. 4 gal 1 qt to quarts — 17 qt
30. 3 yd 1 ft 5 in to inches — 125 in
31. 5 gal 3 qt 1 pt to pints — 47 pt
32. 3 m 57 cm 29 mm to millimeters — 3599 mm

UNITS OF MEASURE

33. How many quarts will a 6-gallon bucket hold?   24 qt

34. How many milliliters will a 2-liter bottle hold?   2000 mL

35. How many cups of coffee does a 4-quart coffeepot hold?   16 c

36. How many cups of hot chocolate will a 1.5-gallon thermos jug hold?   24 c

37. How many inches long is an 8-yard roll of aluminum foil?   288 in

38. Strawberries are sold in 1-pint containers. How many pints must be purchased to have enough for a recipe that calls for 3 cups?   2 (1.5)

39. James Jones knows that his jogging stride is about 1 meter long. The jogging trail he uses is 4.2 kilometers long. How many strides does it take him to go around the trail once?   4200

40. The cafeteria receives 49 cases of milk each day. Each case contains 24 half-pint cartons. How many gallons of milk are received each day?   73.5 gal

41. A soft drink is sold in 355 mL cans. How many liters are in a six-pack?   2.13 L

42. Katie Karanikos baked a chocolate layer cake weighing 1.5 kilograms. How many 75-gram servings can be cut from the cake?   20

43. Joan Baird ordered baseboard molding for the rooms of a new house. Joan needs to complete this chart to determine the total number of feet of molding needed. How much molding is needed?

Length	Width	2 lengths	+ 2 widths	= Perimeter
12 ft	10 ft	24 ft	+ 20 ft	= 44 ft
11 ft	8 ft	22 ft	+ 16 ft	= 38 ft
a. 11 ft	19 ft	22 ft	+ 38 ft	= 60 ft
b. 12 ft	12 ft 2 in	24 ft	+ 24 ft 4 in	= 48 ft 4 in
c. 15 ft	16 ft 8 in	30 ft	+ 33 ft 4 in	= 63 ft 4 in
d. 11 ft 8 in	12 ft 2 in	23 ft 4 in	+ 24 ft 4 in	= 47 ft 8 in
e. 12 ft 10 in	16 ft 10 in	25 ft 8 in	+ 33 ft 8 in	= 59 ft 4 in
f. 16 ft 9 in	24 ft 3 in	33 ft 6 in	+ 48 ft 6 in	= 82 ft
g. 9 ft 4 in	10 ft	18 ft 8 in	+ 20 ft	= 38 ft 8 in
h.		Total		481 ft 4 in

PROBLEM SOLVING: USING THE FOUR-STEP METHOD

The problem-solving process consists of several interrelated actions. The solutions to some problems are obvious and require very little effort. Others require a step-by-step procedure. Using a procedure such as the four-step method will help you to solve word problems.

The Four-Step Method

Step 1: Understand   What is the problem? What is given? What are you asked to do?

Step 2: Plan   What do you need to do to solve the problem? Choose a problem-solving strategy.

Step 3: Work   Carry out the plan. Do any necessary calculations.

Step 4: Answer   Is your answer reasonable? Did you answer the question?

EXAMPLE

The Gordons own several rental homes that need replumbing. It will take 2 plumbers 5 days to do the work. Each plumber works 8 hours a day at $33 per hour. How much will the project cost?

SOLUTION

Step 1: Given   2 plumbers, 5 days, 8 hours, $33 per hour

       Find   The cost per day for 1 plumber.
The cost per day for 2 plumbers.
The cost of 2 plumbers for 5 days.

Step 2: Plan   Find the cost per day for 1 plumber, then multiply by the number of plumbers, and then multiply by the number of days.

Step 3: Work   8 hours per day $\times$ $33 per hour = $264 per day for 1 plumber
2 plumbers $\times$ $264 per day for 1 plumber = $528 per day for 2 plumbers
5 days $\times$ $528 per day for 2 plumbers = $2640 for 2 plumbers for 5 days

Step 4: Answer   It will cost $2640 for 2 plumbers for 5 days.

PROBLEMS

Identify the plan, work, and answer for each problem.

1. It takes 3 electricians 10 days to rewire some apartment buildings. Each electrician earns $37.50 per hour and works $7\frac{1}{2}$ hours per day. How much will the rewiring cost? $8437.50

2. Eric Cortez makes a car payment of $227.15 every month. His car loan is for 5 years. How much will he pay in 5 years? $13,629

3. Jessica Henderson and Kyle Casey spent a total of $213.58 on their prom date. Dinner cost $60.12. How much did everything else cost Jessica and Kyle? $153.46

4. Marcus Johnson purchased 2 shirts at $38 each, a belt for $19.50, jeans for $29.50, shoes for $89.99, and 3 pairs of socks at $6.99 a pair. How much did Marcus spend? $235.96

5. A contractor is building 5 new homes. It will take 4 carpet layers 3 days to install the carpet for all 5 homes. The carpet layers work 8 hours per day and earn $18.00 per hour. How much will it cost for the carpet installation? $1728

6. The same 5 new homes will each have a foyer measuring 12 feet by 12 feet. Wood parquet floors for each foyer cost $55.30 per square yard. What is the cost of the wood parquet floors for the foyers in all 5 homes? $4424

PROBLEM SOLVING: USING THE FOUR-STEP METHOD

7. Beth Anderson charges $2.50 per page for typing rough drafts and an additional 75¢ per page for changes and deletions. A manuscript had 318 pages, of which 165 pages had changes and deletions. What was the total cost of typing the manuscript? $918.75

8. Fred Woo is paying $53.50 per month for a computer. The total cost of the computer was $855.99. How long will it take Fred to pay for the computer?   16 months

9. Mitch Elliot rode his bicycle on a 3-mile path. Approximately how many rotations did Mitch's 26″ bicycle wheels make on this path? (Hint: The circumference of a circle is approximately 3.14 times the diameter and a mile = 5280 feet.)   Approximately 2328 rotations

10. Nicole and Joseph Conti drove to St. Louis, a distance of 781 miles. Their car gets 22 miles per gallon of gasoline. Gasoline costs them $1.36 per gallon. How much did Nicole and Joseph spend for gasoline on their trip? $48.28

11. Joy and Ernie both live in Columbus, Ohio. Joy drove due north for 3 hours at 60 miles per hour. Ernie drove due south for 2 hours at 65 per hour. How far apart were they after their trip?   310 miles

12. Cindee Adams bought 3 boxes of cereal at $2.79 each, a roll of paper towels for 88¢, and 10 pounds of chicken at 65¢ a pound. How much change would Cindee get back from $20? $4.25

13. Thelma Wicker's pound cake is 30 cm long. She slices each cake into 2 cm slices. Thelma is serving 115 people for lunch. How many pound cakes will she need to bake?   8 cakes

Appendix

PROBLEM SOLVING: IDENTIFYING INFORMATION

Before you begin to solve a word problem, first read the problem carefully and answer these questions:

- What are you asked to find?
- What facts are given?
- Are enough facts given? Do you need more information than the problem provides?

Some word problems provide more information than is needed to solve the problem. Others cannot be solved without additional information. Identifying what is wanted, what is given, and what is needed allows you to organize the information and plan your solution.

EXAMPLE Jonathan Klein is a lab technician at Laminates, Ltd. He earns $25.20 per hour. He is single and claims 1 withholding allowance. Last week he worked 40 hours at the regular rate and 4 hours at the weekend rate. He is 28 years old. Find his gross pay for last week.

SOLUTION
A. Wanted: Jonathan Klein's gross pay for last week
B. Facts given: $25.20 hourly rate
                         40 hours worked at regular rate
                         4 hours worked at weekend rate
C. Additional facts needed: Weekend rate

This problem cannot be solved.

EXAMPLE Martha Henderson, age 43, runs 3 miles every day. How many miles does Martha run in a week?

SOLUTION
A. Wanted: Number of miles run in 1 week
B. Facts given: Runs 3 miles every day
C. Additional facts needed: None

This problem can be solved. Multiply the number of miles run per day (3) by the number of days in 1 week (7). The answer is 21 miles.

PROBLEMS

Identify the wanted, given, and needed information. If enough information is given, solve the problem.

1. Kelly Jenkins bought a new car with a $4500 down payment and monthly payments of $375. How much did Kelly pay, in total, for her new car?
   Cannot be solved. Need number of payments.

2. The Great Outdoors is having a sale on sports equipment. The Yosemite dome tent is priced at $99, the GlacierPoint mountain bike is $69, and Shenandoah in-line skates are $49. What is the total cost of the Yosemite dome tent and Yellowstone backpack?
   Cannot be solved. Need cost of backpack.

3. Lisa Smith paid $175 each way to fly round-trip from Atlanta to Denver. Brittany Cruz paid $335 for the round-trip fare. Who paid more? How much more?
   Lisa paid $15 more for the round-trip.

PROBLEM SOLVING: IDENTIFYING INFORMATION

4. The Northside Fruit Farm pays pickers $1.50 per pound to pick blueberries, which are packed in one-pint baskets and sold at market for $2.25 per pint. How many pint baskets need to be sold to pay one worker one day's wage?

   Cannot be solved. Need relationship between pints and pounds and how many pounds a picker picks in a day.

5. Tyler Fulgum paid $95 each for two tickets to a concert. He paid for the tickets with four $50 bills. How much change did he receive? $10

6. How much would four sets of towels cost if they were 25 x 20 inches and priced at three for $9.99?
   $39.96

7. Bill Hale bought a boneless shoulder roast with a $20 bill. He received $3.17 in change. How much did Bill pay per pound for the roast?

   Cannot be solved. Need weight of roast.

8. The party platter cost $65, beverages cost $35.77, and party supplies cost $18.13. Brandon and his friends agreed to share the total cost of food, beverages, and supplies for the party equally. How much did each pay?

   Cannot be solved. Need number of friends.

9. Dana Edwards is 5 feet 2 inches tall and weighs 108 pounds. She grew 3 inches in the past year. How tall was she last year?   4 feet, 11 inches

10. Greg Jones has finished 55 of the 60 math problems on his test. It is now 11:20 A.M. The 1-hour test started at 10:30 A.M. What is the average number of minutes he can spend on each of the remaining problems?   2 minutes

11. A two-drawer file cabinet and a box of files cost $110. What is the cost of the file cabinet?

    Cannot be solved. Need cost of files.

12. A designer fragrance gift set is on sale for 40% off its original retail price of $65. If the retailer discounted it an additional 10% of the sale price, what would the final sale price be? $35.10

13. Matthew Travino sells stereo equipment and receives a weekly salary of $300 plus a 5% commission on sales. Last week his gross pay was $660. What is the dollar amount of stereo equipment sold by Matthew last week? $7200

14. Darien Dromboski was shopping for coffee makers. The Javamaker model was $11.43 more than the BestBrew model and the Coffee Time model was $4.95 less than the BestBrew. How much more than the cost of the Coffee Time was the Javamaker? $16.38

Appendix

PROBLEM SOLVING: USING MORE THAN ONE OPERATION

Some problems require several operations to solve. After deciding which operations to use, you must decide the correct order in which to perform them.

EXAMPLE   The cash price of a new car is $22,885. Marcie Cunningham cannot pay cash, so she is making a down payment of $3300 and 60 monthly payments of $385 each. How much more does it cost to buy the car this way?

SOLUTION

A. Given: Cash price of $22,885
                   $3300 down + 60 payments of $385 each

B. Multiply: To get total of payments
                   60 × $385 = $23,100

   Add: $3300 to total payments
                   $3300 + $23,100 = $26,400

   Subtract: Cash price from total payments
                   $26,400 − $22,885 = $3515

It cost $3515 more to buy the car this way. In this example, the order of operations is very important; that is, multiply, then add, then subtract.

EXAMPLE   Juan Perez bought 2 gallons of milk costing $2.69 per gallon. He gave the cashier a $20 bill. How much change did he receive if there was no sales tax?

SOLUTION

A. Given: Bought 2 gallons of milk at $2.69 per gallon, no sales tax
                   Gave cashier $20.00

B. Multiply: To get total cost
                   2 × $2.69 = $5.38

   Subtract: To find change
                   $20.00 − $5.38 = $14.62

Juan received $14.62 in change. In this example, the order of operations is multiply, then subtract.

PROBLEMS

Give the sequence of operations needed to solve the problems, then solve.

1. Your entertainment budget for the month is $50. If you spent $18.50 at the movies, $12 for tickets to a college basketball game, and $11.75 at a concert, how much is left in your entertainment budget?   +, −, $7.75

2. Steve Sorrells works 9 hours a day 5 days a week. So far this year, he has worked 540 hours. How many weeks has he worked?   ×, ÷, 12

3. The Parent/Teacher Organization (PTO) sells soft drinks and popcorn at home basketball games. Last week they sold 225 cups of soft drinks at $1.00 per cup and 185 bags of popcorn at 75¢ per bag. What were the total sales?   ×, ×, +, $363.75

PROBLEM SOLVING: USING MORE THAN ONE OPERATION

4. Gerry Hanson pays his electric bills through a payment plan of $65 per month regardless of usage. At the end of one year, he is billed for the difference if his usage is more, or sent a refund if his usage is less. His usage for the last three months was $62, $64.35, and $68.20. Is he over or under his payment plan schedule so far this year? By how much?

   +, ÷, compare, −, 15¢ under per month

5. Daniel Dalton sold 16 watermelons for $5 each, 20 for $4 each, and 30 for $3 each. He makes 50% commission for each watermelon he sells. How much money did Daniel make?   ×, ×, ×, +, × $125

6. Henry Mack has a new job as an insurance adjuster and has read 272 pages of a 512-page training manual. It took him two days to read through the remaining pages. If he read the same number of pages each day, how many pages did he read each day?   −, ÷, 120

7. Leah Mattison worked 40 hours for $7.25 per hour. She worked 5 hours for $18.13 an hour. How much money did Leah earn?   ×, ×, +, $380.65

8. In one month, the Bowens spent $95.78, $112.13, $98.66, and $124.33 for groceries. Their monthly food budget is $450. How much money do they have left to spend for food?   +, −, $19.10

9. The temperature in the greenhouse is 25 degrees Celsius at 9:00 A.M. If the temperature increases 1.5 degrees every hour, what will the temperature be at 3:00 P.M.?   −, ×, +, 34 degrees C

10. Daryl Harden walks 3 miles round-trip to work 5 times a week. How far will he walk in one year?   ×, ×, 780 miles

11. Zach McCain assembled a total of 788 circuit boards in 4 days of work. During the first three days, he assembled 201, 196, and 198, respectively. How many did he assemble the last day?   +, −, 193

12. In a one-month reading contest at school, Rick Gonzalez earned 3 half-point certificates, 5 one-point certificates, and 4 two-point certificates. How many points did he earn for the month?   ×, +, 14.5

13. The Athens Historical Society sold 1245 $5 tickets as a fund-raiser. Prizes were a $2,000 handmade quilt, 4 framed prints that cost $500 each, and 10 books that cost $25 each. How much money did the Historical Society make?   ×, +, ×, −, $1975

14. Drew Young sold candy bars at school to raise money for a band trip. He sold 47 $1-candy bars. If his sales totaled $68 dollars, how many $3-candy bars did he sell?   −, ÷, 7

15. Spencer Baird bought 2 sweatshirts for $15.75 each and 2 T-shirts for $8.50 each. How much change did he receive from a $50 bill?   ×, +, −, $1.50

16. Josey Chandler saved $550. After she earned an additional $125, she spent $320 for a chair, $50 for a rug, and $30 for a lamp. How much money did Josey have left?   +, +, −, $275

PROBLEM SOLVING: WRITING AN EQUATION

A word problem can be translated into an equation that is solved by performing the same mathematical operation (adding, subtracting, multiplying, or dividing) to both sides. Solving the equation then leads to the solution of the problem.

To set up the equation, look for words in the problem that suggest which of the four mathematical operations to use.

Words	Symbol	Operation
The total, how many in all, the sum, plus	+	Addition
The difference, how much more, how much smaller, minus	−	Subtraction
The total for a number of equal items, the product	×	Multiplication
The number left over, the quotient	÷	Division

EXAMPLE

In 40 hours at your regular rate of pay plus 10 hours of double time (twice your regular rate of pay), you earn $855. What is your regular rate of pay?

SOLUTION

Use the letter x to stand for your regular rate of pay.

$40x + 10(2x) = \$855.00$

$40x + 20x = \$855.00$

$60x = \$855.00$ (Divide each side by 60.)

$x = \$14.25$

EXAMPLE

A rectangle with a perimeter of 64 mm is 25 mm long. What is the width of the rectangle?

SOLUTION

Let w equal the width of the rectangle.

$w + 25 + w + 25 = 64$

$2w + 50 = 64$ (Subtract 50 from both sides.)

$2w = 14$ (Divide both sides by 2.)

$w = 7$ mm wide

PROBLEMS

1. The sum of 2 consecutive numbers is 47. What is the smaller number?   23

2. One brand of computer scanner can read 83 documents per hour while a second scanner can read 97 documents per hour. How many hours will it take to read 900 documents?   5 hours

3. A jar of mayonnaise costs 97¢. The mayonnaise costs 55¢ more than the jar. How much does each cost?   Jar: 21¢; Mayonnaise: 76¢

4. A robot travels 36 meters around the edge of a rectangular assembly room. If the rectangle is twice as long as it is wide, how long is each side?   12 meters × 6 meters

PROBLEM SOLVING: WRITING AN EQUATION

5. A football field is 100 yards long and has a distance around of 308 yards. How wide is it? 54 yards

6. Ed and Maria Zavala-Waterman make monthly payments of $845 on their $120,000 mortgage. They will have paid $184,200 in interest when their mortgage is paid off. For how many years is their mortgage? 30 years

7. Carol Austin had gross earnings of $804.86 last week. She earns $10.25 per hour plus a 4.5% commission on all sales. She knows she worked 40 hours last week but can't remember her total sales. What were her total sales? $8,774.67

8. Luis Rivera earns $8.10 per hour plus double time for all hours over 40 per week. How much did Luis earn for working 48 hours last week? $453.60

9. Sandy Brubaker has 4 Guernsey cows and 3 Holstein cows that give as much milk in 5 days as 3 Guernsey and 5 Holstein cows give in 4 days. Which kind of cow is the better milk producer, the Guernsey or the Holstein? Holstein

10. The Maren Manufacturing Company building is 6 times as old as the equipment. The building was 40 years old when the equipment was purchased. How old is the equipment? 8 years

11. The sum of 3 consecutive odd numbers is 33. What are the 3 numbers? 9, 11, 13

12. Ingram, Inc. stock sells for $23 $\frac{3}{4}$ a share. The Morrison Brokerage Company charges a flat fee of $45 for every transaction. How many shares could you buy for $900? 36

13. Keesha is working with fabric that is twice as long as it is wide. It is 6$\frac{1}{2}$ yards long. How wide is it? 3$\frac{1}{4}$ yards

14. If the fabric were 4 yards, 6 inches wide, how long would it be? 8 yards, 1 foot or 8$\frac{1}{3}$ yards

15. Tom, Darren, and Kerry have a combined weight of 600 pounds. Kerry weighs 15 pounds more than Darren, while Darren weighs 15 pounds more than Tom. How much does each man weigh? Tom = 185; Darren = 200; Kerry = 215

Glossary

A

accounting The systematic process of recording and reporting the financial position of a business.

actual cash value The value of an item new minus depreciation as a result of wear and tear, or how much the item is worth used.

advertising A paid, non-personal form of communication that businesses use to promote their products.

ageism Discrimination on the basis of age.

Americans with Disabilities Act (ADA) A federal law that requires businesses to provide facilities for people with special needs.

annual percentage rate (APR) The rate at which interest is charged for credit on a yearly basis.

antitrust laws Laws that allow the federal government to break up, regulate, or take over monopolies and trusts.

apprenticeship Learning a trade by working under the guidance of a skilled worker.

aptitudes Talents or abilities that come naturally.

asset Anything of value that a business or individual owns.

autocratic leadership A leadership style in which one person runs everything and makes all decisions without consulting others.

B

baby boom generation People born between 1946 and 1964.

bait and switch Advertising an item at a low price to lure customers into the store and then trying to get them to switch to a more expensive item.

balance of trade The difference in value between how much a country imports and how much it exports.

balance sheet A report of the financial state of a business on a certain date.

bank account A record of how much money a person has put into and taken out of a bank.

bank reconciliation The process of seeing whether one's own checking account records agree with the bank's records.

bank statement A bank's record of all the transactions in a checking account.

bankruptcy A legal process in which a person is relieved of debts but creditors can take some or all of the person's assets.

banner ads Internet ads that are displayed across the top or bottom of the screen.

beneficiary Person who receives part or all of the proceeds from a life insurance policy.

Better Business Bureau (BBB) A nonprofit organization that provides information and handles complaints about local businesses.

blue-chip stocks Stocks in large, well-established companies that have a good track record of success.

body language Non-verbal communication, such as posture, eye contact, facial expressions, and gestures.

bond discount The difference between the amount paid for a bond and its face value.

bonds Written promises, issued by a corporation or the government, to repay a loan with interest on a specific date.

boycott Refuse to buy a company's products or services.

brand name A word or name on a product that helps consumers distinguish it from other products.

breach of contract The failure of a party to live up to the terms of a contract.

break-even point The amount of money a company has to make on a product to pay for the cost of producing it.

bricks-and-mortar Stores, warehouses, and other buildings businesses use.

broker A dealer who specializes in buying and selling stock.

budget A plan of expected income and expenses over a certain period of time.

budget deficit When the government spends more on programs than it collects in taxes, or expenses exceed income.

budget surplus When the government collects more in taxes than it spends on programs, or income exceeds expenses.

budget variance The difference between planned spending and actual spending.

bureaucracy A formal organization consisting of many levels of management.

business Any activity that seeks profit by providing goods or services to others.

business cycle The rise and fall of economic activity over time.

business ethics The rules that govern how businesses should conduct themselves.

business etiquette Acceptable social behavior and manners in business.

byte Amount of memory it takes to store a single computer character.

C

canceled checks Checks written that have been cashed.

capital gain Selling stock for more than it cost to buy it.

capital loss Selling stock for less than it cost to buy it.

capital resources Things such as buildings, materials, and equipment used to produce goods and services.

career An occupation or field in which a person works over a long period of time.

career counselor A person trained to provide information and guidance on choosing and preparing for a career.

career ladder Job levels within an occupation.

career planning The steps necessary to choose and prepare for a career.

cash advance Using a credit card to borrow money rather than to charge a purchase.

cash-value insurance Life insurance that provides both a savings plan and death benefits.

centralized organization An organization that puts authority in one place, with top management.

certificate of deposit (CD) A type of savings account that requires a minimum amount of money deposited in the account for a minimum period of time.

channel of distribution A particular means of directing products from producers to consumers, such as a wholesaler or retailer.

charge account Credit provided by a store or company for customers to buy its products.

check register A checkbook or log used to record checking transactions.

claim A request for payment from an insurer for any damages covered by an insurance policy.

clearance sale A sale to clear out goods that are going out of season or are no longer profitable to make room for new merchandise.

clicks-and-mortar The use of both the Internet and buildings, such as stores and warehouses, to do business.

code of ethics A strict set of guidelines in a profession or company for upholding ethical behavior in the workplace.

coinsurance A percentage of medical expenses an insurance policyholder must pay beyond the deductible.

collateral Something valuable, such as a house or car, used as guarantee for a loan that the lender can take if the borrower doesn't repay the loan.

collection agent A person or business that collects overdue bills.

command economy A system in which a central authority such as the state makes the key economic decisions.

commercial credit Credit used by business.

common stock The primary, or common, form of ownership of a corporation.

comparison shopping Checking the price and quality of a product in more than one store.

compensation The pay and benefits a company offers for a job.

competition The contest between businesses to win customers.

compound interest Interest earned on both the principal amount in an account and the interest already earned on the account, or interest on interest.

compulsory insurance law A law that requires drivers to have a minimum amount of car insurance.

computer-aided design (CAD) Software for designing products with a computer.

conflict of interest When a business puts its interests before the interests of society.

conservation The process of preserving, protecting, and managing resources.

consolidation loan A loan that combines several debts into one loan with lower payments.

consumer A person who selects, purchases, uses, or disposes of goods or services.

consumer advocates Groups and individuals that work to protect, inform, and defend consumers.

consumer credit Credit used by individuals for personal reasons.

Glossary

Consumer Credit Protection Act A federal law, also known as the Truth in Lending Law, that requires creditors to inform consumers of the costs and terms of credit and protects consumers from lost or stolen credit cards.

consumer movement A movement to pass laws protecting consumers from unfair and unsafe business practices.

consumer reporter A radio or TV reporter who reports on issues important to consumers, such as product safety.

consumer rights Consumers' rights to safety, to be heard, to choose, to be informed, to have problems corrected, to consumer education, and to service.

contract A legal agreement between two or more parties to conduct business.

cookies Pieces of information about a computer user, stored on the user's hard drive, that can be accessed by a Web server whenever the user goes on the Internet.

cooperative An organization of businesses owned and operated by the members, who pool their resources and share the benefits.

copayment A fee paid each time a service covered by a health insurance plan, such as a doctor's visit or a prescription, is used.

copyright A legal grant for the sole right to own a creative property, such as a book or video game.

corporate bonds Bond sold by corporations to finance building and equipment.

corporate culture A company's shared values, beliefs, and goals.

corporation A business treated by law as separate from its owners.

cosigner A person who signs a loan for someone else and is responsible for repaying the loan if the borrower doesn't repay it.

coupon rate The rate of interest on a bond.

cover letter A one-page letter accompanying a résumé that tells an employer about an applicant and why the applicant is interested in a job.

credit An agreement to get money, goods, or services now in exchange for a promise to pay in the future.

credit bureau An agency that collects information about consumers of credit.

credit counselor A person who helps consumers with their credit problems.

credit limit The maximum amount a person can spend or charge on a credit account.

credit rating A measure of a person's ability and willingness to pay debts on time.

creditor One who lends money or provides credit.

culture Beliefs, customs, and attitudes of a distinct group of people.

cyber ads Advertisements on the Internet.

D

database A computerized collection of information, usually kept in a list.

debit card A bank card used like a credit card but which takes money directly from a checking account.

debtor One who borrows money or uses credit.

decentralized organization An organization that gives authority to a number of different managers to run their own departments.

deductible The amount of damages that the holder of an insurance policy must pay before the insurance company pays.

deductions Amounts of money taken out of a paycheck for expenses such as taxes, health insurance, retirement, and union dues.

deflation A general decrease in the cost of goods and services.

delegate Give employees the power to run things and make decisions.

demand The amount of goods and services that consumers are willing to buy at various prices.

demand deposits Checks, or orders to a bank to release money from a checking account on demand.

democratic leadership A style of leadership in which managers work with employees to make decisions.

demographics Facts about the population in terms of age, gender, income, and education.

departmentalization Dividing responsibilities in an organization among specific units, or departments.

deposit Money put into a bank account.

depreciation Decline in the value of an item, such as a house or car, because of use.

depression A deep, long-term decline in economic activity.

desktop publishing Writing, designing, and laying out documents on a computer like a professional publisher.

digital workflow Linking all the steps in a process, such as printing, electronically.

direct distribution Selling goods and services directly from producers to consumers without using intermediaries.

direct-mail advertising Advertising sent to people's homes by mail.

discrimination Excluding someone on the basis of age, gender, ethnicity, or other difference.

diversity Variety of people with different backgrounds and identities.

dividends A share of the profits of a corporation paid to stockholders.

dot-com A company that does business on the Internet.

down payment A portion of the total cost of an item that is paid at the time the item is purchased.

E

e-commerce Electronic commerce, or business conducted on the Internet.

economics The study of how society chooses to use resources to produce and distribute goods and services for people's consumption.

electronic funds transfer (EFT) The transfer of money from one account to another using computers.

eleven perils The most common causes of property damage or loss, covered by all homeowner's insurance policies.

embargo A ban on the import or export of a product.

employability skills Qualities that employers look for in a person, including education, experience, character, and ability to work with others.

employment agencies Professional services that help people find jobs.

employment objective A statement in a résumé of one's career goals or interest in a business.

endorsement The signature of the payee on the back of a check, necessary for cashing a check.

entrepreneur A person who recognizes a business opportunity and assumes the risks of starting a business.

entrepreneurial resources The initiative to improve goods and services or create new ones.

entrepreneurship Accepting the risk of starting a business, or a business started by a risk taker.

entry-level job A beginning career job.

Environmental Protection Agency (EPA) A federal agency that enforces rules to protect the environment and control pollution.

Equal Credit Opportunity Act A federal law against denying credit on the basis of gender, age, ethnicity, or other difference.

Equal Employment Opportunity Act A federal law that prevents discriminating against workers on the basis of gender, ethnicity, or other difference.

Equal Pay Act A federal law requiring that men and women be paid the same wages for doing equal work.

equilibrium price The price at which the amount of goods producers supply meets the amount of goods consumers demand.

e-tail Electronic retailing, or selling products on the Internet.

ethics A set of moral principles by which people conduct themselves personally, socially, or professionally.

e-tickets Electronic tickets, or tickets sold using computers.

e-workforce People who work with computers while doing business.

exchange rate The price at which the currency of one country can buy the currency of another country.

expenditures Items you have to spend money on such as food, rent, and clothing, or expenses.

expert system Computer software that stores and uses knowledge that a human expert would have on the same subject.

exports Goods and services one country sells to another country.

extended coverage Coverage added to a basic insurance policy that protects against other types of property damage.

extranet A semiprivate computer network that allows more than one company to access the same information.

F

factors of production The economic resources used to produce goods and services.

Glossary

free trade Few or no limits on trade between countries.

Fair Credit Billing Act A federal law requiring creditors to correct billing mistakes brought to their attention.

Fair Credit Reporting Act A federal law giving people the right to know what is in their credit files at credit bureaus.

Fair Debt Collection Practices Act (FDCPA) A federal law that protects debtors from unfair methods and practices by collection agents.

Federal Deposit Insurance Corporation (FDIC) A federal government agency that insures commercial bank accounts for up to $100,000.

Federal Reserve System The central banking system of the United States, also called the Fed.

finance charge The total amount it costs to finance a loan, including interest and fees, stated in dollars and cents.

financial forecast An estimate of what business conditions will be like in the future.

financial institution An organization for managing money, such as a bank, credit union, or brokerage firm.

financial manager The person in charge of a business's financial planning, funding, and accounting.

financial plan An outline of a business's expenses, needs, and goals, and how it expects to meet them.

financial responsibility law A law requiring drivers to pay for any damages or injuries they cause in an accident.

fiscal year An accounting period in business of one year.

fixed expenses Expenses that occur regularly and must be paid regularly, such as rent and car insurance.

Food and Drug Administration (FDA) A government agency that protects consumers from dangerous or falsely advertised products.

franchise A contractual agreement to use the name and sell the goods or services of an existing company.

fraud Deliberately misleading business practices.

free-rein leadership A style of leadership in which managers and employees are given goals and then left alone to get their jobs done.

G

garnishment of wages A creditor's legal right to take all or part of a debtor's paycheck for an unpaid dept.

generic products Products that are plainly labeled, unadvertised, and sold at lower prices.

goods Material things that can be physically weighed or measured.

grace period An amount of time to pay off a debt without having to pay interest on it.

grade labels Labels that indicate foods have been inspected by the federal government and the quality of the foods.

gross domestic product (GDP) The total value of the goods and services produced in a country in one year.

gross pay The total amount of money earned in a specific period of time before deductions.

group training Learning a new job from an instructor or manager with a group of other employees, like a class.

groupware Computer software that enables members of a team to share information on the same project, also called project management software.

H

hacker A person who breaks into computer systems for illegal purposes.

hardware The physical components of a computer.

health maintenance organization (HMO) A group health program that provides health care at its own center for a fixed fee per month.

hierarchy A formal chain of command with one person at the top.

homeowner's policy An insurance policy designed for homeowners that combines different kinds of home protection.

human relations The ability to communicate with people.

human resources The knowledge, efforts, and skills people bring to their work, also called labor.

human resources management The process of finding, selecting, training, and evaluating employees.

I

imports Goods and services one country buys from another country.

impulse buying Purchasing things on the spur of the moment.

income The amount of money a person earns or receives during a given period of time.

income property Property used to generate an income, such as a farm or apartment building.

income statement A report of a business's net income or net loss over a specific period.

indirect distribution Moving goods from producers to consumers using one or more intermediaries.

inflation A general increase in the cost of goods and services.

inflation risk The risk that the rate of inflation will increase more than the rate of return on an investment.

infomercial A television program, usually 30 minutes long, made to advertise a product.

information technology Hardware and software for creating, processing, storing, and communicating information.

initiative Taking action to get things done.

installment loans Loans repaid in regular payments over a period of time.

insurance Paid protection against losses due to injury or property damage.

integrity Holding to principles like honesty, loyalty, and fairness.

interest A fee charged for the use of money.

interest-bearing account A checking account that earns interest on the balance left in the account.

intermediaries Businesses that act as go-betweens in moving goods from producers to consumers, such as wholesalers, retailers, and distributors.

Internet A collection of tens of thousands of connected computer networks.

internship A program that provides hands-on experience for a beginner in an occupation, usually as a temporary, unpaid trainee.

interstate commerce Business that take place across states, overseen by the federal government.

intranet A private computer network that connects employees from the same company together.

intrastate commerce Business that takes place within a state, overseen by state governments.

investing Putting money to use in order to make money on it.

J

job description A detailed description of the duties, qualifications, and conditions required to do a specific job.

job interview A formal face-to-face discussion between an employer and a potential employee.

job lead Information about a job opening.

journeyworker A skilled craftsperson who has completed an apprenticeship.

junk bonds Corporate bonds that have a low rating and are issued by companies that don't have successful track records.

L

leadership Providing direction and vision.

legal monopolies Companies, such as public utilities, that are allowed to operate without competition.

liability insurance Protection against claims of injury or property damage to others.

licenses Legal permits to conduct business, usually issued by states.

limited liability Financial responsibility of business owners only for what they invested in a business.

line authority An organizational structure in which managers at the top of the line are in charge of those beneath them.

liquidity The ability to quickly turn an investment into cash.

loss leaders Advertised products that sell for a loss to bring customers into a store so they'll buy other things.

M

management plan A business plan that divides a company into different departments run by different managers.

manufacturers Businesses that make finished products out of raw or processed goods.

market A group of customers who share common wants and needs.

Glossary

market economy A system in which economic decisions are made in the marketplace according to the laws of supply and demand.

market research Gathering and studying information about the buying habits of consumers to determine what goods and services to produce.

marketing The process of creating, promoting, and presenting a product to meet the wants and needs of consumers.

marketing concept A plan for how to market a product or service to consumers.

marketing mix The four main elements of marketing, also called the four Ps: product, place, price, and promotion.

mass media Means of mass communication such as TV, radio, and newspapers.

maturity date The date when money invested in a bond or certificate of deposit becomes available to the investor.

Medicaid A health care program provided by state governments for low-income families.

Medicare A health care program provided by the federal government primarily for retired persons.

middle managers Managers who carry out the decisions of top management and oversee specific departments.

mixed economy A combination of a command and a market economy.

monetary system A system in which goods and services are exchanged indirectly using money as a medium.

money Anything that people accept as a standard of payment.

money management The process of planning how to get the most from your money.

money market deposit account A type of savings account offered by banks, savings and loans, and credit unions similar to a money market fund or mutual fund.

money market fund A type of savings account offered by brokerage firms to finance business and government debts.

monopoly Control of an entire industry by one company or a trust.

mortgage Property put up for a loan that the lender can take if the loan is not paid back.

multi-channel retailer A company that uses several means to sell products, such as retail stores, mail-order catalogs, and the Internet.

multinational corporation A company that does business and has facilities in many countries around the world.

municipal bonds Bonds issued by local and state governments to finance government projects.

mutual fund A fund, or pool of money, created by an investment company that raises money from many shareholders and invests it in a variety of stocks and bonds.

N

national debt The total amount of money owed by the federal government.

natural resources Raw materials found in nature used to produce goods.

needs Necessary wants, such as food, shelter, and clothing.

net pay Gross pay minus deductions, also called take-home pay.

networking Meeting and talking to people in different occupations to find out what they do and make connections.

no-fault insurance A law that requires drivers involved in accidents to collect damages from their own insurance companies no matter who is at fault.

nonprofit organization A business whose main purpose is to provide a service rather than to make a profit.

O

Occupational Safety and Health Administration (OSHA) A division of the Department of Labor that sets and enforces work-related health and safety rules.

oligopoly Control of an industry by a small number of companies.

on-the-job training Learning a new job by actually doing it.

operational managers Managers who are responsible for the daily operations of a business, such as supervisors and office managers.

opportunity cost Giving up the opportunity to buy something now in order to buy something else later.

organizational chart A chart that shows how a business is structured and who is in charge of whom.

orientation The process of helping new employees adjust to a company.

outstanding checks Checks that have been written but haven't yet been cashed.

overdraft protection A line of credit offered by banks to cover an overdrawn checking account.

overdrawing Writing checks for more money than there is in a checking account.

owner's equity The difference in value between a business's assets and liabilities, or what a business owns and what it owes.

P

partnership A business owned by two or more persons who share the risks and rewards.

passbook savings account A traditional savings account in which all transactions are recorded in a book that the depositor keeps.

patent A legal grant for the sole right to own an invention.

performance appraisal An evaluation of how well an employee is doing his or her job.

personal digital assistant (PDA) A hand-held computer that can be used as an address book, appointment book, voice recorder, and to access the Internet.

personal property Possessions that can be moved, like furniture, jewelry, and electronic equipment.

policy A contract between an insurance company and policyholder that explains the amount and types of coverage.

pollution Contamination of air, water, and land.

pop-up ads Internet ads that appear briefly when a user logs onto the Internet or clicks on a site.

pre-existing condition A serious health condition diagnosed before a person obtained health insurance and which might not be covered by a policy.

preferred stock A form of ownership of a corporation that gives stockholders certain privileges.

premium The amount an insurance company charges a policyholder for an insurance policy.

principal The actual amount of money owed or deposited in an account, upon which interest is based.

proceeds Money paid from a life insurance policy to a beneficiary.

processors Businesses that change raw goods into more finished products.

producer A business that gathers raw products in their natural state.

product liability The legal responsibility manufacturers have to make a safe product.

profession A field that requires a high level of education, such as law, medicine, or architecture.

profit The amount of money left over after a business has paid for the cost of producing its goods and services.

promotion A move to a higher level job with more authority, responsibility, and pay.

promotional sale A sale that gives you a special buy on a new product or a product that's in season.

property insurance Protection from financial loss on property due to damage or theft.

prosperity The peak of economic activity.

protectionism Limiting trade with other countries to protect businesses at home.

Q

qualifications The education, skills, and experience required to do a particular job.

quota A limit placed on the quantities of a product that can be imported.

R

random access memory (RAM) Computer memory that stores information temporarily and loses it when the computer is turned off.

real estate Land and anything attached to it, such as buildings or natural resources.

real estate agent A person licensed to arrange the buying and selling of homes and other types of real estate.

real property Property attached to land, like a house, business, or garage.

recall An order to take back and repair or replace defective products.

recession A decline in economic activity.

recovery A rise in business activity after a recession or depression.

recruitment Actively looking for the most qualified people to fill a job position.

recycling Collecting products for processing so that they can be used again.

reference A person an employer can contact to find out about a job applicant.

Glossary

referral A personal recommendation to an employer for a job applicant.

refund Return the cost of a product.

relationship marketing Building customer loyalty through good customer relations.

renter's insurance Insurance available to renters, as opposed to homeowners, to cover any loss or damage to personal possessions.

replacement value The full cost of repairing or replacing property by an insurance company regardless of its depreciation value.

repossess To take back collateral put up for a loan, such as a car, if the loan is not paid back.

resource Anything that people can use, such as fuel, labor, or money, to make or obtain what they need or want.

résumé A written summary of one's skills, education, and work experience.

retailer A business that sells goods or services directly to the public.

revenue Government or business income.

revolving account A form of credit which allows one to borrow or charge up to a certain amount of money and pay back a part of the total each month.

rider An addition to an insurance policy that covers specific property or damages.

risk taker Someone willing to take chances in business, considered a key characteristic of an entrepreneur.

S

safety-deposit box A place at a bank for storing valuable items.

savings Money put aside for future use.

savings bonds Bonds sold by the federal government to pay for government projects.

scanner A computerized device that can read images and record or transfer them.

scarcity The shortage of economic resources.

screen ads Internet ads displayed on the right or left of a screen and that can be printed out.

secured loan A loan that is backed by collateral.

self-managed teams Work groups that supervise themselves.

separation Leaving a company because of retirement, resignation, layoff, or termination.

services Tasks that people or machines perform.

shadowing Following a person throughout a workday to see what a job involves.

signature card A record of an account holder's signature used by a bank to verify the person's identity.

simple interest Interest earned only on the money deposited into a savings account, or the principal.

skills Abilities developed through training and experience.

small business An independently owned business that employs fewer than 500 people.

small claims court A court that settles cases involving relatively small amounts of money.

social responsibility The obligation to do what is best for the welfare of society.

software A computer program containing a set of instructions that tells a computer what to do.

sole proprietorship A business owned by only one person.

speculative stocks Stocks in relatively new firms that don't have an established track record of success.

spreadsheet program A computerized worksheet.

standard fire policy Insurance against property damage due to fire or lightning.

standard of living The amount of goods and services the people of a country can buy.

start-ups Businesses just starting out.

statement savings account A traditional savings account in which all transactions are recorded in a statement sent by the bank to the account holder.

stereotype Identify someone by a single trait or as a member of a certain group rather than as an individual.

stock Shares of ownership in a corporation.

stock exchange A marketplace where stocks are bought and sold.

stop payment An order for a bank not to cash a particular check.

subsidies Payments the government gives to businesses to make up for their business losses.

supply The amount of goods and services that producers will provide at various prices.

sweatshops Factories that pay poorly, have unsafe working conditions, and treat workers badly.

T

target marketing Finding and analyzing potential consumers for a product.

tariff A tax placed on imported products to make them more expensive than domestic products.

tax incentives Reductions in taxes government gives to businesses to encourage socially responsible behavior.

telecommuting Using communications technology, such as computers, to keep in touch with the workplace while working away from it.

term insurance Life insurance that covers a person for a specific period of time.

top-level managers Managers responsible for setting goals and planning the future for a company.

trade A field that requires a high level of manual or technical skill, such as carpentry, mechanics, or computer programming.

trademark A legally-protected brand name, trade name, or trade characteristic that distinguishes one product from another.

transfer A move to another job within a company at the same level and pay.

transit advertising Advertising that uses public transportation to display ads.

trust A group of companies that band together to form a monopoly and eliminate competition.

truth-in-lending disclosure A statement creditors must give to consumers informing them of the costs and terms of credit.

U

undeveloped property Unused land intended only for investment purposes.

unit price The cost of an item for a standard unit of measurement, such as an ounce.

unlimited liability Full legal and financial responsibility for a business.

unsecured loan A loan that is not backed by collateral.

usury law A law that restricts the amount of interest that can be charged for credit.

V

variable expenses Expenses that fluctuate and over which you have some control, such as food and entertainment.

variable rate Interest rate on a loan that changes as interest rates in the banking system change.

virtual business A company that does business only on the Internet.

W

wants Things we wish we could have, as opposed to needs.

warranty A legal document that states the rights and responsibilities agreed to by the consumer and the store or manufacturer.

wearable computers Small, lightweight computers that workers can carry with them to assist them on the job.

Web browser A program that makes it easy to search and retrieve information on the Web.

webcast A broadcast, like a TV or a radio broadcast, sent and received over the Internet.

wholesaler A type of business that buys goods in large amounts and resells them to other businesses in smaller lots.

withdrawal Money taken out of a bank account.

withholding Money subtracted from a paycheck for taxes, social security, and other deductions.

Y

yield The rate of return on an investment, or the amount of money an investment earns.

Index

Index

Index

Index

Photo Credits

Cover Photography: Josef Beck/FPG International LLC

Mark Adams/FPG International LLC 481; AFP/Corbis xvii(tr), 2, 95, 503; Courtesy of The Agency 457, 461; Michael Aglialo/International Stock 214; Courtesy of American Energy Systems, Inc. 21, 23, 25; Courtesy of American Honda Motor Company, Inc. 10(b), xv(b); Colin Anderson/Corbis 303; Antman/The Image Works 373; Arizona State Museum 251, 255; Bill Aron/PhotoEdit 190(m), 256(b); Bruce Ayers/Stone 318, 311, 131; Bachmann/PhotoEdit 103; Bill Bachman/Stock Boston 190(l); Phil Banko/Stone 290; Billy Barnes/PhotoEdit 256(m); Cathy Barkataki 171; Courtesy of Susanna Barataki 460; David Barnes/Stock Market 377, 521; Scott Barrow/International Stock 543(t); Eric R Berndt/Photo Network 360; Bettmann/Corbis 55; Courtesy of Dr. Maya Bhaumik 240; Walter Bibikow/FPG International LLC 148; Blacksheep xx(m), 8(t), 52(t), 76(t), 200(t), 214(t), 286(t), 302(t), 336(t), 422(t), 476(t); John Boykin/PhotoEdit 568; Courtesy of Bozart xix(tr1), xix(tr3), xix(tr4); Courtesy of Larisa Brass 321; Robert Brenner/PhotoEdit 31; Bridgeman Art Library, London, New York 185(tr); Paula Bronstein/Stone xxiv; Cleve Bryant/PhotoEdit 491; BusinessWeek 142, 192, 228, 264, 314, 350, 400, 450, 528, 578; Rex A. Butcher/Stone 562, 575; Peter Cade/Stone 423; Al Camapnie/The Image Works 183; Cardstore.com 232, 245; Robert Cardin/Cardin Studio 98, 111; Myrleen Cate/PhotoEdit 52, 356, 569; Center for Creative Leadership 115,117, 119; Paul Chauncey/Stock Market 20; Ron Chappel/FPG International LLC 93 137, 385, 415; Chris Cheadle/Getty Images 448(l); Ken Chernus/FPG International LLC 445; Paul Cherfils/Getty Images 529; Steve Chenn/Corbis 13, 85, 268, 281; Stewart Cohen/Index Stock 386; Courtesy of Christini Technologies 84, 97; Felix Clouzot/Image Bank 354, 369; Connie Coleman/Stone 89; Cosmo Condina/Stone 146,159; Gary Conner/PhotoEdit 269; Courtesy of Cooper, Robertson & Partners 168; Corbis 190(r), 226(l), 237, 257(b), 257(t) 282, 297, 490; R. Crandall/The Image Works 576(br); Guy Crittenden/Index Stock 470, 483; Courtesy of Patty Crown 249; Jim Cummins/CorbisStockMarket 247; Jim Cummins/FPG International LLC 270, 565; Richard Cummins/Corbis 48; Bob Daemmrich/Stock Boston 293(b); James Davis/International Stock 411; Tony Demin/International Stock 51; Stephen Derr/Image Bank 451; George B. Diebold/The Stock Market 147; Doyon Foundation 271, 273, 275, 277; Clark Dunbar/Corbis 239; Courtesy of Amiel Dunn 301; Duomo/Corbis 210, 225; Shaun Egan/Stone 404, 417; John Elk/Stock Boston 157; Amy C. Etra/PhotoEdit 151; Warren Faidley/Corbis 531; Najlah Feanny/Stock Boston 7; Jon Feingersh/Stock Market 162(ml) 405, 441; Gina Fersazzi/Los Angeles Times 149; Myrleen Ferguson Cate/PhotoEdit 3, 74; Tim Flach/Stone xix, 184-185, 464-465; Kevin Flemming/Corbis 365(m); FPG International LLC 39, 169, 286; Charly Franklin/FPG International LLC 112, 115; David Frazier Photolibrary 292(br), 292(tr); Franklin Electronic Publishers 4,17; Robert Frerck/Stone 464(bl); Tony Freeman/PhotoEdit 40, 365(t), 537; Gaetano/Corbis 312(lm), 395; Walter Geiersperger/Corbis Stock Market 500; Getty Images 419, 353, 545; Robert W. Ginn/PhotoEdit 9; Nora Good/Masterfile 78-79; Courtesy of Gore 101; Phillip Gould/Corbis 162(l); Sara Gray/Stone 107; Spencer Grant\PhotoEdit 187, 199, 201, 205, 361, 418, 428(br), 428(m), 428(tr), 429(b), 429(m), 429(t), 433, 495, 514; J Greenberg/The Image Works 121, 293(t); Jeff Greenberg/PhotoEdit 381, 398(tr), 534; Gunter Marx Photography/Corbis 197; David Harry Stewart/Getty Images 448(b); Jordan Harris/Photo Edit 365(m); Cris Hellier/Corbis 185(br); Chip Henderson/Stone 325; Walter Hodges/Stone 262(b), 327; Jack Hollingsworth/Corbis 309; Ed Honowitz/Getty Images 226(br); Kevin Horan/Stone 34, 47; Harry How/Allsport 195; How Stuff Works 342(bm), 342(ml), 342(tr), 343(b), 343(m), 343(t); Terry Husebye/Stone xxii, 15; Image Bank/GettyOne 435; The Image Works 262(l), 559; Index Stock ix, 91, 175, 179, 283, 302, 306(bl) 332, 338, 347, 363, 370, 383, 393; Insurance Institute For Highway Safety 543(m); International Stock 315; Iridian 476; Everett C. Johnson/Pictor 507; Chris Jones/The Stock Market 49; Reed Kaestner/Corbis 459; Zigy Kalunzy/Stone 367; Bonnie Kamin/PhotoEdit 213, 217, 256(t); Courtesy of Gary Kelley 335, 337, 339, 341; Lewis Kemper/Index Stock 523; Courtesy of Sunny Kim 92; John Lamb/Stone xxiv; Courtesy of Wendy Lau 12; Leo de Wys xix (tr2), 203; George D. Lepp/Corbis 436; Alan Levenson/Corbis 409; Alan Levenson/Getty Images 299; Mark Lewis/Stone 493; Rob Lewine/Corbis 241; Liaison 465(tr); A. Lichenstein/The Image Works 43; Michael Lichter/International Stock 420; Dorothy Littell/Stock Boston 463; Betts Loman/PhotoEdit 176; Lew Long/Corbis 320; Tricia Lovar 276, 555, 557; Steven Lunetta/PhotoEdit 234; Dennis MacDonald/PhotoEdit 579; David Madison/Getty Images 576(tr); Courtesy of Mangement Recruiters of Boulder 235; Felicia Martinez/PhotoEdit 357; Don Mason/Stock Market 5, 10; Joe McBride/Corbis 413; Patti McConville/International Stock 448(r), 533; Mendola Ltd./Stock Market 532, 547; Christian Michaels/FPG International LLC 56, 106, 134, 288, 378, 488, 538, 570 ; Chris Minerva/Index Stock 554; David Muench/Corbis 421; Mulvehill/The Image Works 571; Lance Nekson/CorbisStockMarket 388; Michael Newman/PhotEdit 54, 123, 153, 167, 196, 209, 223, 226(tr), 236, 265, 323, 340, 390, 391, 489; Steve Niedorf/Image Bank 45; David Noton/International Stock 27; Jonathan Nourok/PhotoEdit 376; John Nuebauer/PhotoEdit 177; Jim Olive/Pictor xix; A Olney/TSI Imaging/Stone 307; Courtesy of Don Otto 556; Couresty of Mike Owen 42; Panoramic Images xvii, xx(t), 26, 102, 120, 178, 218, 254, 362, 392, 412, 458, 502, 536; Michael Paras/International Stock 526(br); Victor Paris/FPG International LLC 57; Courtesy of Patagonia 53; Courtesy of PEER Africa 358; Jose L Pelaez/Stock Market 143, 181, 478; PhotoEdit 11, 298, 311, 324, 471, 551, 564; Photomorgana/Stock Market 174, 189; Photoworld/FPG International LLC 37; Pictor 87, 105, 109, 132, 140, 231, 243, 262(r), 274, 279, 284, 336, 473, 475, 567, 573; David Pollack/Stock Market 317 431; Peter Poulides/Stone 479; Tom Prettyman/PhotoEdit 8; Richard Price/FPG International LLC 114; Patrick Ramsey/International Stock 155 259, 563; Ramirez/PhotoEdit 306(tr); Sean Ramsay/The Image Works 549, 561; Richard Ransier/Corbis xvi(r), 69; Rick Rappaport xvi(l); Tom Raymond/Getty Images 312(br); Reflections Photolibrary/Corbis 6; Seth Resnick/Stock Boston 548; Reuters NewMedia Inc./Corbis xii, 198, 128, 499, Mark Richards/PhotoEdit 15, 127, 163, 267, 345; Courtesy of Rockwell Automation 285, 287, 289, 291; Otto Rodde/Stock Market 472; Bill Ross/Corbis 517; Michael Rosenfeld/Stone 319; Steven Rubin/The Image Works 193; Rykoff Collection/Corbis 41; Andy Sacks/Getty Images iii, 19, 542(tl), 542(tr); Miguel S. Salmeron/FPG International LLC xx(b), 56(t), 76(t), 106(t), 134(t), 288(t), 378(t), 437, 488 (t), 538(t), 570(t); David J. Sams/Stock Boston 364(b), 364(m); Sanford Angliolo/CorbisStockMarket 553; Bob Schantz/International Stock 86; William Schick/Stock Market 443; Ian Shaw/Stone 498, 511; Benjamin Shearn/FPG International LLC; Jeff Sherman/Getty Images 422(b); Nancy Sheehan/PhotoEdit 253; Rhoda Sidney/PhotoEdit 359; Stephen Simpson/FPG International LLC xix(2); Hygh Sitton/Stone 162(mr); Ariel Skelley/Stock Market 355; Jeff Smith/International Stock 161; Philip & Karen Smith/Getty Images 348(bl); Joseph Sohm/ChromoSohm Inc./Corbis vii, 95, 212, 248, 334; Paul A Souders/Corbis 552; Ted Speigel/Corbis 246, 261; Vince Streano/Corbis; Tom Stewart/Stock Market 504; Bill Ivy/Stone 100; Stock Boston 59; Jan Stromme/PhotoEdit 162(r); Stephen Studd/Stone 50; Courtesy of Summer's Farms of California 374; Sunstar/International Stock 145; SuperStock xii, xix, 24, 35, 104, 154 160, 173, 180, 216, 333, 387, 398(l). 410, 434, 439, 447, 453, 455, 456 462 467, 469, 477, 486, 487 501, 509, 513, 518, 539; Svoboda Stock/International Stock 129; SW Production/Index Stock 535, 406; Adam G. Sylvester/Photo Researchers 348(tr); Allan Tannenbaun/The Image Works 505; Telegraph Colour Library/FPG International LLC 371, 403, 440; John Terence Turner v, 113; Steve Thorton/Corbis 200; Wes Thompsom/Stock Market 515; Bob Torrez/Getty Images 165; Courtesy of Transportation Research Center, Inc. 542(bm); TravelPix/FPG International LLC xxx(bl); Courtesy of The Trustees of The British Museum 185(tl, bl); Randy M. Ury/CorbisStockMarket 527(tr); Steve Uzzell/Stock Rep xv(t); Susan Van Etten/PhotoEdit 215, 219, 401; VCG/FPG International LLC 252; VCG/International Stock 348(tr); Courtesy of Gerado Villalobos 204; Terry Vine/Stone 99, 351; Rudi Von Briel/PhotoEdit 126,139; Courtesy of Helen Walthier 566; Steve Warmowski/Journal-Courier/The Image Works 166; David H Wells/The Image Works 519; Carol Werner/Corbis 384, 397; Carol Werner/Index Stock 398(r); Dana White/PhotoEdit 484, 497; Ken Whitmore/Getty Images 526(bl); Martin Wong 130; Caroline Wood/International Stock 312(tr); Tim Wright/Corbis 543(bl); David Ximeno Tejada/Stone 101, 133, 135, 202, 229, 233, 257(m), 292(ml), 300, 329, 364(tr), 375, 407, 512, 525, 540, 541, 576(bl), 379, 485; Zefa Visual Media/Index Stock 372; Courtesy of Thomas Zuttermeister 506; Zyqmunt Nowak Solins/Stone 18, 33